# FROM INQUIRY
## TO Academic Writing

### A TEXT AND READER

Stuart Greene
April Lidinsky

Second Edition

# Steps to Academic Writing
## A Quick Reference Guide

# FROM INQUIRY TO ACADEMIC WRITING

A Text and Reader

# FROM INQUIRY TO ACADEMIC WRITING

## A Text and Reader

### SECOND EDITION

**Stuart Greene**
*University of Notre Dame*

**April Lidinsky**
*Indiana University South Bend*

Bedford/St. Martin's    BOSTON ■ NEW YORK

**For Bedford/St. Martin's**

*Senior Executive Editor:* Stephen A. Scipione
*Production Editor:* Katherine Caruana
*Senior Production Supervisor:* Jennifer Peterson
*Senior Marketing Manager:* Molly Parke
*Associate Editor:* Shannon Walsh
*Editorial Assistant:* Alyssa Demirjian
*Copyeditor:* Linda McLatchie
*Indexer:* Mary White
*Photo Researcher:* Kathleen Karcher
*Permissions Manager:* Kalina Ingham Hintz
*Senior Art Director:* Anna Palchik
*Text Design:* Jean Hammond
*Cover Design:* Marine Miller
*Cover Art:* Charles Biederman, *#24, Constable*, 1977–1979, painted aluminum,
   41-1/2 × 33-1/8 × 12". Collection of Frederick R. Weisman Art Museum at the
   University of Minnesota, Minneapolis. Biederman Archive, Weisman Art
   Museum, Gift of Charles J. Biederman. L1998.39.168.
*Composition:* Achorn International, Inc.
*Printing and Binding:* RR Donnelley and Sons

*President:* Joan E. Feinberg
*Editorial Director:* Denise B. Wydra
*Editor in Chief:* Karen S. Henry
*Director of Marketing:* Karen R. Soeltz
*Director of Production:* Susan W. Brown
*Associate Director, Editorial Production:* Elise S. Kaiser
*Managing Editor:* Elizabeth M. Schaaf

Library of Congress Control Number: 2011921335

Manufactured in the United States of America.

6   5   4   3   2   1
f    e    d    c    b    a

*For information, write:* Bedford/St. Martin's, 75 Arlington Street, Boston, MA
02116 (617-399-4000)

ISBN-13: 978-0-312-60141-6

**Acknowledgments**
*Acknowledgments and copyrights appear at the back of the book on pages 900–03,*
*which constitute an extension of the copyright page. It is a violation of the law*
*to reproduce these selections by any means whatsoever without the written*
*permission of the copyright holder.*

student writing we use as examples in the rhetoric text, side by side with the examples of professional writing we include.

## ■ A Closer Look at the Thematic Reader

The thematic reader chapters (12 through 17) are organized into disciplinary issues and include many selections that are lengthy and thoroughly documented. They approximate the kinds of reading and writing college students are expected to do in most of their upper-level classes. Although the selections are generally longer and more complex than those found in most other first-year composition readers, students who have had some practice with the reading and writing strategies in the first part of the book are generally more than up to the task of working with these readings. Moreover, our students are usually exhilarated by what they discover in the readings—the kind of "big thinking" they came to college to experience.

As you would expect in a book that emphasizes cross-curricular writing, many of the readings are taken from journals and publications intended for scholarly audiences, and thus model what would traditionally be considered academic writing. Among these are selections by Judith Lorber, Noël Sturgeon, and Shari L. Dworkin and Michael A. Messner, scholars whose texts are influential among their peers in the university and whose ideas are respected and admired by those outside academia. Other selections are drawn from thought-provoking and engaging books on recent *New York Times* best sellers' lists, many of which have been required reading on college campuses. The authors of these books—Stephen Johnson, Thomas L. Friedman, and Deborah Tannen, to name only a few—are intellectuals who use the same kinds of strategies of research and analysis as academic writers, and like academic writers they use those skills to take on big ideas, frame them in interesting new ways, and offer striking examples that present them provocatively to readers. Still other readings—by Eric Schlosser, Barbara Ehrenreich, and Michael Pollan, for example—are brief and accessible, chosen to draw students into the conversation of ideas that longer selections unpack and extend in greater detail.

While all these readings are at some level researched essays—texts that build on ideas others have written—they also provide students with a wide range of rhetorical styles to use as models. Some readings take a journalistic approach, some occasionally dip into autobiographical details, with authors using personal anecdotes to explain their interest in an issue or illustrate an example, while other readings take a more formal tone, relying on research and expertise to build their arguments. We chose these selections in part because of the many different strategies they use to make many different kinds of connections—from the personal to the scholarly, from individual experiences to larger social patterns. This multi-leveled inquiry is at the heart of the thinking and writing we invite students to learn in this book.

We have divided the selections in the reader into six chapters, each focused on an issue broadly associated with a particular discipline:

to revise. Revise a lot. (And we have!) Steve Scipione has been a terrific editor who read our work carefully and who offered sage advice every step of the way. We could not have completed this project without Steve and Leasa and their tireless assistants, Kate Mayhew, Shannon Walsh, and Allie Goldstein. In the marketing department we thank marketing director Karen R. Soeltz, market development manager Karita dos Santos, marketing manager Molly Parke, and her assistants Lindsay Talbot and Laura Horton. The talented production department conscientiously steered the manuscript through a demanding schedule to create the book you hold. We thank Susan W. Brown and Elise S. Kaiser, production manager Elizabeth M. Schaaf, assistant managing editor John Amburg, and especially Katherine Caruana, the book's patient and scrupulous production editor. Linda McLatchie provided exceptionally alert and constructive copyediting; Kalina Hintz and Kathleen Karcher negotiated the complicated process of permissions acquisition. Anna Palchik oversaw the design of the book; Donna Dennison and Marine Miller designed the cover.

*Stuart Greene writes:* I wish to thank the many students and faculty with whom I have worked over the years. Specifically, I would like to thank Kelly Kinney, Stephen Fox, Rebecca Nowacek, and Katherine Weese who served as my assistant directors in the past and who taught me a great deal about the teaching of writing. I would also like to thank Robert Kachur who contributed a great deal to our early iterations of this book. And I will always appreciate the many discussions I have had with John Duffy during these many years and with Connie Mick, a tireless and innovative teacher of writing. Susan Ohmer provided much insight into my understanding of media and student culture. A special thanks to Mike Palmquist with whom I taught writing as "conversation" over twenty years ago and who gave this book direction. Finally, I thank Denise Della Rossa, who has listened to me rehearse these ideas for years. I dedicate this book to her.

*April Lidinsky writes:* I am grateful for the superb pedagogical training I received from Lou Kelly at the University of Iowa, and Kurt Spellmeyer and Hugh English at Rutgers, the State University of New Jersey. My talented colleagues at Indiana University South Bend — particularly Rebecca Brittenham, Mike Keen, Bruce Spitzer, and Becky Torstrick — challenge me to expand my classroom practices in inventive and multi-disciplinary ways. Of course, no one shapes our pedagogy quite like our students, and I am gratified to have shared two decades' worth of classrooms with students whose names and writing projects have stuck with me and influenced my teaching in ways I am sure they cannot imagine. More personally, I am indebted to my parents, JoElla Hunter and Tom Lidinsky, for their model of lifelong reading and learning, and to Ken Smith for his talent for crafting sentences as well as a life of meaning. Our daughters, Grace and Miriam, are passionate thinkers, readers, and writers, and remind me that above all, learning should be joyful and always surprising.

suggestions for what students might pay attention to as they read it. Further, every reading is followed by two kinds of questions, **"Reading as a Writer: Analyzing Rhetorical Choices,"** which asks students to consider the stylistic decisions a writer makes in crafting the piece, and **"Writing as a Reader: Entering the Conversation of Ideas,"** which uses each essay as a launching point for further inquiry, research, and discovery about an issue raised in the text. The questions and assignments in the reader support students by reinforcing the skills and strategies of rhetorical reading and inquiry-based writing presented in the rhetoric.

The book concludes with **Assignment Sequences** for instructors to implement or adapt to their specific needs. They define a subject for inquiry and offer a sequential path through readings and several writing assignments that build on one another. Assignment sequences give students the opportunity to engage in intellectual inquiry that lasts longer than one assignment. Rather than writing a paper and then moving onto a completely new topic, then, each paper students write in a sequence will help them develop the ideas in the next paper, as they consider an issue from many perspectives, and with a range of sources. In other words, these assignment sequences invite students to read, research, and write with the habits of mind and practices of academic writers who are in conversation with other thinkers, and who also bring scholarly analysis to experiences beyond the classroom.

An **Appendix** introduces the basics of documentation in MLA and APA styles.

## ■ New to the Second Edition

We are gratified that the publisher's surveys showed that instructors who used the first edition found our approach to academic writing to be effective and popular with their students. The main change in the second edition is that we have gathered many more readings from a greater variety of sources, making the book more flexible for teachers and, we trust, more current, accessible, and engaging for students. We include about 40 percent more reading selections throughout. Although most of the readings continue to be longer, more challenging, and just more academic than those found in the majority of composition readers, we know that students are and will be wrestling with challenging reading and writing tasks in their other courses, and where better to practice skillful engagement with academic texts than in a writing course? For variety, and to address the wide range of student readiness, we also include shorter selections by academics and public intellectuals that invite a general audience of readers to enter conversations of ideas.

The new readings are most evident in the thematic chapters. Instructors who have examined or used the first edition will now notice these chapters are organized around university disciplines: Education, Media Studies, Business, International Relations, Biology, and Environmental Studies.

Some of the brief new readings include a recent blog entry by Barbara Ehrenreich on the outsourcing of local news items to underpaid newswriters in India (in the International Relations chapter), a three-page analysis by Carmen D. Siering that reveals the anti-feminist bent of the *Twilight* series (Media Studies), and an essay by Pamela Paul on the hidden perils of household cleaning products (Environmental Studies). Such short readings give students a rapid and meaningful entrée to the topics explored by longer pieces in the chapters.

We have also made a number of changes to the rhetoric chapters, many of these revisions involving readings as well. Overall, we tried to increase the range of genres represented as we enhanced the currency of the readings and the immediacy of the topics. A few highlights:

- Chapter 1 on habits of academic writing now concludes with literacy narratives by Richard Rodriguez and Gerald Graff, writers who describe their initiation into academic habits of mind.

- Chapters 2 and 3 now include brief contemporary essays that enact academic conversation. In Chapter 2, Eugene Provenza Jr. responds to E. D. Hirsch's classic manifesto on cultural literacy that precedes it in the chapter; in Chapter 3, two writers respond to the issue of grade inflation.

- Chapter 7 is no longer built around readings on the civil rights era, but around a sequence of short recent essays about whether online writing practices such as texting develop students' sense of audience better than more formal writing instruction.

- Throughout the rhetoric, more student essays have been added, and all of them have been annotated to call out the rhetorical moves the student writers perform in their model essays. For example, in Chapter 5 a student essay on texting and literacy is annotated to show how the student states and supports a thesis.

We have added a section on visual rhetoric to the end of Chapter 8's discussion of rhetorical appeals and logic. We know that students are adept at detecting the appeals of advertisements, but we have provided them with an overtly rhetorical method for performing such analysis, supported with a sample analysis and additional opportunities for practice.

## ■ Available as an E-Book

*From Inquiry to Academic Writing* is available as an e-book in the Course-Smart PDF format. Online, interactive, and at a value price, Bedford e-books can be purchased stand-alone or packaged with a print book. Get an exam copy, adopt for your course, or have students purchase a copy at **bedfordstmartins.com**. Please contact your Bedford/St. Martin's Press representative for more details.

## ■ The Text Is Available Separately

If you are interested in assigning only the rhetoric chapters, they are available without the thematic chapters as *From Inquiry to Academic Writing: A Practical Guide,* Second Edition.

## ■ Additional Resources

We have prepared an instructor's manual, *Resources for Teaching From Inquiry to Academic Writing: A Text and Reader,* Second Edition. The first part of the manual addresses every step of the process of academic writing we set forth in the rhetoric text, with additional comments on the readings integrated in the text chapters. Not only do we discuss many of the issues involved in taking our rhetorical approach to academic argument—problems and questions students and instructors may have—we also suggest background readings on the research informing our approach. The second part of the manual provides concrete strategies for teaching the selections in the thematic reader, and is based on our own experiences working with these readings. We also suggest possible responses to the questions that follow the readings in Part Two.

The instructor's manual is available as a bound volume, but can also be downloaded from the companion site, **bedfordstmartins.com/frominquiry**. Additional resources on the Web site include downloadable templates, worksheets, and summary boxes for students; AuthorLinks that supplement the readings in the book; and connections to the suite of online resources offered by Bedford/St.Martin's, including *Re:Writing*.

## ■ Acknowledgments

We would first like to thank the many reviewers who commented on the proposal, the manuscript, and the first edition. Invariably their comments were useful, and frequently helpful and cheering as well. The list of reviewers includes Angela Adams, Loyola University–Chicago; Steve Adkison, Idaho State University; Teresa Fernandez Arab, University of Kansas; Yesho Atil, Asheville-Buncombe Technical Community College; Paula Bacon, Pace University–Pleasantville; Susan Bailor, Front Range Community College; Mary Ellen Bertolini, Middlebury College; Laurel Bollinger, University of Alabama–Huntsville; Margaret Bonesteel, Syracuse University; James Brill, University of California, Chico; Laurie Britt-Smith, St. Louis University; William Brugger, Brigham Young University–Idaho; Lise Buranen, California State University–Los Angeles; Jeffrey Cebulski, Kennesaw State University; Marie Coffey, San Antonio College; Carolyn Cole, Oklahoma Baptist University; Tami Comstock-Peavy, Arapahoe Community College; Emily Cosper, Delgado Community College; Karen Cox, City College of San Francisco; Ryan Crider, Missouri State University; Calum Cunningham, Fanshawe

College–London; J. Madison Davis, University of Oklahoma–Norman; Anne DeMarzio, University of Scranton; Erin Denney, Community College of San Francisco; Jason DePolo, North Carolina A&T State University; Brock Dethier, Utah State University; Eugenia C. Eberhart, Garden City Community College; Lisa Egan, Brown University; Ed Eleazer, Francis Marion University; Elaine Fredericksen, University of Texas–El Paso; Hannah Furrow, University of Michigan–Flint; Christine A. Geyer, Cazenovia University; Rhoda Greenstone, Long Beach City College; Rima Gulshan, George Mason University; Sinceree Gunn, University of Alabama–Huntsville; Juli E. Hale, King College; Jane Hammons, University of California, Berkeley; Amy Hankins, Blue River Community College; Ann Hartney, Fort Lewis College; Virginia Scott Hendrickson, Missouri State University; Zachery Hickman, University of Miami; Monica Hogan, Johnson County Community College; Jean Incampo, Gateway Community College; T. Christine Jespersen, Western State College of Colorado; Margaret Johnson, Idaho State University; Laura Katsaros, Monmouth University; Karen Keaton Jackson, North Carolina Central University; Therese Jones, Lewis University; Trevor Kearns, Greenfield Community College; Howard Kerner, Polk Community College; Lynn Kilpatrick, Salt Lake Community College; Jeff Klausman, Whatcom Community College; Tamara Kuzmenkov, Tacoma Community College; Erin Lebacqz, University of New Mexico; Lindsay Lewan, Arapahoe Community College; April Lewandowski, Front Range Community College–Westminster; Renee Major, Louisiana State University; Diane L. Maldonado, Point Park University; Loren Loving Marquez, Salisbury University; Mark McBeth, John Jay College; Timothy McGinn, Northwest Arkansas Community College; Amanda McGuire Rzicznek, Bowling Green State University; Erica Messenger, Bowling Green State University–Main; Alyce Miller, Indiana University; Lamata Mitchell, Rock Valley College; Whitney Myers, University of New Mexico; Teddy Norris, St. Charles Community College; Lolly J. Ockerstrom, Park University; Judy Olson, California Sate University, Los Angeles; Jill Onega, University of Alabama–Huntsville; Robert Peltier, Trinity College; Valeries L. Perry, Lewis University; Jeanette Pierce, San Antonio College; Mary Jo Reiff, University of Tennessee; Mary Roma, New York University; David Ryan, University of San Francisco; Daniel Schenker, University of Alabama–Huntsville; Roy Stamper, North Carolina State University; Scott Stevens, Western Washington University; Sarah Stone, University of California–Berkeley; Joseph Sullivan, Marietta College; Gretchen Treadwell, Fort Lewis College; Raymond M. Vince, The University of Tampa; Charles Warren, Salem State College; Patricia Webb, Arizona State University; Susan Garrett Weiss, Goucher College; Worth Weller, Indiana University-Purdue University–Fort Wayne; and Jackie White, Lewis University.

We are also grateful to the many people at Bedford/St. Martin's, starting with president Joan E. Feinberg, editorial director Denise B. Wydra, and editor-in-chief Karen S. Henry. We would especially like to thank Leasa Burton, who believed in this project early on and told us to be prepared to revise. Revise a lot. (And we have!) Steve Scipione has been a terrific editor who read our work carefully and who offered sage advice every step of the way. We could not have completed this project without Steve and Leasa and their tireless assistants, Kate Mayhew, Shannon Walsh, and Allie Goldstein. In the marketing department we thank marketing director Karen R. Soeltz, market development manager Karita dos Santos, marketing manager Molly Parke, and her assistants Lindsay Talbot and Laura Horton. The talented production department conscientiously steered the manuscript through a demanding schedule to create the book you hold. We thank Susan W. Brown and Elise S. Kaiser, production manager Elizabeth M. Schaaf, assistant managing editor John Amburg, and especially Katherine Caruana, the book's patient and scrupulous production editor. Linda McLatchie provided exceptionally alert and constructive copyediting; Kalina Hintz and Kathleen Karcher negotiated the complicated process of permissions acquisition. Anna Palchik oversaw the design of the book; Donna Dennison and Marine Miller designed the cover.

*Stuart Greene writes:* I wish to thank the many students and faculty with whom I have worked over the years. Specifically, I would like to thank Kelly Kinney, Stephen Fox, Rebecca Nowacek, and Katherine Weese who served as my assistant directors in the past and who taught me a great deal about the teaching of writing. I would also like to thank Robert Kachur who contributed a great deal to our early iterations of this book. And I will always appreciate the many discussions I have had with John Duffy during these many years and with Connie Mick, a tireless and innovative teacher of writing. Susan Ohmer provided much insight into my understanding of media and student culture. A special thanks to Mike Palmquist with whom I taught writing as "conversation" over twenty years ago and who gave this book direction. Finally, I thank Denise Della Rossa, who has listened to me rehearse these ideas for years. I dedicate this book to her.

*April Lidinsky writes:* I am grateful for the superb pedagogical training I received from Lou Kelly at the University of Iowa, and Kurt Spellmeyer and Hugh English at Rutgers, the State University of New Jersey. My talented colleagues at Indiana University South Bend—particularly Rebecca Brittenham, Mike Keen, Bruce Spitzer, and Becky Torstrick—challenge me to expand my classroom practices in inventive and multi-disciplinary ways. Of course, no one shapes our pedagogy quite like our students, and I am gratified to have shared two decades' worth of classrooms with students whose names and writing projects have stuck with me and influenced my teaching in ways I am sure they cannot imagine. More personally, I am indebted to my parents, JoElla Hunter and Tom Lidinsky, for their model of lifelong reading and learning, and to Ken Smith for his talent for crafting sentences as well as a life of meaning. Our daughters, Grace and Miriam, are passionate thinkers, readers, and writers, and remind me that above all, learning should be joyful and always surprising.

# Preface for Instructors

A cademic writing is the challenging intellectual price of admission to college. Not only must students learn to write, they also must learn to read—and even to think—in complex new ways. That's where *From Inquiry to Academic Writing* comes in. As it acknowledges and explains the challenges of academic writing, it offers a clear, methodical approach to meeting those challenges. Our students, and many others, have told us that the approach demystifies academic thinking, reading, and writing, while helping them see that the rewards of learning such skills carry over to civic and life issues beyond their college years.

More specifically, *From Inquiry to Academic Writing* is a composition rhetoric and reader that introduces students to college-level inquiry, analysis, and argument. It is based on a first-year composition course where we guide students to produce essays that use evidence and sources in increasingly complex ways. In this book as well as our classes, we present academic writing as a collaborative conversation, undertaken in the pursuit of new knowledge. We teach students to see that academic writing is a social act in which they are expected to work responsibly with the ideas of others. At the same time, we encourage students to see themselves as makers of knowledge who use sources to advance arguments about important academic and cultural issues.

## ▪ A Closer Look at the Rhetoric Text

Broadly speaking, the rhetoric text follows a path that begins with academic thinking and proceeds through academic reading and research, integrating academic writing throughout. Nevertheless, Chapters 1 through 11 are freestanding enough to be taught in any order that suits your course. What unites them is our constant emphasis on the recursive and overlapping nature of these thinking, reading, and writing skills and the centrality of the writing process. Indeed, we assume students will be writing throughout the semester and so we punctuate every chapter with short readings and activities that ask students to pause and attempt the kinds of writing they will need to practice through the various stages of developing their papers.

Chapter 1 presents an overview of academic writing as a process motivated by inquiry, and is followed by chapters that offer strategies for reading critically and working with other writers' ideas. Inevitably, reading and writing processes are intertwined. Thus in Chapter 2 we encourage students to practice "writerly" reading—reading texts as writers who can analyze critically the decisions other writers make—so that they can implement the most appropriate strategies given their own purpose for writing. While Chapters 2 through 5 address the nuts and bolts of getting started on writing, from how to mark a text to forming questions and developing a working thesis, we recognize that this process is rarely linear, and that it benefits from conversation with invested readers. Chapters 6 and 7 help students develop and support their theses by providing a range of strategies for finding and working with sources, for example showing students the ways they can use summary, paraphrase, and synthesis in the service of their purposes as writers. In Chapters 8 and 9 we link "writerly" reading with the ability to practice "readerly" writing, or writing that is self-conscious about the needs of real readers.

Chapter 10 presents revision in the context of peer groups. The responses of classmates can help students determine when they might need to read additional material before shaping more effective research questions, for example, or when a draft indicates that more evidence-gathering will be needed to support a student's argument. Our supporting materials for peer workshops foster productive group interaction at every stage of the peer review process. Finally, in Chapter 11, we provide students with strategies for conducting original research that build upon earlier chapters on using personal experience or writing a researched argument.

As we noted earlier, although the process of developing an academic argument can be messy and unruly, the structured step-by-step pedagogy in the rhetoric text should support students during each stage of the process. Most readings are followed by "Reading as a Writer" questions that send students back into the reading to respond to the rhetorical moves writers make. In every chapter, "Steps to" boxes summarize the major points about each stage of thinking, reading, and writing, offering quick references that bring key information into focus for student review and practice. "Practice Sequences" in each chapter ask students to try out and build on the strategies we have explained or demonstrated. We also provide templates, formulas, and worksheets that students may use to generate ideas or to organize information as they read and write. Your students should feel further supported and encouraged by seeing the abundance of

# Brief Contents

# Contents

## 8 From Ethos to Logos

*Appealing to Your Readers*   199

**Entering the Conversation of Ideas    317**

## 12 Education

*What does it mean to be educated, and who decides?*    319

## 13 Media Studies

*What can we learn from what entertains us?*   419

## 14 Business

*How do we target and train our youngest consumers?*   517

## 15  International Relations

*Who are "we" in relation to "others"?*    606

## 16  Biology

*How do we try to control our bodies?*   697

## 17  Environmental Studies

# FROM INQUIRY TO ACADEMIC WRITING

A Text and Reader

# Starting with Inquiry
*Habits of Mind of Academic Writers*

## WHAT IS ACADEMIC WRITING?

In the strictest sense, *academic writing* is what scholars do to communicate with other scholars in their fields of study, their *disciplines*. It's the research report a biologist writes, the interpretive essay a literary scholar composes, the media analysis a film scholar produces. At the same time, *academic writing* is what you have to learn so that you can participate in the different disciplinary conversations that take place in your courses. You have to learn to *think* like an academic, *read* like an academic, *do research* like an academic, and *write* like an academic—even if you have no plans to continue your education and become a scholar yourself. Learning these skills is what this book is about.

Fair warning: It isn't easy. Initially you may be perplexed by the vocabulary and sentence structure of many of the academic essays you read. Scholars use specialized language to capture the complexity of an issue or to introduce specific ideas from their discipline. Every discipline has its own vocabulary. You probably can think of words and phrases that are not used every day but that are necessary, nevertheless, to express certain ideas precisely. For example, consider the terms *centrifugal force*, *Oedipus complex*, and *onomatopoeia*. These terms carry with them a history of study; when you learn to use them, you also are learning to use the ideas they represent. Such terms help us describe the world specifically rather than generally; they help us better understand how things work and how to make better decisions about what matters to us.

Sentence structure presents another challenge. The sentences in academic writing are often longer and more intricate than the sentences in popular magazines. Academics strive to go beyond what is quick, obvious, and general. They ask questions based on studying a subject from multiple points of view, to make surprising connections that would not occur to someone who has not studied the subject carefully. It follows that academic writers are accustomed to extensive reading that prepares them to examine an issue, knowledgeably, from many different perspectives, and to make interesting intellectual use of what they discover in their research. To become an adept academic writer, you have to learn these practices as well.

Academic writing will challenge you, no doubt. But hang in there. Any initial difficulty you have with academic writing will pay off when you discover new ways of looking at the world and of making sense of it. Moreover, the habits of mind and core skills of academic writing are highly valued in the world outside the academy.

Basically, academic writing entails making an **argument**—text crafted to persuade an audience—often in the service of changing people's minds and behaviors. When you write an academic essay, you have to

- define a situation that calls for some response in writing;
- demonstrate the timeliness of your argument;
- establish a personal investment;
- appeal to readers whose minds you want to change by understanding what they think, believe, and value;
- support your argument with good reasons;
- anticipate and address readers' reasons for disagreeing with you, while encouraging them to adopt your position.

Academic argument is not about shouting down an opponent. Instead, it is the careful expression of an idea or perspective based on reasoning and the insights garnered from a close examination of the arguments others have made on the issue.

The chapters in the first part of this book introduce you to the habits of mind and core skills of academic writing. By **habits of mind**, we mean the patterns of thought that lead you to question assumptions and opinions, explore alternative opinions, anticipate opposing arguments, compare one type of experience to another, and identify the causes and consequences of ideas and events. These forms of **critical thinking** demand an inquiring mind that welcomes complexities and seeks out and weighs many different points of view, a mind willing to enter complex conversations both in and out of the academy. We discuss academic habits of mind in the rest of Chapter 1 and refer to them throughout this book.

Such habits of mind are especially important today, when we are bombarded with appeals to buy this or that product and with information that may or may not be true. For example, in "106 Science Claims and a Truckful of Baloney" (*The Best American Science and Nature Writing*, 2005), William Speed Weed illustrates the extent to which the claims of science vie for our attention alongside the claims of advertising. He notes that advertisers often package their claims as science, but wonders whether a box of Cheerios really can reduce cholesterol.

As readers we have a responsibility to test the claims of both science and advertising in order to decide what to believe and act upon. Weed found that "very few of the 100 claims" he evaluated "proved completely true" and that "a good number were patently false." Testing the truth of claims—learning to consider information carefully and critically and to weigh competing points of view before making our own judgments—gives us power over our own lives.

The habits of mind and practices valued by academic writers are probably ones you already share. You are behaving "academically" when you comparison-shop, a process that entails learning about the product in magazines and on the Internet and then looking at the choices firsthand before you decide which one you will purchase. You employ these same habits of mind when you deliberate over casting a vote in an election. You inform yourself about the issues that are most pressing; you learn about the candidates' positions on these issues; you consider other arguments for and against both issues and candidates; and you weigh those arguments and your own understanding to determine which candidate you will support.

Fundamentally, academic habits of mind are *analytical*. When you consider a variety of factors—the quality and functionality of the item you plan to buy, how it meets your needs, how it compares to similar items before making a shopping choice—you are conducting an **analysis**. That is, you are pausing to examine the reasons why you should buy something, instead of simply handing over your cash and saying, "I want one of those."

To a certain extent, analysis involves breaking something down into its various parts and reflecting on how the parts do or don't work together. For example, when you deliberate over your vote, you may consult one of those charts that newspapers often run around election time: A list of candidates appears across the top of the chart, and a list of issues appears on the side. You can scan the columns to see where each candidate stands on the issues, and you can scan the rows to see how the candidates compare on a particular issue. The newspaper editors have performed a preliminary analysis for you. They've asked, "Who are the candidates?" "What are the issues?" and "Where does each candidate stand on the issues?"; and they have presented the answers to you in a format that can help you make your decision.

But you still have to perform your own analysis of the information before you cast your ballot. Suppose no candidate holds your position on every issue. Whom do you vote for? Which issues are most important to you? Or suppose two candidates hold your position on every issue. Which one do you vote for? What characteristics or experience are you looking for in an elected official? And you may want to investigate further by visiting the candidates' Web sites or by talking with your friends to gather their thoughts on the election.

As you can see, analysis involves more than simply disassembling or dissecting something. It is a process of continually asking questions and looking for answers. Analysis reflects, in the best sense of the word, a *skeptical* habit of mind, an unwillingness to settle for obvious answers in the quest to understand why things are the way they are and how they might be different.

This book will help you develop the questioning, evaluating, and conversational skills you already have into strategies that will improve your ability to make careful, informed judgments about the often conflicting and confusing information you are confronted with every day. With these strategies, you will be in a position to use your writing skills to create change where you feel it is most needed.

The first steps in developing these skills are to recognize the key academic habits of mind and then to refine your practice of them. We explore four key habits of mind in the rest of this chapter:

1. inquiring,
2. seeking and valuing complexity,
3. understanding that academic writing is a conversation, and
4. understanding that writing is a process.

## ACADEMIC WRITERS MAKE INQUIRIES

Academic writers usually study a body of information so closely and from so many different perspectives that they can ask questions that may not occur to people who are just scanning the information. That is, academic writers learn to make **inquiries**. Every piece of academic writing begins with a question about the way the world works, and the best questions lead to rich, complex insights that others can learn from and build on.

You will find that the ability to ask good questions is equally valuable in your daily life. Asking thoughtful questions about politics, popular culture, work, or anything else—questions like What exactly did that candidate mean by "Family values are values for all of us," anyway? What is lost and gained by bringing Tolkien's *Lord of the Rings* trilogy to the screen? What does it take to move ahead in this company?—is the first step in understanding how the world works and how it can be changed.

Inquiry typically begins with **observation**, a careful noting of phenomena or behaviors that puzzle you or challenge your beliefs and values (in a text or in the real world). Observing phenomena prompts an attempt to understand them by **asking questions** (Why does this exist? Why is this happening? Do things have to be this way?) and **examining alternatives** (Maybe this doesn't need to exist. Maybe this could happen another way instead.).

For example, Mark Edmundson, a professor of English at the University of Virginia, *observes* that his students seem to prefer classes they consider "fun" over those that push them to work hard. This prompts him to *ask* how the consumer culture—especially the entertainment culture—has altered the college experience. In his essay "On the Uses of a Liberal Education," he wonders what it means that colleges increasingly see students as customers they need to please with Club Med–style exercise facilities that look "like a retirement spread for the young" more than as minds to be educated. He further *asks* what will happen if we don't change course—if entertaining students and making them feel good about themselves continue to be higher priorities than challenging students to stretch themselves with difficult ideas. Finally, he looks at alternatives to entertainment-style education and *examines those alternatives* to see what they would offer students.

In her reading on the American civil rights movement of the 1950s and 1960s, one of our students *observed* that the difficulties many immigrant groups experienced when they first arrived in the United States are not acknowledged as struggles for civil rights. This student of Asian descent *wondered why* the difficulties Asians faced in assimilating into American culture are not seen as analogous to the efforts of African Americans to gain civil rights (Why are things this way?). In doing so, she *asked* a number of relevant questions: What do we leave out when we tell stories about ourselves? Why reduce the struggle for civil rights to black-and-white terms? How can we represent the multiple struggles of people who have contributed to building our nation? Then she *examined alternatives*—different ways of presenting the history of a nation that prides itself on justice and the protection of its people's civil rights (Maybe this doesn't need to exist. Maybe this could happen another way.). The academic writing you will read—and write yourself—starts with questions and seeks to find rich answers.

## Steps to Inquiry

1 **Observe.** Note phenomena or behaviors that puzzle you or challenge your beliefs and values.

2 **Ask questions.** Consider why things are the way they are.

3 **Examine alternatives.** Explore how things could be different.

### A Practice Sequence: Inquiring

The activities below will help you practice the strategies of observing, asking questions, and examining alternatives.

1 Find an advertisement for a political campaign (you can find many political ads on the Internet), and write down anything about what you observe in the ad that puzzles you or that challenges your beliefs and values. Next, write down questions you might have (Do things have to be this way?). Finally, write down other ways you think the ad could persuade you to vote for this particular candidate (Maybe this could happen another way instead.).

2 Locate and analyze data about the students at your school. For example, you might research the available majors and determine which departments have the highest and lowest enrollments. (Some schools have fact books that can be accessed online; and typically the registrar maintains a database with this information.) Is there anything that puzzles you? Write down any questions you have (Why are things the way they are?). What alternative explanations can you provide to account for differences in the popularity of the subjects students major in?

## ACADEMIC WRITERS SEEK AND VALUE COMPLEXITY

Seeking and valuing complexity are what inquiry is all about. As you read academic arguments (for example, about school choice), observe how the media work to influence your opinions (for example, in political ads), or analyze data (for example, about candidates in an election), you will explore reasons why things are the way they are and how they might be different. When you do so, we encourage you not to settle for simple either/or reasons. Instead, look for multiple explanations.

When we rely on **binary thinking**—imagining there are only two sides to an issue—we tend to ignore information that does not fall tidily into one side or the other. Think of the sound-bite assertions you hear bandied about on talk shows on the pretext of "discussing" a hot-button issue like stem-cell research or abortion: "It's just wrong/right because it is!" Real-world questions (How has the Internet changed our sense of what it means to be a writer? What are the global repercussions of fast food? How do we make sense of terrorism?) don't have easy for-or-against answers. Remember that an **issue** is a subject that can be explored and debated. Issue-based questions, then, need to be approached with a mind open to complex possibilities. (We say more about identifying issues and formulating issue-based questions in Chapter 4.)

If we take as an example the issue of terrorism, we would discover that scholars of religion, economics, ethics, and politics tend to ask very different questions about terrorism and to propose very different approaches for addressing this worldwide problem. This doesn't mean that one approach is right and the others are wrong; it means that complex issues are likely to have multiple explanations, rather than a simple choice between A and B.

In her attempt to explain the popularity of the Harry Potter books and movies, Elizabeth Teare, a professor of English, provides a window on the steps we can take to examine the complexity of a topic. She begins her essay "Harry Potter and the Technology of Magic" with the observations that author J. K. Rowling is one of the ten most influential people in publishing and that her books have "transformed both the technologies of reading and the way we understand those technologies." Motivated by a sense of curiosity, if not puzzlement, Teare formulates a guiding question: "What is it that makes these books—about a lonely boy whose first act on learning he is a wizard is to go shopping for a wand—not only an international phenomenon among children and parents and teachers but also a topic of compelling interest to literary, social, and cultural critics?" Notice that in doing so, she indicates that she will examine this question from the multiple perspectives of literary, social, and cultural critics. To find answers to this question, Teare explores a range of perspectives from a variety of sources, including publishers' Web sites, trade journals, academic studies, and works of fiction for young readers.

One of our students was curious about why a well-known musician, Eminem, was at once so widely popular and so bitterly reviled, a phenomenon he observed in discussions with friends and in reviews of Eminem's music. He set out to understand these conflicting responses by examining the differing perspectives of music critics, politicians, religious evangelists, and his peers; and then he formulated an issue-based question: "How can we explain Eminem's popularity given the ways people criticize Eminem personally and his music?" In looking at this issue, the student opened himself to complexity by resisting simple answers to his question about why Eminem and his music evoked such different and conflicting responses.

## Steps to Seeking and Valuing Complexity

**1** **Reflect on what you observe.** Clarify your initial interest in a phenomenon or behavior by focusing on its particular details. Then reflect on what is most interesting and least interesting to you about these details, and why.

**2** **Examine issues from multiple points of view.** Imagine more than two sides to the issue, and recognize that there may well be other points of view too.

**3** **Ask issue-based questions.** Try to put into words questions that will help you explore why things are the way they are.

---

### A Practice Sequence: Seeking and Valuing Complexity

These activities build on the previous exercises we asked you to complete.

**1** Look again at the political ad. Think about other perspectives that would complicate your understanding of how the ad might persuade voters.

**2** Imagine other perspectives on the data you found on the students in your school. Let's say, for example, that you've looked at data on student majors. How did you explain the popularity of certain majors and the unpopularity of others? How do you think other students would explain these discrepancies? What explanations would faculty members offer?

---

## ACADEMIC WRITERS SEE WRITING AS A CONVERSATION

Another habit of mind at the heart of academic writing is the understanding that ideas always build on and respond to other ideas, just as they do in the best kind of conversations. Of course, conversations in academic writing happen on the page; they are not spoken. Still, these conversations are quite similar to the conversations you have through e-mail and instant messaging: You are responding to something someone else has written (or said) and are writing back in anticipation of future responses.

Academic writing also places a high value on the belief that good, thoughtful ideas come from conversations with others, *many* others. As your exposure to other viewpoints increases, as you take more and different points of view into consideration and build on them, your own ideas will develop more fully and fairly. You already know that to get a full picture of something, often you have to ask for multiple perspectives. When you want to find out what "really" happened at an event when your friends are telling you different stories, you listen to all of them and then evaluate the evidence to draw conclusions you can stand behind—just as academic writers do.

Theologian Martin Marty starts a conversation about hospitality in his book *When Faiths Collide* (2004). *Hospitality* is a word he uses to describe a human behavior that has the potential to bring about real understanding among people who do not share a common faith or culture. As Marty points out, finding common ground is an especially important and timely concern "in a world where strangers meet strangers with gunfire, barrier walls, spiritually land-mined paths, and the spirit of revenge." He believes that people need opportunities to share their stories, their values, and their beliefs; in doing so, they feel less threatened by ideas they do not understand or identify with.

Yet Marty anticipates the possibility that the notion of hospitality will be met with skepticism or incomprehension by those who find the term "dainty." After all, he observes, that there are hospitality suites and hospitality industries suggests current usage of the term is different from historical usage, particularly in the Bible. To counter the incredulity or incomprehension of those who do not immediately understand his use of the term *hospitality*, Marty gives his readers entrée to a conversation with other scholars who understand the complexity and power of the kind of hospitality shown by people who welcome a stranger into their world. The stranger he has in mind may simply be the person who moves in next door; but that person could also be an immigrant, an exile, or a refugee.

Marty brings another scholar, Darrell Fasching, into the conversation to explain that hospitality entails welcoming "the stranger . . . [which] inevitably involves us in a sympathetic passing over into the other's life and stories" (cited in Marty, p. 132). And John Koenig, another scholar Marty cites, traces the biblical sources of the term in an effort to show the value of understanding those we fear. That understanding, Marty argues, might lead to peace among warring factions. The conversation Marty begins on the page helps us see that his views on bringing about peace have their source in other people's ideas. In turn, the fact that he draws on multiple sources gives strength to Marty's argument.

The characteristics that make for effective oral conversation are also in play in effective academic conversation: empathy, respect, and a willingness to exchange and revise ideas. **Empathy** is the ability to understand the perspectives that shape what people think, believe, and value. To express both empathy and respect for the positions of all people involved in the conversation, academic writers try to understand the conditions under which each opinion might be true and then to represent the strengths of that position accurately.

For example, imagine that your firm commitment to protecting the environment is challenged by those who see the value of developing land rich with oil and other resources. In challenging their position, it would serve you well to understand their motives, both economic (lower gas prices, new jobs that will create a demand for new houses) and political (less dependence on foreign oil). If you can demonstrate your knowledge of these factors, those committed to developing resources in protected areas will listen to you. To convey empathy and respect while presenting your own point of view, you might introduce your argument by saying:

> Although it is important to develop untapped resources in remote areas of the United States both to lower gas prices and create new jobs and to eliminate our dependence on other countries' resources, it is in everyone's interest to use alternative sources of power and protect our natural resources.

As you demonstrate your knowledge and a sense of shared values, you could also describe the conditions under which you might change your own position.

People engaging in productive conversation try to create change by listening and responding to one another rather than dominating one another. Instead of trying to win an argument, they focus on reaching a mutual understanding. This does not mean that effective communicators do not take strong positions; more often than not they do. However, they are more likely to achieve their goals by persuading others instead of ignoring them and their points of view. Similarly, writers come to every issue with an agenda. But they realize that they may have to compromise on certain points to carry those that mean the most to them. More important, they understand that their perceptions and opinions may be flawed or limited, and they are willing to revise them when valid new perspectives are introduced.

In an academic community, ideas develop through give-and-take, through a conversation that builds on what has come before and grows stronger from multiple perspectives. You will find this dynamic at work in your classes, when you discuss your ideas: You will build on other people's insights, and they will build on yours. As a habit of mind, paying attention to academic conversations can improve the thinking and writing you do in every class you take.

## Steps to Joining an Academic Conversation

1. **Be receptive to the ideas of others.** Listen carefully and empathetically to what others have to say.

2. **Be respectful of the ideas of others.** When you refer to the opinions of others, represent them fairly and use an evenhanded tone. Avoid sounding scornful or dismissive.

3. **Engage with the ideas of others.** Try to understand how people have arrived at their feelings and beliefs.

4. **Be flexible in your thinking about the ideas of others.** Be willing to exchange ideas and to revise your own opinions.

## A Practice Sequence: Joining an Academic Conversation

The following excerpt is taken from Thomas Patterson's *The Vanishing Voter* (2002), an examination of voter apathy. Read the excerpt and then complete the exercises that follow.

> Does a diminished appetite for voting affect the health of American politics? Is society harmed when the voting rate is low or in decline? As the *Chicago Tribune* said in an editorial, it may be "humiliating" that the United States, the oldest continuous democracy, has nearly the lowest voting rate in the world. But does it have any practical significance? . . .

The increasing number of nonvoters could be a danger to democracy. Although high participation by itself does not trigger radical change, a flood of new voters into the electorate could possibly do it. It's difficult to imagine a crisis big and divisive enough to prompt millions of new voters to suddenly flock to the polls, especially in light of Americans' aversion to political extremism. Nevertheless, citizens who are outside the electorate are less attached to the existing system. As the sociologist Seymour Martin Lipset observed, a society of nonvoters "is potentially more explosive than one in which most citizens are *regularly* involved in activities which give them some sense of participation in decisions which affect their lives."

Voting can strengthen citizenship in other ways, too. When people vote, they are more attentive to politics and are better informed about issues affecting them. Voting also deepens community involvement, as the philosopher John Stuart Mill theorized a century ago. Studies indicate that voters are more active in community affairs than nonvoters are. Of course, this association says more about the type of person who votes as opposed to the effect of voting. But recent evidence, as Harvard University's Robert Putnam notes, "suggests that the act of voting itself encourages volunteering and other forms of government citizenship."

1  In this excerpt, Patterson presents two arguments: that increasing voter apathy is a danger to democracy and that voting strengthens citizenship. With which of these arguments do you sympathize more? Why? Can you imagine reasons that another person might not agree with you? Write them down. Now do the same exercise with the argument you find less compelling.

2  Your instructor will divide the class into four groups and assign each group a position—pro or con—on one of Patterson's arguments. Brainstorm with the members of your group to come up with examples or reasons why your group's position is valid. Make a list of those examples or reasons, and be prepared to present them to the class.

3  Your instructor will now break up the groups into new groups, each with at least one representative of the original groups. In turn with the other members of your new group, take a few moments to articulate your position and the reasons for it. Remember to be civil and as persuasive as possible.

4  Finally, with the other members of your new group, talk about the merits of the various points of view. Try to find common ground ("I understand what you are saying; in fact, it's not unlike the point I was making about . . ."). The point of this discussion is not to pronounce a winner (who made the best case for his or her perspective) but to explore common ground, exchange and revise ideas, and imagine compromises.

## ACADEMIC WRITERS UNDERSTAND THAT WRITING IS A PROCESS

Academic writing is a process of defining issues, formulating questions, and developing sound arguments. This view of writing counters a number of popular myths: that writing depends on inspiration, that writing should happen quickly, that learning to write in one context prepares you to write in other contexts, and that revision is the same as editing. The writing process addresses these myths. First, choosing an idea that matters to you is one way to make your writing matter. And there's a better chance that writing you care about will contribute in a meaningful way to the conversation going on about a given issue in the academic community. Second, writers who invest time in developing and revising their ideas will improve the quality of both their ideas and their language—their ability to be specific and express complexity.

There are three main stages to the writing process: collecting information, drafting, and revising. We introduce them here and expand on them throughout this book.

### ■ Collect Information and Material

Always begin the process of writing an essay by collecting *in writing* the material—the information, ideas, and evidence—from which you will shape your own argument. Once you have read and marked the pages of a text, you have begun the process of building your own argument. The important point here is that you start to put your ideas on paper. Good writing comes from returning to your ideas on your own and with your classmates, reconsidering them, and revising them as your thinking develops. This is not something you can do with any specificity unless you have written down your ideas. The box below shows the steps for gathering information from your reading, the first stage in the process of writing an academic essay. (In Chapter 2, these steps are illustrated and discussed in more detail.)

---

### Steps to Collecting Information and Material

**1 Mark your texts as you read.** Note key terms; ask questions in the margins; indicate connections to other texts.

**2 List quotations you find interesting and provocative.** You might even write short notes to yourself about what you find significant about the quotes.

**3 List your own ideas in response to the reading or readings.** Include what you've observed about the way the author or authors make their arguments.

**4** Sketch out the similarities and differences among the authors whose work you plan to use in your essay. Where would they agree or disagree? How would each respond to the others' arguments and evidence?

## ■ Draft, and Draft Again

The next stage in the writing process begins when you are ready to think about your focus and how to arrange the ideas you have gathered in the collecting stage. Writers often find that writing a first draft is an act of discovery, that their ultimate focus emerges during this initial drafting process. Sometimes it is only at the end of a four-page draft that a writer says, "Aha! This is what I really want to talk about in this essay!" Later revisions of an essay, then, are not simply editing or cleaning up the grammar of a first draft. Instead, they truly involve *re*vision, seeing the first draft again to establish the clearest possible argument and the most persuasive evidence. This means that you do not have to stick with the way a draft turns out the first time. You can—and must!—be willing to rewrite a substantial amount of a first draft if the focus of the argument changes, or if in the process of writing new ideas emerge that enrich the essay. This is why it's important not to agonize over wording in a first draft: It's difficult to toss out a paragraph you've sweated over for hours. Use the first draft to get your ideas down on paper so that you and your peers can discuss what you see there, with the knowledge that you (like your peers) will need to stay open to the possibility of changing an aspect of your focus or argument.

### Steps to Drafting

**1** **Look through the materials** you have collected to see what interests you most and what you have the most to say about.

**2** **Identify what is at issue**, what is open to dispute.

**3** **Formulate a question** that your essay will respond to.

**4** **Select the material you will include**, and decide what is outside your focus.

**5** **Consider the types of readers** who might be most interested in what you have to say.

**6** **Gather more material** once you've decided on your purpose—what you want to teach your readers.

**7** **Formulate a working thesis** that conveys the point you want to make.

**8** **Consider possible arguments** against your position and your response to them.

■ **Revise Significantly**

The final stage, revising, might involve several different drafts as you continue to sharpen your insights and the organization of what you have written. As we discuss in Chapter 10, you and your peers will be reading one another's drafts, offering feedback as you move from the larger issues to the smaller ones. It should be clear by now that academic writing is done in a community of thinkers: That is, people read other people's drafts and make suggestions for further clarification, further development of ideas, and sometimes further research. This is quite different from simply editing someone's writing for grammatical errors and typos. Instead, drafting and revising with real readers, as we discuss in Chapter 10, allow you to participate in the collaborative spirit of the academy, in which knowledge making is a group activity that comes out of the conversation of ideas. Importantly, this process approach to writing in the company of real readers mirrors the conversation of ideas carried on in the pages of academic books and journals.

---

### Steps to Revising

**1** **Draft and revise the introduction and conclusion.**

**2** **Clarify any obscure or confusing passages** your peers have pointed out.

**3** **Provide details and textual evidence** where your peers have asked for new or more information.

**4** **Check to be sure you have included opposing points of view** and have addressed them fairly.

**5** **Consider reorganization.**

**6** **Check to be sure that every paragraph contributes clearly to your thesis or main claim** and that you have included signposts along the way, phrases that help a reader understand your purpose ("Here I turn to an example from current movies to show how this issue is alive and well in pop culture").

**7** **Consider using strategies you have found effective in other reading** you have done for class (repeating words or phrases for effect, asking rhetorical questions, varying your sentence length).

---

The four academic habits of mind we have discussed throughout this chapter—making inquiries, seeking and valuing complexity, understanding writing as a conversation, and understanding writing as a process—are fundamental patterns of thought you will need to cultivate as an academic writer. The core skills we discuss through the rest of the book build on these habits of mind.

## BECOMING ACADEMIC: TWO NARRATIVES

In the following passages, two writers describe their early experiences as readers. Trained as academic writers, Richard Rodriguez and Gerald Graff are well known outside the academy. In this excerpt from *Hunger of Memory*, Rodriguez describes what it was like growing up as a bookish bilingual "scholarship boy" in a Spanish-speaking household. In the other excerpt, from *Beyond the Culture Wars*, Graff narrates how he disliked reading books, especially literature and history books, well into his undergraduate years as an English major. Both of their narratives turn around moments of recognition triggered by exposure to the ideas of others. As you read the selections, consider these questions:

- Where are the turning points in each narrative? What are the most important things the writers seem to learn?

- What incidents or insights did you find most interesting in the narratives? Why?

- What seem to be the key ideas in each narrative? Do these ideas strike you as being potentially useful in your own work as a thinker and writer?

- Do you find that the writers exhibit academic habits of mind (making inquiries, seeking and valuing complexity, seeing writing as a kind of conversation)? If so, where?

### RICHARD RODRIGUEZ

## Scholarship Boy

Richard Rodriguez was born into a Mexican immigrant family in San Francisco, California, and spoke only Spanish until age six. He had a formidable education, receiving a BA from Stanford University and an MA from Columbia University; studying for a PhD at the University of California, Berkeley; and attending the Warburg Institute in London on a Fulbright fellowship. Instead of pursuing a career in academia, he became a journalist. He is perhaps best known for his contributions to PBS's *The NewsHour with Jim Lehrer* and for his controversial opposition to affirmative action and bilingual education. His books include *Hunger of Memory: The Education of Richard Rodriguez* (1981), *Mexico's Children* (1990), *Days of Obligation: An Argument with My Mexican Father* (1992), and *Brown: The Last Discovery of America* (2002).

■ ■ ■

I stand in the ghetto classroom—"the guest speaker"—attempting to lecture on the mystery of the sounds of our words to rows of diffident students. "Don't you hear it? Listen! The music of our words. '*Sumer is*    *1 i-cumen in. . . .'* And songs on the car radio. We need Aretha Franklin's voice to fill plain words with music—her life." In the face of their empty stares, I try to create an enthusiasm. But the girls in the back row turn to watch some boy passing outside. There are flutters of smiles, waves. And someone's mouth elongates heavy, silent words through the barrier of glass. Silent words—the lips straining to shape each voiceless syllable: *"Meet meee late errr."* By the door, the instructor smiles at me, apparently hoping that I will be able to spark some enthusiasm in the class. But only one student seems to be listening. A girl, maybe fourteen. In this gray room her eyes shine with ambition. She keeps nodding and nodding at all that I say; she even takes notes. And each time I ask a question, she jerks up and down in her desk like a marionette, while her hand waves over the bowed heads of her classmates. It is myself (as a boy) I see as she faces me now (a man in my thirties).

The boy who first entered a classroom barely able to speak English, twenty years later concluded his studies in the stately quiet of the reading room in the British Museum. Thus with one sentence I can summarize my academic career. It will be harder to summarize what sort of life connects the boy to the man.     *2*

With every award, each graduation from one level of education to the next, people I'd meet would congratulate me. Their refrain always the same: "Your parents must be very proud." Sometimes then they'd ask me how I managed it—my "success." (How?) After a while, I had several quick answers to give in reply. I'd admit, for one thing, that I went to an excellent grammar school. (My earliest teachers, the nuns, made my success their ambition.) And my brother and both my sisters were very good students. (They often brought home the shiny school trophies I came to want.) And my mother and father always encouraged me. (At every graduation they were behind the stunning flash of the camera when I turned to look at the crowd.)     *3*

As important as these factors were, however, they account inadequately for my academic advance. Nor do they suggest what an odd success I managed. For although I was a very good student, I was also a very bad student. I was a "scholarship boy," a certain kind of scholarship boy. Always successful, I was always unconfident. Exhilarated by my progress. Sad. I became the prized student—anxious and eager to learn. Too eager, too anxious—an imitative and unoriginal pupil. My brother and two sisters enjoyed the advantages I did, and they grew to be as successful as I, but none of them ever seemed so anxious about their schooling. A second-grade student, I was the one who came home and corrected the "simple" grammatical mistakes of our parents. ("Two negatives make a positive.") Proudly I announced—to my family's startled silence—that a teacher had said I was losing all trace of a Spanish accent. I was oddly annoyed when I was unable to get parental help with a homework assign-     *4* ment. The night my father tried to help me with an arithmetic exercise, he kept reading the instructions, each time more deliberately, until I pried the textbook out of his hands, saying, "I'll try to figure it out some more by myself."

When I reached the third grade, I outgrew such behavior. I became more tactful, careful to keep separate the two very different worlds of my day. But then, with ever-increasing intensity, I devoted myself to my studies. I became bookish, puzzling to all my family. Ambition set me apart. When my brother saw me struggling home with stacks of library books, he would laugh, shouting: "Hey, Four Eyes!" My father opened a closet one day and was startled to find me inside, reading a novel. My mother would find me reading when I was supposed to be asleep or helping around the house or playing outside. In a voice angry or worried or just curious, she'd ask: "What do you see in your books?" It became the family's joke. When I was called and wouldn't reply, someone would say I must be hiding under my bed with a book.

(How did I manage my success?)

What I am about to say to you has taken me more than twenty years to admit: *A primary reason for my success in the classroom was that I couldn't forget that schooling was changing me and separating me from the life I enjoyed before becoming a student.* That simple realization! For years I never spoke to anyone about it. Never mentioned a thing to my family or my teachers or classmates. From a very early age, I understood enough, just enough about my classroom experiences to keep what I knew repressed, hidden beneath layers of embarrassment. Not until my last months as a graduate student, nearly thirty years old, was it possible for me to think much about the reasons for my academic success. Only then. At the end of my schooling, I needed to determine how far I had moved from my past. The adult finally confronted, and now must publicly say, what the child shuddered from knowing and could never admit to himself or to those many faces that smiled at his every success. ("Your parents must be very proud. . . .")

At the end, in the British Museum (too distracted to finish my dissertation) for weeks I read, speed-read, books by modern educational theorists, only to find infrequent and slight mention of students like me. (Much more is written about the more typical case, the lower-class student who barely is helped by his schooling.) Then one day, leafing through Richard Hoggart's *The Uses of Literacy*, I found, in his description of the scholarship boy, myself. For the first time I realized that there were other students like me, and so I was able to frame the meaning of my academic success, its consequent price—the loss.

Hoggart's description is distinguished, at least initially, by deep understanding. What he grasps very well is that the scholarship boy must move between environments, his home and the classroom, which are at

cultural extremes, opposed. With his family, the boy has the intense pleasure of intimacy, the family's consolation in feeling public alienation.
Lavish emotions texture home life. *Then*, at school, the instruction bids
him to trust lonely reason primarily. Immediate needs set the pace of his
parents' lives. From his mother and father the boy learns to trust spontaneity and nonrational ways of knowing. *Then*, at school, there is mental
calm. Teachers emphasize the value of a reflectiveness that opens a space
between thinking and immediate action.

Years of schooling must pass before the boy will be able to sketch the    *10*
cultural differences in his day as abstractly as this. But he senses those
differences early. Perhaps as early as the night he brings home an assignment from school and finds the house too noisy for study.

> He has to be more and more alone, if he is going to "get on." He will have,
> probably unconsciously, to oppose the ethos of the hearth, the intense gre-
> gariousness of the working-class family group. Since everything centres
> upon the living-room, there is unlikely to be a room of his own; the bed-
> rooms are cold and inhospitable, and to warm them or the front room, if
> there is one, would not only be expensive, but would require an imaginative
> leap—out of the tradition—which most families are not capable of making.
> There is a corner of the living-room table. On the other side Mother is iron-
> ing, the wireless is on, someone is singing a snatch of song or Father says
> intermittently whatever comes into his head. The boy has to cut himself off
> mentally, so as to do his homework, as well as he can.[1]

The next day, the lesson is as apparent at school. There are even rows
of desks. Discussion is ordered. The boy must rehearse his thoughts and
raise his hand before speaking out in a loud voice to an audience of classmates. And there is time enough, and silence, to think about ideas (big
ideas) never considered at home by his parents.

Not for the working-class child alone is adjustment to the classroom    *11*
difficult. Good schooling requires that any student alter early childhood habits. But the working-class child is usually least prepared for the
change. And, unlike many middle-class children, he goes home and sees
in his parents a way of life not only different but starkly opposed to that
of the classroom. (He enters the house and hears his parents talking in
ways his teachers discourage.)

Without extraordinary determination and the great assistance of oth-    *12*
ers—at home and at school—there is little chance for success. Typically
most working-class children are barely changed by the classroom. The
exception succeeds. The relative few become scholarship students. Of
these, Richard Hoggart estimates, most manage a fairly graceful transition. Somehow they learn to live in the two very different worlds of

---

[1] All quotations in this selection are from Richard Hoggart, *The Uses of Literacy* (London: Chatto
and Windus, 1957), chapter 10.

their day. There are some others, however, those Hoggart pejoratively terms "scholarship boys," for whom success comes with special anxiety. Scholarship boy: good student, troubled son. The child is "moderately endowed," intellectually mediocre, Hoggart supposes—though it may be more pertinent to note the special qualities of temperament in the child. High-strung child. Brooding. Sensitive. Haunted by the knowledge that one *chooses* to become a student. (Education is not an inevitable or natural step in growing up.) Here is a child who cannot forget that his academic success distances him from a life he loved, even from his own memory of himself.

Initially, he wavers, balances allegiance. ("The boy is himself [until he      13
reaches, say, the upper forms] very much of *both* the worlds of home and school. He is enormously obedient to the dictates of the world of school, but emotionally still strongly wants to continue as part of the family circle.") Gradually, necessarily, the balance is lost. The boy needs to spend more and more time studying, each night enclosing himself in the silence permitted and required by intense concentration. He takes his first step toward academic success, away from his family.

From the very first days, through the years following, it will be with      14
his parents—the figures of lost authority, the persons toward whom he feels deepest love—that the change will be most powerfully measured. A separation will unravel between them. Advancing in his studies, the boy notices that his mother and father have not changed as much as he. Rather, when he sees them, they often remind him of the person he once was and the life he earlier shared with them. He realizes what some Romantics also know when they praise the working class for the capacity for human closeness, qualities of passion and spontaneity, that the rest of us experience in like measure only in the earliest part of our youth. For the Romantic, this doesn't make working-class life childish. Working-class life challenges precisely because it is an *adult* way of life.

The scholarship boy reaches a different conclusion. He cannot afford      15
to admire his parents. (How could he and still pursue such a contrary life?) He permits himself embarrassment at their lack of education. And to evade nostalgia for the life he has lost, he concentrates on the benefits education will bestow upon him. He becomes especially ambitious. Without the support of old certainties and consolations, almost mechanically, he assumes the procedures and doctrines of the classroom. The kind of allegiance the young student might have given his mother and father only days earlier, he transfers to the teacher, the new figure of authority. "[The scholarship boy] tends to make a father-figure of his form-master," Hoggart observes.

But Hoggart's calm prose only makes me recall the urgency with which      16
I came to idolize my grammar school teachers. I began by imitating their accents, using their diction, trusting their every direction. The very first facts they dispensed, I grasped with awe. Any book they told me to read,

I read—then waited for them to tell me which books I enjoyed. Their every casual opinion I came to adopt and to trumpet when I returned home. I stayed after school "to help"—to get my teacher's undivided attention. It was the nun's encouragement that mattered most to me. (She understood exactly what—my parents never seemed to appraise so well—all my achievements entailed.) Memory gently caressed each word of praise bestowed in the classroom so that compliments teachers paid me years ago come quickly to mind even today.

The enthusiasm I felt in second-grade classes I flaunted before both    17
my parents. The docile, obedient student came home a shrill and precocious son who insisted on correcting and teaching his parents with the remark: "My teacher told us. . . ."

I intended to hurt my mother and father. I was still angry at them for    18
having encouraged me toward classroom English. But gradually this anger was exhausted, replaced by guilt as school grew more and more attractive to me. I grew increasingly successful, a talkative student. My hand was raised in the classroom; I yearned to answer any question. At home, life was less noisy than it had been. (I spoke to classmates and teachers more often each day than to family members.) Quiet at home, I sat with my papers for hours each night. I never forgot that schooling had irretrievably changed my family's life. That knowledge, however, did not weaken ambition. Instead, it strengthened resolve. Those times I remembered the loss of my past with regret, I quickly reminded myself of all the things my teachers could give me. (They could make me an educated man.) I tightened my grip on pencil and books. I evaded nostalgia. Tried hard to forget. But one does not forget by trying to forget. One only remembers. I remembered too well that education had changed my family's life. I would not have become a scholarship boy had I not so often remembered.

Once she was sure that her children knew English, my mother would    19
tell us, "You should keep up your Spanish." Voices playfully groaned in response. "¡Pochos!" my mother would tease. I listened silently.

After a while, I grew more calm at home. I developed tact. A fourth-    20
grade student, I was no longer the show-off in front of my parents. I became a conventionally dutiful son, politely affectionate, cheerful enough, even—for reasons beyond choosing—my father's favorite. And much about my family life was easy then, comfortable, happy in the rhythm of our living together: hearing my father getting ready for work; eating the breakfast my mother had made me; looking up from a novel to hear my brother or one of my sisters playing with friends in the backyard; in winter, coming upon the house all lighted up after dark.

But withheld from my mother and father was any mention of what    21
most mattered to me: the extraordinary experience of first-learning. Late afternoon: In the midst of preparing dinner, my mother would come up behind me while I was trying to read. Her head just over mine, her breath

warmly scented with food. "What are you reading?" Or, "Tell me all about your new courses." I would barely respond, "Just the usual things, nothing special." (A half smile, then silence. Her head moving back in the silence. Silence! Instead of the flood of intimate sounds that had once flowed smoothly between us, there was this silence.) After dinner, I would rush to a bedroom with papers and books. As often as possible, I resisted parental pleas to "save lights" by coming to the kitchen to work. I kept so much, so often, to myself. Sad. Enthusiastic. Troubled by the excitement of coming upon new ideas. Eager. Fascinated by the promising texture of a brand-new book. I hoarded the pleasures of learning. Alone for hours. Enthralled. Nervous. I rarely looked away from my books—or back on my memories. Nights when relatives visited and the front rooms were warmed by Spanish sounds, I slipped quietly out of the house.

It mattered that education was changing me. It never ceased to matter. My brother and sisters would giggle at our mother's mispronounced words. They'd correct her gently. My mother laughed girlishly one night, trying not to pronounce *sheep* as *ship*. From a distance I listened sullenly. From that distance, pretending not to notice on another occasion, I saw my father looking at the title pages of my library books. That was the scene on my mind when I walked home with a fourth-grade companion and heard him say that his parents read to him every night. (A strange-sounding book—*Winnie the Pooh*.) Immediately, I wanted to know, "What is it like?" My companion, however, thought I wanted to know about the plot of the book. Another day, my mother surprised me by asking for a "nice" book to read. "Something not too hard you think I might like." Carefully I chose one, Willa Cather's *My Ántonia*. But when, several weeks later, I happened to see it next to her bed unread except for the first few pages, I was furious and suddenly wanted to cry. I grabbed up the book and took it back to my room and placed it in its place, alphabetically on my shelf.

"Your parents must be very proud of you." People began to say that to me about the time I was in sixth grade. To answer affirmatively, I'd smile. Shyly I'd smile, never betraying my sense of the irony: I was not proud of my mother and father. I was embarrassed by their lack of education. It was not that I ever thought they were stupid, though stupidly I took for granted their enormous native intelligence. Simply, what mattered to me was that they were not like my teachers.

But, "Why didn't you tell us about the award?" my mother demanded, her frown weakened by pride. At the grammar school ceremony several weeks after, her eyes were brighter than the trophy I'd won. Pushing back the hair from my forehead, she whispered that I had "shown" the *gringos*. A few minutes later, I heard my father speak to my teacher and felt ashamed of his labored, accented words. Then guilty for the shame. I felt such contrary feelings. (There is no simple roadmap through the heart of the scholarship boy.) My teacher was so soft-spoken and her words were edged sharp and clean. I admired her until it seemed to me that she spoke too carefully. Sensing that she was condescending to them, I became nervous. Resentful. Protective. I tried to move my parents away. "You both must be very proud of Richard," the nun said. They responded quickly. (They were proud.) "We are proud of all our children." Then this afterthought: "They sure didn't get their brains from us." They all laughed. I smiled.

## GERALD GRAFF

# Disliking Books

Gerald Graff received his BA in English from the University of Chicago and his PhD in English and American literature from Stanford University. In his distinguished academic career, he has taught at numerous universities and is currently a professor of English and education at the University of Illinois at Chicago. He is probably best known for his pedagogical theories, especially "teaching the controversies," an approach he argues for most famously in his book *Beyond the Culture Wars: How Teaching the Conflicts Can Revitalize American Education* (1993), from which this excerpt is taken. His other well-known books include *Literature Against Itself: Literary Ideas in Modern Society* (1979), *Professing Literature: An Institutional History* (1987), and *Clueless in Academe: How Schooling Obscures the Life of the Mind* (2003).

■  ■  ■

I like to think I have a certain advantage as a teacher of literature because when I was growing up I disliked and feared books. My youthful aversion to books showed a fine impartiality, extending across the whole spectrum of literature, history, philosophy, science, and what by then (the late 1940s) had come to be called social studies. But had I been forced to choose, I would have singled out literature and history as the reading I disliked most. Science at least had some discernible practical use, and you could have fun solving the problems in the textbooks with their clear-cut answers. Literature and history had no apparent application to my experience, and any boy in my school who had cultivated them—I can't recall one who did—would have marked himself as a sissy.

As a middle-class Jew growing up in an ethnically mixed Chicago neighborhood, I was already in danger of being beaten up daily by rougher working-class boys. Becoming a bookworm would have only given them a decisive reason for beating me up. Reading and studying were more permissible for girls, but they, too, had to be careful not to get too intellectual, lest they acquire the stigma of being "stuck up."

In *Lives on the Boundary*, a remarkable autobiography of the making of an English teacher, Mike Rose describes how the "pain and confusion" of his working-class youth made "school and knowledge" seem a saving alternative. Rose writes of feeling "freed, as if I were untying fetters," by his encounters with certain college teachers, who helped him recognize that "an engagement with ideas could foster competence and lead me out into the world."[1] Coming at things from my middle-class perspective, however, I took for granted a freedom that school, knowledge, and engagement with ideas seemed only to threaten.

My father, a literate man, was frustrated by my refusal to read anything besides comic books, sports magazines, and the John R. Tunis and Clair Bee sports novels. I recall his once confining me to my room until I finished a book on the voyages of Magellan, but try as I might, I could do no better than stare bleakly at the pages. I could not, as we would later say, "relate to" Magellan or to any of the other books my father brought home—detective stories, tales of war and heroism, adventure stories with adolescent heroes (the *Hardy Boys*, *Hans Brinker, or The Silver Skates*), stories of scientific discovery (Paul de Kruif's *Microbe Hunters*), books on current events. Nothing worked.

It was understood, however, that boys of my background would go to college and that once there we would get serious and buckle down. For some, "getting serious" meant prelaw, premed, or a major in business to prepare for taking over the family business. My family did not own a business, and law and medicine did not interest me, so I drifted by default into the nebulous but conveniently noncommittal territory of the liberal arts. I majored in English.

At this point the fear of being beaten up if I were caught having anything to do with books was replaced by the fear of flunking out of college if I did not learn to deal with them. But though I dutifully did my homework and made good grades (first at the University of Illinois, Chicago branch, then at the University of Chicago, from which I graduated in 1959), I continued to find "serious" reading painfully difficult and alien. My most vivid recollections of college reading are of assigned classics I failed to finish: *The Iliad* (in the Richmond Lattimore translation); *The Autobiography of Benvenuto Cellini*, a major disappointment after the paperback jacket's promise of "a lusty classic of Renaissance ribaldry"; E. M. Forster's *Passage to India*, sixty agonizing pages of which I managed to slog through before giving up. Even Hemingway, Steinbeck, and Fitzgerald, whose contemporary world was said to be "close to my own experience," left me cold. I saw little there that did resemble my experience.

[1] Mike Rose, *Lives on the Boundary* (New York: Free Press, 1989), pp. 46–47.

Even when I had done the assigned reading, I was often tongue-tied and embarrassed when called on. What was unclear to me was what I was supposed to *say* about literary works, and why. Had I been born a decade or two earlier, I might have come to college with the rudiments of a literate vocabulary for talking about culture that some people older than I acquired through family, high school, or church. As it was, "cultured" phrases seemed effete and sterile to me. When I was able to produce the kind of talk that was required in class, the intellectualism of it came out sounding stilted and hollow in my mouth. If *Cliffs Notes* and other such crib sheets for the distressed had yet come into existence, with their ready-to-copy summaries of widely taught literary works, I would have been an excellent customer. (As it was, I did avail myself of the primitive version then in existence called *Masterplots*.)

What first made literature, history, and other intellectual pursuits seem attractive to me was exposure to critical debates. There was no single conversion experience, but a gradual transformation over several years, extending into my first teaching positions, at the University of New Mexico and then Northwestern University. But one of the first sparks I remember was a controversy over *The Adventures of Huckleberry Finn* that arose in a course during my junior year in college. On first attempt, Twain's novel was just another assigned classic that I was too bored to finish. I could see little connection between my Chicago upbringing and Huck's pre–Civil War adventures with a runaway slave on a raft up the Mississippi.

My interest was aroused, however, when our instructor mentioned that the critics had disagreed over the merits of the last part of the novel. He quoted Ernest Hemingway's remark that "if you read [the novel] you must stop where the nigger Jim is stolen by the boys. This is the real end. The rest is cheating." According to this school of thought, the remainder of the book trivializes the quest for Jim's freedom that has motivated the story up to that point. This happens first when Jim becomes an object of Tom Sawyer's slapstick humor, then when it is revealed that unbeknownst to Huck, the reader, and himself, Jim has already been freed by his benevolent owner, so that the risk we have assumed Jim and Huck to be under all along has been really no risk at all.

Like the critics, our class divided over the question: Did Twain's ending vitiate the book's profound critique of racism, as Hemingway's charge of cheating implied? Cheating in my experience up to then was something students did, an unthinkable act for a famous author. It was a revelation to me that famous authors were capable not only of mistakes but of ones that even lowly undergraduates might be able to point out. When I chose to write my term paper on the dispute over the ending, my instructor suggested I look at several critics on the opposing sides, T. S. Eliot and Lionel Trilling, who defended the ending, and Leo Marx, who sided with Hemingway.

Reading the critics was like picking up where the class discussion had    *11*
left off, and I gained confidence from recognizing that my classmates and
I had had thoughts that, however stumbling our expression of them, were
not too far from the thoughts of famous published critics. I went back
to the novel again and to my surprise found myself rereading it with an
excitement I had never felt before with a serious book. Having the controversy over the ending in mind, I now had some issues *to watch out for*
as I read, issues that reshaped the way I read the earlier chapters as well
as the later ones and focused my attention. And having issues to watch
out for made it possible not only to concentrate, as I had not been able to
do earlier, but to put myself in the text—to read with a sense of personal
engagement that I had not felt before. Reading the novel with the voices
of the critics running through my mind, I found myself thinking of things
that I might say about what I was reading, things that may have belonged
partly to the critics but also now belonged to me. It was as if having a
stock of things to look for and to say about a literary work had somehow
made it possible for me to read one.

One of the critics had argued that what was at issue in the debate    *12*
over *Huckleberry Finn* was not just the novel's value but its cultural significance: If *Huckleberry Finn* was contradictory or confused in its attitude toward race, then what did that say about the culture that had
received the novel as one of its representative cultural documents and
had made Twain a folk hero? This critic had also made the intriguing
observation—I found out only later it was a critical commonplace at that
time—that judgments about the novel's aesthetic value could not be separated from judgments about its moral substance. I recall taking in both
this critic's arguments and the cadence of the phrases in which they were
couched; perhaps it would not be so bad after all to become the sort of
person who talked about "cultural contradictions" and the "inseparabil-
ity of form and content." Perhaps even mere literary-critical talk could
give you a certain power in the real world. As the possibility dawned on
me that reading and intellectual discussion might actually have something to do with my real life, I became less embarrassed about using the
intellectual formulas.

## The Standard Story

It was through exposure to such critical reading and discussion over a    *13*
period of time that I came to catch the literary bug, eventually choosing
the vocation of teaching. This was not the way it is supposed to happen.
In the standard story of academic vocation that we like to tell ourselves,
the germ is first planted by an early experience of literature itself. The
future teacher is initially inspired by some primary experience of a great
book and only subsequently acquires the secondary, derivative skills of

critical discussion. A teacher may be involved in instilling this inspiration, but a teacher who seemingly effaces himself or herself before the text. Any premature or excessive acquaintance with secondary critical discourse, and certainly with its sectarian debates, is thought to be a corrupting danger, causing one to lose touch with the primary passion for literature. . . .

The standard story ascribes innocence to the primary experience of    *14*
literature and sees the secondary experience of professional criticism as corrupting. In my case, however, things had evidently worked the other way around: I had to be corrupted first in order to experience innocence. It was only when I was introduced to a critical debate about *Huckleberry Finn* that my helplessness in the face of the novel abated and I could experience a personal reaction to it. Getting into immediate contact with the text was for me a curiously triangular business; I could not do it directly but needed a conversation of other readers to give me the issues and terms that made it possible to respond.

As I think back on it now, it was as if the critical conversation I needed    *15*
had up to then been withheld from me, on the ground that it could only interfere with my direct access to literature itself. The assumption was that leaving me alone with literary texts themselves, uncontaminated by the interpretations and theories of professional critics, would enable me to get on the closest possible terms with those texts. But being alone with the texts only left me feeling bored and helpless, since I had no language with which to make them mine. On the one hand, I was being asked to speak a foreign language—literary criticism—while on the other hand, I was being protected from that language, presumably for my own safety.

The moral I draw from this experience is that our ability to read well    *16*
depends more than we think on our ability to *talk well* about what we read. Our assumptions about what is "primary" and "secondary" in the reading process blind us to what actually goes on. Many literate people learned certain ways of talking about books so long ago that they have forgotten they ever had to learn them. These people therefore fail to understand the reading problems of the struggling students who have still not acquired a critical vocabulary.

How typical my case was is hard to say, but many of the students I    *17*
teach seem to have grown up as the same sort of nonintellectual, nonbookish person I was, and they seem to view literature with some of the same aversions, fears, and anxieties. That is why I like to think it is an advantage for a teacher to know what it feels like to grow up being indifferent to literature and intimidated by criticism and what it feels like to overcome a resistance to talking like an intellectual.

## A Practice Sequence: Composing a Literacy Narrative

Rodriguez and Graff have written autobiographical *literacy narratives* — their own stories of dealing with some aspects of how they became literate and their relationship with reading. Rodriguez's narrative is part of *Hunger of Memory: The Education of Richard Rodriguez*, a memoir that also explores the politics of language in American culture. Graff's narrative is embedded in his *Beyond the Culture Wars: How Teaching the Conflicts Can Revitalize American Education*, which, as the subtitle suggests, presents arguments and proposals for altering educational practices.

We would like you to write your own literacy narrative. The following practice sequence suggests some strategies for doing so.

1 Reflect on your experiences as a reader. Spend some time jotting down answers to these questions (not necessarily in this order) or to other related questions that occur to you as you write.

- Can you recall the time when you first began to read?
- What are the main types of reading you do? Why?
- How would you describe or characterize yourself as a reader?
- Is there one moment or event that encapsulates who you are as a reader?
- What are your favorite books, authors, and types of books? Why are they favorites?
- In what ways has reading changed you for the better? For the worse?
- What is the most important thing you've learned from reading?
- Have you ever learned something important from reading, only to discover later that it wasn't true, or sufficient? Explain.

2 Write your literacy narrative, focusing on at least one turning point, at least one moment of recognition or lesson learned. Write no fewer than two pages but no more than five pages. See where your story arc takes you. What do you conclude about your own "growing into literacy"?

3 Then start a conversation about literacy. Talk with some other people about their experiences. You might talk with some classmates — and not necessarily those in your writing class — about their memories of becoming literate. You might interview some people you grew up with — a parent, a sibling, a best friend — about their memories of you as a reader and writer and about their own

memories of becoming literate. Compare their memories to your own. Did you all have similar experiences? How were they different? Do you see things the same way? Then write down your impressions and what you think you may have learned.

4 Recast your literacy narrative, incorporating some of the insights you gathered from other people. How does your original narrative change? What new things now have to be accounted for?

5 Like Graff, who takes his own experience as a starting point for proposing new educational policies, can you imagine your insights having larger implications? Explain. Do you think what you've learned from reading Graff's and Rodriguez's literacy narratives has implications for the ways reading is taught in school?

# 2

# From Reading as a Writer to Writing as a Reader

Reading for class and then writing an essay might seem to be separate tasks, but reading is the first step in the writing process. In this chapter we present methods that will help you read more effectively and move from reading to writing your own college essays. These methods will lead you to understand a writer's purpose in responding to a situation, the motivation for asserting a claim in an essay and entering a particular conversation with a particular audience.

## READING AS AN ACT OF COMPOSING: ANNOTATING

Leaving your mark on the page—**annotating**—is your first act of composing. When you mark the pages of a text, you are reading critically, engaging with the ideas of others, questioning and testing those ideas, and inquiring into their significance. **Critical reading** is sometimes called *active reading* to distinguish it from memorization, when you just read for the main idea so that you can "spit it back out on a test." When you read actively and critically, you bring your knowledge, experiences, and interests to a text, so that you can respond to the writer, continuing the conversation the writer has begun.

Experienced college readers don't try to memorize a text or assume they must understand it completely before they respond to it. Instead they read strategically, looking for the writer's claims, for the writer's key ideas and terms, and for connections with key ideas and terms in other texts. They also read to discern what conversation the writer has entered, and how the writer's argument is connected to those he or she makes reference to.

When you annotate a text, your notes in the margins might address the following questions:

- What arguments is this author responding to?
- Is the issue relevant or significant?
- How do I know that what the author says is true?
- Is the author's evidence legitimate? Sufficient?
- Can I think of an exception to the author's argument?
- What would the counterarguments be?

Good readers ask the same kinds of questions of every text they read, considering not just *what* a writer says (the content), but *how* he or she says it given the writer's purpose and audience.

The marks you leave on a page might indicate your own ideas and questions, patterns you see emerging, links to other texts, even your gut response to the writer's argument—agreement, dismay, enthusiasm, confusion. They reveal your own thought processes as you read and signal that you are entering the conversation. In effect, they are traces of your own responding voice.

Developing your own system of marking or annotating pages can help you feel confident when you sit down with a new reading for your classes. Based on our students' experiences, we offer this practical tip: Although wide-tipped highlighters have their place in some classes, it is more useful to read with a pen or pencil in your hand, so that you can do more than draw a bar of color through words or sentences you find important. Experienced readers write their responses to a text in the margins, using personal codes (boxing key words, for example), writing out definitions of words they have looked up, drawing lines to connect ideas on facing pages, or writing notes to themselves ("Connect this to Edmundson on consumer culture"; "Hirsch would disagree big time—see his ideas on memorization in primary grades"; "You call THIS evidence?!"). These notes help you get started on your own writing assignments, and you cannot make them with a highlighter.

Annotating your readings benefits you twice. First, it is easier to participate in class discussions if you have already marked passages that are important, confusing, or linked to specific passages in other texts you have read. It's a sure way to avoid that sinking feeling you get when you return to pages you read the night before but now can't remember at all. Second, by marking key ideas in a text, noting your ideas about them, and making connections to key ideas in other texts, you have begun the process of writing an essay. When you start writing the first draft of your essay, you can quote the passages you have already marked and explain what you find significant about them based on the notes you have already made to yourself. You can make the connections to other texts in the paragraphs of your own essay that you have already begun to make on the pages of your textbook. If you mark your texts effectively, you'll never be at a loss when you sit down to write the first draft of an essay.

Let's take a look at how one of our students marked several paragraphs of Douglas Massey and Nancy Denton's *American Apartheid: Segregation and the Making of the Underclass* (1993). In the excerpt below, the student underlines what she believes is important information and begins to create an outline of the authors' main points.

| | |
|---|---|
| *1. racist attitudes*<br><br>*2. private behaviors*<br><br>*3. & institutional practices*<br>*lead to ghettos*<br>*(authors' claim?)*<br><br>*Ghetto = multistory,*<br>*high-density housing*<br>*projects.*<br>*Post-1950*<br><br>*I remember this hap-*<br>*pening where I grew up,*<br>*but I didn't know the*<br>*government was*<br>*responsible. Is this*<br>*what happened in*<br>*There Are No Children*<br>*Here?* | The spatial isolation of black Americans was achieved by      *1*<br>a conjunction of <u>racist attitudes</u>, <u>private behaviors</u>, and<br><u>institutional practices</u> that disenfranchised blacks from<br>urban housing markets and led to the creation of the <u>ghetto</u>.<br>Discrimination in employment exacerbated black poverty<br>and limited the economic potential for integration, and black<br>residential mobility was systematically blocked by pervasive<br>discrimination and white avoidance of neighborhoods con-<br>taining blacks. <u>The walls of the ghetto were buttressed after</u><br><u>1950</u> by government programs that promoted slum clearance<br>and <u>relocated displaced ghetto residents into multi-story,</u><br><u>high-density housing projects.</u> |
| | In theory, this self-reinforcing cycle of prejudice, dis-      *2*<br>crimination, and segregation was broken during the 1960s<br>by a growing rejection of racist sentiments by whites and a<br>series of court decisions and federal laws that banned dis-<br>crimination in public life. (1) <u>The Civil Rights Act of 1964</u><br><u>outlawed racial discrimination in employment,</u> (2) <u>the Fair</u><br><u>Housing Act of 1968 banned discrimination in housing,</u> and |
| *Authors say situation*<br>*of "spatial isolation"*<br>*remains despite court*<br>*decisions. Does it?* | (3) the <u>*Gautreaux*</u> and <u>*Shannon* court decisions prohibited</u><br><u>public authorities from placing housing projects</u> exclusively<br>in black neighborhoods. Despite these changes, however, the<br><u>nation's largest black communities remained as segregated</u><br><u>as ever in 1980.</u> Indeed, many urban areas displayed a<br>pattern of intense racial isolation that could only be<br>described as <u>hypersegregation</u>. |
| *Subtler racism, not*<br>*on public record.* | Although the racial climate of the United States      *3*<br>improved outwardly during the 1970s, <u>racism still restricted</u><br><u>the residential freedom of black Americans;</u> it just did so in<br>less blatant ways. In the aftermath of the civil rights revolu-<br>tion, few whites voiced openly racist sentiments; realtors<br>no longer refused outright to rent or sell to blacks; and few |
| *Lack of enforcement*<br>*of Civil Rights Act?*<br>*Fair Housing Act?*<br>*Gautreaux and*<br>*Shannon? Why?*<br>*Why not?* | local governments went on record to oppose public housing<br>projects because they would contain blacks. This lack of<br>overt racism, however, did not mean that prejudice and dis-<br>crimination had ended. |

Notice how the student underlines information that helps her understand the argument the authors make.

1. She numbers the three key factors (racist attitudes, private behaviors, and institutional practices) that influenced the formation of ghettos in the United States.

2. She identifies the situation that motivates the authors' analysis: the extent to which "the spatial isolation of black Americans" still exists despite laws and court decisions designed to end residential segregation.

3. She makes connections to her own experience and to another book she has read.

By understanding the authors' arguments and making these connections, the student begins the writing process. She also sets the stage for her own research, for examining the authors' claim that residential segregation still exists.

## READING AS A WRITER: ANALYZING A TEXT RHETORICALLY

When you study how writers influence readers through language, you are analyzing the **rhetoric** (available means of persuasion) of what you read. When you identify a writer's purpose for responding to a situation by composing an essay that puts forth claims meant to sway a particular audience, you are performing **rhetorical analysis**—separating out the parts of an argument to better understand how the argument works as a whole. We discuss each of these elements—*situation, purpose, claims*, and *audience*—as we analyze the following preface from E. D. Hirsch's book *Cultural Literacy: What Every American Needs to Know* (1987). Formerly a professor of English, Hirsch has long been interested in educational reform. That interest developed from his (and others') perception that today's students do not know as much as students did in the past. Although Hirsch wrote the book more than twenty years ago, many observers still believe that the contemporary problems of illiteracy and poverty can be traced to a lack of cultural literacy.

Read the preface. You may want to mark it with your own questions and responses, and then consider them in light of our analysis (following the preface) of Hirsch's rhetorical situation, purpose, claims, and audience.

## E. D. HIRSCH JR.

# Preface to *Cultural Literacy*

E. D. Hirsch Jr., a retired English professor, is the author of many acclaimed books, including *The Schools We Need and Why We Don't Have Them* (1996) and *The Knowledge Deficit* (2006). His book *Cultural Literacy* was a best seller in 1987 and had a profound effect on the focus of education in the late 1980s and 1990s.

■ ■ ■

Rousseau points out the facility with which children lend themselves to our false methods: . . ."The apparent ease with which children learn is their ruin."

—JOHN DEWEY

There is no matter what children should learn first, any more than what leg you should put into your breeches first. Sir, you may stand disputing which is best to put in first, but in the meantime your backside is bare. Sir, while you stand considering which of two things you should teach your child first, another boy has learn't 'em both.

—SAMUEL JOHNSON

To be culturally literate is to possess the basic information needed to thrive in the modern world. The breadth of that information is great, extending over the major domains of human activity from sports to science. It is by no means confined to "culture" narrowly understood as an acquaintance with the arts. Nor is it confined to one social class. Quite the contrary. Cultural literacy constitutes the only sure avenue of opportunity for disadvantaged children, the only reliable way of combating the social determinism that now condemns them to remain in the same social and educational condition as their parents. That children from poor and illiterate homes tend to remain poor and illiterate is an unacceptable failure of our schools, one which has occurred not because our teachers are inept but chiefly because they are compelled to teach a fragmented curriculum based on faulty educational theories. Some say that our schools by themselves are powerless to change the cycle of poverty and illiteracy. I do not agree. They *can* break the cycle, but only if they themselves break fundamentally with some of the theories and practices that education professors and school administrators have followed over the past fifty years.

Although the chief beneficiaries of the educational reforms advocated in this book will be disadvantaged children, these same reforms will also enhance the literacy of children from middle-class homes. The educational goal advocated is that of mature literacy for *all* our citizens.

The connection between mature literacy and cultural literacy may already be familiar to those who have closely followed recent discussions of education. Shortly after the publication of my essay "Cultural Literacy," Dr. William Bennett, then chairman of the National Endowment for the Humanities and subsequently secretary of education in President Ronald Reagan's second administration, championed its ideas. This endorsement from an influential person of conservative views gave my ideas some currency, but such an endorsement was not likely to recommend the concept to liberal thinkers, and in fact the idea of cultural literacy has been attacked by some liberals on the assumption that I must be advocating a list of great books that every child in the land should be forced to read.

But those who examine the Appendix to this book will be able to judge       4
for themselves how thoroughly mistaken such an assumption is. Very few specific titles appear on the list, and they usually appear as words, not works, because they represent writings that culturally literate people have read about but haven't read. *Das Kapital* is a good example. Cultural literacy is represented not by a *prescriptive* list of books but rather by a *descriptive* list of the information actually possessed by literate Americans. My aim in this book is to contribute to making that information the possession of all Americans.

The importance of such widely shared information can best be under-       5
stood if I explain briefly how the idea of cultural literacy relates to currently prevailing theories of education. The theories that have dominated American education for the past fifty years stem ultimately from Jean Jacques Rousseau, who believed that we should encourage the natural development of young children and not impose adult ideas upon them before they can truly understand them. Rousseau's conception of education as a process of natural development was an abstract generalization meant to apply to all children in any time or place: to French children of the eighteenth century or to Japanese or American children of the twentieth century. He thought that a child's intellectual and social skills would develop naturally without regard to the specific content of education. His content-neutral conception of educational development has long been triumphant in American schools of education and has long dominated the "developmental," content-neutral curricula of our elementary schools.

In the first decades of this century, Rousseau's ideas powerfully influ-       6
enced the educational conceptions of John Dewey, the writer who has the most deeply affected modern American educational theory and practice. Dewey's clearest and, in his time, most widely read book on education, *Schools of Tomorrow*, acknowledges Rousseau as the chief source of his educational principles. The first chapter of Dewey's book carries the telling title "Education as Natural Development" and is sprinkled with quotations from Rousseau. In it Dewey strongly seconds Rousseau's opposition to the mere accumulation of information.

Development emphasizes the need of intimate and extensive personal acquaintance with a small number of typical situations with a view to mastering the way of dealing with the problems of experience, not the piling up of information.

Believing that a few direct experiences would suffice to develop the skills that children require, Dewey assumed that early education need not be tied to specific content. He mistook a half-truth for the whole. He placed too much faith in children's ability to learn general skills from a few typical experiences and too hastily rejected "the piling up of information." Only by piling up specific, communally shared information can children learn to participate in complex cooperative activities with other members of their community.

This old truth, recently rediscovered, requires a countervailing theory of education that once again stresses the importance of specific information in early and late schooling. The corrective theory might be described as an anthropological theory of education, because it is based on the anthropological observation that all human communities are founded upon specific shared information. Americans are different from Germans, who in turn are different from Japanese, because each group possesses specifically different cultural knowledge. In an anthropological perspective, the basic goal of education in a human community is acculturation, the transmission to children of the specific information shared by the adults of the group or polis.

Plato, that other great educational theorist, believed that the specific contents transmitted to children are by far the most important elements of education. In *The Republic* he makes Socrates ask rhetorically, "Shall we carelessly allow children to hear any casual tales which may be devised by casual persons, and to receive into their minds ideas for the most part the very opposite of those which we shall wish them to have when they are grown up?" Plato offered good reasons for being concerned with the specific contents of schooling, one of them ethical: "For great is the issue at stake, greater than appears—whether a person is to be good or bad."

Time has shown that there is much truth in the durable educational theories of both Rousseau and Plato. But even the greatest thinkers, being human, see mainly in one direction at a time, and no thinkers, however profound, can foresee the future implications of their ideas when they are translated into social policy. The great test of social ideas is the crucible of history, which, after a time, usually discloses a one-sidedness in the best of human generalizations. History, not superior wisdom, shows us that neither the content-neutral curriculum of Rousseau and Dewey nor the narrowly specified curriculum of Plato is adequate to the needs of a modern nation.

Plato rightly believed that it is natural for children to learn an adult culture, but too confidently assumed that philosophy could devise the one best culture. (Nonetheless, we should concede to Plato that within our culture we have an obligation to choose and promote our best traditions.) On the other side, Rousseau and Dewey wrongly believed that adult culture is "unnatural" to young children. Rousseau, Dewey, and their present-day disciples have not shown an adequate appreciation of the need for transmission of specific cultural information.

In contrast to the theories of Plato and Rousseau, an anthropological   *12* theory of education accepts the naturalness as well as the relativity of human cultures. It deems it neither wrong nor unnatural to teach young children adult information before they fully understand it. The anthropological view stresses the universal fact that a human group must have effective communications to function effectively, that effective communications require shared culture, and that shared culture requires transmission of specific information to children. Literacy, an essential aim of education in the modern world, is no autonomous, empty skill but depends upon literate culture. Like any other aspect of acculturation, literacy requires the early and continued transmission of specific information. Dewey was deeply mistaken to disdain "accumulating information in the form of symbols." Only by accumulating shared symbols, and the shared information that the symbols represent, can we learn to communicate effectively with one another in our national community.

Now let's take a look at the steps to rhetorical analysis.

## ■ Identify the Situation

The **situation** is what moves a writer to write. To understand what motivated Hirsch to write, we need look no further than the situation he identifies in the first paragraph of the preface: "the social determinism that now condemns [disadvantaged children] to remain in the same social and educational condition as their parents." Hirsch wants to make sure his readers are aware of the problem so that they will be motivated to read his argument (and take action). He presents as an urgent problem the situation of disadvantaged children, an indication of what is at stake for the writer and for the readers of the argument. For Hirsch, this situation needs to change.

The urgency of a writer's argument is not always triggered by a single situation; often it is multifaceted. Again in the first paragraph, Hirsch identifies a second concern when he states that poverty and illiteracy reflect "an unacceptable failure of our schools, one which has occurred not because our teachers are inept but chiefly because they are compelled to teach a fragmented curriculum based on faulty educational theories." When he introduces a second problem, Hirsch helps us see the interconnected and complex nature of the situations authors confront in academic writing.

## ■ Identify the Writer's Purpose

The **purpose** for writing an essay may be to respond to a particular situation; it also can be what a writer is trying to accomplish. Specifically, what does the writer want readers to do? Does the writer want us to think about an issue, to change our opinions? Does the writer want to make us aware of a problem that we may not have recognized? Does the writer advocate for some type of change? Or is some combination of all three at work?

Hirsch's main purpose is to promote educational reforms that will produce a higher degree of literacy for all citizens. He begins his argument with a broad statement about the importance of cultural literacy: "Cultural literacy constitutes the only sure avenue of opportunity for disadvantaged children, the only reliable way of combating the social determinism that now condemns them to remain in the same social and educational condition as their parents" (para. 1). As his argument unfolds, his purpose continues to unfold as well. He identifies the schools as a source of the problem and suggests how they must change to promote literacy:

> Some say that our schools by themselves are powerless to change the cycle of poverty and illiteracy. I do not agree. They *can* break the cycle, but only if they themselves break fundamentally with some of the theories and practices that education professors and school administrators have followed over the past fifty years. (para. 1)

The "educational goal," Hirsch declares at the end of paragraph 2, is "mature literacy for *all* our citizens." To reach that goal, he insists, education must break with the past. In paragraphs 5 through 11, he cites the influence of Jean-Jacques Rousseau, John Dewey, and Plato, tracing what he sees as the educational legacies of the past. Finally, in the last paragraph of the excerpt, Hirsch describes an "anthropological view, . . . the universal fact that a human group must have effective communications to function effectively, that effective communications require shared culture, and that shared culture requires transmission of specific information to children." It is here, Hirsch argues, in the "transmission of specific information to children," that schools must do a better job.

## ■ Identify the Writer's Claims

**Claims** are assertions that authors must justify and support with evidence and good reasons. The **thesis**, or **main claim**, is the controlling idea that crystallizes a writer's main point, helping readers track the idea as it develops throughout the essay. A writer's purpose clearly influences the way he or she crafts the main claim of an argument, the way he or she presents all assertions and evidence.

Hirsch's main claim is that "cultural literacy constitutes the only sure avenue of opportunity for disadvantaged children, the only reliable way of combating the social determinism that now condemns them to remain in the same social and educational condition as their parents" (para. 1). Notice that his thesis also points to a solution: making cultural literacy the core of public school curricula. Here we distinguish the main claim, or thesis, from the other claims or assertions that Hirsch makes. For example, at the very outset, Hirsch states that "to be culturally literate is to possess the basic information needed to thrive in the modern world." Although this is an assertion that requires support, it is a **minor claim**; it does not shape what Hirsch writes in the remainder of his essay. His main claim, or thesis, is really his call for reform.

### ■ Identify the Writer's Audience

A writer's language can help us identify his or her **audience**, the readers whose opinions and actions the writer hopes to influence or change. In Hirsch's text, words and phrases like *social determinism, cycle of poverty and illiteracy, educational reforms, prescriptive*, and *anthropological* indicate that Hirsch believes his audience is well educated. References to Plato, Socrates, Rousseau, and Dewey also indicate the level of knowledge Hirsch expects of his readers.

Finally, the way the preface unfolds suggests that Hirsch is writing for an audience that is familiar with a certain **genre**, or type, of writing: the formal argument. Notice how the author begins with a statement of the situation and then asserts his position. The very fact that he includes a preface speaks to the formality of his argument. Hirsch's language, his references, and the structure of the document all suggest that he is very much in conversation with people who are experienced and well-educated readers.

More specifically, the audience Hirsch invokes is made up of people who are concerned about illiteracy in the United States and the kind of social determinism that appears to condemn the educationally disadvantaged to poverty. Hirsch also acknowledges directly "those who have closely followed recent discussions of education," including the conservative William Bennett and liberal thinkers who might be provoked by Bennett's advocacy of Hirsch's ideas (para. 3). Moreover, Hirsch appears to assume that his readers have achieved "mature literacy," even if they are not actually "culturally literate." He is writing for an audience that not only is well educated but also is deeply interested in issues of education as they relate to social policy.

---

### Steps to Analyzing a Text Rhetorically

**1** **Identify the situation.** What motivates the writer to write?

**2** **Identify the writer's purpose.** What does the writer want readers to do or think about?

**3** **Identify the writer's claims.** What is the writer's main claim? What minor claims does he or she make?

**4** **Identify the writer's audience.** What do you know about the writer's audience? What does the writer's language imply about the readers? What about the writer's references? The structure of the essay?

Hirsch's writings on cultural literacy have inspired and provoked many responses to the conversation he initiated more than twenty years ago. Eugene F. Provenzo's book *Critical Literacy: What Every American Needs to Know*, published in 2005, is a fairly recent one. Provenzo examines the source of Hirsch's ideas, his critiques of scholars like John Dewey, the extent to which Hirsch's argument is based on sound research, and the implications of Hirsch's notion of cultural literacy for teaching and learning. Despite the passage of time, Hirsch's book remains relevant in discussions about the purpose of education, demonstrating how certain works become touchstones and the ways academic and cultural conversations can be sustained over time.

## A Practice Sequence: Analyzing a Text Rhetorically

To practice the strategies of rhetorical analysis, we would like you to read "Hirsch's Desire for a National Curriculum," an excerpt from Eugene F. Provenzo's book, using these questions as a guide:

- What motivates Provenzo as a writer?
- What does he want readers to think about?
- What is Provenzo's main point?
- Given the language Provenzo uses, who do you think his main audience is?

## EUGENE F. PROVENZO JR.

# Hirsch's Desire for a National Curriculum

Eugene F. Provenzo Jr. is a professor in the Department of Teaching and Learning in the School of Education at the University of Miami in Coral Gables, Florida. His career as a researcher has been interdisciplinary in nature. Throughout his work, his primary focus has been on education as a social and cultural phenomenon. One of his prime concerns has been the role of the teacher in American society. He is also interested in the impact of computers on contemporary children, education, and culture. He is author or co-author of numerous books, including *Teaching, Learning, and Schooling: A Twenty-first Century Perspective* (2001); *Internet and Online Research for Teachers* (Third Edition, 2004); and *Observing in Schools: A Guide for Students in Teacher Education* (2005).

■ ■ ■

To a large extent, Hirsch, in his efforts as an educational reformer, wants to establish a national curriculum.

*1*

Our elementary schools are not only dominated by the content-neutral ideas of Rousseau and Dewey, they are also governed by approximately sixteen thousand independent school districts. We have viewed this dispersion of educational authority as an insurmountable obstacle to altering the fragmentation of the school curriculum even when we have questioned that fragmentation. We have permitted school policies that have shrunk the body of information that Americans share and these policies have caused our national literacy to decline.

This is an interesting argument when interpreted in a conservative political context. While calling for greater local control, Hirsch and other conservatives call for a curriculum that is controlled not at the state and local level, but at the national level by the federal government.

Putting contradictions like this aside, the question arises as to whether    2 or not Hirsch even has a viable curriculum. In an early review of Hirsch's *Cultural Literacy*, Hazel Whitman Hertzberg criticized the book and its list of 5,000 things every American needs to know for its fragmentation. As she explained:

Hirsch's remedy for curricular fragmentation looks suspiciously like more fragmentation. Outside of the dubious claim that his list represents what literate people know, there is nothing that holds it together besides its arrangement in alphabetical order. Subject-matter organization is ignored. It is not hard to imagine how Hirsch's proposal would have been greeted by educational neoconservatives had it been made by one of those professors of education who he charges are responsible for the current state of cultural illiteracy.

Hertzberg wonders what Hirsch's "hodgepodge of miscellaneous, arbitrary, and often trivial information" would look like if it were put into a coherent curriculum.

In 1988 Hirsch did in fact establish the Core Knowledge Foundation,    3 which had as its purpose the design of a national curriculum. Called the "Core Knowledge Sequence," the sequence offered a curriculum in six content areas: history, geography, mathematics, science, language arts, and fine arts. Hirsch's curriculum was intended to represent approximately half of the total curriculum for K–6 schools. Subsequent curriculum revisions include a curriculum for grades seven and eight as well as one at the preschool level.

Several hundred schools across the United States currently use Hirsch's    4 model. A national conference is held each year, which draws several thousand people. In books like *What Your First Grader Needs to Know* (1991) as well *A First Dictionary of Cultural Literacy: What Our Children Need to Know* (1989) and *The Dictionary of Cultural Literacy* (1993), along with the Core Knowledge Sequence, one finds a fairly conservative but generally useful curriculum that conforms to much of the content already found in local school systems around the country.

Hirsch seems not to recognize that there indeed is a national curric-      5
ulum, one whose standards are set by local communities through their
acceptance and rejection of textbooks and by national accreditation
groups ranging from the National Council of Teachers of Mathematics to
the National Council for Social Studies Teachers and the National Council of Teachers of English. One need only look at standards in different
subject areas in school districts across the country to realize the extent to
which there is indeed a national curriculum.

Whether the current curriculum in use in the schools across the coun-      6
try is adequate is of course open to debate. Creating any curriculum is by
definition a deeply political act, and is, or should be, subject to considerable negotiation and discussion at any level. But to act as though there is
not a de facto national curriculum is simply inaccurate. First graders in
most school districts across the country learn about the weather and the
seasons, along with more basic skills like adding and subtracting. Students do not learn to divide before they learn how to add or multiply.
Local and state history is almost universally introduced for the first time
in either third or fourth grade. It is reintroduced in most states at the seventh or eighth grade levels. Algebra is typically taught in the ninth grade.
Traditions, developmental patterns of students, textbook content, and
national subject standards combine to create a fairly uniform national
curriculum.

Hirsch's complaint that there is no national curriculum is not moti-      7
vated by a desire to establish one but rather a desire to establish a curriculum that reflects his cultural and ideological orientation. It is a
sophisticated assault on more inclusive and diverse models of curriculum and culture—one that represents a major battle in the culture wars
of the last twenty years in the United States.

## WRITING AS A READER: COMPOSING A RHETORICAL ANALYSIS

One of our favorite exercises is to ask our students to choose a single paragraph from a text they have read and to write a rhetorical analysis of it.
Once you are able to identify *how* writers make their arguments, you are
better able to make use of their strategies in your own writing. You may be
amazed by how much you can say or write about a single paragraph in an
essay once you begin to consider such factors as purpose and audience.

For example, one of our students wrote a rhetorical analysis of a paragraph from Sidonie Smith and Julia Watson's *Reading Autobiography: A
Guide for Interpreting Life Narratives* (2001). In the following passage from

Smith and Watson's book, they discuss the concept of *agency*. Scholars in fields such as sociology have sought to explain the relationship between individuals and the institutions that influence their everyday lives—education, capitalism, and politics. Scholars recognize that the values, beliefs, and linguistic practices of a community can exert pressures on and even limit the ways individuals make decisions and take action—that is, the ways they assert a sense of agency. How do individuals create, innovate, and make choices apart from the communities they inhabit or the institutions that have such a significant impact on them? Smith and Watson draw on scholarship in literary criticism to think about what it means to act with a sense of agency in writing autobiography, a form of life narrative.

Note that in the passage, Smith and Watson cite numerous other writers and works, sometimes generally (Catherine Belsey on subject construction) and sometimes very specifically (a direct quotation from an argument by Elizabeth Wingrove). For reasons of space—and because they don't bear on the assignment—the full list of works cited for the passage has been omitted.

## ■ Write a Rhetorical Analysis of a Paragraph

Read this passage, making notes on its rhetorical situation, purpose, main claim, and audience. You may want to underline passages where the writers make the following points explicit:

- the situation to which they are responding
- the purpose of their analysis and argument
- their main claim or thesis
- who they believe their audience is

### SIDONIE SMITH AND JULIA WATSON

## Agency

Sidonie Smith is the Martha Guernsey Colby Collegiate Professor of English and Women's Studies at the University of Michigan. Her fields of specialization include autobiography studies, narrative and human rights, feminist theories, and women's studies in literature. She has additional interests in travel narratives, literature and memory, and postcolonial literatures and theory.

Julia Watson is associate dean in arts and humanities and professor of comparative studies at the Ohio State University. Her interests include life narrative and theory of autobiography, feminist theory and women's writing, twentieth-century postcolonial and multicultural autobiography, and visual autobiography and film.

■ ■ ■

W e like to think of human beings as agents of or actors in their own lives,    *1*
rather than passive pawns in social games or unconscious transmitters
of cultural scripts and models of identity. Consequently, we tend to read
autobiographical narratives as proofs of human agency, relating actions
in which people exercise free choice over the interpretation of their lives
and express their true selves. In fact, traditional autobiography has been
read as a narrative of agency, evidence that subjects can live freely. But we
must recognize that the issue of how subjects claim, exercise, and narrate
agency is far more complicated.

We have noted that discursive systems emergent in social structures shape    *2*
the operations of memory, experience, identity, and embodiment. People
tell stories of their lives through the cultural scripts available to them, and
they are governed by cultural strictures about self-presentation in public. If
individuals are constituted through discursive practices, how, then, can they
be said to control the stories they tell about themselves? Some contemporary investigations of agency are helpful in addressing this question.

## Theories of Agency

Analysts of agency have found the theorist Louis Althusser helpful in    *3*
thinking through these issues. Althusser argued that the subject is a subject of ideology—not in the narrow sense of propaganda but in the broad
sense of the pervasive cultural formations of the dominant class. Althusser
recognized the power of coercive state institutions to conform subjects to
particular behaviors, beliefs, and identities—institutions such as the military and the police. He also recognized that there are less overtly coercive
institutions—social services, educational institutions, the family, literary
and artistic institutions—that "hail" subjects who enter them. By "hail-
ing" Althusser meant the process through which subjects become inter-
pellated, become what institutional discourses and practices make of them.
They are "subjected." Most important, individuals understand themselves
to be "naturally" self-produced because the power of ideology to hail the
subject is hidden, obscured by the very practices of the institution. In this
way, people are invested in and mystified by their own production as subjects, by their own "subjection." That is, they have "false consciousness":
they collude in their own lack of agency by believing that they have it. It is
not enough, then, to say that people exercise free will. The concept of "free
will" is itself embedded in a discourse about the Enlightenment individual,
a historically specific discourse through which subjects understand themselves as intellectually mature and free to make their own choices. To claim
that all humans have something called "free will" in this way is to misunder-
stand an ideological concept as a "natural" aspect of existence.

Other theorists have taken this challenge to agency as a starting point    *4*
from which to rethink its possibility. Political theorist Elizabeth Wingrove,

in rereading Althusser, argues that "agents change, and change their world, by virtue of the systemic operation of multiple ideologies." The key here is the multiplicity of ideologies through which the subject is hailed. These multiple ideologies "expose both the subject and the system to perpetual reconfiguration" (871). In that reconfiguration new possibilities emerge for knowing oneself as a subject and for understanding a system. (See also Catherine Belsey on subject construction.)

French sociologist and theorist Michel de Certeau locates agency in      5
what he terms "transverse tactics." Individuals and groups deploy such tactics to manipulate the spaces in which they are constrained, such as the workplace or the housing project. For instance, a factory worker may superimpose another system (of language or culture) onto the system imposed on him in the factory. Combining systems, he can create "a space in which he can find ways of using the constraining order of the place or of the language" to establish "a degree of plurality and creativity." Such modes of "re-use," then, are interventions that open a space of agency within constrained systems (29–30). For the French theorist Jean-François Lyotard the flexible and uncontrollable networks of language, through which people construct their worlds, spawn unexpected moves and countermoves. As a result language itself holds strategic potential for the formation of new sociopolitical subjects.

For postcolonial theorist Arjun Appadurai, agency in this particular      6
historical moment of global capitalism resides in imagination mobilized as "an organized field of social practices" (327). Imagination negotiates between "sites of agency," namely, the imagined communities in which we participate, and "globally defined fields of possibility" (327). Situated amid multiple forms of imagined worlds, individuals as sites of agency deploy their imaginations as a social fact and a kind of work to navigate the disjunctures of global flows that create radically different self-understandings.

Feminist philosopher Judith Butler situates agency in what she calls the      7
"performativity" of subjectivity. According to Butler, identity is enacted daily through socially enforced norms that surround us. Thus it is through our reenactment of the norms of, say, masculinity or femininity that we know ourselves to be "a heterosexual man" or "a woman." But this enforcement of norms cannot be totally effective since individuals fail to conform fully to them because of the multiplicity of norms we are called to reenact in our everyday lives. The failure to conform signals the "possibility of a variation" of "the rules that govern intelligible identity." And with failure come reconfigurations or changes of identities (*Gender Trouble*, 145).

Like Butler, feminist theorist Teresa de Lauretis defines the unconscious      8
as a potential source of agency. The unconscious is a psychic domain of disidentification ("Eccentric Subjects," 125–27), a repository of all the experiences and desires that have to be repressed in order for the subject to conform to socially enforced norms. As such, it lies at the intersection of the psychic and the social. A repository of the repressed, the unconscious

is also a potential site of agency; its excess is a source of resistance to socially enforced calls to fixed identities. And the anthropologist Sherry B. Ortner situates agency in the ability with which people play the "games" of culture—with their rules and structures—with wit and intelligence. For Ortner, sociocultural structures are always partial rather than total. And thus here is always the possibility of changing the rules—although not of escaping rules altogether.

We have briefly noted several theorizings of agency as multiple: ideologies; transverse tactics and modes of disuse; the flexible network of language; the navigation of imagined communities; performativity; psychic disidentification; the games of culture. These concepts offer critical frameworks for considering how people, in the act of narrating their lives, might change the stories they tell, might gain access to other cultural scripts, might come to understand themselves differently, might, that is, exercise agency. *9*

Now read our student's rhetorical analysis of paragraph 3 from Smith and Watson's piece on agency; we have annotated her analysis to point out the moves she is making in her own writing.

*The student states what she believes is the authors' purpose.*

The particular paragraph that I chose in *Reading Autobiography: A Guide for Interpreting Life Narratives* begins a discussion on the various theories of agency. Its purpose is to investigate the concept of agency in order to determine how individuals can be said to control the stories they tell about themselves. *1*

*The student identifies the audience based on the kind of information the authors provide. She also states their purpose: the context that prompts their discussion.*

The authors assume that the audience has very little or no background about how the concept of agency has been approached in various theories and scholarly interpretations. This is evidenced by the fact that the paragraph essentially introduces and explains a popular theory. By explaining the theory, Smith and Watson are attempting to establish the various contexts in which autobiography is interpreted and understood. *2*

*She underscores the writers' style and method of argument, which makes use of others' ideas. Their use of evidence affects their tone.*

In order to further their own ideas about agency and provide further guides to the study of autobiography, the authors refer to existing analyses and theories. By citing the theorist Louis Althusser, Smith and Watson provide evidence to support and solidify their own claims and develop their own methods. In presenting Althusser's ideas, they are rather objective and matter-of-fact in their style or tone. It is also important to note that this particular paragraph is placed within a larger section that compares and contrasts several theories of agency. *3*

*Finally, the student explains how she would employ a simi- lar tactic in writing her own argument.*

Overall, the paragraph I selected uses other scholarly argu-    *4* ments as evidence and presents an interesting and important the- ory of agency in the study of autobiography. Smith and Watson's use of another's arguments to support and strengthen their own is an effective strategy, and I would certainly use it for similar reasons.

---

## A Practice Sequence: Writing a Rhetorical Analysis of a Paragraph

1 Review your annotations and write a paragraph in which you describe Sidonie Smith and Julia Watson's rhetorical situation, their purpose, their main claim, and their audience.

2 Now write an analysis of a paragraph from Sidonie Smith and Julia Watson's *Reading Autobiography: A Guide for Interpreting Life Narratives*. Choose a substantial paragraph (not paragraph 3!) that you find especially interesting, either for what the authors write or for how they write it. Using quotations from the text, compose one page in which you consider the situation they respond to, their purpose as writers, or their audience.

---

## ■ Write a Rhetorical Analysis of an Essay

By now you should be developing a strong sense of what is involved in ana- lyzing a paragraph rhetorically. You should be ready to take the next steps: performing a rhetorical analysis of a complete text and then sharing your analysis and the strategies you've learned with your classmates.

Read the next text, "Cultural Baggage" by Barbara Ehrenreich, anno- tating it to help you identify her situation, purpose, thesis, and audience. As you read, also make a separate set of annotations—possibly with a dif- ferent color pen or pencil, circled, or keyed with asterisks—in which you comment on or evaluate the effectiveness of her essay. What do you like or dislike about it? Why? Does Ehrenreich persuade you to accept her point of view? What impressions do you have of her as a person? Would you like to be in a conversation with her?

---

### BARBARA EHRENREICH

## Cultural Baggage

Barbara Ehrenreich is a social critic, activist, and political essayist. Her book *Nickel and Dimed: On (Not) Getting By in America* (2001) describes her attempt to live on low-wage jobs; it became a national best seller in the United States. Her book, *Bait and Switch: The (Futile) Pursuit of the American Dream* (2005), explores the shadowy world of the white-collar unemployed. Recent books of cultural analysis by Ehrenreich include

*Bright-Sided: How the Relentless Promotion of Positive Thinking Is Undermining America* and *This Land Is Their Land: Reports from a Divided Nation* (both published in 2009). Ehrenreich has also written for *Mother Jones, The Atlantic, Ms., The New Republic, In These Times,* Salon.com, and other publications. "Cultural Baggage" was originally published in the *New York Times Magazine* in 1992.

■ ■ ■

An acquaintance was telling me about the joys of rediscovering her ethnic and religious heritage. "I know exactly what my ancestors were doing 2,000 years ago," she said, eyes gleaming with enthusiasm, "and *I can do the same things now.*" Then she leaned forward and inquired politely, "And what is your ethnic background, if I may ask?" *1*

"None," I said, that being the first word in line to get out of my mouth. Well, not "none," I backtracked. Scottish, English, Irish—that was something, I supposed. Too much Irish to qualify as a WASP; too much of the hated English to warrant a "Kiss Me, I'm Irish" button; plus there are a number of dead ends in the family tree due to adoptions, missing records, failing memories, and the like. I was blushing by this time. Did "none" mean I was rejecting my heritage out of Anglo-Celtic self-hate? Or was I revealing a hidden ethnic chauvinism in which the Britannically derived serve as a kind of neutral standard compared with the ethnic "others"? *2*

Throughout the 1960s and 70s, I watched one group after another— African Americans, Latinos, Native Americans—stand up and proudly reclaim their roots while I just sank back ever deeper into my seat. All this excitement over ethnicity stemmed, I uneasily sensed, from a past in which *their* ancestors had been trampled upon by *my* ancestors, or at least by people who looked very much like them. In addition, it had begun to seem almost un-American not to have some sort of hyphen at hand, linking one to more venerable times and locales. *3*

But the truth is, I was raised with none. We'd eaten ethnic foods in my childhood home, but these were all borrowed, like the pasties, or Cornish meat pies, my father had picked up from his fellow miners in Butte, Montana. If my mother had one rule, it was militant ecumenism in all manners of food and experience. "Try new things," she would say, meaning anything from sweetbreads to clams, with an emphasis on the "new." *4*

As a child, I briefly nourished a craving for tradition and roots. I immersed myself in the works of Sir Walter Scott. I pretended to believe that the bagpipe was a musical instrument. I was fascinated to learn from a grandmother that we were descended from certain Highland clans and longed for a pleated skirt in one of their distinctive tartans. *5*

But in *Ivanhoe*, it was the dark-eyed "Jewess" Rebecca I identified with, not the flaxen-haired bimbo Rowena. As for clans: Why not call them "tribes," those bands of half-clad peasants and warriors whose idea of cuisine was stuffed sheep gut washed down with whiskey? And then there was the sting of Disraeli's remark—which I came across in my early *6* teens—to the effect that his ancestors had been leading orderly, literate lives when my ancestors were still rampaging through the Highlands daubing themselves with blue paint.

Motherhood put the screws on me, ethnicity-wise. I had hoped that by marrying a man of Eastern European Jewish ancestry I would acquire for my descendants the ethnic genes that my own forebears so sadly lacked. At one point, I even subjected the children to a seder of my own design, including a little talk about the flight from Egypt and its relevance to modern social issues. But the kids insisted on buttering their matzos and snickering through my talk. "Give me a break, Mom," the older one said. "You don't even believe in God."                                              7

After the tiny pagans had been put to bed, I sat down to brood over Elijah's wine. What had I been thinking? The kids knew that their Jewish grandparents were secular folks who didn't hold seders themselves. And if ethnicity eluded me, how could I expect it to take root in my children, who are not only Scottish English Irish, but Hungarian Polish Russian to boot?                                              8

But, then, on the fumes of Manischewitz, a great insight took form in my mind. It was true, as the kids said, that I didn't "believe in God." But this could be taken as something very different from an accusation—a reminder of a genuine heritage. My parents had not believed in God either, nor had my grandparents or any other progenitors going back to the great-great level. They had become disillusioned with Christianity generations ago—just as, on the in-law side, my children's other ancestors had shaken their Orthodox Judaism. This insight did not exactly furnish me with an "identity," but it was at least something to work with: We are the kind of people, I realized—whatever our distant ancestors' religions—who do *not* believe, who do not carry on traditions, who do not do things just because someone has done them before.                                              9

The epiphany went on: I recalled that my mother never introduced a procedure for cooking or cleaning by telling me, "Grandma did it this way." What did Grandma know, living in the days before vacuum cleaners and disposable toilet mops? In my parents' general view, new things were better than old, and the very fact that some ritual had been performed in the past was a good reason for abandoning it now. Because what was the past, as our forebears knew it? Nothing but poverty, superstition, and grief. "Think for yourself," Dad used to say. "Always ask why."                                              10

In fact, this may have been the ideal cultural heritage for my particular ethnic strain—bounced as it was from the Highlands of Scotland across the sea, out to the Rockies, down into the mines, and finally spewed out into high-tech, suburban America. What better philosophy, for a race of migrants, than "Think for yourself"? What better maxim, for a people whose whole world was rudely inverted every thirty years or so, than "Try new things"?                                              11

The more tradition-minded, the newly enthusiastic celebrants of Purim and Kwanzaa and Solstice, may see little point to survival if the                                              12 survivors carry no cultural freight—religion, for example, or ethnic tradition. To which I would say that skepticism, curiosity, and wide-eyed ecumenical tolerance are also worthy elements of the human tradition and are at least as old as such notions as "Serbian" or "Croatian," "Scottish" or "Jewish." I make no claims for my personal line of progenitors except that they remained loyal to the values that may have induced all of our ancestors, long, long ago, to climb down from the trees and make their way into the open plains.

A few weeks ago, I cleared my throat and asked the children, now 13 mostly grown and fearsomely smart, whether they felt any stirrings of ethnic or religious identity, etc., which might have been, ahem, insufficiently nourished at home. "None," they said, adding firmly, "and the world would be a better place if nobody else did, either." My chest swelled with pride, as would my mother's, to know that the race of "none" marches on.

## A Practice Sequence: Writing a Rhetorical Analysis of an Essay

1 Write a brief rhetorical analysis of Barbara Ehrenreich's essay, referring to your notes and citing passages where she indicates her situation, purpose, main claim, and audience.

2 An option for group work: As a class, divide into three or more groups. Each group should answer the following questions in response to their reading of Ehrenreich's essay "Cultural Baggage":

*Group 1:* Identify the situation(s) motivating Ehrenreich to write. Then evaluate: How well does her argument function as a conversation with other authors who have written on the same topic?

*Group 2:* Analyze the audience's identity, perspectives, and conventional expectations. Then evaluate: How well does the argument function as a conversation with the audience?

*Group 3:* Analyze the writer's purpose. Then evaluate: Do you believe Ehrenreich achieves her purpose in this essay? Why or why not?

Then, as a class, share your observations:

- To what extent does the author's ability as a conversationalist—that is, her ability to enter into a conversation with other authors and her audience—affect your evaluation of whether she achieves her purpose in this essay?

- If you were to meet this writer, what suggestions or advice would you give her for making her argument more persuasive?

Much if not all of the writing you do in college will be based on what you have read. This is the case, for example, when you summarize a philosopher's theory, analyze the significance of an experiment in psychology, or, perhaps, synthesize different and conflicting points of view in making an argument about race and academic achievement in sociology.

As we maintain throughout this book, writing and reading are inextricably linked to each other. Good academic writers are also good critical readers: They leave their mark on what they read, identifying issues, making judgments about the truth of what writers tell them, and evaluating the adequacy of the evidence in support of an argument. This is where writing and inquiry begin: understanding our own position relative to the scholarly conversations that we want to enter. Moreover, critical readers try to understand the strategies that writers use to persuade readers to agree with them. At times, these are strategies that we can adapt in advancing our arguments. In the next chapter, we provide some strategies for identifying and evaluating the adequacy of a writer's claims.

# From Identifying Claims to Analyzing Arguments

A **claim** is an assertion of fact or belief that needs to be supported with **evidence**—the information that backs up a claim. A main claim, or **thesis**, summarizes the writer's position on a situation and answers the question(s) the writer addresses. It also encompasses all of the minor claims, along with their supporting evidence, that the writer makes throughout the argument.

As readers, we need to identify a writer's main claim, or thesis, because it helps us organize our own understanding of the writer's argument. It acts as a signpost that tells us, "This is what the essay is about," "This is what I want you to pay attention to," and "This is how I want you to think, change, or act."

When you evaluate a claim, whether it is an argument's main claim or a minor claim, it is helpful to identify the type of claim it is: a claim of fact, a claim of value, or a claim of policy. You also need to evaluate the reasons for and the evidence that supports the claim. Because academic argument should acknowledge multiple points of view, you also should be prepared to identify what, if any, concessions a writer offers his or her readers, and what counterarguments he or she anticipates from others in the conversation.

## IDENTIFYING TYPES OF CLAIMS

To illustrate how to identify a writer's claims, let's take a look at a text by educators Myra and David Sadker that examines gender bias in schools. The text is followed by our analyses of the types of claims (fact, value, and policy) and then, in the next section, of the nature of the arguments (use of evidence, concessions, and counterarguments) the authors present.

## MYRA SADKER AND DAVID SADKER

## Hidden Lessons

Myra Sadker was a professor of education at American University until 1995, the year she died. Dr. Sadker coauthored *Sexism in School and Society*, the first book on gender bias in America's schools, in 1973 and became a leading advocate for equal educational opportunities.

David Sadker is a professor at American University and has taught at the elementary, middle school, and high school levels. David Sadker and his late wife earned a national reputation for their groundbreaking work in confronting gender bias and sexual harassment. "Hidden Lessons" is an excerpt from their book *Failing at Fairness: How Our Schools Cheat Girls* (1994).

■ ■ ■

Sitting in the same classroom, reading the same textbook, listening to the same teacher, boys and girls receive very different educations. From grade school through graduate school female students are more likely to be invisible members of classrooms. Teachers interact with males more frequently, ask them better questions, and give them more precise and helpful feedback. Over the course of years the uneven distribution of teacher time, energy, attention, and talent, with boys getting the lion's share, takes its toll on girls. Since gender bias is not a noisy problem, most people are unaware of the secret sexist lessons and the quiet losses they engender.

Girls are the majority of our nation's schoolchildren, yet they are second-class educational citizens. The problems they face—loss of self-esteem, decline in achievement, and elimination of career options—are at the heart of the educational process. Until educational sexism is eradicated, more than half our children will be shortchanged and their gifts lost to society.

Award-winning author Susan Faludi discovered that backlash "is most powerful when it goes private, when it lodges inside a woman's mind and turns her vision inward, until she imagines the pressure is all in her head, until she begins to enforce the backlash too—on herself."[1] Psychological backlash internalized by adult women is a frightening concept, but what is even more terrifying is a curriculum of sexist school lessons becoming

[1] Editor's note: Journalist Susan Faludi's book *Backlash: The Undeclared War Against American Women* (1991) was a response to the antifeminist backlash against the women's movement.

secret mind games played against female children, our daughters, and to-morrow's women.

After almost two decades of research grants and thousands of hours of classroom observation, we remain amazed at the stubborn persistence of these hidden sexist lessons. When we began our investigation of gender bias, we looked first in the classrooms of one of Washington, D.C.'s elite and expensive private schools. Uncertain of exactly what to look for, we wrote nothing down; we just observed. The classroom was a whirlwind of activity so fast paced we could easily miss the quick but vital phrase or gesture, the insidious incident, the tiny inequity that held a world of meaning. As we watched, we had to push ourselves beyond the blind spots of socialization and gradually focus on the nature of the interaction between teacher and student. On the second day we saw our first example of sexism, a quick, jarring flash within the hectic pace of the school day:

> Two second-graders are kneeling beside a large box. They whisper excit-edly to each other as they pull out wooden blocks, colored balls, counting sticks. So absorbed are these two small children in examining and sorting the materials, they are visibly startled by the teacher's impatient voice as she hovers over them. "Ann! Julia! Get your cottonpickin' hands out of the math box. Move over so the boys can get in there and do their work."

Isolated here on the page of a book, this incident is not difficult to inter-pret. It becomes even more disturbing if you think of it with the teacher making a racial distinction. Picture Ann and Julia as African-American children moved away so white children can gain access to the math mate-rials. If Ann and Julia's parents had observed this exchange, they might justifiably wonder whether their tuition dollars were well spent. But few parents actually watch teachers in action, and fewer still have learned to interpret the meaning behind fast-paced classroom events.

The incident unsettles, but it must be considered within the context of numerous interactions this harried teacher had that day. While she talked to the two girls, she was also keeping a wary eye on fourteen other active children. Unless you actually shadowed the teacher, stood right next to her as we did, you might not have seen or heard the event. After all, it lasted only a few seconds.

It took us almost a year to develop an observation system that would register the hundreds of daily classroom interactions, teasing out the gen-der bias embedded in them. Trained raters coded classrooms in math, reading, English, and social studies. They observed students from differ-ent racial and ethnic backgrounds. They saw lessons taught by women and by men, by teachers of different races. In short, they analyzed Amer-ica's classrooms. By the end of the year we had thousands of observation sheets, and after another year of statistical analysis, we discovered a syn-tax of sexism so elusive that most teachers and students were completely unaware of its influence.

Recently a producer of NBC's *Dateline* contacted us to learn more   *8*
about our discovery that girls don't receive their fair share of education.
Jane Pauley, the show's anchorwoman, wanted to visit classrooms, capture these covert sexist lessons on videotape, and expose them before a
television audience. The task was to extricate sound bites of sexism from
a fifth-grade classroom where the teacher, chosen to be the subject of the
exposé, was aware she was being scrutinized for sex bias.

*Dateline* had been taping in her class for two days when we received   *9*
a concerned phone call. "This is a fair teacher," the producer said. "How
can we show sexism on our show when there's no gender bias in this
teacher's class?" We drove to the NBC studio in Washington, D.C., and
found two *Dateline* staffers, intelligent women concerned about fair treatment in school, sitting on the floor in a darkened room staring at the videotape of a fifth-grade class. "We've been playing this over and over. The
teacher is terrific. There's no bias in her teaching. Come watch."

After about twenty minutes of viewing, we realized it was a case of   *10*
déjà vu: The episodal sexist themes and recurring incidents were all too
familiar. The teacher was terrific, but she was more effective for half of
the students than she was for the other. She was, in fact, a classic example
of the hundreds of skillful well-intentioned professionals we have seen
who inadvertently teach boys better than girls.

We had forgotten how difficult it was to recognize subtle sexism before   *11*
you learn how to look. It was as if the *Dateline* staff members were wearing blinders. We halted the tape, pointed out the sexist behaviors, related
them to incidents in our research, and played the tape again. There is a
classic "aha!" effect in education when people finally "get it." Once the
hidden lessons of unconscious bias are understood, classrooms never
look the same again to the trained observer.

Much of the unintentional gender bias in that fifth-grade class could   *12*
not be shown in the short time allowed by television, but the sound bites
of sexism were also there. *Dateline* chose to show a segregated math
group: boys sitting on the teacher's right side and girls on her left. After
giving the math book to a girl to hold open at the page of examples, the
teacher turned her back to the girls and focused on the boys, teaching
them actively and directly. Occasionally she turned to the girls' side, but
only to read the examples in the book. This teacher, although aware that
she was being observed for sexism, had unwittingly transformed the girls
into passive spectators, an audience for the boys. All but one, that is: The
girl holding the math book had become a prop.

*Dateline* also showed a lively discussion in the school library. With both   *13*
girls' hands and boys' hands waving for attention, the librarian chose
boy after boy to speak. In one interaction she peered through the forest
of girls' hands waving directly in front of her to acknowledge the raised
hand of a boy in the back of the room. Startled by the teacher's attention,
the boy muttered, "I was just stretching."

The next day we discussed the show with future teachers, our students *14* at The American University. They were bewildered. "Those teachers really were sexist. They didn't mean to be, but they were. How could that happen—with the cameras and everyone watching?" When we took those students into classrooms to discover the hidden lessons for themselves, they began to understand. It is difficult to detect sexism unless you know precisely how to observe. And if a lifetime of socialization makes it difficult to spot gender bias even when you're looking for it, how much harder it is to avoid the traps when you are the one doing the teaching.

Now let's consider the types of claims in the Sadkers' argument.

## ■ Identify Claims of Fact

**Claims of fact** are assertions (or arguments) *that a problem or condition has existed, exists, or will exist*. Claims of fact are made by individuals who believe that something is true; but claims are never simply facts, and some claims are more objective, and so easier to verify, than others.

For example, "It's raining in Portland today" is a "factual" claim of fact; it's easily verified. But consider the argument some make that the steel and automotive industries in the United States have depleted our natural resources and left us at a crisis point. This is an assertion that a condition exists. A careful reader must examine the basis for this kind of claim: Are we truly facing a crisis? And if so, are the steel and automotive industries truly responsible? A number of politicians counter this claim of fact by insisting that if the government were to harness the vast natural resources in Alaska, there would be no "crisis." This is also a claim of fact, in this case an assertion that a condition will exist in the future. Again, it is based on evidence, evidence gathered from various sources that indicates sufficient resources in Alaska to keep up with our increasing demands for resources and to allay a potential crisis.

Our point is that most claims of fact are debatable. They may be based on factual information, but they are not necessarily true. Most claims of fact present **interpretations** of evidence derived from **inferences**. That is, a writer will examine evidence (for example, about the quantity of natural resources in Alaska and the rate that industries harness those resources and process them into goods), draw a conclusion based on reasoning (an inference), and offer an explanation based on that conclusion (an interpretation).

So, for example, an academic writer will study the evidence on the quantity of natural resources in Alaska and the rate that industries harness those resources and process them into goods; only after the writer makes an informed decision on whether Alaska's resources are sufficient to keep pace with the demand for them will he or she take a position on the issue.

In the first paragraph of their essay, the Sadkers make the claims of fact that female students are "more likely to be invisible members of classrooms" and that teachers interact differently with female students than they do with male students. The careful reader will want to see how the Sadkers support these claims of fact throughout the essay. Can they convincingly present their argument about "the secret sexist lessons and the quiet losses they engender" in the paragraphs that follow?

## ■ Identify Claims of Value

A claim of fact is different from a **claim of value**, which *expresses an evaluation of a problem or condition that has existed, exists, or will exist*. Is a condition good or bad? Is it important or inconsequential?

For example, an argument that developing the wilderness in Alaska would irreversibly mar the beauty of the land indicates that the writer values the beauty of the land over the possible benefits of development. A claim of value presents a judgment, which is sometimes signaled by a value-laden word like *ugly*, *beautiful*, or *immoral*, but may also be conveyed more subtly by the writer's tone and attitude.

Sadker and Sadker make a claim of value when they suggest that a "majority of our nation's schoolchildren" have become "second-class educational citizens" and point out that the consequences of treating girls differently from boys in school has resulted in a "loss of self-esteem, decline in achievement, and elimination of career options" for girls (para. 2). Of course, the critical reader's task is to question these evaluations: Does gender bias in the classroom affect self-esteem, achievement, and career options? Both of these statements are minor claims, but they make assertions that require support. After all, how do the Sadkers know these things? Whether or not readers are persuaded by these claims depends on the evidence or reasons that the authors use to support them. We discuss the nature of evidence and what constitutes "good reasons" later in this chapter.

## ■ Identify Claims of Policy

A **claim of policy** is an argument for what should be the case, *that a condition should exist*. It is a call for change.

Two recent controversies on college campuses center on claims of policy. One has activists arguing that universities and colleges should have a policy that all workers on campus earn a living wage. The other has activists arguing that universities and colleges should have a policy that prevents them from investing in countries where the government ignores human rights.

Claims of policy are often signaled by words like *should* and *must*: "For public universities to live up to their democratic mission, they *must* provide all their workers with a living wage." Myra and David Sadker make a claim of policy when they assert that "educational sexism" must be eradicated; otherwise, they point out, "more than half our children will be shortchanged and their gifts lost to society" (para. 2).

Not all writers make their claims as explicitly as the Sadkers do; nor does every argument include all three types of claims. But you should be able to identify the three different types of claims. Moreover, you should keep in mind what the situation is and what kind of argument can best address what you see as a problem. Ask yourself: Does the situation involve a question of fact? Does the situation involve a question of value? Does the situation require a change in policy? Or is some combination at work?

## Steps to Identifying Claims

**1** **Ask:** Does the argument assert that a problem or condition has existed, exists, or will exist? If so, it's a claim of fact.

**2** **Ask:** Does the argument express an evaluation of a problem or condition that has existed, exists, or will exist? If so, it's a claim of value.

**3** **Ask:** Does the argument call for change, and is it directed at some future action? If so, it's a claim of policy.

## A Practice Sequence: Identifying Claims

What follows is a series of claims. Identify each one as a claim of fact, value, or policy. Be prepared to justify your categorizations.

1 Taxing the use of fossil fuels will end the energy crisis.

2 We should reform the welfare system to ensure that people who receive support from the government also work.

3 Images of violence in the media create a culture of violence in schools.

4 The increase in homelessness is a deplorable situation that contradicts the whole idea of democracy.

5 Distributing property taxes is the one sure way to end poverty and illiteracy.

6 Individual votes don't really count.

7 Despite the 20 percent increase in the number of females in the workforce over the past forty years, women are still not treated equitably.

8 Affirmative action is a policy that has outlived its usefulness.

9 There are a disproportionate number of black males in American prisons.

10 The media are biased, which means we cannot count on newspapers or television news for the truth.

## ANALYZING ARGUMENTS

Analyzing an argument involves identifying the writer's main and minor claims and then examining (1) the reasons and evidence given in support of each claim, (2) the writer's concessions, and (3) the writer's attempts to handle counterarguments.

### ■ Analyze the Reasons Used to Support a Claim

Stating a claim is one thing; supporting that claim is another. As a critical reader, you need to evaluate whether a writer has provided *good reasons* to support his or her position. Specifically, you will need to decide whether the support for a claim is recent, relevant, reliable, and accurate. As a writer, you will need to use the same criteria when you support your claims.

*Is the source recent?*    Knowledgeable readers of your written arguments not only will be aware of classic studies that you should cite as "intellectual touchstones"; they will also expect you to cite recent evidence, evidence published within five years of when you are writing.

Of course, older research can be valuable. For example, in a paper about molecular biology, you might very well cite James Watson and Francis Crick's groundbreaking 1953 study in which they describe the structure of DNA. That study is an intellectual touchstone that changed the life sciences in a fundamental way.

Or if you were writing about educational reform, you might very well mention E. D. Hirsch's 1987 book *Cultural Literacy*. Hirsch's book did not change the way people think about curricular reform as profoundly as Watson and Crick's study changed the way scientists think about biology, but his term *cultural literacy* continues to serve as useful shorthand for a particular way of thinking about curricular reform that remains influential to this day.

Although citing Hirsch is an effective way to suggest you have studied the history of an educational problem, it will not convince your readers that there is a crisis in education today. To establish that, you would need to use as evidence studies published over the past few years to show, for example, that there has been a steady decline in test scores since Hirsch wrote his book. And you would need to support your claim that curricular reform is the one sure way to bring an end to illiteracy and poverty with data that are much more current than those available to Hirsch in the 1980s. No one would accept the judgment that our schools are in crisis if your most recent citation is more than twenty years old.

*Is the source relevant?*    Evidence that is relevant must have real bearing on your issue. It also depends greatly on what your readers expect. For example, suppose two of your friends complain that they were unable to sell their condominiums for the price they asked. You can claim there is a crisis in the housing market, but your argument won't convince most readers if your only evidence is personal anecdote.

Such *anecdotal evidence* may alert you to a possible topic and help you connect with your readers, but you will need to test the **relevance** of your friends' experience—Is it pertinent? Is it typical of a larger situation or condition?—if you want your readers to take your argument seriously. For example, you might scan real estate listings to see what the asking prices are for properties comparable to your friends' properties. By comparing listings, you are defining the grounds for your argument. If your friends are disappointed that their one-bedroom condominiums sold for less than a three-bedroom condominium with deeded parking in the same neighborhood, it may well be that their expectations were too high.

In other words, if you aren't comparing like things, your argument is going to be seriously flawed. If your friends' definition of what constitutes a "reasonable price" differs dramatically from everyone else's, their experience is probably irrelevant to the larger question of whether the local housing market is depressed.

**Is the source reliable?**    You also need to evaluate whether the data you use to support your argument are reliable. After all, some researchers present findings based on a very small sample of people that can also be rather selective.

For example, a researcher might argue that 67 percent of the people he cited believe that school and residential integration are important concerns. But how many people did this person interview? More important, who responded to the researcher's questions? A reliable claim cannot be based on a few of the researcher's friends.

Let's return to the real estate example. You have confirmed that your friends listed their condominiums at prices that were not out of line with the market. Now what? You need to seek out reliable sources to continue testing your argument. For example, you might search the real estate or business section of your local newspaper to see if there are any recent stories about a softening of the market; and you might talk with several local real estate agents to get their opinions on the subject.

In consulting local newspapers and local agents, you are looking for **authoritative sources** against which to test your anecdotal evidence—the confirmation of experts who report on, study, evaluate, and have an informed opinion on local real estate. Local real estate agents are a source of **expert testimony**, firsthand confirmation of the information you have discovered. You would probably not want to rely on the testimony of a single real estate agent, who may have a bias; instead, talk with several agents to see if a consensus emerges.

**Is the source accurate?**    To determine the accuracy of a study that you want to use to support your argument, you have to do a little digging to find out who else has made a similar claim. For instance, if you want to cite authoritative research that compares the dropout rate for white students with the rate for students of color, you could look at research conducted by the Civil Rights Project. Of course, you don't need to stop your search there. You could also check the resources available through the National Center for Education Statistics. You want to show your readers that you have done a relatively thorough search to make your argument as persuasive as possible.

The accuracy of **statistics**—factual information presented numerically or graphically (for example, in a pie or bar chart)—is difficult to verify. To a certain extent, then, their veracity has to be taken on faith. Often the best you can do is assure yourself that the source of your statistical information is authoritative and reliable—government and major research universities generally are "safe" sources—and that whoever is interpreting the statistical information is not distorting it.

Returning again to our real estate example, let's say you've read a newspaper article that cites statistical information about the condition of the local real estate market (for example, the average price of property and volume of sales this year in comparison to last year). Presumably the author of the article is an expert, but he or she may be interpreting rather than simply reporting on the statistics.

To reassure yourself one way or the other, you may want to check the sources of the author's statistics—go right to your source's sources—which a responsible author will cite. That will allow you to look over the raw data and come to your own conclusions. A further step you could take would be to discuss the article with other experts—local real estate agents—to find out what they think of the article and the information it presents.

Now, let's go back to Myra and David Sadker's essay. How do they develop their assertion that girls are treated differently from boys in classrooms from "grade school through graduate school"? First, they tell us (in paragraph 4) that they have been conducting research continuously for "almost two decades" and that they have accumulated "thousands of hours of classroom observation." This information suggests that their research is both recent and relevant.

But are their studies reliable and accurate? That their research meets the reliability criterion is confirmed by the grants they received over the years: Granting institutions (experts) have assessed their work and determined that it deserved to be funded. Grants confer authority on research. In addition, the Sadkers explain that they observed and refined their analyses over time to achieve accuracy: "As we watched, we had to push ourselves beyond the blind spots of socialization and gradually focus on the nature of the interaction between teacher and student."

In paragraph 7, the authors provide more evidence that the observations that support their claim are accurate. Not only have they observed many instances of gender bias in classrooms; so have trained "raters." The raters add objectivity to the findings because they did not share the Sadkers' interest in drawing a specific conclusion about whether gender bias exists in classrooms. Also the raters observed a wide cross section of students and teachers from "different racial and ethnic backgrounds." At the end of their study, the Sadkers had collected thousands of pieces of data and could feel quite confident about their conclusion—that they had "discovered a syntax of sexism so elusive that most teachers and students were completely unaware of its influence."

---

### Steps to Evaluating Support for a Claim

Ask yourself:

**1 Is the source recent?** Has it been published in the past few years? How have things changed since then? If the source was not published recently, is it still an important part of the conversation worth acknowledging?

**2 Is the source relevant?** Does the evidence have real bearing on the claim? Is it pertinent? Is it typical of a larger situation or condition?

**3 Is the source reliable?** Does the evidence come from recognized experts and authoritative institutions?

**4 Is the source accurate?** Are the data presented in the source sufficient? Have they been gathered, interpreted, and reported responsibly? How do they compare with other data you have found?

---

## ■ Identify Concessions

Part of the strategy of developing a main claim supported with good reasons is to offer a **concession**, an acknowledgment that readers may not agree with every point the writer is making. A concession is a writer's way of saying, "Okay, I can see that there may be another way of looking at the issue or another way to interpret the evidence used to support the argument I am making."

For instance, you may not want your energy costs to go up, but after examining the reasons why it may be necessary to increase taxes on gasoline—to lower usage and conserve fossil fuels—you might concede that a tax increase on gasoline could be useful. The willingness to make concessions is valued in academic writing because it acknowledges both complexity and the importance of multiple perspectives. It also acknowledges the fact that information can always be interpreted in different ways.

The Sadkers make a concession when they acknowledge in the last paragraph of the excerpt that "it is difficult to detect sexism unless you know precisely how to observe." And, they explain, "if a lifetime of socialization makes it difficult to spot gender bias even when you're looking for it, how much harder it is to avoid the traps when you are the one doing the teaching."

Notice that these concessions do not weaken their argument. The authors' evidence appears overwhelmingly to support their thesis. The lesson here is that conceding a point in your argument shows that you have acknowledged there are other ways of seeing things, other interpretations. This is an important part of what it means to enter a conversation of ideas.

Often a writer will signal a concession with phrases like the following:

- "It is true that . . ."
- "I agree with X that Y is an important factor to consider."
- "Some studies have convincingly shown that . . ."

Generally, the writer will then go on to address the concession, explaining how it needs to be modified or abandoned in the light of new evidence or the writer's perspective on the issue.

## ■ Identify Counterarguments

As the term suggests, a **counterargument** is an argument raised in response to another argument. You want to be aware of and acknowledge what your readers may object to in your argument. Anticipating readers' objections is an important part of developing a conversational argument.

For example, if you were arguing in support of universal health care, you would have to acknowledge that the approach departs dramatically from the traditional role the federal government has played in providing health insurance. That is, most people's access to health insurance has depended on their individual ability to afford and purchase this kind of insurance. You would have to anticipate how readers would respond to your proposal, especially readers who do not feel that the federal government should ever play a role in what has heretofore been an individual responsibility.

Anticipating readers' objections demonstrates that you understand the complexity of the issue and are willing at least to entertain different and conflicting opinions.

In the excerpt from "Hidden Lessons," the Sadkers describe the initial response of *Dateline* staffers to what they observed in the classroom they were videotaping: "This is a fair teacher. . . . [T]here's no gender bias in this teacher's class." Two women whom the Sadkers describe as "intelligent" and "concerned about fair treatment in school" agreed: "We've been playing this over and over. The teacher is terrific. There's no bias in her teaching. Come watch" (para. 9).

Notice the Sadkers' acknowledgment that even intelligent, concerned people may not see the problems that the Sadkers spent more than twenty years studying. In addressing the counterargument—that sexism does not exist—the authors are both empathetic to and respectful of what any reasonable person might or might not see. This is in keeping with what we would call a conversational argument: that writers listen to different points of view, that they respect arguments that diverge from their own, and that they be willing to exchange ideas and revise their own points of view.

In an argument that is more conversational than confrontational, writers establish areas of common ground, both to convey different views that are understood and to acknowledge the conditions under which those different views are valid. Writers do this by making concessions and anticipating and responding to counterarguments.

This conversational approach is what many people call a **Rogerian approach to argument**, based on psychologist Carl Rogers's approach to psychotherapy. The objective of a Rogerian strategy is to reduce listeners' sense of threat so that they are open to alternatives. For academic writers, it involves four steps:

1. Conveying to readers that their different views are understood
2. Acknowledging conditions under which readers' views are valid
3. Helping readers see that the writer shares common ground with them
4. Creating mutually acceptable solutions to agreed-on problems

The structure of an argument, according to the Rogerian approach, grows out of the give-and-take of conversation between two people and the topic under discussion. In a written conversation, the give-and-take of face-to-face conversation takes the form of anticipating readers' counterarguments and uses language that is both empathetic and respectful, to put the readers at ease.

---

### Steps to Analyzing an Argument

**1** **Identify the type of claim.** Is it a claim of fact? Value? Policy?

**2** **Analyze the reasons used to support the claim.** Are they recent? Relevant? Reliable? Accurate?

**3** **Identify concessions.** Is there another argument that even the author acknowledges is legitimate?

**4** **Identify counterarguments.** What arguments contradict or challenge the author's position?

---

## AN ANNOTATED STUDENT ARGUMENT

We have annotated the following essay to show the variety of claims the student writer uses, as well as some of the other argumentative moves he performs. The assignment was to write an argument out of personal experience and observation about the cultural impact of a recent innovation. Marques Camp chose to write about the Kindle, an electronic reading device developed by the online retailer Amazon that allows users to download books for a fee. However, the user cannot share the download electronically with other users. Camp touches on a number of issues reflected in his claims.

As you read the essay, imagine how you would respond to his various claims. Which do you agree with, which do you disagree with, and why? What evidence would you present to support or counter his claims? Do you detect a main claim? Do you think his overall essay develops and supports it?

Camp 1

Marques Camp
Professor Fells
English 1020
January 28, 20 —

The End of the World May Be Nigh, and It's the
Kindle's Fault

"Libraries will in the end become cities."
— Gottfried Wilhelm Leibniz, German polymath

*The student presents a claim of fact that others have made.*

The future of written human history will come, as they will have us believe, in the form of the Amazon Kindle, all 10.2 ounces of it, all 2 GB and 532 MHz of it, all 240,000+ titles of it, ready to change the way people read, ready to revolutionize the way people see the world.    *1*

The Kindle is a signpost for our times, the final checkpoint in our long and adventurous journey from the world of printed paper to the twenty-first-century world of digitalization.    *2*

*He lays the basis for a counterargument by questioning whether this is a real threat at all, citing some technological precedents.*

We first saw this paradigm shift with newspapers, where weekly columns were taken over by daily blog posts, where 48-point sans-serif headlines transformed into 12-point Web links. We then moved on into television, where Must-See TV was replaced with On-Demand TV, where consumers no longer sat around in the living room with their families during prime time but rather watched the latest episode of their favorite show commercial-free from the comfortable and convenient confines of their

Camp 2

laptop, able to fast-forward, rewind, and pause with a delightful and devilish sense of programming omnipotence. We are now seeing it, slowly but surely, slay the giant that we never thought could be slain: the world of books.

*In this paragraph, he makes a claim of fact about unequal access to technological innovation and offers a concession to what many see as the value of the Kindle.*

Contrary to popular belief, easier access to a wider quantity of literature is not a universal revolution. The Kindle speaks to the world that measures quantity by the number of cable television channels it has, speed by the connectivity of its wireless networks, and distance by the number of miles a family travels for vacation. Yes, the Kindle is the new paradigm for universal access and literary connectivity. But it is much like a college degree in the sense that it is merely a gateway to a wealth of opportunity. The problem, however, is gaining access to this gateway in the first place.

3

*He supports his claim of fact with evidence based on experience: that sharing books provides something technology cannot offer.*

Books often pass from hand to hand, from friend to friend, from generation to generation, many times with the mutual understanding that remuneration is not necessary — merely the promise of hope that the new reader is as touched and enlightened by the book as the previous one. This transfer serves more than a utilitarian function; symbolically, it represents the passage of hope, of knowledge, of responsibility.

4

*Evidence from observation: not everyone has access to new technologies, but people will always have access to books.*

The book, in many cases, represents the only sort of hope for the poorest among us, the great equalizer in a world full of financial and intellectual capital and highly concentrated access to this capital. The wonderful quality of the book is that its intellectual value is very rarely proportional to its financial value; people often consider their most valuable book to be one they happened to pick up one day for free.

5

*An evaluative claim — that the widening gap between rich and poor is dangerous — adds another layer to the argument.*

The proliferation of the Kindle technology, however, will result in a wider disconnect between the elite and the nonelite — as the old saying goes, the rich will get richer and the poor will get poorer. Unfortunately for the poor, this is no financial disconnect — this is a widening of the gap in the world of ideas. And this is, perhaps, the most dangerous gap of all.

6

*A further evaluative claim — that new technological devices offer little hope to "victims" of illiteracy — is followed by*

The Kindle Revolution, ironically, may end up contributing to the very disease that is antithetical to its implied function: illiteracy. Make no mistake, the Kindle was not designed with the poor in mind. For those in most need of the printed

7

Camp 3

*a claim of fact that books inspire people to create change in the world.*

word, for those who are the most vulnerable victims of the illiteracy threat, the $359 Kindle offers little in the way of hope. One book for a poor person is all he or she needs to be inspired and change the world; with the Kindle, that one book is consolidated and digitized, transformed from a tangible piece of hope and the future into a mere collection of words in the theoretically infinite dimension of cyberspace. A "book" on the Kindle is a book wedged among many other books, separated by nothing more than title, devoid of essence, devoid of uniqueness, devoid of personality, devoid of its unique position in space — precisely what makes a book a "book," as opposed to a mere collection of words. It is no longer singular, no longer serendipitous, no longer distinguishable.

The e-book cannot, like a bound book, pass through multiple hands and eventually settle itself on the right person, ready to be unleashed as a tool to change the world. Due to the restrictions on sharing and reselling e-books with the Kindle, the very nature of reading books transforms from highly communal to individualistic, from highly active to somewhat passive. The Kindle will lead to the mystification of books, wherein they become less unique capsules of thoughts and ideas and experiences and more utility-oriented modes of information-giving. What many Kindle advocates fail to realize is that oftentimes, the transformative quality of books resides less in the actual words comprising the book and more in the actual experience of reading.

*An evaluative claim in which the author observes that technology can make reading passive. Then a claim of fact: that the experience of reading can be transformative.*

8

There is also something to be said for the utter corporeality of books that lies at the heart of Leibniz's metaphor. Libraries are physical testaments to all that we have learned and recorded during human history. The sheer size of libraries, the sheer number of volumes residing in them, tell us, in a spatial sense, of all the theoretical knowledge we have accumulated in the course of our existence, and all the power we have to further shape and define the world we live in. The Kindle and other digital literary technologies are threatening the very connection between the world of ideas and the material world, threatening to take our literal measures of progress and hide them away in

9

*The student offers a final evaluative claim, observing that the Kindle threatens to mask the relationship between ideas and the world.*

Camp 4

*His concluding claim falls just short of making a proposal—but he does suggest that those in positions of power must ensure the proliferation of books.*

the vast database of words and ideas, available only to those with $359 to spare and a credit card for further purchases.

If libraries will indeed become cities, then we need to carefully begin to lay the foundations, book on top of book on top of book, and we are going to have to ensure that we have enough manpower to do it.

*10*

## ANALYZING AND COMPARING ARGUMENTS

As an academic writer, you will often need to compare disparate claims and evidence from multiple arguments addressing the same topic. Rarely, however, will those arguments be simplistic pro/con pairs meant to represent two opposing sides to an issue. Certainly the news media thrive on such black-and-white conflict, but academic writers seek greater complexity and do not expect to find simple answers. Analyzing and comparing essays on the same topic or issue will often reveal the ways writers work with similar evidence to come up with different, and not necessarily opposed, arguments.

The next two selections are arguments about grade inflation. Both are brief, and we recommend you read through them quickly as a prelude to the activity in analyzing and comparing arguments that follows them. As you read, try to note their claims, the reasons used to support them, concessions, and counterarguments.

### STUART ROJSTACZER

## Grade Inflation Gone Wild

A former professor of geophysics at Duke University with a PhD in applied earth sciences, Stuart Rojstaczer has written or coauthored many geological studies in his career as a scientist. He has also published a book, *Gone for Good: Tales of University Life After the Golden Age* (1999), and numerous articles on higher education and grading. He is the creator of gradeinflation.com, where he posts a variety of charts and graphs chronicling his data about grade inflation. This op-ed piece appeared in the *Christian Science Monitor* on March 24, 2009.

■ ■ ■

A bout six years ago, I was sitting in the student union of a small lib-   *1*
eral arts college when I saw a graph on the cover of the student
newspaper that showed the history of grades given at that institution in
the past 30 years.

Grades were up. Way up.   *2*

I'm a scientist by training and I love numbers. So when I looked at that   *3*
graph, I wondered, "How many colleges and universities have data like
this that I can find?" The answer is that a lot of schools have data like this
hidden somewhere. Back then, I found more than 80 colleges and universities with data on grades, mostly by poking around the Web. Then I created a website (gradeinflation.com) so that others could find this data.
I learned that grades started to shoot up nationwide in the 1960s, leveled off in the 1970s, and then started rising again in the 1980s. Private
schools had much higher grades than public schools, but virtually everyone was experiencing grade inflation.

What about today?   *4*

Grades continue to go up regardless of the quality of education. At a   *5*
time when many are raising questions about the quality of US higher education, the average GPA at public schools is 3.0, with many flagship state
schools having average GPAs higher than 3.2. At a private college, the
average is now 3.3. At some schools, it tops 3.5 and even 3.6. "A" is average at those schools! At elite Brown University, two-thirds of all letter
grades given are now A's.

These changes in grading have had a profound influence on college life   *6*
and learning. When students walk into a classroom knowing that they can
go through the motions and get a B+ or better, that's what they tend to do,
give minimal effort. Our college classrooms are filled with students who
do not prepare for class. Many study less than 10 hours a week—that's
less than half the hours they spent studying 40 years ago. Paradoxically,
students are spending more and more money for an education that seems
to deliver less and less content.

With so few hours filled with learning, boredom sets in and students   *7*
have to find something to pass the time. Instead of learning, they drink. A
recent survey of more than 30,000 first-year students across the country
showed that nearly half were spending more hours drinking than they
were studying. If we continue along this path, we'll end up with a generation of poorly educated college graduates who have used their four years
principally to develop an addiction to alcohol.

There are many who say that grade inflation is a complicated issue   *8*
with no easy fix. But there are solutions. At about the same time that I
started to collect data on rising grades, Princeton University began to
actually do something about its grade-inflation problem. Its guidelines
have the effect of now limiting A's on average to 35 percent of students
in a class. Those guidelines have worked. Grades are going back down
at Princeton and academic rigor is making a comeback. A similar suc-

cessful effort has taken place at Wellesley College in Massachusetts. And through a concerted effort on the part of faculty and leadership, grades at Reed College in Oregon have stayed essentially constant for 20 years.

Princeton, Wellesley, and Reed provide evidence that the effort to keep grade inflation in check is not impossible. This effort takes two major steps. First, school officials must admit that there is a problem. Then they must implement policies or guidelines that truly restore excellence. *9*

I asked Dean Nancy Malkiel at Princeton why so few schools seem to be following Princeton's lead. "Because it's hard work," she answered. "Because you have to persuade the faculty that it's important to do the work." *10*

Making a switch will take hard work, but the effort is worthwhile. The alternative is a student body that barely studies and drinks out of boredom. That's not acceptable. Colleges and universities must roll up their sleeves, bring down inflated grades, and encourage real learning. It's not an impossible task. There are successful examples that can be followed. I'm looking forward to the day when we can return to being proud of the education that our nation's colleges and universities provide. *11*

## PHIL PRIMACK

# Doesn't Anybody Get a C Anymore?

Phil Primack is a journalist, editor, and policy analyst who teaches journalism at Tufts University, where he is a senior fellow at the Jonathan M. Tisch College of Citizenship and Public Service. His articles have appeared in many regional and national publications, including the *New York Times*, the *Boston Globe*, and *Columbia Journalism Review*. The following piece appeared in the *Boston Globe* on October 5, 2008.

The student deserved a B-minus. Maybe even a C-plus, I had decided. One paper was especially weak; another was late. But then I began to rationalize. The student had been generally prepared and contributed to class discussion, so I relented and gave what I thought was a very generous B. At least I wouldn't get a complaint about this grade, I figured. Then came the e-mail. *1*

Why such a "low grade," the indignant student wrote. *2*

"Low grade"? Back when I attended Tufts in the late 1960s, a B in certain courses was something I could only dream about. But grade inflation, the steady rise in grade point averages that began in the 1960s, now leaves many students regarding even the once-acceptable B—which has always stood for "good"—as a transcript wrecker, and a C—that is, *3* "average"—as unmitigated disaster. More and more academic leaders may lament grade inflation, but precious few have been willing to act against it, leaving their professors all alone in the minefield between giving marks that reflect true merit and facing the wrath of students for whom entitlement begins with the letter A.

Grade inflation "is a huge problem," says former US senator Hank    4
Brown, who tried to make it a priority issue as president of the University of Colorado in 2006. "Under the current system at a lot of schools, there is no way to recognize the difference between an outstanding job and a good job. Grade inflation hides laziness on the part of the students, and as long as it exists, even faculty who want to do a good job [in grading] don't feel they can."

That's because many professors fear that "tough grading" will trig-    5
ger poor student evaluations or worse, which in turn can jeopardize the academic career track. "In my early years, students would say they liked my class, but the grades were low and the work level high," says retired Duke University professor Stuart Rojstaczer. "I had to get with the program and reduce my own expectations of workload and increase grades in order to have students leave my class with a positive impression to give to other students so they would attend [next year]. I was teaching worse, but the student response was much more positive."

Harvard University is the poster campus for academic prestige—and    6
for grade inflation, even though some of its top officials have warned about grade creep. About 15 percent of Harvard students got a B-plus or better in 1950, according to one study. In 2007, more than half of all Harvard grades were in the A range. Harvard declined to release more current data or officially comment for this article. At the University of Massachusetts at Amherst, the average GPA in 2007 was 3.19 (on a four-point scale), up from 3.02 a decade earlier. That "modest increase" simply reflects better students, UMass spokesman Ed Blaguszewski says in an e-mail. "Since our students have been increasingly well-prepared . . . it makes sense that their UMass grades have crept up. Essentially, the profile of the population has changed over time, so we don't consider this to be grade inflation."

That's certainly the most common argument to explain away grade    7
inflation—smarter students naturally get higher grades. But is it that simple? Privately, many faculty members and administrators say colleges are unwilling to challenge and possibly offend students and their hovering, tuition-paying parents with some tough grade love. And without institutional backing, individual faculty members simply yield to whining students.

But not everywhere. The most cited—and extreme—case of taking on    8
grade inflation is at Princeton University, which in 2004 directed that A's account for less than 35 percent of undergraduate course grades. From 2004 to 2007, A's (A-plus, A, A-minus) accounted for 40.6 percent of

undergraduate course grades, down from 47 percent in the period 2001 to 2004.

Closer to home, Wellesley College calls for the average grade in basic undergraduate courses to be no higher than a B-plus (3.33 GPA). "It's not that we're trying to get grades down, but we're trying to get grades to mean something," says associate dean of the college Adele Wolfson, who teaches chemistry. Wellesley's GPA, which stood at 3.47 in 2002 and was 3.4 when the policy was implemented two years later, fell to 3.3 this year, mainly because of more B grades and fewer A's. "The A has really become the mark of excellence," she says, "which is what it should be." 9

The problem, says Rojstaczer, is that such policies are the exceptions, and that grade inflation will be reduced only through consistent prodding and action by top officials. "In truth, some university leaders are embarrassed that grading is so lax, but they are loath to make any changes," he says in an e-mail. "Grade inflation in academia is like the alcoholic brother you pretend is doing just fine. When someone calls your brother a drunk, you get angry and defend him, although privately you worry. That's where we are with grade inflation: public denial and private concern." 10

## A Practice Sequence: Analyzing and Comparing Arguments

1 To practice these strategies, first break up into small groups to discuss four different concerns surrounding grade inflation:

> *Group 1:* Define what you think grade inflation is.
>
> *Group 2:* Discuss whether you think grade inflation is a problem at the university or college you attend. What evidence can you provide to suggest that it is or is not a problem?
>
> *Group 3:* Why should students or faculty be concerned with grade inflation? What's at stake?
>
> *Group 4:* How would you respond if the administration at your university or college decided to limit the number of A's that faculty could give students?

Reassemble as a class and briefly report on the discussions.

2 Analyze Stuart Rojstaczer's argument in "Grade Inflation Gone Wild," addressing the following questions:

- What evidence does Rojstaczer use to indicate that there is a problem?

- How would you characterize this evidence (for example, scientific, anecdotal), and to what extent are you persuaded by the evidence he provides to suggest that grade inflation has a profound effect on "life and learning"?

- To what extent does he persuade you that a change in policy is necessary or that such a change would make a difference?

**3** Now compare Phil Primack's and Stuart Rojstaczer's strategies for developing an argument.

- How does Primack establish that there is a problem? To what extent is his approach as persuasive as Rojstaczer's?

- What strategies would you identify in either argument as strategies that you might employ to develop your own argument?

- To what extent are you persuaded by the counterargument that Primack introduces?

- What do you think Primack wants you to do or think about in his analysis?

- In the end, does Primack add anything to your understanding of the problem of whether your college or university should introduce a policy to limit grade inflation?

# 4

# From Identifying Issues to Forming Questions

Remember that inquiry is central to the process of composing. As you move from reading texts to writing them, you will discover that writing grows out of answering these questions:

- What are the concerns of the authors I've been reading?
- What situations motivate them to write?
- What frames or contexts do they use to construct their arguments?
- What is my argument in response to their writing?
- What is at stake in my argument?
- Who will be interested in reading what I have to say?
- How can I connect with both sympathetic and antagonistic readers?
- What kinds of evidence will persuade my readers?
- What objections are they likely to raise?

To answer these questions, you must read in the role of writer, with an eye toward

- *identifying an issue* (an idea or a statement that is open to dispute) that compels you to respond in writing
- *understanding the situation* (the factors that give rise to the issue and shape your response)
- *formulating a question* (what you intend to answer in response to the issue)

In Table 4.1, we identify a series of situations and one of the issues and questions that derive from each of them. Notice that the question you

TABLE 4.1    A Series of Situations with Related Issues and Questions

| Situation | Issue | Question |
|---|---|---|
| Different state legislatures are passing legislation to prevent Spanish-speaking students from using their own language in schools. | Most research on learning contradicts the idea that students should be prevented from using their own language in the process of learning a new language. | Under what conditions should students be allowed to use their own language while they learn English? |
| A manufacturing company has plans to move to your city with the promise of creating new jobs in a period of high unemployment. | You feel that this company will compromise the quality of life for the surrounding community because the manufacturing process will pollute the air. | What would persuade the city to prevent this company from moving in, even though the company will provide much-needed jobs? |
| Your school has made an agreement with a local company to supply vending machines that sell drinks and food. The school plans to use its share of the profit to improve the library and purchase a new scoreboard for the football field. | You see that the school has much to gain from this arrangement, but you also know that obesity is a growing problem at the school. | Is there another way for the school to generate needed revenue without putting students' health at risk? |
| An increasing number of homeless people are seeking shelter on your college campus. | Campus security has stepped up its efforts to remove the homeless, even though the shelters off campus are overcrowded. | How can you persuade the school to shelter the homeless and to provide funds to support the needs of the homeless in your city? |

ask defines the area of inquiry as you read; it also can help you formulate your working thesis, the statement that answers your question. (We say more about developing a thesis in Chapter 5.) In this chapter, in addition to further discussing the importance of situation, we look at how you can identify issues and formulate questions to guide your reading and writing.

## IDENTIFYING ISSUES

Below we present several steps to identifying an issue. You don't have to follow them in this particular order, and you may find yourself going back and forth among them as you try to bring an issue into focus.

Keep in mind that issues do not simply exist in the world well formed. Instead, writers construct what they see as issues from the situations they observe. For example, consider legislation to limit downloads from the Internet. If such legislation conflicts with your own practices and sense of freedom, you may have begun to identify an issue: the clash of values over what constitutes fair use and what does not. Be aware that others may not understand your issue and that in your writing you will have to explain carefully what is at stake.

## ■ Draw on Your Personal Experience

You may have been taught that formal writing is objective, that you must keep a dispassionate distance from your subject, and that you should not use *I* in a college-level paper. The fact is, however, that our personal experiences influence how we read, what we pay attention to, and what inferences we draw. It makes sense, then, to begin with you—where you are and what you think and believe.

We all use personal experience to make arguments in our everyday lives. In an academic context, the challenge is to use personal experience to argue a point, to illustrate something, or to illuminate a connection between theories and the sense we make of our daily experience. You don't want simply to tell your story. You want your story to strengthen your argument.

For example, in *Cultural Literacy*, E. D. Hirsch personalizes his interest in reversing the cycle of illiteracy in America's cities. To establish the nature of the problem in the situation he describes, he cites research showing that student performance on standardized tests in the United States is falling. But he also reflects on his own teaching in the 1970s, when he first perceived "the widening knowledge gap [that] caused me to recognize the connection between specific background knowledge and mature literacy." And he injects anecdotal evidence from conversations with his son, a teacher. Those stories heighten readers' awareness that school-aged children do not know much about literature, history, or government. (For example, his son mentions a student who challenged his claim that Latin is a "dead language" by demanding, "What do they speak in Latin America?")

Hirsch's use of his son's testimony makes him vulnerable to criticism, as readers might question whether Hirsch can legitimately use his son's experience to make generalizations about education. But in fact, Hirsch is using personal testimony—his own and his son's—to augment and put a human face on the research he cites. He presents his issue, that schools must teach cultural literacy, both as something personal and as something with which we should all be concerned. The personal note helps readers see Hirsch as someone who has long been concerned with education and who has even raised a son who is an educator.

## ■ Identify What Is Open to Dispute

An issue is something that is open to dispute. Sometimes the way to clarify an issue is to think of it as a *fundamental tension* between two or more conflicting points of view. If you can identify conflicting points of view, an issue may become clear.

Consider E. D. Hirsch, who believes that the best approach to educational reform (the subject he writes about) is to change the curriculum in schools. His position: A curriculum based on cultural literacy is the one sure way to reverse the cycle of poverty and illiteracy in urban areas.

What is the issue? Hirsch's issue emerges in the presence of an alternative position. Jonathan Kozol, a social activist who has written extensively about educational reform, believes that policymakers need to address reform by providing the necessary resources that all students need to learn. Kozol points out that students in many inner-city schools are reading outdated textbooks and that the dilapidated conditions in these schools—windows that won't close, for example—make it impossible for students to learn.

In tension are two different views of the reform that can reverse illiteracy: Hirsch's view that educational reform should occur through curricular changes, and Kozol's view that educational reform demands socioeconomic resources.

## ■ Resist Binary Thinking

As you begin to define what is at issue, try to tease out complexities that may not be immediately apparent. That is, try to resist the either/or mindset that signals binary thinking.

If you considered only what Hirsch and Kozol have to say, it would be easy to characterize the problems facing our schools as either curricular or socioeconomic. But it may be that the real issue combines these arguments with a third or even a fourth, that neither curricular nor socioeconomic changes by themselves can resolve the problems with American schools.

After reading essays by both Hirsch and Kozol, one of our students pointed out that both Hirsch's focus on curriculum and Kozol's socioeconomic focus ignore another concern. She went on to describe her school experience in racial terms. In the excerpt below, notice how this writer uses personal experience (in a new school, she is not treated as she had expected to be treated) to formulate an issue.

> Moving from Colorado Springs to Tallahassee, I was immediately struck by the differences apparent in local home life, school life, and community unity, or lack thereof. Ripped from my sheltered world at a small Catholic school characterized by racial harmony, I was thrown into a large public school where outward prejudice from classmates and teachers and "race wars" were common and tolerated. . . .
>
> In a school where students and teachers had free rein to abuse anyone different from them, I was constantly abused. As the only black student in English honors, I was commonly belittled in front of my "peers" by my teacher. If I developed courage enough to ask a question, I was always answered with the use of improper grammar and such words as "ain't" as my teacher attempted to simplify the mate-

rial to "my level" and to give me what he called "a little learning." After discussing several subjects, he often turned to me, singling me out of a sea of white faces, and asked, "Do *you* understand, Mila?" When asking my opinion of a subject, he frequently questioned, "What do *your* people think about this?" Although he insisted on including such readings as Martin Luther King's "I Have a Dream" speech in the curriculum, the speech's themes of tolerance and equity did not accompany his lesson.

Through her reading, this student discovered that few prominent scholars have confronted the issue of racism in schools directly. Although she grants that curricular reform and increased funding may be necessary to improve education, she argues that scholars also need to address race in their studies of teaching and learning.

Our point is that issues may be more complex than you first think they are. For this student, the issue wasn't one of two positions—reform the curriculum or provide more funding. Instead, it combined a number of different positions, including race ("prejudice" and "race wars") and the relationship between student and teacher ("Do *you* understand, Mila?") in a classroom.

In this passage, the writer uses her experience to challenge binary thinking. Like the student writer, you should examine issues from different perspectives, avoiding either/or propositions that oversimplify the world.

## ■ Build on and Extend the Ideas of Others

Academic writing builds on and extends the ideas of others. As an academic writer, you will find that by extending other people's ideas, you will extend your own. You may begin in a familiar place, but as you read more and pursue connections to other readings, you may well end up at an unexpected destination.

For example, one of our students was troubled when he read Melissa Stormont-Spurgin's description of homeless children. The student uses details from her work (giving credit, of course) in his own:

> The children . . . went to school after less than three hours of sleep. They wore the same wrinkled clothes that they had worn the day before. What will their teachers think when they fall asleep in class? How will they get food for lunch? What will their peers think? What could these homeless children talk about with their peers? They have had to grow up too fast. Their worries are not the same as other children's worries. They are worried about their next meal and where they will seek shelter. Their needs, however, are the same. They need a home and all of the securities that come with it. They also need an education (Stormont-Spurgin 156).

Initially the student was troubled by his own access to quality schools, and the contrast between his life and the lives of the children Stormont-Spurgin describes. Initially, then, his issue was the fundamental tension between his own privileged status, something he had taken for granted, and the struggle that homeless children face every day.

However, as he read further and grew to understand homelessness as a concern in a number of studies, he connected his personal response to a larger conversation about democracy, fairness, and education:

> Melissa Stormont-Spurgin, an author of several articles on educational studies, addresses a very real and important, yet avoided issue in education today. Statistics show that a very high percentage of children who are born into homeless families will remain homeless, or in poverty, for the rest of their lives. How can this be, if everyone actually does have the same educational opportunities? There must be significant educational disadvantages for children without homes. In a democratic society, I feel that we must pay close attention to these disadvantages and do everything in our power to replace them with equality.

Ultimately, the student refined his sense of what was at issue: *Although all people should have access to public education in a democratic society, not everyone has the opportunity to attend quality schools in order to achieve personal success.* In turn, his definition of the issue began to shape his argument:

> Parents, teachers, homeless shelters, and the citizens of the United States who fund [homeless] shelters must address the educational needs of homeless children, while steering them away from any more financial or psychological struggles. Without this emphasis on education, the current trend upward in the number of homeless families will inevitably continue in the future of American society.

The student shifted away from a personal issue—the difference between his status and that of homeless children—to an issue of clashing values: the principle of egalitarian democracy on the one hand and the reality of citizens in a democracy living in abject poverty on the other. When he started to read about homeless children, he could not have made the claim he ends up making, that policymakers must make education a basic human right.

This student offers us an important lesson about the role of inquiry and the value of resisting easy answers. He has built on and extended his own ideas—and the ideas of others—after repeating the process of reading, raising questions, writing, and seeing problems a number of times.

## ■ Read to Discover a Writer's Frame

A more specialized strategy of building on and extending the ideas of others involves reading to discover a writer's **frame**, the perspective through which a writer presents his or her arguments. Writers want us to see the world a certain way, so they frame their arguments much the same way photographers and artists frame their pictures.

For example, if you were to take a picture of friends in front of the football stadium on campus, you would focus on what you would most like to remember—your friends' faces—blurring the images of the people walking behind your friends. Setting up the picture, or framing it, might require using light and shade to make some details stand out more than others. Writers do the same with language.

E. D. Hirsch uses the concept of *cultural literacy* to frame his argument for curricular reform. For Hirsch, the term is a benchmark, a standard: People who are culturally literate are familiar with the body of information that every educated citizen should know. Hirsch's implication, of course, is that people who are not culturally literate are not well educated. But that is not necessarily true. In fact, a number of educators insist that literacy is simply a means to an end—reading to complete an assignment, for example, or to understand the ramifications of a decision—not an end in itself. By defining and using *cultural literacy* as the goal of education, Hirsch is framing his argument; he is bringing his ideas into focus.

When writers use framing strategies, they also call attention to the specific conversations that set up the situation for their arguments. Framing often entails quoting specific theories and ideas from other authors and then using those quotations as a perspective, or lens, through which to examine other material. In his memoir *Hunger of Memory: The Education of Richard Rodriguez* (1982), Richard Rodriguez uses this method to examine his situation as a nonnative speaker of English desperate to enter the mainstream culture, even if it means sacrificing his identity as the son of Mexican immigrants. Reflecting on his life as a student, Rodriguez comes across Richard Hoggart's book *The Uses of Literacy* (1957). Hoggart's description of "the scholarship boy" presents a lens through which Rodriguez can see his own experience. Hoggart writes:

> With his family, the boy has the intense pleasure of intimacy, the family's consolation in feeling public alienation. Lavish emotions texture home life. *Then*, at school, the instruction bids him to trust lonely reason primarily. Immediate needs set the pace of his parents' lives. From his mother and father the boy learns to trust spontaneity and nonrational ways of knowing. *Then*, at school, there is mental calm. Teachers emphasize the value of a reflectiveness that opens a space between thinking and immediate action.
>
> Years of schooling must pass before the boy will be able to sketch the cultural differences in his day as abstractly as this. But he senses those differences early. Perhaps as early as the night he brings home an assignment from school and finds the house too noisy for study. He has to be more and more alone, if he is going to "get on." He will have, probably unconsciously, to oppose the ethos of the hearth, the intense gregariousness of the working-class family group. . . . The boy has to cut himself off mentally, so as to do his homework, as well as he can.

Here is Rodriguez's response to Hoggart's description of the scholarship boy:

> For weeks I read, speed-read, books by modern educational theorists, only to find infrequent and slight mention of students like me. . . . Then one day, leafing through Richard Hoggart's *The Uses of Literacy*, I found, in his description of the scholarship boy, myself. For the first time I realized that there were other students like me, and so I was able to frame the meaning of my academic success, its consequent price—the loss.

Notice how Rodriguez introduces ideas from Hoggart "to frame" his own ideas: "I found, in his description of the scholarship boy, myself. For the first time I realized that there were other students like me, and so I was able to frame the meaning of my academic success, its consequent price—the loss." Hoggart's scholarship boy enables Rodriguez to revisit his own experience with a new perspective. Hoggart's words and idea advance Rodriguez's understanding of the problem he identifies in his life: his inability to find solace at home and within his working-class roots. Hoggart's description of the scholarship boy's moving between cultural extremes—spontaneity at home and reflection at school—helps Rodriguez bring his own youthful discontent into focus.

Rodriguez's response to Hoggart's text shows how another writer's lens can help frame an issue. If you were using Hoggart's term *scholarship boy* as a lens through which to clarify an issue in education, you might ask how the term illuminates new aspects of another writer's examples or your own. And then you might ask, "To what extent does Hirsch's cultural literacy throw a more positive light on what Rodriguez and Hoggart describe?" or "How do my experiences challenge, extend, or complicate the scholarship-boy concept?"

## ■ Consider the Constraints of the Situation

In identifying an issue, you have to understand the situation that gives rise to the issue, including the contexts in which it is raised and debated. One of the contexts is the *audience*. In thinking about your issue, you must consider the extent to which your potential readers are involved in the dialogue you want to enter, and what they know and need to know. In a sense, audience functions as both context and **constraint**, a factor that narrows the choices you can make in responding to an issue. An understanding of your potential readers will help you choose the depth of your discussion; it will also determine the kind of evidence you can present and the language you can use.

Another constraint on your response to an issue is the form that response takes. For example, if you decide to make an issue of government-imposed limits on what you can download from the Internet, your response in writing might take the form of an editorial or a letter to a legislator. In this situation, length is an obvious constraint: Newspapers limit the word count of editorials, and the best letters to legislators tend to be brief and very selective about the evidence they cite. A few personal examples and a few statistics may be all you can include to support your claim about the issue. By contrast, if you were making your case in an academic journal, a very different set of constraints would apply. You would have more space for illustrations and support, for example.

Finally, the situation itself can function as a major constraint. For instance, suppose your topic is the decline of educational standards. It's difficult to imagine any writer making the case for accelerating that decline, or any audience being receptive to the idea that a decline in standards is a good thing.

---

### Steps to Identifying Issues

**1** **Draw on your personal experience.** Start with your own sense of what's important, what puzzles you, or what you are curious about. (Then build your argument by moving on to other sources to support your point of view.)

**2** **Identify what is open to dispute.** Identify a phenomenon or some idea in a written argument that challenges what you think or believe.

**3** **Resist binary thinking.** Think about the issue from multiple perspectives.

**4** **Build on and extend the ideas of others.** As you read, be open to new ways of looking at the issue. The issue you finally write about may be very different from what you set out to write about.

**5** **Read to discover a writer's frame.** What theories or ideas shape the writer's focus? How can these theories or ideas help you frame your argument?

**6** **Consider the constraints of the situation.** Craft your argument to meet the needs of and constraints imposed by your audience and form.

---

## ■ Identify Issues in an Essay

In the following editorial, published in 2002 in *Newsweek*, writer Anna Quindlen addresses her concern that middle-class parents overschedule their children's lives. She calls attention to the ways leisure time helped her develop as a writer and urges parents to consider the extent to which children's creativity depends on having some downtime. They don't always have to have their time scheduled. As you read Quindlen's "Doing Nothing Is Something," note what words and phrases Quindlen uses to identify the situation and to indicate who her audience is. Identify her main claim as one of fact, value, or policy. Finally, answer the questions that follow the selection to see if you can discern how she locates, defines, and advances her issue.

ANNA QUINDLEN

# Doing Nothing Is Something

Anna Quindlen is a best-selling author of novels and children's books, but she is perhaps most widely known for her nonfiction and commentary on current events and contemporary life. She won a Pulitzer Prize in 1992 for her "Public and Private" column in the *New York Times*, and for ten years wrote a biweekly column for *Newsweek*. Some of her novels are *Object Lessons* (1991), *Blessings* (2002), and *Every Last One* (2010). Her nonfiction works and collections include *Living Out Loud* (1988), *Thinking Out Loud* (1994), *Loud and Clear* (2004), and *Good Dog. Stay.* (2007).

■ ■ ■

Summer is coming soon. I can feel it in the softening of the air, but I can see it, too, in the textbooks on my children's desks. The number of uncut pages at the back grows smaller and smaller. The loose-leaf is ragged at the edges, the binder plastic ripped at the corners. An old remembered glee rises inside me. Summer is coming. Uniform skirts in mothballs. Pencils with their points left broken. Open windows. Day trips to the beach. Pickup games. Hanging out.  *1*

How boring it was.  *2*

Of course, it was the making of me, as a human being and a writer. Downtime is where we become ourselves, looking into the middle distance, kicking at the curb, lying on the grass, or sitting on the stoop and staring at the tedious blue of the summer sky. I don't believe you can write poetry, or compose music, or become an actor without downtime, and plenty of it, a hiatus that passes for boredom but is really the quiet moving of the wheels inside that fuel creativity.  *3*

And that, to me, is one of the saddest things about the lives of American children today. Soccer leagues, acting classes, tutors—the calendar of the average middle-class kid is so over the top that soon Palm handhelds will be sold in Toys "R" Us. Our children are as overscheduled as we are, and that is saying something.  *4*

This has become so bad that parents have arranged to schedule times for unscheduled time. Earlier this year the privileged suburb of Ridgewood, New Jersey, announced a Family Night, when there would be no homework, no athletic practices, and no after-school events. This was terribly exciting until I realized that this was not one night a week, but one single night. There is even a free-time movement, and Web site: familylife1st.org. Among the frequently asked questions provided online: "What would families do with family time if they took it back?"  *5*

Let me make a suggestion for the kids involved: How about nothing? It is not simply that it is pathetic to consider the lives of children who don't have a moment between piano and dance and homework to talk about their day or just search for split ends, an enormously satisfying leisure-  *6* time activity of my youth. There is also ample psychological research suggesting that what we might call "doing nothing" is when human beings actually do their best thinking, and when creativity comes to call. Perhaps we are creating an entire generation of people whose ability to think outside the box, as the current parlance of business has it, is being systematically stunted by scheduling.

A study by the University of Michigan quantified the downtime deficit; in the last 20 years American kids have lost about four unstructured hours a week. There has even arisen a global Right to Play movement: in the Third World it is often about child labor, but in the United States it is about the sheer labor of being a perpetually busy child. In Omaha, Nebraska, a group of parents recently lobbied for additional recess. Hooray, and yikes.

How did this happen? Adults did it. There is a culture of adult distrust that suggests that a kid who is not playing softball or attending science-enrichment programs—or both—is huffing or boosting cars: if kids are left alone, they will not stare into the middle distance and consider the meaning of life and how come your nose in pictures never looks the way you think it should, but instead will get into trouble. There is also the culture of cutthroat and unquestioning competition that leads even the parents of preschoolers to gab about prestigious colleges without a trace of irony: this suggests that any class in which you do not enroll your first grader will put him at a disadvantage in, say, law school.

Finally, there is a culture of workplace presence (as opposed to productivity). Try as we might to suggest that all these enrichment activities are for the good of the kid, there is ample evidence that they are really for the convenience of parents with way too little leisure time of their own. Stories about the resignation of presidential aide Karen Hughes unfailingly reported her dedication to family time by noting that she arranged to get home at 5:30 one night a week to have dinner with her son. If one weekday dinner out of five is considered laudable, what does that say about what's become commonplace?

Summer is coming. It used to be a time apart for kids, a respite from the clock and the copybook, the organized day. Every once in a while, either guilty or overwhelmed or tired of listening to me keen about my monumental boredom, my mother would send me to some rinky-dink park program that consisted almost entirely of three-legged races and making things out of Popsicle sticks. Now, instead, there are music camps, sports camps, fat camps, probably thin camps. I mourn hanging out in the backyard. I mourn playing Wiffle ball in the street without a sponsor and matching shirts. I mourn drawing in the dirt with a stick.

Maybe that kind of summer is gone for good. Maybe this is the leading edge of a new way of living that not only has no room for contemplation but is contemptuous of it. But if downtime cannot be squeezed during the school year into the life of frantic and often joyless activity with which our children are saddled while their parents pursue frantic and often joyless activity of their own, what about summer? Do most adults really want to stand in line for Space Mountain or sit in traffic to get to a shore house that doesn't have enough saucepans? Might it be even more enriching for their children to stay at home and do nothing? For those who say they will only watch TV or play on the computer, a piece of technical advice: the cable box can be unhooked, the modem removed. Perhaps it is not too late for American kids to be given the gift of enforced boredom for at least a week or two, staring into space, bored out of their gourds, exploring the inside of their own heads. "To contemplate is to toil, to think is to do," said Victor Hugo. "Go outside and play," said Prudence Quindlen. Both of them were right.

### Reading as a Writer

1. What evidence of Quindlen's personal responses and experiences can you identify?

2. What phenomenon has prompted her to reflect on what she thinks and believes? How has she made it into an issue?

3. Where does she indicate that she has considered the issue from multiple perspectives and is placing her ideas in conversation with those of others?

4. What sort of lens does she seem to be using to frame her argument?

5. What constraints (such as the format of an editorial) seem to be in play in the essay?

### A Practice Sequence: Identifying Issues

This sequence of activities will give you practice in identifying and clarifying issues based on your own choice of reading and collaboration with your classmates.

1 Draw on your personal experience. Reflect on your own responses to what you have been reading in this class or in other classes, or issues that writers have posed in the media. What concerns you most? Choose a story that supports or challenges the claims people are making in what you have read or listened to. What questions do you have? Make some notes in response to these questions, explaining your personal stake in the issues and questions you formulate.

2 Identify what is open to dispute. Take what you have written and formulate your ideas as an issue, using the structure we used in our example of Hirsch's and Kozol's competing arguments:

- Part 1: Your view of a given topic
- Part 2: At least one view that is in tension with your own

If you need to, read further to understand what others have to say about this issue.

3  Resist binary thinking. Share your statement of the issue with one or more peers and ask them if they see other ways to formulate the issue that you may not have thought about. What objections, if any, do they make to your statement in part 1? Write these objections down in part 2 so that you begin to look at the issue from multiple perspectives.

4  Build on and extend the ideas of others. Now that you have formulated an issue from different perspectives, explaining your personal stake in the issue, connect what you think to a broader conversation in what you are reading. Then try making a claim using this structure: "Although some people would argue _____, I think that _____."

5  Read to discover a writer's frame. As an experiment in trying out multiple perspectives, revise the claim you make in exercise 4 by introducing the frame, or lens, through which you want readers to understand your argument. You can employ the same sentence structure. For example, here is a claim framed in terms of race: "Although people should have access to public education, recent policies have worsened racial inequalities in public schools." In contrast, here is a claim that focuses on economics: "Although people should have access to public education, the unequal distribution of tax money has created what some would call an 'economy of education.'" The lens may come from reading you have done in other courses or from conversations with your classmates, and you may want to attribute the lens to a particular author or classmate: "Although some people would argue_____, I use E. D. Hirsch's notion of cultural literacy to show_____."

6  Consider the constraints of the situation. Building on these exercises, develop an argument in the form of an editorial for your local newspaper. This means that you will need to limit your argument to about 250 words. You also will need to consider the extent to which your potential readers are involved in the conversation. What do they know? What do they need to know? What kind of evidence do you need to use to persuade readers?

## FORMULATING ISSUE-BASED QUESTIONS

As we have said, when you identify an issue, you need to understand it in the context of its situation. Ideally, the situation and the issue will be both relevant and recent, making the task of connecting to your audience that much easier when you write about the issue. For example, the student writer who was concerned about long-standing issues of homelessness and lack of educational opportunity connected to his readers by citing recent statistics and giving the problem of homelessness a face: "The children . . . went to school after less than three hours of sleep. They wore the same wrinkled clothes that they had worn the day before." If your issue does not immediately fulfill the criteria of relevance and timeliness, you need to take that into consideration as you continue your reading and research on the issue. Ask yourself, "What is on people's minds these days?" "What do they need to know about?" Think about why the issue matters to you, and imagine why it might matter to others. By the time you write, you should be prepared to make the issue relevant for your readers.

In addition to understanding the situation and defining the issue that you feel is most relevant and timely, you can formulate an issue-based question that can help you think through what you might be interested in writing about. This question should be specific enough to guide inquiry into what others have written. An issue-based question can also help you accomplish the following:

- Clarify what you know about the issue and what you still need to know
- Guide your inquiry with a clear focus
- Organize your inquiry around a specific issue
- Develop an argument, rather than simply collecting information by asking "how," "why," "should," or "the extent to which something is or is not true"
- Consider who your audience is
- Determine what resources you have, so that you can ask a question that you will be able to answer with the resources available to you

A good question develops out of an issue, some fundamental tension that you identify within a conversation. In "Doing Nothing Is Something," Anna Quindlen identifies a problem that middle-class parents need to know about: that overscheduling their children's lives may limit their children's potential for developing their creativity. As she explores the reasons why children do not have sufficient downtime, she raises a question that encourages parents to consider what would happen if they gave their children time to do nothing: "Might it be even more enriching for their children to stay at home and do nothing?" (para. 11). Through identifying what is at issue, you should begin to understand for whom it is an issue — for whom you are answering the question. In turn, the answer to your question will help you craft your thesis.

In the following paragraphs, we trace the steps one of our students took to formulate an issue-based question on the broad topic of language diversity. Although we present the steps in sequence, be aware that they are guidelines only: The steps often overlap, and there is a good deal of room for rethinking and refining along the way.

## ■ Refine Your Topic

Generally speaking, a **topic** is the subject you want to write about. For example, homelessness, tests, and violence are all topics. So are urban homelessness, standardized tests, and video game violence. And so are homelessness in New York City, aptitude tests versus achievement tests, and mayhem in the video game Grand Theft Auto. As our list suggests, even a specific topic needs refining into an issue before it can be explored effectively in writing.

The topic our student wanted to focus on was language diversity, a subject her linguistics class had been discussing. She was fascinated by the extraordinary range of languages spoken in the United States, not just by immigrant groups but by native speakers whose dialects and varieties of English are considered nonstandard. She herself had relatives for whom English was not a first language. She began refining her topic by putting her thoughts into words:

> I want to describe the experience of being raised in a home where non–Standard English is spoken.

> I'd like to know the benefits and liabilities of growing up bilingual.

> I am curious to know what it's like to live in a community of nonnative speakers of English while trying to make a living in a country where the dominant language is English.

Although she had yet to identify an issue, her attempts to articulate what interested her about the topic were moving her toward the situation of people in the United States who don't speak Standard English or don't have English as their first language.

## ■ Explain Your Interest in the Topic

At this point, the student encountered E. D. Hirsch's *Cultural Literacy* in her reading, which had both a provocative and a clarifying effect on her thinking. She began to build on and extend Hirsch's ideas. Reacting to Hirsch's assumption that students should acquire the same base of knowledge and write in Standard Written English, her first, somewhat mischievous thought was, "I wonder what Hirsch would think about cultural literacy being taught in a bilingual classroom?" But then her thinking took another turn, and she began to contemplate the effect of Hirsch's cultural-literacy agenda on speakers whose English is not standard or for whom English is not a first language. She used a demographic fact that she had learned in her linguistics class in her explanation of her interest in the topic: "I'm curious about the consequences of limiting language diversity when the presence of ethnic minorities in our educational system is growing."

## ■ Identify an Issue

The more she thought about Hirsch's ideas, and the more she read about language diversity, the more concerned our student grew. It seemed to her that Hirsch's interest in producing students who all share the same base of knowledge and all write in Standard Written English was in tension with her sense that this kind of approach places a burden on people whose first language is not English. That tension clarified the issue for her. In identifying the issue, she wrote:

> Hirsch's book actually sets some priorities, most notably through his list of words and phrases that form the foundations of what it means to be "American." However, this list certainly overlooks several crucial influences in American culture. Most oversights generally come at the expense of the minority populations.

These two concerns—with inclusion and with exclusion—helped focus the student's inquiry.

## ■ Formulate Your Topic as a Question

To further define her inquiry, the student formulated her topic as a question that pointed toward an argument: "To what extent can E. D. Hirsch's notion of 'cultural literacy' coexist with our country's principles of democracy and inclusion?" Notice that her choice of the phrase *To what extent* implies that both goals do not go hand in hand. If she had asked, "Can common culture coexist with pluralism?" her phrasing would imply that a yes or no answer would suffice, possibly foreclosing avenues of inquiry and certainly ignoring the complexity of the issue.

Instead, despite her misgivings about the implications of Hirsch's agenda, the student suspended judgment, opening the way to genuine inquiry. She acknowledged the usefulness and value of sharing a common language and conceded that Hirsch's points were well taken. She wrote:

> Some sort of unification is necessary. Language, . . . on the most fundamental level of human interaction, demands some compromise and chosen guidelines. . . . How can we learn from one another if we cannot even say hello to each other?

Suspending judgment led her to recognize the complexity of the issue, and her willingness to examine the issue from different perspectives indicated the empathy that is a central component of developing a conversational argument.

## ■ Acknowledge Your Audience

This student's question ("To what extent can E. D. Hirsch's notion of 'cultural literacy' coexist with our country's principles of democracy and inclusion?") also acknowledged an audience. By invoking cultural literacy, she assumed an audience of readers who are familiar with Hirsch's ideas, probably including policymakers and educational administrators. In gesturing toward democracy, she cast her net very wide: Most Americans probably admire the "principles of democracy." But in specifying inclusion as a democratic principle, she wisely linked all Americans who believe in democratic principles, including the parents of schoolchildren, with all people who have reason to feel excluded by Hirsch's ideas, especially nonnative speakers of English, among them immigrants from Mexico and speakers of African American Vernacular English. Thus, this student was acknowledging an audience of policymakers, administrators, parents (both mainstream and marginalized), and those who knew about and perhaps supported cultural literacy.

## Steps to Formulating an Issue-Based Question

**1** **Refine your topic.** Examine your topic from different perspectives. For example, what are the causes of homelessness? What are its consequences?

**2** **Explain your interest in the topic.** Explore the source of your interest in this topic and what you want to learn.

**3** **Identify an issue.** Determine what is open to dispute.

**4** **Formulate your topic as a question.** Use your question to focus your inquiry.

**5** **Acknowledge your audience.** Reflect on what readers may know about the issue, why they may be interested, and what you would like to teach them.

## A Practice Sequence: Formulating an Issue-Based Question

As you start developing your own issue-based question, it might be useful to practice a five-step process that begins with a topic, a word or phrase that describes the focus of your interests. Here, apply the process to the one-word topic homelessness.

**1** Expand your topic into a phrase. "I am interested in the *consequences* of homelessness," "I want to *describe* what it means to be homeless," or "I am interested in discussing the *cause* of homelessness."

**2** Explain your interest in this topic. "I am interested in the consequences of homelessness because it challenges democratic principles of fairness."

3 Identify an issue. "The persistence of homelessness contradicts my belief in social justice."

4 Formulate your topic as a question. "To what extent can we allow homelessness to persist in a democratic nation that prides itself on providing equal opportunity to all?"

5 Acknowledge your audience. "I am interested in the consequences of homelessness because I want people who believe in democracy to understand that we need to work harder to make sure that everyone has access to food, shelter, and employment."

The answer to the question you formulate in step 4 should lead to an assertion, your main claim, or *thesis*. For example, you could state your main claim this way: "Although homelessness persists as a widespread problem in our nation, we must develop policies that eliminate homelessness, ensuring that everyone has access to food, shelter, and employment. This is especially important in a democracy that embraces social justice and equality."

The thesis introduces a problem and makes an assertion that you will need to support: "We must develop policies that eliminate homelessness, ensuring that everyone has access to food, shelter, and employment." What is at issue? Not everyone would agree that policies must be implemented to solve the problem. In fact, many would argue that homelessness is an individual problem, that individuals must take responsibility for lifting themselves out of poverty, homelessness, and unemployment. Of course, you would need to read quite a bit to reach this final stage of formulating your thesis.

Try using the five-step process we describe above to formulate your own topic as a question, or try formulating the following topics as questions:

- Violence in video games
- Recycling
- The popularity of a cultural phenomenon (a book, a film, a performer, an icon)
- Standardized tests
- Professional sports injuries
- Town-gown relationships
- Media and representation
- Government and religion
- Vegetarianism

## AN ACADEMIC ESSAY FOR ANALYSIS

The following essay by William Deresiewicz provides an intriguing academic extension of the homely topic that Anna Quindlen writes about (p. 82): the need for the young to have solitary, unscheduled time. His essay illustrates many of the strategies we have discussed thus far: raising questions, stating a thesis by placing an argument in the stream of a broader conversation, using evidence to support his claims. As you read Deresiewicz's essay, you might use the following questions as a guide:

- What is Deresiewicz's thesis? Would you characterize his claim as one of fact? Value?
- What types of evidence does he use to support his claim?
- What do Deresiewicz's vocabulary and citations indicate about his target audience?
- What does Deresiewicz want his readers to do or think about?

### WILLIAM DERESIEWICZ

## The End of Solitude

William Deresiewicz taught English at Yale University from 1998 to 2008. He is now a contributing writer at *The Nation* and was nominated for a 2009 National Magazine Award for his reviews and criticism. His essay "The End of Solitude" appeared in *The Chronicle of Higher Education* in January 2009 and represents one of many debates about literacy that scholars have waged concerning the benefits and limits of new technologies. Deresiewicz observes that technology fulfills a human impulse to be known, to be connected with others. Posting on MySpace, Twitter, and Facebook enables us to be visible and helps validate who we are as individuals. However, he worries that this instinct to be connected also has an adverse effect: We lose a sense of solitude and the space he believes we all need to have in order to understand who we are, what we believe, and what we value. He worries, too, that a new generation does not see the point of solitude because so many young people equate solitude with loneliness.

■ ■ ■

What does the contemporary self want? The camera has created a culture of celebrity; the computer is creating a culture of connectivity. As the two technologies converge—broadband tipping the Web from text to image, social-networking sites spreading the mesh of interconnection ever wider—the two cultures betray a common impulse. Celebrity and connectivity are both ways of becoming known. This is what the contemporary self wants. It wants to be recognized, wants to be connected: It wants to be visible. If not to the millions, on *Survivor* or

*Oprah*, then to the hundreds, on Twitter or Facebook. This is the quality that validates us, this is how we become real to ourselves—by being seen by others. The great contemporary terror is anonymity. If Lionel Trilling was right, if the property that grounded the self, in Romanticism, was sincerity, and in modernism it was authenticity, then in postmodernism it is visibility.

So we live exclusively in relation to others, and what disappears from our lives is solitude. Technology is taking away our privacy and our concentration, but it is also taking away our ability to be alone. Though I shouldn't say taking away. We are doing this to ourselves; we are discarding these riches as fast as we can. I was told by one of her older relatives that a teenager I know had sent 3,000 text messages one recent month. That's 100 a day, or about one every 10 waking minutes, morning, noon, and night, weekdays and weekends, class time, lunch time, homework time, and toothbrushing time. So on average, she's never alone for more than 10 minutes at once. Which means, she's never alone.   *2*

I once asked my students about the place that solitude has in their lives. One of them admitted that she finds the prospect of being alone so unsettling that she'll sit with a friend even when she has a paper to write. Another said, why would anyone want to be alone?   *3*

To that remarkable question, history offers a number of answers. Man may be a social animal, but solitude has traditionally been a societal value. In particular, the act of being alone has been understood as an essential dimension of religious experience, albeit one restricted to a self-selected few. Through the solitude of rare spirits, the collective renews its relationship with divinity. The prophet and the hermit, the sadhu and the yogi, pursue their vision quests, invite their trances, in desert or forest or cave. For the still, small voice speaks only in silence. Social life is a bustle of petty concerns, a jostle of quotidian interests, and religious institutions are no exception. You cannot hear God when people are chattering at you, and the divine word, their pretensions notwithstanding, demurs at descending on the monarch and the priest. Communal experience is the human norm, but the solitary encounter with God is the egregious act that refreshes that norm. (Egregious, for no man is a prophet in his own land. Tiresias was reviled before he was vindicated, Teresa interrogated before she was canonized.) Religious solitude is a kind of self-correcting social mechanism, a way of burning out the underbrush of moral habit and spiritual custom. The seer returns with new tablets or new dances, his face bright with the old truth.   *4*

Like other religious values, solitude was democratized by the Reformation and secularized by Romanticism. In Marilynne Robinson's interpretation, Calvinism created the modern self by focusing the soul inward, leaving it to encounter God, like a prophet of old, in "profound isolation." To her enumeration of Calvin, Marguerite de Navarre, and Milton as pioneering early-modern selves we can add Montaigne, Hamlet, and even   *5*

Don Quixote. The last figure alerts us to reading's essential role in this transformation, the printing press serving an analogous function in the sixteenth and subsequent centuries to that of television and the Internet in our own. Reading, as Robinson puts it, "is an act of great inwardness and subjectivity." "The soul encountered itself in response to a text, first Genesis or Matthew and then *Paradise Lost* or *Leaves of Grass*." With Protestantism and printing, the quest for the divine voice became available to, even incumbent upon, everyone.

But it is with Romanticism that solitude achieved its greatest cultural salience, becoming both literal and literary. Protestant solitude is still only figurative. Rousseau and Wordsworth made it physical. The self was now encountered not in God but in Nature, and to encounter Nature one had to go to it. And go to it with a special sensibility: The poet displaced the saint as social seer and cultural model. But because Romanticism also inherited the eighteenth-century idea of social sympathy, Romantic solitude existed in a dialectical relationship with sociability—if less for Rousseau and still less for Thoreau, the most famous solitary of all, then certainly for Wordsworth, Melville, Whitman, and many others. For Emerson, "the soul environs itself with friends, that it may enter into a grander self-acquaintance or solitude; and it goes alone, for a season, that it may exalt its conversation or society." The Romantic practice of solitude is neatly captured by Trilling's "sincerity": the belief that the self is validated by a congruity of public appearance and private essence, one that stabilizes its relationship with both itself and others. Especially, as Emerson suggests, one beloved other. Hence the famous Romantic friendship pairs: Goethe and Schiller, Wordsworth and Coleridge, Hawthorne and Melville.

Modernism decoupled this dialectic. Its notion of solitude was harsher, more adversarial, more isolating. As a model of the self and its interactions, Hume's social sympathy gave way to Pater's thick wall of personality and Freud's narcissism—the sense that the soul, self-enclosed and inaccessible to others, can't choose but be alone. With exceptions, like Woolf, the modernists fought shy of friendship. Joyce and Proust disparaged it; D. H. Lawrence was wary of it; the modernist friendship pairs—Conrad and Ford, Eliot and Pound, Hemingway and Fitzgerald—were altogether cooler than their Romantic counterparts. The world was now understood as an assault on the self, and with good reason.

The Romantic ideal of solitude developed in part as a reaction to the emergence of the modern city. In modernism, the city is not only more menacing than ever, it has become inescapable, a labyrinth: Eliot's London, Joyce's Dublin. The mob, the human mass, presses in. Hell is other people. The soul is forced back into itself—hence the development of a more austere, more embattled form of self-validation, Trilling's "authenticity," where the essential relationship is only with oneself. (Just as there are few good friendships in modernism, so are there few good marriages.)

Solitude becomes, more than ever, the arena of heroic self-discovery, a voyage through interior realms made vast and terrifying by Nietzschean and Freudian insights. To achieve authenticity is to look upon these visions without flinching; Trilling's exemplar here is Kurtz. Protestant self-examination becomes Freudian analysis, and the culture hero, once a prophet of God and then a poet of Nature, is now a novelist of self—a Dostoyevsky, a Joyce, a Proust.

But we no longer live in the modernist city, and our great fear is not    9
submersion by the mass but isolation from the herd. Urbanization gave way to suburbanization, and with it the universal threat of loneliness. What technologies of transportation exacerbated—we could live farther and farther apart—technologies of communication redressed—we could bring ourselves closer and closer together. Or at least, so we have imagined. The first of these technologies, the first simulacrum of proximity, was the telephone. "Reach out and touch someone." But through the 1970s and 1980s, our isolation grew. Suburbs, sprawling ever farther, became exurbs. Families grew smaller or splintered apart, mothers left the home to work. The electronic hearth became the television in every room. Even in childhood, certainly in adolescence, we were each trapped inside our own cocoon. Soaring crime rates, and even more sharply escalating rates of moral panic, pulled children off the streets. The idea that you could go outside and run around the neighborhood with your friends, once unquestionable, has now become unthinkable. The child who grew up between the world wars as part of an extended family within a tight-knit urban community became the grandparent of a kid who sat alone in front of a big television, in a big house, on a big lot. We were lost in space.

Under those circumstances, the Internet arrived as an incalculable    10
blessing. We should never forget that. It has allowed isolated people to communicate with one another and marginalized people to find one another. The busy parent can stay in touch with far-flung friends. The gay teenager no longer has to feel like a freak. But as the Internet's dimensionality has grown, it has quickly become too much of a good thing. Ten years ago we were writing e-mail messages on desktop computers and transmitting them over dial-up connections. Now we are sending text messages on our cellphones, posting pictures on our Facebook pages, and following complete strangers on Twitter. A constant stream of mediated contact, virtual, notional, or simulated, keeps us wired in to the electronic hive—though contact, or at least two-way contact, seems increasingly beside the point. The goal now, it seems, is simply to become known, to turn oneself into a sort of miniature celebrity. How many friends do I have on Facebook? How many people are reading my blog? How many Google hits does my name generate? Visibility secures our self-esteem, becoming a substitute, twice removed, for genuine connection. Not long ago, it was easy to feel lonely. Now, it is impossible to be alone.

As a result, we are losing both sides of the Romantic dialectic. What   *11*
does friendship mean when you have 532 "friends"? How does it enhance
my sense of closeness when my Facebook News Feed tells me that Sally
Smith (whom I haven't seen since high school, and wasn't all that friendly
with even then) "is making coffee and staring off into space"? My students told me they have little time for intimacy. And of course, they have
no time at all for solitude.

But at least friendship, if not intimacy, is still something they want. As   *12*
jarring as the new dispensation may be for people in their 30s and 40s, the
real problem is that it has become completely natural for people in their
teens and 20s. Young people today seem to have no desire for solitude,
have never heard of it, can't imagine why it would be worth having. In
fact, their use of technology—or to be fair, our use of technology—seems
to involve a constant effort to stave off the possibility of solitude, a continuous attempt, as we sit alone at our computers, to maintain the imaginative presence of others. As long ago as 1952, Trilling wrote about "the
modern fear of being cut off from the social group even for a moment."
Now we have equipped ourselves with the means to prevent that fear
from ever being realized. Which does not mean that we have put it to
rest. Quite the contrary. Remember my student, who couldn't even write
a paper by herself. The more we keep aloneness at bay, the less are we
able to deal with it and the more terrifying it gets.

There is an analogy, it seems to me, with the previous generation's   *13*
experience of boredom. The two emotions, loneliness and boredom, are
closely allied. They are also both characteristically modern. The *Oxford
English Dictionary*'s earliest citations of either word, at least in the contemporary sense, date from the nineteenth century. Suburbanization, by
eliminating the stimulation as well as the sociability of urban or traditional village life, exacerbated the tendency to both. But the great age of
boredom, I believe, came in with television, precisely because television
was designed to palliate that feeling. Boredom is not a necessary consequence of having nothing to do, it is only the negative experience of that
state. Television, by obviating the need to learn how to make use of one's
lack of occupation, precludes one from ever discovering how to enjoy it.
In fact, it renders that condition fearsome, its prospect intolerable. You
are terrified of being bored—so you turn on the television.

I speak from experience. I grew up in the 1960s and 1970s, the age of   *14*
television. I was trained to be bored; boredom was cultivated within me
like a precious crop. (It has been said that consumer society wants to condition us to feel bored, since boredom creates a market for stimulation.)
It took me years to discover—and my nervous system will never fully
adjust to this idea; I still have to fight against boredom, am permanently
damaged in this respect—that having nothing to do doesn't have to be a
bad thing. The alternative to boredom is what Whitman called idleness: a
passive receptivity to the world.

So it is with the current generation's experience of being alone. That is    *15*
precisely the recognition implicit in the idea of solitude, which is to loneliness what idleness is to boredom. Loneliness is not the absence of company, it is grief over that absence. The lost sheep is lonely; the shepherd
is not lonely. But the Internet is as powerful a machine for the production of loneliness as television is for the manufacture of boredom. If six
hours of television a day creates the aptitude for boredom, the inability
to sit still, a hundred text messages a day creates the aptitude for loneliness, the inability to be by yourself. Some degree of boredom and loneliness is to be expected, especially among young people, given the way our
human environment has been attenuated. But technology amplifies those
tendencies. You could call your schoolmates when I was a teenager, but
you couldn't call them 100 times a day. You could get together with your
friends when I was in college, but you couldn't always get together with
them when you wanted to, for the simple reason that you couldn't always
find them. If boredom is the great emotion of the TV generation, loneliness is the great emotion of the Web generation. We lost the ability to be
still, our capacity for idleness. They have lost the ability to be alone, their
capacity for solitude.

And losing solitude, what have they lost? First, the propensity for in-    *16*
trospection, that examination of the self that the Puritans, and the
Romantics, and the modernists (and Socrates, for that matter) placed at
the center of spiritual life—of wisdom, of conduct. Thoreau called it fishing "in the Walden Pond of [our] own natures," "bait[ing our] hooks with
darkness." Lost, too, is the related propensity for sustained reading. The
Internet brought text back into a televisual world, but it brought it back
on terms dictated by that world—that is, by its remapping of our attention spans. Reading now means skipping and skimming; five minutes on
the same Web page is considered an eternity. This is not reading as
Marilynne Robinson described it: the encounter with a second self in the
silence of mental solitude.

But we no longer believe in the solitary mind. If the Romantics had    *17*
Hume and the modernists had Freud, the current psychological model—
and this should come as no surprise—is that of the networked or social
mind. Evolutionary psychology tells us that our brains developed to
interpret complex social signals. According to David Brooks, that reliable
index of the social-scientific zeitgeist, cognitive scientists tell us that "our
decision-making is powerfully influenced by social context"; neuroscientists, that we have "permeable minds" that function in part through a
process of "deep imitation"; psychologists, that "we are organized by our
attachments"; sociologists, that our behavior is affected by "the power
of social networks." The ultimate implication is that there is no mental
space that is not social (contemporary social science dovetailing here
with postmodern critical theory). One of the most striking things about
the way young people relate to one another today is that they no longer
seem to believe in the existence of Thoreau's "darkness."

The MySpace page, with its shrieking typography and clamorous im-   *18*
agery, has replaced the journal and the letter as a way of creating and
communicating one's sense of self. The suggestion is not only that such
communication is to be made to the world at large rather than to oneself or one's intimates, or graphically rather than verbally, or performa-
tively rather than narratively or analytically, but also that it can be made
completely. Today's young people seem to feel that they can make themselves fully known to one another. They seem to lack a sense of their own
depths, and of the value of keeping them hidden.

If they didn't, they would understand that solitude enables us to secure   *19*
the integrity of the self as well as to explore it. Few have shown this more
beautifully than Woolf. In the middle of *Mrs. Dalloway*, between her navigation of the streets and her orchestration of the party, between the urban
jostle and the social bustle, Clarissa goes up, "like a nun withdrawing," to
her attic room. Like a nun: She returns to a state that she herself thinks of
as a kind of virginity. This does not mean she's a prude. Virginity is classically the outward sign of spiritual inviolability, of a self untouched by the
world, a soul that has preserved its integrity by refusing to descend into
the chaos and self-division of sexual and social relations. It is the mark
of the saint and the monk, of Hippolytus and Antigone and Joan of Arc.
Solitude is both the social image of that state and the means by which
we can approximate it. And the supreme image in *Mrs. Dalloway* of the
dignity of solitude itself is the old woman whom Clarissa catches sight of
through her window. "Here was one room," she thinks, "there another."
We are not merely social beings. We are each also separate, each solitary,
each alone in our own room, each miraculously our unique selves and
mysteriously enclosed in that selfhood.

To remember this, to hold oneself apart from society, is to begin to   *20*
think one's way beyond it. Solitude, Emerson said, "is to genius the stern
friend." "He who should inspire and lead his race must be defended from
traveling with the souls of other men, from living, breathing, reading, and
writing in the daily, time-worn yoke of their opinions." One must protect
oneself from the momentum of intellectual and moral consensus—especially, Emerson added, during youth. "God is alone," Thoreau said, "but
the Devil, he is far from being alone; he sees a great deal of company; he
is legion." The university was to be praised, Emerson believed, if only
because it provided its charges with "a separate chamber and fire"—the
physical space of solitude. Today, of course, universities do everything
they can to keep their students from being alone, lest they perpetrate self-
destructive acts, and also, perhaps, unfashionable thoughts. But no real
excellence, personal or social, artistic, philosophical, scientific, or moral,
can arise without solitude. "The saint and poet seek privacy," Emerson
said, "to ends the most public and universal." We are back to the seer,
seeking signposts for the future in splendid isolation.

Solitude isn't easy, and isn't for everyone. It has undoubtedly never   *21*
been the province of more than a few. "I believe," Thoreau said, "that

men are generally still a little afraid of the dark." Teresa and Tiresias will always be the exceptions, or to speak in more relevant terms, the young people—and they still exist—who prefer to loaf and invite their soul, who step to the beat of a different drummer. But if solitude disappears as a social value and social idea, will even the exceptions remain possible? Still, one is powerless to reverse the drift of the culture. One can only save oneself—and whatever else happens, one can still always do that. But it takes a willingness to be unpopular.

The last thing to say about solitude is that it isn't very polite. Thoreau knew that the "doubleness" that solitude cultivates, the ability to stand back and observe life dispassionately, is apt to make us a little unpleasant to our fellows, to say nothing of the offense implicit in avoiding their company. But then, he didn't worry overmuch about being genial. He didn't even like having to talk to people three times a day, at meals; one can only imagine what he would have made of text-messaging. We, however, have made of geniality—the weak smile, the polite interest, the fake invitation—a cardinal virtue. Friendship may be slipping from our grasp, but our friendliness is universal. Not for nothing does "gregarious" mean "part of the herd." But Thoreau understood that securing one's self-possession was worth a few wounded feelings. He may have put his neighbors off, but at least he was sure of himself. Those who would find solitude must not be afraid to stand alone. 22

### Writing as a Reader

1. Recast Deresiewicz's essay as Anna Quindlen might in her *Newsweek* column. Obviously, her *Newsweek* column is much shorter (an important constraint). She also writes for a more general audience than Deresiewicz, and her tone is quite different. To strengthen your sense of her approach, you may want to browse some of Quindlen's other essays in editions of *Newsweek* or in some of her essay collections listed in the headnote on page 82.

2. Recast Deresiewicz's essay in terms of a writer you read regularly—for example, a columnist in your local newspaper or a blogger in some online venue. Use your imagination. What is the audience, and how will you have to present the issue to engage and persuade them?

# 5

# From Formulating to Developing a Thesis

Academic writing explores complex issues that grow out of relevant, timely conversations in which something is at stake. An academic writer reads as a writer to understand the issues, situations, and questions that lead other writers to make claims. Readers expect academic writers to take a clear, specific, logical stand on an issue, and they evaluate how writers support their claims and anticipate counterarguments. The logical stand is the **thesis**, an assertion that academic writers make at the beginning of what they write and then support with evidence throughout their essay. The illustrations and examples that a writer includes must relate to and support the thesis. Thus, a thesis encompasses all of the information writers use to further their arguments; it is not simply a single assertion at the beginning of an essay.

One of our students aptly described the thesis using the metaphor of a shish kebab: The thesis penetrates every paragraph, holding the paragraphs together, just as a skewer penetrates and holds the ingredients of a shish kebab together. Moreover, the thesis serves as a signpost throughout an essay, reminding readers what the argument is and why the writer has included evidence—examples, illustrations, quotations—relevant to that argument.

An academic thesis

- makes an assertion that is clearly defined, focused, and supported.

- reflects an awareness of the conversation from which the writer has taken up the issue.

- is placed at the beginning of the essay.

- penetrates every paragraph like the skewer in a shish kebab.
- acknowledges points of view that differ from the writer's own, reflecting the complexity of the issue.
- demonstrates an awareness of the readers' assumptions and anticipates possible counterarguments.
- conveys a significant fresh perspective.

It is a myth that writers first come up with a thesis and then write their essays. The reality is that writers use issue-based questions to read, learn, and develop a thesis throughout the process of writing. Through revising and discussing their ideas, writers hone their thesis, making sure that it threads through every paragraph of the final draft. The position writers ultimately take in writing—their thesis—comes at the end of the writing process, after not one draft but many.

## WORKING VERSUS DEFINITIVE THESES

Writers are continually challenged by the need to establish their purpose and to make a clear and specific assertion of it. To reach that assertion, you must first engage in a prolonged process of inquiry, aided by a well-formulated question. The question serves as a tool for inquiry that will help you formulate your **working thesis**, your first attempt at an assertion of your position. A working thesis is valuable in the early stages of writing because it helps you read selectively, in the same way that your issue-based question guides your inquiry. Reading raises questions, helping you see what you know and need to know, and challenging you to read on.

Never accept your working thesis as your final position. Instead, continue testing your assertion as you read and write, and modify your working thesis as necessary. A more definitive thesis will come once you are satisfied that you have examined the issue from multiple perspectives.

For example, one of our students wanted to study representations of femininity in the media. In particular, she focused on why the Barbie doll has become an icon of femininity despite what many cultural critics consider Barbie's "outrageous and ultimately unattainable physical characteristics." Our student's working thesis suggested she would develop an argument about the need for change:

> The harmful implications of ongoing exposure to these unattainable ideals, such as low self-esteem, eating disorders, unhealthy body image, and acceptance of violence, make urgent the need for change.

The student assumed that her research would lead her to argue that Barbie's unattainable proportions have a damaging effect on women's self-image and that something needs to be done about it. However, as she read scholarly research to support her tentative thesis, she realized that a more compelling project would be less Barbie-centric. Instead, she chose to examine the broader phenomenon of how the idea of femininity is created and reinforced by society. That is, her personal interest in Barbie was supplanted by her discoveries about cultural norms of beauty and the power they have to influence self-perception and behavior. In her final draft, this was her definitive thesis:

> Although evidence may be provided to argue that gender is an innate characteristic, I will show that it is actually the result of one's actions, which are then labeled *masculine* or *feminine* according to society's definitions of ideal gender. Furthermore, I will discuss the communication of such definitions through the media, specifically in music videos, on TV, and in magazines, and the harmful implications of being exposed to these ideals.

Instead of arguing for change, the student chose to show her readers how they were being manipulated, leaving it to them to decide what actions they might want to take.

## DEVELOPING A WORKING THESIS: THREE MODELS

What are some ways to develop a working thesis? We suggest three models that may help you organize the information you gather in response to the question guiding your inquiry.

### ■ The Correcting-Misinterpretations Model

This model is used to correct writers whose arguments you believe have misconstrued one or more important aspects of an issue. The thesis typically takes the form of a factual claim. Consider this example and the words we have underlined:

> <u>Although scholars have addressed curriculum</u> to explain low achievement in schools, <u>they have failed to fully appreciate the</u> impact of limited resources to fund up-to-date textbooks, quality teachers, and computers. Therefore, reform in schools must focus on economic need as well as curriculum.

The clause beginning with "Although" lays out the assumption that many scholars make, that curriculum explains low educational achievement; the clause beginning with "they have failed" identifies the error those scholars have made by ignoring the economic reasons for low achievement in schools. Notice that the structure of the sentence reinforces the author's position. He offers the faulty assumption in a subordinate clause, reserving the main clause for his own position. The two clauses also reinforce that there are conflicting opinions here. One more thing: Although it is a common myth that a thesis must be phrased in a single sentence, this example shows that a thesis can be written in two (or more) sentences.

### ■ The Filling-the-Gap Model

The gap model points to what other writers may have overlooked or ignored in discussing a given issue. The gap model typically makes a claim of value. Consider this student's argument that discussions of cultural diversity in the United States are often framed in terms of black and white. Our underlining indicates the gap the writer has identified:

> If America is truly a "melting pot" of cultures, as it is often called, then <u>why is it</u> <u>that stories and events seem only to be in black and white? Why is it that when</u> <u>history courses are taught about the period of the civil rights movement, only the</u> <u>memoirs of African Americans are read,</u> like those of Melba Pattillo Beals and Ida Mae Holland? Where are <u>the works of Maxine Hong Kingston,</u> who tells the story of alienation and segregation in schools through the eyes of a Chinese child? African Americans were denied the right to vote, and many other citizenship rights; but Chinese Americans were denied even the opportunity to become citizens. I am not diminishing the issue of discrimination against African Americans, or belittling the struggles they went through. <u>I simply want to call attention to discrimina-</u> <u>tion against other minority groups and their often-overlooked struggles to achieve</u> <u>equality.</u>

In the student's thesis, the gap in people's knowledge stems from their limited understanding of history. They need to understand that many minority groups were denied their rights.

A variation on the gap model also occurs when a writer suggests that although something might appear to be the case, a closer look reveals something different. For example: "Although it would *appear* that women have achieved equality in the workplace, their paychecks suggest that this is not true."

One of our students examined two poems by the same author that appeared to contradict each other. She noticed a gap others had not seen:

> In both "The Albatross" and "Beauty," Charles Baudelaire chooses to explore the plight of the poet. Interestingly, despite their common author, the two poems' portrayals of the poet's struggles appear contradictory. "The Albatross" seems to give a somewhat sympathetic glimpse into the exile of the poet — the "winged voyager" so awkward in the ordinary world. "Beauty" takes what appears to be a less forgiving stance: The poet here is docile, simply a mirror. Although both pieces depict the poet's struggles, a closer examination demonstrates how the portrayals differ.

In stating her thesis, the student indicates that although readers might expect Baudelaire's images of poets to be similar, a closer examination of his words would prove them wrong.

## ■ The Modifying-What-Others-Have-Said Model

The modification model of thesis writing assumes that mutual understanding is possible. For example, in proposing a change in policy, one student asserts:

> Although scholars have claimed that the only sure way to reverse the cycle of homelessness in America is to provide an adequate education, we need to build on this work, providing school-to-work programs that ensure graduates have access to employment.

Here the writer seeks to modify other writers' claims, suggesting that education alone does not solve the problem of homelessness. The challenge he sets for himself is to understand the complexity of the problem by building on and extending the ideas of others. In effect, he is in a constructive conversation with those whose work he wants to build on, helping readers see that he shares common ground with the other writers and that he hopes to find a mutually acceptable solution to the agreed-on problem.

### Steps to Formulating a Working Thesis: Three Models

**1** **Misinterpretations model:** "Although many scholars have argued about X and Y, a careful examination suggests Z."

**2** **Gap model:** "Although scholars have noted X and Y, they have missed the importance of Z."

**3** **Modification model:** "Although I agree with the X and Y ideas of other writers, it is important to extend/refine/limit their ideas with Z."

### A Practice Sequence: Identifying Types of Theses

Below is a series of working theses. Read each one and then identify the model—misinterpretations, gap, or modification—that it represents.

1 A number of studies indicate that violence on television has a detrimental effect on adolescent behavior. However, few researchers have examined key environmental factors like peer pressure, music, and home life. In fact, I would argue that many researchers have oversimplified the problem.

2 Although research indicates that an increasing number of African American and Hispanic students are dropping out of high school, researchers have failed to fully grasp the reasons why this has occurred.

3  I want to argue that studies supporting single-sex education are relatively sound. However, we don't really know the long-term effects of single-sex education, particularly on young women's career paths.

4  Although recent studies of voting patterns in the United States indicate that young people between the ages of 18 and 24 are apathetic, I want to suggest that not all of the reasons these studies provide are valid.

5  Indeed, it's not surprising that students are majoring in fields that will enable them to get a job after graduation. But students may not be as pragmatic as we think. Many students choose majors because they feel that learning is an important end in itself.

6  Although good teachers are essential to learning, we cannot ignore the roles that race and class play in students' access to a quality education.

7  It is clear that cities need to clean up the dilapidated housing projects that were built over half a century ago; but few, if any, studies have examined the effects of doing so on the life chances of those people who are being displaced.

8  In addition to its efforts to advance the cause of social justice in the new global economy, the university must make a commitment to ending poverty on the edge of campus.

9  Although the writer offers evidence to explain the sources of illiteracy in America, he overstates his case when he ignores other factors, among them history, culture, and economic well-being. Therefore, I will argue that we place the discussion in a broader context.

10  More and more policymakers argue that English should be the national language in the United States. Although I agree that English is important, we should not limit people's right to maintain their own linguistic and cultural identity.

## ESTABLISHING A CONTEXT FOR A THESIS

In addition to defining the purpose and focus of an essay, a thesis must set up a **context** for the writer's claim. The process of establishing a background for understanding an issue typically involves four steps:

1.  Establish that the topic of conversation, the issue, is current and relevant—that it is on people's minds or should be.

2.  Briefly summarize what others have said to show that you are familiar with the topic or issue.

3. Explain what you see as the problem—a misinterpretation, a gap, or a modification that needs to be made in how others have addressed the topic or issue—perhaps by raising the questions you believe need to be answered.

4. State your thesis, suggesting that your view on the issue may present readers with something new to think about as it builds on and extends what others have argued.

You need not follow these steps in this order as long as your readers come away from the first part of your essay knowing why you are discussing a given issue and what your argument is.

## AN ANNOTATED STUDENT INTRODUCTION: PROVIDING A CONTEXT FOR A THESIS

We trace these four steps below in our analysis of the opening paragraphs of a student's essay. She wrote in response to what many call the English-only movement. Specifically, she responds to the effects of Proposition 227 in California, a piece of legislation that prevents non-English-speaking students from using their first language in school. Our discussion of how she provides a context for her thesis follows the excerpt.[1]

---

*NUESTRA CLASE*                                                   1

Jenny Eck
English 200
Professor Walters
March 18, 20 —

*Nuestra Clase*: Making the Classroom a Welcoming Place
for English Language Learners

*Notes the impor-*          With the Latino population growing exponentially and
*tance of the issue.*   Spanish quickly becoming one of the most widely spoken languages in the United States, the question arises of how the
American educational system is meeting the needs of a growing

---

[1] This excerpt follows APA citation style (see Appendix). For brevity, we have omitted the references page at the end of the excerpt.

*NUESTRA CLASE*                                                              2

Hispanic population. What does our educational system do to
address the needs of students whose primary language is not
English?

*Sets the stage with*
*background on*
*Proposition 227.*

In 1998, the state of California passed Proposition 227,
which prohibited bilingual instruction in public schools. Ron
Unz, a former Republican gubernatorial candidate and software
developer, launched the initiative under the name "English for
the Children." Unz argued that the initiative would help Latinos
and other recent immigrants free themselves from bilingual education, which he avowed would hinder the ability of immigrants
to assimilate into American culture (Stritikus, 2002). Supporters
of Proposition 227 assert that bilingual education has failed
English language learners (ELLs) because it does not adequately
equip them with the English language skills essential to success
in school. Eradicating bilingual education, they believe, will
help students learn English more effectively and consequently
achieve more in their educational careers.

*The issue remains*
*relevant.*

Since its passage, Proposition 227 has been hotly
debated. Many researchers claim that its strictures have stunted
the education of Spanish-speaking students (Halcón, 2001;
Stritikus, 2002). Many studies have indicated the harmful
effects of what Gutiérrez and her colleagues describe as "back-

*Represents what*
*others have said in*
*the conversation.*

lash pedagogy" (Gutiérrez, Asato, Santos, & Gotanda, 2002),
which prohibits the use of students' complete linguistic, sociocultural, and academic repertoire. In essence, they claim that
Proposition 227's backlash pedagogy, in attempting to emphasize "colorblindness" in education, has instead eradicated differences that are crucial to students' efforts to become educated.
They argue that by devaluing these differences, the educational
system devalues the very students it is attempting to help.

*Introduces a frame*
*or lens for thinking*
*about the issue.*

A sociocultural theory of learning, with its emphasis
on the significant impact that factors such as language, culture, family, and community have on a student's potential for
educational success (Halcón, 2001), calls attention to growing
concerns that schools may not be meeting the needs of ELLs.
Russian psychologist Lev Vygotsky (1978) introduced this viewpoint to educators when he proposed that development and
learning are firmly embedded in and influenced by society and

2

3

4

culture. With Vygotsky's theory in mind, other researchers have embraced the idea that the failure of minority students is more often than not a systematic failure, rather than an individual failure (Trueba, 1989). Sociocultural theory posits that learning needs to be understood not only in the broader context of the sociocultural lives of students, teachers, and schools, but also in their sociopolitical lives. A sociocultural context takes a student's culture, race, religion, language, family, community, and other similar factors into consideration, while a sociopolitical context takes into account the inherent ideologies and prejudices that exist in society today. In order for teaching to be effective, both sociocultural and sociopolitical factors must be identified and addressed.

*Explains what she sees as the problem.*

Many educators seem to dismiss sociocultural and sociopolitical factors, perhaps not realizing that by ignoring these factors, they are inadvertently privileging the students in their classrooms for whom English is a first language (Larson, 2003). Such a dismissive attitude does not reckon with other studies that have shown how important it is for English language learners to explore and express their bilingual/bicultural identities (McCarthey, García, López-Velásquez, Lin, & Guo, 2004). Some of these other studies have even proposed that schooling acts as a "subtractive process" for minority students, not only denying them opportunities to express their identities, but also divesting them of important social and cultural resources, which ultimately leaves them vulnerable to academic failure (Valenzuela, 1999). These other studies convincingly show that sociocultural factors are essential to the educational success of

*States her thesis.*

English language learners. Therefore, although many educators believe they know the best way to teach these students, I will argue that the educational system, by not taking into account factors that sociocultural theory emphasizes, has mostly failed to create classrooms that embrace cultural differences, and by so doing has failed to create optimal conditions for teaching and learning.

5

## ■ Establish That the Issue Is Current and Relevant

Ideally, you should convey to readers that the issue you are discussing is both current (what's on people's minds) and relevant (of sufficient importance to have generated some discussion and written conversation). In the first sentence, Eck tells readers of a trend she feels they need to be aware of, the dramatic growth of the Hispanic population in the United States. Her issue is what the schools are doing to meet the needs of a growing population of students "whose primary language is not English." At the beginning of the third paragraph, she signals the relevance of the issue when she observes that the passage of Proposition 227 has been "hotly debated."

## ■ Briefly Present What Others Have Said

It is important to introduce who has said what in the conversation you are entering. After all, you are interrupting that conversation to make your contribution, and those who are already in that conversation expect you to have done your homework and acknowledge those who have already made important contributions.

In the second paragraph, Eck sets the stage for her review with a brief history of Proposition 227. Here she describes what was at issue for supporters of the law and what they hoped the law would accomplish. Starting with paragraph 3, Eck acknowledges the researchers who have participated in the debate surrounding Proposition 227 and reviews a number of studies that challenge the premises on which Proposition 227 rested.

In paragraph 4, notice that Eck introduces the frame of sociocultural theory to help her readers see that denying students the use of their native language in the classroom is a problem.

By pointing out the ways that researchers on language learning challenge the assumptions underlying the English-only movement, Eck is doing more than listing sources. She is establishing that a problem, or issue, exists. Moreover, her review gives readers intellectual touchstones, the scholars who need to be cited in any academic conversation about bilingual education. A review is not a catchall for anyone writing on a topic; instead, it should reflect a writer's selection of the most relevant participants in the conversation. Eck's choice of sources, and how she presents them, conveys that she is knowledgeable about her subject. (Of course, it is her readers' responsibility to read further to determine whether she has reviewed the most relevant work and has presented the ideas of others accurately. If she has, readers will trust her, whether or not they end up agreeing with her on the issue.)

## ■ Explain What You See as the Problem

If a review indicates a problem, as Eck's review does, the problem can often be couched in terms of the models we discussed earlier: misinterpretations, gap, or modification. In paragraph 5, Eck identifies what she concludes is a misunderstanding of how students learn a new language. She suggests that the misunderstanding stems from a gap in knowledge (notice our underlining):

> Many educators seem to dismiss sociocultural and sociopolitical factors, perhaps not realizing that by ignoring these factors, they are inadvertently privileging the students in their classrooms for whom English is a first language (Larson, 2003). Such a dismissive attitude does not reckon with other studies that have shown how important it is for English language learners to explore and express their bilingual/bicultural identities (McCarthey, García, López-Velásquez, Lin, & Guo, 2004). Some of these other studies have even proposed that schooling acts as a "subtractive process" for minority students, not only denying them opportunities to express their identities, but also divesting them of important social and cultural resources, which ultimately leaves them vulnerable to academic failure (Valenzuela, 1999).

While Eck concedes that efforts to understand the problems of language learning have been extensive and multifaceted, her review of the research culminates with her assertion that ignoring students' language practices could have devastating results — that educators, by denying students "important social and cultural resources," may be leaving those students "vulnerable to academic failure."

### ▪ State Your Thesis

An effective thesis statement helps readers see the reasoning behind the author's claim; it also signals what readers should look for in the remainder of the essay. Eck closes paragraph 5 with a statement that speaks to both the purpose and the substance of her writing:

> Therefore, although many educators believe they know the best way to teach ELL students, I will argue that the educational system, by not taking into account factors that sociocultural theory emphasizes, has mostly failed to create classrooms that embrace cultural differences, and by so doing has failed to create optimal conditions for teaching and learning.

In your own writing, you can make use of the strategies that Eck uses in her essay. Words like *although* and *though* can set up problem statements: "Although [Though] some people think that nonnative speakers of English can best learn English by not using their first language, the issue is more complex than most people realize." Words like *but*, *however*, and *yet* can serve the same purpose: "One might argue that nonnative speakers of English can best learn English by not using their first language; but [however, yet] the issue is more complex than most people realize."

### Steps to Establishing a Context for a Thesis

**1** **Establish that the issue is current and relevant.** Point out the extent to which others have recognized the problem, issue, or question that you are writing about.

**2** **Briefly present what others have said.** Explain how others have addressed the problem, issue, or question you are focusing on.

**3** **Explain what you see as the problem.** Identify what is open to dispute.

**4** **State your thesis.** Help readers see your purpose and how you intend to achieve it — by correcting a misconception, filling a gap, or modifying a claim others have accepted.

## ■ Analyze the Context of a Thesis

In "Protean Shapes in Literacy Events," cultural anthropologist and linguist Shirley Brice Heath argues that communities of practice shape the ways in which people use reading and writing. Heath points out the problem of holding up a standard of literacy from one community to measure the extent to which another community is or is not literate. Her essay, originally published in 1982, is addressed to a community of scholars who study literacy. As you read the excerpt that follows, you will likely find yourself puzzled by Heath's vocabulary and possibly even excluded from the conversation at times. Our point in reprinting this excerpt is not to initiate you into Heath's academic community but to show, through our annotations, how Heath has applied the strategies we have been discussing in this chapter. As you read, feel free to make your own annotations, and then try to answer the questions — which may involve some careful rereading — that we pose after the excerpt. In particular, watch for signpost words (*but, few, little, however*) that signal the ideas the writer is challenging.

**SHIRLEY BRICE HEATH**

## *From* Protean Shapes in Literacy Events: Ever-Shifting Oral and Literate Traditions

*The first sentence establishes that the issue that interests Heath has been discussed for more than a few years, helping us see the continuing relevance of the area of study.*

Since the mid-1970s, anthropologists, linguists, historians, and psychologists have turned with new tools of analysis to the study of oral and literate societies. They have used discourse analysis, econometrics, theories of schemata and frames, and proposals of developmental performance to consider the possible links between oral and written language, and between

*1*

From the sentence that begins "Much of this research" to the end of the paragraph, Heath reviews some of the relevant literature and points to a problem: that previous work has seen literate and oral cultures as somehow opposed to one another. The author gives us more than a list of sources.

literacy and its individual and societal consequences. Much of this research is predicated on a dichotomous view of oral and literate traditions, usually attributed to researchers active in the 1960s. Repeatedly, Goody and Watt (1963), Ong (1967), Goody (1968), and Havelock (1963) are cited as having suggested a dichotomous view of oral and literate societies and as having asserted certain cognitive, social, and linguistic effects of literacy on both the society and the individual. Survey research tracing the invention and diffusion of writing systems across numerous societies (Kroeber, 1948) and positing the effects of the spread of literacy on social and individual memory (Goody and Watt, 1963; Havelock, 1963, 1976) is cited as supporting a contrastive view of oral and literate social groups. Research which examined oral performance in particular groups is said to support the notion that as members of a society increasingly participate in literacy, they lose habits associated with the oral tradition (Lord, 1965).

In short, existing scholarship makes it easy to interpret a picture which depicts societies existing along a continuum of development from an oral tradition to a literate one, with some societies having a restricted literacy, and others having reached a full development of literacy (Goody, 1968:11). One also finds in this research specific characterizations of oral and written language associated with these traditions.

2

In the first sentence in this paragraph, Heath suggests that a close reading would raise some important unanswered questions about the relationship between orality and literacy.

But a close reading of these scholars, especially Goody (1968) and Goody and Watt (1963), leaves some room for questioning such a picture of consistent and universal processes or products—individual or societal—of literacy. Goody pointed out that in any traditional society, factors such as secrecy, religious ideology, limited social mobility, lack of access to writing materials and alphabetic scripts could lead to restricted literacy. Furthermore, Goody warned that the advent of a writing system did not amount to technological determinism or to sufficient cause of certain changes in either the individual or the society. Goody went on to propose exploring the concrete context of written communication (1968:4) to determine how the

3

potentialities of literacy developed in traditional societies. He brought together a collection of essays based on the ethnography of literacy in traditional societies to illustrate the wide variety of ways in which *traditional*, i.e., pre-industrial but not necessarily preliterate, societies played out their uses of oral and literate traditions.

*The previous paragraph sets up the problem and the gap that Heath believes her research — indicated in the first two sentences of this paragraph — should address.*

Few researchers in the 1970s have, however, heeded Goody's warning about the possible wide-ranging effects of societal and cultural factors on literacy and its uses. In particular, little attention has been given in *modern* complex industrial societies to the social and cultural correlates of literacy or to the work experiences adults have which may affect the maintenance and retention of literacy skills acquired in formal schooling. The public media today give much attention to the decline of literacy skills as measured in school settings and the failure of students to acquire certain

*This sentence indicates the gap: The media focus on one set of concerns when they should be attending to a very different set of issues.*

levels of literacy. However, the media pay little attention to occasions for literacy retention — to the actual uses of literacy in work settings, daily interactions in religious, economic, and legal institutions, and family habits of socializing the young into uses of literacy. In the clamor over the need to increase the teaching of basic skills, there is much emphasis on the positive effects extensive and critical reading can have on im-

*Heath elaborates on what she sees as a troubling gap between what educators know and what they need to know.*

proving oral language. Yet there are scarcely any data comparing the forms and functions of oral language with those of written language produced and used by members of social groups within a complex society. One of the most appropriate sources of data for informing discussions of these issues is that which Goody proposed for traditional societies: the concrete context of written communication. Where, when, how, for whom, and with what results are individuals in different social groups of today's highly industrialized

*In the last four sentences of the excerpt, Heath raises the questions that she wants readers to consider and that guide her own research.*

society using reading and writing skills? How have the potentialities of the literacy skills learned in school developed in the lives of today's adults? Does modern society contain certain conditions which restrict literacy just as some traditional societies do? If so, what are these factors, and are groups with restricted literacy

4

denied benefits widely attributed to full literacy, such as upward socioeconomic mobility, the development of logical reasoning, and access to the information necessary to make well-informed political judgments?

## Reading as a Writer

1. What specific places can you point to in the selection that illustrate what is at issue for Heath?

2. How does Heath use her review to set up her argument?

3. What specific words and phrases does Heath use to establish what she sees as the problem? Is she correcting misinterpretations, filling a gap, or modifying what others have said?

4. What would you say is Heath's thesis? What specifics can you point to in the text to support your answer?

5. What would you say are the arguments Heath wants you to avoid? Again, what specific details can you point to in the text to support your answer?

## A Practice Sequence: Building a Thesis

We would like you to practice some of the strategies we have covered in this chapter. If you have already started working on an essay, exercises 1 through 4 present an opportunity to take stock of your progress, a chance to sort through what you've discovered, identify what you still need to discover, and move toward refining your thesis. Jot down your answer to each of the questions below and make lists of what you know and what you need to learn.

1 Have you established that your issue is current and relevant, that it is or should be on people's minds? What information would you need to do so?

2 Can you summarize briefly what others have said in the past to show that you are familiar with how others have addressed the issue? List some of the key texts you have read and the key points they make.

3 Have you identified any misunderstandings or gaps in how others have addressed the issue? Describe them. Do you have any ideas or information that would address these misunderstandings or help fill these gaps? Where might you find the information you need? Can you think of any sources you should reread to learn more? (For example, have you looked at the works cited or bibliographies in the texts you've already read?)

4  At this point, what is your take on the issue? Try drafting a work-ing thesis statement that will present readers with something new to think about, building on and extending what others have argued. In drafting your thesis statement, try out the three models discussed in this chapter and see if one is an especially good fit:

- *Misinterpretations model*: "Although many scholars have argued about X and Y, a careful examination suggests Z."
- *Gap model*: "Although scholars have noted X and Y, they have missed the importance of Z."
- *Modification model*: "Although I agree with X and Y ideas of other writers, it is important to extend/refine/limit their ideas with Z."

5  If you haven't chosen a topic yet, try a group exercise. Sit down with a few of your classmates and choose one of the following top-ics to brainstorm about as a group. Choose a topic that everyone in the group finds interesting, and work through exercises 1 through 4 in this practice sequence. Here are some suggestions:

- The moral obligation to vote
- The causes or consequences of poverty
- The limits of academic freedom
- Equity in education
- The popularity of _____
- The causes or consequences of teen violence
- Gender stereotypes in the media
- Linguistic diversity
- The uses of a liberal education
- Journalism and truth

## AN ANNOTATED STUDENT ESSAY: STATING AND SUPPORTING A THESIS

We have annotated the following student essay to illustrate the strategies we have discussed in this chapter for stating a thesis that responds to a rele-vant, timely problem in a given context. The assignment was to write an argument focusing on literacy based on research. Veronica Stafford chose to write about her peers' habit of texting and the ways in which this type of social interaction affects their intellectual development. Stafford develops a thesis that provides a corrective to a misconception that she sees in the ongoing conversations about texting. Her approach is a variation on the strategy in which writers correct a misinterpretation. In turn, you will see that she makes claims of fact and evaluation in making an argument for changing her peers' penchant for texting.

As you read the essay, reflect on your own experiences: Do you think the issue she raises is both timely and relevant? How well do you think she places her ideas in conversation with others? How would you respond to her various claims? Which do you agree with and disagree with, and why? What evidence would you present to support or counter her claims? Do you think she offers a reasonable corrective to what she believes is a misconception about texting?

Stafford 1

Veronica Stafford
Professor Wilson
English 1102
April 20—

Texting and Literacy

As students walk to class each day, most do not notice the other people around them. Rather than talking with others, they are texting their friends in the next building, in their dorm, or back home. Although social networking is the most common use for text messages, they are not used solely for socializing. While texting is a quick and easy way to keep up with friends, it threatens other aspects of our lives. When students spend time texting rather than focusing on those other important aspects, texting becomes detrimental. Students' enjoyment of reading, their schoolwork, and their relationships with others are all negatively affected by text messaging.

*The student identifies an issue, or problem, and states her thesis as an evaluative claim that attempts to correct a misconception.*

Due to the mass appeal of text messaging, students pass their free time chatting through their cell phones rather than enjoying a great book. Texting is so widespread because 25% of students under age eight, 89% of students ages eleven to thirteen, and over 95% of students over age fifteen have a cell phone ("Mobile Phones"). On average, 75.6 million text messages are sent in a day, with 54% of the population texting more than five times per day ("Mobile Phones"). In contrast to

*She summarizes research, placing the conversation in a larger context. Her citations also indicate that the problem she identifies is relevant and timely.*

1

2

Stafford 2

the time they spend texting, fifteen- to twenty-four-year-olds read a mere seven minutes per day for fun and only 1.25 hours a week ("To Read" 10), which is less than half the time that seventh-grade students spend texting: 2.82 hours a week (Bryant, Sanders-Jackson and Smallwood). While more than half of the population texts every day, almost as many (43%) have not read a single book in the past year ("To Read" 7). It seems there is a direct correlation between reading and texting because, as text messaging increases in popularity, reading decreases. The National Endowment for the Arts surveyed eighteen- to twenty-four-year-olds and discovered that the enjoyment of reading in this age group is declining the fastest. Inversely, it is the group that sends the most text messages: 142 billion a year ("To Read" 10). From 1992 to 2002, 2.1 million potential readers, aged eighteen to twenty-four years old, were lost ("To Read" 27). As proved by the direct correlation, reading does not have the same appeal because of texting. Students prefer to spend time in the technological world rather than sitting with a book.

*She uses evidence to support her thesis—that we take for granted a mode of communication that actually threatens the development of literacy.*

However, reading well is essential to being successful academically. Although some argue that text messages force students to think quickly and allow them to formulate brief responses to questions, their habit is actually stifling creativity. When a group of twenty students was given a chance to write responses to open-ended questions, the students who owned cell phones with text messaging wrote much less. They also had more grammatical errors, such as leaving apostrophes out of contractions and substituting the letter "r" for the word "are" (Ward). Because of text messages, students perceive writing as a fun way to communicate with friends and not as a way to strongly voice an opinion. Students no longer think of writing as academic, but rather they consider it social. For instance, in Scotland, a thirteen-year-old student wrote this in a school essay about her summer vacation: "My smmr hols wr CWOT. B4 we used 2 go to NY 2C my bro, & 3 kids FTF ILNY, its gr8 . . ." (Ward). She used writing that would appear in a text message for a friend rather than in a report for school. Furthermore,

*She refines her thesis, first stating what people assume is true and then offering a corrective in the second part of her thesis.*

*She also makes a secondary claim related to her thesis.*

3

Stafford 3

*And she elaborates on this claim to point out one of the detrimental effects of texting.*

students who text become so accustomed to reading this type of shorthand lingo that they often overlook it in their own writing (O'Connor). This means that teachers have to spend even longer correcting these bad habits. Regardless, Lily Huang, a writer for *Newsweek*, believes that text messages increase literacy because a student must first know how to spell a word to abbreviate it in texting.

*The student presents a possible counterargument from a published writer and then restates her thesis in an effort to correct a misconception.*

However, texting affects not only the way that students write, but also the way in which they think about language. As a critic of Huang's article writes, "Habitual use of shorthand isn't just about choppy English, but choppy thinking" (Muffie). Writers who text will have trouble thinking creatively, and will especially have trouble composing intricate works like poetry because of the abridged way of thinking to which they are accustomed.

Outside of school, students' interactions with one another are similarly altered. Three in five teens would argue with a friend and one in three would break up with someone through a text message ("Technology Has Tremendous Impact"). Text messaging is now the most popular way for students to arrange to meet with friends, have a quick conversation, contact a friend when bored, or invite friends to a party ("Technology Has Tremendous Impact"). Eight out of ten teens would rather

*She restates an evaluative claim that runs through the essay like the skewer we discussed earlier.*

text than call ("Mobile Phones"). Although it is true that text messaging has made conversations much simpler and faster, it has not improved communication. Texting may make it more convenient to stay in contact with friends, but it does not ensure that the contact is as beneficial as talking in person. Text messages do not incorporate all of the body language and vocal inflections that a face-to-face conversation does. These nonverbal cues are essential to fully comprehending what is

*She provides current research to support her thesis.*

being communicated. Only 7% of a message is verbal. When the message is not communicated face-to-face, 93% of that message is lost ("Importance of Nonverbal"), and this nonverbal message is crucial to maintaining close relationships. According to Don McKay, a contributor to healthinfosource.com, the most important aspect of lasting friendships is effective

Stafford 4

communication. Friends must be able to convey emotions and empathize with others (McKay). However, friends who communicate solely through text messages will miss out on any truly personal interaction because they can never see the other person's posture, body language, or gestures.

*She concludes by restating her premise about the value of reading and her evaluation of texting as a form of communication that erodes what she considers the very definition of literacy.*

All of the negative effects of text messaging additionally deteriorate literacy. The enjoyment of reading leads to avid readers who eagerly absorb written words. A devotion to schoolwork encourages students to read so that they may be informed about important topics. Through book clubs and conversations about great literature, even relationships can foster a love for reading. However, text messaging is detracting from all three. In today's society, literacy is important. Schools focus on teaching English at an early age because of the active role that it forces

*She also concludes with a claim in which she proposes that students need to elevate the way they read and write.*

students to take (Le Guin). While students can passively text message their friends, they need to focus on reading to enjoy it. In order to really immerse themselves in the story, they need to use a higher level of thinking than that of texting. This learning is what causes avid readers to become so successful. Those who read for fun when they are young score better on standardized tests, are admitted to more selective universities, and are able to secure the most competitive jobs ("To Read" 69). The decline in literacy caused by text messaging could inevitably cost a student a selective job. If students spent less time texting and more time reading, it could give them an advantage over their peers. Imagine a scenario between classes without any students' eyes to the ground. Imagine that Notre Dame students are not texting acquaintances hours away. Perhaps instead they are all carrying a pen and notebook and writing a letter to their friends. Maybe they are conversing with those around them. Instead of spending time every week text messaging, they are reading. When those other students text "lol," it no longer is an abbreviation for "laugh out loud," but for "loss of literacy."

5

Stafford 5

## Works Cited

Bryant, J. Alison, Ashley Sanders-Jackson, and Amber M. K.
    Smallwood. "IMing, Text Messaging, and Adolescent Social
    Networks." *Journal of Computer-Mediated Communication*
    11.2 (2006): n. pag Web. 28 Mar. 20--.

Huang, Lily. "The Death of English (LOL)." *Newsweek.* Newsweek,
    2 Aug. 2008. Web. 28 Mar. 20--.

"The Importance of Nonverbal Communication." *EruptingMind
    Self Improvement Tips.* N.p., 2008. Web. 1 Apr. 20--.

Le Guin, Ursula K. "Staying Awake: Notes on the Alleged
    Decline of Reading." *Harper's Magazine.* The Harper's Maga-
    zine Foundation, Feb. 2008. Web. 30 Mar. 20--.

McKay, Don. "Communication and Friendship." *EzineArticles.*
    EzineArticles.com, 22 Feb. 2006. Web. 27 Mar. 20--.

"Mobile Phones, Texting, and Literacy." *National Literacy Trust.*
    NLT, 2008. Web. 1 Apr. 20--.

Muffie. Member comment. "The Death of English (LOL)." *News-
    week.* Newsweek, 18 Aug. 2008. Web. 28 Mar. 20--.

National Endowment for the Arts. *To Read or Not To Read: A
    Question of National Consequence.* Washington, NEA, Nov.
    2007. PDF file.

O'Connor, Amanda. "Instant Messaging: Friend or Foe of Stu-
    dent Writing." *New Horizons for Learning.* New Horizons for
    Learning, Mar. 2005. Web. 27 Mar. 20--.

"Technology Has Tremendous Impact on How Teens Communi-
    cate." *Cellular-news.* Cellular-news, 20 Feb. 2007. Web. 27
    Mar. 20--.

Ward, Lucy. "Texting 'Is No Bar to Literacy.'" *Guardian.co.uk.*
    Guardian News and Media Limited, 23 Dec. 2004. Web.
    2 Apr. 20--.

# 6

# From Finding to Evaluating Sources

In this chapter, we look at strategies for expanding the base of sources you work with to support your argument. The habits and skills of close reading and analysis that we have discussed and that you have practiced are essential for evaluating the sources you find. Once you find sources, you will need to assess the claims the writers make, the extent to which they provide evidence in support of those claims, and the recency, relevance, accuracy, and reliability of the evidence. The specific strategies we discuss here are those you will use to find and evaluate the sources you find in your library's electronic catalog or on the Internet. These strategies are core skills for developing a researched academic argument. They are also essential to avoid being overwhelmed by the torrent of information unleashed at the click of a computer mouse.

Finding sources is not difficult; finding and identifying good sources is challenging. You know how simple it is to look up a subject in an encyclopedia or to use a search engine like Google or Yahoo! to discover basic information on a subject or topic. Unfortunately, this kind of research will only take you so far. What if the information you find doesn't really address your question? True, we have emphasized the importance of thinking about an issue from multiple perspectives—and finding multiple perspectives is easy when you search the Internet. But how do you know whether a perspective is authoritative or trustworthy or even legitimate? Without knowing how to find and identify good sources, you can waste a lot of time reading material that will not contribute to your essay. Our goal is to help you use your time wisely to collect the sources you need to support your argument.

# IDENTIFYING SOURCES

We assume that by the time you visit the library or log on to the Internet to find sources, you are not flying blind. At the very least, you will have chosen a topic to explore (something in general you want to write about), possibly will have identified an issue (a question or problem about the topic that is arguable), and perhaps will even have a working thesis (a main claim that you want to test against other sources) in mind. Let's say you are already interested in the topic of mad cow disease. Perhaps you have identified an issue: Is mad cow disease a significant threat in the United States given the massive scale of factory farming? And maybe you have drafted a working thesis: "Although factory farming is rightly criticized for its often unsanitary practices and lapses in quality control, the danger of an epidemic of mad cow disease in the United States is minimal." The closer you are to having a working thesis, the more purposeful your research will be. With the working thesis above, instead of trying to sift through hundreds of articles about mad cow disease, you can probably home in on materials that examine mad cow disease in relation to epidemiology and agribusiness.

Once you start expanding your research, however, even a working thesis is just a place to begin. As you digest all the perspectives your research yields, you may discover that your thesis, issue, and perhaps even interest in the topic will shift significantly. Maybe you'll end up writing about factory farming rather than mad cow disease. This kind of shift happens more often than you may think. What is important is to follow what interests you and to keep in mind what is going to matter to your readers.

## ■ Consult Experts Who Can Guide Your Research

Before you embark on a systematic hunt for sources, you may want to consult with experts who can help guide your research. The following experts are nearer to hand and more approachable than you may think.

*Your Writing Instructor.*   Your first and best expert is likely to be your writing instructor, who can help you define the limits of your research and the kinds of sources that would prove most helpful. Your writing instructor can probably advise you on whether your topic is too broad or too narrow, help you identify your issue, and perhaps even point you to specific reference works or readings you should consult. He or she can also help you figure out whether you should concentrate mainly on popular or scholarly sources (for more about popular and scholarly sources, see pages 125–26).

*Librarians at Your Campus or Local Library.*   In all likelihood, there is no better repository of research material than your campus or local library, and no better guide to those resources than the librarians who work there. Their job is to help you find what you need (although it's up to you to make the most of what you find). Librarians can give you a map or tour of the library and provide you with booklets or other handouts that instruct you in the specific resources available and their uses. They can explain the catalog system and reference system. And, time allowing, most librarians are willing to give you personal help in finding and using specific sources, from books and journals to indexes and databases.

*Experts in Other Fields.*    Perhaps the idea for your paper originated outside your writing course, in response to a reading assigned in, say, your psychology or economics course. If so, you may want to discuss your topic or issue with the instructor in that course, who can probably point you to other readings or journals you should consult. If your topic originated outside the classroom, you can still seek out an expert in the appropriate field. If so, you may want to read the advice on interviewing we present in Chapter 11.

*Manuals, Handbooks, and Dedicated Web Sites.*    These exist in abundance, for general research as well as for discipline-specific research. They are especially helpful in identifying a wide range of authoritative search tools and resources, although they also offer practical advice on how to use and cite them. Indeed, your writing instructor may assign one of these manuals or handbooks, or recommend a Web site, at the beginning of the course. If not, he or she can probably point you to the one that is best suited to your research.

## ■ Develop a Working Knowledge of Standard Sources

As you start your hunt for sources, it helps to know broadly what kinds of sources are available and what they can help you accomplish. Table 6.1 lists a number of the resources you are likely to rely on when you are looking for material, the purpose and limitations of each type of resource, and some well-known examples. Although it may not help you pinpoint specific resources that are most appropriate for your research, the table does provide a basis for finding sources in any discipline. And familiarizing yourself with the types of resources here should make your conversations with the experts more productive.

## ■ Distinguish Between Primary and Secondary Sources

As you define the research task before you, you will need to understand the difference between primary and secondary sources and figure out which you will need to answer your question. Your instructor may specify which he or she prefers, but chances are you will have to make the decision yourself. A **primary source** is a firsthand, or eyewitness, account, the kind

TABLE 6.1    Standard Types of Sources for Doing Research

| Source | Type of Information | Purpose | Limitations | Examples |
|---|---|---|---|---|
| Abstract | Brief summary of a text and the bibliographic information needed to locate the complete text | To help researchers decide whether they want to read the entire source | | *Biological Abstracts* *Historical Abstracts* *New Testament Abstracts* *Reference Sources in History: An Introductory Guide* |
| Bibliography | List of works, usually by subject and author, with full publication information | For an overview of what has been published in a field and who the principal researchers in the field are | Difficult to distinguish the best sources and the most prominent researchers | *Bibliography of the History of Art* *MLA International Bibliography* |
| Biography | Story of an individual's life and the historical, cultural, or social context in which he or she lived | For background on a person of importance | Lengthy and reflects the author's bias | *Biography and Genealogy Master Index* *Biography Resource Center* *Biography.com* *Literature Resource Center* *Oxford Dictionary of National Biography* |
| Book review | Description and usually an evaluation of a recently published book | To help readers stay current with research and thought in their field and to evaluate scholarship | Reflects the reviewer's bias | ALA *Booklist* *Book Review Digest* *Book Review Index* *Books in Print with Book Reviews on Disc* |
| Database, index | Large collection of citations and abstracts from books, journals, and digests, often updated daily | To give researchers access to a wide range of current sources | Lacks evaluative information | Education Resources Information Center (ERIC) Humanities International Index Index to Scientific & Technical Proceedings |

(*continued on next page*)

**TABLE 6.1**     (*continued*)

| Source | Type of Information | Purpose | Limitations | Examples |
|---|---|---|---|---|
| | | | | United Nations Bibliographic Information System |
| Data, statistics | Measurements derived from studies or surveys | To help researchers identify important trends (e.g., in voting, housing, residential segregation) | Requires a great deal of scrutiny and interpretation | American Fact-Finder |
| | | | | American National Election Studies |
| | | | | Current Index to Statistics |
| | | | | Current Population Survey |
| | | | | *Statistical Abstract of the United States* |
| Dictionary | Alphabetical list of words and their definitions | To explain key terms and how they are used | | *Merriam-Webster's Collegiate Dictionary* |
| | | | | *Oxford English Dictionary* |
| Encyclopedia | Concise articles about people, places, concepts, and things | A starting point for very basic information | Lack of in-depth information | *The CQ Researcher* |
| | | | | Encyclopedia Brittanica Online |
| | | | | *Information Please Almanac* |
| | | | | *McGraw-Hill Encyclopedia of Science & Technology* |
| Internet search engine | Web site that locates online information by keyword or search term | For quickly locating a broad array of current resources | Reliability of information open to question | Google |
| | | | | Yahoo! |
| Newspaper, other news sources | Up-to-date information | To locate timely information | May reflect reporter's or medium's bias | America's Historical Newspapers |
| | | | | LexisNexis Academic |
| | | | | Newspaper Source |
| | | | | ProQuest Historical Newspapers |
| | | | | World News Connection |
| Thesaurus | Alphabetical list of words and their synonyms | For alternative search terms | | *Roget's II: The New Thesaurus* |

of account you find in letters or newspapers or research reports in which the researcher explains his or her impressions of a particular phenomenon. For example, "Hidden Lessons," the Sadkers' study of gender bias in schools, is a primary source. The authors report their own experiences of the phenomenon in the classroom. A **secondary source** is an analysis of information reported in a primary source. For example, even though it may cite the Sadkers' primary research, an essay that analyzes the Sadkers' findings along with other studies of gender dynamics in the classroom would be considered a secondary source.

If you were exploring issues of language diversity and the English-only movement, you would draw on both primary and secondary sources. You would be interested in researchers' firsthand (primary) accounts of language learning and use by diverse learners for examples of the challenges nonnative speakers face in learning a standard language. And you would also want to know from secondary sources what others think about whether national unity and individuality can and should coexist in communities and homes as well as in schools. You will find that you are often expected to use both primary and secondary sources in your research.

## ■ Distinguish Between Popular and Scholarly Sources

To determine the type of information to use, you also need to decide whether you should look for popular or scholarly books and articles. **Popular sources** of information—newspapers like *USA Today* and *The Chronicle of Higher Education*, and large-circulation magazines like *Newsweek* and *Field & Stream*—are written for a general audience. This is not to say that popular sources cannot be specialized: *The Chronicle of Higher Education* is read mostly by academics; *Field & Stream*, by people who love the outdoors. But they are written so that any educated reader can understand them. **Scholarly sources**, by contrast, are written for experts in a particular field. *The New England Journal of Medicine* may be read by people who are not physicians, but they are not the journal's primary audience. In a manner of speaking, these readers are eavesdropping on the journal's conversation of ideas; they are not expected to contribute to it (and in fact would be hard pressed to do so). The articles in scholarly journals undergo **peer review**. That is, they do not get published until they have been carefully evaluated by the author's peers, other experts in the academic conversation being conducted in the journal. Reviewers may comment at length about an article's level of research and writing, and an author may have to revise an article several times before it sees print. And if the reviewers cannot reach a consensus that the research makes an important contribution to the academic conversation, the article will not be published.

When you begin your research, you may find that popular sources provide helpful information about a topic or an issue—the results of a national poll, for example. Later, however, you will want to use scholarly sources to advance your argument. You can see from Table 6.2 that popular

TABLE 6.2   Popular Magazines Versus Scholarly Journals

| CRITERIA | POPULAR MAGAZINES | SCHOLARLY JOURNALS |
|---|---|---|
| Advertisements | Numerous full-page color ads | Few if any ads |
| Appearance | Eye-catching; glossy; pictures and illustrations | Plain; black-and-white graphics, tables, charts, and diagrams |
| Audience | General | Professors, researchers, and college students |
| Author | Journalists | Professionals in an academic field or discipline |
| Bibliography | Occasional and brief | Extensive bibliography at the end of each article; footnotes and other documentation |
| Content | General articles to inform, update, or introduce a contemporary issue | Research projects, methodology, and theory |
| Examples | *Newsweek, National Review, PC World, Psychology Today* | *International Journal of Applied Engineering Research, New England Journal of Medicine* |
| Language | Nontechnical, simple vocabulary | Specialized vocabulary |
| Publisher | Commercial publisher | Professional organization, university, research institute, or scholarly press |

SOURCE: Adapted from materials at the Hesburgh Library, University of Notre Dame.

magazines and scholarly journals can be distinguished by a number of characteristics. Does the source contain advertisements? If so, what kinds of advertisements? For commercial products? Or for academic events and resources? How do the advertisements appear? If you find ads and glossy pictures and illustrations, you are probably looking at a popular magazine. This is in contrast to the tables, charts, and diagrams you are likely to find in an education, psychology, or microbiology journal. Given your experience with rhetorical analyses, you should also be able to determine the makeup of your audience—specialists or nonspecialists—and the level of language you need to use in your writing.

Again, as you define your task for yourself, it is important to consider why you would use one source or another. Do you want facts? Opinions? News reports? Research studies? Analyses? Personal reflections? The extent to which the information can help you make your argument will serve as your basis for determining whether a source of information is of value.

## Steps to Identifying Sources

**1** **Consult experts who can guide your research.** Talk to people who can help you formulate issues and questions.

**2** **Develop a working knowledge of standard sources.** Identify the different kinds of information that different types of sources provide.

**3** **Distinguish between primary and secondary sources.** Decide what type of information can best help you answer your research question.

**4** **Distinguish between popular and scholarly sources.** Determine what kind of information will persuade your readers.

## A Practice Sequence: Identifying Sources

We would now like you to practice using some of the strategies we have discussed so far: talking with experts, deciding what sources of information you should use, and determining what types of information can best help you develop your paper and persuade your readers. We assume you have chosen a topic for your paper, identified an issue, and perhaps formulated a working thesis. If not, think back to some of the topics mentioned in earlier chapters. Have any of them piqued your interest? If not, here are five very broad topics you might work with:

- The civil rights movement
- The media and gender
- Global health
- Science and religion
- Immigration

Once you've decided on a topic, talk to experts and decide which types of sources you should use: primary or secondary, popular or scholarly. Consult with your classmates to evaluate the strengths and weaknesses of different sources of information and the appropriateness of using different types of information. Here are the steps to follow:

**1** Talk to a librarian about the sources you might use to get information about your topic (for example, databases, abstracts, or bibliographies). Be sure to take notes.

**2** Talk to an expert who can provide you with some ideas about current issues in the field of interest. Be sure to take detailed notes.

3 Decide whether you should use primary or secondary sources. What type of information would help you develop your argument?

4 Decide whether you should use popular or scholarly sources. What type of information would your readers find compelling?

## SEARCHING FOR SOURCES

Once you've decided on the types of sources you want to use—primary or secondary, popular or scholarly—you can take steps to locate the information you need. You might begin with a tour of your university or local library, so that you know where the library keeps newspapers, government documents, books, journals, and other sources of information. Notice where the reference desk is: This is where you should head to ask a librarian for help if you get stuck. You also want to find a computer where you can log on to your library's catalog to start your search. Once you have located your sources in the library, you can begin to look through them for the information you need.

You may be tempted to rely on the Internet and a search engine like Google or Yahoo! But keep in mind that the information you retrieve from the Internet may not be trustworthy: Anyone can post his or her thoughts on a Web site. Of course, you can also find excellent scholarly sources on the Internet. (For example, Johns Hopkins University Press manages Project MUSE, a collection of 300-plus academic journals that can be accessed online through institutional subscription.) School libraries also offer efficient access to government records and other sources essential to scholarly writing.

Let's say you are about to start researching a paper on language diversity and the English-only movement. When you log on to the library's site, you find a menu of choices: Catalog, Electronic Resources, Virtual Reference Desk, and Services & Collections. (The wording may vary slightly from library to library, but the means of locating information will be the same.) When you click on Catalog, another menu of search choices appears: Keyword, Title, Author, and Subject (Figure 6.1). The hunt is on.

**Search type:**

| Keyword Anywhere |
| Title begins with... |
| Title Keyword |
| Author (last name first) |
| Author Keyword |
| Subject begins with... |
| Subject Keyword |
| Call Number begins with... |

More Search Options

FIGURE 6.1   Menu of Basic Search Strategies

## ▪ Perform a Keyword Search

A **keyword** is essentially your topic: It defines the topic of your search. To run a keyword search, you can look up information by author, title, or subject. You would search by author to locate all the works a particular author has written on a subject. So, for example, if you know that Paul Lang is an expert on the consequences of the English-only movement, you might begin with an author search. You can use the title search to locate all works with a key word or phrase in the title. The search results are likely to include a number of irrelevant titles, but you should end up with a list of authors, titles, and subject headings to guide another search.

A search by subject is particularly helpful as you begin your research, while you are still formulating your thesis. You want to start by thinking of as many words as possible that relate to your topic. (A thesaurus can help you come up with different words you can use in a keyword search.) Suppose you type in the phrase "English only." A number of different sources appear on the screen, but the most promising is Paul Lang's book *The English Language Debate: One Nation, One Language?* You click on this record, and another screen appears with some valuable pieces of information, including the call number (which tells you where in the library you can find the book) and an indication that the book has a bibliography, something you can make use of once you find the book (Figure 6.2). Notice that the subject listings—*Language policy, English language–Political aspects, English-only movement, Bilingual education*—also give you additional keywords to use in finding relevant information. The lesson here is that it is important to generate keywords to get initial information and then to look

**Full View of Record**

Record 12 out of 18

| | | |
|---|---|---|
| | Author : | Lang, Paul (Paul C.) |
| Source | Title : | The English language debate : one nation, one language? / Paul Lang. |
| | Published : | Springfield, N.J. : Enslow Publishers, c1995. |
| | | 112 p. : ill. ; 24 cm. |

| | | |
|---|---|---|
| ND Has : | All items | |
| | Hesburgh Library General Collection | |
| | P 119.32 .U6 E55 1995 | [ Call number |

Indicates book has a bibliography

| | |
|---|---|
| Notes : | Includes bibliographical references (p. 107-109) and index. |
| Series : | Multicultural issues |
| Subjects : | Language policy – United States – Juvenile literature. |
| | English language – Political aspects – United States – Juvenile literature. |
| Additional list of related subjects | **English-only** movement – United States – Juvenile literature. |
| | Education, Bilingual – United States – Juvenile literature. |
| | **English-only** movement. |
| | English language – Political aspects. |
| | Education, Bilingual. |

Done

FIGURE 6.2    Full-View Bibliographic Entry

at that information carefully for more keywords and to determine if the source has a bibliography. Even if this particular source isn't relevant, it may lead you to other sources that are.

## ■ Try Browsing

Browse is a headings search; it appears in the menu of choices in Figure 6.1 as "Subject begins with . . ." This type of search allows you to scroll through an alphabetical index. Some of the indexes available are the Author Index, the Title Index, and the Library of Congress Subject Headings, a subject index. Browse

- displays an alphabetical list of entries;
- shows the number of records for each entry;
- indicates whether there are cross-references for each entry.

What appears in the window is "Browse List: Choose a field, enter a phrase and click the 'go' button." Figure 6.3 shows the results of a preliminary browse when the words "English-only" are entered. Notice that a list of headings or titles appears on the screen. This is not a list of books, and not all of the entries are relevant. But you can use the list to determine which headings are relevant to your topic, issue, or question.

For your paper on the English-only movement, the first two headings seem relevant: *English-only debate* and *English-only movement*. A further click would reveal the title of a relevant book and a new list of subject headings (Figure 6.4) that differs from those of your initial search. This list gives you a new bibliography from which you can gather new leads and a list of subject headings to investigate.

### Browse List: Subjects

| No. of Recs | Entry |
| --- | --- |
| | English one-act plays - [LC Authority Record] |
| | See: One-act plays, English |
| | English-only debate - [LC Authority Record] |
| | See: English-only movement |
| 4 | English-only movement - [LC Authority Record] |
| 1 | English-only movement — California — Case studies |
| 1 | English-only movement — Colorado |
| 4 | English-only movement — United States |
| 1 | English-only movement — United States — Juvenile literature |
| | English-only question - [LC Authority Record] |
| | See: English-only movement |
| 1 | English — Ontario — Correspondence |
| 1 | English oration |

**FIGURE 6.3**   Preliminary Browse of "English-only" Subject Heading

We suggest that you do a keyword search first and then a browse search to home in on a subject. Especially when you don't know the exact subject, you can do a quick keyword search, retrieve many sets of results, and then begin looking at the subjects that correspond to each title. Once you find a subject that fits your needs, you can click on the direct subject (found in each bibliographic record) and execute a new search that will yield more-relevant results.

## ■ Perform a Journal or Newspaper Title Search

Finally, you can search by journal or newspaper title. For this kind of search, you will need exact information. You can take the name of a journal, magazine, or newspaper cited in your keyword or browse search. The journal or newspaper title search will tell you if your library subscribes to the publication and in what format—print, microform or microfilm, or electronic.

Suppose you want to continue your search in the *New York Times* for information on the English-only movement by searching for articles in the *New York Times*. You would run a basic search under the category "Periodicals": "Periodical Title begins with . . ." That would give you access to a limited number of articles that focused on the debate surrounding the English-only movement. To find more recent articles, you could go to the *New York Times* Web site (nytimes.com), where you could find many potentially useful listings. Recent newspaper articles will lack the depth and complexity of more scholarly studies, but they are undeniably useful in helping you establish the timeliness and relevance of your research. To see the full text of the articles, you must subscribe or pay a nominal fee, although you can usually preview the articles because the Web site will include a few sentences describing the content of each article.

| # | Year | Author | Title |
|---|---|---|---|
| 1 ☐ | 2006 | United States. | English as the official language : hearing before the Subcommittee on Education Reform of the Co <Book> <br> Click for ONLINE ACCESS ( Text version: ) <br> Documents Center Owned: 1  Checked Out: 0 <br> Display full record |
| 2 ☐ | 1996 | United States. | S. 356—Language of Government Act of 1995 : hearings before the Committee on Governmental Affai <Book> <br> Documents Center <br> Display full record |
| 3 ☐ | 1996 | United States. | Hearing on English as the common language : hearing before the Subcommittee on Early Childhood, <Book> <br> Documents Center <br> Display full record |
| 4 ☐ | 1995 | United States. | Hearing on English as a common language : hearing before the Subcommittee on Early Childhood, Yo <Book> <br> Documents Center <br> Display full record |

Done

**FIGURE 6.4**   Results of Browsing Deeper: A New List of Sources

## Steps to Searching for Sources

**1** **Perform a keyword search.** Choose a word or phrase that best describes your topic.

**2** **Try browsing.** Search an alphabetical list by subject.

**3** **Perform a journal or newspaper title search.** Find relevant citations by identifying the exact title of a journal or newspaper, or by subject.

## A Practice Sequence: Searching for Sources

If you tried the practice sequence on identifying sources (p. 127), explore your topic further by practicing the types of searches discussed in this section: a keyword search; a browse; and a journal or newspaper title search (or a subject search).

# EVALUATING LIBRARY SOURCES

The information you collect can and will vary in terms of its relevance and overall quality. You will want to evaluate this information as systematically as possible to be sure that you are using the most appropriate sources to develop your argument. Once you have obtained at least some of the sources you located by searching your library's catalog, you should evaluate the material as you read it. In particular, you want to evaluate the following information for each article or book:

- the author's background and credentials (What is the author's educational background? What has he or she written about in the past? Is this person an expert in the field?)
- the writer's purpose
- the topic of discussion
- the audience the writer invokes and whether you are a member of that audience
- the nature of the conversation (How have others addressed the problem?)
- what the author identifies as a misinterpretation or a gap in knowledge, or an argument that needs modifying
- what the author's own view is
- how the author supports his or her argument (that is, with primary or secondary sources, with facts or opinions)
- the accuracy of the author's evidence (Can you find similar information elsewhere?)

If your topic is current and relevant, chances are your searches are going to turn up a large number of possible sources. How do you go about choosing which sources to rely on in your writing? Of course, if time were not an issue, you would read them all from start to finish. But in the real world, assignments come with due dates. To decide whether a library source merits a close reading and evaluation, begin by skimming each book or article. **Skimming**—briefly examining the material to get a sense of the information it offers—involves four steps:

1. Read the introductory sections.
2. Examine the table of contents and index.
3. Check the notes and bibliographic references.
4. Skim deeper.

## ■ Read the Introductory Sections

Turn to the introductory sections of the text first. Many authors use a preface or an introduction to explain the themes they focus on in a book. An **abstract** serves a similar purpose, but article abstracts are usually only 250 words long. In the introductory sections, writers typically describe the issue that motivated them to write and indicate whether they believe the work corrects a misconception, fills a gap, or builds on and extends the research of others. For example, in the preface to her book *Learning and Not Learning English: Latino Students in American Schools* (2001), Guadalupe Valdés explains that even after two years of language instruction, many students remain at a low level of language competence. In this passage, Valdés makes clear the purpose of her work:

> This book examines the learning of English in American schools by immigrant children. It focuses on the realities that such youngsters face in trying to acquire English in settings in which they interact exclusively with other non-English-speaking youngsters the entire school day. It is designed to fill a gap in the existing literature on non-English-background youngsters by offering a glimpse of the challenges and difficulties faced by four middle-school students enrolled in the United States for the first time when they were 12 or 13 years old. It is my purpose here to use these youngsters' lives and experiences as a lens through which to examine the policy and instructional dilemmas that now surround the education of immigrant children in this country. (p. 2)

If you were looking for sources for a paper on the English-only movement, in particular the consequences of that movement for young students, you might very well find Valdés's words compelling and decide the book is worth a closer reading.

## ■ Examine the Table of Contents and Index

After reading the introductory sections, you will find it useful to analyze the table of contents to see how much emphasis the writer gives to topics that are relevant to your own research. For example, the table of contents to *Learning and Not Learning English* includes several headings that may relate to your interest: "Educating English-Language Learners," "Challenges and Realities," "Implications for Policy and Practice," and the "Politics of Teaching English." You also should turn to the back of the book to examine the **index**, an alphabetical list of the important and recurring concepts in a book, and the page numbers on which they appear. An index also would include the names of authors cited in the book. In the index to Valdés's book, you would find references to "English-language abilities and instruction" with specific page numbers where you can read what the author has to say on this subject. You would also find references to "English-only instruction," "equal educational opportunities," and "sheltered instruction."

## ■ Check the Notes and Bibliographic References

Especially in the initial stages of writing, you should look closely at writers' notes and bibliographies to discern who they feel are the important voices in the field. Frequent citation of a particular researcher's work may indicate that the individual is considered to be an expert in the field you are studying. Notes usually provide brief references to people, concepts, or context; the bibliography includes a long list of related works. Mining Valdés's bibliography, you would find such titles as "Perspectives on Official English," "Language Policy in Schools," "Not Only English," "Language and Power," and "The Cultural Politics of English."

## ■ Skim Deeper

Skimming a book or an article entails briefly looking over the elements we have discussed so far: the preface or abstract, the table of contents and the index, and the notes and bibliography. Skimming also can mean reading chapter titles, headings, and the first sentence of each paragraph to determine the relevance of a book or an article.

Skimming the first chapter of *Learning and Not Learning English*, you would find several topic sentences that reveal the writer's purpose:

"In this book, then, I examine and describe different expressions that both learning and not-learning English took among four youngsters."

"In the chapters that follow . . ."

"What I hope to suggest . . ."

These are the types of phrases you should look for to get a sense of what the writer is trying to accomplish and whether the writer's work will be of use to you.

If, after you've taken these steps, a source still seems promising, you should read it closely, from start to finish, to determine how effectively it can help you answer your research question. Keep in mind all you've learned about critical reading. Those skills are what you'll rely on most as you work through the texts and choose the ones you should use in your paper. Remember the steps of rhetorical analysis: identifying the writer's situation, purpose, claims, and audience. And remember how to identify claims and evaluate the reasons used to support the claims: Is the evidence recent, relevant, accurate, and reliable?

## Steps to Evaluating Library Sources

1 **Read the introductory sections.** Get an overview of the researcher's argument.

2 **Examine the table of contents and index.** Consider the most relevant chapters to your topic and the list of relevant subjects.

3 **Check the notes and bibliographic references.** Identify the authors a researcher refers to (do the names come up in many different books?) and the titles of both books and articles.

4 **Skim deeper.** Read chapter titles and headings and topic sentences to determine the relevance of what you are reading for your own research.

## A Practice Sequence: Evaluating Library Sources

For this exercise, we would like you to choose a specific book or article to examine in order to practice these strategies. If you are far along on your own research, use a book or an article you have identified as potentially useful.

1 Read the introductory sections. What issue is the author responding to? What is the writer's purpose? To correct a misconception? To fill a gap? To build on or extend the work of others?

2 Examine the table of contents and index. What key words or phrases are related to your own research? Which topics does the author focus on? Are you intending to give these topics similar emphasis? (Will you give more or less emphasis?)

3 Check the notes and bibliographic references. Make a list of the sources you think you want to look up for your own research. Do certain sources seem more important than others?

4 Skim deeper. What is the writer's focus? Is that focus relevant to your own topic, issue, question, or working thesis?

## EVALUATING INTERNET SOURCES

Without question, the World Wide Web has revolutionized how research is conducted. It has been a particular boon to experienced researchers who have a clear sense of what they are looking for, giving them access to more information more quickly than ever before. But the Internet is rife with pitfalls for inexperienced researchers. That is, sites that appear accurate and reliable may prove not to be. The sources you find on the Internet outside your school library's catalog pose problems because anyone can post anything he or she wants. Unfortunately, there is no way to monitor the accuracy of what is published on the Internet. Although Internet sources can be useful, particularly because they are current, you must take steps to evaluate them before using information from them.

### ■ Evaluate the Author of the Site

If an author's name appears on a Web site, ask: Who is this person? What is this person's background? Can I contact this person?

One of our students googled "English only" and clicked on the first result, "Language Policy—English Only Movement," which eventually led her to James Crawford's Language Policy Web Site & Emporium. On the site, Crawford explains that he is "a writer and lecturer—formerly the Washington editor of *Education Week*—who specializes in the politics of language."* He notes that "since 1985, I have been reporting on the English Only movement, English Plus, bilingual education, Native American language revitalization, and language rights in the U.S.A." Between 2004 and 2006, he served as executive director of the National Association for Bilingual Education. Perhaps most important, Crawford has authored four books and a number of articles and has testified before Congress on "Official English Legislation." From this biographical sketch, the student inferred that Crawford is credentialed to write about the English-only movement.

Less certain, however, are the credentials of the writer who penned an article titled "Should the National Anthem Be Sung in English Only?" which appeared on another Web site our student visited. Why? Because the writer's name never appears on the site. An anonymous posting is the first clue that you want to move on to a more legitimate source of information.

### ■ Evaluate the Organization That Supports the Site

You have probably noticed that Internet addresses usually end with a suffix: .edu, .gov, .org, or .com. The .edu suffix means the site is associated

---

*Education Week* has been published since 1981 by Editorial Projects in Education, a nonprofit organization that was founded with the help of a Carnegie grant. The publication covers issues related to primary and secondary education. If you are not familiar with a publication and are uncertain about its legitimacy, you can always ask your instructor, a librarian, or another expert to vouch for its reliability.

with a university or college, which gives it credibility. The same holds true for .gov, which indicates a government agency. Both types of sites have a regulatory body that oversees their content. The suffix .org indicates a nonprofit organization; .com, a commercial organization. You will need to approach these Web sites with a degree of skepticism because you cannot be sure that they are as carefully monitored by a credentialed regulatory body. (In fact, even .edu sites may turn out to be postings by a student at a college or university.)

Our student was intrigued by James Crawford's site because he appears to be a credible source on the English-only movement. She was less sure about the reference to the Institute for Language and Education Policy. Is the institute a regulatory body that oversees what appears on the site? How long has the institute existed? Who belongs to the institute? Who sits on its board of directors? As a critical thinker, the student had to ask these questions.

## ■ Evaluate the Purpose of the Site

Information is never objective, so whenever you evaluate a book, an article, or a Web site, you should consider the point of view the writer or sponsor is taking. It's especially important to ask if there is a particular bias among members of the group that sponsors the site. Can you tell what the sponsors of the site advocate? Are they hoping to sell or promote a product, or to influence opinion?

Not all Web sites provide easy answers to these questions. However, James Crawford's Language Policy Web Site & Emporium is quite explicit. In fact, Crawford writes that "the site is designed to encourage discussion of language policy issues, expose misguided school 'reforms,'" and, among other goals, "promote [his] own publications." (Notice "Emporium" in the name of the site.) He is candid about his self-interest, which does raise a question about his degree of objectivity.

What about a site like Wikipedia ("The Free Encyclopedia")? The site appears to exist to convey basic information. Although the popularity of Wikipedia recommends it as a basic resource, you should approach the site with caution because it is not clear whether and how the information posted on the site is regulated. It is prudent to confirm information from Wikipedia by checking on sites that are regulated more transparently rather than take Wikipedia as an authoritative source.

## ■ Evaluate the Information on the Site

In addition to assessing the purpose of a Web site like Wikipedia, you need to evaluate the extent to which the information is recent, accurate, and consistent with information you find in print sources and clearly regulated sites. For example, clicking on "The modern English-only movement" on Wikipedia takes you to a timeline of sorts with a number of links to other sites. But again, what is the source of this information? What is included?

What is left out? You should check further into some of these links, read-ing the sources cited and keeping in mind the four criteria for evaluating a claim — recency, relevance, accuracy, and reliability. Because you cannot be certain that Internet sources are reviewed or monitored, you need to be scrupulous about examining the claims they make: How much and what kind of evidence supports the writer's (or site's) argument? Can you offer counterarguments?

In the last analysis, it comes down to whether the information you find stands up to the criteria you've learned to apply as a critical reader and writer. If not, move on to other sources. In a Web-based world of informa-tion, there is no shortage of material, but you have to train yourself not to settle for the information that is most readily available if it is clearly not credible.

## Steps to Evaluating Internet Sources

**1** **Evaluate the author of the site.** Determine whether the author is an expert.

**2** **Evaluate the organization that supports the site.** Find out what the organization stands for and the extent of its credibility.

**3** **Evaluate the purpose of the site.** What interests are represented on the site? What is the site trying to do? Provide access to legiti-mate statistics and information? Advance an argument? Spread propaganda?

**4** **Evaluate the information on the site.** Identify the type of infor-mation on the site and the extent to which the information is recent, relevant, accurate, and reliable.

## A Practice Sequence: Evaluating Internet Sources

For this exercise, we would like you to work in groups on a common topic. The class can choose its own topic or use one of the topics we suggest on page 127. Then google the topic and agree on a Web site to analyze:

> *Group 1:* Evaluate the author of the site.
>
> *Group 2:* Evaluate the organization that supports the site.
>
> *Group 3:* Evaluate the purpose of the site.
>
> *Group 4:* Evaluate the information on the site.

Next, each group should share its evaluation. The goal is to determine the extent to which you believe you could use the information on this site in writing an academic essay.

# 7

# From Summary to Synthesis
*Using Sources to Build an Argument*

When you start to use sources to build your argument, there are certain strategies for working with the words and ideas of others that you will need to learn. Often you can quote the words of an author directly; but just as often you will restate and condense the arguments of others (paraphrasing and summarizing) or make comparisons to the ideas of others in the process of developing your own argument (synthesizing). We walk you through these more challenging strategies in this chapter. We also briefly discuss plagiarism and ways to avoid it and how to integrate quotations into your writing.

## SUMMARIES, PARAPHRASES, AND QUOTATIONS

In contrast to quotations, which involve using another writer's exact words, paraphrases and summaries are both restatements of another writer's ideas in your own words, but they differ in length:

- A paraphrase is usually about the same length as the original passage.
- A summary generally condenses a significantly longer text, conveying the argument not only of a few sentences but also of entire paragraphs, essays, or books.

In your own writing, you might paraphrase a few sentences or even a few paragraphs, but you certainly would not paraphrase a whole essay (much less a whole book). In constructing your arguments, however, you will often have to summarize the main points of the lengthy texts with which you are in conversation.

Both paraphrasing and summarizing are means to inquiry. That is, the act of recasting someone else's words or ideas into your own language, to suit your argument and reach your readers, forces you to think critically: What does this passage really mean? What is most important about it for my argument? How can I best present it to my readers? It requires making choices, not least of which is the best way to present the information—through paraphrase, summary, or direct quotation. In general, the following rules apply:

- *Paraphrase* when all the information in the passage is important, but the language may be difficult for your readers to understand.

- *Summarize* when you need to present only the key ideas of a passage (or an essay or a book) to advance your argument.

- *Quote* when the passage is so effective—so clear, so concise, so authoritative, so memorable—that you would be hard-pressed to improve on it.

## WRITING A PARAPHRASE

A **paraphrase** is a restatement of all the information in a passage in your own words, using your own sentence structure and composed with your own audience in mind to advance your argument.

- When you paraphrase a passage, start by identifying key words and phrases and substituting synonyms for them. A dictionary or thesaurus can help, but you may also have to reread what led up to the passage to remind yourself of the context. For example, did the writer define terms earlier that he or she uses in the passage and now expects you to know?

- Continue by experimenting with word order and sentence structure, combining and recombining phrases to convey what the writer says without replicating his or her style, in the best sequence for your readers. As you shuffle words and phrases, you should begin arriving at a much better understanding of what the writer is saying. By thinking critically, then, you are clarifying the passage for yourself as much as for your readers.

Let's look at a paraphrase of a passage from science fiction writer and scholar James Gunn's essay "Harry Potter as Schooldays Novel"*:

ORIGINAL PASSAGE

The situation and portrayal of Harry as an ordinary child with an extraordinary talent make him interesting. He elicits our sympathy at every turn. He plays a Cinderella-like role as the abused child of mean-spirited foster parents

---

*Gunn's essay appears in *Mapping the World of Harry Potter: An Unauthorized Exploration of the Bestselling Fantasy Series of All Time*, edited by Mercedes Lackey (Dallas: BenBella, 2006).

who favor other, less-worthy children, and also fits another fantasy role, that of changeling. Millions of children have nursed the notion that they cannot be the offspring of such unremarkable parents; in the Harry Potter books, the metaphor is often literal truth.

## PARAPHRASE

According to James Gunn, the circumstances and depiction of Harry Potter as a normal boy with special abilities captivate us by playing on our empathy. Gunn observes that, like Cinderella, Harry is scorned by his guardians, who treat him far worse than they treat his less-admirable peers. And like another fairy-tale figure, the changeling, Harry embodies the fantasies of children who refuse to believe that they were born of their undistinguished parents (146).

In this paraphrase, synonyms have replaced main words (*circumstances and depiction* for "situation and portrayal," *guardians* for "foster parents"), and the structure of the original sentences has been rearranged. But the paraphrase is about the same length as the original and says essentially the same things as Gunn's original.

Now, compare the paraphrase with this summary:

## SUMMARY

James Gunn observes that Harry Potter's character is compelling because readers empathize with Harry's fairy tale–like plight as an orphan whose gifts are ignored by his foster parents (144–45).

The summary condenses the passage, conveying Gunn's main point without restating the details. Notice how both the paraphrase and the summary indicate that the ideas are James Gunn's, not the writer's — "According to James Gunn," "James Gunn observes" — and signal, with page references, where Gunn's ideas end. *It is essential that you acknowledge your sources*, a subject we come back to in our discussion of plagiarism on page 180. The point we want to make here is that borrowing from the work of others is not always intentional. Many students stumble into plagiarism, especially when they are attempting to paraphrase. Remember that it's not enough to change the words in a paraphrase; you must also change the structure of the sentences. The only sure way to protect yourself is to cite your source.

You may be wondering: "If paraphrasing is so tricky, why bother? What does it add? I can see how the summary of Gunn's paragraph presents information more concisely and efficiently than the original, but the paraphrase doesn't seem to be all that different from the source and doesn't seem to add anything to it. Why not simply quote the original or summarize it?"

Good questions. The answer is that you paraphrase when the ideas in a passage are important but are conveyed in language your readers may have difficulty understanding. When academics write for their peers, they draw on the specialized vocabulary of their disciplines to make their arguments. By paraphrasing, you may be helping your readers, providing a translation of sorts for those who do not speak the language.

Consider this paragraph by George Lipsitz from his academic book *Time Passages: Collective Memory and American Popular Culture*, 1990), and compare the paraphrase that follows it:

## ORIGINAL PASSAGE

The transformations in behavior and collective memory fueled by the contradictions of the nineteenth century have passed through three major stages in the United States. The first involved the establishment and codification of commercialized leisure from the invention of the telegraph to the 1890s. The second involved the transition from Victorian to consumer-hedonist values between 1890 and 1945. The third and most important stage, from World War II to the present, involved extraordinary expansion in both the distribution of consumer purchasing power and in both the reach and scope of electronic mass media. The dislocations of urban renewal, suburbanization, and deindustrialization accelerated the demise of tradition in America, while the worldwide pace of change undermined stability elsewhere. The period from World War II to the present marks the final triumph of commercialized leisure, and with it an augmented crisis over the loss of connection to the past.

## PARAPHRASE

Historian George Lipsitz argues that Americans' sense of the past is rooted in cultural changes dating from the 1800s and has evolved through three stages. In the first stage, technological innovations of the nineteenth century gave rise to widespread commercial entertainment. In the second stage, dating from the 1890s to about 1945, attitudes toward the consumption of goods and services changed. Since 1945, in the third stage, increased consumer spending and the growth of the mass media have led to a crisis in which Americans find themselves cut off from their traditions and the memories that give meaning to them (12).

Notice that the paraphrase is not a word-for-word translation of the original. Instead, the writer has made choices that resulted in a slightly briefer and more accessible restatement of Lipsitz's thinking. (Although this paraphrase is shorter than the original passage, a paraphrase can also be a little longer than the original if extra words are needed to help readers understand the original.)

Notice too that several specialized terms and phrases from the original passage—the "codification of commercialized leisure," "the transition from Victorian to consumer-hedonist values," "the dislocations of urban renewal, suburbanization, and deindustrialization"—have disappeared. The writer not only looked up these terms and phrases in the dictionary but also reread the several pages that preceded the original passage to understand what Lipsitz meant by them.

The paraphrase is not an improvement on the original passage—in fact, historians would probably prefer what Lipsitz wrote—but it may help readers who do not share Lipsitz's expertise understand his point without distorting his argument.

Now compare this summary to the paraphrase:

### SUMMARY

Historian George Lipsitz argues that technological, social, and economic changes dating from the nineteenth century have culminated in what he calls a "crisis over the loss of connection to the past," in which Americans find themselves cut off from the memories of their traditions (12).

Which is better, the paraphrase or the summary? Neither is better or worse in and of itself. Their correctness and appropriateness depend on how the restatements are used in a given argument. That is, the decision to paraphrase or summarize depends entirely on the information you need to convey. Would the details in the paraphrase strengthen your argument? Or is a summary sufficient? In this case, if you plan to focus your argument on the causes of America's loss of cultural memory (the rise of commercial entertainment, changes in spending habits, globalization), then a paraphrase might be more helpful. But if you plan to define *loss of cultural memory*, then a summary may provide enough context for the next stage of your argument.

## Steps to Writing a Paraphrase

1. **Decide whether to paraphrase.** If your readers don't need all the information in the passage, consider summarizing it or presenting the key points as part of a summary of a longer passage. If a passage is clear, concise, and memorable as originally written, consider quoting instead of paraphrasing. Otherwise, and especially if the original was written for an academic audience, you may want to paraphrase the original to make its substance more accessible to your readers.

2. **Understand the passage.** Start by identifying key words, phrases, and ideas. If necessary, reread the pages leading up to the passage, to place it in context.

3. **Draft your paraphrase.** Replace key words and phrases with synonyms and alternative phrases (possibly gleaned from the context provided by the surrounding text). Experiment with word order and sentence structure until the paraphrase captures your understanding of the passage, in your own language, for your readers.

**4** **Acknowledge your source.** That's the only sure way to protect yourself from a charge of plagiarism.

---

### A Practice Sequence: Paraphrasing

**1** In one of the sources you've located in your research, find a sentence of some length and complexity, and paraphrase it. Share the original and your paraphrase of it with a classmate, and discuss the effectiveness of your restatement. Is the meaning clear to your reader? Is the paraphrase written in your own language, using your own sentence structure?

**2** Repeat the activity using a short paragraph from the same source. You and your classmate may want to attempt to paraphrase the same paragraph and then compare results. What differences do you detect?

---

## WRITING A SUMMARY

As you have seen, a **summary** condenses a body of information, presenting the key ideas and acknowledging their source. Summarizing is not an active way to make an argument, but summaries do provide a common ground of information for readers so that you can make your argument more effectively. You can summarize a paragraph, several paragraphs, an essay, a chapter in a book, or even an entire book, depending on the use you plan to make of the information in your argument.

We suggest a method of summarizing that involves

1. describing the author's key claims,
2. selecting examples to illustrate the author's argument,
3. presenting the gist of the author's argument, and
4. contextualizing what you summarize.

We demonstrate these steps for writing a summary following Clive Thompson's article "On the New Literacy."

---

CLIVE THOMPSON

## On the New Literacy

A print journalist at *New York Magazine*, Clive Thompson started his blog, Collision Detection, in September 2002, when he was beginning his year as a Knight Fellow in Science Journalism at MIT. Collision Detection has become one of the most well-regarded blogs on technology and culture. The blog receives approximately 3,000 to 4,000 hits a day. His piece on literacy appeared in *Wired* magazine in 2009.

■  ■  ■

As the school year begins, be ready to hear pundits fretting once again about how kids today can't write—and technology is to blame. Facebook encourages narcissistic blabbering, video and Power-Point have replaced carefully crafted essays, and texting has dehydrated language into "bleak, bald, sad shorthand" (as University College of London English professor John Sutherland has moaned). An age of illiteracy is at hand, right?

Andrea Lunsford isn't so sure. Lunsford is a professor of writing and rhetoric at Stanford University, where she has organized a mammoth project called the Stanford Study of Writing to scrutinize college students' prose. From 2001 to 2006, she collected 14,672 student writing samples—everything from in-class assignments, formal essays, and journal entries to emails, blog posts, and chat sessions. Her conclusions are stirring.

"I think we're in the midst of a literacy revolution the likes of which we haven't seen since Greek civilization," she says. For Lunsford, technology isn't killing our ability to write. It's reviving it—and pushing our literacy in bold new directions.

The first thing she found is that young people today write far more than any generation before them. That's because so much socializing takes place online, and it almost always involves text. Of all the writing that the Stanford students did, a stunning 38 percent of it took place out of the classroom—life writing, as Lunsford calls it. Those Twitter updates and lists of 25 things about yourself add up.

It's almost hard to remember how big a paradigm shift this is. Before the Internet came along, most Americans never wrote anything, ever, that wasn't a school assignment. Unless they got a job that required producing text (like in law, advertising, or media), they'd leave school and virtually never construct a paragraph again.

But is this explosion of prose good, on a technical level? Yes. Lunsford's team found that the students were remarkably adept at what rhetoricians call *kairos*—assessing their audience and adapting their tone and technique to best get their point across. The modern world of online writing, particularly in chat and on discussion threads, is conversational and public, which makes it closer to the Greek tradition of argument than the asynchronous letter and essay writing of 50 years ago.

The fact that students today almost always write for an audience (something virtually no one in my generation did) gives them a different sense of what constitutes good writing. In interviews, they defined good prose as something that had an effect on the world. For them, writing is about persuading and organizing and debating, even if it's over something as quotidian as what movie to go see. The Stanford students were almost always less enthusiastic about their in-class writing because it had no audience but the professor: It didn't serve any purpose other than to get them a grade. As for those texting short-forms and smileys defiling *serious* academic writing? Another myth. When Lunsford examined the work of first-year students, she didn't find a single example of texting speak in an academic paper.

Of course, good teaching is always going to be crucial, as is the mastering of formal academic prose. But it's also becoming clear that online media are pushing literacy into cool directions. The brevity of texting and status updating teaches young people to deploy haiku-like concision. At the same time, the proliferation of new forms of online pop-cultural exegesis—from sprawling TV-show recaps to 15,000-word videogame walkthroughs—has given them a chance to write enormously long and complex pieces of prose, often while working collaboratively with others.    8

We think of writing as either good or bad. What today's young people know is that knowing who you're writing for and why you're writing might be the most crucial factor of all.    9

## ■ Describe the Key Claims of the Text

As you read through a text with the purpose of summarizing it, you want to identify how the writer develops his or her argument. You can do this by what we call "chunking," grouping related material together into the argument's key claims. Here are two strategies to try.

*Notice how paragraphs begin and end.*   Often, focusing on the first and last sentences of paragraphs will alert you to the shape and direction of an author's argument. It is especially helpful if the paragraphs are lengthy and full of supporting information, as much academic writing is.

Because of his particular journalistic forum, *Wired* magazine, Thompson's paragraphs are generally rather short, but it's still worth taking a closer look at the first and last sentences of his opening paragraphs:

> *Paragraph 1:* As the school year begins, be ready to hear pundits fretting once again about how kids today can't write—and technology is to blame. Facebook encourages narcissistic blabbering, video and PowerPoint have replaced carefully crafted essays, and texting has dehydrated language into "bleak, bald, sad shorthand" (as University College of London English professor John Sutherland has moaned). An age of illiteracy is at hand, right?

> *Paragraph 2:* Andrea Lunsford isn't so sure. Lunsford is a professor of writing and rhetoric at Stanford University, where she has organized a mam-

moth project called the Stanford Study of Writing to scrutinize college students' prose. From 2001 to 2006, she collected 14,672 student writing samples—everything from in-class assignments, formal essays, and journal entries to emails, blog posts, and chat sessions. Her conclusions are stirring.

Right away you can see that Thompson has introduced a topic in each paragraph—pundits' criticism of students' use of electronic media in the first, and a national study designed to examine students' literacy in the second—and has indicated a connection between them. In fact, Thompson is explicit in doing so. He asks a question at the end of the first paragraph and then raises doubts as to the legitimacy of critics' denunciation of young people's reliance on blogs and posts to communicate. How will Thompson elaborate on this connection? What major points does he develop?

*Notice the author's point of view and use of transitions.*   Another strategy for identifying major points is to pay attention to descriptive words and transitions. For example, Thompson uses a rhetorical question ("An age of illiteracy is at hand, right?") and then offers a tentative answer ("Andrea Lunsford isn't so sure") that places some doubt in readers' minds.

Notice, too, the words that Thompson uses to characterize the argument in the first paragraph, which he appears to challenge in the second paragraph. Specifically, he describes these critics as "pundits," a word that traditionally refers to an expert or knowledgeable individual. However, the notion of a pundit, someone who often appears on popular talk shows, has also been used negatively. Thompson's description of pundits "fretting," wringing their hands in worry that literacy levels are declining, underscores this negative association of what it means to be a pundit. Finally, Thompson indicates that he does not identify with those who describe students as engaging in "narcissistic blabbering." This is clear when he characterizes the professor as having "moaned."

Once you identify an author's point of view, you will start noticing contrasts and oppositions in the argument—instances where the words are less positive, or neutral, or even negative—which are often signaled by how the writer uses transitions.

For example, Thompson begins with his own concession to critics' arguments when he acknowledges in paragraph 8 that educators should expect students to "[master] formal academic prose." However, he follows this concession with the transition word "but" to signal his own stance in the debate he frames in the first two paragraphs: "online media are pushing literacy into cool directions." Thompson also recognizes that students who write on blogs tend to write short, abbreviated texts. Still, he qualifies his concern with another transition, "at the same time." This transition serves to introduce Thompson's strongest claim: New media have given students "a chance to write enormously long and complex pieces of prose, often while working collaboratively with others."

These strategies can help you recognize the main points of an essay and explain them in a few sentences. For example, you could describe Thompson's key claims in this way:

1.  Electronic media give students opportunities to write more than in previous generations, and students have learned to adapt what they are writing in order to have some tangible effect on what people think and how they act.

2.  Arguably, reliance on blogging and posting on Twitter and Facebook can foster some bad habits in writing.

3.  But at least one major study demonstrates that the benefits of using the new media outweigh the disadvantages. This study indicates that students write lengthy, complex pieces that contribute to creating significant social networks and collaborations.

### ■ Select Examples to Illustrate the Author's Argument

A summary should be succinct, which means you should limit the number of examples or illustrations you use. As you distill the major points of the argument, try to choose one or two examples to illustrate each major point. Here are the examples (in italics) you might use to support Thompson's main points:

1.  Electronic media give students opportunities to write more than in previous generations, and students have learned to adapt what they are writing in order to have some tangible effect on what people think and how they act. *Examples from the Stanford study: Students "defined good prose as something that had an effect on the world. For them, writing is about persuading and organizing and debating"* (para. 7).

2.  Arguably, reliance on blogging and posting on Twitter and Facebook can foster some bad habits in writing. *Examples of these bad habits include critics' charges of "narcissistic blabbering," "bleak, bald, sad shorthand," and "dehydrated language"* (para. 1). *Thompson's description of texting's "haiku-like concision"* (para. 8) *seems to combine praise (haiku can be wonderful poetry) with criticism (it can be obscure and unintelligible).*

3.  But at least one major study demonstrates that the benefits of using the new media outweigh the disadvantages. *Examples include Thompson's point that the writing in the new media constitutes a "paradigm shift"* (para. 5). *Andrea Lunsford observes that students are "remarkably adept at what rhetoricians call* kairos—*assessing their audience and adapting their tone and technique to best get their point across"* (para. 6).

A single concrete example may be sufficient to clarify the point you want to make about an author's argument. Throughout the essay, Thompson derives examples from the Stanford study to support his argument in the final two paragraphs. The most concrete, specific example of how the new media benefit students as writers appears in paragraph 6, where the primary research of the Stanford study describes students' acquisition of important rhetorical skills of developing writing that is opportune (*kairos*) and purposeful. This one example may be sufficient for the purposes of summarizing Thompson's essay.

## ■ Present the Gist of the Author's Argument

When you present the **gist** of an argument, you are expressing the author's central idea in a sentence or two. The gist is not quite the same thing as the author's thesis statement. Instead, it is your formulation of the author's main idea, composed for the needs of your own argument.

Thompson's observations in paragraph 8 represent his thesis: "But it's also becoming clear that online media are pushing literacy into cool directions. . . . [T]he proliferation of new forms of online pop-cultural exegesis—from sprawling TV-show recaps to 15,000-word videogame walkthroughs—has given [students] a chance to write enormously long and complex pieces of prose, often while working collaboratively with others." In this paragraph, Thompson clearly expresses his central ideas in two sentences, while also conceding some of the critics' concerns. However, in formulating the gist of his argument, you want to do more than paraphrase Thompson. You want to use his position to support your own. For example, suppose you want to qualify the disapproval that some educators have expressed in drawing their conclusions about the new media. You would want to mention Thompson's own concessions when you describe the gist of his argument:

GIST

In his essay "On the New Literacy," Clive Thompson, while acknowledging some academic criticism of new media, argues that these media give students opportunities to write more than in previous generations and that students have learned to adapt what they are writing in order to have some tangible effect on what people think and how they act.

Notice that this gist could not have been written based only on Thompson's thesis statement. It reflects knowledge of Thompson's major points, his examples, and his concessions.

## ■ Contextualize What You Summarize

Your summary should help readers understand the context of the conversation:

- Who is the author?
- What is the author's expertise?

- What is the title of the work?
- Where did the work appear?
- What was the occasion of the work's publication? What prompted the author to write the work?
- What are the issues?
- Who else is taking part in the conversation, and what are their perspectives on the issues?

Again, because a summary must be concise, you must make decisions about how much of the conversation your readers need to know. If your assignment is to practice summarizing, it may be sufficient to include only information about the author and the source. However, if you are using the summary to build your own argument, you may need to provide more context. Your practice summary of Thompson's essay should mention that he is a journalist and should cite the title of and page references to his essay. You also may want to include information about Thompson's audience, publication information, and what led to the work's publication. Was it published in response to another essay or book, or to commemorate an important event?

We compiled our notes on Thompson's essay (key claims, examples, gist, context) in a worksheet (Figure 7.1). All of our notes in the worksheet constitute a type of prewriting, our preparation for writing the summary. Creating a worksheet like this can help you track your thoughts as you plan to write a summary. (You can download a template of this worksheet at bedfordstmartins.com/frominquiry.)

| Key Claim(s) | Examples | Gist | Context |
|---|---|---|---|
| 1. Electronic media prompt more student writing than ever before, and students use their writing to make a difference. | The Stanford study: Students "defined good prose as something that had an effect on the world" (para. 7). | In his essay "On the New Literacy," Clive Thompson, while acknowledging some academic criticism of new media, argues that these media give students opportunities to write more than in previous generations and that students have learned to adapt what they are writing in order to have some tangible effect on what people think and how they act. | Thompson is a journalist who has written widely on issues in higher education. His essay "On the New Literacy" appeared in *Wired* in August 2009 (http://www.wired .com/techbiz/people/ magazine/17-09/ st_thompson). Under consideration is the debate that he frames in his opening paragraphs. |
| 2. Arguably, reliance on blogging and posting can foster some bad writing habits. | Complaints of "bleak, bald, sad shorthand" and "narcissistic blabbering" (para. 1); texting can be obscure. | | |
| 3. But one major study shows the benefits of new media on student writing. | A "paradigm shift" (para. 5) to fluency in multiple formats and skill in assessing and persuading audiences. | | |

FIGURE 7.1    Worksheet for Writing a Summary

Here is our summary of Thompson's essay:

*The gist of Thompson's argument.*   In his essay "On the New Literacy," Clive Thompson, while acknowledging some academic criticism of new media, argues that these media give students opportunities to write more than in previous generations and that students have learned to adapt what they are writing in order to have some tangible effect on what people think and how they act. Argu-

*This concession helps to balance enthusiasm based on a single study.*   ably, reliance on blogging and posting on Twitter and Facebook can foster some bad habits in writing. But at least one

*Thompson's main point with example.*   major study demonstrates that the benefits of using the new media outweigh the disadvantages. Students write lengthy, complex pieces that contribute to creating significant social networks and collaborations.

## Steps to Writing a Summary

**1** **Describe the key claims of the text.** To understand the shape and direction of the argument, study how paragraphs begin and end, and pay attention to the author's point of view and use of transitions. Then combine what you have learned into a few sentences describing the key claims.

**2** **Select examples to illustrate the author's argument.** Find one or two examples to support each key claim. You may need only one example when you write your summary.

**3** **Present the gist of the author's argument.** Describe the author's central idea in your own language with an eye to where you expect your argument to go.

**4** **Contextualize what you summarize.** Cue your readers into the conversation. Who is the author? Where and when did the text appear? Why did the author write? Who else is in the conversation?

## A Practice Sequence: Summarizing

**1** Summarize a text that you have been studying for research or for one of your other classes. You may want to limit yourself to an excerpt of just a few paragraphs or a few pages. Follow the four steps we've described, using a summary worksheet for notes, and write a summary of the text. Then share the excerpt and your summary of it with two of your peers. Be prepared to justify your choices in composing the summary. Do your peers agree that your summary captures what is important in the original?

2  With a classmate, choose a brief text of about three pages. Each of you should use the method we describe above to write a summary of the text. Exchange your summaries and worksheets, and discuss the effectiveness of your summaries. Each of you should be prepared to discuss your choice of key claims and examples and your wording of the gist. Did you set forth the context effectively?

## SYNTHESIS VERSUS SUMMARY

A **synthesis** is a discussion that forges connections between the arguments of two or more authors. Like a summary, a synthesis requires you to understand the key claims of each author's argument, including his or her use of supporting examples and evidence. Also like a summary, a synthesis requires you to present a central idea, a *gist*, to your readers. But in contrast to a summary, which explains the context of a source, a synthesis creates a context for your own argument. That is, when you write a synthesis comparing two or more sources, you demonstrate that you are aware of the larger conversation about the issue and begin to claim your own place in that conversation.

Most academic arguments begin with a synthesis that sets the stage for the argument that follows. By comparing what others have written on a given issue, writers position themselves in relation to what has come before them, acknowledging the contributions of their predecessors as they advance their own points of view.

Like a summary, a synthesis requires analysis: You have to break down arguments and categorize their parts to see how they work together. In our summary of Thompson's essay (p. 151), the parts we looked at were the key claims, the examples and evidence that supported them, the central idea (conveyed in the gist), and the context. But in a synthesis, your main purpose is not simply to report what another author has said. Rather, you must think critically about how multiple points of view intersect on your issue, and decide what those intersections mean.

Comparing different points of view prompts you to ask why they differ. It also makes you more aware of *counterarguments*—passages where claims conflict ("writer X says this, but writer Y asserts just the opposite") or at least differ ("writer X interprets this information this way, while writer Y sees it differently"). And it starts you formulating your own counterarguments: "Neither X nor Y has taken this into account. What if they had?"

Keep in mind that the purpose of a synthesis is not merely to list the similarities and differences you find in different sources or to assert your agreement with one source as opposed to others. Instead, it sets up your argument. Once you discover connections among texts, you have to decide what those connections mean to you and your readers. What bearing do they have on your own thinking? How can you make use of them in your argument?

## WRITING A SYNTHESIS

To compose an effective synthesis, you must (1) make connections among ideas in different texts, (2) decide what those connections mean, and (3) formulate the gist of what you've read, much like you did when you wrote a summary. The difference is that in a synthesis, your gist should be a succinct statement that brings into focus not the central idea of one text but the relationship among different ideas in multiple texts.

To help you grasp strategies of writing a synthesis, read the following essays by journalists Cynthia Haven and Josh Keller, which, like Clive Thompson's essay, deal with the effects of new media on the quality of students' writing. We have annotated the Haven and Keller readings not only to comment on their ideas but also to connect their ideas with those of Thompson. Annotating your texts in this manner is a useful first step in writing a synthesis.

Following the Haven and Keller selections, we explain how annotating contributes to writing a synthesis. Then we show how you can use a worksheet to organize your thinking when you are formulating a gist of your synthesis. Finally, we present our own synthesis based on the texts of Thompson, Haven, and Keller.

### CYNTHIA HAVEN

## The New Literacy: Stanford Study Finds Richness and Complexity in Students' Writing

Cynthia Haven was born in Detroit and educated at the University of Michigan. A writer who has received more than a dozen literary and journalism awards, Haven is currently a literary critic at the *San Francisco Chronicle*. She has long been affiliated with Stanford University and is a regular contributor to its magazine, *Stanford Report*, where this article appeared in 2009.

■ ■ ■

*Begins with claims in the first two paragraphs for our consideration.*

Today's kids don't just write for grades anymore *1* They write to shake the world.

Moreover, they are writing more than any previous *2* generation, ever, in history. They navigate in a bewildering new arena where writers and their audiences have merged.

*Cites a study that supports these claims and sets up the terms of a debate: that new media may not be eroding literacy as "conventional wisdom" might suggest.*

These are among the startling findings in the Stanford Study of Writing, spearheaded by Professor Andrea Lunsford, director of Stanford's Program in Writing and Rhetoric. The study refutes conventional wisdom and provides a wholly new context for those who wonder "whether Google is making us stupid and whether Facebook is frying our brains," said Lunsford. 3

The five-year study investigated the writing of Stanford students during their undergraduate careers and their first year afterward, whether at a job or in graduate school. 4

*Observing the way the study employed a random sample helps give legitimacy to the study and support for the study's claims.*

The study began in September 2001, when Lunsford invited a random sample of the freshman class to participate in the study. Of the 243 invited, 189 accepted the invitation—about 12 percent of that year's class. 5

Students agreed to submit the writing they did for all their classes, including multimedia presentations, problem sets, lab reports, and honors theses. They also submitted as much as they wanted of what Lunsford calls "life writing," that is, the writing they did for themselves, their families, their friends, and the world at large. 6

*The volume and range of writing reinforces the initial claim: Today's students are writing more than previous generations.*

Lunsford was unprepared for the avalanche of material that ensued: about 15,000 pieces of writing, including emails in 11 languages, blog postings, private journal entries and poetry. The last, in particular, surprised her: "If there's any closeted group at Stanford, it's poets." 7

Only 62 percent of the writing was for their classwork. 8

While data analysis is ongoing, Lunsford said the study's first goal was "to paint a picture of the writing that these young writers do" and to portray "its richness and complexity." 9

Her conclusion: Although today's kids are "writing more than ever before in history," it may not look like the writing of yesterday. The focus of today's writing is "more about instantaneous communication." It's also about audience. 10

## Writing as Vehicle of Change

*Implied comparison between the current generation, which communicates to create change, and previous generations, who wrote to fulfill classroom assignments.*

For these students, "Good writing changes some- *11* thing. It doesn't just sit on the page. It gets up, walks off the page, and changes something," whether it's a website or a poster for a walkathon.

More than earlier generations, said Lunsford, *12* "Young people today are aware of the precarious nature of our lives. They understand the dangers that await us." Hence, "Writing is a way to get a sense of power."

*Haven provides a representative case example from the study to illustrate one of the conclusions drawn from the research: that students are writing more outside of class to "get something done."*

Twenty-six-year-old Mark Otuteye, one of 36 stu- *13* dents in the study group who agreed to be interviewed once a year, is in many ways representative. While at Stanford, he started a performance poetry group in response to 2003 student protests against growing involvement in Iraq.

"Academic writing seemed to be divorced from a *14* public audience. I was used to communicating not only privately, with emails, but publicly, with websites, blogs, and social networks," said Otuteye, CEO of AES Connect, a social media design company (he's also worked at Google).

"I was used to writing transactionally—not just for *15* private reflection, but writing to actually get something done in the world." For Otuteye, a half-Ghanaian student in the Program in African and African American Studies who went on to get a Stanford master's degree in modern thought and literature (2005) and, with a Marshall Scholarship, a master's degree from the University of Sussex in artificial intelligence (2008), academic writing was often "less important" than his writing for the "real world"—for example, the fliers he put up all over Stanford to promote his poetry group.

Lunsford cautioned that "audiences are very slip- *16* pery," and that, in the Internet age, "in a way the whole world can be your audience. It's inspirational, really, but it's hard to know who they are or what they'll do."

Anyone anywhere can be an overnight pundit *17* with an audience of millions—or can ramble on in

*Haven raises a question that many critics have about students being trapped in a limited view of the world.*

an unregarded cyberspace tirade. A lively blog "conversation" may consist largely of one writer assuming different masks. Does much of this writing, moreover, trap them in a world of other 19-year-olds, their peers?

### Audiences Change over Time

Otuteye noted that the students in the study were already writing for professors, friends, and parents. Moreover, as they transition into the work world after graduation, they begin to see "those audiences begin to mix and overlap. All the communication that they do online, with the exception of email, can become public." [18]

*The case example helps support the claim that new media enable students to learn to value rhetorical skills.*

"The skill of being able to manage multiple, overlapping audiences is a principle of rhetoric, a skill I was able to hone and perfect not only in academic writing, but in the performance writing I did and all the rhetorical activity I was engaged in at Stanford." [19]

He said that even the computer code he writes now follows "the same principles of rhetoric, specifically around audience, that is used in poetry and academic writing." A line of code, he said, could have four or more audiences, including other engineers and computers. [20]

*Is it higher education—not students—that needs to change to meet the demands of new media?*

Lunsford underscored the need for higher education to adapt; for example, students could post their essays online, accommodating their preference for an audience and online discussion. But Lunsford said adaptation must go even further: What does an English professor say when a student approaches her and says, "I know you'd like me to write an essay, but I'd like to make a documentary"? [21]

*This is Haven's own stand. It's clear that these prognosticators were wrong, and they may be wrong again.*

In light of this brave new world, it can be hard to remember that only a few decades ago doomsday prophets were predicting the death of the written word, as telephones and television increased their domination over a culture, and business CEOs dictated their letters into Dictaphones. [22]

In those days, graduation from college largely meant goodbye to writing. An office memo, letters, or "annotated cookbooks" were about the only written expres- [23]

sions of the adult world, said Lunsford, unless they were headed for jobs in the media or in academia. Writing was "instrumental"—designed for a purpose, such as a purchasing agreement, or advertising to sell a product.

## Redefining "Writing"

Today's landscape alters fundamental notions of what writing is. According to Lunsford, "The everyday understanding of writing is usually operational as opposed to epistemic."

*Defines a specialized term, "epistemic."*

Epistemic writing creates knowledge. (Think of all those times when you don't know what to think till you begin writing.) Such epistemic writing is an exploration, rather than declaration. It's the writing that dominates journals, letters, and many blogs. Clearly, the students' sense of agency extends to self-knowledge as well as changing the world.

*But is the writing "three times" as effective? Is it good writing?*

Comparing the Stanford students' writing with their peers from the mid-1980s, Lunsford found that the writing of today's students is about three times as long—they have "the ability to generate more prose."

They are also likely to make different kinds of errors. The number one error 20 years ago was spelling—a problem easily circumvented today by a spell-checker. Today's number one error is using the wrong word—"constraint" instead of "constrained," for example, or using the wrong preposition.

Lunsford recalls one student writing "I feel necrotic" rather than "neurotic."

*Counterargument to Lunsford's position: Students have not mastered the technical aspects of writing. However, the quotation does not really answer the question.*

Some nevertheless insist that writing today is substandard, littered with too many LOLs and OMGs. However, Lunsford noted that Stanford students were adept at different writing for different audiences. Moreover, they are changing the game: For a graphic novel such as Chris Ware's *Jimmy Corrigan: The Smartest Kid on Earth*, "traditional reading strategies do not work. Every single word is important." And websites, though they can be skimmed with a click, can be very labor- and thought-intensive.

24

25

26

27

28

29

"College writers need to be able to retain the best 30 of print literacy, and know how to deploy it for their own purposes," said Lunsford. "They also need and deserve to be exposed to new forms of expression."

With the more playful, inventive and spontaneous 31 forms of writing available to them, are today's students losing the taste for more complex English?

*Concludes with a quotation about how the use of new media does not devalue traditional conceptions of literacy, writing, and classic literature.*

"Every time I pick up Henry James, I have to 32 relearn how to read Henry James. We don't want to lose the ability to do that kind of reading and writing," said Lunsford.

"Thinking about hard things requires hard prose. 33 We can boil things down, prepare for a different audiences, but when it comes to hard things, I don't think it can be worked out in 140 characters."

## JOSH KELLER

# Studies Explore Whether the Internet Makes Students Better Writers

Josh Keller is a reporter for *The Chronicle of Higher Education* in Washington, D.C. The weekly publication focuses on issues in higher education and on news and serves as a job-information source for college and university faculty members, administrators, and students. His piece appeared in 2009.

■ ■ ■

As a student at Stanford University, Mark Otuteye 1 wrote in any medium he could find. He wrote blog posts, slam poetry, to-do lists, teaching guides, e-mail and Facebook messages, diary entries, short stories. He wrote a poem in computer code, and he wrote a computer program that helped him catalog all the things he had written.

*Keller uses the same student example as Haven to make the same point about college writing assignments.*

But Mr. Otuteye hated writing academic papers. 2 Although he had vague dreams of becoming an English professor, he saw academic writing as a "soulless exercise" that felt like "jumping through hoops." When given a writing assignment in class, he says, he would usually adopt a personal tone and more or less ignore the prompt. "I got away with it," says Mr. Otuteye, who graduated from Stanford in 2006. "Most of the time."

The rise of online media has helped raise a new    3
generation of college students who write far more, and in more-diverse forms, than their predecessors did. But the implications of the shift are hotly debated, both for the future of students' writing and for the college curriculum.

*Sums up two opposed points of view on the debate.*

Some scholars say that this new writing is more    4
engaged and more connected to an audience, and that colleges should encourage students to bring lessons from that writing into the classroom. Others argue that tweets and blog posts enforce bad writing habits and have little relevance to the kind of sustained, focused argument that academic work demands.

A new generation of longitudinal studies, which    5
track large numbers of students over several years, is attempting to settle this argument. The "Stanford Study of Writing," a five-year study of the writing lives of Stanford students—including Mr. Otuteye—is probably the most extensive to date.

*Goes beyond Haven to cite an additional study at Michigan State that reached similar conclusions as the Stanford study.*

In a shorter project, undergraduates in a first-year    6
writing class at Michigan State University were asked to keep a diary of the writing they did in any environment, whether blogging, text messaging, or gaming. For each act of writing over a two-week period, they recorded the time, genre, audience, location, and purpose of their writing.

"What was interesting to us was how small a percentage of the total writing the school writing was,"    7
says Jeffrey T. Grabill, the study's lead author, who is director of the Writing in Digital Environments Research Center at Michigan State. In the diaries and in follow-up interviews, he says, students often described their social, out-of-class writing as more persistent and meaningful to them than their in-class work was.

*Additional evidence that supports the Stanford study.*

"Digital technologies, computer networks, the    8
Web—all of those things have led to an explosion in

writing," Mr. Grabill says. "People write more now than ever. In order to interact on the Web, you have to write."

Keller adds the voices of scholars of writing to comment on the value of new media.

Kathleen Blake Yancey, a professor of English at Florida State University and a former president of the National Council of Teachers of English, calls the current period "the age of composition" because, she says, new technologies are driving a greater number of people to compose with words and other media than ever before.    9

"This is a new kind of composing because it's so variegated and because it's so intentionally social," Ms. Yancey says. Although universities may not consider social communication as proper writing, it still has a strong influence on how students learn to write, she says. "We ignore it at our own peril."    10

Unlike Thompson and Haven, Keller provides the counterarguments of scholars who dispute the findings of the Stanford study.

But some scholars argue that students should adapt their writing habits to their college course work, not the other way around. Mark Bauerlein, a professor of English at Emory University, cites the reading and writing scores in the National Assessment of Educational Progress, which have remained fairly flat for decades. It is a paradox, he says: "Why is it that with young people reading and writing more words than ever before in human history, we find no gains in reading and writing scores?"    11

## The Right Writing

Underscores the difficulty of drawing conclusions either way.

Determining how students develop as writers, and why they improve or not, is difficult. Analyzing a large enough sample of students to reach general conclusions about how the spread of new technologies affects the writing process, scholars say, is a monumental challenge.    12

The sheer amount of information that is relevant to a student's writing development is daunting and difficult to collect: formal and informal writing, scraps of notes and diagrams, personal histories, and fleeting conversations and thoughts that never make it onto the printed page.    13

*This summary of the Stanford study suggests that researchers there have responded to the complexity of measuring outcomes of writing in any medium.*

The Stanford study is trying to collect as much of that material as possible. Starting in 2001, researchers at the university began collecting extensive writing samples from 189 students, roughly 12 percent of the freshman class. Students were given access to a database where they could upload copies of their work, and some were interviewed annually about their writing experiences. By 2006 researchers had amassed nearly 14,000 pieces of writing. *14*

Students in the study "almost always" had more enthusiasm for the writing they were doing outside of class than for their academic work, says Andrea A. Lunsford, the study's director. Mr. Otuteye submitted about 700 pieces of writing and became the study's most prolific contributor. *15*

The report's authors say they included nonacademic work to better investigate the links between academic and nonacademic writing in students' writing development. One of the largest existing longitudinal studies of student writing, which started at Harvard University in the late 1990s, limited its sample to academic writing, which prevented researchers from drawing direct conclusions about that done outside of class. *16*

In looking at students' out-of-class writing, the Stanford researchers say they found several traits that were distinct from in-class work. Not surprisingly, the writing was self-directed; it was often used to connect with peers, as in social networks; and it usually had a broader audience. *17*

*Cites the study at George Mason. Writing on blogs is more engaging than writing in school, and it represents the ways students sustain social networks (paras. 17–20).*

The writing was also often associated with accomplishing an immediate, concrete goal, such as organizing a group of people or accomplishing a political end, says Paul M. Rogers, one of the study's authors. The immediacy might help explain why students stayed so engaged, he says. "When you talked to them about their out-of-class writing, they would talk about writing to coordinate out-of-class activity," says Mr. Rogers, an assistant professor of English at George Mason University. "A lot of them were a lot more *18* conscious of the effect their writing was having on other people."

Mr. Rogers believes from interviews with students that the data in the study will help show that students routinely learn the basics of writing concepts wherever they write the most. For instance, he says, students who compose messages for an audience of their peers on a social-networking Web site were forced to be acutely aware of issues like audience, tone, and voice.    19

"The out-of-class writing actually made them more conscious of the things writing teachers want them to think about," the professor says.    20

Mr. Otuteye, who recently started a company that develops Web applications, says he paid close attention to the writing skills of his peers at Stanford as the co-founder of a poetry slam. It was the students who took their out-of-class writing seriously who made the most progress, he says. "Everybody was writing in class, but the people who were writing out of and inside of class, that was sort of critical to accelerating their growth as writers."    21

Although analysis of the Stanford study is still at an early stage, other scholars say they would like to start similar studies. At the University of California, several writing researchers say they are trying to get financial support for a longitudinal study of 300 students on the campuses in Irvine, Santa Barbara, and Davis.    22

## Curricular Implications

The implications of the change in students' writing habits for writing and literature curricula are up for debate. Much of the argument turns on whether online writing should be seen as a welcome new direction or a harmful distraction.    23

*Why does it have to be "either/or"? Isn't it possible that there's a middle ground?*

Mr. Grabill, from Michigan State, says college writing instruction should have two goals: to help students become better academic writers, and to help them become better writers in the outside world. The second, broader goal is often lost, he says, either    24

*Grabill criticizes the critics, pointing out that they have lost sight of an important goal: Students should be able to write to a general, public audience, not just academic readers (paras. 24–30).*

because it is seen as not the college's responsibility, or because it seems unnecessary.

"The unstated assumption there is that if you can write a good essay for your literature professor, you can write anything," Mr. Grabill says. "That's utter nonsense." 25

The writing done outside of class is, in some ways, the opposite of a traditional academic paper, he says. Much out-of-class writing, he says, is for a broad audience instead of a single professor, tries to solve real-world problems rather than accomplish academic goals, and resembles a conversation more than an argument. 26

Rather than being seen as an impoverished, secondary form, online writing should be seen as "the new normal," he says, and treated in the curriculum as such: "The writing that students do in their lives is a tremendous resource." 27

*This seems rather anecdotal.*

Ms. Yancey, at Florida State, says out-of-class writing can be used in a classroom setting to help students draw connections among disparate types of writing. In one exercise she uses, students are asked to trace the spread of a claim from an academic journal to less prestigious forms of media, like magazines and newspapers, in order to see how arguments are diluted. In another, students are asked to pursue the answer to a research question using only blogs, and to create a map showing how they know if certain information is trustworthy or not. 28

*But does this occur—avoiding a "fire wall"?*

The idea, she says, is to avoid creating a "fire wall" between in-class and out-of-class writing. 29

"If we don't invite students to figure out the lessons they've learned from that writing outside of school and bring those inside of school, what will happen is only the very bright students" will do it themselves, Ms. Yancey says. "It's the rest of the population that we're worried about." 30

*One critic concedes that writing in electronic media can help struggling writers, but he also*

Writing in electronic media probably does benefit struggling students in a rudimentary way, says Emory's Mr. Bauerlein, because they are at least forced to string sentences together: "For those kids who 31 *warns that educators should temper their enthusiasm for blogging and other online writing (paras. 32–35).*

wouldn't be writing any words anyway, that's going to improve their very low-level skills."

But he spends more of his time correcting, not integrating, the writing habits that students pick up outside of class. The students in his English courses often turn in papers that are "stylistically impoverished," and the Internet is partly to blame, he says. Writing for one's peers online, he says, encourages the kind of quick, unfocused thought that results in a scarcity of coherent sentences and a limited vocabulary.

*Has he studied this?*

"When you are writing so much to your peers, you're writing to other 17-year-olds, so your vocabulary is going to be the conventional vocabulary of the 17-year-old idiom," Mr. Bauerlein says.

Students must be taught to home in on the words they write and to resist the tendency to move quickly from sentence to sentence, he says. Writing scholars, too, should temper their enthusiasm for new technologies before they have fully understood the implications, he says. Claims that new forms of writing should take a greater prominence in the curriculum, he says, are premature.

"The sweeping nature of their pronouncements to me is either grandiose or flatulent, or you could say that this is a little irresponsible to be pushing for practices so hard that are so new," Mr. Bauerlein says. "We don't know what the implications of these things will be. Slow down!?"

*Another scholar reaffirms a finding in the Stanford study: that electronic media represent a cultural shift that educators must learn to accept and adapt to.*

Deborah Brandt, a professor of English at the University of Wisconsin at Madison who studies the recent history of reading and writing, says the growth of writing online should be seen as part of a broader cultural shift toward mass authorship. Some of the resistance to a more writing-centered curriculum, she says, is based on the view that writing without reading can be dangerous because students will be untethered to previous thought, and reading levels will decline.

*Really, people are not shaped by what they read?*

But that view, she says, is "being challenged by the literacy of young people, which is being developed

32

33

34

35

36

37

primarily by their writing. They're going to be reading, but they're going to be reading to write, and not
to be shaped by what they read."

## ■ Make Connections Among Different Texts

The texts by Thompson, Haven, and Keller all deal with the emergence
of new electronic media and their effects on students' development as
writers. These texts are very much in conversation with one another, as
each author focuses on what research tells us are the benefits of the new
media and the potential ways that electronic media can limit young writers' growth:

- Thompson uses the Stanford study to emphasize the ways that students'
  participation on blogs and the like helps students learn to adapt their
  writing for specific audiences and to write fairly complex texts to affect
  the ways readers think and act.

- Haven provides a more elaborate analysis of the Stanford study to argue
  that we are witnessing a revolution in literacy, the likes of which we have
  not experienced since the development of classical rhetoric.

- Keller offers converging pieces of evidence to support the findings from
  the Stanford study that Thompson and Haven discuss, but additionally he provides a more detailed counterargument that is also based on
  research.

All three authors seem to agree that the introduction of new electronic
media has contributed to a paradigm shift in the uses of writing—to create agency and community—but they seem to vary in the concessions they
make to counterarguments.

Notice how our annotations call out connections. "Keller uses the
same student example as Haven to make the same point about college writing assignments." "Keller adds the voices of scholars of writing to comment on the value of new media." "Unlike Thompson and Haven, Keller
provides the counterarguments of scholars who dispute the findings of the
Stanford study."

With these annotations, we are starting to think critically about the
ideas in the essays. Notice, however, that not all of the annotations make
connections. Some note examples that support the argument that electronic media benefit writers, while others point to examples that provide
compelling evidence for the counterargument. Still other annotations raise
questions about the basis on which researchers and teachers reached their
conclusions. In the end, you should not expect that every annotation will
contribute to your synthesis. Instead, use them to record your responses
and also to spur your thinking.

## ■ Decide What Those Connections Mean

Having annotated the selections, we filled out the worksheet in Figure 7.2, making notes in the grid to help us see the three texts in relation to one another. Our worksheet included columns for

- author and source information
- the gist of each author's arguments
- supporting examples and illustrations
- counterarguments
- our own thoughts

A worksheet like this one can help you concentrate on similarities and differences in the texts to determine what the connections among texts mean. (You can download a template for this worksheet at bedfordstmartins .com/frominquiry.) Of course, you can design your own worksheet as well, tailoring it to your needs and preferences. If you want to take very detailed notes about your authors and sources, for example, you may want to have separate columns for each.

Once you start making connections, including points of agreement and disagreement, you can start identifying counterarguments in the reading—for example, Keller quotes a scholar who cites a national study, the National Assessment of Education Progress, to dampen enthusiasm for the claims that Thompson and Haven give so much attention to. Identifying counterarguments gives you a sense of what is at issue for each author. And determining what authors think in relation to one another can help you realize what is at issue for you. Suppose you are struck by Haven's implicit argument that a revolution in literacy is occurring and that institutions of higher education, not students, need to respond to changes in the nature of literacy and communication. But you also recognize in Keller's analysis that questions persist about studies conducted to assess the development of students' growth and development as writers. How persuasive are the studies conducted at Stanford, Michigan State, and George Mason? What do we really know? And how can we further test the claims experts make about electronic media and paradigm shifts? Turning these ideas and questions over in your mind, you may be able to decide on a topic you want to explore and develop.

## ■ Formulate the Gist of What You've Read

Remember that your gist should bring into focus the relationship among different ideas in multiple texts. Looking at the information juxtaposed on the worksheet, you can begin to construct the gist of your synthesis:

- Clive Thompson cites research conducted at Stanford to challenge prevailing arguments about electronic media's effects on students' literacy.

| Author and Source | Gist of Argument | Examples/ Illustrations | Counterarguments | What I Think |
|---|---|---|---|---|
| Clive Thompson, "On the New Literacy," *Wired* (2009) | Research challenges prevailing arguments about electronic media's effects on students' literacy, suggesting they may be more literate than in the past. | The Stanford study, with its sample of more than 14,000 pieces of writing and randomized sample of student participants. One case example. | Student writing is full of "texting-speak." | The Stanford study is persuasive, especially given the size of the study. Not much counter-evidence. |
| Cynthia Haven, "The New Literacy: Stanford Study Finds Richness and Complexity in Students' Writing," *Stanford Report* (2009) | A study indicates a possible revolution in literacy. Using online social networks to create change, students now write more, more persuasively, and more adaptively than ever before. | Stanford study and case example of one student. | Students who spend most of their time writing on electronic networks do not attend to the technical aspects of communication and have a limited sense of their audience. | This is a more thorough review of the Stanford study. It emphasizes how much more meaningful writing is outside of the classroom. |
| Josh Keller, "Studies Explore Whether the Internet Makes Students Better Writers," *Chronicle of Higher Education* (2009) | Two studies suggest that electronic media, in giving students more opportunities to write and honing their sense of audience, have made them better writers than previous generations. But an emerging body of evidence challenges these recent claims, which force educators to consider what they consider good writing. | Studies at Stanford, Michigan State, and George Mason. Expert opinion from faculty at Florida State and the University of Wisconsin. | Critics like Professor Bauerlein at Emory University argue that literacy is not progressing steadily, as some have observed, at least not based on standardized tests. He suggests that writing solely to one's peers online encourages spontaneous but unfocused thought and a limited vocabulary. | The three studies together are quite powerful. I am not sure that standardized tests developed a generation ago are the best way to measure increases in literacy. And Bauerlein relies on anecdotal evidence to make his argument: that writing in electronic media limits thinking or writing quality. I should check if any studies exist to support Baeurlein. |

**FIGURE 7.2    Worksheet for Writing a Synthesis**

Indeed, despite pundits' complaints, students may be more literate than in the past.

- Cynthia Haven also analyzes the Stanford study, which indicates that we may very well be experiencing a revolution in literacy. Students use electronic media to sustain social networks and create change. As Thompson also points out, students are writing more than ever before and are more adept at applying principles of rhetoric than were students in previous generations. Those in higher education may have to change in order to respond to students' uses of electronic media, not the other way around.

- Josh Keller points to two additional studies of writing to suggest that students are developing literate practices that are more impressive than those of previous generations. This can be attributed to the fact that current students have more opportunities to write and they know what it means to write for an audience. But he also observes that an emerging body of evidence challenges these recent claims, forcing educators to consider what constitutes good writing.

How do you formulate this information into a gist? You can use a transition word such as *although* or *however* to connect ideas that different authors bring together while conveying their differences. Thus, a gist of these essays might read:

### GIST OF A SYNTHESIS

Although Clive Thompson and Cynthia Haven suggest that new electronic media have created a paradigm shift in the ways educators think about writing, journalists such as Josh Keller have also cited evidence that dampens enthusiasm for the benefits of writing on blogs without students' having instruction in formal, academic writing.

Having drafted the gist, we returned to our notes on the worksheet to complete the synthesis, presenting examples and using transitions to signal the relationships among the texts and their ideas. Here is our brief synthesis of the three texts:

*The gist of our synthesis. "Although" signals that Thompson's and Haven's arguments are qualified.*

*Specific example of a key piece of evidence that has sparked debate.*

Although Clive Thompson and Cynthia Haven suggest that new electronic media have created a paradigm shift in the ways educators think about writing, journalists such as Josh Keller have also cited evidence that dampens enthusiasm for the benefits of writing on blogs without students' having instruction in formal, academic writing. In particular, Thompson cites research conducted at Stanford University to challenge prevailing arguments about electronic media's effects on students' literacy. The Stanford study, with its sample of more than 14,000 pieces of writing and randomized sample of student participants, seems very persuasive.

Indeed, despite pundits' complaints, students may be more literate than in the past.

Cynthia Haven also analyzes the Stanford study, indicating that we may very well be experiencing a revolution in literacy. Students use electronic media to sustain social networks and create change. As Thompson also points out, students are writing more than ever before and are more adept at applying principles of rhetoric than were students in previous generations. Those in higher education may have to change in order to respond to students' uses of electronic media, not the other way around.

Finally, Josh Keller points to two additional studies of writing to suggest that students are developing literate practices that are more impressive than those of previous generations. This can be attributed to the fact that current students have more opportunities to write and they know what it means to write for an audience. However, Keller, more than Thompson and Haven, observes that an emerging body of evidence challenges these recent claims, forcing educators to consider what constitutes good writing. Keller's analysis reveals that questions persist about studies conducted to assess the development of students' growth and development as writers. How persuasive are the studies conducted at Stanford, Michigan State, and George Mason? What do we really know, and what do we need to know? Further, how can we test the claims experts make about electronic media and paradigm shifts?

*Transition: Both Thompson and Haven give less attention to the counterargument than they should.*

*Questions set up direction of what is to follow.*

Writing a synthesis, like writing a summary, is principally a strategy for framing your own argument. In writing a synthesis, you are conveying to your readers how various points of view in a conversation intersect and diverge. The larger point of this exercise is to find your own issue—your own position in the conversation—and make your argument for it.

## Steps to Writing a Synthesis

**1** **Make connections between and among different texts.** Annotate the texts you are working with, with an eye to comparing them. As you would for a summary, note major points in the texts, choose relevant examples, and formulate the gist of each text.

**2** **Decide what those connections mean.** Fill out a worksheet to compare your notes on the different texts, track counterarguments, and record your thoughts. Decide what the similarities and differences mean to you and what they might mean to your readers.

**3** **Formulate the gist of what you've read.** Identify an overarching idea that brings together the ideas you've noted, and write a synthesis that forges connections and makes use of the examples you've noted. Use transitions to signal the direction of your synthesis.

## A Practice Sequence: Writing a Synthesis

**1** To practice the strategies for synthesizing that we describe in this chapter, read the following three essays, which focus on the role that electronic media play in conveying information to diverse groups of readers or viewers. As you discuss the strategies the authors use to develop their arguments, consider these questions:

- How would you explain the popularity of blogs, Twitter, and YouTube?

- What themes have the writers focused on as they have sought to enter the conversation surrounding the use of electronic media?

- To what extent do you think the criticisms of new media presented by the authors are legitimate?

- Do blogs, Twitter, and YouTube pose a threat to traditional journalism?

- Do you think that blogs, Twitter, and YouTube add anything to print journalism? If so, what?

**2** To stimulate a conversation, or a debate, we suggest that you break up into four different groups:

*Group 1:* Print journalism

*Group 2:* Blogs

*Group 3:* Twitter

*Group 4:* YouTube

Students in each group should prepare an argument indicating the strengths and limitations of the particular mode of communication that they represent. In preparing the argument, be sure to acknowledge what other modes of communication might add to the ways we learn about news and opinions. One student from each group will present this argument to the other groups.

**3** Based on the discussion you have had in exercise 1 and/or exercise 2, write a synthesis of the three essays using the steps we have outlined in this chapter:

- Summarize each essay.

- Explain the ways in which the authors' arguments are similar or different, using examples and illustrations to demonstrate the similarities and differences.

- Formulate an overall gist that synthesizes the points each author makes.

DAN KENNEDY

## Political Blogs: Teaching Us Lessons About Community

Dan Kennedy, an assistant professor of journalism at Northeastern University, writes on media issues for *The Guardian* and for *CommonWealth* magazine. His blog, Media Nation, is online at medianation.blogspot.com.

■ ■ ■

The rise of blogging as both a supplement and a challenge to traditional journalism has coincided with an explosion of opinion mongering. Blogs—and the role they play in how Americans consume and respond to information—are increasingly visible during our political season, when our ideological divide is most apparent. From nakedly partisan sites such as Daily Kos on the left and Little Green Footballs on the right, to more nuanced but nevertheless ideological enterprises such as Talking Points Memo, it sometimes seems there is no room in blogworld for straight, neutral journalism.

The usual reasons given for this are that reporting is difficult and expensive and that few bloggers know how to research a story, develop and interview sources, and assemble the pieces into a coherent, factual narrative. Far easier, so this line of thinking goes, for bloggers to sit in their pajamas and blast their semi-informed opinions out to the world.

There is some truth to this, although embracing this view wholeheartedly requires us to overlook the many journalists who are now writing blogs, as well as the many bloggers who are producing journalism to a greater or lesser degree. But we make a mistake when we look at the opinion-oriented nature of blogs and ask whether bloggers are capable of being "objective," to use a hoary and now all but meaningless word. The better question to ask is why opinion-oriented blogs are so popular—and what lessons the traditional media can learn from them without giving up their journalistic souls.

Perhaps what's happening is that the best and more popular blogs pro-    4
vide a sense of community that used to be the lifeblood of traditional news organizations and, especially, of newspapers. Recently I reread part of Jay Rosen's book, *What Are Journalists For?*, his 1999 postmortem on the public journalism movement. What struck me was Rosen's description of public journalism's origins, which were grounded in an attempt to recreate a sense of community so that people might discover a reason to read newspapers. "Eventually I came to the conclusion . . . that journalism's purpose was to see the public into fuller existence," Rosen writes. "Informing people followed that."

Rosen's thesis—that journalism could only be revived by reawakening    5
the civic impulse—is paralleled by Robert Putnam's 2000 book, *Bowling Alone*, in which he found that people who sign petitions, attend public meetings, and participate in religious and social organizations are more likely to be newspaper readers than those who do not. "Newspaper readers are older, more educated, and more rooted in their communities than is the average American," Putnam writes.

Unfortunately for the newspaper business, the traditional idea of com-    6
munity, based mainly on geography, remains as moribund today as it was when Rosen and Putnam were analyzing its pathologies. But if old-fashioned communities are on the decline, the human impulse to form communities is not. And the Internet, as it turns out, is an ideal medium for fostering a new type of community in which people have never met, and may not even know each other's real names, but share certain views and opinions about the way the world works. It's interesting that Rosen has become a leading exponent of journalism tied to these communities, both through his PressThink blog and through NewAssignment.net, which fosters collaborations between professional and citizen journalists.


## Attitude First, Facts Second

This trend toward online community-building has given us a mediascape    7
in which many people—especially those most interested in politics and public affairs—want the news delivered to them in the context of their attitudes and beliefs. That doesn't mean they want to be fed a diet of self-reinforcing agit-prop (although some do). It does mean they see their news consumption as something that takes place within their community, to be fit into a pre-existing framework of ideas that may be challenged but that must be acknowledged.

Earlier this year John Lloyd, a contributing editor for the *Financial* 8
*Times*, talked about the decline of just-the-facts journalism on *Open Source*, a Web-based radio program hosted by the veteran journalist Christopher Lydon. It has become increasingly difficult, Lloyd said, to report facts that are not tied to an ideological point of view. The emerging paradigm, he explained, may be "that you can only get facts through by attaching them to a very strong left-wing, right-wing, Christian, atheist position. Only then, only if you establish your bona fides within this particular community, will they be open to facts."

No less a blogging enthusiast than Markos Moulitsas, founder of Daily 9
Kos, has observed that political blogs are a nonentity in Britain, where the newspapers themselves cater to a wide range of different opinions. "You look at the media in Britain, it's vibrant and it's exciting and it's fun, because they're all ideologically tinged," Moulitsas said at an appearance in Boston last fall. "And that's a good thing, because people buy them and understand that their viewpoints are going to be represented."

The notion that journalism must be tied to an ideological community 10
may seem disheartening to traditionalists. In practice, though, journalism based on communities of shared interests and beliefs can be every bit as valuable as the old model of objectivity, if approached with rigor and respect for the truth.

Last year, for instance, Talking Points Memo (TPM) and its related 11
blogs helped break the story of how the U.S. Department of Justice had fired eight U.S. attorneys for what appeared to be politically motivated reasons, a scandal that led to the resignation of Attorney General Alberto Gonzales. TPM's reporting was based in part on information dug up and passed along by its liberal readership. The founder and editor, Joshua Micah Marshall, received a George Polk Award, but it belonged as much to the community he had assembled as it did to him personally.

Of course, we still need neutral, non-opinionated journalism to help us 12
make sense of the world around us. TPM's coverage of the U.S. attorneys scandal was outstanding, but it was also dismissive of arguments that it was much ado about nothing, or that previous administrations had done the same or worse. Liberals or conservatives who get all of their news from ideologically friendly sources don't have much incentive to change their minds.

## Connecting to Communities of Shared Interests

Even news outlets that excel at traditional, "objective" journalism do so 13
within the context of a community. Some might not find liberal bias in the news pages of the *New York Times*, as the paper's conservative critics

would contend, but there's little doubt that the *Times* serves a community of well educated, affluent, culturally liberal readers whose preferences and tastes must be taken into account. Not to be a journalistic relativist, but all news needs to be evaluated within the context in which it was produced, even an old-fashioned, inverted-pyramid-style dispatch from the wires. Who was interviewed? Who wasn't? Why? These are questions that must be asked regardless of the source.

We might now be coming full circle as placeblogs—chatty, conversational blogs that serve a particular geographic community—become more prevalent. Lisa Williams, founder of H2otown, a blog that serves her community of Watertown, Massachusetts, believes that such forums could help foster the sense of community that is a necessary precondition to newspaper readership. Williams also runs a project called Placeblogger.com, which tracks local blogs around the world.    14

"The news creates a shared pool of stories that gives us a way to talk to people who aren't family or close friends or people who we will never meet—in short, our fellow citizens," Williams says by e-mail. "The truth is, people still want those neighbor-to-neighbor contacts, but the traditional ways of doing it don't fit into the lives that people are actually living today. Your core audience is tired, sitting on the couch with their laptop, and watching *Lost* with one eye. Give them someone to sit with."    15

Critics of blogs have been looking at the wrong thing. While traditionalists disparage bloggers for their indulgence of opinion and hyperbole, they overlook the sense of community and conversation that blogs have fostered around the news. What bloggers do well, and what news organizations do poorly or not at all, is give their readers someone to sit with. News consumers—the public, citizens, us—still want the truth. But we also want to share it and talk about it with our like-minded neighbors and friends. The challenge for journalism is not that we'll lose our objectivity; it's that we won't find a way to rebuild a sense of community.    16

JOHN DICKERSON

## Don't Fear Twitter

John Dickerson is *Slate* magazine's chief political correspondent and a political analyst for CBS News. Before joining *Slate,* Dickerson covered politics for *Time* magazine, including four years as the magazine's White House correspondent. Dickerson has also written for the *New York Times* and *Washington Post* and is a regular panelist on *Washington Week in Review*. This essay first appeared in the Summer 2008 issue of *Nieman Reports*.

■  ■  ■

If I were cleverer, this piece on Twitter and journalism would fit in Twitter's 140-character limitation. The beauty of Twitter when properly used—by both the reader and the writer—is that everyone knows what it is. No reader expects more from Twitter than it offers, and no one writing tries to shove more than necessary into a Twitter entry, which is sometimes called a Tweet, but not by me, thank you. [1]

Not many people know what Twitter is, though, so I'm going to go on for a few hundred words. Twitter is a Web site that allows you to share your thoughts instantly and on any topic with other people in the Twitter network as long as you do so in tight little entries of 140 characters or less. If you're wondering how much you can write with that space limitation, this sentence that you're reading right now hits that mark perfectly. [2]

For some, journalism is already getting smaller. Newspapers are shrinking. Serious news is being pushed aside in favor of entertainment and fluff stories. To many journalists and guardians of the trade, the idea that any journalist would willingly embrace a smaller space is horrifying and dumb. One journalism professor drew himself up to his full height and denounced Twitter journalism—or microjournalism, as someone unfortunately called it—as the ultimate absurd reduction of journalism. (I think he may have dislodged his monocle, he was waving his quill pen so violently.) Venerable CBS newsman Roger Mudd had a far lighter touch when he joked to me that he could barely say the word "texting" when he and I were talking about the idea of delivering a couple of sentences and calling it journalism. [3]

We can all agree that journalism shouldn't get any smaller, but Twitter doesn't threaten the traditions of our craft. It adds, rather than subtracts, from what we do. [4]

As I spend nearly all of my time on the road these days reporting on the presidential campaigns, Twitter is the perfect place for all of those asides I've scribbled in the hundreds of notebooks I have in my garage from the campaigns and stories I've covered over the years. Inside each of those notebooks are little pieces of color I've picked up along the way. Sometimes these snippets are too off-topic or too inconsequential to work into a story. Sometimes they are the little notions or sideways thoughts that become the lead of a piece or the kicker. All of them now have found a home on Twitter. [5]

As journalists we take people places they can't go. Twitter offers a little snapshot way to do this. It's informal and approachable and great for conveying a little moment from an event. Here's an entry from a McCain rally during the Republican primaries: "Weare, NH: Audience man to McCain: 'I heard that Hershey is moving plants to Mexico and I'll be damned if I'm going to eat Mexican chocolate.'" In Scranton covering Barack Obama I sent this: "Obama: 'What's John McCain's problem?' Audience member: 'He's too old.' Obama: 'No, no that's not the problem. There are a lot of [6] wise people. . . .'" With so many Democrats making an issue of McCain's age, here was the candidate in the moment seeming to suggest that critique was unfair.

Occasionally, just occasionally, reporters can convey a piece of news       7
that fits into 140 characters without context. If Twitter had been around when the planes hit the World Trade Center, it would have been a perfect way for anyone who witnessed it to convey at that moment what they'd seen or heard. With Twitter, we can also pull back the curtain on our lives a little and show readers what it's like to cover a campaign. ("Wanna be a reporter? On long bus rides learn to sleep in your own hand.")

The risk for journalism, of course, is that people spend all day Twit-       8
tering and reading other people's Twitter entries and don't engage with the news in any other way. This seems a pretty small worry. If written the right way, Twitter entries build a community of readers who find their way to longer articles because they are lured by these moment-by-moment observations. As a reader, I've found that I'm exposed to a wider variety of news because I read articles suggested to me by the wide variety of people I follow on Twitter. I'm also exposed to some keen political observers and sharp writers who have never practiced journalism.

Twitter is not the next great thing in journalism. No one should try to       9
make Twitter do more than it can and no reader should expect too much from a 140-character entry. As for the critics, their worries about Twitter and journalism seem like the kind of obtuse behavior that would make a perfect observational Twitter entry: "A man at the front of the restaurant is screaming at a waiter and gesticulating wildly. The snacks on the bar aren't a four-course meal!"

STEVE GROVE

# YouTube: The Flattening of Politics

Steve Grove directs all news, political programming, and citizen journalism for YouTube. He has been quoted as saying that he regards himself less as an editor than as a curator of the Web site's "chaotic sea of content." A native of Northfield, Minnesota, he worked as a journalist at the *Boston Globe* and ABC News before moving to YouTube.

▪ ▪ ▪

For a little over a year, I've served as YouTube's news and political       1
director—perhaps a perplexing title in the eyes of many journalists. Such wonderment might be expected since YouTube gained its early notoriety as a place with videos of dogs on skateboards or kids falling off of trampolines. But these days, in the 10 hours of video uploaded to

YouTube every minute of every day (yes—every minute of every day), an increasing amount of the content is news and political video. And with YouTube's global reach and ease of use, it's changing the way that politics—and its coverage—is happening.

Each of the 16 one-time presidential candidates had YouTube channels; seven announced their candidacies on YouTube. Their staffs uploaded thousands of videos that were viewed tens of millions of times. By early March of this year, the Obama campaign was uploading two to three videos to YouTube every day. And thousands of advocacy groups and nonprofit organizations use YouTube to get their election messages into the conversation. For us, the most exciting aspect is that ordinary people continue to use YouTube to distribute their own political content; these range from "gotcha" videos they've taken at campaign rallies to questions for the candidates, from homemade political commercials to video mash-ups of mainstream media coverage.

What this means is that average citizens are able to fuel a new meritocracy for political coverage, one unburdened by the gatekeeping "middleman." Another way of putting it is that YouTube is now the world's largest town hall for political discussion, where voters connect with candidates—and the news media—in ways that were never before possible.

In this new media environment, politics is no longer bound by traditional barriers of time and space. It doesn't matter what time it is, or where someone is located—as long as they have the means to connect through the Web, they can engage in the discussion. This was highlighted in a pair of presidential debates we produced with CNN during this election cycle during which voters asked questions of the candidates via YouTube videos they'd submitted online. In many ways, those events simply brought to the attention of a wider audience the sort of exchanges that take place on YouTube all the time. . . .

## News Organizations and YouTube

Just because candidates and voters find all sorts of ways to connect directly on YouTube does not mean there isn't room for the mainstream media, too. In fact, many news organizations have launched YouTube channels, including the Associated Press, the *New York Times*, the BBC, CBS, and the *Wall Street Journal*.

Why would a mainstream media company upload their news content to YouTube?

Simply put, it's where eyeballs are going. Research from the Pew Internet & American Life project found that 37 percent of adult Internet users have watched online video news, and well over half of online adults have used the Internet to watch video of any kind. Each day on YouTube hundreds of millions of videos are viewed at the same time that television viewership is decreasing in many markets. If a mainstream news organization wants its political reporting seen, YouTube offers visibility without a cost. The ones that have been doing this for a while rely on a strategy of building audiences on YouTube and then trying to drive viewers back to their Web sites for a deeper dive into the content. And these organizations can earn revenue as well by running ads against their video content on YouTube.

In many ways, YouTube's news ecosystem has the potential to offer much more to a traditional media outlet. Here are some examples:  *8*

1. **Interactivity:** YouTube provides an automatic focus group for news content. How? YouTube wasn't built as merely a "series of tubes" to distribute online video. It is also an interactive platform. Users comment on, reply to, rank, and share videos with one another and form communities around content that they like. If news organizations want to see how a particular piece of content will resonate with audiences, they have an automatic focus group waiting on YouTube. And that focus group isn't just young people: 20 percent of YouTube users are over age 55—which is the same percentage that is under 18. This means the YouTube audience roughly mirrors the national population.

2. **Partner with Audiences:** YouTube provides news media organizations new ways to engage with audiences and involve them in the programming. Modeled on the presidential debates we cohosted last year, YouTube has created similar partnerships, such as one with the BBC around the mayoral election in London and with a large public broadcaster in Spain for their recent presidential election. Also on the campaign trail, we worked along with Hearst affiliate WMUR-TV in New Hampshire to solicit videos from voters during that primary. Hundreds of videos flooded in from across the state. The best were broadcast on that TV station, which highlighted this symbiotic relationship: On the Web, online video bubbles the more interesting content to the top and then TV amplifies it on a new scale. We did similar arrangements with news organizations in Iowa, Pennsylvania, and on Super Tuesday, as news organizations leveraged the power of voter-generated content. What the news organizations discover is that they gain audience share by offering a level of audience engagement—with opportunities for active as well as passive experiences.

For news media organizations, audience engagement is much easier to achieve by using platforms like YouTube than it is to do on their own. And we just made it easier: Our open API (application programming interface), nicknamed "YouTube Everywhere"—just launched a few months ago—allows other companies to integrate our upload functionality into their online platforms. It's like having a mini YouTube on your  *9*

Web site and, once it's there, news organizations can encourage—and publish—video responses and comments on the reporting they do.

Finally, reporters use YouTube as source material for their stories. With *10* hundreds of thousands of video cameras in use today, there is a much greater chance than ever before that events will be captured—by someone—as they unfold. No need for driving the satellite truck to the scene if someone is already there and sending in video of the event via their cell phone. It's at such intersections of new and old media that YouTube demonstrates its value. It could be argued, in fact, that the YouTube platform is the new frontier in newsgathering. On the election trail, virtually every appearance by every candidate is captured on video—by someone—and that means the issues being talked about are covered more robustly by more people who can steer the public discussion in new ways. The phenomenon is, of course, global, as we witnessed last fall in Burma (Myanmar) after the government shut down news media outlets during waves of civic protests. In time, YouTube was the only way to track the violence being exercised by the government on monks who'd taken to the streets. Videos of this were seen worldwide on YouTube, creating global awareness of this situation—even in the absence of journalists on the scene.

Citizen journalism on YouTube—and other Internet sources—is *11* often criticized because it is produced by amateurs and therefore lacks a degree of trustworthiness. Critics add that because platforms like YouTube are fragmenting today's media environment, traditional newsrooms are being depleted of journalists, and thus the denominator for quality news coverage is getting lower and lower. I share this concern about what is happening in the news media today, but I think there are a couple of things worth remembering when it comes to news content on YouTube.

## Trusting What We See

When it comes to determining the trustworthiness of news content on *12* YouTube, it's important to have some context. People tend to know what they're getting on YouTube, since content is clearly labeled by username as to where it originated. A viewer knows if the video they're watching is coming from "jellybean109" or "thenewyorktimes." Users also know that YouTube is an open platform and that no one verifies the truth of content better than the consumer. The wisdom of the crowd on YouTube is far more likely to pick apart a shoddy piece of "journalism" than it is to elevate something that is simply untrue. In fact, because video is ubiquitous and so much more revealing and compelling than text, YouTube can provide a critical fact-checking platform in today's media environment. And in some ways, it offers a backstop for accuracy since a journalist can't afford to get the story wrong; if they do, it's likely that someone else who was there got it right—and posted it to YouTube.

Scrutiny cuts both ways. Journalists are needed today for the work      *13* they do as much as they ever have been. While the wisdom of crowds might provide a new form of fact checking, and the ubiquity of technology might provide a more robust view of the news, citizens desperately need the Fourth Estate to provide depth, context, and analysis that only comes with experience and the sharpening of the craft. Without the work of journalists, the citizens—the electorate—lose a critical voice in the process of civic decision-making.

This is the media ecosystem in which we live in this election cycle.      *14* Candidates and voters speak directly to one another, unfiltered. News organizations use the Internet to connect with and leverage audiences in new ways. Activists, issue groups, campaigns, and voters all advocate for, learn about, and discuss issues on the same level platform. YouTube has become a major force in this new media environment by offering new opportunities and new challenges. For those who have embraced them—and their numbers grow rapidly every day—the opportunity to influence the discussion is great. For those who haven't, they ignore the opportunity at their own peril.

## AVOIDING PLAGIARISM

Whether you paraphrase, summarize, or synthesize, it is essential that you acknowledge your sources. Academic writing requires you to use and document sources appropriately, making clear to readers the boundaries between your words and ideas and those of other writers. Setting boundaries can be a challenge because so much of academic writing involves interweaving the ideas of others into your own argument. Still, no matter how difficult, you must acknowledge your sources. It's only fair. Imagine how you would feel if you were reading a text and discovered that the writer had incorporated a passage from one of your papers, something you slaved over, without giving you credit. You would see yourself as a victim of plagiarism, and you would be justified in feeling very angry indeed.

In fact, **plagiarism**—the unacknowledged use of another's work, passed off as one's own—is a most serious breach of academic integrity, and colleges and universities deal with it severely. If you are caught plagiarizing in your work for a class, you can expect to fail that class and may even be expelled from your college or university. Furthermore, although a failing grade on a paper or in a course, honestly come by, is unlikely to deter an employer from hiring you, the stigma of plagiarism can come back to haunt you when you apply for a job. Any violation of the principles set forth in Table 7.1 could have serious consequences for your academic and professional career.

TABLE 7.1   Principles Governing Plagiarism

1. All written work submitted for any purpose is accepted as your own work. This means it must not have been written even in part by another person.

2. The wording of any written work you submit is assumed to be your own. This means you must not submit work that has been copied, wholly or partially, from a book, an article, an essay, a newspaper, another student's paper or notebook, or any other source. Another writer's phrases, sentences, or paragraphs can be included only if they are presented as quotations and the source acknowledged.

3. The ideas expressed in a paper or report are assumed to originate with you, the writer. Written work that paraphrases a source without acknowledgment must not be submitted for credit. Ideas from the work of others can be incorporated in your work as starting points, governing issues, illustrations, and the like, but in every instance the source must be cited.

4. Remember that any online materials you use to gather information for a paper are also governed by the rules for avoiding plagiarism. You need to learn to cite electronic sources as well as printed and other sources.

5. You may correct and revise your writing with the aid of reference books. You also may discuss your writing with your peers in a writing group or with peer tutors at your campus writing center. However, you may not submit writing that has been revised substantially by another person.

Even if you know what plagiarism is and wouldn't think about doing it, you can still plagiarize unintentionally. Again, paraphrasing can be especially tricky: Attempting to restate a passage without using the original words and sentence structure is, to a certain extent, an invitation to plagiarism. If you remember that your paper is *your* argument, and understand that any paraphrasing, summarizing, or synthesizing should reflect *your* voice and style, you will be less likely to have problems with plagiarism. Your paper should sound like you. And, again, the surest way to protect yourself is to cite your sources.

## Steps to Avoiding Plagiarism

**1** **Always cite the source.** Signal that you are paraphrasing, summarizing, or synthesizing by identifying your source at the outset — "According to James Gunn," "Clive Thompson argues," "Cynthia Haven and Josh Keller . . . point out." And if possible, indicate the end of the paraphrase, summary, or synthesis with relevant page references to the source. If you cite a source several times in your paper, don't assume that your first citation has you covered; acknowledge the source as often as you use it.

**2** **Provide a full citation in your bibliography.** It's not enough to cite a source in your paper; you must also provide a full citation for every source you use in the list of sources at the end of your paper.

# INTEGRATING QUOTATIONS INTO YOUR WRITING

When you integrate quotations into your writing, bear in mind a piece of advice we've given you about writing the rest of your paper: Take your readers by the hand and lead them step-by-step. When you quote other authors to develop your argument—using their words to support your thinking or to address a counterargument—discuss and analyze the words you quote, showing readers how the specific language of each quotation contributes to the larger point you are making in your essay. When you integrate quotations, then, there are three basic things you want to do: (1) Take an active stance, (2) explain the quotations, and (3) attach short quotations to your own sentences.

## ■ Take an Active Stance

Critical reading requires that you adopt an active stance toward what you read—that you raise questions in response to a text. You should be no less active when you are using other authors' texts to develop your own argument.

Taking an active stance when you are quoting means knowing when to quote. Don't quote when a paraphrase or summary will convey the information from a source more effectively. More important, you have to make fair and wise decisions about what and how much you should quote to make your argument.

- It's not fair (or wise) to quote selectively—choosing only passages that support your argument—when you know you are distorting the argument of the writer you are quoting. You want to show that you understand the writer's argument, and you want to make evenhanded use of it in your own argument.

- It's not wise (or fair to yourself) to flesh out your paper with an overwhelming number of quotations that could make readers think that you do not know your topic well or do not have your own ideas. Don't allow quotations to take over your paragraphs. Remember that your ideas and argument—your thesis—are what is most important to the readers and what justifies a quotation's being included at all.

Above all, taking an active stance when you quote means taking control of your writing. You want to establish your own argument and guide your readers through it, allowing sources to contribute to but not dictate its direction. You are responsible for plotting and pacing your essay. Always keep in mind that your thesis is the skewer that runs through every paragraph, holding all of the ideas together. When you use quotations, then, you must organize them to enrich, substantiate, illustrate, and help support your central claim or thesis.

## ■ Explain the Quotations

When you quote an author to support or advance your argument, make sure that readers know exactly what they should learn from the quotation.

Read the excerpt below from one student's early draft of an argument that focuses on the value of service learning in high schools. The student reviews several relevant studies—but then simply drops in a quotation, expecting readers to know what they should pay attention to in it.

> Other research emphasizes community service as an integral and integrated part of moral identity. In this understanding, community service activities are not isolated events but are woven into the context of students' everyday lives (Yates, 1995); the personal, the moral, and the civic become "inseparable" (Colby, Ehrlich, Beaumont, & Stephens, 2003, p. 15). In their study of minority high schoolers at an urban Catholic school who volunteered at a soup kitchen for the homeless as part of a class assignment, Youniss and Yates (1999) found that the students underwent significant identity changes, coming to perceive themselves as lifelong activists. The researchers' findings are worth quoting at length here because they depict the dramatic nature of the students' changed viewpoints. Youniss and Yates wrote:
>
> > Many students abandoned an initially negative view of homeless people and a disinterest in homelessness by gaining appreciation of the humanity of homeless people and by showing concern for homelessness in relation to poverty, job training, low-cost housing, prison reform, drug and alcohol rehabilitation, care for the mentally ill, quality urban education, and welfare policy. Several students also altered perceptions of themselves from politically impotent teenagers to involved citizens who now and in the future could use their talent and power to correct social problems. They projected articulated pictures of themselves as adult citizens who could affect housing policies, education for minorities, and government programs within a clear framework of social justice. (p. 362)

The student's introduction to the quoted passage provided a rationale for quoting Youniss and Yates at length, but it did not help her readers see how the research related to her argument. The student needed to frame the quotation for her readers. Instead of introducing the quotation by saying "Youniss and Yates wrote," she should have made clear that the study supports the argument that community service can create change. A more appropriate frame for the quotation might have been a summary like this one:

*Frames the quotations, explaining it in the context of the student's argument.*

One particular study underscores my argument that service can motivate change, particularly when that change begins within the students who are involved in service. Youniss and Yates (1999) wrote that over the course of their research, the students developed both an "appreciation of the humanity of homeless people" and a sense that they would someday be able to "use their talent and power to correct social problems" (p. 362).

In the following example, notice that the student writer uses Derrick Bell's text to say something about how the effects of desegregation have been muted by political manipulation.* The writer shapes what he wants readers to focus on, leaving nothing to chance.

The effectiveness with which the meaning of *Brown v. Board of Education* has been manipulated, Derrick Bell argued, is also evidenced by the way in which such thinking has actually been embraced by minority groups. Bell claimed that a black school board member's asking "But of what value is it to teach black children to read in all-black schools?" indicates this unthinking acceptance that whiteness is an essential ingredient to effective schooling for blacks. Bell continued:

> The assumption that even the attaining of academic skills is worthless unless those skills are acquired in the presence of white students illustrates dramatically how a legal precedent, namely the Supreme Court's decision in *Brown v. Board of Education*, has been so constricted even by advocates that its goal—equal educational opportunity—is rendered inaccessible, even unwanted, unless it can be obtained through racial balancing of the school population. (p. 255)

Bell's argument is extremely compelling, particularly when one considers the extent to which "racial balancing" has come to be defined in terms of large white majority populations and small nonwhite minority populations.

Notice that the student's last sentence helps readers understand what the quoted material suggests and why it's important by embedding and extending Bell's notion of racial balancing into his explanation.

In sum, you should always explain the information that you quote so that your readers can see how the quotation relates to your own argument. ("Take your readers by the hand . . .") As you read other people's writing, keep an eye open to the ways writers introduce and explain the sources they use to build their arguments.

## ■ Attach Short Quotations to Your Sentences

The quotations we discussed above are **block quotations**, lengthy quotations of more than five lines that are set off from the text of a paper with

---

*This quotation is from Derrick Bell's *Silent Covenants: Brown v. Board of Education and the Unfulfilled Hopes for Racial Reform* (New York: Oxford UP, 2005).

indention. Make shorter quotations part of your own sentences so that your readers can understand how the quotations connect to your argument and can follow along easily. How do you make a quotation part of your own sentences? There are two main methods:

- Integrate quotations within the grammar of your writing.
- Attach quotations with punctuation.

If possible, use both to make your integration of quotations more interesting and varied.

*Integrate quotations within the grammar of a sentence.*    When you integrate a quotation into a sentence, the quotation must make grammatical sense and read as if it is part of the sentence:

> Fine, Weiss, and Powell (1998) expanded upon what others call "equal status contact theory" by using a "framework that draws on three traditionally independent literatures — those on community, difference, and democracy" (p. 37).

If you add words to the quotation, use square brackets around them to let readers know that the words are not original to the quotation:

> Smith and Wellner (2002) asserted that they "are not alone [in believing] that the facts have been incorrectly interpreted by Mancini" (p. 24).

If you omit any words in the middle of a quotation, use an **ellipsis**, three periods with spaces between them, to indicate the omission:

> Riquelme argues that "Eliot tries . . . to provide a definition by negations, which he also turns into positive terms that are meant to correct misconceptions" (156).

If you omit a sentence or more, make sure to put a period before the ellipsis points:

> Eagleton writes, "What Eliot was in fact assaulting was the whole ideology of middle-class liberalism. . . . Eliot's own solution is an extreme right-wing authoritarianism: men and women must sacrifice their petty 'personalities' and opinions to an impersonal order" (39).

Whatever you add (using square brackets) or omit (using ellipses), the sentence must read grammatically. And, of course, your additions and omissions must not distort the author's meaning.

*Attach quotations with punctuation.*    You also can attach a quotation to a sentence by using punctuation. For example, this passage attaches the run-in quotation with a colon:

> For these researchers, there needs to be recognition of differences in a way that will include and accept all students. Specifically, they asked: "Within multiracial settings, when are young people invited to discuss, voice, critique, and re-view the

very notions of race that feel so fixed, so hierarchical, so damaging, and so accepted in the broader culture?" (p. 132).

In conclusion, if you don't connect quotations to your argument, your readers may not understand why you've included them. You need to explain a significant point that each quotation reveals as you introduce or end it. This strategy helps readers know what to pay attention to in a quotation, particularly if the quotation is lengthy.

---

### Steps to Integrating Quotations into Your Writing

**1** **Take an active stance.** Your sources should contribute to your argument, not dictate its direction.

**2** **Explain the quotations.** Explain what you quote so your readers understand how each quotation relates to your argument.

**3** **Attach short quotations to your sentences.** Integrate short quotations within the grammar of your own sentences, or attach them with appropriate punctuation.

---

### A Practice Sequence: Integrating Quotations

**1** Using several of the sources you are working with in developing your paper, try integrating quotations into your essay. Be sure you are controlling your sources. Carefully read the paragraphs where you've used quotations. Will your readers clearly understand why the quotations are there — the points the quotations support? Do the sentences with quotations read smoothly? Are they grammatically correct?

**2** Working in a small group, agree on a substantial paragraph or passage (from this book or some other source) to write about. Each member should read the passage and take a position on the ideas, and then draft a page that quotes the passage using both strategies for integrating these quotations. Compare what you've written, examining similarities and differences in the use of quotations.

---

## AN ANNOTATED STUDENT RESEARCHED ARGUMENT: SYNTHESIZING SOURCES

The student who wrote the essay "A Greener Approach to Groceries: Community-Based Agriculture in LaSalle Square" did so in a first-year writing class that gave students the opportunity to do service in the local community. For this assignment, students were asked to explore debates about community and citizenship in contemporary America and to focus their research and writing on a social justice–related issue of their choice. The context of the course guided their inquiry as all the students in the course explored community service as a way to engage meaningfully and to develop relationships in the community.

We have annotated her essay to show the ways that she summarized and paraphrased research to show the urgency of the problem of food insecurity that exists around the world and to offer possible solutions. Notice how she synthesizes her sources, taking an active stance in using what she has read to advance her own argument.

Nancy Paul                                                    Paul 1
Professor McLaughlin
English 2102
May 11, 20—

A Greener Approach to Groceries:
Community-Based Agriculture in LaSalle Square

*1*

In our post-9/11 society, there is incessant concern for the security of our future. Billions of dollars are spent tightening borders, installing nuclear detectors, and adjudicating safety measures so that the citizens of the United States can grow and prosper without fear. Unfortunately, for some urban poor, the threat from terrorism is minuscule compared to the cruelty of their immediate environment. Far from the sands of the Afghan plains and encapsulated in the midst of inner-city deterioration, many find themselves in gray-lot deserts devoid of vegetation

*The student's thesis* and reliable food sources. Abandoned by corporate supermarkets, millions of Americans are maimed by a "food insecurity" — the nutritional poverty that cripples them developmentally, physically, and psychologically.

*2*

The midwestern city that surrounds our university has a food-desert sitting just west of the famously lush campus. Known as LaSalle Square, it was once home to the lucrative Bendix plant and has featured both a Target and a Kroger supermar-

*She calls attention to both the immediacy and urgency of the problem* ket in recent years. But previous economic development decisions have driven both stores to the outskirts of town, and without a local supplier, the only food available in the neighborhood is prepackaged and sold at the few small convenience stores. This available food is virtually devoid of nutrition and

Paul 2

inhibits the ability of the poor to prosper and thrive. Thus, an aging strip mall, industrial site, and approximately three acres of an empty grass lot between the buildings anchor — and unfortunately define — the neighborhood.

*She proposes a possible solution.*

While there are multiple ways of providing food to the destitute, I am proposing a co-op of community gardens built on the grassy space in LaSalle Square and on smaller sites within the neighborhood, supplemented by extra crops from Michiana farmers, which would supply fresh fruit and vegetables to be sold or distributed to the poor. Together the co-op could meet the nutritional needs of the people, provide plenty of nutritious food, not cost South Bend any additional money, and contribute to neighborhood revitalization, yielding concrete increases in property values. Far from being a pipe dream, LaSalle Square already hosted an Urban Garden Market this fall, so a co-op would simply build upon the already recognized need and desire for healthy food in the area. Similar coalitions around the world are harnessing the power of community to remedy food insecurity without the aid of corporate enterprise, and South Bend is perfectly situated to reproduce and possibly exceed their successes.

*She places her solution in a larger context to indicate its viability.*

Many, myself previously included, believe that the large-volume, cheap industrialization of food and the welfare system have obliterated hunger in the United States. Supermarkets like Wal-Mart and Kroger seem ubiquitous in our communities, and it is difficult to imagine anyone being beyond their influence. However, profit-driven corporate business plans do not mix well with low-income, high-crime populations, and the gap between the two is growing wider. This polarization, combined with the vitamin deficiency of our high-fructose corn syrup society, has created food deserts in already struggling communities where malnutrition is the enemy *inconnu* of the urban poor.

*More context*

LaSalle Square's food insecurity is typical of many urban areas. The grocery stores that used to serve the neighborhood have relocated to more attractive real estate on the outskirts of the city, and only local convenience stores, stocking basic necessary items and tobacco products, remain profitable. Linda Wolfson, a member of the steering committee for the LaSalle

3

4

5

Paul 3

Square Redevelopment Plan, notes that if the community was
fiscally healthy, it would be reasonable to expect the inhabitants to simply drive the six miles to the strip mall district, but
unfortunately many are marginally employed and do not have
access to cars. For them, it is economically irresponsible to
spend the extra money to get to the supermarket, and so they
feed their families on the cheap soda, chips, and processed food

*Synthesizing helps*
*illustrate the extent*
*of the problem and*
*bolster her view*
*that the poor suffer*
*the most from the*
*problem she identi-*
*fies (Garnett; Smith;*
*Brown and Carter).*

that are readily available at the convenience store. Especially
since high-calorie, low-nutrient, packaged food tends to
be denser, urban mothers find that it helps their children feel
full (Garnett). Sadly, a health investigation released in 2006
concluded that by the age of three, more than one-third of
urban children are obese, due in large part to the consumption
of low-quality food obtained from corner stores (Smith). A
recent analysis of urban stores in Detroit found that only 19%
offer the healthy food array suggested by the FDA food pyramid
(Brown and Carter 5). The food that is offered contains 25%
less nutrient density, and consequently, underprivileged socioeconomic populations consume significantly lower levels of the
micronutrients that form the foundation for proper protein and

*Here she para-*
*phrases findings.*

brain development. In a recent study of poor households, it was
found that two-thirds of children were nutritionally poor and
that more than 25% of women were deficient in iron, vitamin
A, vitamin C, vitamin B6, thiamin, and riboflavin (Garnett). Of
course, some may challenge the relevance of these vitamins
and nutrients since they are not something the average person
consciously incorporates into his or her diet on a daily basis. Yet
modern research, examining the severely homogenous diets of
the poor, has found severe developmental consequences associated with the lack of nutritional substance. For those afflicted,
these deficiencies are not simply inconvenient, but actually
exacerbate their plight and hinder their progress toward a sustainable lifestyle.

    The human body is a complex system that cannot be sus-
tained merely on the simple sugars and processed carbohydrates
that comprise most cheap and filling foodstuffs, and research
shows a relationship between nutritional deficiencies and a host
of cognitive and developmental impairments that are prevalent

6

Paul 4

*Again she both sum-marizes and cites a relevant study to advance her argu-ment.*

in the undernourished families from urban America. Standard-ized tests of impoverished siblings, one of whom received nutri-tional supplements and the other who did not, showed cognitive gains in the well-nourished child as well as increased motor skills and greater interest in social interactions when compared to the other child. In the highly formative toddler years, under-nutrition can inhibit the myelination of nerve fibers, which is responsible for neurotransmitting and proper brain function. Collaborators Emily Tanner from the University of Oxford and Matia Finn-Stevenson from Yale University published a compre-hensive analysis of the link between nutrition and brain development in 2002. Their analysis, which they linked to social policy, indicated that a shortage of legumes and leafy green vegetables, which are nearly impossible to find in corner stores, is the leading cause of the iron-deficiency anemia afflicting 25% of urban children. This extreme form of anemia is characterized by impaired neurotransmission, weaker memory, and reduced attention span (Tanner and Finn-Stevenson 186). For those who do not have access to the vitamins, minerals, and micronutrients found in fruits and vegetables, these maladies are not distant risks, but constant, inescapable threats.

In light of these severe consequences of undernutrition, the term "food insecurity" encapsulates the condition wherein the economically disadvantaged are vulnerable simply because their bodies are unable to receive adequate fuel for optimal functioning. Just as one cannot expect a dry, parched plant to bloom and pollinate a garden, by constraining the development of individuals, food insecurity also constrains the development of the neighborhoods in which the individuals contribute. For the health of a city and its communities, all roadblocks to prog-ress must be removed, and food insecurity must be cut out at its roots so that individuals have the resources for advancement.

As socially conscious citizens and local governments have recognized the prevalence and danger of food insecurity in inner cities, there have been attempts at a remedy. Obviously, the easiest solution is simply to introduce a grocery store that would provide a variety of quality, healthful foods. However, for big-box supermarkets driven by the bottom line, urban areas are

7

8

Paul 5

less than desirable business locales from a standpoint of both profitability and maintenance. It is simply irrational for a supermarket to invest in an urban area with less revenue potential, size constraints, an unattractive locale, and an increased threat of theft and defacement when it is so easy to turn a profit in spacious and peaceful suburbia (Eisenhauer 131). Supermarkets must have significant incentive, beyond humanitarian ends, if they are to take the financial risk of entering a poor, urban marketplace.

*She takes an active stance in citing initiatives that could be applied more effectively to alleviate the problem of food insecurity.*

Certain cities are using the power of Tax Increment Financing (TIF) districts to encourage supermarkets to invest in urban centers. Under these redevelopment laws, tax revenues from retail development or other commercial enterprises are devoted, for a specified number of years, to infrastructural improvement of the district ("TIF Reform"). This approach has been effective in enticing new businesses; in fact, the exterior growth around South Bend is the result of a TIF district established in the late 1980s. LaSalle Square is currently part of a TIF district, but there is discussion as to how the TIF monies should best be applied (Wolfson). It may be possible to use the power of the TIF to encourage another large retailer such as Kroger to establish a presence in the square, but a smaller enterprise may be a better option. Experts indicate that for the destitute and food-insecure, reliance on a corporate entity is not optimal. Elizabeth Eisenhauer, a researcher from the State University of New York, investigated the interplay between supermarkets and

*She paraphrases a researcher's findings.*

the urban poor; she concluded that large big-box stores lack a commitment to the communities they serve and can be relied on only when it is clear they will make a profit, which may or may not happen when TIF benefits expire (131). Even when a portion of proceeds is used in the community, the majority of the cash flow from a supermarket is going to a corporate headquarters elsewhere, not directly supporting the surrounding neighborhood. Likewise, while some employees may be local, the highest-salary management positions are generally given to outsiders, making the stores and their employees set apart, rather than integrated into the neighborhood (Eisenhauer 130). Certainly a supermarket in an urban area will greatly contribute

9

Paul 6

to the reduction of food insecurity, but it is not the only available option, and the city of South Bend is ripe for alternative solutions. The city is primed for a cooperative effort that could shift the paradigm for urban renewal from a quick, corporate solution, to a long-term enterprise built on community contributions and under local control.

*She cites a number of examples as evidence to demonstrate the viability of the solution she offers.*

Around the globe, many destitute urban areas have found the means to reverse nutritional poverty through a literal and figurative grassroots effort. In an effort to avoid packaged, convenience store food, neighbors in the Bronx, San Francisco, Los Angeles, London, and most successfully in Philadelphia, have been planting their own crops right in the heart of the city (Brown and Carter 3-4). Truly farming the food desert, coalitions that link community gardens, local farmers, and urban markets are providing healthy, sustainable food sources without a supermarket. Interestingly, in the process, such coalitions are generating jobs, increasing property value, and, in some cases, actually reversing the effects of poverty. The city of South Bend, uniquely situated in the breadbasket of the United States, is in the perfect position to launch a "greening" effort, modeled after the successes in other parts of the world, which would both solve the problem of food insecurity of LaSalle Square and invigorate the local economy.

*10*

While modern Americans have the tendency to think that food production should be, and always has been, industrialized, countries around the world, especially economically disadvantaged nations, are exemplifying the possibilities of local gardening efforts. Far removed from industrial farms, Cubans grow half their vegetables within the city; vacant land in Russian cities produces 80% of the nation's vegetables, and specifically in Moscow, 65% of families contribute to food production. Singapore has 10,000 urban farmers, and nearly half of the residents of Vancouver grow food in their gardens (Brown and Carter 10). These habits are not simply a novelty; rather, populations that garden tend to be healthier, eating six out of the fourteen vegetable categories more regularly than non-gardeners and also consuming fewer sweet and sugary foods per capita (Brown and Carter 13). These data, compiled by the North American Urban

*11*

*The use of multiple sources would make her case even stronger than using just one source of information, in this case Brown and Carter.*

Paul 7

Agriculture Committee, were synthesized from the *Journal of Public Health Policy* and the *Journal of Nutrition Education* and show the interrelatedness of nutritional access and availability to healthy personal choices. While these trends toward healthful lifestyles and gardening have been gaining ground slowly in the United States, when food insecurity and poverty take their toll, cities are finding that urban agriculture is an increasingly attractive and profitable alternative.

12

American communities have shown that creativity and collaboration can be quite effective at reversing food insecurity. The Garden Project of the Greater Lansing Food Bank has successfully combined gardening and Midwest access to local farms to bring food security to urban residents and senior citizens. Their eighteen community gardens and volunteers provide fresh fruits and vegetables year-round to low-income families, food

*She synthesizes sources to make her point.*

pantries, the elderly, and social service organizations. Completely bypassing the commercial market, the Garden Project has trained 500 families to grow their own food in backyard plots so that they can always have healthy food in the midst of the city (Brown and Carter 1). The gardens are supplemented by a process known as "gleaning," in which volunteers harvest extra crops from local farmers that would otherwise go to waste, and deliver it to residents of subsidized housing ("Gleaning"). In 2008 alone, the Garden Project actively involved 2,500 individual gardeners and was able to provide over 250,000 pounds of produce from gleaning alone, plus the yields of the community plots that were used directly by the gardeners ("GLFB Facts"). This Lansing coalition serves over 5,000 individuals per month, yet only 4,400 reside under the poverty line in the LaSalle Square area (*City-Data.com*). If half of the inhabitants of LaSalle Square became engaged in the gardening effort, a similar collaboration could meet the needs of the region, and greater participation could yield an excess.

13

Similar efforts have demonstrated not only that inner-city food production is achievable but also that it can be cost-effective and self-sufficient, unlike a food bank. Frustrated by the inner-city downturn she describes as "an overgrown dog toilet," industrious London entrepreneur Julie Brown created a

Paul 8

*In this paragraph, she summarizes research to address the possible counter-argument.*

community gardening company aimed at providing unmecha-nized, local, sustainable food. The company, Growing Communi-ties, uses organic box gardens and small farms to supply more than 400 homes with weekly deliveries of organic fruits and veg-etables. After a ten-year investment in local farmers and mini-gardens within the city, Growing Communities is now financially independent and generates over $400,000 per year (Willis 53). Compelled by both capitalism and social concern, Brown's efforts have shown that community-supported agriculture not only is possible but can be profitable as well! Our own commu-nity agriculture program should not be an entrepreneurial endeavor, but Brown's work in London indicates that it need not be a financial burden to the city either. Rather, the co-op would be financially self-sufficient, with the potential to generate rev-enues and fiscal growth in the city.

There are environmental factors that make South Bend       14
an even better place to launch a profitable community agricul-ture program than London. Chiefly, South Bend has many more farms in the immediate vicinity than Ms. Brown could ever have dreamed of in the U.K. While Brown was limited to 25 local farms within 100 miles of the city, South Bend has over 50 farms within 25 miles of LaSalle Square (*Local Harvest*). Offering a broader production base creates more potential for profits by decreasing transportation time and increasing product, thereby making it easier for a coalition to become financially self-sufficient in a shorter time frame than Ms. Brown's ten-year plan.

*She again cites research to address the counterargu-ment.*

Urban Philadelphia has led the way in demonstrating       15
the profitability of community solutions to food insecurity through an offshoot of the Pennsylvania Horticultural Society (PHS) known as Philadelphia Greens. Since the 1970s, this coalition has reclaimed parks, planted trees, and created com-munity gardens, both to revitalize the neighborhood and to serve the nutritionally and economically poor. Through a process that plants trees, builds wooden fences, and gardens the more than 1,000 vacant lots of Philadelphia, PHS combines housing projects and reclaimed space to "green" and reinvigorate the neighborhood ("The Effects"). Since LaSalle Square is essentially a large empty grassy area at the moment, a community agricul-

Paul 9

tural co-op should turn this vacant lot and others in the neighborhood into community gardens, which would work in tandem
with the gleaning from local farms. Similar to the Philadelphia
project, these gardens would simultaneously yield produce and
improve the appearance of the neighborhood.

One PHS project, in the New Kensington neighborhood of
north Philadelphia, was the subject of a recent socioeconomic
study conducted by the University of Pennsylvania's renowned
Wharton School of Business. In the New Kensington area,
PHS recently planted 480 new trees, cleaned 145 side yards,
developed 217 vacant lots, and established 15 new community
gardens. The effort was a model of the collaborative strategy
between PHS and the local community development corporation,

*She summarizes a study and then paraphrases.*

making it the ideal subject of the Wharton study. The findings,
published in 2004, showed significant increases in property values around the PHS greening projects and were the first step in
quantifying the fiscal returns of neighborhood greening beyond
the qualitative benefits of remedying food insecurity. After analyzing the sales records of thousands of New Kensington homes
between 1980 and 2003, the study reported that PHS greening
had led to a $4 million gain in property value from tree plant-
ings alone and a $12 million gain from vacant lot improvements.
Simply greening a vacant lot increased nearby property values
by as much as 30% ("Seeing Green"). While a supermarket might
modestly improve property values for those immediately near
the store, community greening involves multiple plots across an
area, benefiting many more people and properties. The Wharton
study showed that community greening would provide increases
in the value of any property near a green space, up to multiple
millions of dollars. The New Kensington neighborhood covers
1.4 square miles, which is approximately the size of LaSalle
Square, so while the overall property values are lower simply
because South Bend is a smaller city, the gains might be proportional (*City-Data.com*). It is reasonable to believe that cleaning
up LaSalle Square and planting gardens would quantitatively
benefit the fiscal situation of the city and increase assets of the
homeowners while subsequently improving the quality of life
over many acres.

*16*

Paul 10

Certainly there are challenges to the sort of dynami-
cal, community-based solution that I am proposing. Such an
agricultural co-op hinges on the participation of the people it
serves and cannot be successful without the dedicated support
of the neighborhood. It could be noted that lower-income economic groups are less socially involved than their higher-income
counterparts, and some might believe that they are unlikely to
contribute to, or care about, a greening effort. Yet I believe
that there is a distinction between political involvement and
neighborhood interaction. Middle-class Americans are conscious
of gas prices and the fluctuations of the stock market that affect
their job security and ability to provide for their families; yet
the unemployed poor without cars must rely on their neighborhoods to eke out a living. Their sustenance comes not from a
salary, but from odd jobs, welfare, and the munificence of fate.
The battle to put food on the table is more familiar to the poor
than foreign conflict and is one that they fight every day. Therefore, while the poor are less inclined to vote or worry about governmental affairs because of the difficulties associated simply
with daily living, they are acutely aware of their immediate surroundings and how those surroundings challenge or contribute
to their success. This position makes them uniquely inclined to
invest in the betterment of their surroundings since it can have
a dramatic effect on their personal lives. The real success of
the sustainable food movement may come from harnessing the
power of urban communities that can derive great, immediate,
and lasting benefit from neighborhood revitalization.

17

*In this paragraph,
she takes an active
stance in using
research to alleviate
fears that the local
community would
have to start from
scratch with limited
expertise.*

It has been argued that urban growers, especially from
lower socioeconomic classes, do not have the expertise or
knowledge base to generate successful yields that will ensure
food security. Fortunately, agriculture is Indiana's fourth-largest
industry, and the state boasts over 63,000 farms ("A Look"). In
addition to the many inhabitants of LaSalle Square who have a
background in agriculture, there is a wealth of knowledge about
proper planting methods available from the farmers around the
local area. Many of these farmers have already shown a willingness to help by selling or donating their produce to the local
Urban Market. Additionally, national urban agriculture nonprofit

18

groups, such as Master Gardening and Cooperative Extension,
offer free public education to cities beginning community
agriculture programs, and some will even perform on-site training (Brown and Carter 16). By harnessing the assets of local,
gratuitous knowledge and supplementing that knowledge with
national support groups, South Bend has multiple resources
available to train and encourage its burgeoning urban farmers.

The economic and nutritional gains of the people would
only be heightened by the personal well-being that is born of
interpersonal collaboration that crosses racial and social boundaries. Such an effort is ambitious; it will indeed require the time
and talents of many people who care about the health of their
community. But the local community is rich with the necessary
seeds for such a project, which may, in time, blossom and grow
to feed its people.

## Works Cited

Brown, Katherine H., and Anne Carter. *Urban Agriculture and Com-
munity Food Security in the United States: Farming from the City
Center to the Urban Fringe*. Venice, CA: Community Food Security
Coalition, Oct. 2003. PDF file.

*City-Data.com*. Advameg, 2008. Web. 16 Apr. 20—.

"The Effects of Neighborhood Greening." *PHS*. Pennsylvania Horticultural Society, Jan. 2001. Web. 8 Apr. 20—.

Eisenhauer, Elizabeth. "In Poor Health: Supermarket Redlining and
Urban Nutrition." *GeoJournal* 53.2 (2001): 125-33. Print.

Garnett, Tara. "Farming the City." *Ecologist* 26.6 (1996): 299. *Academic Search Premier*. Web. 8 Apr. 20—.

"Gleaning." *Greater Lansing Food Bank*. Greater Lansing Food Bank,
n.d. Web. 15 Apr. 20—.

"GLFB Facts." *Greater Lansing Food Bank*. Greater Lansing Food Bank,
2005. Web. 15 Apr. 20—.

Paul 13

*Local Harvest*. LocalHarvest, 2008. Web. 15 Apr. 20—.

"A Look at Indiana Agriculture." *Agriculture in the Classroom*. USDA-
    CSREES, n.d. PDF file.

"Seeing Green: Study Finds Greening Is a Good Investment." *PHS*.
    Pennsylvania Horticultural Society, 2005. Web. 8 Apr. 20—.

Smith, Stephen. "Obesity Battle Starts Young for Urban Poor." *Boston
    Globe*. NY Times, 29 Dec. 2006. Web. 18 Apr. 20—.

Tanner, Emily M., and Matia Finn-Stevenson. "Nutrition and Brain
    Development: Social Policy Implications." *American Journal of
    Orthopsychiatry* 72.2 (2002): 182-93. *Academic Search Premier*.
    Web. 8 Apr. 20—.

"TIF Reform." *New Rules Project*. Institute for Local Self-Reliance,
    2008. Web. 15 Apr. 20—.

Willis, Ben. "Julie Brown of Growing Communities." *The Ecologist*
    June 2008: 52-55. Print.

Wolfson, Linda. Personal interview. 20 Apr. 20—.

# From Ethos to Logos
*Appealing to Your Readers*

Who you believe your readers are influences how you see a particular situation, define an issue, explain the ongoing conversation surrounding that issue, and formulate a question. You may need to read widely to understand how different writers have dealt with the issue you address. And you will need to anticipate how others might respond to your argument—whether they will be sympathetic or antagonistic—and to compose your essay so that readers will "listen" whether or not they agree with you.

To achieve these goals, you will no doubt use reason in the form of evidence to sway readers. But you can also use other means of persuasion: That is, you can use your own character, by presenting yourself as someone who is knowledgeable, fair, and just; and you can appeal to your readers' emotions. Although you may believe that reason alone should provide the means for changing people's minds, people's emotions also color the way they see the world.

Your audience is more than your immediate reader, your instructor or a peer. Your audience encompasses those you cite in writing about an issue and those you anticipate responding to your argument. This is true no matter what you write about, whether it be an interpretation of the novels of a particular author, an analysis of the cultural work of horror films, the ethics of treating boys and girls differently in schools, or the moral issues surrounding homelessness in America.

In this chapter we discuss different ways of engaging your readers, centering on three kinds of appeals: **ethos**, appeals from character; **pathos**, appeals to emotion; and **logos**, appeals to reason. *Ethos, pathos,* and *logos*

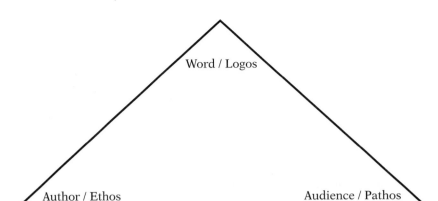

**FIGURE 8.1**   The Rhetorical Triangle

are terms derived from ancient Greek writers, but they are still of great value today when considering how to persuade your audience. Readers will judge your argument on whether or not you present an argument that is fair and just, one that creates a sense of goodwill. All three appeals rely on these qualities.

Figure 8.1, the **rhetorical triangle**, visually represents the interrelationship among ethos, pathos, and logos. Who we think our readers are (pathos: which of their emotions do we appeal to?) influences decisions about the ways we should represent ourselves to them (ethos: how can we come across as fair, credible, and just?). In turn, we use certain patterns of argument (logos: how do we arrange our words to make our case?) that reflect our interpretation of the situation to which we respond and that we believe will persuade readers to accept our point of view. Effective communication touches on each of the three points of the triangle. Your task as a writer is to determine the proper balance of these different appeals in your argument, based on your thesis, the circumstances, and your audience.

## CONNECTING WITH READERS: A SAMPLE ARGUMENT

To see how an author connects with his audience, read the following excerpt from James W. Loewen's book *Lies My Teacher Told Me: Everything Your American History Textbook Got Wrong*. As you read the excerpt, note Loewen's main points, and select key examples that illustrate his argument. As a class, test the claims he makes: To what extent do you believe that what Loewen argues is true? This may entail recalling your own experiences in high school history classes or locating one or more of the books that Loewen mentions.

JAMES W. LOEWEN

# The Land of Opportunity

In addition to *Lies My Teacher Told Me* (1995), James Loewen, who holds a PhD in sociology, has written several other books, including *Lies Across America: What Our Historic Sites Get Wrong* (1999) and *Sundown Towns: A Hidden Dimension of American Racism* (2005). As the titles of these books suggest, Loewen is a writer who questions the assumptions about history that many people take for granted. This is especially true of the following excerpt, from a chapter in which Loewen challenges a common American belief—that everyone has an equal chance in what he calls the "land of opportunity"—by arguing that we live in a class system that privileges some people and raises barriers for others. History textbook writers, he points out, are guilty of complicity in this class system because they leave a great deal of history out of their textbooks.

■ ■ ■

High school students have eyes, ears, and television sets (all too many have their own TV sets), so they know a lot about relative privilege in America. They measure their family's social position against that of other families, and their community's position against other communities. Middle-class students, especially, know little about how the American class structure works, however, and nothing at all about how it has changed over time. These students do not leave high school merely ignorant of the workings of the class structure; they come out as terrible sociologists. "Why are people poor?" I have asked first-year college students. Or, if their own class position is one of relative privilege, "Why is your family well off?" The answers I've received, to characterize them charitably, are half-formed and naïve. The students blame the poor for not being successful. They have no understanding of the ways that opportunity is not equal in America and no notion that social structure pushes people around, influencing the ideas they hold and the lives they fashion.

High school history textbooks can take some of the credit for this state of affairs. Some textbooks cover certain high points of labor history, such as the 1894 Pullman strike near Chicago that President Cleveland broke with federal troops, or the 1911 Triangle Shirtwaist fire that killed 146 women in New York City, but the most recent event mentioned in most books is the Taft-Hartley Act of fifty years ago. No book mentions the Hormel meat-packers' strike in the mid-1980s or the air traffic controllers' strike broken by President Reagan. Nor do textbooks describe any continuing issues facing labor, such as the growth of multinational corporations and their exporting of jobs overseas. With such omissions, textbook authors can construe labor history as something that happened long ago, like slavery, and that, like slavery, was corrected long ago. It logically follows that unions appear anachronistic. The idea that they might be necessary in order for workers to have a voice in the workplace goes unstated.

Textbooks' treatments of events in labor history are never anchored in any analysis of social class. This amounts to delivering the footnotes instead of the lecture! Six of the dozen high school American history textbooks I examined contain no index listing at all for "social class," "social stratification," "class structure," "income distribution," "inequality," or any conceivably related topic. Not one book lists "upper class," "working class," or "lower class." Two of the textbooks list "middle class," but only to assure students that America is a middle-class country. "Except for slaves, most of the colonists were members of the 'middling ranks,'" says *Land of Promise*, and nails home the point that we are a middle-class country by asking students to "Describe three 'middle-class' values that united free Americans of all classes." Several of the textbooks note the explosion of middle-class suburbs after World War II. Talking about the middle class is hardly equivalent to discussing social stratification, however; in fact, as Gregory Mantsios has pointed out, "such references appear to be acceptable precisely because they mute class differences."

Stressing how middle-class we all are is particularly problematic today, because the proportion of households earning between 75 percent and 125 percent of the median income has fallen steadily since 1967. The Reagan-Bush administrations accelerated this shrinkage of the middle class, and most families who left its ranks fell rather than rose. This is the kind of historical trend one would think history books would take as appropriate subject matter, but only four of the twelve books in my sample provide any analysis of social stratification in the United States. Even these fragmentary analyses are set mostly in colonial America. *Land of Promise* lives up to its reassuring title by heading its discussion of social class "Social Mobility." "One great difference between colonial and European society was that the colonists had more social mobility," echoes *The American Tradition*. "In contrast with contemporary Europe, eighteenth-century America was a shining land of equality and opportunity—with the notorious exception of slavery," chimes in *The American Pageant*. Although *The Challenge of Freedom* identifies three social classes—upper, middle, and lower—among whites in colonial society, compared to Europe "there was greater *social mobility*."

Never mind that the most violent class conflicts in American history— Bacon's Rebellion and Shays's Rebellion—took place in and just after colonial times. Textbooks still say that colonial society was relatively classless and marked by upward mobility. And things have gotten rosier since. "By 1815," *The Challenge of Freedom* assures us, two classes had withered away and "America was a country of middle class people and of middle class goals." This book returns repeatedly, at intervals of every fifty years or so, to the theme of how open opportunity is in America. "In the years after 1945, *social mobility*—movement from one social class

3

4

5

to another—became more widespread in America," *Challenge* concludes. "This meant that people had a better chance to move upward in society." The stress on upward mobility is striking. There is almost nothing in any of these textbooks about class inequalities or barriers of any kind to social mobility. "What conditions made it possible for poor white immigrants to become richer in the colonies?" *Land of Promise* asks. "What conditions made/make it difficult?" goes unasked. Textbook authors thus present an America in which, as preachers were fond of saying in the nineteenth century, men start from "humble origins" and attain "the most elevated positions."

Social class is probably the single most important variable in society. From womb to tomb, it correlates with almost all other social characteristics of people that we can measure. Affluent expectant mothers are more likely to get prenatal care, receive current medical advice, and enjoy general health, fitness, and nutrition. Many poor and working-class mothers-to-be first contact the medical profession in the last month, sometimes the last hours, of their pregnancies. Rich babies come out healthier and weighing more than poor babies. The infants go home to very different situations. Poor babies are more likely to have high levels of poisonous lead in their environments and their bodies. Rich babies get more time and verbal interaction with their parents and higher quality day care when not with their parents. When they enter kindergarten, and through the twelve years that follow, rich children benefit from suburban schools that spend two to three times as much money per student as schools in inner cities or impoverished rural areas. Poor children are taught in classes that are often 50 percent larger than the classes of affluent children. Differences such as these help account for the higher school-dropout rate among poor children.

Even when poor children are fortunate enough to attend the same school as rich children, they encounter teachers who expect only children of affluent families to know the right answers. Social science research shows that teachers are often surprised and even distressed when poor children excel. Teachers and counselors believe they can predict who is "college material." Since many working-class children give off the wrong signals, even in first grade, they end up in the "general education" track in high school. "If you are the child of low-income parents, the chances are good that you will receive limited and often careless attention from adults in your high school," in the words of Theodore Sizer's best-selling study of American high schools, *Horace's Compromise*. "If you are the child of upper-middle-income parents, the chances are good that you will receive substantial and careful attention." Researcher Reba Page has provided vivid accounts of how high school American history courses use rote learning to turn off lower-class students. Thus schools have put into practice Woodrow Wilson's recommendation: "We want one class of persons to have a liberal education, and we want another class of persons,

a very much larger class of necessity in every society, to forgo the privilege of a liberal education and fit themselves to perform specific difficult
manual tasks."

As if this unequal home and school life were not enough, rich teenagers then enroll in the Princeton Review or other coaching sessions for the
Scholastic Aptitude Test. Even without coaching, affluent children are
advantaged because their background is similar to that of the test-
makers, so they are comfortable with the vocabulary and subtle sub-
cultural assumptions of the test. To no one's surprise, social class correlates strongly with SAT scores.

All these are among the reasons why social class predicts the rate of
college attendance and the type of college chosen more effectively than
does any other factor, including intellectual ability, however measured.
After college, most affluent children get white-collar jobs, most working-
class children get blue-collar jobs, and the class differences continue. As
adults, rich people are more likely to have hired an attorney and to be
a member of formal organizations that increase their civic power. Poor
people are more likely to watch TV. Because affluent families can save
some money while poor families must spend what they make, wealth differences are ten times larger than income differences. Therefore most
poor and working-class families cannot accumulate the down payment
required to buy a house, which in turn shuts them out from our most
important tax shelter, the write-off of home mortgage interest. Working-
class parents cannot afford to live in elite subdivisions or hire high-quality
day care, so the process of educational inequality replicates itself in the
next generation. Finally, affluent Americans also have longer life expectancies than lower- and working-class people, the largest single cause of
which is better access to health care. Echoing the results of Helen Keller's
study of blindness, research has determined that poor health is not distributed randomly about the social structure but is concentrated in the
lower class. Social Security then becomes a huge transfer system, using
monies contributed by all Americans to pay benefits disproportionately
to longer-lived affluent Americans.

Ultimately, social class determines how people think about social class.
When asked if poverty in America is the fault of the poor or the fault of
the system, 57 percent of business leaders blamed the poor; just 9 percent
blamed the system. Labor leaders showed sharply reversed choices: only
15 percent said the poor were at fault while 56 percent blamed the system. (Some replied "don't know" or chose a middle position.) The largest
single difference between our two main political parties lies in how their
members think about social class: 55 percent of Republicans blamed the
poor for their poverty, while only 13 percent blamed the system for it;
68 percent of Democrats, on the other hand, blamed the system, while
only 5 percent blamed the poor.

Few of these statements are news, I know, which is why I have not documented most of them, but the majority of high school students do not

know or understand these ideas. Moreover, the processes have changed over time, for the class structure in America today is not the same as it was in 1890, let alone in colonial America. Yet in *Land of Promise*, for example, social class goes unmentioned after 1670.

## Reading as a Writer

1. List what you think are Loewen's main points. What appeals does he seem to draw on most when he makes those points: appeals based on his own character (ethos), on the emotions of his reader (pathos), or on the reasonableness of his evidence (logos)? Are the appeals obvious or difficult to tease out? Does he combine them? Discuss your answers with your classmates.

2. Identify what you think is the main claim of Loewen's argument, and choose key examples to support your answer. Compare your chosen claim and examples to those chosen by your classmates. Do they differ significantly? Can you agree on Loewen's gist and his key examples?

3. As a class, test the claims Loewen makes by thinking about your own experiences in high school history classes. Do you remember finding out that something you were taught from an American history textbook was not true? Did you discover on your own what you considered to be misrepresentations in or important omissions from your textbook? If so, did these misrepresentations or omissions tend to support or contradict the claims about history textbooks that Loewen makes?

# APPEALING TO ETHOS

Although we like to believe that our decisions and beliefs are based on reason and logic, in fact they are often based on what amounts to character judgments. That is, if a person you trust makes a reasonable argument for one choice, and a person you distrust makes a reasonable argument for another choice, you are more likely to be swayed by the argument of the person you trust. Similarly, the audience for your argument will be more disposed to agree with you if its members believe you are a fair, just person who is knowledgeable and has good judgment. Even the most well-developed argument will fall short if you do not leave this kind of impression on your readers. Thus, it is not surprising that ethos may be the most important component of your argument.

There are three strategies for evoking a sense of ethos:

1. Establish that you have good judgment.
2. Convey to readers that you are knowledgeable.
3. Show that you understand the complexity of the issue.

These strategies are interrelated: A writer who demonstrates good judgment is more often than not someone who is both knowledgeable about an issue and who acknowledges the complexity of it by weighing the strengths *and* weaknesses of different arguments. However, keep in mind that these characteristics do not exist apart from what readers think and believe.

## ■ Establish That You Have Good Judgment

Most readers of academic writing expect writers to demonstrate good judgment by identifying a problem that readers agree is worth addressing. In turn, good judgment gives writers credibility.

Loewen crafts his introduction to capture the attention of educators as well as concerned citizens when he claims that students leave high school unaware of class structure and as a consequence "have no understanding of the ways that opportunity is not equal in America and no notion that social structure pushes people around, influencing the ideas they hold and the lives they may fashion" (para. 1). Loewen does not blame students, or even instructors, for this lack of awareness. Instead, he writes, "textbooks can take some of the credit for this state of affairs" (para. 2) because, among other shortcomings, they leave out important events in "labor history" and relegate issues facing labor to the past.

Whether an educator—or a general reader for that matter—will ultimately agree with Loewen's case is, at this point, up for grabs, but certainly the possibility that high schools in general, and history textbooks in particular, are failing students by leaving them vulnerable to class-based manipulation would be recognized as a problem by readers who believe America should be a society that offers equal opportunity for all. At this point, Loewen's readers are likely to agree that the problem of omission he identifies may be significant if its consequences are as serious as he believes them to be.

Writers also establish good judgment by conveying to readers that they are fair-minded and just and have the best interests of readers in mind. Loewen is particularly concerned that students understand the persistence of poverty and inequality in the United States and the historical circumstances of the poor, which they cannot do unless textbook writers take a more inclusive approach to addressing labor history, especially "the growth of multinational corporations and their exporting of jobs overseas" (para. 2). It's not fair to deny this important information to students, and it's not fair to the poor to leave them out of official histories of the United States. Loewen further demonstrates that he is fair and just when he calls attention in paragraph 6 to the inequality between rich and poor children in schools, a problem that persists despite our forebears' belief that class would not determine the fate of citizens of the United States.

## ■ Convey to Readers That You Are Knowledgeable

Being thoughtful about a subject goes hand in hand with being knowledgeable about the subject. Loewen demonstrates his knowledge of class issues and their absence from textbooks in a number of ways (not the least of which is his awareness that a problem exists—many people, including educators, may not be aware of this problem).

In paragraph 3, Loewen makes a bold claim: "Textbooks' treatments of events in labor history are never anchored in any analysis of social class." As readers, we cannot help wondering: How does the author know this? How will he support this claim? Loewen anticipates these questions by demonstrating that he has studied the subject through a systematic examination of American history textbooks. He observes that six of the twelve textbooks he examined "contain no index listing at all for 'social class,' 'social stratification,' 'class structure,' 'income distribution,' 'inequality,' or any conceivably related topic" and that "not one book lists 'upper class,' 'working class,' or 'lower class.'" Loewen also demonstrates his grasp of class issues in American history, from the "violent class conflicts" that "took place in and just after colonial times" (para. 5), which contradict textbook writers' assertions that class conflicts did not exist during this period, to the more recent conflicts in the 1980s and early 1990s (paras. 2 and 4).

Moreover, Loewen backs up his own study of textbooks with references to a number of studies from the social sciences to illustrate that "social class is probably the single most important variable in society" (para. 6). Witness the statistics and findings he cites in paragraphs 6 through 10. The breadth of Loewen's historical knowledge and the range of his reading should convince readers that he is knowledgeable, and his trenchant analysis contributes to the authority he brings to the issue and to his credibility.

## ■ Show That You Understand the Complexity of a Given Issue

Recognizing the complexity of an issue helps readers see the extent to which authors know that any issue can be understood in a number of different ways. Loewen acknowledges that most of the history he recounts is not "news" (para. 11) to his educated readers, who by implication "know" and "understand" his references to historical events and trends. What may be news to his readers, he explains, is the extent to which class structure in the United States has changed over time. With the steady erosion of middle-class households since 1967, "class inequalities" and "barriers . . . to social mobility" (para. 5) are limiting more and more Americans' access to even the most fundamental of opportunities in a democratic society—health care and education.

Still, even though Loewen has introduced new thinking about the nature of class in the United States and has demonstrated a provocative play of mind by examining an overlooked body of data (high school history textbooks) that may influence the way class is perceived in America, there are still levels of complexity he hasn't addressed explicitly. Most important, perhaps, is the question of why history textbooks continue to ignore issues of class when there is so much research that indicates its importance in shaping the events history textbooks purport to explain.

---

### Steps to Appealing to Ethos

**1** **Establish that you have good judgment.** Identify an issue your readers will agree is worth addressing, and demonstrate that you are fair-minded and have the best interests of your readers in mind when you address it.

**2** **Convey to readers that you are knowledgeable.** Support your claims with credible evidence that shows you have read widely on, thought about, and understand the issue.

**3** **Show that you understand the complexity of the issue.** Demonstrate that you understand the variety of viewpoints your readers may bring—or may not be able to bring—to the issue.

---

## APPEALING TO PATHOS

An appeal to pathos recognizes that people are moved to action by their emotions as well as by reasonable arguments. In fact, pathos is a vital part of argument that can predispose readers one way or another. Do you want to arouse readers' sympathy? Anger? Passion? You can do that by knowing what readers value.

Appeals to pathos are typically indirect. You can appeal to pathos by using examples or illustrations that you believe will arouse the appropriate emotions and by presenting them using an appropriate tone.

To acknowledge that writers play on readers' emotions is not to endorse manipulative writing. Rather, it is to acknowledge that effective writers use all available means of persuasion to move readers to agree with them. After all, if your thoughtful reading and careful research have led you to believe that you must weigh in with a useful insight on an important issue, it stands to reason that you would want your argument to convince your readers to believe as strongly in what you assert as you do.

For example, if you genuinely believe that the conditions some families are living in are abysmal and unfair, you want your readers to believe it too. And an effective way to persuade them to believe as you do, in addition to convincing them of the reasonableness of your argument and of your own good character and judgment, is to establish a kind of emotional common ground in your writing—the common ground of pathos.

## ■ Show That You Know What Your Readers Value

Let's consider some of the ways James Loewen signals that he knows what his readers value.

In the first place, Loewen assumes that readers feel the same way he does: Educated people should know that the United States has a class structure despite the democratic principles that the nation was founded on. He also expects readers to identify with his unwillingness to accept the injustice that results from that class structure. He believes that women living in poverty should have access to appropriate health care, that children living in poverty should have a chance to attend college, and that certain classes of people should not be written off to "perform specific difficult manual tasks" (para. 7).

Time and again, Loewen cites examples that reveal that the poor are discriminated against by the class structure in the United States not for lack of ability, lack of desire, lack of ambition, or lack of morality, but for no better reason than lack of money—and that such discrimination has been going on for a long time. He expects that his readers also will find such discrimination an unacceptable affront to their values of fair play and democracy and that they will experience the same sense of outrage that he does.

## ■ Use Illustrations and Examples That Appeal to Readers' Emotions

You can appeal to readers' emotions indirectly through the illustrations and examples you use to support your argument.

For instance, in paragraph 2, Loewen contends that textbook writers share responsibility for high school students' not knowing about the continued relevance of class issues in American life. Loewen's readers—parents, educators, historians—may very well be angered by the omissions he points out. Certainly he would expect them to be angry when they read about the effects of economic class on the health care expectant mothers and then their children receive (para. 6) and on their children's access to quality education (paras. 6–8). In citing the fact that social class "correlates strongly with SAT scores" (para. 8) and so "predicts the rate of college attendance and the type of college chosen" (para. 9), Loewen forces his readers to acknowledge that the educational playing field is far from level.

Finally, he calls attention to the fact that accumulated wealth accounts for deep class divisions in our society—that their inability to save prevents the poor from hiring legal counsel, purchasing a home, or taking advantage of tax shelters. The result, Loewen observes, is that "educational inequality replicates itself in the next generation" (para. 9).

Together, these examples strengthen both Loewen's argument and what he hopes will be readers' outrage that history textbooks do not address class issues. Without that information, Americans cannot fully understand or act to change the existing class structure.

### ■ Consider How Your Tone May Affect Your Audience

The **tone** of your writing is your use of language that communicates your attitude toward yourself, your material, and your readers. Of course, your tone is important in everything you write, but it is particularly crucial when you are appealing to pathos.

When you are appealing to your readers' emotions, it is tempting to use loaded, exaggerated, and even intemperate language to convey how you feel (and hope your readers will feel) about an issue. Consider these sentences: "The Republican Party has devised the most ignominious means of filling the pockets of corporations." "These wretched children suffer heartrending agonies that can barely be imagined, much less described." "The ethereal beauty of the Brandenburg concertos thrill one to the deepest core of one's being." All of these sentences express strong and probably sincere beliefs and emotions, but some readers might find them overwrought and coercive and question the writer's reasonableness.

Similarly, some writers rely on irony or sarcasm to set the tone of their work. **Irony** is the use of language to say one thing while meaning quite another. **Sarcasm** is the use of heavy-handed irony to ridicule or attack someone or something. Although irony and sarcasm can make for vivid and entertaining writing, they also can backfire and end up alienating readers. The sentence "Liberals will be pleased to hear that the new budget will be making liberal use of their hard-earned dollars" may entertain some readers with its irony and wordplay, but others may assume that the writer's attitude toward liberals is likely to result in an unfairly slanted argument. And the sentence "In my opinion, there's no reason why Christians and Muslims shouldn't rejoice together over the common ground of their both being deluded about the existence of a God" may please some readers, but it risks alienating those who are uncomfortable with breezy comments about religious beliefs. Again, think of your readers and what they value, and weigh the benefits of a clever sentence against its potential to detract from your argument or offend your audience.

You often find colorful wording and irony in op-ed and opinion pieces, where a writer may not have the space to build a compelling argument using evidence and has to resort to shortcuts to readers' emotions. However, in academic writing, where the careful accumulation and presentation of evidence and telling examples are highly valued, the frequent use of loaded language, exaggeration, and sarcasm is looked on with distrust.

Consider Loewen's excerpt. Although his outrage comes through clearly, he never resorts to hectoring. For example, in paragraph 1, he writes that students are "ignorant of the workings of the class structure" and that their opinions are "half-formed and naïve." But he does not imply that students are ignoramuses or that their opinions are foolish. What they lack, he contends, is understanding. They need to be taught something about class structure that they are not now being taught. And paragraph 1 is about as close to name-calling as Loewen comes. Even textbook writers, who are the target of his anger, are not vilified.

Loewen does occasionally make use of irony, for example in paragraph 5, where he points out inconsistencies and omissions in textbooks: "Never mind that the most violent class conflicts in American history— Bacon's Rebellion and Shays's Rebellion—took place in and just after colonial times. Textbooks still say that colonial society was relatively classless and marked by upward mobility. And things have gotten rosier since." But he doesn't resort to ridicule. Instead, he relies on examples and illustrations to connect with his readers' sense of values and appeal to their emotions.

---

### Steps to Appealing to Pathos

**1** **Show that you know what your readers value.** Start from your own values and imagine what assumptions and principles would appeal to your readers. What common ground can you imagine between your values and theirs? How will it need to be adjusted for different kinds of readers?

**2** **Use illustrations and examples that appeal to readers' emotions.** Again, start from your own emotional position. What examples and illustrations resonate most with you? How can you present them to have the most emotional impact on your readers? How would you adjust them for different kinds of readers?

**3** **Consider how your tone may affect your audience.** Be wary of using loaded, exaggerated, and intemperate language that may put off your readers; and be careful in your use of irony and sarcasm.

---

### A Practice Sequence: Appealing to Ethos and Pathos

Discuss the language and strategies the writers use in the following passages to connect with their audience, in particular their appeals to both ethos and pathos. After reading each excerpt, discuss who you think the implied audience is and whether you think the strategies the writers use to connect with their readers are effective or not.

1  Almost a half century after the U.S. Supreme Court concluded that Southern school segregation was unconstitutional and "inherently unequal," new statistics from the 1998–99 school year show that segregation continued to intensify throughout the 1990s, a period in which there were three major Supreme Court decisions authorizing a return to segregated neighborhood schools and limiting the reach and duration of desegregation orders. For African American students, this trend is particularly apparent in the South, where most blacks live and where the 2000 Census shows a

continuing return from the North. From 1988 to 1998, most of the progress of the previous two decades in increasing integration in the region was lost. The South is still much more integrated than it was before the civil rights revolution, but it is moving backward at an accelerating rate.

—GARY ORFIELD, "Schools More Separate:
Consequences of a Decade of Resegregation"

2 No issue has been more saturated with dishonesty than the issue of racial quotas and preferences, which is now being examined by the Supreme Court of the United States. Many defenders of affirmative action are not even honest enough to admit that they are talking about quotas and preferences, even though everyone knows that that is what affirmative action amounts to in practice.

Despite all the gushing about the mystical benefits of "diversity" in higher education, a recent study by respected academic scholars found that "college diversity programs fail to raise standards" and that "a majority of faculty members and administrators recognize this when speaking anonymously."

This study by Stanley Rothman, Seymour Martin Lipset, and Neil Nevitte found that "of those who think that preferences have some impact on academic standards those believing it negative exceed those believing it positive by 15 to 1."

Poll after poll over the years has shown that most faculty members and most students are opposed to double standards in college admissions. Yet professors who will come out publicly and say what they say privately in these polls are as rare as hens' teeth.

Such two-faced talk is pervasive in academia and elsewhere. A few years ago, in Berkeley, there was a big fight over whether a faculty vote on affirmative action would be by secret ballot or open vote. Both sides knew that the result of a secret ballot would be the direct opposite of the result in a public vote at a faculty meeting.

—THOMAS SOWELL, "The Grand Fraud:
Affirmative Action for Blacks"

3 When the judgment day comes for every high school student— that day when a final transcript is issued and sent to the finest institutions, with every sin of class selection written as with a burning chisel on stone—on that day a great cry will go up throughout the land, and there will be weeping, wailing, gnashing of teeth, and considerable grumbling against guidance counselors, and the cry of a certain senior might be, "WHY did no one tell me that Introduction to Social Poker wasn't a solid academic class?" At another, perhaps less wealthy school, a frustrated and under-nurtured sculptress will wonder, "Why can't I read, and

why don't I care?" The reason for both of these oversights, as they may eventually discover, is that the idea of the elective course has been seriously mauled, mistreated, and abused under the current middle-class high school system. A significant amount of the blame for producing students who are stunted, both cognitively and morally, can be traced back to this pervasive fact. Elective courses, as shoddily planned and poorly funded as they may be, constitute the only formation that many students get in their own special types of intelligences. Following the model of Howard Gardner, these may be spatial, musical, or something else. A lack of stimulation to a student's own intelligence directly causes a lack of identification with the intelligence of others. Instead of becoming moderately interested in a subject by noticing the pleasure other people receive from it, the student will be bitter, jealous, and without empathy. These are the common ingredients in many types of tragedy, violent or benign. Schools must take responsibility for speaking in some way to each of the general types of intelligences. Failure to do so will result in students who lack skills, and also the inspiration to comfort, admire, emulate, and aid their fellow humans.

"All tasks that really call upon the power of attention are interesting for the same reason and to an almost equal degree," wrote Simone Weil in her *Reflections on Love and Faith*, her editor having defined attention as "a suspension of one's own self as a center of the world and making oneself available to the reality of another being." In Parker Palmer's *The Courage to Teach*, modern scientific theorist David Bohm describes "a holistic underlying implicate order whose information unfolds into the explicate order of particular fields." Rilke's euphemism for this "holistic . . . implicate order," which Palmer borrows, is "the grace of great things." Weil's term would be "God." However, both agree that eventual perception of this singular grace, or God, is accessible through education of a specific sort, and for both it is doubtless the most necessary experience of a lifetime. Realizing that this contention is raining down from different theorists, and keeping in mind that the most necessary experience of a lifetime should not be wholly irrelevant to the school system, educators should therefore reach the conclusion that this is a matter worth looking into. I assert that the most fruitful and practical results of their attention will be a wider range of electives coupled with a new acknowledgment and handling of them, one that treats each one seriously.

—Erin Meyers,
"The Educational Smorgasbord as Saving Grace"

## APPEALING TO LOGOS: USING REASON AND EVIDENCE TO FIT THE SITUATION

To make an argument persuasive, you need to be in dialogue with your readers, using your own character (ethos) to demonstrate that you are a reasonable, credible, fair person and appealing to your readers' emotions (pathos), particularly their sense of right and wrong. Both types of appeal go hand in hand with appeals to logos, using converging pieces of evidence—statistics, facts, observations—to advance your claim. Remember that the type of evidence you use is determined by the issue, problem, situation, and readers' expectations. As an author, you should try to anticipate and address readers' beliefs and values. Ethos and pathos are concerned with the content of your argument; logos addresses both form and content.

An argument begins with one or more premises and ends with a conclusion. A **premise** is an assumption that you expect your readers to agree with, a statement that is either true or false—for example, "Alaska is cold in the winter"—that is offered in support of a claim. That claim is the **conclusion** you want your readers to draw from your premises. The conclusion is also a sentence that is either true or false.

For instance, Loewen's major premise is that class is a key factor in Americans' access to health care, education, and wealth. Loewen also offers a second, more specific premise: that textbook writers provide little discussion of the ways class matters. Loewen crafts his argument to help readers draw the following conclusion: "We live in a class system that runs counter to the democratic principles that underlie the founding of the United States, and history textbooks must tell this story. Without this knowledge, citizens will be uninformed."

Whether readers accept this as true depends on how Loewen moves from his initial premises to reach his conclusion—that is, whether we draw the same kinds of inferences, or reasoned judgments, that he does. He must do so in a way that meets readers' expectations of what constitutes relevant and persuasive evidence and guides them one step at a time toward his conclusion.

There are two main forms of argument: deductive and inductive. A **deductive argument** is an argument in which the premises support (or appear to support) the conclusion. If you join two premises to produce a conclusion that is taken to be true, you are stating a **syllogism**. This is the classic example of deductive reasoning through a syllogism:

1.  All men are mortal. (First premise)
2.  Socrates is a man. (Second premise)
3.  Therefore, Socrates is mortal. (Conclusion)

In a deductive argument, it is impossible for both premises to be true and the conclusion to be false. That is, the truth of the premises means that the conclusion must also be true.

By contrast, an **inductive argument** relies on evidence and observation to reach a conclusion. Although readers may accept a writer's premises as true, it is possible for them to reject the writer's conclusion.

Let's consider this for a moment in the context of Loewen's argument. Loewen introduces the premise that class matters, then offers the more specific premise that textbook writers leave class issues out of their narratives of American history, and finally draws the conclusion that citizens need to be informed of this body of knowledge in order to create change:

1. Although class is a key factor in Americans' access to health care, education, and wealth, students know very little about the social structure in the United States.

2. In their textbooks, textbook writers do not address the issue of class, an issue that people need to know about.

3. Therefore, if people had this knowledge, they would understand that poverty cannot be blamed on the poor.

Notice that Loewen's premises are not necessarily true. For example, readers could challenge the premise that "textbook writers do not address issues of class." After all, Loewen examined just twelve textbooks. What if he had examined a different set of textbooks? Would he have drawn the same conclusion? And even if Loewen's evidence convinces us that the two premises are true, we do not have to accept that the conclusion is true.

The conclusion in an inductive argument is never definitive. That is the nature of any argument that deals with human emotions and actions. Moreover, we have seen throughout history that people tend to disagree much more on the terms of an argument than on its form. Do we agree that Israel's leaders practice apartheid? (What do we mean by *apartheid* in this case?) Do we agree with the need to grant women reproductive rights? (When does life begin?) Do we agree that all people should be treated equally? (Would equality mean equal access to resources or to outcomes?)

Deductive arguments are conclusive. In a deductive argument, the premises are universal truths—laws of nature, if you will—and the conclusion must follow from those premises. That is, $a^2$ plus $b^2$ always equals $c^2$, and humans are always mortal.

By contrast, an inductive argument is never conclusive. The premises may or may not be true; and even if they are true, the conclusion may be false. We might accept that class matters and that high school history textbooks don't address the issue of class structure in the United States; but we still would not know that students who have studied social stratification in America will necessarily understand the nature of poverty. It may be that social class is only one reason for poverty; or it may be that textbooks are only one source of information about social stratification in the United States, that textbook omissions are simply not as serious as Loewen claims. That the premises of an argument are true only establishes that the conclusion is probably true and, perhaps, true only for some readers.

Inductive argument is the basis of academic writing; it is also the basis of any appeal to logos. The process of constructing an inductive argument involves three steps:

1. State the premises of your argument.
2. Use credible evidence to show readers that your argument has merit.
3. Demonstrate that the conclusion follows from the premises.

In following these three steps, you will want to determine the truth of your premises, help readers understand whether or not the inferences you draw are justified, and use word signals to help readers fully grasp the connections between your premises and your conclusion.

## ■ State the Premises of Your Argument

Stating a premise establishes what you have found to be true and what you want to persuade readers to accept as truth as well. Let's return to Loewen, who asserts his premise at the very outset of the excerpt: "Middle-class students . . . know little about how the American class structure works . . . and nothing at all about how it has changed over time." Loewen elaborates on this initial premise a few sentences later, arguing that students "have no understanding of the ways that opportunity is not equal in America and no notion that the social structure pushes people around, influencing the ideas they hold and the lives they fashion."

Implicit here is the point that class matters. Loewen makes this point explicit several paragraphs later, where he states that "social class is probably the single most important variable in society" (para. 6). He states his second, more specific premise in paragraph 2: "High school history textbooks can take some of the credit for this state of affairs." The burden of demonstrating that these premises are true is on Loewen. If readers find that either of the premises is not true, it will be difficult, if not impossible, for them to accept his conclusion that with more knowledge, people will understand that poverty is not the fault of the poor (para. 10).

## ■ Use Credible Evidence

The validity of your argument depends on whether the inferences you draw are justified, and whether you can expect a reasonable person to draw the same conclusion from those premises. Loewen has to demonstrate throughout (1) that students do not have much, if any, knowledge about the class structure that exists in the United States and (2) that textbook writers are in large part to blame for this lack of knowledge. He also must help readers understand how this lack of knowledge contributes to (3) his conclusion that greater knowledge would lead Americans to understand that poor people are not responsible for poverty. He can help readers with the order in which he states his premises and by choosing the type and amount of evidence that will enable readers to draw the inferences that he does.

Interestingly, Loewen seems to assume that one group of readers — educators — will accept his first premise as true. He does not elaborate on what students know or do not know. Instead, he moves right to his second premise, which involves first acknowledging what high school history textbooks typically cover, then identifying what he believes are the important events that textbook writers exclude, and ultimately asserting that "treatments of events in labor history are never anchored in any analysis of social class" (para. 3). He supports this point with his own study of twelve textbooks (paras. 3–5) before returning to his premise that "social class is probably the single most important variable in society" (para. 6). What follows is a series of observations about the rich and references to researchers' findings on inequality (paras. 7–9). Finally, he asserts that "social class determines how people think about social class" (para. 10), implying that fuller knowledge would lead business leaders and conservative voters to think differently about the source of poverty. The question to explore is whether or not Loewen supports this conclusion.

## ■ Demonstrate That the Conclusion Follows from the Premises

Authors signal their conclusion with words like *consequently, finally, in sum, in the end, subsequently, therefore, thus, ultimately,* and *as a result.* Here is how this looks in the structure of Loewen's argument:

1. Although class is a key factor in Americans' access to health care, education, and wealth, students know very little about the social structure in the United States.

2. In their textbooks, textbook writers do not address the issue of class, an issue that people need to know about.

3. Ultimately, if people had this knowledge, they would understand that poverty cannot be blamed on the poor.

We've reprinted much of paragraph 9 of Loewen's excerpt below. Notice how Loewen pulls together what he has been discussing. He again underscores the importance of class and achievement ("All these are among the reasons"). And he points out that access to certain types of colleges puts people in a position to accumulate and sustain wealth. Of course, this is not true of the poor "because affluent families can save some money while poor families must spend what they make." This causal relationship ("Because") heightens readers' awareness of the class structure that exists in the United States.

All these are among the reasons why social class predicts the rate of college attendance and the type of college chosen more effectively than does any other factor, including intellectual ability, however measured. After college, most affluent children get white-collar jobs, most working-class children get blue-collar jobs, and the class differences continue. As adults, rich people are more likely to have hired an attorney and to be a member of formal organizations that increase their civic power. Poor people are more likely to watch TV. Because affluent families can save some money while poor families must spend what they make, wealth differences are ten times larger than income differences. Therefore most poor and working-class families cannot accumulate the down payment required to buy a house, which in turn shuts them out from our most important tax shelter, the write-off of home mortgage interest. Working-class parents cannot afford to live in elite subdivisions or hire high-quality day care, so the process of educational inequality replicates itself in the next generation. Finally, affluent Americans also have longer life expectancies than lower- and working-class people, the largest single cause of which is better access to health care. . . .

Once Loewen establishes this causal relationship, he concludes ("Therefore," "Finally") with the argument that poverty persists from one generation to the next.

In paragraph 10, Loewen uses the transition word *ultimately* to make the point that social class matters, so much so that it limits the ways in which people see the world, that it even "determines how people think about social class." (We discuss how to write conclusions in Chapter 9.)

---

### Steps to Appealing to Logos

**1** **State the premises of your argument.** Establish what you have found to be true and what you want readers to accept as well.

**2** **Use credible evidence.** Lead your readers from one premise to the next, making sure your evidence is sufficient and convincing and your inferences are logical and correct.

**3** **Demonstrate that the conclusion follows from the premises.** In particular, use the right words to signal to your readers how the evidence and inferences lead to your conclusion.

---

## RECOGNIZING LOGICAL FALLACIES

We turn now to **logical fallacies**, flaws in the chain of reasoning that lead to a conclusion that does not necessarily follow from the premises, or evidence. Logical fallacies are common in inductive arguments for two reasons: Inductive arguments rely on reasoning about probability, not certainty; and they derive from human beliefs and values, not facts or laws of nature.

Here we list fifteen logical fallacies. In examining them, think about how to guard against the sometimes-faulty logic behind statements you might hear from politicians, advertisers, and the like. That should help you examine the premises on which you base your own assumptions and the logic you use to help readers reach the same conclusions you do.

1. *Erroneous Appeal to Authority.* An authority is someone with expertise in a given subject. An *erroneous authority* is an author who claims to be an authority but is not, or someone an author cites as an authority who is not. In this type of fallacy, the claim might be true, but the fact that an unqualified person is making the claim means there is no reason for readers to accept the claim as true.

Because the issue here is the legitimacy of authority, your concern should be to prove to yourself and your readers that you or the people you are citing have expertise in the subject. An awareness of this type of fallacy has become increasingly important as celebrities offer support for candidates running for office or act as spokespeople for curbing global warming or some other cause. The candidate may be the best person for the office, and there may be very good reasons to control global warming; but we need to question the legitimacy of a nonexpert endorsement.

2. *Ad Hominem.* An ad hominem argument focuses on the person making a claim instead of on the claim itself. (*Ad hominem* is Latin for "to the person.") In most cases, an ad hominem argument does not have a bearing on the truth or the quality of a claim.

Keep in mind that it is always important to address the claim or the reasoning behind it, rather than the person making the claim. "Of course Senator Wiley supports oil drilling in Alaska—he's in the pocket of the oil companies!" is an example of an ad hominem argument. Senator Wiley may have good reasons for supporting oil drilling in Alaska that have nothing to do with his alleged attachment to the oil industry. However, if an individual's character is relevant to the argument, then an ad hominem argument can be valid. If Senator Wiley has been found guilty of accepting bribes from an oil company, it makes sense to question both his credibility and his claims.

3. *Shifting the Issue.* This type of fallacy occurs when an author draws attention away from the issue instead of offering evidence that will enable people to draw their own conclusions about the soundness of an argument. For example:

> Affirmative action proponents accuse me of opposing equal opportunity in the workforce. I think my positions on military expenditures, education, and public health speak for themselves.

The author of this statement does not provide a chain of reasoning that would enable readers to judge his or her stance on the issue of affirmative action.

4. *Either/Or Fallacy.* At times, an author will take two extreme positions to force readers to make a choice between two seemingly contradictory positions. For example:

> Either you support the war in Iraq, or you are against it.

Although the author has set up an either/or condition, in reality one position does not exclude the other. Many people support the troops in Iraq even though they do not support the reasons for starting the war.

5. *Sweeping Generalizations.* When an author attempts to draw a conclusion without providing sufficient evidence to support the conclusion or examining possible counterarguments, he or she may be making sweeping generalizations. For example:

> Despite the women's movement in the 1960s and 1970s, women still do not receive equal pay for equal work. Obviously, any attempt to change the status quo for women is doomed to failure.

As is the case with many fallacies, the author's position may be reasonable, but we cannot accept the argument at face value. Reading critically entails testing assumptions like this one—that any attempt to create change is doomed to failure because women do not receive equal pay for equal work. We could ask, for example, whether inequities persist in the public sector. And we could point to other areas where the women's movement has had measurable success. Title IX, for example, has reduced the dropout rate among teenage girls; it has also increased the rate at which women earn college and graduate degrees.

6. *Bandwagon.* When an author urges readers to accept an idea because a significant number of people support it, he or she is making a bandwagon argument. This is a fairly common mode of argument in advertising; for example, a commercial might attempt to persuade us to buy a certain product because it's popular.

> Because Harvard, Stanford, and Berkeley have all added a multicultural component to their graduation requirements, other institutions should do so as well.

The growing popularity of an idea is not sufficient reason to accept that it is true.

7. *Begging the Question.* This fallacy entails advancing a circular argument that asks readers to accept a premise that is also the conclusion readers are expected to draw:

> We could improve the undergraduate experience with coed dorms because both men and women benefit from living with members of the opposite gender.

Here readers are being asked to accept that the conclusion is true despite the fact that the premises—men benefit from living with women, and women benefit from living with men—are essentially the same as the conclusion. Without evidence that a shift in dorm policy could improve on the undergraduate experience, we cannot accept the conclusion as true. Indeed, the conclusion does not necessarily follow from the premise.

8. *False Analogy.* Authors (and others) often try to persuade us that something is true by using a comparison. This approach is not in and of itself a problem, as long as the comparison is reasonable. For example:

> It is ridiculous to have a Gay and Lesbian Program and a Department of African American Culture. We don't have a Straight Studies Program or a Department of Caucasian Culture.

Here the author is urging readers to rethink the need for two academic departments by saying that the school doesn't have two other departments. That, of course, is not a reason for or against the new departments. What's needed is an analysis that compares the costs (economic and otherwise) of starting up and operating the new departments versus the contributions (economic and otherwise) of the new departments.

9. *Technical Jargon.* If you've ever had a salesperson try to persuade you to purchase a television or an entertainment system with capabilities you absolutely *must* have—even if you didn't understand a word the salesperson was saying about alternating currents and circuit splicers—then you're familiar with this type of fallacy. We found this passage in one of our student's papers:

> You should use this drug because it has been clinically proven that it inhibits the reuptake of serotonin and enhances the dopamine levels of the body's neurotransmitters.

The student's argument may very well be true, but he hasn't presented any substantive evidence to demonstrate that the premises are true and that the conclusion follows from the premises.

10. *Confusing Cause and Effect.* It is challenging to establish that one factor causes another. For example, how can we know for certain that economic class predicts, or is a factor in, academic achievement? How do we know that a new president's policies are the cause of a country's economic well-being? Authors often assume cause and effect when two factors are simply associated with each other:

> The current recession came right after the president was elected.

This fallacy states a fact, but it does not prove that the president's election caused the recession.

11. *Appeal to Fear.* One type of logical fallacy makes an appeal to readers' irrational fears and prejudices, preventing them from dealing squarely with a given issue and often confusing cause and effect:

> We should use whatever means possible to avoid further attack.

The reasoning here is something like this: "If we are soft on defense, we will never end the threat of terrorism." But we need to consider whether there is indeed a threat, and, if so, whether the presence of a threat should lead to action, and, if so, whether that action should include "whatever means possible." (Think of companies that sell alarm systems by pointing to people's vulnerability to harm and property damage.)

12. *Fallacy of Division.* A fallacy of division suggests that what is true of the whole must also be true of its parts:

> Conservatives have always voted against raising the minimum wage, against stem cell research, and for defense spending. Therefore, we can assume that conservative Senator Harrison will vote this way.

The author is urging readers to accept the premise without providing evidence of how the senator has actually voted on the three issues.

13. *Hasty Generalization.* This fallacy is committed when a person draws a conclusion about a group based on a sample that is too small to be representative. Consider this statement:

> Seventy-five percent of the seniors surveyed at the university study just 10 hours a week. We can conclude, then, that students at the university are not studying enough.

What you need to know is how many students were actually surveyed. Seventy-five percent may seem high, but not if the researcher surveyed just 400 of the 2,400 graduating seniors. This sample of students from a total population of 9,600 students at the university is too small to draw the conclusion that students in general are not studying enough.

14. *The Straw Man Argument.* A straw man fallacy makes a generalization about what a group believes without actually citing a specific writer or work:

> Democrats are more interested in running away than in trying to win the war on terrorism.

Here the fallacy is that the author simply ignores a person's actual position and substitutes a distorted, exaggerated, or misrepresented version of that position. This kind of fallacy often goes hand in hand with assuming that what is true of the group is true of the individual, what we call the fallacy of division.

15. *Fallacy of the Middle Ground.* The fallacy of the middle ground assumes that the middle position between two extreme positions must be correct. Although the middle ground may be true, the author must justify this position with evidence.

> E. D. Hirsch argues that cultural literacy is the only sure way to increase test scores, and Jonathan Kozol believes schools will improve only if state legislators increase funding; but I would argue that school reform will occur if we change the curriculum *and* provide more funding.

This fallacy draws its power from the fact that a moderate or middle position is often the correct one. Again, however, the claim that the moderate or middle position is correct must be supported by legitimate reasoning.

# ANALYZING THE APPEALS
# IN A RESEARCHED ARGUMENT

Now that you have studied the variety of appeals you can make to connect with your audience, we would like you to read a paper on urban health problems by Meredith Minkler and analyze her strategies for appealing to her readers. The paper is long and carefully argued, so we suggest you take detailed notes about her use of appeals to ethos, pathos, and logos as you read. You may want to refer to the Practice Sequence questions on page 236 to help focus your reading. Ideally, you should work through the text with your classmates, in groups of three or four, appointing one student to record and share each group's analysis of Minkler's argument.

## MEREDITH MINKLER

## Community-Based Research Partnerships: Challenges and Opportunities

Meredith Minkler is a professor of health and social behavior at the School of Public Health, University of California, Berkeley. She is an activist and researcher whose work explores community partnerships, community organizing, and community-based participatory research. With more than one hundred books and articles to her credit, she is coeditor of the influential *Community Based Participatory Research for Health* (2003). The following article appeared in *The Journal of Urban Health* in 2005.

■ ■ ■

### Abstract
*The complexity of many urban health problems often makes them ill suited to traditional research approaches and interventions. The resultant frustration, together with community calls for genuine partnership in the research process, has highlighted the importance of an alternative paradigm. Community-based participatory research (CBPR) is presented as a promising collaborative approach that combines systematic inquiry, participation, and action to address urban health problems. Following a brief review of its basic tenets and historical roots, key ways in which CBPR adds value to urban health research are introduced and illustrated. Case study examples from diverse international settings are used to illustrate some of the difficult ethical challenges that may arise in the course of CBPR partnership approaches. The concepts of partnership synergy and cultural humility, together with protocols such as Green et al.'s guidelines for appraising CBPR projects, are highlighted as useful tools for urban health researchers seeking to apply this collaborative approach and to deal effectively with the difficult ethical challenges it can present.*

### Keywords
*Community-based participatory research, Ethical issues in research, Participatory action research, Partnership, Urban health.*

## Introduction

The complexity of urban health problems has often made them poorly     *1*
suited to traditional "outside expert"–driven research and intervention
approaches.[1] Together with community demands for authentic partnerships in research that are locally relevant and "community based" rather
than merely "community placed," this frustration has led to a burgeoning
of interest in an alternative research paradigm.[1,2] Community-based participatory research (CBPR) is an overarching term that increasingly is used
to encompass a variety of approaches to research that have as their cen-
terpiece three interrelated elements: participation, research, and action.[3]
As defined by Green et al.[4] for the Royal Society of Canada, CBPR may
concisely be described as "systematic investigation with the participation of those affected by an issue for purposes of education and action or
affecting social change." The approach further has been characterized as

> [A] collaborative process that equitably involves all partners in the research
> process and recognizes the unique strengths that each brings. CBPR begins
> with a research topic of importance to the community with the aim of com-
> bining knowledge and action for social change to improve community
> health and eliminate health disparities.[5,6]

This article briefly describes CBPR's roots and core principles and     *2*
summarizes the value added by this approach to urban health research.
Drawing on examples from a variety of urban health settings nationally
and internationally, it discusses and illustrates several of the key challenges faced in applying this partnership approach to inquiry and action.
The article concludes by suggesting that despite such challenges and
the labor-intensive nature of this approach, CBPR offers an exceptional
opportunity for partnering with communities in ways that can enhance
both the quality of research and its potential for helping address some of
our most intractable urban health problems.

## Historical Roots and Core Principles

The roots of CBPR may be traced in part to the action research school de-     *3*
veloped by the social psychologist Kurt Lewin[7] in the 1940s, with its emphasis on the active involvement in the research of those affected by the
problem being studied through a cyclical process of fact finding, action,
and reflection. But CBPR is most deeply grounded in the more revolutionary approaches to research that emerged, often independently from
one another, from work with oppressed communities in South America,
Asia, and Africa in the 1970s.[3,8,9] Brazilian adult educator Paulo Freire[9]
provided critical grounding for CBPR in his development of a dialogi-
cal method accenting co-learning and action based on critical reflection.

Freire,[9] Fals-Borda,[10] and other developing countries' scholars developed their alternative approaches to inquiry as a direct counter to the often "colonizing" nature of research to which oppressed communities were subjected, with feminist and postcolonialist scholars adding further conceptual richness.[11,12]

Among the tenets of participatory action approaches to research outlined by McTaggart[13] are that it is a political process, involves lay people in theory-making, is committed to improving social practice by changing it, and establishes "self-critical communities." As Israel et al.[6] adds, other core principles are that CBPR "involves systems development and local community capacity development," is "a co-learning process" to which community members and outside researchers contribute equally, and "achieves a balance between research and action." CBPR reflects a profound belief in "partnership synergy." As described by Lasker et al.[14]:

> [T]he synergy that partners seek to achieve through collaboration is more than a mere exchange of resources. By combining the individual perspectives, resources, and skills of the partners, the group creates something new and valuable together—something that is greater than the sum of its parts.

Moreover, CBPR embodies a deep commitment to what Tervalon and Murray-Garcia[15] have called cultural humility. As they point out, although we can never become truly competent in another's culture, we can demonstrate a "lifelong commitment to self evaluation and self-critique," to redress power imbalances and "develop and maintain mutually respectful and dynamic partnerships with communities."[15] Although the term *cultural humility* was coined primarily in reference to race and ethnicity, it also is of value in helping us understand and address the impacts of professional cultures (which tend to be highly influenced by white, western, patriarchal belief systems), as these help shape interactions between outside researchers and their community partners.[15]

CBPR is not a method per se but an orientation to research that may employ any of a number of qualitative and quantitative methodologies. As Cornwall and Jewkes[16] note, what is distinctive about CBPR is "the attitudes of researchers, which in turn determine how, by and for whom research is conceptualized and conducted [and] the corresponding location of power at every stage of the research process." The accent placed by CBPR on individual, organizational, and community empowerment also is a hallmark of this approach to research.

With the increasing emphasis on partnership approaches to improving urban health, CBPR is experiencing a rebirth of interest and unprecedented new opportunities for both scholarly recognition and financial support. In the United States, for example, the Institute of Medicine[17] recently named "community-based participatory research" as one of eight new areas in which all schools of public health should be offering training.

Although the renewed interest in CBPR provides a welcome contrast to      8
more traditional top-down research approaches, it also increases the dangers of co-optation as this label is loosely applied to include research and intervention efforts in search of funding that do not truly meet the criteria for this approach. The sections below illustrate some of the value added to urban research when authentic partnership approaches are taken seriously and then briefly highlight some of the ethical challenges such work may entail.

## The Value Added to Urban Health Research by a CBPR Approach

CBPR can enrich and improve the quality and outcomes of urban health      9
research in a variety of ways. On the basis of the work of many scholars and institutions,[4,6,8,18] and as summarized by the National Institutes of Health (http://grants.nih.gov/grants/guide/pa-files/PAR-05-026.html), some of its primary contributions may be characterized and illustrated as follows.

### CBPR Can Support the Development of Research Questions That Reflect Health Issues of Real Concern to Community Members

Ideally, CBPR begins with a research topic or question that comes from      10
the local community, as when the nongovernmental organization (NGO) Alternatives for Community and Environment (ACE) in the low-income Roxbury section of Boston, reached out to Harvard University's School of Public Health and other potential partners to study and address the high rates of asthma in their neighborhood. Collaborative studies using air-monitoring and other approaches yielded data supporting the hypothesis that Roxbury was indeed a hot spot for pollution contributing to asthma. This in turn paved the way for a variety of policy and community education actions and outcomes.[19]

Although having a community partner such as ACE identify an issue      11
and catalyze a research partnership may be the ideal, it is often the privileged outside researcher who initiates a CBPR project. In these instances too, however, a genuine commitment to high-level community involvement in issue selection, with NGOs and formal and informal community leaders engaged as equal partners, can help ensure that the research topic decided upon really is of major concern to the local population.

### CBPR Can Improve Our Ability to Achieve Informed Consent, and to Address Issues of "Costs and Benefits" on the Community, and Not Simply the Individual Level[20]

With its accent on equitable community involvement in all stages of the      12
research process,[6] CBPR often finds creative means of ensuring informed consent. The "One Hand, One Heart" study in urban and rural Tibet,

which included a randomized controlled clinical trial of an indigenous medicine to prevent maternal hemorrhaging, actively involved local midwives and other community partners on the research team who played a key role in helping find locally translatable concepts to improve informed consent. Their help in early ethnographic work thus revealed that the concept of disclosing risk was highly problematic, because such disclosure was believed to disturb the wind element responsible for emotions, potentially leading to emotional upset and other adverse outcomes. By reframing risk disclosure as "safety issues," needed information could be conveyed in a far more culturally acceptable manner.[21]

CBPR also offers an important potential opening for extending the gaze of our ethical review processes such that we examine and address risks and benefits for the community. In Toronto, Travers and Flicker[20] have pioneered in developing such guidelines, pointing out the importance of having us ask such questions as "Will the methods used be sensitive and appropriate to various communities?" "What training or capacity building opportunities will you build in?" and "How will you balance scientific rigor and accessibility?" The strong philosophical fit between questions such as these and CBPR's commitments to equitable partnership and community capacity building reflect another source of value added to urban health research through this approach.

### CBPR Can Improve Cultural Sensitivity and the Reliability and Validity of Measurement Tools Through High-Quality Community Participation in Designing and Testing Study Instruments

Particularly in survey research, community advisory boards (CABs) and other partnership structures can improve measurement instruments by making sure that questions are worded in ways that will elicit valid and reliable responses. In a study of urban grandparents raising grandchildren due to the crack cocaine epidemic, the author and her colleagues used validated instruments, such as those for depressive symptomatology. However, they also learned from CAB members how to word other questions about sensitive topics. Rather than asking a standard (and disliked) question about income, for example, the CAB encouraged us to rephrase the question as "How much money is available to help you in raising this child?" When this alternate wording was used, a wealth of detailed income data was obtained, which improved our understanding of the challenges faced by this population.[22]

### CBPR Can Uncover Lay Knowledge Critical to Enhancing Understanding of Sensitive Urban Health Problems

Through the cultural humility and partnership synergy involved in deeply valuing lay knowledge and working in partnership with community residents, CBPR can uncover hidden contributors to health and social problems. The high rates of HIV/AIDS in India and the often sensitive

*13*

*14*

*15*

nature of this subject among young men led the Deepak Charitable Trust to develop a research committee for a study in the industrial area of Nandesari, in Gujarat, comprised of several male village health workers and other young men from the area. Working closely with a medical anthropologist, the research committee planned the research, including developing a sampling plan and the phrasing of culturally sensitive questions. Their insider knowledge helped reveal that AIDS itself was not perceived as a major problem by the young men in this area. Instead, men who were engaging in high-risk behaviors wanted to find sex partners at least partly to avoid "thinning of the semen" and sexual dysfunction and fatigue, which were believed to be long-term consequences of masturbation and nocturnal emissions. These fears appeared to be contributing to high rates of unprotected intercourse with sex workers at the area's many truck stops and with other sex partners.[23] This insider knowledge both strengthened the research and led to subsequent interventions to help dispel such misinformation.

### By Increasing Community Trust and Ownership, CBPR Can Improve Recruitment and Retention Efforts

In a participatory epidemiology project on diabetes in an urban Aboriginal community in Melbourne, Australia, a marked increase in recruitment was experienced following the hiring of a community codirector and the changing of the project's name to one chosen by the local community.[24] Similarly, a 69% response rate achieved in a CBPR study of the health and working conditions of the largely immigrant hotel room cleaner population (many of them undocumented) in several of San Francisco's major tourist hotels was heavily attributed to the hiring and training of a core group of 25 room cleaners as key project staff. That high response rate, together with the high quality of data collected, made a substantial contribution when results later were presented and used to help negotiate a new contract.[25]

### CBPR Can Help Increase Accuracy and Cultural Sensitivity in the Interpretation of Findings

Even highly engaged community members of the research team may not wish to be involved in the labor-intensive data analysis phase of a research project,[26] nor do all methodological approaches lend themselves to such involvement. Yet when applicable and desired, community involvement in data analysis can make real contributions to our understanding of the themes and findings that emerge. In a US study of and with people with disabilities on the contentious topic of death with dignity legislation in their community, the author and an "insider/outsider" member of the research team met on alternate Saturdays with a subcommittee of the CAB to engage in joint data analysis. Using redacted transcripts, and applying lessons learned in qualitative data interpretation, the diverse CAB members came up with far richer codes and themes than outside researchers could have achieved alone.[27]

### CBPR Can Increase the Relevance of Intervention Approaches and Thus the Likelihood of Success

One of the strengths of CBPR is its commitment to action as part of the research process. But without strong community input, researchers not infrequently design interventions that are ill suited to the local context in which they are applied. In the Gujarat case study mentioned above, partnership with local community members helped in the design of culturally relevant interventions, such as street theater performed by locally recruited youth at *melas* (or fairs), and the dissemination of study findings through the 15 local credit and savings groups that often provided platforms for discussing reproductive health and related issues. Both these approaches provided critical means of information dissemination on this culturally and emotionally charged topic.[23]

## Ethical and Other Challenges in Community-Based Participatory Research

Engaging in urban health research with diverse community partners can indeed enrich both the quality and the outcomes of such studies. At the same time, CBPR is fraught with ethical and related challenges, several of which are now highlighted.

### "Community Driven" Issue Selection

A key feature of CBPR involves its commitment to ensuring that the research topic comes from the community. Yet many such projects "paradoxically ... would not occur without the initiative of someone outside the community who has the time, skill, and commitment, and who almost inevitably is a member of a privileged and educated group."[28] In such instances, outside researchers must pay serious attention to community understandings of what the real issue or topic of concern is.

In South Africa, for example, high rates of cervical cancer in the Black and Colored populations led Mosavel et al.[29] to propose an investigation of this problem. In response to community feedback, however, they quickly broadened their initial topic to "cervical health," a concept which "acknowledged the fact that women's health in South Africa extends well beyond the risk of developing cervical cancer, and includes HIV-AIDS and STDs, sexual violence, and multiple other social problems." In other instances, the outside researcher as an initiator of a potential CBPR project needs to determine whether the topic he or she has identified really is of concern to the local community—and whether outsider involvement is welcome. The Oakland, California–based Grandmother Caregiver Study mentioned above grew out of the interests of my colleague and me in studying the strengths of as well as the health and social problems faced by the growing number of urban African American grandmothers who were raising grandchildren in the context of a major drug epidemic. As privileged white women, however, we had to determine first whether this was a topic of local concern and, if so, whether there might be a role for us in working with the community to help study and address it. We began by enlisting the support of an older African American colleague with deep ties in the community, who engaged with us in a frank discussion with two prominent African American NGOs. It was only after getting their strong support for proceeding that we wrote a grant, with funds for these organizations, which in turn helped us pull together an outstanding CAB that was actively involved in many stages of the project.[21,26]

We were lucky in this case that a topic we as outsiders identified turned out to represent a deep concern in the local community. Yet not infrequently "the community" is in fact deeply divided over an issue. Indeed, as Yoshihama and Carr[30] have argued, "communities are not places that researchers enter but are instead a set of negotiations that inherently entail multiple and often conflicting interests." In such situations, outside researchers can play a useful role in helping community partners think through who "the community" in fact is in relation to a proposed project and the pros and cons of undertaking the project to begin with. The holding of town hall meetings and other forums may then be useful in helping achieve consensus on an issue that is truly of, by, and for the community, however it is defined.[26]

### Insider–Outsider Tensions

Urban health researchers in many parts of the world have written poignantly about the power dynamics and other sources of insider–outsider tensions and misunderstandings in CBPR and related partnership efforts. Ugalde[31] points out how in Latin America participants may be exploited as cheap sources of labor or may become alienated from their communities because of their participation. In her work with Native American and other marginalized groups in New Mexico, Wallerstein[32] further illustrates how even outsiders who pride ourselves on being trusted community friends and allies often fail to appreciate the extent of the power that is embedded in our own, often multiple sources of privilege, and how it can affect both process and outcomes in such research.

One major source of insider–outsider tensions involves the differential reward structures for partners in CBPR. For although a major aim of such research is to benefit the local community, the outside researchers typically stand to gain the most from such collaborations, bringing in grants, getting new publications, and so forth. The common expectation that community partners will work for little or no pay and the fact that receipt of compensation may take months if the funds are coming through a ministry of health or a university are also sources of under-standable resentment.[6,26]

To address these and other sources of insider–outsider tensions in work with indigenous communities in both urban and rural areas, research-ers in New Zealand,[33] Australia,[34] the United States,[35] and Canada[36] have worked with their community partners to develop ethical guidelines for their collaborative work, including protocols that address

1. negotiating with political and spiritual leaders in the community to obtain their input and their approval for the proposed research,
2. ensuring equitable benefits to participants (e.g., appropriate train-ing and hiring of community members) in return for their contribu-tions and resources,
3. developing agreements about the ownership and publication of find-ings, and the early review of findings by key community leaders.

Although such protocols cannot begin to address all of the conflicts that may arise in CBPR, they can play a critical role in helping pave the way for the continued dialogue and negotiation that must be an integral part of the process.

### Constraints on Community Involvement

Outside researchers committed to a CBPR approach not infrequently ex-press frustration at the difficulty moving from the goal of heavy commu-nity partner involvement in the research process to the reality. As Diaz and Simmons[37] found in their Reproductive Health Project in Brazil, de-spite a strong commitment to involving the most marginalized and vul-nerable classes (in this case, women who were users of the public sector services being studied), such individuals often "are least likely to be in a position to donate their time and energy." Further, and even when outside researchers are careful to provide child care and transportation, there are differential costs of participation by gender.[30]

Still another set of challenges may arise when community desires with respect to research design and methods clash with what outsider re-searchers consider to be "good science." In an oft-cited CBPR study with a local Mohawk community in Québec, Chataway[38] describes how com-munity members at first strongly objected to the idea of using a ques-tionnaire approach which they saw as "putting their thoughts in boxes." Through respectful listening on both sides, the value of such an approach was realized and a more qualitative methodology developed, through which community members would then be actively involved in helping analyze and interpret the quantitative findings that emerged. As such case studies illustrate, CBPR does not condone an abandonment of one's own scientific standards and knowledge base. But it does advocate a genuine co-learning process through which lay and professional ways of knowing both are valued and examined for what they can contribute.[26]

### *Dilemmas in the Sharing and Release of Findings*

A crucial step in CBPR involves returning data to the community and     29
enabling community leaders and participants to have an authentic role in
deciding how that data will be used. As Travers and Flicker[20] suggest,
ethical research review processes that ask questions such as "Are there
built-in mechanisms for how unflattering results will be dealt with?"
should be employed at the front end of our CBPR projects. In addition
to the formal IRB process they propose, which offers a critical next step
for the field, CBPR partners can look to a variety of formal or informal
research protocols and particularly to the detailed guidelines for health
promotion research developed by Green et al.,[4,39] which help partnerships decide in advance how potentially difficult issues concerning the
sharing and release of findings and other matters will be handled.

### *Challenges in the Action Dimensions of CBPR*

Numerous ethical challenges lastly may arise in relation to the critical     30
action component of CBPR. In some instances, community partners may
wish to move quickly into action, whereas academic and other outside research partners may want to "put the breaks on" until findings have been
published or other steps brought to fruition. In other cases, the nature
of funding (e.g., from a government body) may constrain action on the
policy level that is prohibited or discouraged by the funder. And in still
other instances, including the Brazilian Reproductive Health Project[37]
cited above, community members may not wish to be associated with a
CBPR project that appears connected to a broader political agenda.

Participation in the action phase of CBPR projects may sometimes     31
present risks to community participants, as when immigrant hotel room
cleaners in the San Francisco study took part in a Labor Day sit-in and in
some cases faced arrest.[25] And for both professionally trained researchers
and their community partners, actions that involve challenging powerful
corporate or other entrenched interests may have negative consequences
for those involved. At the same time, CBPR's fundamental commitment
to action and to redressing power imbalances makes this aspect of the
work a particularly important contributor to urban health improvement
through research.

## Conclusion

Difficult ethical challenges may confront urban health researchers who     32
engage in CBPR. Yet this approach can greatly enrich the quality of our
research, helping ensure that we address issues of genuine community
concern and use methods and approaches that are culturally sensitive
and that improve the validity and reliability of our findings. Moreover,
through its commitment to action as an integral part of the research
process, CBPR can help in translating findings as we work with commu-

nity partners to help address some of our most intractable urban health problems.

## Acknowledgement

Many current and former community and academic partners have con- 33 tributed to my understanding of the advantages and pitfalls of collaborative urban health research and I am deeply grateful. Particular thanks are extended to Nina Wallerstein, Kathleen M. Roe, Barbara Israel, Lawrence W. Green, and Ronald Labonte, who have greatly stimulated my own thinking and scholarship in this area. I am grateful to former students, Rima Shaw and Caroline Bell, as well as other individuals who have shared some of the cases drawn upon in this paper. My gratitude is extended to Claire Murphy for assistance with manuscript preparation.

## References

1. Minkler M, Wallerstein N. *Community Based Participatory Research for Health.* San Francisco, CA: Jossey-Bass; 2003.

2. Green LW, Mercer SL. Can public health researchers and agencies reconcile the push from funding bodies and the pull from communities? *Am J Public Health.* 2001;91:1926–1929.

3. Hall BL. From margins to center: the development and purpose of participatory action research. *Am Sociol.* 1992;23:15–28.

4. Green LW, George A, Daniel M, et al. *Study of Participatory Research in Health Promotion.* Ottawa, Ontario: Royal Society of Canada; 1995.

5. Community Health Scholars Program. *The Community Health Scholars Program: Stories of Impact.* Ann Arbor, MI; 2002.

6. Israel BA, Schulz AJ, Parker EA, Becker AB. Review of community-based research: assessing partnership approaches to improve public health. *Annu Rev Public Health.* 1998;19:173–202.

7. Lewin K. Action research and minority problems. *J Soc Issues.* 1946;2:34–46.

8. Brown LD, Tandon R. Ideology and political economy in inquiry: action research and participatory research. *J Appl Behav Sci.* 1983; 19:277–294.

9. Freire P. *Pedagogy of the Oppressed.* New York, NY: Seabury Press; 1970.

10. Fals-Borda O. The application of participatory action-research in Latin America. *Int Sociol.* 1987;2:329–347.

11. Maguire P. *Doing Participatory Research: A Feminist Approach.* Amherst, MA: Center for International Education; 1987.

12. Duran E, Duran B. *Native American Postcolonial Psychology.* Albany, NY: State University of New York Press; 1995.

13. McTaggart R. Sixteen tenets of participatory action research. In: Wadsworth Y, ed. *Everyday Evaluation on the Run.* Sydney, Australia: Allen & Unwin; 1997:79.

14. Lasker RD, Weiss ES, Miller R. Partnership synergy: a practical framework for studying and strengthening the collaborative advantage. *Milbank Q.* 2001;79:179–205, III–IV.

15. Tervalon M, Murray-Garcia J. Cultural humility vs. cultural competence: a critical distinction in defining physician training outcomes in medical education. *J Health Care Poor Underserved.* 1998; 9:117–125.

16. Cornwall A, Jewkes R. What is participatory research? *Soc Sci Med.* 1995;41:1667–1676.

17. Gebbie K, Rosenstock L, Hernandez LM. *Who Will Keep the Public Healthy? Educating Public Health Professionals for the 21st Century.* Washington, DC: Institute of Medicine; 2002.

18. O'Fallon LR, Dearry A. Community-based participatory research as a tool to advance environmental health sciences. *Environ Health Perspect.* 2002;110:155–159.

19. Loh P, Sugerman-Brozan J. Environmental justice organizing for environmental health: case study on asthma and diesel exhaust in Roxbury, Massachusetts. *Environ Health Perspect.* 2002;584: 110–124.

20. Travers R, Flicker S. Ethical issues in community based research. In: *Urban Health Community-Based Research Series Workshop.* Wellesley, MA; 2004.

21. Bell C. *One HEART (Health Education and Research in Tibet) Community Based Participatory Research on Top of the World.* Unpublished manuscript, University of California, Berkeley, School of Public Health; 2004.

22. Roe KM, Minkler M, Saunders FF. Combining research, advocacy and education: the methods of the Grandparent Caregiving Study. *Health Educ Q.* 1995;22:458–475.

23. Shah R. *A Retrospective Analysis of an HIV Prevention Program for Men in Gujarat, India.* Unpublished manuscript, University of California, Berkeley, School of Public Health; 2004.

24. Thompson SJ. Participatory epidemiology: methods of the Living With Diabetes Project. *Intl Q Community Health Educ.* 2000; 19:3–18.

25. Lee P, Krause N, Goetchius C. Participatory action research with hotel room cleaners: from collaborative study to the bargaining table. In: Minkler M, Wallerstein N, eds. *Community Based Participatory Research for Health.* San Francisco, CA: Jossey-Bass; 2003: 390–404.

26. Minkler M. Ethical challenges for the "outside" researcher in community based participatory research. *Health Educ Behav.* 2004;31: 684–701.

27. Fadem P, Minkler M, Perry M, et al. Ethical challenges in community based participatory research: a case study from the San Francisco Bay Area disability community. In: Minkler M, Wallerstein N, eds. *Community Based Participatory Research for Health.* San Francisco, CA: Jossey-Bass; 2003.

28. Reason P. *Participation in Human Inquiry.* London, UK: Sage; 1994.

29. Mosavel M, Simon C, van Stade D, Buchbinder M. *Community Based Participatory Research (CBPR) in South Africa: Engaging Multiple Constituents to Shape the Research Question.* Unpublished manuscript; 2004.

30. Yoshihama M, Carr ES. Community participation reconsidered: feminist participatory action research with Hmong women. *J Community Pract.* 2002;10:85–103.

31. Ugalde A. Ideological dimensions of community participation in Latin American health programs. *Soc Sci Med.* 1985;21:41–53.

32. Wallerstein N. Power between evaluator and community: research relationships within New Mexico's healthier communities. *Soc Sci Med.* 1999;49:39–53.

33. Cram F. Rangahau Maori: Tona tika, tona pono: The validity and integrity of Maori research. In: Tolich M, ed. *Research Ethics in Aotearoa New Zealand.* Longman, Auckland: Pearson Education; 2001:35–52.

34. Anderson I. Ethics and health research in Aboriginal communities. In: Daly J, ed. *Ethical Intersections: Health Research, Methods and Researcher Responsibility.* St. Leonards, New South Wales: Allen & Unwin; 1996:153–165.

35. Turning Point, National Association of County and City Health Officials. Thirteen policy principles for advancing collaborative activity among and between tribal communities and surrounding jurisdictions. In: Minkler M, Wallerstein N, eds. *Community Based Participatory Research for Health.* San Francisco, CA: Jossey-Bass; 2003:436, Appendix E.

36. Stuart CA. Care and concern: an ethical journey in participatory action research. *Can J Couns.* 1998;32:298–314.

37. Diaz M, Simmons R. When is research participatory? Reflections on a Reproductive Health Project in Brazil. *J Women's Health.* 1999;8:175–184.

38. Chataway CJ. Examination of the constraints of mutual inquiry in a participatory action research project. *J Soc Issues.* 1997;53: 747–765.

39. Green LW, George MA, Daniel M, et al. Guidelines for participatory research in health promotion. In: Minkler M, Wallerstein N, eds. *Community Based Participatory Research for Health.* San Francisco, CA: Jossey-Bass; 2003:419, Appendix C.

## A Practice Sequence: Analyzing the Appeals in a Researched Argument

1 Make a list of the major premises that inform Minkler's argument, and examine the evidence she uses to support them. To what extent do you find her evidence credible? Do you generally agree or disagree with the conclusions she draws? Be prepared to explain your responses to your class or peer group.

2 Note instances where Minkler appeals to ethos, pathos, and logos. How would you describe the ways she makes these three types of appeals? How does she present herself? What does she seem to assume? How does she help you understand the chain of reasoning by which she moves from premises to conclusion?

3 Working in groups of three or four, compose a letter to Minkler in which you take issue with her argument. This does not mean your group has to disagree with her entire argument, although of course you may. Rather, present your group's own contribution to the conversation in which she is participating. You may want to ask her to further explain one or more of her points, or suggest what she might be leaving out, or add your own take or evidence to her argument. As a group, you will have to agree on your focus. In the letter, include a summary of Minkler's argument or the part of it on which your group is focusing. Pay close attention to your own strategies for appealing to her—how you present yourselves, how you appeal to her values and emotions, and how you present your reasons for your own premises and conclusion.

## ANALYZING VISUAL RHETORIC: ADVERTISEMENTS

This section focuses on visual rhetoric; that is, how visual images communicate and create an argument designed to move a specific audience to think or act in a specific way. Every day we view films and television, read

FIGURE 8.2    Feeding America Advertisement

magazines, browse the Internet, and walk the aisles of stores where signage and packaging encourage us to buy products we may not need. Everywhere we are confronted by visual images that aim to persuade us.

To examine the strategies you can use to understand how images and texts convey meaning, we would like you to analyze a public service announcement (PSA) for Feeding America, distributed by the Ad Council, a nonprofit institution founded in 1942 for the purpose of bringing attention to social issues. The long horizontal advertisement shows a blurry group of children in the background playing street hockey. In the foreground to the right is a bright red alarm bell attached to a wooden telephone pole. The text reads, "School may be out for summer but lunch is always in session." A sentence in smaller text below it reads, "If your kids rely on free school meals, call your Feeding America member food bank or visit FeedingAmerica.org/SummerMeals." Examine the advertisement (Figure 8.2) and try to answer the questions below.

1.  Record what you think is the ad's overall message. What does the Ad Council want you to do or think about? What appeals does the ad seem to draw on most: appeals based on our cultural relationship to children (ethos), on the emotional reaction of potential viewers/readers (pathos), or on the ways text and image work together to convey an argument (logos)? Do you find that the appeals overlap and are difficult to tease out? Discuss with your classmates.

2.  Formulate what you think is the ad's argument, and point out specific details that seem to support it. Compare your ideas with those of your classmates. Do they differ significantly? Can you agree on what the argument is?

3.  As a class, test the assumption that the ad makes: When school is in session, policies are in place to insure federally funded schools feed

children in need. Less certain is the extent to which children in need receive sufficient nutrition during the summer when school is out.

Let's begin with the assumption that everything in an advertisement appears for a specific reason in a particular place to direct your attention in an exact sequence. The "economy of the genre," its constraints, dictate that the message come across quickly in a limited space.

## ■ Notice Where the Ad Appears

Analyzing an ad begins with noting where the ad appears. In this case, the Ad Council posted the Feeding America ad on billboards in a wide range of cities across the United States. An ad on a billboard will reach many people whose assumptions about hunger in America will vary, as will their levels of education, race, gender, and ethnicity. Therefore, it's worthwhile to consider how an ad about hunger will connect with such a wide range of possible viewers who will clearly interpret the ad in different ways and act upon its message differently. It is also worth considering the Ad Council's choice to post the ad in urban areas, as opposed to rural towns in the United States. Does the Ad Council assume there are greater hunger issues in urban areas? Is this a fair assumption? And equally important, can we assume that the people who should have access to the information on the ad will actually see it and get the support they require?

Imagine for a moment that the ad had appeared in an issue of *Time* magazine, which has the largest circulation of any news weekly in the United States. As a news magazine, not an entertainment magazine such as *People*, *Time* aims to reach a broad, educated, even affluent, readership interested in keeping up with current events. Knowing your readers' demographics is important because producers of ads always have a target audience in mind when they design and place an ad. They assume that the audience shares certain beliefs and values, and that the ad will move the audience to think and act in particular ways.

As you compare the effects of posting an ad on a billboard versus placing an ad in a widely-read magazine, you will inevitably discuss how a particular advertisement will travel from one medium to another. Certainly this Feeding America ad could appear in other weekly news magazines such as *Newsweek*. How effective would it be in a weekly tabloid? A fashion magazine? Or some place more public, such as in a bus terminal or waiting area in a public service office?

## ■ Identify What Draws Your Attention

The second step is to examine the main image or text that captures your attention. In the Feeding America ad, our attention is drawn to the central image of four children playing street hockey on a summer day. Their appearance suggests that they are healthy, happy, and well-cared for. The seemingly carefree scene of children playing with friends is familiar to most viewers.

## ■ Reflect on What Draws Your Attention

Then reflect on what draws your attention to this image or text. Is there something startling or shocking about the image or text, about the situation depicted? Something puzzling that holds your attention? Something about the use of color, the size of the image or text, or the font that catches your eye?

The Feeding America ad draws our attention to the center of the page where images of children, though blurred and in the background, catch our gaze. Evidently the ad was composed to emphasize the children's presence in our imagination. Who are these children? Where are they from? What are they like? Are they like us?

We are puzzled by the alarm bell in the foreground to the right. (In the original full-color ad, the alarm bell is bright red and demands our attention.) What does the designer want us to understand by juxtaposing children playing during the summer with an image that for many of us represents school? It's difficult to grasp the significance of these juxtapositions without further inquiry, in this case without looking at the text in the foreground of the ad. We assume that the designer expects readers to look there next, because of its size and the distinct way the letters are drawn — like children's chalk writing on the sidewalk. Finally, our eyes are drawn to the Feeding America logo. What is Feeding America and what values does it espouse?

## ■ Consider the Ethos of the Ad

The fourth step is to evaluate the ethos of the creator or sponsor of the ad. Ethos works in visual rhetoric just as it does in written rhetoric. Like writing, images are meant to convey how their composers or sponsors wish to be perceived. Thus, especially if you don't recognize a sponsor's logo or brand, it's important to ask: What is the sponsor's mission? What values does the sponsor embrace? What is the sponsor's track record? You need to know such things to determine how willing you are to believe what the ad promotes. In this case, you might find it helpful to go to the Feeding America Web site (listed in the ad) or to do a simple search on the Internet to see whether the organization has been discussed in blogs about hunger. Has Feeding America done significant work in the area of hunger? Is it a charity? If so, is it a reputable charity?

## ■ Analyze the Pathos in the Ad

The fifth step is to analyze the pathos in the ad — how images and text appeal to your emotions. An appeal to pathos is meant to evoke emotions such as empathy (which might prompt us to identify with an image) or out-rage (which might spur us to act in a certain way). In this case, the image of children playing outdoors with friends on a neighborhood street is likely to appeal to many of us, evoking as it does idyllic childhood memo-ries. Its nostalgic appeal invites us into an apparently calm, innocent world of peaceful play.

### ■ Understand the Logos of the Ad

The sixth and final step requires that we understand the entire composi-tion of the ad—what the cluster of images and text convey. What is the logic of the ad? How do the images and text work together to persuade us? What is the takeaway message?

The text in the Feeding America ad helps clarify the meaning of the central images of the children and the alarm bell. The alarm bell ties the image in the background to the foregrounded text—"School may be out for summer, but lunch is always in session." Food insecurity is a problem everyday for children in need. But where do these children get their food when school is not in session?

Hunger is not readily visible to most of us. Images of playfulness, even childlike innocence, can mask the deprivation that any of the people sur-rounding us may experience in their own lives. The text makes the appeal in the ad explicit. Those living in hunger are all around us.

The smaller text answers the question of where children in need can receive the nutrition they require. Children who are eligible for free lunch during the school year are also eligible to receive free meals during the summer.

Translating the discrete images and text into a coherent argument re-quires inductive reasoning, moving from specific pieces of evidence to a major premise. We would conclude that the argument in the ad goes some-thing like this:

1. Hunger in America is a reality in the lives of many children and families.

2. Food insecurity exists for children year round—whether school is in session or not.

3. Feeding America can help children and families gain access to the nu-trition they require.

There are other ways to formulate the argument, and we invite you to dis-cuss these alternatives as a class. Our main point, though, is that visual images make claims on us as viewers in much the same ways as any writ-ten text does. Having the tools of visual rhetoric can help you discern how images and text work together to produce an argument.

## Steps to Visual Analysis

**1** **Notice where the ad appears.** What is its target audience? To what extent does the placement of the ad in a magazine or newspaper or on a billboard determine the potential viewers of the ad?

**2** **Identify what draws your attention.** Where does your eye go? To an image, some text, some odd juxtaposition?

**3** **Reflect on what draws your attention.** Is there something startling or shocking about the image or text, about the situation depicted? Something puzzling that holds your attention? Something about the use of color, the size of the image or text, or the font that catches your eye?

**4** **Consider the ethos of the ad.** Evaluate the legitimacy, or ethos, of the ad's sponsor. For example, what do you know about the corporation or institution sponsoring the ad? To what extent do you share its values?

**5** **Analyze the pathos in the ad.** How do the images and text appeal to your emotions? What does the image or text make you feel or think about?

**6** **Understand the logos of the ad.** What is the logic of the ad? Taken together, what do the cluster of images and text convey? How are the different images and text related to the claim that the ad is making?

## A Practice Sequence: Analyzing the Rhetoric of an Advertisement

To practice these strategies, we would like you to choose and analyze the following ad for Microsoft (Figure 8.3). The photograph is of a girl in a robe and slippers sitting on her bed looking at a laptop. The text above the image reads, "You have your best ideas in the shower. Now you can work in the next room." Below the image the text reads, "Office and an online workspace from Microsoft let you work from almost anywhere inspiration finds you. It's easier than ever to store, view, and share all your important documents from pretty much anywhere you happen to be. That's because Microsoft Office works so easily with a free online workspace from Microsoft. So work no longer requires clothes, just Internet access. Buy it for your PC this holiday season." Text at the bottom of the ad reads, "Office2007.com Microsoft Office Real life tools." (Other advertisements for analysis appear on pages 244–246.)

First, evaluate the ethos that the ad tries to project. Do some research on the Internet to find out what Microsoft, which designs and manufactures computer software, represents as a company. In doing this research, write a brief summary of the company's values. Do you share those values? Are you confident in the company's ability to produce a good product that you want to use?

Second, reflect on and write about what the images and text make you feel about your own experiences working from home. In what ways do you identify with the message that the workplace extends into personal space?

Third, work in small groups to identify the logic of the narrative that the images and text convey. What do you see as the main premise of the ad? How did you arrive at your conclusion? Report your group's findings to the class. Be sure to present the evidence to support your claim.

**FIGURE 8.3    Microsoft Advertisement**

■ **Further Ads for Analysis: Figures 8.4–8.6.**

The "It's Only Another Beer"
Black and Tan

8 oz. pilsner lager
8 oz. stout lager
1 frosty mug
1 icy road
1 pick-up truck
1 10-hour day
1 tired worker
A few rounds with the guys

Mix ingredients.
Add 1 totalled vehicle.

Never underestimate 'just a few.'
Buzzed driving is drunk driving.

Ad Council

U.S. Department of Transportation

**FIGURE 8.4  Drinking and driving PSA**    The image is of a full beer glass representing a mixture of light and dark beers. The main text heading reads: The "It's Only Another Beer" Black and Tan. A list of "ingredients" follows: 8 oz. pilsner lager. 8 oz. stout lager. 1 frosty mug. 1 icy road. 1 pick-up truck. 1 10-hour day. 1 tired worker. A few rounds with the guys. Mix ingredients. Add 1 totalled vehicle. Never underestimate 'just a few.' Buzzed driving is drunk driving. Sponsors appear at the bottom of the page: AdCouncil.org and U.S. Department of Transportation.

**FIGURE 8.5   Exercise PSA**   The image is of a poster pinned to a wall in public space, with a representation of a bulging human waistline lying on the ground. The text on the poster reads: Lost   Spare Tire   Last seen before parking farther away from store and walking. Take a small step to get healthy. Get started at www.smallstep.gov. At the bottom of the poster the sponsors are listed: AdCouncil.org, www.smallstep.gov, and the U.S. Department of Health & Human Services.

**FIGURE 8.6   Health Care PSA**   A tongue depressor appears against a plain white background next to a headline that reads: open up and say anything. The text underneath it reads: want better health care? start asking more questions. to your doctor. to your pharmacist. to your nurse. what are the test results? what about side effects? don't fully understand your prescriptions? don't leave confused. because the most important question is the one you should have asked. go to *www.ahrq.gov/questionsaretheanswer* or call *1-800-931-AHRQ (2477)* for the 10 questions every patient should ask. questions are the answer. The sponsors appear at the bottom of the ad: Ad Council, the U.S. Department of Health & Human Services, and AHRQ Agency for Healthcare Research and Quality.

# 9

# From Introductions to Conclusions
*Drafting an Essay*

I n this chapter, we describe strategies for crafting introductions that set up your argument. We then describe the characteristics of well-formulated paragraphs that will help you build your argument. Finally, we provide you with some strategies for writing conclusions that reinforce what is new about your argument, what is at stake, and what readers should do with the knowledge you convey.

## DRAFTING INTRODUCTIONS

The introduction is where you set up your argument. It's where you identify a widely held assumption, challenge that assumption, and state your thesis. Writers use a number of strategies to set up their arguments. In this section we look at five of them:

- Moving from a general topic to a specific thesis (inverted-triangle introduction)
- Introducing the topic with a story (narrative introduction)
- Beginning with a question (interrogative introduction)
- Capturing readers' attention with something unexpected (paradoxical introduction)
- Identifying a gap in knowledge (minding-the-gap introduction)

Remember that an introduction need not be limited to a single paragraph. It may take several paragraphs to effectively set up your argument.

Keep in mind that you have to make these strategies your own. That is, we can suggest models, but you must make them work for your own argument. You must imagine your readers and what will engage them. What tone do you want to take? Playful? Serious? Formal? Urgent? The attitude you want to convey will depend on your purpose, your argument, and the needs of your audience.

## ■ The Inverted-Triangle Introduction

An **inverted-triangle introduction**, like an upside-down triangle, is broad at the top and pointed at the base. It begins with a general statement of the topic and then narrows its focus, ending with the point of the paragraph (and the triangle), the writer's thesis. We can see this strategy at work in the following introduction from a student's essay. The student writer (1) begins with a broad description of the problem she will address, (2) then focuses on a set of widely held but troublesome assumptions, and (3) finally, responding to what she sees as a pervasive problem, presents her thesis.

*The student begins with a general set of assumptions about education that she believes people readily accept.*

In today's world, many believe that education's sole purpose is to communicate information for students to store and draw on as necessary. By storing this information, students hope to perform well on tests. Good test scores assure good grades. Good grades eventually lead to acceptances into good colleges, which ultimately guarantee good jobs. Many teachers and students, convinced that education exists as a tool to secure good jobs,

*She then cites author bell hooks, to identify an approach that makes use of these assumptions—the "banking system" of education, a term hooks borrows from educator Paulo Freire.*

rely on the *banking system*. In her essay "Teaching to Transgress," bell hooks defines the *banking system* as an "approach to learning that is rooted in the notion that all students need to do is consume information fed to them by a professor and be able to memorize and store it" (185). Through the banking system, students focus solely on facts, missing the important themes and life

*The student then points to the banking system as the problem. This sets up her thesis about the "true purpose" of education.*

lessons available in classes and school materials. The banking system misdirects the fundamental goals of education. Education's true purpose is to prepare students for the real world by allowing them access to pertinent life knowledge available in their studies. Education should then entice students to apply this pertinent life knowledge to daily life struggles through praxis. In addition to her definition of the banking system, hooks offers the idea of praxis from the work of Paulo Freire. When incorporated into education, *praxis*, or "action and reflection upon the world in order to change it" (185), offers an advantageous educational tool that enhances the true purpose of education and overcomes the banking system.

The strategy of writing an introduction as an inverted triangle entails first identifying an idea, an argument, or a concept that people appear to accept as true; next, pointing out the problems with that idea, argument, or concept; and then, in a few sentences, setting out a thesis—how those problems can be resolved.

## ■ The Narrative Introduction

Opening with a short **narrative**, or story, is a strategy many writers use successfully to draw readers into a topic. A narrative introduction relates a sequence of events and can be especially effective if you think you need to coax indifferent or reluctant readers into taking an interest in the topic. Of course, a narrative introduction delays the declaration of your argument, so it's wise to choose a short story that clearly connects to your argument, and get to the thesis as quickly as possible (within a few paragraphs) before your readers start wondering "What's the point of this story?"

Notice how the student writer uses a narrative introduction to her argument in her essay titled "Throwing a Punch at Gender Roles: How Women's Boxing Empowers Women."

*The student's entire first paragraph is a narrative that takes us into the world of women's boxing and foreshadows her thesis.*

Glancing at my watch, I ran into the gym, noting to myself that being late to the first day of boxing practice was not the right way to make a good first impression. I flew down the stairs into the basement, to the room the boxers have lovingly dubbed "The Pit." What greeted me when I got there was more than I could ever have imagined. Picture a room filled with boxing gloves of all sizes covering an entire wall, a mirror covering another, a boxing ring in a corner, and an awesome collection of framed newspaper and magazine articles chronicling the boxers whose pictures were hanging on every wall. Now picture that room with seventy-plus girls on the floor doing push-ups, sweat dripping down their faces. I was immediately struck by the discipline this sport would take from me, but I had no idea I would take so much more from it.

*With her narrative as a backdrop, the student identifies a problem, using the transition word yet to mark her challenge to the conditions she observes in the university's women's boxing program.*

The university offers the only nonmilitary-based college-level women's boxing program in America, and it also offers women the chance to push their physical limits in a regulated environment. Yet the program is plagued with disappointments. I have experienced for myself the stereotypes female boxers face and have dealt with the harsh reality that boxing is still widely recognized as only a men's sport. This paper will show that the women's boxing program at Notre Dame serves as a much-needed outlet for females to come face-to-face with aspects of themselves they

*The writer then states her thesis (what her paper "will show"): Despite the problems of stereotyping, women's boxing offers women significant opportunities for growth.*

would not typically get a chance to explore. It will also examine how viewing this sport as a positive opportunity for women at ND indicates that there is growing hope that very soon more activities similar to women's boxing may be better received by society in general. I will accomplish these goals by analyzing scholarly journals, old *Observer* [the school newspaper] articles, and survey questions answered by the captains of the 2003 women's boxing team of ND.

The student writer uses a visually descriptive narrative to introduce us to the world of women's college boxing; then, in the second paragraph, she steers us toward the purpose of the paper and the methods she will use to develop her argument about what women's boxing offers to young women and to the changing world of sports.

## ■ The Interrogative Introduction

An **interrogative introduction** invites readers into the conversation of your essay by asking one or more questions, which the essay goes on to answer. You want to think of a question that will pique your readers' interest, enticing them to read on to discover how your insights shed light on the issue. Notice the question Daphne Spain, a professor of urban and environmental planning, uses to open her essay "Spatial Segregation and Gender Stratification in the Workplace."

*Spain sets up her argument by asking a question and then tentatively answering it with a reference to a published study.*

*In the third sentence, she states her thesis — that men and women have very little contact in the workplace.*

*Finally, she outlines the effects that this lack of contact has on women.*

To what extent do women and men who work in different occupations also work in different space? Baran and Teegarden propose that occupational segregation in the insurance industry is "tantamount to spatial segregation by gender" since managers are overwhelmingly male and clerical staff are predominantly female. This essay examines the spatial conditions of women's work and men's work and proposes that working women and men come into daily contact with one another very infrequently. Further, women's jobs can be classified as "open floor," but men's jobs are more likely to be "closed door." That is, women work in a more public environment with less control of their space than men. This lack of spatial control both reflects and contributes to women's lower occupational status by limiting opportunities for the transfer of knowledge from men to women.

By the end of this introductory paragraph, Spain has explained some of the terms she will use in her essay (*open floor* and *closed door*) and has offered in her final sentence a clear statement of her thesis.

In "Harry Potter and the Technology of Magic," literature scholar Elizabeth Teare begins by contextualizing the Harry Potter publishing phenomenon. Then she raises a question about what is fueling this success story.

*In her first four sentences, Teare describes something she is curious about and she hopes readers will be curious about—the growing popularity of the Harry Potter books.*

The July/August 2001 issue of *Book* lists J. K. Rowling as one of the ten most influential people in publishing. She shares space on this list with John Grisham and Oprah Winfrey, along with less famous but equally powerful insiders in the book industry. What these industry leaders have in common is an almost magical power to make books succeed in the marketplace, and this magic, in addition to that performed with wands, Rowling's novels appear to practice. Opening weekend sales charted like those of a blockbuster movie (not to mention the blockbuster movie itself), the reconstruction of the venerable *New York Times* bestseller lists, the creation of a new nation's worth of web sites in the territory of cyberspace, and of course the legendary inspiration of tens of millions of child readers—the Harry Potter books have transformed both the technologies of reading and the way we

*In the fifth sentence, Teare asks the question she will try to answer in the rest of the essay.*

understand those technologies. What is it that makes these books—about a lonely boy whose first act on learning he is a wizard is to go shopping for a wand—not only an international phenomenon among children and parents and teachers but also a topic of compelling interest to literary, social,

*Finally, in the last sentence, Teare offers a partial answer to her question— her thesis.*

and cultural critics? I will argue that the stories the books tell, as well as the stories we're telling about them, enact both our fantasies and our fears of children's literature and publishing in the context of twenty-first-century commercial and technological culture.

In the final two sentences of the introduction, Teare raises her question about the root of this "international phenomenon" and then offers her thesis. By the end of the opening paragraph, then, the reader knows exactly what question is driving Teare's essay and the answer she proposes to explain throughout the essay.

## ■ The Paradoxical Introduction

A **paradoxical introduction** appeals to readers' curiosity by pointing out an aspect of the topic that runs counter to their expectations. Just as an interrogative introduction draws readers in by asking a question, a paradoxical introduction draws readers in by saying, in effect, "Here's something completely surprising and unlikely about this issue, but my essay will go on to show you how it is true." In this passage from "'Holding Back': Negotiating a Glass Ceiling on Women's Muscular Strength," sociologist

Shari L. Dworkin points to a paradox in our commonsense understanding of bodies as the product of biology, not culture.

*In the first sentence, Dworkin quotes from a study to identify the thinking that she is going to challenge.*

*Notice how Dworkin signals her own position "However" relative to commonly held assumptions.*

*Dworkin ends by stating her thesis, noting a paradox that will surprise readers.*

Current work in gender studies points to how "when examined closely, much of what we take for granted about gender and its causes and effects either does not hold up, or can be explained differently." These arguments become especially contentious when confronting nature/culture debates on gendered *bodies*. After all, "common sense" frequently tells us that flesh and blood bodies are about biology. However, bodies are also shaped and constrained through cumulative social practices, structures of opportunity, wider cultural meanings, and more. Paradoxically, then, when we think that we are "really seeing" naturally sexed bodies, perhaps we are seeing the effect of internalizing gender ideologies—carrying out social practices—and this constructs our vision of "sexed" bodies.

Dworkin's strategy in the first three sentences is to describe common practice, the understanding that bodies are biological. Then, in the sentences beginning "However" and "Paradoxically," she advances the surprising idea that our bodies—not just the clothes we wear, for example—carry cultural gender markers. Her essay then goes on to examine women's weight lifting and the complex motives driving many women to create a body that is perceived as muscular but not masculine.

## ■ The Minding-the-Gap Introduction

This type of introduction takes its name from the British train system, the voice on the loudspeaker that intones "Mind the gap!" at every stop, to call riders' attention to the gap between the train car and the platform. In a **minding-the-gap introduction**, a writer calls readers' attention to a gap in the research on an issue and then uses the rest of the essay to fill in the "gap." A minding-the-gap introduction says, in effect, "Wait a minute. There's something missing from this conversation, and my research and ideas will fill in this gap."

For example, in the introductory paragraphs to their book *Men's Lives*, Michael S. Kimmel and Michael A. Messner explain how the book is different from other books that discuss men's lives, and how it serves a different purpose.

*The authors begin with an assumption and then challenge it. A transition word (but) signals the challenge.*

This is a book about men. But, unlike other books about men, which line countless library shelves, this is a book about men as men. It is a book in which men's experiences are not taken for granted as we explore the "real" and significant accomplishments of men, but a book in which those experiences are treated as significant and important in themselves.

*The authors follow with a question that provokes readers' interest and points to the gap they summarize in the last sentence.*

But what does it mean to examine men "as men"? Most courses in a college curriculum are about men, aren't they? But these courses routinely deal with men only in their public roles, so we come to know and understand men as scientists, politicians, military figures, writers, and philosophers. Rarely, if ever, are men understood through the prism of gender.

Kimmel and Messner use these opening paragraphs to highlight both what they find problematic about the existing literature on men and to introduce readers to their own approach.

## Steps to Drafting Introductions: Five Strategies

1 **Use an inverted triangle.** Begin with a broad situation, concept, or idea, and narrow the focus to your thesis.

2 **Begin with a narrative.** Capture readers' imagination and interest with a story that sets the stage for your argument.

3 **Ask a question that you will answer.** Provoke readers' interest with a question, and then use your thesis to answer the question.

4 **Present a paradox.** Begin with an assumption that readers accept as true, and formulate a thesis that not only challenges that assumption but may very well seem paradoxical.

5 **Mind the gap.** Identify what readers know and then what they don't know (or what you believe they need to know).

## A Practice Sequence: Drafting an Introduction

1 Write or rewrite your introduction (which, as you've seen, may involve more than one paragraph), using one of the strategies described above. Then share your introduction with one of your peers and ask the following questions:

- To what extent did the strategy compel you to want to read further?
- To what extent is my thesis clear?
- How effectively do I draw a distinction between what I believe others assume to be true and my own approach?
- Is there another way that I might have made my introduction more compelling?

After listening to the responses, try a second strategy and then ask your peer which introduction is more effective.

**2** If you do not have your own introduction to work on, revise the introduction below from one of our students' essays, combining two of the strategies we describe above.

> News correspondent Pauline Frederick once commented, "When a man gets up to speak people listen then look. When a woman gets up, people look; then, if they like what they see, they listen." Ironically, the harsh reality of this statement is given life by the ongoing controversy over America's most recognizable and sometimes notorious toy, Barbie. Celebrating her 40th birthday this year, Barbie has become this nation's most beleaguered soldier (a woman no less) of idolatry who has been to the front lines and back more times than the average "Joe." This doll, a piece of plastic, a toy, incurs both criticism and praise spanning both ends of the ideological spectrum. Barbie's curvaceous and basically unrealistic body piques the ire of both liberals and conservatives, each contending that Barbie stands for the distinct view of the other. One hundred and eighty degrees south, others praise Barbie's (curves and all) ability to unlock youthful imagination and potential. M. G. Lord explains Barbie best: "To study Barbie, one sometimes has to hold seemingly contradictory ideas in one's head at the same time. . . . The doll functions like a Rorschach test: people project wildly dissimilar and often opposing meanings on it. . . . And her meaning, like her face, has not been static over time." In spite of the extreme polarity, a sole unconscious consensus manifests itself about Barbie. Barbie is "the icon" of womanhood and the twentieth century. She is the American dream. Barbie is "us." The question is always the same: What message does Barbie send? Barbie is a toy. She is the image of what we see.

## DEVELOPING PARAGRAPHS

In your introduction, you set forth your thesis. Then, in subsequent paragraphs, you have to develop your argument. Remember our metaphor: If your thesis, or main claim, is the skewer that runs through each paragraph in your essay, then these paragraphs are the "meat" of your argument. The paragraphs that follow your introduction carry the burden of evidence in your argument. After all, a claim cannot stand on its own without supporting evidence. Generally speaking, each paragraph should include a topic sentence that brings the main idea of the paragraph into focus, be unified around the main idea of the topic sentence, and adequately develop the idea. At the same time, a paragraph does not stand on its own; as part of your overall argument, it can refer to what you've said earlier, gesture toward where you are heading, and connect to the larger conversation to which you are contributing.

We now ask you to read an excerpt from "Reinventing 'America': Call for a New National Identity," by Elizabeth Martínez, and answer some

questions about how you think the author develops her argument, paragraph by paragraph. Then we discuss her work in the context of the three
key elements of paragraphs: *topic sentences*, *unity*, and *adequate development*. As you read, pay attention to how, sentence by sentence, Martínez
develops her paragraphs. We also ask that you consider how she makes
her argument provocative, impassioned, and urgent for her audience.

ELIZABETH MARTÍNEZ

## *From* Reinventing "America": Call for a New National Identity

Elizabeth Martínez is a Chicana activist who since 1960 has worked in and
documented different movements for change, including the civil rights,
women's, and Chicano movements. She is the author of six books and numerous articles. Her best-known work is *500 Years of Chicano History in
Pictures* (1991), which became the basis of a two-part video she scripted
and codirected. Her latest book is *De Colores Means All of Us: Latina Views
for a Multi-Colored Century* (1998). In "Reinventing 'America,'" Martínez
argues that Americans' willingness to accept a "myth" as "the basis for [the]
nation's self-defined identity" has brought the country to a crisis.

■ ■ ■

For some fifteen years, starting in 1940, 85 percent of all U.S. elemen-      1
tary schools used the Dick and Jane series to teach children how to
read. The series starred Dick, Jane, their white middle-class parents,
their dog Spot, and their life together in a home with a white picket
fence.

"Look, Jane, look! See Spot run!" chirped the two kids. It was a house      2
full of glorious family values, where Mom cooked while Daddy went to
work in a suit and mowed the lawn on weekends. The Dick and Jane
books also taught that you should do your job and help others. All this
affirmed an equation of middle-class whiteness with virtue.

In the mid-1990s, museums, libraries, and eighty Public Broadcast-      3
ing Service (PBS) stations across the country had exhibits and programs
commemorating the series. At one museum, an attendant commented,
"When you hear someone crying, you know they are looking at the Dick
and Jane books." It seems nostalgia runs rampant among many Euro-
Americans: a nostalgia for the days of unchallenged White Supremacy—both moral and material—when life was "simple."

We've seen that nostalgia before in the nation's history. But today it sig-      4
nifies a problem reaching a new intensity. It suggests a national identity
crisis that promises to bring in its wake an unprecedented nervous breakdown for the dominant society's psyche.

Nowhere is this more apparent than in California, which has long been      5
on the cutting edge of the nation's present and future reality. Warning

sirens have sounded repeatedly in the 1990s, such as the fierce battle over new history textbooks for public schools, Proposition 187's ugly denial of human rights to immigrants, the 1996 assault on affirmative action that culminated in Proposition 209, and the 1997 move to abolish bilingual education. Attempts to copycat these reactionary measures have been seen in other states.

The attack on affirmative action isn't really about affirmative action. 6 Essentially it is another tactic in today's war on the gains of the 1960s, a tactic rooted in Anglo resentment and fear. A major source of that fear: the fact that California will almost surely have a majority of people of color in 20 to 30 years at most, with the nation as a whole not far behind.

Check out the February 3, 1992, issue of *Sports Illustrated* with its 7 double-spread ad for *Time* magazine. The ad showed hundreds of new-born babies in their hospital cribs, all of them Black or brown except for a rare white face here and there. The headline says, "Hey, whitey! It's your turn at the back of the bus!" The ad then tells you, read *Time* magazine to keep up with today's hot issues. That manipulative image could have been published today; its implication of shifting power appears to be the recurrent nightmare of too many potential Anglo allies.

Euro-American anxiety often focuses on the sense of a vanishing na- 8 tional identity. Behind the attacks on immigrants, affirmative action, and multiculturalism, behind the demand for "English Only" laws and the rejection of bilingual education, lies the question: with all these new people, languages, and cultures, what will it mean to be an American? If that question once seemed, to many people, to have an obvious, universally applicable answer, today new definitions must be found. But too often Americans, with supposed scholars in the lead, refuse to face that need and instead nurse a nostalgia for some bygone clarity. They remain trapped in denial.

An array of such ostriches, heads in the sand, began flapping their 9 feathers noisily with the publication of Allan Bloom's 1987 best-selling book, *The Closing of the American Mind*. Bloom bemoaned the decline of our "common values" as a society, meaning the decline of Euro-American cultural centricity (shall we just call it cultural imperialism?). Since then we have seen constant sniping at "diversity" goals across the land. The assault has often focused on how U.S. history is taught. And with reason, for this country's identity rests on a particular narrative about the historical origins of the United States as a nation.

## The Great White Origin Myth

Every society has an origin narrative that explains that society to itself 10 and the world with a set of stories and symbols. The origin myth, as scholar-activist Roxanne Dunbar Ortiz has termed it, defines how a society understands its place in the world and its history. The myth provides the basis for a nation's self-defined identity. Most origin narratives can be called myths because they usually present only the most flattering view of a nation's history; they are not distinguished by honesty.

Ours begins with Columbus "discovering" a hemisphere where some 80 million people already lived but didn't really count (in what became the United States, they were just buffalo-chasing "savages" with no grasp of real estate values and therefore doomed to perish). It continues with the brave Pilgrims, a revolution by independence-loving colonists against a decadent English aristocracy, and the birth of an energetic young republic that promised democracy and equality (that is, to white male landowners). In the 1840s, the new nation expanded its size by almost one-third, thanks to a victory over that backward land of little brown people called Mexico. Such has been the basic account of how the nation called the United States of America came into being as presently configured.

The myth's omissions are grotesque. It ignores three major pillars of our nationhood: genocide, enslavement, and imperialist expansion (such nasty words, who wants to hear them?—but that's the problem). The massive extermination of indigenous peoples provided our land base; the enslavement of African labor made our economic growth possible; and the seizure of half of Mexico by war (or threat of renewed war) extended this nation's boundaries north to the Pacific and south to the Rio Grande. Such are the foundation stones of the United States, within an economic system that made this country the first in world history to be born capitalist. . . .

## Racism as Linchpin of the U.S. National Identity

A crucial embellishment of the origin myth and key element of the national identity has been the myth of the frontier, analyzed in Richard Slotkin's *Gunfighter Nation*, the last volume of a fascinating trilogy. He describes Theodore Roosevelt's belief that the West was won thanks to American arms, "the means by which progress and nationality will be achieved." That success, Roosevelt continued, "depends on the heroism of men who impose on the course of events the latent virtues of their 'race.'" Roosevelt saw conflict on the frontier producing a series of virile "fighters and breeders" who would eventually generate a new leadership class. Militarism thus went hand in hand with the racialization of history's protagonists. . . .

The frontier myth embodied the nineteenth-century concept of Manifest Destiny, a doctrine that served to justify expansionist violence by means of intrinsic racial superiority. Manifest Destiny was Yankee conquest as the inevitable result of a confrontation between enterprise and progress (white) versus passivity and backwardness (Indian, Mexican).

*11*

*12*

*13*

*14*

"Manifest" meant "God-given," and the whole doctrine is profoundly rooted in religious conviction going back to the earliest colonial times. In his short, powerful book *Manifest Destiny: American Expansion and the Empire of Right*, Professor Anders Stephanson tells how the Puritans reinvented the Jewish notion of chosenness and applied it to this hemisphere so that territorial expansion became God's will. . . .

## Manifest Destiny Dies Hard

The concept of Manifest Destiny, with its assertion of racial superiority    15
sustained by military power, has defined U.S. identity for 150 years. . . .

Today's origin myth and the resulting concept of national identity make    16
for an intellectual prison where it is dangerous to ask big questions about this society's superiority. When otherwise decent people are trapped in such a powerful desire not to feel guilty, self-deception becomes unavoidable. To cease our present falsification of collective memory should, and could, open the doors of that prison. When together we cease equating whiteness with Americanness, a new day can dawn. As David Roediger, the social historian, has said, "[Whiteness] is the empty and therefore terrifying attempt to build an identity on what one isn't, and on whom one can hold back."

Redefining the U.S. origin narrative, and with it this country's national    17
identity, could prove liberating for our collective psyche. It does not mean Euro-Americans should wallow individually in guilt. It does mean accepting collective responsibility to deal with the implications of our real origin. A few apologies, for example, might be a step in the right direction. In 1997, the idea was floated in Congress to apologize for slavery; it encountered opposition from all sides. But to reject the notion because corrective action, not an apology, is needed misses the point. Having defined itself as the all-time best country in the world, the United States fiercely denies the need to make a serious official apology for anything. . . . To press for any serious, official apology does imply a new origin narrative, a new self-image, an ideological sea-change.

Accepting the implications of a different narrative could also shed light    18
on today's struggles. In the affirmative-action struggle, for example, opponents have said that that policy is no longer needed because racism ended with the Civil Rights Movement. But if we look at slavery as a fundamental pillar of this nation, going back centuries, it becomes obvious that racism could not have been ended by 30 years of mild reforms. If we see how the myth of the frontier idealized the white male adventurer as the central hero of national history, with the woman as sunbonneted helpmate, then we might better understand the dehumanized ways in which women have continued to be treated. A more truthful origin narrative could also help break down divisions among peoples of color by revealing common experiences and histories of cooperation.

**Reading as a Writer**

1. To what extent does the narrative Martínez begins with make you want to read further?
2. How does she connect this narrative to the rest of her argument?
3. How does she use repetition to create unity in her essay?
4. What assumptions does Martínez challenge?
5. How does she use questions to engage her readers?

## ■ Use Topic Sentences to Focus Your Paragraphs

The **topic sentence** states the main point of a paragraph. It should

- provide a partial answer to the question motivating the writer.
- act as an extension of the writer's thesis and the question motivating the writer's argument.
- serve as a guidepost, telling readers what the paragraph is about.
- help create unity and coherence both within the paragraph and within the essay.

Elizabeth Martínez begins by describing how elementary schools in the 1940s and 1950s used the Dick and Jane series not only to teach reading but also to foster a particular set of values—values that she believes do not serve all children enrolled in America's schools. In paragraph 4, she states her thesis, explaining that nostalgia in the United States has created "a national identity crisis that promises to bring in its wake an unprecedented nervous breakdown for the dominant society's psyche." This is a point that builds on an observation she makes in paragraph 3: "It seems nostalgia runs rampant among many Euro-Americans: a nostalgia for the days of unchallenged White Supremacy—both moral and material—when life was 'simple.'" Martínez often returns to this notion of nostalgia for a past that seems "simple" to explain what she sees as an impending crisis.

Consider the first sentence of paragraph 5 as a topic sentence. With Martínez's key points in mind, notice how she uses the sentence to make her thesis more specific. Notice too, how she ties in the crisis and breakdown she alludes to in paragraph 4. Essentially, Martínez tells her readers that they can see these problems at play in California, an indicator of "the nation's present and future reality."

> *Nowhere is this more apparent than in California, which has long been on the cutting edge of the nation's present and future reality.* Warning sirens have sounded repeatedly in the 1990s, such as the fierce battle over new history textbooks for public schools, Proposition 187's ugly denial of human rights to immigrants, the 1996 assault on affirmative action that culminated in Proposition 209, and the 1997 move to abolish bilingual education. *Attempts to copycat these reactionary measures have been seen in other states.*

The final sentence of paragraph 5 sets up the remainder of the essay.

As readers, we expect each subsequent paragraph to respond in some way to the issue Martínez has raised. She meets that expectation by formulating a topic sentence that appears at the beginning of the paragraph. The topic sentence is what helps create unity and coherence in the essay.

## ■ Create Unity in Your Paragraphs

Each paragraph in an essay should focus on the subject suggested by the topic sentence. If a paragraph begins with one focus or major point of discussion, it should not end with another. Several strategies can contribute to the unity of each paragraph.

*Use details that follow logically from your topic sentence and maintain a single focus — a focus that is clearly an extension of your thesis.*   For example, in paragraph 5, Martínez's topic sentence ("Nowhere is this more apparent than in California, which has long been on the cutting edge of the nation's present and future reality") helps to create unity because it refers back to her thesis (*this* refers to the "national identity crisis" mentioned in paragraph 4) and limits the focus of what she includes in the paragraph to "the fierce battle over new history textbooks" and recent pieces of legislation in California that follow directly from and support the claim of the topic sentence.

*Repeat key words to guide your readers.*   A second strategy for creating unity is to repeat (or use synonyms for) key words within a given paragraph. You can see this at work in paragraph 12 (notice the words we've underscored), where Martínez explains that America's origin narrative omits significant details:

> The myth's omissions are grotesque. It ignores three major pillars of our nationhood: genocide, enslavement, and imperialist expansion (such nasty words, who wants to hear them?—but that's the problem). The massive extermination of indigenous peoples provided our land base; the enslavement of African labor made our economic growth possible; and the seizure of half of Mexico by war (or threat of renewed war) extended this nation's boundaries north to the Pacific and south to the Rio Grande. Such are the foundation stones of the United States, within an economic system that made this country the first in world history to be born capitalist. . . .

Specifically, Martínez tells us that the origin narrative ignores "three major pillars of our nationhood: genocide, enslavement, and imperialist expansion." She then substitutes *extermination* for "genocide," repeats *enslavement*, and substitutes *seizure* for "imperialist expansion." By connecting words in a paragraph, as Martínez does here, you help readers understand that the details you provide are all relevant to the point you want to make.

*Use transition words to link ideas from different sentences.*   A third strategy for creating unity within paragraphs is to establish a clear relationship among different ideas by using **transition words** or phrases. Transition words or phrases signal to your readers the direction your ideas are taking. Table 9.1 lists common transition words and phrases grouped by function—that is, for adding a new idea, presenting a contrasting idea, or drawing a conclusion about an idea.

Martínez uses transition words and phrases throughout the excerpt here. In several places, she uses the word *but* to make a contrast—to draw a distinction between an idea that many people accept as true and an alternative idea that she wants to pursue. Notice in paragraph 17 how she signals the importance of an official apology for slavery—and by implication genocide and the seizure of land from Mexico:

> . . . A few apologies, for example, might be a step in the right direction. In 1997, the idea was floated in Congress to apologize for slavery; it encountered opposition from all sides. <u>But</u> to reject the notion because corrective action, not an apology, is needed misses the point. Having defined itself as the all-time best country in the world, the United States fiercely denies the need to make a serious official apology for anything. . . . To press for any serious, official apology does imply a new origin narrative, a new self-image, an ideological sea-change.

Similarly, in the last paragraph, Martínez counters the argument that affirmative action is not necessary because racism no longer exists:

> . . . In the affirmative-action struggle, for example, opponents have said that that policy is no longer needed because racism ended with the Civil Rights Movement. <u>But</u> if we look at slavery as a fundamental pillar of this nation, going back centuries, it becomes obvious that racism could not have been ended by 30 years of mild reforms. . . .

There are a number of ways to rephrase what Martínez is saying in paragraph 18. We could substitute *however* for "but." Or we could combine the two sentences into one to point to the relationship between the two competing ideas: *Although some people oppose affirmative action, believing that racism no longer exists, I would argue that racism remains a fundamental pillar of this nation.* Or we could pull together Martínez's different points to draw a logical conclusion using a transition word like *therefore.* Martínez observes that our country is in crisis as a result of increased immigration. *Therefore, we need to reassess our conceptions of national*

TABLE 9.1    Common Transition Words and Phrases

| Adding an Idea | Presenting a Contrasting Idea | Drawing a Logical Conclusion |
| --- | --- | --- |
| also, and, further, more-over, in addition to, in support of, similarly | although, alternatively, as an alternative, but, by way of contrast, despite, even though, however, in contrast to, neverthe-less, nonetheless, rather than, yet | as a result, because of, consequently, finally, in sum, in the end, subse-quently, therefore, thus |

*identity to account for the diversity that increased immigration has created.* We can substitute any of the transition words in Table 9.1 for drawing a logical conclusion.

The list of transition words and phrases in Table 9.1 is hardly exhaustive, but it gives you a sense of the ways to connect ideas so that readers understand how your ideas are related. Are they similar ideas? Do they build on or support one another? Are you challenging accepted ideas? Or are you drawing a logical connection from a number of different ideas?

## ■ Use Critical Strategies to Develop Your Paragraphs

To develop a paragraph, you can use a range of strategies, depending on what you want to accomplish and what you believe your readers will need in order to be persuaded by what you argue. Among these strategies are using examples and illustrations; citing data (facts, statistics, evidence, details); analyzing texts; telling a story or an anecdote; defining terms; making comparisons; and examining causes and evaluating consequences.

*Use examples and illustrations.*    Examples make abstract ideas concrete through illustration. Using examples is probably the most common way to develop a piece of writing. Of course, Martínez's essay is full of examples. In fact, she begins with an example of a series of books—the Dick and Jane books—to show how a generation of schoolchildren were exposed to white middle-class values. She also uses examples in paragraph 5, where she lists several pieces of legislation (Propositions 187 and 209) to develop the claim in her topic sentence.

*Cite data.*    **Data** are factual pieces of information. They function in an essay as the bases of propositions. In the first few paragraphs of the excerpt, Martínez cites statistics ("85 percent of all U.S. elementary schools used the Dick and Jane series to teach children how to read") and facts ("In the mid-1990s, museums, libraries, and eighty Public Broadcasting Service . . . stations across the country had exhibits and programs commemorating the series") to back up her claim about the popularity of the Dick and Jane series and the nostalgia the books evoke.

*Analyze texts.*    Analysis is the process of breaking something down into its elements to understand how they work together. When you analyze a text, you point out parts of the text that have particular significance to your argument and explain what they mean. By *texts*, we mean both verbal and visual texts. In paragraph 7, Martínez analyzes a visual text, an advertisement that appeared in *Sports Illustrated*, to reveal "its implication of shifting power"—a demographic power shift from Anglos to people of color.

*Tell narratives or anecdotes.*    Put simply, a narrative is an account of something that happened. More technically, a narrative relates a sequence of events that are connected in time; and an **anecdote** is a short narrative that recounts a particular incident. An anecdote, like an example, can bring an abstraction into focus. Consider Martínez's third paragraph, where the anecdote about the museum attendant brings her point about racially charged nostalgia among white Americans into memorable focus: The tears of the museum-goers indicate just how profound their nostalgia is.

By contrast, a longer narrative, in setting out its sequence of events, often opens up possibilities for analysis. Why did these events occur? Why did they occur in this sequence? What might they lead to? What are the implications? What is missing?

In paragraph 11, for example, Martínez relates several key events in the origin myth of America. Then, in the next paragraph, she explains what is omitted from the myth, or narrative, and builds her argument about the implications and consequences of those omissions.

**Define terms.**   A definition is an explanation of what something is and, by implication, what it is not. The simplest kind of definition is a synonym, but for the purpose of developing your argument, a one-word definition is rarely enough.

When you define your terms, you are setting forth meanings that you want your readers to agree on, so that you can continue to build your argument on the foundation of that agreement. You may have to stipulate that your definition is part of a larger whole to develop your argument. For example: "Nostalgia is a bittersweet longing for things of the past; but for the purposes of my essay, I focus on white middle-class nostalgia, which combines a longing for a past that never existed with a hostile anxiety about the present."

In paragraph 10, Martínez defines the term *origin narrative*—a myth that explains "how a society understands its place in the world and its history . . . the basis for a nation's self-defined identity." The "Great White Origin Myth" is an important concept in her developing argument about a national crisis of identity.

**Make comparisons.**   Technically, a **comparison** shows the similarities between two or more things, and a **contrast** shows the differences. In practice, however, it is very difficult, if not impossible, to develop a comparison that does not make use of contrast. Therefore, we use the term *comparison* to describe the strategy of comparing *and* contrasting.

Doubtless you have written paragraphs or even whole essays that take as a starting point a version of this sentence: "X and Y are similar in some respects and different in others." This neutral formulation is seldom helpful when you are developing an argument. Usually, in making your comparison—in setting forth the points of similarity and difference—you have to take an evaluative or argumentative stance.

Note the comparison in this passage:

Although there are similarities between the current nostalgias for Dick and Jane books and for rhythm and blues music of the same era—in both cases, the object of nostalgia can move people to tears—the nostalgias spring from emotional responses that are quite different and even contradictory. I will argue that the Dick and Jane books evoke a longing for a past that is colored by a fear of the present, a longing for a time when white middle-class values were dominant and unquestioned. By contrast, the nostalgia for R&B music may indicate a yearning for a past when multicultural musicians provided white folks with a sweaty release on the dance floor from those very same white-bread values of the time.

The writer does more than list similarities and differences; he offers an analysis of what they mean and is prepared to argue for his interpretation.

Certainly Elizabeth Martínez takes an evaluative stance when she compares versions of American history in paragraphs 11 and 12. In paragraph 11, she angrily relates the sanitized story of American history, setting up a contrast in paragraph 12 with the story that does not appear in history textbooks, a story of "genocide, enslavement, and imperialist expansion." Her evaluative stance comes through clearly: She finds the first version repugnant and harmful, its omissions "grotesque."

*Examine causes and evaluate consequences.*    In any academic discipline, questions of cause and consequence are central. Whether you are analyzing the latest election results in a political science course, reading about the causes of the Vietnam War in a history course, or speculating about the long-term consequences of global warming in a science course, questions of why things happened, happen, or will happen are inescapable.

Examining causes and consequences usually involves identifying a phenomenon and asking questions about it until you gather enough information to begin analyzing the relationships among its parts and deciding which are most significant. You can then begin to set forth your own analysis of what happened and why.

Of course, this kind of analysis is rarely straightforward, and any phenomenon worthy of academic study is bound to generate a variety of conversations about its causes and consequences. In your own thinking and research, avoid jumping to conclusions and continue to sift evidence until plausible connections present themselves. Be prepared to revise your thinking—perhaps several times—in light of new evidence.

In your writing, you also want to avoid oversimplifying. A claim like this—"The answer to curbing unemployment in the United States is to restrict immigration"—does not take into account corporate outsourcing of jobs overseas or the many other possible causes of unemployment. At the very least, you may need to explain the basis and specifics of your analysis and qualify your claim: "Recent studies of patterns of immigration and unemployment in the United States suggest that unrestricted immigration is a major factor in the loss of blue-collar job opportunities in the Southwest." Certainly this sentence is less forceful and provocative than the other one, but it does suggest that you have done significant and focused research and respect the complexity of the issue.

Throughout her essay, Martínez analyzes causes and consequences. In paragraph 8, for example, she speculates that the *cause* of "attacks on immigrants, affirmative action, and multiculturalism" is "Euro-American anxiety," "the sense of a vanishing national identity." In paragraph 13, she concludes that a *consequence* of Theodore Roosevelt's beliefs about race and war was a "militarism [that] went hand in hand with the racialization of history's protagonists." In paragraph 16, the topic sentence itself is a statement about causes and consequences: "Today's origin myth and the resulting concept of national identity make for an intellectual prison where it is dangerous to ask big questions about this society's superiority."

Having shown where and how Martínez uses critical strategies to develop her paragraphs, we must hasten to add that these critical strategies usually work in combination. Although you can easily develop an entire paragraph (or even an entire essay) using comparison, it is almost impossible to do so without relying on one or more of the other strategies. What if you need to tell an anecdote about the two authors you are comparing? What if you have to cite data about different rates of economic growth to clarify the main claim of your comparison? What if you are comparing different causes and consequences?

Our point is that the strategies described here are methods for exploring your issue in writing. How you make use of them, individually or in combination, depends on which can help you best communicate your argument to your readers.

## Steps to Developing Paragraphs

1 **Use topic sentences to focus your paragraphs.** Remember that a topic sentence partially answers the question motivating you to write; acts as an extension of your thesis; indicates to your readers what the paragraph is about; and helps create unity both within the paragraph and within the essay.

2 **Create unity in your paragraphs.** The details in your paragraph should follow logically from your topic sentence and maintain a single focus, one tied clearly to your thesis. Repetition and transition words also help create unity in paragraphs.

3 **Use critical strategies to develop your paragraphs.** Use examples and illustrations; cite data; analyze texts; tell stories or anecdotes; define terms; make comparisons; and examine causes and evaluate consequences.

> ### A Practice Sequence: Working with Paragraphs
>
> We would like you to work in pairs on paragraphing. The objective of this exercise is to gauge the effectiveness of your topic sentences and the degree to which your paragraphs are unified and fully developed.
>
> Make a copy of your essay and cut it up into paragraphs. Shuffle the paragraphs to be sure they are no longer in the original order, and then exchange cut-up drafts with your partner. The challenge is to put your partner's essay back together again. When you both have finished, compare your reorderings with the original drafts. Were you able to reproduce the original organization exactly? If not, do the variations make sense? If one or the other of you had trouble putting the essay back together, talk about the adequacy of your topic sentences, ways to revise topic sentences in keeping with the details in a given paragraph, and strategies for making paragraphs more unified and coherent.

## DRAFTING CONCLUSIONS

In writing a conclusion to your essay, you are making a final appeal to your audience. You want to convince readers that what you have written is a relevant, meaningful interpretation of a shared issue. You also want to remind them that your argument is reasonable. Rather than summarize all of the points you've made in the essay—assume your readers have carefully read what you've written—pull together the key components of your argument in the service of answering the question "So what?" Establish why your argument is important: What will happen if things stay the same? What will happen if things change? How effective your conclusion is depends on whether or not readers feel that you have adequately addressed "So what?"—that you have made clear what is significant and of value.

In building on the specific details of your argument, you can also place what you have written in a broader context. (What are the sociological implications of your argument? How far-reaching are they? Are there political implications? Economic implications?) Finally, explain again how your ideas contribute something new to the conversation by building on, extending, or even challenging what others have argued.

In her concluding paragraph, Elizabeth Martínez brings together her main points, puts her essay in a broader context, indicates what's new in her argument, and answers the question "So what?":

> Accepting the implications of a different narrative could also shed light on today's struggles. In the affirmative-action struggle, for example, opponents have said that that policy is no longer needed because racism ended with the

Civil Rights Movement. But if we look at slavery as a fundamental pillar of this nation, going back centuries, it becomes obvious that racism could not have been ended by 30 years of mild reforms. If we see how the myth of the frontier idealized the white male adventurer as the central hero of national history, with the woman as sunbonneted helpmate, then we might better understand the dehumanized ways in which women have continued to be treated. A more truthful origin narrative could also help break down divisions among peoples of color by revealing common experiences and histories of cooperation.

Let's examine this concluding paragraph:

1. Although Martínez refers back to important events and ideas she has discussed, she does not merely summarize. Instead, she suggests the implications of those important events and ideas in her first sentence (the topic sentence), which crystallizes the main point of her essay: Americans need a different origin narrative.

2. Then she puts those implications in the broader context of contemporary racial and gender issues.

3. She signals what's new in her argument with the word *if* (if we look at slavery in a new way, if we look at the frontier myth in a new way).

4. Finally, her answers to why this issue matters culminate in the last sentence. This last sentence connects and extends the claim of her topic sentence, by asserting that a "more truthful origin narrative" could help heal divisions among peoples of color who have been misrepresented by the old origin myth. Clearly, she believes the implications of her argument matter: A new national identity has the potential to heal a country in crisis, a country on the verge of a "nervous breakdown" (para. 4).

Martínez also does something else in the last sentence of the concluding paragraph: She looks to the future, suggesting what the future implications of her argument could be. Looking to the future is one of five strategies for shaping a conclusion. The others we discuss are echoing the introduction, challenging the reader, posing questions, and concluding with a quotation. Each of these strategies appeals to readers in different ways; therefore, we suggest you try them all out in writing your own conclusions. Also, remember that some of these strategies can be combined. For example, you can write a conclusion that challenges readers, poses a question, looks to the future, and ends with a quotation.

## ■ Echo the Introduction

Echoing the introduction in your conclusion helps readers come full circle. It helps them see how you have developed your idea from beginning to end. In the following example, the student writer begins with a voice speaking from behind an Islamic veil, revealing the ways that Western culture mis-understands the symbolic value of wearing the veil. The writer repeats this visual image in her conclusion, quoting from the Koran: "Speak to them from behind a curtain."

Notice that the author begins with "a voice from behind the shrouds of an Islamic veil" and then echoes this quotation in her conclusion: "Speak to them from behind a curtain."

*Introduction:* A voice from behind the shrouds of an Islamic veil exclaims: "I often wonder whether people see me as a radical, fundamentalist Muslim terrorist packing an AK-47 assault rifle inside my jean jacket. Or maybe they see me as the poster girl for oppressed womanhood everywhere." In American culture where shameless public exposure, particularly of females, epitomizes ultimate freedom, the head-to-toe covering of a Muslim woman seems inherently oppressive. Driven by an autonomous national attitude, the inhabitants of the "land of the free" are quick to equate the veil with indisputable persecution. Yet Muslim women reveal the enslaving hijab as a symbolic display of the Islamic ideals — honor, modesty, and stability. Because of an unfair American assessment, the aura of hijab mystery cannot be removed until the customs and ethics of Muslim culture are genuinely explored. It is this form of enigmatic seclusion that forms the feminist controversy between Western liberals, who perceive the veil as an inhibiting factor against free will, and Islamic disciples, who conceptualize the veil as a sacred symbol of utmost morality.

*Conclusion:* By improperly judging an alien religion, the veil becomes a symbol of oppression and devastation, instead of a representation of pride and piety. Despite Western images, the hijab is a daily revitalization and reminder of the Islamic societal and religious ideals, thereby upholding the conduct and attitudes of the Muslim community. Americans share these ideals yet fail to recognize them in the context of a different culture. By sincerely exploring the custom of Islamic veiling, one will realize the vital role the hijab plays in shaping Muslim culture by sheltering women, and consequently society, from the perils that erupt from indecency. The principles implored in the Koran of modesty, honor, and stability construct a unifying and moral view of the Islamic Middle Eastern society when properly investigated. As it was transcribed from Allah, "Speak to them from behind a curtain. This is purer for your hearts and their hearts."

Notice how the conclusion echoes the introduction in its reference to a voice speaking from behind a curtain.

## ■ Challenge the Reader

By issuing a challenge to your readers, you create a sense of urgency, provoking them to act to change the status quo. In this example, the student writer explains the unacceptable consequences of preventing young women from educating themselves about AIDS and the spread of a disease that has already reached epidemic proportions.

*Here the author cites a final piece of research to empha-size the extent of the problem.*

*Here she begins her explicit challenge to readers about what they have to do to protect themselves or their students from infection.*

> The changes in AIDS education that I am suggesting are necessary and relatively simple to make. Although the current curriculum in high school health classes is helpful and informative, it simply does not pertain to young women as much as it should. AIDS is killing women at an alarming rate, and many people do not realize this. According to Daniel DeNoon, AIDS is one of the six leading causes of death among women aged 18–45, and women "bear the brunt of the worldwide AIDS epidemic." For this reason, DeNoon argues, women are one of the most important new populations that are contracting HIV at a high rate. I challenge young women to be more well-informed about AIDS and their link to the dis-ease; otherwise, many new cases may develop. As the epidemic continues to spread, women need to realize that they can stop the spread of the disease and protect themselves from infection and a number of related complications. It is the responsibility of health educators to present this to young women and inform them of the powerful choices that they can make.

## ■ Look to the Future

Looking to the future is particularly relevant when you are asking readers to take action. To move readers to action, you must establish the persis-tence of a problem and the consequences of letting a situation continue unchanged. In the concluding paragraph below, the student author points out a number of things that teachers need to do to involve parents in their children's education. She identifies a range of options before identify-ing what she believes is perhaps the most important action teachers can take.

*The second through fifth sentences present an array of options.*

> First and foremost, teachers must recognize the ways in which some parents are positively contributing to their children's aca-demic endeavors. Teachers must recognize nontraditional methods of participation as legitimate and work toward supporting parents in these tasks. For instance, teachers might send home sugges-tions for local after-school tutoring programs. Teachers must also try to make urban parents feel welcome and respected in their school. Teachers might call parents to ask their opinion about a certain difficulty their child is having, or invite them to talk about something of interest to them. One parent, for instance, spoke highly of the previous superintendent who had let him use

his work as a film producer to help with a show for students during homeroom. If teachers can develop innovative ways to utilize parents' talents and interests rather than just inviting them to be passively involved in an already-in-place curriculum, more parents might respond. Perhaps, most importantly, if teachers want parents to be involved in their students' educations, they must make the parents feel as though their opinions and concerns have real weight. When parents such as those interviewed for this study voice concerns and questions over their child's progress, it is imperative that teachers acknowledge and answer them.

*In the last two sentences, the writer looks to the future with her recommendations.*

## ■ Pose Questions

Posing questions stimulates readers to think about the implications of your argument and to apply what you argue to other situations. This is the case in the following paragraph, in which the student writer focuses on immigration and then shifts readers' attention to racism and the possibility of hate crimes. It's useful to extrapolate from your argument, to raise questions that test whether what you write can be applied to different situations. These questions can help readers understand what is at issue.

*The first question.*

*Other speculative questions follow from possible responses to the writer's first question.*

Also, my research may apply to a broader spectrum of sociological topics. There has been recent discussion about the increasing trend of immigration. Much of this discussion has involved the distribution of resources to immigrants. Should immigrants have equal access to certain economic and educational resources in America? The decision is split. But it will be interesting to see how this debate will play out. If immigrants are granted more resources, will certain Americans mobilize against the distribution of these resources? Will we see another rise in racist groups such as the Ku Klux Klan in order to prevent immigrants from obtaining more resources? My research can also be used to understand global conflict or war. In general, groups mobilize when their established resources are threatened by an external force. Moreover, groups use framing processes to justify their collective action to others.

## ■ Conclude with a Quotation

A quotation can add authority to your argument, indicating that others in positions of power and prestige support your stance. A quotation also can add poignancy to your argument, as it does in the following excerpt, in which the quotation amplifies the idea that people use Barbie to advance their own interests.

> The question still remains, what does Barbie mean? Is she the spokeswoman for the empowerment of women, or rather is she performing the dirty work of conservative patriarchy? I do not think we will ever know the answer. Rather, Barbie is the undeniable "American Icon." She is a toy, and she is what we want her to be. A test performed by Albert M. Magro at Fairmont State College titled "Why Barbie Is Perceived as Beautiful" shows that Barbie is the epitome of what we as humans find beautiful. The test sought to find human preferences on evolutionary changes in the human body. Subjects were shown a series of photos comparing different human body parts, such as the size and shape of the eyes, and asked to decide which feature they preferred: the primitive or derived (more evolved traits). The test revealed that the subjects preferred the derived body traits. Ironically, it is these preferred evolutionary features that are utilized on the body of Barbie. Barbie is truly an extension of what we are and what we perceive. Juel Best concludes his discourse on Barbie with these words: "Toys do not embody violence or sexism or occult meanings. People must assign toys their meanings." Barbie is whoever we make her out to be. Barbie grabs hold of our imaginations and lets us go wild.

*The writer quotes an authority to amplify the idea that individually and collectively, we project significance on toys.*

## Steps to Drafting Conclusions: Five Strategies

**1** **Pull together the main claims of your essay.** Don't simply repeat points you make in the paper. Instead, show readers how the points you make fit together.

**2** **Answer the question "So what?"** Show your readers why your stand on the issue is significant.

**3** **Place your argument in a larger context.** Discuss the specifics of your argument, but also indicate its broader implications.

**4** **Show readers what is new.** As you synthesize the key points of your argument, explain how what you argue builds on, extends, or challenges the thinking of others.

**5** **Decide on the best strategy for writing your conclusion.** Will you echo the introduction? Challenge the reader? Look to the future? Pose questions? Conclude with a quotation? Choose the best strategy or strategies to appeal to your readers.

### A Practice Sequence: Drafting a Conclusion

1 Write your conclusion, using one of the strategies described in this section. Then share your conclusion with a classmate. Ask this person to address the following questions:

   - Did I pull together the key points of the argument?
   - Did I answer "So what?" adequately?
   - Are the implications I want readers to draw from the essay clear?

After listening to the responses, try a second strategy, and then ask your classmate which conclusion is more effective.

2 If you do not have a conclusion of your own, analyze each example conclusion above to see how well each appears to (1) pull together the main claim of the essay, (2) answer "So what?" (3) place the argument in a larger context, and (4) show readers what is new.

# From Revising to Editing
*Working with Peer Groups*

Academic writing is a collaborative enterprise. By reading and commenting on your drafts, your peers can support your work as a writer. And you can support the work of your peers by reading their drafts with a critical but constructive eye.

In this chapter, we set out the differences between revising and editing, discuss the peer editing process in terms of the composition pyramid, present a model peer editing session, and then explain the writer's and reader's responsibilities through early drafts, later drafts, and final drafts, providing opportunities for you to practice peer response on three drafts of a student paper.

## REVISING VERSUS EDITING

We make a distinction between revising and editing. By **revising**, we mean making changes to a paper to reflect new thinking or conceptualizing. If a reader finds that the real focus of your essay comes at the end of your draft, you need to revise the paper with this new focus in mind. Revising differs from **editing**, which involves minor changes to what will be the final draft of a paper—replacing a word here and there, correcting misspellings, or substituting dashes for commas to create emphasis, for example.

When you're reading a first or second draft, the niceties of style, spelling, and punctuation are not priorities. After all, if the writer had to change the focus of his or her argument, significant changes to words, phrases, and punctuation would be inevitable. Concentrating on editing errors early on, when the writer is still trying to develop an argument with evidence, organize information logically, and anticipate counterarguments, is inefficient and even counterproductive.

Here are some characteristics of revising and editing that can guide how you read your own writing and the comments you offer to other writers:

| REVISING | EDITING |
|---|---|
| Treats writing as a work in progress | Treats writing as an almost-finished product |
| Focuses on new possibilities both within and beyond the text | Addresses obvious errors and deficiencies |
| Focuses on new questions or goals | Focuses on the text alone |
| Considers both purpose and readers' needs | Considers grammar, punctuation, spelling, and style |
| Encourages further discovery | Polishes up the essay |

Again, writing is a process, and revising is an integral part of that process. Your best writing will happen in the context of real readers' responding to your drafts. Look at the acknowledgments in any academic book, and you will see many people credited with having improved the book through their comments on drafts and ideas. All academic writers rely on conversations with others to strengthen their work.

## THE PEER EDITING PROCESS

We emphasize that the different stages of writing—early, later, and final—call for different work from both readers and writers because writers' needs vary with each successive draft. These stages correspond to what has been called the composition pyramid (Figure 10.1).* The composition pyramid represents elements of writing that can help you decide what to pay attention to at different stages of writing.

1. The top of this inverted pyramid corresponds to the early stages of writing. At this point, members of the writing group should identify the situation the writer is responding to (for example, homelessness, inequality, or air pollution), the issue the writer has defined (for example, the economic versus the social costs of homelessness), the

*We thank Susannah Brietz-Monta and Anthony Monta for this idea.

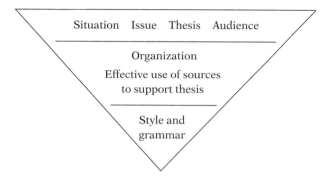

**FIGURE 10.1**   The Composition Pyramid

thesis or argument the writer advances, and the extent to which the writer addresses a given audience appropriately.

2. The middle portion of the pyramid corresponds to a later stage of the writing process, the point at which members of the group should move on to discuss the extent to which the writer has organized the argument logically and used sources effectively to support the thesis. Has the writer integrated quotations smoothly into the paper? Is the evidence relevant, recent, and credible?

## Steps in the Peer Editing Process

**1** The writer distributes copies of the draft to each member of the writing group. (Ideally, the group should not exceed four students.)

**2** The writer distributes a cover letter, setting an agenda for each member of the group.

**3** The members read the cover letter.

**4** The writer then reads the draft aloud, while members follow along, underlining passages and making notes to prepare themselves to discuss the draft.

**5** Members ask questions that help the writer identify concepts that need further elaboration or clarification.

**6** Discussion focuses on the strengths and weaknesses of the draft appropriate to the stage of writing and the writer's concerns. (Even in the early stage, readers and the writer should sustain discussion for at least ten minutes before the next student takes a turn as writer.)

3. Finally, the bottom of the pyramid corresponds to the final stages of drafting. As the writer's focus shifts to grammar and style, so should the group's. Questions to ask: Is this specific language appropriate to the intended audience? Has the writer presented the argument in ways that will compel readers—even those who disagree—to listen?

## PEER GROUPS IN ACTION: A SAMPLE SESSION

Let's take a look at one writing group in action to see the potential of this approach to writing. One student, Brett Preacher, worked collaboratively with three other students, Caitlin, Meghan, and Daimon, on a paper about whether the movie *Million Dollar Baby* portrays poverty accurately. Brett explained to his group that he had struggled to find ways to advance his argument at the same time that he was trying to synthesize different authors' points of view. Moreover, he was worried that he didn't do the assignment:

> BRETT: That was the assignment, to argue whether the movie portrays poverty justly or unjustly. That was the assignment, what we were supposed to do, and I didn't do that at all.
>
> CAITLIN: Well, I didn't do that either, but I used hooks's "Seeing and Making Culture: Representing the Poor" and Freedman's *From Cradle to Grave: The Human Face of Poverty in America*.
>
> BRETT: Yeah, well, I kind of quit. I strayed off the movie at the end. I basically quit talking about the movie about halfway through the paper, so basically the whole second half of my paper is the weak part. I just kind of quit talking about *Million Dollar Baby*.

Brett restated his understanding of the assignment before reading his draft aloud. This is a valuable starting point because a writer's interpretation of the assignment—the task, the purpose, the audience—helps the peer readers understand why the writer is taking a particular approach. If the readers disagree with the writer's interpretation, they should discuss their differences before the writer shares the draft, to determine an appropriate response to the assignment.

## AN ANNOTATED STUDENT DRAFT

Here we reprint Brett's draft, with annotations on passages that elicited comments from his peer editors. Following the draft, we present their discussion in more detail.

Brett Preacher

Professor Tindall

English 200

October 10, 20—

### Representing Poverty in *Million Dollar Baby*

In "Seeing and Making Culture: Representing the Poor,"
bell hooks discusses the extent to which the media describe the
poor as all nihilistic and longing for material worth. This image
is slightly expressed in the movie *Million Dollar Baby* through
Maggie's family. In the only scenes where her family makes an
appearance, they present themselves as white trash by worrying
that their welfare will be taken away and trying to make an easy
dollar off a crippled Maggie. Jonathan Friedman, however, seems
to capture the essence of the movie much more accurately in a
chapter out of his book *Cradle to the Grave*, called "The Human
Face of Poverty in America." In this chapter, Friedman presents
many stories that support his argument that perseverance can
help people rise from a life of poverty. This argument is portrayed perfectly by Maggie throughout the movie.

In the movie, Maggie strives to become a professional
boxer to support herself rather than succumb to a life of poverty
as her family did. Through drive and determination, Maggie
strives to rise out of poverty despite all the doubt and negativity directed toward her. With nothing more than her wages and
tips from her waitressing job, she saves her money, sacrificing
much along the way to pay for her trainer. Her family, however,
represents the other side of the spectrum and looks for nothing
more than an easy way out of their welfare-sustained lifestyle.
Rather than working to better themselves, they depend on
welfare, and after putting Maggie down repeatedly about her
career, they try to sign her savings over to themselves when she
gets injured. Through her hard work and determination, Maggie
achieves her dream in the end, helping to support the argument
Friedman makes. Jonathan Friedman catches the face of poverty
precisely by arguing that perseverance can put anyone out of a
life of poverty.  Most people, however, cannot fathom this idea
until they have witnessed something similar.

In her essay, hooks describes the generalizations that
the media have of the poor, which convey stereotypes.

*Brett's point is not
clear. His group
member Caitlin won-
ders if he is saying
the film does, or does
not, support hooks's
argument.*

*Brett introduces
some examples
related to the char-
acter Maggie, and he
could include more;
but he needs to
decide what point he
wants to make. Is he
saying that the film
portrays poverty in a
realistic way?*

*Brett no longer
focuses on the film*

*1*

*2*

*3*

Preacher 2

*at the end, a prob-*
*lem that even he*
*recognizes. Daimon*
*points out that*
*Brett doesn't talk*
*enough about the*
*film throughout the*
*paper.*

Friedman observes that it takes money, organization, and laws to maintain a social structure, but none of it works if there are not opportunities for people to meet and help each other along the way. For example, he tells the story about Nitza, a young homeless mother with four children. She is forced to put her children into foster care for three years until she works her way out of poverty and can support her family. Friedman's point is that there is not enough opportunity to maintain the social structure that we desire. At the same time, we see that Nitza succeeds because she is motivated to change her circumstances.

Unable to identify Brett's key claim, his writing group members asked a number of questions that they hoped would guide Brett toward making an explicit claim about whether the film *Million Dollar Baby* represents poverty in a fair way:

> CAITLIN: So what you are saying is that the film does and doesn't support hooks's argument that the media misrepresent the poor?
> MEGHAN: You give a lot of examples here, like about Maggie. You could expand those into a paper. But what point do you want to make?
> BRETT: Yeah, each example could be in a different paragraph.
> CAITLIN: Those could be your main points, you know?

Caitlin believed that Brett's point may have been more implicit than explicit, that the film *Million Dollar Baby* "does and doesn't support hooks's argument that the media misrepresent the poor." Caitlin's suggestion underscores the complexity of what Brett was trying to argue—that the film does and doesn't represent poverty in a fair way—and poses a challenge that Meghan appeared to understand. Meghan suggested to Brett that he formulate different paragraphs to advance the point that *Million Dollar Baby* offers a contradictory image of poverty that is at once realistic and unrealistic. Caitlin agreed when she said that "those could be your main points." (Actually, that's just one key claim.)

However, Daimon recognized that Brett would have to develop his discussion of the film to clarify whether it offers two conflicting images of poverty:

> DAIMON: It's just you don't talk about *Million Dollar Baby* enough, and I think that's what the essay is supposed to be about. Not so much about the other two. You can use the other two, but not so much as you did.
> BRETT: Just tie in *Million Dollar Baby* a little more, you think?
> CAITLIN: Well, because you talk a lot, it does fit with your paper, but it doesn't . . . it's supposed to be about *Million Dollar Baby*. . . . Do you think the film portrays poverty in a realistic way?

MEGHAN: Yeah, give examples of the way the film describes Maggie's family. It's like they depend on her to get themselves out of poverty.

And then Caitlin steered Brett back to the point she made earlier—that Brett could revise his paper to address the complicated way the film represents poverty:

CAITLIN: That could be the issue. There are contradictory images of poverty and how people deal.
BRETT: Yeah, well, I don't know. I'm going to have to think about that.

Brett's draft reflects his first attempt to get his ideas down. It's fine for a first draft to be exploratory. When writers formulate a working thesis or when they fail to formulate a thesis, readers in a peer group can offer support, noting strengths or pointing to places of greatest interest in an effort to sustain the writer's energy for writing. Caitlin helped Brett generate a plan for taking the next step by pointing out how he could define the issue—"There are contradictory images of poverty and how people deal."

A peer group can also ask questions to help a writer set new goals. A good strategy is to paraphrase particular parts of the draft so that the writer can hear how you, the reader, have understood what he or she is trying to say. This is what Caitlin did when she said, "So what you are saying is that the film does and doesn't support hooks's argument that the media misrepresent the poor?"

## WORKING WITH EARLY DRAFTS

### ■ Understand the Writer's Responsibilities

When you present an early draft of your essay to your writing group, you want the group to focus on top-level pyramid concerns—situation, issue, thesis, and audience. You should explain this and any other concerns you have in a cover letter. Use the template in Figure 10.2 as a model for what needs explaining in the letter to your readers.

1. What is your question (or assignment)?
2. What is the issue motivating you to write?
3. How have published writers addressed the issue about which you are writing?
4. What is your working thesis?
5. Who is your audience, and what kind of response do you want from your readers?
6. What do you think is working best?
7. What specific aspect of the essay are you least satisfied with at this time?
8. What kind of feedback do you especially want today?

**FIGURE 10.2    The Writer's Cover Letter: Early Drafts**

During the session, it's important to be open to suggestions. Although you don't have to incorporate every suggestion your group makes when you revise your draft, be sure you at least understand the members' comments and concerns. If you don't understand what the members are saying about your draft, ask them to clarify or give you an example.

Finally, if you decide not to take someone's suggestion, have a good reason for doing so. If a suggested change means you won't be addressing the terms of the assignment or that you would no longer be interested in the issue, it's fine to say no.

## ■ Understand the Reader's Responsibilities

Your task as a reader is to follow along as the early draft is read, paying special attention to the concerns the writer has explained in the cover letter and focusing on the top of the pyramid: situation, issue, thesis, and audience. Take notes directly on the draft copy, circling or underlining sections you find confusing or have questions about, so that you can refer to them specifically in the discussion.

When it's your turn to talk, have a conversation about your reactions to the draft—where the draft amused, confused, or persuaded you, for example. Don't just jump in and start telling the writer what he or she should be doing in the paper. Your role as a reader is to give the writer a live audience: Your responses can help the writer decide what parts of the paper are working and what parts need serious revision. There are times, however, when you should play the role of *deferring reader*, putting off certain comments. You don't want to overwhelm the writer with problems no matter how many questions the essay raises.

Offer both positive and negative remarks. Start by pointing out what is working well in the paper, so the writer knows where he or she is on the right track. This also leaves the writer more open to constructive criticism. But don't shy away from telling the writer what should be working better. It's your job as a reader to offer honest and specific responses to the draft, so the writer can develop it into an effective piece of writing. Figure 10.3 lists key questions you should ask as a reader of an early draft.

---

1. Are the questions and issues that motivate the writer clear?
2. Has the writer effectively related the conversation that published writers are engaged in?
3. What is at issue?
4. What is the writer's thesis?
5. Is the writer addressing the audience's concerns effectively?
6. What passages of the draft are most effective?
7. What passages of the draft are least effective?

---

**FIGURE 10.3   A Reader's Questions: Early Drafts**

## ■ Analyze an Early Draft

Keep these questions in mind as you read the following excerpt from a student's early draft. After reading a number of scholarly articles on the civil rights movement, Tasha Taylor decided to address what she sees as the difference between scholars' understanding of the movement and more popular treatments in textbooks and photographs. She also tries to tie in the larger question of historical memory to her analysis of southern blacks' struggle for equality—what people remember about the past and what they forget. In fact, she begins her essay with a quotation she believes summarizes what she wants to argue ("The struggle of man against power is the struggle of memory against forgetting").

As you read Taylor's essay, take detailed notes, and underline passages that concern you. Then write a paragraph or two explaining what she could do to strengthen the draft. Keep in mind that this is an early draft, so focus on the top level of the pyramid: the situation or assignment; the issue; the thesis; and the audience.

Taylor 1

Tasha Taylor
Professor Winters
English 111
October 23, 20—

Memory Through Photography

The struggle of man against power is the struggle of
memory against forgetting.

—Milan Kundera

Ask the average American what the key components of the
civil rights movement are, and most people will probably recall
Martin Luther King Jr. speaking of a dream in front of the Lincoln
Memorial, Rosa Parks riding a bus, a few court decisions, and perhaps
a photograph of Elizabeth Eckford cowering before an angry mob
in front of Central High School in Little Rock. Few people are aware
A. Philip Randolph planned the march on Washington. Few could
describe Rosa Parks's connection to the civil rights movement
(for example, the fact that she had been a member of the NAACP
since 1943) before her legendary refusal to give up her seat in
December 1955, which led to the Montgomery Bus Boycott. Few recognize the years of struggle that existed between the *Brown v. Board*

Taylor 2

*of Education* decision and the actual desegregation of schools. Few consider the fate of Elizabeth Eckford after the federal troops were sent to protect her and the other members of the Little Rock Nine had left Central High or the months of abuse (physical and emotional) that they endured in the name of integration. What most people know is limited to textbooks they read in school or the captions under photographs that describe where a particular event occurred.

Why is it that textbooks exclusively feature the stories of larger than life figures like Martin Luther King? Why is it that we remember things the way we do? Historical events "have little meaning without human interpretation, without our speaking about them within the contexts of our lives and our culture, without giving them names and meanings" (Kolker xix). Each person experiencing the exact same event will carry a different memory from that event. Trying to decipher what memories reveal about each person is a fascinating yet difficult endeavor, because each retelling of a memory and each additional memory alters existing ones.

The story that photographs and textbooks tell us does not even begin to describe the depth of the movement or the thousands who risked their lives and the lives of their families to make equality a reality. Embracing this selective memory as a nation prevents understanding and acknowledgment of the harsh reality of other images from the civil rights movement (demonstrators being plowed down by fire hoses, beatings, and the charred bodies of bombing victims) which are key aspects of understanding who we are as a society. The question therefore is why. Why is it that textbook writers and publishers have allowed so much of this history to be skewed and forgotten? How can it be that barely 50 years after these events so many have been forgotten or diluted?

## Reading as a Writer

1. What is working well in Taylor's draft?
2. What is Taylor's thesis or argument?
3. To what extent does she connect her analysis of the civil rights movement and historical memory?

4. What parts of her analysis could Taylor explain further? (What do you still need to know?)

5. What would you suggest Taylor do next?

## WORKING WITH LATER DRAFTS

### ■ Understand the Writer's Responsibilities

At a later stage, after you've had the opportunity to take readers' suggestions and do further research, you should be able to state your thesis more definitively than you did in your earlier draft. You also should be able to support your thesis with evidence, anticipating possible counterarguments. Ideally, your readers will still provide constructive criticism, offering their support, as in the first draft, but they will also question and challenge more than before.

Here, too, you want to help readers focus on your main concerns, which you should explain in a cover letter. You may still need to work on one or two top-level pyramid concerns, but your focus will likely be midlevel concerns—organization and the effective use of sources. Use the list of questions in Figure 10.4 to help you write your cover letter.

### ■ Understand the Reader's Responsibilities

In a later draft, your focus as a reader should be on midlevel concerns in the composition pyramid: places in the writer's text that are confusing,

---

1. What is your research question?

2. What is the issue motivating you to write?

3. What is your thesis?

4. How do you go about identifying a gap in readers' knowledge, modifying others' ideas, or trying to correct readers' misunderstandings?

5. To what extent do you distinguish your argument from the information you quote, summarize, or paraphrase from the sources you have read?

6. To what extent have you organized your ideas in ways that will help readers follow the logic of your argument?

7. To what extent have you anticipated potential counterarguments to your thesis?

8. What do you think is working best?

9. What specific aspect of the essay are you least satisfied with at this time?

---

**FIGURE 10.4   The Writer's Cover Letter: Later Drafts**

1. To what extent is it clear what questions and issues motivate the writer?

2. What is the writer's thesis?

3. How effectively does the writer establish the conversation — identify a gap in people's knowledge, attempt to modify an existing argument, or try to correct some misunderstanding?

4. How effectively does the writer distinguish between his or her ideas and the ideas he or she summarizes, paraphrases, or quotes?

5. How well does the writer help you follow the logic of his or her argument?

6. To what extent are you persuaded by the writer's argument?

7. To what extent does the writer anticipate possible counterarguments?

8. To what extent does the writer make clear how he or she wants readers to respond?

9. What do you think is working best? Explain by pointing to specific passages in the writer's draft.

10. What specific aspect of the draft is least effective? Explain by pointing to a specific passage in the writer's draft.

**FIGURE 10.5    A Reader's Questions: Later Drafts**

that require better transitions, or that could use sources more effectively. You can challenge writers at this stage of the composing process, perhaps playing the role of *naive reader*, suggesting places in the draft where the writer has left something out or isn't clear. The naive reader's comments tend to take the form of questions: "Do you mean to suggest that everyone who learns to write well succeeds in life? What kind of success are you talking about?" Closely related to the naive reader is the *devil's advocate reader.* This reader's comments also challenge the writer, often taking the form of a question like this: "But why couldn't this be attributed to the effects of socialization rather than heredity?" Figure 10.5 offers questions for reading later drafts.

## ■ Analyze a Later Draft

Now read the following excerpt from Taylor's second draft. You will see that she begins with her discussion of historical memory. She also has included an analysis of a book of photographs that Nobel Prize–winning author Toni Morrison compiled. Take notes as you read the draft and write a paragraph in which you describe what you see as some of the strengths of what Taylor has written and what she can do to make other elements stronger. In particular, focus on the middle level of the composition pyramid—on organization and the effective use of sources and evidence to support her thesis.

Taylor 1

Tasha Taylor
Professor Winters
English 111
November 14, 20—

Memory Through Photography

The struggle of man against power is the struggle of
memory against forgetting.

—Milan Kundera

Memory is such an integral part of what it is to be human, yet
is something so often taken for granted: people assume that their
memories are accurate to protect themselves from the harsh realities
of the atrocities committed by ordinary people. Even the pictures
used to represent the much-celebrated civil rights movement give
us a false sense of security and innocence. For example, the Ku Klux
Klan is most often depicted by covered faces and burning crosses; the
masks allow us to remove ourselves from responsibility. Few could
describe Rosa Parks's connection to the civil rights movement (for
example, the fact that she had been a member of the NAACP since
1943) before her legendary refusal to give up her seat in December
1955, which led to the Montgomery Bus Boycott. Few recognize the
years of struggle that existed between the *Brown v. Board of Education* decision and the actual desegregation of schools. Few consider
the fate of Elizabeth Eckford after the federal troops were sent to
protect her and the other members of the Little Rock Nine had left
Central High or the months of abuse (physical and emotional) that
they endured in the name of integration. What most people know is
limited to textbooks they read in school or the captions under photographs that describe where a particular event occurred.

It is important, therefore, to analyze what is remembered and
even more importantly to recognize what it is forgotten: to question
why it is that it is forgotten, what that says about society today,
how far it has come and how much it has unwittingly fallen back
into old patterns such as prejudice and ignorance. The discrepancies
in cultural memory are due more to a society's desire to remember
itself in the best light and protect itself from the reality of its brutality and responsibility. Such selective memory only temporarily heals

Taylor 2

the wounds of society; lack of awareness does not cause healing. Although there have been many recent moves to increase awareness, they are tainted by unavoidable biases and therefore continue to perpetuate a distorted memory.

Images play a central role in the formation of cultural memory because people can point to photographs and claim them as concrete evidence: "Images entrance us because they provide a powerful illusion of owning reality. If we can photograph reality or paint or copy it, we have exercised an important kind of power" (Kolker 3). A picture of black and white children sitting at a table together is used to reinforce the cultural perception that the problems of racism are over, that it has all been fixed.

In her book *Remember*, Toni Morrison strives to revitalize the memory of school integration through photographs. The book is dedicated to Denise McNair, Carole Robertson, Addie Mae Collins, and Cynthia Wesley, the four girls killed in the 16th Street Baptist Church bombing in 1963. Morrison writes, "Things are better now. Much, much better. But remember why and please remember us" (Morrison 72). The pictures are of black and white children happily eating together, solemnly saluting the flag together, and holding hands. The photographs of the four murdered girls show them peacefully and innocently smiling as if everything really is better now. In reality, according to the United States Bureau of Alcohol, Tobacco and Firearms, between 1995 and 1997 there were 162 incidents of arson or bombing in African American houses of worship. There are a few images of people protesting integration, but they are also consistent with the cultural memory (protesters are shown simply holding signs and yelling, not beating and killing innocent children). Finally, the captions are written in a child's voice. Yet it is not a child's voice at all it is merely a top down view of children that serves to perpetuate a distorted cultural memory.

The photographs used to suggest how things are much, much better now are misleading. For example, the last photograph is of a black girl and a white girl holding hands through a bus window, which was transporting them to an integrated school. The caption reads: "Anything can happen. Anything at all. See?" (71). It is a very powerful image of how the evil of Jim Crow and segregation exists in a distant past and the nation has come together and healed.

Taylor 3

However, Morrison neglects to point out that the picture was taken in Boston, Massachusetts, not the deep south, the heart of racism. Children holding hands in Boston is much less significant than if they were in Birmingham where that action would be concrete evidence of how far we as a nation have come.

Morrison also glorifies of Martin Luther King, Jr. and Rosa Parks pointing to them as epitomizing the movement. Unfortunately, she perpetuates the story that one needs to be special or somehow larger than life to affect change. Paul Rogat Loeb writes in *Soul of a Citizen*:

> Once we enshrine our heroes, it becomes hard for mere mortals to measure up in our eyes . . . in our collective amnesia we lose the mechanisms through which grassroots social movements of the past successfully shifted public sentiment and challenged entrenched institutional power. Equally lost are the means by which their participants managed to keep on, sustaining their hope and eventually prevailing in circumstances at least as difficult as those we face today. (Loeb 36, 38)

Placing a select few on pedestals and claiming them as next to divine heroes of the movement does society a disservice; people fail to realize that ordinary people can serve as agents of change.

Morrison's book ignores the thousand of ordinary people who risked their lives for the cause to bring about equality. The caption besides the picture of Rosa Parks in *Remember* reads "because if I ever feel helpless or lonely I just have to remember that all it takes is one person" (Morrison 62). Ironically, Morrison gives credit for the Montgomery Bus Boycott to one person, ignoring the months of planning and involved dozens of planners. Even the photograph presents Rosa Parks in a position of power. It is a low-angle shot up at Parks that makes her appear larger than life and authoritative. The photographs of Martin Luther King, Jr. also further the impression of power with a close up shot of his face as he stands above thousands of participants in the March on Washington. Although these photographs were selected to perpetuate the hero illusion, it is more inspiring to remember the ordinary people who took a stand and were able to accomplish extraordinary feats because of their dedication and persistence rather than glorify extraordinary people who were destined for greatness.

## Reading as a Writer

1.  What is Taylor's thesis or argument?
2.  How well does she help you follow the logic of her argument with transitions?
3.  How effectively does she distinguish between her ideas and the ideas she summarizes, paraphrases, or quotes?
4.  To what extent are you persuaded by her argument?
5.  What should Taylor do next?

# WORKING WITH FINAL DRAFTS

## ■ Understand the Writer's Responsibilities

Your final draft should require editing, not revising. At this stage, readers should focus on errors in style and grammar in the text, not on the substance of your work. Here, too, indicate your main concerns in a cover letter (Figure 10.6).

## ■ Understand the Reader's Responsibilities

Once a writer's ideas are developed and in place, readers should turn their attention to the bottom level of the composition pyramid, to matters of style and grammar. At this stage, details are important: Is this the best word to use? Would this sentence be easier to follow if it was broken into two sentences? Which spelling is correct—*Freedman* or *Friedman*? Are citations handled consistently? Should this question mark precede or follow the quotation mark? The *grammatically correct reader* evaluates and makes judgments about the writer's work. This reader may simply indicate with a mark of some sort that there's a problem in a sentence or paragraph, or may even correct the writer's work. Figure 10.7 is a list of questions a reader should ask of a final draft.

## ■ Analyze a Near-Final Draft

Now read Taylor's near-final draft and write a paragraph detailing what she can do to strengthen it. Again, you will see that Taylor has made sub-

---

1.  What is your unique perspective on your issue?
2.  To what extent do the words and phrases you use reflect who you believe your readers are?
3.  Does your style of citation reflect accepted conventions for academic writing?
4.  What do you think is working best?
5.  What specific aspect of the essay are you least satisfied with at this time?

---

FIGURE 10.6    The Writer's Cover Letter: Final Drafts

1. How does the writer go about contributing a unique perspective on the issue?

2. To what extent does the writer use words and phrases that are appropriate for the intended audience?

3. To what extent does the style of citation reflect accepted conventions for academic writing?

4. What do you think is working best?

5. What specific aspect of the essay are you least satisfied with at this time?

FIGURE 10.7    A Reader's Questions: Final Drafts

stantial changes. She compares Morrison's book of photographs to a Spike Lee documentary that she watched with her class. As you read the essay, focus on the bottom level of the composition pyramid: Does the writer use appropriate language? Does she adhere to appropriate conventions for using and citing sources? (See the Appendix for information on MLA and APA formats.)

Taylor 1

Tasha Taylor

Professor Winters

English 111

December 5, 20—

Memory Through Photography

Memory is such an integral part of what it is to be human, yet it is something so often taken for granted: people assume that their memories are accurate to protect themselves from the harsh realities of the atrocities committed by ordinary people. Even the pictures used to represent the much-celebrated civil rights movement give us a false sense of security and innocence. For example, the Ku Klux Klan is most often depicted by covered faces and burning crosses; the masks allow us to remove ourselves from responsibility. Few could describe Rosa Parks's connection to the civil rights movement before her legendary refusal to give up her seat in December 1955, which led to the Montgomery Bus Boycott (for example, the fact that she had been a member of the NAACP since 1943). Few recognize the years of struggle that existed between the 1954 *Brown v. Board of Education* decision and the actual desegregation of schools. Few consider the fate of Elizabeth Eckford after the federal troops sent to protect her and the other members of the Little Rock Nine had left

Taylor 2

Central High or the months of abuse (physical and emotional) that they endured in the name of integration. What most people know is limited to the textbooks they read in school or the captions under photographs that describe where a particular event occurred.

It is important, then, to analyze what is remembered, and even more important to recognize what is forgotten: to question why it is that it is forgotten, what that says about society today, how far it has come and how much it has unwittingly fallen back into old patterns of prejudice and ignorance. The discrepancies in cultural memory are due more to society's desire to remember itself in the best light and protect itself from the reality of its brutality and responsibility. Such selective memory only temporarily heals the wounds of society; lack of awareness does not cause healing. Although there have been many recent moves to increase awareness, they are tainted by unavoidable biases and therefore continue to perpetuate a distorted memory.

Images play a central role in the formation of cultural memory because people can point to photographs and claim them as concrete evidence: "Images entrance us because they provide a powerful illusion of owning reality. If we can photograph reality or paint or copy it, we have exercised an important kind of power" (Kolker 3). A picture of black and white children sitting at a table together is used to reinforce the cultural perception that the problems of racism are over, that they have all been fixed.

In her book *Remember,* Toni Morrison strives to revitalize the memory of school integration through photographs. The book is dedicated to Denise McNair, Carole Robertson, Addie Mae Collins, and Cynthia Wesley, the four girls killed in the 16th Street Baptist Church bombing in 1963. Morrison writes: "Things are better now. Much, much better. But remember why and please remember us" (72). The pictures are of black and white children happily eating together, solemnly saluting the flag together, and holding hands. The photographs of the four murdered girls show them peacefully and innocently smiling as if everything really is better now. In reality, according to the United States Bureau of Alcohol, Tobacco and Firearms, between 1995 and 1997 there were 162 incidents of arson or bombing in African American houses of worship. There are a few images of people protesting integration, but they are also consistent with the cultural memory (protesters are shown simply holding signs and yelling, not beating and killing innocent children). Finally, the captions are written in a child's voice. Yet it is not a child's voice at all; it is merely a top-down view of children that serves to perpetuate a distorted cultural memory.

The photographs used to suggest how things are much, much better now are misleading. For example, the last photograph, taken through a bus window, is of a black girl and a white girl holding hands; the bus was transporting them to an integrated school. The caption reads: "Anything can happen. Anything at all. See?" (Morrison 71). It is a very powerful image of how the evil of Jim Crow and segregation exists in a distant past and the nation has come together and healed. However, Morrison neglects to point out that the picture was taken in Boston, not in the Deep South, the heart of racism. Children holding hands in Boston is much less significant than if they were in Birmingham, where that action would be concrete evidence of how far we as a nation have come.

Morrison also glorifies Martin Luther King Jr. and Rosa Parks, pointing to them as epitomizing the movement. Unfortunately, she perpetuates the story that one needs to be special or somehow larger than life to effect change. Paul Rogat Loeb writes in *Soul of a Citizen*:

> Once we enshrine our heroes, it becomes hard for mere mortals to measure up in our eyes. . . . In our collective amnesia we lose the mechanisms through which grassroots social movements of the past successfully shifted public sentiment and challenged entrenched institutional power. Equally lost are the means by which their participants managed to keep on, sustaining their hope and eventually prevailing in circumstances at least as difficult as those we face today. (36, 38)

Placing a select few on pedestals and claiming them as next-to-divine heroes of the movement does society a disservice; people fail to realize that ordinary people can serve as agents of change.

Morrison's book ignores the thousands of ordinary people who risked their lives for the cause to bring about equality. The caption beside the picture of Rosa Parks in *Remember* reads "Because if I ever feel helpless or lonely I just have to remember that all it takes is one person" (Morrison 62). Ironically, Morrison gives credit for the Montgomery Bus Boycott to one person, ignoring the months

Taylor 4

of planning that involved dozens of planners. Even the photograph presents Rosa Parks in a position of power. It is a low-angle shot up at Parks that makes her appear larger than life and authoritative. The photographs of Martin Luther King Jr. also further the impression of power with a close-up shot of his face as he stands above thousands of participants in the March on Washington. Although these photographs were selected to perpetuate the hero illusion, it is more inspiring to remember the ordinary people who took a stand and were able to accomplish extraordinary feats because of their dedication and persistence rather than to glorify extraordinary people who were destined for greatness.

In contrast, Spike Lee's 1998 documentary titled *4 Little Girls* is a stirring depiction of the lives and deaths of the girls who died in the 1963 16th Street Baptist Church bombing. In his film, Spike Lee looks behind what some would call "societal amnesia" to disclose the harsh realities of the civil rights movement. Lee interviews family members and friends of the murdered girls, revealing the pain and anger that they grapple with more than forty years after the tragedy. Lee includes not only images of the bombed church but also the charred and nearly unrecognizable bodies of the murdered girls. These disturbing images underscore the reality of their deaths without appearing sensationalist. The film does an exceptional job of reminding the viewer of the suffering and mindless hate that were prevalent during the civil rights movement. 8

However, the documentary is also biased. For instance, the girls were not little; they were fourteen, not really little girls. Lee chose to describe them as little to elicit emotion and sympathy for their tragic deaths. They were victims. They had not marched through the streets demanding equality; instead, Denise McNair, Carole Robertson, Addie Mae Collins, and Cynthia Wesley were simply attending Sunday school and were ruthlessly murdered. Victimizing Denise, Carole, Addie Mae, and Cynthia is not detrimental to the cultural memory in and of itself. The problem is that the victimization of the four girls is expanded to encompass the entire black community, undermining the power and achievement of the average black citizen. We need to remember the people who struggled to gain employment for blacks in the labor movement of the 1940s and 1950s that initiated the civil rights movement. 9

Taylor 5

One can argue that despite the presence of misleading images in Spike Lee's film and Toni Morrison's book, at least some of the story is preserved. Still, it is easy to fall victim to the cliché: those who do not remember history are doomed to repeat it. Just because a portion of the story is remembered, it does not mean that society is immune to falling back into its old habits. This cultural amnesia not only perpetuates the injustices of the time but leaves open the possibility that these atrocities can occur again. If people believe the government can simply grant black equality, then they may believe that it can also take it away. In essence memory is about power: "The struggle of man against power is the struggle of memory against forgetting" (Kundera). Those who are remembered hold power over the forgotten. Their legacy is lost and so is their ability to inspire future generations through their memory.

*10*

Taylor 6

Works Cited

*4 Little Girls*. Dir. Spike Lee. 40 Acres & A Mule Filmworks, 1997. Film.

Kolker, Robert. *Film, Form, and Culture*. New York: McGraw Hill, 1998. Print.

Kundera, Milan. *QuotationsBook*. QuotationsBook, 2007. Web. 22 Nov. 20—.

Loeb, Paul Rogat. *Soul of a Citizen: Living with Conviction in a Cynical Time*. New York: St. Martin's/Griffin, 1999. Print.

Morrison, Toni. *Remember*. Boston: Houghton Mifflin, 2004. Print.

United States. Dept. of the Treasury. Bureau of Alcohol, Tobacco and Firearms. "Arson and Explosives: Incidents Report 1994." *ATF.gov*. US Dept. of Justice, 1995. Web. 15 Nov. 20—.

## Reading as a Writer

1. What would you say is Taylor's argument?
2. To what extent does she provide transitions to help you understand how her analysis supports her argument?

3. To what extent does she integrate quotations appropriately into the text of her argument?

4. To what extent does the style of citation reflect accepted conventions for academic writing?

5. If Taylor had more time to revise, what would you suggest she do?

## FURTHER SUGGESTIONS FOR PEER EDITING GROUPS

Monitoring your own writing group can help ensure that the group is both providing and receiving the kinds of responses the members need. Here is a list of questions you might ask of one another after a session:

- What topics were discussed?
- Were most questions and comments directed at the level of ideas? Structure? Language?
- Were topics always brought up with a question or a comment?
- Who initiated talk more frequently—the writer or the readers?
- What roles did different group members play?
- Did each author open with specific questions or concerns?
- Did the readers begin by giving specific reactions?

After answering these questions, identify two things that are working well in your group. Then identify two things that you could improve. How would you go about making those improvements?

When we asked our students what they thought contributed to effective conversation in their writing groups, here is what they told us:

- Honest and spontaneous expression
- Free interaction among members
- High levels of personal involvement
- Members' commitment to insight and change
- The sense that self-disclosure is safe and highly valued
- Members' willingness to take responsibility for the group's effectiveness
- Members' belief that the group is important
- Members' belief that they are primary agents of help for one another
- Members' focus on communication within the group over other discussions

# 11

# Other Methods of Inquiry
## Interviews and Focus Groups

Sometimes to advance your argument you may need to do original research. By **original research**, we mean using primary sources of evidence you gather yourself. (Another common term for this type of investigation is *field research*.) Remember that primary sources of evidence include firsthand or eyewitness accounts like those found in letters or newspapers, or in research reports in which the researcher explains his or her impressions of a particular phenomenon—for example, gender relations in classroom interactions. (In contrast, a secondary source is an analysis of information contained in primary sources.)

The type of original research we discuss in this chapter relies on people—interviewees and members of focus groups—as primary sources of information. To inquire into gender dynamics in college science classrooms, then, you might conduct interviews with young women to understand their perceptions of how gender affects teaching. Or you might convene a focus group to put a variety of perspectives into play on questions about gendered teaching practices. The pages that follow present strategies for conducting interviews and setting up focus groups that can generate multiple responses to your research questions.

When you conduct research, keep in mind that you are not setting out to prove anything; instead, the process of inquiry will enable you to answer the questions *you* ask, address problems, and move readers to rethink their positions. Good critical readers know that the arguments they produce as writers are influenced by what they choose to discuss and how they construe the evidence they provide.

Although there is really no way to avoid the limitations of writing from one point of view, writers can provide readers with multiple sources of information so that they can make their own judgments about what to believe or not believe. In fact, this is the argument we make above in studying inequities in education. Relying on a single source of data will inevitably limit your field of vision. Multiple sources of information add complexity and texture to your analysis, conveying to readers the thoroughness of your approach.

## WHY DO ORIGINAL RESEARCH?

We can think of four reasons (all of which overlap to some extent) why you might do original research for a writing class.

*To Increase Your Ability to Read Critically.*    When you do original research, you learn, at a basic and pragmatic level, how the studies you consult in a researched argument come into being. You're on the ground floor of knowledge making.

As a critical reader, you know it's important to ask questions like these: What is the source of the author's claim? Why should I believe the author? What is the source of the author's authority? What are the possible counterarguments? When you are doing original research, you are in the position of that author, with a real stake in establishing your own authority. By coming to understand what it takes to establish your own authority, you are in a better position to evaluate how effectively other researchers establish theirs.

Let's say your research question concerns gender differences in math education. You might read a study that asserts that girls and young women are being shortchanged in math classes, impeding their ability to go into math-related fields. You would want to ask about the nature of the data used to support this claim. If the author of the study states that 56 percent of the female students interviewed said they were discouraged from going into math-related fields, you might wonder where the figure of 56 percent came from. How many girls and young women were interviewed? How was this sample selected? What were the students asked? Questions like these inform your own use of interviews and focus groups.

*To Increase Your Own Research Skills.*    Doing original research broadens your own range of research methods. By developing a repertoire of research methods, you will be better able to explore questions that may be too complex to answer by examining texts alone. One scholar put it this way: "I couldn't see what a text was doing without looking at the worlds in which these texts served as significant activities."* After all, it is one thing to

---

*C. Bazerman, *Shaping Written Knowledge: The Genre and Activity of the Scientific Article in Science* (Madison: University of Wisconsin Press, 1988), p. 4.

read a research report and understand its purpose, its intended audience, the nature of its claims, and the like. But it is quite another to watch scientists at work and begin to understand how they have come to know what they know. The discovery of DNA, for example, was the result of an arduous process that involved much risk, collaboration, chance, error, and competition. The neat structure of a scientific report could mislead you into thinking that science is a linear process that begins with a question, moves on to an experiment, and ends with an answer. Real research is messier than that. Original research takes us behind the words we read, introducing levels of complexity.

*To Broaden Your Scope of Inquiry.*   Doing original research may also broaden the scope of your inquiry. First, it is useful to use different research methods than the ones you are accustomed to using. Learning to interview and run focus groups, at the very least, can give you insight and practice for nonacademic applications—market research, for example. Second, it can make you aware of how people outside your field address the questions you raise. Consider, for example, the different perspectives an educator, a sociologist, and an economist would bring to the question of educational inequities. An educator might study educational inequities as a curricular problem and therefore analyze the content of different curricula within and across schools. A sociologist might visit students' homes, noting the presence or absence of books or asking parents how they go about preparing their children for school. An economist might examine income levels in both wealthy and impoverished neighborhoods. The point is that each field brings its own perspective to a problem, adding complexity and richness to your own discussion of that problem.

*To Make a Unique Contribution to a Conversation of Ideas.*   Finally, doing original research affords you the opportunity to make a unique contribution to a conversation of ideas. Instead of relying exclusively on texts others have written as evidence for your claims, you can offer your own data to address a question or problem, data that others do not have available. For instance, if you wanted to examine claims that primary school teachers pay more attention to boys in class than to girls, you could review the relevant literature and then add to that literature a study that systematically analyzes the ways in which teachers in different classrooms treat boys and girls.

## GETTING STARTED: WRITING A PROPOSAL

A **proposal** is a formal plan that outlines your objectives for conducting a research project, specifies the methods you intend to use, and describes what you expect the implications of the work to be. The proposal is a tool that helps guide you through various stages of the project. The most immediate benefit of writing a proposal is that through the act of writing—by setting forth an outline of your project—your thinking will become more focused and precise.

At a minimum, a research proposal should include three sections: purpose, method, and discussion and implications. You may also want to include additional sections with materials that provide concrete support for your proposal—some of the tools that will help you get the job done. You should arrange your plan and use headings so that readers can find information quickly.

## ■ Describe Your Purpose

In the purpose section of your proposal, formulate the question that is motivating your study. Inquiry begins with a good question.

- A good question can help you think through the issue you want to write about.
- It is specific enough to guide your inquiry and to be answered with the tools and resources you have available and have decided to use.
- It does not limit the answer to yes, no, or either/or.
- It asks how, why, should, or the extent to which.
- It conveys a clear idea of who you are answering the question for—your audience.

In your purpose section (usually the introduction), you should summarize the issue and explain how it has led to the question driving your research. You also should explain why you are interested in this issue area, why it is important, and what is at stake. Ask yourself why others should be interested in your effort to answer the question.

## ■ Define Your Method

In the method section, you list and describe the tools and strategies you will use to conduct your research. Some of the tools and strategies of original research are

- conducting interviews or focus groups
- taking notes
- recording on audio- or videotape a particular activity or activities
- doing background, historical, or archival work
- observing and coming to terms with your own impressions

In addition to identifying your method, you need to discuss the appropriateness of your tools and strategies, why they are the best means for answering your research question. Given the objectives you have set for yourself and the constraints of doing the research, are some methods better than others?

## ■ Discuss Your Implications

It may seem a little premature to talk about what you hope to find in your study, but it is important to address "So what?"—to explain what you believe is the significance of your study. Place your argument in the context of the conversation you want to join, and explain how your study can contribute to that conversation. Write about how your study will build on, challenge, or extend other studies in your area of research. And, finally, identify what you believe is going to be new about your findings.

## ■ Include Additional Materials That Support Your Research

Depending on your instructor and the level of formality of your proposal, you may be asked to include additional materials that reveal other dimensions of your research. Those materials may include (1) an annotated bibliography, (2) scripts of the questions you are planning to ask in interviews and focus groups, and (3) the consent forms you will ask interviewees or participants in your focus groups to sign.

*Annotated Bibliography.*  An **annotated bibliography** is a list of sources (arranged alphabetically by author) that you plan to consult and make use of in your research paper. Typically you provide a citation (author, date, title of source, and publication information) and a short summary of the source. You can present all your sources in one long list or organize them by type of source (books, journals, and so forth). An excerpt from a student's annotated bibliography in APA style is shown in Figure 11.1.

*Questions You Plan to Ask.*  Including a list (or lists) of the questions you expect to ask those you plan to interview or survey will help you focus your thinking. What personal information do you need to know? What information about your issue? What opinions and recommendations would be helpful? Each list should include at least five good questions but can include many more. A sample set of questions to ask the parents of homeless children appears in Figure 11.2.

*Consent Forms.*  Whenever you plan to solicit information in an interview or focus group, you need to get the interviewee's or participants' permission to make use of that information in your research paper. We have included a sample consent form for an interview in Figure 11.3.

Bibliography

*Books*

Dupper, D. R. (2003). *School social work: Skills and interventions for effective practice.* Hoboken, NJ: John Wiley & Sons.

> This book provides a general overview of the duties and responsibilities of school social workers. It explains various social problems that many students encounter, and evaluates intervention and prevention programs.

Kryder-Coe, J. H., Salamon, L. H., & Molnar, J. M. (Eds.). (1991). *Homeless children and youth: A new American dilemma.* New Brunswick, NJ: Transaction.

> This book examines the impact of child homelessness on society, the causes of child homelessness, and society's response to child homelessness. Part of the book focuses on the developmental and educational consequences of homelessness on children.

Vostanis, P., & Cumella, S. (Eds.). (1999). *Homeless children: Problems and needs.* London, England: Jessica Kingsley.

> This book is a collection of articles examining the various aspects of life for homeless children. One article focuses specifically on problems surrounding education for homeless youth.

*Journal Articles*

All of the following journal articles focus on the educational and developmental needs of homeless youth. They relate this issue to the effectiveness of the McKinney-Vento Homeless Assistance Act (1987), to the current and future work of school counselors and social workers, and to the development of community programs.

Markward, M. J., & Biros, E. (2001). McKinney revisited: Implications for school social work. *Children & Schools, 23*(3), 182-187. Retrieved from http://puck.naswpressonline.org/v1=933544/cl=17/nw=1/rpsv/journal/journal4_home.htm.

> This article examines the extent to which the McKinney-Vento Act has affected homeless children and youth. It discusses the implications the act has had for school social work.

**FIGURE 11.1   An Excerpt from a Student's Annotated Bibliography**

> Moroz, K. J., & Segal, E. A. (1990). Homeless children: Intervention strategies for school social workers. *Social Work in Education,* *12*(2), 134-143.
>> This article investigates the various effects of homelessness on children. The authors propose a model for intervention for school social workers that would connect them with community services.

**FIGURE 11.1**   (*continued*)

## ▪ Establish a Timeline

To write a proposal, you'll need to draw up a schedule for your research. This timeline should include the dates when you expect to finish the proposal, when you will conduct interviews and focus groups, when you hope to have a draft, and when you will complete the project. As you develop your timeline, you need to be realistic about when you can actually complete the different stages of collecting your data and writing. You can anticipate that events will prevent everything from going as planned.

---

**Parent(s)**
1. a. Describe your current living and family situation (parents, siblings, how long homeless, where living, where child attends school).
   b. Describe your child.
   c. Describe your relationship with your child.

2. a. Do you think homelessness is affecting your child's schooling?
   b. If so, tell me how (grades, friends, attendance, transportation).

3. Tell me about enrolling your child in school. What was the process like? Were there any problems? Conditions? Challenges?

4. a. Do you feel that your child's right to an education has been recognized?
   b. Why or why not? What experiences can you point to to support your answer?

5. Describe the relationship between your child and his or her teachers.

6. a. What types of support services is your child currently being offered in school and in the community?
   b. How effective are those services?
   c. How supportive of your child's educational and developmental growth do you feel your child's school has been?
   d. What about the Center for the Homeless?
   e. Do you have any recommendations for these sources of help or requests for other types of help or services for your child that are not currently offered?

7. How do you envision your child's future?

---

**FIGURE 11.2**   **Sample Interview Questions**

You are invited to participate in a study of homelessness and education conducted by Mary Ronan, an undergraduate at the University of Notre Dame, during the next few months. If you decide to participate, you will

1. provide up to two interviews with the researcher,

2. allow the researcher to use excerpts from the interviews in publications about research with the understanding that your identity will not be revealed at any time.

Participation is completely voluntary. You may choose to stop participating at any time prior to completion of the project. Should you have any questions at any time, you are welcome to contact the researcher by phone or e-mail. Your decision to participate will have no effect on or prejudice your future relationship with the University of Notre Dame. One possible benefit of participating in the study is that you will have the opportunity to learn about the implications of homelessness on education.

If you are willing to participate in this research, please read and sign the consent form below. You will be given a copy of this form to keep.

### CONSENT FORM

*I agree to participate in all of the procedures above. I understand that my identity will be protected during the study and that others will not have access to the interviews I provide. I also understand that my name will not be revealed when data from the research are presented in publications. I have read the above and give the researcher, Mary Ronan, permission to use excerpts from transcripts of tapes without identifying me as the writer or speaker.*

_____     _____
*Date*                                                           *Signature*

                                                                 _____
                                                                 *Signature of Researcher*
                                                                 *[Telephone number]/[E-mail address]*

FIGURE 11.3    Sample Interview Consent Form

People cannot always meet you when you would like them to, and you may have to change your own schedule. Therefore, be sure to contact participants well in advance of the time you would like to speak with them in interviews or focus groups.

## Steps to Writing a Proposal

**1** **Describe your purpose.** Summarize your issue, describing how it has led you to the question motivating your research.

**2** **Define your method.** What tools and strategies are you planning to use? Why are they appropriate and sufficient for your purposes?

**3** **Discuss your implications.** What is the context of the conversation you are entering? What significant information do you expect your study to uncover?

**4** **Include additional materials that support your research.** These may include an annotated bibliography, a series of interview questions, and blank consent forms.

## AN ANNOTATED STUDENT PROPOSAL

Our student Mary Ronan submitted a formal proposal for a study of the education of a homeless child. Ronan's proposal was exceptionally well prepared, thorough, and thoughtful, and she included a number of additional materials: an annotated bibliography; sample questions for the teachers, students, and parents she planned to interview; and sample consent forms. We reprint only the main part of her proposal, the part that includes her purpose, methods, and discussion and implications sections, for you to consider as a model for proposal writing. Notice how Ronan summarizes her issue and explains how it led to her research, and how she makes her readers understand why her research is important.

CASE STUDY OF ONE HOMELESS CHILD                                    1

Research Paper Proposal:
A Case Study of One Homeless Child's Education and Lifestyle
Mary Ronan

*Identifies a pressing concern that readers should be aware of.*

    In 2000, the Urban Institute estimated that 1.35 million children experience homelessness over the course of a year (Urban Institute, 2000). The U.S. Department of Education estimated that the number of children and youth in homeless situations increased from approximately 841,700 to 930,000 in 2000 (U.S. Department of Education, 2000). It also determined that preschool and elementary-aged children make up the largest numbers of children experiencing homelessness (U.S. Department of Education, 2000). Homelessness as experienced by school-aged children is clearly increasing.

*Provides a definition of a key concept to clarify the focus of research.*

    Homeless children and youth are defined as "those individuals who lack a fixed, regular, and adequate nighttime residence" (McKinney-Vento Homeless Assistance Act, 1987).

CASE STUDY OF ONE HOMELESS CHILD                                    2

This includes children who live in shelters, cars, motels, and numerous other inadequate housing situations. The McKinney-Vento Act states that each child of a homeless individual and each homeless youth must have equal access to the same free, appropriate public education as provided to other children. It states specifically that homelessness alone is not a sufficient reason to separate these students from the mainstream school environment.

*Explains why the increase in home-lessness is such a pressing problem for educators and reviews research to determine what we know.*

Homelessness has serious implications for children's developmental and academic growth. Developmental problems include withdrawal, aggression, short attention span, sleep disorders, speech delays, regressive behaviors, immature motor behavior, immature peer interaction, and inappropriate social interaction with adults (Baumohl, 1996; Pawlas, 1994). These developmental problems lead to academic problems, which are especially evident in reading and math. The majority of home-less students read below grade level and score below grade level in mathematics (Pawlas, 1994; Stormont-Spurgin & De Reus, 1995; Walsh & Buckley, 1994; Ziesemer & Marcoux, 1992). Homeless students have higher rates of school transfer, special education services, and grade retention (Baumohl, 1996; Walsh & Buckley, 1994). Homeless students face barriers to school enrollment and attendance. These students often do not have the documents required for school enrollment; as a result, many children are turned away from attending school until this issue is resolved (U.S. Department of Education, 2000). Transporta-tion to and from school is the biggest problem for homeless youth (U.S. Department of Education, 2000). These barriers directly and negatively affect the success of homeless students in school.

3

A stable lifestyle for these children is crucial to their mental, emotional, physical, and social well-being. "Stability is central to children's growth and development, and times of tran-sition are times of risk" (Baumohl, 1996, p. 118). Homelessness creates great risks for the developmental and academic growth of youth; these risks need to be confronted. "Children who have lost their homes live the experience of having, as they describe it, 'nowhere to go' " (Walsh & Buckley, 1994, p. 2).

4

CASE STUDY OF ONE HOMELESS CHILD                 3

# 5

*Identifies a gap: what we still need to know that research has not focused on.*

Communities need to examine how they are reacting and responding to the struggles and needs of homeless students. Despite the obstacles that homeless students face, schools are an ideal setting for developing and organizing the educational and social services they need (Wall, 1996). Comprehensive services including both educators and social workers can be done both within and outside the school system (Wall, 1996). If these homeless children's lives are to improve, they will require the help of schools and social agencies, both working as parts of a community that is sensitive and responsive to these students' needs. It is clear that society understands the importance of caring for homeless students, but to what extent have schools and social service agencies carried out their suggestions or plans?

*Formulates the question motivating the writer's research.*

# 6

*Further defines the gap in what is necessary to address the problem the writer identifies.*

The McKinney-Vento Homeless Assistance Act defines homeless youth and explains the rights of students facing homelessness. It provides specific guidelines for how schools and social service agencies are to care for homeless students' educational needs. Yet Congress has not adequately funded state or local efforts to implement this legislation. In 2003, Congress appropriated $55 million for educational programs under the McKinney-Vento Act. However, this appropriation is $15 million less than the authorized amount of $70 million (National Coalition for the Homeless, 2004). Is the country doing everything it can to ensure the rights of homeless children as stated in the McKinney-Vento Homeless Assistance Act?

### Purpose

*Provides a more specific version of the question motivating this research. Develops a rationale for conducting further research and answers the question "What's at stake?"*

The question this research is attempting to answer is "To what extent are schools and social service agencies, working as parts of larger communities, creating a stable lifestyle that will improve homeless students' developmental and educational growth?" There has not been much research examining how effectively schools and social service agencies are creating stability in homeless students' lives. In order to better the lives of these children, research must be done investigating and evaluating the current services offered.

CASE STUDY OF ONE HOMELESS CHILD                                    4

The developmental and academic lives of students are                    8
threatened by the lack of stability resulting from homelessness.
This issue is a very important one as the numbers of homeless
children continue to increase each year. Answering this question will provide valuable information to both schools and social
agencies about how to better care for the specific needs and
rights of homeless students. Moreover, this research will lead to
a greater sense of community caring for those who live in poverty. It may inspire future research and the creation of programs
that better aid homeless students.

### Methods

*Describes the approach to answering the research question.*

    I will take a case study approach in order to better                    9
understand this issue and attempt to answer my research question. My case study will focus on one child from the South Bend
Center for the Homeless. I will interview the child, his or her
parents, teacher, school social worker, and others who play a
role in creating stability in this child's life. I will take notes as

*Explains what the approach will help uncover and how she will build on others' work to offer a perspective that others have neglected.*

well as audio-record the interviews. These interviews will allow
me to explore the connections between homelessness and education as explained by the voices of those who witness or are
affected by homelessness every day.

    I will also be using archival information, including both                    10
journal articles and books, from the library. I will explore what
other researchers have contributed to this issue and what they
are currently saying about it. I will also examine present-day
statistics involving homelessness, youth, and education and will
study the plans of various government and community programs
and policies, particularly the McKinney-Vento Homeless Assistance Act. This will help me to further develop and answer my
own questions about homelessness and education.

    Utilizing these various methods will provide me with a                    11
broad range of information and resources that will aid me in
completing my research. Directly discussing this education issue
with participants will lead to an honest and realistic perspective. It is the true stories of those who are faced with the issue
of homelessness on a daily basis that will bring this important
issue to the surface.

CASE STUDY OF ONE HOMELESS CHILD                                    5

## Discussion and Implications

*Elaborates on what we can learn from the study and why it matters.*

In America, over 800,000 children are homeless. In South Bend, over 300 children live in one of three homeless shelters. It is believed that 50% of these local children will grow up to be homeless. Many homeless children do not attend school regularly. Studies have found that those who do attend school do not perform as well as their peers and have difficulties socializing with others. A school should be a permanent safe-haven for these students. A school should be one place that these students might be able to consider their home. Why then do problems involving homeless youth and education continue to exist?

*12*

Homelessness traps the young in a vicious cycle from which they may never be able to escape. If they are continuously moving from shelter to shelter, they are continuously moving from school to school. As a result, their attendance may drop; their performance may not be at grade level; they may be stereotyped and labeled by others based on their temporary lifestyle. Without the psychological, social, and mental benefits a strong formal education imparts, the homeless child seems to be left to the fate of his or her parents. The cycle of homelessness continues for another generation.

*13*

*Further explains the positive changes the research can bring about.*

Perhaps as a result of this study, there will be more community and school action and involvement to support homeless students. Perhaps there will be better busing systems so that these students can remain enrolled in the same school for longer periods. Perhaps school social workers can work toward finding more permanent living arrangements for their homeless students. Perhaps more mentoring and tutoring programs can be formed to aid homeless students. Much can be done and should be done to better the lives of these students.

*14*

# INTERVIEWING

An **interview** is a face-to-face conversation in which you ask questions to collect information or opinions that relate to your research question. It's certainly possible to conduct an interview by phone, especially if the interviewee is not local, but a face-to-face conversation, in which you can note physical details and body language, is preferable.

The ways writers incorporate interviews into their writing appears almost seamless; but keep in mind that a finished text hides the process involved in conducting a successful interview. What you don't see is the planning that occurs. Writers have to make appointments with each of the people they interview; they have to develop a script, or list of questions, before actually conducting the interview; and they have to test the questions to be sure that they work—that is, that the answers give them the information they are looking for. In other words, the key to a successful interview is preparation. The following information should help you plan for your interview and prepare you for writing down your results.

## ■ Plan the Interview

You'll want to do some preliminary research to identify people who can help you understand more about your subject: What kind of expertise or experience do they have? Then you have to contact them to find out if they are willing to be interviewed. Begin by explaining your project and why you want to interview them (you may want to send them a copy of your proposal). Let them know how much of their time you are requesting: Half an hour? An hour? (More than an hour is probably excessive.) If you are planning to record the interview—always a wise idea—make sure the person consents to being recorded. Then make the necessary arrangements. For example, you may need to reserve a room where you can conduct your interview without being disturbed.

Obviously it is crucial to find out in your first contact whether your candidates actually have expertise in an area relevant to your study. If they lack that expertise, consider asking if they can recommend someone who has it.

It's important to set up appointments with people early on. To keep on schedule, list the names of people who have agreed to be interviewed:

Interviewee 1: _____ Contacted? _____(y/n)

Interviewee 2: _____ Contacted? _____(y/n)

## ■ Prepare Your Script

You should now begin to work on your script in earnest. If you submitted a series of questions with your proposal, you may have received some response to them from your instructor or classmates. Perhaps they suggested refinements or proposed additional questions. If you agree with their suggestions, now is the time to incorporate them. As you work on your script, keep the following points in mind.

*Try to establish common ground.*   In any conversation, you want to establish common ground, and an interview is no different. Do you have any interests in common with the person that may ease you into the interview?

Order your questions so that you begin by establishing common ground and then move on to the issues you want to learn more about.

*Start with nonthreatening questions.*   For example, "How long have you been working at the homeless shelter?" "What prompted you to work at a homeless shelter?" "What role do you play with the children at the homeless shelter?"

*Ask filter questions.*   Filter questions help you determine what the person you are interviewing knows or has experienced. For instance, you might ask a worker at a homeless shelter if he or she works with children. If not, does he or she work with parents? Of course, if you've done your homework, you will know where to start the interview.

*Beware of yes/no questions.*   Try not to ask questions that encourage simple yes or no responses. Work on rephrasing yes/no questions in your script so that you're more likely to get an enlightening answer. For example, don't ask "Do you think that the children at the homeless shelter can overcome the obstacles they face?" Instead, ask something like this: "How do you think children at the homeless shelter can overcome the obstacles they face?"

*Try funneling.*   *Funneling* means moving from more-general questions — "What challenges have you faced as an educator in the homeless shelter?" — to more-specific ones — "How did you respond to those challenges?"

*Rehearse and then revise the script.*   After you've reworked your script, rehearse it with your writing group or some friends to see how it works. You want to develop a sense of how an interviewee is going to respond to your questions. Is the wording clear? Are you getting the information you need? If not, what other questions should you ask? How did the order and pacing of the questions make your stand-in interviewees feel? How long did the interview take? After the rehearsal, revise the script to improve the content, order, and pacing of your questions.

## ■ Conduct the Interview

On the day of an interview, contact your interviewee again to make sure he or she remembers the time of the interview and knows how to find the location where it will take place. See to it that your tape recorder or video camera is charged and functioning and has sufficient recording capacity for the interview. Be on time. Start by having the person sign a simple consent form (see Figure 11.3). It should specify how you will use the material and should indicate that the interviewee knows you will be recording the interview and agrees to let you use quotes from the interview in your paper.

Once you begin asking questions, if at all possible, take notes and record the conversation. Be flexible with the script as you go. Pursue new questions that are raised by what the interviewee tells you. If the interviewee's answers are vague, evasive, or misdirected, try rephrasing your questions to be more specific about the information you need. If you think the interviewee is implying something that is of special interest to you, ask for clarification. This kind of reflective query may shake loose some interesting new material.

Toward the end of the interview, check your script for important questions you may have forgotten to ask. If there are several, try to ask only the most important ones in the time remaining.

## ■ Make Sense of the Interview

Conducting an interview is only part of the challenge; you then have to make sense of what was said. That process involves four steps:

1. *Familiarize yourself with the conversation.* If you recorded the interview, listen to or watch it a couple of times to become really familiar with what was said. Read through your notes several times too.

2. *Transcribe the interview.* Being familiar with the conversation will make it easier to transcribe. Keep in mind that transcription takes more time than you think, so plan accordingly. An hour-long interview usually takes about three hours to transcribe.

3. *Analyze the interview.* Read through the interview again. Look for answers to the questions motivating your research, and look for recurring patterns or themes. Make a list of those ideas relevant to the issues you intend to focus on, especially evidence that might support your argument.

4. *Find one good source.* Using the themes you identify in your analysis as a guide, find one good source that relates to your interview in some way. Maybe your subject's story fits into an educational debate (for example, public versus private education). Or maybe your subject's story counters a common conception about education (that inner-city schools are hopelessly inadequate). You're looking for a source you can link to your interview in an interesting and effective way.

## ■ Turn Your Interview into an Essay

Try to lay out on paper, in paragraphs, the material you've collected that pertains to the focus of your paper. In a first draft, you might take these steps:

1. State your argument, or the purpose of your essay. What do you want to teach your readers?

2. Begin writing your supporting evidence for your thesis. What examples from your reading, observations, or interviews do you want to offer your readers? How do those examples illuminate your claim?

3. Place quotations from more than one source in as many paragraphs as you can, so that you can play the quotations off against one another. What is significant about the ways you see specific quotations "in conversation" with one another? How do these conversations between quotations help you build your own point?

4. Consider possible counterarguments to the point you want to make.

5. Help readers understand what is at stake in adopting your position.

---

### Steps to Interviewing

**1** **Plan the interview.** After you've identified candidates through research, contact them to explain your project and set up appointments if they are willing to participate.

**2** **Prepare your script.** Draft your questions, rehearse them with your classmates or friends, and then make revisions based on their responses.

**3** **Conduct the interview.** Be flexible with your script as you go, making sure to take good notes even if you are recording the interview.

**4** **Make sense of the interview.** Review the recording and your notes of the interview, transcribe the interview, analyze the transcript, and connect the conversation to at least one good source.

**5** **Turn your interview into an essay.** State your argument, organize your evidence, use quotes to make your point, consider counterarguments, and help your readers understand what's at stake.

---

## USING FOCUS GROUPS

Focus groups can provide you with an original source of evidence to complement (or complicate, contradict, or extend) the evidence you find in books and articles. Conducting a focus group is much like conducting an interview. According to Bruce L. Berg, in *Qualitative Research Methods for the Social Sciences*, a **focus group** "may be defined as an interview style designed for small groups . . . addressing a particular topic of interest or relevance to the group and the researcher." College administrators often speak with groups of students to understand the nature of a problem—for instance, whether writing instruction is as effective as it should be beyond a first-year writing course, or whether technology is used to best effect in classes across the curriculum. One advantage of a focus group, as opposed to an interview, is that once one person starts talking, others join in. It is generally easier to get a conversation going in a focus group than to get an interview started with a single person.

A typical focus group session is guided by a facilitator, or moderator. The moderator's job is much like the interviewer's: to draw out information from the participants on topics of importance to a given investigation. The informal atmosphere of the focus group is intended to encourage participants to speak freely and completely about their behaviors, attitudes, and opinions. Interaction among group members often takes the form of brainstorming, generating a larger number of ideas, issues, topics, and even solutions to problems than could be produced through individual conversations.

The following are several basic tasks necessary to orchestrating a focus group.

## ■ Select Participants for the Focus Group

Focus groups should consist of five to seven participants, in addition to you, the moderator. Think carefully about the range of participants you'll need in order to gather the information you're hoping to find. Depending on your issue, you might choose participants based on gender, ethnicity, major, year in school, living situation, or some other factor. Do you want a wide range of participants? Or do you want to control the focus of the conversation by looking at just one particular group of people? For instance, if you wanted to find out if technology is serving students' needs, would you talk only to people in the sciences? Or would you want a cross section of disciplines represented? Or if your question is whether colleges and universities should take race and ethnicity into consideration when selecting students from the applicant pool, would you limit participation to the admissions staff? Where should you look for input on the purpose of giving preference to minority students or the advantages of a diverse campus?

## ■ Plan the Focus Group

Planning is as important for a focus group as it is for an interview. Make specific arrangements with participants about the time and place of the focus group session, and be clear about how much time it will take, usually thirty minutes. You should tape-record or videotape the session, in addition to any notes you take. Jot down important information during the session, and allow yourself time to make more extensive notes as soon as it is over. You will need to get permission from respondents to use the information they give you and ensure their anonymity. (In your essay, you can refer to participants by letter, number, or some other designation.) Make a sheet with your signature that spells this out clearly, and make sure all your participants sign it before the session. You should include a state-

You are invited to participate in a study of academic writing at the university over the next four years. You were selected from a random sample of all first-year students. If you decide to participate, you will

1.  provide the researcher with copies of the writing you complete for every class and the assignment, when available.

2.  attend up to four focus group sessions during a given academic year.

3.  allow the researcher to use excerpts from the writing you complete and the focus group sessions in publications about research with the understanding that your identity will not be revealed at any time.

In all, out-of-class participation will take no more than four hours during an academic year.

Participation is completely voluntary; you may stop participating at any time prior to completion of the project. Should you have any questions at any time, you are welcome to contact the researcher at the address below or via e-mail. Your decision to participate or not will have no effect on your grade in any course or prejudice your future relationship with the university. One benefit of participating in the study is that you will have the opportunity to learn important information about writing.

If you are willing to participate in this research, please read and sign the consent form below. You will be given a copy of this form to keep.

### CONSENT FORM

*I agree to participate in all of the procedures above. I understand that my identity will be protected during the study and that instructors will not have access to the statements I make in focus group sessions. I also understand that my name will not be revealed when data from the research are presented in publications. (Tapes from this study will be kept for five years and then destroyed.) I have read the above and give the researcher, Stuart Greene, and his coauthors permission to use excerpts from what I write or transcripts of tapes without identifying me as the writer or speaker.*

_____          _____

*Date*                                   *Signature*

                                         _____

                                         *Signature of Researcher*
                                         *[Telephone number]/[E-mail address]*

**FIGURE 11.4    Sample Consent Form for a Focus Group**

ment pointing out that people have the right not to participate. We have included sample consent forms in Figures 11.4 and 11.5.

### ■ Prepare Your Script

Many of the guidelines for designing interview questions (see pp. 308–09) apply equally well to focus group questions. So, for example, you might start by establishing common ground or with a couple of nonthreatening

Should colleges and universities take race and ethnicity into consideration when selecting new freshmen from the applicant pool? What is the purpose of giving preference to minority status in admissions? What does a diverse campus offer its students? These are some of the issues I want to discuss in today's focus group. But before we start, let me tell you about the assignment and your involvement.

The focus group is an interview style designed for small groups of five to seven participants. Focus group interviews are guided discussions that address a particular topic of interest or relevance to the group and the researcher. The informality of the focus group structure is intended to encourage participants to speak freely about their behaviors, attitudes, and opinions. For the purposes of my research, focus groups are a way to include multiple perspectives in my paper.

This session will be recorded so that I can prove my research. No names will be used in any drafts or in my final paper; instead, I will use letters (A, B, C) to identify different speakers. Two focus groups — one for minority students at Notre Dame and another for nonminority students — are being held so that I can obtain opinions and viewpoints from both sides of the issue and discuss their similarities and differences in my report. Some things to keep in mind during the session:

- Because I need to transcribe the dialogue, try not to talk over another person.
- Feel free to agree or disagree with a question, statement, or another person's answer.
- Focus on the discussion, not the question.
- Avoid going off on tangents.
- Be open and honest in all your responses.

Thank you for taking the time to be involved in my research. By signing below you give me permission to use the comments you provide for my paper. You understand that in no way will your identity be revealed, except by your minority or nonminority status. If you would like a copy of the results of the focus groups, please include your e-mail address, and the documents will be sent to you.

Name _____    Male Female (circle one)

Ethnicity _____    Class of _____

E-mail address _____

**FIGURE 11.5    Sample Consent Form for a Focus Group**

questions. For variety, and to keep the discussion moving, use both open-ended and closed-ended (yes/no answer) questions. Consider asking participants for definitions, impressions, examples, their ideas of others' perceptions, and the like. Also, you might quote from key passages in the scholarly research you will be using and ask for the group's responses to these "expert" theories. Not only will this be interesting; it also will help you organize and integrate your focus group evidence with evidence from library sources in your essay. Ask a wider range of questions than you think you might need so that you can explore side issues if they arise.

## ■ Conduct the Focus Group

On the day you conduct the focus group, contact those who have agreed to participate to remind them of when and where it will happen. Show up ahead of time to make sure that your tape recorder or video camera is in good working order and that the room has sufficient seating for the participants. And don't forget your script. Here are three other guidelines.

*Ask questions that draw people out.*   During the focus group, be ready to draw out participants with follow-up questions ("Can you offer an example?" "Where do you think this impression comes from?"). Encourage all participants to speak; don't allow one member to dominate the discussion. (You may need to ask a facilitating question like "Do the rest of you agree with X's statement?" or "How would you extend what X has said?" or "Has anyone had a different experience?")

*Limit the time of a focus group session.*   It's a good idea to limit the session to twenty to thirty minutes. When deciding how long the session should last, remember that it will take approximately three times longer to transcribe it. You must transcribe the session so that you can read through the participants' comments and quote them accurately.

*Notice nonverbal interactions.*   The tape recorder or video camera will give you a record of what was said, but be sure to notice nonverbal interactions and responses in your session, taking notes of body language, reluctance or eagerness to speak, and dynamics among group members that either open up or shut down conversation. These responses should be part of the data you analyze.

## ■ Interpret the Data from the Focus Group

Once you transcribe your focus group session, decide how you will refer anonymously to your participants. You then need to interpret the significance of the way participants talk about issues, as well as the information they relate. Interpret the nonverbal communication in the group as well as the verbal communication.

In making claims based on focus group data, remember that data from focus group interviews are not the same as data from individual interviews. They reflect collective thinking, ideas shared and negotiated by the group. Also, although you might speculate that data from a focus group are indicative of larger trends, be careful about the kinds of claims you make. One first-year student's idea is not necessarily every first-year student's idea.

The principal aim of doing original research is to make a contribution to a conversation using primary material as evidence to support your argument. For instance, when you conduct interviews or focus group discussions, you are collecting information (or data) that can offer a unique perspective. And doing original research also can enable you to test others' claims or assumptions and broaden your scope of inquiry beyond secondary materials. An effective piece of original research still relies on secondary materials, particularly as you find ways to locate what you discover in the context of what other authors have observed and argued. Moreover, there is the value of using multiple sources of information to support your claims—using your observations and the findings of others to say something about your subject. Also important, the research methods you choose depend on the question you ask. A focus on the types of educational opportunities available to the homeless lends itself more to close observation, interviews, and perhaps focus groups.

Finally, we want to end with an ethical reminder: *Be fair to your sources.* Throughout this chapter, we have included a number of forms on which you can base your own consent forms when you conduct interviews and focus groups. When people give you their consent to use their words, it is incumbent on you—really it is essential—that you represent as faithfully as possible what people have said. As a researcher, you are given a kind of power over the people you interview and write about, using what they tell you for your own purposes. You cannot abuse the trust they place in you when they consent to be part of your research. It is important that they understand why you're doing the research and how your theories and assumptions will likely figure into your interpretation of the information you gather. You must also be aware of how their words will be construed by those who read what you write.

---

## Steps for Conducting a Focus Group

**1** **Select participants for the focus group.** Identify the range of your five to seven participants. Are you looking for diverse perspectives or a more specialized group?

**2** **Plan the focus group.** Make sure that you have a specified time and place and that your participants are willing to sign consent forms.

**3** **Prepare your script.** Prepare a variety of open-ended and closed-ended questions; consider quoting research you are interested in using in your paper to get participants' responses; and try to rehearse and revise.

**4** **Conduct the focus group.** Record the session; ask questions that draw people out; limit the time of the session; and notice nonverbal interactions. And don't forget the consent forms.

**5** **Interpret the data from the focus group.** Transcribe and analyze the data, including nonverbal communications; draw conclusions, but be careful not to overgeneralize from your small sample.

# Entering
# the Conversation
# of Ideas

# Education

*What does it mean to be educated, and who decides?*

S tudents don't always get a chance to step back and reflect on the many elements that shape the educational system—elements that at this very moment affect what you are learning, how you are learning it, and the kind of educated person you will be when you graduate. The readings in this chapter take a range of inventive approaches to two central questions: What does it mean to be educated? Who decides?

Some of these authors invite you to reflect on your own educational experiences, both good and bad. For example, Jonathan Kozol and Gloria Anzaldúa draw on specific examples of early education to demonstrate the ways that school settings can empower or disempower their students. They also describe political and social debates around bilingualism, integration, and education that illuminate some classroom dynamics, helping us reflect on what Kozol provocatively calls the "educational apartheid" of the present. Although public education is widely thought to be the most crucial element of a democracy, clearly not all public education in the United States is equal. These writers use interviews with students and personal experiences to argue that many American schools fall far short of their democratic potential. Deborah Tannen, a professor of linguistics, examines classroom dynamics through another lens, noticing the way girls and boys are socialized into different speech patterns that can affect learning environments at all levels of education. Like Kozol and Anzaldúa, Tannen analyzes specific examples of instructors and students interacting in a classroom, in order to help us see conversational patterns that limit both males and females, though in different ways. Keep your own experiences in mind as you consider the ways these authors explain these educational problems and possible solutions.

Beverly Daniel Tatum and Peggy McIntosh extend this conversation, mulling over what McIntosh calls the "myth of meritocracy," or the falsity of the "American dream" idea that if we just work hard enough, we can succeed. These authors focus on the larger social dynamics—particularly social dynamics around racial differences—that shape the way others respond to us. Tatum's essay, pointedly titled "Why Are All the Black Kids Sitting Together in the Cafeteria?" provides tools for analyzing social dynamics of high schools that may be very familiar to you, and visible in your college setting, too. Tatum's interviews with students invite us to see with fresh eyes how school environments might more often than not reinforce racial stereotyping rather than providing tools for resisting these inequitable assumptions. While McIntosh looks beyond the school environment, we hope you will think about school dynamics when she describes how challenging it was for her, as a white woman, to see clearly the many small, unconscious, everyday racial assumptions that we make about ourselves and others, which often reinforce racial hierarchies. Neither Tatum nor McIntosh is interested in blame; instead, they try to demonstrate the potential of living with our eyes wide open and envisioning ways we can learn both inside and outside school to act more equitably.

James Loewen's essay focuses more specifically on the curricula taught in high schools, and in particular on high school history classes, which he claims are often designed not only to bore students but also to teach them outright lies. Loewen's central complaint is that many of the facts and dates that bloat most history textbooks are incorrect; more importantly, they ignore the sometimes unpleasant truths of this nation's founding and development. Many adults lament how little today's students know about history, but Loewen blames teachers and textbook writers for students' lack of knowledge and inability to ask critical questions about the past and the present. Loewen claims, "We've got to do better."

That same sentiment pervades the college-level curricular analyses by Gerald Graff and Mark Edmundson, who are similarly concerned by the way students are rewarded for simply echoing back the information they are presented in their classes, rather than challenging the history of and assumptions behind what counts as "important knowledge" in different disciplines. Graff focuses on the lack of coherence in most college educations, in which students learn pieces of disconnected information in various disciplines without ever really seeing the big picture. He suggests this system is as absurd as trying "to learn the game of baseball by being shown a series of rooms in which you see each component of the game separately: pitchers going through their windups in one room; hitters swinging their bats in the next. . . . But since you see them separately you get no clear idea of what the game actually looks like or why the players do what they do." His metaphor should get you thinking, as should Edmundson's attack on what he calls the "lite" college education experience, in which instructors and campuses cater mostly to the pleasure of the student consumer. He suggests that something is wrong when college students "shop" for classes they will "enjoy" rather than aiming to be challenged by them. Like Graff, Edmundson argues for courses that stretch students beyond their comfort zones. What is education for, these writers wonder, if not to change us?

All the writers in this chapter push us to ask what it means in contemporary culture to be educated, and who has access to which kinds of education. These readings invite you to question common assumptions about how classrooms operate, from teacher-student dynamics to the material that has been designated "important knowledge." These readings should help you see your past and present educational experiences through fresh eyes, to consider the relationship between education and social power, and to ask an important question: What do *you* think it should mean to be an educated person in the contemporary United States?

MARK EDMUNDSON

# On the Uses of a Liberal Education: As Lite Entertainment for Bored College Students

Mark Edmundson is a professor of English at the University of Virginia. He has published many scholarly articles on literary and cultural criticism and has written books for academic specialists on the politics of reading and writing. Edmundson's popular press books on the business of teaching and learning include the acclaimed *Teacher: The One Who Made the Difference* (2003), about a quirky high school philosophy teacher who inspired Edmundson, a self-described "jock," to become a teacher himself.

In this piece, you will hear Edmundson's very distinctive voice, which can be funny as well as sharply critical. As you read, consider both his argument that higher education caters too much to the consumerist tendencies of students, and the way he makes this argument, through specific examples of himself, his students, and his campus.

How on target do you think he is about student culture? Consider, for example, how you and your friends talk about "good" versus "bad" professors, perhaps in terms of those who are "fun" or "boring."

Because this is an article for a general readership, Edmundson does not quote other scholars at length or cite them in a bibliography or a works cited page. However, he does draw on a wide range of literary and historical references and assumes that his readers know what he means when he refers to Adorno and Horkheimer in paragraph 48, or when he lists Lenin, Trotsky, Freud, and Blake in paragraph 52. As a reader, you might assess what it feels like to be put in the position of being expected to know these names. (For example, do you usually look up names and words you don't know? How might your willingness—or unwillingness—to do this "extra" work be connected to Edmundson's argument?)

The bulk of Edmundson's evidence comes from his personal observations and exchanges with students, and as you read, you should weigh the strengths and weaknesses of these kinds of examples. What kinds of examples draw you in and make you think about your own school experiences? In his conclusion, he challenges professors and students to embrace exuberance, despite the cultural tendency simply to shrug and mutter "Whatever." This provocative essay aims to get under your skin so that such a response isn't likely.

■ ■ ■

Today is evaluation day in my Freud class, and everything has changed. *1* The class meets twice a week, late in the afternoon, and the clientele, about fifty undergraduates, tends to drag in and slump, looking disconsolate and a little lost, waiting for a jump start. To get the discussion moving, they usually require a joke, an anecdote, an off-the-wall question—When you were a kid, were your Halloween getups ego costumes, id costumes, or superego costumes? That sort of thing. But today, as soon as I flourish the forms, a buzz rises in the room. Today they write their assessments of the course, their assessments of *me*, and they are without a doubt wide-awake. "What is your evaluation of the instructor?" asks question number eight, entreating them to circle a number between five (excellent) and one (poor). Whatever interpretive subtlety they've acquired during the term is now out the window. Edmundson: one to five, stand and shoot.

And they do. As I retreat through the door—I never stay around for this phase of the ritual—I look over my shoulder and see them toiling away like the devil's auditors. They're pitched into high writing gear, even the ones who struggle to squeeze out their journal entries word by word, stoked on a procedure they have by now supremely mastered. They're playing the informed consumer, letting the provider know where he's come through and where he's not quite up to snuff.

But why am I so distressed, bolting like a refugee out of my own class-room, where I usually hold easy sway? Chances are the evaluations will be much like what they've been in the past—they'll be just fine. It's likely that I'll be commended for being "interesting" (and I am commended, many times over), that I'll be cited for my relaxed and tolerant ways (that happens, too), that my sense of humor and capacity to connect the arcana of the subject matter with current culture will come in for some praise (yup). I've been hassled this term, finishing a manuscript, and so haven't given their journals the attention I should have, and for that I'm called—quite civilly, though—to account. Overall, I get off pretty well.

Yet I have to admit that I do not much like the image of myself that emerges from these forms, the image of knowledgeable, humorous detachment and bland tolerance. I do not like the forms themselves, with their number ratings, reminiscent of the sheets circulated after the TV pilot has just played to its sample audience in Burbank. Most of all I dislike the attitude of calm consumer expertise that pervades the responses. I'm disturbed by the serene belief that my function—and, more important, Freud's, or Shakespeare's, or Blake's—is to divert, entertain, and interest. Observes one respondent, not at all unrepresentative: "Edmundson has done a fantastic job of presenting this difficult, important & controversial material in an enjoyable and approachable way."

Thanks but no thanks. I don't teach to amuse, to divert, or even, for that matter, to be merely interesting. When someone says she "enjoyed" the course—and that word crops up again and again in my evaluations—somewhere at the edge of my immediate complacency I feel encroaching self-dislike. That is not at all what I had in mind. The off-the-wall questions and the sidebar jokes are meant as lead-ins to stronger stuff—in the case of the Freud course, to a complexly tragic view of life. But the affability and the one-liners often seem to be all that land with the students; their journals and evaluations leave me little doubt.

I want some of them to say that they've been changed by the course. I want them to measure themselves against what they've read. It's said that some time ago a Columbia University instructor used to issue a harsh two-part question. One: What book did you most dislike in the course? Two: What intellectual or characterological flaws in you does that dislike point to? The hand that framed that question was surely heavy. But at least it compels one to see intellectual work as a confrontation between two people, student and author, where the stakes matter. Those Columbia students were being asked to relate the quality of an *encounter*, not rate the action as though it had unfolded on the big screen.

Why are my students describing the Oedipus complex and the death drive as being interesting and enjoyable to contemplate? And why am I coming across as an urbane, mildly ironic, endlessly affable guide to this intellectual territory, operating without intensity, generous, funny, and loose?

Because that's what works. On evaluation day, I reap the rewards of my partial compliance with the culture of my students and, too, with the culture of the university as it now operates. It's a culture that's gotten little exploration. Current critics tend to think that liberal-arts education is in crisis because universities have been invaded by professors with peculiar ideas: deconstruction, Lacanianism, feminism, queer theory. They believe that genius and tradition are out and that P.C., multiculturalism, and identity politics are in because of an invasion by tribes of tenured radicals, the late millennial equivalents of the Visigoth hordes that cracked Rome's walls.

But mulling over my evaluations and then trying to take a hard, extended look at campus life both here at the University of Virginia and around the country eventually led me to some different conclusions. To me, liberal-arts education is as ineffective as it is now not chiefly because there are a lot of strange theories in the air. (Used well, those theories *can* be illuminating.) Rather, it's that university culture, like American culture writ large, is, to put it crudely, ever more devoted to consumption and entertainment, to the using and using up of goods and images. For someone growing up in America now, there are few available alternatives to the cool consumer worldview. My students didn't ask for that view, much less create it, but they bring a consumer weltanschauung to school, where it exerts a powerful, and largely unacknowledged, influence. If we want to understand current universities, with their multiple woes, we might try leaving the realms of expert debate and fine ideas and turning to the classrooms and campuses, where a new kind of weather is gathering.

From time to time I bump into a colleague in the corridor and we have what I've come to think of as a Joon Lee fest. Joon Lee is one of the best students I've taught. He's endlessly curious, has read a small library's worth, seen every movie, and knows all about showbiz and entertainment. For a class of mine he wrote an essay using Nietzsche's Apollo and Dionysus to analyze the pop group The Supremes. A trite, cultural-studies bonbon? Not at all. He said striking things about conceptions of race in America and about how they shape our ideas of beauty. When I talk with one of his other teachers, we run on about the general splendors of his work and presence. But what inevitably follows a JL fest is a mournful reprise about the divide that separates him and a few other remarkable students from their contemporaries. It's not that some aren't nearly as bright—in terms of intellectual ability, my students are all that I could ask for. Instead, it's that Joon Lee has decided to follow his interests and let them make him into a singular and rather eccentric man; in his charming way, he doesn't mind being at odds with most anyone.

It's his capacity for enthusiasm that sets Joon apart from what I've come to think of as the reigning generational style. Whether the students are sorority/fraternity types, grunge aficionados, piercer/tattooers, black or white, rich or middle class (alas, I teach almost no students from truly poor backgrounds), they are, nearly across the board, very, very self-contained. On good days they display a light, appealing glow; on bad days, shuffling disgruntlement. But there's little fire, little passion to be found.

This point came home to me a few weeks ago when I was wandering across the university grounds. There, beneath a classically cast portico, were two students, male and female, having a rip-roaring argument. They were incensed, bellowing at each other, headstrong, confident, and wild. It struck me how rarely I see this kind of full-out feeling in students anymore. Strong emotional display is forbidden. When conflicts arise, it's generally understood that one of the parties will say something sarcastically propitiating ("whatever" often does it) and slouch away.

How did my students reach this peculiar state in which all passion seems to be spent? I think that many of them have imbibed their sense of self from consumer culture in general and from the tube in particular. They're the progeny of 100 cable channels and omnipresent Blockbuster outlets. TV, Marshall McLuhan famously said, is a cool medium. Those who play best on it are low-key and nonassertive; they blend in. Enthusiasm, à la Joon Lee, quickly looks absurd. The form of character that's most appealing on TV is calmly self-interested though never greedy, attuned to the conventions, and ironic. Judicious timing is preferred to sudden self-assertion. The TV medium is inhospitable to inspiration, improvisation, failures, slipups. All must run perfectly.

Naturally, a cool youth culture is a marketing bonanza for producers of the right products, who do all they can to enlarge that culture and keep it grinding. The Internet, TV, and magazines now teem with what I call persona ads, ads for Nikes and Reeboks and Jeeps and Blazers that don't so much endorse the capacities of the product per se as show you what sort of person you will be once you've acquired it. The Jeep ad that features hip, outdoorsy kids whipping a Frisbee from mountaintop to mountaintop isn't so much about what Jeeps can do as it is about the kind of people who own them. Buy a Jeep and be one with them. The ad is of little consequence in itself, but expand its message exponentially and you have the central thrust of current consumer culture—buy in order to be.

Most of my students seem desperate to blend in, to look right, not to make a spectacle of themselves. (Do I have to tell you that those two students having the argument under the portico turned out to be acting

in a role-playing game?) The specter of the uncool creates a subtle tyranny. It's apparently an easy standard to subscribe to, this Letterman-like,
Tarantino-like cool, but once committed to it, you discover that matters
are rather different. You're inhibited, except on ordained occasions, from
showing emotion, stifled from trying to achieve anything original. You're
made to feel that even the slightest departure from the reigning code will
get you genially ostracized. This is a culture tensely committed to a laid-
back norm.

Am I coming off like something of a crank here? Maybe. Oscar Wilde, 16
who is almost never wrong, suggested that it is perilous to promiscuously
contradict people who are much younger than yourself. Point taken. But
one of the lessons that consumer hype tries to insinuate is that we must
never rebel against the new, never even question it. If it's new—a new
need, a new product, a new show, a new style, a new generation—it must
be good. So maybe, even at the risk of winning the withered, brown laurels
of crankdom, it pays to resist newness-worship and cast a colder eye.

Praise for my students? I have some of that too. What my students are, 17
at their best, is decent. They are potent believers in equality. They help out
at the soup kitchen and volunteer to tutor poor kids to get a stripe on their
résumés, sure. But they also want other people to have a fair shot. And in
their commitment to fairness they are discerning; there you see them at
their intellectual best. If I were on trial and innocent, I'd want them on
the jury.

What they will not generally do, though, is indict the current system. 18
They won't talk about how the exigencies of capitalism lead to a reserve
army of the unemployed and nearly inevitable misery. That would be getting too loud, too brash. For the pervading view is the cool consumer perspective, where passion and strong admiration are forbidden. "To stand in
awe of nothing, Numicus, is perhaps the one and only thing that can make
a man happy and keep him so," says Horace in the *Epistles,* and I fear that
his lines ought to hang as a motto over the university in this era of high
consumer capitalism.

It's easy to mount one's high horse and blame the students for this 19
state of affairs. But they didn't create the present culture of consumption.
(It was largely my own generation, that of the Sixties, that let the counterculture search for pleasure devolve into a quest for commodities.) And
they weren't the ones responsible, when they were six and seven and eight
years old, for unplugging the TV set from time to time or for hauling off
and kicking a hole through it. It's my generation of parents who sheltered
these students, kept them away from the hard knocks of everyday life,
making them cautious and overfragile, who demanded that their teachers,
from grade school on, flatter them endlessly so that the kids are shocked if
their college profs don't reflexively suck up to them.

Of course, the current generational style isn't simply derived from cul- 20
ture and environment. It's also about dollars. Students worry that taking
too many chances with their educations will sabotage their future pros-

pects. They're aware of the fact that a drop that looks more and more like one wall of the Grand Canyon separates the top economic tenth from the rest of the population. There's a sentiment currently abroad that if you step aside for a moment, to write, to travel, to fall too hard in love, you might lose position permanently. We may be on a conveyor belt, but it's worse down there on the filth-strewn floor. So don't sound off, don't blow your chance.

But wait. I teach at the famously conservative University of Virginia. *21* Can I extend my view from Charlottesville to encompass the whole country, a whole generation of college students? I can only say that I hear comparable stories about classroom life from colleagues everywhere in America. When I visit other schools to lecture, I see a similar scene unfolding. There are, of course, terrific students everywhere. And they're all the better for the way they've had to strive against the existing conformity. At some of the small liberal-arts colleges, the tradition of strong engagement persists. But overall, the students strike me as being sweet and sad, hovering in a nearly suspended animation.

Too often now the pedagogical challenge is to make a lot from a little. *22* Teaching Wordsworth's "Tintern Abbey," you ask for comments. No one responds. So you call on Stephen. Stephen: "The sound, this poem really flows." You: "Stephen seems interested in the music of the poem. We might extend his comment to ask if the poem's music coheres with its argument. Are they consistent? Or is there an emotional pain submerged here that's contrary to the poem's appealing melody?" All right, it's not usually that bad. But close. One friend describes it as rebound teaching: they proffer a weightless comment, you hit it back for all you're worth, then it comes dribbling out again. Occasionally a professor will try to explain away this intellectual timidity by describing the students as perpetrators of postmodern irony, a highly sophisticated mode. Everything's a slick counterfeit, a simulacrum, so by no means should any phenomenon be taken seriously. But the students don't have the urbane, Oscar Wilde–type demeanor that should go with this view. Oscar was cheerful, funny, confident, strange. (Wilde, mortally ill, living in a Paris flophouse: "My wallpaper and I are fighting a duel to the death. One or the other of us has to go.") This generation's style is considerate, easy to please, and a touch depressed.

Granted, you might say, the kids come to school immersed in a con- *23* sumer mentality—they're good Americans, after all—but then the university and the professors do everything in their power to fight that dreary mind-set in the interest of higher ideals, right? So it should be. But let us look at what is actually coming to pass.

Over the past few years, the physical layout of my university has been *24* changing. To put it a little indecorously, the place is looking more and more like a retirement spread for the young. Our funds go to construction, into new dorms, into renovating the student union. We have a new aquatics center and ever-improving gyms, stocked with StairMasters and Nautilus machines. Engraved on the wall in the gleaming aquatics building is a line by our founder, Thomas Jefferson, declaring that everyone ought to get about two hours' exercise a day. Clearly even the author of the Declaration of Independence endorses the turning of his university into a sports-and-fitness emporium.

But such improvements shouldn't be surprising. Universities need to    25
attract the best (that is, the smartest *and* the richest) students in order to survive in an ever more competitive market. Schools want kids whose parents can pay the full freight, not the ones who need scholarships or want to bargain down the tuition costs. If the marketing surveys say that the kids require sports centers, then, trustees willing, they shall have them. In fact, as I began looking around, I came to see that more and more of what's going on in the university is customer driven. The consumer pressures that beset me on evaluation day are only a part of an overall trend.

From the start, the contemporary university's relationship with stu-    26
dents has a solicitous, nearly servile tone. As soon as someone enters his junior year in high school, and especially if he's living in a prosperous zip code, the informational material—the advertising—comes flooding in. Pictures, testimonials, videocassettes, and CD ROMs (some bidden, some not) arrive at the door from colleges across the country, all trying to capture the student and his tuition cash. The freshman-to-be sees photos of well-appointed dorm rooms; of elaborate phys-ed facilities; of fine dining rooms; of expertly kept sports fields; of orchestras and drama troupes; of students working alone (no overbearing grown-ups in range), peering with high seriousness into computers and microscopes; or of students arrayed outdoors in attractive conversational garlands.

Occasionally—but only occasionally, for we usually photograph rather    27
badly; in appearance we tend at best to be styleless—there's a professor teaching a class. (The college catalogues I received, by my request only, in the late Sixties were austere affairs full of professors' credentials and course descriptions; it was clear on whose terms the enterprise was going to unfold.) A college financial officer recently put matters to me in concise, if slightly melodramatic, terms: "Colleges don't have admissions offices anymore, they have marketing departments." Is it surprising that someone who has been approached with photos and tapes, bells and whistles, might come in thinking that the Freud and Shakespeare she had signed up to study were also going to be agreeable treats?

How did we reach this point? In part the answer is a matter of demo-    28
graphics and (surprise) of money. Aided by the G.I. bill, the college-going population in America dramatically increased after the Second World War. Then came the baby boomers, and to accommodate them, schools continued to grow. Universities expand easily enough, but with tenure locking faculty in for lifetime jobs, and with the general reluctance of administrators to eliminate their own slots, it's not easy for a university to contract. So after the baby boomers had passed through—like a fat meal digested by a boa constrictor—the colleges turned to energetic promotional strate-

gies to fill the empty chairs. And suddenly college became a buyer's market. What students and their parents wanted had to be taken more and more into account. That usually meant creating more comfortable, less challenging environments, places where almost no one failed, everything was enjoyable, and everyone was nice.

Just as universities must compete with one another for students, so *29* must the individual departments. At a time of rank economic anxiety, the English and history majors have to contend for students against the more success-insuring branches, such as the sciences and the commerce school. In 1968, more than 21 percent of all the bachelor's degrees conferred in America were in the humanities; by 1993, that number had fallen to about 13 percent. The humanities now must struggle to attract students, many of whose parents devoutly wish they would study something else.

One of the ways we've tried to stay attractive is by loosening up. We *30* grade much more softly than our colleagues in science. In English, we don't give many Ds, or Cs for that matter. (The rigors of Chem 101 create almost as many English majors per year as do the splendors of Shakespeare.) A professor at Stanford recently explained grade inflation in the humanities by observing that the undergraduates were getting smarter every year; the higher grades simply recorded how much better they were than their predecessors. Sure.

Along with softening the grades, many humanities departments have *31* relaxed major requirements. There are some good reasons for introducing more choice into curricula and requiring fewer standard courses. But the move, like many others in the university now, jibes with a tendency to serve—and not challenge—the students. Students can also float in and out of classes during the first two weeks of each term without making any commitment. The common name for this time span—shopping period— speaks volumes about the consumer mentality that's now in play. Usually, too, the kids can drop courses up until the last month with only an innocuous "W" on their transcripts. Does a course look too challenging? No problem. Take it pass-fail. A happy consumer is, by definition, one with multiple options, one who can always have what he wants. And since a course is something the students and their parents have bought and paid for, why can't they do with it pretty much as they please?

A sure result of the university's widening elective leeway is to give students *32* more power over their teachers. Those who don't like you can simply avoid you. If the clientele dislikes you en masse, you can be left without students, period. My first term teaching I walked into my introduction to poetry course and found it inhabited by one student, the gloriously named Bambi Lynn Dean. Bambi and I chatted amiably awhile, but for all that she and the pleasure of her name could offer, I was fast on the way to meltdown. It was all a mistake, luckily, a problem with the scheduling book. Everyone was waiting for me next door. But in a dozen years of teaching I haven't forgotten that feeling of being ignominiously marooned. For it happens to others, and not always because of scheduling glitches. I've seen older colleagues go through hot embarrassment at not having enough students sign up for their courses: they graded too hard, demanded too much, had beliefs too far out of keeping with the existing disposition. It takes only a few such instances to draw other members of the professoriat further into line.

And if what's called tenure reform—which generally just means the 33 abolition of tenure—is broadly enacted, professors will be yet more vulnerable to the whims of their customer-students. Teach what pulls the kids in, or walk. What about entire departments that don't deliver? If the kids say no to Latin and Greek, is it time to dissolve classics? Such questions are being entertained more and more seriously by university administrators.

How does one prosper with the present clientele? Many of the most 34 successful professors now are the ones who have "decentered" their classrooms. There's a new emphasis on group projects and on computer-generated exchanges among the students. What they seem to want most is to talk to one another. A classroom now is frequently an "environment," a place highly conducive to the exchange of existing ideas, the students' ideas. Listening to one another, students sometimes change their opinions. But what they generally can't do is acquire a new vocabulary, a new perspective, that will cast issues in a fresh light.

The Socratic method—the animated, sometimes impolite give-and- 35 take between student and teacher—seems too jagged for current sensibilities. Students frequently come to my office to tell me how intimidated they feel in class; the thought of being embarrassed in front of the group fills them with dread. I remember a student telling me how humiliating it was to be corrected by the teacher, by me. So I asked the logical question: "Should I let a major factual error go by so as to save discomfort?" The student—a good student, smart and earnest—said that was a tough question. He'd need to think about it.

Disturbing? Sure. But I wonder, are we really getting students ready 36 for Socratic exchange with professors when we push them off into vast lecture rooms, two and three hundred to a class, sometimes face them with only grad students until their third year, and signal in our myriad professorial ways that we often have much better things to do than sit in our offices and talk with them? How bad will the student-faculty ratios have to become, how teeming the lecture courses, before we hear students righteously complaining, as they did thirty years ago, about the impersonality of their schools, about their decline into knowledge factories? "This is a firm," said Mario Savio at Berkeley during the Free Speech protests of the Sixties, "and if the Board of Regents are the board of directors . . . then . . . the faculty are a bunch of employees and we're the raw material. But we're a bunch of raw material that don't mean . . . to be made into any product."

Teachers who really do confront students, who provide significant chal- 37 lenges to what they believe, *can* be very successful, granted. But sometimes such professors generate more than a little trouble for themselves. A con-

troversial teacher can send students hurrying to the deans and the counselors, claiming to have been offended. ("Offensive" is the preferred term
of repugnance today, just as "enjoyable" is the summit of praise.) Colleges
have brought in hordes of counselors and deans to make sure that everything is smooth, serene, unflustered, that everyone has a good time. To
the counselor, to the dean, and to the university legal squad, that which is
normal, healthy, and prudent is best.

An air of caution and deference is everywhere. When my students
come to talk with me in my office, they often exhibit a Franciscan humility. "Do you have a moment?" "I know you're busy. I won't take up much of
your time." Their presences tend to be very light; they almost never change
the temperature of the room. The dress is nondescript: clothes are in
earth tones; shoes are practical—cross-trainers, hiking boots, work shoes,
Dr. Martens, with now and then a stylish pair of raised-sole boots on one
of the young women. Many, male and female both, peep from beneath the
bills of monogrammed baseball caps. Quite a few wear sports, or even corporate, logos, sometimes on one piece of clothing but occasionally (and dis-
concertingly) on more. The walk is slow; speech is careful, sweet, a bit weary,
and without strong inflection. (After the first lively week of the term, most
seem far in debt to sleep.) They are almost unfailingly polite. They don't
want to offend me; I could hurt them, savage their grades.

Naturally, there are exceptions, kids I chat animatedly with, who offer
a joke, or go on about this or that new CD (almost never a book, no). But
most of the traffic is genially sleepwalking. I have to admit that I'm a touch
wary, too. I tend to hold back. An unguarded remark, a joke that's taken
to be off-color, or simply an uncomprehended comment can lead to difficulties. I keep it literal. They scare me a little, these kind and melancholy
students, who themselves seem rather frightened of their own lives.

Before they arrive, we ply the students with luscious ads, guaranteeing them a cross between summer camp and lotusland. When they get
here, flattery and nonstop entertainment are available, if that's what they
want. And when they leave? How do we send our students out into the
world? More and more, our administrators call the booking agents and
line up one or another celebrity to usher the graduates into the millennium. This past spring, Kermit the Frog won himself an honorary degree
at Southampton College on Long Island; Bruce Willis and Yogi Berra took
credentials away at Montclair State; Arnold Schwarzenegger scored at the
University of Wisconsin–Superior. At Wellesley, Oprah Winfrey gave the
commencement address. (*Wellesley*—one of the most rigorous academic
colleges in the nation.) At the University of Vermont, Whoopi Goldberg
laid down the word. But why should a worthy administrator contract the
likes of Susan Sontag, Christopher Hitchens, or Robert Hughes—someone who might actually say something, something disturbing, something
"offensive"—when he can get what the parents and kids apparently want
and what the newspapers will softly commend—more lite entertainment,
more TV?

Is it a surprise, then, that this generation of students—steeped in con-    *41*
sumer culture before going off to school, treated as potent customers by
the university well before their date of arrival, then pandered to from
day one until the morning of the final kiss-off from Kermit or one of his
kin—are inclined to see the books they read as a string of entertainments
to be placidly enjoyed or languidly cast down? Given the way universities are now administered (which is more and more to say, given the way
that they are currently marketed), is it a shock that the kids don't come to
school hot to learn, unable to bear their own ignorance? For some measure
of self-dislike, or self-discontent—which is much different than simple
depression—seems to me to be a prerequisite for getting an education that
matters. My students, alas, usually lack the confidence to acknowledge
what would be their most precious asset for learning: their ignorance.

Not long ago, I asked my Freud class a question that, however hoary, never    *42*
fails to solicit intriguing responses: Who are your heroes? Whom do you
admire? After one remarkable answer, featuring T. S. Eliot as hero, a series
of generic replies rolled in, one gray wave after the next: my father, my best
friend, a doctor who lives in our town, my high school history teacher. Virtually all the heroes were people my students had known personally, people
who had done something local, specific, and practical, and had done it for
them. They were good people, unselfish people, these heroes, but most of
all they were people who had delivered the goods.

My students' answers didn't exhibit any philosophical resistance to the    *43*
idea of greatness. It's not that they had been primed by their professors
with complex arguments to combat genius. For the truth is that these students don't need debunking theories. Long before college, skepticism became their habitual mode. They are the progeny of Bart Simpson and
David Letterman, and the hyper-cool ethos of the box. It's inane to say that
theorizing professors have created them, as many conservative critics like
to do. Rather, they have substantially created a university environment in
which facile skepticism can thrive without being substantially contested.

Skeptical approaches have *potential* value. If you have no all-    *44*
encompassing religious faith, no faith in historical destiny, the future of
the West, or anything comparably grand, you need to acquire your vision of
the world somewhere. If it's from literature, then the various visions literature offers have to be inquired into skeptically. Surely it matters that
women are denigrated in Milton and in Pope, that some novelistic voices
assume an overbearing godlike authority, that the poor are, in this or that
writer, inevitably cast as clowns. You can't buy all of literature wholesale if
it's going to help draw your patterns of belief.

But demystifying theories are now overused, applied mechanically.    *45*
It's all logocentrism, patriarchy, ideology. And in this the student environment—laid-back, skeptical, knowing—is, I believe, central. Full-out debunking is what plays with this clientele. Some have been doing it nearly
as long as, if more crudely than, their deconstructionist teachers. In the

context of the contemporary university, and cool consumer culture, a useful intellectual skepticism has become exaggerated into a fundamentalist caricature of itself. The teachers have buckled to their students' views.

At its best, multiculturalism can be attractive as well-deployed theory. 46 What could be more valuable than encountering the best work of far-flung cultures and becoming a citizen of the world? But in the current consumer environment, where flattery plays so well, the urge to encounter the other can devolve into the urge to find others who embody and celebrate the right ethnic origins. So we put aside the African novelist Chinua Achebe's abrasive, troubling *Things Fall Apart* and gravitate toward hymns on Africa, cradle of all civilizations.

What about the phenomenon called political correctness? Raising the 47 standard of civility and tolerance in the university has been—who can deny it?—a very good thing. Yet this admirable impulse has expanded to the point where one is enjoined to speak well—and only well—of women, blacks, gays, the disabled, in fact of virtually everyone. And we can owe this expansion in many ways to the student culture. Students now do not wish to be criticized, not in any form. (The culture of consumption never criticizes them, at least not *overtly*.) In the current university, the movement for urbane tolerance has devolved into an imperative against critical reaction, turning much of the intellectual life into a dreary Sargasso Sea. At a certain point, professors stopped being usefully sensitive and became more like careful retailers who have it as a cardinal point of doctrine never to piss the customers off.

To some professors, the solution lies in the movement called cultural 48 studies. What students need, they believe, is to form a critical perspective on pop culture. It's a fine idea, no doubt. Students should be able to run a critical commentary against the stream of consumer stimulations in which they're immersed. But cultural-studies programs rarely work, because no matter what you propose by way of analysis, things tend to bolt downhill toward an uncritical discussion of students' tastes, into what they like and don't like. If you want to do a Frankfurt School–style analysis of *Braveheart,* you can be pretty sure that by mid-class Adorno and Horkheimer will be consigned to the junk heap of history and you'll be collectively weighing the charms of Mel Gibson. One sometimes wonders if cultural studies hasn't prospered because, under the guise of serious intellectual analysis, it gives the customers what they most want—easy pleasure, more TV. Cultural studies becomes nothing better than what its detractors claim it is—Madonna studies—when students kick loose from the critical perspective and groove to the product, and that, in my experience teaching film and pop culture, happens plenty.

On the issue of genius, as on multiculturalism and political correct- 49 ness, we professors of the humanities have, I think, also failed to press back against our students' consumer tastes. Here we tend to nurse a pair of—to put it charitably—disparate views. In one mode, we're inclined to a programmatic debunking criticism. We call the concept of genius into question. But in our professional lives per se, we aren't usually disposed against the idea of distinguished achievement. We argue animatedly about the caliber of potential colleagues. We support a star system, in which some professors are far better paid, teach less, and under better conditions than the rest. In our own profession, we are creating a system that is the mirror image of the one we're dismantling in the curriculum. Ask a professor what she thinks of the work of Stephen Greenblatt, a leading critic of Shakespeare, and you'll hear it for an hour. Ask her what her views are on Shakespeare's genius and she's likely to begin questioning the term along with the whole "discourse of evaluation." This dual sensibility may be intellectually incoherent. But in its awareness of what plays with students, it's conducive to good classroom evaluations and, in its awareness of where and how the professional bread is buttered, to self-advancement as well.

My overall point is this: It's not that a left-wing professorial coup has  *50* taken over the university. It's that at American universities, left-liberal politics have collided with the ethos of consumerism. The consumer ethos is winning.

Then how do those who at least occasionally promote genius and high lit-  *51* erary ideals look to current students? How do we appear, those of us who take teaching to be something of a performance art and who imagine that if you give yourself over completely to your subject you'll be rewarded with insight beyond what you individually command?

I'm reminded of an old piece of newsreel footage I saw once. The  *52* speaker (perhaps it was Lenin, maybe Trotsky) was haranguing a large crowd. He was expostulating, arm waving, carrying on. Whether it was flawed technology or the man himself, I'm not sure, but the orator looked like an intricate mechanical device that had sprung into fast-forward. To my students, who mistrust enthusiasm in every form, that's me when I start riffing about Freud or Blake. But more and more, as my evaluations showed, I've been replacing enthusiasm and intellectual animation with stand-up routines, keeping it all at arm's length, praising under the cover of irony.

It's too bad that the idea of genius has been denigrated so far, because  *53* it actually offers a live alternative to the demoralizing culture of hip in which most of my students are mired. By embracing the works and lives of extraordinary people, you can adapt new ideals to revise those that came courtesy of your parents, your neighborhood, your clan—or the tube. The aim of a good liberal-arts education was once, to adapt an observation by the scholar Walter Jackson Bate, to see that "we need not be the passive victims of what we deterministically call 'circumstances' (social, cultural, or reductively psychological-personal), but that by linking ourselves through what Keats calls an 'immortal free-masonry' with the great we can become freer—freer to be ourselves, to be what we most want and value."

But genius isn't just a personal standard; genius can also have political  *54* effect. To me, one of the best things about democratic thinking is the conviction that genius can spring up anywhere. Walt Whitman is born into the working class and thirty-six years later we have a poetic image of America that gives a passionate dimension to the legalistic brilliance of the Constitution. A democracy needs to constantly develop, and to do so it requires the most powerful visionary minds to interpret the present and to propose possible shapes for the future. By continuing to notice and praise genius, we create a culture in which the kind of poetic gamble that Whitman made—a gamble in which failure would have entailed rank humiliation, depression, maybe suicide—still takes place. By rebelling against established ways of seeing and saying things, genius helps us to apprehend how malleable the present is and how promising and fraught with danger is the future. If we teachers do not endorse genius and self-overcoming, can we be surprised when our students find their ideal images in TV's latest persona ads?

A world uninterested in genius is a despondent place, whose sad deni-   55
zens drift from coffee bar to Prozac dispensary, unfired by ideals, by the glowing image of the self that one might become. As Northrop Frye says in a beautiful and now dramatically unfashionable sentence, "The artist who uses the same energy and genius that Homer and Isaiah had will find that he not only lives in the same palace of art as Homer and Isaiah, but lives in it at the same time." We ought not to deny the existence of such a place simply because we, or those we care for, find the demands it makes intimidating, the rent too high.

What happens if we keep trudging along this bleak course? What hap-   56
pens if our most intelligent students never learn to strive to overcome what they are? What if genius, and the imitation of genius, become silly, outmoded ideas? What you're likely to get are more and more one-dimensional men and women. These will be people who live for easy pleasures, for comfort and prosperity, who think of money first, then second, and third, who hug the status quo; people who believe in God as a sort of insurance policy (cover your bets); people who are never surprised. They will be people so pleased with themselves (when they're not in despair at the general pointlessness of their lives) that they cannot imagine humanity could do better. They'll think it their highest duty to clone themselves as frequently as possible. They'll claim to be happy, and they'll live a long time.

It is probably time now to offer a spate of inspiring solutions. Here   57
ought to come a list of reforms, with due notations about a core curriculum and various requirements. What the traditionalists who offer such solutions miss is that no matter what our current students are given to read, many of them will simply translate it into melodrama, with flat characters and predictable morals. (The unabated capitalist culture that conservative critics so often endorse has put students in a position to do little else.) One can't simply wave a curricular wand and reverse acculturation.

Perhaps it would be a good idea to try firing the counselors and sending   58
half the deans back into their classrooms, dismantling the football team and making the stadium into a playground for local kids, emptying the fraternities, and boarding up the student-activities office. Such measures

would convey the message that American colleges are not northern out-posts of Club Med. A willingness on the part of the faculty to defy student conviction and affront them occasionally—to be usefully offensive—also might not be a bad thing. We professors talk a lot about subversion, which generally means subverting the views of people who never hear us talk or read our work. But to subvert the views of our students, our customers, that would be something else again.

Ultimately, though, it is up to individuals—and individual students in particular—to make their own way against the current sludgy tide. There's still the library, still the museum, there's still the occasional teacher who lives to find things greater than herself to admire. There are still fellow students who have not been cowed. Universities are inefficient, cluttered, archaic places, with many unguarded corners where one can open a book or gaze out onto the larger world and construe it freely. Those who do as much, trusting themselves against the weight of current opinion, will have contributed something to bringing this sad dispensation to an end. As for myself, I'm canning my low-key one-liners; when the kids' TV-based tastes come to the fore, I'll aim and shoot. And when it's time to praise genius, I'll try to do it in the right style, full-out, with faith that finer artistic spirits (maybe not Homer and Isaiah quite, but close, close), still alive somewhere in the ether, will help me out when my invention flags, the students doze, or the dean mutters into the phone. I'm getting back to a more exuberant style; I'll be expostulating and arm waving straight into the millennium, yes I will.

■ ■ ■

## Reading as a Writer: Analyzing Rhetorical Choices

1.  How would you describe Edmundson's ethos, or self-representation, in this essay? How would you characterize his tone and attitude? Find three pas-sages that you think best illustrate the author's self-representation, and discuss how this contributes to, or detracts from, the argument he makes in this essay.

2.  Edmundson writes at length about what he thinks is wrong with univer-sity culture, but he also makes recommendations for change. What does he want students and professors to do differently? How practical do you find Edmundson's suggestions? Explain why you do—or do not—agree with his suggestions for change.

## Writing as a Reader: Entering the Conversation of Ideas

1.  Edmundson and Deborah Tannen both describe specific classroom dy-namics in detail as they make their cases about some of the shortcomings of contemporary education. How do you think these very different authors would analyze each other's classroom examples and conclusions based on those examples? What do you think of these perspectives and insights?

Write an essay in which you place yourself and these authors in conversation about the connection between classroom dynamics and the goals of education.

2. The college students Edmundson analyzes may seem at first to have little in common with the primary and secondary school children Jonathan Kozol describes in his essay. However, both authors address the goals of education and the methods that work best to meet those goals. Write an essay in which you draw on the authors' arguments about educational goals and methods in order to take your own position on these issues. Feel free to draw on examples from your own education as you develop your argument.

## GERALD GRAFF

# Other Voices, Other Rooms

Gerald Graff, a professor of English and education at the University of Illinois at Chicago, has become a leading voice in debates about current directions in college education. He is the author of several books on this topic, including *Clueless in Academe: How Schooling Obscures the Life of the Mind* (2003), a text whose subtitle has raised eyebrows and hackles. While Graff himself teaches in a mainstream university, he is interested in asking difficult questions about the standard curriculum taught in most colleges, how teachers impart this material, and, ultimately, the purposes of this kind of education. Graff is perhaps most famous for coining the concept of "teaching the controversy," by which he means that instructors should teach students the conflicts around issues in specific fields in order to show how knowledge comes to be established in a context of swirling conversations. Too often, he argues, students are taught isolated bits of knowledge in different courses and are never given access to the bigger picture, much less the tools to challenge the values and assumptions implicit in the ideas they are learning.

As you read, keep your own educational experiences in mind, particularly the ways students learn to "psych out each course" in order to succeed in classes with completely different standards and expectations. How accurately do his classroom examples capture your own experiences? How often do instructors explain the origins of the disciplinary conventions you are expected to learn and display in papers and on exams? Given his complaints about the ways most educators fail to explain the larger contexts of intellectual debates, how would you evaluate Graff's strategy of arguing his point? Where does he provide the context for his ideas that he demands of others?

After discussing examples that come from academic experience, Graff ends with a baseball metaphor that may help bring into focus the significance of the ways he sees the current educational system failing students. Do you think this metaphor accurately captures the process of American higher education? Ultimately, what do you—and Graff—think education is for?

An undergraduate tells of an art history course in which the instructor    *1*
observed one day, "As we now know, the idea that knowledge can be objective is a positivist myth that has been exploded by postmodern thought." It so happens the student is concurrently enrolled in a political science course in which the instructor speaks confidently about the objectivity of his discipline as if it had not been "exploded" at all. What do you do? the student is asked. "What else can I do?" he says: "I trash objectivity in art history, and I presuppose it in political science."

A second undergraduate describes a history teacher who makes a point    *2*
of stressing the superiority of Western culture in developing the ideas of freedom, democracy, and free-market capitalism that the rest of the world is now rushing to imitate. She also has a literature teacher who describes such claims of Western supremacy as an example of the hegemonic ideology by which the United States arrogates the right to police the world. When asked which course she prefers, she replies, "Well, I'm getting an A in both."

To some of us these days, the moral of these stories would be that students have become cynical relativists who care less about convictions than    *3*
about grades and careers. In fact, if anything is surprising, it is that more students do not behave in this cynical fashion, for the established curriculum encourages it. The disjunction of the curriculum is a far more powerful source of relativism than any doctrine preached by the faculty.

One of the oddest things about the university is that it calls itself a    *4*
community of scholars yet organizes its curriculum in a way that conceals the links of the community from those who are not already aware of them. The courses being given at any moment on a campus represent any number of rich potential conversations within and across the disciplines. But since students experience these conversations only as a series of monologues, the conversations become actual only for the minority who can reconstruct them on their own. No self-respecting educator would deliberately design a system guaranteed to keep students dependent on the whim of the individual instructor. Yet this is precisely the effect of a curriculum composed of courses that are not in dialogue with one another.

## Ships in the Night

The problem deepens when teachers are further apart. A student today can    *5*
go from a course in which the universality of Western culture is taken for granted (and therefore not articulated) to a course in which it is taken for granted (and therefore not articulated) that such claims of universality are fallacious and deceptive. True, for the best students the resulting cognitive dissonance is no great problem. The chance to try on a variety of clashing ideas, to see what they feel like, is one of the most exciting opportunities an education can provide; it can be especially rewarding for students who come to the university with already developed skills at summarizing and

weighing arguments and synthesizing conflicting positions on their own. Many students, however, become confused or indifferent and react as the above two students did by giving their teachers whatever they seem to want even though it is contradictory.

Then, too, when their teachers' conflicting perspectives do not enter 6 into a common discussion, students may not even be able to infer what is wanted. Like everyone else, teachers tend to betray their crucial assumptions as much in what they do *not* say, what they take to go without saying, as in what they say explicitly. To students who are not at home in the academic intellectual community, the significance of these silences and exclusions is likely to be intimidating, if it does not elude them entirely.

Furthermore, in an academic environment in which there is increas- 7 ingly less unspoken common ground, it may not even be clear to students that their teachers are in conflict, for different words may be used by several teachers for the same concepts or the same words for different concepts. If students do not know that "positivism" has in some quarters become a derogatory buzzword for any belief in objectivity, they may not become aware that the art history and political science teachers in the above example are in disagreement. A student who goes from one humanist who speaks of "traditional moral themes" to another who speaks of "patriarchal discursive practices" may not become aware that the two teachers are actually referring to the same thing. Students in such cases are being exposed to some of the major cultural debates of their time, but in a way that makes it difficult to recognize them *as* debates.

Note, too, that the instructors in these situations are protected by the 8 insularity of their classrooms, which makes it unnecessary, if not impossible, for them to confront the challenges to their assumptions that would be represented by their colleagues. Professors do not expect such immunity from peer criticism when they publish their work or appear at professional conferences. It is only in the classroom that such immunity is taken for granted as if it were a form of academic freedom. Since students enjoy no such protection, one can hardly blame them if they, too, protect themselves by compartmentalizing the contradictions to which they are exposed, as my first student did when he became an objectivist in one course and an antiobjectivist in the other.

I recall a semester late in college when I took a course in modern 9 poetry taught by a New Critic, a follower of T. S. Eliot, and a course in seventeenth-century English literature taught by an older scholar who resented Eliot and the New Critics, who had attacked John Milton for his grandiloquence and lack of irony. Three days a week between ten and eleven I listened with dutiful respect to the New Critic's theories of irony and paradox, and between eleven and twelve I listened with dutiful respect to the argument that these New Critical theories had no application whatsoever to Milton, Dryden, and their contemporaries. What was really odd, however, is that I hardly focused at the time on the fact that my two teachers were in disagreement.

Was I just ridiculously slow to comprehend the critical issues that were    *10*
at stake? Perhaps so, but since no one was asking me to think about the relationship between the two courses, I did not. If my teachers disagreed, this
was their business—a professional dispute that did not concern me. Each
course was challenging enough on its own terms, and to have raised the
question of how they related would have only risked needlessly multiplying difficulties for myself. Then, too, for me to ask my teachers about their
differences might have seemed impertinent and ill-mannered—who was I
to impugn their authority? Only later did it dawn on me that studying different centuries and clashing theories without having them brought together had made things much *harder* since it removed the element of
contrast.

Contrast is fundamental to understanding, for no subject, idea, or text    *11*
is an island. In order to become intelligible "in itself," it needs to be seen in
its relation to other subjects, ideas, and texts. When this relation of interdependence is obscured because different courses do not communicate, subjects, ideas, and texts become harder to comprehend, if not unintelligible.
We think we are making things simpler for students by abstracting periods, texts, and authors from their relationships with other periods, texts,
and authors so that we can study them closely in a purified space. But the
very act of isolating an object from its contrasting background and relations makes it hard to grasp. Since we cannot talk about everything all at
once, subjects do have to be distinguished and to that extent isolated from
one another. But this isolation does not have to preclude connections and
relations. It is hard to grasp the modernity of modern literature unless one
can compare it with something that is not modern.

That is why teachers in modern periods need nonmodernists (and vice    *12*
versa) in order to make their subjects intelligible to their students, just as
teachers who defend the culture of the West need the teachers who criticize it (and vice versa). Without the criticisms, after all, there would be no
need to defend the West to begin with. Insofar as neither a defense nor a
critique of tradition makes sense apart from the dialogue these positions
are engaged in, a curriculum which removes that dialogue from view defeats the goals of traditionalists and revisionists alike. It is true that fundamental conflicts like these may turn out to be nonnegotiable. But no one
knows this in advance, and even if a dispute proves to be nonnegotiable, to
learn that this is the case is not worthless.

I noted earlier that among the factors that make academic culture    *13*
more confusing today than in the past is not only that there is more controversy but that there is even controversy about what can legitimately be
considered controversial. Traditionalists are often angry that there should
even *be* a debate over the canon, while revisionists are often angry that
there should even be a debate over "political correctness," or the relevance
of ideology and politics to their subjects. A recent feminist critic says she
finds it "astonishing" that it still needs repeating at this late date that "the
perspective assumed to be 'universal' which has dominated knowledge...
has actually been male and culture-bound."[1] Since the feminist argument,

however, is that we still fail to see how culture-bound our thinking is, it is hard to see why this critic should be astonished that she still needs to make the point. Another political critic writes that "we are perhaps already weary of the avalanche of papers, books, and conferences entitled 'The Politics of X,' and we have recently begun to question that most hallowed of all political slogans on the left, 'everything is political.'"[2] Yet the idea of politics that this critic and her audience are already "weary of" is one that most people have not yet encountered and might well find incomprehensible. The "advanced" academic and the layperson (or the traditional academic) are so far apart that what is already old news to one has not yet become intelligible to the other.

Imagine how this affects students who, at the moment they are negotiating the difficult transition from the lay culture to the academic culture, must also negotiate the unpredictable and unfathomable discrepancies between academic departments and factions. When there is no correlation of the different discourses to which students are exposed, it becomes especially difficult for them to infer which assumptions are safe and which are likely to be challenged. The problem is that knowledge of what is and is not considered potentially or legitimately controversial cannot be learned a priori; you cannot get it out of E. D. Hirsch's *Dictionary of Cultural Literacy*. Such knowledge comes only through interaction with a community, and that interaction is precisely what is prevented by a disconnected system of courses. Then, too, assumptions about what is and is not potentially controversial tend to change from one moment to the next and one subcommunity to the next, and they are changing at a faster rate today than in the past.    *14*

Thomas S. Kuhn in *The Structure of Scientific Revolutions* describes moments of crisis or "paradigm shift" in the sciences, when "a law that cannot even be demonstrated to one group of scientists may . . . seem intuitively obvious to another."[3] The fate of Kuhn's own book is an interesting case in point. Even as his sociological account of scientific paradigm change has been treated as virtual holy writ by many literary theorists (for a while it seemed almost obligatory to begin every book or essay with a respectful bow to Kuhn), his work has often been ignored or dismissed by scientists and philosophers of science, who accuse him of subverting the concept of objective truth in reducing scientific discovery to "mob psychology." As the controversy over Kuhn has revealed, both the literati and the scientists have remained largely walled up within their clashing assumptions about objectivity, the smugness of which might have been punctured had these parties been forced to argue with each other in their teaching. This mutual smugness has persisted in the sniper fire that continues to be exchanged over the concept of objectivity and the extent to which knowledge is independent of the social situation of the knower; revisionists sneer at the concept and traditionalists sneer at the very idea of questioning it.    *15*

The question neither group seems to ask is what it must be like to be a student caught in the crossfire between these conflicting views of    *16* objectivity, each one prone to present itself as "intuitively obvious" and uncontroversial. A rhetoric scholar, Gregory Colomb, has studied the disorientation experienced by a bright high school graduate who, after doing well in a humanities course as a freshman at the University of Chicago, tried to apply her mastery to a social science course, only to come up with a grade of C.[4] Imagine trying to write an academic paper when you sense that almost anything you say can be used against you and that the intellectual moves that got you an A in existentialist philosophy may get you a C minus and a dirty look in Skinnerian behaviorism.

Consider the fact that the passive voice that is so standard in sociology writing ("it will be contended in this paper . . .") has been perennially rebuked in English courses.[5] Or consider something so apparently trivial as the convention of using the present tense to describe actions in literature and philosophy and the past tense to describe them in history. Plato *says* things in literary and philosophical accounts while in historical accounts he *said* them. Experienced writers become so accustomed to such tense shifting that it seems a simple matter, but it reflects deep-rooted and potentially controversial differences between disciplines. Presumably, Plato speaks in the present in literary and philosophical contexts because ideas there are considered timeless; only when we move over to history does it start to matter that the writer is dead.[6] We English teachers write "tense shift" in the margin when student writers betray uncertainty about this convention, but how do we expect them to "get" it when they pass from the very different time zones of history and philosophy/English with no engagement of the underlying issues? [17]

One of the most frequent comments teachers make on student papers is "What's your evidence?" But nobody would ever finish a piece of writing if it were necessary to supply evidence for everything being said, so in order to write, one must acquire a sense of which statements have to be supported by evidence (or further argument) and which ones a writer can get away with because they are already taken for granted by the imagined audience. What happens, then, when a writer has no way of knowing whether an assumption that he or she got away with audience A will also be conceded by audience B? It is no wonder that students protect themselves from the insecurity of such a situation by "psyching out" each course as it comes—and then forgetting about it as soon as possible after the final exam in order to clear their minds for the seemingly unrelated demands of the next set of courses. [18]

It is not only ideas and reasoning processes but the recall of basic information as well that figure to be impaired by disjunctive curricular organization. To use the jargon of information theory, an information system that is experienced as an unrelated series of signals will be weak in the kind of redundancy that is needed for information to be retained. Faced with a curriculum overloaded with data and weak in redundancy, students may find it difficult to know which items of information they are supposed to remember. Then, too, a student may be exposed to the same informa- [19]

tion in several courses while failing to recognize it as "the same," since it is contextualized differently in each course. When students fail to identify a cultural literacy item on a test, the problem may be not that they don't know the information but that they don't know they know it; they may have learned it in a context whose relevance to the test question they don't recognize. What is learned seems so specific to a particular course that it is difficult for students to see its application beyond.

The critic Kenneth Burke once compared the intellectual life of a culture to a parlor in which different guests are forever dropping in and out. As the standard curriculum represents the intellectual life, however, there is no parlor; the hosts congregate in separate rooms with their acolytes and keep their differences and agreements to themselves. Making one's way through the standard curriculum is rather like trying to comprehend a phone conversation by listening at only one end.[7] You can manage it up to a point, but this is hardly the ideal way to do it.

To venture a final comparison, it is as if you were to try to learn the game of baseball by being shown a series of rooms in which you see each component of the game separately: pitchers going through their windups in one room; hitters swinging their bats in the next; then infielders, outfielders, umpires, fans, field announcers, ticket scalpers, broadcasters, hotdog vendors, and so on. You see them all in their different roles, but since you see them separately you get no clear idea of what the game actually looks like or why the players do what they do. No doubt you would come away with a very imperfect understanding of baseball under these conditions. Yet it does not seem far-fetched to compare these circumstances with the ones students face when they are exposed to a series of disparate courses, subjects, and perspectives and expected not only to infer the rules of the academic-intellectual game but to play it competently themselves.

NOTES

1. Gayle Green, "The Myth of Neutrality, Again?" in *Shakespeare Left and Right*, ed. Ivo Kamps (New York: Routledge, 1991), p. 24.

2. Diana Fuss, *Essentially Speaking: Feminism, Nature and Difference* (New York: Routledge, 1989), p. l05.

3. Thomas S. Kuhn, *The Structure of Scientific Revolutions*, 2d ed. (Chicago: University of Chicago Press, 1970), p. 150.

4. Gregory Colomb, *Disciplinary "Secrets" and the Apprentice Writer: The Lessons for Critical Thinking* (Upper Montclair, N.J.: Montclair State College, Institute for Critical Thinking, 1988), pp. 2–3.

5. For this point I am indebted to an unpublished talk by Susan Lowry.

6. I am indebted for this point to Susan H. McLeod, "Writing across the Curriculum: An Introduction," forthcoming in *Writing across the Curriculum: A Guide to Developing Programs*, ed. McLeod and Margot Soven (Newberry Park, Calif.: Sage, 1992).

7. I adapt an observation made in a somewhat different context by Mary Louise Pratt, "Humanities for the Future: Reflections on the Western Culture Debate at Stanford," in *Politics of Liberal Education* (Durham: Duke University Press, 1992), p. 19.

■ ■ ■

Reading as a Writer: Analyzing Rhetorical Choices

1.  In his essay, Graff shifts between detailed descriptions of classroom experiences that are probably pretty familiar to you, and more abstract claims about the many shortcomings he sees in contemporary university education. In his opening paragraphs, he makes just this move between description of college experiences and the more abstract idea that "cognitive dissonance" (para. 5) is common for students. What does he mean by "cognitive dissonance"? Locate other places in the essay where this idea recurs, and be ready to discuss how this idea contributes to his argument.

2.  What is the effect of saving the metaphor about learning baseball for the final paragraph of the essay? What does that metaphor help you re-see in the many examples Graff cites throughout his piece? What would be gained or lost, do you think, if Graff's essay opened, rather than closed, with this metaphor?

Writing as a Reader: Entering the Conversation of Ideas

1.  Graff and Mark Edmundson are fairly critical of contemporary education. While they are both professors who are the beneficiaries of the current system, they both argue that most professors ought to change their current strategies. Write an essay in which you use ideas from both authors to propose a new kind of "ideal" professor, based on these writers' perspectives. Give examples of how such a professor would teach, and what kinds of information he or she would teach. How might students have to change their learning strategies to meet these new standards? Is this a vision of education you would support? Why or why not?

2.  James W. Loewen, Graff, and Deborah Tannen have different perspectives on the value of conflict in the classroom. Placing these writers in conversation with one another, write an essay in which you compare their ideas about the place of conflict in education. Given the evidence each author presents, and perhaps your own educational experiences, where do you stand in this conversation about conflict and learning?

## DEBORAH TANNEN

# How Male and Female Students Use Language Differently

Deborah Tannen is a professor of linguistics at Georgetown University who is well known by both scholars and generalist readers with an interest in the ways people talk to one another. As a linguistic researcher, Tannen is curious about the relationship between the speech patterns we develop as a result of our socialization and the ways we are heard and misheard in the classroom, the workplace, our families, and our culture. This selection is from Tannen's book *You Just Don't Understand: Women and Men in Conver-*

*sation* (1990), which spent almost four years on the *New York Times* best seller list.

Tannen uses a writing style influenced by journalism. How does she express complex ideas within often short, punchy sentences? Pay attention to places where you see her moving smoothly between scholarly references to sociologists, anthropologists, and linguists, and personal anecdotes and observations about classroom behavior. Tannen argues that most classroom dynamics are "fundamentally male" and are characterized by an understanding that "the pursuit of knowledge is believed to be achieved by ritual opposition: public display followed by argument and challenge" (para. 5). How does this claim line up with your own experiences—good and bad—in the classroom?

Critics sometimes complain that Tannen's examples are too selective and that she makes generalizing claims from too little evidence, though she also has many admirers among academics, book award committees, and the millions of readers who purchase her books. It's difficult to be neutral about Tannen's work, because she asks us to question and analyze the ways we interact with others, and this feels very personal—as it should. This selection focuses on linguistic dynamics in the classroom, but you may find that her insights will make you reconsider conversations you have had in almost every part of your life.

W hen I researched and wrote . . . *You Just Don't Understand: Women and Men in Conversation*, the furthest thing from my mind was reevaluating my teaching strategies. But that has been one of the direct benefits of having written the book.

The primary focus of my linguistic research always has been the language of everyday conversation. One facet of this is conversational style: how different regional, ethnic, and class backgrounds, as well as age and gender, result in different ways of using language to communicate. *You Just Don't Understand* is about the conversational styles of women and men. As I gained more insight into typically male and female ways of using language, I began to suspect some of the causes of the troubling facts that women who go to single-sex schools do better in later life, and that when young women sit next to young men in classrooms, the males talk more. This is not to say that all men talk in class, nor that no women do. It is simply that a greater percentage of discussion time is taken by men's voices.

The research of sociologists and anthropologists such as Janet Lever, Marjorie Harness Goodwin, and Donna Eder has shown that girls and boys learn to use language differently in their sex-separate peer groups. Typically, a girl has a best friend with whom she sits and talks, frequently telling secrets. It's the telling of secrets, the fact and the way that they talk to each other, that makes them best friends. For boys, activities are central: Their best friends are the ones they do things with. Boys also tend to play in larger groups that are hierarchical. High-status boys give orders and push low-status boys around. So boys are expected to use language to seize center stage: by exhibiting their skill, displaying their knowledge, and challenging and resisting challenges.

These patterns have stunning implications for classroom interaction. 4 Most faculty members assume that participating in class discussion is a necessary part of successful performance. Yet speaking in a classroom is more congenial to boys' language experience than to girls', since it entails putting oneself forward in front of a large group of people, many of whom are strangers and at least one of whom is sure to judge speakers' knowledge and intelligence by their verbal display.

Another aspect of many classrooms that makes them more hospitable 5 to most men than to most women is the use of debatelike formats as a learning tool. Our educational system, as Walter Ong argues persuasively in his book *Fighting for Life* (Cornell University Press, 1981), is fundamentally male in that the pursuit of knowledge is believed to be achieved by ritual opposition: public display followed by argument and challenge. Father Ong demonstrates that ritual opposition—what he calls "adversativeness" or "agonism"—is fundamental to the way most males approach almost any activity. (Consider, for example, the little boy who shows he likes a little girl by pulling her braids and shoving her.) But ritual opposition is antithetical to the way most females learn and like to interact. It is not that females don't fight, but that they don't fight for fun. They don't *ritualize* opposition.

Anthropologists working in widely disparate parts of the world have found 6 contrasting verbal rituals for women and men. Women in completely unrelated cultures (for example, Greece and Bali) engage in ritual laments: spontaneously produced rhyming couplets that express their pain, for example, over the loss of loved ones. Men do not take part in laments. They have their own, very different verbal ritual: a contest, a war of words in which they vie with each other to devise clever insults.

When discussing these phenomena with a colleague, I commented that 7 I see these two styles in American conversation: Many women bond by talking about troubles, and many men bond by exchanging playful insults and put-downs, and other sorts of verbal sparring. He exclaimed: "I never thought of this, but that's the way I teach: I have students read an article, and then I invite them to tear it apart. After we've torn it to shreds, we talk about how to build a better model."

This contrasts sharply with the way I teach: I open the discussion of 8 readings by asking, "What did you find useful in this? What can we use in our own theory building and our own methods?" I note what I see as weaknesses in the author's approach, but I also point out that the writer's discipline and purposes might be different from ours. Finally, I offer personal anecdotes illustrating the phenomena under discussion and praise students' anecdotes as well as their critical acumen.

These different teaching styles must make our classrooms wildly dif-  *9*
ferent places and hospitable to different students. Male students are more
likely to be comfortable attacking the readings and might find the inclusion of personal anecdotes irrelevant and "soft." Women are more likely to
resist discussion they perceive as hostile, and, indeed, it is women in my
classes who are most likely to offer personal anecdotes.

A colleague who read my book commented that he had always taken for  *10*
granted that the best way to deal with students' comments is to challenge
them; this, he felt it was self-evident, sharpens their minds and helps them
develop debating skills. But he had noticed that women were relatively
silent in his classes, so he decided to try beginning discussion with relatively open-ended questions and letting comments go unchallenged. He
found, to his amazement and satisfaction, that more women began to
speak up.

Though some of the women in his class clearly liked this better, per-  *11*
haps some of the men liked it less. One young man in my class wrote in a
questionnaire about a history professor who gave students questions to
think about and called on people to answer them: "He would then play
devil's advocate . . . i.e., he debated us. . . . That class *really* sharpened me intellectually. . . . We as students do need to know how to defend ourselves."
This young man valued the experience of being attacked and challenged
publicly. Many, if not most, women would shrink from such "challenge,"
experiencing it as public humiliation.

A professor at Hamilton College told me of a young man who was up-  *12*
set because he felt his class presentation had been a failure. The professor was puzzled because he had observed that class members had listened
attentively and agreed with the student's observations. It turned out that
it was this very agreement that the student interpreted as failure: since no
one had engaged his ideas by arguing with him, he felt they had found them
unworthy of attention.

So one reason men speak in class more than women is that many of  *13*
them find the "public" classroom setting more conducive to speaking,
whereas most women are more comfortable speaking in private to a small
group of people they know well. A second reason is that men are more
likely to be comfortable with the debatelike form that discussion may take.
Yet another reason is the different attitudes toward speaking in class that
typify women and men.

Students who speak frequently in class, many of whom are men, as-  *14*
sume that it is their job to think of contributions and try to get the floor to
express them. But many women monitor their participation not only to get
the floor but to avoid getting it. Women students in my class tell me that if
they have spoken up once or twice, they hold back for the rest of the class
because they don't want to dominate. If they have spoken a lot one week,
they will remain silent the next. These different ethics of participation are,

of course, unstated, so those who speak freely assume that those who remain silent have nothing to say, and those who are reining themselves in
assume that the big talkers are selfish and hoggish.

When I looked around my classes, I could see these differing ethics *15*
and habits at work. For example, my graduate class in analyzing conversation had twenty students, eleven women and nine men. Of the men, four
were foreign students: two Japanese, one Chinese, and one Syrian. With the
exception of the three Asian men, all the men spoke in class at least occasionally. The biggest talker in the class was a woman, but there were also
five women who never spoke at all, only one of whom was Japanese. I
decided to try something different.

I broke the class into small groups to discuss the issues raised in the *16*
readings and to analyze their own conversational transcripts. I devised
three ways of dividing the students into groups: one by the degree program
they were in, one by gender, and one by conversational style, as closely as
I could guess it. This meant that when the class was grouped according to
conversational style, I put Asian students together, fast talkers together,
and quiet students together. The class split into groups six times during
the semester, so they met in each grouping twice. I told students to regard
the groups as examples of interactional data and to note the different ways
they participated in the different groups. Toward the end of the term, I gave
them a questionnaire asking about their class and group participation.

I could see plainly from my observation of the groups at work that *17*
women who never opened their mouths in class were talking away in the
small groups. In fact, the Japanese woman commented that she found it
particularly hard to contribute to the all-woman group she was in because
"I was overwhelmed by how talkative the female students were in the
female-only group." This is particularly revealing because it highlights
that the same person who can be "oppressed" into silence in one context
can become the talkative "oppressor" in another. No one's conversational
style is absolute; everyone's style changes in response to the context and
others' styles.

Some of the students (seven) said they preferred the same-gender groups; *18*
others preferred the same-style groups. In answer to the question "Would
you have liked to speak in class more than you did?" six of the seven who
said yes were women; the one man was Japanese. Most startlingly, this
response did not come only from quiet women; it came from women who
had indicated they had spoken in class never, rarely, sometimes, and often.
Of the eleven students who said the amount they had spoken was fine,
seven were men. Of the four women who checked "fine," two added qualifications indicating it wasn't completely fine: One wrote in "maybe more,"
and one wrote, "I have an urge to participate but often feel I should have
something more interesting/relevant/wonderful/intelligent to say!!"

I counted my experiment a success. Everyone in the class found the *19*
small groups interesting, and no one indicated he or she would have pre-

ferred that the class not break into groups. Perhaps most instructive, however, was the fact that the experience of breaking into groups, and of talking about participation in class, raised everyone's awareness about classroom participation. After we had talked about it, some of the quietest women in the class made a few voluntary contributions, though sometimes I had to ensure their participation by interrupting the students who were exuberantly speaking out.

Americans are often proud that they discount the significance of cul- 20 tural differences: "We are all individuals," many people boast. Ignoring such issues as gender and ethnicity becomes a source of pride: "I treat everyone the same." But treating people the same is not equal treatment if they are not the same.

The classroom is a different environment for those who feel comfort- 21 able putting themselves forward in a group than it is for those who find the prospect of doing so chastening, or even terrifying. When a professor asks, "Are there any questions?" students who can formulate statements the fastest have the greatest opportunity to respond. Those who need significant time to do so have not really been given a chance at all, since by the time they are ready to speak, someone else has the floor.

In a class where some students speak out without raising hands, those who 22 feel they must raise their hands and wait to be recognized do not have equal opportunity to speak. Telling them to feel free to jump in will not make them feel free; one's sense of timing, of one's rights and obligations in a classroom, are automatic, learned over years of interaction. They may be changed over time, with motivation and effort, but they cannot be changed on the spot. And everyone assumes his or her own way is best. When I asked my students how the class could be changed to make it easier for them to speak more, the most talkative woman said she would prefer it if no one had to raise hands, and a foreign student said he wished people would raise their hands and wait to be recognized.

My experience in this class has convinced me that small-group inter- 23 action should be part of any class that is not a small seminar. I also am convinced that having the students become observers of their own interaction is a crucial part of their education. Talking about ways of talking in class makes students aware that their ways of talking affect other students, that the motivations they impute to others may not truly reflect others' motives, and that the behaviors they assume to be self-evidently right are not universal norms.

The goal of complete equal opportunity in class may not be attainable, 24 but realizing that one monolithic classroom-participation structure is not equal opportunity is itself a powerful motivation to find more-diverse methods to serve diverse students—and every classroom is diverse.

■ ■ ■

## Reading as a Writer: Analyzing Rhetorical Choices

1. Given that Tannen is concerned with classroom dynamics, why does she open her essay with a discussion of sociologists and anthropologists? How do the framing ideas of those experts contribute to her descriptions of classroom dynamics? In particular, how does she use the concept of "ritual opposition" to help build her argument?

2. How would you describe Tannen's own style of making an argument? Are there aspects of both "female" and "male" conversational styles, as she defines them? How successfully do you think she addresses readers who might disagree with her?

## Writing as a Reader: Entering the Conversation of Ideas

1. Both Tannen and James W. Loewen notice that the way we learn is connected to what we learn. How might Tannen's insights help explain some of the dynamics Loewen describes in his essay? What can Loewen's ideas about the shortcomings of history textbooks and classrooms help us see in Tannen's text? Compose an essay that places these two writers' ideas in conversation as you propose an approach to teaching and learning history that would satisfy the demands for "inclusivity" that both writers desire. What are the strengths and possible shortfalls of what you propose?

2. Tannen's insights about gendered classroom conversational patterns may help bring aspects of Beverly Daniel Tatum's essay into clearer focus. Write an essay in which you use Tannen's insights about gender and conversational style to analyze some of the vocal exchanges you find most interesting in Tatum's essay. How might the sociological and anthropological ideas about gender dynamics that Tannen cites in her essay help you analyze both the problems and the solutions Tatum describes in her essay?

## PEGGY McINTOSH

# White Privilege: The Invisible Knapsack

Peggy McIntosh is associate director of the Wellesley College Center for Research on Women. She has written many well-known articles on multicultural and gender-equitable curricula and is a sought-after lecturer on these topics. The ideas in this very influential essay, which are drawn from conference presentations in 1986 and 1987, were published as a working paper in 1988 and reprinted in the winter 1990 issue of *Independent School*.

When McIntosh first spoke out about white privilege, she was among the first scholars developing an analysis of "whiteness" as a racial category, which involves in part examining the ways European-Americans have become an "invisible norm" against which other racial categories are often measured. In this article, McIntosh traces her own shift from simply seeing nonwhites as "disadvantaged" to seeing her own whiteness as an unearned "privilege." As she explains early in her essay,

> I have come to see white privilege as an invisible package of un-
> earned assets that I can count on cashing in each day, but about
> which I was "meant" to remain oblivious. White privilege is like
> an invisible weightless knapsack of special provisions, maps, pass-
> ports, codebooks, visas, clothes, tools, and blank checks. (para. 3)

Perhaps the most striking feature of this essay, rare in scholarly writing, is the long personal list in the middle of the piece in which she details
the unearned advantages she experiences in her daily life. This strategy of
connecting concrete, daily experiences to larger systems of power enables
readers to "see" freshly advantages that might come from social class,
nationality, educational status, gender, sexuality, or able-bodied status. In
other words, McIntosh's approach is one we might all use to analyze many
different aspects of our daily lives.

In her final paragraph, she leaves readers with the provocative question, "What will we do with such knowledge?" In this piece, McIntosh takes
risks and reveals her previous ignorance and her slow learning process; in
so doing, she invites readers to take similar risks and to begin this important work, as well.

■ ■ ■

Through work to bring materials from women's studies into the rest of    1
the curriculum, I have often noticed men's unwillingness to grant that
they are overprivileged, even though they may grant that women are disadvantaged. They may say they will work to raise women's status, in the
society, the university, or the curriculum, but they can't or won't support
the idea of lessening men's status. Denials that amount to taboos surround
the subject of advantages that men gain from women's disadvantages. These
denials protect male privilege from being fully acknowledged, lessened, or
ended.

Thinking through unacknowledged male privilege as a phenomenon,    2
I realized that, since hierarchies in our society are interlocking, there was
most likely a phenomenon of white privilege that was similarly denied and
protected. As a white person, I realized I had been taught about racism as
something that puts others at a disadvantage, but had been taught not to see
one of its corollary aspects, white privilege, which puts me at an advantage.

I think whites are carefully taught not to recognize white privilege, as    3
males are taught not to recognize male privilege. So I have begun in an untu-
tored way to ask what it is like to have white privilege. I have come to see
white privilege as an invisible package of unearned assets that I can count
on cashing in each day, but about which I was "meant" to remain oblivious.
White privilege is like an invisible weightless knapsack of special provi-
sions, maps, passports, codebooks, visas, clothes, tools, and blank checks.

Describing white privilege makes one newly accountable. As we in    4
women's studies work to reveal male privilege and ask men to give up some
of their power, so one who writes about having white privilege must ask,
"Having described it, what will I do to lessen or end it?"

After I realized the extent to which men work from a base of un-   5
acknowledged privilege, I understood that much of their oppressiveness
was unconscious. Then I remembered the frequent charges from women
of color that white women whom they encounter are oppressive. I
began to understand why we are just seen as oppressive, even when we
don't see ourselves that way. I began to count the ways in which I enjoy
unearned skin privilege and have been conditioned into oblivion about its
existence.

My schooling gave me no training in seeing myself as an oppressor, as   6
an unfairly advantaged person, or as a participant in a damaged culture. I
was taught to see myself as an individual whose moral state depended on
her individual moral will. My schooling followed the pattern my colleague
Elizabeth Minnich has pointed out: Whites are taught to think of their lives
as morally neutral, normative, and average, and also ideal, so that when we
work to benefit others, this is seen as work that will allow "them" to be more
like "us."

## Daily Effects of White Privilege

I decided to try to work on myself at least by identifying some of the daily   7
effects of white privilege in my life. I have chosen those conditions that
I think in my case attach somewhat more to skin-color privilege than to
class, religion, ethnic status, or geographic location, though of course all
these other factors are intricately intertwined. As far as I can tell, my African American coworkers, friends, and acquaintances with whom I come
into daily or frequent contact in this particular time, place, and line of work
cannot count on most of these conditions.

1. I can, if I wish, arrange to be in the company of people of my race
   most of the time.
2. I can avoid spending time with people whom I was trained to mistrust
   and who have learned to mistrust my kind or me.
3. If I should need to move, I can be pretty sure of renting or purchasing
   housing in an area which I can afford and in which I would want to
   live.
4. I can be pretty sure that my neighbors in such a location will be neutral or pleasant to me.
5. I can go shopping alone most of the time, pretty well assured that I
   will not be followed or harassed.
6. I can turn on the television or open to the front page of the paper and
   see people of my race widely represented.
7. When I am told about our national heritage or about "civilization," I
   am shown that people of my color made it what it is.

8. I can be sure that my children will be given curricular materials that testify to the existence of their race.

9. If I want to, I can be pretty sure of finding a publisher for this piece on white privilege.

10. I can be pretty sure of having my voice heard in a group in which I am the only member of my race.

11. I can be casual about whether or not to listen to another person's voice in a group in which s/he is the only member of his/her race.

12. I can go into a music shop and count on finding the music of my race represented, into a supermarket and find the staple foods which fit with my cultural traditions, into a hairdresser's shop and find someone who can cut my hair.

13. Whether I use checks, credit cards, or cash, I can count on my skin color not to work against the appearance of financial reliability.

14. I can arrange to protect my children most of the time from people who might not like them.

15. I do not have to educate my children to be aware of systemic racism for their own daily physical protection.

16. I can be pretty sure that my children's teachers and employers will tolerate them if they fit school and workplace norms; my chief worries about them do not concern others' attitudes toward their race.

17. I can talk with my mouth full and not have people put this down to my color.

18. I can swear, or dress in secondhand clothes, or not answer letters, without having people attribute these choices to the bad morals, the poverty, or the illiteracy of my race.

19. I can speak in public to a powerful male group without putting my race on trial.

20. I can do well in a challenging situation without being called a credit to my race.

21. I am never asked to speak for all the people of my racial group.

22. I can remain oblivious of the language and customs of persons of color who constitute the world's majority without feeling in my culture any penalty for such oblivion.

23. I can criticize our government and talk about how much I fear its policies and behavior without being seen as a cultural outsider.

24. I can be pretty sure that if I ask to talk to the "person in charge," I will be facing a person of my race.

25. If a traffic cop pulls me over or if the IRS audits my tax return, I can be sure I haven't been singled out because of my race.

26. I can easily buy posters, postcards, picture books, greeting cards, dolls, toys, and children's magazines featuring people of my race.

27. I can go home from most meetings of organizations I belong to feeling somewhat tied in, rather than isolated, out-of-place, outnumbered, unheard, held at a distance, or feared.

28. I can be pretty sure that an argument with a colleague of another race is more likely to jeopardize her/his chances for advancement than to jeopardize mine.

29. I can be pretty sure that if I argue for the promotion of a person of another race, or a program centering on race, this is not likely to cost me heavily within my present setting, even if my colleagues disagree with me.

30. If I declare there is a racial issue at hand, or there isn't a racial issue at hand, my race will lend me more credibility for either position than a person of color will have.

31. I can choose to ignore developments in minority writing and minority activist programs, or disparage them, or learn from them, but in any case, I can find ways to be more or less protected from negative consequences of any of these choices.

32. My culture gives me little fear about ignoring the perspectives and powers of people of other races.

33. I am not made acutely aware that my shape, bearing, or body odor will be taken as a reflection on my race.

34. I can worry about racism without being seen as self-interested or self-seeking.

35. I can take a job with an affirmative action employer without having my co-workers on the job suspect that I got it because of my race.

36. If my day, week, or year is going badly, I need not ask of each negative episode or situation whether it had racial overtones.

37. I can be pretty sure of finding people who would be willing to talk with me and advise me about my next steps, professionally.

38. I can think over many options, social, political, imaginative, or professional, without asking whether a person of my race would be accepted or allowed to do what I want to do.

39. I can be late to a meeting without having the lateness reflect on my race.

40. I can choose public accommodation without fearing that people of my race cannot get in or will be mistreated in the places I have chosen.

41. I can be sure that if I need legal or medical help, my race will not work against me.

42. I can arrange my activities so that I will never have to experience feelings of rejection owing to my race.

43. If I have low credibility as a leader, I can be sure that my race is not the problem.

44. I can easily find academic courses and institutions which give attention only to people of my race.

45. I can expect figurative language and imagery in all of the arts to testify to experiences of my race.

46. I can choose blemish cover or bandages in "flesh" color and have them more or less match my skin.

47. I can travel alone or with my spouse without expecting embarrassment or hostility in those who deal with us.

48. I have no difficulty finding neighborhoods where people approve of our household.

49. My children are given texts and classes which implicitly support our kind of family unit and do not turn them against my choice of domestic partnership.

50. I will feel welcomed and "normal" in the usual walks of public life, institutional and social.

## Elusive and Fugitive

I repeatedly forgot each of the realizations on this list until I wrote it down. 8 For me white privilege has turned out to be an elusive and fugitive subject. The pressure to avoid it is great, for in facing it I must give up the myth of meritocracy. If these things are true, this is not such a free country; one's life is not what one makes it; many doors open for certain people through no virtues of their own.

In unpacking this invisible knapsack of white privilege, I have listed 9 conditions of daily experience that I once took for granted. Nor did I think of any of these perquisites as bad for the holder. I now think that we need a more finely differentiated taxonomy of privilege, for some of these varieties are only what one would want for everyone in a just society, and others give license to be ignorant, oblivious, arrogant, and destructive.

I see a pattern running through the matrix of white privilege, a pattern 10 of assumptions that were passed on to me as a white person. There was one main piece of cultural turf; it was my own turf, and I was among those who could control the turf. My skin color was an asset for any move I was educated to want to make. I could think of myself as belonging in major ways and of making social systems work for me. I could freely disparage, fear, neglect, or be oblivious to anything outside of the dominant cultural forms. Being of the main culture, I could also criticize it fairly freely.

In proportion as my racial group was being made confident, com- 11 fortable, and oblivious, other groups were likely being made unconfident, uncomfortable, and alienated. Whiteness protected me from many kinds of hostility, distress, and violence, which I was being subtly trained to visit, in turn, upon people of color.

For this reason, the word "privilege" now seems to me misleading. We [12] usually think of privilege as being a favored state, whether earned or conferred by birth or luck. Yet some of the conditions I have described here work systematically to over-empower certain groups. Such privilege simply confers dominance because of one's race or sex.

## Earned Strength, Unearned Power

I want, then, to distinguish between earned strength and unearned power. [13] Conferred privilege can look like strength when it is in fact permission to escape or to dominate. But not all of the privileges on my list are inevitably damaging. Some, like the expectation that neighbors will be decent to you, or that your race will not count against you in court, should be the norm in a just society. Others, like the privilege to ignore less powerful people, distort the humanity of the holders as well as the ignored groups.

We might at least start by distinguishing between positive advantages, [14] which we can work to spread, and negative types of advantage, which unless rejected will always reinforce our present hierarchies. For example, the feeling that one belongs within the human circle, as Native Americans say, should not be seen as privilege for a few. Ideally it is an unearned entitlement. At present, since only a few have it, it is an unearned advantage for them. This paper results from a process of coming to see that some of the power that I originally saw as attendant on being a human being in the United States consisted in unearned advantage and conferred dominance.

I have met very few men who are truly distressed about systemic, unearned male advantage and conferred dominance. And so one question for [15] me and others like me is whether we will be like them, or whether we will get truly distressed, even outraged, about unearned race advantage and conferred dominance, and, if so, what we will do to lessen them. In any case, we need to do more work in identifying how they actually affect our daily lives. Many, perhaps most, of our white students in the United States think that racism doesn't affect them because they are not people of color; they do not see "whiteness" as a racial identity. In addition, since race and sex are not the only advantaging systems at work, we need similarly to examine the daily experience of having age advantage, or ethnic advantage, or physical ability, or advantage related to nationality, religion, or sexual orientation.

Difficulties and dangers surrounding the task of finding parallels are [16] many. Since racism, sexism, and heterosexism are not the same, the advantages associated with them should not be seen as the same. In addition, it is hard to disentangle aspects of unearned advantage that rest more on social class, economic class, race, religion, sex, and ethnic identity than on other factors. Still, all of the oppressions are interlocking, as the members of the Combahee River Collective pointed out in their "Black Feminist Statement" of 1977.

One factor seems clear about all of the interlocking oppressions. They *17* take both active forms, which we can see, and embedded forms, which as a member of the dominant groups one is taught not to see. In my class and place, I did not see myself as a racist because I was taught to recognize racism only in individual acts of meanness by members of my group, never in invisible systems conferring unsought racial dominance on my group from birth.

Disapproving of the systems won't be enough to change them. I was *18* taught to think that racism could end if white individuals changed their attitude. But a "white" skin in the United States opens many doors for whites whether or not we approve of the way dominance has been conferred on us. Individual acts can palliate, but cannot end, these problems.

To redesign social systems, we need first to acknowledge their colos- *19* sal unseen dimensions. The silences and denials surrounding privilege are the key political tool here. They keep the thinking about equality or equity incomplete, protecting unearned advantage and conferred dominance by making these subjects taboo. Most talk by whites about equal opportunity seems to me now to be about equal opportunity to try to get into a position of dominance while denying that systems of dominance exist.

It seems to me that obliviousness about white advantage, like oblivi- *20* ousness about male advantage, is kept strongly inculturated in the United States so as to maintain the myth of meritocracy, the myth that democratic choice is equally available to all. Keeping most people unaware that freedom of confident action is there for just a small number of people props up those in power and serves to keep power in the hands of the same groups that have most of it already.

Although systemic change takes many decades, there are pressing ques- *21* tions for me and, I imagine, for some others like me if we raise our daily consciousness on the perquisites of being light-skinned. What will we do with such knowledge? As we know from watching men, it is an open question whether we will choose to use unearned advantage, and whether we will use any of our arbitrarily awarded power to try to reconstruct power systems on a broader base.

■ ■ ■

## Reading as a Writer: Analyzing Rhetorical Choices

1. McIntosh divides her essay into subsections. Read back through each of the subsections and describe the purpose of each subsection (including that remarkable, long list in the middle). How do the ideas and examples in each subsection contribute to the larger goal of her essay? What other ways of organizing these ideas might you propose, and with what possible effect on readers?

2. Explain in your own words the distinction McIntosh makes in paragraphs 13 and 14 between "earned strength" and "unearned power." What specific examples of these does she urge readers to work against, and how? What

other suggestions and strategies for change can you add, based on your experiences and hopes?

## Writing as a Reader: Entering the Conversation of Ideas

1. How do our educational systems work to preserve or undo the kinds of race and class divisions McIntosh examines in her text? Draw on the ideas in McIntosh's text and connect them to concepts in one or two essays by Beverly Daniel Tatum, Gloria Anzaldúa, or Jonathan Kozol. Write an essay in which you use specific examples and ideas in the texts you select to build an argument about what American education currently accomplishes in relation to class and race differences. What do you think it should accomplish?

2. While both McIntosh and Beverly Daniel Tatum focus primarily on the small daily interactions that constitute and perpetuate assumptions about racial identity, these authors also bring gender into their analysis of these situations. Write an essay in which you consider how each author's insights about gender contribute to the observations and analysis they make about racial identity and power. You may include your own experiential insights in your essay as you build an argument about what we can learn from the ways gender dynamics often intersect with race dynamics. How hopeful are these authors, and are you, about changing these dynamics, based on their concluding statements and your own experiences?

## BEVERLY DANIEL TATUM

# "Why Are All the Black Kids Sitting Together in the Cafeteria?"

Beverly Daniel Tatum is a clinical psychologist and president of Spelman College in Atlanta. Her research often focuses on racial identity development and the role of race in education, including the concrete experiences of race dynamics in the classroom. She is the author of several books, the most recent of which are *Can We Talk About Race? And Other Conversations in an Era of School Resegregation* (2007) and *"Why Are All the Black Kids Sitting Together in the Cafeteria?": A Psychologist Explains the Development of Racial Identity* (revised, 2003). Like many of the scholars in this book, she is an expert in her field, but she chooses language that is welcoming to any informed and interested reader.

This excerpt comes from her 2003 book and hinges on a concrete example of the gathering patterns of kids in mixed high schools. Her title alone should get you thinking and talking with your peers. If you attended a high school with a diverse population, how would you answer her question? Tatum is aware that many Americans are uncomfortable talking about race and the effects of racial categorization, and so she offers her readers a set of tools for analyzing specific examples, like the cafeteria table example. She invites readers to see "racial identity formation" in a series of stages that we can analyze and reconsider. If cultural stereotypes are learned, as she argues, what will help us learn to think more open-mindedly about the potential of all people? Tatum's particular concern is the way schools—and high schools, in particular, in this excerpt—seem to be places where old patterns prevail more often than not.

As you read, evaluate the way Tatum frames both problems and solutions. Consider her claims and proposals in the context of your own experiences. How might your own racial identity, and even your gender, affect your insights and responses? This is a reading that might feel very close to home, which is not always comfortable. Tatum would argue, though, that facing discomfort head-on is better than never even asking obvious but difficult questions such as "Why are all the black kids sitting together in the cafeteria?"

■ ■ ■

Walk into any racially mixed high school cafeteria at lunch time and you will instantly notice that in the sea of adolescent faces, there is an identifiable group of Black students sitting together. Conversely, it could be pointed out that there are many groups of White students sitting together as well, though people rarely comment about that. The question on the tip of everyone's tongue is "Why are the Black kids sitting together?" Principals want to know, teachers want to know, White students want to know, the Black students who aren't sitting at the table want to know.

How does it happen that so many Black teenagers end up at the same cafeteria table? They don't start out there. If you walk into racially mixed elementary schools, you will often see young children of diverse racial backgrounds playing with one another, sitting at the snack table together, crossing racial boundaries with an ease uncommon in adolescence. Moving from elementary school to middle school (often at sixth or seventh grade) means interacting with new children from different neighborhoods than before, and a certain degree of clustering by race might therefore be expected, presuming that children who are familiar with one another would form groups. But even in schools where the same children stay together from kindergarten through eighth grade, racial grouping begins by the sixth or seventh grade. What happens?

One thing that happens is puberty. As children enter adolescence, they begin to explore the question of identity, asking "Who am I? Who can I be?" in ways they have not done before. For Black youth, asking "Who am I?" includes thinking about "Who am I ethnically and/or racially? What does it mean to be Black?"

As I write this, I can hear the voice of a White woman who asked me, "Well, all adolescents struggle with questions of identity. They all become more self-conscious about their appearance and more concerned about what their peers think. So what is so different for Black kids?" Of course, she is right that all adolescents look at themselves in new ways, but not all adolescents think about themselves in racial terms.

The search for personal identity that intensifies in adolescence can in-  5
volve several dimensions of an adolescent's life: vocational plans, religious
beliefs, values and preferences, political affiliations and beliefs, gender
roles, and ethnic identities. The process of exploration may vary across these
identity domains. James Marcia described four identity "statuses" to characterize the variation in the identity search process: (1) *diffuse*, a state in
which there has been little exploration or active consideration of a particular domain, and no psychological commitment; (2) *foreclosed*, a state in
which a commitment has been made to particular roles or belief systems,
often those selected by parents, without actively considering alternatives;
(3) *moratorium*, a state of active exploration of roles and beliefs in which
no commitment has yet been made; and (4) *achieved*, a state of strong personal commitment to a particular dimension of identity following a period
of high exploration.[1]

An individual is not likely to explore all identity domains at once; there-  6
fore it is not unusual for an adolescent to be actively exploring one dimension while another remains relatively unexamined. Given the impact of
dominant and subordinate status, it is not surprising that researchers have
found that adolescents of color are more likely to be actively engaged in an
exploration of their racial or ethnic identity than are White adolescents.[2]

Why do Black youths, in particular, think about themselves in terms  7
of race? Because that is how the rest of the world thinks of them. Our self-
perceptions are shaped by the messages that we receive from those around
us, and when young Black men and women enter adolescence, the racial
content of those messages intensifies. A case in point: If you were to ask my
ten-year-old son, David, to describe himself, he would tell you many things:
that he is smart, that he likes to play computer games, that he has an older
brother. Near the top of his list, he would likely mention that he is tall for
his age. He would probably not mention that he is Black, though he certainly knows that he is. Why would he mention his height and not his racial
group membership? When David meets new adults, one of the first questions they ask is "How old are you?" When David states his age, the inevitable reply is "Gee, you're tall for your age!" It happens so frequently that I
once overheard David say to someone, "Don't say it, I know. I'm tall for my
age." Height is salient for David because it is salient for others.

When David meets new adults, they don't say, "Gee, you're Black for  8
your age!" If you are saying to yourself, of course they don't, think again.
Imagine David at fifteen, six-foot-two, wearing the adolescent attire of the
day, passing adults he doesn't know on the sidewalk. Do the women hold
their purses a little tighter, maybe even cross the street to avoid him? Does
he hear the sound of the automatic door locks on cars as he passes by? Is
he being followed around by the security guards at the local mall? As he
stops in town with his new bicycle, does a police officer hassle him, asking
where he got it, implying that it might be stolen? Do strangers assume he
plays basketball? Each of these experiences conveys a racial message. At
ten, race is not yet salient for David, because it is not yet salient for society.
But it will be.

## Understanding Racial Identity Development

Psychologist William Cross, author of *Shades of Black: Diversity in African American Identity*, has offered a theory of racial identity development that I have found to be a very useful framework for understanding what is happening not only with David, but with those Black students in the cafeteria.[3] According to Cross's model, referred to as the psychology of nigrescence, or the psychology of becoming Black, the five stages of racial identity development are *pre-encounter, encounter, immersion/emersion, internalization,* and *internalization-commitment*. For the moment, we will consider the first two stages as those are the most relevant for adolescents.

In the first stage, the Black child absorbs many of the beliefs and values of the dominant White culture, including the idea that it is better to be White. The stereotypes, omissions, and distortions that reinforce notions of White superiority are breathed in by Black children as well as White. Simply as a function of being socialized in a Eurocentric culture, some Black children may begin to value the role models, lifestyles, and images of beauty represented by the dominant group more highly than those of their own cultural group. On the other hand, if Black parents are what I call race-conscious—that is, actively seeking to encourage positive racial identity by providing their children with positive cultural images and messages about what it means to be Black—the impact of the dominant society's messages are reduced.[4] In either case, in the pre-encounter stage, the personal and social significance of one's racial group membership has not yet been realized, and racial identity is not yet under examination. At age ten, David and other children like him would seem to be in the pre-encounter stage. When the environmental cues change and the world begins to reflect his Blackness back to him more clearly, he will probably enter the encounter stage.

Transition to the encounter stage is typically precipitated by an event or series of events that force the young person to acknowledge the personal impact of racism. As the result of a new and heightened awareness of the significance of race, the individual begins to grapple with what it means to be a member of a group targeted by racism. Though Cross describes this process as one that unfolds in late adolescence and early adulthood, research suggests that an examination of one's racial or ethnic identity may begin as early as junior high school.

In a study of Black and White eighth graders from an integrated urban junior high school, Jean Phinney and Steve Tarver found clear evidence for the beginning of the search process in this dimension of identity. Among the forty-eight participants, more than a third had thought about the effects of ethnicity on their future, had discussed the issues with family and friends, and were attempting to learn more about their group. While White students in this integrated school were also beginning to think about ethnic identity, there was evidence to suggest a more active search among Black students, especially Black females.[5] Phinney and Tarver's research is consistent with my own study of Black youth in predominantly White communities, where the environmental cues that trigger an examination of racial identity often become evident in middle school or junior high school.[6]

Some of the environmental cues are institutionalized. Though many     13
elementary schools have self-contained classrooms where children of vary-ing performance levels learn together, many middle and secondary schools use "ability grouping," or tracking. Though school administrators often defend their tracking practices as fair and objective, there usually is a rec-ognizable racial pattern to how children are assigned, which often repre-sents the system of advantage operating in the schools.[7] In racially mixed schools, Black children are much more likely to be in the lower track than in the honors track. Such apparent sorting along racial lines sends a mes-sage about what it means to be Black. One young honors student I inter-viewed described the irony of this resegregation in what was an otherwise integrated environment, and hinted at the identity issues it raised for him.

> It was really a very paradoxical existence, here I am in a school that's
> 35 percent Black, you know, and I'm the only Black in my classes. . . . That
> always struck me as odd. I guess I felt that I was different from the other
> Blacks because of that.

In addition to the changes taking place within school, there are     14
changes in the social dynamics outside school. For many parents, puberty raises anxiety about interracial dating. In racially mixed communities, you begin to see what I call the birthday party effect. Young children's birthday parties in multiracial communities are often a reflection of the communi-ty's diversity. The parties of elementary school children may be segregated by gender but not by race. At puberty, when the parties become sleepovers or boy-girl events, they become less and less racially diverse.

Black girls, especially in predominantly White communities, may grad-     15
ually become aware that something has changed. When their White friends start to date, they do not. The issues of emerging sexuality and the societal messages about who is sexually desirable leave young Black women in a very devalued position. One young woman from a Philadelphia suburb described herself as "pursuing White guys throughout high school" to no avail. Since there were no Black boys in her class, she had little choice. She would feel "really pissed off" that those same White boys would date her White friends. For her, "that prom thing was like out of the question."[8]

Though Black girls living in the context of a larger Black community     16
may have more social choices, they too have to contend with devaluing messages about who they are and who they will become, especially if they are poor or working-class. As social scientists Bonnie Ross Leadbeater and Niobe Way point out,

> The school drop-out, the teenage welfare mother, the drug addict, and
> the victim of domestic violence or of AIDS are among the most prevalent
> public images of poor and working-class urban adolescent girls. . . . Yet,

despite the risks inherent in economic disadvantage, the majority of poor urban adeolescent girls do not fit the stereotypes that are made about them.[9]

Resisting the stereotypes and affirming other definitions of themselves is part of the task facing young Black women in both White and Black communities.

As was illustrated in the example of David, Black boys also face a devalued status in the wider world. The all too familiar media image of a young Black man with his hands cuffed behind his back, arrested for a violent crime, has primed many to view young Black men with suspicion and fear. In the context of predominantly White schools, however, Black boys may enjoy a degree of social success, particularly if they are athletically talented. The culture has embraced the Black athlete, and the young man who can fulfill that role is often pursued by Black girls and White girls alike. But even these young men will encounter experiences that may trigger an examination of their racial identity.

Sometimes the experience is quite dramatic. *The Autobiography of Malcolm X* is a classic tale of racial identity development, and I assign it to my psychology of racism students for just that reason. As a junior high school student, Malcolm was a star. Despite the fact that he was separated from his family and living in a foster home, he was an A student and was elected president of his class. One day he had a conversation with his English teacher, whom he liked and respected, about his future career goals. Malcolm said he wanted to be a lawyer. His teacher responded, "That's no realistic goal for a nigger," and advised him to consider carpentry instead.[10] The message was clear: You are a Black male, your racial group membership matters, plan accordingly. Malcolm's emotional response was typical—anger, confusion, and alienation. He withdrew from his White classmates, stopped participating in class, and eventually left his predominately white Michigan home to live with his sister in Roxbury, a Black community in Boston.

No teacher would say such a thing now, you may be thinking, but don't be so sure. It is certainly less likely that a teacher would use the word *nigger*, but consider these contemporary examples shared by high school students. A young ninth-grade student was sitting in his homeroom. A substitute teacher was in charge of the class. Because the majority of students from this school go on to college, she used the free time to ask the students about their college plans. As a substitute she had very limited information about their academic performance, but she offered some suggestions. When she turned to this young man, one of few Black males in the class, she suggested that he consider a community college. She had recommended four-year colleges to the other students. Like Malcolm, this student got the message.

In another example, a young Black woman attending a desegregated school to which she was bussed was encouraged by a teacher to attend the upcoming school dance. Most of the Black students did not live in the neighborhood and seldom attended the extracurricular activities. The young woman indicated that she wasn't planning to come. The well-intentioned teacher was persistent. Finally the teacher said, "Oh come on, I know you people love to dance." This young woman got the message, too.

## Coping with Encounters: Developing an Oppositional Identity

What do these encounters have to do with the cafeteria? Do experiences    22
with racism inevitably result in so-called self-segregation? While certainly a desire to protect oneself from further offense is understandable, it is not the only factor at work. Imagine the young eighth-grade girl who experienced the teacher's use of "you people" and the dancing stereotype as a racial affront. Upset and struggling with adolescent embarrassment, she bumps into a White friend who can see that something is wrong. She explains. Her White friend responds, in an effort to make her feel better perhaps, and says, "Oh, Mr. Smith is such a nice guy, I'm sure he didn't mean it like that. Don't be so sensitive." Perhaps the White friend is right, and Mr. Smith didn't mean it, but imagine your own response when you are upset, perhaps with a spouse or partner. He or she asks what's wrong and you explain why you are offended. Your partner brushes off your complaint, attributing it to your being oversensitive. What happens to your emotional thermostat? It escalates. When feelings, rational or irrational, are invalidated, most people disengage. They not only choose to discontinue the conversation but are more likely to turn to someone who will understand their perspective.

In much the same way, the eighth-grade girl's White friend doesn't get    23
it. She doesn't see the significance of this racial message, but the girls at the "Black table" do. When she tells her story there, one of them is likely to say, "You know what, Mr. Smith said the same thing to me yesterday!" Not only are Black adolescents encountering racism and reflecting on their identity, but their White peers, even when they are not the perpetrators (and sometimes they are), are unprepared to respond in supportive ways. The Black students turn to each other for the much needed support they are not likely to find anywhere else.

In adolescence, as race becomes personally salient for Black youth,    24
finding the answer to questions such as, "What does it mean to be a young Black person? How should I act? What should I do?" is particularly important. And although Black fathers, mothers, aunts, and uncles may hold the answers by offering themselves as role models, they hold little appeal for most adolescents. The last thing many fourteen-year-olds want to do is to grow up to be like their parents. It is the peer group, the kids in the cafeteria, who hold the answers to these questions. They know how to be Black. They have absorbed the stereotypical images of Black youth in the popular culture and are reflecting those images in their self-presentation.

Based on their fieldwork in U.S. high schools, Signithia Fordham and    25
John Ogbu identified a common psychological pattern found among African American high school students at this stage of identity development.[11]
They observed that the anger and resentment that adolescents feel in
response to their growing awareness of the systematic exclusion of Black
people from full participation in U.S. society leads to the development of
an oppositional social identity. This oppositional stance both protects one's
identity from the psychological assault of racism and keeps the dominant
group at a distance. Fordham and Ogbu write:

> Subordinate minorities regard certain forms of behavior and certain activi-
> ties or events, symbols, and meanings as *not appropriate* for them because
> those behaviors, events, symbols, and meanings are characteristic of white
> Americans. At the same time they emphasize other forms of behavior as more
> appropriate for them because these are *not* a part of white Americans' way of
> life. To behave in the manner defined as falling within a white cultural frame
> of reference is to "act white" and is negatively sanctioned.[12]

Certain styles of speech, dress, and music, for example, may be em-    26
braced as "authentically Black" and become highly valued, while attitudes
and behaviors associated with Whites are viewed with disdain. The peer
group's evaluation of what is Black and what is not can have a powerful
impact on adolescent behavior.

Reflecting on her high school years, one Black woman from a White    27
neighborhood described both the pain of being rejected by her Black classmates and her attempts to conform to her peers' definition of Blackness:

> "Oh you sound White, you think you're White," they said. And the idea of
> sounding White was just so absurd to me. . . . So ninth grade was sort of trau-
> matic in that I started listening to rap music, which I really just don't like.
> [I said] I'm gonna be Black, and it was just that stupid. But it's more than just
> how one acts, you know. [The other Black women there] were not into me for
> the longest time. My first year there was hell.

Sometimes the emergence of an oppositional identity can be quite dra-    28
matic, as the young person tries on a new persona almost overnight. At the
end of one school year, race may not have appeared to be significant, but
often some encounter takes place over the summer and the young person
returns to school much more aware of his or her Blackness and ready to
make sure that the rest of the world is aware of it, too. There is a certain "in
your face" quality that these adolescents can take on, which their teachers
often experience as threatening. When a group of Black teens are sitting
together in the cafeteria, collectively embodying an oppositional stance,
school administrators want to know not only why they are sitting together,
but what can be done to prevent it.

We need to understand that in racially mixed settings, racial grouping    29
is a developmental process in response to an environmental stressor, racism. Joining with one's peers for support in the face of stress is a positive
coping strategy. What is problematic is that the young people are operating

with a very limited definition of what it means to be Black, based largely
on cultural stereotypes.

## Oppositional Identity Development and Academic Achievement

Unfortunately for Black teenagers, those cultural stereotypes do not usually    *30*
include academic achievement. Academic success is more often associated
with being White. During the encounter phase of racial identity development, when the search for identity leads toward cultural stereotypes and
away from anything that might he associated with Whiteness, academic
performance often declines. Doing well in school becomes identified as
trying to be White. Being smart becomes the opposite of being cool.

While this frame of reference is not universally found among adoles-    *31*
cents of African descent, it is commonly observed in Black peer groups.
Among the Black college students I have interviewed, many described
some conflict or alienation from other African American teens because of
their academic success in high school. For example, a twenty-year-old female from a Washington, D.C., suburb explained:

> It was weird, even in high school a lot of the Black students were, like, "Well,
> you're not really Black." Whether it was because I became president of the
> sixth-grade class or whatever it was, it started pretty much back then. Junior
> high, it got worse. I was then labeled certain things, whether it was "the oreo"
> or I wasn't really Black.

Others described avoiding situations that would set them apart from    *32*
their Black peers. For example, one young woman declined to participate
in a gifted program in her school because she knew it would separate her
from the other Black students in the school.

In a study of thirty-three eleventh-graders in a Washington, D.C.,    *33*
school, Fordham and Ogbu found that although some of the students had
once been academically successful, few of them remained so. These students also knew that to be identified as a "brainiac" would result in peer
rejection. The few students who had maintained strong academic records
found ways to play down their academic success enough to maintain some
level of acceptance among their Black peers.[13]

Academically successful Black students also need a strategy to find ac-    *34*
ceptance among their White classmates. Fordham describes one such strategy as *racelessness*, wherein individuals assimilate into the dominant group
by de-emphasizing characteristics that might identify them as members of
the subordinate group.[14] Jon, a young man I interviewed, offered a classic
example of this strategy as he described his approach to dealing with his
discomfort at being the only Black person in his advanced classes. He said,
"At no point did I ever think I was White or did I ever want to be White....
I guess it was one of those things where I tried to de-emphasize the fact

that I was Black." This strategy led him to avoid activities that were associated with Blackness. He recalled, "I didn't want to do anything that was traditionally Black, like I never played basketball. I ran cross-country. . . . I went for distance running instead of sprints." He felt he had to show his White classmates that there were "exceptions to all these stereotypes." However, this strategy was of limited usefulness. When he traveled outside his home community with his White teammates, he sometimes encountered overt racism. "I quickly realized that I'm Black, and that's the thing that they're going to see first, no matter how much I try to de-emphasize my Blackness."

A Black student can play down Black identity in order to succeed in school and mainstream institutions without rejecting his Black identity and culture.[15] Instead of becoming raceless, an achieving Black student can become an *emissary*, someone who sees his or her own achievements as advancing the cause of the racial group. For example, social scientists Richard Zweigenhaft and G. William Domhoff describe how a successful Black student, in response to the accusation of acting White, connected his achievement to that of other Black men by saying, "Martin Luther King must not have been Black, then, since he had a doctoral degree, and Malcolm X must not have been Black since he educated himself while in prison." In addition, he demonstrated his loyalty to the Black community by taking an openly political stance against the racial discrimination he observed in his school.[16]

It is clear that an oppositional identity can interfere with academic achievement, and it may be tempting for educators to blame the adolescents themselves for their academic decline. However, the questions that educators and other concerned adults must ask are, How did academic achievement become defined as exclusively White behavior? What is it about the curriculum and the wider culture that reinforces the notion that academic excellence is an exclusively White domain? What curricular interventions might we use to encourage the development of an empowered emissary identity?

An oppositional identity that disdains academic achievement has not always been a characteristic of Black adolescent peer groups. It seems to be a post-desegregation phenomenon. Historically, the oppositional identity found among African Americans in the segregated South included a positive attitude toward education. While Black people may have publicly deferred to Whites, they actively encouraged their children to pursue education as a ticket to greater freedom.[17] While Black parents still see education as the key to upward mobility, in today's desegregated schools the models of success—the teachers, administrators, and curricular heroes—are almost always White.

Black Southern schools, though stigmatized by legally sanctioned segregation, were often staffed by African American educators, themselves visible models of academic achievement. These Black educators may have presented a curriculum that included references to the intellectual legacy of other African Americans. As well, in the context of a segregated school, it was a given that the high achieving students would all be Black. Academic achievement did not have to mean separation from one's Black peers.

## The Search for Alternative Images

This historical example reminds us that an oppositional identity discouraging academic achievement is not inevitable even in a racist society. If young people are exposed to images of African American academic achievement in their early years, they won't have to define school achievement as something for Whites only. They will know that there is a long history of Black intellectual achievement.

This point was made quite eloquently by Jon, the young man I quoted earlier. Though he made the choice to excel in school, he labored under the false assumption that he was "inventing the wheel." It wasn't until he reached college and had the opportunity to take African American studies courses that he learned about other African Americans besides Martin Luther King, Malcolm X, and Frederick Douglass—the same three men he had heard about year after year, from kindergarten to high school graduation. As he reflected on his identity struggle in high school, he said:

> It's like I went through three phases. . . . My first phase was being cool, doing whatever was particularly cool for Black people at the time, and that was like in junior high. Then in high school, you know, I thought being Black was basically all stereotypes, so I tried to avoid all of those things. Now in college, you know, I realize that being Black means a variety of things.

Learning his history in college was of great psychological importance to Jon, providing him with role models he had been missing in high school. He was particularly inspired by learning of the intellectual legacy of Black men at his own college:

> When you look at those guys who were here in the Twenties, they couldn't live on campus. They couldn't eat on campus. They couldn't get their hair cut in town. And yet they were all Phi Beta Kappa. . . . That's what being Black really is, you know, knowing who you are, your history, your accomplishments. . . . When I was in junior high, I had White role models. And then when I got into high school, you know, I wasn't sure but I just didn't think having White role models was a good thing. So I got rid of those. And I basically just, you know, only had my parents for role models. I kind of grew up thinking that we were on the cutting edge. We were doing something radically different than everybody else. And not realizing that there are all kinds of Black people doing the very things that I thought we were the only ones doing. . . . You've got to do the very best you can so that you can continue the great traditions that have already been established.

This young man was not alone in his frustration over having learned little about his own cultural history in grade school. Time and again in the research interviews I conducted, Black students lamented the absence of courses in African American history or literature at the high school level and indicated how significant this new learning was to them in college, how excited and affirmed they felt by this newfound knowledge. Sadly, many Black students never get to college, alienated from the process of education long before high school graduation. They may never get access to the information that might have helped them expand their definition of what it means to be Black and, in the process, might have helped them stay in school. Young people are developmentally ready for this information in adolescence. We ought to provide it. . . .

## An Alternative to the Cafeteria Table

The developmental need to explore the meaning of one's identity with oth-  43
ers who are engaged in a similar process manifests itself informally in school corridors and cafeterias across the country. Some educational institutions have sought to meet this need programmatically. Several colleagues and I recently evaluated one such effort, initiated at a Massachusetts middle school participating in a voluntary desegregation program known as the Metropolitan Council for Educational Opportunity (METCO) program.[18] Historically, the small number of African American students who are bussed from Boston to this suburban school have achieved disappointing levels of academic success. In an effort to improve academic achievement, the school introduced a program, known as Student Efficacy Training (SET), that allowed Boston students to meet each day as a group with two staff members. Instead of being in physical education or home economics or study hall, they were meeting, talking about homework difficulties, social issues, and encounters with racism. The meeting was mandatory and at first the students were resentful of missing some of their classes. But the impact was dramatic. Said one young woman,

> In the beginning of the year, I didn't want to do SET at all. It took away my study and it was only METCO students doing it. In the beginning all we did was argue over certain problems or it was more like a rap session and I didn't think it was helping anyone. But then when we looked at records . . . I know that last year out of all the students, sixth through eighth grade, there was, like, six who were actually good students. Everyone else, it was just pathetic, I mean, like, they were getting like Ds and Fs. . . . The eighth grade is doing much better this year. I mean, they went from Ds and Fs to Bs and Cs and occasional As. . . . And those seventh-graders are doing really good, they have a lot of honor roll students in seventh grade, both guys and girls. Yeah, it's been good. It's really good.

Her report is borne out by an examination of school records. The op-  44
portunity to come together in the company of supportive adults allowed these young Black students to talk about the issues that hindered their performance—racial encounters, feelings of isolation, test anxiety, homework dilemmas—in the psychological safety of their own group. In the process,

the peer culture changed to one that supported academic performance rather than undermined it, as revealed in these two students' comments:

> Well, a lot of the Boston students, the boys and the girls, used to fight all the time. And now, they stopped yelling at each other so much and calling each other stupid.

> It's like we've all become like one big family, we share things more with each other. We tease each other like brother and sister. We look out for each other with homework and stuff. We always stay on top of each other 'cause we know it's hard with African American students to go to a predominantly White school and try to succeed with everybody else.

The faculty, too, were very enthusiastic about the outcomes of the intervention, as seen in the comments of these two classroom teachers: 45

> This program has probably produced the most dramatic result of any single change that I've seen at this school. It has produced immediate results that affected behavior and academics and participation in school life.

> My students are more engaged. They aren't battling out a lot of the issues of their anger about being in a White community, coming in from Boston, where do I fit, I don't belong here. I feel that those issues that often came out in class aren't coming out in class anymore. I think they are being discussed in the SET room, the kids feel more confidence. The kids' grades are higher, the homework response is greater, they're not afraid to participate in class, and I don't see them isolating themselves within class. They are willing to sit with other students happily. . . . I think it's made a very positive impact on their place in the school and on their individual self-esteem. I see them enjoying themselves and able to enjoy all of us as individuals. I can't say enough, it's been the best thing that's happened to the METCO program as far as I'm concerned.[19]

Although this intervention is not a miracle cure for every school, it does highlight what can happen when we think about the developmental needs of Black adolescents coming to terms with their own sense of identity. It might seem counterintuitive that a school involved in a voluntary desegregation program could improve both academic performance and social relationships among students by *separating* the Black students for one period every day. But if we understand the unique challenges facing adolescents of color and the legitimate need they have to feel supported in their identity development, it makes perfect sense. 46

Though they may not use the language of racial identity development theory to describe it, most Black parents want their children to achieve an internalized sense of personal security, to be able to acknowledge the reality of racism and to respond effectively to it. Our educational institutions should do what they can to encourage this development rather than impede it. When I talk to educators about the need to provide adolescents with identity-affirming experiences and information about their own cultural groups, they sometimes flounder because this information has not been part of their own education. Their understanding of adolescent de- 47 velopment has been limited to the White middle-class norms included in most textbooks, their knowledge of Black history limited to Martin Luther King, Jr., and Rosa Parks. They sometimes say with frustration that parents should provide this kind of education for their children. Unfortunately Black parents often attended the same schools the teachers did and have the same informational gaps. We need to acknowledge that an important part of interrupting the cycle of oppression is constant re-education, and sharing what we learn with the next generation.

NOTES

1. J. Marcia, "Development and validation of ego identity status," *Journal of Personality and Social Psychology* 3 (1966): 551–58.

2. For a review of the research on ethnic identity in adolescents, see J. Phinney, "Ethnic identity in adolescents and adults: Review of research," *Psychological Bulletin* 108, no. 3 (1990): 499–514. See also "Part I: Identity development," in B. J. R. Leadbeater and N. Way (Eds.), *Urban girls: Resisting stereotypes, creating identities* (New York: New York University Press, 1996).

3. W. E. Cross, Jr., *Shades of Black: Diversity in African-American identity* (Philadelphia: Temple University Press, 1991).

4. For an expanded discussion of "race-conscious" parenting, see B. D. Tatum, *Assimilation blues*, ch. 6.

5. J. S. Phinney and S. Tarver, "Ethnic identity search and commitment in Black and White eighth graders," *Journal of Early Adolescence* 8, no. 3 (1988): 265–77.

6. See B. D. Tatum, "African-American identity, academic achievement, and missing history," *Social Education* 56, no. 6 (1992): 331–34; B. D. Tatum, "Racial identity and relational theory: The case of Black women in White communities," in *Work in progress, no. 63* (Wellesley MA: Stone Center Working Papers, 1992); B. D. Tatum, "Out there stranded? Black youth in White communities," pp. 214–33 in H. McAdoo (Ed.), *Black families*, 3d ed. (Thousand Oaks, CA: Sage, 1996).

7. For an in-depth discussion of the negative effects of tracking in schools, see J. Oakes, *Keeping track: How schools structure inequality* (New Haven: Yale University Press, 1985).

8. For further discussion of the social dynamics for Black youth in White communities, see Tatum, "Out there stranded?"

9. Leadbeater and Way, *Urban girls*, p. 5.

10. A. Haley and Malcolm X, *The autobiography of Malcolm X* (New York: Grove Press, 1965), p. 36.

11. S. Fordham and J. Ogbu, "Black students' school success: Coping with the burden of 'acting White,'" *Urban Review* 18 (1986): 176–206.

12. Ibid., p. 181.

13. For an expanded discussion of the "trying to be White" phenomenon, see Fordham and Ogbu, "Black students' school success," and S. Fordham, "Racelessness as a factor in Black students' school success: Pragmatic strategy or Pyrrhic victory?" *Harvard Educational Review* 58, no. 1 (1988): 54–84.

14. Fordham, "Racelessness as a factor in Black students' school success." See also S. Fordham, *Blacked out: Dilemmas of race, identity, and success at Capital High* (Chicago: University of Chicago Press, 1996).

15. For further discussion of this point, see R. Zweigenhaft and G. W Domhoff, *Blacks in the White establishment? A study of race and class in America* (New Haven: Yale University Press, 1991), p. 155.

16. Ibid.

17. Ibid., p. 156.

18. The Metropolitan Council for Educational Opportunity (METCO) program was established in 1966 under the state's Racial Imbalance Law passed by the Massachusetts General Court in 1965. METCO was established to provide (1) the opportunity for an integrated public school education for urban Black children and other children of color from racially unbalanced schools in Boston by placing them in suburban schools, (2) a new learning experience for suburban children, and (3) a closer understanding and cooperation between urban and suburban parents and other citizens in the Boston metropolitan area. Thirty-four suburban communities participate in the METCO program.

19. For a more complete description of the program and its evaluation, see B. D. Tatum, P. C. Brown, P. Elliott, and T. Tatum, "Student efficacy training: An evaluation of one middle school's programmatic response to the Eastern Massachusetts Initiative" (presented at the American Educational Research Association Annual Meeting, April 9,1996, New York).

■ ■ ■

## Reading as a Writer: Analyzing Rhetorical Choices

1. Tatum launches her essay with a pointed question in her title and in her first paragraph: "Why are the Black kids sitting together?" While the rest of her essay is a response to this big question, Tatum uses questions throughout her essay. Using an easy-to-see pen, mark all the questions in this essay. At what points in her argument do they appear, and what functions do they serve? What conclusions can you draw about the effect of question-asking strategies in persuasive writing?

2. Tatum moves between citing experts (particularly in psychology and education) and presenting interviews with students. Locate the places where she shifts between experts and students, and discuss how exactly she makes these connections. How effectively does she explain and analyze the ideas in quotations from both experts and students? To what extent are the students she interviews experts, as well?

## Writing as a Reader: Entering the Conversation of Ideas

1. Tatum and James W. Loewen approach racial inequity and school curricula from different perspectives and with different kinds of examples, yet they share a commitment to making school a place where future citizens can fully develop the skills they will need to succeed in increasingly diverse environments. Write a paper in which you place these two scholars in conversation, exploring how each envisions both the problems and the solutions when they examine racial inequity in the school setting. Where do you stand in this conversation about the role schools can (and should) play in fostering equity within the curriculum and school environment?

2. While Tatum focuses on adolescents and Ann duCille focuses on children, both authors are concerned with the many ways cultural "norms" in the United States still perpetuate very narrow ideas about what it means to be African American in the United States. Write an essay in which you draw on ideas and specific examples from both authors in order to consider how much of our "education" about race in American culture often happens in

such small, seemingly innocuous exchanges. (If you like, you might find it interesting to develop and include in your essay a Peggy McIntosh–style list that helps you enumerate some of the concrete, daily ways we are "educated" into assumptions about racial identity.) Based on these writers' ideas, what conclusions can you draw about the most effective ways we might change this "education"?

## GLORIA ANZALDÚA

# How to Tame a Wild Tongue

Gloria Anzaldúa was born in South Texas and was a sixth-generation Tejana and a prolific writer. She died in 2004 at age 62 of complications from diabetes. Her personal experiences of racism, sexism, and linguistic prejudice during her childhood in Texas often provide poignant and pointed examples for the arguments she makes about identity and language in her academic writing. She is best known for coediting with Cherríe Moraga an anthology of writing by women titled *This Bridge Called My Back: Writings by Radical Women of Color* (1981). She became famous for helping others see that having a mixed identity could be a source of strength and great insight, and her term "new mestiza" captured the promise she saw in "complex, heterogeneous people" (para. 13), who may be in a good position to challenge simplistic binary thinking.

As you will notice in this piece, which is an excerpt from her book *Borderlands/La Frontera* (1987), Anzaldúa often moves between languages and dialects in her writing, rarely translating as she switches quickly from English to Spanish to Tex-Mex or Pachuco (or *caló*), a variant of Mexican Spanish. As you read, consider what it feels like to ride this linguistic roller coaster, perhaps not always fully understanding what is going on. What effects might Anzaldúa's tactics have on her readers, and how might these effects be related to her argument in this essay?

Anzaldúa brings together personal experience, history, quotations, and theories about identity in this rich essay. Pay attention to the connections she establishes—or asks her readers to establish—among all these pieces, and consider where she leaves her readers at the end. What does she want us to see differently? Some of her phrases and claims are both poetic and challenging. What does she mean by "linguistic terrorism," for example, or by the assertion "I am my language," particularly since she speaks many languages? Anzaldúa's voice is alternately personable, in-your-face, abstract, and thought-provoking. Whether or not you are multilingual, how might her insights help you understand the connections between the ways you speak and the many identities you might have?

"Were going to have to control your tongue," the dentist says, pulling out all the metal from my mouth. Silver bits plop and tinkle into the basin. My mouth is a motherlode.

The dentist is cleaning out my roots. I get a whiff of the stench when I gasp. "I can't cap that tooth yet, you're still draining," he says.

"We're going to have to do something about your tongue," I hear the anger rising in his voice. My tongue keeps pushing out the wads of cotton, pushing back the drills, the long thin needles. "I've never seen anything as strong or as stubborn," he says. And I think, how do you tame a wild tongue, train it to be quiet, how do you bridle and saddle it? How do you make it lie down?

"Who is to say that robbing a people of its language is less violent than war?"

—Ray Gwyn Smith[1]

I remember being caught speaking Spanish at recess—that was good for    1
three licks on the knuckles with a sharp ruler. I remember being sent to the corner of the classroom for "talking back" to the Anglo teacher when all I was trying to do was tell her how to pronounce my name. "If you want to be American, speak 'American.' If you don't like it, go back to Mexico where you belong."

"I want you to speak English. *Pa'hallar buen trabajo tienes que saber*    2
*hablar el inglés bien. Qué vale toda tu educación si todavía hablas inglés con un* 'accent,'" my mother would say, mortified that I spoke English like a Mexican. At Pan American University, I and all Chicano students were required to take two speech classes. Their purpose: to get rid of our accents.

Attacks on one's form of expression with the intent to censor are a vio-    3
lation of the First Amendment. *El Anglo con cara de inocente nos arrancó la lengua.* Wild tongues can't be tamed, they can only be cut out.

## Overcoming the Tradition of Silence

*Ahogadas, escupimos el oscuro.*
*Peleando con nuestra propia sombra*
*el silencio nos sepulta.*

*En boca cerrada no entran moscas.* "Flies don't enter a closed mouth" is    4
a saying I kept hearing when I was a child. *Ser habladora* was to be a gossip and a liar, to talk too much. *Muchachitas bien criadas*, well-bred girls don't answer back. *Es una falta de respeto* to talk back to one's mother or father. I remember one of the sins I'd recite to the priest in the confession box the few times I went to confession: talking back to my mother, *hablar pa' 'tras, repelar. Hociocona, repelona, chismosa*, having a big mouth, questioning, carrying tales are all signs of being *mal criada*. In my culture they are all words that are derogatory if applied to women—I've never heard them applied to men.

The first time I heard two women, a Puerto Rican and a Cuban, say    5
the word "*nosotras*," I was shocked. I had not known the word existed. Chicanas use *nosotros* whether we're male or female. We are robbed of our female being by the masculine plural. Language is a male discourse.

And our tongues have become
dry   the wilderness has
dried out our tongues   and
we have forgotten speech.
—IRENA KLEPFISZ[2]

Even our own people, other Spanish speakers *nos quieren poner*   6
*candados en la boca.* They would hold us back with their bag of *reglas de
academia.*

"*Pocho,* cultural traitor, you're speaking the oppressor's language by   7
speaking English, you're ruining the Spanish language," I have been accused by various Latinos and Latinas. Chicano Spanish is considered by
the purist and by most Latinos deficient, a mutilation of Spanish.

But Chicano Spanish is a border tongue which developed naturally.   8
Change, *evolución, enriquecimiento de palabras nuevas por invención o adop-
ción* have created variants of Chicano Spanish, *un nuevo lenguaje. Un lenguaje que corresponde a un modo de vivir.* Chicano Spanish is not incorrect,
it is a living language.

For a people who are neither Spanish nor live in a country in which   9
Spanish is the first language; for a people who live in a country in which
English is the reigning tongue but who are not Anglo; for a people who
cannot entirely identify with either standard (formal, Castilian) Spanish or
standard English, what recourse is left to them but to create their own language? A language which they can connect their identity to, one capable
of communicating the realities and values true to themselves—a language
with terms that are neither *español ni inglés*, but both. We speak a patois, a
forked tongue, a variation of two languages.

Chicano Spanish sprang out of the Chicanos' need to identify ourselves   10
as a distinct people. We needed a language with which we could communicate with ourselves, a secret language. For some of us, language is
a homeland closer than the Southwest—for many Chicanos today live in
the Midwest and the East. And because we are a complex, heterogeneous
people, we speak many languages. Some of the languages we speak are

1. Standard English
2. Working class and slang English
3. Standard Spanish
4. Standard Mexican Spanish
5. North Mexican Spanish dialect
6. Chicano Spanish (Texas, New Mexico, Arizona, and California have
   regional variations)
7. Tex-Mex
8. *Pachuco* (called *caló*)

My "home" tongues are the languages I speak with my sister and broth-   11
ers, with my friends. They are the last five listed, with 6 and 7 being closest

to my heart. From school, the media, and job situations, I've picked up standard and working class English. From Mamagrande Locha and from reading Spanish and Mexican literature, I've picked up Standard Spanish and Standard Mexican Spanish. From *los recién llegados*, Mexican immigrants, and *braceros*, I learned the North Mexican dialect. With Mexicans I'll try to speak either Standard Mexican Spanish or the North Mexican dialect. From my parents and Chicanos living in the Valley, I picked up Chicano Texas Spanish, and I speak it with my mom, younger brother (who married a Mexican and who rarely mixes Spanish with English), aunts, and older relatives.

With Chicanas from *Nuevo México* or *Arizona* I will speak Chicano    12
Spanish a little, but often they don't understand what I'm saying. With most California Chicanas I speak entirely in English (unless I forget). When I first moved to San Francisco, I'd rattle off something in Spanish, unintentionally embarrassing them. Often it is only with another Chicana *tejano* that I can talk freely.

Words distorted by English are known as anglicisms or *pochismos*.    13
The *pocho* is an anglicized Mexican or American of Mexican origin who speaks Spanish with an accent characteristic of North Americans and who distorts and reconstructs the language according to the influence of English.[3] Tex-Mex, or Spanglish, comes most naturally to me. I may switch back and forth from English to Spanish in the same sentence or in the same word. With my sister and my brother Nune and with Chicano *tejano* contemporaries I speak in Tex-Mex.

From kids and people my own age I picked up *Pachuco*. *Pachuco* (the    14
language of the zoot suiters) is a language of rebellion, both against Standard Spanish and Standard English. It is a secret language. Adults of the culture and outsiders cannot understand it. It is made up of slang words from both English and Spanish. *Ruca* means girl or woman, *vato* means guy or dude, *chale* means no, *simón* means yes, *churro* is sure, talk is *periquiar*, *pigionear* means petting, *que gacho* means how nerdy, *ponte águila* means watch out, death is called *la pelona*. Through lack of practice and not having others who can speak it, I've lost most of the *Pachuco* tongue.

## Chicano Spanish

Chicanos, after 250 years of Spanish/Anglo colonization, have developed    15
significant differences in the Spanish we speak. We collapse two adjacent vowels into a single syllable and sometimes shift the stress in certain words such as *maíz/maiz, cohete/cuete*. We leave out certain consonants when they appear between vowels: *lado/lao, mojado/mojao*. Chicanos from South Texas pronounce *f* as *j* as in *jue (fue)*. Chicanos use "archaisms," words that are no longer in the Spanish language, words that have been evolved out. We say *semos, truje, haiga, ansina,* and *naiden*. We retain the "archaic" *j*, as

in *jalar*, that derives from an earlier *h* (the French *halar* or the Germanic *halon* which was lost to standard Spanish in the sixteenth century), but which is still found in several regional dialects such as the one spoken in South Texas. (Due to geography, Chicanos from the Valley of South Texas were cut off linguistically from other Spanish speakers. We tend to use words that the Spaniards brought over from Medieval Spain. The majority of the Spanish colonizers in Mexico and the Southwest came from Extremadura—Hernán Cortés was one of them—and Andalucía. Andalucians pronounce *ll* like a *y*, and their *d*'s tend to be absorbed by adjacent vowels: *tirado* becomes *tirao*. They brought *el lenguaje popular, dialectos y regionalismos*.)[4]

Chicanos and other Spanish speakers also shift *ll* to *y* and *z* to *s*.[5] We     16
leave out initial syllables, saying *tar* for *estar*, *toy* for *estoy*, *hora* for *ahora* (*cubanos* and *puertorriqueños* also leave out initial letters of some words). We also leave out the final syllable such as *pa* for *para*. The intervocalic *y*, the *ll* as in *tortilla, ella, botella*, gets replaced by *tortia* or *toriya, ea, botea*. We add an additional syllable at the beginning of certain words: *atocar* for *tocar*, *agastar* for *gastar*. Sometimes we'll say *lavaste las vacijas*, other times *lavates* (substituting the *ates* verb endings for the *aste*).

We use anglicisms, words borrowed from English: *bola* from ball, *car-*     17
*peta* from carpet, *máchina de lavar* (instead of *lavadora*) from washing machine. Tex-Mex argot, created by adding a Spanish sound at the beginning or end of an English word such as *cookiar* for cook, *watchar* for watch, *parkiar* for park, and *rapiar* for rape, is the result of the pressures on Spanish speakers to adapt to English.

We don't use the word *vosotros/as* or its accompanying verb form. We     18
don't say *claro*, (to mean yes), *imagínate*, or *me emociona*, unless we picked up Spanish from Latinas, out of a book, or in a classroom. Other Spanish-speaking groups are going through the same, or similar, development in their Spanish.

## Linguistic Terrorism

> *Deslenguadas. Somos los del español deficiente.* We are your linguistic nightmare, your linguistic aberration, your linguistic *mestisaje*, the subject of your *burla*. Because we speak with tongues of fire we are culturally crucified. Racially, culturally, and linguistically *somos huérfanos*—we speak an orphan tongue.

Chicanas who grew up speaking Chicano Spanish have internalized     19
the belief that we speak poor Spanish. It is illegitimate, a bastard language. And because we internalize how our language has been used against us by the dominant culture, we use our language differences against each other.

Chicana feminists often skirt around each other with suspicion and     20
hesitation. For the longest time I couldn't figure it out. Then it dawned on

me. To be close to another Chicana is like looking into the mirror. We are afraid of what we'll see there. *Pena.* Shame. Low estimation of self. In childhood we are told that our language is wrong. Repeated attacks on our native tongue diminish our sense of self. The attacks continue throughout our lives.

Chicanas feel uncomfortable talking in Spanish to Latinas, afraid of    *21* their censure. Their language was not outlawed in their countries. They had a whole lifetime of being immersed in their native tongue; generations, centuries in which Spanish was a first language, taught in school, heard on radio and TV, and read in the newspaper.

If a person, Chicana or Latina, has a low estimation of my native    *22* tongue, she also has a low estimation of me. Often with *mexicanas y latinas* we'll speak English as a neutral language. Even among Chicanas we tend to speak English at parties or conferences. Yet, at the same time, we're afraid the other will think we're *agringadas* because we don't speak Chicano Spanish. We oppress each other trying to out-Chicano each other, vying to be the "real" Chicanas, to speak like Chicanos. There is no one Chicano language just as there is no one Chicano experience. A monolingual Chicana whose first language is English or Spanish is just as much a Chicana as one who speaks several variants of Spanish. A Chicana from Michigan or Chicago or Detroit is just as much a Chicana as one from the Southwest. Chicano Spanish is as diverse linguistically as it is regionally.

By the end of this century, Spanish speakers will comprise the biggest    *23* minority group in the United States, a country where students in high schools and colleges are encouraged to take French classes because French is considered more "cultured." But for a language to remain alive it must be used.[6] By the end of this century English, and not Spanish, will be the mother tongue of most Chicanos and Latinos.

So, if you want to really hurt me, talk badly about my language. Ethnic    *24* identity is twin skin to linguistic identity—I am my language. Until I can take pride in my language, I cannot take pride in myself. Until I can accept as legitimate Chicano Texas Spanish, Tex-Mex, and all the other languages I speak, I cannot accept the legitimacy of myself. Until I am free to write bilingually and to switch codes without having always to translate, while I still have to speak English or Spanish when I would rather speak Spanglish, and as long as I have to accommodate the English speaker rather than having them accommodate me, my tongue will be illegitimate.

I will no longer be made to feel ashamed of existing. I will have my    *25* voice: Indian, Spanish, white. I will have my serpent's tongue—my woman's voice, my sexual voice, my poet's voice. I will overcome the tradition of silence.

> My fingers
> move sly against your palm
> Like women everywhere, we speak in code. . . .
> —MELANIE KAYE/KANTROWITZ[7]

## *"Vistas," Corridos, y Comida:* My Native Tongue

In the 1960s, I read my first Chicano novel. It was *City of Night* by John  26
Rechy, a gay Texan, son of a Scottish father and a Mexican mother. For
days I walked around in stunned amazement that a Chicano could write
and could get published. When I read *I Am Joaquín*[8] I was surprised to see
a bilingual book by a Chicano in print. When I saw poetry written in Tex-
Mex for the first time, a feeling of pure joy flashed through me. I felt like
we really existed as a people. In 1971, when I started teaching High School
English to Chicano students, I tried to supplement the required texts with
works by Chicanos, only to be reprimanded and forbidden to do so by the
principal. He claimed that I was supposed to teach "American" and English literature. At the risk of being fired, I swore my students to secrecy
and slipped in Chicano short stories, poems, a play. In graduate school,
while working toward a Ph.D., I had to "argue" with one advisor after the
other, semester after semester, before I was allowed to make Chicano literature an area of focus.

Even before I read books by Chicanos or Mexicans, it was the Mexican  27
movies I saw at the drive-in—the Thursday night special of $1.00 a car-
load—that gave me a sense of belonging. *"Vámonos a las vistas,"* my mother
would call out and we'd all—grandmother, brothers, sister, and cousins—
squeeze into the car. We'd wolf down cheese and bologna white bread
sandwiches while watching Pedro Infante in melodramatic tearjerkers like
*Nosotros los pobres,* the first "real" Mexican movie (that was not an imitation of European movies). I remember seeing *Cuando los hijos se van* and
surmising that all Mexican movies played up the love a mother has for her
children and what ungrateful sons and daughters suffer when they are not
devoted to their mothers. I remember the singing-type "westerns" of Jorge
Negrete and Miquel Aceves Mejía. When watching Mexican movies, I felt
a sense of homecoming as well as alienation. People who were to amount
to something didn't go to Mexican movies, or *bailes,* or tune their radios to
*bolero, rancherita,* and *corrido* music.

The whole time I was growing up, there was *norteño* music sometimes  28
called North Mexican border music, or Tex-Mex music, or Chicano music,
or *cantina* (bar) music. I grew up listening to *conjuntos,* three- or four-
piece bands made up of folk musicians playing guitar, *bajo sexto,* drums,
and button accordion, which Chicanos had borrowed from the German
immigrants who had come to Central Texas and Mexico to farm and build
breweries. In the Rio Grande Valley, Steve Jordan and Little Joe Hernández
were popular, and Flaco Jiménez was the accordion king. The rhythms of
Tex-Mex music are those of the polka, also adapted from the Germans,
who in turn had borrowed the polka from the Czechs and Bohemians.

I remember the hot, sultry evenings when *corridos*—songs of love and  29
death on the Texas-Mexican borderlands—reverberated out of cheap am-
plifiers from the local *cantinas* and wafted in through my bedroom window.

*Corridos* first became widely used along the South Texas/Mexican bor- ³⁰
der during the early conflict between Chicanos and Anglos. The *corridos*
are usually about Mexican heroes who do valiant deeds against the Anglo
oppressors. Pancho Villas song, "*La cucaracha*," is the most famous one.
*Corridos* of John F. Kennedy and his death are still very popular in the Valley. Older Chicanos remember Lydia Mendoza, one of the great border *corrido* singers who was called *la Gloria de Tejas*. Her "*El tango negro*," sung
during the Great Depression, made her a singer of the people. The ever-
present *corridos* narrated one hundred years of border history, bringing
news of events as well as entertaining. These folk musicians and folk songs
are our chief cultural myth-makers, and they made our hard lives seem
bearable.

I grew up feeling ambivalent about our music. Country-western and ³¹
rock-and-roll had more status. In the fifties and sixties, for the slightly educated and *agringado* Chicanos, there existed a sense of shame at being
caught listening to our music. Yet I couldn't stop my feet from thumping
to the music, could not stop humming the words, nor hide from myself the
exhilaration I felt when I heard it.

There are more subtle ways that we internalize identification, espe- ³²
cially in the forms of images and emotions. For me food and certain smells
are tied to my identity, to my homeland. Woodsmoke curling up to an immense blue sky; woodsmoke perfuming my grandmother's clothes, her skin.
The stench of cow manure and the yellow patches on the ground; the crack
of a .22 rifle and the reek of cordite. Homemade white cheese sizzling in a
pan, melting inside a folded *tortilla*. My sister Hilda's hot, spicy *menudo*,
*chile colorado* making it deep red, pieces of *panza* and hominy floating on
top. My brother Carito barbequing *fajitas* in the backyard. Even now and
3,000 miles away, I can see my mother spicing the ground beef, pork, and
venison with *chile*. My mouth salivates at the thought of the hot steaming
*tamales* I would be eating if I were home.

### *Si le preguntas a mi mamá, "¿Qué eres?"*

> Identity is the essential core of who
> we are as individuals, the conscious
> experience of the self inside.
> —GERSHEN KAUFMAN[9]

*Nosotros los* Chicanos straddle the borderlands. On one side of us, we ³³
are constantly exposed to the Spanish of the Mexicans, on the other side
we hear the Anglos' incessant clamoring so that we forget our language.
Among ourselves we don't say *nosotros los americanos, o nosotros los espa-
ñoles, o nosotros los hispanos*. We say *nosotros los mexicanos* (by *mexicanos* we do not mean citizens of Mexico; we do not mean a national identity,

but a racial one). We distinguish between *mexicanos del otro lado* and *mexicanos de este lado*. Deep in our hearts we believe that being Mexican has nothing to do with which country one lives in. Being Mexican is a state of soul—not one of mind, not one of citizenship. Neither eagle nor serpent, but both. And like the ocean, neither animal respects borders.

> *Dime con quien andas y te diré quien eres.*
> (Tell me who your friends are and I'll tell you who you are.)
> —Mexican Saying

*Si le preguntas a mi mamá, "¿Qué eres?" te dirá, "Soy mexicana."* My  34
brothers and sister say the same. I sometimes will answer *"soy mexicana"* and at others will say *"soy Chicana" o "soy tejana."* But I identified as *"Raza"* before I ever identified as *"mexicana" or "Chicana."*

As a culture, we call ourselves Spanish when referring to ourselves as  35
a linguistic group and when copping out. It is then that we forget our predominant Indian genes. We are 70–80 percent Indian.[10] We call ourselves Hispanic[11] or Spanish-American or Latin American or Latin when linking ourselves to other Spanish-speaking peoples of the Western hemisphere and when copping out. We call ourselves Mexican-American[12] to signify we are neither Mexican nor American, but more the noun "American" than the adjective "Mexican" (and when copping out).

Chicanos and other people of color suffer economically for not accul-  36
turating. This voluntary (yet forced) alienation makes for psychological conflict, a kind of dual identity—we don't identify with the Anglo-American cultural values and we don't totally identify with the Mexican cultural values. We are a synergy of two cultures with various degrees of Mexicanness or Angloness. I have so internalized the borderland conflict that sometimes I feel like one cancels out the other and we are zero, nothing, no one. *A veces no soy nada ni nadie. Pero hasta cuando no lo soy, lo soy.*

When not copping out, when we know we are more than nothing, we  37
call ourselves Mexican, referring to race and ancestry; *mestizo* when affirming both our Indian and Spanish (but we hardly ever own our Black) ancestry; Chicano when referring to a politically aware people born and/or raised in the United States; *Raza* when referring to Chicanos; *tejanos* when we are Chicanos from Texas.

Chicanos did not know we were a people until 1965 when Cesar Chavez  38
and the farmworkers united and *I Am Joaquín* was published and *la Raza Unida* party was formed in Texas. With that recognition, we became a distinct people. Something momentous happened to the Chicano soul—we became aware of our reality and acquired a name and a language (Chicano Spanish) that reflected that reality. Now that we had a name, some of the fragmented pieces began to fall together—who we were, what we were, how we had evolved. We began to get glimpses of what we might eventually become.

Yet the struggle of identities continues, the struggle of borders is our  39
reality still. One day the inner struggle will cease and a true integration
take place. In the meantime, *tenémos que hacer la lucha. ¿Quién está prote-
giendo los ranchos de mi gente? ¿Quién está tratando de cerrar la fisura entre
la India y el blanco en nuestra sangre? El Chicano, si, el Chicano que anda
como un ladrón en su propia casa.*

*Los Chicanos,* how patient we seem, how very patient. There is the  40
quiet of the Indian about us.[13] We know how to survive. When other races
have given up their tongue we've kept ours. We know what it is to live
under the hammer blow of the dominant *norteamericano* culture. But more
than we count the blows, we count the days the weeks the years the centuries the aeons until the white laws and commerce and customs will rot in
the deserts they've created, lie bleached. *Humildes* yet proud, *quietos* yet
wild, *nosotros los mexicanos-Chicanos* will walk by the crumbling ashes as
we go about our business. Stubborn, persevering, impenetrable as stone,
yet possessing a malleability that renders us unbreakable, we, the *mestizas*
and *mestizos,* will remain.

NOTES

1. Ray Gwyn Smith, *Moorland Is Cold Country,* unpublished book.
2. Irena Klepfisz, "*Di rayze aheym*/The Journey Home," in *The Tribe of Dina: A Jewish Women's Anthology,* Melanie Kaye/Kantrowitz and Irena Klepfisz, eds. (Montpelier, VT: Sinister Wisdom Books, 1986), 49.
3. R. C. Ortega, *Dialectología Del Barrio,* trans. Hortencia S. Alwan (Los Angeles, CA: R. C. Ortega Publisher & Bookseller, 1977), 132.
4. Eduardo Hernandéz-Chávez, Andrew D. Cohen, and Anthony F. Beltramo, *El Lenguaje de los Chicanos: Regional and Social Characteristics of Language Used By Mexican Americans* (Arlington, VA: Center for Applied Linguistics, 1975), 39.
5. Hernandéz-Chávez, xvii.
6. Irena Klepfisz, "Secular Jewish Identity: Yidishkayt in America," in *The Tribe of Dina,* Kaye/Kantrowitz and Klepfisz, eds., 43.
7. Melanie Kaye/Kantrowitz, "Sign," in *We Speak In Code: Poems and Other Writings* (Pittsburgh, PA: Motheroot Publications, Inc., 1980), 85.
8. Rodolfo Gonzales, *I Am Joaquín/Yo Soy Joaquín* (New York, NY: Bantam Books, 1972). It was first published in 1967.
9. Gershen Kaufman, *Shame: The Power of Caring* (Cambridge, MA: Schenkman Books, Inc., 1980), 68.
10. John R. Chávez, *The Lost Land: The Chicano Images of the Southwest* (Albuquerque, NM: University of New Mexico Press, 1984), 88–90.
11. "Hispanic" is derived from *Hispanis* (*España,* a name given to the Iberian Peninsula in ancient times when it was a part of the Roman Empire) and is a term designated by the U.S. government to make it easier to handle us on paper.
12. The Treaty of Guadalupe Hidalgo created the Mexican-American in 1848.
13. Anglos, in order to alleviate their guilt for dispossessing the Chicano, stressed the Spanish part of us and perpetrated the myth of the Spanish Southwest. We have accepted the fiction that we are Hispanic, that is Spanish, in order to accommodate ourselves to the dominant culture and its abhorrence of Indians. Chávez, 88–91.

■ ■ ■

## Reading as a Writer: Analyzing Rhetorical Choices

1. Anzaldúa tosses her readers right into the sound of "the border," and readers who are not fluent in Spanish, or in the other community-specific variants of borderland languages that she includes, have to figure out how to respond to her prose. What different effects might this prose have on a variety of readers? How might these differing responses be related to Anzaldúa's overall argument?

2. Anzaldúa makes a case for the connection between identity and language. Locate at least three specific places where she makes this argument, and evaluate the evidence she provides for her claims. To what extent do you agree with her claim that we are our language? What might be limiting or liberating about this idea?

## Writing as a Reader: Entering the Conversation of Ideas

1. Both Deborah Tannen and Anzaldúa are fascinated by the connections between the ways we speak and who we are. As Anzaldúa declares, "I am my language" (para. 27). Write an essay in which you consider how each author would evaluate the strengths and possible blind spots in the other's argument about the ways language is related to our identities. Where do you stand in this conversation?

2. Anzaldúa and Peggy McIntosh both aim to illuminate what McIntosh calls the "colossal unseen dimensions" of our cultural identities that we often ignore and fail to analyze. Placing these authors in conversation with each other, write an essay in which you evaluate the strategies each author uses to teach readers to see what is in the "invisible knapsack" of assumptions about cultural identities. Where might these authors agree, or disagree, about what we should all do in order to create more equitable communities? What do these practices have to do with education?

---

## JAMES W. LOEWEN

# *From* Lies My Teacher Told Me: Everything Your American History Textbook Got Wrong

James W. Loewen is a professor of sociology who taught for twenty years at the University of Vermont and now continues his research and teaching in Washington, D.C., where his academic focus is on the history and the sociology of U.S. race relations. He is a popular campus lecturer, well known for surprising his audiences with historical facts most of us never learned and teaching us why we should care about what gets left out of history books, and what those books get wrong.

This reading is drawn from Loewen's best-known book, *Lies My Teacher Told Me: Everything Your American History Textbook Got Wrong* (1996). The epigraphs leading into the introduction will give you a sense of his tone, as he moves from serious quotations to his own witty twist on a familiar saying: "Those who don't remember the past are condemned to repeat the eleventh grade." As a writer, Loewen is very sensitive to his readers' responses, which is evident in his empathy with bored high school students in his first paragraph. As you read, pay particular attention to the ways he anticipates readers who might be skeptical, and consider why he might offer such extensive and detailed footnotes to support his claims.

While Loewen finds depressing how little most American students know about our country's history and how incurious most of them are, he does not blame the students themselves. Rather, he examines the ways textbooks present partial stories (and often pure "lies") as if they *are* the whole story, so that students rarely bother to ask what might lie underneath claims that America was first settled in 1620, for example. Pay attention to what you find especially surprising in this "new" look at these "old" facts, and carefully consider Loewen's claims about why this information matters—beyond his threat that we might all be condemned to repeat the eleventh grade!

## Introduction: Something Has Gone Very Wrong

> It would be better not to know so many things than to know so many things that are not so.
>
> —Felix Okoye[1]

> American history is longer, larger, more various, more beautiful, and more terrible than anything anyone has ever said about it.
>
> —James Baldwin[2]

> Concealment of the historical truth is a crime against the people.
>
> —Gen. Petro G. Grigorenko,
> Samizdat letter to a history journal, c. 1975, USSR[3]

> Those who don't remember the past are condemned to repeat the eleventh grade.
>
> —James W. Loewen

High school students hate history. When they list their favorite subjects, history invariably comes in last: Students consider history "the most irrelevant" of twenty-one subjects commonly taught in high school.

---

[1] Felix Okoye, *The American Image of Africa: Myth and Reality* (Buffalo, N.Y.: Black Academy Press, 1971), 3.

[2] James Baldwin, "A Talk to Teachers," *Saturday Review*, December 21, 1963, reprinted in Rick Simonson and Scott Walker, eds., *Multicultural Literacy* (St. Paul, Minn.: Graywolf Press, 1988), 11.

[3] Gen. Petro G. Grigorenko, quoted in Robert Slusser, "History and the Democratic Opposition," in Rudolf L. Tökés, ed., *Dissent in the USSR* (Baltimore: Johns Hopkins University Press, 1975), 329–53.

*Bor-r-ring* is the adjective they apply to it. When students can, they avoid it, even though most students get higher grades in history than in math, science, or English.[4] Even when they are forced to take classes in history, they repress what they learn, so every year or two another study decries what our seventeen-year-olds don't know.[5]

African American, Native American, and Latino students view history with a special dislike. They also learn history especially poorly. Students of color do only slightly worse than white students in mathematics. If you'll pardon my grammar, nonwhite students do more worse in English and most worse in history.[6] Something intriguing is going on here: surely history is not more difficult for minorities than trigonometry or Faulkner. Students don't even know they are alienated, only that they "don't *like* social studies" or "aren't any good at history." In college, most students of color give history departments a wide berth.

Many history teachers perceive the low morale in their classrooms. If they have a lot of time, light domestic responsibilities, sufficient resources, and a flexible principal, some teachers respond by abandoning the overstuffed textbooks and reinventing their American history courses. All too many teachers grow disheartened and settle for less. At least dimly aware that their students are not requiting their own love of history, these teachers withdraw some of their energy from their courses. Gradually they end up going through the motions, staying ahead of their students in the textbooks, covering only material that will appear on the next test.

College teachers in most disciplines are happy when their students have had significant exposure to the subject before college. Not teachers in history. History professors in college routinely put down high school history courses. A colleague of mine calls his survey of American history "Iconoclasm I and II," because he sees his job as disabusing his charges of what they learned in high school. In no other field does this happen. Mathematics professors, for instance, know that non-Euclidean geometry is rarely taught in high school, but they don't assume that Euclidean geometry was

---

[4]I use the term *history* as encompassing social studies, as do most researchers and students. When the distinction is important, I will make it. Robert Reinhold, Harris Poll, reported in *New York Times*, July 3, 1971, and quoted in Herbert Aptheker, *The Unfolding Drama* (New York: International, 1978), 146; Terry Borton, *The Weekly Reader National Survey on Education* (Middletown, Conn.: Field Publications, 1985), 14, 16; Mark Schug, Robert Todd, and R. Beery, "Why Kids Don't Like Social Studies," *Social Education* 48 (May 1984): 382–87; Albert Shanker, "The 'Efficient' Diploma Mill," paid column in *New York Times*, February 14, 1988; Joan M. Shaughnessy and Thomas M. Haladyna, "Research on Student Attitudes Toward Social Studies," *Social Education* 49 (November 1985): 692–95. National grade averages in *1992 ACT Assessment Results, Summary Report, Mississippi* (Iowa City: ACT, 1993), 7.

[5]Diane Ravitch and Chester E. Finn, Jr., *What Do Our 17-Year-Olds Know?* (New York: Harper and Row, 1987); National Geographic Society, *Geography: An International Gallup Survey* (Washington, D.C.: National Geographic Society, 1988).

[6]Richard L. Sawyer, "College Student Profiles: Norms for the ACT Assessment, 1980–81" (Iowa City: ACT, 1980). Sawyer finds larger differences by race and income in social studies than in English, mathematics, and the natural sciences.

*mistaught.* Professors of English literature don't presume that *Romeo and Juliet* was misunderstood in high school. Indeed, history is the only field in which the more courses students take, the stupider they become.

Perhaps I do not need to convince you that American history is impor-    5
tant. More than any other topic, it is about *us.* Whether one deems our present society wondrous or awful or both, history reveals how we arrived at this point. Understanding our past is central to our ability to understand ourselves and the world around us. We need to know our history, and according to C. Wright Mills, we know we do.[7]

Outside of school, Americans show great interest in history. Historical    6
novels, whether by Gore Vidal (*Lincoln, Burr,* et al.) or Dana Fuller Ross (*Idaho!, Utah!, Nebraska!, Oregon!, Missouri!,* and on! and on!) often become bestsellers. The National Museum of American History is one of the three big draws of the Smithsonian Institution. The series "The Civil War" attracted new audiences to public television. Movies based on historical incidents or themes are a continuing source of fascination, from *Birth of a Nation* through *Gone with the Wind* to *Dances with Wolves* and *JFK.*

Our situation is this: American history is full of fantastic and impor-    7
tant stories. These stories have the power to spellbind audiences, even audiences of difficult seventh-graders. These same stories show what America has been about and are directly relevant to our present society. American audiences, even young ones, need and want to know about their national past. Yet they sleep through the classes that present it.

What has gone wrong?    8

We begin to get a handle on this question by noting that the teaching    9
of history, more than any other discipline, is dominated by textbooks.[8] And students are right: the books are boring.[9] The stories that history textbooks tell are predictable; every problem has already been solved or is about to be solved. Textbooks exclude conflict or real suspense. They leave out anything that might reflect badly upon our national character. When they try for drama, they achieve only melodrama, because readers know that everything will turn out fine in the end. "Despite setbacks, the United States overcame these challenges," in the words of one textbook. Most authors of

---

[7] Years ago Mills discerned that Americans feel a need to locate themselves in social structure in order to understand the forces that shape their society and themselves. See C. Wright Mills, *The Sociological Imagination* (New York: Oxford University Press, 1959), 3–20.

[8] Paul Goldstein, *Changing the American Schoolbook* (Lexington, Mass.: D. C. Heath, 1978). Goldstein says textbooks are the organizing principle for more than 75 percent of classroom time. In history, the proportion is even higher.

[9] Mel Gabler's right-wing textbook critics and I concur that textbooks are boring. Mrs. W. Kelley Haralson writes, "The censoring of emotionalism from history texts during the last half century has resulted in history textbooks which are boring to students." "Objections [to *The American Adventure*]" (Longview, Tex.: Educational Research Analysts, n.d.), 4. We part company in our proposed solutions, however, for the only emotion that Gabler and his allies seem to want to add is pride.

history textbooks don't even try for melodrama. Instead, they write in a tone that if heard aloud might be described as "mumbling lecturer." No wonder students lose interest.

Textbooks almost never use the present to illuminate the past. They *10* might ask students to consider gender roles in contemporary society as a means of prompting students to think about what women did and did not achieve in the suffrage movement or in the more recent women's movement. They might ask students to prepare household budgets for the families of a janitor and a stockbroker as a means of prompting thinking about labor unions and social classes in the past and present. They might, but they don't. The present is not a source of information for writers of history textbooks.

Conversely, textbooks seldom use the past to illuminate the present. *11* They portray the past as a simple-minded morality play. "Be a good citizen" is the message that textbooks extract from the past. "You have a proud heritage. Be all that you can be. After all, look at what the United States has accomplished." While there is nothing wrong with optimism, it can become something of a burden for students of color, children of working-class parents, girls who notice the dearth of female historical figures, or members of any group that has not achieved socioeconomic success. The optimistic approach prevents any understanding of failure other than blaming the victim. No wonder children of color are alienated. Even for male children from affluent white families, bland optimism gets pretty boring after eight hundred pages.

Textbooks in American history stand in sharp contrast to other teach- *12* ing materials. Why are history textbooks so bad? Nationalism is one of the culprits. Textbooks are often muddled by the conflicting desires to promote inquiry and to indoctrinate blind patriotism. "Take a look in your history book, and you'll see why we should be proud," goes an anthem often sung by high school glee clubs. But we need not even look inside.[10] The titles themselves tell the story: *The Great Republic, The American Way, Land of Promise, Rise of the American Nation*.[11] Such titles differ from the titles of all other textbooks students read in high school or college. Chemistry books, for example, are called *Chemistry* or *Principles of Chemistry*, not *Rise of the Molecule*. And you can tell history textbooks just from their covers, graced as they are with American flags, bald eagles, the Statue of Liberty.

Between the glossy covers, American history textbooks are full of *13* information—overly full. These books are huge. The specimens in my

---

[10]"It's a Great Country," sung with pride by a high school choir from Webster Groves, Missouri, in a CBS News videotape, *Sixteen in Webster Groves* (New York: Carousel Films, 1966).

[11]In the aftermath of the Vietnam War, Harcourt Brace renamed this last one *Triumph of the American Nation*. This is the Rambo approach to history: We may have lost the war in Southeast Asia, but we'll win it on the book jackets!

collection of a dozen of the most popular textbooks average four and a half pounds in weight and 888 pages in length. No publisher wants to lose an adoption because a book has left out a detail of concern to a particular geographical area or a particular group. Textbook authors seem compelled to include a paragraph about every U.S. president, even Chester A. Arthur and Millard Fillmore. Then there are the review pages at the end of each chapter. *Land of Promise*, to take one example, enumerates 444 chapter-closing "Main Ideas." In addition, the book lists literally thousands of "Skill Activities," "Key Terms," "Matching" items, "Fill in the Blanks," "Thinking Critically" questions, and "Review Identifications," as well as still more "Main Ideas" at the ends of the various sections within each chapter. At year's end, no student can remember 444 main ideas, not to mention 624 key terms and countless other "factoids." So students and teachers fall back on one main idea: to memorize the terms for the test following each chapter, then forget them to clear the synapses for the next chapter. No wonder so many high school graduates cannot remember in which century the Civil War was fought![12]

None of the facts is remembered, because they are presented simply as one damn thing after another. While textbook authors tend to include most of the trees and all too many twigs, they neglect to give readers even a glimpse of what they might find memorable: the forests. Textbooks stifle meaning by suppressing causation. Students exit history textbooks without having developed the ability to think coherently about social life.    *14*

Even though the books bulge with detail, even though the courses are so busy they rarely reach 1960, our teachers and our textbooks still leave out most of what we need to know about the American past. Some of the factoids they present are flatly wrong or unverifiable. In sum, startling errors of omission and distortion mar American histories.    *15*

Errors in history textbooks often go uncorrected, partly because the history profession does not bother to review textbooks. Occasionally outsiders do: Frances FitzGerald's 1979 study, *America Revised*, was a bestseller, but it made no impact on the industry. In pointing out how textbooks ignored or distorted the Spanish impact on Latin America and the colonial United States, FitzGerald predicted, "Text publishers may now be on the verge of rewriting history." But she was wrong—the books have not changed.[13]    *16*

History can be imagined as a pyramid. At its base are the millions of primary sources—the plantation records, city directories, speeches, songs, photographs, newspaper articles, diaries, and letters that document times past. Based on these primary materials, historians write secondary works—books and articles on subjects ranging from deafness on Martha's Vineyard to Grant's tactics at Vicksburg. Historians produce hundreds of these works every year, many of them splendid. In theory, a few historians, work-    *17*

---

[12]Ravitch and Finn, *What Do Our 17-Year-Olds Know?*, 49.
[13]Frances FitzGerald, *America Revised* (New York: Vintage, 1980 [1979]), 93–97.

ing individually or in teams, then synthesize the secondary literature into tertiary works—textbooks covering all phases of U.S. history.

In practice, however, it doesn't happen that way. Instead, history text- *18* books are clones of each other. The first thing editors do when recruiting new authors is to send them a half-dozen examples of the competition. Often a textbook is written not by the authors whose names grace its cover, but by minions deep in the bowels of the publisher's offices. When historians do write textbooks, they risk snickers from their colleagues—tinged with envy, but snickers nonetheless: "Why are you devoting time to pedagogy rather than original research?"

The result is not happy for textbook scholarship. Many history text- *19* books list up-to-the-minute secondary sources in their bibliographies, yet the narratives remain totally traditional—unaffected by recent research.[14]

What would we think of a course in poetry in which students never *20* read a poem? The editor's voice in an English literature textbook might be as dull as the voice in a history textbook, but at least in the English textbook the voice stills when the book presents original works of literature. The omniscient narrator's voice of history textbooks insulates students from the raw materials of history. Rarely do authors quote speeches, songs, diaries, or letters. Students need not be protected from this material. They can just as well read one paragraph from William Jennings Bryan's "Cross of Gold" speech as read *American Adventures*'s two paragraphs *about* it.

Textbooks also keep students in the dark about the nature of history. *21* History is furious debate informed by evidence and reason. Textbooks encourage students to believe that history is facts to be learned. "We have not avoided controversial issues," announces one set of textbook authors; "instead, we have tried to offer reasoned judgments" on them—thus removing the controversy! Because textbooks employ such a godlike tone, it never occurs to most students to question them. "In retrospect I ask myself, why *didn't* I think to ask, for example, who *were* the original inhabitants of the Americas, what was *their* life like, and how did it change when Columbus arrived," wrote a student of mine in 1991. "However, back then everything was presented as if it were the full picture," she continued, "so I never thought to doubt that it was."

As a result of all this, most high school seniors are hamstrung in their *22* efforts to analyze controversial issues in our society. (I know because I encounter these students the next year as college freshmen.) We've got to do better. Five-sixths of all Americans never take a course in American history beyond high school. What our citizens "learn" in high school forms much of what they know about our past. . . .

[14] James Axtell, "Europeans, Indians, and the Age of Discovery in American History Textbooks," *American Historical Review* 92 (1987): 627. Essays such as Axtell's, which review college-level textbooks, rarely appear in history journals. Almost never are high school textbooks reviewed.

# The Truth About the First Thanksgiving

Considering that virtually none of the standard fare surrounding Thanksgiving contains an ounce of authenticity, historical accuracy, or cross-cultural perception, why is it so apparently ingrained? Is it necessary to the American psyche to perpetually exploit and debase its victims in order to justify its history?

—MICHAEL DORRIS[15]

European explorers and invaders discovered an inhabited land. Had it been pristine wilderness then, it would possibly be so still, for neither the technology nor the social organization of Europe in the 16th and 17th centuries had the capacity to maintain, of its own resources, outpost colonies thousands of miles from home.

—FRANCIS JENNINGS[16]

The Europeans were able to conquer America not because of their military genius, or their religious motivation, or their ambition, or their greed. They conquered it by waging unpremeditated biological warfare.

—HOWARD SIMPSON[17]

It is painful to advert to these things. But our forefathers, though wise, pious, and sincere, were nevertheless, in respect to Christian charity, under a cloud; and, in history, truth should be held sacred, at whatever cost . . . especially against the narrow and futile patriotism, which, instead of pressing forward in pursuit of truth, takes pride in walking backwards to cover the slightest nakedness of our forefathers.

—COL. THOMAS ASPINWALL[18]

Over the last few years, I have asked hundreds of college students, "When  23 was the country we now know as the United States first settled?" This is a generous way of phrasing the question; surely "we now know as" implies that the original settlement antedated the founding of the United States. I initially believed—certainly I had hoped—that students would suggest 30,000 B.C., or some other pre-Columbian date.

They did not. Their consensus answer was "1620."  24

Obviously, my students' heads have been filled with America's origin  25 myth, the story of the first Thanksgiving. Textbooks are among the retailers of this primal legend.

[15]Michael Dorris, "Why I'm Not Thankful for Thanksgiving" (New York: Council on Interracial Books for Children *Bulletin* 9, no. 7, 1978), 7.

[16]Francis Jennings, *The Invasion of America: Indians, Colonialism, and the Cant of Conquest* (Chapel Hill: University of North Carolina Press, 1975), 15.

[17]Howard Simpson, *Invisible Armies: The Impact of Disease on American History* (Indianapolis: Bobbs-Merrill, 1980), 2.

[18]Col. Thomas Aspinwall, quoted in Jennings, *The Invasion of America*, 175.

Part of the problem is the word *settle*. "Settlers" were white, a student  *26*
once pointed out to me. "Indians" didn't settle. Students are not the only
people misled by *settle*. The film that introduces visitors to Plimoth Planta-
tion tells how "they went about the work of civilizing a hostile wilderness."
One recent Thanksgiving weekend I listened as a guide at the Statue of
Liberty talked about European immigrants "populating a wild East Coast."
As we shall see, however, if Indians hadn't already settled New England,
Europeans would have had a much tougher job of it.

Starting the story of America's settlement with the Pilgrims leaves  *27*
out not only the Indians but also the Spanish. The very first non-Native
settlers in "the country we now know as the United States" were African
slaves left in South Carolina in 1526 by Spaniards who abandoned a settlement attempt. In 1565 the Spanish massacred the French Protestants who
had settled briefly at St. Augustine, Florida, and established their own fort
there. Some later Spanish settlers were our first pilgrims, seeking regions
new to them to secure religious liberty: these were Spanish Jews, who
settled in New Mexico in the late 1500s.[19] Few Americans know that one-
third of the United States, from San Francisco to Arkansas to Natchez to
Florida, has been Spanish longer than it has been "American," and that
Hispanic Americans lived here before the first ancestor of the Daughters of
the American Revolution ever left England. Moreover, Spanish culture left
an indelible mark on the American West. The Spanish introduced horses,
cattle, sheep, pigs, and the basic elements of cowboy culture, including its
vocabulary: *mustang, bronco, rodeo, lariat,* and so on.[20] Horses that escaped
from the Spanish and propagated triggered the rapid flowering of a new
culture among the Plains Indians. "How refreshing it would be," wrote
James Axtell, "to find a textbook that began on the West Coast before treating the traditional eastern colonies."[21]

Beginning the story in 1620 also omits the Dutch, who were living in  *28*
what is now Albany by 1614. Indeed, 1620 is not even the date of the first
permanent British settlement, for in 1607, the London Company sent settlers to Jamestown, Virginia.

No matter. The *mythic* origin of "the country we now know as the  *29*
United States" is at Plymouth Rock, and the year is 1620. Here is a representative account from *The American Tradition*:

> After some exploring, the Pilgrims chose the land around Plymouth Har-
> bor for their settlement. Unfortunately, they had arrived in December and

---

[19] Kathleen Teltsch, "Scholars and Descendants Uncover Hidden Legacy of Jews in
Southwest," *New York Times*, November 11, 1990, A30; "Hidden Jews of the Southwest,"
*Groundrock*, Spring 1992.

[20] Alfred W. Crosby, Jr., *The Columbian Exchange: Biological and Cultural Consequences of 1492* (Westport, Conn.: Greenwood, 1972), 83. Our cowboy culture's Spanish
origin explains why it is so similar to the gaucho tradition of Argentina.

[21] James Axtell, "Europeans, Indians, and the Age of Discovery in American History
Textbooks," 630.

were not prepared for the New England winter. However, they were aided by friendly Indians, who gave them food and showed them how to grow corn. When warm weather came, the colonists planted, fished, hunted, and prepared themselves for the next winter. After harvesting their first crop, they and their Indian friends celebrated the first Thanksgiving.[22]

My students also remember that the Pilgrims had been persecuted in    30
England for their religious beliefs, so they had moved to Holland. They sailed on the *Mayflower* to America and wrote the Mayflower Compact, the forerunner to our Constitution, according to my students. Times were rough, until they met Squanto, who taught them how to put a small fish as fertilizer in each little cornhill, ensuring a bountiful harvest. But when I ask my students about the plague, they just stare back at me. "What plague? The Black Plague?" No, I sigh, that was three centuries earlier. . . .

About the plagues the textbooks tell even less. Only three of the twelve    31
textbooks even mention Indian disease as a factor at Plymouth or anywhere in New England.[23] *Life and Liberty* does quite a good job. *The American Way* is the only book that draws the appropriate geopolitical inference about the Plymouth outbreak, but it doesn't discuss any of the other plagues that beset Indians throughout the hemisphere. According to *Triumph of the American Nation*: "If the Pilgrims had arrived at Plymouth a few years earlier, they would have found a busy Indian village surrounded by farmland. As it was, an epidemic had wiped out most of the Indians. Those who survived had abandoned the village." "Fortunately for the Pilgrims," *Triumph* goes on, "the cleared fields remained, and a brook of fresh water flowed into the harbor." These four sentences exemplify what Michael W. Apple and Linda K. Christian-Smith call dominance through mentioning.[24] The passage can hardly offend Pilgrim descendants, yet it gives the publisher deniability—*Triumph* cannot be accused of omitting the plague. But the sentences bury the plague within a description of the beautiful harbor at Plymouth. Therefore, even though gory details of disease and death are exactly the kinds of things that high school students remember best, the plague won't "stick." I know, because I never remembered the plague, and my college textbook mentioned it—in a fourteen-word passage nestled within a paragraph about the Pilgrims' belief in God.[25]

In colonial times, everyone knew about the plague. Even before the    32
*Mayflower* sailed, King James of England gave thanks to "Almighty God in his great goodness and bounty towards us" for sending "this wonder-

---

[22]The passage is basically accurate, although the winter of 1620–21 was not particularly harsh and probably did not surprise the British, and Indians did not assist them until spring.

[23]A paragraph in *The American Pageant* does tell of the 90 percent toll throughout the hemisphere but leaves out any mention of the plague at Plymouth.

[24]Michael W. Apple and Linda K. Christian-Smith, *The Politics of the Textbook* (New York: Routledge, 1991), 66.

[25]Richard Hofstadter, William Miller, and Daniel Aaron, *The American Republic* (Englewood Cliffs, N.J.: Prentice-Hall, 1959), 47–48.

ful plague among the salvages [*sic*]."[26] Two hundred years later the oldest American history in my collection—J. W. Barber's *Interesting Events in the History of the United States*, published in 1829—still recalled the plague.

> A few years before the arrival of the Plymouth settlers, a very mortal sickness raged with great violence among the Indians inhabiting the eastern parts of New England. "Whole towns were depopulated. The living were not able to bury the dead; and their bodies were found lying above ground, many years after. The Massachusetts Indians are said to have been reduced from 30,000 to 300 fighting men. In 1633, the small pox swept off great numbers."[27]

Today it is no surprise that not one in a hundred of my college students has ever heard of the plague. Unless they have read *Life and Liberty*, students could scarcely come away from these books thinking of Indians as people who made an impact on North America, who lived here in considerable numbers, who *settled*, in short, and were then killed by disease or arms. Textbook authors have retreated from the candor of Barber. Treatments like that in *Triumph* guarantee our collective amnesia.

Having mistreated the plague, the textbooks proceed to mistreat the Pilgrims. Their arrival in Massachusetts poses another historical controversy that textbook authors take pains to duck. The textbooks say the Pilgrims intended to go to Virginia, where there existed a British settlement already. But "the little party on the *Mayflower*," explains *American History*, "never reached Virginia. On November 9, they sighted land on Cape Cod." How did the Pilgrims wind up in Massachusetts when they set out for Virginia? "Violent storms blew their ship off course," according to some textbooks; others blame an "error in navigation." Both explanations may be wrong. Some historians believe the Dutch bribed the captain of the *Mayflower* to sail north so the Pilgrims would not settle near New Amsterdam. Others hold that the Pilgrims went to Cape Cod on purpose.[28]

Bear in mind that the Pilgrims numbered only about 35 of the 102 settlers aboard the *Mayflower*; the rest were ordinary folk seeking their fortunes in the new Virginia colony. George Willison has argued that the Pilgrim leaders, wanting to be far from Anglican control, never planned to

---

[26] Quoted in Ziner, *Squanto*, 147.

[27] J. W. Barber, *Interesting Events in the History of the United States* (New Haven: Barber, 1829), 30. Barber does not cite the authority he quotes.

[28] Even though "Virginia" then included most of New Jersey, the *Mayflower* nonetheless landed hundreds of miles northeast. Historians who support the "on purpose" theory include George F. Willison, *Saints and Strangers* (New York: Reynal and Hitchcock, 1945); Lincoln Kinnicutt, "The Settlement at Plymouth Contemplated before 1620," *Publications of the American Historical Association*, 1920, 211–21; and Neal Salisbury, *Manitou and Providence* (New York: Oxford University Press, 1982), 109, 270. Leon Clark Hills, *History and Genealogy of the Mayflower Planters* (Baltimore: Genealogical Publ. Co., 1975), and Francis R. Stoddard, *The Truth about the Pilgrims* (New York: Society of Mayflower Descendants, 1952), 19–20, support the "Dutch bribe" theory, based on primary source material by Nathanial Morton. Historians at Plimoth Plantation support the theories of pilot error or storm.

settle in Virginia. They had debated the relative merits of Guiana, in South America, versus the Massachusetts coast, and, according to Willison, they intended a hijacking.

Certainly the Pilgrims already knew quite a bit about what Massa- 35 chusetts could offer them, from the fine fishing along Cape Cod to that "wonderful plague," which offered an unusual opportunity for British settlement. According to some historians, Squanto, an Indian from the village of Patuxet, Massachusetts, had provided Ferdinando Gorges, a leader of the Plymouth Company in England, with a detailed description of the area. Gorges may even have sent Squanto and Capt. Thomas Dermer as advance men to wait for the Pilgrims, although Dermer sailed away when the Pilgrims were delayed in England. In any event, the Pilgrims were familiar with the area's topography. Recently published maps that Samuel de Champlain had drawn when he had toured the area in 1605 supplemented the information that had been passed on by sixteenth-century explorers. John Smith had studied the region and named it "New England" in 1614, and he even offered to guide the Pilgrim leaders. They rejected his services as too expensive and carried his guidebook along instead.[29]

These considerations prompt me to believe that the Pilgrim leaders 36 probably ended up in Massachusetts on purpose. But evidence for any conclusion is soft. Some historians believe Gorges took credit for landing in Massachusetts after the fact. Indeed, the *Mayflower* may have had no specific destination. Readers might be fascinated if textbook authors presented two or more of the various possibilities, but, as usual, exposing students to historical controversy is taboo. Each textbook picks just one reason and presents it as fact.

Only one of the twelve textbooks adheres to the hijacking possibility. 37 "The New England landing came as a rude surprise for the bedraggled and tired [non-Pilgrim] majority on board the *Mayflower*," says *Land of Promise*. "[They] had joined the expedition seeking economic opportunity in the Virginia tobacco plantations." Obviously, these passengers were not happy at having been taken elsewhere, especially to a shore with no prior English settlement to join. "Rumors of mutiny spread quickly." *Promise* then ties this unrest to the Mayflower Compact, giving its readers a fresh interpretation of why the colonists adopted the agreement and why it was so democratic: "To avoid rebellion, the Pilgrim leaders made a remarkable concession to the other colonists. They issued a call for every male on board, regardless of religion or economic status, to join in the creation of a 'civil body politic.'" The compact achieved its purpose: the majority acquiesced.

---

[29]Ziner, *Squanto*, 147; Kinnicutt, "The Settlement at Plymouth Contemplated before 1620"; Almon W. Lauber, *Indian Slavery in Colonial Times within the Present Limits of the United States* (Williamstown, Mass.: Corner House, 1970 [1913]), 156–59; Stoddard, *The Truth about the Pilgrims*, 16.

Actually, the hijacking hypothesis does not show the Pilgrims in such a 38 bad light. The compact provided a graceful solution to an awkward problem. Although hijacking and false representation doubtless were felonies then as now, the colony did survive with a lower death rate than Virginia, so no permanent harm was done. The whole story places the Pilgrims in a somewhat dishonorable light, however, which may explain why only one textbook selects it.

The "navigation error" story lacks plausibility: the one parameter of 39 ocean travel that sailors could and did measure accurately in that era was latitude—distance north or south from the equator. The "storms" excuse is perhaps still less plausible, for if a storm blew them off course, when the weather cleared they could have turned southward again, sailing out to sea to bypass any shoals. They had plenty of food and beer, after all.[30] But storms and pilot error leave the Pilgrims pure of heart, which may explain why the other eleven textbooks choose one of the two.

Regardless of motive, the Mayflower Compact provided a democratic 40 basis for the Plymouth colony. Since the framers of our Constitution in fact paid the compact little heed, however, it hardly deserves the attention textbook authors lavish on it. But textbook authors clearly want to package the Pilgrims as a pious and moral band who laid the antecedents of our democratic traditions. Nowhere is this motive more embarrassingly obvious than in John Garraty's *American History*. "So far as any record shows, this was the first time in human history that a group of people consciously created a government where none had existed before." Here Garraty paraphrases a Forefathers' Day speech, delivered in Plymouth in 1802, in which John Adams celebrated "the only instance in human history of that positive, original social compact." George Willison has dryly noted that Adams was "blinking several salient facts—above all, the circumstances that prompted the compact, which was plainly an instrument of minority rule."[31] Of course, Garraty's paraphrase also exposes his ignorance of the Republic of Iceland, the Iroquois Confederacy, and countless other polities antedating 1620. Such an account simply invites students to become ethnocentric.

In their pious treatment of the Pilgrims, history textbooks introduce 41 the archetype of American exceptionalism. According to *The American Pageant*, "This rare opportunity for a great social and political experiment may never come again." *The American Way* declares, "The American people have created a unique nation." How is America exceptional? Surely we're

---

[30] The *Mayflower* sailed south for half a day, until encountering "dangerous shoals," according to several of our textbooks. Then the captain and the Pilgrim leadership insisted on returning to Provincetown and eventually New Plymouth. Conspiracy theorists take this to be a charade to dissuade the majority from insisting on Virginia. See Willison, *Saints and Strangers*, 145, 466; Kinnicutt, "The Settlement at Plymouth Contemplated before 1620"; and Salisbury, *Manitou and Providence*, 109, 270.

[31] Willison, *Saints and Strangers*, 421–22.

exceptionally *good*. As Woodrow Wilson put it, "America is the only ideal-
istic nation in the world."[32] And the goodness started at Plymouth Rock,
according to our textbooks, which view the Pilgrims as Christian, sober,
democratic, generous to the Indians, God-thanking. Such a happy portrait
can be painted only by omitting the facts about the plague, the possible
hijacking, and the Indian relations.

For that matter, our culture and our textbooks underplay or omit     *42*
Jamestown and the sixteenth-century Spanish settlements in favor of
Plymouth Rock as the archetypal birthplace of the United States. Virginia,
according to T. H. Breen, " ill-served later historians in search of the mythic
origins of American culture."[33] Historians could hardly tout Virginia as
moral in intent; in the words of the first history of Virginia written by a
Virginian: "The chief Design of all Parties concern'd was to fetch away the
Treasure from thence, aiming more at sudden Gain, than to form any regular Colony."[34] The Virginians' relations with the Indians were particularly
unsavory: in contrast to Squanto, a volunteer, the British in Virginia took
Indian prisoners and forced them to teach colonists how to farm.[35] In 1623
the British indulged in the first use of chemical warfare in the colonies
when negotiating a treaty with tribes near the Potomac River, headed by
Chiskiack. The British offered a toast "symbolizing eternal friendship,"
whereupon the chief, his family, advisors, and two hundred followers
dropped dead of poison.[36] Besides, the early Virginians engaged in bicker-
ing, sloth, even cannibalism. They spent their early days digging random
holes in the ground, haplessly looking for gold instead of planting crops.
Soon they were starving and digging up putrid Indian corpses to eat or
renting themselves out to Indian families as servants — hardly the heroic
founders that a great nation requires.[37]

Textbooks indeed cover the Virginia colony, and they at least mention     *43*
the Spanish settlements, but they devote 50 percent more space to Massachusetts. As a result, and due also to Thanksgiving, of course, students are
much more likely to remember the Pilgrims as our founders.[38] They are then
embarrassed when I remind them of Virginia and the Spanish, for when
prompted students do recall having heard of both. But neither our culture
nor our textbooks give Virginia the same archetypal status as Massachu-

---

[32] Speech in Sioux Falls, September 8, 1919, in *Addresses of President Wilson* (Washington, D.C.: Government Printing Office, 1919), 86.

[33] T. H. Breen, "Right Man, Wrong Place," *New York Review of Books*, November 20,
1986, 50.

[34] Written by Robert Beverley in 1705 and quoted in Wesley Frank Craven. *The Legend of the Founding Fathers* (Westport, Conn.: Greenwood, 1983 [1956]), 5–8.

[35] Axtell, *The European and the Indian*, 292–95.

[36] J. Leitch Wright, Jr., *The Only Land They Knew* (New York: Free Press, 1981), 78.

[37] Kupperman, *Settling with the Indians*, 173; James Truslow Adams, *The March of
Democracy*, vol. 1 (New York: Scribner's, 1933), 12.

[38] I encountered most of these students in New England, but many of them came
from suburbs of Philadelphia, Washington, D.C., and New Jersey. I suspect that replies
from the rest of the United States would be similar, except perhaps the Far West.

setts. That is why almost all my students know the name of the Pilgrims' ship, while almost no students remember the names of the three ships that brought the British to Jamestown. (For the next time you're on *Jeopardy*, they were the *Susan Constant*, the *Discovery*, and the *Goodspeed*.)

Despite having ended up many miles from other European enclaves, the Pilgrims hardly "started from scratch" in a "wilderness." Throughout southern New England, Native Americans had repeatedly burned the underbrush, creating a parklike environment. After landing at Provincetown, the Pilgrims assembled a boat for exploring and began looking around for their new home. They chose Plymouth because of its beautiful cleared fields, recently planted in corn, and its useful harbor and "brook of fresh water." It was a lovely site for a town. Indeed, until the plague, it had been a town, for "New Plimoth" was none other than Squanto's village of Patuxet! The invaders followed a pattern: throughout the hemisphere Europeans pitched camp right in the middle of Native populations—Cuzco, Mexico City, Natchez, Chicago. Throughout New England, colonists appropriated Indian cornfields for their initial settlements, avoiding the backbreaking labor of clearing the land of forest and rock.[39] (This explains why, to this day, the names of so many towns throughout the region—Marshfield, Springfield, Deerfield—end in *field*.) "Errand into the wilderness" may have made a lively sermon title in 1650, a popular book title in 1950, and an archetypal textbook phrase in 1990, but it was never accurate. The new settlers encountered no wilderness: "In this bay wherein we live," one colonist noted in 1622, "in former time hath lived about two thousand Indians."[40]

Moreover, not all the Native inhabitants had perished, and the survivors now facilitated British settlement. The Pilgrims began receiving Indian assistance on their second full day in Massachusetts. A colonist's journal tells of sailors discovering two Indian houses:

> Having their guns and hearing nobody, they entered the houses and found the people were gone. The sailors took some things but didn't dare stay. . . . We had meant to have left some beads and other things in the houses as a sign of peace and to show we meant to trade with them. But we didn't do it because we left in such haste. But as soon as we can meet with the Indians, we will pay them well for what we took.

It wasn't only houses that the Pilgrims robbed. Our eyewitness resumes his story:

> We marched to the place we called Cornhill, where we had found the corn before. At another place we had seen before, we dug and found some more corn, two or three baskets full, and a bag of beans. . . . In all we had about ten bushels, which will be enough for seed. It was with God's help that we found

[39]Gary Nash, *Red, White, and Black* (Englewood Cliffs, N.J.: Prentice-Hall, 1974), 139, describes the same process in Pennsylvania.

[40]Emmanuel Altham letter quoted in Sydney V. James, ed., *Three Visitors to Early Plymouth* (Plymouth: Plimoth Plantation, 1963), 29.

this corn, for how else could we have done it, without meeting some Indians who might trouble us.

From the start, the Pilgrims thanked God, not the Indians, for assistance that the latter had (inadvertently) provided—setting a pattern for later thanksgivings. Our journalist continues:

> The next morning, we found a place like a grave. We decided to dig it up. We found first a mat, and under that a fine bow. . . . We also found bowls, trays, dishes, and things like that. We took several of the prettiest things to carry away with us, and covered the body up again.[41]

A place "like a grave"!

Although Karen Kupperman says the Pilgrims continued to rob graves *47* for years,[42] more help came from a live Indian, Squanto. Here my students return to familiar turf, for they have all learned the Squanto legend. *Land of Promise* provides a typical account:

> Squanto had learned their language, he explained, from English fishermen who ventured into the New England waters each summer. Squanto taught the Pilgrims how to plant corn, squash, and pumpkins. Would the small band of settlers have survived without Squanto's help? We cannot say. But by the fall of 1621, colonists and Indians could sit down to several days of feast and thanksgiving to God (later celebrated as the first Thanksgiving).

What do the books leave out about Squanto? First, how he learned En- *48* glish. According to Ferdinando Gorges, around 1605 a British captain stole Squanto, who was then still a boy, along with four Penobscots, and took them to England. There Squanto spent nine years, three in the employ of Gorges. At length, Gorges helped Squanto arrange passage back to Massachusetts. Some historians doubt that Squanto was among the five Indians stolen in 1605.[43] All sources agree, however, that in 1614 a British slave raider seized Squanto and two dozen fellow Indians and sold them into slavery in Málaga, Spain. What happened next makes Ulysses look like a homebody. Squanto escaped from slavery, escaped from Spain, and made his way back to England. After trying to get home via Newfoundland, in

---

[41]Could there be a fairy tale parallel to this Pilgrim incident? Like Goldilocks, the Pilgrims broke-and-entered, trespassed, vandalized, and stole, and like Goldilocks, educators forgive them because they are Aryan. The Goldilocks tale makes her victims less than human, and the shadowy way our histories represent Indians makes the Pilgrims' victims also less than human. My thanks to Toni Cade Bambara for this analysis of Goldilocks.

[42]Kupperman, *Settling with the Indians*, 125.

[43]All five had names other than Squanto or Tisquantum, but Indians sometimes went by different names in different tribes. Squanto's biographer, Feenie Ziner, believes he was one of the five. Ferdinando Gorges stated in 1658 that Squanto was among those abducted in 1605 and lived with him in England for three years, which convinced Lincoln Kinnicutt ("The Settlement at Plymouth Contemplated before 1620," 212–13) but not historians at Plimoth Plantation or Salisbury (*Manitou and Providence*, 265–66), although Salisbury seems more positive in "Squanto: Last of the Patuxets." See also Lauber, *Indian Slavery in Colonial Times*, 156–59.

1619 he talked Thomas Dermer into taking him along on his next trip to Cape Cod.

It happens that Squanto's fabulous odyssey provides a "hook" into the plague story, a hook that our textbooks choose not to use. For now Squanto set foot again on Massachusetts soil and walked to his home village of Patuxet, only to make the horrifying discovery that "he was the sole member of his village still alive. All the others had perished in the epidemic two years before."[44] No wonder Squanto threw in his lot with the Pilgrims.

Now *that* is a story worth telling! Compare the pallid account in *Land of Promise*: "He had learned their language from English fishermen."

As translator, ambassador, and technical advisor, Squanto was essential to the survival of Plymouth in its first two years. Like other Europeans in America, the Pilgrims had no idea what to eat or how to raise or find it until Indians showed them. William Bradford called Squanto "a special instrument sent of God for their good beyond their expectation. He directed them how to set their corn, where to take fish, and to procure other commodities, and was also their pilot to bring them to unknown places for their profit." Squanto was not the Pilgrims' only aide: in the summer of 1621 Massasoit sent another Indian, Hobomok, to live among the Pilgrims for several years as guide and ambassador.[45]

"Their profit" was the primary reason most *Mayflower* colonists made the trip. As Robert Moore has pointed out, "Textbooks neglect to analyze the profit motive underlying much of our history."[46] Profit too came from the Indians, by way of the fur trade, without which Plymouth would never have paid for itself. Hobomok helped Plymouth set up fur trading posts at the mouth of the Penobscot and Kennebec rivers in Maine; in Aptucxet, Massachusetts; and in Windsor, Connecticut.[47] Europeans had neither the skill nor the desire to "go boldly where none dared go before." They went to the Indians.[48]

All this brings us to Thanksgiving. Throughout the nation every fall, elementary school children reenact a little morality play, *The First Thanksgiving*, as our national origin myth, complete with Pilgrim hats made out of construction paper and Indian braves with feathers in their hair: Thanksgiving is the occasion on which we give thanks to God as a nation for the

[44]Simpson, *Invisible Armies*, 6.

[45]William Bradford, *Of Plimouth Plantation*, 99. See also, inter alia, Salisbury, "Squanto: Last of the Patuxets," 228–46.

[46]Robert Moore, *Stereotypes, Distortions, and Omissions in U.S. History Textbooks* (New York: CIBC, 1977), 19.

[47]Robert M. Bartlett, *The Pilgrim Way* (Philadelphia: Pilgrim Press, 1971), 265; and Loeb, *Meet the Real Pilgrims*, 65.

[48]Charles Hudson et al., "The Tristan de Luna Expeditions, 1559–61," in Jerald T. Milanich and Susan Milbrath, eds., *First Encounters* (Gainesville: University of Florida Press, 1989), 119–34, supplies a vivid illustration of European dependence on Indians for food. They tell of the little-known second Spanish expedition (after De Soto) into what is now the southeastern United States. Because the Indians retreated from them and burned their crops, the Europeans almost starved.

blessings that He [*sic*] hath bestowed upon us. More than any other celebration, more even than such overtly patriotic holidays as Independence Day and Memorial Day, Thanksgiving celebrates our ethnocentrism. We have seen, for example, how King James and the early Pilgrim leaders gave thanks for the plague, which proved to them that God was on their side. The archetypes associated with Thanksgiving—God on our side, civilization wrested from wilderness, order from disorder, through hard work and good Pilgrim character traits—continue to radiate from our history textbooks. More than sixty years ago, in an analysis of how American history was taught in the 1920s, Bessie Pierce pointed out the political uses to which Thanksgiving is put: "For these unexcelled blessings, the pupil is urged to follow in the footsteps of his forbears, to offer unquestioning obedience to the law of the land, and to carry on the work begun."[49]

Thanksgiving dinner is a ritual, with all the characteristics that Mircea Eliade assigns to the ritual observances of origin myths:

1. It constitutes the history of the acts of the founders, the Supernaturals.

2. It is considered to be true.

3. It tells how an institution came into existence.

4. In performing the ritual associated with the myth, one "'experiences' knowledge of the origin" and claims one's patriarchy.

5. Thus one "lives" the myth, as a religion.[50]

My Random House dictionary lists as its main heading for the Plymouth colonists not *Pilgrims* but *Pilgrim Fathers*. The Library of Congress similarly catalogs its holdings for Plymouth under *Pilgrim Fathers*, and of course *fathers* is capitalized, meaning "fathers of our country," not of Pilgrim children. Thanksgiving has thus moved from history into the field of religion, "civil religion," as Robert Bellah has called it. To Bellah, civil religions hold society together. Plymouth Rock achieved iconographic status around 1880, when some enterprising residents of the town rejoined its two pieces on the waterfront and built a Greek templet around it. The templet became a shrine, the Mayflower Compact became a sacred text, and our textbooks began to play the same function as the Anglican *Book of Common Prayer*, teaching us the meaning behind the civil rite of Thanksgiving.[51]

[49]Bessie L. Pierce, *Public Opinion and the Teaching of History in the United States* (New York: Alfred A. Knopf, 1926), 113–14. See also Alice B. Kehoe, "'In fourteen hundred and ninety two, Columbus sailed . . .': The Primacy of the National Myth in U.S. Schools," in Peter Stone and Robert MacKenzie, eds., *The Excluded Past* (London: Unwin Hyman, 1990), 207.

[50]Mircea Eliade, *Myth and Reality* (New York: Harper and Row, 1963), 18–19.

[51]Robert N. Bellah, "Civil Religion in America," *Daedalus*, winter 1967, 1–21. See Hugh Brogan, *The Pelican History of the U.S.A.* (Harmondsworth, Eng.: Penguin, 1986), 37, re Plymouth Rock. See also Michael Kammen, *Mystic Chords of Memory* (New York: Alfred A. Knopf, 1991), 207–10.

The religious character of Pilgrim history shines forth in an introduc-   *55*
tion by Valerian Paget to William Bradford's famous chronicle *Of Plimoth Plantation*: "The eyes of Europe were upon this little English handful of unconscious heroes and saints, taking courage from them step by step. For their children's children the same ideals of Freedom burned so clear and strong that . . . the little episode we have just been contemplating, resulted in the birth of the United States of America, and, above all, of the estab-lishment of the humanitarian ideals it typifies, and for which the Pilgrims offered their sacrifice upon the altar of the Sonship of Man."[52] In this invo-cation, the Pilgrims supply not only the origin of the United States, but also the inspiration for democracy in Europe and perhaps for all goodness in the world today! I suspect that the original colonists, Separatists and Anglicans alike, would have been amused.

The civil ritual we practice marginalizes Indians. Our archetypal image   *56*
of the first Thanksgiving portrays the groaning boards in the woods, with the Pilgrims in their starched Sunday best next to their almost naked Indian guests. As a holiday greeting card puts it, "I is for the Indians we in-vited to share our food." The silliness of all this reaches its zenith in the handouts that schoolchildren have carried home for decades, complete with captions such as, "They served pumpkins and turkeys and corn and squash. The Indians had never seen such a feast!" When the Native Ameri-can novelist Michael Dorris's son brought home this "information" from his New Hampshire elementary school, Dorris pointed out that "the *Pilgrims* had literally never seen 'such a feast,' since all foods mentioned are exclu-sively indigenous to the Americas and had been provided *by* [or with the aid of] the local tribe."[53]

This notion that "we" advanced peoples provided for the Indians,   *57*
exactly the converse of the truth, is not benign. It reemerges time and again in our history to complicate race relations. For example, we are told that white plantation owners furnished food and medical care for their slaves, yet every shred of food, shelter, and clothing on the plantations was raised, built, woven, or paid for by black labor. Today Americans believe as part of our political understanding of the world that we are the most generous nation on earth in terms of foreign aid, overlooking the fact that the net dollar flow from almost every Third World nation runs *toward* the United States.

The true history of Thanksgiving reveals embarrassing facts. The Pil-   *58*
grims did not introduce the tradition; Eastern Indians had observed au-tumnal harvest celebrations for centuries. Although George Washington did set aside days for national thanksgiving, our modern celebrations date back only to 1863. During the Civil War, when the Union needed all the

---

[52]Valerian Paget, introduction to *Bradford's History of the Plymouth Settlement, 1608–1650* (New York: McBride, 1909), xvii.

[53]Dorris, "Why I'm Not Thankful for Thanksgiving," 9. The addition is mine, in the interest of accuracy.

patriotism that such an observance might muster, Abraham Lincoln proclaimed Thanksgiving a national holiday. The Pilgrims had nothing to do with it; not until the 1890s did they even get included in the tradition. For that matter, no one used the term *Pilgrims* until the 1870s.[54]

The ideological meaning American history has ascribed to Thanksgiving compounds the embarrassment. The Thanksgiving legend makes Americans ethnocentric. After all, if our culture has God on its side, why should we consider other cultures seriously? This ethnocentrism intensified in the middle of the last century. In *Race and Manifest Destiny*, Reginald Horsman has shown how the idea of "God on our side" was used to legitimate the open expression of Anglo-Saxon superiority vis-à-vis Mexicans, Native Americans, peoples of the Pacific, Jews, and even Catholics.[55] Today, when textbooks promote this ethnocentrism with their Pilgrim stories, they leave students less able to learn from and deal with people from other cultures.    *59*

On occasion, we pay a more direct cost: censorship. In 1970, for example, the Massachusetts Department of Commerce asked the Wampanoags to select a speaker to mark the 350th anniversary of the Pilgrims' landing. Frank James "was selected, but first he had to show a copy of his speech to the white people in charge of the ceremony. When they saw what he had written, they would not allow him to read it."[56] James had written:    *60*

> Today is a time of celebrating for you . . . but it is not a time of celebrating
> for me. It is with heavy heart that I look back upon what happened to my
> People. . . . The Pilgrims had hardly explored the shores of Cape Cod four days
> before they had robbed the graves of my ancestors, and stolen their corn,
> wheat, and beans. . . . Massasoit, the great leader of the Wampanoag, knew
> these facts; yet he and his People welcomed and befriended the settlers . . .
> little knowing that . . . before 50 years were to pass, the Wampanoags . . .
> and other Indians living near the settlers would be killed by their guns or
> dead from diseases that we caught from them. . . . Although our way of life
> is almost gone and our language is almost extinct, we the Wampanoags still
> walk the lands of Massachusetts. . . . What has happened cannot be changed,
> but today we work toward a better America, a more Indian America where
> people and nature once again are important.[57]

What the Massachusetts Department of Commerce censored was not some incendiary falsehood but historical truth. Nothing James would have said, had he been allowed to speak, was false, excepting the word *wheat*. Our textbooks also omit the facts about grave robbing, Indian enslavement,    *61*

[54]Plimoth Plantation, "The American Thanksgiving Tradition, or How Thanksgiving Stole the Pilgrims" (Plymouth, Mass.: n.d., photocopy); Stoddard, *The Truth about the Pilgrims*, 13.

[55]Reginald Horsman, *Race and Manifest Destiny* (Cambridge, Mass.: Harvard University Press, 1981), 5.

[56]Arlene Hitshfelder and Jane Califf, "Celebration or Mourning? It's All in the Point of View" (New York: Council on Interracial Books for Children *Bulletin* 10, no. 6, 1979), 9.

[57]Frank James, "Frank James' Speech" (New York: Council on Interracial Books for Children *Bulletin* 10, no. 6, 1979), 13.

the plague, and so on, even though they were common knowledge in colonial New England. For at least a century Puritan ministers thundered their interpretation of the meaning of the plague from New England pulpits. Thus our popular history of the Pilgrims has not been a process of gaining perspective but of deliberate forgetting. Instead of these important facts, textbooks supply the feel-good minutiae of Squanto's helpfulness, his name, the fish in the cornhills, sometimes even the menu and the number of Indians who attended the prototypical first Thanksgiving.

I have focused here on untoward detail only because our histories have *62* suppressed everything awkward for so long. The Pilgrims' courage in setting forth in the late fall to make their way on a continent new to them remains unsurpassed. In their first year the Pilgrims, like the Indians, suffered from diseases, including scurvy and pneumonia; half of them died. It was not immoral of the Pilgrims to have taken over Patuxet. They did not cause the plague and were as baffled as to its origin as the stricken Indian villagers. Massasoit was happy that the Pilgrims were using the bay, for the Patuxet, being dead, had no more need for the site. Pilgrim-Indian relations started reasonably positively. Plymouth, unlike many other colonies, usually paid the Indians for the land it took. In some instances Europeans settled in Indian towns because Indians had *invited* them, as protection against another tribe or a nearby competing European power.[58] In sum, U.S. history is no more violent and oppressive than the history of England, Russia, Indonesia, or Burundi—but neither is it exceptionally less violent.

The antidote to feel-good history is not feel-bad history but honest and *63* inclusive history. If textbook authors feel compelled to give moral instruction, the way origin myths have always done, they could accomplish this aim by allowing students to learn both the "good" and the "bad" sides of the Pilgrim tale. Conflict would then become part of the story, and students might discover that the knowledge they gain has implications for their lives today. Correctly taught, the issues of the era of the first Thanksgiving could help Americans grow more thoughtful and more tolerant, rather than more ethnocentric.

Origin myths do not come cheaply. To glorify the Pilgrims is danger- *64* ous. The genial omissions and the invented details with which our textbooks retail the Pilgrim archetype are close cousins of the overt censorship practiced by the Massachusetts Department of Commerce in denying Frank James the right to speak. Surely, in history, "truth should be held sacred, at whatever cost."

---

[58]Willison, *Saints and Strangers*; Salisbury, *Manitou and Providence*, 114–17; Wright, *The Only Land They Knew*, 220. Salisbury, *Manitou and Providence*, 120–25, tells of the militaristic and coercive nature of Plymouth's dealings with the Indians, however, right from the first.

■ ■ ■

Reading as a Writer: Analyzing Rhetorical Choices

1.  How are the ideas Loewen sets up in the first section of the reading ("Introduction: Something Has Gone Very Wrong") illustrated in the second section ("The Truth About the First Thanksgiving")? Locate several specific passages that demonstrate the connections you see between these sections, and be prepared to explain your ideas to a small group or the class.

2.  How and where does Loewen anticipate counterarguments? How effectively do you think he addresses the concerns of readers who might disagree with him? What conclusions can you draw from Loewen as you think about effective strategies for addressing resistant readers in your own writing?

Writing as a Reader: Entering the Conversation of Ideas

1.  Although they each point to different kinds of evidence, both Loewen and Gloria Anzaldúa are interested in the shortfalls of American education. Write an essay in which you place in conversation the examples each author presents to build your own argument about the traits of an effective education for Americans. Include evidence from your own experience if it strengthens your point.

2.  Both Loewen and Daniel Hade are interested in considering the many effects of learning partial or even incorrect histories in textbooks and historical children's books. Write an essay in which you examine how each author would evaluate the other's evidence, and the proposals each makes for change. What kinds of readers, and what kinds of students, do these writers call us to be, and why? What effects might these changes have beyond the classroom? Where do you stand in this conversation about changing our view of the past in order to see the present differently?

## JONATHAN KOZOL

# *From* Still Separate, Still Unequal: America's Educational Apartheid

Jonathan Kozol is an award-winning writer and public lecturer who focuses on social injustice in the United States, an interest that began in the 1960s, when he taught in the Boston public school system. This first experience of learning about the lives of the country's poor and undereducated led him to investigate and write extensively about Americans who suffer from what he calls social and educational "apartheid" in the United States, which keeps many people in a cycle of poverty that he believes is nearly impossible to break. An Internet search of Kozol's name will demonstrate how widely he is quoted and how often he appears in the media as an expert on social inequality.

This essay, published in *Harper's Magazine* in September 2005, was adapted from his book *The Shame of the Nation: The Restoration of Apartheid Schooling in America* (2005). While Kozol uses many different sources to support his argument, the essay is written in the style of magazine journalism, and so he does not use footnotes. You might keep track of all the different kinds of sources in this piece, though, to see what connections you can make between Kozol's central argument and the voices he includes here. Kozol makes his case in part by juxtaposing the words of the powerless and the powerful and by contextualizing these individual speakers with statistics and facts that demonstrate what he believes is a profoundly unjust system of keeping the haves and have-nots separated through a variety of policies and belief systems.

Before you read, you might consider what you know about the No Child Left Behind policy, which plays a role in Kozol's examination of urban school systems. You might even do a bit of research about the strong feelings held by supporters and opponents of this policy, so that you have a sense of this high-stakes conversation before you read Kozol's analysis. Also keep your own schooling experience in mind, and think about your childhood sense of what other kids had or didn't have. Kozol taps into a discussion about education that is linked to almost every other kind of social division in our country. What does he hope to illuminate, and what solutions does he propose? Just as important, where do you place yourself in this conversation about what it means to learn and grow as an American?

Many Americans who live far from our major cities and who have no firsthand knowledge of the realities to be found in urban public schools seem to have the rather vague and general impression that the great extremes of racial isolation that were matters of grave national significance some thirty-five or forty years ago have gradually but steadily diminished in more recent years. The truth, unhappily, is that the trend, for well over a decade now, has been precisely the reverse. Schools that were already deeply segregated twenty-five or thirty years ago are no less segregated now, while thousands of other schools around the country that had been integrated either voluntarily or by the force of law have since been rapidly resegregating.

In Chicago, by the academic year 2002–2003, 87 percent of public-school enrollment was black or Hispanic; less than 10 percent of children in the schools were white. In Washington, D.C., 94 percent of children were black or Hispanic; less than 5 percent were white. In St. Louis, 82 percent of the student population were black or Hispanic; in Philadelphia and Cleveland, 79 percent; in Los Angeles, 84 percent; in Detroit, 96 percent; in Baltimore, 89 percent. In New York City, nearly three quarters of the students were black or Hispanic.

Even these statistics, as stark as they are, cannot begin to convey how deeply isolated children in the poorest and most segregated sections of these cities have become. In the typically colossal high schools of the Bronx, for instance, more than 90 percent of students (in most cases, more than 95 percent) are black or Hispanic. At John F. Kennedy High School in 2003, 93 percent of the enrollment of more than 4,000 students were black and Hispanic; only 3.5 percent of students at the school were white. At Harry S. Truman High School, black and Hispanic students represented 96 percent of the enrollment of 2,700 students; 2 percent were white. At Adlai Stevenson High School, which enrolls 3,400 students, blacks and Hispanics made up 97 percent of the student population; a mere eight-tenths of 1 percent were white.

A teacher at P.S. 65 in the South Bronx once pointed out to me one of    4 the two white children I had ever seen there. His presence in her class was something of a wonderment to the teacher and to the other pupils. I asked how many white kids she had taught in the South Bronx in her career. "I've been at this school for eighteen years," she said. "This is the first white student I have ever taught."

One of the most disheartening experiences for those who grew up in    5 the years when Martin Luther King Jr. and Thurgood Marshall were alive is to visit public schools today that bear their names, or names of other honored leaders of the integration struggles that produced the temporary progress that took place in the three decades after *Brown v. Board of Education*, and to find out how many of these schools are bastions of contemporary segregation. It is even more disheartening when schools like these are not in deeply segregated inner-city neighborhoods but in racially mixed areas where the integration of a public school would seem to be most natural, and where, indeed, it takes a conscious effort on the part of parents or school officials in these districts to avoid the integration option that is often right at their front door.

In a Seattle neighborhood that I visited in 2002, for instance, where    6 approximately half the families were Caucasian, 95 percent of students at the Thurgood Marshall Elementary School were black, Hispanic, Native American, or of Asian origin. An African-American teacher at the school told me—not with bitterness but wistfully—of seeing clusters of white parents and their children each morning on the corner of a street close to the school, waiting for a bus that took the children to a predominantly white school.

"At Thurgood Marshall," according to a big wall poster in the school's    7 lobby, "the dream is alive." But school-assignment practices and federal court decisions that have countermanded long-established policies that previously fostered integration in Seattle's schools make the realization of the dream identified with Justice Marshall all but unattainable today. In San Diego there is a school that bears the name of Rosa Parks in which 86 percent of students are black and Hispanic and only some 2 percent are white. In Los Angeles there is a school that bears the name of Dr. King that is 99 percent black and Hispanic, and another in Milwaukee in which black and Hispanic children also make up 99 percent of the enrollment. There is a high school in Cleveland that is named for Dr. King in which black students make up 97 percent of the student body, and the graduation rate is only 35 percent. In Philadelphia, 98 percent of children at a high school named for Dr. King are black. At a middle school named for Dr. King in Boston, black and Hispanic children make up 98 percent of the enrollment.

In New York City there is a primary school named for Langston Hughes (99 percent black and Hispanic), a middle school named for Jackie Robinson (96 percent black and Hispanic), and a high school named for Fannie Lou Hamer, one of the great heroes of the integration movement in the South, in which 98 percent of students are black or Hispanic. In Harlem there is yet another segregated Thurgood Marshall School (also 98 percent black and Hispanic), and in the South Bronx dozens of children I have known went to a segregated middle school named in honor of Paul Robeson in which less than half of 1 percent of the enrollment was Caucasian.

There is a well-known high school named for Martin Luther King Jr. in New York City too. This school, which I've visited repeatedly in recent years, is located in an upper-middle-class white neighborhood, where it was built in the belief—or hope—that it would draw large numbers of white students by permitting them to walk to school, while only their black and Hispanic classmates would be asked to ride the bus or come by train. When the school was opened in 1975, less than a block from Lincoln Center in Manhattan, "it was seen," according to the *New York Times*, "as a promising effort to integrate white, black and Hispanic students in a thriving neighborhood that held one of the city's cultural gems." Even from the start, however, parents in the neighborhood showed great reluctance to permit their children to enroll at Martin Luther King, and, despite "its prime location and its name, which itself creates the highest of expectations," notes the *Times*, the school before long came to be a destination for black and Hispanic students who could not obtain admission into more successful schools. It stands today as one of the nation's most visible and problematic symbols of an expectation rapidly receding and a legacy substantially betrayed.

Perhaps most damaging to any serious effort to address racial segregation openly is the refusal of most of the major arbiters of culture in our northern cities to confront or even clearly name an obvious reality they would have castigated with a passionate determination in another section of the nation fifty years before—and which, moreover, they still castigate today in retrospective writings that assign it to a comfortably distant and allegedly concluded era of the past. There is, indeed, a seemingly agreed-upon convention in much of the media today not even to use an accurate descriptor like "racial segregation" in a narrative description of a segregated school. Linguistic sweeteners, semantic somersaults, and surrogate vocabularies are repeatedly employed. Schools in which as few as 3 or 4 percent of students may be white or Southeast Asian or of Middle Eastern origin, for instance—and where every other child in the building is black or Hispanic—are referred to as "diverse." Visitors to schools like these discover quickly the eviscerated meaning of the word, which is no longer a proper adjective but a euphemism for a plainer word that has apparently become unspeakable.

School systems themselves repeatedly employ this euphemism in describing the composition of their student populations. In a school I visited in the fall of 2004 in Kansas City, Missouri, for example, a document distributed to visitors reports that the school's curriculum "addresses the needs of children from diverse backgrounds." But as I went from class to class, I did not encounter any children who were white or Asian—or Hispanic, for that matter—and when I was later provided with precise statistics for the demographics of the school, I learned that 99.6 percent of students there were African American. In a similar document, the school board of another district, this one in New York State, referred to "the diversity" of its student population and "the rich variations of ethnic backgrounds." But when I looked at the racial numbers that the district had reported to the state, I learned that there were 2,800 black and Hispanic children in the system, 1 Asian child, and 3 whites. Words, in these cases, cease to have real meaning; or, rather, they mean the opposite of what they say.     *11*

High school students whom I talk with in deeply segregated neighborhoods and public schools seem far less circumspect than their elders and far more open in their willingness to confront these issues. "It's more like being hidden," said a fifteen-year-old girl named Isabel[1] I met some years ago in Harlem, in attempting to explain to me the ways in which she and her classmates understood the racial segregation of their neighborhoods and schools. "It's as if you have been put in a garage where, if they don't have room for something but aren't sure if they should throw it out, they put it there where they don't need to think of it again."     *12*

I asked her if she thought America truly did not "have room" for her or other children of her race. "Think of it this way," said a sixteen-year-old girl sitting beside her. "If people in New York woke up one day and learned that we were gone, that we had simply died or left for somewhere else, how would they feel?"     *13*

"How do you think they'd feel?" I asked.     *14*

"I think they'd be relieved," this very solemn girl replied.     *15*

Many educators make the argument today that given the demographics of large cities like New York and their suburban areas, our only realistic goal should be the nurturing of strong, empowered, and well-funded schools in segregated neighborhoods. Black school officials in these situations have sometimes conveyed to me a bitter and clear-sighted recognition that they're being asked, essentially, to mediate and render functional an uncontested separation between children of their race and children of white people living sometimes in a distant section of their town and some-     *16*

---

[1] The names of children mentioned in this article have been changed to protect their privacy.

times in almost their own immediate communities. Implicit in this mediation is a willingness to set aside the promises of *Brown* and—though never
stating this or even thinking of it clearly in these terms—to settle for the
promise made more than a century ago in *Plessy v. Ferguson*, the 1896
Supreme Court ruling in which "separate but equal" was accepted as a tol-
erable rationale for the perpetuation of a dual system in American society.

Equality itself—equality alone—is now, it seems, the article of faith 17
to which most of the principals of inner-city public schools subscribe. And
some who are perhaps most realistic do not even dare to ask for, or expect,
complete equality, which seems beyond the realm of probability for many
years to come, but look instead for only a sufficiency of means—"adequacy"
is the legal term most often used today—by which to win those practical
and finite victories that appear to be within their reach. Higher standards,
higher expectations, are repeatedly demanded of these urban principals,
and of the teachers and students in their schools, but far lower standards—
certainly in ethical respects—appear to be expected of the dominant society that isolates these children in unequal institutions.

"Dear Mr. Kozol," wrote the eight-year-old, "we do not have the things 18
you have. You have Clean things. We do not have. You have a clean bathroom. We do not have that. You have Parks and we do not have Parks. You
have all the thing and we do not have all the thing. Can you help us?"

The letter, from a child named Alliyah, came in a fat envelope of twenty- 19
seven letters from a class of third-grade children in the Bronx. Other letters that the students in Alliyah's classroom sent me registered some of
the same complaints. "We don't have no gardens," "no Music or Art," and
"no fun places to play," one child said. "Is there a way to fix this Problem?"
Another noted a concern one hears from many children in such over-
crowded schools: "We have a gym but it is for lining up. I think it is not
fair." Yet another of Alliyah's classmates asked me, with a sweet misspell-
ing, if I knew the way to make her school into a "good" school—"like the
other kings have"—and ended with the hope that I would do my best to
make it possible for "all the kings" to have good schools.

The letter that affected me the most, however, had been written by a 20
child named Elizabeth. "It is not fair that other kids have a garden and new
things. But we don't have that," said Elizabeth. "I wish that this school was
the most beautiful school in the whole why world."

"The whole why world" stayed in my thoughts for days. When I later 21
met Elizabeth, I brought her letter with me, thinking I might see whether,
in reading it aloud, she'd change the "why" to "wide" or leave it as it was.
My visit to her class, however, proved to be so pleasant, and the children
seemed so eager to bombard me with their questions about where I lived,
and why I lived there rather than in New York, and who I lived with, and how
many dogs I had, and other interesting questions of that sort, that I decided
not to interrupt the nice reception they had given me with questions about
usages and spelling. I left "the whole why world" to float around unedited

and unrevised in my mind. The letter itself soon found a resting place on the wall above my desk.

In the years before I met Elizabeth, I had visited many other schools 22 in the South Bronx and in one northern district of the Bronx as well. I had made repeated visits to a high school where a stream of water flowed down one of the main stairwells on a rainy afternoon and where green fungus molds were growing in the office where the students went for counseling. A large blue barrel was positioned to collect rainwater coming through the ceiling. In one makeshift elementary school housed in a former skating rink next to a funeral establishment in yet another nearly all-black-and-Hispanic section of the Bronx, class size rose to thirty-four and more; four kindergarten classes and a sixth-grade class were packed into a single room that had no windows. The air was stifling in many rooms, and the children had no place for recess because there was no outdoor playground and no indoor gym.

In another elementary school, which had been built to hold 1,000 chil- 23 dren but was packed to bursting with some 1,500, the principal poured out his feelings to me in a room in which a plastic garbage bag had been attached somehow to cover part of the collapsing ceiling. "This," he told me, pointing to the garbage bag, then gesturing around him at the other indications of decay and disrepair one sees in ghetto schools much like it elsewhere, "would not happen to white children."

Libraries, once one of the glories of the New York City school system, 24 were either nonexistent or, at best, vestigial in large numbers of the elementary schools. Art and music programs had also for the most part disappeared. "When I began to teach in 1969," the principal of an elementary school in the South Bronx reported to me, "every school had a full-time licensed art and music teacher and librarian." During the subsequent decades, he recalled, "I saw all of that destroyed."

School physicians also were removed from elementary schools dur- 25 ing these years. In 1970, when substantial numbers of white children still attended New York City's public schools, 400 doctors had been present to address the health needs of the children. By 1993 the number of doctors had been cut to 23, most of them part-time—a cutback that affected most severely children in the city's poorest neighborhoods, where medical facilities were most deficient and health problems faced by children most extreme. Teachers told me of asthmatic children who came into class with chronic wheezing and who at any moment of the day might undergo more serious attacks, but in the schools I visited there were no doctors to attend to them.

In explaining these steep declines in services, political leaders in New 26 York tended to point to shifting economic factors, like a serious budget crisis in the middle 1970s, rather than to the changing racial demographics of the student population. But the fact of economic ups and downs from year to year, or from one decade to the next, could not convincingly explain the permanent shortchanging of the city's students, which took place routinely in good economic times and bad. The bad times were seized upon politically to justify the cuts, and the money was never restored once the crisis years were past.

"If you close your eyes to the changing racial composition of the   27
schools and look only at budget actions and political events," says Noreen Connell, the director of the nonprofit Educational Priorities Panel in New York, "you're missing the assumptions that are underlying these decisions." When minority parents ask for something better for their kids, she says, "the assumption is that these are parents who can be discounted. These are kids who just don't count—children we don't value."

This, then, is the accusation that Alliyah and her classmates send our   28
way: "You have . . . We do not have." Are they right or are they wrong? Is this a case of naive and simplistic juvenile exaggeration? What does a third-grader know about these big-time questions of fairness and justice? Physical appearances apart, how in any case do you begin to measure something so diffuse and vast and seemingly abstract as having more, or having less, or not having at all?

Around the time I met Alliyah in the school year 1997–1998, New   29
York's Board of Education spent about $8,000 yearly on the education of a third-grade child in a New York City public school. If you could have scooped Alliyah up out of the neighborhood where she was born and plunked her down in a fairly typical white suburb of New York, she would have received a public education worth about $12,000 a year. If you were to lift her up once more and set her down in one of the wealthiest white suburbs of New York, she would have received as much as $18,000 worth of public education every year and would likely have had a third-grade teacher paid approximately $30,000 more than her teacher in the Bronx was paid.

The dollars on both sides of the equation have increased since then,   30
but the discrepancies between them have remained. The present per-pupil spending level in the New York City schools is $11,700, which may be compared with a per-pupil spending level in excess of $22,000 in the well-to-do suburban district of Manhasset, Long Island. The present New York City level is, indeed, almost exactly what Manhasset spent per pupil eighteen years ago, in 1987, when that sum of money bought a great deal more in services and salaries than it can buy today. In dollars adjusted for inflation, New York City has not yet caught up to where its wealthiest suburbs were a quarter-century ago.

Gross discrepancies in teacher salaries between the city and its afflu-   31
ent white suburbs have remained persistent as well. In 1997 the median salary for teachers in Alliyah's neighborhood was $43,000, as compared with $74,000 in suburban Rye, $77,000 in Manhasset, and $81,000 in the town of Scarsdale, which is only about eleven miles from Alliyah's school. Five years later, in 2002, salary scales for New York City's teachers rose to levels that approximated those within the lower-spending districts in the suburbs, but salary scales do not reflect the actual salaries that teachers

typically receive, which are dependent upon years of service and advanced degrees. Salaries for first-year teachers in the city were higher than they'd been four years before, but the differences in median pay between the city and its upper-middle-income suburbs had remained extreme. The overall figure for New York City in 2002–2003 was $53,000, while it had climbed to $87,000 in Manhasset and exceeded $95,000 in Scarsdale.

"There are expensive children and there are cheap children," writes 32 Marina Warner, an essayist and novelist who has written many books for children, "just as there are expensive women and cheap women." The governmentally administered diminishment in value of the children of the poor begins even before the age of five or six, when they begin their years of formal education in the public schools. It starts during their infant and toddler years, when hundreds of thousands of children of the very poor in much of the United States are locked out of the opportunity for preschool education for no reason but the accident of birth and budgetary choices of the government, while children of the privileged are often given veritable feasts of rich developmental early education.

In New York City, for example, affluent parents pay surprisingly large 33 sums of money to enroll their youngsters, beginning at the age of two or three, in extraordinary early-education programs that give them social competence and rudimentary pedagogic skills unknown to children of the same age in the city's poorer neighborhoods. The most exclusive of the private preschools in New York, which are known to those who can afford them as "Baby Ivies," cost as much as $24,000 for a full-day program. Competition for admission to these pre-K schools is so extreme that private counselors are frequently retained, at fees as high as $300 an hour, to guide the parents through the application process.

At the opposite extreme along the economic spectrum in New York are 34 thousands of children who receive no preschool opportunity at all. Exactly how many thousands are denied this opportunity in New York City and in other major cities is almost impossible to know. Numbers that originate in governmental agencies in many states are incomplete and imprecise and do not always differentiate with clarity between authentic pre-K programs that have educative and developmental substance and those less expensive child-care arrangements that do not. But even where states do compile numbers that refer specifically to educative preschool programs, it is difficult to know how many of the children who are served are of low income, since admissions to some of the state-supported programs aren't determined by low income or they are determined by a complicated set of factors of which poverty is only one.

There are remarkable exceptions to this pattern in some sections of 35 the nation. In Milwaukee, for example, virtually every four-year-old is now enrolled in a preliminary kindergarten program, which amounts to a full year of preschool education, prior to a second kindergarten year for five-year-olds. More commonly in urban neighborhoods, large numbers of low-income children are denied these opportunities and come into their kindergarten year without the minimal social skills that children need in order to participate in class activities and without even such very modest early-learning skills as knowing how to hold a crayon or a pencil, identify perhaps a couple of shapes and colors, or recognize that printed pages go from left to right.

Three years later, in third grade, these children are introduced to what are known as "high-stakes tests," which in many urban systems now determine whether students can or cannot be promoted. Children who have been in programs like those offered by the "Baby Ivies" since the age of two have, by now, received the benefits of six or seven years of education, nearly twice as many as the children who have been denied these opportunities; yet all are required to take, and will be measured by, the same examinations. Which of these children will receive the highest scores? The ones who spent the years from two to four in lovely little Montessori programs and in other pastel-painted settings in which tender and attentive and well-trained instructors read to them from beautiful storybooks and introduced them very gently for the first time to the world of numbers and the shapes of letters, and the sizes and varieties of solid objects, and perhaps taught them to sort things into groups or to arrange them in a sequence, or to do those many other interesting things that early childhood specialists refer to as pre-numeracy skills? Or the ones who spent those years at home in front of a TV or sitting by the window of a slum apartment gazing down into the street? There is something deeply hypocritical about a society that holds an eight-year-old inner-city child "accountable" for her performance on a high-stakes standardized exam but does not hold the high officials of our government accountable for robbing her of what they gave their own kids six or seven years earlier.

Perhaps in order to deflect these recognitions, or to soften them somewhat, many people, even while they do not doubt the benefit of making very large investments in the education of their own children, somehow—paradoxical as it may seem—appear to be attracted to the argument that money may not really matter that much at all. No matter with what regularity such doubts about the worth of spending money on a child's education are advanced, it is obvious that those who have the money, and who spend it lavishly to benefit their own kids, do not do it for no reason. Yet shockingly large numbers of well-educated and sophisticated people whom I talk with nowadays dismiss such challenges with a surprising ease. "Is the answer really to throw money into these dysfunctional and failing schools?" I'm often asked. "Don't we have some better ways to make them 'work'?" The question is posed in a variety of forms. "Yes, of course, it's not a perfectly fair system as it stands. But money alone is surely not the sole response. The values of the parents and the kids themselves must have a role in this as well—you know, housing, health conditions, social factors." "Other factors"—a term of overall reprieve one often hears—"have got to be considered, too." These latter points are obviously true but always seem to have the odd effect of substituting things we know we cannot change in the short run for obvious solutions like cutting class size and constructing new school buildings or providing universal preschool that we actually could put in place right now if we were so inclined.

Frequently these arguments are posed as questions that do not invite   *38*
an answer because the answer seems to be decided in advance. "Can you really buy your way to better education for these children?" "Do we know enough to be quite sure that we will see an actual return on the investment that we make?" "Is it even clear that this is the right starting point to get to where we'd like to go? It doesn't always seem to work, as I am sure that you already know," or similar questions that somehow assume I will agree with those who ask them.

Some people who ask these questions, although they live in wealthy   *39*
districts where the schools are funded at high levels, don't even send their children to these public schools but choose instead to send them to expensive private day schools. At some of the well-known private prep schools in the New York City area, tuition and associated costs are typically more than $20,000 a year. During their children's teenage years, they sometimes send them off to very fine New England schools like Andover or Exeter or Groton, where tuition, boarding, and additional expenses rise to more than $30,000. Often a family has two teenage children in these schools at the same time, so they may be spending more than $60,000 on their children's education every year. Yet here I am one night, a guest within their home, and dinner has been served and we are having coffee now; and this entirely likable, and generally sensible, and beautifully refined and thoughtful person looks me in the eyes and asks me whether you can really buy your way to better education for the children of the poor.

As racial isolation deepens and the inequalities of education finance re-   *40*
main unabated and take on new and more innovative forms, the principals of many inner-city schools are making choices that few principals in public schools that serve white children in the mainstream of the nation ever need to contemplate. Many have been dedicating vast amounts of time and effort to create an architecture of adaptive strategies that promise incremental gains within the limits inequality allows....

Corporate leaders, when they speak of education, sometimes pay lip-   *41*
service to the notion of "good critical and analytic skills," but it is reasonable to ask whether they have in mind the critical analysis of *their* priorities. In principle, perhaps some do; but, if so, this is not a principle that seems to have been honored widely in the schools I have been visiting. In all the various business-driven inner-city classrooms I have observed in the past five years, plastered as they are with corporation brand names and managerial vocabularies, I have yet to see the two words "labor unions." Is this an oversight? How is that possible? Teachers and principals themselves, who are almost always members of a union, seem to be so beaten down that they rarely even question this omission.

It is not at all unusual these days to come into an urban school in which   *42*
the principal prefers to call himself or herself "building CEO" or "building

manager." In some of the same schools teachers are described as "classroom managers."[2] I have never been in a suburban district in which principals were asked to view themselves or teachers in this way. These terminologies remind us of how wide the distance has become between two very separate worlds of education.

It has been more than a decade now since drill-based literacy methods like Success for All began to proliferate in our urban schools. It has been three and a half years since the systems of assessment that determine the effectiveness of these and similar practices were codified in the federal legislation, No Child Left Behind, that President Bush signed into law in 2002. Since the enactment of this bill, the number of standardized exams children must take has more than doubled. It will probably increase again after the year 2006, when standardized tests, which are now required in grades three through eight, may be required in Head Start programs and, as President Bush has now proposed, in ninth, tenth, and eleventh grades as well.

The elements of strict accountability, in short, are solidly in place; and in many states where the present federal policies are simply reinforcements of accountability requirements that were established long before the passage of the federal law, the same regimen has been in place since 1995 or even earlier. The "tests-and-standards" partisans have had things very much their way for an extended period of time, and those who were convinced that they had ascertained "what works" in schools that serve minorities and children of the poor have had ample opportunity to prove that they were right.

What, then, it is reasonable to ask, are the results?

The achievement gap between black and white children, which narrowed for three decades up until the late years of the 1980s—the period in

---

[2]A school I visited three years ago in Columbus, Ohio, was littered with "Help Wanted" signs. Starting in kindergarten, children in the school were being asked to think about the jobs that they might choose when they grew up. In one classroom there was a poster that displayed the names of several retail stores: J. C. Penney, Wal-Mart, Kmart, Sears, and a few others. "It's like working in a store," a classroom aide explained. "The children are learning to pretend they're cashiers." At another school in the same district, children were encouraged to apply for jobs in their classrooms. Among the job positions open to the children in this school, there was an "Absence Manager" and a "Behavior Chart Manager," a "Form Collector Manager," a "Paper Passer Outer Manager," a "Paper Collecting Manager," a "Paper Returning Manager," an "Exit Ticket Manager," even a "Learning Manager," a "Reading Corner Manager," and a "Score Keeper Manager." I asked the principal if there was a special reason why those two words "management" and "manager" kept popping up throughout the school. "We want every child to be working as a manager while he or she is in this school," the principal explained. "We want to make them understand that, in this country, companies will give you opportunities to work, to prove yourself, no matter what you've done." I wasn't sure what she meant by "no matter what you've done," and asked her if she could explain it. "Even if you have a felony arrest," she said, "we want you to understand that you can be a manager someday."

which school segregation steadily decreased—started to widen once more in the early 1990s when the federal courts began the process of resegregation by dismantling the mandates of the *Brown* decision. From that point on, the gap continued to widen or remained essentially unchanged; and while recently there has been a modest narrowing of the gap in reading scores for fourth-grade children, the gap in secondary school remains as wide as ever.

The media inevitably celebrate the periodic upticks that a set of scores    47 may seem to indicate in one year or another in achievement levels of black and Hispanic children in their elementary schools. But if these upticks were not merely temporary "testing gains" achieved by test-prep regimens and were instead authentic education gains, they would carry over into middle school and high school. Children who know how to read—and read with comprehension—do not suddenly become nonreaders and hopelessly disabled writers when they enter secondary school. False gains evaporate; real gains endure. Yet hundreds of thousands of the inner-city children who have made what many districts claim to be dramatic gains in elementary school, and whose principals and teachers have adjusted almost every aspect of their school days and school calendars, forfeiting recess, canceling or cutting back on all the so-called frills (art, music, even social sciences) in order to comply with state demands—those students, now in secondary school, are sitting in subject-matter classes where they cannot comprehend the texts and cannot set down their ideas in the kind of sentences expected of most fourth-and fifth-grade students in the suburbs. Students in this painful situation, not surprisingly, tend to be most likely to drop out of school.

In 48 percent of high schools in the nation's 100 largest districts, which    48 are those in which the highest concentrations of black and Hispanic students tend to be enrolled, less than half the entering ninth-graders graduate in four years. Nationwide, from 1993 to 2002, the number of high schools graduating less than half their ninth-grade class in four years has increased by 75 percent. In the 94 percent of districts in New York State where white children make up the majority, nearly 80 percent of students graduate from high school in four years. In the 6 percent of districts where black and Hispanic students make up the majority, only 40 percent do so. There are 120 high schools in New York, enrolling nearly 200,000 minority students, where less than 60 percent of entering ninth-graders even make it to twelfth grade.

The promulgation of new and expanded inventories of "what works,"    49 no matter the enthusiasm with which they're elaborated, is not going to change this. The use of hortatory slogans chanted by the students in our segregated schools is not going to change this. Desperate historical revisionism that romanticizes the segregation of an older order (this is a common theme of many separatists today) is not going to change this. Skinnerian instructional approaches, which decapitate a child's capability for critical reflection, are not going to change this. Posters about "global competition"

will certainly not change this. Turning six-year-olds into examination soldiers and denying eight-year-olds their time for play at recess will not
change this.

"I went to Washington to challenge the soft bigotry of low expecta- *50*
tions," said President Bush in his campaign for reelection in September
2004. "It's working. It's making a difference." Here we have one of those
deadly lies that by sheer repetition is at length accepted by surprisingly
large numbers of Americans. But it is not the truth; and it is not an innocent misstatement of the facts. It is a devious appeasement of the heartache
of the parents of the black and brown and poor, and if it is not forcefully
resisted it will lead us further in a very dangerous direction.

Whether the issue is inequity alone or deepening resegregation or the *51*
labyrinthine intertwining of the two, it is well past the time for us to start
the work that it will take to change this. If it takes people marching in the
streets and other forms of adamant disruption of the governing civilities,
if it takes more than litigation, more than legislation, and much more than
resolutions introduced by members of Congress, these are prices we should
be prepared to pay. "We do not have the things you have," Alliyah told me
when she wrote to ask if I would come and visit her school in the South
Bronx. "Can you help us?" America owes that little girl and millions like
her a more honorable answer than they have received.

■ ■ ■

## Reading as a Writer: Analyzing Rhetorical Choices

1. How would you describe Kozol's relationship to the people who are the
   subject of his essay? How does this relationship work to his advantage, or
   disadvantage, as he builds his argument? Be prepared to point to and explain several passages that support your responses to these questions.

2. Who is Kozol's audience (or audiences), and how can you tell? You might
   find it helpful to look for the counterarguments Kozol addresses, the kinds
   of sources he uses to make his argument, and the examples he uses to
   illustrate his points. Based on your findings, you could also consider who
   might be shut out of his audience, and why this matters.

## Writing as a Reader: Entering the Conversation of Ideas

1. Kozol and Beverly Daniel Tatum both focus on conversational exchanges
   between those in power and those without power within educational settings. Write an essay in which you analyze the similarities and differences
   in the points they raise and the conclusions they draw. What are the problems and the potential each author sees in education in the United States
   when it comes to racial equity? Where do you stand on the issues they raise
   and the conclusions they draw? Feel free to include a few of your own specific experiences and insights as you take a stance on this important topic.

2. In his essay, Kozol notes that certain school districts claim a diverse population, but he reveals what he calls "the eviscerated meaning of the word" (para. 10). Ann duCille is also interested in the ways that terms related to multiculturalism and diversity are often euphemisms for something else. Drawing on both Kozol's and duCille's points about how the language of diversity and multiculturalism is often used and misused, write an essay in which you examine the significance of this dynamic in the contemporary United States. Include your analysis of Kozol's and duCille's examples as well as examples from your own experience that will help you make your point.

# Media Studies

*What can we learn from what entertains us?*

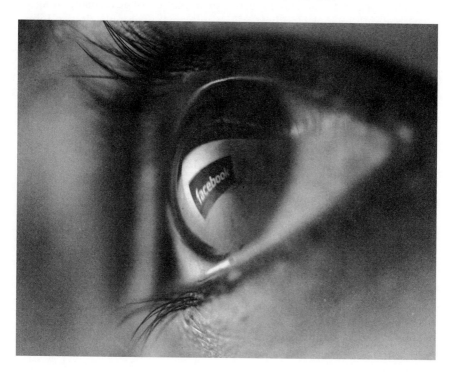

Who among us can resist a premise like that of Steven Johnson's title "Why Games Are Good for You"? Johnson, like the other authors in this chapter, believes that popular culture, far from being too "lite" to take seriously, is the very ground we should be exploring carefully if we wish to make sense of our lives today. In the many pastimes, entertainments, and guilty pleasures that tempt us every day, these writers discover meanings that may surprise you. When scholars study "fun"—online avatars, movies, and Facebook, to name just a few of the guilty pleasures analyzed in these texts—we learn how every cultural artifact, no matter how seemingly insignificant, carries meaning that shapes our lives in often quite significant ways.

Some of the authors in this chapter focus specifically on television and films, such as Neil Postman, who draws on John Dewey's concept of "collateral learning" in order to convince us that we learn far more from television than we might think—and it isn't all good. That concept of "collateral learning" is evident (if not named) in bell hooks's essay about ideas we learn about poverty from television and films, and also in Julie D. O'Reilly's analysis of female superheroes in cartoons and movies. Like O'Reilly, several other authors in this chapter focus on the ways popular culture "teaches" ideas about gender roles that are severely limiting for women and men, as in Carmen D. Siering's analysis of the smash-hit *Twilight* book and film series and in Jean Kilbourne's examination of advertising images.

Other authors look closely at online culture; for example, Steven Johnson analyzes video game culture, and Katherine Bessière, A. Fleming Seay, and Sara Kiesler examine avatar-creation among World of Warcraft players in an essay with the telling title "The Ideal Elf." These pieces, as well as S. Craig Watkins's analysis about racial assumptions and identity communities on MySpace and Facebook, based on hundreds of surveys and interviews with college students, should get you thinking and talking about your own online practices, and what they can tell you—and us—about what "we" believe.

The readings in this chapter acknowledge the possibilities of technology and popular culture, but they also help us understand that the past is always with us in our concerns for the present and hopes for the future. Whether you see media culture today as the end of culture as we know it, the same old stuff, or something entirely new—or perhaps all three—these readings raise provocative questions about the significance of our "just-for-fun" pastimes.

NEIL POSTMAN

# Television as Teacher

Neil Postman, who died in 2003, was a popular and controversial scholar and critic who asked tough questions about the negative effects of popular culture, most notably in his 1985 book about American television, titled *Amusing Ourselves to Death: Public Discourse in an Age of Show Business*, from which this excerpt is taken. Postman had an EdD, or doctorate in education, and much of his professional life was spent reimagining school curricula to foster more independent, critical thinking. You can hear his critique of standard education in the title of his book on reinventing education, cowritten with Charles Weingartner in 1969, *Teaching as a Subversive Activity*.

Postman takes the same no-holds-barred approach in his analysis of contemporary media, particularly in his claim that reasoned analysis is increasingly supplanted by shallow images, thereby hindering the ways we learn about the world. Postman argues that television, in particular, mixes information and entertainment so thoroughly that viewers have come to expect even newscasts to be entertaining. While Postman made this claim in 1985, we believe his ideas still have the power to shake us up if we apply them to even the most recent forms of media "edutainment." Postman opens this piece with a reflection on the origins of *Sesame Street*, a television show you might have a history with as well. Like many of the writers in this book, Postman argues *against* popular opinion. He disagrees with people who believe that *Sesame Street* teaches kids to enjoy learning and, by association, to enjoy school. Instead, Postman claims, "As a television show, and a good one, *Sesame Street* does not encourage children to love school or anything about school. It encourages them to love television" (para. 5).

In the analysis that follows, Postman posits some tongue-in-cheek "commandments" that television programming follows, which run counter to the purposes of education. However, he observes that those same commandments are increasingly central to classroom experiences. Postman then offers as an extended example a specific math and science project called *The Voyage of the Mimi*, which brings television into the classroom as part of a teaching unit. In the years since Postman wrote this piece, television has played increasingly larger roles in the classroom, as have other forms of visual media. As you read, consider how Postman's ideas help you analyze your own experiences with education-as-entertainment, both inside and outside the classroom.

■ ■ ■

There could not have been a safer bet when it began in 1969 than that *Sesame Street* would be embraced by children, parents, and educators. Children loved it because they were raised on television commercials, which they intuitively knew were the most carefully crafted entertainments on television. To those who had not yet been to school, even to those who had just started, the idea of being *taught* by a series of commercials did not seem peculiar. And that television should entertain them was taken as a matter of course.

Parents embraced *Sesame Street* for several reasons, among them   2
that it assuaged their guilt over the fact that they could not or would not restrict their children's access to television. *Sesame Street* appeared to justify allowing a four- or five-year-old to sit transfixed in front of a television screen for unnatural periods of time. Parents were eager to hope that television could teach their children something other than which breakfast cereal has the most crackle. At the same time, *Sesame Street* relieved them of the responsibility of teaching their pre-school children how to read—no small matter in a culture where children are apt to be considered a nuisance. They could also plainly see that in spite of its faults, *Sesame Street* was entirely consonant with the prevailing spirit of America. Its use of cute puppets, celebrities, catchy tunes, and rapid-fire editing was certain to give pleasure to the children and would therefore serve as adequate preparation for their entry into a fun-loving culture.

As for educators, they generally approved of *Sesame Street*, too.   3
Contrary to common opinion, they are apt to find new methods congenial, especially if they are told that education can be accomplished more efficiently by means of the new techniques. (That is why such ideas as "teacher-proof" textbooks, standardized tests, and, now, micro-computers have been welcomed into the classroom.) *Sesame Street* appeared to be an imaginative aid in solving the growing problem of teaching Americans how to read, while, at the same time, encouraging children to love school.

We now know that *Sesame Street* encourages children to love school   4
only if school is like *Sesame Street*. Which is to say, we now know that *Sesame Street* undermines what the traditional idea of schooling represents. Whereas a classroom is a place of social interaction, the space in front of a television set is a private preserve. Whereas in a classroom, one may ask a teacher questions, one can ask nothing of a television screen. Whereas school is centered on the development of language, television demands attention to images. Whereas attending school is a legal requirement, watching television is an act of choice. Whereas in school, one fails to attend to the teacher at the risk of punishment, no penalties exist for failing to attend to the television screen. Whereas to behave oneself in school means to observe rules of public decorum, television watching requires no such observances, has no concept of public decorum. Whereas in a classroom, fun is never more than a means to an end, on television it is the end in itself.

Yet *Sesame Street* and its progeny, *The Electric Company*, are not to   5
be blamed for laughing the traditional classroom out of existence. If the classroom now begins to seem a stale and flat environment for learning, the inventors of television itself are to blame, not the Children's Television Workshop. We can hardly expect those who want to make good television shows to concern themselves with what the classroom is for. They are concerned with what television is for. This does not mean that *Sesame Street* is

not educational. It is, in fact, nothing but educational—in the sense that every television show is educational. Just as reading a book—any kind of book—promotes a particular orientation toward learning, watching a television show does the same. *The Little House on the Prairie, Cheers*, and *The Tonight Show* are as effective as *Sesame Street* in promoting what might be called the television style of learning. And this style of learning is, by its nature, hostile to what has been called book-learning or its handmaiden, school-learning. If we are to blame *Sesame Street* for anything, it is for the pretense that it is any ally of the classroom. That, after all, has been its chief claim on foundation and public money. As a television show, and a good one, *Sesame Street* does not encourage children to love school or anything about school. It encourages them to love television.

Moreover, it is important to add that whether or not *Sesame Street* teaches children their letters and numbers is entirely irrelevant. We may take as our guide here John Dewey's observation that the content of a lesson is the least important thing about learning. As he wrote in *Experience and Education*: "Perhaps the greatest of all pedagogical fallacies is the notion that a person learns only what he is studying at the time. Collateral learning in the way of formation of enduring attitudes . . . may be and often is more important than the spelling lesson or lesson in geography or history. . . . For these attitudes are fundamentally what count in the future."[1] In other words, the most important thing one learns is always something about *how* one learns. As Dewey wrote in another place, we learn what we do. Television educates by teaching children to do what television-viewing requires of them. And that is as precisely remote from what a classroom requires of them as reading a book is from watching a stage show.

Although one would not know it from consulting various recent proposals on how to mend the educational system, this point—that reading books and watching television differ entirely in what they imply about learning—is the primary educational issue in America today. America is, in fact, the leading case in point of what may be thought of as the third great crisis in Western education. The first occurred in the fifth century B.C., when Athens underwent a change from an oral culture to an alphabet-writing culture. To understand what this meant, we must read Plato. The second occurred in the sixteenth century, when Europe underwent a radical transformation as a result of the printing press. To understand what this meant, we must read John Locke. The third is happening now, in America, as a result of the electronic revolution, particularly the invention of television. To understand what this means, we must read Marshall McLuhan.

We face the rapid dissolution of the assumptions of an education organized around the slow-moving printed word, and the equally rapid emergence of a new education based on the speed-of-light electronic image. The classroom is, at the moment, still tied to the printed word, although that connection is rapidly weakening. Meanwhile, television forges ahead, making no concessions to its great technological predecessor, creating

new conceptions of knowledge and how it is acquired. One is entirely justified in saying that the major educational enterprise now being undertaken
in the United States is not happening in its classrooms but in the home, in
front of the television set, and under the jurisdiction not of school administrators and teachers but of network executives and entertainers. I don't
mean to imply that the situation is a result of a conspiracy or even that
those who control television want this responsibility. I mean only to say
that, like the alphabet or the printing press, television has by its power to
control the time, attention, and cognitive habits of our youth gained the
power to control their education.

This is why I think it accurate to call television a curriculum. As I   9
understand the word, a curriculum is a specially constructed information
system whose purpose is to influence, teach, train, or cultivate the mind
and character of youth. Television, of course, does exactly that, and does it
relentlessly. In so doing, it competes successfully with the school curriculum. By which I mean, it damn near obliterates it.

Having devoted an earlier book, *Teaching as a Conserving Activity*, to a   10
detailed examination of the antagonistic nature of the two curriculums—
television and school—I will not burden the reader or myself with a repetition of that analysis. But I would like to recall two points that I feel I did
not express forcefully enough in that book and that happen to be central
to this one. I refer, first, to the fact that television's principal contribution
to educational philosophy is the idea that teaching and entertainment are
inseparable. This entirely original conception is to be found nowhere in
educational discourses, from Confucius to Plato to Cicero to Locke to
John Dewey. In searching the literature of education, you will find it said
by some that children will learn best when they are interested in what they
are learning. You will find it said—Plato and Dewey emphasized this—that
reason is best cultivated when it is rooted in robust emotional ground. You
will even find some who say that learning is best facilitated by a loving
and benign teacher. But no one has ever said or implied that significant
learning is effectively, durably, and truthfully achieved when education
is entertainment. Education philosophers have assumed that becoming
acculturated is difficult because it necessarily involves the imposition of
restraints. They have argued that there must be a sequence to learning,
that perseverance and a certain measure of perspiration are indispensable,
that individual pleasures must frequently be submerged in the interests of
group cohesion, and that learning to be critical and to think conceptually
and rigorously do not come easily to the young but are hard-fought victories. Indeed, Cicero remarked that the purpose of education is to free the
student from the tyranny of the present, which cannot be pleasurable for
those, like the young, who are struggling hard to do the opposite—that is,
accommodate themselves to the present.

Television offers a delicious and, as I have said, original alternative to   11
all of this. We might say there are three commandments that form the philosophy of the education which television offers. The influence of these

commandments is observable in every type of television programming—from *Sesame Street* to the documentaries of *Nova* and *The National Geographic* to *Fantasy Island* to MTV. The commandments are as follows:

### Thou shalt have no prerequisites

Every television program must be a complete package in itself. No previous knowledge is to be required. There must not be even a hint that learning is hierarchical, that it is an edifice constructed on a foundation. The learner must be allowed to enter at any point without prejudice. This is why you shall never hear or see a television program begin with the caution that if the viewer has not seen the previous programs, this one will be meaningless. Television is a nongraded curriculum and excludes no viewer for any reason, at any time. In other words, in doing away with the idea of sequence and continuity in education, television undermines the idea that sequence and continuity have anything to do with thought itself.

### Thou shalt induce no perplexity

In television teaching, perplexity is a superhighway to low ratings. A perplexed learner is a learner who will turn to another station. This means that there must be nothing that has to be remembered, studied, applied, or, worst of all, endured. It is assumed that any information, story, or idea can be made immediately accessible, since the contentment, not the growth, of the learner is paramount.

### Thou shalt avoid exposition like the ten plagues visited upon Egypt

Of all the enemies of television-teaching, including continuity and perplexity, none is more formidable than exposition. Arguments, hypotheses, discussions, reasons, refutations, or any of the traditional instruments of reasoned discourse turn television into radio or, worse, third-rate printed matter. Thus, television-teaching always takes the form of story-telling, conducted through dynamic images and supported by music. This is as characteristic of *Star Trek* as it is of *Cosmos*, of *Diff'rent Strokes* as of *Sesame Street*, of commercials as of *Nova*. Nothing will be taught on television that cannot be both visualized and placed in a theatrical context.

The name we may properly give to an education without prerequisites, perplexity, and exposition is entertainment. And when one considers that save for sleeping there is no activity that occupies more of an American youth's time than television-viewing, we cannot avoid the conclusion that a massive reorientation toward learning is now taking place. Which leads to the second point I wish to emphasize: The consequences of this reorientation are to be observed not only in the decline of the potency of the classroom but, paradoxically, in the refashioning of the classroom into a place where both teaching and learning are intended to be vastly amusing activities.

[Elsewhere I have] referred to the experiment in Philadelphia in which the classroom is reconstituted as a rock concert. But this is only the silliest example of an attempt to define education as a mode of entertainment. Teachers, from primary grades through college, are increasing the visual stimulation of their lessons; are reducing the amount of exposition their students must cope with; are relying less on reading and writing assignments; and are reluctantly concluding that the principal means by which student interest may be engaged is entertainment. With no difficulty I could fill the remaining pages of this chapter with examples of teachers' efforts—in some instances, unconscious—to make their classrooms into second-rate television shows. But I will rest my case with *The Voyage of the Mimi*, which may be taken as a synthesis, if not an apotheosis, of the New Education. *The Voyage of the Mimi* is the name of an expensive science and mathematics project that has brought together some of the most prestigious institutions in the field of education—the United States Department of Education, the Bank Street College of Education, the Public Broadcasting System, and the publishing firm Holt, Rinehart and Winston. The project was made possible by a $3.65 million grant from the Department of Education, which is always on the alert to put its money where the future is. And the future is *The Voyage of the Mimi*. To describe the project succinctly, I quote from four paragraphs in *The New York Times* of August 7, 1984:

> Organized around a twenty-six-unit television series that depicts the adventures of a floating whale-research laboratory, [the project] combines television viewing with lavishly illustrated books and computer games that simulate the way scientists and navigators work. . . .
>
> *The Voyage of the Mimi* is built around fifteen-minute television programs that depict the adventures of four young people who accompany two scientists and a crusty sea captain on a voyage to monitor the behavior of humpback whales off the coast of Maine. The crew of the converted tuna trawler navigates the ship, tracks down the whales, and struggles to survive on an uninhabited island after a storm damages the ship's hull. . . .
>
> Each dramatic episode is men followed by a fifteen-minute documentary on related themes. One such documentary involved a visit by one of the teen-age actors to Ted Taylor, a nuclear physicist in Greenport, L.I., who has devised a way of purifying sea water by freezing it.
>
> The television programs, which teachers are free to record off the air and use at their convenience, are supplemented by a series of books and computer exercises that pick up four academic themes that emerge naturally from the story line: map and navigational skills, whales and their environment, ecological systems, and computer literacy.

The television programs have been broadcast over PBS; the books and computer software have been provided by Holt, Rinehart and Winston; the educational expertise by the faculty of the Bank Street College. Thus, *The Voyage of the Mimi* is not to be taken lightly. As Frank Withrow of the Department of Education remarked, "We consider it the flagship of what we are doing. It is a model that others will begin to follow." Everyone involved in the project is enthusiastic, and extraordinary claims of its benefits come trippingly from their tongues. Janice Trebbi Richards of Holt, Rinehart and Winston asserts, "Research shows that learning increases when information is presented in a dramatic setting, and television can do this better than any other medium." Officials of the Department of Education claim that the appeal of integrating three media—television, print, and computers—lies in their potential for cultivating higher-order thinking skills. And Mr. Withrow is quoted as saying that projects like *The Voyage of the Mimi* could mean great financial savings, that in the long run "it is cheaper than anything else we do." Mr. Withrow also suggested that there are many ways of financing such projects. "With *Sesame Street*," he said, "it took five or six years, but eventually you can start bringing in the money with T-shirts and cookie jars."

We may start thinking about what *The Voyage of the Mimi* signifies [18] by recalling that the idea is far from original. What is here referred to as "integrating three media" or a "multi-media presentation" was once called "audio-visual aids," used by teachers for years, usually for the modest purpose of enhancing student interest in the curriculum. Moreover, several years ago, the Office of Education (as the Department was then called) supplied funds to WNET for a similarly designed project called *Watch Your Mouth*, a series of television dramatizations in which young people inclined to misuse the English language fumbled their way through a variety of social problems. Linguists and educators prepared lessons for teachers to use in conjunction with each program. The dramatizations were compelling—although not nearly as good as *Welcome Back, Kotter*, which had the unassailable advantage of John Travolta's charisma—but there exists no evidence that students who were required to view *Watch Your Mouth* increased their competence in the use of the English language. Indeed, since there is no shortage of mangled English on everyday commercial television, one wondered at the time why the United States government would have paid anyone to go to the trouble of producing additional ineptitudes as a source of classroom study. A videotape of any of David Susskind's programs would provide an English teacher with enough linguistic aberrations to fill a semester's worth of analysis.

Nonetheless, the Department of Education has forged ahead, appar- [19] ently in the belief that ample evidence—to quote Ms. Richards again— "shows that learning increases when information is presented in a dramatic setting, and that television can do this better than any other medium." The most charitable response to this claim is that it is misleading. George Comstock and his associates have reviewed 2,800 studies on the general topic of television's influence on behavior, including cognitive processing, and are unable to point to persuasive evidence that "learning increases when information is presented in a dramatic setting."[2] Indeed, in studies conducted by Cohen and Salomon; Meringoff; Jacoby, Hoyer, and Sheluga; Stauffer, Frost, and Rybolt; Stern; Wilson; Neuman; Katz, Adoni, and Parness; and Gunter, quite the opposite conclusion is justified.[3] Jacoby et al.

found, for example, that only 3.5 percent of viewers were able to answer successfully twelve true/false questions concerning two thirty-second segments of commercial television programs and advertisements. Stauffer et al. found in studying students' responses to a news program transmitted via television, radio, and print, that print significantly increased correct responses to questions regarding the names of people and numbers contained in the material. Stern reported that 51 percent of viewers could not recall a single item of news a few minutes after viewing a news program on television. Wilson found that the average television viewer could retain only 20 percent of the information contained in a fictional televised news story. Katz et al. found that 21 percent of television viewers could not recall any news items within one hour of broadcast. On the basis of his and other studies, Salomon has concluded that "the meanings secured from television are more likely to be segmented, concrete, and less inferential, and those secured from reading have a higher likelihood of being better tied to one's stored knowledge and thus are more likely to be inferential."[4] In other words, so far as many reputable studies are concerned, television viewing does not significantly increase learning, is inferior to and less likely than print to cultivate higher-order, inferential thinking.

But one must not make too much of the rhetoric of grantsmanship. We *20* are all inclined to transform our hopes into tenuous claims when an important project is at stake. Besides, I have no doubt that Ms. Richards can direct us to several studies that lend support to her enthusiasm. The point is that if you want money for the redundant purpose of getting children to watch even more television than they already do—and dramatizations at that—you have to escalate the rhetoric to Herculean proportions.

What is of greatest significance about *The Voyage of the Mimi* is that *21* the content selected was obviously chosen because it is eminently *televisible*. Why are these students studying the behavior of humpback whales? How critical is it that the "academic themes" of navigational and map-reading skills be learned? Navigational skills have never been considered an "academic theme" and in fact seem singularly inappropriate for most students in big cities. Why has it been decided that "whales and their environment" is a subject of such compelling interest that an entire year's work should be given to it?

I would suggest that *The Voyage of the Mimi* was conceived by some- *22* one's asking the question, What is television good for?, not, What is education good for? Television is good for dramatizations, shipwrecks, seafaring adventures, crusty old sea captains, and physicists being interviewed by actor-celebrities. And that, of course, is what we have got in *The Voyage of the Mimi*. The fact that this adventure sit-com is accompanied by lavishly illustrated books and computer games only underscores that the television presentation controls the curriculum. The books whose pictures the students will scan and the computer games the students will play are dictated by the content of the television shows, not the other way around. Books, it would appear, have now become an audio-visual aid; the principal carrier of the content of education is the television show, and its principal claim for a preeminent place in the curriculum is that it is entertaining. Of course, a television production can be used to stimulate interest in lessons, or even as the focal point of a lesson. But what is happening here is that the content of the school curriculum is being determined by the character of television, and even worse, that character is apparently not included as part of what is studied. One would have thought that the school room is the proper place for students to inquire into the ways in which media of all kinds—including television—shape people's attitudes and perceptions. Since our students will have watched approximately sixteen thousand hours of television by high school's end, questions should have arisen, even in the minds of officials at the Department of Education, about who will teach our students how to look at television, and when not to, and with what critical equipment when they do. *The Voyage of the Mimi* project bypasses these questions; indeed, hopes that the students will immerse themselves in the dramatizations in the same frame of mind used when watching *St. Elsewhere* or *Hill Street Blues*. (One may also assume that what is called "computer literacy" does not involve raising questions about the cognitive biases and social effects of the computer, which, I would venture, are the most important questions to address about new technologies.)

    *The Voyage of the Mimi*, in other words, spent $3.65 million for the purpose of using media in exactly the manner that media merchants want them to be used—mindlessly and invisibly, as if media themselves have no epistemological or political agenda. And, in the end, what will the students have learned? They will, to be sure, have learned something about whales, perhaps about navigation and map reading, most of which they could have learned just as well by other means. Mainly, they will have learned that learning is a form of entertainment or, more precisely, that anything worth learning can take the form of an entertainment, and ought to. And they will not rebel if their English teacher asks them to learn the eight parts of speech through the medium of rock music. Or if their social studies teacher sings to them the facts about the War of 1812. Or if their physics comes to them on cookies and T-shirts. Indeed, they will expect it and thus will be well prepared to receive their politics, their religion, their news, and their commerce in the same delightful way.

NOTES

    1. J. Dewey, *Experience and Education*. The Kappa Delta Pi Lectures (London: Collier Books, 1963): 48.

    2. G. Comstock, S. Chaffee, N. Katzman, M. McCombs, and D. Roberts, *Television and Human Behavior* (New York: Columbia University Press, 1978).

    3. A. Cohen and G. Salomon, "Children's Literate Television Viewing: Surprises and Possible Explanations." *Journal of Communication* 29 (1979): 156–63; L. M. Meringoff, "What Pictures Can and Can't Do for Children's Story Comprehension," paper

presented at the annual meeting of the American Educational Research Association, April 1982; J. Jacoby, W. D. Hoyer, and D. A. Sheluga, *Miscomprehension of Televised Communications* (New York: The Educational Foundation of the American Association of Advertising Agencies, 1980); J. Stauffer, R. Frost, and W. Rybolt, "Recall and Learning from Broadcast News: Is Print Better?," *Journal of Broadcasting* (Summer 1981): 253–62; A. Stern, "A Study for the National Association for Broadcasting," in M. Barret (ed.). *The Politics of Broadcasting. 1971–1972* (New York: Thomas Y. Crowell, 1973); C. E. Wilson, "The Effect of a Medium on Loss of Information," *Journalism Quarterly* 51 (Spring 1974): 111–15; W. R. Neuman, "Patterns of Recall Among Television News Viewers," *Public Opinion Quarterly* 40 (1976): 118–25; E. Katz, H. Adoni, and P. Parness, "Remembering the News: What the Pictures Add to Recall," *Journalism Quarterly* 54 (1977): 233–42; B. Gunter, "Remembering Television News: Effects of Picture Content," *Journal of General Psychology* 102 (1980): 127–33.

4. G. Salomon, *Interaction of Media, Cognition, and Learning* (San Francisco: Jossey-Bass, 1979): 81.

■ ■ ■

## Reading as a Writer: Analyzing Rhetorical Choices

1. At the end of paragraph 7, Postman refers briefly to Marshall McLuhan, an influential media theorist, and in paragraph 8 describes some of McLuhan's theories. You will understand the ways Postman uses McLuhan's ideas as a springboard for his own arguments if you look up McLuhan's ideas to get a broader sense of his research. How do McLuhan's ideas provide a context for Postman's analysis of specific television examples?

2. Postman devotes many paragraphs to a close analysis of *The Voyage of the Mimi*. Citing specific details in his analysis of this show, explain how Postman uses this example to illustrate his larger argument. What do you conclude about strategies of using extended examples effectively?

## Writing as a Reader: Entering the Conversation of Ideas

1. Both Postman and bell hooks are interested in what Postman refers to as "collateral learning" (para. 6), a term coined by John Dewey that describes the cultural values and standards we learn while engaged in often entertaining pastimes. Choose a "test case" from popular culture (a film or an episode of a television show, for example) that you could usefully analyze through the lenses of these two writers' ideas. What do these writers help you bring into focus in your test case? What can we learn from analyzing popular culture this way?

2. Like Postman, Mark Edmundson is concerned about students' expectation that education be entertaining. Compose an essay in which you place these writers in conversation with each other, drawing on their ideas and examples in order to demonstrate the problem of and, perhaps, solutions to education-as-entertainment. Bring your own voice into the conversation as you consider whether, based on your personal experience, you agree that this is a problem, and why (or why not).

# Seeing and Making Culture: Representing the Poor

bell hooks is the pen name of Gloria Watkins, a cultural critic, scholar, and prolific writer. She has a wide range of intellectual interests, and her many books on race, gender, politics, and popular culture are taught frequently in both undergraduate and graduate courses. She is well known for her collaborations with prominent scholars such as Cornel West (quoted in this essay) on projects related to activism and spirituality. Recently, she coedited a collection of essays on the aftermath of Hurricane Katrina, *What Lies Beneath: Katrina, Race, and the State of the Nation* (2007). This selection, taken from *Outlaw Culture: Resisting Representations* (1994), focuses on images of poverty in popular culture and what they tell us about "our" assumptions about "the poor."

Despite bell hooks's publishing success, some scholars have criticized her for refusing to follow the "rules" of academic publishing. For example, although she quotes and engages with numerous scholars in her writing, she does not use footnotes in her work because she believes many readers find them off-putting, and she is interested in making her ideas accessible to readers who are not necessarily academics. As you read, you might pay attention to the many different strategies she uses as a writer to invite readers to think about some challenging ideas—what Americans really think about poverty. Where does she use personal experiences to illustrate her arguments? How does she introduce other scholars into the conversation of her essay? You might mark some of the challenging phrases in this piece, such as some of the quotations by Cornel West in paragraph 1 or anthropologist Carol Stack's ideas about the "ethic of liberal individualism" (para. 11); then work with your peers (and, if necessary, look up information) to make sure you understand these terms. By noticing how hooks moves between personal examples and scholarly references in her sentences, you can learn how to make these moves in your own writing.

hooks also cites specific popular culture representations of poverty in this essay, such as *Pretty Woman* and *Menace II Society*. While hooks's essay is as pertinent now as when she published it in 1994, we acknowledge that these references are now a bit dated. As you read this piece, think about more recent representations of poverty in television shows, films, or even news coverage (such as the coverage of Hurricane Katrina), and be ready to discuss the ways hooks's ideas help you make sense of those images and the stories that accompany them. What do the examples you come up with tell us about what we believe about poverty and those who are poor?

In this essay, hooks is interested both in illuminating what she considers to be problematic in attitudes toward poverty in the United States, and in proposing solutions. Pay close attention to her closing paragraphs and assess what you think about the solutions she suggests for developing less punishing attitudes toward poverty among people who are poor and those who are not. What values can poverty teach us all?

Cultural critics rarely talk about the poor. Most of us use words such    *1*
as "underclass" or "economically disenfranchised" when we speak about
being poor. Poverty has not become one of the new hot topics of radical
discourse. When contemporary Left intellectuals talk about capitalism, few
if any attempts are made to relate that discourse to the reality of being poor
in America. In his collection of essays *Prophetic Thought in Post-modern
Times,* black philosopher Cornel West includes a piece entitled "The Black
Underclass and Black Philosophers" wherein he suggests that black intellectuals within the "professional-managerial class in U.S. advanced capitalist
society" must "engage in a kind of critical self-inventory, a historical situ-
ating and positioning of ourselves as persons who reflect on the situation
of those more disadvantaged than us even though we may have relatives and
friends in the black underclass." West does not speak of poverty or being
poor in his essay. And I can remember once in conversation with him referring to my having come from a "poor" background; he corrected me and
stated that my family was "working class." I told him that technically we
*were* working class, because my father worked as a janitor at the post office,
however the fact that there were seven children in our family meant that
we often faced economic hardship in ways that made us children at least
think of-ourselves as poor. Indeed, in the segregated world of our small
Kentucky town, we were all raised to think in terms of the haves and the
have-nots, rather than in terms of class. We acknowledged the existence of
four groups: the poor, who were destitute; the working folks, who were
poor because they made just enough to make ends meet; those who worked
and had extra money; and the rich. Even though our family was among the
working folks, the economic struggle to make ends meet for such a large
family always gave us a sense that there was not enough money to take
care of the basics. In our house, water was a luxury and using too much
could be a cause for punishment. We never talked about being poor. As
children we knew we were not supposed to see ourselves as poor but we
felt poor.

I began to *see* myself as poor when I went away to college. I never had    *2*
any money. When I told my parents that I had scholarships and loans to
attend Stanford University, they wanted to know how I would pay for getting there, for buying books, for emergencies. We were not poor, but there
was no money for what was perceived to be an individualistic indulgent
desire; there were cheaper colleges closer to family. When I went to college and could not afford to come home during breaks, I frequently spent
my holidays with the black women who cleaned in the dormitories. Their
world was my world. They, more than other folks at Stanford, knew where
I was coming from. They supported and affirmed my efforts to be educated, to move past and beyond the world they lived in, the world I was
coming from.

To this day, even though I am a well-paid member of what West calls    *3*
the academic "professional-managerial class," in everyday life, outside
the classroom, I rarely think of myself in relation to class. I mainly think

about the world in terms of who has money to spend and who does not. Like many technically middle-class folks who are connected in economic responsibility to kinship structures where they provide varying material support for others, the issue is always one of money. Many middle-class black folks have no money because they regularly distribute their earnings among a larger kinship group where folks are poor and destitute, where elder parents and relatives who once were working class have retired and fallen into poverty.

Poverty was no disgrace in our household. We were socialized early on, by grandparents and parents, to assume that nobody's value could be measured by material standards. Value was connected to integrity, to being honest and hardworking. One could be hardworking and still be poor. My mother's mother Baba, who did not read or write, taught us—against the wishes of our parents—that it was better to be poor than to compromise one's dignity, that it was better to be poor than to allow another person to assert power over you in ways that were dehumanizing or cruel.

I went to college believing there was no connection between poverty and personal integrity. Entering a world of class privilege which compelled me to think critically about my economic background, I was shocked by representations of the poor learned in classrooms, as well as by the comments of professors and peers that painted an entirely different picture. They almost always portrayed the poor as shiftless, mindless, lazy, dishonest, and unworthy. Students in the dormitory were quick to assume that anything missing had been taken by the black and Filipina women who worked there. Although I went through many periods of shame about my economic background (even before I educated myself for critical consciousness about class by reading and studying Marx, Gramsci, Memmi, and the like), I contested stereotypical negative representations of poverty. I was especially disturbed by the assumption that the poor were without values. Indeed one crucial value that I had learned from Baba, my grandmother, and other family members was not to believe that "schooling made you smart." One could have degrees and still not be intelligent or honest. I had been taught in a culture of poverty to be intelligent, honest, to work hard, and always to be a person of my word. I had been taught to stand up for what I believed was right, to be brave and courageous. These lessons were the foundation that made it possible for me to succeed, to become the writer I always wanted to be, and to make a living in my job as an academic. They were taught to me by the poor, the disenfranchised, the underclass.

Those lessons were reinforced by liberatory religious traditions that affirmed identification with the poor. Taught to believe that poverty could be the breeding ground of moral integrity, of a recognition of the significance of communion, of sharing resources with others in the black church, I was prepared to embrace the teachings of liberatory theology, which emphasized solidarity with the poor. That solidarity was meant to be expressed not simply through charity, the sharing of privilege, but in the assertion of one's power to change the world so that the poor would have their needs met, would have access to resources, would have justice and beauty in their lives.

Contemporary popular culture in the United States rarely represents 7 the poor in ways that display integrity and dignity. Instead, the poor are portrayed through negative stereotypes. When they are lazy and dishonest, they are consumed with longing to be rich, a longing so intense that it renders them dysfunctional. Willing to commit all manner of dehumanizing and brutal acts in the name of material gain, the poor are portrayed as seeing themselves as always and only worthless. Worth is gained only by means of material success.

Television shows and films bring the message home that no one can 8 truly feel good about themselves if they are poor. In television sitcoms the working poor are shown to have a healthy measure of self-contempt; they dish it out to one another with a wit and humor that we can all enjoy, irrespective of our class. Yet it is clear that humor masks the longing to change their lot, the desire to "move on up" expressed in the theme song of the sitcom *The Jeffersons*. Films which portray the rags-to-riches tale continue to have major box-office appeal. Most contemporary films portraying black folks—*Harlem Nights, Boomerang, Menace II Society,* to name only a few—have as their primary theme the lust of the poor for material plenty and their willingness to do anything to satisfy that lust. *Pretty Woman* is a perfect example of a film that made huge sums of money portraying the poor in this light. Consumed and enjoyed by audiences of all races and classes, it highlights the drama of the benevolent, ruling-class person (in this case a white man, played by Richard Gere) willingly sharing his resources with a poor white prostitute (played by Julia Roberts). Indeed, many films and television shows portray the ruling class as generous, eager to share, as unattached to their wealth in their interactions with folks who are not materially privileged. These images contrast with the opportunistic avaricious longings of the poor.

Socialized by film and television to identify with the attitudes and val- 9 ues of privileged classes in this society, many people who are poor, or a few paychecks away from poverty, internalize fear and contempt for those who are poor. When materially deprived teenagers kill for tennis shoes or jackets they are not doing so just because they like these items so much. They also hope to escape the stigma of their class by appearing to have the trappings of more privileged classes. Poverty, in their minds and in our society as a whole, is seen as synonymous with depravity, lack, and worthlessness. No one wants to be identified as poor. Teaching literature by African American women writers at a major urban state university to predominantly black students from poor and working-class families, I was bombarded by their questioning as to why the poor black women who were abused in families in the novels we read did not "just leave." It was amazing to me that these students, many of whom were from materially disadvantaged backgrounds, had no realistic sense about the economics of housing or jobs in this society. When I asked that we identify our class backgrounds, only one student—a young single parent—was willing toidentify herself as poor. We talked later about the reality that although she was not the only poor person in the class, no one else wanted to identify with being poor for fear this stigma would mark them, shame them in ways that would go beyond our class. Fear of shame-based humiliation is a primary factor leading no one to want to identify themselves as poor. I talked with young black women receiving state aid, who have not worked in years, about the issue of representation. They all agree that they do not want to be identified as poor. In their apartments they have the material possessions that indicate success (a VCR, a color television), even if it means that they do without necessities and plunge into debt to buy these items. Their self-esteem is linked to not being seen as poor.

If to be poor in this society is everywhere represented in the language we  *10* use to talk about the poor, in the mass media, as synonymous with being nothing, then it is understandable that the poor learn to be nihilistic. Society is telling them that poverty and nihilism are one and the same. If they cannot escape poverty, then they have no choice but to drown in the image of a life that is valueless. When intellectuals, journalists, or politicians speak about nihilism and the despair of the underclass, they do not link those states to representations of poverty in the mass media. And rarely do they suggest by their rhetoric that one can lead a meaningful, contented, and fulfilled life if one *is* poor. No one talks about our individual and collective accountability to the poor, a responsibility that begins with the politics of representation.

When white female anthropologist Carol Stack looked critically at the  *11* lives of black poor people more than twenty years ago and wrote her book *The Culture of Poverty,* she found a value system among them which emphasized the sharing of resources. That value system has long been eroded in most communities by an ethic of liberal individualism, which affirms that it is morally acceptable not to share. The mass media has been the primary teacher bringing into our lives and our homes the logic of liberal individualism, the idea that you make it by the privatized hoarding of resources, not by sharing them. Of course, liberal individualism works best for the privileged classes. But it has worsened the lot of the poor who once depended on an ethic of communalism to provide affirmation, aid, and support.

To change the devastating impact of poverty on the lives of masses of  *12* folks in our society we must change the way resources and wealth are distributed. But we must also change the way the poor are represented. Since many folks will be poor for a long time before those changes are put in place that address their economic needs, it is crucial to construct habits of seeing and being that restore an oppositional value system affirming that one can live a life of dignity and integrity in the midst of poverty. It is precisely this dignity Jonathan Freedman seeks to convey in his book *From Cradle to Grave: The Human Face of Poverty in America,* even though he does not critique capitalism or call for major changes in the distribution of wealth and resources. Yet any efforts to change the face of poverty in the United States must link a shift in representation to a demand for the redistribution of wealth and resources.

Progressive intellectuals from privileged classes who are themselves    *13*
obsessed with gaining material wealth are uncomfortable with the insistence that one can be poor, yet lead a rich and meaningful life. They fear
that any suggestion that poverty is acceptable may lead those who have to
feel no accountability towards those who have not, even though it is unclear
how they reconcile their pursuit with concern for and accountability towards the poor. Their conservative counterparts, who did much to put in
place a system of representation that dehumanized the poor, fear that if
poverty is seen as having no relation to value, the poor will not passively
assume their role as exploited workers. That fear is masked by their insistence that the poor will not seek to work if poverty is deemed acceptable,
and that the rest of us will have to support them. (Note the embedded
assumption that to be poor means that one is not hardworking.) Of course,
there are many more poor women and men refusing menial labor in low-
paid jobs than ever before. This refusal is not rooted in laziness but in the
assumption that it is not worth it to work a job where one is systematically
dehumanized or exploited only to remain poor. Despite these individuals,
the vast majority of poor people in our society want to work, even when
jobs do not mean that they leave the ranks of the poor.

Witnessing that individuals can be poor and lead meaningful lives, I    *14*
understand intimately the damage that has been done to the poor by a dehumanizing system of representation. I see the difference in self-esteem between my grandparents' and parents' generations and that of my siblings,
relatives, friends, and acquaintances who are poor, who suffer from a deep-
seated, crippling lack of self-esteem. Ironically, despite the presence of more
opportunity than that available to an older generation, low self-esteem
makes it impossible for this younger generation to move forward even as
it also makes their lives psychically unbearable. That psychic pain is most
often relieved by some form of substance abuse. But to change the face of
poverty so that it becomes, once again, a site for the formation of values, of
dignity and integrity, as any other class positionality in this society, we would
need to intervene in existing systems of representation.

Linking this progressive change to radical/revolutionary political    *15*
movements (such as eco-feminism, for example) that urge all of us to live
simply could also establish a point of connection and constructive interaction. The poor have many resources and skills for living. Those folks who
are interested in sharing individual plenty as well as working politically
for redistribution of wealth can work in conjunction with individuals who
are materially disadvantaged to achieve this end. Material plenty is only one
resource. Literacy skills are another. It would be exciting to see unemployed folks who lack reading and writing skills have available to them
community-based literacy programs. Progressive literacy programs connected to education for critical consciousness could use popular movies as
a base to begin learning and discussion. Theaters all across the United
States that are not used in the day could be sites for this kind of program
where college students and professors could share skills. Since many individuals who are poor, disadvantaged, or destitute are *already* literate, read-

ing groups could be formed to educate for critical consciousness, to help folks rethink how they can organize life both to live well in poverty and to move out of such circumstances. Many of the young women I encounter—black and white—who are poor and receiving state aid (and some of whom are students or would-be students) are intelligent, critical thinkers struggling to transform their circumstances. They are eager to work with folks who can offer guidance, know-how, concrete strategies. Freedman concludes his book with the reminder that

> it takes money, organization, and laws to maintain a social structure but none of it works if there are not opportunities for people to meet and help each other along the way. Social responsibility comes down to something simple—the ability to respond.

Constructively changing ways the poor are represented in every aspect of life is one progressive intervention that can challenge everyone to look at the face of poverty and not turn away.

■ ■ ■

## Reading as a Writer: Analyzing Rhetorical Choices

1. bell hooks includes personal anecdotes in this selection. Use a pen or highlighter to mark all the places where she makes use of personal experiences, and discuss with your classmates the relationship you see between these personal experiences and the larger point she is making about perceptions of poverty in the United States. What do you notice about the structure of this essay? What conclusions can you draw about effective strategies for using personal experiences in scholarly writing?

2. In paragraphs 6, 7, and 8, hooks lays out various cultural attitudes about the relationship between poverty and personal integrity. What do you notice about the order of the ideas in these paragraphs and about the examples she offers? Discuss the way she structures her argument here, and consider how some more recent examples from popular culture would fit with the claims she makes in this section. How do these ideas relate to the solutions she proposes in her final paragraphs?

## Writing as a Reader: Entering the Conversation of Ideas

1. Both hooks and Carmen D. Siering are concerned with the ways popular culture often reinforces stereotypes, whether those stereotypes are about poverty or about gender roles. Using specific examples from current popular culture (books, television, movies, and so on), write an essay in which you draw on insights from both authors in order to analyze the way your examples reinforce common stereotypes, counteract them, or (as is often the case) do both. What do you conclude?

2. hooks, like Jonathan Kozol, is committed to understanding the many subtle ways we learn who "counts" in our society and who doesn't. Both writers draw on examples of school dynamics that teach students far more

than what is in their textbooks. Compose an essay that places these authors in conversation about the ways school settings can teach students, perhaps inadvertently, about who "counts," by analyzing some specific school examples in each text. What connections do you see, and what can you conclude? If you like, describe and analyze some specific examples from your own classroom or campus experiences to help establish your point.

## CARMEN D. SIERING

# Taking a Bite out of *Twilight*

Carmen D. Siering is an assistant professor of English and women's studies at Ball State University. She won a Distinguished Dissertation award for her doctoral thesis, "Rhetorical Vision: Resistance, Fantasy, and the Work of Texts in Creating and Sustaining Subculture." Among her research interests are the ways girls and women consume popular culture, so it is not surprising that Siering finds compelling material to work with in Stephenie Meyer's blockbuster *Twilight* series. She examines possible reasons why both teenage girls and their mothers ("Twi-Moms") are "swooning" over this book and film series, and she contextualizes these fantasy stories in the very real contemporary debates about sex education, feminism, and what we believe about equality in romantic relationships.

Debates about the reasons for Stephenie Meyer's success are raging through blogs about publication trends, book groups, feminism, and teen culture. Some critics simply dismiss the series, but the incredible sales success of the books and films means that when Siering "takes a bite out of *Twilight*," as her title claims, she is also taking a stance against millions of fans who are devoted to Meyer's romantic story. As you read Siering's critique of this series, then, watch carefully for places where she anticipates readers who might disagree with her, and evaluate how effectively she disarms the opposition. Where does she offer multiple perspectives on an aspect of the series? How does she contrast the books and the films, and how does this contrast allow her to develop her ideas?

This article was published in 2009 in *Ms.*, a feminist magazine founded in 1971, at the peak of the modern women's movement. According to the *Ms.* Web site, "*Ms.* was the first national magazine to make feminist voices audible, feminist journalism tenable, and a feminist worldview available to the public" (www.msmagazine.com/about.asp). You might find it interesting to browse the *Ms.* Web site. What have you heard about feminism? What strikes you about the stories highlighted on the *Ms.* Web site? Siering's opening anecdote is a useful introduction to feminist analysis: Why do fans most often divide into Team Edward or Team Jacob? Siering asks us, "Why not Team Bella?" The answer to that question goes far beyond Meyer's series, which is Siering's point.

In Stephenie Meyer's *Twilight* saga, a wildly popular four-book series
of young adult novels, the protagonist, Bella Swan—by all accounts a
very average human girl—has two suitors. They are hardly average themselves—one is the unimaginably beautiful vampire Edward, the other a
loyal and devoted werewolf, Jacob. Fans of the books, and now a movie
version, often break into "teams," aligning themselves with the swain they
hope Bella will choose in the end: Team Edward or Team Jacob.

But few young readers ask, "Why not Team Bella?" perhaps because
the answer is quite clear: There can be no Team Bella. Even though Bella
is ostensibly a hero, in truth she is merely an object in the *Twilight* world.
Bella is a prize, not a person, someone to whom things happen, not an active participant in the unfolding story.

On the surface, the *Twilight* saga seems to have something to please
everyone. Moms are reading the books and swooning over Edward right
alongside their teen and tween daughters. Librarians and teachers are
delighted to see students with their heads tucked into books, and since
*Twilight's* romantic sensuality is wrapped up in an abstinence message, all
the kissing and groping appear to be harmless. Of course booksellers and
movie exhibitors are happy: In 2008, the novels sold more than 22 million copies worldwide, and the first in a series of films based on the novels
grossed more than $35 million on opening day. But feminists might not be
quite as happy after critically analyzing how *Twilight* deals with a young
woman and her place in the world.

While *Twilight* is presented as a love story, scratch the surface and you
will find an allegorical tale about the dangers of unregulated female sexuality. While Edward's first scent of Bella nearly sends him into a homicidal
frenzy, he is ultimately shown to be capable of controlling his bloodlust
as well as the more human, sexual kind. Bella, on the other hand, is never
able to do the same. From their very first kiss, she is fighting to control her
awakening sexuality. Edward must restrain her, sometimes physically, to
keep her from ravishing him, and he frequently chastises her when she
becomes, in his opinion, too passionate.

The message of abstinence presented in the books is overt, with Edward
as the keeper of the couple's purity. There are those who might applaud the
depiction of a young man showing such self-restraint, but shouldn't the
decision about when a couple is ready to move forward sexually be one
they make together? Of course there are extenuating circumstances when
one person in the relationship happens to be a vampire afraid of commit-
ting homicide in the midst of passion, but in *Twilight* it is typically Edward
who is allowed to initiate intimacy or break things up when he feels they
are getting out of hand. Bella is frequently reprimanded for physically
desiring the man she loves. The overriding message is that young women
are incapable of understanding or controlling their own sexuality; it takes
a man to keep them in check.

Bella is also depicted as being in need of someone to take charge, someone to take care of her. We see that Bella needs protection as she stumbles

through the world, literally damaging herself due to her clumsiness and bad luck, or figuratively falling into danger due to her naiveté. In fact, Bella can hardly get through a chapter without Edward jumping in to save her in some way. It seems that in Meyer's view, the world is too dangerous for Bella to navigate on her own; she needs a man—in fact a *supernatural* man—to protect her.

Edward isn't just protective, though, but often *over*-protective of Bella,    7 and in this way their relationship should serve as a cautionary tale for young women. Edward is jealous of Bella's relationships with other boys, going so far as to disable her car to keep her at home. He is condescending, assuming that he knows what is best for her in every situation. And there are many situations in which Bella is infantilized, including when Edward writes her a lullaby—a piece of music typically associated with infants and children, not someone you consider your equal, sexually or otherwise.

Maybe it's difficult for Edward to see Bella as an equal because Bella    8 has almost no personality. Meyer writes on her website that she "left out a detailed description of Bella in the book so that the reader could more easily step into her shoes." But Meyer fails to give Bella much of an interior life as well; Bella is a blank slate, with few thoughts or actions that don't center on Edward. Outside of him and occasional outings with werewolf Jacob, Bella doesn't do anything more than go to school, cook and clean for her dad, write to her mother, read and romanticize over Victorian literature, and find fault with her clothing. She has no other interests, no goals, few friends: Bella does nothing that suggests she is a person in her own right. If Meyer hopes that readers see themselves as Bella, what is it she is suggesting to them about the significance of their own lives?

Some fans may argue that Bella is a strong character and that she    9 makes her own decisions, but the few decisions she does make are usually shown to be bad ones, and they nearly always lead to someone (generally Edward) having to save her. Even the decision to keep her baby in *Breaking Dawn*, the final book in the series, nearly proves fatal. Bella comes to the brink of death in childbirth and Edward saves her once again—this time by turning her into a vampire.

Meyer insists on her website that Bella is not an unfeminist character,   10 since "the foundation of feminism . . . is being able to choose." She writes, "When I hear or read theories about Bella being an anti-feminist character, those theories are usually predicated by her choices. In the beginning, she chooses romantic love over everything else. Eventually, she chooses to marry at an early age and then chooses to keep an unexpected and dangerous baby." What Meyer fails to acknowledge is that all of the choices Bella makes are *Meyer's* choices—choices perhaps based on her own background as a member of the highly patriarchal Morman church.

In *Breaking Dawn*, Meyer finally allows Bella's subordination to end   11 as she takes her proper place: in the patriarchal structure. When Bella becomes a wife and mother, Meyer allows her to receive her heart's desire—to live forever by Edward's side, to be preternaturally beautiful and graceful, to be strong and be able to defend herself. Being a wife and mother is the choice Meyer has made for herself, for Bella, and, by extension, for her readers as well. It is she, after all, who wrote that she hoped readers could step into Bella's shoes.

The *Twilight* saga has become something of a bonding phenomenon [12] among mothers and daughters. But reading the books together and mutually swooning over Edward isn't enough. As influential adults, mothers (and teachers and librarians) have an obligation to start a conversation concerning the darker themes and anti-feminist rhetoric in these tales. There is plenty to work with, from the dangers of losing yourself in an obsessive relationship to the realities of owning one's sexuality.

Director Catherine Hardwicke's film version of *Twilight* remains true to [13] the novel, but there are subtle changes that make it much more feminist-friendly. Kristen Stewart's Bella is more outspoken and forthright, and Robert Pattinson's Edward is much less condescending and overbearing. Their relationship seems to be built on equality and friendship, and includes scenes of *mutual* sexual frustration and restraint. Here is a Bella we can root for, a Bella who stands just a little bit more on her own and is a part of the action. It will be interesting to see if the next film in the *Twilight* series, to be directed by a man this time, Chris Weitz, will take a similar path. Or, once again, will Bella be left without a team of her own?

■ ■ ■

## Reading as a Writer: Analyzing Rhetorical Choices

1. In this piece, Siering is aware that she is arguing against prevailing public opinion about these best-selling books. Locate places in her essay where she seems to anticipate readers who disagree with her, and assess how successful you think she is at responding. How does her analysis of the film adaptations affect her critique of *Twilight* and its fans?

2. Siering does not rely on jargon to make her point; however, because her article appears in the feminist magazine *Ms.*, she does not define some of her terms. Look up definitions of *feminism* and *abstinence-only education*, and discuss what you find. How does this additional information add to your understanding of Siering's argument?

## Writing as a Reader: Entering the Conversation of Ideas

1. The supernatural aspect of the *Twilight* series could open up possibilities for nontraditional (or nonstereotypical) gender dynamics, but Siering sees little of this. In her analysis of female superheroes, Julie D. O'Reilly similarly discovers that real-world gender stereotypes often remain in place even in fantasy fiction. Choose as a "test case" an example of a supernatural or fantasy text (a book, a movie, or an episode of a television show) to analyze through the insights of Siering and O'Reilly. Explain the significance of your findings.

2. Many of the advertisements Jean Kilbourne analyzes in her essay are aimed at the *Twilight* demographic. Write an essay in which you apply

Kilbourne's analysis of the ways advertising "sells" an image of women as vulnerable and insecure to Siering's representation of gender dynamics in the *Twilight* series. How might Kilbourne's ideas about sexualized violence in the media also apply to *Twilight*? Feel free to draw on additional examples from the *Twilight* books or movies as you build your point.

## JULIE D. O'REILLY

# The Wonder Woman Precedent: Female (Super)Heroism on Trial

Julie D. O'Reilly is professor of communication and women's and gender studies at Heidelberg University in Ohio. Her research focuses on gender issues in popular culture, and in particular the depiction of strong female characters in novels and on television, such as Buffy the Vampire Slayer and the comic heroines she examines in this article. This essay appeared in 2005 in *The Journal of American Culture*, a scholarly journal whose premise is that we can learn a lot by taking even "light" aspects of popular culture seriously. Thus, this article opens with an exchange between characters on the animated series *Powerpuff Girls* and then rockets back in time to the origins of Wonder Woman as a female superhero who has paved a bumpy road, O'Reilly argues, for other female characters to follow.

As you read, keep track of O'Reilly's key argument about the distinctions between the ways male and female superheroes are "put to the test" in their respective narratives, and consider how each new example she includes helps develop her overall point. Where do you see O'Reilly moving between her detailed analysis of specific shows, and "signposting" statements about her larger argument? Which examples do you find most compelling, and why? As a class, try to come up with "test cases" of other female superheroes, and then examine the extent to which O'Reilly's argument applies to those characters, too.

In her final three paragraphs, O'Reilly shifts from her close reading of examples to answer the larger question readers might have about scholarly analysis of popular culture: "So what?" In other words, skeptics may well wonder why academics are spending time analyzing comic book characters or television shows. How effectively does O'Reilly address the "So what?" question here? What do these "light" forms of entertainment tell us about our attitudes toward women and power, and what might be the implications be for our larger culture? O'Reilly is part of a much larger scholarly conversation about the importance of taking forms of entertainment seriously as a means of understanding contemporary culture. She reminds us that while in these stories it is superheroes who are "on trial," our own assumptions are on trial as well.

# Introduction

> FEMME FATALE: Surely you've noticed. Female superheroes aren't nearly as revered as male superheroes.
>
> BUBBLES: Sure they are. There's Supergirl. Batgirl.
>
> FEMME FATALE: Shhh. They're so lame. Merely extensions of their male counterparts. Who besides you is a heroine in her own right?
>
> BLOSSOM: Huh! There's Wonder Woman and . . . eh . . . um . . . um . . . Wonder Woman . . .
>
> BUTTERCUP: She's right! There is no one else.

The above exchange was included in a 2002 episode titled "Equal Fights" of the animated series *Powerpuff Girls* (1998–), which follows the adventures of three diminutive superheroes. In this episode, the Girls—Bubbles, Blossom, and Buttercup—encounter Femme Fatale, a criminal who carries a ♀-shaped gun and demands that the teller of the bank she is robbing fill the loot sack with only Susan B. Anthony coins. When the Powerpuff Girls capture Femme Fatale, this villain, in an attempt to evade punishment for her crimes, appeals to the Girls in the name of female solidarity: "Sending me to jail would be a blow for all of womankind . . . including you" ("Equal Fights"). Femme Fatale's ploy works, for a time; the Girls become angry with all men, from the mayor they have willingly assisted in the past to a male classmate who accidentally knocks down a female playmate during a game of catch. By the episode's end, though, the Girls have realized that Femme Fatale must pay for her crimes because, as Susan B. Anthony taught by example, equal rights for all do not include special privileges for some.

Unfortunately, not all representations of superheroes promote the same equal-opportunity perspective on heroism. While most hero stories include a series of trials designed to prove the hero's worthiness (Bongco 94), many female superheroes have the privilege of demonstrating their abilities or defending their roles as heroes in a manner not afforded their male counterparts. And Wonder Woman, the "heroine in her own right" named by Blossom, set the precedent.

Although Wonder Woman, who debuted in *All-Star Comics* in 1941, challenged previous notions regarding the subordination of female superheroes to men (Inness 144), she was still not equal to her male counterparts. In Wonder Woman's first comic book story line, the Amazon princess Diana must compete in and win a series of physical challenges that culminate in a frightening and potentially deadly game of "bullets and bracelets" (i.e., deflecting gunshots with her wristbands) to prove to the Amazon Queen—her mother—that she is a "Wonder Woman" worthy to venture into man's world to "fight for liberty and freedom and all womankind" ("Introducing" 15). In contrast, in the first Superman comic book story line published three years earlier, Clark Kent decides to don a cape and enforce justice—a decision that is neither questioned nor challenged. He becomes a hero simply because he chooses to be: "Early, Clark decided he must turn his titanic strength into channels that would benefit mankind. And so was created . . . Superman!" ("Superman" 11).

Thus, Wonder Woman's legacy is one of deference, or at the least, limited agency; Superman's is one of assumed autonomy. Because of these respective positions of submission or dominance, the resolution of heroic trials, in their various forms, differs significantly based on the gender of the hero. Female superheroes on trial must prove their merit to a sanctioning institution, while male superheroes on trial affect the outcome on their own behalf.

The use of the narrative device of the "hero on trial" extends beyond the superhero comic book genre to portrayals of such superpowered characters on television. Like Wonder Woman, the sister witches of *Charmed* (1998–) and the title character of *Buffy the Vampire Slayer* (1997–2003) face examination to justify possession of their conferred powers. Unlike Wonder Woman, the teenage Clark Kent of *Smallville* (2001–) and Jake Foley of *Jake 2.0* (2003) defy those who presume authority over their powers.

## Wonder Woman: Trial by Gunfire

As noted above, Wonder Woman, who was known to her Amazon sisters as Diana, is given her superhero status by her mother, Queen Hippolyte, after Diana triumphs over her fellow Amazons in a series of physical contests that concludes with her surviving gunshots from point-blank range. While Diana does rebel against her mother by entering the contests—her mother has forbidden her participation, thus Diana competes masked— she does not become Wonder Woman until her mother bestows that moniker upon her. Upon Diana's victory, Hippolyte announces, "You've won and I'm proud of you! In America you'll indeed be a 'Wonder Woman,' for I have taught you well!" ("Introducing" 16). Thus Wonder Woman was born and achieved rapid popularity (Inness 144), much to the delight of child fans such as Juanita Coulson, author of "Of (Super)Human Bondage": "While America was riding a historical roller coaster toward Pearl Harbor, to my delight a costumed marvel appeared just for us girls. (Or so I naively thought at the time.)" (229). The "costumed marvel" about which Coulson writes may have seemed, at the time of Wonder Woman's debut, to be just for girls, but Wonder Woman actually was created by a man—William Moulton Marston—possibly for men.

Marston, a Harvard-educated psychologist who wrote the comic book's issues under the name Charles Moulton until his death in 1947, has been hailed by some as a women's liberation pioneer (O'Neil 51); Marston once wrote that "without doubt, the female sex is assuming day by day a more dominant role in world affairs" (qtd. in O'Neil 51). In fact, Marston even predicted to the *New York Times* in 1937 that the coming century would bring the genesis of an American matriarchy in which women would gain political and economic control (Behrens 7).

Despite Marston's feminist-leaning rhetoric, some critics do not view his  8
creation of Wonder Woman as a step toward women's liberation. Marston's
creation of Wonder Woman as both a strong and alluring woman has led
numerous scholars to consider the feminist implications of the comic
books (Smith 129). For example, Richard Reynolds suggests in *Super
Heroes: A Modern Mythology* that Moulton designed Wonder Woman's physical appearance and costume to appeal to men's sexual domination fantasies (34). Likewise, Bradford W. Wright explains in *Comic Book Nation: The
Transformation of Youth Culture in America,* "The [Wonder Woman] stories
were rife with suggestive sadomasochistic images like bondage, masters
and slaves, and men groveling at the feet of women" (21). Just as comic
book scholars have been hesitant to proclaim Wonder Woman as a feminist icon, so too was Marston's wife reluctant to align her husband with
feminism; when speaking of her late husband's creation, she noted, "He
wouldn't have called it 'feminism.' He just would have called it a personal
expression of the female character" (qtd. in O'Neil 51).

Marston's "personal expression of the female character" included a  9
woman facing a potentially deadly physical challenge—a trial by gunfire—
and has continued through the retelling of Wonder Woman's origin. In a
relaunch of the *Wonder Woman* comic book in 1987, Princess Diana still
must face gunfire, although the test is no longer called "bullets and bracelets," but "fac[ing] the flashing thunder" ("The Princess" 30). Central to
Wonder Woman's legend, then, is the questioning of her status as a hero
because she is subject to the approval or disapproval of her Amazon mother
and sisters. As Phyllis Chesler notes in her interpretive essay "The Amazon
Legacy," Amazons are reared to be subservient to female authority.

This theme of the Amazons' sanctioning (or disallowing) Wonder  10
Woman's position as their ambassador to a man's world carries through
to her television representations as well. The contest to determine Wonder
Woman's worthiness was incorporated into the 1975 live-action telefilm
*The New Original Wonder Woman,* which served as the pilot of her epony-
mous television series (1976–1979). More recently, a 2002 episode of the
animated series *Justice League* (2001–) also featured Wonder Woman facing judgment by the Amazons. However, in this more recent depiction of
the character, the trial is not a physical one; there are no bracelets required.
Instead, this trial is a formal proceeding to determine if Diana has upheld
Amazon law and proved herself worthy as the Amazons' representative.

In the two-part episode titled "Paradise Lost," Wonder Woman returns  11
to her island home feeling guilty that she last left without her mother's
approval. Upon her arrival, she finds that her mother and her Amazon sisters have been turned to stone by the evil Faust, a henchman of Hades. To
save her mother's and sisters' lives, Diana must, of course, strike a Faust-
ian bargain; if she recovers the artifacts that serve as the key to the underworld, her loved ones will survive, but the gates of hell will be opened.
Because she cannot battle Hades alone, Wonder Woman accepts the help
of fellow Justice League members Superman, the Flash, and the Martian

Manhunter. The superhero quartet indeed saves the day, both defeating Hades and saving the Amazons, and Queen Hippolyte is appropriately grateful to the male members of the League, noting that they "are all truly heroes" ("Paradise Lost. Pt. 2"). For Diana, however, Hippolyte has these words: "As your mother, I am overjoyed that you have finally returned to us. But as your Queen, I am obliged to uphold the laws . . . and, in bringing these outsiders to our island, you have broken our most sacred law [that men shall never set foot on the island]. . . . It is with a heavy heart that I must exile you" ("Paradise Lost. Pt. 2"). Despite the protests of Superman and the Flash, Wonder Woman dutifully accepts her mother's judgment.

As these examples demonstrate, the multiple variations of Wonder   12
Woman, from her comic book debut to a contemporary television appearance, all contain a challenging of her agency and her resulting deference to authority despite her superhuman abilities. With Wonder Woman as the prototype for female superheroes, Marston's legacy does not seem to be a clear depiction of women's empowerment, or the potential thereof, but instead of their submission to and acceptance of a series of trials put forth by those who would sanction their position as heroes. That those who govern Wonder Woman's power and put her on trial are other women only underscores the notion that female superheroes operate according to a different code of heroism than their male counterparts, a code with built-in limitations.

## The Charmed Ones: Trial by Demon for Hire

For Piper, Phoebe, and Paige, the sister witches of *Charmed*, one such limi-   13
tation of heroism is invisibility. While the sisters themselves are not invisible, their magical abilities and any effects are to remain unseen; their mission as "the Charmed Ones" to protect innocents must be fulfilled with minimal magical evidence, in accordance with the law agreed upon by the guardians of both good (the Elders) and evil (demon leaders). Although the sisters have a long history of "cleaning up" their own "magical messes" when such exposure occurs, the "Cleaners" intervene when, in a sixth-season episode promoted as "Charmed on Trial" by the Warner Brothers network, the sisters' vanquishing of a demon is caught on tape by a police officer.

The Cleaners are two white-suited gentlemen who were created by and   14
operate under the auspices of the "Tribunal," a council made up of both Elders and demons to ensure magic's secrecy "at whatever cost" ("Crimes and Witch-Demeanors"). The potential cost in this case is Darryl Morris, the sisters' police-inspector friend and confidant who assisted them in the vanquishing. The Cleaners have changed past events to make it appear that Darryl shot a helpless victim instead of the demon-possessed man he was forced to kill in self-defense. To save Darryl from execution for this

alleged crime, the Charmed Ones must convince the Tribunal to reverse the Cleaners' actions.

When the sisters' trial before the Tribunal begins, they learn that the opposing counsel is Barbas, the Demon of Fear, whom they previously defeated and sent to a hell dimension. Barbas has made a deal with the Tribunal; if the Charmed Ones are found guilty, he will be reprieved. Although the sisters protest Barbas's presence because he has made multiple attempts on their lives, he counters that his past is not in question. Instead, he explains, "What is in question here is these three witches' so-called right to be continually cleaning up after their own magical asses" ("Crimes and Witch-Demeanors"). Through the course of the trial, as Barbas replays the sisters' magical mistakes via holographic images, he convinces the members of the Tribunal that in addition to considering a reversal of the Cleaners' actions, they should decide the "fate of the Charmed Ones and if they should be allowed to practice magic again."

Although the Charmed Ones believe that Barbas orchestrated the magical exposure in question, they are not able to prove it before the Tribunal passes judgment. The Tribunal declares that the sisters may continue to practice magic, but that Darryl must die because "the trail of exposure must end with him." Paige responds in outrage, "If this is the thanks that we get for all of our good work . . . if this is the way the system works, then you can keep our stupid powers" ("Crimes and Witch-Demeanors"). Before the Tribunal can respond to Paige's words or Piper's announcement that they "quit," Leo (an Elder) and Chris (the sisters' Whitelighter, a guardian angel) arrive with evidence of Barbas's treachery. The Tribunal then reverses the actions of the Cleaners—Darryl is saved—but the Tribunal has further words for the Charmed Ones. Because Barbas noted that Phoebe has been using her powers for "personal gain" (employing her power of premonition to determine if she has a future with potential romantic partners), the Tribunal strips Phoebe of her active powers, noting that she can "earn them back" if she and her sisters are more careful with their abilities. While Paige and Piper protest this pronouncement, Phoebe acquiesces, telling her sisters, "It's okay. I mean, it might be kind of refreshing to not rely on my powers so much anymore, you know? Besides, they're not the only ones who think I have been misusing them."

Phoebe's repentant attitude toward the Tribunal's final judgment contrasts with the anger she expressed during the proceedings. She had noted, "if all the good we've done in the last six years isn't good enough, then nothing is." Apparently, for the Charmed Ones, their multiple years of heroism are not "good enough" to allow them to make decisions about when it is appropriate to use their powers or which actions are appropriate when such powers are observed by others. The Charmed Ones, then, like Wonder Woman, accept this restricting of their agency with little (or in Phoebe's case, almost no) protest; they are still heroes, but it is a heroism delineated by others—in this case, the four members of the Tribunal, two of whom are evil, and Barbas, who is decidedly evil. Once again, the identity of female superheroes' accusers reinforces the idea that heroism for women has its limitations.

## Buffy Summers: Trial by Vampire

Just as Princess Diana is chosen from among the Amazons and Piper,   18
Phoebe, and Paige are designated "the Charmed Ones," so too is Buffy Summers the "Chosen One." Viewers learn in the first episode of the series that "[i]nto each generation, a Slayer is born. One girl, in all the world. One born with the . . . strength and skill to hunt the vampires, to stop the spread of evil" (qtd. in Golden and Holder 2). Unfortunately for Buffy, along with her Slayer strength and skill comes oversight by the Watchers Council. This Council, similar in power to Wonder Woman's Amazon sisters or the Tribunal faced by the Charmed Ones, officially sanctions the Slayer's powers and provides her with a mentor called a Watcher. The institutional power of the Watchers Council becomes apparent in the third season of *Buffy*, when the Council subjects the title character to a potentially fatal test on her eighteenth birthday.

This test, called the "Tento de Cruciamentum" (Latin for "Test of Tor-   19
ture"), pits Buffy against "a psychotic vampire [named Zachary Kralik] with mother issues" (Golden, Bissette, and Sniegoski 134). While under normal circumstances, facing a vampire—even one this monstrous— would be only minimally challenging to Buffy, the Cruciamentum requires that she face this creature without her Slayer skills. The Council has ordered her Watcher, Giles, to inject her with an organic compound that renders her "normal"—without her knowledge. When Giles has doubts about the test and his role in it, he shares the following exchange with Quentin, the head of the Watchers Council:

> GILES: It's an archaic exercise in cruelty. To lock her in this . . . tomb . . .
> weakened, defenseless. And to unleash "that" [Kralik] on her . . .
> QUENTIN: A Slayer is not just physical prowess. She must have cunning,
> imagination, a confidence derived from self-reliance. And believe me,
> once this is all over, your Buffy will be stronger for it.
> GILES: Or she'll be dead for it. ("Helpless")

When Buffy begs Giles to help her discover why she has lost her Slayer   20
skills, noting that she "can't be helpless like that," Giles decides to defy the Council's orders and tell Buffy about the Cruciamentum ("Helpless"). However, after Kralik kidnaps Buffy's mother, the Slayer has no choice but to go through with the test. She succeeds in rescuing her mother and killing Kralik, much to the Council's satisfaction. Despite Quentin's earlier prediction to Giles, Buffy survives the Cruciamentum shaken, not stronger, although the experience does cause her to more fully embrace her Slayer powers.

The Cruciamentum is recalled in the fifth season of *Buffy* when Buffy  21
must once again face a visit from the Council. After her prior experience
with this institution, Buffy is understandably wary of its members' arrival,
commenting that "they put me through that test, and it almost killed
me. . . . Honestly, I really can't handle almost being killed right now"
("Checkpoint"). This time, the Council claims to have knowledge that will
help Buffy defeat her current foe, Glory; however, before the Council will
offer Buffy that intelligence, she must face a review. As Quentin explains to
Giles, "We've discovered information about this creature, your Glory. . . .
And it won't be handed over until we are convinced that you and your
Slayer are prepared for it."

Buffy resists the review, which consists of an examination of her abili-  22
ties and the role that her friends play in her duties as Slayer. Quentin counters this resistance by outlining the Council's authority:

> I think your Watcher hasn't reminded you lately of the roles and statuses of the
> players in our little game. The Council fights evil; the Slayer is the instrument
> by which we fight. The Council remains; the Slayers change. It has been that
> way since the beginning. . . . We can help you. We have information that will
> help. Pass the review, and we give it to you without reservation. ("Checkpoint")

To underscore the Council's authority and coerce Buffy into participating, Quentin threatens to close the magic shop run by Giles and deport
the English Watcher immediately. After struggling through the beginning
phases of the review, Buffy realizes that she is in the privileged position in
her power relationship with the Council:

> There isn't going to be a review. . . . No interrogations. No questions you know
> I can't answer. No hoops. No jumps. . . . See, I've had a lot of people talking
> at me the last few days. Everyone just lining up to tell me how unimportant I
> am. And I've finally figured out why. Power. I have it. They don't. This bothers
> them. . . . You're Watchers. Without a Slayer, you're pretty much just watching
> *Masterpiece Theatre*. . . . So here's how it's going to work. You're going to tell me
> everything you know, and then you're going to go away. ("Checkpoint")

Quentin complies and provides Buffy with his information; thus armed,
Buffy can prepare to defeat Glory.

Therefore, in *Buffy the Vampire Slayer*, the title character undergoes  23
trials by the Watchers Council, an institution that attempts to sanction her
role as the Slayer. Through these trials, though, Buffy learns that she has
had power over the Council all along—although this realization is made
after a number of years—an autonomy not realized by Wonder Woman or
the Charmed Ones. Buffy's reversal of the power differential in her relationship with the Council indicates a greater degree of autonomy for a
superpowered woman on television, a level of agency more often exhibited
by similarly powered male characters. However, it is important to note
that the "Charmed on Trial" episode aired more than three years after this
fifth-season episode of *Buffy*. Wonder Woman's precedent, then, seems to
have had a more lasting effect than Buffy's.

# Clark Kent and Jake Foley: Mock Trials

As noted in the introduction, Superman's comic book debut featured his    24
alter ego, Clark Kent, choosing to use his powers to enforce justice—a
choice neither authorized nor contested by any societal or supernatural institution. Clark Kent decides to become Superman; therefore, he is
Superman. Just as Wonder Woman, as the archetypal female superhero,
set a precedent of deference or limited agency for future superpowered
women, so too did Superman, as the archetypal male superhero, set a precedent of assumed autonomy for future superpowered men. Based on these
opposing power positions, the trials experienced by male superheroes differ significantly from those experienced by their female counterparts.

Superman's implicit autonomy, which was established in his comic    25
book appearances, has also been depicted in his television representations, such as the *Adventures of Superman* (1952–1957) and *Lois & Clark:
The New Adventures of Superman* (1993–1997). This characteristic can be
seen in its emergent stage in Superman's most recent television vehicle,
*Smallville*. On *Smallville*, a teenage Clark Kent struggles with the dual burdens of adolescence and heroism while attending high school and doing
chores on the family farm. Although Clark knows of his alien origins (the
spaceship that brought young Clark to Earth is hidden in the family's root
cellar), he values his family and friends and calls Smallville "home." However, just as Clark settles even more comfortably into his life in Smallville
by finally beginning a romantic relationship with true love Lana Lang, a
voice from Clark's past disrupts the pastoral harmony.

As the second season of *Smallville* draws to a close, a voice tells Clark,    26
"It is time" ("Calling"); the voice, which emanates from the hidden spaceship, belongs to Jor-El, Clark's biological father—or more precisely, to Jor-
El's "memory" or "will," as Jor-El is no longer alive. Jor-El informs Clark
that by day's end, Clark must "return to [Jor-El]" so that his "destiny will
be fulfilled" ("Exodus"). In a later episode, it is revealed that this encounter with Jor-El is the "first test to see if [Clark] was ready to begin his
journey"—that is, the fulfillment of his destiny ("Exile"). Although Clark
pleads with Jor-El that "[e]verything and everyone [he] love[s] is here! In
Smallville!" and asserts that he wants to create his own future, Jor-El is
adamant, telling Clark that he has no choice in the matter. When Clark
relates this encounter to his adoptive parents, Jonathan and Martha Kent,
they assure Clark that his future is indeed his own. Jonathan explains,
"Clark, you choose your own destiny. Nobody can decide that for you, son"
("Exodus"). While Martha and Jonathan fail to realize the extent of Jor-El's
power, Clark is able to resist his biological father's commands—at a price.

Later that day, Jor-El demands obedience, but Clark refuses. Jor-El    27
then marks Clark's chest with a symbol of his ancestors, a symbol that
Clark fears will control him. To avoid such control, Clark destroys the
spaceship that links him to Jor-El. The resulting explosion causes an automobile accident for the Kents, and Martha miscarries. When Clark con-

fesses to Jonathan that his actions caused the explosion, Jonathan is angry and reminds Clark that such actions have consequences. Clark, unable to face said consequences, puts on a red kryptonite ring (the ring weakens his conscience and causes him to lose inhibition), jumps on a motorcycle, and leaves Smallville. As Clark speeds away, Jor-El's voice can be heard: "You will obey me, Kal-El [Clark's birth name]." When the third season resumes the story line, viewers learn that Clark has been leading a life of crime and excess in Metropolis. By refusing to succumb to Jor-El's demands for obedience and leaving Smallville, Clark determines the outcome of his own trial.

Although Clark does not emerge from his trial unscathed—he bears [28] the physical mark with which Jor-El branded him and the emotional scars of the experience—he has taken an important first step in establishing his autonomy. By destroying the ship, Clark defies both Jor-El (he is attempting to sever their connection) and the Kents (he had lied to them about Jor-El's continued demands; he told them that Jor-El only contacted him once). While this act of defiance could be seen as a typical stage of adolescence—all teenagers must test boundaries as they mature—it is important to note that the similarly aged Buffy initially does not assume the same position of independence.

Like Clark, Jake Foley, the NSA computer technician turned "ultimate [29] human upgrade" (and agent) in the short-lived *Jake 2.0*, assumes a position of autonomy when he affects the outcome of his own trial. This trial commences when an emergency board of inquiry convenes to determine the future of Jake's special operations unit. The board threatens to disband the unit if the agents in question cannot explain their actions on a recent South American mission. The mission in question aligns Jake, romantically and otherwise, with a former CIA agent named Angela. In an effort to avenge her sister's death, Angela plans to kill the leaders of a country with "an abominable human rights record" ("The Spy"). Although Jake offers Angela asylum and all but convinces her to turn herself in (when she has the opportunity to shoot the man responsible for her sister's death, she hesitates to pull the trigger), Jake's immediate superior follows protocol and turns over Angela to local authorities.

The board of inquiry not only questions Jake's actions on this mission, [30] but also his involvement in the mission itself; the board members note that his skills were not vital to the operation. (Jake has enhanced physical abilities and can interface with any computerized technology.) In response, one of Jake's superiors explains, "Jake isn't an appliance. He's a member of our intelligence community being trained for advanced field work. He goes on missions" ("The Spy"). However, the board is not convinced of the necessity of Jake's presence on the South American mission, nor are they convinced that the special ops unit acted appropriately. The board members therefore announce that they will review the evidence; in the interim, the team members will be restricted to desk duty and will be under surveillance.

Such an outcome is unacceptable to Jake. He berates the board mem- *31* bers for their hypocrisy: trying to cover up that the United States was selling biological weapons in South America (Angela's sister died as the result of a biological weapon, so Angela stole vials of said weapon to wreak her revenge). When the board declares Jake out of line, he uses his abilities to ready the trial's transcripts for e-mailing to a national wire service— or so he tells the board. (He later reveals that he was going to send the transcripts to a dummy e-mail account.) The fear of exposure causes the board to reverse its decision and return Angela to the United States. One of the board members even notes of Jake's team that such an "unorthodox unit cannot be measured by traditional notions of intelligence work" ("The Spy").

The board members, although angry with Jake for his defiance, ulti- *32* mately respect his act of contempt. One member remarks, "Did you see the way he stood up to us? As a soldier." Although the board vows to control Jake in the future—"a man like that bent to your will could accomplish anything"—at this point, Jake's autonomous position is assured. By using his abilities, Jake is able to assume a position of power over those who would attempt to limit his agency, to use him as "an appliance." His insurrection is viewed in heroic terms—as the action of a soldier—and he is in effect praised by his superiors instead of punished, an advantage that Wonder Woman was never afforded by the Amazons.

## Female (Super)Heroism on Trial

The use of the narrative of superheroes on trial, as noted by the examples *33* above, varies by gender. For female superheroes, the trials are imposed upon them by the institutions that sanction their power as a way to limit their agency, thus exposing their weaknesses. In contrast, male superheroes use their powers to affect the outcome of such trials in their favor, therefore underscoring their autonomy.

What really is on trial, then, is a female superhero's ability to be a fully *34* recognized subject, the "heroine in her own right" whom the Powerpuff Girls' Blossom struggled to name. As "most people see femininity and aggression as mutually exclusive" (Grindstaff 169), the "female superhero" may be viewed as an oxymoron because she is both feminine and aggressive. Therefore, the trials that these female superheroes undergo may be a way to perpetuate the "masculine gaze," which depicts viewing "the female form as a prototypically masculine-subject/feminine-object relationship" (Cirksena and Cuklanz 32). The trials serve as a periodic repositioning of superpowered women from the active subjects they must be in order to function as heroes to the more passive—or at least submissive—objects they must become to undergo these trials. For example, in Buffy's "helpless" days preceding the Cruciamentum, she is depicted in a red-hooded cloak—à la Little Red Riding Hood—an incongruous image for a Slayer who already has staved off more than one apocalyptic "wolf" and even death (she was resuscitated after drowning). Similarly, by the time of the Watchers Council's second visit, the Council's impending examination erodes Buffy's self-confidence: "They're going to expect me to be like a Slayer and know stuff, but I'm just me . . . and I don't know anything" ("Checkpoint"). When faced with the Watchers Council's trials, Buffy initially regresses from powerful action hero to frightened young woman.

This repositioning of female superheroes from subject to object may  35 stem in part from Marston's creation of Wonder Woman "as a feminine character with all the strength of a Superman plus all the allure of a good and beautiful woman" (Smith 129). The depiction of female superheroes as both strong and beautiful underscores the binary of the masculine-subject/feminine-object relationship. Reynolds offers this description of the binary: "The costumed heroine may be frankly the object of sexual attraction, and therefore (for many male readers) will constitute the object of their gaze, as well as the subject or protagonist through which they engage with the action of the text" (37). The trials that female superheroes undergo provide a narrative representation of the duality of the female superhero, an objectified character who still drives the story line. The continued use of this narrative of female superheroes on trial indicates that depictions of female superheroes have not fully broken from the idea that feminine characters cannot be aggressive, despite Gloria Steinem's assertion in her 1995 essay on Wonder Woman that "only the villains bought the idea that 'masculine' meant aggression and 'feminine' meant submission" (qtd. in Behrens 7).

Additionally, the trials of female superheroes may serve as a reminder  36 of the ever-present threat of replacement. As Wonder Woman, the Charmed Ones, and Buffy are each part of an ancient female lineage—the Amazons, the Halliwell witches, and the Slayers—they are not unique. While Diana won the "bullets and bracelets" challenge to be proclaimed "the strongest and most agile of all the Amazons" ("Introducing" 9), had she failed, one of her Amazon sisters would have fulfilled her role as Wonder Woman in America. (In fact, in a 1994 issue of the comic book, an Amazon named Artemis defeats Princess Diana in a test of skills to win the right to the costume and moniker of "Wonder Woman" [Daniels 191].) Similarly, after Prue, the eldest Halliwell sister, dies, half sister Paige Matthews takes Prue's place in "the power of three." Likewise, Buffy's role as the Slayer is a transient one; in fact, she meets her replacement when, after drowning (and presumably in the minutes before her resuscitation), the next Slayer is called. The trials of these female superheroes emphasize the successive nature of their power; while each female superhero may be unique to her generation, others have come before and probably will come after. The institutions that sanction their power determine their status (or nonstatus) as heroes; they cannot, like Superman, self-proclaim their heroism.

Despite the threat of replacement, the trials of female superheroes  37 may also offer them the chance to gain a degree of autonomy, although to gain this independence, they must first go through the hoops and jumps that Buffy berates the Watchers Council for trying to impose upon her. These hoops and jumps may allow a female superhero to define or redefine her role as a hero and to resist a position as the instrument of some presumably more powerful institution or tradition, whether matriarchal or patriarchal in origin. Although Wonder Woman remains submissive to her mother and Amazon sisters and Phoebe succumbs to the judgment of the Tribunal, Buffy, as noted above, emerges from her trials with a greater sense of independence. In Buffy's case, it was the second trial of the Watchers Council that led her to comprehend the power that her role as Slayer commands (although it was a long time in coming—five seasons); she reverses the previous power relationship she shared with the Council members by outlining *her* terms to them. While it could certainly be argued that Buffy could have reached this realization without undergoing any such trials (without the interference of a sanctioning institution), her actions demonstrate an improvement over the head-bowed-in-shame apologetic mode that Wonder Woman often adopts.

So, to paraphrase Maxine Sheets-Johnstone's essay "Female Muscularity and the Comics," what are we to make of twentieth- and twenty-first-century comic book females and their television counterparts? On the positive side, more female characters are being incorporated into action films and TV shows, genres previously reserved for males (Samanta and Franzman 28). Negatively, though, physically powerful female characters seem to be accepted only within the realms of science fiction and fantasy (28). If, as Laurie Fierstein suggests in *Picturing the Modern Amazon*, "comics art and narrative is intended to be outrageous and entertaining, to grant popular culture a haven for the expression of imagination and fantasy without inhibitions and reality checks" (qtd. in Fierstein and Frueh 138), then televised depictions of female superheroes that owe a debt to comic books are failing in their intentions. As Chesler notes, Wonder Woman is "grounded in reality" because "it [the comic strip] clearly portrays the fact that women have to be better and stronger than men to be given a chance in a man's world." Or, as a 27-year-old viewer of *Buffy* remarked, "you can take it out of the context of vampires and just think of it as all the usual bulls– [sic] women have to deal with" (qtd. in Rogers 60).

Television series that employ the narrative of female superheroes on trial clearly depict inhibitions and reality checks for women. Just as women may have to accomplish more than men, both personally and professionally, to be successful, as Chesler suggests, so too do female superheroes. Therefore, it is not surprising that the media icon of a successful career woman in the 1970s was the "Superwoman" (Faludi 76–77); the use of this icon suggests that women requiring superpowers to make it in a man's world was not a difficult concept for the media to sell to women of that decade—or perhaps of this one. In the June 24, 2002, comic strip "Cathy" by Cathy Guisewite, Cathy's then-friend Irving describes the pressure that "men are under today" (D5). He tells Cathy that men are "supposed to be tough business people, brilliant investors, nurturing parents, sensitive spouses, community leaders, fabulous athletes with abs of steel and great hair!!" He continues by saying that men are "expected to be like a . . . a . . ." When Cathy attempts to finish his sentence with "Female!" he completes his thought with "Superhero!" to which Cathy replies, "Same thing." As this example illustrates, the narrative of the female superhero on trial continues to allegorically represent the successful contemporary woman who, in her attempts to do and be all, undergoes her own share of trials as she encounters numerous individuals, institutions, and ideologies that may attempt to limit her agency.

Wonder Woman, William Moulton Marston's incarnation of the first *40* superwoman, led to a number of female superheroes (Reynolds 80) and is still seen by some as the symbol of feminine power and heroism that Marston apparently envisioned. As artist and author Jill Thompson, a *Wonder Woman* comic book illustrator, commented, "Wonder Woman's on equal footing with the other heroes. She's just as strong, just as powerful as all these guys" (qtd. in Behrens 7). Wonder Woman is just as strong as her male counterparts, physically speaking—she certainly holds her own in battle in *Justice League* episodes—but she and many of her more recent sisters, such as the Charmed Ones and Buffy, are put to the test in different ways than are their male counterparts. Until the use of this narrative technique to limit women's roles as fully recognized subjects—as heroines in their own right—is discontinued, the "equal fights" described by the Powerpuff Girls will continue to be absent from superhero television series.

WORKS CITED

Behrens, Web. "Wonder Woman Going Strong at 60." *Chicago Tribune* 28 Dec. 2001, sec. 2: 7.

Bongco, Mila. *Reading Comics: Language, Culture, and the Concept of the Superhero in Comic Books*. New York: Garland, 2000.

"Calling." Dir. Terrence O'Hara. Writ. Kenneth Biller. Perf. Tom Welling. *Smallville*. WB. 13 May 2003.

"Checkpoint." Dir. Nick Marck. Writ. Jane Espenson and Doug Petrie. Perf. Sarah Michelle Gellar. *Buffy the Vampire Slayer*. WB. 23 Jan. 2001.

"Crimes and Witch-Demeanors." Dir. John T. Kretchmer. Writ. Henry Alonso Myers. Perf. Holly Marie Combs, Alyssa Milano, and Rose McGowan. *Charmed*. WB. 25 Apr. 2004.

Chesler, Phyllis. "The Amazon Legacy: An Interpretive Essay." *Wonder Woman*. A *Ms.* Book. New York: Holt, 1972. N. pag.

Cirksena, Kathryn, and Lisa Cuklanz. "Male Is to Female as ____ Is to ____: A Guided Tour of Five Feminist Frameworks for Communication Studies." Ed. Lana F. Rakow. *Women Making Meaning: New Feminist Directions in Communication*. New York: Routledge, 1992. 18–44.

Coulson, Juanita. "Of (Super)Human Bondage." *The Comic-Book Book*. Ed. Don Thompson and Dick Lupoff. New Rochelle, NY: Arlington, 1973. 227–55.

Daniels, Les. *Wonder Woman: The Complete History*. San Francisco: Chronicle Books, 2000.

"Equal Fights." Dir. Randy Myers and Craig McCracken. Writ. Lauren Faust. *Powerpuff Girls*. Cartoon Network. 23 Mar. 2002.

"Exile." Dir. Greg Beeman. Writ. Al Gough and Miles Millar. Perf. Tom Welling. *Smallville*. WB. 1 Oct. 2003.

"Exodus." Dir. Greg Beeman. Writ. Al Gough and Miles Millar. Perf. Tom Welling. *Smallville*. WB. 20 May 2003.

Faludi, Susan. *Backlash: The Undeclared War Against American Women*. New York: Doubleday, 1991.

Fierstein, Laurie, and Joanna Frueh. "Comments on the Comics." *Picturing the Modern Amazon*. Ed. Joanna Frueh, Laurie Fierstein, and Judith Stein. New York: Rizzoli, 1999. 137–49.

Golden, Christopher, Stephen R. Bissette, and Thomas E. Sniegoski. *Buffy the Vampire Slayer: The Monster Book*. New York: Pocket Books, 2000.

Golden, Christopher, and Nancy Holder. *Buffy the Vampire Slayer: The Watcher's Guide*. New York: Pocket Books, 1998.

Grindstaff, Laura. "Sometimes Being a Bitch Is All a Woman Has to Hold on to." *Reel Knockouts: Violent Women in the Movies*. Ed. Martha McCaughey and Neal King. Austin: U of Texas P, 2001. 147–71.

Guisewite, Cathy. "Cathy." Cartoon. *The Blade* [Toledo] 24 June 2002: D5.

"Helpless." Dir. James A. Contner. Writ. David Fury. Perf. Sarah Michelle Gellar. *Buffy the Vampire Slayer*. WB. 19 Jan. 1999.

Inness, Sherrie A. "Tough Girls in Comic Books: Beyond Wonder Woman." *Tough Girls: Women Warriors and Wonder Women in Popular Culture*. Philadelphia: U of Pennsylvania P, 1999. 138–59.

"Introducing Wonder Woman." *Wonder Woman Archives*. Vol. 1. Stories by William Moulton Marston and Harry G. Peter. New York: DC Comics, 1998. 8–16.

*The New Original Wonder Woman* (Telefilm). Dir. Leonard Horn. Writ. Stanley Ralph Ross. Perf. Lynda Carter. ABC. 7 Nov. 1975.

O'Neil, Dennis, ed. *Secret Origins of the Super DC Heroes*. New York: Warner Books, 1976.

"Paradise Lost." Dir. Dan Riba. Writ. Joseph Kuhr. *Justice League*. Cartoon Network. 24 Mar. 2002.

"Paradise Lost. Pt. 2." Dir. Dan Riba. Writ. Joseph Kuhr. *Justice League*. Cartoon Network. 30 Mar. 2002.

"The Princess and the Power." *Wonder Woman*. Script, co-plot, and pencils Greg Potter and George Pérez. Inks Bruce Patterson. New York: DC Comics, 1987.

Reynolds, Richard. *Super Heroes A Modern Mythology*. Jackson: UP of Mississippi, 1992.

Rogers, Adam. "Hey, Ally, Ever Slain a Vampire?" *Newsweek* 2 Mar 1998: 60.

Samanta, Anamika, and Erin Franzman. "Women in Action." *HUES: Hear Us Emerging Sisters* 4.3 (1998): 28.

Sheets-Johnstone, Maxine. "Female Muscularity and the Comics." *Picturing the Modern Amazon*. Ed. Joanna Frueh, Joanna Fierstein, and Judith Stein. New York: Rizzoli, 1999. 120–36.

Smith, Matthew J. "The Tyranny of the Melting Pot Metaphor: Wonder Woman as the Americanized Immigrant." *Comics & Ideology*, Ed. Matthew P. McAllister, Edward H. Sewell, Jr., and Ian Gordon. New York: Peter Lang, 2001. 129–50.

"The Spy Who Really Liked Me." Dir. David Straiton. Writ. Mark Wilding. Perf. Christopher Gorham. *Jake 2.0*. UPN. 19 Nov. 2003.

"Superman, Champion of the Oppressed!" *Superman: The Action Comics Archives*. Vol 1. Writ. Jerry Siegel. Art Joe Shuster. New York: DC Comics, 1997. 9–23.

Wright, Bradford W. *Comic Book Nation: The Transformation of Youth Culture in America*. Baltimore: Johns Hopkins UP, 2001.

■ ■ ■

## Reading as a Writer: Analyzing Rhetorical Choices

1. While O'Reilly opens with a reference to the Powerpuff Girls, in her second paragraph she shifts to a fairly lengthy analysis of Wonder Woman as a character. How does O'Reilly's examination of the origins of Wonder Woman serve the larger purpose of her essay? What does this background add to her argument?

2. What are the key distinctions O'Reilly makes between male and female superheroes? She includes examples from several different shows; choose a few to focus on and examine how she uses the details from each show to build her point about the unique aspects she sees in narratives about female superheroes. What point is she making about the difference between male and female superheroes?

## Writing as a Reader: Entering the Conversation of Ideas

1. While O'Reilly's essay is not about education, she argues, as does Neil Postman, that television teaches viewers a lot about what to expect in the real world. In other words, both O'Reilly and Postman are interested in a term coined by John Dewey, "collateral learning," which describes the cultural values and standards we learn while engaged in often entertaining pastimes. Choose a "test case" from popular culture (a film or an episode of a television show, for example) that you could usefully analyze through the lenses of these two writers' ideas. What do these writers help you bring into focus in your test case? What can we learn from analyzing popular culture this way?

2. O'Reilly's analysis of gender expectations in superhero fantasy narratives is interesting to consider next to Shari L. Dworkin and Michael A. Messner's article "Just Do . . . What? Sport, Bodies, Gender." Compose an essay in which you make an argument about what these fantasy and real-world examples tell us about current beliefs about gender, strength, and power.

---

JEAN KILBOURNE

## "Two Ways a Woman Can Get Hurt": Advertising and Violence

Jean Kilbourne, EdD, is an award-winning author and educator who is best known for her lively campus lectures on the effects of media images on young people. Her academic interests stem from personal experience. Although Kilbourne was a superb student when she came of age in the 1960s, she found that she was rewarded more for her looks than for her intelligence. Later, after she began working in journalism and education, she noticed the absurd arguments that advertisements often make, many of them insulting to women's intelligence and self-esteem. Once she found her personal and professional interests intersecting, Kilbourne began collecting and analyzing advertisements, eventually shaping them into a lecture series and then a film titled *Killing Us Softly: Advertising's Image of Women* (1979). This film, its three subsequent versions, and other films Kilbourne has produced on anorexia and on tobacco and alcohol addiction are taught frequently in college classes today. Kilbourne has also published many articles and several books on these topics, including the book from which this essay is excerpted, *Deadly Persuasion: Why Women and Girls Must Fight the Addictive Power of Advertising* (1999).

The first thing you may notice about Kilbourne's essay is that it is filled with advertising images. Before you read, flip through the essay to see if you can get a sense of Kilbourne's argument simply from the advertisements she includes. As you read, keep returning to these images, testing them against Kilbourne's argument and the information she presents from other scholars about violence in our culture (particularly sexualized violence) and the power of the media. Kilbourne's is an important voice among the many media critics who have discussed the ways advertising images normalize—and even make appealing—sexual and violent situations that most often threaten women and children. Pay close attention to the connections Kilbourne makes between the media and social problems. Note the passages you find most and least convincing, and ask yourself why. Getting in the habit of evaluating evidence this way will help you immeasurably when you decide on the kinds of evidence you want to include in your own writing.

Kilbourne is sometimes criticized for being too selective in her choice of images and evidence, and too narrow in her analysis. Throughout the essay, you will hear her addressing her critics, anticipating claims that she is simply reading too much into these images or taking advertising too seriously. Often she provides more than one interpretation of an image—for example, saying about the subject of one advertisement, "I suppose this could be a woman awaiting her lover, but it could as easily be a girl being preyed upon" (para. 33). Note the way she builds her claims about images on the research of experts in the fields of anthropology, addiction, gendered violence, and media criticism, and also the way she cites newspaper reports of crimes and trends she finds so dangerous.

Given our visually rich media culture, you are likely to find many familiar ideas and images in Kilbourne's essay, and you also are likely to find yourself strongly agreeing or disagreeing—or perhaps both—with her as she builds her case about the "deadly" power of the advertising industry. Even if you do not agree with her on every point, Kilbourne's strategy of analyzing the ways advertising makes dangerous behaviors seem "normal" and even appealing is one that all consumers can use to make sense of marketing claims and popular culture.

# Two Ways A Woman Can Get Hurt.

(Heartbreaker)   (Soap and water shave)

Skintimate® Shave Gel Ultra Protection formula contains 75% moisturizers, including vitamin E, to protect your legs from nicks, cuts and razor burn. So while guys may continue to be a pain, shaving most definitely won't.

SKINTIMATE® SHAVE GEL
LOVE YOUR LEGS

Sex in advertising is more about disconnection and distance than connection and closeness. It is also more often about power than passion, about violence than violins. The main goal, as in pornography, is usually power over another, either by the physical dominance or preferred status of men or what is seen as the exploitative power of female beauty and female sexuality. Men conquer and women ensnare, always with the essential aid of a product. The woman is rewarded for her sexuality by the man's wealth, as in an ad for Cigarette boats in which the woman says, while lying in a man's embrace clearly after sex, "Does this mean I get a ride in your Cigarette?"

Sex in advertising is pornographic because it dehumanizes and objectifies people, especially women, and because it fetishizes products, imbues them with an erotic charge—which dooms us to disappointment since products never can fulfill our sexual desires or meet our emotional needs. The poses and postures of advertising are often borrowed from pornography, as are many of the themes, such as bondage, sadomasochism, and the sexual exploitation of children. When a

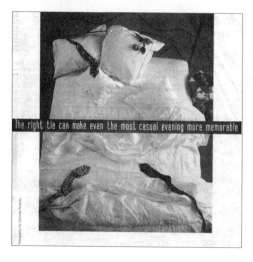

The right tie can make even the most casual evening more memorable

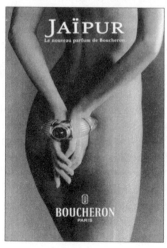

JAÏPUR
Le nouveau parfum de Boucheron

BOUCHERON
PARIS

beer ad uses the image of a man licking the high-heeled boot of a woman clad in leather, when bondage is used to sell neckties in *The New York Times,* perfume in *The New Yorker,* and watches on city buses, and when a college magazine promotes an **S&M Ball,** pornography can be considered mainstream.

Most of us know all this by now and I suppose some consider it kinky 3 good fun. Pornography is more dangerously mainstream when its glorification of rape and violence shows up in mass media, in films and television shows, in comedy and music videos, and in advertising. Male violence is subtly encouraged by ads that encourage men to be forceful and dominant, and to value sexual intimacy more than emotional intimacy. "Do you want to be the one she tells her deep, dark secrets to?" asks a three-page ad for men's cologne. "Or do you want to be her deep, dark secret?" The last page advises men, "Don't be such a good boy." There are two iden-

tical women looking adoringly at the man in the ad, but he isn't looking at either one of them. Just what is the deep, dark secret? That he's sleeping with both of them? Clearly the way to get beautiful women is to ignore them, perhaps mistreat them.

"Two ways a woman can get hurt," says an ad for shaving gel, featuring a razor and a photo of a handsome man. My first thought is that the man is a batterer or date rapist, but the ad informs us that he is merely a "heartbreaker." The gel will protect the woman so that "while guys may continue to be a pain, shaving most definitely won't." Desirable men are painful—heartbreakers at best.

Wouldn't it be wonderful if, realizing the importance of relationships in 5 all of our lives, we could seek to learn relational skills from women and to help men develop these strengths in themselves? In fact, we so often do the opposite. The popular culture usually trivializes these abilities in women, mocks men who have real intimacy with women (it is almost always married men in ads and cartoons who are jerks), and idealizes a template for relation-

ships between men and women that is a recipe for disaster: a template that views sex as more important than anything else, that ridicules men who are not in control of their women (who are "pussy-whipped"), and that disparages fidelity and commitment (except, of course, to brand names).

Indeed the very worst kind of 6 man for a woman to be in an intimate relationship with, often a truly dangerous man, is the one considered most sexy and desirable in the popular culture. And the men capable of real intimacy (the ones we tell our deep, dark secrets to) constantly have their very masculinity impugned. Advertising often

encourages women to be attracted to hostile and indifferent men while encouraging boys to become these men. This is especially dangerous for those of us who have suffered from "condemned isolation" in childhood: like heat-seeking missiles, we rush inevitably to mutual destruction.

Men are also encouraged to never take no for an answer. Ad after ad implies that girls and women don't really mean "no" when they say it, that women are only teasing when they resist men's advances. "NO" says an ad showing a man leaning over a woman against a wall. Is she screaming or laughing? Oh, it's an ad for deodorant and the second word, in very small print, is "sweat." Sometimes it's "all in good fun," as in the ad for Possession shirts and shorts featuring a man ripping the clothes off a woman who seems to be having a good time.

And sometimes it is more sinister. A perfume ad running in several teen magazines features a very young woman, with eyes blackened by makeup or perhaps something else, and the copy, "Apply generously to your neck so he can smell the scent as you shake your head 'no.'" In other words, he'll understand that you don't really mean it and he can respond to the scent like any other animal.

Sometimes there seems to be no question but that a man should force a woman to have sex. A chilling newspaper ad for a bar in Georgetown features a closeup of a cocktail and the headline, "If your date won't listen to reason, try a Velvet Hammer." A vodka ad pictures a wolf hiding in a flock of sheep, a hideous grin on its face. We all know what wolves do to sheep. A campaign for Bacardi Black rum features shadowy figures almost obliterated by darkness and captions such as "Some people embrace the night because the rules of the day do not apply." What it doesn't say is that people who are above the rules do enormous harm to other people, as well as to themselves.

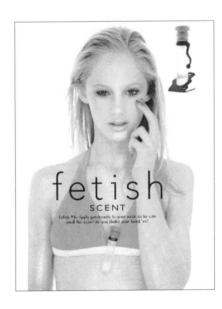

Sip exotic cocktails, dine and dance to Swing Era music at Georgetown's top nightspot. 1232 36th St., N.W. Reservation call 342-0009. Free valet parking. Jackets required.

F. SCOTT'S

These ads are particu- 10 larly troublesome, given that between one-third and three-quarters of all cases of sexual assault involve alcohol consumption by the perpetrator, the victim, or both.[1] "Make strangers your friends, and your friends a lot stranger," says one of the ads in a Cuervo campaign that uses colorful cartoon beasts and emphasizes heavy drinking. This ad is especially disturbing when we consider the role of alcohol in date rape, as is another ad in the series that says, "The night began with a bottle of Cuervo and ended with a vow of silence." Over half of all reported rapes on college campuses occur when either the victim or the assailant has been drinking.[2] Alcohol's role has different meaning for men and women, however. If a man is drunk when he commits a rape, he is considered less responsible. If a woman is drunk (or has had a drink or two or simply met the man in a bar), she is considered more responsible.

In general, females are still held responsible and hold each other 11 responsible when sex goes wrong—when they become pregnant or are the victims of rape and sexual assault or cause a scandal. Constantly exhorted to be sexy and attractive, they discover when assaulted that that very sexiness is evidence of their guilt, their lack of "innocence." Sometimes the ads play on this by "warning" women of what might happen if they use the product. "Wear it but beware it," says a perfume ad. Beware what exactly? Victoria's Secret tempts young women with blatantly sexual ads promising that their lingerie will make them irresistible. Yet when a young woman accused William Kennedy Smith of raping her, the fact that she wore Victoria's Secret panties was used against her as an indication of her immorality. A jury acquitted Smith, whose alleged history of violence against women was not permitted to be introduced at trial.

It is sadly not surprising that the jury was composed mostly of women. 12 Women are especially cruel judges of other women's sexual behavior, mostly because we are so desperate to believe we are in control of what happens to us. It is too frightening to face the fact that male violence against women is irrational and commonplace. It is reassuring to believe that we can avoid it by being good girls, avoiding dark places, staying out of bars, dressing "innocently." An ad featuring two young women talking intimately at a coffee shop says, "Carla and Rachel considered themselves open-minded and

[1] Wilsnack, Plaud, Wilsnack, and Klassen, 1997, 262.
[2] Abbey, Ross, and McDuffie, 1991. Also Martin, 1992, 230–37.

non-judgmental people. Although they did agree Brenda was a tramp." These terrible judgments from other women are an important part of what keeps all women in line.

If indifference in a man is sexy, then violence is sometimes downright *13* erotic. Not surprisingly, this attitude too shows up in advertising. "Push my buttons," says a young woman, "I'm looking for a man who can totally floor me." Her vulnerability is underscored by the fact that she is in an elevator, often a dangerous place for women. She is young, she is submissive (her eyes are downcast), she is in a dangerous place, and she is dressed provocatively. And she is literally asking for it.

"Wear it out and make it scream," *14* says a jeans ad portraying a man sliding his hands under a woman's transparent blouse. This could be a seduction, but it could as easily be an attack. Although the ad that ran in the Czech version of *Elle* portraying three men attacking a woman seems unambiguous, the terrifying image is being used to sell jeans *to women*. So someone must think that women would find this image compelling or attractive. Why would we? Perhaps it is simply designed to get our attention, by shocking us and by arousing unconscious anxiety. Or perhaps the intent is more subtle and it is

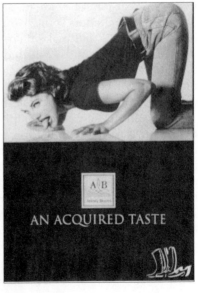

designed to play into the fantasies of domination and even rape that some women use in order to maintain an illusion of being in control (we are the ones having the fantasies, after all, we are the directors).

A camera ad features a woman's torso wrapped in plastic, her hands *15* tied behind her back. A smiling woman in a lipstick ad has a padlocked chain around her neck. An ad for MTV shows a vulnerable young woman,

her breasts exposed, and the simple copy "Bitch." A perfume ad features a man shadow-boxing with what seems to be a woman.

Sometimes women are shown dead or in *16* the process of being killed. "Great hair never dies," says an ad featuring a female corpse lying on a bed, her breasts exposed. An ad in the Italian version of *Vogue* shows a man aiming a gun at a nude woman wrapped in plastic, a leather briefcase covering her face. And an ad for Bitch skateboards, for God's sake, shows a cartoon version of a similar scene, this time clearly targeting young people. We believe we are not affected by these images, but most of us experience visceral shock when we pay conscious attention to them. Could they be any less shocking to us on an unconscious level?

Most of us become numb to these images, just as we become numb *17* to the daily litany in the news of women being raped, battered, and killed.

ÉGOÏSTE
"PLATINUM"
**CHANEL**

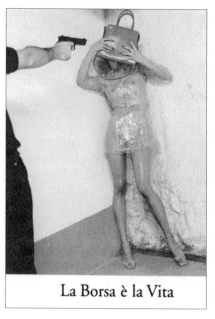

La Borsa è la Vita

According to former surgeon general Antonia Novello, battery is the single greatest cause of injury to women in America, more common than automobile accidents, muggings, and stranger rapes combined, and more than one-third of women slain in this country die at the hands of husbands or boyfriends.[3] Throughout the world, the biggest problem for most women is simply surviving at home. The Global Report on Women's Human Rights concluded that "domestic violence is a leading cause of female injury in almost every country in the world and is typically ignored by the state or only erratically punished."[4] Although usually numb to these facts on a conscious level, most women live in a state of subliminal terror, a state that, according to Mary Daly, keeps us divided both from each other and from our most passionate, powerful, and creative selves.[5]

**bitch skateboards**

Ads don't directly cause violence, of course. But the violent images contribute to the state of terror. And objectification and disconnection create a climate in which there is widespread and increasing violence. Turning a human being into a thing, an object, is almost always the first step toward justifying violence against that person. It is very difficult, perhaps impossible, to be violent to someone we think of as an equal, someone we have empathy with, but it is very easy to abuse a thing. We see this with racism, with homophobia. The person becomes an object and violence is inevitable. This step is already taken with women. The violence, the abuse, is partly the chilling but logical result of the objectification. *18*

An editorial in *Advertising Age* suggests that even some advertisers are concerned about this: "Clearly it's time to wipe out sexism in beer ads; for the brewers and their agencies to wake up and join the rest of America in realizing that sexism, sexual harassment, and the cultural portrayal of women in advertising are inextricably linked."[6] Alas, this editorial was written in 1991 and nothing has changed. *19*

It is this link with violence that makes the objectification of women a more serious issue than the objectification of men. Our economic system constantly requires the development of new markets. Not surprisingly, men's bodies are the latest territory to be exploited. Although we are growing more used to it, in the beginning the male sex object came as a surprise. In 1994 a "gender bender" television commercial in which a bevy of women office *20*

---

[3] Novello, 1991. Also Blumenthal, 1995.
[4] Wright, 1995, A2.
[5] Weil, 1999, 21.
[6] Brewers can help fight sexism, 1991, 28.

workers gather to watch a construction worker doff his shirt to quaff a Diet Coke led to so much hoopla that you'd have thought women were mugging men on Madison Avenue.[7]

There is no question that men are used as sex objects in ads now as [21] never before. We often see nude women with fully clothed men in ads (as in art), but the reverse was unheard of, until recently. These days some ads do feature clothed and often aggressive women with nude men. And women sometimes blatantly objectify men, as in the Metroliner ad that says, " 'She's reading Nietzsche,' Harris noted to himself as he walked towards the café car for a glass of cabernet. And as he passed her seat, Maureen looked up from her book and thought, 'Nice buns.' "

Although these ads are often funny, it is never a good thing for human [22] beings to be objectified. However, there is

a world of difference between the objectification of men and that of women. The most important difference is that there is no danger for most men, whereas objectified women are always at risk. In the Diet Coke ad, for instance, the women are physically separated from the shirtless man. He is the one in control. His body is powerful, not passive. Imagine a true role reversal of this ad: A group of businessmen gather to leer at a beautiful woman worker on her break, who removes her shirt before drinking her Diet Coke. This scene would be frightening, not funny, as the Diet Coke ad is. And why is the Diet Coke ad funny? Because we know it doesn't describe any truth. However, the ads featuring images of male violence against women do describe a truth, a truth we are all aware of, on one level or another.

When power is unequal, when one group is oppressed and discrimi- [23] nated against *as a group*, when there is a context of systemic and historical oppression, stereotypes and prejudice have different weight and meaning. As Anna Quindlen said, writing about "reverse racism": "Hatred by the powerful, the majority, has a different weight—and often very different effects—than hatred by the powerless, the minority."[8] When men objectify women, they do so in a cultural context in which women are constantly objectified and in which there are consequences—from economic discrimination to violence—to that objectification.

For men, though, there are no such consequences. Men's bodies are [24] not routinely judged and invaded. Men are not likely to be raped, harassed,

[7]Kilbourne, 1994, F13.
[8]Quindlen, 1992, E17.

or beaten (that is to say, men presumed to be heterosexual are not, and very few men are abused in these ways by women). How many men are frightened to be alone with a woman in an elevator? How many men cross the street when a group of women approach? Jackson Katz, who writes and lectures on male violence, often begins his workshops by asking men to describe the things they do every day to protect themselves from sexual assault. The men are surprised, puzzled, sometimes amused by the question. The women understand the question easily and have no trouble at all coming up with a list of responses. We don't list our full names in the phone directory or on our mailboxes, we try not to be alone after dark, we carry our keys in our hands when we approach our cars, we always look in the back seat before we get in, we are wary of elevators and doorways and bushes, we carry pepper sprays, whistles, Mace.

Nonetheless, the rate of sexual assault in the United States is the high-    25
est of any industrialized nation in the world.[9] According to a 1998 study by the federal government, one in five of us has been the victim of rape or attempted rape, most often before our seventeenth birthday.[10] And more than half of us have been physically assaulted, most often by the men we live with. In fact, three of four women in the study who responded that they had been raped or assaulted as adults said the perpetrator was a current or former husband, a cohabiting partner, or a date. The article reporting the results of this study was buried on page twenty-three of my local newspaper, while the front page dealt with a long story about the New England Patriots football team.

A few summers ago, a Diet Pepsi commercial featured Cindy Crawford    26
being ogled by two boys (they seemed to be about twelve years old) as she got out of her car and bought a Pepsi from a machine. The boys made very suggestive comments, which in the end turned out to be about the Pepsi's can rather than Ms. Crawford's. There was no outcry: the boys' behavior was acceptable and ordinary enough for a soft-drink commercial.

Again, let us imagine the reverse: a sexy man gets out of a car in the    27
countryside and two preteen girls make suggestive comments, seemingly about his body, especially his buns. We would fear for them and rightly so. But the boys already have the right to ogle, to view women's bodies as property to be looked at, commented on, touched, perhaps eventually hit and raped. The boys have also learned that men ogle primarily to impress other men (and to affirm their heterosexuality). If anyone is in potential danger in this ad, it is the woman (regardless of the age of the boys). Men are not seen as *property* in this way by women. Indeed if a woman does whistle at a man or touches his body or even makes direct eye contact, it is still *she* who is at risk and the man who has the power.

[9]Blumenthal, 1995, 2.
[10]Tjaden and Thoennes, 1998.

"I always lower my eyes to see if a man is worth following," says the  28
woman in an ad for men's pants. Although the ad is offensive to everyone,
the woman is endangering only herself.

"Where women are women and men are roadkill," says an ad for  29
motorcycle clothing featuring an angry-looking African-American woman.

Women are sometimes hostile and
angry in ads these days, especially
women of color who are often seen
as angrier and more threatening than
white women. But, regardless of color,
we all know that women are far more
likely than men to end up as roadkill—and, when it happens, they are
blamed for being on the road in the
first place.

Even little girls are sometimes held  30
responsible for the violence against
them. In 1990 a male Canadian judge
accused a three-year-old girl of being
"sexually aggressive" and suspended
the sentence of her molester, who was
then free to return to his job of baby-
sitter.[11] The deeply held belief that all
women, regardless of age, are really
temptresses in disguise, nymphets, sexually insatiable and seductive, conveniently transfers all blame and responsibility onto women.

All women are vulnerable in a culture in which there is such wide-  31
spread objectification of women's bodies, such glorification of disconnection, so much violence against women, and such blaming of the victim.

When everything and everyone is sexualized, it is the powerless who are most at
risk. Young girls, of course, are especially
vulnerable. In the past twenty years or so,
there have been several trends in fashion
and advertising that could be seen as cultural reactions to the women's movement,
as perhaps unconscious fear of female
power. One has been the obsession with
thinness. Another has been an increase
in images of violence against women.
Most disturbing has been the increasing sexualization of children, especially
girls. Sometimes the little girl is made up
and seductively posed. Sometimes the language is suggestive. "Very cherry," says the

[11]Two men and a baby, 1990, 10.

ad featuring a sexy little African-American girl who is wearing a dress with cherries all over it. A shocking ad in a gun magazine features a smiling little girl, a toddler, in a bathing suit that is tugged up suggestively in the rear.[12] The copy beneath the photo says, "short BUTTS from FLEMING FIREARMS." Other times girls are juxtaposed with grown women, as in the ad for underpants that says "You already know the feeling."

This is not only an American phenomenon. A growing national obses-    32 sion in Japan with schoolgirls dressed in uniforms is called "Loli-con," after Lolita.[13] In Tokyo hundreds of "image clubs" allow Japanese men to act out their fantasies with make-believe schoolgirls. A magazine called *V-Club* featuring pictures of naked elementary-school girls competes with another called *Anatomical Illustrations of Junior High School Girls*. Masao Miyamoto, a male psychiatrist, suggests that Japanese men are turning to girls because they feel threatened by the growing sophistication of older women.[14]

In recent years, this sexualization of little girls has become even more    33 disturbing as hints of violence enter the picture. A three-page ad for Prada clothing features a girl or very young woman with a barely pubescent body, clothed in what seem to be cotton panties and perhaps a training bra, viewed through a partially opened door. She seems surprised, startled, worried, as if she's heard a strange sound or glimpsed someone watching her. I suppose this could be a woman awaiting her lover, but it could as easily be a girl being preyed upon.

[12]Herbert, 1999, WK 17.
[13]Schoolgirls as sex toys, 1997, 2E.
[14]*Ibid.*

The 1996 murder *34* of six-year-old Jon-Benet Ramsey was a gold mine for the media, combining as it did child pornography and violence. In November of 1997 *Advertising Age* reported in an article entitled "JonBenet keeps hold on magazines" that the child had been on five magazine covers in October, "enough to capture the Cover Story lead for the month. The pre-adolescent beauty queen, found slain in her home last Christmas, garnered 6.5 points. The case earned a *triple play* [italics mine] on the *National Enquirer,* and one-time appearances on *People* and *Star.*"[15] Imagine describing a six-year-old child as "pre-adolescent."

Sometimes the models in ads are children, other times they just look *35* like children. Kate Moss was twenty when she said of herself, "I look twelve."[16] She epitomized the vacant, hollow-cheeked look known as "heroin chic" that was popular in the mid-nineties. She also often looked vulnerable, abused, and exploited. In one ad she is nude in the corner of a huge sofa, cringing as if braced for an impending sexual assault. In another,

[15]Johnson, 1997, 42.
[16]Leo, 1994, 27.

she is lying nude on her stomach, pliant, available, androgynous enough to appeal to all kinds of pedophiles. In a music video she is dead and bound to a chair while Johnny Cash sings "Delia's Gone."

It is not surprising that Kate Moss [36] models for Calvin Klein, the fashion designer who specializes in breaking taboos and thereby getting himself public outrage, media coverage, and more bang for his buck. In 1995 he brought the federal government down on himself by running a campaign that may have crossed the line into child pornography.[17] Very young models (and others who just seemed young) were featured in lascivious print ads and in television commercials designed to mimic child porn. The models were awkward, self-conscious. In one commercial, a boy stands in what seems to be a finished basement. A male voiceover tells him he has a great body and asks him to take off his shirt. The boy seems embarrassed but he complies. There was a great deal of protest, which brought the issue into national consciousness but which also gave Klein the publicity and free media coverage he was looking for. He pulled the ads but, at the same time, projected that his jeans sales would almost double from $115 million to $220 million that year, partly because of the free publicity but also because the controversy made his critics seem like prudes and thus positioned Klein as the daring rebel, a very appealing image to the majority of his customers.

[17]Sloan, 1996, 27.

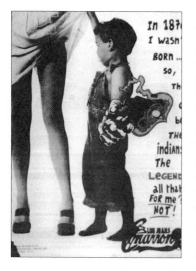

Having learned from this, in 1999 Klein launched a very brief advertising campaign featuring very little children frolicking in their underpants, which included a controversial billboard in Times Square.[18] Although in some ways this campaign was less offensive than the earlier one and might have gone unnoticed had the ads come from a department store catalog rather than from Calvin Klein, there was the expected protest and Klein quickly withdrew the ads, again getting a windfall of media coverage. In my opinion, the real obscenity of this campaign is the whole idea of people buying designer underwear for their little ones, especially in a country in which at least one in five children doesn't have enough to eat.

Although boys are sometimes sexualized in an overt way, they are more often portrayed as sexually precocious, as in the Pepsi commercial featuring the young boys ogling Cindy Crawford or the jeans ad portraying a very little boy looking up a woman's skirt. It may seem that I am reading too much into this ad, but imagine if the genders were reversed. We would fear for a little girl who was unzipping a man's fly in an ad (and we would be shocked, I would hope). Boys are vulnerable to sexual abuse too, but cultural attitudes make it difficult to take this seriously. As a result, boys are less likely to report abuse and to get treatment.

Many boys grow up feeling that they are unmanly if they are not always "ready for action," capable of and interested in sex with any woman who is available. Advertising doesn't cause this attitude, of course, but it contributes to it. A Levi Strauss commercial that ran in Asia features the shock of a schoolboy who discovers that the seductive young woman who has slipped a note into the jeans of an older student is his teacher. And an ad for BIC pens pictures a young boy wearing X-ray glasses while ogling the derriere of an older woman. Again, these ads would be unthinkable if the genders were reversed. It is increasingly difficult in such a toxic environment to see children, boys or girls, as *children.*

In the past few years there has been a proliferation of sexually grotesque toys for boys, such as a Spider Man female action figure whose exaggerated breasts have antennae coming out of them and a female Spawn figure with carved skulls for breasts. Meantime even children have easy access to pornography in video games and on the World Wide Web,

[18]Associated Press, 1999, February 18.

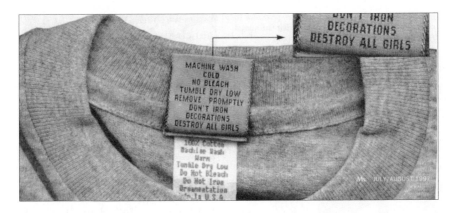

which includes explicit photographs of women having intercourse with groups of men, with dogs, donkeys, horses, and snakes; photographs of women being raped and tortured; some of these women made up to look like little girls.

It is hard for girls not to learn self-hatred in an environment in which there is such widespread and open contempt for women and girls. In 1997 a company called Senate distributed clothing with inside labels that included, in addition to the usual cleaning instructions, the line "Destroy all girls."[19] A Senate staffer explained that he thought it was "kind of cool." Given all this, it's not surprising that when boys and girls were asked in a recent study to write an essay on what it would be like to be the other gender, many boys wrote they would rather be dead. Girls had no trouble writing essays about activities, power, freedom, but boys were often stuck, could think of nothing.

It is also not surprising that, in such an environment, sexual harassment is considered normal and ordinary. According to an article in the journal *Eating Disorders*:

> In our work with young women, we have heard countless accounts of this contempt being expressed by their male peers: the girls who do not want to walk down a certain hallway in their high school because they are afraid of being publicly rated on a scale of one to ten; the girls who are subjected to barking, grunting, and mooing calls and labels of "dogs, cows, or pigs" when they pass by groups of male students; those who are teased about not measuring up to buxom, bikini-clad [models]; and the girls who are grabbed, pinched, groped, and fondled as they try to make their way through the school corridors.
>
> Harassing words do not slide harmlessly away as the taunting sounds dissipate. . . . They are slowly absorbed into the child's identity and developing sense of self, becoming an essential part of whom she sees herself to be.

[19]Wire and *Times* staff reports, 1997, D1.

Harassment involves the use of words as weapons to inflict pain and assert power. Harassing words are meant to instill fear, heighten bodily discomfort, and diminish the sense of self.[20]

It is probably difficult for those of us who are older to understand [43] how devastating and cruel and pervasive this harassment is, how different from the "teasing" some of us might remember from our own childhoods (not that that didn't hurt and do damage as well). A 1993 report by the American Association of University Women found that 76 percent of female students in grades eight to eleven and 56 percent of male students said they had been sexually harassed in school.[21] One high-school junior described a year of torment at her vocational school: "The boys call me slut, bitch. They call me a 10-timer, because they say I go with 10 guys at the same time. I put up with it because I have no choice. The teachers say it's because the boys think I'm pretty."[22]

High school and junior high school have always been hell for those [44] who were different in any way (gay teens have no doubt suffered the most, although "overweight" girls are a close second), but the harassment is more extreme and more physical these days. Many young men feel they have the right to judge and touch young women and the women often feel they have no choice but to submit. One young woman recalled that "the guys at school routinely swiped their hands across girls' legs to patrol their shaving prowess and then taunt them if they were slacking off. If I were running late, I'd protect myself by faux shaving—just doing the strip between the bottom of my jeans and the top of my cotton socks."[23]

Sexual battery, as well as inappropriate sexual gesturing, touching, [45] and fondling, is increasing not only in high schools but in elementary and middle schools as well.[24] There are reports of sexual assaults by students on other students as young as eight. A fifth-grade boy in Georgia repeatedly touched the breasts and genitals of one of his fellow students while saying, "I want to get in bed with you" and "I want to feel your boobs."[25] Authorities did nothing, although the girl complained and her grades fell. When her parents found a suicide note she had written, they took the board of education to court.

A high-school senior in an affluent suburban school in the Boston area [46] said she has been dragged by her arms so boys could look up her skirt and that boys have rested their heads on her chest while making lewd comments.[26] Another student in the same school was pinned down on a lunch table while a boy simulated sex on top of her. Neither student reported

[20]Larkin, Rice, and Russell, 1996, 5–26.
[21]Daley and Vigue, 1999, A12.
[22]Hart, 1998, A12.
[23]Mackler, 1998, 56.
[24]Daley and Vigue, 1999, A1, A12.
[25]Shin, 1999, 32.
[26]Daley and Vigue, 1999, A12.

any of the incidents, for fear of being ostracized by their peers. In another school in the Boston area, a sixteen-year-old girl, who had been digitally raped by a classmate, committed suicide.[27]

According to Nan Stein, a researcher at Wellesley College:                    47

> Schools may in fact be training grounds for the insidious cycle of domestic violence. . . . The school's hidden curriculum teaches young women to suffer abuse privately, that resistance is futile. When they witness harassment of others and fail to respond, they absorb a different kind of powerlessness—that they are incapable of standing up to injustice or acting in solidarity with their peers. Similarly, in schools boys receive permission, even training, to become batterers through the practice of sexual harassment.[28]

This pervasive harassment of and contempt for girls and women con-    48
stitute a kind of abuse. We know that addictions for women are rooted in trauma, that girls who are sexually abused are far more likely to become addicted to one substance or another. I contend that all girls growing up in this culture are sexually abused—abused by the pornographic images of female sexuality that surround them from birth, abused by all the violence against women and girls, and abused by the constant harassment and threat of violence. Abuse is a continuum, of course, and I am by no means implying that cultural abuse is as terrible as literally being raped and assaulted. However, it hurts, it does damage, and it sets girls up for addictions and self-destructive behavior. Many girls turn to food, alcohol, cigarettes, and other drugs in a misguided attempt to cope.

As Marian Sandmaier said in *The Invisible Alcoholics: Women and*    49
*Alcohol Abuse in America*, "In a culture that cuts off women from many of their own possibilities before they barely have had a chance to sense them, that pain belongs to all women. Outlets for coping may vary widely, and may be more or less addictive, more or less self-destructive. But at some level, all women know what it is to lack access to their own power, to live with a piece of themselves unclaimed."[29]

Today, every girl is endangered, not just those who have been physi-    50
cally and sexually abused. If girls from supportive homes with positive role models are at risk, imagine then how vulnerable are the girls who have been violated. No wonder they so often go under for good—ending up in abusive marriages, in prison, on the streets. And those who do are almost always in the grip of one addiction or another. More than half of women in prison are addicts and most are there for crimes directly related to their addiction.[30] Many who are there for murder killed men who had been battering them for years. Almost all of the women who are homeless or in prisons and mental institutions are the victims of male violence.

[27]Vigue and Abraham, 1999, B6.
[28]Stein, 1993, 316–17.
[29]Sandmaier, 1980, xviii.
[30]Snell, 1991.

Male violence exists within the same cultural and sociopolitical con- *51* text that contributes to addiction. Both can be fully understood only within this context, way beyond individual psychology and family dynamics. It is a context of systemic violence and oppression, including racism, classism, heterosexism, weightism, and ageism, as well as sexism, all of which are traumatizing in and of themselves. Advertising is only one part of this cultural context, but it is an important part and thus is a part of what traumatizes.

All right, you might think, these ads are shocking. They are probably *52* not good for us. But just what is the relationship of all these sexist and violent ads to addiction? Am I blaming advertisers for everything now? No. But I do contend that ads that contribute to a climate of disconnection also contribute to addiction. Ads that objectify women and sexualize children also play a role in the victimization of women and girls that often leads to addiction. When women are shown in positions of powerlessness, submission, and subjugation, the message to men is clear: women are always available as the targets of aggression and violence, women are inferior to men and thus deserve to be dominated, and women exist to fulfill the needs of men.

There is a further connection between images that legitimize male *53* domination of females and addiction. In his classic essay "The Cybernetics of Self" Gregory Bateson describes the fundamental belief of Western culture that we can dominate, control, and have power over almost every aspect of our experience.[31] We can get rid of pain, we can dominate people who threaten us, we can win in any interaction, we can be invulnerable. Bateson theorizes that this belief is fundamentally erroneous and leads to addiction, which he sees as a disordered attempt to get to a more "correct" state of mind, one in which we permit dependency, vulnerability, and mutuality. Bateson argues that we have no culturally sanctioned, nonaddictive way to achieve this state.

Claudia Bepko takes Bateson's theory further by arguing that the *54* stage is set for addiction by the overriding belief system maintaining that men have power and women are the objects of that power.[32] This assumption is as erroneous as is the assumption that we can control our emotions. But our entire culture is predicated on this illusion of male dominance, and our institutions are set up in ways that perpetuate it. According to Bepko, being socialized in an erroneous belief system leads to addiction because incongruity may arise between what one believes and how one actually feels. A man who feels he must be dominant but who actually feels vulnerable might use an addictive substance to lessen his feeling of vulnerability or to enhance his sense of dominance. A woman forced to show dependence who really feels powerful might use a drug or other substance either to enhance or disqualify the impulse to be powerful (as the old

[31]Bateson, 1972.
[32]Bepko, 1989.

Jefferson Airplane song says, "One pill makes you larger and one pill makes you small"). Thus gender-role socialization both shapes and is continually challenged by addictive behavior.

Bepko describes what she calls "the yin and yang of addiction." Both   55 men and women become addicted and suffer, but their individual addictions arise from their different positions in the world and have different effects. Men operate within a context in which both autonomy and entitlement to be taken care of are assumed; women within a context in which both dependency on a man and emotional and physical nurturing and caretaking are assumed. The contradictions in these prescriptions obviously create a bind: the male is independent but taken care of and the woman is dependent but the caretaker. Addiction is one response to the pain created by these contradictions.

Although the critical issues are dependency and control, these have   56 radically different meanings and outcomes for women and men. Since money, sexuality, size, strength, and competitive work convey power and status for men, gambling, sexual addictions, and work addiction tend to be predominantly male forms of compulsive behavior (although women are catching up as gender roles change). Women are still socialized to be physically and emotionally nurturing, so eating disorders, obsessive shopping or cleaning, self-mutilation, and compulsive behavior in relationships are common female forms of addictive behavior, as is prescription drug abuse, which reflects the cultural belief that women's emotions need to be subdued and controlled. A man is more likely to engage in addictive behavior that involves having power over others, whereas a woman's attempt at control is often focused on her own body.

It would be foolish to suggest that advertising is *the cause* of violence   57 against women—or of alcoholism or eating disorders or any other major problem. These problems are complex and have many contributing factors. There is no doubt that flagrant sexism and sex role stereotyping abound in all forms of the media. There is abundant information about this. It is far more difficult to document the effects of these stereotypes and images on the individuals and institutions exposed to them because, as I've said, it is difficult to separate media effects from other aspects of the socialization process and almost impossible to find a comparison group (just about everyone in America has been exposed to massive doses of advertising).

But, at the very least, advertising helps to create a climate in which   58 certain attitudes and values flourish, such as the attitude that women are valuable only as objects of men's desire, that real men are always sexually aggressive, that violence is erotic, and that women who are the victims of sexual assault "asked for it." These attitudes have especially terrible consequences for women abused as children, most of whom grow up feeling like objects and believing they are responsible for their own abuse. These are the very women who are likely to mutilate and starve themselves, to smoke, to become addicted to alcohol and other drugs. As Judith Herman wrote in her classic book *Father-Daughter Incest*:

These women alone suffered the consequences of their psychological impairment. Almost always, their anger and disappointment were expressed in self-destructive action: in unwanted pregnancies, in submission to rape and beatings, in addiction to alcohol and drugs, in attempted suicide.

. . . Consumed with rage, they nevertheless rarely caused trouble to anyone but themselves. In their own flesh, they bore repeated punishment for the crimes committed against them in their childhood.[33]

Addictions are not incidental in the lives of women. Most often they 59 are caused by (or at least related to) disturbances in relationships in childhood, often violent disturbances. They are fueled by a culture that sexualizes children, objectifies, trivializes, and silences women, disparages our interest in and skill at relating, and constantly threatens us with violence. Feeling isolated and disconnected, a girl or a woman reaches out to a substance to numb her pain, to be sure, but also to end her isolation, to relate, to connect. She reaches for alcohol or other drugs, she reaches for cigarettes, she reaches for men who don't love her, or she reaches for food. The advertisers are ready for her.

[33]Herman and Hirschman, 1981, 107–8.

BIBLIOGRAPHY

Abbey, A., Ross, L., and McDuffie, D. (1991). Alcohol's role in sexual assault. In Watson, R., ed. *Addictive behaviors in women.* Totowa, NJ: Humana Press.

Associated Press (1999, February 18). Calvin Klein retreats on ad. *Boston Globe,* A7.

Bateson, G. (1972). The cybernetics of self. In *Steps to an ecology of mind.* New York: Chandler Publishing.

Bepko, C. (1989). Disorders of power: Women and addiction in the family. In McGoldrick, M., Anderson, C. M., and Walsh, F., eds. (1989). *Women in families: A framework for family therapy.* New York: W. W. Norton, 406–26.

Blumenthal, S. J. (1995, July). *Violence against women.* Washington, DC: Department of Health and Human Services.

Brewers can help fight sexism (1991, October 28). *Advertising Age,* 28.

Daley, B., and Vigue, D. I. (1999, February 4). Sex harassment increasing amid students, officials say. *Boston Globe,* A1, A12.

Hart, J. (1998, June 8). Northampton confronts a crime, cruelty. *Boston Globe,* A1, A12.

Herbert, B. (1999, May 2). America's littlest shooters. *New York Times,* WK17.

Herman, J. L., and Hirschman, L. (1981). *Father-daughter incest.* Cambridge, MA: Harvard University Press.

Johnson, J. A. (1997, November 10). JonBenet keeps hold on magazines. *Advertising Age,* 42.

Kilbourne, J. (1994, May 15). 'Gender bender' ads: Same old sexism. *New York Times,* F13.

Larkin, J., Rice, C., and Russell, V. (1996, Spring). Slipping through the cracks: Sexual harassment. *Eating Disorders: The Journal of Treatment and Prevention,* vol. 4, no. 1, 5–26.

Leo, J. (1994, June 13). Selling the woman-child. *U.S. News and World Report,* 27.

Mackler, C. (1998). Memoirs of a (sorta) ex-shaver. In Edut, O., ed. (1998). *Adios, Barbie.* Seattle, WA: Seal Press, 55–61.

Martin, S. (1992). The epidemiology of alcohol-related interpersonal violence. *Alcohol, Health and Research World,* vol. 16, no. 3, 230–37.

Novello, A. (1991, October 18). Quoted by Associated Press, AMA to fight wife-beating. *St. Louis Post Dispatch*, 1, 15.

Quindlen, A. (1992, June 28). All of these you are. *New York Times*, E17.

Sandmaier, M. (1980). *The invisible alcoholics: Women and alcohol abuse in America.* New York: McGraw-Hill.

Schoolgirls as sex toys. (1997, April 16) *New York Times*, 2E.

Shin, A. (1999, April/May). Testing Title IX. *Ms.*, 32.

Sloan, P. (1996, July 8). Underwear ads caught in bind over sex appeal. *Advertising Age*, 27.

Snell, T. L. (1991). *Women in prison.* Washington, DC: U.S. Department of Justice.

Stein, N. (1993). No laughing matter: Sexual harassment in K–12 schools. In Buchwald, E., Fletcher, P. R., and Roth, M. (1993). *Transforming a rape culture.* Minneapolis, MN: Milkweed Editions, 311–31.

Tjaden, R., and Thoennes, N. (1998, November). *Prevalence, incidence, and consequences of violence against women: Findings from the National Violence Against Women Survey.* Washington, DC: U.S. Department of Justice.

Two men and a baby (1990, July/August). *Ms.*, 10.

Vigue, D. I., and Abraham, Y. (1999, February 7). Harassment a daily course for students. *Boston Globe*, B1, B6.

Weil, L. (1999, March). Leaps of faith. *Women's Review of Books*, 21.

Wilsnack, S. C., Plaud, J. J., Wilsnack, R. W., and Klassen, A. D. (1997). Sexuality, gender, and alcohol use. In Wilsnack, R. W., and Wilsnack, S. C., eds. *Gender and alcohol: Individual and social perspectives.* New Brunswick, NJ: Rutgers Center of Alcohol Studies, 262.

Wire and *Times* Staff Reports (1997, May 20). Orange County skate firm's 'destroy all girls' tags won't wash. *Los Angeles Times*, D1.

Wright, R. (1995, September 10). Brutality defines the lives of women around the world. *Boston Globe*, A2.

■ ■ ■

## Reading as a Writer: Analyzing Rhetorical Choices

1. Kilbourne spends much of the essay explaining why she finds certain advertisements harmful to women, but she also hints at the damage they do to men. Locate those passages, and, in class, discuss how you could develop her argument that men also are harmed by advertising. How would the essay be different if she had included more material on men?

2. Like many writers who analyze the effects of the media, Kilbourne seeks to show how media images influence us, but she does not establish a simplistic cause-and-effect relationship between the images we see and the ways we act. How *does* she explain the relationship between images and ideas/actions? Locate several places in her essay where she explains this relationship, and discuss what you think of the claims she makes.

## Writing as a Reader: Entering the Conversation of Ideas

1. Kilbourne and bell hooks use similar strategies of inviting readers to see familiar images (in advertising or on the screen) through new lenses and to consider the ways viewers are positioned to value (or devalue) people on the screen. Choose a film or a series of related advertisements as a "test

case" to analyze through the lenses of Kilbourne's and hooks's ideas, in order to see what your test case teaches viewers about gender and class norms. As you draw your own conclusions about your findings, keep in mind what these authors say about why it is important to take these images seriously.

2. While they take different approaches, Kilbourne and Judith Lorber both analyze the ways representations of male and female bodies foster assumptions about extreme differences between the sexes that are both artificial and damaging. Write an essay in which you place these authors in conversation, noting ways their different insights about women's and men's bodies help you understand the larger significance of what we believe about women and men in our culture.

## STEVEN JOHNSON

# Why Games Are Good for You

Steven Johnson writes about science and culture. His book *Interface Culture: How New Technology Transforms the Way We Create and Communicate* (1997) is considered one of the most important early texts to explain the impact of cybertechnology on human perception and communication, a subject to which he frequently returns. Johnson became more widely known with the publication of his best-selling book *Everything Bad Is Good for You: How Today's Popular Culture Is Actually Making Us Smarter* (2005), in which he defends the value of computer games, among other popular "time-wasting" pastimes. This reading is excerpted from *Everything Bad Is Good for You*. You will immediately grasp Johnson's interest in sailing against the current of popular opinion. In response to those who claim the sky is falling, Johnson argues that "the weather has never been better. It just takes a new kind of barometer to tell the difference."

The pages that follow are Johnson's barometer. As you read his analysis of pop culture pastimes, consider the games you found most absorbing as a child. Do you agree with Johnson about the kinds of skills those games taught you? What about the time you spend today on technological recreation—are you wasting time or getting smarter? Because Johnson is writing for a general audience, he does not use scholarly citations, but he does refer explicitly to the ideas of others in his main text and detailed notes. As you read, notice the many kinds of experts he refers to, and how he deploys their ideas to serve his larger purpose.

Leisure studies—which focuses on the ways we spend our free time—is a rich area of research. The question driving Johnson's analysis here about the purposes games serve is part of this ongoing conversation. What "work" does our play accomplish? Johnson has answers that may surprise you.

Y ou can't get much more conventional than the conventional wisdom    *1*
that kids today would be better off spending more time reading books,
and less time zoning out in front of their video games. The latest edition
of *Dr. Spock* — "revised and fully expanded for a new century" as the cover
reports — has this to say of video games: "The best that can be said of them
is that they may help promote eye-hand coordination in children. The
worst that can be said is that they sanction, and even promote aggression
and violent responses to conflict. But what can be said with much greater
certainty is this: most computer games are a colossal waste of time." But
where reading is concerned, the advice is quite different: "I suggest you
begin to foster in your children a love of reading and the printed word
from the start. . . . What is important is that your child be an avid reader."[1]

In the middle of 2004, the National Endowment for the Arts released    *2*
a study that showed that reading for pleasure had declined steadily among
all major American demographic groups. The writer Andrew Solomon
analyzed the consequences of this shift: "People who read for pleasure are
many times more likely than those who don't to visit museums and attend
musical performances, almost three times as likely to perform volunteer
and charity work, and almost twice as likely to attend sporting events.
Readers, in other words, are active, while nonreaders — more than half
the population — have settled into apathy. There is a basic social divide
between those for whom life is an accrual of fresh experience and knowledge, and those for whom maturity is a process of mental atrophy. The
shift toward the latter category is frightening."[2]

The intellectual nourishment of reading books is so deeply ingrained    *3*
in our assumptions that it's hard to contemplate a different viewpoint. But
as [Marshall] McLuhan famously observed, the problem with judging new
cultural systems on their own terms is that the presence of the recent past
inevitably colors your vision of the emerging form, highlighting the flaws
and imperfections. Games have historically suffered from this syndrome,
largely because they have been contrasted with the older conventions
of reading. To get around these prejudices, try this thought experiment.
Imagine an alternate world identical to ours save one techno-historical
change: video games were invented and popularized *before* books. In this
parallel universe, kids have been playing games for centuries — and then

---

[1] Benjamin Spock and Steven J. Parker, *Dr. Spock's Baby and Child Care* (New York:
Pocket Books, 1998), p. 625.

[2] Andrew Solomon, "The Closing of the American Book," *The New York Times*, July 10,
2004. Solomon is a thoughtful and eloquent writer, but this essay by him contains a
string of bizarre assertions, none of them supported by facts or common sense. Consider
this passage: "My last book was about depression, and the question I am most frequently
asked is why depression is on the rise. I talk about the loneliness that comes of spending
the day with a TV or a computer or video screen. Conversely, literary reading is an entry
into dialogue; a book can be a friend, talking not at you, but to you." Begin with the fact
that most video games contain genuine dialogue, where your character must interact
with other onscreen characters, in contrast to books, in which the "dialogue" between

these page-bound texts come along and suddenly they're all the rage. What would the teachers, and the parents, and the cultural authorities have to say about this frenzy of reading? I suspect it would sound something like this:

> Reading books chronically understimulates the senses. Unlike the long-standing tradition of gameplaying—which engages the child in a vivid, three-dimensional world filled with moving images and musical soundscapes, navigated and controlled with complex muscular movements—books are simply a barren string of words on the page. Only a small portion of the brain devoted to processing written language is activated during reading, while games engage the full range of the sensory and motor cortices.

> Books are also tragically isolating. While games have for many years engaged the young in complex social relationships with their peers, building and exploring worlds together, books force the child to sequester him- or herself in a quiet space, shut off from interaction with other children. These new "libraries" that have arisen in recent years to facilitate reading activities are a frightening sight: dozens of young children, normally so vivacious and socially interactive, sitting alone in cubicles, reading silently, oblivious to their peers.

> Many children enjoy reading books, of course, and no doubt some of the flights of fancy conveyed by reading have their escapist merits. But for a sizable percentage of the population, books are downright discriminatory. The reading craze of recent years cruelly taunts the 10 million Americans who suffer from dyslexia—a condition that didn't even exist as a condition until printed text came along to stigmatize its sufferers.

> But perhaps the most dangerous property of these books is the fact that they follow a fixed linear path. You can't control their narratives in any fashion—you simply sit back and have the story dictated to you. For those of us raised on interactive narratives, this property may seem astonishing. Why would anyone want to embark on an adventure utterly choreographed by another person? But today's generation embarks on such adventures millions of times a day. This risks instilling a general passivity in our children, making them feel as though they're powerless to change their circumstances. Reading is not an active, participatory process; it's a submissive one. The book readers of the younger generation are learning to "follow the plot" instead of learning to lead.

It should probably go without saying, but it probably goes better with saying, that I don't agree with this argument. But neither is it exactly right to say that its contentions are untrue. The argument relies on a kind of amplified selectivity: it foregrounds certain isolated properties of books,

---

reader and text is purely metaphorical. When you factor in the reality that most games are played in social contexts—together with friends in shared physical space, or over network connections—you get the sense that Solomon hasn't spent any time with the game form he lambastes. So that by the time he asserts, "Reading is harder than watching television or playing video games," you have to ask: Which video game, exactly, is he talking about? Certainly, reading *Ulysses* is harder than playing *PacMan*, but is reading Stephen King harder than playing *Zelda* or *SimCity*? Hardly.

and then projects worst-case scenarios based on these properties and their potential effects on the "younger generation." But it doesn't bring up any of the clear benefits of reading: the complexity of argument and storytelling offered by the book form; the stretching of the imagination triggered by reading words on a page; the shared experience you get when everyone is reading the same story.

A comparable sleight of hand is at work anytime you hear someone  5 bemoaning today's video game obsessions and their stupefying effects on tomorrow's generations. Games are not novels, and the ways in which they harbor novelistic aspirations are invariably the least interesting thing about them. You can judge games by the criteria designed to evaluate novels: Are the characters believable? Is the dialogue complex? But inevitably, the games will come up wanting. Games are good at novelistic storytelling the way Michael Jordan was good at playing baseball. Both could probably make a living at it, but their world-class talents lie elsewhere.

Before we get to those talents, let me say a few words about the vir-  6 tues of reading books. For the record, I think those virtues are immense ones—and not just because I make a living writing books. We should all encourage our kids to read more, to develop a comfort with and an appetite for reading. But even the most avid reader in this culture is invariably going to spend his or her time with other media—with games, television, movies, or the Internet. And these other forms of culture have intellectual or cognitive virtues in their own right—different from, but comparable to, the rewards of reading.

What are the rewards of reading, exactly? Broadly speaking, they  7 fall into two categories: the information conveyed by the book, and the mental work you have to do to process and store that information. Think of this as the difference between acquiring information and exercising the mind. When we encourage kids to read for pleasure, we're generally doing so because of the mental exercise involved. In Andrew Solomon's words: "[Reading] requires effort, concentration, attention. In exchange, it offers the stimulus to and the fruit of thought and feeling." Spock says: "Unlike most amusements, reading is an activity requiring active participation. We must do the reading ourselves—actively scan the letters, make sense of the words, and follow the thread of the story." Most tributes to the mental benefits of reading also invoke the power of imagination; reading books forces you to concoct entire worlds in your head, rather than simply ingest a series of prepackaged images. And then there is the slightly circular—though undoubtedly true—argument for the long-term career benefits: being an avid reader is good for you because the educational system and the job market put a high premium on reading skills.

To summarize, the cognitive benefits of reading involve these facul-  8 ties: effort, concentration, attention, the ability to make sense of words, to follow narrative threads, to sculpt imagined worlds out of mere sentences on the page. Those benefits are themselves amplified by the fact that society places a substantial emphasis on precisely this set of skills.

The very fact that I am presenting this argument to you in the form     9
of a book and not a television drama or a video game should make it clear
that I believe the printed word remains the most powerful vehicle for conveying complicated information—though the *electronic* word is starting
to give printed books a run for their money. The argument that follows is
centered squarely on the side of mental exercise—and not content. I aim
to persuade you of two things:

1. By almost all the standards we use to measure reading's cognitive
   benefits—attention, memory, following threads, and so on—the nonliterary popular culture has been steadily growing more challenging over
   the past thirty years.

2. Increasingly, the nonliterary popular culture is honing *different* mental
   skills that are just as important as the ones exercised by reading books.

Despite the warnings of Dr. Spock, the most powerful examples of both     10
these trends are found in the world of video games. Over the past few years,
you may have noticed the appearance of a certain type of story about gaming culture in mainstream newspapers and periodicals. The message of that
story ultimately reduces down to: Playing video games may not actually be
a *complete* waste of time. Invariably these stories point to some new study
focused on a minor side effect of gameplaying—often manual dexterity
or visual memory—and explain that heavy gamers show improved skills
compared to non-gamers.[3] (The other common let's-take-games-seriously

---

[3] I don't dwell on the manual dexterity question here, but it's worth noting how the
control systems for these games have grown strikingly more complex over the past decade
or so. Compare the original *Legend of Zelda* (July 1987), on the original NES, to the current
*Zelda*, on the GameCube (March 2003). In sixteen years, games have changed as follows:

| THEN | NOW |
|---|---|
| *Controller* | *Controller* |
| 4 direction buttons | 2 joysticks + 4 direction buttons |
| 2 action buttons | 7 action buttons |
| Each button has a single function. | Each combo of buttons has a unique function. |
| | |
| *Perspective* | *Perspective* |
| Static overhead view | Dynamic player-controlled "camera" view |
| You always have complete vision. | Your vision is limited. You must control it. |
| The game is "flat" (two-dimensional). | The game is "virtual" (three-dimensional). |
| | |
| *Gameplay* | *Gameplay* |
| Movement is in one of four directions. | Movement is in any direction, including up and down. |
| | |
| Fighting: 2 buttons | Fighting: More than 10 different button combos. Requires accurate timing and coordination. |
| | |
| Objects: Press a single button. | Objects: Assign a button, learn unique controls to use each object. Requires timing, training. |

story is financial, usually pointing to the fact that the gaming industry now pulls in more money than Hollywood.)

Now, I have no doubt that playing today's games does in fact improve  *11*
your visual intelligence and your manual dexterity, but the virtues of gaming run far deeper than hand-eye coordination. When I read these ostensibly positive accounts of video games, they strike me as the equivalent of writing a story about the merits of the great novels and focusing on how reading them can improve your spelling. It's true enough, I suppose, but it doesn't do justice to the rich, textured experience of novel reading. There's a comparable blindness at work in the way games have been covered to date. For all the discussion of gaming culture that you see, the actual experience of playing games has been strangely misrepresented. We hear a lot about the content of games: the carnage and drive-by killings and adolescent fantasies. But we rarely hear accurate descriptions about what it actually *feels like* to spend time in these virtual worlds. I worry about the experiential gap between people who have immersed themselves in games, and people who have only heard secondhand reports, because the gap makes it difficult to discuss the meaning of games in a coherent way. It reminds me of the way the social critic Jane Jacobs felt about the thriving urban neighborhoods she documented in the sixties: "People who know well such animated city streets will know how it is. People who do not will always have it a little wrong in their heads—like the old prints of rhinoceroses made from travelers' descriptions of the rhinoceroses."

So what does the rhinoceros actually look like?[4] The first and last thing  *12*
that should be said about the experience of playing today's video games, the thing you almost never hear in the mainstream coverage, is that games are fiendishly, sometimes maddeningly, *hard.*

The dirty little secret of gaming is how much time you spend not  *13*
having fun. You may be frustrated; you may be confused or disoriented;

[4]Henry Jenkins has painted perhaps the most accurate picture of the rhinoceros of pop culture over the past decade: "Often, our response to popular culture is shaped by a hunger for simple answers and quick actions. It is important to take the time to understand the complexity of contemporary culture. We need to learn how to be safe, critical, and creative users of media. We need to evaluate the information and entertainment we consume. We need to understand the emotional investments we make in media content. And perhaps most importantly, we need to learn not to treat differences in taste as mental pathologies or social problems. We need to think, talk, and listen. When we tell students that popular culture has no place in classroom discussions, we are signaling to them that what they learn in school has little to do with the things that matter to them at home. When we avoid discussing popular culture at the dinner table, we may be suggesting we have no interest in things that are important to our children. When we tell our parents that they wouldn't understand our music or our fashion choices, we are cutting them off from an important part of who we are and what we value. We do not need to share each other's passions. But we do need to respect and understand them." "Encouraging Conversations About Popular Culture and Media Convergence: An Outreach Program for Parents, Students, and Teachers, March–May 2000." http://web.mit .edu/21fms/www/faculty/henry3/resourceguide.html.

you may be stuck. When you put the game down and move back into the real world, you may find yourself mentally working through the problem you've been wrestling with, as though you were worrying a loose tooth. If this is mindless escapism, it's a strangely masochistic version. Who wants to escape to a world that irritates you 90 percent of the time?

Consider the story of Troy Stolle, a construction site worker from Indianapolis profiled by the technology critic Julian Dibbell. When he's not performing his day job as a carpenter building wooden molds, Stolle lives in the virtual world of *Ultima Online*, the fantasy-themed game that allows you to create a character—sometimes called an avatar—and interact with thousands of other avatars controlled by other humans, connected to the game over the Net. (Imagine a version of Dungeons & Dragons where you're playing with thousands of strangers from all over the world, and you'll get the idea.) *Ultima* and related games like *EverQuest* have famously developed vibrant simulated economies that have begun to leak out into the real world. You can buy a magic sword or a plot of land—entirely made of digital code, mind you—for hundreds of dollars on eBay. But earning these goods the old-fashioned within-the-gameworld way takes time—a lot of time. Dibbell describes the ordeal Stolle had to go through to have his avatar, named Nils Hansen, purchase a new house in the *Ultima* world:

> Stolle had had to come up with the money for the deed. To get the money, he had to sell his old house. To get that house in the first place, he had to spend hours crafting virtual swords and plate mail to sell to a steady clientele of about three dozen fellow players. To attract and keep that clientele, he had to bring Nils Hansen's blacksmithing skills up to Grandmaster. To reach that level, Stolle spent six months doing nothing but smithing: He clicked on hillsides to mine ore, headed to a forge to click the ore into ingots, clicked again to turn the ingots into weapons and armor, and then headed back to the hills to start all over again, each time raising Nils' skill level some tiny fraction of a percentage point, inching him closer to the distant goal of 100 points and the illustrious title of Grandmaster Blacksmith.
>
> Take a moment now to pause, step back, and consider just what was going on here: Every day, month after month, a man was coming home from a full day of bone-jarringly repetitive work with hammer and nails to put in a full night of finger-numbingly repetitive work with "hammer" and "anvil"—and paying $9.95 per month for the privilege. Ask Stolle to make sense of this, and he has a ready answer: "Well, it's not work if you enjoy it." Which, of course, begs the question: Why would anyone enjoy it?[5]

Why? Anyone who has spent more than a few hours trying to complete a game knows the feeling: You get to a point where there's a sequence of tasks you know you have to complete to proceed further into the world, but the tasks themselves are more like chores than entertainment, something you *have* to do, not something you want to do: building roads and laying power lines, retreating through a tunnel sequence to find an object

[5] Julian Dibbell, "The Unreal-Estate Boom," *Wired,* January 2003.

you've left behind, conversing with characters when you've already memorized their lines. And yet a large part of the population performing these tasks every day is composed of precisely the demographic group most averse to doing chores. If you practically have to lock kids in their room to get them to do their math homework, and threaten to ground them to get them to take out the trash, then why are they willing to spend six months smithing in *Ultima*? You'll often hear video games included on the list of the debased instant gratifications that abound in our culture, right up there with raunchy music videos and fast food. But compared to most forms of popular entertainment, games turn out to be all about *delayed* gratification—sometimes so long delayed that you wonder if the gratification is ever going to show.

The clearest measure of the cognitive challenges posed by modern  16
games is the sheer size of the cottage industry devoted to publishing game guides, sometimes called walk-throughs, that give you detailed, step-by-step explanations of how to complete the game that is currently torturing you. During my twenties, I'd wager that I spent somewhere shockingly close to a thousand dollars buying assorted cheat sheets, maps, help books, and phone support to assist my usually futile attempt to complete a video game. My relationship to these reference texts is intimately bound up with my memory of each game, so that the *Myst* sequel *Riven* brings to mind those hours on the automated phone support line, listening to a recorded voice explain that the lever has to be rotated 270 degrees before the blue pipe will connect with the transom, while the playful *Banjo-Kazooie* conjures up a cheery atlas of vibrant level maps, like a child's book where the story has been replaced with linear instruction sets: jump twice on the mushroom, then grab the gold medallion in the moat. Admitting just how much money I spent on these guides sounds like a cry for help, I know, but the great, looming racks of these game guides at most software stores are clear evidence that I am not alone in this habit. The guidebook for the controversial hit game *Grand Theft Auto* alone has sold more than 1.6 million copies.

Think about the existence of these guides in the context of other forms  17
of popular entertainment. There are plenty of supplementary texts that accompany Hollywood movies or Billboard chart-toppers: celebrity profiles, lyrics sheets, reviews, fan sites, commentary tracks on DVDs. These texts can widen your understanding of a film or an album, but you'll almost never find yourself *needing* one. People don't walk into theaters with guidebooks that they consult via flashlight during the film. But they regularly rely on these guides when playing a game. The closest cultural form to the game guide is the august tradition of CliffsNotes marketed as readers' supplements to the Great Books. There's nothing puzzling about the existence of CliffsNotes: we accept both the fact that the Great Books are complicated, and the fact that millions of young people are forced more or less against their will to at least pretend to read them. Ergo: a thriving market for CliffsNotes. Game guides, however, confound our expectations:

because we're not used to accepting the complexity of gaming culture, and because nobody's forcing the kids to master these games.

The need for such guides is a relatively new development: You didn't    18 need ten pages to explain the *PacMan* system, but two hundred pages barely does justice to an expanding universe like *EverQuest* or *Ultima*. You need them because the complexity of these worlds can be overwhelming: You're stuck in the middle of a level, with all the various exits locked and no sign of a key. Or the password for the control room you thought you found two hours ago turns out not to work. Or the worst case: You're wandering aimlessly through hallways, like those famous tracking shots from *The Shining*, and you've got no real idea what you're supposed to be doing next.

This aimlessness, of course, is the price of interactivity. You're more    19 in control of the narrative now, but your supply of information about the narrative—whom you should talk to next, where that mysterious package has been hidden—is only partial, and so playing one of these games is ultimately all about filling in that information gap. When it works, it can be exhilarating, but when it doesn't—well, that's when you start shelling out the fifteen bucks for the cheat sheet. And then you find yourself hunched over the computer screen, help guide splayed open on the desk, flipping back and forth between the virtual world and the level maps, trying to find your way. After a certain point—perhaps when the level maps don't turn out to be all that helpful, or perhaps when you find yourself reading the help guides over dinner—you start saying to yourself: Remind me why this is fun?

So why does anyone bother playing these things? Why do we use the    20 word "play" to describe this torture? I'm always amazed to see what our brains are willing to tolerate to reach the next level in these games. Several years ago I found myself on a family vacation with my seven-year-old nephew, and on one rainy day I decided to introduce him to the wonders of *SimCity 2000*, the legendary city simulator that allows you to play Robert Moses to a growing virtual metropolis. For most of our session, I was controlling the game, pointing out landmarks as I scrolled around my little town. I suspect I was a somewhat condescending guide—treating the virtual world as more of a model train layout than a complex system. But he was picking up the game's inner logic nonetheless. After about an hour of tinkering, I was concentrating on trying to revive one particularly rundown manufacturing district. As I contemplated my options, my nephew piped up: "I think we need to lower our industrial tax rates." He said it as naturally, and as confidently, as he might have said, "I think we need to shoot the bad guy."

The interesting question here for me is not whether games are, on the    21 whole, more complex than most other cultural experiences targeted at kids today—I think the answer to that is an emphatic yes. The question is why kids are so eager to soak up that much information when it is delivered to them in game form. My nephew would be asleep in five seconds if you popped him down in an urban studies classroom, but somehow an hour of playing *SimCity* taught him that high tax rates in industrial areas can stifle development. That's a powerful learning experience, for reasons we'll explore in the coming pages. But let's start with the more elemental question of desire. Why does a seven-year-old soak up the intricacies of industrial economics in game form, when the same subject would send him screaming for the exits in a classroom?

The quick explanations of this mystery are not helpful. Some might   22
say it's the flashy graphics, but games have been ensnaring our attention since the days of *Pong*, which was—graphically speaking—a huge step backward compared with television or movies, not to mention reality. Others would say it's the violence and sex, and yet games like *SimCity*—and indeed most of the best-selling games of all time—have almost no violence and sex in them. Some might argue that it's the interactivity that hooks, the engagement of building your own narrative. But if active participation alone functions as a drug that entices the mind, then why isn't the supremely *passive* medium of television repellant to kids?

Why do games captivate? I believe the answer involves a deeper prop-   23
erty that most games share—a property that will be instantly familiar to anyone who has spent time in this world, but one that is also strangely absent from most outside descriptions. To appreciate this property you need to look at game culture through the lens of neuroscience. There's a logical reason to use that lens, of course: If you're trying to figure out why cocaine is addictive, you need a working model of what cocaine is, and you need a working model of how the brain functions. The same goes for the question of why games are such powerful attractors. Explaining that phenomenon without a working model of the mind tells only half the story.

. . . Cultural critics like to speculate on the cognitive changes induced   24
by new forms of media, but they rarely invoke the insights of brain science and other empirical research in backing up those claims. All too often, this has the effect of reducing their arguments to mere superstition. If you're trying to make sense of a new cultural form's effect on the way we view the world, you need to be able to describe the cultural object in some detail, and also demonstrate how that object transforms the mind that is apprehending it. In some instances, you can measure that transformation through traditional modes of intelligence testing; in some cases, you can measure changes by looking at brain activity directly, thanks to modern scanning technology; and in cases where the empirical research hasn't yet been done, you can make informed speculation based on our understanding of how the brain works.

To date, there has been very little direct research into the question of   25
how games manage to get kids to learn without realizing that they're learning. But a strong case can be made that the power of games to captivate involves their ability to tap into the brain's natural reward circuitry. Because of its central role in drug addiction, the reward circuits of the brain have been extensively studied and mapped in recent years. Two insights that have emerged from this study are pertinent to the understanding of games. First, neuroscientists have drawn a crucial distinction between the way the brain

seeks out reward and the way it delivers pleasure. The body's natural pain-killers, the opioids, are the brain's pure pleasure drugs, while the reward system revolves around the neurotransmitter dopamine interacting with specific receptors in a part of the brain called the nucleus accumbens.

The dopamine system is a kind of accountant: keeping track of 26 expected rewards, and sending out an alert—in the form of lowered dopamine levels—when those rewards don't arrive as promised. When the pack-a-day smoker deprives himself of his morning cigarette; when the hotshot Wall Street trader doesn't get the bonus he was planning on; when the late-night snacker opens the freezer to find someone's pilfered all the Ben & Jerry's—the disappointment and craving these people experience is triggered by lowered dopamine levels.

The neuroscientist Jaak Panksepp calls the dopamine system the 27 brain's "seeking" circuitry, propelling us to seek out new avenues for reward in our environment. Where our brain wiring is concerned, the craving instinct triggers a desire to explore. The system says, in effect: "Can't find the reward you were promised? Perhaps if you just look a little harder you'll be in luck—it's got to be around here somewhere."

How do these findings connect to games? Researchers have long sus- 28 pected that geometric games like *Tetris* have such a hypnotic hold over us (longtime *Tetris* players have vivid dreams about the game) because the game's elemental shapes activate modules in our visual system that execute low-level forms of pattern recognition—sensing parallel and per-pendicular lines, for instance. These modules are churning away in the background all the time, but the simplified graphics of *Tetris* bring them front and center in our consciousness. I believe that what *Tetris* does to our visual circuitry, most video games do to the reward circuitry of the brain.

Real life is full of rewards, which is one reason why there are now so 29 many forms of addiction. You can be rewarded by love and social con-nection, financial success, drug abuse, shopping, chocolate, and watching your favorite team win the Super Bowl. But supermarkets and shopping malls aside, most of life goes by without the potential rewards available to you being clearly defined. You know you'd like that promotion, but it's a long way off, and right now you've got to deal with getting this memo out the door. Real-life reward usually hovers at the margins of day-to-day existence—except for the more primal rewards of eating and making love, both of which exceed video games in their addictiveness.

In the gameworld, reward is everywhere. The universe is literally teem- 30 ing with objects that deliver very clearly articulated rewards: more life, access to new levels, new equipment, new spells. Game rewards are fractal; each scale contains its own reward network, whether you're just learning to use the controller, or simply trying to solve a puzzle to raise some extra cash, or attempting to complete the game's ultimate mission. Most of the crucial work in game interface design revolves around keeping players noti-fied of potential rewards available to them, and how much those rewards are currently needed. Just as *Tetris* streamlines the fuzzy world of visual reality to a core set of interacting shapes, most games offer a fictional world where rewards are larger, and more vivid, more clearly defined, than life.

This is true even of games that have been rightly celebrated for their 31 open-endedness. *SimCity* is famous for not forcing the player along a pre-ordained narrative line; you can build any kind of community you want: small farming villages, vast industrial Coketowns, high-centric edge cities or pedestrian-friendly neighborhoods. But the game has a subtle reward architecture that plays a major role in the game's addictiveness: the software withholds a trove of objects and activities until you've reached certain predefined levels, either of population, money, or popularity. You can build pretty much any kind of environment you want playing *SimCity*, but you can't build a baseball stadium until you have fifty thousand residents. Similarly, *Grand Theft Auto* allows players to drive aimlessly through a vast urban environment, creating their own narratives as they explore the space. But for all that open-endedness, the game still forces you to complete a series of pre-defined missions before you are allowed to enter new areas of the city. The very games that are supposed to be emblems of unstructured user control turn out to dangle rewards at every corner.

"Seeking" is the perfect word for the drive these designs instill in their 32 players. You want to win the game, of course, and perhaps you want to see the game's narrative completed. In the initial stages of play, you may just be dazzled by the game's graphics. But most of the time, when you're hooked on a game, what draws you in is an elemental form of desire: the desire to *see the next thing*. You want to cross that bridge to see what the east side of the city looks like, or try out that teleportation module, or build an aquarium on the harbor. To someone who has never felt that sort of compulsion, the underlying motivation can seem a little strange: You want to build the aquarium not, in the old mountaineering expression, because it's there, but rather because it's not there, or not there *yet*. It's not there, but you know—because you've read the manual or the game guide, or because the interface is flashing it in front of your eyes—you know that if you just apply yourself, if you spend a little more time cultivating new residents and watching the annual budget, the aquarium will eventually be yours to savor.

In a sense, neuroscience has offered up a prediction here, one that 33 games obligingly confirm. If you create a system where rewards are both clearly defined and achieved by exploring an environment, you'll find human brains drawn to those systems, even if they're made up of virtual characters and simulated sidewalks. It's not the subject matter of these games that attracts—if that were the case, you'd never see twenty-somethings following absurd rescue-the-princess storylines like the best-selling *Zelda* series on the Nintendo platform. It's the reward system that draws those players in, and keeps their famously short attention spans locked on the screen. No other form of entertainment offers that cocktail of reward and exploration: We don't "explore" movies or television or music in anything but the most figurative sense of the word. And while there are rewards to those other forms—music in fact has been shown to trigger opioid release in the brain—they don't come in the exaggerated, tantalizing packaging that video games wrap around them.

You might reasonably object at this point that I have merely dem-  34
onstrated that video games are the digital equivalent of crack cocaine. Crack also has a powerful hold over the human brain, thanks in part to its manipulations of the dopamine system. But that doesn't make it a good thing. If games have been unwittingly designed to lock into our brain's reward architecture, then what positive value are we getting out of that intoxication? . . .

Here again, you have to shed your expectations about older cultural  35
forms to make sense of the new. Game players are not soaking up moral counsel, life lessons, or rich psychological portraits. They are not having emotional experiences with their Xbox, other than the occasional adrenaline rush. The narratives they help create now rival pulp Hollywood fare, which is an accomplishment when measured against the narratives of *Pac-Man* and *Pong*, but it's still setting the bar pretty low. With the occasional exception, the actual *content* of the game is often childish or gratuitously menacing—though, again, not any more so than your average summer blockbuster. Complex social and historical simulations like *Age of Empires* or *Civilization* do dominate the game charts, and no doubt these games do impart some useful information about ancient Rome or the design of mass transit systems. But much of the roleplay inside the gaming world alternates between drive-by shooting and princess rescuing.

De-emphasizing the content of game culture shouldn't be seen as a  36
cop-out. We ignore the content of many activities that are widely considered to be good for the brain or the body. No one complains about the simplistic, militaristic plot of chess games. ("It always ends the same way!") We teach algebra to children knowing full well that the day they leave the classroom, ninety-nine percent of those kids will never again directly employ their algebraic skills. Learning algebra isn't about acquiring a specific tool; it's about building up a mental muscle that will come in handy elsewhere. You don't go to the gym because you're interested in learning how to operate a StairMaster; you go to the gym because operating a StairMaster does something laudable to your body, the benefits of which you enjoy during the many hours of the week when you're not on a StairMaster.

So it is with games. It's not *what* you're thinking about when you're  37
playing a game, it's *the way* you're thinking that matters. The distinction is not exclusive to games, of course. Here's John Dewey, in his book *Experience and Education*: "Perhaps the greatest of all pedagogical fallacies is the notion that a person learns only that particular thing he is studying at the time. Collateral learning in the way of formation of enduring attitudes, of likes and dislikes, may be and often is much more important than the spelling lesson or lesson in geography or history that is learned. For these attitudes are fundamentally what count in the future."[6]

---

[6]John Dewey, *Experience and Education* (London: Collier, 1963), p. 48.

This is precisely where we need to make our portrait of the rhinoceros  *38*
as accurate as possible: defining the collateral learning that goes beyond
the explicit content of the experience. Start with the basics: Far more than
books or movies or music, games force you to make *decisions.* Novels may
activate our imagination, and music may conjure up powerful emotions,
but games force you to decide, to choose, to prioritize. All the intellectual
benefits of gaming derive from this fundamental virtue, because learning how to think is ultimately about learning to make the right decisions:
weighing evidence, analyzing situations, consulting your long-term goals,
and then deciding. No other pop cultural form directly engages the brain's
decision-making apparatus in the same way. From the outside, the primary
activity of a gamer looks like a fury of clicking and shooting, which is why
so much of the conventional wisdom about games focuses on hand-eye
coordination. But if you peer inside the gamer's mind, the primary activity turns out to be another creature altogether: making decisions, some of
them snap judgments, some long-term strategies.

■ ■ ■

### Reading as a Writer: Analyzing Rhetorical Choices

1.  Why do you think Johnson opens with the debate that pits the playing of video
    games against the practice of reading? Where exactly does he dive in with his
    own perspective on debate? What is the "sleight of hand" he refers to in para-
    graph 5? How do his examples in the following paragraphs complicate this sim-
    plistic debate about the relative virtues of video games and reading? What are
    your thoughts on this debate?

2.  Johnson has a very distinctive voice on the page, and often addresses the reader
    as "you"—practice that is unconventional in researched writing. Locate at least
    three sentences in which you think Johnson's voice is particularly distinctive,
    and discuss what happens in those sentences that captures your attention.
    What insights (about tone, word choice, rhetorical strategy) might you apply
    to your own writing?

### Writing as a Reader: Entering the Conversation of Ideas

1.  Johnson and S. Craig Watkins share an interest in paying close attention
    to activities widely thought of as "time-wasters." They draw different con-
    clusions about what we can learn from the ways people (especially young
    people) use online time and video games. Compose an essay in which you
    use insights from both authors to make a point about the positive and
    negative aspects of online time and video games, using specific examples
    to illustrate your points, as these authors do. What is the significance of
    your findings?

2.  Johnson argues that "everything bad is good for you"; Eric Schlosser, on
    the other hand, argues almost the opposite in his attack on advertising to
    "Kid Kustomers." Using the strategies these authors employ, write an essay
    in which you argue against the prevailing opinion that some aspect of

popular culture is either "good" or "bad" for us. As Johnson and Schlosser do, be sure to offer concrete and detailed examples, and explain why readers should care about this issue.

## KATHERINE BESSIÈRE, A. FLEMING SEAY, AND SARA KIESLER

# The Ideal Elf: Identity Exploration in World of Warcraft

These three authors, Katherine Bessière, A. Fleming Seay, and Sara Kiesler, research the relationship between humans and computers in a variety of settings. Their publications, written with various collaborators, use social science and behavioral science theory and methods to analyze the significance of human interactions with technology and to examine the wide-ranging effects of emerging technologies on communities. This essay, a quantitative analysis that appeared in the academic journal *CyberPsychology & Behavior* in 2007, examines the ways players use avatars in massively multiplayer online role-playing games (MMORPGs).

The authors focus on World of Warcraft (WoW) players and consider the freedom and possibilities that come with creating an online character with "collaborators who have no prior knowledge of the player or his real-life situation" (para. 3). Using fifty-one WoW players' responses to survey questions, the authors assess the significance in the self-reported differences among the players' actual selves, their WoW characters, and their description of their ideal selves. Before you read this piece, you might think about and discuss your expectations on this topic, based either on your own experiences with creating characters for WoW or similar games or on watching your friends participate. As you will see, some of the authors' expectations were fulfilled, and others were not; readers are allowed to watch them puzzle through their findings.

This essay is structured like a traditional social science paper, with sections for the hypotheses, methods, and results. How does the structure of the piece affect your experience of reading it? Pay attention to your response as you read the different presentations of data in the "Results" section, including the two charts. Which formats do you find most persuasive, and why? As you read the "Discussion" section, evaluate the authors' conclusions, as well as the limitations they see in their own study (every study has limitations of one sort or another). Given your own experiences with online games, what expectations do you have for this kind of study in different demographics? How might the authors' conclusions be applied to other online characterizations of ourselves, such as on Facebook, dating services, or other screen presences?

# Abstract

In this study, we examine the identity exploration possibilities presented by online multiplayer games in which players use graphics tools and character-creation software to construct an avatar, or character. We predicted World of Warcraft players would create their main character more similar to their ideal self than the players themselves were. Our results support this idea; a sample of players rated their character as having more favorable attributes that were more favorable than their own self-rated attributes. This trend was stronger among those with lower psychological well-being, who rated themselves comparatively lower than they rated their character. Our results suggest that the game world allows players the freedom to create successful virtual selves regardless of the constraints of their actual situation.

# Introduction

The massively multiplayer online role-playing game (MMORPG) is a per- *1* sistent, immersive online world in which people create and enact characters who pursue adventure, success in war, and other social and nonsocial goals. Like quilting and reality TV, MMORPGs are entertaining and provide an escape from everyday cares.[1,2] The games involve competition and collaborations that enhance gamers' enjoyment.[3] The games also offer players the opportunity for personal expression and competence building through the construction of their character and the character's achievement over time. In the current research, we focus on this last, potentially self-enhancing value of MMORPGs. We report survey results from a sample of players that suggest the players' characters express aspects of the players' ideal selves with implications for their sense of well-being.

## *Character and identity in MMORPGs*

MMORPGs have several critical features that affect players' psychologi- *2* cal experience, among which are the characters that players create as an embodied representation of themselves. As players gain experience in the game, their characters accumulate knowledge, skills, and resources, gaining instrumental value over time. Players also feel psychologically connected to their character, often keeping the same one for months or years. Characters also are the medium through which players experience social interaction in the game. MMORPGs are intensely competitive, often in (virtually) violent ways involving death and destruction, and characters cannot survive alone. Players rely on other players' characters for training, information, and resources, forming groups and intergroup collaborations. Players' reliance on others gives rise to robust communities in which players transact their relationships through their virtual characters not only in the game but also through instant messaging, Web forums, e-mail, and voice over IP networks.

Sherry Turkle[4] has argued that online environments offer people the 3
option of creating multiple representations of themselves and exploring
new aspects of themselves (see also Reid[5]). Previous research on online
groups suggests that in some cases the representations people make of
themselves online are an amalgamation of their actual and ideal selves—
that is, that the virtual self is a somewhat idealized actual self.[6,7] From
these ideas, we argue that MMORPGs are a mode by which the player,
through a constructed character, can enact aspects of his or her ideal self—
the physical or psychological self the player wishes to be. For instance, a
young player can create a character who is more mature, braver, stronger,
or more outgoing than the player feels he himself is. This fantasy-creation
process is supported by the fact that the player has an audience and collaborators who have no prior knowledge of the player or his real-life situation.

We propose that those who are dissatisfied with aspects of themselves 4
are more likely than those who are content with the way they are to engage
in virtual self-enhancement through their character. Some evidence suggests that those with a more marginalized self-identity seek affirmation
in their use of the Internet,[7] and those scoring higher in depression are
more likely to use the Internet for escape.[8] The chance to exist in a persistent online world where their character can interact with others freely
and anonymously may give the former group a means to escape poor self-
evaluation by eschewing negative traits and enacting a better virtual self.

### Character creation in World of Warcraft

This study was conducted among players of a popular MMORPG titled 5
World of Warcraft (WoW). In WoW, each player creates at least one character (most players have one primary character) that serves as the player's
physical representative in the digital world. The character-creation process involves making decisions about the appearance, profession, and personality of the character. Once created, the character travels around the
virtual world, gaining skills, experience, and riches and defeating monsters, discovering new locations, and interacting with other players' characters. Players are referred to by their character's name, and they interact
with others as that character. This process and the anonymity offered by
the game allows players, as their character, to escape real-world norms
and expectations and to act out roles and try out personas that range from
enhanced versions of their real-life self to alter-egos who behave in rep-
rehensible ways. In these respects, WoW players' characters are virtual
selves.

### Hypotheses

We predicted, first, that WoW players would create characters who repre- 6
sent aspects of both themselves and their ideal selves. In other words, the
difference between the attributes of a player's virtual (character) and ideal
selves, henceforth called the *character discrepancy*, will be smaller than the

difference between the attributes of a player's real and ideal selves, henceforth called the *self discrepancy*.

**Hypothesis 1:** Players will view their character as being more similar to their ideal self than they themselves are, thus making the character discrepancy smaller than the self discrepancy.

Based on previous research, we also argued that those with poorer 7 psychological well-being and larger self discrepancies would be more likely to idealize their character.

**Hypothesis 2:** Those scoring less positively on measures of psychological well-being will create characters who are closer to their ideal self and less like their actual self than will those scoring more positively on measures of psychological well-being.

## Method

We administered a survey via the Internet to a sample of players of WoW 8 as part of a laboratory study of the game. E-mails soliciting participation in the online survey were sent to a listserv at a local university and to a local gaming group. Participants received no compensation for completing this survey.

### Participants

Sixty-eight participants responded to the e-mail query for WoW players 9 and subsequently completed the survey. From the answers to filtering questions about their play, we determined that 17 respondents were not WoW players. They were dropped from the sample, leaving 51 valid participants. The valid participants' ages ranged from 18 to 27 years old with a mean of 21 years. Participants were primarily male (43 men, 8 women).

### Measures

The survey was conducted in the spring of 2005. Respondents were asked a 10 battery of questions about WoW, their actual self, their character, and their ideal self. An adjective rating method, a version of the Big Five Personality Inventory, was used to assess the different self and character views.[9] The Big Five traits consist of 44 items in five categories: conscientiousness (e.g., thorough, reliable, organized; Cronbach's $\alpha = 0.88$), extraversion (e.g., talkative, energetic, assertive; Cronbach's $\alpha = 0.87$), neuroticism (depressed, worried, nervous; Cronbach's $\alpha = 0.85$), agreeableness (e.g., trusting, forgiving, kind; Cronbach's $\alpha = 0.69$), and openness to experience (e.g., creative, artistic, inventive; Cronbach's $\alpha = 0.82$). Participants rated how similar each personality characteristic was to their actual and ideal selves. They used the same rating scale to evaluate their primary WoW character. Each measure (actual self, ideal self, and character ratings) was separated by a battery of other questions on different pages to encourage independence of responses.

When the participants rated their actual self, the question was worded, [11] "Please think of yourself and answer the following questions. 'I see myself as someone who _____.'" When they rated their ideal self, they were told, "Now think of yourself as you would like to be, ideally, and answer the following questions. 'Ideally, I would like to be someone who _____.'" When they rated their main WoW character, the question was worded, "Please think of your main character in World of Warcraft and answer the following questions. 'I see my main character in World of Warcraft as someone who _____.'" Participants rated themselves and their character on the 44 characteristics using seven-point Likert-type scales ranging front "disagree strongly" to "agree strongly."

To measure psychological well-being, we used two measures. One mea- [12] sure was the 12-item Center for Epidemiologic Studies Depression Scale (CES-D).[10] Participants reported how frequently in the past week they had experienced symptoms of depression, including "I felt that everything I did was an effort," "My sleep was restless," and "I had trouble keeping my mind on what I was doing" (Cronbach's $\alpha = 0.60$). The second measure was a subset of items from the Positive Affect Negative Affect Scale (PANAS).[11] Eleven items indicate the participant's current confidence in his or her abilities and intelligence, or self-esteem (Cronbach's $\alpha = 0.85$). These two measures, depression and self-esteem, were not correlated with each other in any meaningful way ($r = 0.30$).

## Results

Our first prediction was that the character discrepancy would be smaller [13] than the self discrepancy. We began this analysis by verifying that players created their character more like themselves than like other players' selves. We found the expected main effect showing that each participant's character was more similar to the participant's actual self than to a random other participant's actual self ($F [1,36] = 5.3, p = 0.02$).

Next we turned to the question of whether a player's character was [14] viewed as more ideal than the player's actual self. We tested this hypothesis using a paired $t$-test to examine whether the differences between the self discrepancy and the character discrepancy were significant. The hypothesis was supported for three of the five personality dimensions: conscientiousness (paired $t = 5, p < 0.001$), extraversion (paired $t = 3.2, p < 0.01$), and neuroticism (paired $t = 4.89, p < 0.0001$). These effects can be seen in Figure 13.1.

The hypothesis was not supported for the personality dimension of [15] agreeableness. There was no difference between agreeableness ratings of the actual self and the virtual character (means: actual = 3.56, character =

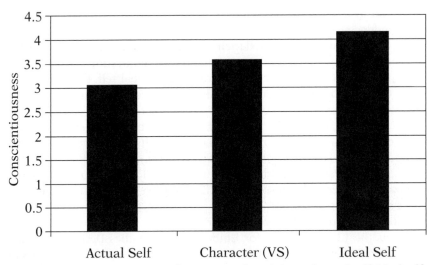

**FIGURE 13.1**  Big Five personality ratings of participants' actual self, ideal self, and character. Figure shows ratings of conscientiousness. Other trait ratings are similar; see text.

3.60, ideal = 4.0). The hypothesis also was not supported for the dimension openness to experience, a measure of artistic talent, creativity, and reflection. Instead, the character rating for openness to experience was lower than ratings of either the actual or the ideal self, and the character discrepancy was significantly larger than the self discrepancy (paired $t$ = 3.8, $p$ < 0.001). Although unexpected, this result makes sense. Characters in WoW typically do not enact a creative role; they act at the behest of the player. These results suggest that participants did not simply rate their characters positively across all personality dimensions but did so selectively for the Big Five characteristics most relevant to the virtual world.

Our second hypothesis was that those with poorer psychological well-being would be more likely to see their character as realizing aspects of their ideal self. If so, there should be an interaction between players' psychological well-being and their discrepancy scores. To test this hypothesis, we conducted mixed-model analyses of variance on the personality dimensions. The target of the rating (actual self, ideal self, character) is the within-subjects variable, and level of well-being (depression or self-esteem) is a continuous between-subjects variable.  16

Using depression scores to group participants, the hypothesis was supported for three of the Big Five personality dimensions. When participants rated their own or their character's conscientiousness, there was a main effect (such that their character ratings fell between their actual and ideal self ratings; $F$ [2, 89] = 50, $p$ < 0.001), a main effect of level of depression (such that ratings of conscientiousness by those high in depression were lower; $F$ [1, 46] = 9.3, $p$ < 0.01), and also a significant interaction such  17 that those with higher depression showed a significantly larger disparity between their self discrepancy and character discrepancy ($F$ [2, 92] = 5.3, $p < 0.01$. Similarly, the main effects and interaction were significant for neuroticism (main effect of rating target, $F$ [2,92] = 57, $p < 0.001$; main effect of depression, $F$ [2, 46] = 12, $p < 0.01$; interaction $F$ [2, 92] = 8.7, $p < 0.001$) and for agreeableness (main effect of rating target, $F$ [2, 89] = 24, $p < 0.001$; main effect of depression, $F$ [2, 47] = 2.8, $p < 0.10$; interaction $F$ [2, 89] = 4.7, $p = 0.01$). The first of these interaction effects is illustrated in Figure 2a, using the depression scores split at the median into high and low depression groups and showing effects on ratings of actual, ideal, and character conscientiousness. The figure uses line graphs so that the slopes for both groups can be seen easily.

a. Participants divided into groups scoring above and below the median of depression.

b. Participants divided into groups scoring above and below the median of self-esteem.

From Figure 13.2A, it can be seen that the reason for the significant interaction effect derives from two phenomena. First, those with lower depression scores do not rate their character as more ideal than they rate their actual self. Only those with higher depression scores do so. Second, both groups rate their character as equally close to their ideal self. Thus, there is no evidence that the characters of those with high depression scores have different traits from the characters of those with low depression scores. Nor is there any evidence that their ideal selves differ. Instead, it seems that those with high depression scores, as compared with low depression scores, (a) have much lower actual-self views and (b) create characters who are equally close to their ideal. Those with high depression scores thus create characters who are equivalent to the actual-self scores of those who have lower depression scores. [18]

We found a similar pattern using self-esteem as the moderator variable. Hypothesis 2 was confirmed with significant interaction effects for four of the Big Five personality dimensions: conscientiousness ($F$ [2, 89] = 4.7, $p = 0.01$), neuroticism ($F$ [2, 89] = 3.6, $p < 0.05$), agreeableness ($F$ [2, 86] = 4.9, $p = 0.001$), and openness to experience ($F$ [2, 89] = 2.9, $p = 0.05$). Figure 13.2B shows the pattern, using conscientiousness as an example. As when depression is the moderator variable, the reason for the interaction is that those with low self-esteem scores had much lower actual-self ratings but rated their character as close to their ideal as did those with high self-esteem. [19]

## Discussion

Our data suggest that MMORPG virtual worlds offer players the opportunity to create idealized characters as virtual, alternative selves. On average, participants rated their virtual character as being more conscientious, [20]

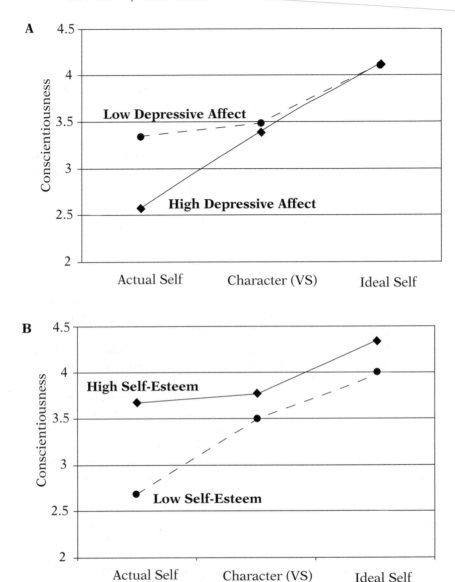

**FIGURE 13.2**   Big Five personality ratings of participants' actual self, ideal self, and character, divided into high and low well-being participant groups. Figures show ratings of conscientiousness. Other trait ratings are similar; see text.

mal about the proportions of Barbie's body. Rather, he asserts, "she has the ideal that Western culture has insisted upon since the 1920s: long legs, long arms, small waist, high round bosom, and long neck" (22). The irony is that BillyBoy may be right. "Unrealistic" or not, Barbie's weight and measurements (which if proportionate to those of a woman 5'6" tall would be something like 110 pounds and a top-heavy 39–18–33) are not much different from those of the beauty queens to whom Bert Parks used to sing "Here she is, Miss America. Here she is, our ideal."[6] If Barbie is a monster, she is our monster, our ideal.

"But is Barbie bad?" Someone asked me the other day if a black doll 37 that looks like a white doll isn't better than no black doll at all. I must admit that I have no ready answer for this and a number of other questions posed by my own critique. Although, as I acknowledged in the beginning, the dolls I played with as a child were white, I still remember the first time I saw a black doll. To me, she was the most beautiful thing I had ever seen; I wanted her desperately, and I was never again satisfied with white Betsy Wetsy and blonde, blue-eyed Patty Play Pal. She was something else, something *Other*, like me, and that, I imagine, was the source of her charm and my desire.

If I did not consciously note my own absence in the toys I played with, 38 that absence, I suspect, had a profound effect on me nevertheless. We have only to read Toni Morrison's chilling tale *The Bluest Eye* to see the effect of the white beauty myth on the black child. And while they were by no means as dire for me as for Morrison's character Pecola Breedlove, I was not exempt from the consequences of growing up black in a white world that barely acknowledged my existence. I grew up believing I was ugly: my kinky hair, my big hips, the gap between my teeth. I have spent half my life smiling with my hand over my mouth to hide that gap, a habit I only began to get over in graduate school when a couple of Nigerian men told me that in their culture, where my body type is prized much more than Barbie's, such gaps are a sign of great beauty. I wonder what it would have meant for me as a child to see a black doll — or any doll — with big hips and a gap between her two front teeth.

Today, for $24.99, Mattel reaches halfway around the world and gives 39 little girls — black like me — Nigerian Barbies to play with. Through the wonders of plastic, dyes, and mass production, the company brings into the homes of African American children a Nigeria that I as a young child did not even know existed. The problem is that Mattel's Nigeria does not exist either. The would-be ethnic dolls of the world Mattel sells, like their "traditional, blond, blue-eyed" all-American girl prototype, have no gaps,

---

[6]In response to criticism from feminists in particular, the Miss America Pageant has attempted to transform itself from a beauty contest to a talent competition, whose real aim is to give college scholarships to smart, talented women (who just happen to look good in bathing suits and evening gowns). As part of its effort to appear more concerned with a woman's IQ than with her bra size, the pageant did away with its long-standing practice of broadcasting the chest, waist, and hip measurements, as well as the height and weight, of each contestant.

extraverted, and less neurotic than they themselves were. Furthermore, these trends were more prominent among those who were more depressed or had lower self-esteem. Those with higher levels of well-being did not rate their character much better than they rated themselves, whereas those with lower levels of well-being rated themselves significantly lower than they rated their character. We believe these results support the idea that despite the many rules, constraints, and difficulties of the game world, its anonymity and fantasy free players from the yoke of their real-life history and social situation, allowing them to be more like the person they wish they were.

Our survey was limited to players of WoW, and the sample consisted 21 mainly of male college and graduate students. Whereas evidence of idealized selves in other domains is consistent with our findings,[12] more research is needed to expand the scope of this study. There also remains much to learn about the process of choosing a character and imbuing it with personality. For instance, do players choose roles for their characters that reflect their own personality (for instance, clerics rather than warriors if they themselves are mild mannered)? Do characters become more idealized over time? It is possible that the process is gradual as players gain the technical and social skills for success in the virtual world.

The ability to create characters who embody aspects of players' ideal 22 selves may have implications for players' psychological well-being. Self-discrepancy theory[13] suggests that psychological well-being is closely related to a person's actual self (me as I am) versus his or her ideal self (me as I would like to be). People with larger actual–ideal self discrepancies have higher depression and lower self-esteem.[13,14] McKenna and Bargh[7,12] have proposed that enacting an ideal self online may reduce some people's actual–ideal self discrepancy and increase their feelings of self-confidence and self-worth. In therapy, visual imagery techniques can help drug addicts create ideal self-representations, which in turn help them reject the addictive selves.[15] In like manner, it seems possible that players whose characters display desirable qualities could imagine themselves as different and reduce their ideal–actual self discrepancies, with positive consequences for their psychological health. This process might depend on many factors, such as the extent to which players actually tried to emulate their characters' better traits.

REFERENCES

1. Seay, A.F., Jerome, W.J., Lee, K.S., & Kraut, R.E. (2004). Project Massive: A study of online gaming communities. In Proceedings of the 2004 Conference on Human Factors in Computing Systems. New York: ACM Press, pp. 1421–1424.

2. Williams, D. (2004). *Trouble in River City: The social life of video games.* Unpublished doctoral dissertation. Ann Arbor, University of Michigan.

3. Ducheneaut, N., & Moore, R.J. (2004). Social side of gaming: A study of interaction patterns in a massively multiplayer online game. Proceedings of the 2004 ACM Conference on Computer Supported Cooperative Work (CSCW04). New York: ACM Press.

4. Turkle, S. (1997). Multiple subjectivity and virtual community at the end of the Freudian century. *Sociological Inquiry* 67:72–84.

5. Reid, E. (1998). The self and the Internet: Variations on the illusion of one self. In: Gackenbach, J. (ed.) *Psychology and the Internet.* San Diego: Academic Press, pp. 29–42.

6. Lawson, K. (2000). Beyond corporeality: The virtual self in postmodern times. *Journal of Psychological Practice* 6:35–43.

7. McKenna, K.Y.A., & Bargh, J. (2000). Plan 9 from cyberspace: The implications of the Internet for personality and social psychology. *Personality and Social Psychology Review* 4:57–75.

8. Bessière, K, Kiesler, S., Kraut, R., & Boneva, B. (2007). *Effects of Internet use and social resources on changes in depression.* Unpublished manuscript. Carnegie Mellon University, Pittsburgh.

9. John, O., Donahue, E., & Kentle, R. (1991). *The Big Five Inventory,* v. 4a & 54. Berkeley: University of California, Berkeley Institute of Personality and Social Research.

10. Radloff, L.S. (1991). The use of the center for epidemiologic studies depression scale in adolescents and young adults. *Journal of Youth and Adolescence* 20:149–166.

11. Watson, D., Clark, L.A., & Tellegen, A. (1988). Development and validation of brief measures of positive and negative affect: The PANAS scales. *Journal of Personality and Social Psychology* 54:1063–1070.

12. McKenna, K.Y.A., & Bargh, J. (1998). Coming out in the age of the Internet: Identity "demarginalization" through virtual group participation. *Journal of Personality and Social Psychology* 75:681–694.

13. Higgins, E.T. (1987). Self-discrepancy: A theory relating self and affect. *Psychological Review* 94:319–340.

14. Moretti, M.M., & Higgins, E.T. (1990). Relating self-discrepancy to self-esteem: The contribution of discrepancy beyond actual-self ratings. *Journal of Experimental Social Psychology* 26:108–123.

15. Avants, S.K., Margolin, A., & Singer, J.L. (1994). Self-reevaluation therapy: A cognitive intervention for the chemically dependent patient. *Psychology of Addictive Behaviors* 8:214–222.

■ ■ ■

## Reading as a Writer: Analyzing Rhetorical Choices

1. This essay contains technical language and methods of presenting data that might seem quite foreign to some readers. What might be lost or gained by communicating this information in a less technical way? Where do you see the authors interpreting their data for wider audiences, and how effectively do you think they answer the "So what?" question readers might ask about the value of researching online game avatars?

2. Reread the final two paragraphs, in which the authors explain the limitations of their study and the potential uses of these data. What implications do you see in their findings when it comes to other online self-representations, such as on social networks, dating sites, or other screen presences? What role does gender play in this mix of screen identities?

## Writing as a Reader: Entering the Conversation of Ideas

1. The authors of "The Ideal Elf" share with Steven Johnson an interest in taking games seriously as a means of understanding cultural values. Choose as a "test case" a particular online game (and, perhaps, your expe-

riences playing it) and write an essay in which you use these authors' insights to analyze the dynamics between the game's options and the players. What can we learn about cultural values by analyzing the game in this way?

2. In "The Ideal Elf," the authors consider what we can learn from the distinction between real players and online avatars or other screen identities. S. Craig Watkins's field research in the selection in this book includes many college students' responses to the ways people interpret online identities. Drawing on ideas from both readings, compose an essay in which you make an argument about the significance you see in the ways college students use online screen presence to create particular kinds of identities. You may include specific examples from your own experiences if they help you build your point.

## S. CRAIG WATKINS

# *From* The Young and the Digital

S. Craig Watkins is a professor of radio-TV-film at the University of Texas at Austin, and is a leading researcher on the ways young people today use the many forms of social media. His publications include *Hip Hop Matters: Politics, Pop Culture, and the Struggle for the Soul of a Movement* (2005) and *Representing: Hip Hop Culture and the Production of Black Cinema* (1998). His most recent research is on the dynamics of online spaces, where young people form communities, create identities, and resist or reinstate the values of the dominant culture. Watkins complements his analysis of social media with fieldwork in what he calls the "digital trenches," conducting hundreds of surveys and in-depth interviews with young people, teachers, and parents in order to understand the richness and complexity of these online communities.

What follows is an excerpt from Watkins's 2009 book, *The Young and the Digital: What the Migration to Social Network Sites, Games, and Anytime, Anywhere Media Means for Our Future.* In this selection from a chapter titled "Digital Gates: How Race and Class Distinctions Are Shaping the Digital World," Watkins challenges readers to think about the ways class and race distinctions manifest themselves online, even though, as he notes, Americans are not very skilled at discussing these differences. Further, Watkins observes that race is an "'inconvenient truth' for evangelists of the social Web" (para. 5), who are often invested in the idea that the Web offers an equal playing field for all participants. Instead, Watkins argues in this piece, online space often reasserts the real-world divides we see in gated communities, and functions as "digital gates." His close analysis of the ways college students describe MySpace versus Facebook should invite you to consider how you and your friends think about—and talk about—those spaces. Watkins blogs at theyoungandthedigital.com, so if you find his work compelling, it is easy—and fitting, given his topic—to stay updated on his latest thoughts.

■ ▨ ▨

I used to have MySpace but got rid of it because it felt too open. You feel safer with a thing like Facebook . . . It doesn't feel as if you're vulnerable to the outside creepy world. It's just your friends.

— Doug, twenty-one-year-old college student

In the summer of 2007, blogger danah boyd posted an informal essay *1* titled "Viewing American Class Divisions through Facebook and MySpace." Based primarily on her observations of MySpace and Facebook profiles, boyd ponders how class antagonisms influence young people's use of social-network sites. By her own admission, boyd was uncomfortable with the argument and the sociological vocabulary she was in search of to articulate her main thesis: that the class divisions that shape American cultural life off-line are clearly discernible in the communities that form online in MySpace and Facebook. "Americans aren't so good at talking about class," she writes, adding, "it's uncomfortable, and to top it off, we don't have the language for marking class in a meaningful way."[1] She is right, partially.

Sustaining a serious public conversation about the class cleavages *2* in American life is a constant challenge, but not for the reason usually cited—that Americans rarely if ever think in terms of class. The truth is nearly every facet of our daily lives—the clothes we wear, the foods we eat, the schools we attend, the neighborhoods we live in, and the company we keep—bears the visible marks of social class and the ever-deepening cleavages between the economically mobile and the economically vulnerable.

"Facebook kids," the blogger writes, "come from families who empha- *3* size education and going to college."[2] Users of Facebook, boyd asserts, tend to be white and come, more often than not, from a world of middle-class comfort. Drawing from some of the more familiar social cliques among young people, boyd equates the "preps" and the "jocks" with Facebook. MySpace kids, in contrast, come from the other side of the cultural divide. According to boyd, they are the "kids whose parents didn't go to college, who are expected to get a job when they finish high school."[3] Latino, black, and youth from working-class and immigrant households, she maintains, are more likely to be users of MySpace.

In the end, boyd's essay is consistent with a concept—the digital *4* divide—that gained momentum as far back as the late 1990s as academic and policy-oriented researchers began to ponder how social inequalities impact engagement with the Internet. Some of the most vigorous champions of all things digital—the social Web, blogs, wikis, virtual worlds, user-generated content, and social-network sites—can be intolerant of disapproving analysis. Truth be told, technology enthusiasts pay only scant attention to matters of social inequality. After access to computers and the Internet were widened significantly, the continued gap between the technology rich and the technology poor quickly receded to the background.

Race is a kind of "inconvenient truth" for evangelists of the social *5* Web. Early in the Web's history, the anonymity of computer-mediated communication suggested to many commentators that longstanding spheres of social division, discord, and discrimination—most notably race and gender—would be rendered meaningless in the digital world. It was that logic that made the *New Yorker* cartoon about the dog and the Internet so famous. The cartoon implies that if being a dog on the Internet does not matter, certainly being black, Latino, or female would not matter either. Despite the utopian view that the Web provides a place and a way to escape the social burdens and divisions of the off-line world, this has never been true. All of the optimism notwithstanding, the digital world has never existed in a bubble, insulated from the social tensions and economic inequalities that are integral to the making and remaking of the social world. Life online has always been intricately though never predictably connected to life off-line. Social inequalities still matter in the physical world. And as we are learning, they also matter in the virtual world. Nowhere is this clearer than in the rise and use of social-network sites.

Right around the time that boyd wrote her essay, my research assistant 6 and I were assessing the data from the surveys and interviews we were collecting. . . . the use of social-network sites is the premiere online activity among young people between the ages of fifteen and twenty-four. Along with noticing how pervasive the use of social sites is among college students, we detected something else: a decisive preference for Facebook over MySpace among college students. When we asked college students, "Which social-network site do you visit MOST OFTEN?"—among white students, more than eight out of ten, or 84 percent, preferred Facebook. By contrast, 66 percent of those who identified as Latino preferred Facebook. In our survey Latino students were more likely to name MySpace as their preferred site.

What started out in 2005 and 2006 as a steady move to Facebook 7 among American college students has become, by the time of this writing in 2009, a massive migration and cultural rite of passage. As twenty-two-year-old Sara told us, "In college you are almost expected to use Facebook." Though many of the young college students we spoke with around this time, in 2007 and 2008, began using MySpace before Facebook, they had either deleted their MySpace profile or seldom bothered to use what at the time was the world's most populated social-network site. Within months of its debut, MySpace leaped ahead of Friendster, one of the first online social-network sites, to attract a large concentration of American youth. Soon after its launch in 2004, Facebook replaced MySpace as the new digital destination for the college set. By 2007 high school students bound for college were also showing a stronger preference for Facebook.

While identifying emergent themes and trends from our survey, we 8 noticed that the findings from a separate study conducted around the same time, in early 2007, parallel some of the results from our study. After surveying 1,060 students, ages eighteen and nineteen, Eszter Hargittai, a professor of communication studies, found that a majority of the students, four out of five, used Facebook. About one-third of the sample used MySpace frequently. But when Hargittai broke her data down by gender, race, and class, a number of interesting results surfaced. Similar to many studies, and as I note above, Hargittai found that women use social-network sites more frequently than men. But Hargittai's most interesting findings revolve around the racial and class differences her data tracked.

A majority of white students, 83 percent, preferred Facebook, whereas   9 a little more than half, 57 percent, reported using MySpace. Eighty percent of the African American students used Facebook, and about 58 percent used MySpace. Hargittai reports some significant differences among students of Latino and Asian origins. "Hispanic students," she writes, "are significantly less likely to use Facebook (60% compared to 75% or more for other groups), whereas they are much more likely than others to use MySpace (73% among Hispanic students compared to 58% or less among all others)."[4] Students of Asian origins showed clear differences too. Whereas 84 percent of the Asian students in Hargittai's sample used Facebook, 39 percent reported using MySpace.

Hargittai's study also shows pronounced differences across class,   10 which she measures by parents' level of education. High levels of education attainment are often associated with higher levels of employment and income. In fact, you can tell a lot about a family's habits, activities, and lifestyle based on parental education. Past studies of children and teens' use of television and video games, for instance, show a strong correlation with parental education. Children growing up in low-education households tend to watch more television and play more video games than children in households with highly educated parents.[5] Hargittai's study finds similar results. "The most pronounced finding," Hargittai writes, "is that students whose parents have less than a high school degree are significantly less likely to be on Facebook and are significantly more likely to be MySpace users."[6] A close look at her results reveals that the more schooling parents attain, the less likely their children are to use MySpace.

Both the survey I led and the one conducted by Hargittai confirm that   11 something truly interesting is happening with race, class, and education as it relates to young people's engagement with social-network sites. But neither study answers the all-important question: Why does racial identification appear to influence which sites students prefer?

Fortunately, we were complementing our surveys with in-depth con-   12 versations, going out into the digital trenches to talk directly with young people about their use of social-network sites.

What we learned is quite revealing.   13

Right away, the interviews illuminated the constantly evolving ways teens   14 and young twenty-somethings use the social Web. Talk to them and you quickly learn that they harbor intense views, both favorable and unfavorable, toward social-network sites. Some young people are incredibly passionate about MySpace. "I use it all of the time," twenty-six-year-old Avani told us. "It's fun, exciting, and easy to meet people. I think people interact more on MySpace [than Facebook]." Loyalty to Facebook is just as strong. Frances, a twenty-two-year-old communication major, said, "It's a much simpler site to use." With assurance, Jonathan declared, "Facebook is for people who already have friends, whereas MySpace is for people who are looking for friends."

In all of our in-depth conversations we asked each person to use adjec- 15 tives that, in their view, best describe MySpace and Facebook. Over the course of more than two hundred conversations with white college students, we heard all kinds of words. The preference for Facebook is undeniable. In Table 13.1 I list the adjectives that they use most often to describe MySpace and Facebook. Notice anything? The language they used to characterize MySpace is strikingly hostile. Words like creepy, crowded, uneducated, and fake reveal a considerable degree of bad feeling toward the MySpace site and community. By comparison, they maintain a largely favorable view of Facebook, consistently describing the platform as trustworthy, selective, educated, and authentic. "Addictive" was another common word used to describe Facebook. Along with the adjectives, young people offered a variety of stories that explain in colorful detail how they make sense of the digital media landscape and, more specifically, the two most popular social-network sites in the United States.

**TABLE 13.1** Adjectives college students use to describe MySpace and Facebook

| MYSPACE | FACEBOOK |
| --- | --- |
| Crowded | Selective |
| Trashy | Clean |
| Creepy | Trustworthy |
| Busy | Simple |
| General Public | College |
| Uneducated | Educated |
| Fake | Authentic |
| Open | Private |
| Immature | Mature |
| Predators | Stalker-friendly |
| Crazy | Addictive |

After analyzing the in-depth conversations, we drilled the preference *16* among young white collegians for Facebook over MySpace down to two main factors—aesthetics and demographics. Aesthetics refers to the look, style, and manner in which personal profiles are designed and presented. The second factor, demographics, refers to the individuals and communities that tend to use both sites. Aesthetics point to the system features of social sites, while demographics alludes to system users. Together, both factors illuminate the sharp and powerful differences race and class make in the online communities young people participate in.

Visit MySpace and Facebook and the first thing you will likely notice is that *17* the design, look, and feel of the personal profiles on each site are worlds apart. MySpace's system features encourage customization and personalization, a kind of digital wild style. The color, design, and mood of MySpace pages vary significantly. Twenty-six-year-old Avani said, "With MySpace there's a lot you can do with HTML." Facebook profiles, on the other hand, maintain a relatively standard look. Compared to MySpace, the tone and style of Facebook seems antistyle. From the very beginning of its launch, MySpace carefully cultivated a demeanor that is personal, whimsical, and, at times, oppositional. Facebook, on me other hand, has maintained a relatively stable and uniform presentation even as it expands the scope of its services. Though the content—pictures, wall posts, and use of applications—may vary on Facebook, the presentation of it all does not. These two contrasting styles engender strong views from users of social-network sites, especially those in college who believe Facebook is the superior platform.

Gerry, a nineteen-year-old sophomore, told us that "Facebook just *18* looks cleaner. Not now, with all the new applications and stuff, but it still looks cleaner than MySpace and a lot more organized, as opposed to MySpace . . . with all the background and fonts, and things." In his words, MySpace "feels very cluttered and kind of schizophrenic to look at a page . . . it really makes your head spin." Sarah, a twenty-one-year-old communication studies major, agreed. "Oh, MySpace is horrible. It takes forever to download a MySpace page and you never know if you are looking at a real person or not."

Throughout our conversations with them, college students repeatedly *19* expressed their dislike with the often overzealous design of MySpace profiles and the time it takes to download them. MySpace, said twenty-one-year-old Matthew, reminds him of the "dark, dark days of the Internet." When asked to elaborate he said, "I don't like the fact that the designs of MySpace pages are for the most part dreadful. They remind me of back when I was seven and eight and people had just learned how to create Web pages. And they had flashing texts and bubbles."

Likewise, twenty-two-year-old Brandon expressed irritation with the *20* customizable features of MySpace.

"The big difference I suppose is HTML. There's no HTML writing in   *21*
Facebook as opposed to MySpace," Brandon observed. Like many other
college students, he believes the ability to write in MySpace undermines
the quality of the user experience. "I think it makes Facebook so much
better in the sense that you're never being plagued by someone else's bad
code."

Initially, the dissatisfaction with the customized profiles on MySpace   *22*
caught me by surprise. A hallmark feature of the social Web is the ability
to not only read Web-based content, but write content too. In the age of
do-it-yourself (DIY) media, the fact that we are both consumers and cre-
ators of content redefines the rules of media engagement by redefining the
rules of media production and consumption. And yet, it turns out that the
customization and personalization of MySpace profiles through creative
layouts, music, video, and graphics is a major source of annoyance and
cultural friction for many college students.

Nineteen-year-old Shelby was not impressed with MySpace, a social   *23*
site she believes is filled with phony names, phony profiles, and in her
words, "glittery, gaudy-as-shit layouts." The repeated characterization of
MySpace as "trashy," "messy," "busy," and "gaudy" unveils a widespread
belief among young collegians that the profiles crafted on the platform are
unrefined, unsophisticated, and unappealing. All of this is in sharp contrast to the generally glowing praise showered on Facebook profiles, which,
according to twenty-four-year-old Kevin, "is much better organized and
easy to use." Another young woman described Facebook as "pretty, simple,
and classy."

Beneath the preference for the more uniform interface of Facebook   *24*
lies a more complex tale about the influence of race, class, and geography
in the digital world. The triumph of Facebook over MySpace across Campus USA is not purely about aesthetic judgments or the desire for a simple
and easily navigable platform. Matters of taste, French sociologist Pierre
Bourdieu reminds us, do not develop in a vacuum but rather in relation to
people's social class position. Bourdieu, widely recognized as a pioneering thinker and theorist in the "sociology of culture," used the terrain of
culture or, more precisely, what we do in our everyday lives, to examine
expressions of social inequality. Bourdieu made a career of studying what
he calls the "distinctions — tastes, lifestyle, manners, and values — members of the middle class diligently practice in order to maintain clear
boundaries between themselves and the classes they view as less cultured,
sophisticated, and desirable.[7] Sociologists following in the tradition of
Bourdieu refer to these practices as boundary-maintenance work.

Bourdieu carefully illustrates how the accumulation of middle-class   *25*
cultural capital — education, and a taste for the high arts and the other presumed finer things of life — does more than serve the psyche of the bour-
geois classes; it also enables them to reinforce their position of privilege.
Many of the distinctions college students make in relation to social-network

sites are not merely about taste; they are also about the preservation of social status and privilege.

As we probed deeper into the use of social-network sites, it became   26
increasingly clear that young Facebookers' abandonment of MySpace is not simply about avoiding "bad code"; it is also about avoiding "bad people." . . .

Despite all of the hype about how the digital age is changing our lives, it   27
has not changed one essential aspect of human life—who we form our strongest social ties with. Similar to life B.W.—before the Web—our most intimate bonds online tend to be formed with like-minded people. Indeed, the young people we surveyed and spoke with are attracted to online communities that connect them to people who are like them in some notable way—age, education, region, race, or class. In order to understand what is happening online, you have to understand what is happening off-line. One place to start understanding what is driving young people toward homogeneous online communities is a consideration of what author Bill Bishop has tagged the Big Sort, a reference to the geographic transformation of American neighborhoods.

The Big Sort, according to Bishop, began around 1970 as Americans   28
underwent a massive social experiment that changed one of the most basic features of everyday life—where and with whom we live. The change in geography, Bishop maintains, is "really a sorting by lifestyle," as Americans now more than ever gravitate toward counties and communities that reflect their values, beliefs, and ways of life. Thinking further about the Big Sort and how it is remapping American neighborhoods, Bishop writes, "We have come to expect living arrangements that don't challenge our cultural expectations."[8] Many Americans, especially the ones who enjoy a degree of economic mobility, are choosing to live near people who think, live, and look like them.

Social-network sites do not cause social divisions. The young and   29
the digital have grown up in a world in which the geographic sorting by race, lifestyle, and ideological values—a rather extraordinary development—has become ordinary. Bishop is correct when he writes, "Kids have grown up in neighborhoods of like-mindedness, so homogenous groups are considered normal."[9] The vast majority of the young people we meet go online to have fun by sharing their lives and communicating with their peers. And yet, the choices they make regarding who they interact with online are not immune to the social forces that are shaping their off-line lives. Like the Big Sort, the online sorting among young Facebook users is shaped by a general suspicion of difference, a split along lifestyle, and, finally, the wish to reside in communities with like-minded people.

The digital gating practices of young, white college students are especially   30
interesting when you consider how often we hear that race does not matter to Generation Digital. In his 2008 book, *The Way We'll Be: The Zogby*

*Report on the Transformation of the American Dream*, pollster John Zogby writes that the generation he calls the "First Globals," Americans between the ages of eighteen and twenty-nine, are "the most outward-looking . . . generation in American history." On the question that has challenged America for more than two centuries—race—Zogby says, "The nation's youth are leading the way into a more accepting future."[10] From MTV's embrace of black pop to the selling of hip hop, this generation certainly came of age in a cultural milieu in which racial signifiers were not only visible, but also elaborately marketed entertainment. This generation personally experienced a racial milestone in 2008, the historic presidential election of Barack Obama. Liberals and conservatives alike argued that by embracing Obama's message of "CHANGE," young whites provided evidence of a generation no longer burdened by our nation's racial past. Meanwhile, our conversations with young whites show that some view MySpace and Facebook, in part, through a racially coded lens. Race, it turns out, still matters.

"MySpace," said nineteen-year-old Thomas, "is on crack. There is too much glitter and music." Twenty-two-year-old Veronica also drew a connection between MySpace and the notorious drug. "My favorite is Facebook because MySpace is absolutely on crack and overwhelming," she said. The reference to crack, a drug associated primarily with the black urban poor, is certainly not race neutral. Add to this a sentiment like "MySpace is too ghetto," and the racial marking of the digital world is apparent. Likewise, the belief that MySpace is sullied with profiles that feature "glittery, gaudy-as-shit layouts" and "too much glitter and music" invoke another racially marked term—*bling*—a popular slang derived from the larger-than-life fantasies played out in hip-hop songs, videos, and style. *31*

Starting around the early 1990s, hip-hop music, fashion, movies, and marketing campaigns were made as much for young white consumers, especially suburban males, as black and Latino consumers. So, why would a generation that grew up consuming hip hop be turned off by the "bling aesthetics" that pervade MySpace culture? To answer that question, you have to understand the difference between "old media" (think television) and "new media" (think social-network sites). *32*

Television and social-network sites represent two fundamentally different kinds of mediated experiences. Whereas television is about watching and consuming, social-network sites are primarily about doing and sharing. Facebook users share themselves daily through wall posts, news feeds, blogs, photos, gifts, and other activities. This kind of constant connectivity establishes varying degrees of community and intimacy. By the time they arrived in college, the late teens and young twenty-somethings we met were a little less concerned with the quantity of their online social networks and more concerned with what the quality of those networks say about them and the people they are associated with. It is one thing for young whites to listen to music inspired by the hood, and something *33* entirely different to establish a degree of intimacy with people they believe come from the hood. This is the crucial difference between "old media" and "new media."

Whereas the use of old media platforms like television maintains  34 distance from black and Latino youth, new media platforms like social-network sites offer a greater possibility for closeness. Back when television was dominant, young whites could consume black style and expressive culture from a distance. Social-network sites afford young whites the opportunity to interact with actual black people. However, by avoiding MySpace, the users of Facebook elect to avoid sharing their lives and experiencing a modicum of intimacy with "real" black and Latino youth in the computer-mediated spaces they frequent. Instead of venturing to bridge, some young whites choose instead to bond with each other inside their digital gates.

Social and mobile media may be changing how we connect, but as we move  35 into the digital future, it does not appear to be significantly altering who we connect to.

In one of the first "virtual-field studies" exploring the role of race in  36 computer-mediated social worlds, two social psychologists from Northwestern University, Paul Eastwick and Wendi Gardner, found evidence of racial bias in the online world There.com.[11] The experimenters created two avatars, one with light skin and the other with dark skin. Modeling one of their investigations on a classic "compliance technique" experiment called "Face-in-the-Door" condition, Eastwick and Gardner made a large request of There.com participants that was sure to be refused. It was the response to the second, more moderate request that the researchers were really interested in. Previous studies found that the moderate request usually leads to greater compliance from study participants. It turns out that the participants believe that the requester has made a concession and, thus, are more likely to reciprocate. Researchers believe that the participant's decision to agree is based on their assessment of the requester.

As expected, Eastwick and Gardner noticed that the more moder-  37 ate request led to greater compliance. But when they examined the responses to the light- and dark-skinned avatars, a statistically significant difference emerged. Among the light-skinned avatars, 20 percent more people said yes to the second request. Among the dark-skinned avatars, only 8 percent more of There.com participants said yes. The researchers concluded that the social influence of race might have been a factor, though they were unsure of the precise nature of the effect. Did participants respond based on their perception of the avatars' appearance (skin color) or their perceptions of the person controlling the avatar? Either way, Eastwick and Gardner write, "the virtual world may not prove to be a perfect utopian getaway from the real world."[12] The racial perceptions and biases we develop in our off-line lives, they conclude, likely creep in to our online lives.

NOTES

1. danah boyd, "Viewing American Class Divisions through Facebook and MySpace," June 24, 2007, www.zephoria.org/thoughts/archives/2007/06/24/viewing_america.html.
2. Ibid.
3. Ibid.
4. Eszter Hargittai, "Whose Space? Differences among Users and Non-Users of Social Network Sites." *Journal of Computer-Mediated Communication* 13, no. 1 (2007), http://jcmc.indiana.edu/vol13/issue1/hargittai.html.
5. Donald F. Roberts et al., *Kids & Media & the New Millennium* (Menlo Park, CA: The Henry J. Kaiser Family Foundation, 1999).
6. Hargittai, "Whose Space?"
7. Pierre Bourdieu, *Distinction: A Social Critique of the Judgment of Taste* (Cambridge, MA: Harvard University Press, 1984).
8. Bill Bishop, *The Big Sort: Why the Clustering of Like-Minded America Is Tearing Us Apart* (Boston: Houghton Mifflin, 2008), 213.
9. Ibid.
10. John Zogby, *The Way We'll Be: The Zogby Report on the Transformation of the American Dream* (New York: Random House, 2008), 115.
11. Paul W. Eastwick and Wendi L. Gardner, "Is It a Game? Evidence for Social Influence in the Virtual World," *Social Influence* 4, no. I (January 2009): 18–32.
12. Ibid., 29.

■ ■ ■

## Reading as a Writer: Analyzing Rhetorical Choices

1  On page 509, Watkins includes a table with lists of "Adjectives college students use to describe MySpace and Facebook." Watkins could have easily presented this information in paragraph form; what is the effect of presenting it as two lists?

2. In the title of the chapter from which this selection is taken, "Digital Gates," Watkins plays on the ideas of both "gated communities" and the "digital divide." Look up both of these terms to be sure you understand the history behind them. Discuss how both of these terms help Watkins develop his point about the dynamics he sees in online culture, and in particular in social networking.

## Writing as a Reader: Entering the Conversation of Ideas

1. This chapter begins with an analysis of television screen entertainment, in Neil Postman's essay, and concludes with Watkins's analysis of the screen pastime of social networking. Compose an essay that places these authors in conversation to reflect on the similarities and differences you see in these early (1985) and recent (2009) media analyses. What can you conclude about the direction we are headed? Feel free to draw on specific examples from screen culture to help you make your point.

2. Both Watkins and Peggy McIntosh are interested in the many subtle ways assumptions about race and racial identity are built into everyday life. At first, the consequences of these assumptions may seem harmless, but they quickly add up over the course of a day, a week, a college experience, and a lifetime. Write an essay in which you use both authors' insights to explain the significance you see in the way these assumptions work through everyday interchanges. What conclusions can you draw? Include examples from your own experiences, if you like.

# Business

*How do we target and train our youngest consumers?*

M ost of us recognize both the pleasure and the problems of American culture's belief that "to be is to buy"—that who we are is connected in some way to what we wear, smell like, eat, drive, and own. Most of us are able to resist the lure of commercial sloganeering a bit (that is, we know we are not literally our Abercrombie & Fitch shirts), and yet we give

517

in as well (otherwise, companies like Abercrombie & Fitch would not be so successful). What happens, however, when our very youngest consumers get hit with these powerful messages?

The readings in this chapter examine the sales pitches we aim directly at children, whether we're selling them fast food, toys, stories, or—more abstractly but more importantly—*ideas* about cultural values and norms that are much harder to point to than the pile of fast-food plastic toys that most American children have accumulated at some point in their lives. We all know that companies try to "hook" kids with their products, just as we know that grocery stores place candy at the height of toddlers for a reason. These readings go much further, however, in helping us see the implications and influence of the marketplace on education and children's literature, as well as on children's media in the age of globalization. In this chapter, you'll be able to consider from many different perspectives the significance of what we are teaching "kid kustomers" (as Eric Schlosser calls them) to want and to value.

Several of the writers take on the more obvious ways corporations target children, but they reveal additional layers of complexity in their analysis, as in Eric Schlosser's insights into fast-food marketing to kids and Ann duCille's illumination of the ways multicultural Barbies sell children (and the adults who purchase them) a problematic and limited version of cultural "difference." Katha Pollitt takes on cartoon culture in her pithy analysis, "The Smurfette Principle," which invites an eye-opening gender analysis of familiar children's movies and television shows. Other authors examine aspects of children's culture that seem on the surface to be nothing but good news, such as the American Girl and Harry Potter book series (in essays by Daniel Hade and Elizabeth Teare) or the effects of environmentalist themes and globalization on children's media (in essays by Noël Sturgeon and David Buckingham).

In every essay, these authors suggest that there is more than meets the eye in the ideas and stories we are "selling" to our youngest consumers. What kind of future adults are we producing in our product-saturated culture? What does this mean for who we are, in our own eyes, and in the eyes of the world?

ERIC SCHLOSSER

# Kid Kustomers

Eric Schlosser has won numerous awards for his exposé-style journalism, which has appeared in *The Atlantic, Rolling Stone, Vanity Fair, The Nation,* and *The New Yorker,* among other magazines. He has published several best-selling books, including *Reefer Madness: Sex, Drugs, and Cheap Labor in the American Black Market* (2003) and, with Charles Wilson, *Chew on This: Everything You Don't Want to Know About Fast Food* (2006), which introduces middle school readers to the history of the fast-food industry and the agribusiness and animal-raising practices that the industry fosters. *Chew on This* evolved from *Fast Food Nation: The Dark Side of the All-American Meal* (2001), from which this reading is taken. *Fast Food Nation* has been assigned for campuswide reading at many universities, and it inspired a 2006 film version, starring Greg Kinnear. Schlosser's expertise on America's food industry has made him a popular lecturer on and off campus. He also has addressed Congress about the risk to the food supply from bioterrorism.

Schlosser's interest in the fast-food industry extends to the industry's marketing campaigns and their focus on children, the "kid kustomers" who are featured in this reading. Think back to your own childhood encounters with clever, kid-appealing fast-food packaging. How did the toys, the packaging, and the commercials affect your association with fast food? Do Schlosser's insights change your thinking about marketing campaigns by fast-food restaurants? If so, how?

Like any good writer, Schlosser uses a number of specific examples to persuade his readers. Keep track of the facts, statistics, and examples he uses, and consider how you might use similar strategies in your own writing. While this reading is just a small part of Schlosser's book *Fast Food Nation,* in these paragraphs he weaves together strands of an argument about past and present attitudes toward fast food, the intersection of dining and consumer culture, and the effects of aggressive marketing to children. As a public intellectual, Schlosser has helped ignite a conversation about what we eat, and why, that is likely to continue for a long time. It's a conversation that could change the way you eat and the way you spend money, as well as the way you think.

■ ■ ■

Twenty-five years ago, only a handful of American companies directed their marketing at children—Disney, McDonald's, candy makers, toy makers, manufacturers of breakfast cereal. Today children are being targeted by phone companies, oil companies, and automobile companies, as well as clothing stores and restaurant chains. The explosion in children's advertising occurred during the 1980s. Many working parents, feeling guilty about spending less time with their kids, started spending more money on them. One marketing expert has called the 1980s "the decade of the child consumer."[1] After largely ignoring children for years, Madison Avenue began to scrutinize and pursue them. Major ad agencies now have children's divisions, and a variety of marketing firms focus solely on kids. These groups tend to have sweet-sounding names: Small Talk, Kid Connection, Kid2Kid, the Gepetto Group, Just Kids, Inc. At least three industry publications—*Youth Market Alert, Selling to Kids,* and *Marketing to Kids Report*—cover the latest ad campaigns and market research. The growth in children's advertising has been driven by efforts to increase not just current, but also future, consumption. Hoping that nostalgic childhood memories of a brand will lead to a lifetime of purchases, companies now plan "cradle-to-grave" advertising strategies. They have come to believe what Ray Kroc and Walt Disney realized long ago—a person's "brand loyalty" may begin as early as the age of two.[2] Indeed, market research has found that children often recognize a brand logo before they can recognize their own name.[3]

The discontinued Joe Camel ad campaign, which used a hip cartoon    2 character to sell cigarettes, showed how easily children can be influenced by the right corporate mascot. A 1991 study published in the *Journal of the American Medical Association* found that nearly all of America's six-year-olds could identify Joe Camel, who was just as familiar to them as Mickey Mouse.[4] Another study found that one-third of the cigarettes illegally sold to minors were Camels.[5] More recently, a marketing firm conducted a survey in shopping malls across the country, asking children to describe their favorite TV ads. According to the CME KidCom Ad Traction Study II, released at the 1999 Kids' Marketing Conference in San Antonio, Texas, the Taco Bell commercials featuring a talking chihuahua were the most popular fast food ads.[6] The kids in the survey also liked Pepsi and Nike commercials, but their favorite television ad was for Budweiser.

The bulk of the advertising directed at children today has an immedi-    3 ate goal. "It's not just getting kids to whine," one marketer explained in *Selling to Kids,* "it's giving them a specific reason to ask for the product."[7] Years ago sociologist Vance Packard described children as "surrogate sales-

[1]James U. McNeal, *Kids as Customers: A Handbook of Marketing to Children.* Lanham, MD: Lexington Books, 1992, p. 6.

[2]Cited in "Brand Aware," *Children's Business,* June 2000.

[3]See "Brand Consciousness," *IFF on Kids: Kid Focus,* no. 3.

[4]Paul Fischer et al., "Brand Logo Recognition by Children Aged 3 to 6 Years: Mickey Mouse and Old Joe the Camel," *Journal of the American Medical Association,* December 11, 1991.

[5]See Judann Dagnoli, "JAMA Lights New Fire Under Camel's Ads," *Advertising Age,* December 16, 1991.

[6]Cited in "Market Research Ages 6–17: Talking Chihuahua Strikes Chord with Kids," *Selling to Kids,* February 3, 1999.

[7]Quoted in "Market Research: The Old Nagging Game Can Pay Off for Marketers," *Selling to Kids,* April 15, 1998.

men" who had to persuade other people, usually their parents, to buy what they wanted.[8] Marketers now use different terms to explain the intended response to their ads—such as "leverage," "the nudge factor," "pester power." The aim of most children's advertising is straightforward: get kids to nag their parents and nag them well.

James U. McNeal, a professor of marketing at Texas A&M University, is considered America's leading authority on marketing to children. In his book *Kids As Customers* (1992), McNeal provides marketers with a thorough analysis of "children's requesting styles and appeals."[9] He classifies juvenile nagging tactics into seven major categories. A *pleading* nag is one accompanied by repetitions of words like "please" or "mom, mom, mom." A *persistent* nag involves constant requests for the coveted product and may include the phrase "I'm gonna ask just one more time." *Forceful* nags are extremely pushy and may include subtle threats, like "Well, then, I'll go and ask Dad." *Demonstrative* nags are the most high-risk, often characterized by full-blown tantrums in public places, breath-holding, tears, a refusal to leave the store. *Sugar-coated* nags promise affection in return for a purchase and may rely on seemingly heartfelt declarations like "You're the best dad in the world." *Threatening* nags are youthful forms of blackmail, vows of eternal hatred and of running away if something isn't bought. *Pity* nags claim the child will be heartbroken, teased, or socially stunted if the parent refuses to buy a certain item. "All of these appeals and styles may be used in combination," McNeal's research has discovered, "but kids tend to stick to one or two of each that prove most effective . . . for their own parents."

McNeal never advocates turning children into screaming, breath-holding monsters. He has been studying "Kid Kustomers" for more than thirty years and believes in a more traditional marketing approach.[10] "The key is getting children to see a firm . . . in much the same way as [they see] mom or dad, grandma or grandpa," McNeal argues.[11] "Likewise, if a company can ally itself with universal values such as patriotism, national defense, and good health, it is likely to nurture belief in it among children."

Before trying to affect children's behavior, advertisers have to learn about their tastes.[12] Today's market researchers not only conduct surveys of children in shopping malls, they also organize focus groups for kids as young as two or three. They analyze children's artwork, hire children to

[8]Max Boas and Steve Chain, *Big Mac: The Unauthorized Story of McDonald's*. New York: Dutton, 1976. Vance Packard, *The Hidden Persuaders*. New York: D. McKay Co., 1957, pp. 158–61.

[9]McNeal, *Kids As Customers*, pp. 72–75.

[10]Ibid., p. 4.

[11]Ibid., p. 98.

[12]For a sense of the techniques now being used by marketers, see Tom McGee, "Getting Inside Kids' Heads," *American Demographics*, January 1997.

run focus groups, stage slumber parties and then question children into the night. They send cultural anthropologists into homes, stores, fast food restaurants, and other places where kids like to gather, quietly and surreptitiously observing the behavior of prospective customers. They study the academic literature on child development, seeking insights from the work of theorists such as Erik Erikson and Jean Piaget. They study the fantasy lives of young children, then apply the findings in advertisements and product designs.

Dan S. Acuff—the president of Youth Market System Consulting 7 and the author of *What Kids Buy and Why* (1997)—stresses the importance of dream research. Studies suggest that until the age of six, roughly 80 percent of children's dreams are about animals.[13] Rounded, soft creatures like Barney, Disney's animated characters, and the Teletubbies therefore have an obvious appeal to young children. The Character Lab, a division of Youth Market System Consulting, uses a proprietary technique called Character Appeal Quadrant Analysis to help companies develop new mascots. The technique purports to create imaginary characters who perfectly fit the targeted age group's level of cognitive and neurological development.

Children's clubs have for years been considered an effective means of 8 targeting ads and collecting demographic information; the clubs appeal to a child's fundamental need for status and belonging. Disney's Mickey Mouse Club, formed in 1930, was one of the trailblazers. During the 1980s and 1990s, children's clubs proliferated, as corporations used them to solicit the names, addresses, zip codes, and personal comments of young customers. "Marketing messages sent through a club not only can be personalized," James McNeal advises, "they can be tailored for a certain age or geographical group."[14] A well-designed and well-run children's club can be extremely good for business. According to one Burger King executive, the creation of a Burger King Kids Club in 1991 increased the sales of children's meals as much as 300 percent.[15]

The Internet has become another powerful tool for assembling data 9 about children. In 1998 a federal investigation of Web sites aimed at children found that 89 percent requested personal information from kids; only 1 percent required that children obtain parental approval before supplying the information.[16] A character on the McDonald's Web site told children that Ronald McDonald was "the ultimate authority in everything."[17]

---

[13]Cited in Dan S. Acuff and Robert H. Reiher, *What Kids Buy and Why: The Psychology of Marketing to Kids*. New York: Free Press, 1997, pp. 45–46.

[14]McNeal, *Kids As Customers*, p. 175.

[15]Cited in Karen Benezra, "Keeping Burger King on a Roll," *Brandweek*, January 15, 1996.

[16]Cited in "Children's Online Privacy Proposed Rule Issued by FTC," press release, Federal Trade Commission, April 20, 1999.

[17]Quoted in "Is Your Kid Caught Up in the Web?" *Consumer Reports*, May 1997.

The site encouraged kids to send Ronald an e-mail revealing their favorite menu item at McDonald's, their favorite book, their favorite sports team—and their name.[18] Fast food Web sites no longer ask children to provide personal information without first gaining parental approval; to do so is now a violation of federal law, thanks to the Children's Online Privacy Protection Act, which took effect in April of 2000.

Despite the growing importance of the Internet, television remains [10] the primary medium for children's advertising. The effects of these TV ads have long been a subject of controversy. In 1978, the Federal Trade Commission (FTC) tried to ban all television ads directed at children seven years old or younger. Many studies had found that young children often could not tell the difference between television programming and television advertising. They also could not comprehend the real purpose of commercials and trusted that advertising claims were true. Michael Pertschuk, the head of the FTC, argued that children need to be shielded from advertising that preys upon their immaturity. "They cannot protect themselves," he said, "against adults who exploit their present-mindedness."[19]

The FTC's proposed ban was supported by the American Academy of [11] Pediatrics, the National Congress of Parents and Teachers, the Consumers Union, and the Child Welfare League, among others. But it was attacked by the National Association of Broadcasters, the Toy Manufacturers of America, and the Association of National Advertisers. The industry groups lobbied Congress to prevent any restrictions on children's ads and sued in federal court to block Pertschuk from participating in future FTC meetings on the subject. In April of 1981, three months after the inauguration of President Ronald Reagan, an FTC staff report argued that a ban on ads aimed at children would be impractical, effectively killing the proposal. "We are delighted by the FTC's reasonable recommendation," said the head of the National Association of Broadcasters.[20]

The Saturday-morning children's ads that caused angry debates twenty [12] years ago now seem almost quaint. Far from being banned, TV advertising aimed at kids is now broadcast twenty-four hours a day, closed-captioned and in stereo. Nickelodeon, the Disney Channel, the Cartoon Network, and the other children's cable networks are now responsible for about 80 percent of all television viewing by kids.[21] None of these networks existed before 1979. The typical American child now spends about twenty-one hours a week watching television—roughly one and a half months of TV

[18]See Matthew McAllester, "Life in Cyberspace: What's McDonald's Doing with Kids' E-mail Responses?" *Newsday*, July 20, 1997.

[19]Quoted in Linda E. Demkovich, "Pulling the Sweet Tooth of Children's TV Advertising," *National Journal*, January 7, 1978.

[20]Quoted in A. O. Sulzberger, Jr., "FTC Staff Urges End to Child-TV Ad Study," *New York Times*, April 3, 1981.

[21]Cited in Steve McClellan and Richard Tedesco, "Children's TV Market May Be Played Out," *Broadcasting & Cable*, March 1, 1999.

every year.[22] That does not include the time children spend in front of a screen watching videos, playing video games, or using the computer. Outside of school, the typical American child spends more time watching television than doing any other activity except sleeping.[23] During the course of a year, he or she watches more than thirty thousand TV commercials.[24] Even the nation's youngest children are watching a great deal of television. About one-quarter of American children between the ages of two and five have a TV in their room.[25]

## Perfect Synergy

Although the fast food chains annually spend about $3 billion on televi-   *13*
sion advertising, their marketing efforts directed at children extend far beyond such conventional ads.[26] The McDonald's Corporation now operates more than eight thousand playgrounds at its restaurants in the United States.[27] Burger King has more than two thousand.[28] A manufacturer of "playlands" explains why fast food operators build these largely plastic structures: "Playlands bring in children, who bring in parents, who bring in money."[29] As American cities and towns spend less money on children's recreation, fast food restaurants have become gathering spaces for families with young children. Every month about 90 percent of American children between the ages of three and nine visit a McDonald's.[30] The seesaws, slides, and pits full of plastic balls have proven to be an effective lure. "But when it gets down to brass tacks," a *Brandweek* article on fast food notes, "the key to attracting kids is toys, toys, toys."[31]

The fast food industry has forged promotional links with the nation's   *14*
leading toy manufacturers, giving away simple toys with children's meals and selling more elaborate ones at a discount. The major toy crazes of recent years—including Pokémon cards, Cabbage Patch Kids, and Tamogotchis—have been abetted by fast food promotions. A successful promotion easily

[22]Cited in "Policy Statement: Media Education," American Academy of Pediatrics, August 1999.

[23]Cited in "Policy Statement: Children, Adolescents, and Television," American Academy of Pediatrics, October 1995.

[24]Cited in Mary C. Martin, "Children's Understanding of the Intent of Advertising: A Meta-Analysis," *Journal of Public Policy & Marketing*, Fall 1997.

[25]Cited in Lisa Jennings, "Baby, Hand Me the Remote," *Scripps Howard News Service*, October 13, 1999.

[26]Interview with Lynn Fava, Competitive Media Reporting.

[27]Cited in "Fast Food and Playgrounds: A Natural Combination," promotional material, Playlandservices, Inc.

[28]Ibid.

[29]Ibid.

[30]Cited in Rod Taylor, "The Beanie Factor," *Brandweek*, June 16, 1997.

[31]Sam Bradley and Betsey Spethmann, "Subway's Kid Pack: The Ties That Sell," *Brandweek*, October 10, 1994.

doubles or triples the weekly sales volume of children's meals. The chains often distribute numerous versions of a toy, encouraging repeat visits by small children and adult collectors who hope to obtain complete sets. In 1999 McDonald's distributed eighty different types of Furby. According to a publication called *Tomart's Price Guide to McDonald's Happy Meal Collectibles,* some fast food giveaways are now worth hundreds of dollars.[32]

Rod Taylor, a *Brandweek* columnist, called McDonald's 1997 Teenie   15 Beanie Baby giveaway one of the most successful promotions in the history of American advertising.[33] At the time McDonald's sold about 10 million Happy Meals in a typical week. Over the course of ten days in April of 1997, by including a Teenie Beanie Baby with each purchase, McDonald's sold about 100 million Happy Meals. Rarely has a marketing effort achieved such an extraordinary rate of sales among its intended consumers. Happy Meals are marketed to children between the ages of three and nine; within ten days about four Teenie Beanie Baby Happy Meals were sold for every American child in that age group. Not all of those Happy Meals were purchased for children. Many adult collectors bought Teenie Beanie Baby Happy Meals, kept the dolls, and threw away the food.

The competition for young customers has led the fast food chains to   16 form marketing alliances not just with toy companies, but with sports leagues and Hollywood studios. McDonald's has staged promotions with the National Basketball Association and the Olympics. Pizza Hut, Taco Bell, and KFC signed a three-year deal with the NCAA. Wendy's has linked with the National Hockey League. Burger King and Nickelodeon, Denny's and Major League Baseball, McDonald's and the Fox Kids Network have all formed partnerships that mix advertisements for fast food with children's entertainment. Burger King has sold chicken nuggets shaped like Teletubbies. McDonald's now has its own line of children's videos starring Ronald McDonald. *The Wacky Adventures of Ronald McDonald* is being produced by Klasky-Csupo, the company that makes *Rugrats* and *The Simpsons.* The videos feature the McDonaldland characters and sell for $3.49. "We see this as a great opportunity," a McDonald's executive said in a press release, "to create a more meaningful relationship between Ronald and kids."[34]

All of these cross-promotions have strengthened the ties between Hol-   17 lywood and the fast food industry. In the past few years, the major studios have started to recruit fast food executives. Susan Frank, a former director of national marketing for McDonald's, later became a marketing executive at the Fox Kids Network. She now runs a new family-oriented cable

[32]Meredith Williams, *Tomart's Price Guide to McDonald's Happy Meal Collectibles* (Dayton, Ohio: Tomart Publications, 1995).

[33]The story of McDonald's Teenie Beanie Baby promotion can be found in Taylor, "The Beanie Factor."

[34]Quoted in "McDonald's Launches Second Animated Video in Series Starring Ronald McDonald," press release, McDonald's Corporation, January 21, 1999.

network jointly owned by Hallmark Entertainment and the Jim Henson Company, creator of the Muppets. Ken Snelgrove, who for many years worked as a marketer for Burger King and McDonald's, now works at MGM. Brad Ball, a former senior vice president of marketing at McDonald's, is now the head of marketing for Warner Brothers. Not long after being hired, Ball told the *Hollywood Reporter* that there was little difference between selling films and selling hamburgers.[35] John Cywinski, the former head of marketing at Burger King, became the head of marketing for Walt Disney's film division in 1996, then left the job to work for McDonald's. Forty years after Bozo's first promotional appearance at a McDonald's, amid all the marketing deals, giveaways, and executive swaps, America's fast food culture has become indistinguishable from the popular culture of its children.

In May of 1996, the Walt Disney Company signed a ten-year global *18* marketing agreement with the McDonald's Corporation. By linking with a fast food company, a Hollywood studio typically gains anywhere from $25 million to $45 million in additional advertising for a film, often doubling its ad budget. These licensing deals are usually negotiated on a perfilm basis; the 1996 agreement with Disney gave McDonald's exclusive rights to that studio's output of films and videos. Some industry observers thought Disney benefited more from the deal, gaining a steady source of marketing funds.[36] According to the terms of the agreement, Disney characters could never be depicted sitting in a McDonald's restaurant or eating any of the chain's food. In the early 1980s, the McDonald's Corporation had turned away offers to buy Disney; a decade later, McDonald's executives sounded a bit defensive about having given Disney greater control over how their joint promotions would be run.[37] "A lot of people can't get used to the fact that two big global brands with this kind of credibility can forge this kind of working relationship," a McDonald's executive told a reporter. "It's about their theme parks, their next movie, their characters, their videos. . . . It's bigger than a hamburger. It's about the integration of our two brands, long-term."[38]

The life's work of Walt Disney and Ray Kroc had come full-circle, uniting in perfect synergy. McDonald's began to sell its hamburgers and french *19* fries at Disney's theme parks. The ethos of McDonaldland and of Disneyland, never far apart, have finally become one. Now you can buy a Happy Meal at the Happiest Place on Earth.

[35]See T. L. Stanley, *Hollywood Reporter,* May 26, 1998.

[36]See Thomas R. King, "Mickey May Be the Big Winner in Disney-McDonald's Alliance," *Wall Street Journal,* May 24, 1996.

[37]See Monci Jo Williams, "McDonald's Refuses to Plateau," *Fortune,* November 12, 1984.

[38]Quoted in James Bates, "You Want First-Run Features with Those Fries?" *Newsday,* May 11, 1997.

■ ■ ■

## Reading as a Writer: Analyzing Rhetorical Choices

1. What assumptions does Schlosser make about his readers and their sympathies? Mark several places in the essay that alert you to the kind of audience Schlosser assumes he is writing for, and be ready to explain how the wording in those places supports your thinking. What are the benefits and risks of targeting an audience in this way?

2. How persuasive do you find Schlosser's use of sources? Locate the sources that seem most and least persuasive and explain why. How and where does he address counterarguments or anticipate antagonistic readers?

## Writing as a Reader: Entering the Conversation of Ideas

1. Both Schlosser and David Buckingham are fascinated by the way children's media and marketing reach around the globe. Choose a toy or a film with widespread marketing to analyze through the lenses of these authors' ideas, and consider the possible positives and negatives of connecting children through this kind of marketing. What kinds of stories and values are being "sold" to kids this way? What do you conclude?

2. Schlosser, like Elizabeth Teare, is interested in the expanding role corporations play in our daily lives, even in a personal activity like reading books. Write an essay in which you draw on these authors' ideas to make an argument about the role corporations do play and ought to play in our lives. To what extent does the age of the consumer (a child or an adult) matter as you examine this topic? Support your claims with examples from the texts and, if you like, your own experiences.

---

ANN duCILLE

# *From* Multicultural Barbie and the Merchandising of Difference

Ann duCille has served as the chair and director of the Center for African American Studies at Wesleyan University. She has published widely on black women writers and on race and popular culture, particularly in her book *Skin Trade* (1996), which won the Myers Center Award for the Study of Human Rights in 1997. The essay here originally appeared in the spring 1994 issue of *differences: A Journal of Feminist Cultural Studies*. In this piece about Barbie, you'll hear one of duCille's key interests in popular culture—the ways we all help establish cultural norms through producing and consuming goods and ideas.

A quick look through duCille's MLA-style works cited list at the end of the essay shows that she draws on a range of academic conversations to frame her analysis of Barbie. She responds not only to scholars who write about Barbie but also to those who write about adolescent self-image,

raising African American children, and various aspects of multiculturalism and diversity. As you read duCille's essay, keep track of when and how
she draws on those she calls "Barbiologists" and those whose ideas give context to her broader analysis of culture. You will have to make similar moves
in your own writing as you use various sources to help you build your
own point.

While she draws on many other scholars' ideas to help her build her
point, duCille also invites readers to identify with her personal experiences, particularly in the opening and closing sections of the essay. How
effectively do these personal anecdotes—her own and others'—draw you
into the piece? How might they shed new light on toys you played with as
a child, toys you may have forgotten about? Considering the way culture
teaches us to pay attention to both race and physical appearance as we
think about who we are, duCille ends her essay by asking, "Is Barbie bad?"
Her answer: "Barbie is just a piece of plastic, but what she says about the
economic base of our society—what she suggests about gender and race in
our world—ain't good." DuCille's essay invites you to reconsider your own
experiences with "the ideological work of child's play" (para. 5). If you ask
the kinds of questions duCille asks of Barbie, you should discover similarly
eye-opening answers.

The white missionaries who came to Saint Aug's from New England were
darling to us. They gave Bessie and me these beautiful china dolls that probably were very expensive. Those dolls were white, of course. You couldn't get
a colored doll like that in those days. Well, I loved mine, just the way it was,
but do you know what Bessie did? She took an artist's palette they had also
given us and sat down and mixed the paints until she came up with a shade of
brown that matched her skin. Then she painted that white doll's face! None of
the white missionaries ever said a word about it. Mama and Papa just smiled.
(Sarah Delany)

This is my doll story (because every black journalist who writes about
race gets around to it sometime). Back when I started playing with Barbie,
there were no Christies (Barbie's black friend, born in 1968) or black Barbies
(born in 1980, brown plastic poured into blond Barbie's mold). I had two
blonds, which I bought with Christmas money from girls at school.
I cut off their hair and dressed them in African-print fabric. They lived
together (polygamy, I guess) with a black G.I. Joe bartered from the Shepp
boys, my downstairs neighbors. After an "incident" at school (where all of the
girls looked like Barbie and none of them looked like me), I galloped down
our stairs with one Barbie, her blond head hitting each spoke of the banister,
thud, thud, thud. And galloped up the stairs, thud, thud, thud, until her head
popped off, lost to the graveyard behind the stairwell. Then I tore off each
limb, and sat on the stairs for a long time twirling the torso like a baton. (Lisa
Jones)

Growing up in the 1950s, in the shadow of the second world war, it
was natural for children—including little black children like my

two brothers and me—to want to play war, to mimic what we heard on the radio, what we watched in black and white on our brand new floor model Motorola. In these war games, everyone wanted to be the Allied troops—the fearless, conquering white male heroes who had made the world safe for democracy, yet again, and saved us all from yellow peril. No one, of course, wanted to play the enemy—who most often was not the Germans or the Italians but the Japanese. So the enemy became or, more rightly, remained invisible, lurking in bushes we shot at with sticks we pretended were rifles and stabbed at with make-believe bayonets. "Take that," we shouted, liberally peppering our verbal assaults with racial epithets. "And that! And that!" It was all in fun—our venom and vigor. All's fair in wars of words. We understood little of what we said and nothing of how much our child's play reflected the sentiments of a nation that even in its finer, pre-war moments had not embraced as citizens its Asian immigrants or claimed as countrymen and women their American-born offspring.

However naively imitative, our diatribe was interrupted forever one 2 summer afternoon by the angry voice of our mother, chastising us through the open window. "Stop that," she said. "Stop that this minute. It's not nice. You're talking about the Japanese. *Japanese*, do you understand? And don't let me ever hear you call them anything else." In the lecture that accompanied dinner that evening, we were made to understand not the history of Japanese-Americans, the injustice of internment, or the horror of Hiroshima, but simply that there were real people behind the names we called; that name-calling always hurts somebody, always undermines someone's humanity. Our young minds were led on the short journey from "Jap" to "nigger"; and if we were too young then to understand the origins and fine points of all such pejoratives, we were old enough to know firsthand the pain of one of them.

I cannot claim that this early experience left me free of prejudice, but 3 it did assist me in growing up at once aware of my own status as "different" and conscious of the exclusion of others so labeled. It is important to note, however, that my sense of my own difference was affirmed and confirmed not simply by parental intervention but also by the unrelenting sameness of the tiny, almost exclusively white town in which I was raised. There in the country confines of East Bridgewater, Massachusetts, the adults who surrounded me (except for my parents) were all white, as were the teachers who taught me, the authors who thrilled me (and instilled in me a love of literature), and the neighborhood children who called me nigger one moment and friend the next. And when my brothers and I went our separate ways into properly gendered spheres, the dolls I played with—like almost everything else about my environment—were also white: Betsy Wetsy, Tiny Tears, and Patty Play Pal.

It seems remarkable to me now, as I remember these childish things 4 long since put away, that, for all the daily reminders of my blackness, I did not take note of its absence among the rubber-skin pinkness of Betsy

Wetsy, the bald-headed whiteness of Tiny Tears, and the blue-eyed blond-ness of Patty Play Pal. I was never tempted like Sarah Delany to paint the dolls I played with brown like me or to dress them in African-print fabric like Lisa Jones. (Indeed, I had no notion of such fabrics and little knowledge of the "dark continent" from which they came.) Caught up in fantasy, completely given over to the realm of make-believe, for most of my childhood I neither noticed nor cared that the dolls I played with did not look like me. The make-believe world to which I willingly surrendered more than just my disbelief was thoroughly and profoundly white. That is to say, the "me" I invented, the "I" I imagined, the Self I day-dreamed in technicolor fantasies was no more black like me than the dolls I played with. In the fifties and well into the sixties of my childhood, the black Other who was my Self, much like the enemy Other who was the foreign body of our war games, could only be imagined as faceless, far away, and utterly unfamiliar.

As suggested by my title, I am going to use the figure of multicultural 5 Barbie to talk about the commodification of race and gender difference. I wanted to back into the present topic, however, into what I have to say about Barbie as a gendered, racialized icon of contemporary commodity culture, by reaching into the past—into the admittedly contested terrain of the personal—to evoke the ideological work of child's play. More than simple instruments of pleasure and amusement, toys and games play cru-cial roles in helping children determine what is valuable in and around them. Dolls in particular invite children to replicate them, to imagine themselves in their dolls' images. What does it mean, then, when little girls are given dolls to play with that in no way resemble them? What did it mean for me that I was nowhere in the toys I played with?

If the Japan and the Africa of my youth were beyond the grasp (if not 6 the reach) of my imagination, children today are granted instant global gratification in their play—immediate, hands-on access to both Self and Other. Or so we are told by many of the leading fantasy manufactur-ers—Disney, Hasbro, and Mattel, in particular—whose contributions to multicultural education include such play things as Aladdin (movie, video, and dolls), G.I. Joe (male "action figures" in black and white), and Barbie (now available in a variety of colors and ethnicities). Disneyland's river ride through different nations, like Mattel's Dolls of the World Collection, instructs us that "It's a Small World After All." Those once distant lands of Africa, Asia, Australia, and even the Arctic regions of the North Pole (yes, Virginia, there is an Eskimo Barbie) are now as close to home as the local Toys R Us and F.A.O. Schwarz. And lo and behold, the inhabi-tants of these foreign lands—from Disney's Princess Jasmine to Mattel's Jamaican Barbie—are just like us, dye-dipped versions of archetypal white American beauty. It is not only a small world after all, but, as the Grammy award–winning theme from *Aladdin* informs us, "it's a whole new world."

Many of the major toy manufacturers have taken on a global perspec- 7
tive, a kind of nearsightedness that constructs this whole new world as
small and cultural difference as consumable. Perhaps nowhere is this uni-
versalizing myopia more conspicuous than in the production, marketing,
and consumption of Barbie dolls. By Mattel's reckoning, Barbie enjoys 100
percent brand name recognition among girls ages three to ten, ninety-six
percent of whom own at least one doll, with most owning an average of
eight. Five years ago, as Barbie turned thirty, *Newsweek* noted that nearly
500 million Barbies had been sold, along with 200 million G.I. Joes—
"enough for every man, woman, and child in the United States and Europe"
(Kantrowitz 59–60). Those figures have increased dramatically in the past
five years, bringing the current world-wide Barbie population to 800 million. In 1992 alone, $1 billion worth of Barbies and accessories were sold.
Last year, Barbie dolls sold at an average of one million per week, with
overall sales exceeding the $1 billion all-time high set the year before. As
the *Boston Globe* reported on the occasion of Barbie's thirty-fifth birthday
on March 9, 1994, nearly two Barbie dolls are sold every second somewhere in the world; about fifty percent of the dolls sold are purchased here
in the United States (Dembner 16).

The current Barbie boom may be in part the result of new, multicul- 8
turally oriented developments both in the dolls and in their marketing. In
the fall of 1990, Mattel, Inc. announced a new marketing strategy to boost
its sales: the corporation would "go ethnic" in its advertising by launching
an ad campaign for the black and Hispanic versions of the already popular doll. Despite the existence of black, Asian, and Latina Barbies, prior
to the fall of 1990 Mattel's print and TV ads featured only white dolls. In
what *Newsweek* described as an attempt to capitalize on ethnic spending
power, Mattel began placing ads for multicultural Barbies in such Afrocen-
tric publications as *Essence* magazine and on such Latin-oriented shows
as *Pepe Plata* after market research revealed that most black and Hispanic
consumers were unaware of the company's ethnic dolls. This targeted
advertising was a smart move, according to the industry analysts cited by
*Newsweek,* because "Hispanics buy about $170 billion worth of goods each
year, [and] blacks spend even more." Indeed, sales of black Barbie dolls
reportedly doubled in the year following this new ethnically-oriented ad
campaign.[1] But determined to present itself as politically correct as well as
financially savvy, Mattel was quick to point out that ethnic audiences, who
are now able to purchase dolls who look like them, also have profited from
the corporation's new marketing priorities. Barbie is a role model for all of
her owners, according to product manager Deborah Mitchell, herself an

---

[1]Mattel introduced the Shani doll—a black, Barbie-like doll—in 1991, which also
may have contributed to the rise in sales, particularly since the company engaged the
services of a PR firm that specializes in targeting ethnic audiences.

African American. "Barbie allows little girls to dream," she asserted—to which the *Newsweek* reporter added (seemingly without irony): "now, ethnic Barbie lovers will be able to dream in their own image" (Berkwitz 48).

Dream in their own image? The *Newsweek* columnist inadvertently  *9* put his finger on precisely what is so troubling to many parents, feminist scholars, and cultural critics about Barbie and dolls like her. Such toys invite, inspire, and even demand a potentially damaging process not simply of imagining but of interpellation. When little girls fantasize themselves into the conspicuous consumption, glamour, perfection, and, some have argued, anorexia of Barbie's world, it is rarely, if ever, "in their own image that they dream."[2] Regardless of what color dyes the dolls are dipped in or what costumes they are adorned with, the image they present is of the same mythically thin, long-legged, luxuriously-haired, buxom beauty. And while Mattel and other toy manufacturers may claim to have the best interests of ethnic audiences in mind in peddling their integrated wares, one does not have to be a cynic to suggest that profit remains the motivating factor behind this merchandising of difference.[3]

Far from simply playing with the sixty or so dolls I have acquired in  *10* the past year, then, I take them very seriously. In fact, I regard Barbie and similar dolls as Louis Althusser might have regarded them: as objects that do the dirty work of patriarchy and capitalism in the most insidious way—in the guise of child's play. But, as feminists have protested almost from the moment she hit the market, Barbie is not simply a child's toy or just a teenage fashion doll; she is an icon—perhaps *the* icon—of true white womanhood and femininity, a symbol of the far from innocent ideological stuff of which the (Miss) American dream and other mystiques of race and gender are made.

Invented by Ruth Handler, one of the founders of Mattel, and named  *11* after her daughter, Barbie dolls have been a very real force in the toy market since Mattel first introduced them at the American Toy Fair in 1959. In fact, despite the skepticism of toy store buyers—who at the time were primarily men—the first shipment of a half million dolls and a million

---

[2]Of course, the notion of "dreaming in one's own image" is always problematic since dreams, by definition, engage something other than the "real."

[3]Olmec Toys, a black-owned company headed by an African American woman named Yla Eason, markets a line of black and Latina Barbie-like dolls called the Imani Collection. Billed on their boxes as "African American Princess" and "Latin American Fantasy," these dolls are also presented as having been designed with the self images of black children in mind. "We've got one thing in mind with all our products," the blurbs on the Imani boxes read: "let's build self-esteem. Our children gain a sense of self importance through toys. So we make them look like them." Given their obvious resemblance to Barbie dolls—their long, straight hair and pencil-thin plastic bodies—Imani dolls look no more "like them," like "real" black children, than their prototype. Eason, who we are told was devastated by her son's announcement that he couldn't be a superhero because he wasn't white, may indeed want to give black children toys to play with that "look like them." Yet, in order to compete in a market long dominated by Mattel and Hasbro, her company, it seems, has little choice but to conform to the Barbie mold.

costumes sold out immediately (Larcen A7). The first Barbies, which were modeled after a sexy German doll and comic strip character named Lilli, were all white, but in 1967 Mattel premiered a black version of the doll called "Colored Francie." "Colored Francie," like white "Francie Fairchild" introduced the year before, was supposed to be Barbie's "MODern" younger cousin. As a white doll modeled and marketed in the image of Hollywood's Gidget, white Francie had been an international sensation, but Colored Francie was not destined to duplicate her prototype's success. Although the "black is beautiful" theme of both the civil rights and black power movements may have suggested a ready market for a beautiful black doll, Colored Francie in fact did not sell well.

Evelyn Burkhalter, owner, operator, and curator of the Barbie Hall of *12* Fame in Palo Alto, California—home to 16,000 Barbie dolls—attributes Colored Francie's commercial failure to the racial climate of the times. Doll purchasing patterns, it seems, reflected the same resistance to integration that was felt elsewhere in the nation. In her implied family ties to white Barbie, Colored Francie suggested more than simple integration. She implied miscegenation: a make-believe mixing of races that may have jeopardized the doll's real market value. Cynthia Roberts, author of *Barbie: Thirty Years of America's Doll* (1989), maintains that Colored Francie flopped because of her straight hair and Caucasian features (44), which seemingly were less acceptable then than now. No doubt Mattel's decision to call its first black Barbie "Colored Francie" also contributed to the doll's demise. The use of the outmoded, even racist term "colored" in the midst of civil rights and black power activism suggested that while Francie might be "MODern," Mattel was still in the dark(y) ages. In any case, neither black nor white audiences bought the idea of Barbie's colored relations, and Mattel promptly took the doll off the market, replacing her with a black doll called Christie in 1968.

While a number of other black dolls appeared throughout the late six- *13* ties and seventies—including the Julia doll, modeled after the TV character played by black singer and actress Diahann Carroll—it was not until 1980 that Mattel introduced black dolls that were called Barbie like their white counterparts. Today, Barbie dolls come in a virtual rainbow coalition of colors, races, ethnicities, and nationalities—most of which look remarkably like the prototypical white Barbie, modified only by a dash of color and a change of costume. It is these would-be multicultural "dolls of the world"—Jamaican Barbie, Nigerian and Kenyan Barbie, Malaysian Barbie, Chinese Barbie, Mexican, Spanish, and Brazilian Barbie, et cetera, et cetera, et cetera—that interest me. For me these dolls are at once a symbol and a symptom of what multiculturalism has become at the hands of contemporary commodity culture: an easy and immensely profitable way off the hook of Eurocentrism that gives us the face of cultural diversity without the particulars of racial difference.

If I could line up across the page the ninety "different" colors, cultures, *14* and other incarnations in which Barbie currently exists, the fact of her unrelenting sameness (or at least similarity) would become immediately apparent. Even two dolls might do the trick: "My First Barbie" in white and "My First Barbie" in black, for example, or white "Western Fun Barbie" and black "Western Fun Barbie." Except for their dye jobs, the dolls are identical: the same body, size, shape, and apparel. Or perhaps I should say *nearly* identical because in some instances — with black and Asian dolls in particular — coloring and other subtle changes (stereotypically slanted eyes in the Asian dolls, thicker lips in the black dolls) suggest differently coded facial features.

In other instances, when Barbie moves across cultural as opposed to    15
racial lines, it is costume rather than color that distinguishes one ethnic group or nation from another. Nigeria and Jamaica, for instance, are represented by the same basic brown body, dolled-up in different native garbs — or Mattel's interpretation thereof.[4] With other costume changes, this generic black body becomes Western Fun Barbie or Marine Barbie or Desert Storm Barbie, and even Presidential Candidate Barbie, who, by the way, comes with a Nancy Reagan–red taking-care-of-business suit as well as a red, white, and blue inaugural ball gown. Much the same is true of the generic Asian doll — sometimes called Kira — who reappears in a variety of different dress-defined ethnicities. In other words, where Barbie is concerned, clothes not only make the woman, they mark the racial and/or cultural difference.

Such difference is marked as well by the cultural history and language    16
lessons that accompany each doll in Mattel's international collection. The back of Jamaican Barbie's box tells us, for example, "*How-you-du* (Hello) from the land of Jamaica, a tropical paradise known for its exotic fruit, sugar cane, breathtaking beaches, and reggae beat!" The box goes on to explain that most Jamaicans have ancestors from Africa. Therefore, "even though our official language is English, we speak patois, a kind of '*Jamaica Talk*,' filled with English and African words." The lesson ends with a brief glossary (eight words) and a few more examples of this "Jamaica Talk," complete with translations: "*A hope yu wi come-a Jamaica!* (I hope you will come to Jamaica!)" and "*Teck care a yusself, mi fren!* (Take care of yourself, my friend!)." A nice idea, I suppose, but for me these quick-and-dirty ethnographies only enhance the extent to which these would-be multicultural dolls treat race and ethnic difference like collectibles, contributing more to commodity culture than to the intercultural awareness they claim to inspire.

---

[4]After many calls to the Jamaican Embassy in Washington, D.C., and to various cultural organizations in Jamaica, I have determined that Jamaican Barbie's costume — a floor-length granny-style dress with apron and headrag — bears some resemblance to what is considered the island's traditional folk costume. I am still left wondering about the decision-making process, however: why the doll representing Jamaica is figured as a maid, while the doll representing Great Britain, for example, is presented as a lady — a blonde, blue-eyed Barbie doll dressed in a fancy riding habit with boots and hat.

Is the current fascination with the black or colored body—especially *17* the female body—a contemporary version of the primitivism of the 1920s? Is multiculturalism to postmodernism what primitivism was to modernism? It was while on my way to a round table discussion on precisely this question that I bought my first black Barbie dolls in March of 1993. As carbon copies of an already problematic original, these colorized Mattel toys seemed to me the perfect tools with which to illustrate the point I wanted to make about the collapse of multiculturalism into an easy pluralism that simply adds what it constructs as the Other without upsetting the fundamental precepts and paradigms of Western culture or, in the case of Mattel, without changing the mold.

Not entirely immune to such critiques, Mattel sought expert advice *18* from black parents and early childhood specialists in the development and marketing of its newest line of black Barbie dolls. Chief among the expert witnesses was clinical psychologist Darlene Powell Hopson, who coauthored with her husband Derek S. Hopson a study of racism and child development entitled *Different and Wonderful: Raising Black Children in a Race-Conscious Society* (1990). As part of their research for the book, the Hopsons repeated a ground-breaking study conducted by black psychologists Kenneth and Mamie Clark in the 1940s.

The Clarks used black and white dolls to demonstrate the negative *19* effects of racism and segregation on black children. When given a choice between a white doll and a black doll, nearly 70 percent of the black children in the study chose the white doll. The Clarks' findings became an important factor in *Brown v. the Board of Education* in 1954. More recently, some scholars have called into question not necessarily the Clarks' findings but their interpretation: the assumption that, in the realm of make-believe, a black child's choosing a white doll necessarily reflects a negative self concept.[5] For the Hopsons, however, the Clarks' research remains compelling. In 1985 they repeated the Clarks' doll test and found that an alarming 65 percent of the black children in their sample chose a white doll over a black one. Moreover, 76 percent of the children interviewed said that the black dolls "looked bad" to them (Hopson xix).

In addition to the clinical uses they make of dolls in their experiments, *20* the Hopsons also give considerable attention to what they call "doll play" in their book, specifically mentioning Barbie. "If your daughter likes 'Barbie' dolls, by all means get her Barbie," they advise black parents. "But also choose Black characters from the Barbie world. *You do not want your child to grow up thinking that only White dolls, and by extension White people, are*

---

[5]See among others Morris Rosenberg's books *Conceiving the Self* (1979) and *Society and the Adolescent Self-Image* (1989) and William E. Cross's *Shades of Black: Diversity in African American Identity* (1991), all of which challenge the Clarks' findings. Cross argues, for example, that the Clarks confounded or conflated two different issues: attitude toward race in general and attitude toward the self in particular. How one feels about race is not necessarily an index of one's self-esteem.

*attractive and nice*" (Hopsons 127, emphasis original). (Note that "Barbie," unmodified in the preceding passage, seems to mean *white* Barbie dolls.) The Hopsons suggest that parents should not only provide their children with black and other ethnic dolls but that they should get involved in their children's doll play. "Help them dress and groom the dolls while you compliment them both," they advise, offering the following suggested routine: "'This is a beautiful doll. It looks just like you. Look at her hair. It's just like yours. Did you know your nose is as pretty as your doll's?'" (119). They also suggest that parents use "complimentary words such as *lovely, pretty, or nice* so that [the] child will learn to associate them with his or her own image" (124).

Certainly it is important to help children feel good about themselves. 21 One might argue, however, that the "just like you" simile and the beautiful doll imagery so central to these suggestions for what the Hopsons call positive play run the risk of transmitting to the child a colorized version of the same old beauty myth. Like Barbie dolls themselves, they make beauty—and by implication worth—a matter of physical characteristics.

In spite of their own good intentions, the Hopsons, in linking play 22 with "beautiful" dolls to positive self-imagining, echoed Mattel's own marketing campaign. It is not surprising, then, that the Hopsons' findings and the interventional strategies they designed for using dolls to instill ethnic pride caught the attention of Mattel. In 1990 Darlene Hopson was asked to consult with the corporation's product manager Deborah Mitchell and designer Kitty Black-Perkins—both African Americans—in the development of a new line of "realistically sculpted" black fashion dolls. Hopson agreed and about a year later Shani and her friends Asha and Nichelle became the newest members of Barbie's ever-expanding family.

Shani means "marvelous" in Swahili, according to the dolls' press kit. 23 But as *Village Voice* columnist Lisa Jones has noted, the name has other meanings as well: "startling, a wonder, a novelty" (36). My own research indicates that while Shani is a Swahili female name meaning marvelous, the Kiswahili word "shani" translates as "an adventure, something unusual" (Stewart 120). So it seems that Mattel's new play thing is not just marvelous, too marvelous for words, but, as her name also suggests, she is difference incarnate—a novelty, a new enterprise, or, perhaps, as the black female Other so often is, an exotic. Mattel, it seems to me, both plays up and plays on what it presents as the doll's exotic black-is-beautiful difference. As the back of her package reads:

> Shani means marvelous in the Swahili language . . . and marvelous she is! With her friends Asha and Nichelle, Shani brings to life the special style and beauty of the African American woman.
>
> Each one is beautiful in her own way, with her own lovely skin shade and unique facial features. Each has a different hair color and texture, perfect for braiding, twisting, and creating fabulous hair styles! Their clothes, too, reflect the vivid colors and ethnic accents that showcase their *exotic looks* and fashion flair!

Shani, Asha, and Nichelle invite you into their glamorous world to share the fun and excitement of being a top model. Imagine appearing on magazine covers, starring in fashion shows, and going to Hollywood parties as you, Shani, Asha, and Nichelle live your dreams of beauty and success, loving every marvelous minute! (emphasis added)

While these words attempt to convey a message of black pride—after the fashion of the Hopsons' recommendations for positive play—that message is clearly tied to bountiful hair, lavish and exotic clothes, and other outward and visible signs not of brains but of beauty, wealth, and success. Shani may be a top fashion model, but don't look for her (or, if Mattel's own oft-articulated theory of Barbie as role model holds, yourself or your child) at M.I.T.

Like any other proud, well-to-do parents of a debutante, Mattel gave 24 Shani her own coming out party at the International Toy Fair in February of 1991. This gala event included a tribute to black designers and an appearance by En Vogue singing the Negro National Anthem, "Lift Every Voice and Sing!"—evidently the song of choice of the doll Mattel describes as "tomorrow's African American woman." Also making their debuts were Shani's friends Asha and Nichelle, notable for the different hues in which their black plastic skin comes—an innovation due in part to Darlene Hopson's influence. Shani, the signature doll of the line, is what we call in the culture "brown-skinned"; Asha is honey-colored (some would say "highyella"); and Nichelle is deep mahogany. Their male friend Jamal, added in 1992, completes the collection.

For the un(make-)believing, the three-to-one ratio of the Shani quar- 25 tet—three black females to one black male—may be the most realistic thing about these dolls. In the eyes and the advertising of Mattel, however, Shani and her friends are the most authentic black female thing the mainstream toy market has yet produced. "Tomorrow's African American woman" (an appellation which, as Lisa Jones has noted, both riffs and one-ups *Essence*'s "Today's Black Woman") has broader hips, fuller lips, and a broader nose, according to product manager Deborah Mitchell. Principal designer Kitty Black-Perkins, who has dressed black Barbies since their birth in 1980, adds that the Shani dolls are also distinguished by their unique, culturally-specific clothes in "spice tones, [and] ethnic fabrics," rather than "fantasy colors like pink or lavender" (qtd. in Jones 36)—evidently the colors of the faint of skin.

The notion that fuller lips, broader noses, wider hips, and higher der- 26 rières somehow make the Shani dolls more realistically African American raises many difficult questions about authenticity, truth, and the ever-problematic categories of the real and the symbolic, the typical and the stereotypical. Just what are we saying when we claim that a doll does or does not "look black"? How does black look? What would it take to make a doll look authentically African American? What preconceived, prescriptive ideals of legitimate blackness are inscribed in such claims of authenticity? How can doll manufacturers or any other image makers—the film industry, for example—attend to cultural, racial, and phenotypical differences without merely engaging the same simplistic big-lips/broad-hips stereotypes that make so many of us—blacks in particular—grit our (pearly white) teeth? What would it take to produce a line of dolls that more fully reflects the wide variety of sizes, shapes, colors, hair styles, occupations, abilities, and disabilities that African Americans—like all people—come in? In other words: what price difference? . . .

## The Body Politic(s) of Barbie

> Barbie's body is a consumer object itself, a vehicle for the display of clothing and the spectacular trappings of a wealthy teenage fantasy life. Her extraordinary body exists not simply as an example of the fetishized female form typical of those offered up to the male gaze, but as a commodity vehicle itself whose form seduces the beholder and sells accessories, the real source of corporate profit. Like Lay's chips, no one can buy just one outfit for the doll. Barbie is the late capitalist girl incarnate. (McCombie)

In focusing thus far on the merchandising of racial, perhaps more    27
so than gender, difference, I do not mean to imply that racial and gender identities are divisible, even in dolls. Nor, in observing that most if not all of Mattel's "dolls of the world" look remarkably like what the company calls the "traditional, blond, blue-eyed Barbie," do I mean to suggest that the seemingly endless recapitulation of the white prototype is the only way in which these dolls are problematic. In fact, the most alarming thing about Barbie may well be the extent to which she functions as what M. G. Lord calls a teaching tool for femininity, whatever her race or ethnicity. Lord, the author of *Forever Barbie: The Unauthorized Biography of a Real Doll*, due out later this year, describes Barbie as a "space-age fertility icon. She looks like a modern woman, but she's a very primitive totem of female power" (qtd. in Dembner 1).

Barbie has long had the eye and ire of feminists, who, for the most    28
part, have reviled her as another manifestation of the damaging myths of female beauty and the feminine body that patriarchy perpetuates through such vehicles as popular and commodity culture. A counter narrative also exists, however, one in which Barbie is not an empty-headed, material girl bimbo, for whom math class is tough, but a feminist heroine, who has been first in war (a soldier who served in the Gulf, she has worn the colors of her country as well as the United Colors of Benetton), first in peace (she held her own summit in 1990 and she's a long-time friend of UNICEF, who "loves all the children of the world"), and always first in the hearts of her country (Americans buy her at the rate of one doll every second). While time does not allow me to reiterate or to assess here all the known critiques and defenses of Barbie, I do want to discuss briefly some of the gender ideals that I think are encoded in and transmitted by this larger-than-life little woman and what Barbie's escalating popularity says about contemporary American culture.

In *Touching Liberty: Abolition, Feminism, and the Politics of the Body* 29
(1993), Karen Sanchez-Eppler argues that all dolls are intended to teach
little girls about domesticity (133). If such tutelage is Barbie's not so secret
mission, her methodology is far more complex and contradictory than that
of the Betsy Wetsy and Tiny Tears baby dolls I played with thirty-five years
ago. Those dolls invoked and evoked the maternal, as they and the baby
bottles and diapers with which they were packaged invited us to nestle,
nurse, and nurture. Barbie's curvaceous, big-busted, almost fully female
body, on the other hand, summons not the maternal but the sexual, not the
nurturant mother but the sensuous woman. As Mel McCombie has argued,
rather than rehearsing parenting, as a baby doll does, Barbie's adult body
encourages children to dress and redress a fashion doll that yields lessons
about sexuality, consumption, and teenage life (3). Put another way, we
might say that Barbie is literally and figuratively a titillating toy.

Bodacious as they may be, however, Barbie's firm plastic breasts have 30
no nipples—nothing that might offend, nothing that might suggest her
own pleasure. And if her protruding plastic mounds signify a simmering
sensuality, what are we to make of her missing genitalia? McCombie suggests that Barbie's genital ambiguity can be read as an "homage to 'good
taste'" and as a "reflection of the regnant mores for teenage girls—to be
both sexy and adult yet remain virginal" (4). I agree that her body invites
such readings, but it also seems to me that there is nothing ambiguous
about Barbie's crotch. It's missing in inaction. While male dolls like Ken
and Jamal have bumps "down there" and in some instances simulated
underwear etched into the plastic, most Barbies come neither with draw-
ers nor with even a hint of anything that needs covering, even as "it" is
already covered or erased. As an icon of idealized femininity, then, Barbie is locked into a never-never land in which she must be always already
sexual without the possibility of sex. Conspicuously sensual on top but
definitively nonsexual below, her plastic body indeed has inscribed within
it the very contradictory, whore/madonna messages with which patriarchy
taunts and even traumatizes young women in particular.

This kind of speculation about Barbie's breasts has led the doll's cre- 31
ator, Ruth Handler, to chide adults for their nasty minds. "In my opinion
people make too much of breasts," Handler has complained. "They are just
part of the body" (qtd. in BillyBoy 20). Mrs. Handler has a point (or maybe
two). I feel more than just a little ridiculous myself as I sit here contemplating the body parts and sex life of a piece of plastic. What is fascinating,
however, what I think is worth studying, what both invites and resists theorizing, is not the lump of molded plastic that is Barbie, but the imaginary
life that is not—that is *our* invention. Barbie as a cultural artifact may be
able to tell us more about ourselves and our society—more about society's
attitudes toward its women—than anything we might say about the doll
her- or, rather, *itself.*

In the nineteenth century, Alexis de Tocqueville and others argued 32
that you could judge the character, quality, and degree of advancement
of a civilization by the status and treatment of its women. What is the

status of women in soon to be twenty-first-century America, and can Barbie serve as a barometer for measuring that status? Barbie, it seems to me, is a key player in the process of socialization—of engendering and racialization—that begins in infancy and is furthered by almost everything about our society, including the books children read, the toys they play with, and the cartoons they watch on television.

While changing channels one Saturday morning, I happened upon a 33 cartoon, just a glimpse of which impelled me to watch on. At the point that I tuned in, a big, gray, menacingly male bulldog was barking furiously at a pretty, petite, light-colored cat, who simply batted her long lashes, meowed coquettishly, and rubbed her tiny feline body against his huge canine leg in response. The more the dog barked and growled, the softer the cat meowed, using her slinky feline body and her feminine wiles to win the dog over. Her strategy worked; before my eyes—and, I imagine, the eyes of millions of children—the ferocious beast was transformed into a lovesick puppy dog, who followed the cat everywhere, repeatedly saving her from all manner of evil and danger. Time and time again, the bulldog rescued the helpless, accident-prone pussy from falling girders, oncoming traffic, and other hazards to which she, in her innocent frailty, was entirely oblivious. By the end, the once ferocious bulldog was completely domesticated, as his no longer menacing body became a kind of bed for the cat to nestle in.

There are, of course, a number of ways to read the gender and racial 34 politics of this cartoon. I suppose that the same thought process that theorizes Barbie as a feminist heroine for whom men are mere accessories might claim the kitty cat, too, as a kind of feminist feline, who uses her feminine wiles to get her way. What resonates for me in the cartoon, however, are its beauty and the beast, light/dark, good/evil, female/male, race and gender codes: light, bright, cat-like femininity tames menacing black male bestiality. Make no mistake, however; it is not wit that wins out over barbarism but a mindless, can't-take-care-of-herself femininity.

Interestingly enough, these are the kinds of messages of which fairy 35 tales and children's stories are often made. White knights rescue fair damsels in distress from dark, forbidding evils of one kind or another. As Darlene and Derek Hopson argue: "Some of the most blatant and simplistic representations of white as good and black as evil are found in children's literature," where evil black witches and good white fairies—heroes in white and villains in black—abound (121).

What Barbie dolls, cartoons like the one outlined above, and even the 36 seemingly innocent fairy tales we read to our children seem to me to have in common are the mythologies of race and gender that are encoded in them. Jacqueline Urla and Alan Swedlund maintain that Barbie's body type constructs the bodies of other women as deviant and perpetuates an impossible standard of beauty. Attempting to live up to the Barbie ideal, others argue, fosters eating and shopping disorders in teenage girls—nightmares instead of dreams. BillyBoy, one of Barbie's most ardent supporters, defends his heroine against such charges by insisting that there is nothing abnor-

no big ears, no chubby thighs or other "imperfections." For a modest price, I can dream myself into Barbie's perfect world, so long as I dream myself in her image. It may be a small world, a whole new world, but there is still no place for me as *me* in it.

This, then, is my final doll story. Groucho Marx said that he wouldn't    40
want to belong to a club that would have him as a member. In that same vein, I am not so sure that most of us would want to buy a doll that "looked like us." Indeed, efforts to produce and market such truer-to-life dolls have not met with much commercial success. Cultural critics like me can throw theoretical stones at her all we want, but part of Barbie's infinite appeal is her very perfection, the extent to which she is both product and purveyor of the dominant white Western ideal of beauty.

And what of black beauty? If Colored Francie failed thirty years ago in    41
part because of her Caucasian features, what are we to make of the current popularity and commercial success of Black Barbie and Shani, straight hair and all? Have we progressed to a point where "difference" makes no difference? Or have we regressed to such a degree that "difference" is only conceivable as similarity—as a mediated text that no matter what its dye job ultimately must be readable as white. Listen to our language: we "*tolerate* difference"; we practice "racial tolerance." Through the compound fractures of interpellation and universalization, the Other is reproduced not in her own image but in ours. If we have gotten away from "Us" and "Them," it may be only because Them R Us.

Is Barbie bad? Barbie is just a piece of plastic, but what she says about    42
the economic base of our society—what she suggests about gender and race in our world—ain't good.

NOTE

*I am particularly pleased to be publishing this essay in* differences, *since its genesis was at a roundtable discussion on multiculturalism and postmodernism, sponsored by the Pembroke Center for Teaching and Research on Women at Brown University, in March of 1993. I wish to thank the many friends and colleagues who have encouraged this project, especially Indira Karamcheti and her four-year-old daughter Gita, who introduced me to the miniature Barbies that come with McDonald's "Happy Meals," and Erness Brody, who, with her daughter Jennifer Brody, is a veteran collector of vintage dolls. I owe a special debt to fellow "Barbiologists" M. G. Lord, Mel McCombie, Jacqueline Urla, and Eric Swedlund, who have so generously shared their research, and to Darlene Powell Hopson for talking with me about her work with Mattel. I wish to acknowledge as well the work of Erica Rand, an art historian at Bates College, who is also working on Barbie.*

WORKS CITED

Berkwitz, David N. "Finally, Barbie Doll Ads Go Ethnic." *Newsweek* 13 Aug. 1990: 48.
BillyBoy. *Barbie: Her Life and Times.* New York: Crown, 1987.
Cross, William E., Jr. *Shades of Black: Diversity in African American Identity.* Philadelphia: Temple UP, 1991.
Delany, Sarah, and Delany, A. Elizabeth. *Having Our Say: The Delany Sisters' First 100 Years.* New York: Kodansha, 1993.
Dembner, Alice. "Thirty-five and Still a Doll." *Boston Globe* 9 Mar. 1994: 1+.
Jones, Lisa. "A Doll Is Born." *Village Voice* 26 Mar. 1991: 36.

Kantrowitz, Barbara. "Hot Date: Barbie and G.I. Joe." *Newsweek* 20 Feb. 1989: 59–60.

Hopson, Darlene Powell and Derek S. *Different and Wonderful: Raising Black Children in a Race-Conscious Society.* New York: Simon, 1990.

Larcen, Donna. "Barbie Bond Doesn't Diminish with Age." *Hartford Courant* 17 Aug. 1993: A6–7.

Lord, M. G. *Forever Barbie: The Unauthorized Biography of a Real Doll.* New York: Morrow, 1994.

McCombie, Mel. "Barbie: Toys Are Us." Unpublished essay.

Morrison, Toni. *The Bluest Eye.* New York: Washington Square, 1970.

Roberts, Cynthia. *Barbie: Thirty Years of America's Doll.* Chicago: Contemporary, 1989.

Rosenberg, Morris. *Conceiving the Self.* New York: Basic, 1979.

———. *Society and the Adolescent Self-Image.* Middletown: Wesleyan UP, 1989.

Sanchez-Eppler, Karen. *Touching Liberty: Abolition, Feminism, and the Politics of the Body.* Berkeley: U of California P, 1993.

Stewart, Julia. *African Names.* New York: Carol, 1993.

Urla, Jacqueline, and Alan Swedlund. "The Anthropometry of Barbie: Unsettling Ideals of the Feminine in Popular Culture." *Deviant Bodies.* Ed. Jennifer Terry and Jacqueline Urla. Bloomington: Indiana UP, [1995].

■ ■ ■

## Reading as a Writer: Analyzing Rhetorical Choices

1. List the key phrases duCille uses to build her argument in her early paragraphs (you might look in particular at paragraphs 5, 9 and 10), and be ready to explain them in your own words. Be sure you look up words that are new to you. For example, what do you think duCille means by "the commodification of race and gender difference" in paragraph 5? Work in pairs or groups to help make sense of some of these challenging phrases that are important to duCille's argument about Barbie.

2. Find two passages where duCille uses a specific doll as an example to illustrate her larger argument. What words and phrases does she use to move between her detailed descriptions of the dolls and their packaging, and her analysis of those details? How persuasive do you find her claims, based on the evidence in these passages? Explain your answer.

## Writing as a Reader: Entering the Conversation of Ideas

1. DuCille and Noël Sturgeon examine the ways that attitudes toward racial differences are constructed through children's popular culture. Select as a test case a children's film not covered by Sturgeon that you can analyze through both duCille's and Sturgeon's insights about race and gender. How do these authors' ideas help illuminate aspects of this film that audiences might miss? What significance do you see in this "hidden" story?

2. DuCille's emphasis on women's bodies and the marketplace intersects with the concerns of Jean Kilbourne and Sharlene Nagy Hesse-Biber. Write an essay in which you use insights from duCille and one or both of these other writers in order to analyze a specific product (and perhaps its advertising) that relies on gender—feminine or masculine—for its marketing. What do you conclude?

KATHA POLLITT

# The Smurfette Principle

Katha Pollitt is a prize-winning poet, critic, and columnist who is best known for her "Subject to Debate" column in *The Nation* magazine. This piece first appeared in the "Hers" column in the *New York Times* in April 1991. Pollitt writes frequently about gender politics, media trends, American domestic and foreign policies, and popular culture. Many of her essays are gathered in two collections: *Reasonable Creatures: Essays on Women and Feminism* (1994) and *Virginity or Death! And Other Social and Political Issues of Our Time* (2006).

In "The Smurfette Principle," Pollitt uses her own experiences as a parent of a 3-year-old daughter as the springboard for asking larger cultural questions about the media stories we are "selling" to girls and to boys. Disney's *The Little Mermaid* is the story Pollitt focuses on in her opening example, and she mulls over the reasons that Ariel the mermaid holds such appeal to her spunky daughter, when the story ultimately shows how the "happy" ending with a wedding is made possible by the heroine giving up her voice. Pollitt contextualizes this Disney film historically, reflecting on the ways Ariel is an improvement over the much more passive *Cinderella* story she grew up with. However, Pollitt finds more bad news than good when she examines the high ratio of male to female characters in most children's books, movies, and television. She also discovers, by looking through many examples, that male characters are most often cast as active and outgoing and that female characters are most often stereotyped as quiet, hair bow–wearing sidekicks, helpers, or little sisters to the boys—even when the characters are friendly, fuzzy monsters.

Where does Pollitt explain her title phrase, the "Smurfette principle," a term she coins here in order to label a pattern she sees in stories marketed to children? Pollitt lists and describes many examples from children's popular culture to illustrate this principle at work. Many of those examples may be familiar to you, but you may be able to list many more that either fulfill or refute her point. This is a short essay, but Pollitt covers a lot of ground, so keep your eyes open as you read this lively but dense piece. How is her closing paragraph related to her opening one? What intellectual distance have we traveled, as readers, by the time we reach the end? What does she want us to *do*? These last three questions are questions you should ask of every essay you write, too. Whether or not you agree that the gender roles Pollitt notices in children's media are a problem, her strategy of asking questions and looking for patterns in popular culture should inspire you to draw some conclusions of your own about your past and present entertainment favorites.

This Christmas, I finally caved in: I gave my 3-year-old daughter, Sophie, *1* her very own cassette of *The Little Mermaid*. Now, she, too, can sit transfixed by Ariel, the perky teen-ager with the curvy tail who trades her voice for a pair of shapely legs and a shot at marriage to a prince. ("On land it's much preferred for ladies not to say a word," sings the cynical sea witch, "and she who holds her tongue will get her man." Since she's the villain, we're not meant to notice that events prove her correct.)

Usually when parents give a child some item they find repellent, they *2* plead helplessness before a juvenile filibuster. But *The Little Mermaid* was my idea. Ariel may look a lot like Barbie, and her adventure may be limited to romance and over with the wedding bells, but unlike, say, Cinderella or Sleeping Beauty, she's active, brave, and determined, the heroine of her own life. She even rescues the prince. And that makes her a rare fish, indeed, in the world of preschool culture.

Take a look at the kids' section of your local video store. You'll find that *3* features starring boys, and usually aimed at them, account for 9 out of 10 offerings. Clicking the television dial one recent week—admittedly not an encyclopedic study—I came across not a single network cartoon or puppet show starring a female. (Nickelodeon, the children's cable channel, has one of each.) Except for the crudity of the animation and the general air of witlessness and hype, I might as well have been back in my own 1950s childhood, nibbling Frosted Flakes in front of Daffy Duck, Bugs Bunny, Porky Pig, and the rest of the all-male Warner Brothers lineup.

Contemporary shows are either essentially all-male, like *Garfield*, or *4* are organized on what I call the Smurfette principle: a group of male buddies will be accented by a lone female, stereotypically defined. In the worst cartoons—the ones that blend seamlessly into the animated cereal commercials—the female is usually a little-sister type, a bunny in a pink dress and hair ribbons who tags along with the adventurous bears and badgers. But the Smurfette principle rules the more carefully made shows, too. Thus, Kanga, the only female in *Winnie-the-Pooh*, is a mother. Piggy, of *Muppet Babies*, is a pint-size version of Miss Piggy, the camp glamour queen of the Muppet movies. April, of the wildly popular *Teen-Age Mutant Ninja Turtles*, functions as a girl Friday to a quartet of male superheroes. The message is clear. Boys are the norm, girls the variation; boys are central, girls peripheral; boys are individuals, girls types. Boys define the group, its story, and its code of values. Girls exist only in relation to boys.

Well, commercial television—what did I expect? The surprise is that *5* public television, for all its superior intelligence, charm, and commitment to worthy values, shortchanges preschool girls, too. Mister Rogers lives in a neighborhood populated mostly by middle-aged men like himself, *Shining Time Station* features a cartoon in which the male characters are train engines and the female characters are passenger cars. And then there's *Sesame Street*. True the human characters are neatly divided between the genders (and among the races, too, which is another rarity). The film clips, moreover, are just about the only place on television in which you regularly see girls having fun together: practicing double Dutch, having a sleep-over. But the Muppets are the real stars of *Sesame Street*, and the important ones—the ones with real personalities, who sing on the musical videos, whom kids identify with and cherish in dozens of licensed products—are all male. I know one little girl who was so outraged and heartbroken when she realized that even Big Bird—her last hope—was a boy that she hasn't watched the show since.

Well, there's always the library. Some of the best children's books ever  6 written have been about girls—Madeline, Frances the badger. It's even possible to find stories with funny, feminist messages, like *The Paperbag Princess*. (She rescues the prince from a dragon, but he's so ungrateful that she decides not to marry him, after all.) But books about girls are a subset in a field that includes a much larger subset of books about boys (12 of the 14 storybooks singled out for praise in last year's Christmas roundup in *Newsweek*, for instance) and books in which the sex of the child is theoretically unimportant—in which case it usually "happens to be" male. Dr. Seuss's books are less about individual characters than about language and imaginative freedom—but, somehow or other, only boys get to go on beyond Zebra or see marvels on Mulberry Street. Frog and Toad, Lowly Worm, Lyle the Crocodile, all could have been female. But they're not.

Do kids pick up on the sexism in children's culture? You bet. Pre-  7 schoolers are like medieval philosophers: the text—a book, a movie, a TV show—is more authoritative than the evidence of their own eyes. "Let's play weddings," says my little niece. We grownups roll our eyes, but face it: it's still the one scenario in which the girl is the central figure. "Women are nurses," my friend Anna, a doctor, was informed by her then 4-year-old, Molly. Even my Sophie is beginning to notice the back-seat role played by girls in some of her favorite books. "Who's that?" she asks every time we reread *The Cat in the Hat*. It's Sally, the timid little sister of the resourceful boy narrator. She wants Sally to matter, I think, and since Sally is really just a name and a hair ribbon, we have to say her name again and again.

The sexism in preschool culture deforms both boys and girls. Little  8 girls learn to split their consciousness, filtering their dreams and ambitions through boy characters while admiring the clothes of the princess. The more privileged and daring can dream of becoming exceptional women in a man's world—Smurfettes. The others are being taught to accept the more usual fate, which is to be a passenger car drawn through life by a masculine train engine. Boys, who are rarely confronted with stories in which males play only minor roles, learn a simpler lesson: Girls just don't matter much.

How can it be that 25 years of feminist social change have made so  9 little impression on preschool culture? Molly, now 6 and well aware that women can be doctors, has one theory: Children's entertainment is mostly made by men. That's true, as it happens, and I'm sure it explains a lot. It's also true that, as a society, we don't seem to care much what goes on with kids, as long as they are reasonably quiet. Marshmallow cereal, junky toys, endless hours in front of the tube—a society that accepts all that is not going to get in a lather about a little gender stereotyping. It's easier to focus on the bright side. I had *Cinderella*, Sophie has *The Little Mermaid*—that's progress, isn't it?

"We're working on it," Dulcy Singer, the executive producer of *Sesame* 10 *Street*, told me when I raised the sensitive question of those all-male Muppets. After all, the show has only been on the air for a quarter of a century; these things take time. The trouble is, our preschoolers don't have time. My funny, clever, bold, adventurous daughter is forming her gender ideas right now. I do what I can to counteract the messages she gets from her entertainment, and so does her father—Sophie watches very little television. But I can see we have our work cut out for us. It sure would help if the bunnies took off their hair ribbons, and if half of the monsters were fuzzy, blue—and female.

■ ■ ■

## Reading as a Writer: Analyzing Rhetorical Choices

1. Do a "reverse outline" of this short piece, summarizing in a phrase or two the work each paragraph does. What do you notice about the way Pollitt organizes her examples and her argument? In what ways does she use examples from the past and present? What relationship do you see between her opening and closing paragraphs? What conclusions can you draw about some effective ways to structure an argument?

2. Locate the definition of the "Smurfette principle" and explain it in your own words. What is the significance of this idea, according to Pollitt? Which examples do you think best illustrate this idea? To what extent do your childhood entertainment favorites fulfill this dynamic? How much has changed—or not—in children's media culture, based on examples you can think of?

## Writing as a Reader: Entering the Conversation of Ideas

1. Pollitt and Ann duCille are concerned that only certain kinds of "femininity" are being marketed to little girls. Compose an essay in which you place yourself and these writers in conversation about a toy, a television show, or a movie that is explicitly marketed to girls. What values, norms, and ideals does this example teach young girls? What significance do you see for girls and for the broader culture, given the insights you glean from Pollitt and duCille?

2. Pollitt's analysis of kids' television and movies as cultural "teachers" is similar to the way Neil Postman discusses the "collateral learning" about culture that accompanies many forms of entertainment. Write an essay in which you bring both authors' insights together to analyze a specific example of children's media that interests you. You might choose to focus

on a television show that is intended to be educational, as a way to focus your ideas about the incidental messages children could be learning along with the main educational messages. What conclusions can you draw about children's media?

## ELIZABETH TEARE

# Harry Potter and the Technology of Magic

Elizabeth Teare has taught literature at Yale (where she earned her doctorate) and the University of Dayton. She has written about famous Victorian authors like William Thackeray and Matthew Arnold, but, as this essay makes clear, she is also interested in contemporary children's literature. She presented a draft of this piece at the 1999 Modern Language Association convention; it was later published in *The Ivory Tower and Harry Potter: Perspectives on a Literary Phenomenon* (2002), a collection edited by Lana A.Whited.

J. K. Rowling's Harry Potter series has spawned a rich body of criticism, as book reviewers, scholars, parents, and young readers have responded to the unprecedented success of the books and films. Teare's essay, then, is in conversation with people who hold a wide range of perspectives on what they think is very good and very bad about Harry Potter. Some critics claim that the books' magical theme sends an "anti-Christian" message; others find the books exemplary for their modeling of moral and philosophical virtues. Teare joins in this conversation with another perspective, looking at the "twenty-first-century commercial and technological culture" (para. 1) that shapes consumerist themes in many children's books and the marketing of merchandise associated with children's books and films. Teare notes the way Rowling pokes fun at commodity culture in her fiction—through her teasing portrayal of the empty-headed celebrity author Gilderoy Lockhart, for example—but Teare argues that the books spend as much time encouraging children to participate as consumers as they do criticizing adults who fall prey to the allure of money.

As you read, pay attention to Teare's strategy of moving between her own argument and the details of the novels themselves. Notice in particular her analysis of Lockhart in paragraphs 15 through 17. You might also focus on the ways she draws on other writers' ideas to develop her own, citing Jack Zipes (para. 11) and Ellen Seiter (para. 14), for example. In Teare's footnotes, you will see hints of other conversations about the Harry Potter phenomenon and children's literature and consumer culture.

Whether or not you are a fan of J. K. Rowling's series, this essay models some ways to analyze any fiction you enjoy. While we don't often think of novels as making arguments, Teare's point is that fiction—even fiction aimed at children—can teach readers values that shape their relation to culture. What values have *you* learned from the childhood books you read? Teare inspires us to revisit those stories and ask questions that may reveal surprising aspects of those childhood favorites.

The July/August 2001 issue of *Book* lists J. K. Rowling as one of the ten *1* most influential people in publishing.[1] She shares space on this list with John Grisham and Oprah Winfrey, along with less famous but equally powerful insiders in the book industry. What these industry leaders have in common is an almost magical power to make books succeed in the marketplace, and this magic, in addition to that performed with wands, Rowling's novels appear to practice. Opening weekend sales charted like those of a blockbuster movie (not to mention the blockbuster movie itself), the reconstruction of the venerable *New York Times* bestseller lists, the creation of a new nation's worth of web sites in the territory of cyberspace, and of course the legendary inspiration of tens of millions of child readers—the Harry Potter books have transformed both the technologies of reading and the way we understand those technologies. What is it that makes these books—about a lonely boy whose first act on learning he is a wizard is to go shopping for a wand—not only an international phenomenon among children and parents and teachers but also a topic of compelling interest to literary, social, and cultural critics? I will argue that the stories the books tell, as well as the stories we're telling about them, enact both our fantasies and our fears of children's literature and publishing in the context of twenty-first-century commercial and technological culture.

The classics of children's fantasy literature are Luddite, or at best *2* ambivalent, in their attitudes toward modern commodity culture. The great example is Tolkien, whose hobbits destroy the One Ring and Sauron's industrial hell to restore Middle Earth to pastoral, precapitalist serenity (though, Tolkien acknowledges, that serenity is ultimately doomed). In C. S. Lewis's Narnia, too, the arrival of industry heralds the Fall. The same principles hold true in fantasies set in more contemporary worlds. Magic in Diana Wynne Jones and Susan Cooper and Elizabeth Goudge is natural and inborn or, if man-made, is antique, given as a gift or found. Magic cannot be bought or sold: anyone who tries to commodify it is doomed to the kind of horrible fate best portrayed by Roald Dahl. The acquisitive children who accompany Charlie through the chocolate factory all get their appropriate comeuppance; James's aunts are crushed by the giant peach when they try to exhibit it for profit.

Philip Pullman's recent *His Dark Materials* trilogy comes closest to *3* celebrating the complicated technologies of its alternate universes. Each volume of the trilogy is named for the marvelous instrument its heroes receive or construct: *The Golden Compass, The Subtle Knife, The Amber Spyglass*. All three novels celebrate the inventive technologies Pullman's parallel universes have developed, particularly the aeronautic devices: balloons, witches' broomsticks (actually pine branches), zeppelins, "gyropters," and the extraordinary "intention craft" directed by its pilot's desires.[2]

---

[1]Abramson et al., "People Who Decide What America Reads," 39.
[2]Philip Pullman, *The Golden Compass*, 218.

As the story develops, however, all these inventions are used for, and often destroyed in, a vividly described and bloody universal war. The Subtle Knife turns out to be draining consciousness from the universe and letting in soul-sucking specters. And paradise is a world inhabited by gentle and civilized quadrupeds whose most elaborate technologies are fishing nets and the wheel.

Ursula Le Guin has recently made explicit the opposition of children's  *4* fantasy literature to commodity culture. In her new collection of stories, she not only adds to her chronicle of what she carefully notes is the "non-industrial society" of her Earthsea archipelago but also includes, in her Foreword, a powerful critique of what she calls "commodified fantasy." According to Le Guin, the "mills of capitalism" take advantage of modern "long[ing] for the unalterable . . . stability, ancient truths, immutable sim-plicities" of fantasy by providing readers with empty imitations. Le Guin writes, "Commodified fantasy takes no risks: It invents nothing, but imi-tates and trivializes. It proceeds by depriving the old stories of their intel-lectual and ethical complexity, turning their action to violence, their actors to dolls, and their truth-telling to sentimental platitude. Heroes brandish their swords, lasers, [and] wands, as mechanically as combine harvesters, reaping profits. . . . The passionately conceived ideas of the great story-tellers are copied, stereotyped, reduced to toys, molded in bright-colored plastic, advertised, sold, broken, junked, replaceable, interchangeable."[3] The metaphor in Le Guin's last sentence is particularly powerful, evok-ing the world of tie-in marketing campaigns and the "bright-colored plas-tic" toys in McDonald's Happy Meals. In returning to Earthsea in *Tales of Earthsea* and the new novel *The Other Wind*, Le Guin argues by example for a return to the "nonindustral" practice of fantasy writing. And by implication she raises questions about the Harry Potter books, with their burgeoning industry of bright plastic tie-in merchandise. Are Rowling's novels too, as they have been published and marketed, only "commodified fantasy"?

As with the plots of the fantasy genre, so with the stories we tell our-  *5* selves about their place in children's culture. The producers and consum-ers of children's literature have traditionally constructed their cultural position in opposition to capitalist enterprise. Books last. They are reread. It doesn't matter that their covers get torn. Child readers, according to advocates of book culture, are better children than those who clamor for the newest video games. And publishers are better, more wholesome, than the manufacturers who flood the children's market with toys like Pokémon and participate in an interlocking system of cartoons and video games and movies and plastic toys and clothing and accessories and trading cards, all designed to encourage continued consumption in search of the rare miss-ing card, like the golden ticket to Willy Wonka's factory.

[3]Ursula Le Guin, *Tales of Earthsea*, 267, xiii–xiv.

In the last twenty years, however, this pastoral vision of children's 6 book culture has become as endangered as Tolkien's Shire. Books have lost children's attention, and therefore market share, to other media that present narrative fantasies: movies, video, and video games. Pokémon is only one of the most visible examples. But it is not only the competition. Children's publishing is itself increasingly tainted. The rise of the franchise series—Animorphs, Goosebumps, the Baby Sitters Club, even the educationally "historical" American Girl—works to create the same kind of desire for mass-produced similarity and for serial acquisition that Pokémon does. (And even Pokémon has a franchised series of books.) Increasingly, too, successful children's books are part of their own systems of tie-ins. Read the American Girls and buy the dolls, their outfits and furniture (displayed behind glass in the Chicago flagship store as if they are valuable museum artifacts), the matching doll-and-owner American Girl jackets, tickets to the American Girl revue. Nancy Drew never carried all this baggage. Disney, of course, is the merchandising master of this game.

Then Harry Potter appeared on the scene, initially offering a strong 7 counternarrative to the Disney story and allowing its publishers, particularly Bloomsbury in the United Kingdom and Scholastic in the United States, to retake the high ground and redirect the story they tell about themselves. Much of the power of the Harry Potter story is in the way it seems to resist the pressures of children's commodity culture. Account after account in the press features a parent describing the change in her child (most often it is a mother and son), who has learned to love reading by reading these books: "they took my non-reader and turned him into a reader."[4] Such stories also feature children who loudly resist Harry Potter tie-in products that might trammel their imaginations. In October 1999, when Rowling's book tour took her to Washington, D.C., the *Washington Post* featured an article about the challenges faced by parents who couldn't buy ready-made Albus Dumbledore and Hermione Granger Halloween costumes and were forced, joyfully, to help their children make their own. The same article, published well before Rowling's film and product-licensing deal with Warner Brothers, quotes a boy who perfectly embodies adult fantasies of children's contented innocence and resistance to commercial exploitation of the book. "'I don't think they should make TV shows because then when you imagine stuff from the book, then it will be much different,' says Sam Piazza, 10, of Silver Spring."[5]

Rowling's authorial biography has been pressed into service to sup- 8 port this noncommercial narrative. According to legend, Rowling was a single mother on the dole when she developed the Harry Potter stories, writing in cafés while her daughter napped. She has protested this account

[4]Linton Weeks, "Sheer Sorcery."
[5]Libby Copeland, "Sew-cery: Young Fans Conjure Some Wizardly Costumes."

of herself as an unworldly and suffering romantic genius, but she is also quoted, on the Scholastic web site as well as in numerous articles, as saying that all she wants to do is write, whether or not she is paid: "I have always written and I know that I always will; I would be writing even if I hadn't been published."[6] The publishers have matched this story of commercial innocence with one of technological innocence. They have hardly advertised, they claim; the books are a grassroots phenomenon, built on the innocent desire and pleasure of children. Rowling has endorsed this idea, claiming "she was hard-pressed to answer the question she often asked as a child. Why? 'I suppose it's mainly word of mouth,' she offered of the books' success in the London *Guardian*. 'I think children just tell one another about it.'"[7]

Supporters of the innocence myth point to experiences like that of *9* Politics and Prose, an independent bookstore in Washington, D.C., which cited "unprecedented interest" as the reason for a special "crowd control strategy" put in place when Rowling appeared there to sign *Harry Potter and the Prisoner of Azkaban*. Elements of the strategy include the following: "2) We will give out 500 tickets, no more than 4 per person standing in line. We are sure that Ms. Rowling will be able to sign 500 books. . . . 3) Ms. Rowling will start to sign at 4 P.M. and she will sign NO MORE THAN ONE BOOK FOR EACH PERSON. She will sign until 6 P.M."[8] In fact, Rowling signed nine hundred books in two hours, for admirers who had lined up as early as 8 A.M. and who "clapped and cheered as though [Rowling] were Literate Spice."[9]

Linton Weeks of the *Washington Post*, who coined this Spice Girls *10* simile, aptly captures the conflicts that lie behind the narrative of Harry Potter's innocence and suggest the fundamental question. Are the Harry Potter books a real alternative to children's commodity culture, or are they just the most cleverly packaged part of it? Rowling's celebrity is more like that of Oprah Winfrey herself than that of Oprah's Book Club authors—it is Winfrey, after all, with whom Rowling shares space on the *Book* list. And with the flood of Harry Potter products released into the marketplace since the Warner licensing agreement, it is much more difficult to differentiate between Harry Potter and the Powerpuff girls. The release of the movie, with its ubiquitous advertising, has blurred the distinction further.

Children's literature critic Jack Zipes has argued that "it is exactly *11* because the success of the Harry Potter novels is so great and reflects certain troubling sociocultural trends that we must try to evaluate the phenomenon." Zipes argues that the Harry Potter books are so successful because they are so "formulaic," that they could not succeed unless they were. There is something wonderfully paradoxical about the phenomena

[6]"Meet J. K. Rowling," Scholastic Press Harry Potter Web Site.
[7]Marc Shapiro, *J. K. Rowling: The Wizard behind Harry Potter*, 83.
[8]Politics and Prose bookstore, e-mail to subscribers.
[9]Linton Weeks, "Charmed, I'm Sure."

surrounding the phenomenon of the Harry Potter books. For anything to become a phenomenon in Western society, it must become *conventional*; it must be recognized and categorized as unusual, popularly accepted, praised, or condemned, worthy of everyone's attention; it must conform to the standards of exception set by the mass media and promoted by the culture industry in general. To be phenomenal means that a person or commodity must conform to the tastes of hegemonic groups that determine what makes up a phenomenon. It is impossible to be phenomenal without conforming to conventionality.[10] Zipes admits with pleasure Rowling's wit and humor, but he resists the argument that her books are something special. Their much-touted exceptionality is in fact a sign of their entanglement in the commodified culture industry they are believed to transcend. Zipes points out that the Harry Potter books, especially in hardback, are too expensive for children to buy for themselves, so they must be purchased by reasonably well-off adults; he doubts that as many children have actually read the books as have been exposed to them. The seeming success among children of the conventional Harry Potter books is for Zipes another sign that middle-class parents are "turning [their children] into commodities" by providing them with the cultural signs, like books, that adults think signal parenting success (xi).

Zipes's skepticism about the "Harry Potter phenomenon'" is justified [12] on several counts. The publishers and marketers of Harry Potter are of course steeped in the commercial technologies they affect to despise. They couldn't buy publicity like their celebrated lack of publicity, which has garnered them everything from Rowling's 1999 "Woman of the Year" honors from *Glamour* to raves on air and in print from George Will.[11] And the novels' publishers, especially Scholastic, have made ample use of the non-print technologies the books are said to resist. The elaborate Scholastic web site encourages young visitors to play Harry Potter trivia games and to post entries identifying the character they most admire. To play some games, they must register their "personally identifiable information," which Scholastic in a lengthy privacy notice acknowledges the company may use "to provide parents, via e-mail or other means, with information about materials, activities, or other things that may be of interest to parents or their children, including products or services of third parties."[12] There is a page for teachers and parents, too, suggesting topics of discussion for class reading groups and home discussion. It is worth pointing out that, despite the elegant interactive design of the web page, the questions it actually poses are as inane and moralizing as those in any old-fashioned junior-high literature anthology: "In *The Prisoner of Azkaban*, when Harry has the opportunity to kill the character responsible for his parents' death,

[10]Jack Zipes, *Sticks and Stones: The Troublesome Success of Children's Literature from Slovenly Peter to Harry Potter,* 172, 171, 175.

[11]"1999 Women of the Year"; George Will, "Harry Potter: A Wizard's Return."

[12]"Privacy Notice," Scholastic Web Site.

he chooses not to do it. How does that separate him once and for all from his archenemy, Voldemort?"[13] A question like this could as easily appear on a dittoed handout from the 1970s as on a flickering screen in the 2000s. Such familiarity might reconcile parents who worry about the hours their children spend at the computer—if it doesn't induce despair about the unimaginative, coercive questions children now face not only at school but in the broad "cultural pedagogy" sponsored by corporations.[14]

More problematic is the relation in which the Harry Potter books find    *13* themselves to Internet commerce. In late spring 1999, as the first U.S. volume gained popularity, eager American consumers discovered that they could order copies of the second and third volumes directly from Britain over the Internet, from Amazon.com's U.K. affiliate. Scholastic immediately moved up the publication dates of its own second and third volumes and made sure the fourth and subsequent books would be published simultaneously in the United Kingdom and the United States. Scholastic also challenged Amazon.com for violating international territorial publishing rights. Amazon has argued in return that buying a book from a British web site is legally just like Americans buying it in a British bookstore when they are visiting the country. Web sites based in Britain display, though not prominently, a warning that they can ship only one copy to a customer overseas. The Association of American Publishers is now involved, and Rowling's books are providing a test case for the role of traditional territorial rights in the age of e-commerce. In this context, it is impossible to understand the Harry Potter books solely as texts, apart from their status as commodities.

It is possible, however, to take a more optimistic point of view than    *14* Zipes's on the way the books as commodities function in children's culture. In *Sold Separately: Children and Parents in Consumer Culture*, Ellen Seiter argues that "[c]hildren are creative in their appropriation of consumer goods and media, and the meanings they make with these materials are not necessarily and not completely in line with a materialist ethos."[15] In the second half of this essay, I will argue that the Harry Potter books themselves attempt to make their own "creative . . . appropriation" of the problem of "consumer goods and media" in both book culture and children's culture. When Zipes concedes that "[p]erhaps it is because the novels are a hodgepodge of . . . popular entertainments that [Rowling's] novels are so appealing," he glimpses an important part of Rowling's method. Unlike

---

[13]In "Conflict," "Harry Potter Discussion Guides," Scholastic Web Site.

[14]Shirley R. Steinberg and Joe L. Kincheloe, eds., *Kinderculture: The Corporate Construction of Childhood*, 4.

[15]Ellen Seiter, *Sold Separately: Children and Parents in Consumer Culture*, 10. Zipes cites this passage from Seiter but counters that children's "creative . . . appropriation," like that of adults, is ultimately only "a false freedom of choice, for all our choices are prescribed and dictated by market systems" (Zipes, *Sticks and Stones*, 4).

Ursula Le Guin, who turns away from "commodified fantasy," Rowling works such fantasy into her fiction. The Harry Potter books offer instructions on how to live in commodity culture, with Rowling advocating, though not always consistently or successfully, resistance to the consumerist pressures both children and adults face. Their engagement with these issues is indeed one reason the novels are "so appealing."

Rowling wittily addresses questions of contemporary book culture 15 in the books themselves, particularly in *Harry Potter and the Chamber of Secrets*. This second novel in the series features celebrity author Gilderoy Lockhart, whom we first meet at a book-signing in wizard London's largest bookstore, Flourish and Blotts. Lockhart's appearance prefigures the crowds that have grown around Rowling's. Lockhart's appeal is sexual, not innocent—most of the crowd is middle-aged witches—but the long line, newspaper photographer, and cheering crowd are recognizable from any collection of articles about Rowling or, indeed, any media celebrity.

Lockhart embodies empty celebrity. He views anything that happens 16 around him as "all publicity." Like many another dim celebrity with a rudimentary sense of his own market power, Lockhart spends hours answering fan mail and signing pictures. Rowling strikes a satiric blow against the book culture into which she has been swept as Lockhart is gradually revealed as a fraud, detested by Hogwarts faculty and students alike. His spells usually fail. His franchise of autobiographical adventures, from *Gadding with Ghouls* to *Travels with Trolls* to *A Year with the Yeti*, is faked, its heroic stories stolen from less photogenic witches and wizards. Explaining this literary theft to Harry, Lockhart invokes a doctrine of "common sense" for understanding and manipulating book culture. Lockhart's cynical sense of what makes a book valuable takes on a darker tone when he decides that Harry and Ron's knowledge of his fraud is too great a threat to his success. He attacks them magically, trying to wipe out their memories rather than help them rescue Ron's sister, Ginny, from the Chamber of Secrets. To save his reputation, Lockhart is prepared not only to destroy the boys' minds but also to abandon Ginny to certain death. Here, celebrity is villainy (*Chamber of Secrets*, 63, 297).

When Lockhart's spell backfires and he loses his own identity, the 17 pleased reader echoes the dismissive comment of Professor Minerva McGonagall: "that's got *him* out from under our feet" (*Chamber of Secrets*, 295). The pleasure of unmasking Lockhart aligns Rowling's readers with Harry himself, one of the first characters to see through Lockhart's façade. Harry's resistance to Lockhart's media obsession highlights an important theme running through all the books. His distaste for the trappings of fame thrust upon him—photo ops, groupies, journalistic puff pieces—constantly reminds the reader of his boyish modesty and good taste. Through Harry, Rowling builds into her novels the possibility of resistance to celebrity book culture, as Harry models the kind of "creative appropriation" possible for children faced with such cultures in the real world.

Another sign of Rowling's knowing use of the commodification of *18*
books is the 2001 publication of two of "Harry's favorite books" in support
of the U.K. charity Comic Relief, to create "a fund set up in Harry Potter's
name . . . specifically to help children in need throughout the world." Both
*Fantastic Beasts and Where to Find Them* and *Quidditch through the Ages*
are carefully and imaginatively designed to use and comment on the conventions of twenty-first-century publishing. Both books claim to be published by wizard presses (Obscurus and Whizz Hard) "in association with"
Scholastic and to be sold in both wizard and Muggle bookstores. On the
back covers, below the ISBN number and UPC bar code, the price appears
in both Muggle and wizard money: "$3.99 US (14 Sickles 3 Knuts)." Each
"special edition" features a foreword by wizard Albus Dumbledore, famous
headmaster of Hogwarts; *Quidditch through the Ages* also offers a page of
endorsements by several authors the devoted Harry Potter reader will recognize. The most wittily self-referential of these blurbs comes from "Gilderoy Lockhart, author *Magical Me,*" who remarks that "Mr. Whisp shows
a lot of promise. If he keeps up the good work, he may well find himself
sharing a photoshoot with me one of these days!" Rowling's resurrection
of Lockhart gives added bite to her parody of both the form and the content of publishing's promotional ephemera.

*Quidditch through the Ages* claims to be a Hogwarts library book, with *19*
a list of borrowers, including Harry, Ron, Hermione, and the heroic Cedric
Diggory, noted in the front. *Fantastic Beasts and Where to Find Them* offers
a more significant conceit: it is presented as a facsimile of Harry's own
book. According to Dumbledore's foreword, "You hold in your hands a
duplicate of Harry Potter's own copy of *Fantastic Beasts,* complete with his
and his friends' informative notes in the margins. Although Harry seemed
a trifle reluctant to allow this book to be reprinted in its present form, our
friends at Comic Relief feel that his small additions will add to the entertaining tone of the book" (viii). The "small additions" include games of
hangman and tic-tac-toe, Quidditch graffiti, and annotations that allude
to Harry's adventures with giant spiders, dragons, merpeople, werewolves,
and others. The additions are indeed "entertaining," making the reader
who gets the jokes feel especially clever. They also allude again to the role
of celebrity in book culture: the fact that *Fantastic Beasts* bears "Harry's
signature," even as a joke, does make it more appealing (and hence valuable) to its readers, as does Rowling's signature on individual volumes of
the novels themselves. The market for signed copies of the Harry Potter
books is strong enough that a Virginia man was able to bilk twenty eBay
auction-site buyers out of hundreds of dollars for fraudulent signed first
editions. Such fraud is possible because "legitimate first-edition, first-print
Harry Potter books go for more than $3,000 on the open market," accord-
ing to Matt Duffy of *Auction Watch*.[16] Rowling parodies her fans' interest

---

[16]Matt Duffy, "Alleged Harry Potter Fraud on eBay."

in books as collectible commodities when she attaches Harry's signature to the charity books at the same time as she uses that interest to generate more money for the Comic Relief fund to which she has also attached his signature and her own.

Most critics who have weighed in on the Harry Potter phenomenon to date have placed the books firmly in the Luddite tradition of children's fantasy. The September 20, 1999, cover article in *Time* concludes with a celebratory contrast between Warner Brothers' plans for "fantastical" special effects for the then upcoming movie—"Technology is now incredible," says the producer—and the "interesting" fact that the wizard world of the books "contains no technology at all. Light is provided by torches and heat by massive fireplaces. Who needs electricity when you have plenty of wizards and magic wands? . . . Technology is for Muggles, who rely on contraptions because they cannot imagine the conveniences of magic. Who wouldn't choose a wizard's life?"[17] The train to Hogwarts, powered by a "scarlet steam engine," serves as a transition from the crowds at Kings Cross to what Alison Lurie calls the "pre-industrial" world of Hogwarts, where students write on rolls of parchment with quills.[18] And full-blooded wizards who have no day-to-day contact with the nonmagical Muggle world can hardly understand—though they are often fascinated by the ingenuity of—telephones or cars or the "escapators" they've heard of in the tube stations they don't need to use.

Certainly the contrast between Harry and his Muggle relatives reinforces the distance between their commercial, technological world and his purer one. His stupid cousin Dudley Dursley, in particular, who receives stacks of video games one birthday, represents all children obsessed with acquiring and discarding the electronic toys with which his playroom is littered: "Nearly everything . . . was broken. . . . Other shelves were full of books. They were the only things in the room that looked as though they'd never been touched" (*Sorcerer's Stone*, 37–38). Dudley is clearly a nonreader, the figure against whom all children who side with Harry Potter—particularly the formerly nonreading boys to whom the series famously appeals—will set themselves. (Dudley, besides being thuggish, is fat. He clearly descends from Dahl's Augustus Gloop, whose gluttony Rowling can make even more contemptible by implicitly calling on current concern about obesity and inactivity among couch-potato kids.) The Dursleys, Dudley's parents and Harry's guardians, are the kind of materialistic adults who would riot at Toys R Us for the latest Pokémon figure for their darling boy, while giving Harry old socks or fifty-pence pieces as Christmas presents.

Harry's idol, headmaster Albus Dumbledore, stakes out the anti-Dursley position most clearly when he explains to Harry his reasons for destroying

[17]Paul Gray, "Wild about Harry: The Exploits of a Young Wizard Have Enchanted Kids," 72.

[18]Alison Lurie, "Not for Muggles."

the Sorcerer's Stone of the first novel's title: "As much money and life as you could want! The two things most human beings would choose above all—the trouble is, humans do have a knack of choosing precisely those things that are worst for them" (*Sorcerer's Stone*, 297). Readers who see Rowling's fantasy world as more pure than our reality can turn to such Dumbledorean paradoxes, worthy of Tolkien's Gandalf or Susan Cooper's Merriman, for evidence. The problem with such a reading, however, is that Dumbledore does not represent the majority of Rowling's wizard world. In fact, he resists its desires, turning down a nomination to be Minister of Magic. Dumbledore is considered, even by admiring students, to be "a bit mad" and "off his rocker" (*Sorcerer's Stone*, 123, 302).

The virtuous Dumbledore apart, the wizard world more generally is  23 much like ours: highly commercialized and obsessed with its technologies. Gringott's, the wizard bank, is fully international (Bill Weasley works for its branch in Egypt); it also seems to have no competition. This monopoly troubles no one in the world of the novels, perhaps because Rowling takes care to make the bank a model of integrity and capitalist morality. Over its doors is engraved a poem warning patrons (and potential thieves) that they will "pay dearly" for "the sin of greed" (*Sorcerer's Stone*, 72).

In *Harry Potter and the Goblet of Fire*, the reader learns about interna-  24 tional wizard commerce as well. The Ministry of Magic, which in the earlier books has been concerned with domestic British issues, is revealed to have important international responsibilities. Percy Weasley begins working for the Department of International Cooperation, whose concerns include an effort "to standardize cauldron thickness" (for safety reasons) and to prevent the illegal import of flying carpets (56).

The first set piece of *Goblet of Fire* is also a scene of international magi-  25 cal commerce, when the Weasley family, Hermione, and Harry attend the World Cup of Quidditch. This international sporting event, like the Triwizard Tournament that follows it, not to mention the Olympics, is in theory intended to create wholesome "ties between young witches and wizards of different nationalities." In practice, the World Cup, again like the Olympics or World Cup soccer, is a richly productive site for commercial enterprise. As they approach the stadium, Harry and his friends are besieged by commodity culture: "Salesmen were Apparating every few feet, carrying trays and pushing carts full of extraordinary merchandise." The schlocky souvenirs they "push" are irresistible to the children, who arrive at the game with "their moneybags considerably lighter." The Quidditch stadium, too, is a commercial vehicle, with a "gigantic blackboard . . . flashing advertisements across the field" (*Goblet of Fire*, 187, 93, 94). Rowling is at her most playful in creating the excesses of wizardly mass production, but the humor loses some of its force when the reader remembers that "collectible figures" like those the children buy are part of the vast array of Harry Potter merchandise now available. Though these figures, easily found in bookstore children's sections and on the same Internet sites that sell the books, do not fly or stroll, some of them cost more than one hundred dollars.

Money is always a concern and often a worry in Rowling's world, as we might expect, since expensive accessories of magic—spellbooks, cauldrons, potion ingredients, wands—must be purchased before any magic can be performed. The commercial mystique of wands is especially great. Although, as A. O. Scott points out, Rowling's wands appear to be "artisanal handcrafts,"[19] that fact is used primarily to enhance their market value. Venerable wand merchant and authority Mr. Ollivander himself tells Harry that "no two Ollivander wands are alike" and that "of course, you will never get such good results with another wizard's wand" (*Sorcerer's Stone*, 82–84). Magic wands, like Muggle cars or computers, are marketed to match their buyer's personality, and settling for second-hand will make you a lesser wizard. While wizardly technologies may not look like the commodities we are used to, they are nonetheless marketed and consumed as ours are.

Rowling builds her strongest critique of the importance of money to children on the story of Ron Weasley and his wand, a saga that extends through the first three volumes of the series. The Weasleys, supporting seven children on a Ministry of Magic salary, are not only poorer than most wizards but also famous for their poverty, as the wealthy and sneering Draco Malfoy constantly points out. Because of his poverty, Ron faces a series of what he perceives as humiliations—hand-me-down textbooks, hideous second-hand dress robes, the constant awareness of Harry's comparative wealth—that remind the reader how sensitive children are to the pressures of consumerism. The most important of Ron's humiliations by far is his wand.

Although Mr. Ollivander has made it clear that successful wizards must have custom-fitted wands, Ron begins his Hogwarts career with his brother Charlie's worn-out wand. Worse, when that wand is damaged at the beginning of the second novel, Ron doesn't dare ask his parents for a new one. Through *Chamber of Secrets*, Ron struggles in his classes as his wand, though "patched up . . . with some borrowed Spellotape . . . seems to be damaged beyond repair. It [keeps] crackling and sparking at odd moments" and causes him disaster after disaster both in class and out (95). This wand turns out to have some value, when its tendency to backfire is what foils Lockhart's memory charm on the way to the Chamber of Secrets, but Ron cannot see or recognize that value. He gets his own wand only by luck, when his father wins the lottery at the beginning of *Prisoner of Azkaban*.

[19]A. O. Scott, "A Dialogue on Harry Potter."

Ron's sufferings, along with the more serious anxieties of his loving, 29 courageous parents and older brothers, Fred and George, talented inventors and budding entrepreneurs with no capital, allow Rowling to comment on the difficulties faced by people who don't have enough money to provide their children with the commodities that trigger self-esteem in capitalist culture. Here, she is making a serious critique. She undermines that critique, however, when she cannot bear to deprive the Weasleys of the commodities and capital that according to Harry their niceness "deserves" (*Prisoner of Azkaban*, 9). In the third novel, Mr. Weasley wins the lottery; in the fourth, Harry himself gives Fred and George his Triwizard Tournament prize money, on the condition that they also replace Ron's embarrassing dress robes (*Goblet of Fire*, 733). Harry as hero is generous and superior to the lure of gold, in part because he has plenty already, but he is also a means for Rowling to sidestep the most painful consequences, for both adults and children, of her magical world's commodity culture.

Rowling's children are fully exposed to the temptations of commerce 30 in the magic world. They love to buy, and a visit to the local village is an occasion to stock up on nose-biting teacups, dungbombs, and "shelves upon shelves of the most succulent-looking sweets imaginable" (*Prisoner of Azkaban*, 197). (What Dudley Dursley is despised for desiring, Harry and his friends eat constantly.) One particular brand of candy, Chocolate Frogs, increases its appeal by including Famous Witch and Wizard trading cards. Although Ron has about five hundred cards, he continues constantly to consume Chocolate Frogs in his search for the rare Agrippa and Ptolemy. Though they most closely resemble baseball cards, Rowling's Witches and Wizards cannot help recalling Pokémon and the more wizardly Magic: The Gathering, as well as the Harry Potter game cards now available at bookstore checkout counters.

And the most important accoutrement of wizard childhood, the 31 broomstick, is the most like Muggle toys. The brand of broomstick one rides is a status symbol, and the best model of one year, Harry's Nimbus 2000, can be made obsolete by the next year's Nimbus 2001, acquired by arch-rival Draco Malfoy. The best broomstick, the "state-of-the-art . . . streamlined, superfine" Firebolt (this is the broom's advertising copy, provided by Rowling), is an object of awed desire, too expensive and exclusive to have a price tag. Naturally responding to this tempting display, Harry realizes he has "never wanted anything as much in his whole life" (*Prisoner of Azkaban*, 51–52). Harry disciplines this desire because "he had a very good broom already," and of course he is rewarded by receiving a Firebolt from the mysterious benefactor later revealed to be the adult who cares the most about Harry—his godfather, Sirius Black. The value of this loving gift only increases in the fourth book, when Harry uses his prized Firebolt to win the first challenge of the Triwizard Tournament. In the case of broomsticks, at least, the novels endorse the value of (high-quality, expensive) consumer goods and of the purchase of those goods as a sign of adult nurturing of children.

Like her account of celebrity book culture, Rowling's depiction of 32 her consuming children is gently satiric. Unlike the adults, however, the children in her world are not punished when they succumb to the lure of commodities. Neither, in our world, are either the children or the adults whose commodities of choice are the Harry Potter books. The adult readers, critics, and publishers concerned with the definition of culture, in particular, have found in Rowling's narratives a story that allows them both to participate in the messy world of millennial commerce and technology and to hold themselves apart from it. The novels' uneven, interesting, and compromised depiction of children and commodity culture offers a useful arena in which such concerns can be thought about, though not satisfactorily resolved.

BIBLIOGRAPHY

Abramson, Marla, Jennifer Clarson, Matthew Flamm, and Kristin Cloberdanz. "Ten People Who Decide What America Reads." *Book Magazine,* July/August 2001, 36–41.
Copeland, Libby. "Sew-cery: Young Fans Conjure Some Wizardly Costumes." *Washington Post,* October 20, 1999, Style.
Duffy, Matt. "Alleged Harry Potter Fraud on eBay." *Auction Watch Daily,* April 9, 2001. <http://www.auctionwatch.com/awdaily/dailynews/april01/1-040901.html>.
Gray, Paul. "Wild about Harry: The Exploits of a Young Wizard Have Enchanted Kids." *Time,* September 20, 1999, 66+.
Le Guin, Ursula K. *Tales of Earthsea.* New York: Harcourt, 2001.
Lurie, Alison. "Not for Muggles." *New York Review of Books,* December 16, 1999. <http://www.nybooks.com/nyrev/WWWarchdisplay.cgi?19991216006R>.
"1999 Women of the Year." *Glamour,* December 1999, 168.
Politics and Prose Bookstore. Washington, D.C. E-mail to subscribers. October 18, 1999.
Pullman, Philip. *The Golden Compass.* New York: Random House, 2000.
Rowling, J. K. *Fantastic Beasts and Where to Find Them, by Newt Scamander.* New York: Scholastic, 2001.
———. *Harry Potter and the Chamber of Secrets.* London: Bloomsbury, 1998. New York: Scholastic, 1999.
———. *Harry Potter and the Goblet of Fire.* London: Bloomsbury, 2000. New York: Scholastic, 2000.
———. *Harry Potter and the Prisoner of Azkaban.* London: Bloomsbury, 1999. New York: Scholastic, 1999.
———. *Harry Potter and the Sorcerer's Stone.* New York: Scholastic, 1998.
Scholastic Press Harry Potter Web Site. <http://www.scholastic.com/harrypotter/jkinterview.htm>.
Scott, A. O. "A Dialogue on Harry Potter." *Slate.* <http://slate.msn.com//code/BookClub.asp>.
Seiter, Ellen. *Sold Separately: Children and Parents in Consumer Culture.* New Brunswick, N.J.: Rutgers University Press, 1993.
Shapiro, Marc. *J. K. Rowling: The Wizard behind Harry Potter.* New York: St. Martin's Griffin, 2000.
Steinberg, Shirley R., and Joe L. Kincheloe, eds. *Kinderculture: The Corporate Construction of Childhood.* Boulder, Colo.: HarperCollins/Westview Press, 1997.

Weeks, Linton. "Charmed, I'm Sure." *Washington Post,* October 20, 1999, Style.

———. "Sheer Sorcery." *Washington Post,* September 9, 1999, Style.

Will, George. "Harry Potter: A Wizard's Return." *Washington Post,* July 4, 2000, Op-ed.

Zipes, Jack. "The Phenomenon of Harry Potter, or Why All the Talk?" In *Sticks and Stones: The Troublesome Success of Children's Literature from Slovenly Peter to Harry Potter,* 170–89. New York: Routledge, 2000.

■ ■ ■

## Reading as a Writer: Analyzing Rhetorical Choices

1. Read the first paragraph of Teare's essay carefully, taking note of how she organizes her introduction to her topic and issue. What is the central question fueling her essay? Locate and underline her thesis statement. Try to paraphrase her thesis, making sure you express all the different parts of the argument she promises to make in the essay. After you have read the essay once, return to reread the last two sentences of the opening paragraph. Discuss with your classmates where in her essay—and how effectively—Teare answers her own question and presents evidence for her argument.

2. How does Teare use other critics' ideas to advance her own argument? You might focus on the passages she quotes from author Ursula Le Guin and critic Jack Zipes. Draw a box around the passages where Teare quotes or paraphrases their ideas, and underline the passages where she connects their ideas to her own larger argument. What can you conclude about effective strategies for using other people's ideas to advance your own argument in your writing?

## Writing as a Reader: Entering the Conversation of Ideas

1. Teare and Steven Johnson are interested in the way children enjoy becoming experts at their pastimes, whether that means knowing every detail in a series of books or mastering all the stages in a video game. Write an essay in which you draw on these authors' ideas and your own insights to consider the appeal to children of expertise that adults often see as useless. How might this type of expertise be positive or negative? You might draw on reviews of the Harry Potter books that address the "problem" of children becoming obsessed with a series of books, or on articles on children's game culture that address an obsession with game playing.

2. Teare's essay is primarily about the Harry Potter books, but she also examines the toy culture that has sprung up around the series. The marketing of children's toys—and the ideas that are sold to children along with the toys—is also the subject of essays by Ann duCille and Eric Schlosser. Write an essay in which you evaluate these authors' arguments about toy culture, and develop an argument about its positive and/or negative aspects, drawing on specific examples from the readings and toys currently on the market.

DANIEL HADE

# Lies My Children's Books Taught Me: History Meets Popular Culture in the American Girls Books

Daniel Hade is a professor of language and literacy education at Penn State University's College of Education. He has edited the *Journal of Children's Literature* and has published on the topic of children and reading, particularly in school contexts. Before becoming a university professor, he taught fifth grade and worked as an elementary school library and media specialist. Thus, he brings multiple perspectives to his research on the effects of social contexts on children's reading experiences, from the physical spaces they read in to the attitudes of teachers toward children's literature. Hade is part of a vibrant community of literature and education scholars who study the "cultural work" performed by children's literature. These scholars investigate the values and ideals that children's literature teaches its young readers, whether or not these values are evident on the surface of the story. In this piece, Hade takes on the wildly popular American Girl book series and the Pleasant Company in an essay that was included in a collection of essays titled *Voices of the Other: Children's Literature in the Postcolonial Context* (2000).

Whether or not you own a pricey American Girl doll or any of the "historically accurate" accessories that accompany them, you likely have some knowledge of this company, its flagship stores in major American cities, its thick catalog of merchandise aimed directly at girls, its popular *American Girl Magazine*, and, yes, the book series devoted to each American Girl character. In this essay, Hade seems to be aware that he is taking on a corporate Goliath. He opens by rehearsing the many successes of the company but begins raising flags of concern in paragraphs 6 through 8, when he notes that schools and museums are using the American Girl line to teach history to children. He sums up the positives and negatives of his argument this way: "The success of the Pleasant Company and the popularity of its books, dolls, and other products is based upon a shrewd packaging and selling of history. But what is this history that they are selling?" (para. 8).

In the paragraphs that follow, Hade walks readers through many examples aimed at convincing readers that the historical inaccuracies he finds in the Kirsten and Samantha books are more than simple factual errors. He argues, "Filled with historical errors, misrepresentations, and overgeneralizations, the books put forth a romantic America, where all needs are met by opportunity, where poverty and oppression can be easily solved by the initiative of a young child, and an American Girl childhood is innocent and safe" (para. 34). Where is the danger here? And what is the problem of allowing only certain kinds of girls to star in these stories? Hade offers some answers that should start you thinking about the ways we use history. His concluding comparison of the Pleasant Company's packaging of history to Colonial Williamsburg may open up further discussions about the effects of turning our complicated histories into "a commodity to be bought and sold" (para. 35).

We give girls chocolate cake with vitamins. Our books are exciting, our magazine is fun, and our dolls are pretty. But most importantly, they all give girls a sense of self and an understanding of where they came from and who they are today.

— PLEASANT T. ROWLAND, President of the Pleasant Company

In 1985, the Pleasant Company was founded by Pleasant Rowland for 1 the purpose of providing girls in the United States, age seven and up, with books and dolls that would bring American history and the roles girls played in that history alive. Since that time the company has become one of the fastest-growing companies in the United States, selling millions of copies of their books and millions of dollars' worth of dolls. In the process the Pleasant Company has become an important source of historical information and ideas for girls in the United States.

The American Girl Collection (consisting of books, dolls, and acces- 2 sories) consists of five characters, each a nine-year-old girl, each from a different period of American history. Felicity Merriman lives in Virginia in 1774, just before the American Revolution. Kirsten Larson is an immigrant from Sweden. She and her family live in Minnesota in 1854. Addie Walker is an escaped slave living in Philadelphia in 1864. Samantha Parkington, an orphan, lives in 1904 in a community outside New York City with her wealthy grandmother. Molly McIntire lives in 1944 New York City with her mother; her father is away in the military fighting during World War II. Josephina Montoya, a character added to the collection in 1997, is a Hispanic girl growing up in New Mexico in 1824. These six girls are "The American Girls."

Six books have been written about each girl, except for Josephina, 3 who so far has three books, As of January 1998, the series consists of thirty-three books. The books for each girl follow an identical formula. For example, the books about Samantha are titled: *Meet Samantha: An American Girl; Samantha Learns a Lesson: A School Story; Samantha's Surprise: A Christmas Story; Happy Birthday Samantha! A Springtime Story; Samantha Saves the Day: A Summer Story;* and *Changes for Samantha: A Winter Story.* One need only substitute the name of any of the other girls for Samantha to have the titles of the books about them. Apparently, the lives of American girls can all be pressed into the same formula of seasons, school, birthdays, and Christmas.

According to Jeanne Brady (3), as of 1993 over 10 million copies of 4 these books have been sold. Current numbers are difficult to come by, but a conservative estimate would suggest sales of at least 30 million copies of the books. Three of the titles from the series appear in the most recent (1995) *Publisher's Weekly* list of the 100 all-time best-selling children's books in hard copy: *Meet Samantha* with 1,300,000 copies, *Meet Addie* with 1,200,000 copies, and *Meet Kirsten* with 1,100,000 copies. We should note that these numbers do not reflect sales of the less expensive soft-cover editions.

In addition to the books, a doll for each character is available, along 5 with what the company describes as "historically accurate" accessories. The dolls are expensive, costing a minimum of $82. Accessories for each doll are extensive and also expensive. To purchase all of the accessories for just a single doll, it would require an expenditure of just under $1,000. And this figure does not include the doll-care products, background scenery, or the highly expensive line of clothing available in which the young contemporary girl can dress like her doll. (Outfits range from $60 to over $100 apiece.) The dolls and the accessories are available only through a catalogue, an oversized and high-gloss publication. If a young girl owns two or more dolls, and many contemporary American girls do, it is easy to imagine purchases of American Girl products ranging into the thousands of dollars. Since the early 1990s, the Pleasant Company has been on *Inc Magazine*'s list of fastest-growing privately owned companies in the United States, a testament to the appeal of the company's products for girls.

But the American Girl phenomenon is more than just dolls and books. 6 The *American Girl Magazine* has over 500,000 subscribers. American Girl clubs meet regularly across the country, usually in bookstores, where scores of girls, each clutching her own American Girl doll meet to hear stories, make crafts, and learn about new products the Pleasant Company is developing. School libraries and classrooms routinely stock multiple copies of these books for the purposes of promoting history to girls. The Pleasant Company provides dolls and some accessories for free loan to classrooms, along with lesson plans for teachers and free giveaways such as bookmarks for the children. In addition to the free materials, the company offers reading journals, wall charts, and other educational materials for sale. It assures teachers that these materials are highly motivational and not only will help children understand history, but will also help build self-esteem, especially among female students.

Among its more recent ventures, the Pleasant Company has taken to 7 sponsoring social events across the United States. In many American cities, girls can attend "Samantha's Ice Cream Socials." Girls are invited to dress up in their very best party dresses and join in turning old-fashioned ice-cream freezers, folding fancy Victorian napkins, singing songs, viewing a video about 1904 America, and participating in door-prize drawings. Also, historical museums in Williamsburg, Virginia; Scandia, Minnesota; Washington, D.C; and Portsmouth, New Hampshire, in partnership with the Pleasant Company, provide programs related to the American Girls. The programs are expensive—tickets range from $15 to $25 per person. Somehow, it seems strange to attract children to a historical museum to learn about people who only exist in books.

Virtually no girl over the age of seven in the United States does not 8 know about these American Girls, their stories, and, of course, the dolls and other paraphernalia associated with the books, whether they can afford to own one of the dolls or not. It should come as little surprise that the Pleasant Company has won many awards from the business community for excellence and innovation in marketing and advertising. The success of the Pleasant Company and the popularity of its books, dolls, and other products is based upon a shrewd packaging and selling of history. But what is this history that they are selling?

## Historically Accurate?

> It was my hope to prolong and protect those fleeting years of childhood when girls are old enough to read and still love to play. The American Girls Collection was created to give girls an understanding of their past and a sense of pride in the traditions they share with girls of yesterday.
>
> —Pleasant T. Rowland, President of the Pleasant Company

As the Pleasant Company catalogue and its World Wide Web pages state,  9 the purpose of the American Girl books, dolls, and paraphernalia is to provide contemporary American girls with an understanding of their past and to help them develop a sense of pride in the connections they share with American girls of the past. In attempting to do this, the Pleasant Company assures parents and girls that their materials are thoroughly researched and historically accurate.

But how accurate are the books? At the end of each book is a section  10 of five to six pages called "A Peek into the Past." Here is a paragraph from *Meet Kirsten*:

> Immigrating to America in 1854 was certainly dangerous, but it was exciting, too. If Kirsten's family had stayed in Sweden, she would never have seen the ocean or even a town more than 20 miles from the place she was born, Because they became immigrants, she traveled halfway around the world. She saw machines she had never dreamed of, like trains and paddle-wheel boats. She saw long stretches of open prairie and miles of rich farmland. And at the end of her journey, she had a new home in a new land, with a life full of opportunity ahead of her. (61)

Above this paragraph is a map showing how immigrants came from  11 Sweden to the United States. The map shows a route leaving from Malmö, Sweden, sailing past Denmark, through the English Channel, and across the Atlantic Ocean to New York City.

There are at least five historical errors on this page.[1] First, Kirsten's  12 name is spelled incorrectly. In Sweden the name is Kersten, with an "e." "Kirsten" is the Danish and Norwegian spelling, Also Kirsten's (*sic*) last name is spelled incorrectly. It should be Larsson, with two "s"s. After the family had been in the United States a while, the name would likely have been shortened to Larson. The book misses an opportunity to provide contemporary American girls with a real connection to the past—how and why family names were often changed after immigration to the United

States. Instead, the books give an inaccurate impression that family names in the United States are the same as the families' European ancestors.

Second, the passage claims Kirsten would never have seen the ocean [13] had she not emigrated from Sweden, While this may technically be true that she would not have seen the *ocean*, Sweden is bound on three sides by the Skagerrak, the Kattegat, and the North Sea. Since the book is silent on what part of Sweden Kirsten comes from, it is misleading to state she would never have had the opportunity to see the ocean, the sea, or a large body of water.

Third, the passage states that Kirsten would never have traveled more [14] than twenty miles from the place she was born. Again, this is highly misleading. It is possible Kirsten might never have traveled more than twenty miles from the place she was born, but to imply that no Swedes moved about the country during the nineteenth century is false. In Småland, where many of the Swedish emigrants came from, poverty was widespread and people moved all about the province looking for what little work existed.[2]

Fourth, the route shown in the book for emigrating from Sweden to [15] the United States would not have been available to Kirsten's family. Direct passage from Sweden to the United States wasn't available until early in the twentieth century, nearly fifty years after the Larsons (*sic*) made their trip. Instead, the Larsons would have traveled to Gothenburg, taken a boat to Hull, England, traveled on a train to Liverpool, and departed on a ship for the United States from there.

Fifth, the passage states that Kirsten would never have seen a train had [16] she not come to the United States. In the story itself, Kirsten is astonished and frightened (Shaw, *Meet Kirsten* 28) when she rides a train for the first time, in New York. Contrary to what the book suggests, Sweden had trains in the nineteenth century. Had Kirsten remained in Sweden, she would certainly have seen a train there and probably would have ridden on trains in Sweden as well. If the book had accurately described the route Kirsten's family would have taken to the United States, readers would know that trains would not have been unknown to Kirsten; she would have ridden one in England.

Misspelled names, inaccurate routes, and misleading statements about [17] what life was like in Sweden may seem like just a few insignificant details, but the effect upon the message is quite significant. These errors support one of the great myths of United States history—that the United States was a land of opportunity, that it was the *new* world, a land of progress filled with new ideas, new vitality, and new technology as opposed to a Europe that was old, tired, and behind the times.

Interestingly, the Pleasant Company has compared its books and mate- [18] rials to school history textbooks, noting that its materials are more motivating for children, especially girls, to learn history. James W. Loewen, in *Lies My Teacher Told Me* (1995), argues that American history textbooks fail to teach American children much real history in part because the textbooks perpetuate a feel-good, progress-oriented version of American history, while ignoring real historical issues. In effect the books are too busy telling the students how great the United States was and still is to give them much real history. The American Girls books perpetuate these same errors.

## Who Gets to Be an American Girl?

If book sales and social events are an appropriate measure of popularity, then Samantha could well be the most popular of the American Girls. Samantha Parkington is an orphan living with her rich grandmother in a wealthy community outside New York City in 1904. The books about Samantha show an idyllic childhood filled with material comfort, servants to take care of the menial work, vacations in the country, and a life of leisure. Contrasted against Samantha in these stories is Nellie O'Malley, a servant girl of Samantha's age, who, the reader is often told, is Samantha's friend. While some children in 1904 may have lived a life such as Samantha's, certainly most American children did not. For every Samantha there were scores of Nellies. According to Jacob A. Riis's *How the Other Half Lives* (1971), at the turn of the century, over 75 percent of the children living in New York City lived in extreme poverty. Milton Meltzer in *Cheap Raw Material* (1994) and Russell Freedman is *Kids at Work* (1994) state that millions of children worked sixty hours a week or more in factories, mills, and food-processing plants. Though the vast majority of children living in the United States in 1904 lived a life far different from Samantha, it is not their lives that the Pleasant Company holds up for contemporary American girls to study, connect with, and feel a sense of pride in past accomplishment. It is rather the life of a very privileged, wealthy girl of leisure that is the life of an American Girl. How the Samantha stories depict the differences between the lives of the privileged Samantha and the servant girl Nellie I will explore below.

Briefly, the six stories about Samantha are as follows, In *Meet Samantha* (Adler), readers are introduced to Samantha Parkington, a nine-year-old orphan who lives with her wealthy grandmother in the affluent city of Mount Bedford outside New York City. Samantha is lonely, living with her grandmother and the many servants of the household, because there are no children with whom she can play. She discovers that the neighbors have hired a new servant girl, Nellie, who is Samantha's age. Samantha learns that Nellie's family is very poor and that Nellie has been hired out as a servant so she can send money back to her impoverished family who live and work in New York City. Samantha's seamstress, Jessie, an African American woman and a confidant of Samantha, announces she is leaving, but will not tell Samantha the reason why. With Nellie as a guide, Samantha steals away at night and visits Jessie in her home in the "colored" part of town and learns that Jessie has had a baby. Samantha, who misses Jessie very much, arranges for Jessie to return to work at her grandmother's house. However, Samantha then learns that Nellie is being returned to the city because Nellie's employers believe her to be weak and sickly. At the end of the story, Samantha gives Nellie her expensive china doll and a basket filled with food.

When the second book, *Samantha Learns a Lesson* (Adler), opens, we learn that Samantha's grandmother has arranged for Nellie's entire family to come to work for different wealthy families in Mount Bedford. Nellie, in addition to her duties as a servant, is also attending public school. She has a difficult time of it, so Samantha, who attends an exclusive private school, begins to tutor her. Samantha enters a speaking contest, the topic of which is "Progress in America." She wins the contest with a speech about how American factories can make anything well and cheaply. Later Nellie, who has worked in a textile mill, sets Samantha straight on the realities of working in the factories—long hours, low wages, and unhealthy working conditions. Samantha revises her speech at her next public performance, speaking about the poor working conditions in American factories. Nellie gets promoted a grade in public school, thanks to Samantha's tutoring.

In the next three books, *Samantha's Surprise* (Schur), *Happy Birthday, Samantha!*, and *Samantha Saves the Day* (Tripp), Samantha celebrates Christmas, enjoys her own birthday party, and summers at her grandmother's large and comfortable summer home next to a mountain lake. Except for a very brief appearance in *Samantha's Surprise*, Nellie is absent from the books. Though we have been told Nellie is Samantha's friend, Nellie does not figure in Samantha's experiences with Christmas, nor is she a guest at her birthday party. She merits neither a Christmas present from Samantha nor an invitation to Samantha's party.

In the last book of the Samantha series, *Changes for Samantha* (Tripp), circumstances have changed for both Samantha and Nellie. Samantha's grandmother has remarried and is traveling with her new husband. Samantha has gone to live in New York City with her wealthy Uncle Gard and Aunt Cornelia. Nellie and her two younger sisters also live in New York City at an orphanage. Nellie's parents have died in an influenza epidemic. Nellie is being trained to be a maid and will soon be sent out West on an orphan train. It was common at that time for orphans to be loaded on trains in the East and sent West. The trains would stop periodically and persons looking for help on the farm, in the home, or in small businesses would take on one or more of the orphans. Brothers and sisters were often split. Samantha helps Nellie and her sisters escape from the orphanage. She hides them in the attic of her house until they are discovered by the housekeeper. To the delight of all, Uncle Gard and Aunt Cornelia decide to adopt Nellie and her sisters.

At the beginning of the last book, *Changes for Samantha* (Tripp), Samantha states that "Nellie is my very best friend in Mount Bedford" (6). Though readers are told throughout the series of books that Nellie is Samantha's friend, their relationship actually seems more like caretaking than a friendship between equals. Samantha gives Nellie her doll and some food when she learns Nellie may have to leave Mount Bedford. She tutors Nellie after Nellie is humiliated at school. Samantha smuggles food into the orphanage for Nellie and her sisters. And finally, Samantha helps Nellie and her sisters escape the orphanage. When Nellie has a problem, Samantha as her benefactor helps her out.

What Samantha doesn't do with Nellie is play. In fact Samantha's   25
grandmother is careful to point that out to Samantha in *Samantha Learns a Lesson*, "You are helping Nellie," she tells Samantha, "not playing with her. There is a difference" (34). Samantha takes care of Nellie, tries to help Nellie solve her problems, but we do not see the two girls playing together. We do see Samantha play, but she plays with girls who are her social equal. Actually, Nellie has little time to play. When she is not in school, she works. What this suggests is that the relationship Samantha and Nellie have isn't a friendship; it's the relationship a parent has with a child or the relationship the privileged have with the less fortunate.

Nellie's part in the relationship is to make Samantha feel better. When   26
Nellie is about to be sent back from Mount Bedford to the factory in New York City, it is Nellie who reassures Samantha that she will be fine and asks Samantha not to worry about her. Nellie's problems become Samantha's to fix and Samantha can then feel good about helping someone less fortunate than she is. While the last book ends with a happy-ever-after feeling with Samantha and Nellie becoming sisters, one wonders if Samantha will continue to see her new sister as "poor Nellie."

At the time of the Samantha stories, according to Meltzer's *Cheap*   27
*Raw Material*, over 2,000,000 children were working in the nation's mills, factories, farms, and food-processing plants. In some parts of the country children made up as much as 25 percent of the labor force. In New York City alone over 100,000 children were working long hours at low pay in dangerous and unsanitary working conditions. At the end of *Happy Birthday, Samantha!* readers learn that nearly all children in 1904 had time to play. This would have been news to the hundreds of thousands of children, like Nellie O'Malley, working at that time.

At the end of the second Samantha book, *Samantha Learns a Lesson*,   28
in the "Peek into the Past" section, we read: "But in the poor neighborhoods of large cities some children did not go to school at all because they had to work. Even though there were laws that said children should not work, some poor children disobeyed them so they could earn money to help their families" (58–59).

This statement is misleading at best. According to Meltzer there were   29
no national laws prohibiting child labor and only a few states in 1904 had laws prohibiting child labor. These laws had many loopholes for certain industries and were rarely enforced. It was a long struggle to get the country to adopt child labor laws. Laws passed in 1916 and 1918 were challenged immediately in the courts by industry and were eventually declared unconstitutional by the Supreme Court of the United States. It

wasn't until 1938 that a permanent national law on child labor was passed. Even so, to this day millions of children in the United States continue to work on farms, in sweat shops, fast-food restaurants, and scores of other businesses.

It is outrageous to suggest, as the Samantha books do, that the problem of child labor was the responsibility of the children themselves. By stating that it was the children who disobeyed the laws, the books obscure the truth that it was employers who were prohibited from hiring children (where such laws existed), and it was employers who were responsible for the wretched working conditions. But then the American Girl books often seem confused, if not indifferent, to causes of historical events.    30

In his book *Lies My Teacher Told Me*, James W. Loewen argues that among the reasons American history is so poorly known by Americans is that history textbook never talk about causes. Events just happen, situations just seem to occur. The Samantha stories are no better than the bland history told by the school textbooks. From the Samantha stories we don't know why children have to work. We don't know why Samantha's family is rich or what is the source of their wealth. There is no discussion why it is that the Parkingtons are rich, but the O'Malleys are poor, a missed opportunity to discuss the roles of both class and ethnicity in shaping who was rich and who was poor in America. Instead of real discussions of history, readers are given fairy-tale solutions to complex problems: Grandmother finds employment for the O'Malleys so Samantha will not lose her "friend." Uncle Gard and Aunt Cornelia agree to adopt the orphaned O'Malley children, sparing them the ordeal of separation and life as servants, but most importantly, again, sparing Samantha the loss of her "friend."    31

So who is an American Girl? According to the Pleasant Company, the few privileged girls such as Samantha are American Girls, but the poor, such as Nellie, are not. The Samantha stories are told from Samantha's point of view, readers know of Samantha's desires and dreams, they know how she makes sense of her world, and how she imagines other children live. It is Samantha who has a doll made after her and it is Samantha that contemporary American girls are asked to identify with, and to pretend to be like, There is no Nellie doll and we know Nellie's thoughts, feelings, and wishes only through Samantha. Nellie is an object of the reader's pity and sympathy, not a subject for readers to admire. What readers of the Samantha books are not asked to do is to admire the struggle girls like Nellie endured, the strength of character girls such as Nellie required to survive in the face of desperate conditions in a society that cared little for the welfare of poor children. American Girls such as Nellie were true heroes and it is a matter of gross public amnesia that their stories are not better known.    32

There is a co-opting of history occurring in the American Girls books; the history of the struggles of America's working poor is silenced by a wealthy elite, like Samantha's family, who secured and held onto their privilege all too often through the labor of children, After all, though    33

Samantha and her family are horrified by the conditions of child labor, though her Aunt Cornelia is portrayed as a socially conscious woman not afraid to work for causes such as women's suffrage, Samantha and her family do nothing to work to abolish child labor, even though groups such as the National Child Labor Committee were active in New York City in 1904, even though her "best friend" has been a child laborer.

Though extremely popular, a commercial success, and marketed as an 34 attempt to tell girls something about the experience of growing up female at different moments of American history, the books fail in showing an accurate and authentic view of the American past. Filled with historical errors, misrepresentations, and overgeneralizations, the books put forth a romantic America, where all needs are met by opportunity, where poverty and oppression can be easily solved by the initiative of a young child, and an American Girl childhood is innocent and safe. Instead of providing real connection with the real past, the books and accompanying merchandise provide connection with conspicuous consumption. Popular culture is being sold under the guise of history and literature.

Pleasant Rowland was inspired to create the American Girls after a 35 trip to Williamsburg, Virginia, a kind of living history theme park, where people dress up in the costumes of colonial America and plenty of amusements are provided for children. This seems fitting, for just as the Williamsburg theme park turns history into a commodity to be bought and sold, the Pleasant Company has done the same with its books, dolls, paraphernalia, and events. Instead of creating a tie to the past and a greater understanding of the struggles girls (and most Americans) endured, these books show a sanitized version of the United States. Ultimately, the goal of these books, the dolls and accessories, and the associated programs seems to be to connect American girls, not with their history, but with the ultimate American goal—consuming stuff.

NOTES

1. My information about Swedish emigration comes from displays at the Emigrant Institute in Växjo, Sweden.

2. My own ancestors were Swedish emigrants during the nineteenth century. My research into family history and conversations I have held with a Swedish genealogist all confirm that during the extreme poverty of the nineteenth century, poor Swedes did move about the country looking for work.

BIBLIOGRAPHY

Adler, Susan. *Meet Samantha: An American Girl*. Middleton, WI: Pleasant Company, 1986.
———. *Samantha Learns a Lesson: A School Story*. Middleton, WI: Pleasant Company, 1986.
Brady, Jeanne, "Reading the American Dream: The History of the American Girl Collection." *Teaching and Learning with Literature* 4 (1994): 2–6.
Freedman, Russell. *Kids at Work: Lewis Hine and the Crusade Against Child Labor*. New York: Clarion, 1994.

Loewen, James W. *Lies My Teacher Told Me: Everything Your American History Textbook Got Wrong.* New York: New Press, 1995.

Meltzer, Milton. *Cheap Raw Material: How Our Youngest Workers Are Exploited and Abused.* New York: Viking, 1994.

Pleasant Company. "American Girl Home Page." URL: www.americangirl.com.

Pleasant Company. "Holiday Catalogue." Middleton, WI: 1996.

Pleasant Company. "July Catalogue." Middleton, WI: 1997.

Pleasant Company. "Spring Catalogue." Middleton, WI: 1997.

*Publisher's Weekly.* "Top All-Time Best-Selling Children's Books Hardcover." URL: www.bookwire.com/pw/articles/children's/

Riis, Jacob A. *How the Other Half Lives.* 1890. New York: Dover, 1971.

Schur, Maxine Rose. *Samantha's Sunrise: A Christmas Story.* Middleton, WI: Pleasant Company, 1986.

Shaw, Janet. *Meet Kirsten: An American Girl.* Middleton, WI: Pleasant Company, 1986.

Tripp, Valerie. *Changes for Samantha: A Winter Story.* Middleton, WI: Pleasant Company, 1988.

———. *Happy Birthday, Samantha! A Springtime Story.* Middleton, WI: Pleasant Company, 1987.

———. *Samantha Saves the Day: A Summer Story.* Middleton, WI: Pleasant Company, 1988.

■ ■ ■

## Reading as a Writer: Analyzing Rhetorical Choices

1. Where and how do you see Hade anticipate and address readers who might disagree with him? Point to specific passages where you see him conceding the positive aspects of the American Girl series and also to places where he explicitly tries to persuade readers about the negative aspects he sees in these books. What conclusions can you draw about effective strategies a writer can use to convince the opposition?

2. Hade concludes his essay with a comparison between the Pleasant Company's "sanitized version of the United States" and the version of history depicted in Colonial Williamsburg (para. 35). To what extent do you think this comparison is fair and useful? (You might visit the Colonial Williamsburg Web site as you gather evidence for your answer.) What is the effect of ending with this kind of example, when the essay is mostly concerned with children's literature?

## Writing as a Reader: Entering the Conversation of Ideas

1. Both Hade and Elizabeth Teare build arguments about the values they see being promoted by children's book series (the American Girl series and the Harry Potter series) that are linked to lucrative franchises. Write an essay in which you draw on both authors' insights in order to analyze the values being sold via Web sites devoted to these franchises. In your essay, be sure to describe and analyze specific examples of language and images on the American Girl and Harry Potter Web sites that support your point. What is the significance of your findings?

2. In paragraphs 18 and 31, Hade explicitly refers to James W. Loewen's argument about the "feel-good" version of history found in many

American history textbooks, and the effects this sanitization can have on our understandings of who we are. Compose an essay in which you place Hade and Loewen in conversation with each other more fully, analyzing how Loewen's insights shed light on the particular case Hade is making against the historical claims of the American Girl books. What conclusions do you and these authors draw about the implications of telling history this way, in terms of understanding the diversity of our past and present and our relationship to the rest of the world?

NOËL STURGEON

## "The Power Is Yours, Planeteers!": Race, Gender, and Sexuality in Children's Environmentalist Popular Culture

Noël Sturgeon is a professor of women's studies and American studies at Washington State University; her research interests include social movements, theories of globalization and transnationalism, and environmental cultural studies. She has published many articles and books, including *Environmentalism in Popular Culture: Gender, Sexuality, Race, and the Politics of the Natural* (2009) and *Ecofeminist Natures: Race, Gender, Feminist Theory, and Political Action* (1997). This piece, on representations of environmental issues in popular culture marketed to children, first appeared in an anthology titled *New Perspectives on Environmental Justice: Gender, Sexuality, and Activism* (2004), edited by Rachel Stein.

You will notice right away that Sturgeon opens with a paradoxical claim. It may seem to be a good thing that "starting in the late 1990s, environmentalism [became] a new moral framework for children's popular culture" (para. 1). However, Sturgeon urges readers to look more closely at these moral tales, to see the stereotypes these seemingly good-for-us stories might be reinforcing, and to consider the damage these simplifying stereotypes can cause. She urges readers to think carefully about "what stories are being told, what values are being promoted, which actors get to have agency, and what solutions are being offered" (para. 8). Pay particular attention to the argument Sturgeon makes about nuclear families in these stories, as well as the sexism, racism, and homophobia implicit in the stories.

Like many authors in our book, Sturgeon suspects that some readers will resist her interpretations of what are, after all, popular forms of entertainment. In paragraph 17, she directly addresses such potential detractors and suggests film scenes her readers could analyze to test her claims. In paragraph 28, she again poses questions she imagines skeptical readers might ask about why she is "picking" on children's media that at least feature the environment. Her answer may surprise you.

Whether or not you read the *Animorphs* book series, enjoyed Disney films such as *Pocahontas* or *The Lion King*, or are familiar with all of Sturgeon's examples, her critique of seemingly environmentally minded entertainment will open your eyes to aspects of these stories that you may have missed. You can find many recent examples of this genre that are fascinating to examine through the lens of Sturgeon's ideas. The blockbuster film *Avatar* is a good place to begin. Discuss!

■ ■ ■

Starting in the late 1990s, environmentalism has become a new moral  *1* framework for children's popular culture. But we should not rush to celebrate this because the messages contained in these environmentalist stories are often counter to what environmental justice activists are fighting for, and they contain problematic notions about what is "natural" that environmental justice practitioners need to think about. Instead of the recognition central to environmental justice that social equality and environmental sustainability are interconnected, these stories contain habits of thinking that naturalize social inequality and disconnect environmental problems from their corporate causes. I take a feminist environmental justice approach to analyze these children's cultural objects, an approach that fits into what T. V. Reed has called "environmental justice ecocriticism" (Reed 2002). While most environmental justice criticism, rightly, focuses directly on issues in and around the movement against environmental racism, we also need an approach that critiques the wider world of cultural values that reinforce environmental inequalities. Such an approach is useful in delegitimating stories — in literature, film, and popular culture — that directly and indirectly naturalize inequality, by paying attention to questions of gender and sexuality as well as race and class issues. In this essay, I point out the toxic effect of promoting ideas about what constitute "natural" men and women, "natural" families, "natural" racial/ethnic identities, and "natural" sexuality. These are mainstream environmentalist stories I am looking at, but because they are liberal stories that ostensibly want to promote racial and gender equality, those of us who support environmental justice issues want to be particularly wary of underlying messages that contradict their moderately progressive surface. We need to be aware of how these dominant cultural messages may undermine the understanding of environmental justice issues we want to promote.

The plots of the recent spate of environmentalist children's films, TV  *2* shows, and stories fit into a dominant Western cultural logic that "nature" is the foundation of truth and that only certain (patriarchal) gender relations and certain kinds of racial identities (such as presenting people of color as closer to nature) are "natural." For dominant U.S. culture, seeing something as "natural" (whether it is gendered characteristics, racialized identities, or corporate competition) is a way of rendering it to the realm of the unquestioned. Mainstream environmentalists, in their emphasis on wilderness, species extinction, and in general seeing the environment as excluding human beings, often fall into service to this dominant Western logic of seeing the natural as pure, unchanging, untainted by social influence and without history. This kind of mainstream environmentalism avoids environmental justice issues, which deal primarily with problems of human and community health using a broader, less reified definition of the environment and identifying power relations as central to the cause of environmental problems. Given the historical role these mainstream ideas about nature and what is natural have played in justifying unequal social relations, and given the close relationship between justifying social inequality and supporting a form of global capitalist economy that ruthlessly exploits the environment, environmental justice supporters must be very careful about accepting such arguments, in mainstream culture or in their own political and cultural contexts. Though it may sometimes go against our own unquestioned assumptions, we must be very careful of fostering cultural arguments or movement practices that accept the "naturalization" of gender and sexual relations or racial and ethnic identities. We may feel like we care more about one or the other of these aspects, but it is important to note that, in the children's stories discussed here as well as other dominant cultural products, these two aspects (sexism/heterosexism and racism) often reinforce one another.

In this essay, two aspects of these problematic environmentalist stories   *3* in children's culture are examined. One is the association continually created between homosexuality, evil, and environmental destruction, coupled with an anxiety about the successful reproduction of white, middle-class, nuclear families. In these stories, it is the white, middle-class, nuclear family form that is presented as "normal" and "natural" without any critique of its complicity in the overconsumption of corporate products in an environmentally destructive system in which the toxins, waste, pollution, and radiation produced are visited on the poor, the people of color, and the tribal peoples of the world. The patriarchal white, middle-class, nuclear family, organized in the 1950s specifically as a unit of increasing post–World War II consumption situated in environmentally problematic suburbs, was presented at the time as the antithesis to the extended family located in the immigrant communities of inner cities, rural close-knit communities, or tribal reservations (May 1999). The insistence that this family form is natural, normal, and the best for the planet that can be found in these children's stories goes against the argument of most environmental justice activists that healthy empowered communities, strong extended families, tribal sovereignty, participatory democratic politics, and interconnections with the land through sustainable practices are the social and economic forms we will need to create social justice and environmental health. Thus what I call in this essay the "heterosexist" family is meant to point to a particular emphasis of these stories on the "normal," "natural" status of a white, middle-class, nuclear family in which men have most of the power.

The second theme examined in this essay is the idea that environ-   *4* mentalism is best achieved through the work of gender-balanced, multicultural kids' teams like *The Animorphs* and the Planeteers of the cartoon *Captain Planet*. These stories work to "naturalize" racial/ethnic differences in a particular way. The multicultural kids' teams present all cultures as equally responsible for environmental problems, and their enemies are never corporations, or the military, or governments. Further, despite the evenhandedness of these racially balanced environmentalist kids' groups, white, male, and middle-class characters have the most power; people of color, especially women of color, are seen as closer to nature and less powerful. We may want to welcome environmentalism coupled with a certain promotion of liberal racial equality as a predominant theme in children's popular culture so that we could raise concerns about the role of inequality in creating environmental problems. Unfortunately, the logic of these stories ends up "naturalizing" white middle-class values and economic practices instead.

## Bringing Up Baby to Reduce, Reuse, and Recycle

How and why did environmentalism become such a common framework for children's culture? As a new parent over a decade ago, I was exposed suddenly and rather overwhelmingly to U.S. kinderculture. One of the things I was struck by was the importance of environmentalism as a theme in just about every aspect of my son's life. This environmental emphasis popped up everywhere: on unbreakable plastic plates and fast-food containers, on T-shirts and backpacks, in books and museum exhibits, in elementary science curricula and field trips—let alone in the movies and TV shows I will be concentrating on in this essay. 5

The appearance of this emphasis in my son's life, however, should not be accepted simply as the positive influence of environmentalism, but approached with a critical eye. Of course, as Susan Davis, among others, points out, there is a long-standing Western middle-class practice of using images from nature to educate children (Davis 1995).[1] But the thematic narratives U.S. children, especially from three to ten years of age, encountered in the 1990s were about saving nature, not just identifying with Moles who like to boat and Toads who like to drive automobiles. Something new was going on; what did it signify? 6

One of the pervasive qualities of this environmentalist material and popular kinderculture is the peculiarly American stories about nature that are being told.[2] The parochial status of these tropes about nature does not, however, make them incidental or marginal to processes of globalization. Rather, these U.S.-inflected children's cultural forms are sold and consumed around the world; further, they are frequently tales about a global world, a U.S. dream of a common planet and an undifferentiated childhood experience. This is particularly true of the movies and TV shows I will concentrate on here, which are objects that travel cross-culturally more easily than environmentalist museum exhibits or primary 7 school practices. So in a strong but not totalizing way, I want to empha-size that these cultural objects reflect and reinforce a project of U.S. cul-tural hegemony that aims to assist the opening of global markets and the imposition on other cultures of the equation between liberal democracy, post-industrial economies, and free-market ideologies.[3] These are exactly the kinds of messages that environmental justice activists seek to counter.

Given the status of these objects as carriers of dominant raced, gen- 8 dered, classed, sexed, and naturalized stories that are part of global contests for cultural, political, and economic hegemony, it is crucially important to examine what stories are being told, what values are being promoted, which actors get to have agency, and what solutions are being offered. What lessons are being learned, and what kind of environmentalism has become the medium of these messages? What connections are made for children between environmentalism and social justice, between nature and morality?

I will first discuss the theme of "naturalizing" the nuclear family, 9 which is presented as a solution to environmental problems, and then I will look at the theme of multicultural kids' teams presented as examples of the best environmental activists.

## Saving the Planet Is Saving the Family

One of my favorite examples of the theme of offering the nuclear family as 10 the answer to environmental disruption is in *White Fang 2*. The ending of this 1994 movie neatly encapsulates several themes that I want to discuss. The main character, a young white man named Henry Casey, comes from a broken family, travels to the Alaskan wilderness, and ends up fighting against greedy miners (who are environmentally destructive) on behalf of what appear to be Northwest Coast Indians, along with his animal side-kick, the wolf White Fang. At the end, after the miners have been defeated, one of the young women of the tribe (who also happens to have, coinciden-tally, a female wolf sidekick) declares her love for the young white man, her willingness to form a family with him. The touching scene in which this happens shows her calling him as he walks away (supposedly leav-ing forever) and then, in classic Hollywood style, the two are shown run-ning slowly towards each other for a heartfelt (but relatively chaste, given the PG rating) kiss. At the same time, intercut comically and ludicrously with the two human lovers, the two wolves also run together and kiss. The movie closes with a charming scene in which the female wolf has pup-pies, and White Fang is, in very unwolflike ways, behaving like a proud daddy.

Some of the themes found in this movie we could easily predict, given 11 their long-standing involvement in the U.S. cultural imaginary, such as the figure of feminized nature and natural femininity, especially in its mater-nal form, or the naturally ecological noble savage. However, in the present

historical inflection, these aspects are almost always combined, as represented in *White Fang 2* by the Northwest Coast Indian woman, or in *Pocahontas* by the title character. Earth Mothers are almost inevitably brown
women, especially indigenous women, thus ensuring that nature and
natural wisdom are feminized and raced simultaneously. These movies
have been made after civil rights and women's movements have challenged
many cultural stereotypes, and their makers, generally liberal-minded
folks, clearly want to do the right thing. Postfeminist and civil rights–era
inflections mean that these figures are also presented as tribally specific,
independent, choosing beings, even if their choices are still narrowed to
nice white guys such as Henry Casey in *White Fang 2* and Captain John
Smith in *Pocahontas*.

This female noble savage trope does not, however, prevent the bad  *12*
guys in these stories from sometimes being imagined as racial and sexual
others. Sometimes the villain is orientalized, but more frequently the bad
guy is a sexualized other, a nonreproductive, unnatural upper-class twit,
the kind of campy, limp-wristed, unpatriotic male closet queen long seen
as subversive to the naturalized patriarchal American nuclear family, the
only legitimate reproductive unit in the Cold War era. Figures like Scar
in *The Lion King* or Governor Ratcliff in *Pocahontas* represent the deeply
problematic idea that gay men in particular are threatening to the "natural" family.

These days, the U.S. religious right wing anxiously and hysterically  *13*
argues that civil rights, feminism, and gay liberation movements have
destroyed the suburban Cold War family unit. Though the liberal makers
of many of the environmentalist cultural items I am talking about here
may reject this conservative position, a similar anxious message about the
collapse of the "traditional" nuclear family (ignoring the limited historical,
raced, and classed characteristics of this family form) is strongly promul-
gated throughout these children's stories. Those cultural, economic, and
social factors that "threaten" nuclear families also involved challenges to
masculinist power within the family and to images of white normality and
superiority. The instability of the nuclear family is thus presented by these
stories as a crisis, one that can only be solved by reinstating a "natural"
order. Over and over, the plots of these movies involve nature in the task of
saving young white boys (and sometimes white girls) from "broken" family circumstances. In particular, mothers are peculiarly absent; if an alien
came down and watched kid's films in the 1990s, she would be convinced
that there was a 95 percent chance of a kid's mother having met a fatal
accident around the time the child was seven or eight. (An incomplete list
of recent popular U.S. children's films in which the mother has died, or
the child is completely orphaned, would include *Alaska, Free Willy, Finding Nemo, Fly Away Home, Beauty and the Beast, The Lion King, James and
the Giant Peach, Anastasia, Once Upon a Forest, Harry Potter, Spider-Man,
Jurassic Park 2, Star Wars, Batman, X-Men, Aladdin, The Black Stallion,
Babe,* and *A Little Princess.*)

Responding to this postfeminist absence of the "good maternal *14* woman," nature is deployed in many of these films to reconstitute the heterosexist patriarchal family, again and again, in movies like *Alaska* and *Free Willy*, in *Fly Away Home* and *Wild America*, in *White Fang 2* and *Homeward Bound*, in *The Emerald Forest* and *Jungle to Jungle*. Sometimes the nature that accomplishes this healing of the broken family is an animal character, such as the geese in *Fly Away Home* that teach the young girl who has lost her mother to accept a new family with her father and stepmother, or the orphaned bear cub in *Alaska* that helps bring two kids together with their missing dad. But as often, the nature that accomplishes this reconstitution of the nuclear family is a combination of an indigenous figure and an animal, as in *Free Willy*'s Native American character Randolph, who along with the whale, Willy, helps the white boy Jesse accept his foster family, or in *Jungle to Jungle* in which the white boy has "gone native" and, with the help of a friendly tarantula, instructs his wayward father in how to get back together with his mother, or in *White Fang 2* mentioned above. A related figure to White Fang and Willy the Whale is the baboon/African-shaman character Rafiki in *The Lion King*, who reinscribes the boy/lion Hamlet/cub Simba properly into the patriarchal legacy he initially rejects, and thereby recovers the (environmentally sound) circle of life from its dangerous and deadly nonreproductive state.

In equating the restoration of natural harmony with the restoration of *15* the two-parent, suburban family, then, this kind of environmentalism naturalizes the nuclear family. In perfect symmetry to this dominant message of mainstream environmentalist popular culture that protected and valued nature equals white heterosexist reproduction (meant on both biological and social levels), the figure of the evil male homosexual often inhabits the ecovillains of these films. One of the best illustrations of this figure is the character Scar, the evil uncle in *The Lion King*, voiced by Jeremy Irons, who depends on his past history of playing sexually perverse, socially dangerous male characters to animate his depiction of Scar. This is clearly evidenced in a famous interchange with the lion cub Simba, in which, when Simba says, "You're so weird, Uncle Scar," Irons replies, "You have no idea," the exact same line he spoke in the exact same plummy overtones as the sexually ambivalent Claus Van Bulow in the film *Reversal of Fortune* (with enough style to win an Oscar nomination).

There is a segment from *The Lion King* that chillingly demonstrates *16* the way in which racialized and sexualized identities inhabit the depiction of environmental villainy. This is the scene where the nasty hyenas, voiced by Whoopi Goldberg and Cheech Marin to lend them the proper "ghetto" feel, are given a demonstration of Scar's desire to become king in Simba's father's place. Scar's musical number begins with a thoroughly campy intro, in which he prances about in classic drag queen style, and ends disturbingly with a scene of goose-stepping hyenas borrowed almost image by image from Leni Riefenstahl's film promoting Hitler, *Triumph of the Will*. Scar is figured here first as an evil homosexual, and then as a

Hitler worshiped by hyenas with "ghetto" voices. My narrative description of this scene does nothing to convey the emotional power of these images and sounds for kids and their accompanying parents, carried by the high production values of these movies. The audacity of the use of the Riefenstahl images to depict a campy gay male figure as a Hitler in league with untrustworthy and moronic people of color is appalling. Here, Hitler as the embodiment of evil is equated with Scar's "unnatural" sexuality and his anti-nature power politics—quite contrary to the history of the Nazis' deadly combination of racism, the slaughter of Jewish, gay, and disabled peoples, their celebration of heterosexist reproductive family forms, and their deep love of nature.[4]

In case it seems that the importance of this evil gay male figure is exaggerated in my argument, I can point to other examples. For instance, in the film *Ferngully*, subtitled *The Last Rainforest*, and a specifically pro-environmentalist film, there is the evil character Hexxus, voiced by another sexually ambivalent actor, Tim Curry (best known and most well-loved as the actor who played the "sweet transvestite from Transylvania," Dr. Frankenfurter, in *The Rocky Horror Picture Show*). Hexxus is not only campy and creepy; he is very, very black, both in color and in his mutable features. In his signature musical number, "Toxic Love" (the title alone gives away the sensibility), Hexxus oozes dangerous and nasty dark sexuality tied to a stomping rock beat. (Once again, the high quality of the music and images makes this movie, like *The Lion King*, a product that is intensely pleasurable. Try to watch the two scenes I have just referenced from a critical perspective without tapping your feet.) There's another one of these evil gay male figures in *Pocahontas*, the nasty imperialist Governor Ratcliffe, who is more concerned about the state of his hair than the people he callously orders to kill as "savages." He carries a little dog around with him on a velvet pillow, and his valet is always close behind with a mirror. *17*

That people of color, particularly indigenous people, should be exploited as natural resources for white environmentalism is an old story in U.S. environmentalist history, a story the environmental justice and Third World environmentalist movements are determined to disrupt. But the persistence of combining this story with the notion that part of restoring natural balance involves promoting heterosexist patriarchal family forms as the only means to healthy reproduction (of white people in particular) points to our dominant culture's constant confusion between "nature" and the naturalization of social inequality. In fact, successful environmental strategies may require us to rethink entire modes of production and reproduction built on this nuclear family form. But our children, particularly the U.S. white male children like my son who will grow up privileged in multiple ways, will not learn to think through these connections between environmental destruction, middle-class consumerism, and racism if all they have are these particular environmentalist stories to go on. We need instead stories of other kinds of reproduction, that don't depend on these heterosexist, racist, and naturalized tropes.[5] *18*

In these films, not only is the white nuclear family naturalized, but kids *19* are given the responsibility to fight environmental problems on their own without adults. Often they do this work in racially balanced, gender equal kids' teams. What kind of environmental and social messages are contained in promoting multicultural kids' teams as the ultimate ecowarriors?

## Combining Powers: Liberal Multiculturalism or Environmental Justice?

Of course, and ironically, my criticisms would come as a shock to the pro- *20* ducers of much of this environmental children's culture, who clearly want to create liberal messages about racial and gender equality (they don't yet care much about equality for those that challenge sexual norms). Everywhere in this material, there is an insistence on a certain notion of easily achievable multiculturalism and gender equality, a diversity just as naturally achieved as biodiversity is imagined to be. Yet, as environmental justice activists know, achieving collaboration across racial differences in U.S. society is no easy task for coalition politics.

In popular culture texts, this diversity is often represented by groups *21* of five or six teenagers with particular patterns that unfortunately ensure the reinstantiation of white middle-class men in the position of leadership. Thus the Animorphs (characters in popular books as well as a less popular TV show) are teenagers who are given the power to acquire animal DNA and morph into animals in order to fight against the invasion of mind-controlling sluglike communards called "Yeerks." Like the Power Rangers, the Animorphs are a group of five kinds: two white boys, one white girl, one boy of color, and one girl of color. This is a liberal form of multiculturalism, of course, in which racial differences are seen as naturally necessary to an effective team, like certain notions of ecosystems in stasis, in which differences never have competing interests or signal histories of genocide, slavery, rape, or exploitation but instead are examples of good managerial theory.[6] Just as static notions of biodiversity (sometimes found in mainstream environmentalism) only make sense within depictions of ecosystems as closed, circular, in balance, and without history, the easy necessity of racial and gender diversity of these kids' teams exist within a homogenous middle-class existence in which the favorite place for the kids to meet is the suburban mall (a kind of closed ecosystem in itself!).

These discourses of mainstream biocentric environmentalism and *22* liberal multiculturalism effectively combine in these children's stories to eviscerate power-laden histories of socially constructed difference. For example, in the *Animorphs* books, Cassie, the African American girl in the team, is figured as closer to nature by her ability to befriend animals (both of her parents are vets), and by her comfort with her body (she is the most controlled and graceful morpher, given her natural affinity with animals).

When faced with the Animorphs' risky attempt to free two members of the enslaved alien species Hork-Bajir, who are almost always defined in the books by the adjective "enslaved," Cassie responds not by referencing abolitionist discourses one would assume to be easily deployed by a fourteen-year-old African American girl. Instead, Cassie passionately wants to save them because they are a breeding pair of an endangered species (Applegate 1997, 72).

This liberal multiculturalism serves a more distinctively post–Cold 23 War purpose in the service of a globalizing environmentalism in the *Captain Planet* TV series. Here our group of five teenagers hew pretty much to the pattern mentioned above (one white U.S. guy, one black African guy, one brown South American guy, one white Russian girl, and one "Asian" [in other words, generically Asian] girl), but this pattern of biodiversity is very much about globally significant cultural diversity, a quasi-U.N. version of multiculturalism. When we learn that *Captain Planet* is a product of Turner Enterprises, we aren't surprised by the program's support of the idea of an international strike force against global environmental problems.

Despite, or rather through this cultural diversity, the Planeteers are 24 a United Nations clearly led by the United States while dependent on the work, body, and knowledge of a brown woman. Gaia, voiced in the first Captain Planet by the distinctive tones of Whoopi Goldberg, is a brown woman who is the spirit of Earth and the source of the Planeteers' abilities. Once again, the Mother Earth figure is a woman of color. But for the animating life force of Earth personified, Gaia is curiously powerless, dependent on the work of the five teenagers she gives rings to so they can call up the powers of fire, water, earth, wind, and the fifth element, heart. (Of course the U.S. alpha male, the white Wheeler, has the power of fire; the African male, Kwame, naturally has the power of earth; and the geopolitically marginal brown male, the South American Ma-Ti, is given the feminized power of heart.)

When the Planeteers are in deep trouble, however, they combine their 25 powers and call up a real superhero, Captain Planet, who, despite his blue skin and green hair, is a typical wisecracking suburban white guy straight out of sitcom land. For example, when faced with a mutant giant octopus created by toxic dumping off Japanese coastal waters, Captain Planet says, "I've got to stop that super-squid before it turns the city into sushi!" And, zipping into the sky, he calls out, "Calamari, dudes!" The character Captain Planet, to quote from the "Mission to Save Planet Earth" section of the show's Web page, is meant to be "a metaphor for that which can be accomplished by teamwork," and thus he "symbolizes that the whole is indeed greater than the sum of its parts." But it seems that this particular whole created by the unification of the "world's cultures and ethnic diversity" is—far from being anything like the "sum of its parts"—a good old American white male adolescent superhero. The notion of the world's cultures "combining powers" may seem like a nice metaphor for political coalition, but not if its purpose is creating a unity that looks and acts like a southern California surfer dude with body paint.

In some ways, it may seem supercritical to pick on *Captain Planet*, [26] which is a thoroughly self-conscious environmental cultural product, and a very successful one (especially according to its own promotional material), having garnered several media and educational awards, and reaching over 7 million people a week in the United States alone while being distributed in over sixty countries during its heyday in the mid-1990s.[7] Further, *Captain Planet* is unusual and commendable as a media product in its effort to provide action-oriented information, political inspiration, and organizational linkages. At the end of every episode is a thirty-second bit called "Planeteer Alert," which focuses on a specific problem, for instance, the safe disposal of household wastes, and gives kids tips on how they can be environmentally conscious consumers and citizens.

*Captain Planet* has also set up a number of links with other institu- [27] tions in a position to influence kids and their parents, a process that the producers call "combining powers" (which is what the Planeteers do when they summon Captain Planet). The Captain Planet Foundation makes the shows available to teachers for classroom use, and has collaborated with such organizations as the American Public Transit Association, the EPA, and the U.S. Fish and Wildlife Service. (With the latter, it has held a program called "Earth Day with the Braves," neatly combining Turner's environmentalism with his love of baseball while ignoring the Atlanta Braves' use of Native American stereotypes.) The Captain Planet Foundation also funds numerous children's grassroots environmental efforts.[8]

So why pick on *Captain Planet*? After all, wouldn't we rather have [28] environmentalist messages than nonenvironmentalist ones? Messages of multiculturalism rather than messages of bigotry? Messages in which women play important roles rather than ones in which they are powerless or invisible? Messages that allow agency to non-Western peoples rather than ones that assume the only teenagers with power are middle-class U.S. suburbanites?

But its very status as the most radical example of children's environ- [29] mentalist popular culture shows the deep dependence of these stories on problematic tropes of powerless (but proto-feminist) brown indigenous women, exoticized pure nature like Gaia's Hope Island, and naturalized differences operating in conflict-free teams.

*Captain Planet's* attempt to produce a liberal message is also beholden [30] to certain assumptions about the necessity to preserve corporate America's good reputation. As the producers explain:

> The use of villains to delineate good and evil is common in action-adventure series. However, given that we deal with real life issues, we were concerned children might come to the conclusion that if their parents worked in a polluting industry they were somehow villains. Although our show is basically realistic, our eco-villains are intentionally exaggerated so that they are clearly

operating outside of the law. They are symbolic of the environmental problems rather than representative of the actions of individuals. We are careful not to be critical of business/industry, but to encourage responsible business practices and a balance between the needs of people, environment/wildlife, and industry.[9]

Like every one of the environmentalist objects of children's popular and material culture I have encountered, then, Captain Planet presents solutions that are almost entirely restricted to individual lifestyle changes, to legitimating the rule of law rather than challenging business as usual. Environmental catastrophes always happen "outside the law" rather than the reality in which legal parameters often protect polluting corporations or governments. Ecovillains are nasty male queens, dark spirits, mustachioed men with accents, brittle and demented white female scientists, or mutant human/animal paranoids with delusions of grandeur. Though children get the notion that trees are cut down and animals killed because of greedy behavior, it is almost always the greedy behavior of a single ecovillain. Never are the ecovillains corporations, or militaries, or governments, or white patriarchal science—the real ecovillains on our planet, the ones the environmental justice movement is presently confronting. Gaia lives on a pure tropical island far away from urban sites of environmental struggle. Solutions that romanticize ecological noble savages lock both nature and people of color in an imagined preindustrial past, but they are almost the only solutions offered, along with the idea that recycling and disposing of toxic waste "properly" (rather than identifying the source of the waste and preventing it from being made) are important tasks for children acting alone without responsible adults.

## Conclusion

In a story like *Captain Planet,* which, like other examples of children's environmentalist popular culture, wants to equate environmentalism with social equality, how do we evaluate the notion that "The Power Is Yours"? There are a number of ways to read the show's slogan, and to speculate about its likely results as an internalized message. We might start by thinking about who gets to be Planeteers, who most easily can imagine themselves as global citizens, empowered to combine powers with others on a planetwide scale. That this story might be most invested in interpellating privileged Western children comes as no surprise. And it may be an appropriate strategy, given the inordinate amount of the world's resources these children will consume over their lifetime. So perhaps this message will have unforeseen radical results. After all, one of the important demographic actors in the 1960s movements were privileged children like myself, who, having been brought up on the notion that we were empowered to promote Truth, Justice, and the American Way, realized with shock that it was up to us to follow the lead of those less privileged and to force our country and our parents to correct deeply held hypocrisies. Perhaps the Planeteers of tomorrow will someday rebel against the corporate forces that are destroying the planet and causing suffering for so many of the world's peoples. Perhaps the megamedia empires, like Turner Enterprises, will take responsibility for the misleading stories they are promoting, in which environmental damage can be cured by constructing a suburban nuclear middle-class family or by promoting superficial multiculturalism. A utopian hope, but maybe one day the multinationals will wish they never told these kids that "The Power Is Yours," allowing the liberal, superficial, and individualistic solutions presently offered to be rejected for collective, social, and revolutionary action.

But another, more pessimistic reading of this message is possible. It 33 is clear that the dominance of the environmentalist theme is not centrally about environmentalism at all, but about producing morally uplifting and privilege-maintaining stories that legitimate the notion that especially for white middle-class children, the Power Is Theirs to do what they will with the world. Like the idea of easy multicultural kids' teams, the "environment" is a safe issue when freed from questions of power. Given the Planeteers' superpowers, their incapacity for wrongdoing, and the overwhelming priority for saving an otherwise doomed nature, the privileged kids that identify with them might feel fully justified in imposing putatively environmentalist solutions undemocratically on less powerful non-Planeteers.

And what about the kids who don't so easily identify as Planeteers? 34 Certainly the kids being poisoned by lead in the cities, the kids who are malnourished by corporately produced salinification and erosion, the kids who are drinking pesticide-laced water at migrant farmworkers camps, the kids who are living on uranium tailings on Navajo land—are Captain Planet's producers worried about whether *they* will start holding *their* parents responsible for "polluting industries"? Will these kids be satisfied with the idea that nature will be restored if they all form happy, consuming nuclear families? It is less likely that these kids, in a post-feminist, post–civil rights environmental justice era, will not know the shape and character of the real ecovillains. These kids can't wait, and in fact aren't waiting, for an awakened force of white middle-class Planeteers to take on the combined problems of environmental destruction and social inequalities.

Looking critically at environmentalist children's popular culture 35 underscores the difficulty of telling stories about saving nature from the point of view of dominant U.S. culture without engaging in problematic stories about social difference, which depend upon the naturalization of social inequalities via the invocation of the "natural order," nature as truth, foundation, all that is right and valuable. And these themes are particular to our present historical and political context, showing the traces of recent social movement critiques while transposing them onto justifications of white, male, straight, liberal capitalist hegemony—that is, they tend to be post-feminist, post–civil rights stories about environmentalist new world orders. But even when apparently promoting the kind of environmentalist values shared by environmental justice activists, for instance, struggling against toxic waste or mining on Native American lands, these stories often portray people of color either stereotypically or as the villains. Even more disturbingly, they combine homophobic and racist portrayals in ways that distract audiences from remembering that the ecovillains of the real world are corporations, militaries, and governments (Seager 1993).

Rather than thinking the Power Is Yours, or Ours, or Theirs, or the planet's, we must think about powers that arise out of struggle and contest, which are justified on the basis of participatory democratic practices rather than what is natural. Rather than look to superpowered teams that naturalize U.S. white male middle-class leadership, we need to think about combining powers in political coalitions that go against the present "natural" order. And this is what the environmental justice movement, in its refusal to depend only on biocentric environmentalist arguments about saving a "pure" nature, has the potential to do.

NOTES

1. Some listeners have asked me whether I would include in this criticism nature-based spiritual and cultural practices such as those found in many indigenous cultures, which use animals and natural entities as significant characters in educational stories and spiritual practices. But I think there is a fundamental difference between stories from cultures that do not display a Western culture-nature dualism and the way in which animals are used as characters in moral stories for young children in Eurocentric cultures.

2. These conclusions are tentative. There is no research, as far as I am aware, of the frequency of environmentalist themes in children's education and culture worldwide and cross-culturally. There is some work done in the United States, mostly prompted by conservative concerns that kids were being "brainwashed" by environmentalists in the public schools. This research does not cover popular culture. I am therefore forced to make tentative statements here, backed up by my attention to this phenomenon in the United States and Europe over a period of ten years of personal observation and, it should be said, with the assistance of my son, who parried my constant questions and critical observations with his own as well as bringing me numerous examples of this material as he came to understand my interest in it. So I thank Hart Sturgeon-Reed for his research assistance. Thanks are also due to T. V. Reed for many useful editing suggestions. I would also like to thank the Center for Cultural Studies at UCSC, Patsy Hallen and Peter Newman of the Institute for the Study of Technology and Policy at Murdoch University, and the many audiences whose comments contributed to this final version. This essay is dedicated to Zoë Sofoulis, who taught me a lot about the problems with Planeteer tendencies, especially my own.

3. One of the things I would do if I were to pursue this project is to explore the reception of these children's products in different cultural contexts, in which I would expect to find them the subject of surprising and different narrative reconstructions and oppositional practices. And this should be true not only in international contexts, but in subjugated cultural contexts internal to the United States.

4. Audiences to this essay as a talk have disputed my characterization of *The Lion King* as homophobic by pointing out that *The Lion King*, whose famous musical team included the openly gay Sir Elton John, portrays a happy and helpful gay male couple in the loving and committed relationship of Timon, the meerkat, and Pumba, the warthog. Though I think this is an accurate reading of a relationship that should have been far scarier to Jerry Falwell than the proclivities of the purple Teletubby, Tinky Winky, it remains true that the central resolution of the plot requires the restoration of Simba to the throne and to a heterosexual, nuclear family form quite unlike that of real lions.

5. One could see the movie *Babe*, for instance, as a counterexample to most of these other films. In *Babe*, the story of a pig who wants to be a sheepdog, an argument against naturalizing social orders, "racial" identities, or social roles is clearly, charmingly, and humorously presented. Containing strong statements against the exploitation of animals as workers or as meat as well as the importance of certain participatory democratic practices, the film deserves a more complex treatment in light of the framework of my arguments than I can give here, but it can serve as one example of a different way of imagining the connection between environmentalism and social equality that doesn't naturalize the dominant order. Though I strongly believe in this positive reading of *Babe*, the movie is alarmingly sexist in its portrayal of the farm wife. For another analysis of the nonnaturalizing effect of *Babe*, as well as other interesting insights into the message of the movie, see Plumwood 2002, esp. 600–606.

6. I've written elsewhere about the dangers of assuming that racial balance in numbers is the solution to creating effective antiracist coalition politics (Sturgeon 1997).

7. From "Mission to Save Planet Earth," Captain Planet Web page, http://www. turner .com/planet/static/mission.html (1998, 2002).

8. Captain Planet Foundation Web page, http://www.captainplanetfdn.org (2002).

9. From "Mission to Save Planet Earth," Captain Planet Web page, http://www.turner .com/planet/static/mission.html (1998, 2002). The last sentence I quote here was on the page in 1998, but was removed in the 2002 page.

REFERENCES

Applegate, K. A. 1997. *The Change*. Vol. 13 of *The Animorphs*. New York: Scholastic.
Davis, S. 1995. "Touch the Magic." In *Uncommon Ground*, ed. William Cronon. New York: Norton.
May, E. 1999. *Homeward Bound: American Families in the Cold War Era*. 2nd ed. New York: Basic Books.
Plumwood, V. 2002. *Environmental Culture: The Ecological Crisis of Reason*. London: Routledge.
Reed, T. V. 2002. "Toward an Environmental Justice Ecocriticism." In *The Environmental Justice Reader*, ed. Joni Adamson, Mei Mei Evans, and Rachel Stein. Tucson: University of Arizona Press.
Seager, J. 1993. *Earth Follies: Coming to Feminist Terms with the Global Environmental Crisis*. New York: Routledge.
Sturgeon, N. 1997. *Ecofeminist Natures: Race, Gender, Feminist Theory, and Political Action*. New York: Routledge.

■ ■ ■

## Reading as a Writer: Analyzing Rhetorical Choices

1. Sturgeon does a lot of work in her very first paragraph to set up her task and the framing theory for her essay. Reread that paragraph closely and

prepare to explain in your own words the paradoxical problem she sees in the fact that environmental themes are increasingly evident in children's popular culture. Why isn't this a good thing, according to Sturgeon? What definitions and theories does she set out in this first paragraph? What does she plan to teach her readers? Finally, how effectively do the examples in her essay illustrate these ideas?

2. Sturgeon uses the terms "environmental justice" and "environmental justice ecocriticism" early in her essay. Look up these terms so that you have a better understanding of the ways scholars use these ideas in conversations that push ecological discussions in new directions. Why do you think she so often places the word *natural* in quotation marks?

## Writing as a Reader: Entering the Conversation of Ideas

1. While Sturgeon addresses gender stereotypes only briefly in her analysis of environmentally minded children's entertainment, her analysis of the roles that women of color often play in those films is interesting to place next to Ann duCille's analysis of representations of women of color in toys. Choose an environmentally themed children's film not mentioned in Sturgeon's essay and use both Sturgeon's and duCille's insights to analyze the extent to which the film reinforces or unsettles race and gender stereotypes. Be sure to describe and explain specific examples from the film as you make your point.

2. Sturgeon's argument about the ways children's media culture tends to reinforce gender assumptions about active men and passive women picks up on issues Jim Tarter raises in his analysis of gender assumptions in recognizing the environmental causes of cancer. How do these authors' ideas enrich and extend one another? Write an essay in which you connect these authors' insights in order to make an argument about the role gender assumptions can play in our understanding of the power we can—and should—have over our environment. What does each author think—and what do *you* think—we should do differently?

## DAVID BUCKINGHAM

# Childhood in the Age of Global Media

David Buckingham is a professor of education at the University of London, where he teaches at the Institute of Education and directs the Centre for the Study of Children, Youth, and Media. He is a leader in using classroom-based research and cultural studies insights in media education and youth interaction with media. He has edited, written, and cowritten many books on this topic, including *After the Death of Childhood* (2000), *Computer Games: Text, Narrative, and Play* (2006), and *Digital Generations: Children, Young People, and the New Media* (2006).

While Buckingham is a British scholar, his insights about children's media literacy in an increasingly "shrinking" world will speak to American readers and are intended for *all* readers who have an interest in the impact of global media. One of the hallmarks of Buckingham's style of argument is his consistent movement between positive and negative potentials in his examples, whether he is analyzing the global spread of Pokémon or the phenomenon of Harry Potter's popularity in China. As you read, listen for phrases that indicate weighing of potential positives and potential negatives, and notice how Buckingham resists easy praise or blame of the media examples he analyzes. Buckingham is curious about the "contradictions and paradoxes" (para. 21) in these examples and in other scholars' ideas about them, too.

Buckingham's essay brings together insights about the ways the global market adapts to local contexts (a dynamic he and other scholars refer to as "glocalization") and insights about the effects of global media on childhood. What might be lost and gained from children's access to the wider world? To what extent does marketing harmfully or beneficially shape that access and the perspectives about "others" for the children participating in the media? How do children passively consume or actively resist these messages—or do both? Tellingly, Buckingham concludes with "a series of questions." After reading his essay, you may have others to add to his list, based on your own insights and experiences in our dynamic media marketplace.

■ ■ ■

# Abstract

This paper provides a critical overview of debates about the role of media in globalisation, with specific reference to the position of children. The paper begins with a broad-ranging discussion of relevant literature in the field. It argues that, while the economic "logic" of globalisation may lead to a homogenisation of cultural products, it has also led to the emergence of a "modernist" discourse about childhood that has paradoxical consequences in terms of children's rights. The paper then moves on to a discussion of three case studies, drawing partly on the author's empirical research: Disney, which is often cited as a defining instance of "cultural imperialism"; Pokémon, which serves as an illustration of the "multi-media intertextuality" of contemporary children's media; and the contrasting examples of "public serviced" productions such as *Teletubbies* and *Sesame Street*. In each case, the paper suggests that the reception and use of such cultural products cannot simply be "read off" from an analysis of their production context, or their textual characteristics; and that, in practice, the production, circulation, and consumption of children's media entails a complex relationship between global and local imperatives. The media may be producing a global "children's culture" that transcends national differences, but this may not necessarily be disadvantageous for children themselves.

In most regions of the world, the media are now an inescapable fact of contemporary childhoods. In most industrialised countries, children spend more time with media of various kinds than they spend in school, or with their family or friends. Even in the rural areas of developing countries, the advent of electronic media is often an early harbinger of "modernisation"; and growing numbers of children have access to globally- and locally-produced media material. However, the role of the media—and, more broadly, of children's consumer culture—has typically been neglected by sociologists of childhood: Definitive overviews of the field often make little or no mention of the issue (e.g., James et al., 1998). As Sonia Livingstone (1998, p. 438) has argued, the new sociological child appears to live a "natural," *non-mediated* childhood: This is "a carefree child playing hopscotch with friends in a nearby park, not a child with music on the headphones watching television in her bedroom."

Historically, research on children's relationships with media has been dominated by psychological perspectives. Broadly behaviourist studies of the media's effects on behaviour or attitudes—most notably in relation to "violence"—have partly given way to a more constructivist approach, in which the child is seen as an active processor of meaning, rather than a passive victim (Singer and Singer, 2002; van Evra, 2004). In general, however, researchers in this field continue to employ a developmentalist approach, in which children are seen to be gradually progressing towards a state of adult rationality. The focus here is on the interaction between the individual child and the screen, in isolation from broader interpersonal and social processes.

In recent years, however, researchers in the fields of Media and Cultural Studies have been developing a more sociological account of children's uses and interpretations of media (see, for example, Gillespie, 1995; Buckingham, 2000; Livingstone, 2002). This research seeks to explore children's perspectives, and to analyse their interactions with media, on their own terms. In the process, it draws attention to children's *competence* as media users—their "media literacy"—and the ways in which media use is embedded in the contexts and relationships of everyday life. However, it also recognises that children's dealings with media are framed by the operations of the media industries, and by the constraints exerted by textual meanings: children are by no means simply free to make their own meanings in any way they choose. Understanding the power of the media thus requires us to theorise and account for the complex relationship between structure and agency in defining childhood (Buckingham and Sefton-Green, 2004).

In this essay, I intend to apply this kind of approach to analysing the place of the media in children's experiences of globalisation. As I shall argue, children are not merely passive victims of all-powerful media representations; but neither are they completely free agents. Both economically and culturally, the media play a profoundly ambiguous role in terms of globalisation: they provide powerful and pleasurable forms of "children's culture" that appeal to children living in very different circumstances around the world; yet they also provide symbolic resources with which children come to define their own meanings and identities.

## Media and Globalisation

Like the trade in material goods, the trade in cultural goods is undoubt-  5 edly a key factor in the contemporary reconfiguration of relations between the global and the local. Nevertheless, there are some starkly opposing accounts of this process, which beg broader questions about our understanding of the power of the media and of the ways in which it is exercised.

Thus, on the one hand, we have theories of *cultural imperialism*, which  6 point the finger of blame directly at the United States, as the world's leading superpower. As the title of one influential early book expressed it, *The Media Are American* (Tunstall, 1977). From this perspective, US media are powerful agents of cultural homogenisation: they eradicate local or indigenous cultures by imposing a singular ideology and world-view. This development is seen as an inevitable consequence of capitalist expansion, as corporations restlessly seek out new markets, and as economies of scale result in a steady growth of monopolisation. Rather than relying simply on physical occupation, the US is now seen to sustain its hegemony through a process of ideological and cultural domination, or "Coca-colonisation" (Wagnleitner, 1994).

This kind of argument has been widely criticised by many scholars. It  7 is argued that the flow of cultural goods is not so straightforwardly unidirectional; and that *economic* power does not necessarily result in a form of *ideological* domination. Tomlinson (1991), for example, argues that such arguments effectively infantilise consumers, implying that they are somehow powerless to resist colonial ideologies; and he points to evidence from audience research that shows the diverse ways in which global audiences respond to (and, in many situations, resist) US-made cultural products (e.g., Liebes and Katz, 1990). Researchers also point to the dominance of home-grown media products in domestic markets (Silj, 1988); the historical and continuing popularity of non-US cultural products around the world (French paintings, Chinese food, Latin American music) (Cowen, 2002); and the emergence of new "cosmopolitan" global cultures (Hannerz, 1996).

In more recent years, the cultural imperialism thesis has effectively  8 given way to a much more optimistic account of the global spread of media. Rather than the global replacing the local, the two have been seen to merge in a process of "glocalisation" (Robertson, 1994; Featherstone, 1995); and, it is argued, this process also has a very long history, rather than being a development unique to contemporary capitalism. Advocates of this approach point to the flourishing of local cultural production in many regions of the world; and to the global dissemination of non-US

media products, ranging from Brazilian *telenovelas* to Japanese animation to Jamaican reggae music (Cowen, 2002). They also proclaim the new
forms of "hybridity"—or "new ethnicities"—that emerge as global media
forms (such as hip-hop: Bennett, 2000) are merged with local idioms and
traditions. From this perspective, globalisation actively produces cultural
diversity, rather than homogeneity; and cultural identities are accordingly
fluid and open to change.

However, critics have begun to point to some of the difficulties with    9
this more optimistic approach. They question the emphasis on "hybridity,"
arguing that this is not equally available to all, and that it may be merely a
characteristic of the intelligentsia rather than of the population as a whole
(Cohen, 1997); they critique the commodification that continues to charac-
terise the global trade in culture, for instance in the marketing of so-called
"world music" (Feld and Keil, 1992); and they challenge the superficial-
ity (or "ethnic chic") of some such developments (Leshkowich and Jones,
2003). It is certainly possible to argue that this more optimistic account
neglects the economic dimension of the media—that is, their function as
a means of generating profit for already-wealthy nations, which was a key
concern of the cultural imperialism thesis—and slides into a somewhat
easy form of celebration that is characteristic of some postmodern cultural theory.

## Global Childhoods

What happens when children enter this picture? The global scale of mar-    10
keting to children typically provokes an additional anxiety, which is essentially about cultural continuity. According to the critics, what we are seeing
is the construction of a homogenised global children's culture, in which
cultural differences are being flattened out and erased, and in which parents' attempts to sustain their cultural values are increasingly in vain. The
media are seen to have disrupted the process of socialisation, upsetting the
smooth transmission of values from one generation to the next. For authors
such as McChesney (2002) and Kline (1993), this is an inevitable consequence of commercialisation: neo-liberal economics are, in their view,
inherently incompatible with the "real" needs and interests of children.
Within the media production sector, there are also frequent calls for government intervention to support indigenous children's production against
the pressure of the global market (von Feilitzen and Carlsson, 2002).

Such arguments almost inevitably have an element of conservatism,    11
and often seem to rely on judgments about cultural value that are asserted
rather than fully justified (see Buckingham, 2000, Chapter 7). By contrast,
it could be argued that the media are responsible for a *modernisation* of
childhood, or at least for the growing dominance of a moder*nist* discourse
about childhood. For example, the global success of the children's channel Nickelodeon provides a symptomatic instance of the ways in which

market values have come to be aligned with liberal political arguments about children's rights. . . . The statements of Nickelodeon executives and the rhetoric of its on-screen publicity proclaim its role as an agent of empowerment—a notion of the channel as a "kid-only" zone, giving voice to kids, taking the kids' point of view, as the friend of kids; and the interests of "kids" are frequently defined here as being in opposition to the interests of adults (see Hendershot, 2004).

This "modernist" discourse has increasingly been adopted by expo-  12
nents of more traditional children's media, not least in public service television. This is certainly the case in the UK (see Buckingham et al., 1999);
but it is also apparent, for example, in the (possibly unlikely) case of the
Minimax channel in post-communist Hungary (Lustyik, 2003). It might
even be possible to talk here about the emergence of a globalised "modernist style" in children's culture, that seeks to address children across cultural boundaries—in the same way that critics have talked about "youth
culture" as a global phenomenon (Buckingham, 2004). The Japanese business consultant Kenichi Ohmae (1995), for example, asserts that children's
exposure to such a global culture means that they now have more in common with their peers in other cultures than they do with their own parents.

Of course, we should not forget that many children in the major-  13
ity world—particularly in the more isolated rural areas of poorer countries—still do not have access to many forms of media communication.
Such children and their families may lack the economic resources to purchase manufactured toys or printed media, and may lack electricity, let
alone access to broadcast signals; and as such, their ability to "buy into" a
globalised children's culture is distinctly limited (for example, see Punch,
2003, on rural Bolivia). Yet as modern technologies steadily extend their
reach across the globe, the media that these children are likely to encounter first will not be those produced in their own countries, but those produced in the wealthy nations of the West.

## The Economic Case

There is certainly an economic logic to the globalisation of children's cul-  14
ture. The children's market is potentially large, but it is also by its nature
quite fragmented. In terms of age, children are quite clearly divided (and
divide themselves) into age segments. What appeals to a five-year-old is
unlikely to appeal to a 10-year-old.[1] The market is also clearly divided in
terms of gender. Particularly for younger children, this is a very "pink and
blue" market, and there are significant risks in attempting to cross the line,
in order to appeal to both groups. It used to be the received wisdom among
marketers that the way to succeed was to appeal to boys first: girls were
quite likely to buy into boy culture, although boys were less likely to buy
into girl culture (Schneider, 1992). Analyses of contemporary toy advertis-

ing would suggest that—despite decades of second-wave feminism—this continues to be the case (Griffiths, 2002).

While the picture is (perhaps increasingly) complicated, the fact *15* remains that the children's market is strongly segmented; and one way for producers to deal with this—to develop economies of scale—is to build markets globally, to amass "niche" markets into a larger global market. This tendency is also reinforced by the vertical and horizontal integration of the media and cultural industries. "Vertical integration" refers to the way in which the market is coming to be dominated by a small number of global players, who integrate hardware, software, and means of distribution; and these are largely the same players who dominate the adult market (Westcott, 2002). For example, in the case of specialist children's TV channels, the market is dominated by Disney (who have significant interests in the adult market via subsidiaries like Touchstone and Buena Vista, and own the ABC network in the US), Nickelodeon (owned by Viacom), Cartoon Network (owned by AOL Time Warner), and Fox Kids (Murdoch). It is these US-based companies that dominate the children's market: these four companies run more than thirty branded children's channels across Europe, for example, although none of them invests to any significant degree in local production. This is by no means a risk-free market, and local producers are responding to the challenge; but in homes where children have access to cable/satellite, these US-owned channels are achieving a growing market share.

These companies are also increasingly operating across media platforms ("horizontal integration"). Nearly all the major children's "crazes" of *16* the last twenty years (Ninja Turtles, Power Rangers, Pokémon, Beyblades, Harry Potter, Yugioh) have worked on the principle of what the industry calls "integrated marketing," or "multimedia synergy." For example, Pokémon was first a computer game, then a TV series, a trading card game, a series of movies, and a whole range of merchandise, from clothes and toys to food and bags and all sorts of unlikely paraphernalia. Again, horizontal integration on this scale requires global marketing: it would be much harder to achieve in one country alone.

As this implies, there is an economic logic to the globalisation of *17* the children's market; and to this extent, the cultural imperialism thesis appears to be correct. Yet *economic* domination does not necessarily translate directly into *ideological* or *cultural* domination. Sam Punch . . . shows how, as individuals move across cultures, the purchase of certain commodities (such as clothes) may accompany changes in attitudes; but even here, the direction of any causal relationship between these things is not necessarily easy to establish. In the cultural sphere, globalisation is often a paradoxical phenomenon. As I intend to show, children's culture is characterised not so much by a one-way process of domination, but by an unpredictable and contested relationship between the global and the local—often expressed in the notion of "glocalization" (Robertson, 1994).

In the following sections of this article, I explore this further by focussing on some specific examples: I begin with two instances of commercial culture, Disney and Pokémon, and conclude by looking briefly at a couple of "public service" productions.

## Uncle Walt and His Evil Empire

For critics of commercialism, Disney is the "bad brand" of children's culture. It is the McDonald's, the Nike of childhood. Historically, it is hard to ignore the political intentions of the Disney corporation. Uncle Walt's involvement in far-right politics is quite well documented (Roth, 1996); and critics have seen some of the early films as little more than ideological propaganda in the service of US foreign policy. Eric Smoodin's (1994) collection, for example, contains some trenchant critiques of the role of Disney movies promoting cultural imperialism in Latin America: the Donald Duck film *The Three Caballeros* is singled out for particular criticism (Burton-Carvajal, 1994; Piedra, 1994), alongside some of the lesser-known travelogues and educational films (Cartwright and Goldfarb, 1994). [18]

Donald Duck was also the subject of a famous early critique by Ariel Dorfman and Armand Mattelart (1975), whose book *Reading Donald Duck* was written in Chile in the wake of the United States' involvement in the overthrow of the Allende government. They argued that, far from being a harmless fantasy of childhood innocence, Donald was actually a vehicle for the propagation of capitalist ideology and US interests and values. That critique has certainly been questioned, however. Martin Barker's (1990) book on comics takes Dorfman and Mattelart to task for a kind of conspiracy theory that overemphasises the closeness of the relationship between government and business; and, perhaps more importantly, for oversimplifying the ways in which people read these comics—in effect, for assuming that children would simply swallow whole the values that the comics were seen to represent. [19]

Even so, for many adults—particularly middle-class adults—outside North America, Disney is synonymous with the unacceptable face of US capitalism. My own research on this was undertaken as part of a global project, published in the book *Dazzled by Disney?* (Wasko et al., 2001). For the older adults (many of them parents) whom we interviewed, Disney was seen as safe, sanitized, predictable, inauthentic, and somewhat "corny" (Buckingham, 2001). It was full of objectionable stereotypes and cheap moralism; and it was leading children away from true (that is, national) cultural traditions towards a homogeneous, mass-produced consumer culture. Disney was all about brainwashing, seducing the innocent—and in this sense, the debate about Disney was tied up with broader arguments about the changing symbolic value of childhood. This is a view that is also apparent in some of the academic criticism, for example in the work of Henry Giroux (2001)—although for our British respondents, it was very [20] much reinforced by a sense of Disney as quintessential *American*, as somehow inherently alien. Their resentment of Disney—as of McDonald's—was often inextricably connected with their rejection of the United States' political role as a global superpower.

However, this criticism was not without its contradictions and paradoxes. Some of the younger adult participants we interviewed (who were mostly undergraduates) were more inclined to admit to enjoying Disney: they expressed a kind of aesthetic appreciation of the animation and the spectacle, and talked about the emotional appeal of Disney's construction of childhood. Even for the older adults, there was a certain amount of ambivalence, even tinged with a degree of nostalgia. It may be that the symbolic importance of Disney as a bearer of US capitalist values tends to provoke a principled critical discourse, even where that discourse might not actually reflect how individuals respond to the films themselves.

Nevertheless, this sense of Disney's "Americanness" was not at all an issue for the children we interviewed. When I asked one group of six year olds where they thought Disney films came from, they were quite unsure (despite the US accents). In the end, they opted for France, on the grounds that one of them had been to Disneyland Paris. A similar finding was apparent from Kirsten Drotner's (2001) research for the same project in Denmark. Her chapter in the book is named after a quote from one of her respondents: "Donald seems so Danish." To some extent, she is suggesting that the Americanness—the alienness—of Disney went unnoticed by the young Danes whom she interviewed, partly because the comics are translated and the movies are dubbed (which obviously is not the case in the UK). However, she also suggests that they read the comics selectively: The good aspects of Donald (his unconventional, politically incorrect style) were read as Danish, as reflecting some kind of national character, while his bad qualities were seen as American, and hence as "other."

On one level, of course, this invisibility could be seen precisely as testimony to the power of Disney's cultural imperialism—that, if the media are American, then we are all American too. It could be that Americanness is the default position, something so universal and so unquestioned that it has become effectively invisible. On the other hand, it could be argued that, as they increasingly engage with world markets, Disney and other cultural producers are having to suppress elements that might be perceived to be too culturally specific in favour of those that seem to speak to some universal, trans-cultural notion of childhood.

There are some elements of truth in both arguments. In fact, what our research and Drotner's shows is that audiences read selectively, taking aspects of the text that seem to them to confirm a positive self-image or cultural identity, and setting that against other aspects of the text that they perceive as problematic or undesirable. And it is these latter aspects that they often seem to define as "American"—as plastic, fake, kitschy, or indeed as ideologically suspect. Obviously, this is also an historical process: It would certainly be interesting now to map young people's changing perceptions of the US, as they are mediated through popular culture, in the wake of George Bush's so-called "war on terror."

However, the actual texts that are being produced for the global market 25 are also more complex. Politically speaking, the key Disney movies of the last couple of decades have moved quite a long way from *The Three Caballeros*. McQuillan and Byrne (1999) read the Disney of the 1980s and 1990s as a set of parables for US foreign policy—so *The Lion King* is about South Africa, *Aladdin* is about the Middle East, *Mulan* is about China, and so on. On one level, it is possible to read all these texts as being about global ideological colonization—and, if you add in *Pocahontas,* about internal colonisation as well. One might argue that they are all about recuperating and sanitising "other" cultures and the challenges they might represent. However, I believe it makes more sense to see them as liberal texts, even as confused liberal texts—as texts which do at least recognise other cultures, and which try to construct some kind of dialogue with them. If we see such films merely as a more subtle form of propaganda (as critics like Giroux are wont to do), then we miss much of their ambivalence and complexity.

## Gotta Catch 'Em All

Pokémon provides an interesting contrast with Disney, on several levels. 26 Walt Disney always maintained that his films were intended for a family audience, and not just for children; and while this was essentially a financial decision on Disney's part, it is possible to argue that the films tell children and adults rather different stories about childhood (Forgacs, 1992). By contrast, Pokémon was largely inaccessible, impenetrable even, to the majority of adults; and that in itself partly explains some of its appeal to children.

My own research on Pokémon was part of another global project, 27 which involved researchers from Japan and the US as well as from the UK, France, Israel, and Australia. This research is collected in Joseph Tobin's book *Pikachu's Global Adventure: The Rise and Fall of Pokémon* (Tobin, 2004). Among other things, we were interested in how Pokémon was produced and marketed as a global phenomenon, and how it was perceived and used by children. As I have noted, Pokémon began life as a computer game, which was produced by Nintendo, but it rapidly spun off into a TV series, movies, books and comics, a trading card game, toys, plus the usual range of clothing, food, lunchboxes, stickers, and countless other products. In many ways, it was a classic example of integrated marketing. The Pokémon brand became a means to market a whole range of licensed goods to a very diverse range of audiences: soft toys for younger children, TV cartoons for a slightly older age group, the Game Boy game for the oldest, pre-teens and younger teenagers. There was also appeal to girls as well as boys, with girl-friendly themes and characters as well as the more predictable boy-oriented ones: so Pokémon was about collecting, about nurturing as well as competing, about feeling as well as fighting. For a while at least, it managed very effectively to cut across the divisions and segments in the children's market.

It was also very successful globally. This needs to be understood, firstly, 28 in terms of the emergence of Japan as a global cultural power—which has become an increasingly important factor in global media markets (see Allison, 2000). This phenomenon is most obviously apparent in the rise of *manga* (the Japanese comic book) and its move from being a "cult" medium, or a medium just for children, to something more mainstream; and it is also evident in the global marketing of Japanese "cuteness" *(kawai'sa)*, in the form of Hello Kitty, Sailor Moon, and even the Tamagotchi (Yano, 2004). Pokémon clearly combines elements of both these forms.

Our research considered how Japanese producers used other coun- 29 tries as a kind of springboard into local markets around the world. In Asia, where there can be resistance to Japanese products, Nintendo marketed Pokémon products via Hong Kong; while it also used the United States, and US franchise holders, to push into other Western markets. So the Pokémon card game was actually produced by a US company, the sinisterly-named Wizards of the Coast, who were also responsible for a similar game for older children, *Magic the Gathering*. Likewise, the version of the TV series that is exported globally is a re-versioned one from the US, not the Japanese original: It is an "Americanised" version of a Japanese cultural product.

This "glocalisation" involved two things. Firstly, at the point of dis- 30 tribution, there is a process that the industry calls "localising." Thus, the distributors employed people in the US to adapt the TV cartoons for the US market, which involved editing out material that was seen to be too culturally strange or specific. Hirofumi Katsuno and Jeffrey Maret (2004) compared the Japanese and US versions of Pokémon cartoons and found some quite unexpected (or at least quite bizarre) differences here, in terms of what was seen to be palatable to a US market—particularly to do with the removal of anything remotely sexual or "violent."

At the same time, at the point of production, there was a process Koi- 31 chi Iwabushi (2004) calls "deodorising": that is, anything that was seen as too Japanese (the "odour" of Japan) was removed. So, for example, the characters are given Westernised names, the characteristic *anime* visual style (for example, of the faces) is relatively muted, there is no written language, no religious references, and some of the settings are rendered less obviously Japanese. There was therefore a distinct effort to create a product that would be exportable, both at the point of local distribution and at the point of production.

To some extent, as Kenichi Ohmae (1995) suggests, this may facili- 32 tate the creation of a common global culture among children. We observed several instances of children communicating and playing with Pokémon across social and cultural differences: Its extensive, specialised mythology provided a kind of common language that transcended cultural barriers.

Yet what was interesting was that—unlike my brief experience with Disney—the "Japaneseness" of Pokémon was something that children definitely recognised and enjoyed. It was strange, but strange-exotic—and, indeed, profoundly cool (see McGray, 2002). Of course, "cool" has a limited shelf-life; and our project also tracked the complicated reasons why children appeared to drop Pokémon as quickly as they had taken it up. Even so, it would be interesting to consider how the continuing rise of Japan in the cultural sphere might play out in terms of children's global awareness.

## Glocalisation as Public Service

This phenomenon of "glocalisation" is not entirely new, nor are the pro-   33
cesses I am describing confined to the more obviously commercialised end of children's media. My final two examples suggest that public service media companies may also be engaging in similar attempts to reach the global market—in both cases, of pre-school children.

The US series *Sesame Street* is now more than 35 years old. Produced   34
by a not-for-profit company, and screened in the US on public television, its success and survival have crucially depended on global marketing. Just as with Pokémon, there are global Sesame Street franchises, and an enormous range of spin-off merchandise—although because of its educational cachet, these tend to be the kinds of products middle-class parents are less likely to object to.

Interestingly, *Sesame Street* was also the subject of a forceful ideologi-   35
cal critique from Armand Mattelart, the co-author of *Reading Donald Duck* (Mattelart and Waksman, 1978). He saw *Sesame Street*, like Disney, as the bearer of a set of US ideological values, and as part of a broader cultural imperialism. Just as Disney's appeal to childhood allowed it to profess an essential innocence, he argued, so the educational intentions of *Sesame Street* served as a kind of alibi. According to Mattelart, the programme was actually putting across a specific set of social values and capitalist ideologies that children were assumed to simply swallow whole. Perhaps surprisingly, this argument was also made in the UK as well, albeit in slightly different terms. There was a great controversy in the late 1960s when the BBC refused to buy *Sesame Street*, not so much on ideological grounds as on the basis of its style of pedagogy. The use of what were seen as "advertising techniques" for drilling children in letter and number recognition was seen as somehow at odds with the more child-centred, play-oriented British tradition of pre-school education (see Buckingham et al., 1999).

In fact, however, *Sesame Street* has frequently worked with local pro-   36
ducers around the world to insert local content. Alongside Big Bird and Elmo and Kermit, the programmes typically include locally-produced documentary inserts that feature children in the country where the programme is screened. There has also been some research looking at how,

for example, *Sesame Street* in Israel incorporated material about Israeli and Palestinian children, and the consequences of this in terms of their attitudes towards each other (Fisch, 2001).

Ironically, in recent years the BBC has been engaged in a very similar ₃₇ enterprise. Its ground-breaking pre-school series of the late 1990s, *Teletubbies*, was clearly produced with a global audience in mind; and indeed, it has become increasingly imperative for the BBC to earn revenue from overseas sales, even though it is primarily funded by compulsory taxation (the license fee). An investment on the scale of *Teletubbies* would not have been possible without assured overseas revenue, not just from programme sales but also from ancillary merchandising—and, as with the other texts I have discussed, the scale and diversity of the merchandising is quite phenomenal (Buckingham, 2002).

Like *Sesame Street*, *Teletubbies* also offers the facility for local broad- ₃₈ casters to insert local content. For example, despite resistance on the part of the Norwegian public broadcasters to buying it (on grounds that were not dissimilar to the BBC's concerns about *Sesame Street*), the programme is now screened in Norway, and includes not just Norwegian voice-overs and dubbing but also documentary material featuring Norwegian children. Again, this could be seen as an example of glocalisation, a productive meeting of the global and the local. Nevertheless, there are questions to be raised about what is and is not culturally specific here. It may be that cultural specificity is not simply a matter of content, but also of form—or in educational terms, it is not just about the curriculum of the programme, but also about its pedagogy. *Teletubbies* has a very different style of pedagogy compared with *Sesame Street*; and while I would hesitate to label one essentially British and the other essentially "American," there clearly are cultural differences here that would be worth investigating more closely.

## Conclusion: Harry Potter Goes Global

The forms that this "glocalisation" takes—and its consequences for chil- ₃₉ dren's sense of cultural identity—are therefore diverse and variable. The notion of cultural imperialism does to some extent describe what is taking place here, at least at an economic level; but it fails to account for the diversity and complexity of how children use and interpret cultural texts. On the other hand, there are reasons to be cautious about the postmodern emphasis on hybridity and fragmentation: access to global markets is not equally open to all, and consumers are clearly not free to choose their cultural identities from an infinite range of global possibilities.

Yet the global marketing of children's culture constantly throws up ₄₀ new paradoxes. The current worldwide success of Harry Potter is a striking case in point. Harry Potter seems to me at least to be highly culturally specific. It is distinctly British, indeed essentially English: it draws on a middle-class British tradition of school stories, although it could also be seen to reflect some rather more contemporary concerns and anxieties in British culture (Blake, 2002). Nevertheless, it clearly has global appeal: like the other phenomena I have discussed, it is effectively a global brand, which is used to sell a whole range of media and merchandise—books, films, computer games, posters, toys, clothing, gifts, and paraphernalia of all kinds—to children around the world.

The reasons for this remain to be established. How, for example, do we   41 explain the success of Harry Potter in China? What is it that Chinese children, whose lives are very different in many ways from those of children in Britain, seem to recognise in Harry Potter? Does this point to the existence of some kind of universal, global childhood—or is it that these texts are interpreted in such different ways in different cultures that they effectively become very different things? Does Harry Potter, for all the apparently old-fashioned nature of the story, somehow represent *a modernist* conception of childhood, which transcends cultural differences?

And so I conclude with a series of questions. Is Kenichi Ohmae cor-   42 rect: Is global marketing really creating a common culture of childhood? Is it helping children to communicate across cultural differences—or is it simply eradicating those differences? And even if it is, is that something we should necessarily regret?

## NOTE

1. To some extent, the reverse is also true, but there is also a strong aspirational element at work here: children frequently aspire to consume things that seem on the face of it to be targeted at a somewhat older audience. This is particularly an issue for children in the immediate pre-teen age group, for whom the category of the "teenager" is seen to embody a degree of freedom from adult constraints (de Block, 2000).

## REFERENCES

Allison, A. (2000) A challenge to Hollywood: Japanese character goods hit the US, *Japanese Studies*, 20(1), 67–88.

Barker, M. (1990) *Comics: Ideology, Power, and the Critics*, Manchester: Manchester University Press.

Bennett, A. (2000) *Popular Music and Youth Culture*, London: Palgrave Macmillan.

Blake (2002) *The Irresistible Rise of Harry Potter: Kid-Lit in a Globalised World*, London: Verso.

Buckingham, D. (2000) *After the Death of Childhood: Growing Up in the Age of Electronic Media*, Cambridge: Polity.

Buckingham, D. (2001) Disney dialectics: Debating the politics of children's media culture, in J. Wasko, M. Phillips, and E. Meehan (eds) *Dazzled by Disney*, London: Leicester University Press, 269–96.

Buckingham, D. (2002) Child-centred television? *Teletubbies* and the educational imperative, in D. Buckingham (ed.) *Small Screens: Television for Children*, London: Leicester University Press.

Buckingham, D. (2004) *Young People and Media*, Briefing paper for the United Nations Workshop on Global Media-Driven Youth Culture, New York.

Buckingham, D., and Sefton-Green, J. (2004) Gotta catch 'em all: Structure, agency, and pedagogy in children's media culture, in J. Tobin (ed.) *Pikachu's Global Adventure: The Rise and Fall of Pokémon*, Durham, NC: Duke University Press, 12–33.

Buckingham, D., Davies, H., Jones, K., and Kelley, P. (1999) *Children's Television In Britain: History, Discourse, and Policy*, London: British Film Institute.

Burton-Carvajal, J. (1994) "Surprise package": Looking southward with Disney, in E. Smoodin (ed.) *Disney Discourse: Producing the Magic Kingdom*, New York: Routledge, 131–47.

Cartright, L., and Goldfarb, B. (1994) Cultural contagion: On Disney's health education films for Latin America, in E. Smoodin (ed.) *Disney Discourse: Producing the Magic Kingdom*, New York: Routledge, 169–80.

Cohen, P. (1997) *Rethinking the Youth Question*, London: Macmillan.

Cowen, T. (2002) *Creative Destruction: How Globalisation Is Changing the World's Cultures*, Princeton, NJ: Princeton University Press.

de Block, L. (1998) From childhood pleasures to adult identities, *English and Media Magazine*, 38, 24–29.

Dorfman, A., and Mattelart, A. (1975) *How to Read Donald Duck: Imperialist Ideology in the Disney Comics*, New York: International General.

Drotner, K. (2001) "Donald Seems So Danish": Disney and the formation of cultural identity, in J. Wasko, M. Phillips, and E. Meehan (eds) *Dazzled by Disney*, London: Leicester University Press, 102–20.

Feld, S., and Keil, C. (1992) *Music Grooves*, Chicago, IL: University of Chicago.

Featherstone, M. (1995) *Undoing Culture*, London: Sage.

Fisch, S. (2001) *G Is for Growing: Thirty Years of Research on Children and Sesame Street*, Mahwah, NJ: Erlbaum.

Forgacs, D. (1992) Disney animation and the business of childhood, *Screen*, 33(4), 361–74.

Gillespie, M. (1995) *Television, Ethnicity, and Cultural Change*, London: Routledge.

Giroux, H. (2001) *The Mouse that Roared: Disney and the End of Innocence*, New York: Rowman and Littlefield.

Griffiths, M. (2002) Pink worlds and blue worlds: A portrait of infinite polarity, in D. Buckingham (ed.) *Small Screens: Television for Children*, London: Leicester University Press.

Hannerz, U. (1996) *Transnational Connections: People, Culture, Places*, London: Routledge.

Hendershot, H. (2004) *Nickelodeon Nation: The History, Politics, and Economics of America's Only TV Channel for Kids*, New York: New York University Press.

Iwabushi, K. (2004) How "Japanese" is Pokémon?, in J. Tobin (ed.) *Pikachu's Global Adventure: The Rise and Fall of Pokémon*, Durham, NC: Duke University Press, 53–79.

James, A., Jenks, C., and Prout, A. (1998) *Theorizing Childhood*, Cambridge: Polity.

Katsuno, H., and Maret, J. (2004) Localizing the Pokémon TV series for the US market, in J. Tobin (ed.) *Pikachu's Global Adventure: The Rise and Fall of Pokémon*, Durham, NC: Duke University Press, 80–107.

Kline, S. (1993) *Out of the Garden: Toys and Children's Culture in the Age of TV Marketing*, London: Verso.

Leshkowich, A., and Jones, C. (2003) What happens when Asian chic becomes chic in Asia?, *Fashion Theory*, 7(3–4), 281–99.

Liebes, T., and Katz, E. (1990) *The Export of Meaning*, Oxford: Oxford University Press.

Livingstone, S. (1998) Mediated childhoods: A comparative approach to young people's changing media environment in Europe, *European Journal of Communication*, 13(4), 435–56.

Livingstone, S. (2002) *Young People and New Media*, London: Sage.

Lustyik, K. (2003) *The Transformation of Children's Television from Communism to Global Capitalism in Hungary*, Boulder, CO: University of Colorado.

McGray, D. (2002) Japan's gross national cool, *Foreign Policy*, May–June.

McQuillan, M, and Byme, E. (1999) *Deconstructing Disney*, London: Pluto.

Mattelart, A., and Waksman, D. (1978) *Plaza Sezamo* and an alibi for the author's real intentions, *Screen Education*, 27, 56–62.

McChesney, R. (2002) Media globalisation: Consequences for the rights of children, in C. von Feilitzen and U. Carlsson (eds) *Children, Young People, and Media Globalisation*, Goteborg, Sweden: UNESCO International Clearinghouse on Children, Youth, and Media, 33–42.

Ohmae, K. (1995) *The End of the Nation State*, New York: HarperCollins.

Piedra, J. (1994) Pato Donald's gender ducking, in E. Smoodin (ed.) *Disney Discourse: Producing the Magic Kingdom*, New York: Routledge, 148–68.

Punch, S. (2003) Childhoods in the majority world: Miniature adults or tribal children?, *Sociology*, 37(2), 277–95.

Robertson, R. (1994) Globalisation or glocalisation?, *Journal of International Communication*, 1(1), 33–52.

Roth, M. (1996) A short history of Disney fascism, *Jump Cut*, 40, 15–20.

Schneider, C. (1992) *Children's Television*, New York: Contemporary Books.

Silj, A. (1988) *East of Dallas: The European Challenge to American Television*, London: British Film Institute.

Singer, D., and Singer, J. (2002) *Handbook of Children and the Media*, New York: Sage.

Smoodin, E. (ed.) (1994) *Disney Discourse: Producing the Magic Kingdom*, New York: Routledge.

Tobin, J. (ed.) (2004) *Pikachu's Global Adventure: The Rise and Fall of Pokémon*, Durham, NC: Duke University Press.

Tomlinson, J. (1991) *Cultural Imperialism*, Baltimore, MD: Johns Hopkins University Press.

Tunstall, J. (1977) *The Media Are American*, London: Constable.

van Evra, J. (2004) *Television and Child Development*, Mahwah, NJ: Erlbaum.

von Feilitzen, C. and Carlsson, U. (eds) (2002) *Children, Young People, and Media Globalisation*, Goteborg, Sweden: UNESCO International Clearinghouse on Children, Youth, and Media.

Wagnleitner, R. (1994) *Coca-colonisation and the Cold War: The Cultural Mission of the US in Austria After the Second World War*, Chapel Hill, NC: Duke University Press.

Wasko, J., Phillips, M., and Meehan, E. (eds) (2001) *Dazzled by Disney*, London: Leicester University Press.

Westcott, T. (2002) Globalisation of children's TV and the strategies of the "big three," in C. von Feilitzen and U. Carlsson (eds) *Children, Young People, and Media Globalisation*, Goteborg, Sweden: UNESCO International Clearinghouse on Children, Youth, and Media, 69–76.

Yano, C. (2004) Kitty litter: Japanese cute at home and abroad, in J. Goldstein, D. Buckingham, and G. Brougere (eds) *Toys, Games, and Media*, Mahwah, NJ: Erlbaum.

■ ■ ■

## Reading as a Writer: Analyzing Rhetorical Choices

1. Buckingham contextualizes his arguments thoroughly in the research of others. Use a distinctive color of ink to mark the sentences where Buckingham quotes other scholars. Once you have done this, look back over his essay and see what you notice about where and how Buckingham uses other scholars' ideas to develop his own argument. What conclusions can you draw about using other writers' ideas in your own writing?

2. Buckingham refers to "glocalization" throughout his essay. Look up several definitions of this term, and mark all the references to this concept in Buckingham's essay. Discuss the ways he uses this term to develop his own argument about the potential positives and negatives of the marketing of children's media.

Writing as a Reader: Entering the Conversation of Ideas

1. Buckingham and Eric Schlosser examine the significance of the ways marketers reach children. Write an essay in which you place these writers in conversation in order to discover the patterns and tactics these authors observe in marketing to children. What significance do they—and you—find? What kind of citizens are these children being trained to become, and what do you think of this development?

2. Both Buckingham and Elizabeth Teare use the marketing of Harry Potter books and merchandise as a key example in larger arguments about the values being sold to children. Place these authors' ideas about this marketing in conversation with each other and with your own ideas about the values the Harry Potter franchise "sells," in order to make an argument about the strengths and weaknesses you see in this global marketing phenomenon.

# 15

# International Relations
*Who are "we" in relation to "others"?*

The readings in this chapter confront the enormous and challenging question of who "we" are in relation to "others" in what one of the writers
in this chapter, Thomas Friedman, calls the rapidly "flattening" world. It
is often hard to get our minds around the complex economic and political
issues in this age of multiculturalism and globalization. Although most of
us see and hear plenty of media sound bites on these topics, it is not always

easy to understand how they affect us personally. Through their concrete, sometimes shocking, and often quite funny examples, the authors in this chapter demonstrate how thoroughly our daily lives are shaped by international dynamics.

For example, Barbara Ehrenreich suggests that when local stories for a Pasadena, California, newspaper are being outsourced to reporters in India, we may want to think about how well-prepared Americans are for the global marketplace. Thomas Friedman similarly puts a face on outsourcing—or many faces, really, in his interviews with the workers of these outsourced jobs who answer phone calls from American customers or do Americans' taxes from the other side of the world. Is this a problem, an opportunity, or both—and for whom? Fareed Zakaria helps us further understand where "we" are in this global economy by showing the historical context of global power shifts and by proposing that we consider what seems to be a post-American economy as an opportunity for "the rise of the rest."

In his essay about the rise of soccer's popularity in the United States, Franklin Foer uses a different lens for examining the ways our daily experiences are shaped by larger forces. Foer's essay brings to light some of the internal divisions in American identity, or what he calls "the American culture wars." Michael Kimmel looks at the darker side of globalism and nationalism in his essay "Gender, Class, and Terrorism," which asks us to consider a tragedy like 9/11 alongside the 1995 bombing of the Alfred P. Murrah Federal Building in Oklahoma City. In the context of popular media that often pit "us" against "them," Kimmel asks us to look at the many parallels between people who feel disenfranchised in their own countries and those who feel adrift in our rapidly shrinking global environment. What inspires so much fear in today's world? And why do so many respond with violence?

Kwame Anthony Appiah uses philosophical insights to help us think about ourselves as "cosmopolitan" citizens of the world, but he also points out many reasons that we struggle to achieve this ideal—reasons you will recognize. For example, Appiah suggests that a simple debate about whether *Million Dollar Baby* or *Sideways* is a better movie reveals a lot about relational ethics in this age of globalization, as do the foods we eat, or refuse to eat. (Americans eat pigs, for example, but refuse to eat cats. Why?) Martha Nussbaum and Cynthia Scott continue the conversation about cosmopolitan, national, and local identities by focusing on what happens in the classroom—and what should happen—as we shape the next generation of global citizens. In the chapter's final reading, an excerpt from Marjane Satrapi's graphic novel *Persepolis*, we are reminded through arresting images and text just how much is at stake when we teach young people to see themselves and "others" through oppositional lenses. Who are you—and who are we—in today's world? Your answers will be woven in among the voices in this chapter.

BARBARA EHRENREICH

# Your Local News — Dateline Delhi

Barbara Ehrenreich is one of the best-known journalists publishing social commentary in the United States today. She earned a PhD in cell biology but has a voracious appetite for learning and writing about topics far beyond science. She has published and lectured on the state of health care, the history of women as healers, the anxieties of the middle class, women's participation in the torture at Abu Ghraib, and the history of dancing, to name just a few of the topics she has addressed. In addition to the many books she has written, cowritten, and edited, she writes prolifically for newspapers and magazines, including the *New York Times Magazine*, the *Washington Post Magazine*, *The Atlantic*, *The Nation*, and *The New Republic*. She also has an active news analysis blog, *Barbara's Blog: Barbara Ehrenreich Comments About Working in America*, from which this piece was taken. You can read her blog at http://ehrenreich.blogs.com/barbaras_blog/.

In this piece, Ehrenreich offers her personal and professional insights into outsourcing, starting with a news item about a newspaper in Pasadena, California, that has begun outsourcing the writing of even its most local stories. She notes with wry humor that if reporters in India need to write about potholes in Pasadena's pavement, "there's always Google Earth." She then widens the frame of her focus to show the historical trends in outsourcing, pointing to a series of turning points when outsourcing pushed a wider and wider range of jobs out of the United States. Where, she wonders, will this trend stop?

As you read, pay attention to the ways Ehrenreich connects specific examples of outsourcing to the larger thread of her piece. What do you think she is arguing, ultimately? What does outsourcing have to do with international relations, the focus of this chapter? Where and how does she use rhetorical questions and humor to draw her readers into a subject that is sobering, if not frightening, to many?

In the precarious economy of the United States today, most of us have experienced outsourcing or know someone who has either lost or gained work because of outsourcing trends. Keep your own experiences and knowledge in mind as you read Ehrenreich's perspective. How would you enter this conversation?

The world may be flat, as *New York Times* columnist Thomas Friedman has written, but I always liked to think I was standing on a bit of a hill. Now comes the news that pasadenanow.com, a local news site, is recruiting reporters in India. The Web site's editor points out that he can get two Indian reporters for a mere $20,800 a year—and no, they won't be commuting from New Delhi. Since Pasadena's city council meetings can be observed on the Web, the Indian reporters will be able to cover local poli-

tics from half the planet away. And if they ever feel a need to see the potholes of Pasadena, there's always Google Earth.

Excuse me, but isn't this more or less what former *New York Times*  2
reporter Jayson Blair was fired for—pretending to report from sites around
the country while he was actually holed up in his Brooklyn apartment? Or
will pasadenanow.com be honest enough to give its new reporters datelines
in Delhi (or wherever they live)?

I should have seen it coming. In the eighties, US companies began out-  3
sourcing the manufacturing of everything from garments to steel, leaving
whole cities to die. Education was the recommended solution for the unemployed because in the globalized future Americans would be the world's
brains while Mexicans and Malaysians would provide the hands.

So no one really complained when the back office and call center jobs  4
migrated to India in the nineties: Who needed them? We would still be the
brains of global business. When the IT jobs started drifting away, we were
at first assured that only the more "routine" ones were outsourceable. As
for all the laid-off techies, they were smart enough to develop new skills,
right?

But no one can pretend any longer that we have a global monopoly on  5
intellect and innovation. Look at the "telemedicine" trend, which has radiologists in India and Lebanon reading CT scans for hospitals in Altoona
and Chicago. Or—and this was never supposed to happen—the growing
outsourcing of R & D, with scores of companies opening labs in India or
China—"Chindia," as they are known in the biz lit. A Microsoft manager
told the *Financial Times* that "the question is how you make [the Chinese]
truly creative, truly innovative." Whoops—weren't we supposed to be the
innovators?

Still, writing was believed to be safe, the last stronghold of Western  6
creativity. Explaining the outsourcing of almost every newspaper function, including copyediting, the billionaire CEO of a consortium of Irish
newspapers wrote: "With the exception of the magic of writing and editing news . . . almost every other function, except printing, is location-
indifferent." But the magic has clearly been fading, starting three years ago
when Reuters began outsourcing its Wall Street coverage to Bangalore. Is
there nothing an actual, on-site American can do better than anyone else?

In the Pasadena case, I can't even complain, as US-based Reuters  7
workers did when their jobs were outsourced, that the quality of journalism will suffer as a result. One of the Indian reporters just hired by
pasadenanow.com has a degree from the Graduate School of Journalism at
UC Berkeley, which is one of the three or four best j-schools in the country.
I have taught there myself and know that the students are scarily smart.
Too bad that these reporters couldn't get real on-site journalism jobs, at
normal American wages, but American newspapers are axing good journalists even as I write.

No, I don't resent the Indians for moving in on the kind of work I do. I  8
just hope the next time some managers get the idea of cost saving through

outsourcing they go for the CEO's job. That's where the big bucks are, and there's no reason to think a Chinese or Indian person couldn't do a CEO's work, whatever it may be, perfectly adequately, and at less than a tenth of the price. As for me, I'm retraining as a massage therapist, at least until they figure out how to do that from Mumbai.

■ ■ ■

### Reading as a Writer: Analyzing Rhetorical Choices

1.  Ehrenreich seems to assume that her readers have come across the concept of outsourcing before; how well can you explain this practice in your own words? Based on this piece, what do you think it means? Look up the term *outsourcing* at a few trustworthy sites and discuss what you find with your peers. How do these further definitions enhance your understanding of Ehrenreich's piece?

2.  This article appeared on Ehrenreich's blog, but she has shaped it as carefully as a more formal essay. Do a "reverse outline" of this piece, noting briefly in the margins how each paragraph contributes to the larger point she is making. What do you notice about the way it is structured? What organizational strategies might you wish to try in your own writing?

### Writing as a Reader: Entering the Conversation of Ideas

1.  In her opening sentence, Ehrenreich refers to Thomas Friedman's concept of the world as "flat." Write an essay that takes this conversation further, reflecting on what each writer would say about some of the specific examples the other uses, and the interpretation each author might make of the other's argument. Where do these writers' ideas converge and diverge? What do these similarities and differences suggest to you about the conversation about globalization and work?

2.  Ehrenreich's ideas about the outsourcing of American news media are interesting to consider in light of David Buckingham's discussion of "glocalization," or the way globalization adapts to local contexts. Compose an essay in which you analyze these authors' ideas about the potential positive and negative effects of globalization on media, focusing especially on the implications of outsourcing local news coverage. You might find out how many of your local newspaper's stories are locally written and then analyze this information as you make your argument.

### FAREED ZAKARIA

## The Rise of the Rest

Fareed Zakaria has a PhD in political science from Harvard and has been the editor of *Newsweek International* since 2000. He is well known for the political columns he writes for *Newsweek* and the *Washington Post*, and he is a frequent guest on political analysis television shows. His many awards for columns and leading essays include his October 2001 *Newsweek* cover story, "Why They Hate Us." In addition to his columns, he has written several best-selling books, including *The Future of Freedom* (2003) and *The Post-American World* (2008), from which this reading is taken. Included here is the first chapter, "The Rise of the Rest," and two sections from the second chapter, "The Rise of Nationalism" and "The Last Superpower."

In Zakaria's opening line, you can hear that he is interested in helping us see the world in a new way: "This is a book not about the decline of America but rather about the rise of everyone else." In the paragraphs that follow, Zakaria lists at length various kinds of evidence that we are on the cusp of the third great "tectonic power shift" of the last 500 years. As he describes these three power shifts, test your own knowledge of history against his claims, and see what comes into focus for you in this description.

Zakaria's general approach is to look back in *history* to see how we arrived at this globalizing moment, to examine the *present* through myriad examples and data, and to begin to consider the globalized *future* with "the rise of the rest." As you read, pay particular attention to how and where he makes these moves backward and forward in time, to see how Zakaria uses this historical contextualization to make his argument. Which examples do you find most compelling, and why?

Like many of the authors in this book, Zakaria hopes to reveal aspects of contemporary life that we might miss if we fail to understand certain contexts or to make particular connections. He does not have a crystal ball to reveal the future, but he argues that if we look carefully at the evidence around us, we will see that the United States has to make some changes in order to have a place in the new world order. Will the United States be willing to "globalize itself"? Zakaria provides evidence that should help us ponder possible answers to a very big question that will affect all our lives.

■  ■  ■

This is a book not about the decline of America but rather about the 1 rise of everyone else. It is about the great transformation taking place around the world, a transformation that, though often discussed, remains poorly understood. This is natural. Changes, even sea changes, take place gradually. Though we talk about a new era, the world seems to be one with which we are familiar. But in fact, it is very different.

There have been three tectonic power shifts over the last five hundred 2 years, fundamental changes in the distribution of power that have reshaped international life — its politics, economics, and culture. The first was the rise of the Western world, a process that began in the fifteenth century and accelerated dramatically in the late eighteenth century. It produced modernity as we know it: science and technology, commerce and capitalism, the agricultural and industrial revolutions. It also produced the prolonged political dominance of the nations of the West.

The second shift, which took place in the closing years of the nine-  3
teenth century, was the rise of the United States. Soon after it industrialized, the United States became the most powerful nation since imperial
Rome, and the only one that was stronger than any likely combination of
other nations. For most of the last century, the United States has dominated global economics, politics, science, and culture. For the last twenty
years, that dominance has been unrivaled, a phenomenon unprecedented
in modern history.

We are now living through the third great power shift of the modern  4
era. It could be called "the rise of the rest." Over the past few decades,
countries all over the world have been experiencing rates of economic
growth that were once unthinkable. While they have had booms and busts,
the overall trend has been unambiguously upward. This growth has been
most visible in Asia but is no longer confined to it. That is why to call this
shift "the rise of Asia" does not describe it accurately. In 2006 and 2007,
124 countries grew at a rate of 4 percent or more. That includes more than
30 countries in Africa, two-thirds of the continent. Antoine van Agtmael,
the fund manager who coined the term "emerging markets," has identified
the 25 companies most likely to be the world's next great multinationals.
His list includes four companies each from Brazil, Mexico, South Korea,
and Taiwan; three from India; two from China; and one each from Argentina, Chile, Malaysia, and South Africa.

Look around. The tallest building in the world is now in Taipei, and  5
it will soon be overtaken by one being built in Dubai. The world's richest man is Mexican, and its largest publicly traded corporation is Chinese. The world's biggest plane is built in Russia and Ukraine, its leading
refinery is under construction in India, and its largest factories are all in
China. By many measures, London is becoming the leading financial center, and the United Arab Emirates is home to the most richly endowed
investment fund. Once quintessentially American icons have been appropriated by foreigners. The world's largest Ferris wheel is in Singapore. Its
number one casino is not in Las Vegas but in Macao, which has also overtaken Vegas in annual gambling revenues. The biggest movie industry, in
terms of both movies made and tickets sold, is Bollywood, not Hollywood.
Even shopping, America's greatest sporting activity, has gone global.
Of the top ten malls in the world, only one is in the United States; the
world's biggest is in Beijing. Such lists are arbitrary, but it is striking that
only ten years ago, America was at the top in many, if not most, of these
categories.

It might seem strange to focus on growing prosperity when there are  6
still hundreds of millions of people living in desperate poverty. But in fact,
the share of people living on a dollar a day or less plummeted from 40 percent in 1981 to 18 percent in 2004, and is estimated to fall to 12 percent by
2015. China's growth alone has lifted more than 400 million people out
of poverty. Poverty is falling in countries housing 80 percent of the world's
population. The 50 countries where the earth's poorest people live are
basket cases that need urgent attention. In the other 142—which include

China, India, Brazil, Russia, Indonesia, Turkey, Kenya, and South Africa—
the poor are slowly being absorbed into productive and growing economies. For the first time ever, we are witnessing genuinely global growth.
This is creating an international system in which countries in all parts of
the world are no longer objects or observers but players in their own right.
It is the birth of a truly global order.

A related aspect of this new era is the diffusion of power from states  7
to other actors. The "rest" that is rising includes many nonstate actors.
Groups and individuals have been empowered, and hierarchy, centraliza-
tion, and control are being undermined. Functions that were once controlled by governments are now shared with international bodies like the
World Trade Organization and the European Union. Nongovernmental
groups are mushrooming every day on every issue country. Corporations
and capital are moving from place to place, finding the best location in
which to do business, rewarding some governments while punishing others. Terrorists like Al Qaeda, drug cartels, insurgents, and militias of all
kinds are finding space to operate within the nooks and crannies of the
international system. Power is shifting away from nation-states, up, down,
and sideways. In such an atmosphere, the traditional applications of
national power, both economic and military, have become less effective.

The emerging international system is likely to be quite different from  8
those that have preceded it. One hundred years ago, there was a multipolar
order run by a collection of European governments, with constantly shifting alliances, rivalries, miscalculations, and wars. Then came the bipolar
duopoly of the Cold War, more stable in many ways, but with the superpowers reacting and overreacting to each other's every move. Since 1991,
we have lived under an American imperium, a unique, unipolar world in
which the open global economy has expanded and accelerated dramatically. This expansion is now driving the next change in the nature of the
international order.

At the politico-military level, we remain in a single-superpower world.  9
But in every other dimension—industrial, financial, educational, social, cultural—the distribution of power is shifting, moving away from American
dominance. That does not mean we are entering an anti-American world.
But we are moving into a *post-American world*, one defined and directed
from many places and by many people.

What kinds of opportunities and challenges do these changes pre-  10
sent? What do they portend for the United States and its dominant position?
What will this new era look like in terms of war and peace, economics and
business, ideas and culture?

In short, what will it mean to live in a post-American world? . . .  11

## The Rise of Nationalism

In a globalized world, almost all problems spill over borders. Whether  12
it's terrorism, nuclear proliferation, disease, environmental degradation,

economic crisis, or water scarcity, no issue can be addressed without significant coordination and cooperation among many countries. But while economics, information, and even culture might have become globalized, formal political power remains firmly tethered to the nation-state, even as the nation-state has become less able to solve most of these problems unilaterally. And increasingly, nation-states are becoming less willing to come together to solve common problems. As the number of players—governmental and nongovernmental—increases and each one's power and confidence grows, the prospects for agreement and common action diminish. This is the central challenge of the rise of the rest—to stop the forces of global growth from turning into the forces of global disorder and disintegration.

The rise of pride and confidence among other nations, particularly the *13* largest and most successful ones, is readily apparent. For me, it was vividly illustrated a few years ago in an Internet café in Shanghai, where I was chatting with a young Chinese executive. He was describing the extraordinary growth that was taking place in his country and a future in which China would be modern and prosperous. He was thoroughly Westernized in dress and demeanor, spoke excellent English, and could comfortably discuss the latest business trends or gossip about American pop culture. He seemed the consummate product of globalization, the person who bridges cultures and makes the world a smaller, more cosmopolitan place. But when we began talking about Taiwan, Japan, and the United States, his responses were filled with bile. He explained in furious tones that were Taiwan to dare to declare independence, China should instantly invade it. He said that Japan was an aggressor nation that could never be trusted. He was sure that the United States deliberately bombed the Chinese embassy during the Kosovo war in 1999, to terrify the Chinese people with its military might. And so on. I felt as if I were in Berlin in 1910, speaking to a young German professional, who in those days would have also been both thoroughly modern and thoroughly nationalist.

As economic fortunes rise, so does nationalism. This is understand- *14* able. Imagine that you lived in a country that had been poor and unstable for centuries. And then, finally, things turn and your nation is on the rise. You would be proud and anxious to be seen. This desire for recognition and respect is surging throughout the world. It may seem paradoxical that globalization and economic modernization are breeding political nationalism, but that is so only if we view nationalism as a backward ideology, certain to be erased by the onward march of progress.

Nationalism has always perplexed Americans. When the United States *15* involves itself abroad, it always believes that it is genuinely trying to help other countries better themselves. From the Philippines and Haiti to Vietnam and Iraq, the natives' reaction to U.S. efforts has taken Americans by surprise. Americans take justified pride in their own country—we call it patriotism—and yet are genuinely startled when other people are proud and possessive of theirs.

In the waning days of Britain's rule in India, its last viceroy, Lord Louis 16
Mountbatten, turned to the great Indian leader Mahatma Gandhi and said
in exasperation, "If we just leave, there will be chaos." Gandhi replied, "Yes,
but it will be *our* chaos." That sense of being governed by one's "own," without interference, is a powerful feeling in emerging countries, especially
those that were once colonies or quasi-colonies of the West.

Zbigniew Brzezinski recently called attention to what he terms a "global 17
political awakening." He pointed to rising mass passions, fueled by various forces—economic success, national pride, higher levels of education,
greater information and transparency, and memories of the past. Brzezinski noted the disruptive aspects of this new force. "The population of much
of the developing world is politically stirring and in many places seething
with unrest," he wrote. "It is acutely conscious of social injustice to an
unprecedented degree . . . [and this] is creating a community of shared
perceptions and envy that can be galvanized and channeled by demagogic
political or religious passions. These energies transcend sovereign borders
and pose a challenge both to existing states as well as to the existing global
hierarchy, on top of which America still perches."[1]

In many countries outside the Western world, there is pent-up frus- 18
tration with having had to accept an entirely Western or American narrative of world history—one in which they either are miscast or remain
bit players. Russians have long chafed at the standard narrative about
World War II, in which Britain and the United States heroically defeat
the forces of fascist Germany and Japan. Given mainstream U.S. historical accounts, from Stephen Ambrose to Ken Burns, Americans could
be forgiven for believing that Russia played a minor part in the decisive
battles against Hitler and Tojo. In fact, the eastern front was the central
arena of World War II. It involved more land combat than all other theaters of the war put together and resulted in thirty million deaths. It was
where three-quarters of all German forces fought and where Germany
incurred 70 percent of its casualties. The European front was in many
ways a sideshow, but in the West it is treated as the main event. As the
writer Benjamin Schwarz has pointed out, Stephen Ambrose "lavishes
[attention] on the U.S.-British invasion of Sicily, which drove 60,000 Germans from the island, but completely ignores Kursk—the largest battle
in history, in which at least 1.5 million Soviets and Germans fought, and
which occurred at exactly the same time. . . . [M]uch as it may make us
squirm, we must admit that the struggle against Nazi Germany . . . was
primarily, as the great military historian John Erickson called it, 'Stalin's
war.'"[2]

Or consider the perspective on the same war from another spot on the 19
map. An Indian friend explained to me, "For Britain and America, World
War II is a heroic struggle in which freedom triumphs over evil. For us, it
was a battle to which Britain committed India and its armed forces without bothering to consult us. London told us to die for an idea of freedom
that it was at that very moment brutally denying to us."

Such divergent national perspectives have always existed, but today, *20* thanks to greater education, information, and confidence, they are widely disseminated on new news networks, cable channels, and Internet sites of the emerging world. Many of the "rest" are dissecting the narratives, arguments, and assumptions of the West and countering them with a different view of the world. "When you tell us that we support a dictatorship in Sudan to have access to its oil," a young Chinese official told me in 2006, "what I want to say is, 'And how is that different from your support for a medieval monarchy in Saudi Arabia?' We see the hypocrisy, we just don't say anything, yet."

After the Cold War ended, there was a general hope and expectation *21* that China and Russia would move inexorably into the post–World War II Western political and economic system. When George H. W. Bush spoke of "a new world order," he meant simply that the old Western one would be extended worldwide. Perhaps this view stemmed from the postwar experience with Japan and Germany, both of which rose to the heights of economic power and yet were accommodating, cooperative, and largely silent members of the existing order. But perhaps those were special circumstances. The two countries had unique histories, having waged aggressive wars and become pariahs as a consequence, and they faced a new threat from Soviet communism and relied on American military power for their protection. The next round of rising powers might not be so eager to "fit in."

We still think of a world in which a rising power must choose between *22* two stark options: integrate into the Western order, or reject it, becoming a rogue nation and facing the penalties of excommunication. In fact, rising powers appear to be following a third way: entering the Western order but doing so on their own terms—thus reshaping the system itself. As the political scientists Naazneen Barma, Ely Ratner, and Steven Weber point out, in a world where everyone feels empowered, countries can choose to bypass this Western "center" entirely and forge their own ties with one another.[3] In a post-American world, there may be no center to integrate into. U.S. Secretary of State James Baker suggested in 1991 that the world was moving toward a hub-and-spoke system, with every country going through the United States to get to its destination. The twenty-first-century world might be better described as one of point-to-point routes, with new flight patterns being mapped every day. (This is true even in a physical sense: in just ten years, the number of Russian visitors to China increased more than fourfold, from 489,000 in 1995 to 2.2 million in 2005.) The focus has shifted. Countries are increasingly interested in themselves—the story of their rise—and pay less attention to the West and the United States. As a result, the urgent discussions on the presidential campaign trail throughout 2007 about the need to lessen anti-Americanism are somewhat off-point. The world is moving from anger to indifference, from anti-Americanism to post-Americanism.

The fact that new powers are more strongly asserting their interests is *23* the reality of the post-American world. It also raises the political conundrum of how to achieve international objectives in a world of many actors, state and nonstate. According to the old model of getting things done, the United States and a few Western allies directed the show while the Third World either played along or stayed outside the box and remained irrelevant as a result. Nongovernmental players were too few and too weak to worry about. Now, look at something like trade negotiations, and you see the developing world acting with greater and greater force. Where they might once have taken any deal offered by the West or ignored the process altogether, countries like Brazil and India play hardball until they get the deal of their choice. They have heard Western CEOs explain [in an analysis of the economies of Brazil, Russia, India, and China] where the future lies. They have read the Goldman Sachs BRIC report. They know that the balance of power has shifted.

The Kyoto accord (now treated as sacred because of President Bush's  24 cavalier rejection of them) is in fact a treaty marked by its adherence to the old worldview. Kyoto assumed that if the West came together and settled on a plan, the Third World would adopt the new framework and the problem would be solved. That may be the way things have been done in international affairs for decades, but it makes little sense today. China, India, Brazil, and other emerging powers will not follow along with a Western-led process in which they have not participated. What's more, governments on their own can do only so much to tackle a problem like climate change. A real solution requires creating a much broader coalition that includes the private sector, nongovernmental groups, cities and localities, and the media. In a globalized, democratized, and decentralized world, we need to get to individuals to alter their behavior. Taxes, tariffs, and wars are the old ways to do this, but states now have less room to maneuver on these fronts. They need more subtle and sophisticated ways to effect change.

The traditional mechanisms of international cooperation are relics of  25 another era. The United Nations system represents an outdated configuration of power. The permanent members of the UN Security Council are the victors of a war that ended sixty years ago. The body does not include Japan or Germany, the world's second- and third-largest economies (at market exchange rates), or India, the world's largest democracy, or any Latin American or African country. The Security Council exemplifies the antique structure of global governance more broadly. The G-8 does not include China, already the world's fourth-largest economy, or India and South Korea, the twelfth and thirteenth. By tradition, the IMF is always headed by a European and the World Bank by an American. This "tradition," like the customs of an old segregated country club, may be charming and amusing to insiders, but to outsiders it is bigoted and outrageous.

A further complication: When I write of the rise of nationalism, I am  26 describing a broader phenomenon—the assertion of identity. The nation-state is a relatively new invention, often no more than a hundred years old. Much older are the religious, ethnic, and linguistic groups that live within nation-states. And these bonds have stayed strong, in fact grown, as economic interdependence has deepened. In Europe, the Flemish and French in Belgium remain as distinct as ever. In Britain, the Scots have elected a ruling party that proposes ending the three-hundred-year-old Acts of Union that created the United Kingdom of England, Scotland, and Wales. In India, national parties are losing ground to regional ones. In Kenya, tribal distinctions are becoming more important. In much of the world, these core identities—deeper than the nation-state—remain the defining features of life. It is why people vote, and what they die for. In an open world economy, these groups know that they need the central government less and less. And in a democratic age, they gain greater and greater power if they stay together as a group. This twin ascendancy of identity means that, when relating to the United States or the United Nations or the world at large, Chinese and Indian nationalism grows. But within their own countries, sub-nationalism is also growing. What is happening on the global stage—the rise of identity in the midst of economic growth—is also happening on the local stage. The bottom line: It makes purposeful national action far more difficult.

As power becomes diversified and diffuse, legitimacy becomes even 27 more important—because it is the only way to appeal to all the disparate actors on the world stage. Today, no solution, no matter how sensible, is sustainable if it is seen as illegitimate. Imposing it will not work if it is seen as the product of one country's power and preferences, no matter how powerful that country. The massacres in Darfur, for example, are horrific, and yet military intervention there—the most effective way of stopping it—would succeed only if sanctioned by the major powers as well as Sudan's African neighbors. If the United States acted alone or with a small coalition—invading its third Muslim country in five years—the attempt would almost certainly backfire, providing the Sudanese government with a fiery rallying cry against "U.S. imperialism." The Bush administration's foreign policy record offers a perfect illustration of the practical necessity of legitimacy. And yet, beyond Bush's failures, the dilemma remains: If many countries need to cooperate to get things done, how to make this happen in a world with more players, many of them more powerful?

## The Last Superpower

Many observers and commentators have looked at the vitality of this 28 emerging world and concluded that the United States has had its day. Andy Grove, the founder of Intel, puts it bluntly. "America is in danger of following Europe down the tubes," he says, "and the worst part is that nobody knows it. They're all in denial, patting themselves on the back as the *Titanic* heads straight for the iceberg full speed ahead." Thomas Friedman describes watching waves of young Indian professionals get to work for the night shift at Infosys in Bangalore. "Oh, my God, there are so many of them, and they just keep coming, wave after wave. How in the world can it possibly be good for my daughters and millions of other Americans that these Indians can do the same jobs as they can for a fraction of the wages?"[4]

"Globalization is striking back," writes Gabor Steingart, an editor at Germany's leading news magazine, *Der Spiegel*, in a bestselling book. As its rivals have prospered, he argues, the United States has lost key industries, its people have stopped saving money, and its government has become increasingly indebted to Asian central banks.[5]

What's puzzling, however, is that these trends have been around for a while—and they have actually helped America's bottom line. Our the past twenty years, as globalization and outsourcing have accelerated dramatically, America's growth rate has averaged just over 3 percent, a full percentage point higher than that of Germany and France. (Japan averaged 2.3 percent over the same period.) Productivity growth, the elixir of modern economics, has been over 2.5 percent for a decade now, again a full percentage point higher than the European average. Even American exports held up, despite a decade-long spike in the value of the dollar that ended recently. In 1980, U.S. exports represented 10 percent of the world total; in 2007, that figure was still almost 9 percent. According to the World Economic Forum, the United States remains the most competitive economy in the world and ranks first in innovation, ninth in technological readiness, second in company spending for research and technology, and second in the quality of its research institutions. China does not come within thirty countries of the United States in any of these, and India breaks the top ten on only one count: market size. In virtually every sector that advanced industrial countries participate in, U.S. firms lead the world in productivity and profits.

The United States' share of the global economy has been remarkably steady through wars, depressions, and a slew of other powers rising. With 5 percent of the world's population, the United States has generated between 20 and 30 percent of world output for 125 years. There will surely be some slippage of America's position over the next few decades. This is not a political statement but a mathematical one. As other countries grow faster, America's relative economic weight will fall. But the decline need not be large-scale, rapid, or consequential, as long as the United States can adapt to new challenges as well as it adapted to those it confronted over the last century. In the next few decades, the rise of the emerging nations is likely to come mostly at the expense of Western Europe and Japan, which are locked in a slow, demographically determined decline.

America will face the most intense economic competition it has ever faced. The American economic and social system knows how to respond and adjust to such pressures. The reforms needed are obvious but because they mean some pain now for long-term gain, the political system cannot make them. The more difficult challenge that the United States faces is international. It will confront a global order quite different from the one it is used to operating in. For now, the United States remains the most powerful player. But every year the balance shifts.

For the roughly two decades since 1989, the power of the United States has defined the international order. All roads have led to Washington, and American ideas about politics, economics, and foreign policy have been the starting points for global action. Washington has been the most powerful outside actor on every continent in the world, dominating the Western Hemisphere, remaining the crucial outside balancer in Europe and East Asia, expanding its role in the Middle East and Central and South Asia, and everywhere remaining the only country that can provide the muscle for any serious global military operation. For every country—from Russia and China to South Africa and India—its most important relationship in the world has been the relationship with the United States.

That influence reached its apogee with Iraq. Despite the reluctance, opposition, or active hostility of much of the world, the United States was able to launch an unprovoked attack on a sovereign country and to enlist dozens of countries and international agencies to assist it during and after the invasion. It is not just the complications of Iraq that have unwound this order. Even had Iraq been a glorious success, the method of its execution would have made utterly clear the unchallenged power of the United States—and it is this exercise of unipolarity that has provoked a reaction around the world. The unipolar order of the last two decades is waning not because of Iraq but because of the broader diffusion of power across the world.

On some matters, unipolarity seems already to have ended. The European Union now represents the largest trade bloc on the globe, creating bipolarity, and as China and then other emerging giants gain size, the bipolar realm of trade might become tripolar and then multipolar. In every realm except military, similar shifts are underway. In general, however, the notion of a multipolar world, with four or five players of roughly equal weight, does not describe reality today or in the near future. Europe cannot act militarily or even politically as one. Japan and Germany are hamstrung by their past. China and India are still developing. Instead, the international system is more accurately described by Samuel Huntington's term "uni-multipolarity," or what Chinese geopoliticians call "many powers and one superpower." The messy language reflects the messy reality. The United States remains by far the most powerful country but in a world with several other important great powers and with greater assertiveness and activity from all actors. This hybrid international system—more democratic, more dynamic, more open, more connected—is one we are likely to live with for several decades. It is easier to define what it is not than what it is, easier to describe the era it is moving away from than the era it is moving toward—hence *the post-American world*.

The United States occupies the top spot in the emerging system, but it is also the country that is most challenged by the new order. Most other great powers will see their role in the world expand. That process is already underway. China and India are becoming bigger players in their neighborhoods and beyond. Russia has ended its post-Soviet accommodation and is becoming more forceful, even aggressive. Japan, though not a rising power, is now more willing to voice its views and positions to its neighbors. Europe acts on matters of trade and economics with immense strength and purpose. Brazil and Mexico are becoming more vocal on Latin American issues. South Africa has positioned itself as a leader of the African continent. All these countries are taking up more space in the international arena than they did before.

For the United States, the arrow is pointing in the opposite direction. 36 Economics is not a zero-sum game—the rise of other players expands the pie, which is good for all—but geopolitics is a struggle for influence and control. As other countries become more active, America's enormous space for action will inevitably diminish. Can the United States accommodate itself to the rise of other powers, of various political stripes, on several continents? This does not mean becoming resigned to chaos or aggression; far from it. But the only way for the United States to deter rogue actions will be to create a broad, durable coalition against them. And that will be possible only if Washington can show that it is willing to allow other countries to become stakeholders in the new order. In today's international order, progress means compromise. No country will get its way entirely. These are easy words to write or say but difficult to implement. They mean accepting the growth in power and influence of other countries, the prominence of interests and concerns. This balance—between accommodation and deterrence—is the chief challenge for American foreign policy in the next few decades.

I began . . . by arguing that the new order did not herald American 37 decline, because I believe that America has enormous strengths and that the new world will not throw up a new superpower but rather a diversity of forces that Washington can navigate and even help direct. But still, as the rest of the world rises, in purely economic terms, America will experience relative decline. As others grow faster, its share of the pie will be smaller (though the shift will likely be small for many years). In addition, the new nongovernmental forces that are increasingly active will constrain Washington substantially.

This is a challenge for Washington but also for everyone else. For 38 almost three centuries, the world has been undergirded by the presence of a large liberal hegemon—first Britain, then the United States. These two superpowers helped create and maintain an open world economy, protecting trade routes and sea lanes, acting as lenders of last resort, holding the reserve currency, investing abroad, and keeping their own markets open. They also tipped the military balance against the great aggressors of their ages, from Napoleon's France, to Germany, to the Soviet Union. For all its abuses of power, the United States has been the creator and sustainer of the current order of open trade and democratic government—an order that has been benign and beneficial for the vast majority of humankind. As things change, and as America's role changes, that order could begin to fracture. The collapse of the dollar—to the point where there was no global reserve currency—would be a problem for the world just as much as for America. And solving common problems in an era of diffusion and decentralization could turn out to be far more difficult without a superpower.

Some Americans have become acutely conscious of the changing world.   *39* American business is increasingly aware of the shifts taking place around the world and is responding to them rapidly and unsentimentally. Large U.S.-based multinationals almost uniformly report that their growth now relies on penetrating new foreign markets. With annual revenue growth of 2–3 percent a year in the United States and 10–15 percent a year abroad, they know they have to adapt to a post-American world—or else lose out in it. A similar awareness is visible in America's universities, where more and more students study and travel abroad and interact with foreign students. Younger Americans live comfortably with the knowledge that the latest trends—in finance, architecture, art, technology—might originate in London, Shanghai, Seoul, Tallinn, or Mumbai.

But this outward orientation is not yet common in American society   *40* more broadly. The American economy remains internally focused, though this is changing, with trade making up 28 percent of GDP (compared with 38 percent for Germany). Insularity has been one of nature's blessings to America, bordered as it is by two vast oceans and two benign neighbors. America has not been sullied by the machinations and weariness of the Old World and has always been able to imagine a new and different order—whether in Germany, Japan, or even Iraq. But at the same time, this isolation has left Americans quite unaware of the world beyond their borders. Americans speak few languages, know little about foreign cultures, and remain unconvinced that they need to rectify this. Americans rarely benchmark to global standards because they are sure that their way must be the best and most advanced. The result is that they are increasingly suspicious of this emerging global era. There is a growing gap between America's worldly business elite and cosmopolitan class, on the one hand, and the majority of the American people, on the other. Without real efforts to bridge it, this divide could destroy America's competitive edge and its political future.

Popular suspicions are fed and encouraged by an irresponsible national   *41* political culture. In Washington, new thinking about a new world is sorely lacking. It is easy enough to criticize the Bush administration for its arrogance and unilateralism, which have handicapped America abroad. But the problem is not confined to Bush, Cheney, Rumsfeld, or the Republicans, even though they have become the party of chest-thumping machismo, proud to be despised abroad. Listen to some Democrats in Washington, and you hear a weaker unilateralism—on trade, labor standards, and various pet human rights issues. On terrorism, both parties continue to speak in language entirely designed for a domestic audience with no concern for the poisonous effect it has everywhere else. American politicians constantly and promiscuously demand, label, sanction, and condemn whole countries for myriad failings. Over the last fifteen years, the United States has placed sanctions on half the world's population. We are the only country in the world to issue annual report cards on every other country's behavior. Washington, D.C., has become a bubble, smug and out of touch with the world outside.

The 2007 Pew Global Attitudes Survey showed a remarkable increase  *42* worldwide in positive views about free trade, markets, and democracy. Large majorities in countries from China and Germany to Bangladesh and Nigeria said that growing trade ties between countries were good. Of the forty-seven countries polled, however, the one that came in dead last in terms of support for free trade was the United States. In the five years the survey has been done, no country has seen as great a drop-off as the United States.

Or take a look at the attitudes toward foreign companies. When  *43* asked whether they had a positive impact, a surprisingly large number of people in countries like Brazil, Nigeria, India, and Bangladesh said yes. Those countries have typically been suspicious of Western multinationals. (South Asia's unease has some basis; after all, it was initially colonized by a multinational corporation, the British East India Company.) And yet, 73 present in India, 75 percent in Bangladesh, 70 percent in Brazil, and 82 percent in Nigeria now have positive views of these companies. The figure for America, in contrast, is 45 percent, which places us in the bottom five. We want the world to accept American companies with open arms, but when they come here—that's a different matter. Attitudes on immigration represent an even larger reversal. On an issue where the United States has been the model for the world, the country has regressed toward an angry defensive crouch. Where we once wanted to pioneer every new technology, we now look at innovation fearfully, wondering how it will change things.

The irony is that the rise of the rest is a consequence of American ideas  *44* and actions. For sixty years, American politicians and diplomats have traveled around the world pushing countries to open their markets, free up their politics, and embrace trade technology. We have urged peoples in distant lands to take up the challenge of competing in the global economy, freeing up their currencies, and developing new industries. We counseled them to be unafraid of change and learn the secrets of our success. And it worked: The natives have gotten good at capitalism. But now we are becoming suspicious of the very things we have long celebrated—free markets, trade, immigration, and technological change. And all this is happening when the tide is going our way. Just as the world is opening up, America is closing down.

Generations from now, when historian write about these times, they  *45* might note that, in the early decades of the twenty-first century, the United States succeeded in its great and historic mission—it globalized the world. But along the way, they might write, it forgot to globalize itself.

NOTES

1. Zbigniew Brzezinski, "The Dilemma of the Last Sovereign," *American Interest* 1, no. 1 (Autumn 2005).

2. Benjamin Schwarz, review of Stephen E. Ambrose, *The Good Fight*, in *Atlantic Monthly*, June 2001, p. 103

3. Naazneen Barma et al., "The World without the West," *National Interest*, no. 90 (July/Aug. 2007): 23–30.

4. Thomas L. Friedman, *The World Is Flat: A Brief History of the Twenty-first Century* (New York: Farrar, Straus and Giroux, 2006), 226. Andy Grove's statement is quoted in Clyde Prestowitz, *Three Billion New Capitalists: The Great Shift of Wealth and Power to the East* (New York: Basic Books, 2005), 8.

5. Gabor Steingart, *The War for Wealth: Why Globalization Is Bleeding the West of Its Prosperity* (New York: McGraw-Hill, 2008).

■ ■ ■

### Reading as a Writer: Analyzing Rhetorical Choices

1. Zakaria is careful to point out that the evidence he presents "does not mean we are entering an anti-American world. But we are moving into a *post-American world*, one defined and directed from many places and by many people" (para. 9). What is the significance of phrasing his argument this way? How do his examples illustrate his definition?

2. Part of Zakaria's argumentative strategy is to situate the present in relation to the past. Which historical details that Zakaria includes are most surprising and interesting to you? How does this history relate to his larger point about where we are now and what might come next?

### Writing as a Reader: Entering the Conversation of Ideas

1. Zakaria, like many of the other writers in this chapter, is interested in analyzing the economic shifts that are coming with globalization, and not only from a U.S. perspective. Write an essay in which you link Zakaria's insights about the United States' role in a "post-American world" to ideas on this topic raised by Barbara Ehrenreich, Thomas Friedman, or Kwame Anthony Appiah. What do the writers you choose have to say about what might be next for the United States, based on the evidence they provide? What path do you think the United States should take, and why, given this evidence?

2. Both Zakaria and James W. Loewen are interested in the many effects of telling history in biased, self-interested ways. Locate specific examples in each author's text where the author raises the problem of biased history (Zakaria calls this "an entirely Western or American narrative of world history" [para. 18]) in terms of how we understand ourselves and our role in the world. Compose an essay in which you explain the significance of these examples, and the possible solutions each author proposes. Where do you stand in this debate?

## THOMAS L. FRIEDMAN

# While I Was Sleeping

Thomas L. Friedman is an award-winning journalist who has written for the *New York Times* since 1981. Over the years, he has served as bureau chief in Beirut and Israel, chief economic correspondent in the Washington bureau, and chief White House correspondent. He has won three Pulitzer Prizes for his international reporting and columns. He is also the author of many best-selling books about international relations, including the book from which this excerpt is taken, *The World Is Flat: A Brief History of the Twenty-first Century* (2005, expanded ed. 2006). Friedman's provocative title is meant to catch us by surprise. *The World Is Flat* examines the daily realities and possible long-term effects of globalization on our economy, politics, and the way we think of our place in the world. Friedman argues that if we don't pay attention to rapidly shifting trends in technology, outsourcing, and the economy, we could find the twenty-first century passing us by. The title of this reading—"While I Was Sleeping"—suggests how easily that might happen.

Friedman claims that he was "sleeping" while the world was flattening (para. 17), but he is certainly wide awake in this text. Like many well-trained journalists, he is able to grasp a complex situation and offer readers concrete examples that illustrate the many parts they must understand in order to understand the whole. This clarity, along with Friedman's careful analysis of the significance of each situation he describes, helps readers make sense of what could otherwise be an abstract—perhaps even boring—topic. Given this risk, pay attention to your responses to the anecdotes Friedman uses to open this text. What is the effect of his moving quickly from Christopher Columbus's journal to a description of playing golf in downtown Bangalore, "India's Silicon Valley" (para. 3)? How does Friedman's strategy of introducing us to individuals in each setting help us see global economic implications in more human terms?

Whether you come to his writing with a comfortable understanding of the global economy, or only vague notions about this topic, Friedman will help you understand the human face of the rapidly changing world workforce. His goal is to help us understand the exciting new opportunities created by technology, as well as the potential costs. Whose jobs, and whose lives, are at stake in Globalization 3.0? Friedman offers answers worth thinking about.

■  ■  ■

Your Highnesses, as Catholic Christians, and princes who love and promote the holy Christian faith, and are enemies of the doctrine of Mahomet, and of all idolatry and heresy, determined to send me, Christopher Columbus, to the above-mentioned countries of India, to see the said princes, people, and territories, and to learn their disposition and the proper method of converting them to our holy faith; and furthermore directed that I should not proceed by land to the East, as is customary, but by a Westerly route, in which direction we have hitherto no certain evidence that anyone has gone.

— Entry from the journal of CHRISTOPHER COLUMBUS on his voyage of 1492

No one ever gave me directions like this on a golf course before: "Aim at either Microsoft or IBM." I was standing on the first tee at the KGA Golf Club in downtown Bangalore, in southern India, when my playing partner pointed at two shiny glass-and-steel buildings off in the distance, just behind the first green. The Goldman Sachs building wasn't done yet; otherwise he could have pointed that out as well and made it a threesome. HP and Texas Instruments had their offices on the back nine, along the tenth hole. That wasn't all. The tee markers were from Epson, the printer company, and one of our caddies was wearing a hat from 3M. Outside, some of the traffic signs were also sponsored by Texas Instruments, and the Pizza Hut billboard on the way over showed a steaming pizza, under the headline "Gigabites of Taste!"

No, this definitely wasn't Kansas. It didn't even seem like India. Was this the New World, the Old World, or the Next World? 2

I had come to Bangalore, India's Silicon Valley, on my own Columbus-like journey of exploration. Columbus sailed with the *Niña*, the *Pinta*, and the *Santa María* in an effort to discover a shorter, more direct route to India by heading west, across the Atlantic, on what he presumed to be an open sea route to the East Indies—rather than going south and east around Africa, as Portuguese explorers of his day were trying to do. India and the magical Spice Islands of the East were famed at the time for their gold, pearls, gems, and silk—a source of untold riches. Finding this shortcut by sea to India, at a time when the Muslim powers of the day had blocked the overland routes from Europe, was a way for both Columbus and the Spanish monarchy to become wealthy and powerful. When Columbus set sail, he apparently assumed the Earth was round, which was why he was convinced that he could get to India by going west. He miscalculated the distance, though. He thought the Earth was a smaller sphere than it is. He also did not anticipate running into a landmass before he reached the East Indies. Nevertheless, he called the aboriginal peoples he encountered in the new world "Indians." Returning home, though, Columbus was able to tell his patrons, King Ferdinand and Queen Isabella, that although he never did find India, he could confirm that the world was indeed round. 3

I set out for India by going due east, via Frankfurt. I had Lufthansa business class. I knew exactly which direction I was going thanks to the GPS map displayed on the screen that popped out of the armrest of my airline seat. I landed safely and on schedule. I too encountered people called Indians. I too was searching for the source of India's riches. Columbus was searching for hardware—precious metals, silk, and spices—the source of wealth in his day. I was searching for software, brainpower, complex algorithms, knowledge workers, call centers, transmission protocols, breakthroughs in optical engineering—the sources of wealth in our day. Columbus was happy to make the Indians he met his slaves, a pool of free manual labor. 4

I just wanted to understand why the Indians I met were taking our work, why they had become such an important pool for the outsourcing of service and information technology work from America and other industrialized countries. Columbus had more than one hundred men on his three ships; I had a small crew from the Discovery Times channel that 5 fit comfortably into two banged-up vans, with Indian drivers who drove barefoot. When I set sail, so to speak, I too assumed that the world was round, but what I encountered in the real India profoundly shook my faith in that notion. Columbus accidentally ran into America but thought he had discovered part of India. I actually found India and thought many of the people I met there were Americans. Some had actually taken American names, and others were doing great imitations of American accents at call centers and American business techniques at software labs.

Columbus reported to his king and queen that the world was round, 6 and he went down in history as the man who first made this discovery. I returned home and shared my discovery only with my wife, and only in a whisper.

"Honey," I confided, "I think the world is flat."                                     7

How did I come to this conclusion? I guess you could say it all started 8 in Nandan Nilekani's conference room at Infosys Technologies Limited. Infosys is one of the jewels of the Indian information technology world, and Nilekani, the company's CEO, is one of the most thoughtful and respected captains of Indian industry. I drove with the Discovery Times crew out to the Infosys campus, about forty minutes from the heart of Bangalore, to tour the facility and interview Nilekani. The Infosys campus is reached by a pockmarked road, with sacred cows, horse-drawn carts, and motorized rickshaws all jostling alongside our vans. Once you enter the gates of Infosys, though, you are in a different world. A massive resort-size swimming pool nestles amid boulders and manicured lawns, adjacent to a huge putting green. There are multiple restaurants and a fabulous health club. Glass-and-steel buildings seem to sprout up like weeds each week. In some of those buildings, Infosys employees are writing specific software programs for American or European companies; in others, they are running the back rooms of major American- and European-based multinationals—everything from computer maintenance to specific research projects to answering customer calls routed there from all over the world. Security is tight, cameras monitor the doors, and if you are working for American Express, you cannot get into the building that is managing services and research for General Electric. Young Indian engineers, men and women, walk briskly from building to building, dangling ID badges. One looked like he could do my taxes. Another looked like she could take my computer apart. And a third looked like she designed it!

After sitting for an interview, Nilekani gave our TV crew a tour of Info- 9 sys's global conferencing center—ground zero of the Indian outsourcing industry. It was a cavernous wood-paneled room that looked like a tiered classroom from an Ivy League law school. On one end was a massive wall-size screen and overhead there were cameras in the ceiling for teleconferencing. "So this is our conference room, probably the largest screen in Asia—this is forty digital screens [put together]," Nilekani explained proudly, pointing to the biggest flat-screen TV I had ever seen. Infosys, he said, can hold a virtual meeting of the key players from its entire global supply chain for any project at any time on that supersize screen. So their American designers could be on the screen speaking with their Indian software writers and their Asian manufacturers all at once. "We could be sitting here, somebody from New York, London, Boston, San Francisco, all live. And maybe the implementation is in Singapore, so the Singapore person could also be live here. . . . That's globalization," said Nilekani. Above the screen there were eight clocks that pretty well summed up the Infosys workday: 24/7/365. The clocks were labeled US West, US East, GMT, India, Singapore, Hong Kong, Japan, Australia.

"Outsourcing is just one dimension of a much more fundamental 10 thing happening today in the world," Nilekani explained. "What happened over the last [few] years is that there was a massive investment in technology, especially in the bubble era, when hundreds of millions of dollars were invested in putting broadband connectivity around the world, undersea cables, all those things." At the same time, he added, computers became cheaper and dispersed all over the world, and there was an explosion of software—e-mail, search engines like Google, and proprietary software that can chop up any piece of work and send one part to Boston, one part to Bangalore, and one part to Beijing, making it easy for anyone to do remote development. When all of these things suddenly came together around 2000, added Nilekani, they "created a platform where intellectual work, intellectual capital, could be delivered from anywhere. It could be disaggregated, delivered, distributed, produced, and put back together again—and this gave a whole new degree of freedom to the way we do work, especially work of an intellectual nature. . . . And what you are seeing in Bangalore today is really the culmination of all these things coming together."

We were sitting on the couch outside of Nilekani's office, waiting for 11 the TV crew to set up its cameras. At one point, summing up the implications of all this, Nilekani uttered a phrase that rang in my ear. He said to me, "Tom, the playing field is being leveled." He meant that countries like India are now able to compete for global knowledge work as never before—and that America had better get ready for this. America was going to be challenged, but, he insisted, the challenge would be good for America because we are always at our best when we are being challenged. As I left the Infosys campus that evening and bounced along the road back to Bangalore, I kept chewing on that phrase: "The playing field is being leveled."

What Nandan is saying, I thought, is that the playing field is being flat- 12 tened. . . . Flattened? Flattened? My God, he's telling me the world is flat!

Here I was in Bangalore—more than five hundred years after Colum- 13 bus sailed over the horizon, using the rudimentary navigational technologies of his day, and returned safely to prove definitively that the world was round—and one of India's smartest engineers, trained at his country's top technical institute and backed by the most modern technologies of his day, was essentially telling me that the world was *flat*—as flat as that screen on which he can host a meeting of his whole global supply chain. Even more interesting, he was citing this development as a good thing, as a new milestone in human progress and a great opportunity for India and the world—the fact that we had made our world flat!

In the back of that van, I scribbled down four words in my notebook: *14* "The world is flat." As soon as I wrote them, I realized that this was the underlying message of everything that I had seen and heard in Bangalore in two weeks of filming. The global competitive playing field was being leveled. The world was being flattened.

As I came to this realization, I was filled with both excitement and *15* dread. The journalist in me was excited at having found a framework to better understand the morning headlines and to explain what was happening in the world today. Clearly, it is now possible for more people than ever to collaborate and compete in real time with more other people on more different kinds of work from more different corners of the planet and on a more equal footing than at any previous time in the history of the world—using computers, e-mail, networks, teleconferencing, and dynamic new software. That is what Nandan was telling me. That was what I discovered on my journey to India and beyond. And that is what this book is about. When you start to think of the world as flat, a lot of things make sense in ways they did not before. But I was also excited personally, because what the flattening of the world means is that we are now connecting all the knowledge centers on the planet together into a single global network, which—if politics and terrorism do not get in the way—could usher in an amazing era of prosperity and innovation.

But contemplating the flat world also left me filled with dread, profes- *16* sional and personal. My personal dread derived from the obvious fact that it's not only the software writers and computer geeks who get empowered to collaborate on work in a flat world. It's also al-Qaeda and other terrorist networks. The playing field is not being leveled only in ways that draw in and superempower a whole new group of innovators. It's being leveled in a way that draws in and superempowers a whole new group of angry, frustrated, and humiliated men and women.

Professionally, the recognition that the world was flat was unnerving *17* because I realized that this flattening had been taking place while I was sleeping, and I had missed it. I wasn't really sleeping, but I was otherwise engaged. Before 9/11, I was focused on tracking globalization and exploring the tension between the "Lexus" forces of economic integration and the "Olive Tree" forces of identity and nationalism—hence my 1999 book, *The Lexus and the Olive Tree*. But after 9/11, the olive tree wars became all-consuming for me. I spent almost all my time traveling in the Arab and Muslim worlds. During those years I lost the trail of globalization.

I found that trail again on my journey to Bangalore in February 2004. *18* Once I did, I realized that something really important had happened while I was fixated on the olive groves of Kabul and Baghdad. Globalization had gone to a whole new level. If you put *The Lexus and the Olive Tree* and this book together, the broad historical argument you end up with is that there have been three great eras of globalization. The first lasted from 1492—when Columbus set sail, opening trade between the Old World and the New World—until around 1800. I would call this era Globalization 1.0. It shrank the world from a size large to a size medium. Globalization 1.0 was about countries and muscles. That is, in Globalization 1.0 the key agent of change, the dynamic force driving the process of global integration was how much brawn—how much muscle, how much horsepower, wind power, or, later, steam power—your country had and how creatively you could deploy it. In this era, countries and governments (often inspired by religion or imperialism or a combination of both) led the way in breaking down walls and knitting the world together, driving global integration. In Globalization 1.0, the primary questions were: Where does my country fit into global competition and opportunities? How can I go global and collaborate with others through my country?

The second great era, Globalization 2.0, lasted roughly from 1800 to    *19* 2000, interrupted by the Great Depression and World Wars I and II. This era shrank the world from a size medium to a size small. In Globalization 2.0, the key agent of change, the dynamic force driving global integration, was multinational companies. These multinationals went global for markets and labor, spearheaded first by the expansion of the Dutch and English joint-stock companies and the Industrial Revolution. In the first half of this era, global integration was powered by falling transportation costs, thanks to the steam engine and the railroad, and in the second half by falling telecommunication costs—thanks to the diffusion of the telegraph, telephones, the PC, satellites, fiber-optic cable, and the early version of the World Wide Web. It was during this era that we really saw the birth and maturation of a global economy, in the sense that there was enough movement of goods and information from continent to continent for there to be a global market, with global arbitrage in products and labor. The dynamic forces behind this era of globalization were breakthroughs in hardware—from steamships and railroads in the beginning to telephones and mainframe computers toward the end. And the big questions in this era were: Where does my company fit into the global economy? How does it take advantage of the opportunities? How can I go global and collaborate with others through my company? *The Lexus and the Olive Tree* was primarily about the climax of this era, an era when the walls started falling all around the world, and integration, and the backlash to it, went to a whole new level. But even as the walls fell, there were still a lot of barriers to seamless global integration. Remember, when Bill Clinton was elected president in 1992, virtually no one outside of government and the academy had e-mail, and when I was writing *The Lexus and the Olive Tree* in 1998, the Internet and e-commerce were just taking off.

Well, they took off—along with a lot of other things that came together    *20* while I was sleeping. And that is why I argue in this book that around the year 2000 we entered a whole new era: Globalization 3.0. Globalization

3.0 is shrinking the world from a size small to a size tiny and flattening the playing field at the same time. And while the dynamic force in Globalization 1.0 was countries globalizing and the dynamic force in Globalization 2.0 was companies globalizing, the dynamic force in Globalization 3.0—the thing that gives it its unique character—is the newfound power for *individuals* to collaborate and compete globally. And the lever that is enabling individuals and groups to go global so easily and so seamlessly is not horsepower, and not hardware, but software—all sorts of new applications—in conjunction with the creation of a global fiber-optic network that has made us all next-door neighbors. Individuals must, and can, now ask, Where do *I* fit into the global competition and opportunities of the day, and how can *I*, on my own, collaborate with others globally?

But Globalization 3.0 not only differs from the previous eras in how it *21* is shrinking and flattening the world and in how it is empowering individuals. It is different in that Globalization 1.0 and 2.0 were driven primarily by European and American individuals and businesses. Even though China actually had the biggest economy in the world in the eighteenth century, it was Western countries, companies, and explorers who were doing most of the globalizing and shaping of the system. But going forward, this will be less and less true. Because it is flattening and shrinking the world, Globalization 3.0 is going to be more and more driven not only by individuals but also by a much more diverse—non-Western, nonwhite—group of individuals. Individuals from every corner of the flat world are being empowered. Globalization 3.0 makes it possible for so many more people to plug and play, and you are going to see every color of the human rainbow take part.

(While this empowerment of individuals to act globally is the most im- *22* portant new feature of Globalization 3.0, companies—large and small— have been newly empowered in this era as well. . . .)

Needless to say, I had only the vaguest appreciation of all this as I left *23* Nandan's office that day in Bangalore. But as I sat contemplating these changes on the balcony of my hotel room that evening, I did know one thing: I wanted to drop everything and write a book that would enable me to understand how this flattening process happened and what its implications might be for countries, companies, and individuals. So I picked up the phone and called my wife, Ann, and told her, "I am going to write a book called *The World Is Flat.*" She was both amused and curious—well, maybe *more* amused than curious! Eventually, I was able to bring her around, and I hope I will be able to do the same with you, dear reader. Let me start by taking you back to the beginning of my journey to India, and other points east, and share with you some of the encounters that led me to conclude the world was no longer round—but flat.

Jaithirth "Jerry" Rao was one of the first people I met in Bangalore—and *24* I hadn't been with him for more than a few minutes at the Leela Palace hotel before he told me that he could handle my tax returns and any other accounting needs I had—from Bangalore. No thanks. I demurred, I already have an accountant in Chicago. Jerry just smiled. He was too polite to say it—that he may already be my accountant, or rather my accountant's accountant, thanks to the explosion in the outsourcing of tax preparation.

"This is happening as we speak," said Rao, a native of Mumbai, formerly    25
Bombay, whose Indian firm, MphasiS, has a team of Indian accountants able to do outsourced accounting work from any state in America and the federal government. "We have tied up with several small and medium-sized CPA firms in America."

"You mean like my accountant?" I asked. "Yes, like your accountant,"    26
said Rao with a smile. Rao's company has pioneered a work flow software program with a standardized format that makes the outsourcing of tax returns cheap and easy. The whole process starts, Jerry explained, with an accountant in the United States scanning my last year's tax returns, plus my W-2, W-4, 1099, bonuses, and stock statements—everything—into a computer server, which is physically located in California or Texas. "Now your accountant, if he is going to have your taxes done overseas, knows that you would prefer not to have your surname be known or your Social Security number known [to someone outside the country], so he can choose to suppress that information," said Rao. "The accountants in India call up all the raw information directly from the server in America [using a password], and they complete your tax returns, with you remaining anonymous. All the data stays in the U.S. to comply with privacy regulations. . . . We take data protection and privacy very seriously. The accountant in India can see the data on his screen, but he cannot take a download of it or print it out—our program does not allow it. The most he could do would be to try to memorize it, if he had some ill intention. The accountants are not allowed to even take a paper and pen into the room when they are working on the returns."

I was intrigued at just how advanced this form of service outsourcing    27
had become. "We are doing several thousand returns," said Rao. What's more, "Your CPA in America need not even be in their office. They can be sitting on a beach in California and e-mail us and say, 'Jerry, you are really good at doing New York State returns, so you do Tom's returns. And Sonia, you and your team in Delhi do the Washington and Florida returns.' Sonia, by the way, is working out of her house in India, with no overhead [for the company to pay]. 'And these others, they are really complicated, so I will do them myself.'"

In 2003, some 25,000 U.S. tax returns were done in India. In 2004, the    28
number was 100,000. In 2005, it is expected to be 400,000. In a decade, you will assume that your accountant has outsourced the basic preparation of your tax returns—if not more.

"How did you get into this?" I asked Rao.    29

"My friend Jeroen Tas, a Dutchman, and I were both working in Cali-    30
fornia for Citigroup," Rao explained. "I was his boss and we were coming back from New York one day together on a flight and I said that I was plan-

ning to quit and he said, 'So am I.' We both said, 'Why don't we start our own business?' So in 1997–98, we put together a business plan to provide high-end Internet solutions for big companies. . . . Two years ago, though, I went to a technology convention in Las Vegas and was approached by some medium-size [American] accounting firms, and they said they could not afford to set up big tax outsourcing operations to India, but the big guys could, and [the medium guys] wanted to get ahead of them. So we developed a software product called VTR—Virtual Tax Room—to enable these medium-size accounting firms to easily outsource tax returns."

These midsize firms "are getting a more level playing field, which they were denied before," said Jerry. "Suddenly they can get access to the same advantages of scale that the bigger guys always had."    31

Is the message to Americans, "Mama, don't let your kids grow up to be accountants"? I asked.    32

Not really, said Rao. "What we have done is taken the grunt work. You know what is needed to prepare a tax return? Very little creative work. This is what will move overseas."    33

"What will stay in America?" I asked.    34

"The accountant who wants to stay in business in America will be the one who focuses on designing creative complex strategies, like tax avoidance or tax sheltering, managing customer relationships," he said. "He or she will say to his clients, 'I am getting the grunt work done efficiently far away. Now let's talk about how we manage your estate and what you are going to do about your kids. Do you want to leave some money in your trusts?' It means having the quality-time discussions with clients rather than running around like chickens with their heads cut off from February to April, and often filing for extensions into August, because they have not had the quality time with clients."    35

Judging from an essay in the journal *Accounting Today* (June 7, 2004), this does, indeed, seem to be the future. L. Gary Boomer, a CPA and CEO of Boomer Consulting in Manhattan, Kansas, wrote, "This past [tax] season produced over 100,000 [outsourced] returns and has now expanded beyond individual returns to trusts, partnerships and corporations. . . . The primary reason that the industry has been able to scale up as rapidly as it has over the past three years is due to the investment that these [foreign-based] companies have made in systems, processes and training." There are about seventy thousand accounting grads in India each year, he added, many of whom go to work for local Indian firms starting at $100 a month. With the help of high-speed communications, stringent training, and standardized forms, these young Indians can fairly rapidly be converted into basic Western accountants at a fraction of the cost. Some of the Indian accounting firms even go about marketing themselves to American firms through teleconferencing and skip the travel. Concluded Boomer, "The accounting profession is currently in transformation. Those who get caught in the past and resist change will be forced deeper into    36 commoditization. Those who can create value through leadership, relationships and creativity will transform the industry, as well as strengthen relationships with their existing clients."

What you're telling me, I said to Rao, is that no matter what your profession—doctor, lawyer, architect, accountant—if you are an American, you better be good at the touchy-feely service stuff, because anything that can be digitized can be outsourced to either the smartest or the cheapest producer, or both. Rao answered, "Everyone has to focus on what exactly is their value-add." 37

But what if I am just an average accountant? I went to a state university. I had a B+ average. Eventually I got my CPA. I work in a big accounting firm, doing a lot of standard work. I rarely meet with clients. They keep me in the back. But it is a decent living and the firm is basically happy with me. What is going to happen to me in this system? 38

"It is a good question," said Rao. "We must be honest about it. We are in the middle of a big technological change, and when you live in a society that is at the cutting edge of that change [like America], it is hard to predict. It's easy to predict for someone living in India. In ten years we are going to be doing a lot of the stuff that is being done in America today. We can predict our future. But we are behind you. You are defining the future. America is always on the edge of the next creative wave. . . . So it is difficult to look into the eyes of that accountant and say this is what is going to be. We should not trivialize that. We must deal with it and talk about it honestly. . . . Any activity where we can digitize and decompose the value chain, and move the work around, will get moved around. Some people will say, 'Yes, but you can't serve me a steak.' True, but I can take the reservation for your table sitting anywhere in the world, if the restaurant does not have an operator. We can say, 'Yes, Mr. Friedman, we can give you a table by the window.' In other words, there are parts of the whole dining-out experience that we can decompose and outsource. If you go back and read the basic economics textbooks, they will tell you: Goods are traded, but services are consumed and produced in the same place. And you cannot export a haircut. But we are coming close to exporting a haircut, the appointment part. What kind of haircut do you want? Which barber do you want? All those things can and will be done by a call center far away." 39

As we ended our conversation, I asked Rao what he is up to next. He was full of energy. He told me he'd been talking to an Israeli company that is making some big advances in compression technology to allow for easier, better transfers of CAT scans via the Internet so you can quickly get a second opinion from a doctor half a world away. 40

A few weeks after I spoke with Rao, the following e-mail arrived from Bill Brody, the president of Johns Hopkins University, whom I had just interviewed for this book: 41

> Dear Tom, I am speaking at a Hopkins continuing education medical meeting for radiologists (I used to be a radiologist). . . . I came upon a very fascinating situation that I thought might interest you. I have just learned that in many

small and some medium-size hospitals in the US, radiologists are outsourcing reading of CAT scans to doctors in India and Australia!!! Most of this evidently occurs at night (and maybe weekends) when the radiologists do not have sufficient staffing to provide in-hospital coverage. While some radiology groups will use teleradiology to ship images from the hospital to their home (or to Vail or Cape Cod, I suppose) so that they can interpret images and provide a diagnosis 24/7, apparently the smaller hospitals are shipping CAT scan images to radiologists abroad. The advantage is that it is day-time in Australia or India when it is nighttime here—so after-hours coverage becomes more readily done by shipping the images across the globe. Since CAT (and MRI) images are already in digital format and available on a network with a standardized protocol, it is no problem to view the images anywhere in the world. . . . I assume that the radiologists on the other end . . . must have trained in [the] US and acquired the appropriate licenses and credentials. . . . The groups abroad that provide these after-hours readings are called "Nighthawks" by the American radiologists that employ them.
Best,
Bill

. . . Some of the signs of flattening I encountered back home, though, _42_ had nothing to do with economics. On October 3, 2004, I appeared on the CBS News Sunday morning show *Face the Nation*, hosted by veteran CBS correspondent Bob Schieffer. CBS had been in the news a lot in previous weeks because of Dan Rather's *60 Minutes* report about President George W. Bush's Air National Guard service that turned out to be based on bogus documents. After the show that Sunday, Schieffer mentioned that the oddest thing had happened to him the week before. When he walked out of the CBS studio, a young reporter was waiting for him on the sidewalk. This isn't all that unusual, because as with all the Sunday-morning shows, the major networks—CBS, NBC, ABC, CNN, and Fox—always send crews to one another's studios to grab exit interviews with the guests. But this young man, Schieffer explained, was not from a major network. He politely introduced himself as a reporter for a Web site called InDC Journal and asked whether he could ask Schieffer a few questions. Schieffer, being a polite fellow, said sure. The young man interviewed him on a device Schieffer did not recognize and then asked if he could take his picture. A picture? Schieffer noticed that the young man had no camera. He didn't need one. He turned his cell phone around and snapped Schieffer's picture.

"So I came in the next morning and looked up this Web site and there _43_ was my picture and the interview and there were already three hundred comments about it," said Schieffer, who, though keenly aware of online journalism, was nevertheless taken aback at the incredibly fast, low-cost, and solo manner in which this young man had put him up in lights.

I was intrigued by this story, so I tracked down the young man from _44_ InDC Journal. His name is Bill Ardolino, and he is a very thoughtful guy. I conducted my own interview with him online—how else?—and began by asking about what equipment he was using as a one-man network/newspaper.

"I used a minuscule MP3 player/digital recorder (three and a half inches    45
by two inches) to get the recording, and a separate small digital camera
phone to snap his picture," said Ardolino. "Not quite as sexy as an all-in-one
phone/camera/recorder (which does exist), but a statement on the ubiquity and miniaturization of technology nonetheless. I carry this equipment
around D.C. at all times because, hey, you never know. What's perhaps
more startling is how well Mr. Schieffer thought on his feet, after being
jumped on by some stranger with interview questions. He blew me away."

Ardolino said the MP3 player cost him about $125. It is "primarily    46
designed to play music," he explained, but it also "comes prepackaged as a
digital recorder that creates a WAV sound file that can be uploaded back to a
computer. . . . Basically, I'd say that the barrier to entry to do journalism that
requires portable, ad hoc recording equipment is [now] about $100—$200
to $300 if you add a camera, $400 to $500 for a pretty nice recorder and
a pretty nice camera. [But] $200 is all that you need to get the job done."

What prompted him to become his own news network?    47

"Being an independent journalist is a hobby that sprang from my    48
frustration about biased, incomplete, selective, and/or incompetent information gathering by the mainstream media," explained Ardolino, who
describes himself as a "center-right libertarian." "Independent journalism and its relative, blogging, are expressions of market forces—a need
is not being met by current information sources. I started taking pictures
and doing interviews of the antiwar rallies in D.C., because the media was
grossly misrepresenting the nature of the groups that were organizing the
gatherings—unrepentant Marxists, explicit and implicit supporters of terror, etc. I originally chose to use humor as a device, but I've since branched
out. Do I have more power, power to get my message out, yes. The Schieffer interview actually brought in about twenty-five thousand visits in
twenty-four hours. My peak day since I've started was fifty-five thousand
when I helped break 'Rathergate.' . . . I interviewed the first forensics expert
in the Dan Rather National Guard story, and he was then specifically picked
up by the *Washington Post, Chicago Sun-Times, Globe, NYT*, etc., within
forty-eight hours.

"The pace of information gathering and correction in the CBS fake    49
memo story was astounding," he continued. "It wasn't just that CBS News
'stonewalled' after the fact, it was arguably that they couldn't keep up
with an army of dedicated fact-checkers. The speed and openness of the
medium is something that runs rings around the old process. . . . I'm a
twenty-nine-year-old marketing manager [who] always wanted to write for
a living but hated the AP style book. As überblogger Glenn Reynolds likes
to say, blogs have given the people a chance to stop yelling at their TV and
have a say in the process. I think that they serve as sort of a 'fifth estate'
that works in conjunction with the mainstream media (often by keeping
an eye on them or feeding them raw info) and potentially function as a
journalism and commentary farm system that provides a new means to
establish success.

"Like many facets of the topic that you're talking about in your book, 50 there are good and bad aspects of the development. The splintering of media makes for a lot of incoherence or selective cognition (look at our country's polarization), but it also decentralizes power and provides a better guarantee that the *complete* truth *is* out there . . . somewhere . . . in pieces."

On any given day one can come across any number of stories, like the 51 encounter between Bob Schieffer and Bill Ardolino, that tell you that old hierarchies are being flattened and the playing field is being leveled. As Micah L. Sifry nicely put it in *The Nation* magazine (November 22, 2004): "The era of top-down politics—where campaigns, institutions and journalism were cloistered communities powered by hard-to-amass capital—is over. Something wilder, more engaging and infinitely more satisfying to individual participants is arising alongside the old order."

I offer the Schieffer-Ardolino encounter as just one example of how 52 the flattening of the world has happened faster and changed rules, roles, and relationships more quickly than we could have imagined. And, though I know it is a cliché, I have to say it nevertheless: *You ain't seen nothin' yet.* We are entering a phase where we are going to see the digitization, virtualization, and automation of almost everything. The gains in productivity will be staggering for those countries, companies, and individuals who can absorb the new technological tools. And we are entering a phase where more people than ever before in the history of the world are going to have access to these tools—as innovators, as collaborators, and, alas, even as terrorists. You say you want a revolution? Well, the real information revolution is about to begin. I call this new phase Globalization 3.0 because it followed Globalization 2.0, but I think this new era of globalization will prove to be such a difference of degree that it will be seen, in time, as a difference in kind. That is why I introduced the idea that the world has gone from round to flat. Everywhere you turn, hierarchies are being challenged from below or transforming themselves from top-down structures into more horizontal and collaborative ones.

"Globalization is the word we came up with to describe the changing 53 relationships between governments and big businesses," said David Rothkopf, a former senior Department of Commerce official in the Clinton administration and now a private strategic consultant. "But what is going on today is a much broader, much more profound phenomenon." It is not simply about how governments, business, and people communicate, not just about how organizations interact, but is about the emergence of completely new social, political, and business models. "It is about things that impact some of the deepest, most ingrained aspects of society right down to the nature of the social contract," added Rothkopf. "What happens if the political entity in which you are located no longer corresponds to a job that takes place in cyberspace, or no longer really encompasses workers collaborating with other workers in different corners of the globe, or no longer really captures products produced in multiple places simultaneously? Who regulates the work? Who taxes it? Who should benefit from those taxes?"

If I am right about the flattening of the world, it will be remembered  54
as one of those fundamental changes—like the rise of the nation-state or
the Industrial Revolution—each of which, in its day, noted Rothkopf, produced changes in the role of individuals, the role and form of governments,
the way we innovated, the way we conducted business, the role of women,
the way we fought wars, the way we educated ourselves, the way religion
responded, the way art was expressed, the way science and research were
conducted, not to mention the political labels we assigned to ourselves and
to our opponents. "There are certain pivot points or watersheds in history
that are greater than others because the changes they produced were so
sweeping, multifaceted, and hard to predict at the time," Rothkopf said.

If the prospect of this flattening—and all of the pressures, dislocations,  55
and opportunities accompanying it—causes you unease about the future,
you are neither alone nor wrong. Whenever civilization has gone through
one of these disruptive, dislocating technological revolutions—like Guten-
berg's introduction of the printing press—the whole world has changed
in profound ways. But there is something about the flattening of the
world that is going to be qualitatively different from other such profound
changes: the speed and breadth with which it is taking hold. The introduction of printing happened over a period of decades and for a long time
affected only a relatively small part of the planet. Same with the Industrial Revolution. This flattening process is happening at warp speed and
directly or indirectly touching a lot more people on the planet at once. The
faster and broader this transition to a new era, the more likely is the potential for disruption, as opposed to an orderly transfer of power from the old
winners to the new winners.

To put it another way, the experiences of the high-tech companies  56
in the last few decades who failed to navigate the rapid changes brought
about in their marketplace by these types of forces may be a warning to all
the businesses, institutions, and nation-states that are now facing these
inevitable, even predictable, changes but lack the leadership, flexibility,
and imagination to adapt—not because they are not smart or aware, but
because the speed of change is simply overwhelming them.

And that is why the great challenge for our time will be to absorb these  57
changes in ways that do not overwhelm people but also do not leave them
behind. None of this will be easy. But this is our task. It is inevitable and
unavoidable. [I hope] to offer a framework for how to think about it and
manage it to our maximum benefit.

■ ■ ■

## Reading as a Writer: Analyzing Rhetorical Choices

1.  What is the effect of Friedman's decision to begin this piece with an excerpt
    from Christopher Columbus's journal? Why does he open his first para-

graph with sentences that contrast so much in tone? What connections do you find between the content of the Columbus excerpt and Friedman's anecdote about golf course directions? Discuss the strategies Friedman uses to catch his readers' interest in paragraphs 1 through 6, leading up to his confiding to his wife, "I think the world is flat" (para. 7).

2. What do you think Friedman means by the statement "the world is flat"? Identify several passages that help you define and understand the way he uses this statement.

### Writing as a Reader: Entering the Conversation of Ideas

1. How do Friedman and Kwame Anthony Appiah conceive of the possibilities and challenges of being a global citizen? Write an essay in which you play their ideas off one another. What skills and knowledge do you think are necessary to being a "good" global citizen?

2. How do you think Friedman's ideas about the flattening of the world apply to Michael Kimmel's ideas in "Gender, Class, and Terrorism"? Compose an essay in which you consider how flattening might account for some of the behaviors Kimmel describes in his essay. Be sure to quote and analyze specific passages in each text as you explain to your reader what you find significant about the authors' ideas.

## FRANKLIN FOER

# *From* How Soccer Explains the World: An Unlikely Theory of Globalization

Franklin Foer is the editor of *The New Republic*, a magazine that covers a broad spectrum of political and cultural topics. He has worked as a journalist, publishing in *U.S. News & World Report*, *Slate*, the *New York Times*, the *Washington Post*, and *Spin*. This reading is taken from *How Soccer Explains the World: An Unlikely Theory of Globalization* (2004), a book that brought Foer to the attention of many sports fans. Although soccer does not have the same hold on Americans that it has on people in other parts of the world, Foer uses soccer—"its fans, its players, and strategies" (para. 4)—to address larger issues. Foer writes in a tradition of sports reporting that goes far beyond describing the plays and scores of the game. Like other writers who look at the business and influence of sports such as golf, tennis, and football, Foer is interested in the culture of sport, and how and why it has such a grip on the imaginations of fans.

In this reading, we reproduce the prologue and last chapter of Foer's book about soccer. In the prologue, he lays out his rationale for his "unlikely" method of using soccer as a way to examine a series of national and global dynamics. As you read, consider what he accomplishes there by proposing that soccer can be used "as a way of thinking about how people would identify themselves in this new era" of globalization (para. 4). How are these ideas in conversation with the material that follows on "How Soccer Explains the American Culture Wars"?

Foer includes autobiographical anecdotes in this section, humorously describing his own shameful childhood soccer career in the early 1980s, before suburban soccer leagues became so highly organized and before the term "soccer mom" was coined to describe the necessary parental support system for this pastime. Although Foer does not use MLA style to cite sources in the text, notice the ways he includes the ideas and comments of others to give context to the "culture war" that raged over soccer in the 1980s. How does the anxiety Foer describes here about soccer seeming "un-American" apply to current political and cultural conversations in which we Americans are encouraged to think of ourselves as different from others for a variety of reasons? How does Foer explain the political and cultural conflicts that soccer has come to exemplify? What solutions does he offer, if any? Finally, what does imported goat cheese (para. 28) have to do with soccer? Read on, and see if you can make other connections between soccer and globalization. As Foer demonstrates, if you can offer clear and persuasive examples, any connection can be fair game.

■ ■ ■

## Prologue

At about the time that I started working on this book, in the fall of 2001, *1* the consensus on globalization changed considerably—for obvious reasons. It was no longer possible to speak so breathlessly, so messianically of the political promise of economic interdependence. And there was another problem. The world's brief experiment in interdependence didn't come close to delivering the advertised result of prosperity. [I] use the metaphor of soccer to address some of the nagging questions about this failure: Why have some nations remained poor, even though they had so much foreign investment coursing through them? How dangerous are the multinational corporations that the Left rails against?

This is not to dredge up the tired old Marxist criticisms of corporate *2* capitalism—the big question of the book is less economic than cultural. The innovation of the anti-globalization left is its embrace of traditionalism: its worry that global tastes and brands will steamroll indigenous cultures. Of course, soccer isn't the same as Bach or Buddhism. But it is often more deeply felt than religion, and just as much a part of the community's fabric, a repository of traditions. During Franco's rule, the clubs Athletic Bilbao and Real Sociedad were the only venues where Basque people could express their cultural pride without winding up in jail. In English industrial towns like Coventry and Derby, soccer clubs helped glue together small cities amid oppressive dinginess.

By the logic of both its critics and proponents, the global culture should *3* have wiped away these local institutions. Indeed, traveling the world, it's hard not to be awed by the power of mega-brands like the clubs Manchester United and Real Madrid, backed by Nike and Adidas, who have cultivated support across continents, prying fans away from their old allegiances. But that homogenization turned out to be more of an exception than I had anticipated. Wandering among lunatic fans, gangster owners, and crazed Bulgarian strikers, I kept noticing the ways that globalization had failed to diminish the game's local cultures, local blood feuds, and even local corruption. In fact, I began to suspect that globalization had actually increased the power of these local entities—and not always in such a good way.

On my travels, I tried to use soccer—its fans, its players, and 4 strategies—as a way of thinking about how people would identify themselves in this new era. Would they embrace new, more globalized labels? Would people stop thinking of themselves as English and Brazilian and begin to define themselves as Europeans and Latin Americans? Or would those new identities be meaningless, with shallow roots in history? Would people revert back to older identities, like religion and tribe? If soccer is an object lesson, then perhaps religion and tribe have too much going for them. . . .

The story begins bleakly and grows progressively more optimistic. In the 5 end, I found it hard to be too hostile toward globalization. For all its many faults, it has brought soccer to the far corners of the world and into my life.

## How Soccer Explains the American Culture Wars

### *I.*

My soccer career began in 1982, at the age of eight. This was an entirely 6 different moment in the history of American soccer, well before the youth game acquired its current, highly evolved infrastructure. Our teams didn't have names. We had jersey colors that we used to refer to ourselves: "Go Maroon!" Our coach, a bearded German named Gunther, would bark at us in continental nomenclature that didn't quite translate into English. Urging me to stop a ball with my upper body, he would cry out, "Use your breasts, Frankie!"

That I should end up a soccer player defied the time-tested laws of 7 sporting heredity. For generations, fathers bequeathed their sporting loves unto their sons. My father, like most men of his baby boom age, had grown up madly devoted to baseball. Why didn't my dad adhere to the practice of handing his game to his son? The answer has to do with the times and the class to which my parents belonged, by which I mean, they were children of the sixties and we lived in the yuppie confines of Upper Northwest Washington, D.C., a dense aggregation of Ivy League lawyers with aggressively liberal politics and exceptionally protective parenting styles. Nearly everyone in our family's social set signed up their children to play soccer. It was the fashionable thing to do. On Monday mornings, at school, we'd each walk around in the same cheaply made pair of white shorts with the logo of our league, Montgomery Soccer Inc.

Steering your child into soccer may have been fashionable, but it wasn't 8 a decision to be made lightly. When my father played sandlot baseball, he could walk three blocks to his neighborhood diamond. With soccer, this simply wasn't possible. At this early moment in the youth soccer boom, the city of Washington didn't have any of its own leagues. My parents would load up our silver Honda Accord and drive me to fields deep in suburban Maryland, 40-minute drives made weekly across a landscape of oversized hardware stores and newly minted real estate developments. In part, these drives would take so long because my parents would circle, hopelessly lost, through neighborhoods they had never before visited and would likely never see again.

As I later discovered, my parents made this sacrifice of their leisure 9 time because they believed that soccer could be transformational. I suffered from a painful, rather extreme case of shyness. I'm told that it extended beyond mere clinging to my mother's leg. On the sidelines at halftime, I would sit quietly on the edge of the other kids' conversations, never really interjecting myself. My parents had hoped that the game might necessitate my becoming more aggressive, a breaking through of inhibitions.

The idea that soccer could alleviate shyness was not an idiosyncratic 10 parenting theory. It tapped into the conventional wisdom among yuppie parents. Soccer's appeal lay in its opposition to the other popular sports. For children of the sixties, there was something abhorrent about enrolling kids in American football, a game where violence wasn't just incidental but inherent. They didn't want to teach the acceptability of violence, let alone subject their precious children to the risk of physical maiming. Baseball, where each batter must stand center stage four or five times a game, entailed too many stressful, potentially ego-deflating encounters. Basketball, before Larry Bird's prime, still had the taint of the ghetto.

But soccer represented something very different. It was a tabula 11 rasa, a sport onto which a generation of parents could project their values. Quickly, soccer came to represent the fundamental tenets of yuppie parenting, the spirit of *Sesame Street* and Dr. Benjamin Spock. Unlike the other sports, it would foster self-esteem, minimize the pain of competition while still teaching life lessons. Dick Wilson, the executive director of the American Youth Soccer Organization since the early seventies, described the attitude this way: "We would like to provide the child a chance to participate in a less competitive, win-oriented atmosphere. . . . We require that teams be balanced; and that teams not remain intact from year to year, that they be dissolved and totally reconstituted in the next season. This is done to preclude the adults from building their own dynasty 'win at all cost' situations."

This was typical of the thinking of a generation of post-'60s parenting *12* theories, which were an extension of the counterculture spirit—Theodor Adorno's idea that strict, emotionally stultifying homes created authoritarian, bigoted kids. But for all the talk of freedom, the sixties parenting style had a far less laissez-faire side, too. Like the 1960s consumer movement which brought American car seatbelts and airbags, the soccer movement felt like it could create a set of rules and regulations that would protect both the child's body and mind from damage. Leagues like the one I played in handed out "participation" trophies to every player, no matter how few games his (or her) team won. Other leagues had stopped posting the scores of games or keeping score altogether. Where most of the world accepts the practice of heading the ball as an essential element of the game, American soccer parents have fretted over the potential for injury to the brain. An entire industry sprouted to manufacture protective headgear, not that different-looking from a boxer's sparring helmet, to soften the blows. Even though very little medical evidence supports this fear, some youth leagues have prohibited headers altogether.

This reveals a more fundamental difference between American youth *13* soccer and the game as practiced in the rest of the world. In every other part of the world, soccer's sociology varies little: It is the province of the working class. Sure, there might be aristocrats, like Gianni Agnelli, who take an interest, and instances like Barca, where the game transcendently grips the community. But these cases are rare. The United States is even rarer: It inverts the class structure of the game. Here, aside from Latino immigrants, the professional classes follow the game most avidly and the working class couldn't give a toss about it. Surveys, done by the sporting goods manufacturers, consistently show that children of middle class and affluent families play the game disproportionately. Half the nation's soccer participants come from households earning over $50,000. That is, they come from the solid middle class and above.

Elites have never been especially well liked in postwar American *14* politics—or at least they have been easy to take swipes at. But the generation of elites that adopted soccer has been an especially ripe target. That's because they came through college in the sixties and seventies, at a time when the counterculture self-consciously turned against the stultifying conformity of what it perceived as traditional America. Even as this group shed its youthful radical politics, it kept some of its old ideals, including its resolute cosmopolitanism and suspicions of middle America, "flyover country." When they adopted soccer, it gave the impression that they had turned their backs on the American pastime. This, naturally, produced even more disdain for them—and for their sport.

Pundits have employed many devices to sum up America's cultural *15* divisions. During the 1980s, they talked about the "culture war"—the battle over textbooks, abortion, prayer in school, affirmative action, and funding of the arts. This war pitted conservative defenders of tradition and morality against liberal defenders of modernity and pluralism. More recently this debate has been described as the split between "red and blue America"—the two colors used to distinguish partisan preference in maps charting presidential election voting. But another explanatory device has yet to penetrate political science departments and the national desks of newspapers. There exists an important cleavage between the parts of the country that have adopted soccer as its pastime and the places that haven't. And this distinction lays bare an underrated source of American cultural cleavage: globalization.

## II.

Other countries have greeted soccer with relative indifference. The Indian 16 subcontinent and Australia come to mind. But the United States is perhaps the only place where a loud portion of the population actively disdains the game, even campaigns against it. This anti-soccer lobby believes, in the words of USA Today's Tom Weir, "that hating soccer is more American than apple pie, driving a pickup, or spending Saturday afternoons channel surfing with the remote control." Weir exaggerates the pervasiveness of this sentiment. But the cadre of soccer haters has considerable sway. Their influence rests primarily with a legion of prestigious sportswriters and commentators, who use their column inches to fulminate against the game, especially on the occasions of World Cups.

Not just pundits buried in the C Section of the paper, but people with 17 actual power believe that soccer represents a genuine threat to the American way of life. The former Buffalo Bills quarterback Jack Kemp, one of the most influential conservatives of the 1980s, a man once mentioned in the same breath as the presidency, holds this view. In 1986, he took to the floor of the United States Congress to orate against a resolution in support of an American bid to host the World Cup. Kemp intoned, "I think it is important for all those young out there, who someday hope to play real football, where you throw it and kick it and run with it and put it in your hands, a distinction should be made that football is democratic, capitalism, whereas soccer is a European socialist [sport]."

Lovers of the game usually can't resist dismissing these critics as xeno- 18 phobes and reactionaries intoxicated with a sense of cultural superiority, the sporting wing of Pat Buchanan's America First conservatism. For a time, I believed this myself. But over the years I've met too many conservatives who violently disagree with Kemp's grafting of politics onto the game. And I've heard too many liberals take their shots at soccer, people who write for such publications as the Village Voice and couldn't be plausibly grouped in the troglodyte camp of American politics. So if hatred of soccer has nothing to do with politics, conventionally defined, why do so many Americans feel threatened by the beautiful game?

For years, I have been collecting a file on this anti-soccer lobby. The 19 person whose material mounts highest in my collection is the wildly popular radio shock jock Jim Rome. Rome arrived on the national scene in the mid-nineties and built an audience based on his self-congratulatory flouting of social norms. Rome has created his own subculture that has enraptured a broad swath of American males. They are united by their own vernacular, a Walter Winchell–like form of slang that Rome calls "smack," derived in part from the African American street and in part from the fraternity house. An important part of this subculture entails making fun of the people who aren't members of it. Rome can be cruelly cutting to callers who don't pass his muster, who talk the wrong kind of smack or freeze up on air. These put-downs form a large chunk of his programs. The topics of his rants include such far-ranging subject matter as the quackery of chiropractors, cheap seafood restaurants, and, above all, soccer.

Where specific events trigger most soccer hating—a World Cup, news 20 of hooligan catastrophes that arrive over the wires—Rome doesn't need a proximate cause to break into a tirade. He lets randomly rip with invective. "My son is not playing soccer. I will hand him ice skates and a shimmering sequined blouse before I hand him a soccer ball. Soccer is not a sport, does not need to be on my TV, and my son will not be playing it." In moments of honesty, he more or less admits his illogic. "If it's incredibly stupid and soccer is in any way related, then soccer must be the root cause [of the stupidity]," he said in one segment, where he attacked the sporting goods manufacturer Umbro for putting out a line of clothing called Zyklon, the same name as the Auschwitz gas. (Zyklon translates as cyclone. By his logic, the words "concentration" or "camp" should be purged from conversational English for their Holocaust associations.) He often inadvertently endorses some repulsive arguments. One segment ripped into African soccer teams for deploying witch doctors. "So you can add this to the laundry list of reasons why I hate soccer," he frothed.

Such obvious flaws make it seem he is proud of his crassness, and that 21 would be entirely in keeping with character. These arguments would be more easily dismissed were they the product of a single demented individual. But far smarter minds have devolved down to Rome's level. Allen Barra, a sportswriter for the *Wall Street Journal,* is one of these smarter minds. Usually, Barra distinguishes himself from his colleagues by making especially rarified, sharp arguments that follow clearly from the facts and have evidence backing his provocative claims. But on soccer, he slips from his moorings. He writes, "Yes, OK, soccer is the most 'popular' game in the world. And rice is the most 'popular' food in the world. So what? Maybe other countries can't afford football, basketball and baseball leagues: maybe if they could afford these other sports, they'd enjoy them even more."

Unlike Rome, Barra has some sense of why he flies off the handle on 22 this subject. It has to do with his resentment of the game's yuppie promoters. He argues, "Americans are such suckers when it comes to something with a European label that many who have resisted thus far would give in to trendiness and push their kids into youth soccer programs." And more than that, he worries that the soccer enthusiasts want the U.S. to "get with the rest of the world's program."

As Barra makes clear, the anti-soccer lobby really articulates the same  23
fears as Eurico Miranda and Alan Garrison, a phobia of globalization. To
understand their fears, it is important to note that both Barra and Rome
are proud aficionados of baseball. The United States, with its unashamedly
dynamic culture, doesn't have too many deeply rooted, transgenerational
traditions that it can claim as its own. Baseball is one of the few. That's
one reason why the game gets so much nostalgia-drenched celebration in
Kevin Costner movies and Stephen Jay Gould books.

But Major League Baseball, let's face it, has been a loser in globaliza-  24
tion. Unlike the NBA or NFL, it hasn't made the least attempt to market
itself to a global audience. And the global audience has shown no hunger
for the game. Because baseball has failed to master the global economy, it
has been beat back by it. According to the Sporting Goods Manufacturers
Association of America, the number of teens playing baseball fell 47 percent between 1987 and 2000. During that same period, youth soccer grew
exponentially. By 2002, 1.3 million more kids played soccer than Little
League. And the demographic profile of baseball has grown ever more lily
white. It has failed to draw African Americans and attracts few Latinos
who didn't grow up playing the game in the Caribbean. The change can
also be registered in the ballot box that matters most. Nielsen ratings show
that, in most years, a World Series can no longer draw the same number of
viewers as an inconsequential Monday night game in the NFL.

It's not surprising that Americans should split like this over soccer.  25
Globalization increasingly provides the subtext for the American cultural
split. This isn't to say America violently or even knowingly divides over
globalization. But after September 11 opened new debates over foreign
policy, two camps in American politics have clearly emerged. One camp
believes in the essential tenets of the globalization religion as preached by
European politicians, that national governments should defer to institutions like the UN and WTO. These tend to be people who opposed the war
in Iraq. And this opinion reflects a worldview. These Americans share cultural values with Europeans—an aggressive secularism, a more relaxed
set of cultural mores that tolerates gays and pot smoking—which isn't surprising, considering that these Americans have jobs and tourist interests
that put them in regular contact with the other side of the Atlantic. They
consider themselves to be part of a cosmopolitan culture that transcends
national boundaries.

On the other side, there is a group that believes in "American exception-  26
alism," an idea that America's history and singular form of government has
given the nation a unique role to play in the world; that the U.S. should be
above submitting to international laws and bodies. They view Europeans as
degraded by their lax attitudes, and worry about the threat to American culture posed by secular tolerance. With so much relativism seeping into the
American way of life, they fret that the country has lost the self-confidence
to make basic moral judgments, to condemn evil. Soccer isn't exactly perni-

cious, but it's a symbol of the U.S. junking its tradition to "get with the rest of the world's program."

There are many conservatives who hate relativism, consider the French 27 wussy, and still adore soccer. But it's not a coincidence that the game has become a small touchstone in this culture war.

### III.

I wish that my side, the yuppie soccer fans, were blameless victims in these 28 culture wars. But I've been around enough of America's soccer cognoscenti to know that they invite abuse. They are inveterate snobs, so snobbish, in fact, that they think nothing of turning against their comrades. According to their sneering critique, their fellow fans are dilettantes without any real understanding of the game; they are yuppies who admire soccer like a fine slab of imported goat cheese; they come from neighborhoods with spectacularly high Starbucks-per-capita, so they lack any semblance of burning working-class passion.

This self-loathing critique can be easily debunked. I've seen the coun- 29 terevidence with my own eyes. In the spring of 2001, the U.S. national team played Honduras in Washington's Robert Francis Kennedy stadium. This vital World Cup qualifying match had generated the packed, exuberant stadium that the occasion deserved. Fans wore their nation's jersey. Their singing and stomping caused the steel and concrete to undulate like the Mexican wave. In a country with lesser engineering standards, it would have been time to worry about a stadium collapse. On the field, stewards scampered to pick up scattered sneakers. Fans had removed them and thrown them at the opposing goalkeeper, a small gesture of homage to the madness of Glasgow and the passion of Barcelona. They mercilessly booed the linesman, softening him up by insulting his slut of a mother. It might not have quite ascended to the atmospheric wonders of a game played by the English national team, but it wasn't far from that mark.

There is, however, an important difference between a home game in 30 London and Washington. The majority of English fans will root for England. In Washington, more or less half the stadium wore the blue-and-white Honduran jersey, and they were the ones who shouted themselves hoarse and heaved their shoes. The American aspiration of appearing in the World Cup rested on this game. But on that day, the Washington stadium might as well have been in Tegucigalpa.

Traveling through Europe, you hear the same complaint repeated over 31 and over: Americans are so "hypernationalistic." But is there any country in the world that would tolerate such animosity to their national team in their own national capital? In England or France or Italy, this would have been cause for unleashing hooligan hell.

Nor were the American fans what you'd expect of a hegemonic power. 32 The *Washington Post* had published a message from the national soccer federation urging us to wear red shirts as a sign of support—and to clearly distinguish ourselves from the Hondurans. But most American soccer fans don't possess a red USA jersey and aren't about to go down to the sporting goods store to buy one. They do, however, own red Arsenal, Man U., and Ajax jerseys, or, in my case, an old Barcelona one, that they collected on continental travels. While we were giving a patriotic boost, we couldn't help revealing our Europhilic cosmopolitanism.

I mention this scene because many critics of globalization make    33
America the wicked villain in the tale. They portray the U.S. forcing Nike, McDonald's, and *Baywatch* down the throats of the unwilling world, shredding ancient cultures for the sake of empire and cash. But that version of events skirts the obvious truth: Multinational corporations are just that, multinational; they don't represent American interests or American culture. Just as much as they have changed the tastes and economies of other countries, they have tried to change the tastes and economy of the United States. Witness the Nike and Budweiser campaigns to sell soccer here. No other country has been as subjected to the free flows of capital and labor, so constantly remade by migration, and found its national identity so constantly challenged. In short, America may be an exception, but it is not exceptionally immune to globalization. And we fight about it, whether we know it or not, just like everyone else.

■ ■ ■

## Reading as a Writer: Analyzing Rhetorical Choices

1.  This excerpt from Foer's book *How Soccer Explains the World: An Unlikely Theory of Globalization* includes the prologue and the final chapter. Where and how are the ideas Foer sets out in the prologue developed in the chapter about "the American culture wars"? Mark and prepare to talk about specific sentences where you see these connections.

2.  Like some of the other authors in this chapter, Foer uses his own experiences to develop his argument. Witness his description of his "soccer career" at the start of the second section. Using two different colored pens, mark in one color along the edges of the text where Foer draws on personal experience, and in the second color where he provides other kinds of evidence for his claims. What do you notice about the organization of the reading? How does using these two different approaches to his topic help Foer make his point?

## Writing as a Reader: Entering the Conversation of Ideas

1.  Foer describes a division between pro-soccer Americans and anti-soccer Americans. Kwame Anthony Appiah also examines the ways different cultural groups perceive themselves in opposition to others. Write an essay in which you draw on both authors' insights about how and why cultural groups tend to see themselves in terms of "us" versus "them." Explain to

your readers what you think might be lost and perhaps gained by seeing the world this way. How does each author—and how do you—suggest we can overcome or at least understand our differences?

2.  Both Foer and David Buckingham are interested in the effects of globalization at the local level, a dynamic Buckingham (and other writers) call "glocalization." Using ideas and examples from both authors, write an essay in which you weigh the positive and negative effects of glocalization on the ways we as Americans see ourselves in relation to the world, and how others see us. If you like, draw on a specific extended example of your own choosing to make your argument, as Foer uses soccer to make his point about globalization.

## MICHAEL S. KIMMEL

# Gender, Class, and Terrorism

Michael Kimmel is a professor of sociology at the State University of New York at Stony Brook and is known internationally for his research and writing on men and masculinity. He is part of a growing group of academics who have followed feminist theorists in thinking about gender as a cultural construct, distinct from biological gender. Kimmel is a spokesperson for NOMAS (National Organization for Men Against Sexism) and describes himself as a "profeminist man," arguing that it is in men's best interest, as well as women's, to work for gender equality.

Kimmel has written many articles and books on the topic of men's socialization that are considered landmark texts in masculinity studies, including *Manhood in America: A Cultural History* (1996), and *Guyland: The Perilous World Where Boys Become Men* (2008). As a sociologist, Kimmel is interested in the many aspects of everyday life that teach boys to become men who follow specific social scripts that privilege toughness, violence, and displays of power and confidence. This is a key theme in his essay "Gender, Class, and Terrorism," which appeared in the sixth edition of *Men's Lives* (2004), which Kimmel coedited with Michael A. Messner. For example, look at paragraph 24, where Kimmel describes Mohammed Atta, one of the pilots who crashed a plane into the World Trade Center on 9/11, pointing out that Atta's father urged him as a boy to "toughen up." While Kimmel does not formally cite his sources, he builds his argument on existing research on masculinity and violence, referring to insights from Barbara Ehrenreich, Peter Marsden, and Lothar Machtan, among others.

Before you read, you might think (and talk with your classmates) about your expectations about an essay on gender and terrorism. What kinds of examples do you expect? Consider the images of terrorists you usually see in the media and the explanations you have heard or read about what motivates terrorists. Keep them in mind as you read. Think about Kimmel's strategy in organizing the essay as he does. What surprises do you find, and what do you make of your responses?

Like many scholars of contemporary culture, Kimmel hopes to teach us something beyond what we might read in *Newsweek* or *Time*. Although the debate he enters here—why people use terrorist tactics that are as deadly to themselves as to others—is certainly a debate we hear in the media, Kimmel uses his sociological insights about masculinity to frame the issue in new ways, to help us make connections we otherwise may not see or *want* to see.

■ ■ ■

The events of September 11 [2001] have sent scholars and pundits alike   *1* scrambling to make sense of those seemingly senseless acts. While most analyses have focused on the political economy of globalization or the perversion of Islamic teachings by Al Qaeda, several commentators have raised gender issues.

Some have reminded us that in our haste to lionize the heroes of the   *2* World Trade Center collapse, we ignored the many women firefighters, police officers, and rescue workers who also risked their lives. We've been asked to remember the Taliban's vicious policies toward women; indeed, even Laura Bush seems to be championing women's emancipation.

A few have asked us to consider the other side of the gender coin:   *3* men. Some have rehearsed the rather tired old formulae about masculine bloodlust or the drive for domination and conquest, with no reference to the magnificent humanity displayed by so many on September 11. In an article in *Slate*, the Rutgers anthropologist Lionel Tiger trotted out his old male-bonding thesis but offered no understanding of why Al Qaeda might appeal to some men and not others. Only the journalist Barbara Ehrenreich suggests that there may be a link between the misogyny of the Taliban and the masculinity of the terrorists.

As for myself, I've been thinking lately about a letter to the editor of a   *4* small, upstate–New York newspaper, written in 1992 by an American GI after his return from service in the Gulf War. He complained that the legacy of the American middle class had been stolen by an indifferent government. The American dream, he wrote, has all but disappeared; instead, most people are struggling just to buy next week's groceries.

That letter writer was Timothy McVeigh from Lockport, N.Y. Two years   *5* later, he blew up the Murrah federal building in Oklahoma City in what is now the second-worst act of terrorism ever committed on American soil.

What's startling to me are the ways that McVeigh's complaints were   *6* echoed in some of the fragmentary evidence that we have seen about the terrorists of September 11, and especially in the portrait of Mohammed Atta, the suspected mastermind of the operation and the pilot of the first plane to hit the World Trade Center.

Looking at these two men through the lens of gender may shed some   *7* light on both the method and the madness of the tragedies they wrought.

McVeigh was representative of the small legion of white supremacists—   *8* from older organizations like the John Birch Society, the Ku Klux Klan, and the American Nazi Party, to newer neo-Nazi, racist-skinhead, white-power groups like Posse Comitatus and the White Aryan Resistance, to radical militias.

These white supremacists are mostly younger (in their early 20s), *9* lower-middle-class men, educated at least through high school and often beyond. They are the sons of skilled workers in industries like textiles and tobacco, the sons of the owners of small farms, shops, and grocery stores. Buffeted by global political and economic forces, the sons have inherited little of their fathers' legacies. The family farms have been lost to foreclosure, the small shops squeezed out by Wal-Marts and malls. These young men face a spiral of downward mobility and economic uncertainty. They complain that they are squeezed between the omnivorous jaws of global capital concentration and a federal bureaucracy that is at best indifferent to their plight and at worst complicit in their demise.

As one issue of *The Truth at Last*, a white-supremacist magazine, put it: *10*

> Immigrants are flooding into our nation willing to work for the minimum wage (or less). Super-rich corporate executives are flying all over the world in search of cheaper and cheaper labor so that they can lay off their American employees. . . . Many young White families have no future! They are not going to receive any appreciable wage increases due to job competition from immigrants.

What they want, says one member, is to "take back what is rightfully *11* ours."

Their anger often fixes on "others"—women, members of minority *12* groups, immigrants, gay men, and lesbians—in part because those are the people with whom they compete for entry-level, minimum-wage jobs. Above them all, enjoying the view, hovers the international Jewish conspiracy.

What holds together these "paranoid politics"—antigovernment, *13* anti–global capital but pro–small capitalist, racist, sexist, anti-Semitic, homophobic—is a rhetoric of masculinity. These men feel emasculated by big money and big government—they call the government "the Nanny State"—and they claim that "others" have been handed the birthright of native-born white men.

In the eyes of such downwardly mobile white men, most white Ameri- *14* can males collude in their own emasculation. They've grown soft, feminized, weak. White supremacists' Web sites abound with complaints about the "whimpering collapse of the blond male"; the "legions of sissies and weaklings, of flabby, limp-wristed, non-aggressive, non-physical, indecisive, slack-jawed, fearful males who, while still heterosexual in theory and practice, have not even a vestige of the old macho spirit."

American white supremacists thus offer American men the restora- *15* tion of their masculinity—a manhood in which individual white men control the fruits of their own labor and are not subject to emasculation by Jewish-owned finance capital or a black- and feminist-controlled welfare state. Theirs is the militarized manhood of the heroic John Rambo, a manhood that celebrates their God-sanctioned right to band together in armed militias if anyone, or any government agency, tries to take it away from them. If the state and the economy emasculate them, and if the masculinity of the "others" is problematic, then only "real" white men can rescue America from a feminized, multicultural, androgynous melting pot.

Sound familiar? For the most part, the terrorists of September 11 come   *16* from the same class, and recite the same complaints, as American white supremacists.

Virtually all were under twenty-five, educated, lower middle class or   *17* middle class, downwardly mobile. The journalist Nasra Hassan interviewed families of Middle Eastern suicide bombers (as well as some failed bombers themselves) and found that none of them had the standard motivations ascribed to people who commit suicide, such as depression.

Although several of the leaders of Al Qaeda are wealthy—Osama bin   *18* Laden is a multimillionaire, and Ayman al-Zawahiri, the fifty-year-old doctor thought to be bin Laden's closest adviser, is from a fashionable suburb of Cairo—many of the hijackers were engineering students for whom job opportunities had been dwindling dramatically. (Judging from the minimal information I have found, about one-fourth of the hijackers had studied engineering.) Zacarias Moussaoui, who did not hijack one of the planes but is the first man to be formally charged in the United States for crimes related to September 11, earned a degree at London's South Bank University. Marwan al-Shehhi, the chubby, bespectacled twenty-three-year-old from the United Arab Emirates who flew the second plane into the World Trade Center, was an engineering student, while Ziad Jarrah, the twenty-six-year-old Lebanese who flew the plane that crashed in Pennsylvania, had studied aircraft design.

Politically, these terrorists opposed globalization and the spread of   *19* Western values; they opposed what they perceived as corrupt regimes in several Arab states (notably Saudi Arabia and Egypt), which they claimed were merely puppets of American domination. "The resulting anger is naturally directed first against their rulers," writes the historian Bernard Lewis, "and then against those whom they see as keeping those rulers in power for selfish reasons."

Central to their political ideology is the recovery of manhood from the   *20* emasculating politics of globalization. The Taliban saw the Soviet invasion and westernization of Afghanistan as humiliations. Bin Laden's October 7 videotape describes the "humiliation and disgrace" that Islam has suffered "for more than eighty years." And over and over, Nasra Hassan writes, she heard the refrain: "The Israelis humiliate us. They occupy our land, and deny our history."

Terrorism is fueled by a fatal brew of antiglobalization politics, convoluted Islamic theology, and virulent misogyny. According to Ehrenreich,   *21* while these formerly employed or self-employed males "have lost their traditional status as farmers and breadwinners, women have been entering the market economy and gaining the marginal independence conferred by even a paltry wage." As a result, "the man who can no longer make a living, who has to depend on his wife's earnings, can watch Hollywood sexpots on pirated videos and begin to think the world has been turned upside down."

The Taliban's policies thus had two purposes: to remasculinize men and   22
to refeminize women. Another journalist, Peter Marsden, has observed that those policies "could be seen as a desperate attempt to keep out that other world, and to protect Afghan women from influences that could weaken the society from within." The Taliban prohibited women from appearing in public unescorted by men, from revealing any part of their body, and from going to school or holding a job. Men were required to grow their beards, in accordance with religious images of Muhammad, yes; but also, perhaps, because wearing beards has always been associated with men's response to women's increased equality in the public sphere, since beards symbolically reaffirm biological differences between men and women, while gender equality tends to blur those differences.

The Taliban's policies removed women as competitors and also shored   23
up masculinity, since they enabled men to triumph over the humiliations of globalization and their own savage, predatory, and violently sexual urges that might be unleashed in the presence of uncovered women.

All of these issues converged in the life of Mohammed Atta, the terrorist   24
about whom the most has been written and conjectured. Currently, for example, there is much speculation about Atta's sexuality. Was he gay? Was he a repressed homosexual, too ashamed of his sexuality to come out? Such innuendoes are based on no more than a few circumstantial tidbits about his life. He was slim, sweet-faced, neat, meticulous, a snazzy dresser. The youngest child of an ambitious lawyer father and a pampering mother, Atta grew up shy and polite, a mama's boy. "He was so gentle," his father said. "I used to tell him, 'Toughen up, boy!'"

When such revelations are offered, storytellers seem to expect a reaction   25
like "Aha! So that explains it!" (Indeed, in a new biography of Adolf Hitler, *The Hidden Hitler,* Lothar Machtan offers exactly that sort of explanation. He argues that many of Hitler's policies—such as the killing of longtime colleague and avowed homosexual Ernst Rohm, or even the systematic persecution and execution of gay men in concentration camps—were, in fact, prompted by a desire to conceal his own homosexuality.)

But what do such accusations actually explain? Do revelations about   26
Hitler's or Atta's possible gay propensities raise troubling connections between homosexuality and mass murder? If so, then one would also have to conclude that the discovery of Shakespeare's "gay" sonnet explains the Bard's genius at explicating Hamlet's existential anguish, or that Michelangelo's sexuality is the decisive factor in his painting of God's touch in the Sistine Chapel.

Such revelations tell us little about the Holocaust or September 11.   27
They do, however, address the consequences of homophobia—both official and informal—on young men who are exploring their sexual identities. What's relevant is not the possible fact of Hitler's or Atta's gayness, but

the shame and fear that surround homosexuality in societies that refuse to acknowledge sexual diversity.

Even more troubling is what such speculation leaves out. What unites   28
Atta, McVeigh, and Hitler is not their repressed sexual orientation but gender—their masculinity, their sense of masculine entitlement, and their thwarted ambitions. They accepted cultural definitions of masculinity, and needed someone to blame when they felt that they failed to measure up. (After all, being called a mama's boy, a sissy, and told to toughen up are demands for gender conformity, not matters of sexual desire.) Gender is the issue, not sexuality.

All three failed at their chosen professions. Hitler was a failed   29
artist—indeed, he failed at just about every job he ever tried except dictator. McVeigh, a business-college dropout, found his calling in the military during the Gulf War, where his exemplary service earned him commendations; but he washed out of Green Beret training—his dream job—after only two days. And Atta was the odd man out in his family. His two sisters both became doctors—one a physician and one a university professor. His father constantly reminded him that he wanted "to hear the word 'doctor' in front of his name. We told him, your sisters are doctors and their husbands are doctors and you are the man of the family."

Atta decided to become an engineer, but his degree meant little in a   30
country where thousands of college graduates were unable to find good jobs. After he failed to find employment in Egypt, he went to Hamburg, Germany, to study architecture. He was "meticulous, disciplined, and highly intelligent, an ordinary student, a quiet, friendly guy who was totally focused on his studies," according to another student in Hamburg.

But his ambitions were constantly undone. His only hope for a good   31
job in Egypt was to be hired by an international firm. He applied and was continually rejected. He found work as a draftsman—highly humiliating for someone with engineering and architectural credentials and an imperious and demanding father—for a German firm involved with razing low-income Cairo neighborhoods to provide more scenic vistas for luxury tourist hotels.

Defeated, humiliated, emasculated, a disappointment to his father   32
and a failed rival to his sisters, Atta retreated into increasingly militant Islamic theology. By the time he assumed the controls of American Airlines Flight 11, he evinced a hysteria about women. In the message he left in his abandoned rental car, he made clear what mattered to him in the end. "I don't want pregnant women or a person who is not clean to come and say good-bye to me," he wrote. "I don't want women to go to my funeral or later to my grave." Of course, Atta's body was instantly incinerated, and no burial would be likely.

The terrors of emasculation experienced by lower-middle-class men   33
all over the world will no doubt continue, as they struggle to make a place for themselves in shrinking economies and inevitably shifting cultures. They may continue to feel a seething resentment against women, whom

they perceive as stealing their rightful place at the head of the table, and against the governments that displace them. Globalization feels to them like a game of musical chairs, in which, when the music stops, all the seats are handed to others by nursemaid governments.

The events of September 11, as well as of April 19, 1995 (the Oklahoma City bombing), resulted from an increasingly common combination of factors—the massive male displacement that accompanies globalization, the spread of American consumerism, and the perceived corruption of local political elites—fused with a masculine sense of entitlement. Someone else—some "other"—had to be held responsible for the terrorists' downward mobility and failures, and the failure of their fathers to deliver their promised inheritance. The terrorists didn't just get mad. They got even. 34

Such themes were not lost on the disparate bands of young white supremacists. American Aryans admired the terrorists' courage and chastised their own compatriots. "It's a disgrace that in a population of at least 150 million White/Aryan Americans, we provide so few that are willing to do the same [as the terrorists]," bemoaned Rocky Suhayda, the chairman of the American Nazi Party. "A bunch of towel head/sand niggers put our great White Movement to shame." 35

It is from such gendered shame that mass murderers are made. 36

■ ■ ■

## Reading as a Writer: Analyzing Rhetorical Choices

1. What effect do you think Kimmel hopes to achieve with his comparisons of Timothy McVeigh, Mohammed Atta, and Adolf Hitler? What similarities does he mention? How are these comparisons important to Kimmel's argument?

2. Circle any words that are unfamiliar to you—perhaps *misogyny* or *emasculation*. Look them up so that you feel comfortable explaining them in your own words. Based on his vocabulary and examples, who is Kimmel's audience?

## Writing as a Reader: Entering the Conversation of Ideas

1. How do Kimmel's insights about us-versus-them dynamics compare to Kwame Anthony Appiah's insights? Compose an essay in which you draw on both authors' ideas and examples in order to make an argument about how and why cultural groups tend to see themselves in terms of "us" versus "them." Explain to your readers what you think might be lost and perhaps gained by seeing the world this way. How does each author—and how do you—suggest we can overcome or at least understand our differences?

2. Both Kimmel and Franklin Foer are interested in the relationship between the expected behaviors of American men and masculine behaviors in other countries and cultures. Write an essay in which you draw on each author's

insights and examples to make an argument about how and why you think we often focus on "what it means to be a man" when it comes to defining cultures. What do discussions about masculinity reveal and perhaps conceal about cultures? What significance do you see in your findings?

## KWAME ANTHONY APPIAH

# Moral Disagreement

Kwame Anthony Appiah grew up in Ghana and received his advanced degrees at Cambridge University in England. He is the Laurence S. Rockefeller University Professor of Philosophy at the University Center for Human Values at Princeton University, where he teaches and does research in philosophy, ethics and identity, African and African American cultural and literary studies, and the philosophical foundations of liberalism. He has published extensively on these topics and has also written three novels and an autobiographical reflection on philosophy titled *In My Father's House: Africa in the Philosophy of Culture* (1992).

This reading is taken from a chapter of Appiah's book *Cosmopolitanism: Ethics in a World of Strangers* (2006), which explores the challenge of acting ethically in a world that is both "shrinking" and increasingly characterized by clashing civilizations. Appiah brings his philosophical training to bear on the impact of globalization, terrorism, and other economic and political realities that shape modern life, in order to understand what our obligations to others should be in this rapidly changing environment. In this book, Appiah joins in conversation with George Lakoff, Martha Nussbaum, and other contemporary scholars who study the role of ethics in a politically charged world.

If all this sounds too scholarly or too abstract to be interesting, you may be surprised by the pop culture examples and lively tone that characterize Appiah's writing. Pay attention to the way he draws ethical questions out of an imagined debate between fans of the film *Million Dollar Baby* and those who prefer *Sideways*. Appiah relies on this rhetorical strategy—moving from smaller personal examples to larger theoretical ones—repeatedly in this reading. Notice the way he applies this strategy sometimes within a sentence and at other times to organize a larger passage. This is a writing tactic you can try as well.

Notice, too, the effect of dividing this chapter into many short sections with catchy titles like "Red Peppers on Wednesdays" and "Gross Points." How do the short sections and titles help keep you focused and interested? Appiah sets out to teach us "big ideas" about our moral universe, but he does so through many small examples of what it means to be "cosmopolitan" in today's environment.

You might test the applicability of Appiah's ideas by discussing with your classmates the international news headlines on the day you read and think about this piece. To what extent does Appiah offer tools for analyzing what unites and divides world citizens *today*? What will it take for us to become truly "cosmopolitan"?

■ ■ ■

# Through Thick and Thin

You don't need to leave home to have disagreements about questions of *1* value. In a crowd of people leaving a movie theater, someone thinks *Million Dollar Baby* superior to *Sideways*, but her companion demurs. "How can you respect a movie that tells you that the life of a quadriplegic is so worthless that you ought to kill her if she asks you to?" In a lively discussion after a barroom brawl, some say that the bystander who intervened was courageous, others that he was reckless and should just have called the cops. In a classroom discussion of abortion, one student says that first-trimester abortions are bad for the mother and the fetus, but that they ought to be legal, if the mother chooses. Another thinks that killing a fetus isn't even as bad as killing a grown-up cat. A third claims all abortion is murder. If we are to encourage cosmopolitan engagement, moral conversation between people *across* societies, we must expect such disagreements: after all, they occur *within* societies.

But moral conflicts come in different varieties. To begin with, our vo- *2* cabulary of evaluation is enormously multifarious. Some terms—"good," "ought"—are, as philosophers often put it, rather *thin*. They express approval, but their application is otherwise pretty unconstrained: good soil, good dog, good argument, good idea, good person. Knowing what the word means doesn't tell you much about what it applies to. Of course, there are certain acts that you can't imagine thinking are good. That's because you can't make sense of approving of them, though not because it's somehow built into the meaning of the word "good" that, say, snatching food from a starving child doesn't count.

Much of our language of evaluation, however, is much "thicker" than *3* this. To apply the concept of "rudeness," for example, you have to think of the act you're criticizing as a breach of good manners or as lacking the appropriate degree of concern for the feelings of others. I say, *"Thank you,"* ironically, when you accidentally step on my foot, implying that you did it deliberately. That's rude. Thanking a person, without irony, for something that he's done for you isn't. "Courage" is a term of praise. But its meaning is more substantive than a thin term like "right" or "good": To be courageous requires that you do something that strikes us as risky or dangerous, something where you have something to lose. Opening the front door could be courageous: but only if you had agoraphobia or knew that the secret police had rung the doorbell.

Thin concepts are something like placeholders. When notions of right *4* and wrong are actually at work, they're thickly enmeshed in the complications of particular social contexts. In that sense, as the distinguished American political theorist Michael Walzer says, morality starts out thick. It's when you're trying to find points of agreement with others, say, that you start to abstract out the thin concepts that may underlie the thick ones.[1]

---

[1] Michael Walzer, *Thick and Thin: Moral Arguments at Home and Abroad* (Notre Dame: University of Notre Dame Press, 1994).

Thin concepts seem to be universal; we aren't the only people who have   5
the concepts of right and wrong, good and bad; every society, it seems, has
terms that correspond to these thin concepts, too. Even thick concepts like
rudeness and courage are ones that you find pretty much everywhere. But
there are thicker concepts still that really are peculiar to particular societies. And the most fundamental level of disagreement occurs when one
party to a discussion invokes a concept that the other simply doesn't have.
This is the kind of disagreement where the struggle is not to agree but just
to understand.

## Family Matters

Sometimes, familiar values are intertwined with unfamiliar customs   6
and arrangements. People everywhere have ideas about your responsibility to your children, for instance. But who are your children? I grew up
in two societies that conceived of family in rather different ways. In part,
because these societies—Akan society in Ghana and the English world of
my mother's kin—have been in touch with one another for several centuries, these differences are diminishing. Still, an important difference
remains.

Consider the Akan idea of the *abusua*. This is a group of people related   7
by common ancestry, who have relations of love and obligation to one
another; the closer in time your shared ancestors, roughly speaking, the
stronger the bonds. Sounds, in short, like a family. But there is an important difference between an *abusua* and a family. For your membership in
an *abusua* depends only on who your mother is. Your father is irrelevant.
If you are a woman, then your children are in your *abusua*, and so are the
descendants of your daughters, and their daughters, on to the end of time.
Membership in the *abusua* is shared like mitochondrial DNA, passing only
through women. So I am in the same *abusua* as my sister's children but
not in the same one as my brother's children. And, since I am not related
to my father through a woman, he is not a member of my *abusua* either.

In short, the conception of the family in Akan culture is what anthro-   8
pologists call *matrilineal*. A hundred years ago, in most lives, your mother's
brother—your senior maternal uncle or *wɔfa*—would have played the role
a father would have been expected to play in England. He was responsible,
with the child's mother, for making sure that his sister's children—the
word is *wɔfase*—were fed, clothed, and educated. Many married women
lived with their brothers, visiting their husbands on a regular timetable.
Of course, a man took an interest in his children, but his obligations to
his children were relatively less demanding: rather like being an English
uncle, in fact.

Visitors are often somewhat surprised that the word that you would   9
most naturally use to refer to your brother or sister—which is *nua*—is
also the word for the children of your mother's *sisters*. And, in fact, people

sometimes will tell you, in Ghanaian English, that someone is "my sister, same father, same mother," which you might have thought was a couple of qualifications too many. (If someone tells you that a woman is his junior mother, on the other hand, he's referring to his mother's younger sister.)

When I was a child all this was changing. More men were living with *10* their wives and children and not supporting their sisters' children. But my father still got the school reports of his sisters' children, sent them pocket money, discussed, with their mothers, their schooling, paid the bills at the family house of his *abusua*. He also regularly ate with his favorite sister, while his children and wife—that's us—ate together at home.

There are, in short, different ways of organizing family life. Which one *11* makes sense to you will depend, in good measure, on the concepts with which you grew up. As long as a society has a way of assigning responsibilities for the nurture of children that works and makes sense, it seems to me, it would be odd to say that one way was the right way of doing it, and all the others wrong. We feel, rightly, that a father who is delinquent in his child support payments is doing something wrong. Many Asante, especially in the past, would feel the same about a delinquent *wɔfa*. Once you understand the system, you'll be likely to agree: and it won't be because you've given up any of your basic moral commitments. There are thin, universal values here—those of good parenting—but their expression is highly particular, thickly enmeshed with local customs and expectations and the facts of social arrangements.

## Red Peppers on Wednesdays

But there are other local values that scarcely correspond to anything you *12* might recognize as important. My father, for example, wouldn't eat "bush meat," animals killed in the forest. This included venison, and, he used to tell us, when he once ate it by accident in England, his skin broke out in a rash the next day. Had you asked him why he wouldn't eat bush meat, though, he wouldn't have said he didn't like it or that he was allergic to it. He would have told you—if he thought it was any of your business—that it was *akyiwadeɛ* for him, because he was of the clan of the Bush Cow. Etymologically *akyiwadeɛ* means something like "a thing you turn your back on," and, if you had to guess at the translation of it, you would presumably suggest "taboo." That is, of course, a word that came into English from a Polynesian language, where it was used to refer to a class of things that people of certain groups strenuously avoided.

As in Polynesia, in Asante doing one of these forbidden things leaves *13* you "polluted," and there are various remedies, ways of "cleansing" yourself. We all have experience with the sense of revulsion, and the desire to cleanse ourselves, but that doesn't mean that we really have the concept of *akyiwadeɛ*. Because to have that idea—that thick concept—you have to think that there are things that you ought not to do because of your clan membership, or because they are taboo to a god to whom you owe allegiance. Now, you might say that there's a rationale of sorts for a member of the Bush Cow clan's not eating bush meat. Your clan animal is, symbolically, a relative of yours; so, for you, eating it (and its relatives) is a bit like eating a person. And perhaps this is one rationalization that a member of the clan might offer. But the list of *akyiwadeɛ* in traditional Asante society far exceeds anything that you can make sense of in this sort of way. One shrine god named Edinkra—mentioned in the 1920s by Captain Rattray, the colonial anthropologist who first wrote extensively about Asante traditions—had among its taboos red peppers on Wednesdays.

Now, I don't claim that you can't learn what *akyiwadeɛ* means: indeed, I hope you pretty much grasp how the word is used on the basis of what I've told you already, and if you read the complete works of Captain Rattray, you'd know a lot more about Akan taboos, certainly enough to grasp the concept. Nevertheless, this isn't an idea that plays any role in your actual thinking. There are acts we avoid that we rather loosely call "taboo," of course: the prohibition on incest, for example. But you don't really think incest is to be avoided because it is taboo. Your thought is exactly the other way round: it's "taboo" because there are good reasons not to do it.    14

Some *akyiwadeɛ*, like the one that prohibited my father from eating venison, are specific to particular kinds of people, as is evidenced in a proverb that makes a metaphor of the fact:    15

> Nnipa gu ahodoɔ mmiɛnsa, nanso obiara wɔ n'akyiwadeɛ: ɔhene, ɔdehyeɛ na akoa. Ɔhene akyiwadɛ ne akyinnyeɛ, ɔdehyeɛ deɛ ne nsamu, na akoa deɛ ne nkyeraseɛ.
> *People fall into three kinds, but everyone has his own taboo: the ruler, the royal, and the slave. The ruler's taboo is disagreement, the royal's is disrespect, and the slave's is the revealing of origins.*

As a result, even if you were in Asante, many taboos wouldn't affect you, since you don't belong to an Asante clan and don't have obligations to shrine gods. But there are many things all Asantes "turn their backs on" and would expect everyone else to as well. Given that some of them have to do with contact with menstruating women or men who have recently had sex, they can affect strangers, even if strangers don't act on them. Once you know about the taboos, they can raise questions as to how you should act. Since, for example, shaking hands with a menstruating woman is taboo to a chief, some visitors to the Asante court have a decision to make about whether to come to a meeting.

I have deliberately not used the word "moral" to describe these taboos. They are certainly values: They guide acts, thoughts, and feelings. They are unlike what we would think of as moral values, however, in at least three ways. First, they don't always apply to everybody. Only members of the Ekuona clan have the obligation to avoid bush meat. Second, you are polluted if you break a taboo, even if you do it by accident. So, whereas with an offense against morality, "I didn't mean to do it" counts as a substantial defense,    16 with taboo breaking, the reply must be, "It doesn't matter what you meant to do. You're polluted. You need to get clean." Oedipus was no better off for having broken the incest taboo unknowingly. A final difference between taboos and moral demands is that breaches of them pollute mostly *you*: They aren't fundamentally about how you should treat other people; they're about how you should keep yourself (ritually) clean.

Now, all around the world many people have believed in something 17 like *akyiwadeɛ*, and the analogous term, *tabu* or whatever, is certainly a powerful part of evaluative language. But—at least nowadays—while the avoidance of taboos is still important to people, it isn't as important as many other sorts of values. That's partly because, as I said, while breaches of taboo produce pollution, that pollution can usually be ritually cleansed. The laws of kashrut for Orthodox Jews in our country are like this, too: obedience to them is important, and so is a commitment to obeying them if you can. If you break them accidentally, however, the right response is not guilt but the appropriate ritual form of purification. Moral offenses—theft, assault, murder—on the other hand, are not expiated by purification. Now there are historical trends that help explain why a concern with *akyiwadeɛ* plays a smaller part in contemporary life in my hometown than it would have done when my father was growing up. One reason is that even more people now are Christian and Muslim, and these taboos are associated with earlier forms of religion. Our earlier religious ideas survive, as I've noted, even in the lives of devout believers in these global faiths. They just have less weight than they had before they were competing with Jehovah and Allah. In the old days, you had reason to fear the wrath of the gods or the ancestors if you broke taboos—that was part of why it was important to make peace with them by cleansing yourself. But these powers have less respect in the contemporary world. . . .

Another reason is that the forms of identity—the clan identities, 18 for example—with which they are often associated are just a good deal less significant than they used to be. People still mostly know their clans. And in the past, when you showed up in a strange town in another part of the Akan world, you could have sought hospitality from the local leaders of your clan. Now, however, there are hotels; travel is commoner (so the demands of clan hospitality could easily become oppressive); and clans, like the families of which they are a part, recede in importance anyway when so many people live away from the places where they were born.

Equally important, I think, most people in Kumasi know now that 19 our taboos are local: that strangers do not know what is and is not taboo and that, if they do, they have taboos of their own. So increasingly people think of taboos as "things *we* don't do." The step from "what *we* don't do" to "what we *happen* not to do" can be a small one; and then people can come to think of these practices as the sort of quaint local custom that one observes without much enthusiasm and, in the end, only when it doesn't cause too much fuss.

## Gross Points

The *akyiwadeɛ* is, as we've seen, thickly enmeshed in all sorts of customs   *20* and factual beliefs (not least the existence of irascible ancestors and shrine gods), and one response to such alien values is just to dismiss them as primitive and irrational. But if that is what they are, then the primitive and the irrational are pervasive here, too. Indeed, the affect, the sense of repugnance, that underlies *akyiwadeɛ* is surely universal: That's one reason it's not difficult to grasp. Many Americans eat pigs but won't eat cats. It would be hard to make the case that cats are, say, dirtier or more intelligent than pigs. And since there are societies where people *will* eat cats, we know that it is possible for human beings to eat them with pleasure and without danger. Most American meat eaters who refuse to eat cats have only the defense that the very thought of it fills them with disgust. Indeed, all of us have things that we find contact with polluting: touching them makes us feel dirty; eating them would nauseate us. We're likely to run off to wash our hands or wash out our mouths if we come into contact with them. Mostly, when we have these responses, we defend them as rational: Cockroaches and rats and other people's saliva or vomit do actually carry diseases, we say; cats and dogs taste horrible. Yet these reactions are not really explained by the stories we tell. Flies carry most of the same risks as cockroaches, but usually produce less "pollution." And people are disgusted by the idea of drinking orange juice that has had a cockroach in it, even if they know that the cockroach was rigorously cleansed of all bacteria by being autoclaved in advance. They're reluctant to eat chocolate shaped like dog feces, even if they know exactly what it is.

Psychologists (notably Paul Rozin, who has conducted many experi-   *21* ments along these lines) think that this capacity for disgust is a fundamental human trait, one that evolved in us because distinguishing between what you will and will not eat is an important cognitive task for an omnivorous species like our own. Disgust goes with nausea, because it is a response that developed to deal with food that we should avoid. But that capacity for disgust, like all our natural capacities, can be built on by culture. Is it the *same* capacity that makes some men in many cultures feel polluted when they learn they have shaken hands with a menstruating woman? Or that makes most Americans squirm in disgust at the thought of incest? I don't think we yet know. The pervasiveness of these taboo responses does suggest, however, that they draw on something deep in human nature.[2]

Most people in this country, both secular and religious, think that   *22* the attitudes of some of their contemporaries to certain sexual acts— masturbation and homosexuality, for instance, or even consensual adult

[2] See Paul Rozin, "Food Is Fundamental, Fun, Frightening, and Far-reaching," *Social Research* 66 (1999): 9–30. I am grateful to John Haidt for a discussion of these issues.

incest—are simply versions of taboos found in many cultures around the world. In the so-called Holiness Code, at the end of Leviticus, for example, eating animals that have died of natural causes requires you to wash yourself and your clothes, and even then you will be unclean until the evening (Leviticus 17:15–16). Priests, "the sons of Aaron," are told at Leviticus 22:5–8 that if they touch people or "any swarming thing" that is polluting, they must bathe and wait until sunset before they can eat the "sacred donations." The same chapters proscribe the consuming of blood, bodily self-mutilation (tattoos, shaving for priests, cutting gashes in one's flesh, though not, of course, male circumcision), and seeing various of one's relatives naked, while prescribing detailed rules for certain kinds of sacrifice. For most modern Christians, these regulations are parts of Jewish law that Christ freed people from. But the famous proscriptions of a man's "lying with a man as with a woman" are to be found alongside these passages, along with commands to avoid incest and bestiality, which most Christians still endorse.[3]

Earlier in Leviticus, we find an extensive set of proscriptions on contact, both direct and indirect, with menstruating women and rules for cleansing oneself from that form of pollution; as well as rules that indicate that male ejaculation is polluting, so that, even after a man has bathed, he is ritually unclean until evening.[4] Like Akan traditions, these rules are embedded in metaphysical beliefs: They are repeatedly said to be laws given by God to Moses for the Israelites, and often they have religious explanations embedded in them. The prohibition on consuming blood is explained thus:

> For the life of the flesh is in the blood. And as for Me, I have given it to you on the altar to ransom your lives, for it is the blood that ransoms in exchange for life. Therefore have I said to the Israelites: no living person among you shall consume blood, nor shall the sojourner who sojourns in your midst consume blood.[5]

Leviticus should remind us that appeals to values do not come neatly parceled out according to kinds. You might think that failing to respect your parents is a bad thing, but that it's bad in a way that's different from adultery; different, too, from sex with an animal; different, again, from incest with your daughter-in-law. I confess that I do not think sex between men, even if they lie with one another "as with a woman," is bad at all. But all of these acts are proscribed in succession by the Holiness Code; in fact (in Leviticus 20:9–13) all of them are deemed worthy of death.

Among those who take them seriously, these prohibitions evoke a deep, visceral response; they're also entangled in beliefs about metaphysical or religious matters. The combination of these two features is what makes

---

[3] Leviticus 18:22 and 20:13.
[4] Menstruation: Leviticus 15:19–28. Male ejaculation: Leviticus 15:16–18.
[5] Leviticus 17:11–13. . . . The proscription itself is in the preceding verse.

them so difficult to discuss with people who share neither the response nor the metaphysics. Yet even with values we do not take seriously, there is something to be hoped for: namely, understanding. Nor do you have to share a value to feel how it might motivate someone. We can be moved by Antigone's resolve to bury her brother's corpse, even if (unlike those Indians and Greeks that Darius scandalized) we couldn't care less about how cadavers are disposed of, and think she shouldn't really, either.

And while taboos can lead to genuine disagreements about what to    26
do, many people readily understand that such values vary from place to place. Asante people largely accept now that others don't feel the power of our taboos; we know that they may have their own. And, most importantly, these local values do not, of course, stop us from also recognizing, as we do, kindness, generosity, and compassion, or cruelty, stinginess, and inconsiderateness—virtues and vices that are recognized widely among human societies. So, too, scattered among the various abominations in Leviticus we come across, from time to time, appeals to values that are universal and that discipline the demands made by the taboos. Leviticus 19 commands us to leave a share of our crops for the poor, to avoid lying and dissembling, fraud, and theft; not to speak ill of the deaf or put a stumbling block in the way of the blind; not to slander our relatives. Indeed, it makes the impossibly demanding command that "you shall love your fellow man as yourself" (Leviticus 19:18). There are values here that not all of us recognize; there are many we all do.

## Terms of Contention

Cosmopolitans suppose that all cultures have enough overlap in their    27
vocabulary of values to begin a conversation. But they don't suppose, like some universalists, that we could all come to agreement if only we had the same vocabulary. Despite what they say in Japan, almost every American knows what it is to be polite, a thickish concept. That doesn't mean that we can't disagree about when politeness is on display. A journalist interviews a foreign dictator, someone who is known for his abuses of human rights. She speaks deferentially, frequently calling him Your Excellency. She says, "Some people have suggested that you have political prisoners in your jails," when everybody knows that this is so. "What do you say, Your Excellency, to the accusations of torture by your secret police?" "Nonsense," he replies. "Lies made up by people who want to confuse foreigners about the progress we are making in my country." She moves on. Is this politeness? Or is it a craven abdication of the journalist's obligation to press for the truth? Can it be both? If it is politeness, is it appropriate, in these circumstances, to be polite? You can imagine such a conversation proceeding for a long while without resolution.

Politeness is a value term from the repertory of manners, which we    28
usually take to be less serious than morals. But this sort of controversy also surrounds the application of more straightforwardly ethical terms—like

"brave"—and more centrally moral ones—like "cruel." Like most terms for virtues and vices, "courage" and "cruelty" are what philosophers call "open-textured": two people who both know what they mean can reasonably disagree about whether they apply in a particular case.[6] Grasping what the words mean doesn't give you a rule that will definitively decide whether it applies in every case that might come along. Nearly half a century ago, the philosopher of law H. L. A. Hart offered as an example of open texture, a bylaw that prohibits "vehicles" in a public park. Does it apply to a two-inch-long toy car in a child's pocket? "Vehicle" has an open texture. There are things to be said on either side. Of course, in the context of the rule, it may be clear that the idea was to stop people from driving around, disturbing the peace. Let the child bring in the toy. But doesn't that rationale suggest that a skateboard is a vehicle? There need be no reason to think that those who made the rule had any answer to this question in mind. Our language works very well in ordinary and familiar cases. Once things get interesting, even people who know the language equally well can disagree.

The open texture of our evaluative language is even more obvious. 29 One of my great-uncles once led a cavalry charge against a machine-gun emplacement, armed with a sword. Brave? Or just foolhardy? (You may have guessed that this uncle was Asante; actually, he was English, fighting against the Ottomans in the First World War. Great-Uncle Fred called his autobiography *Life's a Gamble,* so you can tell he was willing to take risks.) Aristotle argued that courage involved an *intelligent* response to danger, not just ignoring it. Perhaps, in the circumstances and given his aims, that saber charge *was* the smartest thing to do. Still, even if we got as full a story as we could ask for about the exact circumstances, you and I might end up disagreeing.

Several years ago, an international parliament of religious leaders 30 issued what they called a "universal declaration of a global ethic." The credo's exhortations had the quality of those horoscopes that seem wonderfully precise while being vague enough to suit all comers. "We must not commit any kind of sexual immorality": a fine sentiment, unless we don't agree about what counts as sexual immorality. "We must put behind us all forms of domination and abuse": but societies that, by our lights, subject women to domination and abuse are unlikely to recognize themselves in that description. They're convinced that they're protecting women's honor and chastity. "We must strive for a just social and economic order, in which everyone has an equal chance to reach full potential as a human being": a Randian will take this to be an endorsement of unfettered capitalism, as a Fabian will take it to be an endorsement of socialism.

---

[6] H. L. A. Hart introduced the idea of "open texture" to discussions of jurisprudence in *The Concept of Law* (Oxford: Clarendon Press, 1997), chap. 6. He borrowed the idea of open texture from F. Waismann, who thought open texture was an irreducible feature of language. The example of the bylaw about vehicles in the park is Hart's; see his "Positivism and the Separation of Law and Morals," *Harvard Law Review* 71 (1958): 593–629.

And so it goes with our most central values. Is it cruel to kill cattle in   *31*
slaughterhouses where live cattle can smell the blood of the dead? Or to
spank children in order to teach them how to behave? The point is not that
we couldn't argue our way to one position or the other on these questions;
it's only to say that when we disagree, it won't always be because one of us
just doesn't understand the value that's at stake. It's because applying value
terms to new cases requires judgment and discretion. Indeed, it's often
part of our understanding of these terms that their applications are *meant*
to be argued about. They are, to use another piece of philosopher's jargon,
*essentially contestable.* For many concepts, as W. B. Gallie wrote in introducing the term, "proper use inevitably involves endless disputes about
their proper use on the part of users."[7] Evaluative language, I've been
insisting, aims to shape not just our acts but our thoughts and our feelings.
When we describe past acts with words like "courageous" and "cowardly,"
"cruel" and "kind," we are shaping what people think and feel about what
was done—and shaping our understanding of our moral language as well.
Because that language is open-textured and essentially contestable, even
people who share a moral vocabulary have plenty to fight about. . . .

[7] W.B. Gallie, "Essentially Contested Concepts" *Proceedings of the Aristotelian Society* 56 (1956) : 169.

■ ■ ■

### Reading as a Writer: Analyzing Rhetorical Choices

1.  Explain in your own words what Appiah means by the terms *thick* and
    *thin* as applied to the concept of morality, and give several examples of
    each category. What benefit do you see in using these metaphors of depth
    (thickness and thinness) for explaining different kinds of morality?

2.  What do you think is the purpose of the long list of taboos Appiah includes
    in the "Gross Points" section of this reading? What effect do you think he
    hopes to have on his readers by describing the different things that disgust
    people in different cultures? How is this strategy connected to the overall
    argument he is making?

### Writing as a Reader: Entering the Conversation of Ideas

1.  Both Appiah and Fareed Zakaria demonstrate the problems of and offer
    some solutions to thinking about the place of the United States in the glob-
    alized world. Write an essay in which you place these writers in conversa-
    tion, considering what each would think of the way the other frames the
    problems and possible solutions. Where do you stand in this debate?

2.  Appiah and Ann duCille use quite different kinds of examples and evidence
    to explore a similar idea—the ways we understand cultural differences.
    Compose an essay in which you use both authors' ideas and some selected
    examples from each text to show what we can learn from the desire and
    anxiety that can arise when we try to cross cultures. What is the signifi-
    cance of your findings for citizens in an increasingly globalized world?

# Patriotism and Cosmopolitanism

Martha Nussbaum is a well-known American philosopher who has taught at Harvard University and Brown University and currently is the Ernst Freund Distinguished Service Professor of Law and Ethics at the University of Chicago. She has published widely and is read and cited frequently in discussions on ancient Greek and Roman philosophy; however, because she is also interested in applying her insights to contemporary political, religious, and ethical debates, her work reaches far beyond the discipline of philosophy. As you will see in this essay, she is skilled at helping readers analyze specific, current examples of philosophical dilemmas in action. Nussbaum has published voluminously on the ways our daily experiences and values are shaped by our assumptions about ethics, goodness, fairness, and what constitutes a "good education." Her book-length arguments include *Cultivating Humanity: A Classical Defense of Reform in Liberal Education* (1997), *Sex and Social Justice* (1999), and, most recently, *From Disgust to Humanity: Sexual Orientation and Constitutional Law* (2010).

This piece on "Patriotism and Cosmopolitanism" appeared in the *Boston Review* in 1994 and launched a series of responses, one of which, by Cynthia C. Scott, we include next. Nussbaum begins by quoting philosopher Richard Rorty's defense of patriotism in a widely cited *New York Times* op-ed and proceeds to lead readers through what she sees as the values and shortcomings of Rorty's stance. Nussbaum moves back in history (all the way to the Stoics, third-century B.C.E. philosophers who tied ethics to logic) and forward to classroom applications of the ideals of patriotism and cosmopolitanism. Nussbaum proposes applying the Stoics' insights to our present selves. In paragraph 6, she suggests an activity you might try—mapping yourself in the center of concentric circles of all the communities to which you belong, starting with your family and moving outward into all the groups to which you feel an affiliation.

The many scholars from a range of disciplines who responded to Nussbaum's essay all ponder the central question of this text: What does it mean, *right now*, to be a "citizen of the world"? Try answering this question before and after you read Nussbaum's piece. Philosophers take on big ideas, but their daily applications are as concrete as what we learn in the classroom, how we vote, and how we speak to one another.

■ ■ ■

In a by now well-known op-ed piece in *The New York Times* (13 February 1994), philosopher Richard Rorty urges Americans, especially the American left, not to disdain patriotism as a value, and indeed to give central importance to "the emotion of national pride" and "a sense of shared national identity." Rorty argues that we cannot even criticize ourselves well unless we also "rejoice" in our American identity and define ourselves fundamentally in terms of that identity. Rorty seems to hold that the primary alternative to a politics based on patriotism and national identity is what he calls a "politics of difference," one based on internal divisions among America's ethnic, racial, religious, and other sub-groups. He nowhere considers the possibility of a more international basis for political emotion and concern. . . .

Proponents of nationalism in politics and in education frequently 2 make a thin concession to cosmopolitanism. They may argue, for example, that although nations should in general base education and political deliberation on shared national values, a commitment to basic human rights should be part of any national educational system, and that this commitment will in a sense serve to hold many nations together. This seems to be a fair comment on practical reality; and the emphasis on human rights is certainly necessary for a world in which nations interact all the time on terms, let us hope, of justice and mutual respect.

But is it sufficient? As students here grow up, is it sufficient for them 3 to learn that they are above all citizens of the United States, but that they ought to respect the basic human rights of citizens of India, Bolivia, Nigeria, and Norway? Or should they, as I think—in addition to giving special attention to the history and current situation of their own nation—learn a good deal more than is frequently the case about the rest of the world in which they live, about India and Bolivia and Nigeria and Norway and their histories, problems, and comparative successes? Should they learn only that citizens of India have equal basic human rights, or should they also learn about the problems of hunger and pollution in India, and the implications of these problems for larger problems of global hunger and global ecology? Most important, should they be taught that they are above all citizens of the United States, or should they instead be taught that they are above all citizens of a world of human beings, and that, while they themselves happen to be situated in the United States, they have to share this world of human beings with the citizens of other countries? I shall shortly suggest four arguments for the second conception of education, which I shall call cosmopolitan education. But first I introduce a historical digression, which will trace cosmopolitanism to its origins, in the process recovering some excellent arguments that originally motivated it as an educational project.

Asked where he came from, the ancient Greek Cynic philosopher Diogenes 4 replied, "I am a citizen of the world." He meant by this, it appears, that he refused to be defined by his local origins and local group memberships, so central to the self-image of a conventional Greek male; he insisted on defining himself in terms of more universal aspirations and concerns. The Stoics who followed his lead developed his image of the *kosmou politês* or world citizen more fully, arguing that each of us dwells, in effect, in two communities—the local community of our birth, and the community of human argument and aspiration that "is truly great and truly common, in which we look neither to this corner nor to that, but measure the boundaries of our nation by the sun" (Seneca, *De Otio*). It is this community that is, most fundamentally, the source of our moral obligations. With respect to the most basic moral values such as justice, "we should regard all human beings as our fellow citizens and neighbors" (Plutarch, *On the Fortunes of Alexander*). We should regard our deliberations as, first and foremost, deliberations about human problems of people in particular concrete situations, not problems growing out of national identity that is altogether unlike that of others. Diogenes knew that the invitation to think as a world citizen was, in a sense, an invitation to be an exile from the comfort of patriotism and its easy sentiments, to see our own ways of life from the point of view of justice and the good. The accident of where one is born is just that, an accident; any human being might have been born in any nation. Recognizing this, his Stoic successors held, we should not allow differences of nationality or class or ethnic membership or even gender to erect barriers between us and our fellow human beings. We should recognize humanity wherever it occurs, and give its fundamental ingredients, reason and moral capacity, our first allegiance and respect.

This clearly did not mean that the Stoics were proposing the abolition 5 of local and national forms of political organization and the creation of a world state. The point was more radical still: that we should give our first allegiance to no mere form of government, no temporal power, but to the moral community made up by the humanity of all human beings. The idea of the world citizen is in this way the ancestor and source of Kant's idea of the "kingdom of ends," and has a similar function in inspiring and regulating moral and political conduct. One should always behave so as to treat with equal respect the dignity of reason and moral choice in every human being. . . .

. . . The Stoics stress that to be a citizen of the world one does not need 6 to give up local identifications, which can frequently be a source of great richness in life. They suggest that we think of ourselves not as devoid of local affiliations, but as surrounded by a series of concentric circles. The first one is drawn around the self; the next takes in one's immediate family; then follows the extended family; then, in order, one's neighbors or local group, one's fellow city-dwellers, one's fellow countrymen—and we can easily add to this list groupings based on ethnic, linguistic, historical, professional, gender, and sexual identities. Outside all these circles is the largest one, that of humanity as a whole. Our task as citizens of the world will be to "drawn the circles somehow toward the center" (Stoic philosopher Hierocles), making all human beings more like our fellow city-dwellers, and so on. In other words, we need not give up our special affections and identifications, whether ethnic or gender-based or religious. We need not think of them as superficial, and we may think of our identity as in part constituted by them. We may and should devote special attention to them in education. But we should work to make all human beings part of our community of dialogue and concern, base our political deliberations on that interlocking commonality, and give the circle that defines our humanity a special attention and respect.

This means, in educational terms, that the student in the United States,   7
for example, may continue to regard herself as in part defined by her particular loves—for her family, her religious and/or ethnic and/or racial community or communities, even for her country. But she must also, and centrally, learn to recognize humanity wherever she encounters it, undeterred by traits that are strange to her, and be eager to understand humanity in its "strange" guises. She must learn enough about the different to recognize common aims, aspirations, and values, and enough about these common ends to see how variously they are instantiated in the many cultures and many histories. Stoic writers insist that the vivid imagining of the different is an essential task of education; and that requires in turn, of course, a mastery of many facts about the different. Marcus Aurelius gives himself the following advice, which might be called the basis for cosmopolitan education: "Accustom yourself not to be inattentive to what another person says, and as far as possible enter into that person's mind" (VI.53). "Generally," he concludes, "one must first learn many things before one can judge another's action with understanding." . . . I would like to see education adopt this cosmopolitan Stoic stance; however, I shall now return to the present day and offer four arguments for making world citizenship, rather than democratic/national citizenship, education's central focus.

1. **Through cosmopolitan education, we learn more about ourselves**. One of the greatest barriers to rational deliberation in politics is the unexamined feeling that one's own current preferences and ways are neutral and natural. An education that takes national boundaries as morally salient too often reinforces this kind of irrationality, by lending to what is an accident of history a false air of moral weight and glory. By looking at ourselves in the lens of the other, we come to see what in our practices is local and non-necessary, what more broadly or deeply shared. Our nation is appallingly ignorant of most of the rest of the world. I think that this means that it is also, in many crucial ways, ignorant of itself.

To give just one example of this—since 1994 is the United Nations'   9
International Year of the Family—if we want to understand our own history and our choices where the structure of the family and of child-rearing is involved, we are immeasurably assisted by looking around the world to see in what configurations families exist, and through what strategies children are in fact being cared for. (This would include a study of the history of the family, both in our own and in other traditions.) Such a study can show us, for example, that the two-parent nuclear family, in which the mother is the primary homemaker and the father the primary breadwinner, is by no means a pervasive style of child-rearing in today's world. The extended family, clusters of families, the village, women's associations—all these groups

and still others are in various places regarded as having major child-rearing responsibilities. Seeing this, we can begin to ask question—for example, how much child abuse there is in a family that involves grandparents and other relatives in child-rearing, as compared with the relatively isolated Western-style nuclear family; how many different structures of child care have been found to support women's work, and how well each of these is functioning. If we do not undertake this kind of educational project, we risk assuming that the options familiar to us are the only ones there are, and that they are somehow "normal" and "natural" for the human species as such. Much the same can be said about conceptions of gender and sexuality, about conceptions of work and its division, about schemes of property holding, about the treatment of childhood and old age.

2. **We make headway solving problems that require international** *10* **cooperation**. The air does not obey national boundaries. This simple fact can be, for children, the beginning of the recognition that, like it or not, we live in a world in which the destinies of nations are closely intertwined with respect to basic goods and survival itself. The pollution of third-world nations who are attempting to attain our high standard of living will, in some cases, end up in our air. No matter what account of these matters we will finally adopt, any intelligent deliberation about ecology—as, also, about the food supply and population—requires global planning, global knowledge, and the recognition of a shared future.

To conduct this sort of global dialogue, we need not only knowledge of *11* the geography and ecology of other nations—something that would already entail much revision in our curricula—but also a great deal about the people with whom we shall be taking, so that in talking with them we may be capable of respecting their traditions and commitments. Cosmopolitan education would supply the background necessary for this type of deliberation.

3. **We recognize moral obligations to the rest of the world that** *12* **are real, and that otherwise would go unrecognized.** What are Americans to make of the fact that the high living standard we enjoy is one that very likely cannot be universalized, at least given the present costs of pollution controls and the present economic situation of developing nations, without ecological disaster? We need to educate our children to be troubled by this fact. Otherwise we are educating a nation of moral hypocrites, who talk the language of universalizability but whose universe has a self-servingly narrow scope.

This point may appear to presuppose universalism, rather than being *13* an argument in its favor. But here one may note that the values on which Americans may most justly pride themselves are in a deep sense, Stoic values: respect for human dignity and the opportunity for each person to pursue happiness. If we really do believe that all human beings are created equal and endowed with certain inalienable rights, we are morally required to think about what that conception requires us to do with and for the rest of the world.

Once again, that does not mean that one may not permissibly give *14* one's own sphere a special degree of concern. Politics, like child care, will be poorly done if each thinks herself equally responsible for all, rather than giving the immediate surroundings special attention and care. To give one's own sphere special care is justifiable in universalist terms, and I think that this is its most compelling justification. To take one example, we do not really think that our own children are morally more important than other people's children, even though almost all of us who have children would give our own children far more love and care than we give other people's children. It is good for children, on the whole, that things should work out this way, and that is why our special care is good rather than selfish. Education may and should reflect those special concerns—spending more time, for example, within a given nation, on that nation's history and politics. But my argument does entail that we should not confine our thinking to our own sphere—that in making choices in both political and economic matters we should most seriously consider the right of other human beings to life, liberty, and the pursuit of happiness, and work to acquire the knowledge that will enable us to deliberate well about those rights. I believe that this sort of thinking will have large-scale economic and political consequences.

**4. We make a consistent and coherent argument based on dis-** *15* **tinctions we are really prepared to defend.** Let me now return to the defense of shared values in Richard Rorty's *New York Times* article. In his eloquent appeals to the common there is something that makes me very uneasy. On the one hand Rorty seems to argue well when he insists on the centrality to democratic deliberation of certain values that bind all citizens together. But why should these values, which instruct us to join hands across boundaries of ethnicity and class and gender and race, lose steam when they get to the borders of the nation? By conceding that a morally arbitrary boundary such as the boundary of the nation has a deep and formative role in our deliberations, we seem to be depriving ourselves of any principled way of arguing to citizens that they should in fact join hands across these other barriers.

For one thing, the very same groups exist both outside and inside. Why *16* should we think of people from China as our fellows the minute they dwell in a certain place, namely the United States, but not when they dwell in a certain other place, namely China? What is it about the national boundary that magically converts people toward whom our education is both incurious and indifferent into people to whom we have duties of mutual respect? I think, in short, that we undercut the very case for multicultural respect within a nation by failing to make a broader world respect central to education. Richard Rorty's patriotism may be a way of bringing all Americans together; but patriotism is very close to jingoism, and I'm afraid I don't see in Rorty's argument any proposal for coping with this very obvious danger.

Furthermore, the defense of shared national values, as I understand *17* it, requires appealing to certain basic features of human personhood that obviously also transcend national boundaries. So if we fail to educate children to cross those boundaries in their minds and imaginations, we are tacitly giving them the message that we don't really mean what we say. We say that respect should be accorded to humanity as such, but we really mean that Americans as such are worthy of special respect. And that, I think, is a story that Americans have told for far too long.

Becoming a citizen of the world is often a lonely business. It is, in effect, as *18* Diogenes said, a kind of exile—from the comfort of local truths, from the warm nestling feeling of patriotism, from the absorbing drama of pride in oneself and one's own. In the writings of Marcus Aurelius (as in those of his American followers Emerson and Thoreau) one sometimes feels a boundless loneliness, as if the removal of the props of habit and local boundaries had left life bereft of a certain sort of warmth and security. If one begins life as a child who loves and trusts its parents, it is tempting to want to reconstruct citizenship along the same lines, finding in an idealized image of a nation a surrogate parent who will do one's thinking for one. Cosmopolitanism offers no such refuge; it offers only reason and the love of humanity, which may seem at time less colorful than other sources of belonging.

■ ■ ■

## Reading as a Writer: Analyzing Rhetorical Choices

1.  Nussbaum's essay is a response to philosopher Richard Rorty, as she points out in the first paragraph. You might choose to look up his 1994 *New York Times* op-ed to get a fuller understanding of their conversation. Even without reading his piece, however, you should be able to grasp his argument. Mark the places in her essay where Nussbaum explicitly refers to Rorty's ideas. How exactly do references to his ideas help her make her own point? How might you apply this strategy in your own writing?

2.  In paragraph 3, Nussbaum includes this signposting sentence: "But first I introduce a historical digression. . . ." The next four paragraphs explain aspects of Stoic philosophy. How does this historical background help Nussbaum make her larger point in this essay?

## Writing as a Reader: Entering the Conversation of Ideas

1.  Nussbaum and Kwame Anthony Appiah both wrestle with the tensions we often feel between our relationship to our immediate communities and our country, and our relationship to the larger world. Compose an essay in

which you draw on ideas from both writers on this topic to make your own argument for balancing ourselves as citizens of a nation and as "citizens of the world." Given Nussbaum's and Appiah's ideas, what education do you think people need in order to be citizens of both a country and the world?

2. Nussbaum and David Buckingham are interested in the challenges and possibilities of teaching children who they are in relation to "others." How might Buckingham's ideas about "glocalization" fit next to Nussbaum's model of the self in concentric circles of communities? How do Nussbaum's proposals for reforming education fit next to Buckingham's analysis of children's globalized media? Write an essay in which you tie insights from these authors together with your own ideas about tools for teaching children about their place in the world. What is at stake for us, and for the next generation?

## CYNTHIA C. SCOTT

## Education and Cosmopolitanism

Cynthia C. Scott is a literature student at San Francisco State University. She freelances as a journalist, writing frequently online about popular culture and fiction writing. Scott is one of many scholars who responded to Martha Nussbaum's essay on "Patriotism and Cosmopolitanism" (see page 667), in which Nussbaum wrestles with the tensions between our national and global identities, and how we can best teach children about their place in this increasingly "shrinking" world. While many of those responding to Nussbaum's essay are themselves famous and widely published authors, we thought it might be useful to hear a student's reactions to Nussbaum's proposal to reform school curriculum to better educate "citizens of the world."

As you read, take note of the way Scott engages explicitly with Nussbaum, responding both to specific strengths she sees in Nussbaum's argument and to the weaknesses. Scott is certainly sympathetic to many of the ideals about world citizenship that Nussbaum promotes; however, Scott reminds readers of the real limitations of K–12 classrooms, curricula, money, and teacher resources. She also invites readers to remember what the social dynamics are like at most schools, including the cliques and self-segregation at cafeteria tables. Most students, whether they are in primary school or in high school, do crave a sense of belonging. Can we realistically teach young people about belonging to the "world" when more immediate, local, and personal communities call them?

In this essay, Scott tests the philosophical idealism of Nussbaum's essay against what she sees as the practical limitations of most American schools. Based on your own school experiences and your own idealism, where do you stand in this debate?

Martha Nussbaum writes in her essay "Patriotism and Cosmopoli- 1
tanism," "Our nation is appallingly ignorant of most of the rest of
the world" (670). I agree. And I agree also that students should be taught
more about the world beyond their borders. The question that remains
isn't what but how. Nussbaum believes that a cosmopolitan education, in
which students are taught that they are, above all, "citizens of the world,"
will help produce the kind of adults that will see the commonality in other
human beings, and will stress to make them "more like our fellow city-
dwellers" (669).

Yet, I have issues as to how such an education might be taught and its 2
social impact on students. A laudable as Nussbaum's goal is, integrating
a cosmopolitan education in any meaningful way collides with the realities of a time- and cash-strapped public educational system. Even if the
integration of cosmopolitanism in schools was possible, I see nothing in
it that will prevent it from having the same ramifications as a patriotic or
nationalistic one.

Since Nussbaum believes that students should be taught about other 3
countries, "their histories, problems, and comparative successes" (668), a
fundamental change in curricula would be needed, a fact to which Nussbaum readily accedes. It would require a change in the textbooks which
are taught in class, as well as a change in the subjects discussed. As Nussbaum writes, students ought to be taught not only about the rest of the
world, but also about "the problems of hunger and pollution . . . and the
implications of these problems for larger problems of global hunger and
global ecology" (668).

She sees an obvious advantage in a cosmopolitan education for local 4
concerns. By examining the rest of the world, American students can learn
more about their own, such a child-rearing practices or that the two-parent
nuclear family is "by no means a pervasive style of child-rearing in today's
world" (670). There are obvious benefits to a cosmopolitan education, but
there are also disadvantages. Since the world is an immensely vast place
(in spite of twentieth-century technology which has made it seem "small"),
full of nations and peoples with distinct cultural and historical realities,
the job of any teacher to give attention to them all would be daunting, to
say the least.

Certainly, on the collegiate level, this problem would be easily resolved, 5
but what about the grade school level? How much attention should a world
history teacher pay to each country or region in the short amount of time
allotted during the school year? If she devotes an equal amount of time to
each country or region, it would mean that the particular complexities of
those nations, such as how each culture evolved, or important local and
worldwide events which helped shape its political foundation, will have to
be left out or glossed over.

A particularly dedicated cosmopolitan teacher would want to instill 6
in her students the belief that no one country or culture is above all, or

superior. Yet, a dedicated instructor, given time constraints and amount of instruction, would also be forced to decide which countries or cultures should have priority class time, if she wanted to provide her students with more than a shallow knowledge of history, literature, politics, and so on. Unfortunately, this is the case with much of grade-level education today. This certainly wouldn't engender respect for "traditions and commitments," nor would it help create the kind of global dialogue Nussbaum insists is needed to solve international problems. And yet, giving one culture primacy over others (i.e., Western civilization over African, Asian, or Native Indian as is the case now) is not only not the answer, but it contradicts Nussbaum's ideal cosmopolitan education.

Of course, the simplest answer to this dilemma is to restructure grade  7 school courses in the same manner as college-level courses. But how much more money would be needed for the extra teachers and textbooks to cover the added courses? Where would those funds come from, especially in poverty-stricken neighborhoods? Since there is a shortage of educators and some public school districts barely have enough funds for books or paper, only middle-class and private schools would be able to afford to institute a cosmopolitan education in any meaningful way.

The way in which public schools are funded will have to be completely  8 restructured, a move I would favor with or without cosmopolitanism as its thrust. No doubt, a true cosmopolitan would argue for an egalitarian educational system, but Nussbaum fails to address the fundamental problems in public education to make that possible. Charter schools and vouchers might be attractive to cosmopolitans, but each has its flaw and, where vouchers are concerned, is at the center of boisterous debates about its efficacy.

Another issue concerning a cosmopolitan education is the impact it  9 will have on the social structure within the classroom and on campus. Will it help create an open environment where students will respect and find commonality among each other as fellow human beings? Nussbaum's reply would be an unquestionable yes. She quotes Marcus Aurelius as the model for an ideal cosmopolitan education: "Accustom yourself not to be inattentive to what another person says, and as far as possible enter into that person's mind. . . . Generally, one must first learn many things before one can judge another's action with understanding" (670).

Yet, she later writes that the "cosmopolitan Stoic stance" could be  10 abused if it was taken "to deny the fundamental importance of the separateness of people and of fundamental personal liberties." She adds that even the Stoics were not always great practitioners of cosmopolitan values and that "their thought is not always a good basis for a scheme of democratic deliberation and education."

That is the thorn in the crown, isn't it? Can a school environment  11 based on cosmopolitan values ensure that a child who rejects cosmopolitanism over patriotism, or who decides that he or she is African American or Latina or lesbian and gay above all others will be readily accepted and respected? What place will an ethnocentric particularist or national-ist have in a cosmopolitan classroom? Even Nussbaum wouldn't be able to offer any guarantees that a cosmopolitan school won't regress into the kind of separatist conventions that already divide many schools today.

Cosmopolitanism might also begin to question the sense of belong-   *12* ing or how students belong on a school campus. Nussbaum believes that students should be taught that they are "citizens of the world" first, that is, they belong to the human race before all else. There is a strain, as she says, of loneliness in this type of belonging. "In the writings of Marcus Aurelius (as in those of his American followers Emerson and Thoreau) one some-times feels a boundless loneliness, as if the removal of the props of habit and local boundaries had left life bereft of a certain sort of warmth and security" (673).

Perhaps this loneliness exists because belonging to humanity is an   *13* abstract, if noble, ideal, when the desire of wanting to belong, whether to a family, a group, or another individual, arises out of the desire for intimacy and the warmth and security that come with it. Students, particularly teenagers, form into cliques out of that desire to belong, to be a part of the world, in a sense, to not feel as if they are alone. In these cliques they form a sense of individuality, apart from their parents, and a self-expression that can be accepted and encouraged.

The danger they hold is when they do not respect other cliques, but   *14* that could be less about their not understanding the commonality in one another (they are all teens after all), but in that they cannot or do not under-stand the security or warmth each group may provide to its individuals (and isn't that also true for nations?). In other words, the high school jock might not get why somebody would want to the join the chess club, or why black students might want to sit with each other in the lunchroom cafeteria.

Perhaps a cosmopolitan education can address those issues, as it may   *15* be able to address all fundamental problems within modern-day class-rooms. Still, I find it difficult that students would adopt cosmopolitanism as a philosophical way of life. It would require them to reprioritize a funda-mental way in which they develop into adults, which is to say, not seeking out the common in broad, abstract terms, but in the immediate, intimate terms of the local, the here and now.

■ ■ ■

## Reading as a Writer: Analyzing Rhetorical Choices

1. Scott's essay is a direct response to Martha Nussbaum's "Patriotism and Cosmopolitanism." Using two different colored pens, mark the sentences in which Scott expresses agreement with Nussbaum, and those in which she disagrees with her. What is the relationship between these passages and places where Scott develops her own argument? What can you con-clude about effective ways to use another's ideas to develop your own?

2.  Evaluate the evidence Scott uses to discuss the limitations of K–12 educa-
    tion, and the social dynamics of school settings. Based on your experience
    (and perhaps research), are her claims representative? What examples
    can you produce that would confirm or refute her representation of high
    schoolers' desire to belong, whether to immediate groups or to larger
    coalitions?

### Writing as a Reader: Entering the Conversation of Ideas

1.  Scott, like Marjane Satrapi in *Persepolis*, explores the way school settings
    can be used to teach children about national identity and their relation-
    ship to "others"—with both negative and potentially positive results. In
    an essay of your own that draws on the examples in Scott's and Satrapi's
    texts, make an argument for an approach to teaching children about who
    they are in relation to "others" of all kinds. Include the ideals you would
    want students to learn, as well as some specific practical skills that would
    help them achieve these ideals. At what ages should children learn these
    skills, and why?

2.  Scott shares Beverly Daniel Tatum's interest in the potential of schools to
    draw out the best in all students, and the real limitations that often keep
    them from doing so. The two writers illuminate the actual social dynam-
    ics and interactions at many high schools among students, among teach-
    ers, and between students and teachers. Using the ideals and examples in
    Scott's and Tatum's essays, compose an essay in which you make an argu-
    ment for the kinds of "belonging" that schools should foster in students,
    and explain your reasoning. You may include your own experiences if they
    help you illuminate your argument.

## MARJANE SATRAPI

## *From* Persepolis

Marjane Satrapi is an Iranian-born French graphic novelist. She turned her
best-selling memoir *Persepolis* into a film for which she was nominated for
an Academy Award for best director for an animated film. Her witty graphic
novels, which have been translated into several languages, take on politics
and cultural issues from her perspective as both an insider and an outsider
to Iranian culture. She now lives and writes in Paris. Her best-selling books
include *Persepolis: The Story of a Childhood* (2003), *Persepolis 2: The Story of
a Return* (2004), *Embroideries* (2005), and *Chicken with Plums* (2006). This
excerpt, from the first *Persepolis* volume, includes the introduction, which
provides some history for understanding the Iranian revolution, and two
chapters, "The Veil" and "The Bicycle."

Satrapi's text is autobiographical, but even true stories involve a lot of selection about which details to include and which to leave out. As you read, then, notice how Satrapi depicts herself as a child in specific relation to the unfolding revolution. How and why do you think Satrapi uses humor—visual and textual—to make her point, even when this story is largely a tragic one? What insights can readers gain from learning about revolution from the perspective of a child who only partially understands what is happening? Do you think this text makes an argument, and if so, what is it?

Satrapi, like a growing number of other writers/artists, uses the genre of the "comic" graphic novel form to explore serious issues. Art Spiegelman, author of the *Maus* graphic novel series based on his family's experiences during and after the Holocaust, is often cited as a major influence in this movement. While Satrapi's text may seem quite different from other readings we include in this chapter, consider it as one more rich voice in the chorus of writers struggling to depict who we are in relation to our homeland and in the eyes of others.

■ ■ ■

## Introduction

In the second millennium B.C., while the Elam nation was developing *1* a civilization alongside Babylon, Indo-European invaders gave their name to the immense Iranian plateau where they settled. The word "Iran" was derived from "Ayryana Vaejo," which means "the origin of the Aryans." These people were semi-nomads whose descendants were the Medes and the Persians. The Medes founded the first Iranian nation in the seventh century B.C.; it was later destroyed by Cyrus the Great. He established what became one of the largest empires of the ancient world, the Persian Empire, in the sixth century B.C. Iran was referred to as Persia—its Greek name—until 1935 when Reza Shah, the father of the last Shah of Iran, asked everyone to call the country Iran.

Iran was rich. Because of its wealth and its geographic location, it *2* invited attacks: From Alexander the Great, from its Arab neighbors to the west, from Turkish and Mongolian conquerors, Iran was often subject to foreign domination. Yet the Persian language and culture withstood these invasions. The invaders assimilated into this strong culture, and in some ways they became Iranians themselves.

In the twentieth century, Iran entered a new phase. Reza Shah decided *3* to modernize and westernize the country, but meanwhile a fresh source of wealth was discovered: oil. And with the oil came another invasion. The West, particularly Great Britain, wielded a strong influence on the Iranian economy. During the Second World War, the British, Soviets, and

Americans asked Reza Shah to ally himself with them against Germany. But Reza Shah, who sympathized with the Germans, declared Iran a neutral zone. So the Allies invaded and occupied Iran. Reza Shah was sent into exile and was succeeded by his son, Mohammad Reza Pahlavi, who was known simply as the Shah.

In 1951, Mohammed Mossadeq, then prime minister of Iran, national-    4
ized the oil industry. In retaliation, Great Britain organized an embargo on all exports of oil from Iran. In 1953, the CIA, with the help of British intelligence, organized a coup against him. Mossadeq was overthrown and the Shah, who had earlier escaped from the country, returned to power. The Shah stayed on the throne until 1979, when he fled Iran to escape the Islamic revolution.

Since then, this old and great civilization has been discussed mostly in    5
connection with fundamentalism, fanaticism, and terrorism. As an Iranian who has lived more than half of my life in Iran, I know that this image is far from the truth. This is why writing *Persepolis* was so important to me. I believe that an entire nation should not be judged by the wrongdoings of a few extremists. I also don't want those Iranians who lost their lives in prisons defending freedom, who died in the war against Iraq, who suffered under various repressive regimes, or who were forced to leave their families and flee their homeland to be forgotten.

One can forgive but one should never forget.    6

Marjane Satrapi
Paris, September 2002

# THE VEIL

THIS IS ME WHEN I WAS 10 YEARS OLD. THIS WAS IN 1980.

AND THIS IS A CLASS PHOTO. I'M SITTING ON THE FAR LEFT SO YOU DON'T SEE ME. FROM LEFT TO RIGHT: GOLNAZ, MAHSHID, NARINE, MINNA.

IN 1979 A REVOLUTION TOOK PLACE. IT WAS LATER CALLED "THE ISLAMIC REVOLUTION".

THEN CAME 1980: THE YEAR IT BECAME OBLIGATORY TO WEAR THE VEIL AT SCHOOL.

WEAR THIS !

WE DIDN'T REALLY LIKE TO WEAR THE VEIL, ESPECIALLY SINCE WE DIDN'T UNDERSTAND WHY WE HAD TO.

IT'S TOO HOT OUT!

EXECUTION IN THE NAME OF FREEDOM.

GIVE ME MY VEIL BACK!

YOU'LL HAVE TO LICK MY FEET!

OOH! I'M THE MONSTER OF DARKNESS.

GIDDYAP!

EVERYWHERE IN THE STREETS THERE WERE DEMONSTRATIONS FOR AND AGAINST THE VEIL.

AT ONE OF THE DEMONSTRATIONS, A GERMAN JOURNALIST TOOK A PHOTO OF MY MOTHER.

I WAS REALLY PROUD OF HER. HER PHOTO WAS PUBLISHED IN ALL THE EUROPEAN NEWSPAPERS.

AND EVEN IN ONE MAGAZINE IN IRAN, MY MOTHER WAS REALLY SCARED.

HAVE YOU SEEN THIS?

DON'T WORRY, DARLING.

SHE DYED HER HAIR,

AND WORE DARK GLASSES FOR A LONG TIME.

I REALLY DIDN'T KNOW WHAT TO THINK ABOUT THE VEIL. DEEP DOWN I WAS VERY RELIGIOUS BUT AS A FAMILY WE WERE VERY MODERN AND AVANT-GARDE.

I WAS BORN WITH RELIGION.

AT THE AGE OF SIX I WAS ALREADY SURE I WAS THE LAST PROPHET. THIS WAS A FEW YEARS BEFORE THE REVOLUTION.

O' Celestial light!

BEFORE ME THERE HAD BEEN A FEW OTHERS.

I AM THE LAST PROPHET.

A WOMAN?

I WANTED TO BE A PROPHET...

BECAUSE OUR MAID DID NOT EAT WITH US.

BECAUSE MY FATHER HAD A CADILLAC.

AND, ABOVE ALL, BECAUSE MY GRANDMOTHER'S KNEES ALWAYS ACHED.

COME HERE MARJI! HELP ME TO STAND UP.

DON'T WORRY. SOON YOU WON'T HAVE ANY MORE PAIN. YOU'LL SEE.

LIKE ALL MY PREDECESSORS I HAD MY HOLY BOOK.

THE FIRST THREE RULES CAME FROM ZARATHUSTRA. HE WAS THE FIRST PROPHET IN MY COUNTRY BEFORE THE ARAB INVASION.

YOU MUST BASE EVERYTHING ON THESE THREE RULES: BEHAVE WELL, SPEAK WELL, ACT WELL.

I ALSO WANTED US TO CELEBRATE THE TRADITIONAL ZARATHUSTRIAN HOLIDAYS. LIKE THE FIRE CEREMONY,

BEFORE THE PERSIAN NEW YEAR, NOROUZ, ON MARCH 21ST, THE FIRST DAY OF SPRING.

ONLY MY GRANDMOTHER KNEW ABOUT MY BOOK.

RULE NUMBER SIX: EVERY-BODY SHOULD HAVE A CAR.

RULE NUMBER SEVEN: ALL MAIDS SHOULD EAT AT THE TABLE WITH THE OTHERS.

RULE NUMBER EIGHT: NO OLD PER-SON SHOULD HAVE TO SUFFER.

IN THAT CASE, I'LL BE YOUR FIRST DISCIPLE.

REALLY?

BUT TELL ME HOW YOU'LL ARRANGE FOR OLD PEOPLE NOT TO SUFFER?

IT WILL SIMPLY BE FORBIDDEN.

# THE BICYCLE

"AFTER A LONG SLEEP OF 2500 YEARS, THE REVOLUTION HAS FINALLY AWAKENED THE PEOPLE."

"2500 YEARS OF TYRANNY AND SUBMISSION" AS MY FATHER SAID.

FIRST OUR OWN EMPERORS.

THEN THE ARAB INVASION FROM THE WEST.

FOLLOWED BY THE MONGOLIAN INVASION FROM THE EAST.

AND FINALLY MODERN IMPERIALISM.

IT WILL BE 75°F IN THE SHADE.

SHHH! WAIT A SECOND!

THEY BURNED DOWN THE REX CINEMA TONIGHT.

OH MY GOD.

THE DOORS HAD BEEN LOCKED FROM THE OUTSIDE A FEW MINUTES BEFORE THE FIRE.

THE POLICE WERE THERE.

THEY FORBADE PEOPLE TO RESCUE THOSE LOCKED INSIDE.

THEN THEY ATTACKED THEM.

THE FIREMEN DIDN'T ARRIVE UNTIL FORTY MINUTES LATER.

THE BBC SAID THERE WERE 400 VICTIMS. THE SHAH SAID THAT A GROUP OF RELIGIOUS FANATICS PERPETRATED THE MASSACRE. BUT THE PEOPLE KNEW THAT IT WAS THE SHAH'S FAULT!!!

### Reading as a Writer: Analyzing Rhetorical Choices

1. How does the graphic novel format affect the way you read this text? What are the advantages and possible limitations of telling the story this way? Discuss particular frames in which the images and the words, or the relationship between them, are of particular interest to you.

2. While Satrapi offers us a quick version of the history leading up to the Iranian revolution in her introduction, in "The Bicycle" section her character refers to many philosophers and revolutionaries, such as René Descartes, Che Guevara, Fidel Castro, Leon Trotsky, and Karl Marx. Divide the task of looking up information on these figures with your classmates, and report back on what you find. What is significant about the fact that Satrapi depicts herself as a child who knows enough about these figures to name them but who is confused about many aspects of the unfolding revolution?

### Writing as a Reader: Entering the Conversation of Ideas

1. Satrapi, like Michael S. Kimmel, is interested in the us-versus-them mentality that can foster hatred between countries and also between citizens of the same country. Write an essay in which you apply some of Kimmel's insights to the dynamics in Iran that Satrapi captures in this excerpt from *Persepolis*. To what extent does gender play a role in both writers' analysis of the uses of fear and violence as a tactic in establishing a sense of identity in relation to others?

2. Both Satrapi and bell hooks consider the way imaginative texts inform our ideas about "others." Satrapi uses a graphic novel to explore the idea of "enemies" inside or beyond national borders, and hooks describes film and television examples that persuade viewers to understand the poor in particular ways. Compose an essay in which you reflect on the power of imaginative texts to persuade, teach, and influence us to define ourselves in relation to others. How might these insights apply to academic writing, if at all?

# 16

# Biology

*How do we try to control our bodies?*

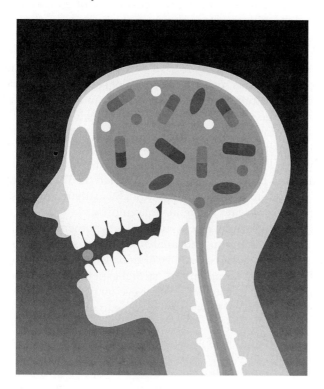

The readings in this chapter focus on biology, but not in the sense of memorizing cell division or plant categorization. Instead, they invite us to think about the fascinating places where biology meets culture, revealing the many intersections where our flesh runs into cultural expectations of what it means to be feminine, masculine, successful, or even perfect. How do we try to exert power over our bodies, and how *should* we? The authors take on questions that are physical and specific—drawn from our daily experiences of studying, exercising, consuming food and popular culture, and just moving around in the world. But these same questions are also philosophical and perhaps difficult to wrap our minds around—questions about whether or not we *should* manipulate our bodies as much as we are able to do with drugs, surgery, or even plastination after death.

Some of the authors focus on the various ways we use drugs to manipulate our moods, mental acuity, and muscles. For example, Margaret Talbot looks at the significance of brain-boosting drugs, which are gaining popularity on college campuses and raising the bar for academic performance (particularly when students are also cramming in socializing activities). Dutch authors Toine Pieters and Stephen Snelders take a historical and cross-cultural approach to analyzing the ways "happy pills" have been used and understood over the course of the last century. Matthew Petrocelli, Trish Oberweis, and Joseph Petrocelli, coauthors of a fascinating study of recreational steroid use, base their conclusions about the uses and abuses of these drugs on in-depth interviews of "gym rats" who put their health at risk to try to achieve a "ripped" body type that pushes the limits of biology.

Those same body-conscious men are the focus of several other essays in this chapter, defying assumptions that only women in our culture are anxious about body image. Judith Lorber, a leading sociologist of gender, reveals how often our assumptions about the biological differences between men and women are really produced by *culture*, not biology, through daily habits and practices that can be altered, with potentially revolutionary results for both men and women. Shari L. Dworkin and Michael A. Messner pick up on this line of thought in their analysis of sports culture, one of the key ways we define masculinity.

Other authors examine some recent cultural phenomena that they believe deserve our close attention and analysis. Sharlene Nagy Hesse-Biber pushes beyond the usual discussions of eating disorders to show how the "Cult of Thinness" is spreading to "straight men, gays, lesbians, and ethnic women." Virginia L. Blum trains her eye on popular cosmetic-surgery television shows to reveal how we have come to see cutting up our bodies as a normal part of "being our best." Finally, Nancy N. Chen invites us to consider the afterlife of bodies by analyzing the worldwide tours of *BodyWorlds, Inc.* exhibits, in which skinned, plastinated corpses help us see bodies, and their relation to cultural attitudes, in surprising ways.

These readings will take you from flesh to philosophy, from your daily workout routine to the largest questions of what it means to be human. We're certain you will have strong responses to these ideas, and we invite you to dive into this raucous conversation.

# *From* Brain Gain: The Underground World of "Neuroenhancing" Drugs

Margaret Talbot is a staff writer at *The New Yorker*, where this article first appeared in 2009. Talbot has also written for *The New Republic* and *The Atlantic* on a wide range of topics, including changing attitudes toward women's work and family life, the intersection of politics and moral debates, and children's culture. This article on neuroenhancing drugs is part of an unfolding conversation among scholars and public intellectuals about the increasingly large role that prescription medication plays in many people's lives. You may be aware of the debates about whether we are overmedicating patients for depression or attention deficit disorder. In this article, Talbot takes up a more recent side effect of our medically fascinated culture—the nonmedical use of prescription drugs such as Adderall and Ritalin to enhance academic performance, particularly at the college level. In this piece, Talbot describes the stressful dynamics of college life that may be familiar to you—balancing academic demands with other pressures on your time, whether from work or socializing. As you read, compare Talbot's examples to your own experiences and the ways you and your peers struggle to stay on top of the competing demands of contemporary life and college coursework.

Talbot uses an extended example of a pseudonymous student, "Alex," to make a broader point about the ways many college campuses "have become laboratories for experimentation with neuroenhancement" (para. 2). Pay attention to the strategies Talbot uses to move from her close-up example of Alex to her big-picture analysis of the implications of college students' increasing use of prescription brain-boosting drugs. How is one person's decision to use drugs in this way more than "a private act," as Talbot claims in paragraph 12? Talbot brings in experts who weigh in on both the negatives and the positives of this issue. She also contextualizes this kind of recreational drug use in a long history of people using (or abusing) caffeine and nicotine in order to stay awake and focused at school and at work. What do you make of these comparisons?

If, as Talbot claims, "every era . . . has its defining drug" (para. 26), she invites us to consider the significance of the current use (or abuse) of brain-boosting drugs. What do they tell us about what we—and our professors and our employers—expect? What does it take to be competitive right now, and do you agree with the direction we are heading toward? Talbot offers multiple perspectives on an issue that is probably affecting your life right now and will surely affect your future.

A young man I'll call Alex recently graduated from Harvard. As a history major, Alex wrote about a dozen papers a semester. He also ran a student organization, for which he often worked more than forty hours a week; when he wasn't on the job, he had classes. Weeknights were devoted to all the schoolwork that he couldn't finish during the day, and weekend nights were spent drinking with friends and going to dance parties. "Trite as it sounds," he told me, it seemed important to "maybe appreciate my own youth." Since, in essence, this life was impossible, Alex began taking Adderall to make it possible.

Adderall, a stimulant composed of mixed amphetamine salts, is commonly prescribed for children and adults who have been given a diagnosis of attention-deficit hyperactivity disorder. But in recent years Adderall and Ritalin, another stimulant, have been adopted as cognitive enhancers: drugs that high-functioning, overcommitted people take to become higher-functioning and more overcommitted. (Such use is "off label," meaning that it does not have the approval of either the drug's manufacturer or the Food and Drug Administration.) College campuses have become laboratories for experimentation with neuroenhancement, and Alex was an ingenious experimenter. His brother had received a diagnosis of A.D.H.D., and in his freshman year Alex obtained an Adderall prescription for himself by describing to a doctor symptoms that he knew were typical of the disorder. During his college years, Alex took fifteen milligrams of Adderall most evenings, usually after dinner, guaranteeing that he would maintain intense focus while losing "any ability to sleep for approximately eight to ten hours." In his sophomore year, he persuaded the doctor to add a thirty-milligram "extended release" capsule to his daily regimen.

Alex recalled one week during his junior year when he had four term papers due. Minutes after waking on Monday morning, around seven-thirty, he swallowed some "immediate release" Adderall. The drug, along with a steady stream of caffeine, helped him to concentrate during classes and meetings, but he noticed some odd effects; at a morning tutorial, he explained to me in an e-mail, "I alternated between speaking too quickly and thoroughly on some subjects and feeling awkwardly quiet during other points of the discussion." Lunch was a blur: "It's always hard to eat much when on Adderall." That afternoon, he went to the library, where he spent "too much time researching a paper rather than actually writing it—a problem, I can assure you, that is common to all intellectually curious students on stimulants." At eight, he attended a two-hour meeting "with a group focussed on student mental-health issues." Alex then "took an extended-release Adderall" and worked productively on the paper all night. At eight the next morning, he attended a meeting of his organization; he felt like "a zombie," but "was there to insure that the semester's work didn't go to waste." After that, Alex explained, "I went back to my room to take advantage of my tired body." He fell asleep until noon, waking "in time to polish my first paper and hand it in."

I met Alex one evening last summer, at an appealingly scruffy bar in  *4*
the New England city where he lives. Skinny and bearded, and wearing
faded hipster jeans, he looked like the lead singer in an indie band. He
was ingratiating and articulate, and smoked cigarettes with an ironic air of
defiance. Alex was happy enough to talk about his frequent use of Adderall at Harvard, but he didn't want to see his name in print; he's involved
with an Internet start-up, and worried that potential investors might dis-
approve of his habit.

After we had ordered beers, he said, "One of the most impressive fea-  *5*
tures of being a student is how aware you are of a twenty-four-hour work
cycle. When you conceive of what you have to do for school, it's not in terms
of nine to five but in terms of what you can physically do in a week while
still achieving a variety of goals in a variety of realms—social, romantic,
sexual, extracurricular, résumé-building, academic commitments." Alex
was eager to dispel the notion that students who took Adderall were "academic automatons who are using it in order to be first in their class, or in
order to be an obvious admit to law school or the first accepted at a consulting firm." In fact, he said, "it's often people"—mainly guys—"who are
looking in some way to compensate for activities that are detrimental to
their performance." He explained, "At Harvard, at least, most people are
to some degree realistic about it. . . . I don't think people who take Adderall are aiming to be the top person in the class. I think they're aiming to
be among the best. Or maybe not even among the best. At the most basic
level, they aim to do better than they would have otherwise." He went on,
"Everyone is aware of the fact that if you were up at 3 A.M. writing this
paper it isn't going to be as good as it could have been. The fact that you
were partying all weekend, or spent the last week being high, watching
*Lost*—that's going to take a toll."

Alex's sense of who uses stimulants for so-called "nonmedical" pur-  *6*
poses is borne out by two dozen or so scientific studies. In 2005, a team
led by Sean Esteban McCabe, a professor at the University of Michigan's
Substance Abuse Research Center, reported that in the previous year 4.1
percent of American undergraduates had taken prescription stimulants
for off-label use; at one school, the figure was twenty-five percent. Other
researchers have found even higher rates: a 2002 study at a small college
found that more than thirty-five percent of the students had used prescription stimulants nonmedically in the previous year.

Drugs such as Adderall can cause nervousness, headaches, sleepless-  *7*
ness, and decreased appetite, among other side effects. An F.D.A. warning on Adderall's label notes that "amphetamines have a high potential for
abuse" and can lead to dependence. (The label also mentions that adults
using Adderall have reported serious cardiac problems, though the role of
the drug in those cases is unknown.) Yet college students tend to consider
Adderall and Ritalin benign, in part because they are likely to know peers
who have taken the drugs since childhood for A.D.H.D. Indeed, McCabe

reports, most students who use stimulants for cognitive enhancement obtain them from an acquaintance with a prescription. Usually, the pills are
given away, but some students sell them.

According to McCabe's research team, white male undergraduates at    8
highly competitive schools—especially in the Northeast—are the most
frequent collegiate users of neuroenhancers. Users are also more likely to
belong to a fraternity or a sorority, and to have a G.P.A. of 3.0 or lower.
They are ten times as likely to report that they have smoked marijuana in
the past year, and twenty times as likely to say that they have used cocaine.
In other words, they are decent students at schools where, to be a great
student, you have to give up a lot more partying than they're willing to
give up.

The BoredAt Web sites—which allow college students to chat idly    9
while they're ostensibly studying—are filled with messages about Adderall. Posts like these, from the BoredAtPenn site, are typical: "I have some
Adderall—I'm sitting by room 101.10 in a grey shirt and headphones"; "I
have Adderall for sale 20mg for $15"; "I took Adderall at 8 p.m., it's 6:30
a.m. and I've barely blinked." On the Columbia site, a poster with an e-mail
address from CUNY complains that her friends take Adderall "like candy,"
adding, "I don't want to be at a disadvantage to everyone else. Is it really
that dangerous? Will it fuck me up? My grades weren't that great this year
and I could do with a bump." A Columbia student responds, "It's probably not a good idea if you're not prescribed," but offers practical advice
anyway: "Keep the dose normal and don't grind them up or snort them."
Occasional dissents ("I think there should be random drug testing at every
exam") are drowned out by testimonials like this one, from the Bored-
AtHarvard site: "I don't want to be a pusher or start people on something
bad, but Adderall is AMAZING."

Alex remains enthusiastic about Adderall, but he also has a slightly    10
jaundiced critique of it. "It only works as a cognitive enhancer insofar as
you are dedicated to accomplishing the task at hand," he said. "The number of times I've taken Adderall late at night and decided that, rather than
starting my paper, hey, I'll organize my entire music library! I've seen
people obsessively cleaning their rooms on it." Alex thought that generally
the drug helped him to bear down on his work, but it also tended to produce writing with a characteristic flaw. "Often, I've looked back at papers
I've written on Adderall, and they're verbose. They're belaboring a point,
trying to create this airtight argument, when if you just got to your point
in a more direct manner it would be stronger. But with Adderall I'd produce two pages on something that could be said in a couple of sentences."
Nevertheless, his Adderall-assisted papers usually earned him at least a B.
They got the job done. As Alex put it, "Productivity is a good thing."

Last April, the scientific journal *Nature* published the results of an infor-    11
mal online poll asking whether readers attempted to sharpen "their
focus, concentration, or memory" by taking drugs such as Ritalin and Pro-

vigil—a newer kind of stimulant, known generically as modafinil, which was developed to treat narcolepsy. One out of five respondents said that they did. A majority of the fourteen hundred readers who responded said that healthy adults should be permitted to take brain boosters for non-medical reasons, and sixty-nine percent said that mild side effects were an acceptable risk. Though a majority said that such drugs should not be made available to children who had no diagnosed medical condition, a third admitted that they would feel pressure to give "smart drugs" to their kids if they learned that other parents were doing so. . . .

If Alex, the Harvard student, . . . [considers his] use of neuroenhancers a 12 private act, Nicholas Seltzer sees his habit as a pursuit that aligns him with a larger movement for improving humanity. Seltzer has a B.A. from U.C. Davis and a master's degree in security policy from George Washington University. But the job that he obtained with these credentials—as a researcher at a defense-oriented think tank, in northern Virginia—has not left him feeling as intellectually alive as he would like. To compensate, he writes papers in his spare time on subjects like "human biological evolution and warfare." He also primes his brain with artificial challenges; even when he goes to the rest room at the office, he takes the opportunity to play memory or logic games on his cell phone. Seltzer, who is thirty, told me that he worried that he "didn't have the mental energy, the endurance, the—I don't know what to properly call this—the *sponginess* that I seem to recall having when I was younger."

Suffice it to say that this is not something you notice when you talk to 13 Seltzer. And though our memory is probably at its peak in our early twenties, few thirty-year-olds are aware of a deficit. But Seltzer is the Washington-wonk equivalent of those models and actors in L.A. who discern tiny wrinkles long before their agent does. His girlfriend, a technology consultant whom he met in a museum, is nine years younger, and he was already thinking about how his mental fitness would stand up next to hers. He told me, "She's twenty-one, and I want to stay young and vigorous and don't want to be a burden on her later in life." He didn't worry about visible signs of aging, but he wanted to keep his mind "nimble and healthy for as long as possible."

Seltzer considers himself a "transhumanist," in the mold of the Oxford 14 philosopher Nick Bostrom and the futurist writer and inventor Ray Kurzweil. Transhumanists are interested in robots, cryogenics, and living a really, really long time; they consider biological limitations that the rest of us might accept, or even appreciate, as creaky obstacles to be aggressively surmounted. On the ImmInst forums—"ImmInst" stands for "Immortality Institute"—Seltzer and other members discuss life-extension strategies and the potential benefits of cognitive enhancers. Some of the forum members limit themselves to vitamin and mineral supplements. Others use Adderall or modafinil or, like Seltzer, a drug called piracetam, which was first marketed by a Belgian pharmaceutical company in 1972 and, in recent years, has become available in the U.S. from retailers that sell supplements. Although not approved for any use by the F.D.A., piracetam has been used experimentally on stroke patients—to little effect—and on patients with a rare neurological condition called progressive myoclonus epilepsy, for whom it proved helpful in alleviating muscle spasms. Data on piracetam's benefits for healthy people are virtually nonexistent, but many users believe that the drug increases blood flow to the brain.

From the time I first talked to Seltzer, it was clear that although he 15 felt cognitive enhancers were of practical use, they also appealed to him on an aesthetic level. Using neuroenhancers, he said, "is like customizing yourself—customizing your brain." For some people, he went on, it was important to enhance their mood, so they took antidepressants; but for people like him it was more important "to increase mental horsepower." He added, "It's fundamentally a choice you're making about how you want to experience consciousness." Whereas the nineties had been about "the personalization of technology," this decade was about the personalization of the brain—what some enthusiasts have begun to call "mind hacking."

Of course, the idea behind mind-hacking isn't exactly new. Fortifying 16 one's mental stamina with drugs of various kinds has a long history. Sir Francis Bacon consumed everything from tobacco to saffron in the hope of goosing his brain. Balzac reputedly fuelled sixteen-hour bouts of writing with copious servings of coffee, which, he wrote, "chases away sleep, and gives us the capacity to engage a little longer in the exercise of our intellects." Sartre dosed himself with speed in order to finish *Critique of Dialectical Reason*. My college friends and I wrote term papers with the sweaty-palmed assistance of NoDoz tablets. And, before smoking bans, entire office cultures chugged along on a collective nicotine buzz—at least, if *Mad Men* is to be believed. Seltzer and his interlocutors on the ImmInst forum are just the latest members of a seasoned cohort, even if they have more complex pharmaceuticals at their disposal.

I eventually met Seltzer in an underground food court not far from 17 the Pentagon. We sat down at a Formica table in the dim light. Seltzer was slim, had a shaved head, and wore metal-frame glasses; matching his fastidious look, he spoke precisely, rarely stumbling over his words. I asked him if he had any ethical worries about smart drugs. After a pause, he said that he might have a concern if somebody popped a neuroenhancer before taking a licensing exam that certified him as, say, a brain surgeon, and then stopped using the drug. Other than that, he couldn't see a problem. He said that he was a firm believer in the idea that "we should have a fair degree of liberty to do with our bodies and our minds as we see fit, so long as it doesn't impinge on the basic rights, liberty, and safety of others." He argued, "Why would you *want* an upward limit on the intellectual capabilities of a human being? And, if you have a very nationalist viewpoint, why wouldn't you want our country to have the advantage over other countries, particularly in what some people call a knowledge-based economy?" He went on, "Think about the complexity of the intellectual tasks that people need to accomplish today. Just trying to understand what Congress is doing is not a simple thing! The complexity of understanding the gamut of scientific and technical and social issues is difficult. If we had a tool that enabled more people to understand the world at a greater level of sophistication, how can we prejudice ourselves against the notion, simply because we don't like athletes to do it? To me, it doesn't seem like the same question. And it deserves its own debate."

Seltzer had never had a diagnosis of any kind of learning disorder. 18 But he added, "Though I wouldn't say I'm dyslexic, sometimes when I type prose, after I look back and read it, I've frequently left out words or interposed words, and sometimes I have difficulty concentrating." In graduate school, he obtained a prescription for Adderall from a doctor who didn't ask a lot of questions. The drug helped him, especially when his ambitions were relatively low. He recalled, "I had this one paper, on nuclear strategy. The professor didn't look favorably on any kind of creative thinking." On Adderall, he pumped out the paper in an evening. "I just bit my tongue, regurgitated, and got a good-enough grade."

On the other hand, Seltzer recalled that he had taken piracetam to 19 write an essay on "the idea of harmony as a trope in Chinese political discourse"—it was one of the papers he was proudest of. He said, "It was really an intellectual challenge to do. I felt that the piracetam helped me to work within the realm of the abstract, and make the kind of associations that I needed—following this idea of harmony from an ancient religious belief as it was translated throughout the centuries into a very important topic in political discourse."

After a hiatus of several years, Seltzer had recently resumed taking 20 neuroenhancers. In addition to piracetam, he took a stack of supplements that he thought helped his brain functioning: fish oils, five antioxidants, a product called ChocoMind, and a number of others, all available at the health-food store. He was thinking about adding modafinil, but hadn't yet. For breakfast every morning, he concocted a slurry of oatmeal, berries, soy milk, pomegranate juice, flaxseed, almond meal, raw eggs, and protein powder. The goal behind the recipe was efficiency: to rely on "one goop you could eat or drink that would have everything you need nutritionally for your brain and body." He explained, "Taste was the last thing on my mind; I wanted to be able to keep it down—that was it." (He told me this in the kitchen of his apartment; he lives with a roommate, who walked in while we were talking, listened perplexedly for a moment, then put a frozen pizza in the oven.)

Seltzer's decision to take piracetam was based on his own online read- 21 ing, which included medical-journal abstracts. He hadn't consulted a doctor. Since settling on a daily regimen of supplements, he had sensed an improvement in his intellectual work and his ability to engage in stimulating conversation. He continued, "I feel I'm better able to articulate my thoughts. I'm sure you've been in the zone—you're having a really exciting debate with somebody, your brain feels alive. I feel that more. But I don't want to say that it's this profound change."

I asked him if piracetam made him feel smarter, or just more alert and    22 confident—a little better equipped to marshal the resources he naturally had. "Maybe," he said. "I'm not sure what being smarter means, entirely. It's a difficult quality to measure. It's the gestalt factor, all these qualities coming together—not only your ability to crunch some numbers, or remember some figures or a sequence of numbers, but also your ability to maintain a certain emotional state that is conducive to productive intellectual work. I do feel I'm more intelligent with the drugs, but I can't give you a number of I.Q. points."

The effects of piracetam on healthy volunteers have been studied even    23 less than those of Adderall or modafinil. Most peer-reviewed studies focus on its effects on dementia, or on people who have suffered a seizure or a concussion. Many of the studies that look at other neurological effects were performed on rats and mice. Piracetam's mechanisms of action are not understood, though it may increase levels of the neurotransmitter acetylcholine. In 2008, a committee of the British Academy of Medical Sciences noted that many of the clinical trials of piracetam for dementia were methodologically flawed. Another published review of the available studies of the drug concluded that the evidence "does not support the use of piracetam in the treatment of people with dementia or cognitive impairment," but suggested that further investigation might be warranted. I asked Seltzer if he thought he should wait for scientific ratification of piracetam. He laughed. "I don't want to," he said. "Because it's working."

It makes no sense to ban the use of neuroenhancers. Too many people are    24 already taking them, and the users tend to be educated and privileged people who proceed with just enough caution to avoid getting into trouble. Besides, [University of Pennsylvania neurologist] Anjan Chatterjee is right that there is an apt analogy with plastic surgery. In a consumer society like ours, if people are properly informed about the risks and benefits of neuroenhancers, they can make their own choices about how to alter their minds, just as they can make their own decisions about shaping their bodies.

Still, even if you acknowledge that cosmetic neurology is here to stay,    25 there is something dispiriting about the way the drugs are used—the kind of aspirations they open up, or don't. Jonathan Eisen, an evolutionary biologist at U.C. Davis, is skeptical of what he mockingly calls "brain doping." During a recent conversation, he spoke about colleagues who take neuroenhancers in order to grind out grant proposals. "It's weird to me that people are taking these drugs to write grants," he said. "I mean, if you came up with some really interesting paper that was *spurred* by taking some really interesting drug—magic mushrooms or something—that would make more sense to me. In the end, you're only as good as the ideas you've come up with."

But it's not the mind-expanding sixties anymore. Every era, it seems, 26 has its own defining drug. Neuroenhancers are perfectly suited for the anxiety of white-collar competition in a floundering economy. And they have a synergistic relationship with our multiplying digital technologies: the more gadgets we own, the more distracted we become, and the more we need help in order to focus. The experience that neuroenhancement offers is not, for the most part, about opening the doors of perception, or about breaking the bonds of the self, or about experiencing a surge of genius. It's about squeezing out an extra few hours to finish those sales figures when you'd really rather collapse into bed; getting a B instead of a B-minus on the final exam in a lecture class where you spent half your time texting; cramming for the G.R.E.s at night, because the information-industry job you got after college turned out to be deadening. Neuroenhancers don't offer freedom. Rather, they facilitate a pinched, unromantic, grindingly efficient form of productivity.

This winter, I spoke again with Alex, the Harvard graduate, and found 27 that, after a break of several months, he had gone back to taking Adderall—a small dose every day. He felt that he was learning to use the drug in a more "disciplined" manner. Now, he said, it was less about staying up late to finish work he should have done earlier, and more "about staying focussed on work, which makes me want to work longer hours." What employer would object to that?

■ ■ ■

### Reading as a Writer: Analyzing Rhetorical Choices

1. Talbot offers an extended example of the Harvard student "Alex" in order to illuminate some of the reasons that college students use neuroenhancing drugs. What strengths and weaknesses can you see in using an extended example to illustrate a larger trend? How effectively do you think Talbot ties this example to her larger argument throughout her essay?

2. After reading this piece carefully, list the different perspectives on brain-boosting drugs that Talbot lays out in her essay. Does she seem to take sides on this issue? Provide evidence from the text for your responses.

### Writing as a Reader: Entering the Conversation of Ideas

1. Talbot's examples of neuroenhancing drug use focus on the way men use these mind-altering substances, just as Matthew Petrocelli, Trish Oberweis, and Joseph Petrocelli's study of recreational steroid use focuses on men. What can these two essays tell us about our expectations of men

in today's culture? Compose an essay that brings together examples and insights from both readings in order to make a larger point about our current expectations for men, in mind and body. What is at stake for these men and for our culture, given the ideas you present to your reader?

2. While they may seem to make an unlikely pair, both Talbot and Virginia Blum analyze the significance of our cultural manipulation of bodies in order to achieve whatever is perceived to be the next standard of perfection. Write an essay in which you connect examples and ideas from each essay in order to examine our present attitudes toward what we can and should do to perfect our bodies. What counts as perfection in mind and body? According to these authors, and to you, what is the significance of the direction in which we seem to be heading?

## TOINE PIETERS AND STEPHEN SNELDERS

# Psychotropic Drug Use: Between Healing and Enhancing the Mind

Toine Pieters and Stephen Snelders both conduct research at the Vrije Universiteit Medisch Centrum in Amsterdam. Pieters focuses on biotechnology and, in particular, the intersections of medicine and ethics. He published *Interferon: The Science and Selling of a Miracle Drug* in 2005. His coauthor, Stephen Snelders, is a Dutch historian with a research interest in biology and social transformation. He is the past editor of *Pan Forum*, a research journal of psychotropic studies. He is also the author of *The Devil's Anarchy: The Other Loose Roving Way of Life and Very Remarkable Travels of Jan Erasmus Reyning, Buccaneer* (2004), a study of seventeenth-century Dutch pirate culture.

In this 2009 article from the journal *Neuroethics*, Pieters and Snelders offer a pithy history of "happy pills" and the ways psychotropic drugs have been seen in both positive and negative ways by popular culture. Their focus is not on the treatment of serious mental illnesses but on the varying popular perceptions of drugs that make people "feel better about living in a modern world" (para. 4). Most of their article takes a historical look at shifting twentieth-century attitudes about these drugs. They argue, "Doctors, patients, and other consumers had to learn how to use and cope with new generations of psychotropics between laboratory, bedside, and the household, *redefining the boundaries* between healing and soothing the mind, and fulfilling fashionable desires of comfort, convenience, and pleasure" (para. 6, emphasis in original). Pieters and Snelders include Dutch, British, German, and American history in their analysis. To what extent does this international focus offer perspective on this topic? As you read, pay attention to the different kinds of data and evidence Pieters and Snelders offer their readers. How do they use quotations from historical drug advertisements, for example, to help strengthen their claims that attitudes toward these medications have shifted over time?

Keep your own knowledge and experiences of these drugs in mind as you read, considering how the historical and international perspective expands your ideas about the role of these drugs in modern life. Like most scholars, Pieters and Snelders are not out to argue that these drugs are either bad or good. Instead, they argue that a historical and international perspective adds a lot to our understanding of the way we use these drugs and why. After you have learned more, what do *you* think?

■ ■ ■

## Abstract

The making and taking of psychotropic drugs, whether on medical prescription or as self-medication, whether marketed by pharmaceutical companies or clamoured for by an anxious population, has been an integral part of the twentieth century. In this modern era of speed, uncertainty, pleasure, and anguish the boundaries between healing and enhancing the mind by chemical means have been redefined. Long before Prozac would become a household name for an "emotional aspirin" did consumers embrace the idea and practice of taking psychotropics not only to treat mental illness but also to make them feel better about living in a modern world. The Freudian promise that each individual can remake him- or herself in the pursuit of health and happiness was helpful in promoting and legitimizing the idea and practice of seeking wellness on prescription. We will argue that the modern consumer-driven political culture of medicine will continue to transverse the boundaries of therapy and enhancement of the mind into the largely unexplored territories of human cognition and behaviour. However exciting, this endeavour will come at the cost of further widening the problem of iatrogenic addiction in the age of happiness pills as "Botox" for the mind.

## Introduction

In his best-selling 2001 novel *The Corrections* the American author Jonathan Franzen concocts a futuristic story about the arrival of a new generation of personality optimizers. "The action is effectively instantaneous. That's the glory of it . . . compared with up to 4 weeks for some of the dinosaurs they are still using. . . . Go on Zoloft today and you're lucky to feel better a week from Friday" [1]    *1*

Despite still rising consumption figures of Zoloft- and Prozac-like    *2* selective serotonin reuptake inhibitors, the heydays of what has been labeled the antidepressant era are over.[1] From the turn of the century the

[1] Worldwide it concerns a market of more than $25 billion (8% of the total global therapeutic drug market) with average yearly growth figures of about 10%; IMS Health 2008.

SSRI's have gradually passed in American, British, and Dutch public perceptions from remarkably safe and effective medicines to allegedly dangerous and addictive drugs. In a similar fashion as Valium and Librium the SSRI's have been associated with an epidemic of iatrogenic addiction. This rather dramatic re-evaluation of what in the 1990s still counted as wonder drugs for the mind coincides with most of these drugs having run out of their patents [2–8].

On the basis of the cyclical dynamics of the careers of psychotropic  3 drugs it seems to be only a matter of time before the SSRI's will be replaced by a new generation of more sophisticated medicines with the promise of more instantaneous and selective mood-affecting effects. The marketing of this new generation of personalized prescription drugs will focus on the prospect of creating yet another horizon of healing and enhancing the mind. In doing so the 1932 vision of Aldous Huxley in *Brave New World* will once again be reiterated: pharmaceutical companies will provide us with first cure and then joy, peace, loving-kindness, and beauty in a pill [9].

The making and taking of psychotropic drugs, whether on medical  4 prescription or as self-medication, whether marketed by pharmaceutical companies or clamoured for by an anxious population, has been an integral part of the twentieth century [10, 11]. In this modern era of speed, uncertainty, pleasure, and anguish the boundaries between healing and enhancing the mind by chemical means have been redefined once and again [12, 13]. Long before Prozac would become a household name for an "emotional aspirin" did consumers embrace the idea and practice of taking psychotropics not to treat a mental illness but to make them feel better about living in a modern world.

In 1912 the German psychiatrist Max Seige pointed to the repetitious  5 quality of the reports on psychotropic drugs in medical journals. In his view it always started with very optimistic reports about promising therapeutic results in a wide range of psychiatric conditions, soon followed by communications about the occurrence of side effects or therapeutic claims that failed to materialize and gradually resulting in a reduction of the range of indications and uses [14]. Whether we focus on the introduction and use of the first synthetic psychotropic chloral at the end of the nineteenth century or the introduction and use of barbiturates like Veronal and Luminal at the beginning of the twentieth century, Siege-like cycles of therapeutic optimism and disappointment manifest themselves [15, 16]. These early examples of modern wonder drugs for the mind became the first rehearsals of the post–World War II scenario seen with psychotropic drugs like Miltown, Valium, or Prozac that acquired a great public following in the psychiatric home-care of the middle classes, seeking relief for the daily discomforts of mental ills and other nervous problems [10, 17–19].

In this article we will show how new diagnostic, therapeutic, and  6 recreational categories and the categorized patients and consumers have emerged hand in hand and changed as social and material conditions changed. Doctors, patients, and other consumers had to learn how to use and cope with new generations of psychotropics between laboratory, bedside, and the household, *redefining the boundaries* between healing and soothing the mind, and fulfilling fashionable desires of comfort, convenience, and pleasure. The question is how and in what sense these boundaries have shifted over time and to what consequences. As part of the cyclical dynamics of psychotropic drug development and use we will point out a parallel spiraling of medically controlled legal ("on prescription") drug markets and criminally controlled illegal drug markets.

## The Emergence of a Mass Market for Prescription-Only Psychotropics

Hysteria was the most fashionable diagnosis for middle-class women in   7
the latter part of the nineteenth century and neurasthenia would develop into the standard diagnosis for functional nervous disorders in the early twentieth century. Both conditions were characterized by overstrained, restless nerves and took on prominence against the background of a modern industrial society in rapid flux. Not only in psychiatric practice but within medicine as a whole, synthetic drugs like chloral hydrate and subsequently the barbiturates became widely used, the family doctor's familiar recourse in dealing with common symptoms from insomnia to anxiety and the vapours [11, 16, 18].

   The relative high pricing of the barbiturates did not prevent them from   8
becoming the most popular hypnotics and sedatives of the first half of the twentieth century. This was due not only to the successful efforts of the pharmaceutical industry to project a modern scientific image on the barbiturates but also to the growing economic strength of the middle classes, and to the expanding health insurance industry with its reimbursement of prescription drugs. Moreover, the enthusiastic acclaim for the barbiturates coincided with the growing disrepute of the opiates and the patent medicines associated with them. The International Opium Convention at The Hague (1912) and the passing of the Harrison Act in the United States (1915), followed by similar restrictive opiate legislation in other countries, created a gap in family medicine cabinets. Doctors and lay consumers in search for psychoactive substances with sedative and hypnotic properties increasingly drifted towards the barbiturates. Barbiturate brand names like Veronal, Verpnal, or Medinal (barbital) and Luminal (phenobarbital) and later Seconal (secobarbital) and Amytal (amobarbital) became household words [20–23].

   It would last until the 1930s before the critical appraisal of the barbi-   9
turates as dangerous drugs could be heard in the public sphere with alarming media reports on the statistics of barbiturate deaths among the middle

classes. In response the supply of barbiturates was increasingly restricted under different national drug acts, with Britain and Germany taking the lead. In both countries Veronal and subsequently Luminal became prescription-only drugs, which officially could be dispensed only by licensed pharmacists and chemists. The foundations were laid for the emergence of a new mass market for prescription-only psychoactive medicines [23].

Whether in Amsterdam, Berlin, London, or Washington sedatives, hypnotics, and stimulants, available in dozens of formulae and brands, were lavishly supplied on medical prescription. The liberal supply on the licit market, however, did not prevent the emergence of an illicit market. By the end of the 1930s the American Food and Drug Administration (FDA) began to issue public warnings against the perceived parallel exponential growth of the volume of so-called legitimate use and the volume of so-called illicit abuse of barbiturates and amphetamines. The latter was attributed to abuse among youths and young adults and associated with an alarming increase in traffic accidents [19, 23]. *10*

But regardless of the new wave of legislative concerns in the USA, the Second World War triggered an enormous increase in the demand for psychotropics. The armies of servicemen returning home with barbiturate and amphetamine experiences and supplies found receptive ground among the anxious and traumatised population of the Western countries. And the post-war period of reconstruction and Cold War–related stress and fears did little to ease demand. Moreover, new career paths were explored. Pentothal and Amytal, for instance, began to make a name for themselves as "truth serum" not only within military quarters but also in the fields of forensic medicine and psychoanalysis [19, 23]. *11*

The war-related surge of demand was a probable factor in the persistent growth of the use of barbiturates and amphetamines. Another factor was the supply chain. US production capacity rose exponentially. In 1950 drug companies produced more than 25 barbiturate and 10 amphetamine pills for every American citizen (pop. 151.3 million). This quantity was claimed to be far beyond "legitimate medical needs" and to match that of the opiates at the turn of the nineteenth century. Likewise there are strong indications that in Britain the supply of barbiturates and amphetamines lawfully manufactured or imported also greatly exceeded the requirements of what was called "legitimate medical use." The prescription-only alliance between pharmaceutical companies, government, doctors, patients, and pharmacists led paradoxically to an overproduction and oversupply of upper and downer pills that disappeared into an illegal market. An American estimate was that half of the legitimate production was meant for the illicit market with its distribution channels through saloons, taxi drivers, and truck stops [19, 23]. *12*

Given increasing visibility by the rise of scientific medicine and marketing practices of industry, and used in contexts that were increasingly subjected to media attention, psychotropic drugs became important *13* focal points of cultural mediation and imagination in medical and public spheres. The growing armoury of sedatives, hypnotics, and stimulants was perceived as invigorating a healthy mind and making it more resistant against the demands of the increasing pace of modern urban life—the housewife's and white collar man's upper and/or downer friend. As such the use of synthetic psychotropics became endemic in the first part of the twentieth century and would continue to support the fabric of social life in an expanding post-war Western consumer culture.

The Second World War further heightened a sense of the value of psychosomatic medicine. Psychiatrists had reported extensively about soldier's experiences that stress, fear, neurotic anxiety, and the emotions in general could produce any number of physical ailments [24]. The popular media helped to spread the belief in the psychological nature of illness and encouraged ideas about the healing potential of Freudian psychoanalysis. Nowhere was the shift in the public perception of the diagnosis and therapy of mental illnesses so dramatic as in the United States. The post-war promise of psychoanalysis was that it could change undesirable states of mind and forms of conduct into less undesirable or even desirable ones. Self-awareness was promoted as a means to the end of engendering a better and healthier self and a better society. With a kind of iatrogenic effect, the psychologization of health and illness resulted in the growth of the need for therapy and not only of the therapeutic talk variety. General practitioners began hearing from all sides that they needed to recognize concealed mental health problems and patients became much more willing to accept a diagnosis for a nervous illness, and a matching prescription for a psychotropic medication [19, 25, 26].

According to historian Nicolas Rasmussen, in the early 1950s American family doctors embraced amphetamines as psychiatric medications for their distressed and neurotic patients suffering from overstrained nerves [19]. The amphetamine stimulants were referred to as psychic energizers, cementing the notion that mood problems in terms of mild and minor depression with symptoms such as insomnia, anxiety, and disturbance of appetite were both commonplace and easily treatable. As part of an eclectic and pragmatic medical practice upper (stimulants) and downer (sedatives and hypnotics) pills, and psychoanalytic approaches were eagerly combined to treat what was considered an epidemic of neurotic anxiety [19, 25].

The pharmaceutical industry was rather helpful in developing, producing, and marketing pills that did the job of energizing and soothing in one. They started promoting a new flexible concept of mood depression, in which insufficiently vigorous pursuit of pleasure and material reward due to an inability to cope with a speedy and tense society was recognized as a medical problem [19]. As a treatment for this condition a combination of dexamphetamine and amylabarbitone, under the trade name Dexamyl, became extremely popular in America, Britain, and the Netherlands alike [26].

## Towards a New Chemistry of the Mind

In the post-war period a new generation of chemists and pharmacolo-    17
gists worked hand in hand with the pharmaceutical industry to improve
the efficiency of the industrial screening programs for therapeutic drugs.
From a technical point of view, companies developed in their laboratories
increasingly sophisticated capacities to attach successively different side
chains to a chemical nucleus and systematically map the pharmacologi-
cal properties of the resulting large series of compounds. At the same time
science-based direct marketing helped to create a buzz around new would-
be wonder drugs for body and mind. The post-war international economic
boom with its vibrant consumerism and consumer desire, in combination with the performance-driven ideologies and cultures of the cold war,
strongly stimulated demand for medicines. In conjunction with the post-
war beliefs in the continuation of breakthroughs in modern medicine this
would bring about the culture of a pill for every ill in the 1960s [25–28].

The testing of the effects of the psychotropic compounds in academic    18
and industrial laboratories was matched by the testing of individuals and
groups in household, street, or nightlife settings. Each user or group of
users selected from the wide range of compounds and affects a few as valuable and interesting. In their urge for self-testing, housewives, businessmen, workers, and youth subcultures (e.g., beatniks) alike all more or less
freely explored new territories ranging from healing, tuning, to enhancing
the mind. At least, until these upper and downer pills came to be seen as
a habit-forming health risk and the growing problem of addiction on prescription was regarded as a social menace to society. But before this would
materialize a new generation of psychotropics was ready to take off and
spawn new cycles of promise and hope [18, 25, 26].

The introduction of chlorpromazine (Thorazine/Largactil) in the early    19
1950s is widely acknowledged as marking the beginning of a major psy-
chopharmacological revolution. Together with the drug reserpine, chlorpromazine transformed the prospects for the treatment of mental illness
and rejuvenated the materia medica for the mind. Both new medications
had a powerful impact not only on the atmosphere in the asylums—from
places of chronic unrest mental hospitals turned into peaceful care
centres—but also on a growing therapeutic optimism in the consulting
room of psychiatrists and general practitioners alike. Expectations ran high
about the arrival of a new penicillin-like era of healing the mind [10, 29,
30]. Popular texts on this revolution in the neurosciences and psychopharmacology like Paul de Kruif's *A Man against Insanity* (1957) or Robert S.
de Ropp's *Drugs and the Mind* (1957) became bestsellers [29, 31].

Right from the beginning the pharmaceutical industry was most    20
helpful in emphasizing the qualities of chlorpromazine (Largactil®) and
reserpine (Serpasil®) as the first modern wonder drugs for the mind
and differentiating them from the conventional sedatives. This is nicely
reflected in some of the 1950s drug ads. Whereas in the case of chlorprom-

azine Van Gogh's painting *The Round of the Prisoners* was used to promote its special relief-producing effect, in the case of reserpine the image of a pill superimposed on a brain with the caption "different from the barbiturates" served to underline the new combination between sedation and mental *recovery*. In order to capture this new therapeutic profile and distinguish it from sedation proper, scientists would begin to label chlorpromazine and reserpine as major tranquillizers from 1956 onwards [10].

The differentiation of the "new" tranquillizers was given impetus by 21 the observation that both chlorpromazine and reserpine counteracted the psychosis induced by another new promising synthetic molecule, the hallucinogenic drug LSD. In suggesting a relationship between chemical and clinical psychosis this observation opened up a horizon of drugs with wondrous potential for brain research, psychiatry, and psychothepy. A horizon which in 1957 was still described as "pharmaco-psychiatry" would become publicly known as "chemistry of madness" by the end of the 1960s [10, 32].

Being the experimental tool par excellence because of its efficacy in 22 extremely small dosages counting in micrograms, LSD paved the way for a productive alliance between the neurosciences, pharmacology, psychiatry, and clinical epidemiology. This would turn the so-called "neurotransmitter revolution in medicine" into an addictive form brain medicine for scientists, doctors, and consumers alike: the chemically transformable mind. The questions about the ability of restoring the balance between psyche and soma, which from the 1920s had been mainly articulated in a Freudian psychological sense, would in the following decades increasingly come to be defined in biological and chemical terms. Mental *discovery* was superimposed on mental *recovery* by chemical means.

The scientific claims of a chemical transformable mind appealed to 23 the imagination of the avant-garde of the Beat Generation and were further popularized by the gurus of the Sixties counterculture. They spoke of unlimited possibilities for the transformation of mind and body, psyche and soma. The evolutionary jump towards a mental Superman seemed at hand with a revolutionary molecule such as LSD.

In the American context Aldous Huxley played an important role in 24 advocating democratic access to the new generation of mind-altering substances. He and other authors publicly heralded the advances on the neuropharmacological frontier and promoted using psychotronic drugs for relieving poverty, monotony, pain, and limitation [32].

The pharmaceutical industry was quick to capitalize on the success of 25 the new miracle drugs for the mind. The major tranquillizers like chlorpromazine were portrayed in the mass media as modern penicillin-like weapons which had created a revolution in the doctoring of madness. The marketers rapidly secured the name minor tranquillizer to position a new generation of hypnotics and sedatives as novel technologies of the self to strengthen self-consciousness and counter negative feelings like fear, guilt, or shame that were associated with an epidemic of psychosomatic health problems. Most advertisements of minor tranquillizers repeated the mantra that in every patient and every illness the individual management of anxiety and tension is essential to recovery. In itself this kind of self-remaking message was far from new and mirrored the claims of psycho-analytic therapy. But the accompanying message of a chemical adjustment of the psychosomatic balance was new [10, 25]. As part of this shifting message *the boundaries* between healing and soothing the mind, and ful-filling fashionable desires of comfort, convenience, and pleasure would be redefined accordingly. And between medical and non-medical uses of psychotropics.

## Mother's Little Helpers

Neurotic anxiety became the signature illness of the 1950s and 1960s. 26 Psychoanalytic psychiatry helped to place anxiety in the public eye as a treatable condition, but the age of anxiety was shaped by the actions of many different social groups: from researchers, doctors, and patients to journalists, politicians, and drug salesmen. The latter, in particular, pro-pagandized the symmetries of illness and remedy and thereby helped to create new notions of illness and cure. The drug companies jumped on the anxiety bandwagon and helped to forge a productive alliance between con-sumer demand, psychic anguish, and medicine. With the aim of casting the widest possible net for potential customers, drug advertisers tended to conflate psychosomatic illness from stomachaches to heart troubles with the familiar daily problems of frustrations with work, household, or other activities and relationships. According to the historian David Herzberg the minor tranquillizers were presented as consumer goods that would bring comfort and convenience to consumers' psychic and emotional lives—the latest new personal technology for pursuing happiness and achieving the good life [25].

The successful marketing of Miltown/Equanil (meprobamate) set 27 the stage for the "happiness pills" era. Whereas the intense excitement in the late 1950s about Miltown as the first minor tranquillizer was for the greater part an Anglo-American affair, the introduction in 1960 of Librium by the Swiss pharmaceutical company Hoffman-La Roche was global news. The black-green capsules with the benzodiazepine compound chlor-diazepoxide—synthesized in 1955 and trade named Librium—became available as medication for anxieties and tensions [23]. Librium promised to be an anxiolytic without the problems of dependence and overdosing associated with the first minor tranquillizer meprobamate (Miltown) and the conventional sedatives and hypnotics [18, 33, 34].

The extensive worldwide information campaign of Roche, directed at 28 specialists and general practitioners alike, and the inflationary spiral of stories in the media about a new medicinal drug with miraculous calming effects in small doses and no manifest side effects, turned Librium into an overnight sensation. The 1960 phrase in *Life* magazine—"The drug that tames wild cats—What will it do for nervous women?"—turned into a self-fulfilling prophecy. Roche set a new global marketing standard for blockbuster drugs. Not only did they decide in favour of a single brand name but they also chose to market an all-embracing revolutionary treatment concept: a comprehensible and practical system of symptom identification, diagnostics, mode of action, and therapy. At the centre was the flexible and for both general practitioners and specialists understandable and manageable concept of chemically restoring the balance between body and mind, through a specific switcher mechanism, the so-called "limbic system." In print promotions Librium was portrayed as an instant limbic stabilizer "whatever the diagnosis." But Librium was not presented as the one and only compound to make this new chemotherapeutic approach of nervous problems feasible. This cleared the way for the introduction of supplementary tranquillizers with different therapeutic profiles. And Roche led the way in 1963 by bringing out the more potent and anxiety-specific benzodiazepine analogue diazepam under the trade name Valium [23, 35, 36].

Librium turned out to be only the prelude to the frenzy or "Valiummania" [37]. Marketed as the most potent safe and sane anxiolytic of the day, the pill with the telltake "V" rapidly surpassed Librium as the best-selling tranquillizer in Western countries. In 1965 Roche introduced yet another benzo, the sleeping-pill Mogadon (nitrazepam). This drug, in contrast to the "traditional hypnotics" (i.e., the barbiturates), was claimed to be reliable and safe and did not lead to narcosis, coma, or death in case of an overdose. The British and American Roche advertisements brought home the message of the superiority of Mogadon in a rather candid way: "Some patients stay on barbiturates until the day they die . . ." [38].

With the fast-growing popularity of the benzos the therapeutic areas in which they were applied seemed to multiply unchecked [23]. Sleeplessness, nervousness, overexertion, stomach and back pains, hypertension and heart problems, and even psychotic disorders such as schizophrenia and manic depression became indications for administration of members of the extending "benzo-family." They were touted as the answer to everything, including the "normal" emotional reactions to life's everyday challenges. In Germany and the Netherlands the following aphorism became popular among physicians: "Wenn man nicht weiss, wie, was, warum, dann gibt man immer Valium" (*When you don't know how to treat your next patient then it is time for Valium*) [39].

Doctors and patients alike eagerly sought out the new drugs. *Fortune* magazine announced that the US was on the verge of a "choose-your-mood society" that would allow "essentially normal people" to cope with and overcome the everyday stresses of their lives [25]. Popular representations of tranquillizers as a pill for every ill mirrored the consumption statistics. From the early 1960s up to the late 1970s Librium, Valium, Mogadon, and other benzos led the drug list in Western countries. The benzo-family together with the limbic concept of therapeutic action beautifully suited the interaction between general practitioners and their distressed patients, the needs and expectations each brought to the short office visit, offering a little help in their pursuit of everyday happiness. This was in spite of the accumulation of reports on side effects, observed as early as 1961 by the American medical internist Leo Hollister: tolerance, dependence, drowsiness, reduced alertness, and other reactions leading to traffic accidents [23].

The promise of a psychoactive magic bullet, with a controllable and specific effect on the chemistry of the brain, a "peace-of-mind" pill, was kept neither by the benzodiazepines or LSD nor by any of the other new synthetic compounds. On the contrary, the chemical effects of the drugs on the mind turned out to be remarkably *non*-specific and addictive. Apart from medical side effects, cultural and social "side effects" became manifest. 32

In 1966 when the psychologist Leslie Farber wrote his essay "Ours Is the Addicted Society," the Rolling Stones produced their classic hit "Mother's Little Helper," epitomizing the critique of middle-class tranquillizer addiction, alienation, and hypocrisy. Historian Susan Speaker shows how the critique on the making and taking of benzos in the United States was tied up with their becoming a symbolic focal point for articulating and addressing social anxieties and tensions but also expectations regarding "The Good Life" [37]. These expectations were redefined by the young American middle-class baby boom generation, who lavished themselves with new spirits of peace and happiness during the "Summer of Love" in 1967. While criticizing tranquillizer use of the elderly the hippie generation and their young heroes of popular music seemed saturated in drug allusions of yet another kind. The development of hippy and psychedelic movements co-evolved with an upsurge of LSD, cannabis, and heroin use. With the promise of a spiritual enhancement of the mind the consumption of these drugs proliferated among the burgeoning youth cultures in Western countries. 33

The parallel spiralling of the medical and non-medical consumption of psychotropics at the end of the 1960s evoked politically consequential public opposition to both kinds of drug use. A rhetorical mix of direct harms to the middle-class youth, anxieties about the collective future of a drug-infused society, perceived criminal behaviour of deviant groups, social costs of addiction, and the war on drugs provoked a worldwide backlash on psychotropic drug use. In the course of the 1970s (inter-)national narcotics laws were strengthened in an attempt to contain (i.e., benzodiazepines), restrict (i.e., amphetamines), or prohibit (i.e., cannabis, LSD, and heroin) the consumption of psychotropics [21–23]. 34

## Appetite for New Chemical Wonders for the Mind

Regardless of the public portrayal and perception of most psychotropics as addictive and/or dangerous drugs, the desire for and expectations of new molecules that might transform and enhance the chemistry of the mind continued to grow. The forceful antipsychiatry movement of the 35

1970s might have temporarily succeeded in halting the growth of the consumption of the so-called "chemical straightjackets of conformity" (psychotropic medication on prescription) but by encouraging a shared drive for self-development and self-expression they also helped to further open up a horizon of achieving wellness by chemical means, giving impetus to a rehearsal of the era of happiness pills. In search for equality and appreciation of the "other," the deviant, the protagonists of this critical movement did anything but halt the historical process of individual empowerment and a growing consciousness of self-control by any available means.

Setting out to make schizophrenia and mania intelligible, the anti- 36 psychiatry movement ended up not only destigmatizing madness and psychiatry, but making its language available and in some ways glorifying it. Paradoxically this not only helped to make madness more acceptable, but fed into a growing public interest in the pathological aspects of "normal" people. Medical consumers showed an increased willingness to read unhappiness and malaise in terms of an expanding repertoire of inconvenient and undesirable symptoms that called for treatment. It helped turn everyone into a potential patient with a mental illness. This was not a passive patient but an assertive consumer participant who sought to educate him- or herself in order to negotiate more effectively a treatment with medical authority, or circumvent it altogether and seek feel-good pills by any affordable way in the pursuit of happiness [10, 25, 35, 40].

The growing popularity of biological theories of mental disorders and 37 rising expectations surrounding the bio-revolution in medicine whetted the appetite for new wonder drugs for the mind. In the mid-eighties, in the continuing search for happiness through chemistry, a new generation of youngsters began to experiment with the psychedelic MDMA under the universal brand-name ecstasy [41].

In the climate of the neo-liberal, no-nonsense political economics of 38 the Reagan and Thatcher era, young urban professionals and students in London, New York, and Amsterdam eagerly started to combine a new raving form of electronic dance music, "acid house," with the drug ecstasy. They eagerly distanced themselves from the heroin-associated, depressing no-future ideology of the punk generation. With the new hug drug in their pockets hundreds and later on crowds of thousands of young people gathered in dodgy warehouses or disused industrial sites to dance away the night. The euphoric explosion of unlicensed ecstasy-fuelled rave parties in the summers of 1988 and 1989 was earmarked as the Second Summer of Love. The new optimistic dance culture drew parallels with the hedonism and freedom of the Summer of Love in San Francisco two decades earlier. Ecstasy served as illegal chemical means of mass "self-enlightenment" between dusk and dawn; as such this and other drugs became a personal technology for constituting immediacy in delivering pleasures between street and medicine cabinet [41–43].

Apparently alarmed by media reports about serious health effects, 39 the public fear of a distortion of public order, and fuelled by the war on drugs, politicians and government would eagerly climb down on the "drug-infected" house scene. Simultaneously, the social appetite for daily chemical "self-control"—in terms of the immediate delivery of comforts and conveniences tuned to a specific state of mind or performance—on prescription was whetted by the promise and hope for once again a new generation of psychotropics. The desire for chemical forms of self-control and self-betterment pervaded both medical and public domains. Once again enveloping and interfering spirals of medical and non-medical use of psychotropics became manifest.

The introduction and international circulation by the American Psy-    40 chiatric Association of operational diagnostic criteria for psychiatric disorders in a series of manuals from the DSM-III in 1980 up to the DSM-IVR in the 1990s acted as an important catalyst of identifying and differentiating treatable forms of mental illness in the consulting room. The steady growth in the number of mental disorders in what became widely regarded as the "diagnostic bible" of psychiatry helped to medicalize additional territories of human emotions, behaviour, and cognition. Previously "normal" human traits like shyness, aggression as antisocial behavior, or attention deficit became a sickness. In the process the need and demand for medical treatments was stimulated [4, 44, 50].

The pharmaceutical industry was first in recognizing the marketing    41 potential of using the DSM as well as the rising tide of bio-optimism and the growing appetite for mind-altering pills. According to the historian Edward Shorter, the FDA was rather helpful in setting rather ambiguous placebo-guided testing standards for new drugs [44]. The American drug company Eli Lilly would lead the way. Its new antidepressant Prozac (flouxetine) was launched in 1987. Prozac was presented as a revolution in the psychopharmacology of depression. Based on the latest scientific evidence, a lowering of the brain neurotransmitter serotonin had been demonstrated in depression. And flouxetine was claimed to selectively restore the serotonin levels in the brain back to normal. This relatively simple mechanistic model of mood levels and brain molecules promised a rather straightforward therapeutic trajectory in what was officially pronounced "the decade of the brain." By prescribing a compound like flouxetine that lacked the nasty side effects of the older tricyclic antidepressants or the addiction problems of the benzos, doctors would be able to provide their patients with an all-in-one safe and effective depression and anxiety therapy [3].

The marketing message of once again a revolution in brain chemis-    42 try and the promise of a therapeutic breakthrough was picked up rather swiftly. The cycle of events following the introduction of Prozac even took Lilly's marketers by surprise. In celebrating Prozac as a wonder drug that effects miraculous changes in personality and social performance—lowering inhibitions and increasing outgoing, confident behaviour—Peter Kramer's "Listening to Prozac" helped to create a worldwide pill-taking hype. Kramer claimed that consumers had entered a new era of cosmetic psychopharmacology. The choice to become a Prozac consumer was presented as one's own choice of mood self-control and engineering wellness. It was not so much the therapeutic contract between a patient and a doctor that would make this mind pill do its work but the individual consumer's belief in the superior therapeutic power of a clean brain medicine [25, 45].

However fictional, this image of self-choice and self-repair had a great sex appeal. Prozac started off as a promising vehicle for popularizing the new brain sciences and yet another generation of chemical consumer goods to achieve wellness on prescription. In 1994 Prozac was the second best-selling medication worldwide, just behind the drug for the treatment of ulcer problems, Zantac. Both Prozac and serotonin became household words — the epitome of modern interventions in the brain and of modern feel-good tools. Moreover, Prozac marked the re-emergence of the pill-for-every-ill culture that was heralded in the 1950s and 1960s. As far as the United States, the UK, and the Netherlands are concerned, the consumption of psychotropics on prescription regained its forceful growth pattern in the 1990s, after a cyclical downturn in the late 1970s and 1980s [19, 23, 25, 39].

In the meantime depression prevalence rates co-evolved and continued to rise. The age of anxiety and blaming society gave way to the age of depression and blaming your own brain. In a similar way as neurotic anxiety in the 1950s and 1960s depression has grown to epidemic proportions in modern, developed Western countries in particular. Within two decades the percentage of the population having depression that requires treatment has risen fivefold on average: in 2009 more than 5% of the general population [5, 8].

Prozac's brand image of personal self-repair and its apparent disregard of the therapeutic contract between a patient and a doctor fitted in rather well in the medicine-on-demand culture in the US. However, this very same brand image turned Prozac into an early loser on the fast-growing Dutch market for antidepressants [45]. Dutch doctors preferred to prescribe therapeutic family members of Prozac like Paxil and Zoloft that did not pose a potential threat to their authority in the consulting room. Moreover, by the end of 1990s optimistic reports about promising therapeutic results in a wide range of psychiatric conditions were drowned out by communications about the occurrence of side effects or therapeutic claims that failed to materialize. As in the case of most consumer goods, mass consumption deprived Prozac of its unique selling point as a personal optimizer to tinker with your own "neurochemical" identity. This romantic and personal connotation was lost as part of the consumerism on the medical market [25]. Contrary to Kramer's claims of the arrival of a new era of personal optimizers, Prozac and the other members of the therapeutic group of SSRI's turned out to be rather unspecific middle-of-the-road feel-good pills. The generic capacity of lifting moods in average consumers should earn these pills the label "Botox for the mind" in the age of happiness pills.

## Conclusion

As we have shown throughout the twentieth century, social and cultural 46
factors, promise, hope, fashion, and taboo have been of major influence
on psychotropic use. This also holds for the familiarity with mental disorders, their recognition and acceptance, and ultimately the choice of treatment. What is recognized and accepted as mental illness and what is not?
Are the consumers familiar with the possibilities of diagnosis and treatment? What expectations do they have of drug treatment? These aspects
are influenced by publicity and media attention.

This is a dynamic process. Pharmaceutical companies have been of 47
importance in this process. The drug marketers have continued to look
for new markets by researching and influencing needs in the consulting
rooms and translating them into treatment options. By information supply to physicians and more and more to potential consumers, drug companies have stimulated the consumption of psychotropics. Despite the
importance that their impact may have, it still depends on the cooperation
of physicians and consumers.

Depression, the drug company Pfizer once advertised, is the most 48
democratic of all disorders. It can affect everyone at any moment, for
shorter or longer duration, without a recognisable course. This kind of
"democratisation" of mental disorders and the application of psychotropic
drugs, however, is not a unique selling point of the pharmaceutical industry. Exemplary in this case is the massive use of cognitive-enhancing drugs
(e.g., amphetamines) in the Second World War, the Cold War period, and
yet again in 2009 by both ill (e.g., ADHD sufferers) and healthy individuals
(recently coined by *Nature* as "professor's little helper") both on prescription and through other channels [46].

According to the vision of the future presented by the Dutch Health 49
Council (*Gezondheidsraad*) in 2002, human emotions, thoughts, and
behaviour will become treatable and controllable. The health council predicted that a regular market for self-medication would develop outside of
medicine, a market where consumers will be able to buy drugs to improve
their mood or cognitive achievements. According to the council these
future consumers should take responsibility, together with a "platform
against addiction" and the pharmaceutical industry, for security, reliability, and handling the risk of addiction to the drugs [47]. The boundaries
between treatment in a therapeutic sense, to get someone "back to normal," and enhancement, of making someone *better* than he or she is, will
continue to be redefined in this scenario.

However courageous the proposition of a public health–focussed plat- 50
form against addiction in a world dominated by a war against drugs, this
vision disqualifies itself by proving historically uninformed. Despite historical changes in neuropsychopharmacological semantics and a progressive process of standardizing mental illness and pills, we do not support
fashionable views of a paradigm shift in consumer demand and behaviour

regarding healing and enhancing the mind [6. 48, 49]. In our article we have argued that redefining boundaries between healing and enhancing the mind is not a new phenomenon in itself and the same holds for the practice of achieving wellness by chemical means. We have shown continuous dynamics of enveloping and interfering spirals of medical and non-medical uses of psychotropics as a means to healing and enhancing the mind. It is no surprise then that Huxley's subtle and challenging early warning of a dystopia of happiness pills in his *Brave New World* classic has been reiterated once again. And as far as we are concerned, this philosophical masterpiece should continue to be used as a source of inspiration for the much-needed public debates on how to proceed with our efforts to explore new territories of chemically intervening in human behaviour and cognition.

ACKNOWLEDGEMENTS

We would like to thank the following colleagues for their comments on preliminary versions of the manuscript: Prof. Dr. Trudy Dehue, Professor of the History of Psychology, Groningen University, the Netherlands; Prof. Dr. Charles Kaplan, Professor and Associates Dean of Research at the University of Houston, College of Social Work; and Prof. D. Frans J. Meijman, Professor of Medical Science Communication and its History, VU Amsterdam Medical Center, The Netherlands.

REFERENCES

1. Franzen, Jonathan. 2001. *The corrections*. London: Fourth Estate.
2. Fukuyama, Francis. 2002. *Our posthuman future*. London: Profile Books.
3. Healy, David. 2004. *Let them eat Prozac*. New York: New York University Press.
4. Horwitz, Allen V., and Jerome C. Wakefield. 2007. *The loss of sadness: How psychiatry transformed normal sorrow into depressive disorder*. Oxford: Oxford University Press.
5. Barber, Charles. 2008. *Comfortably numb: How psychiatry is medicating a nation*. New York: Pantheon Books.
6. Moncrieff, Joanna. 2008. *The myth of the chemical cure: A critique of psychiatric drug treatment*. London: Palgrave.
7. Critser, Greg. 2005. *Generation Rx: How prescription drugs are altering American lives, minds, and bodies*. Houghton Mifflin.
8. Dehue, Trudy. 2008. *De deprssie epidemie*. Amsterdam: Augustus.
9. Huxley, Aldous. 1932. *Brave new world*. New York: Harper and Brothers.
10. Pieters, Toine, and Stephen Snelders. 2005. Mental ills and the hidden history of drug treatment practices. In *Psychiatric cultures compared. Psychiatry and mental health care in the twentieth century: Comparisons and approaches*, eds. Marijke Gijswijt-Hofstra, Harry Oosterhuis, Joost Vijselaar, and Hugh Freeman, 381–401. Amsterdam: Amsterdam University Press.
11. Snelders, Stephen, Charles Kaplan, and Toine Pieters. 2006. On cannabis, chloral hydrate, and career cycles of psychotropic drugs in medicine. *Bulletin of the History of Medicine* 80: 95–114.
12. Bourke, Joanna. 2005. *Fear: A cultural history*. London: Virago.
13. Tomlinson, John. 2007. *The culture of speed: The coming of immediacy*. London: Sage.
14. Seige, Max. 1912. Klinische Erfahrungen mit Neuronal. *Deutsche Medizinische Wochenschrift* 38: 1828.

15. Pieters, Toine. 2004. *Historische trajecten in de farmacie: Medicijnen tussen confectie en maatwerk*. Hilversum: Uitgeverij Verloren.

16. Weber, Matthias M. 1999. *Dei Entwicklung der Psychopharmakologie im Zeitalter der naturwissenschaftlichen Medizin. Ideeengeschichte eines psychiatrischen Therapiesystems*. München: Urban & Vogel.

17. Pieters, Toine, and Stephen Snelders. 2008. Surviving the Seige cycle and managing a double bind: The case of Halcion in the Netherlands. In *Ways of regulating: Therapeutic agents between plants, shops, and consulting rooms*, eds. Jeanne-Paul Gaudilliere, Volker Hess. Max-Planck-Institut für Wissenschaftsgeschichte, Preprint 363, Berlin.

18. Shorter, Edward. 1997. *A history of psychiatry: From the era of the asylum to the age of Prozac*. New York: Wiley.

19. Rasmussen, Nicholas. 2008. *On speed: The many lives of amphetamine*. New York: New York University Press.

20. Hodgson, Barbara. 2001. *In the arms of Morpheus: The tragic history of laudanum, morphine, and patent medicine*. New York: Firefly Books.

21. Davenport-Hines, Richard. 2002. *The pursuit of oblivion*. New York: Norton & Company.

22. Courtwright, David T. 2001. *Forces of habit: Drugs and the making of the modern world*. Cambridge: Harvard University Press.

23. Pieters, Toine, and Stephen Snelders. 2007. From King Kong pills to mother's little helpers—career cycles of two families of psychotropic drugs: The barbiturates and benzodiazepines. *Canadian Bulletin of Medical History* 241: 93–112.

24. Shepard, Ben. 2000. *A war of nerves: Soldiers and psychiatrists (1914–1994)*. London: Cape.

25. Herzberg, David. 2009. *Happy pills in America: From Miltown to Prozac*. Baltimore: The Johns Hopkins University Press.

26. Healy, David. 2002. *The creation of psychopharmacology*. Cambridge: Harvard University Press.

27. Greene, Jeremy A. 2007. *Prescribing by numbers: Drugs and the definition of disease*. Baltimore: The Johns Hopkins University Press.

28. Lesch, John E. 2007. *The first miracle drugs: How the sulfa drugs transformed medicine*. Oxford: Oxford University Press.

29. De Kruijf, Paul 1957. *A man against insanity*. New York: Grove Press.

30. Swazey, Judith P. 1974. *Chlorpromazine in psychiatry: A study of therapeutic innovation*. Cambridge (MA): MIT.

31. De Ropp, Robert S. 1957. *Drugs and the mind*. New York: Grove.

32. Campbell, Nancy. D. 2007. *Discovering addiction: The science and politics of substance abuse research*. Ann Arbor: The University of Michigan.

33. Baenninger, Alex, Jorge A. Costa e Silva, Ian Hindmarch, Hans-Juergen Moeller, and Karl Rickels. 2004. *Good chemistry: The life and legacy of Valium inventor Leo Sternbach*. New York: McGraw Hill.

34. Healy, David. 1997. *The Antidepressant Era*. Cambridge: Harvard University Press.

35. Tone, Andrea. 2005. Listening to the past: History, psychiatry and anxiety. *Canadian Journal of Psychiatry* 50: 373–80.

36. Tone, Andrea. 2007. Tranquillizers on trial: Psychopharmacology in the age of anxiety. In *Medicating modern America: Prescription drugs in history*, eds. Andrea Tone and Elizabeth Siegel Watkins, 156–83. New York: New York University Press.

37. Speaker, Susan L. 1997. From "Happiness Pills" to "National Nightmare": Changing culture assessment of minor tranquillizers in America, 1955–1980. *Journal of the History of Medicine* 52: 338–76.

38. Medawar, Charles. 1992. *Power and dependence*. London: Social Audit.

39. Pieters, Toine, and Stephen Snelders. 2005. Antidepressiva van 1950 tot heden. Een halve eeuw op chemische wolken. *Maandblad voor Geestelijke volksgezondheid* 60: 207–22.

40. Grob, Gerald N. 1994. *The mad among us: A history of the care of America's mentally ill*. Cambridge: Harvard University Press.

41. Iversen, Lesley. 2008. *Speed > Ecstacy > Ritalin: The science of amphetamines*. Oxford: Oxford University Press.

42. Collin, Matthew. 1997. *Altered State: The story of ecstacy culture and acid house*. London: Serpent's Tail.

43. Reynolds, Simon. 1999. *Generation ecstasy: Into the world of the techno and rave culture*. New York: Routledge.

44. Shorter, Edward. 2008. *Before Prozac: The troubled history of mood disorders in psychiatry*. New York: Oxford University Press.

45. Pieters, Toine, and Mineke te Hennepe Mineke de Lange. 2002. *Pillen & Psyche: culturele eb– en vloedbewegingen. Medicamenteus ingrijpen in de psyche*. Den Haag: Rathenau Instituutwerkdocument 87.

46. Sahakian, Barbara, and Sharon Morein-Zamir. 2007. Professor's little helper. *Nature* 450: 1157–59.

47. Gezondheidsraad. 2002. *De toeksomst van ons zelf*. Den Haag: Gezondheidsraad. Publicatie nr. 2002/13.

48. Fukuyama, Francis. 2002. *Our posthuman future: Consequences of the biotechnology revolution*. London: Profile Books.

49. Rose, Nikolas. 2007. *The politics of life itself*. Princeton: Princeton University Press.

50. Kutchins, Herb, and Stuart A. Kirk. 1997. *Making us crazy: DSM—The psychiatric bible and the creation of mental disorders*. London: Constable.

■ ■ ■

## Reading as a Writer: Analyzing Rhetorical Choices

1. In their historical overview of attitudes toward "happy pills," Pieters and Snelders offer quotations from popular advertisements for these drugs from several different decades. Find and highlight these passages, and explain how Pieters and Snelders use the language in those advertisements to capture the attitude toward drugs at that time. How would you compare attitudes in the 1930s, the 1950s, the 1960s, and the late 1980s?

2. After you have read this article once, take another look at the introductory and concluding paragraphs, and explain in your own words what these authors aim to teach their readers about the uses of psychotropic drugs. How do their many historical examples feed into their larger point?

## Writing as a Reader: Entering the Conversation of Ideas

1. Pieters and Snelders, like Margaret Talbot, are interested in our shifting attitudes toward manipulating our minds with drugs. Write an essay that connects the examples and arguments in these essays in order to explain the significance you see in these contemporary attitudes toward drugs. What do these examples tell us about who we think we "should" be? What conclusions can you draw about where we seem to be headed?

2. Pieters and Snelders are fascinated by the ways we use drugs to help us achieve shifting cultural standards. Matthew Petrocelli, Trish Oberweis, and Joseph Petrocelli have a similar interest in their analysis of

recreational steroid use. Drawing on both essays, compose an essay that takes your readers from specific examples to a larger point about the use of drugs as a tool to meet cultural standards for normality or perfection. What do you make of the fact that these standards keep changing? What conclusions can you draw?

## JUDITH LORBER

# *From* Believing Is Seeing: Biology as Ideology

Judith Lorber is an internationally renowned scholar and one of the most widely read gender theorists writing today. She is a professor emerita of sociology and women's studies at Brooklyn College and the Graduate School, City University of New York. Her acclaimed book *Gender Inequality: Feminist Theories and Politics* is currently in its fourth edition (2009). This essay is reprinted from a 1992 lecture, and in it she explains an idea central to her research: that the behaviors we think of as "natural" to men and women, and that often make men and women seem like opposites to each other, are actually cultural inventions. Lorber, along with other sociologists of gender, argues that most of the ideas we hold about men's and women's "oppositional" attributes are not traceable to biological differences but are the result of a social need to justify divisions of labor and activity. Further, she notes that this division of assumptions about men and women most often favors traits perceived to be masculine over those perceived to be feminine. In this essay, she uses examples from sports and technology and what she calls the "bathroom problem" (think about where the lines are longest!) to help us reconsider our assumptions about gender.

In all her writing, Lorber is interested in helping her readers see with fresh eyes the many small *cultural* activities we engage in every day that reproduce these oppositional gender categories so that they come to seem natural. She argues, "It is the taken-for-grantedness of such everyday gendered behavior that gives credence to the belief that the widespread differences in what women and men do must come from biology" (para. 9). Here, she opens with some historical background on changing understandings of biological differences between male and female humans, noting that as those understandings changed, we can see culture stepping in to rejustify gender differences, even if they do not make sense biologically. So, for example, Lorber asks us to rethink our assumptions about who should compete against whom in athletic competitions. (For some sports, weight class may be a better categorization method than sex parts, for example.) She also helps us revisit any assumptions we might have about who might be "naturally" better at technology, offering historical examples that reveal why certain gender myths are launched at particular moments in history, to open or close doors of opportunity to particular groups.

As you read, pay attention to places where Lorber anticipates skeptical readers, as in paragraph 12, where she clarifies: "I am not saying that physical differences between male and female bodies don't exist, but that these differences are socially meaningless until social practices transform them into social facts." Lorber's point is that gender assumptions are so central to our understanding of what is "normal" that it can be confusing—even downright frightening—to reimagine the world without these limiting stereotypes in our heads. In particular, if the male body is still the universal standard, as she argues (para. 14), what might the world look like if we free ourselves from the assumption that masculine standards are best? A world of possibility might open up for both men and women to imagine ourselves as humans, instead of lumping ourselves into limiting categories of "men" and "women." Lorber's examples offer ways to think about what such a future could look like for all of us.

■ ▨ ▧

Until the eighteenth century, Western philosophers and scientists *1* thought that there was one sex and that women's internal genitalia were the inverse of men's external genitalia: the womb and vagina were the penis and scrotum turned inside out (Laqueur 1990). Current Western thinking sees women and men as so different physically as to sometimes seem two species. The bodies, which have been mapped inside and out for hundreds of years, have not changed. What has changed are the justifications for gender inequality. When the social position of all human beings was believed to be set by natural law or was considered God-given, biology was irrelevant; women and men of different classes all had their assigned places. When scientists began to question the divine basis of social order and replaced faith with empirical knowledge, what they saw was that women were very different from men in that they had wombs and menstruated. Such anatomical differences destined them for an entirely different social life from men.

In actuality, the basic bodily material *is* the same for females and *2* males, and except for procreative hormones and organs, female and male human beings have similar bodies (Naftolin and Butz 1981). Furthermore, as has been known since the middle of the nineteenth century, male and female genitalia develop from the same fetal tissue, and so infants can be born with ambiguous genitalia (Money and Ehrhardt 1972). When they are, biology is used quite arbitrarily in sex assignment. Suzanne Kessler (1990) interviewed six medical specialists in pediatric intersexuality and found that whether an infant with XY chromosomes and anomalous genitalia was categorized as a boy or a girl depended on the size of the penis—if a penis was very small, the child was categorized as a girl, and sex-change surgery was used to make an artificial vagina. In the late nineteenth century, the presence or absence of ovaries was the determining criterion of gender assignment for hermaphrodites because a woman who could not procreate was not a complete woman (Kessler 1990, 20).

Yet in Western societies, we see two discrete sexes and two distin- *3* guishable genders because our society is built on two classes or people, "women" and "men." Once the gender category is given, the attributes of the person are also gendered: Whatever a "woman" is has to be "female"; whatever a "man" is has to be "male." Analyzing the social processes that construct the categories we call "female and male," "woman and men," and "homosexual and heterosexual" uncovers the ideology and power differentials congealed in these categories (Foucault 1978). This article will . . . show how myriad physiological differences are transformed into similar-appearing, gendered social bodies. My perspective goes beyond accepted feminist views that gender is a cultural overlay that modifies physiological sex differences. That perspective assumes either that there are two fairly similar sexes distorted by social practices into two genders with purpose-fully different characteristics or that there are two sexes whose essential differences are rendered unequal by social practices. I am arguing that bodies differ in many ways physiologically, but they are completely trans-formed by social practices to fit into the salient categories of a society, the most pervasive of which are "female" and "male" and "women" and "men."

Neither sex nor gender [is a] pure [category]. Combinations of incon-    4 gruous genes, genitalia, and hormonal input are ignored in sex categoriza-tion, just as combinations of incongruous physiology, identity, sexuality, appearance, and behavior are ignored in the social construction of gen-der statuses. Menstruation, lactation, and gestation do not demarcate women from men. Only some women are pregnant and then only some of the time; some women do not have a uterus or ovaries. Some women have stopped menstruating temporarily, others have reached menopause, and some have had hysterectomies. Some women breastfeed some of the time, but some men lactate (Jaggar 1983, 165fn). Menstruation, lacta-tion, and gestation are individual experiences of womanhood (Levesque-Lopman 1988), but not determinants of the social category "woman," or even "female." Similarly, "men are not always sperm-producers, and in fact, not all sperm-producers are men. A male-to-female transsexual, prior to surgery, can be socially a woman, though still potentially (or actually) capable of spermatogenesis" (Kessler and McKenna [1978] 1985, 2).

When gender assignment is contested in sports, where the categories    5 of competitors are rigidly divided into women and men, chromosomes are now used to determine in which category the athlete is to compete. How-ever, an anomaly common enough to be found in several women at every major international sports competition are XY chromosomes that have not produced male anatomy or physiology because of a genetic defect. Because these women are women in every way significant for sports com-petition, the prestigious International Amateur Athletic Federation has urged that sex be determined by simple genital inspection (Kolata 1992). Transsexuals would pass this test, but it took a lawsuit for Renée Richards, a male-to-female transsexual, to be able to play tournament tennis as a woman, despite his male sex choromosomes (Richards 1983). Oddly, nei-ther basis for gender categorization—chromosomes nor genitalia—has anything to do with sports prowess (Birrell and Cole 1990).

In the Olympics, in cases of chromosomal ambiguity, women must undergo "a battery of gynecological and physical exams to see if she is 'female enough' to compete. Men are not tested" (Carlson 1991, 26). The purpose is not to categorize women and men accurately, but to make sure men don't enter women's competitions, where, it is felt, they will have the advantage of size and strength. This practice sounds fair only because it is assumed that all men are similar in size and strength and different from all women. Yet in Olympics boxing and wrestling matches, men are matched within weight classes. Some women might similarly successfully compete with some men in many sports. Women did not run in marathons until about twenty years ago. In twenty years of marathon competition, women have reduced their finish times by more than one-and-one half hours; they are expected to run as fast as men in that race by 1998 and might catch up with men's running times in races of other lengths within the next 50 years because they are increasing their fastest speeds more rapidly than are men (Fausto-Sterling 1985, 213–18).

The reliance on only two sex and gender categories in the biological and social sciences is as epistemologically spurious as the reliance on chromosomal or genital test to group athletes. Most research designs do not investigate whether physical skills or physical abilities are really more or less common in women and men (Epstein 1988). They start out with two social categories ("women," "men"), assume they are biologically different ("female," "male"), look for similarities among them and differences between them, and attribute what they have found for the social categories to sex differences (Gelman, Collman, and Maccoby 1986). These designs rarely question the categorization of their subjects into two and only two groups, even though they often find more significant within-group differences than between-group differences (Hyde 1990). The social construction perspective on sex and gender suggests that instead of starting with the two presumed dichotomies in each category—female, male; woman, man—it might be more useful in gender studies to group patterns of behavior and only then look for identifying markers of the people likely to enact such behaviors. . . .

## Dirty Little Secrets

. . . Technology constructs gendered skills. Meta-analysis of studies of gender differences in spatial and mathematical ability have found that men have a large advantage in ability to mentally rotate an image, a moderate advantage in a visual perception of horizontality and vertically and in mathematical performance, and a small advantage in ability to pick a figure out of a field (Hyde 1990). It could be argued that these advantages explain why, within the short space of time that computers have become ubiquitous in offices, schools, and homes, work on them and with them has become gendered: Men create, program, and market computers, make war and produce science and art with them; women microwire them in computer factories and enter data in computerized offices; boys play games, socialize, and commit crimes with computers; girls are rarely seen in computer clubs, camps, and classrooms. But women were hired as computer programmers in the 1940s because

> the work seemed to resemble simple clerical tasks. In fact, however, programming demanded complex skills in abstract logic, mathermatics, electrical circuitry, and machinery, all of which . . . women used to perform in their work. Once programming was recognized as "intellectually demanding," it became attractive to men. (Donato 1990, 170)

A woman mathematician and pioneer in data processing, Grace M. Hopper, was famous for her work on programming language (Perry and Greber 1990, 86). By the 1960s, programming was split into more and less skilled specialties, and the entry of women into the computer field in the 1970s and 1980s was confined to the lower-paid specialties. At each stage, employers invoked women's and men's purportedly natural capabilities for the jobs for which they were hired (Cockburn 1983, 1985; Donato 1990; Hartmann 1987; Hartmann, Kraut, and Tilly 1986; Kramer and Lehman 1990; Wright et al. 1987; Zimmerman 1983).

It is the taken-for-grantedness of such everyday gendered behavior 9 that gives credence to the belief that the widespread differences in what women and men do must come from biology. To take one ordinarily unremarked scenario: In modern societies, if a man and woman who are a couple are in a car together, he is much more likely to take the wheel than she is, even if she is the more competent driver. Molly Haskell calls this taken-for-granted phenomenon "the dirty little secret of marriage: the husband-lousy-driver syndrome" (1989, 26). Men drive cars whether they are good drivers or not because men and machines are a "natural" combination (Scharff 1991). But the ability to drive gives one mobility; it is form of social power.

In the early days of the automobile, feminist co-opted the symbolism 10 of mobility as emancipation: "Donning goggles and dusters, wielding tire irons and tool kits, taking the wheel, they announced their intention to move beyond the bounds of women's place" (Scharff 1991, 68). Driving enabled them to campaign for women's suffrage in parts of the United States not served by public transportation, and they effectively used motorcades and speaking from cars as campaign tactics (Scharff 1991, 67–88). Sandra Gilbert also notes that during World War I, women's ability to drive was physically, mentally, and even sensually liberating:

> For nurses and ambulance drivers, women doctors and women messengers, the phenomenon of modern battle was very different from that experienced by entrenched combatants. Finally given a change to take the wheel, these post-Victorian girls raced motorcars along foreign rods like adventurers exploring new lands, while their brothers dug deeper into the mud of France. . . .

Retrieving the wounded and the dead from deadly positions, these once-decorous daughters had at last been allowed to prove their valor, and they swooped over the wastelands of the war with the energetic love of Wagnerian Valkyries, their mobility alone transporting countless immobilized heroes to safe havens. (1983, 438–39)

Not incidentally, women in the United States and England got the vote for their war efforts in World War I.

## Social Bodies and the Bathroom Problem

People of the same racial ethnic group and social class are roughly the same size and shape—but there are many varieties of bodies. People have different genitalia, different secondary sex characteristics, different contributions to procreation, different orgasmic experiences, different patterns of illness and aging. Each of us experiences our bodies differently, and these experiences change as we grow, age, sicken, and die. The bodies of pregnant and nonpregnant women, short and tall people, those with intact and functioning limbs and those whose bodies are physically challenged are all different. But the salient categories of a society group these attributes in ways that ride roughshod over individual experiences and more meaningful clusters of people. *11*

I am not saying that physical differences between male and female bodies don't exist, but that these differences are socially meaningless until social practices transform them into social facts. West Point Military Academy's curriculum is designed to produce leaders, and physical competence is used as a significant measure of leadership ability (Yoder 1989). When women were accepted as West Point cadets, it became clear that the tests of physical competence, such as rapidly scaling an eight-foot wall, had been constructed for male physiques—pulling oneself up and over using upper-body strength. Rather than devise tests of physical competence for women, West Point provided boosters that mostly women used—but that lost them test points—in the case of the wall, a platform. Finally, the women themselves figured out how to use their bodies successfully. Janice Yoder describes this situation: *12*

> I was observing this obstacle one day, when a woman approached the wall in the old prescribed way, got her fingertips grip, and did an unusual thing: she walked her dangling legs up the wall until she was in a position where both her hands and feet were atop the wall. She then simply pulled up her sagging bottom and went over. She solved the problem by capitalizing on one of women's physical assets: lower-body strength. (1989, 530)

In short, if West Point is going to measure leadership capability by physical strength, women's pelvises will do just as well as men's shoulders.

The social transformation of female and male physiology into a condition of inequality is well illustrated by the bathroom problem. Most *13* buildings that have gender-segregated bathrooms have an equal number for women and for men. Where there are crowds, there are always long lines in front of women's bathrooms but rarely in front of men's bathrooms. The cultural, physiological, and demographic combinations of clothing, frequency of urination, menstruation, and child care add up to generally greater bathroom use by women than men. Thus, although an equal number of bathrooms seems fair, equity would mean more women's bathrooms or allowing women to use men's bathrooms for a certain amount of time (Molotch 1988).

The bathroom problem is the outcome of the way gendered bodies are  *14* differentially evaluated in Western cultures: Men's social bodies are the measure of what is "human." *Gray's Anatomy*, in use for 100 years, well into the twentieth century, presented the human body as male. The female body was shown only where it differed from the male (Laqueur 1990, 166–67). Denise Riley says that if we envisage women's bodies, men's bodies, and human bodies "as a triangle of identifications, then it is rarely an equilateral triangle in which both sexes are pitched at matching distances from the apex of the human" (1988, 197). Catharine MacKinnon also contends that in Western society, universal "humanness" is male because

> virtually every quality that distinguishes men from women is already affirmatively compensated in this society. Men's physiology defines most sports, their needs define auto and health insurance coverage, their socially defined biographies define workplace expectations and successful career patterns, their perspectives and concerns define quality in scholarship, their experiences and obsessions define merit, their objectification of life defines art, their military service defines citizenship, their presence defines family, their inability to get along with each other—their wars and rulerships—define history, their image defines god, and their genitals define sex. For each of their differences from women, what amounts to an affirmative action plan is in effect, otherwise known as the structure and values of American society. (1987, 36)

## The Paradox of Human Nature

Gendered people do not emerge from physiology or hormones but from  *15* the exigencies of the social order, mostly, from the need for a reliable division of the work of food production and the social (not physical) reproduction of new members. The moral imperatives of religion and cultural representations reinforce the boundary lines among genders and ensure that what is demanded, what is permitted, and what is tabooed for the people in each gender is well-known and followed by most. Political power, control of scarce resources, and, if necessary, violence uphold the gendered social order in the face of resistance and rebellion. Most people, however, voluntarily go along with their society's prescriptions for those of their gender status because the norms and expectations get built into their sense of worth and identity as a certain kind of human being and because they believe their society's way is the natural way. These beliefs emerge from the imagery that pervades the way we think, the way we see and hear and speak, the way we fantasize, and the way we feel. There is no core or bedrock human nature below these endlessly looping processes of the social production of sex and gender, self and other, identity and psyche, each of which is a "complex cultural construction" (Butler 1990, 36). The paradox of "human nature" is that it is *always* a manifestation of cultural meanings, social relationships, and power politics—"not biology, but culture, becomes destiny" (Butler 1990, 8).

Feminist inquiry has long questioned the conventional categories of social science, but much of the current work in feminist sociology has not gone beyond adding the universal category "women" to the universal category "men." Our current debates over the global assumptions of only two categories and the insistence that they must be nuanced to include race and class are steps in the direction I would like to see feminist research go, but race and class are *also* global categories (Collins 1990; Spelman 1988). Deconstructing sex, sexuality, and gender reveals many possible categories embedded in the social experiences and social practices of what Dorothy Smith calls the "everyday/everynight world" (1990, 31–57). These emergent categories group some people together for comparison with other people without prior assumptions about who is like whom. Categories can be broken up and people regrouped differently into new categories for comparison. This process of discovering categories from similarities and differences in people's behavior or responses can be more meaningful for feminist research than discovering similarities and differences between "females" and "males" or "women" and "men" because the social construction of the conventional sex and gender categories already assumes differences between them and similarities among them. When we rely only on the conventional categories of sex and gender, we end up finding what we looked for—we see what we believe, whether it is that "females" and "males" are essentially different or that "women" and "men" are essentially the same.

REFERENCES

Birrell, Susan J., and Sheryl L. Cole. 1990. Double fault: Renée Richards and the construction and naturalization of difference. *Sociology of Sport Journal* 7:1–21.

Butler, Judith. 1990. *Gender trouble: Feminism and the subversion of identity*. New York and London: Routledge & Kegan Paul.

Carlson, Alison. 1991. When is a woman not a woman? *Women's Sport and Fitness* March:24–29.

Cockburn, Cynthia. 1983. *Brothers: Male dominance and technological change*. London: Pluto.

———. 1985. *Machinery of dominance: Women, men, and technical know-how*. London: Pluto.

Collins, Patricia Hill. 1990. *Black feminist thought: Knowledge, consciousness, and the politics of empowerment*. Boston: Unwin Hyman.

Donato, Katharine M. 1990. Programming for change? The growing demand for women systems analysts. In *Job queues, gender queues: Explaining women's inroads into male occupations*, written and edited by Barbara F. Reskin and Patricia A. Roos. Philadelphia: Temple University Press.

Epstein, Cynthia Fuchs. 1988. *Deceptive distinctions: Sex, gender, and the social order*. New Haven, CT: Yale University Press.

Fausto-Sterling, Anne. 1985. *Myths of gender: Biological theories about women and men*. New York: Basic Books.

Foucault, Michel. 1978. *The history of sexuality: An introduction*. Translated by Robert Hurley. New York: Pantheon.

Gelman, Susan A., Pamela Collman, and Eleanor E. Maccoby, 1986. Inferring properties from categories versus inferring categories from properties: The case of gender. *Child Development* 57:396–404.

Gilbert, Sandra M. 1983. Soldier's heart: Literary men, literary women, and the Great War. *Signs: Journal of Women in Culture and Society* 8:422–50.

Hartmann, Heidi I., ed. 1987. *Computer chips and paper clips: Technology and women's employment*. Vol. 2. Washington, DC: National Academy Press.

Hartmann, Heidi I., Robert E. Kraut, and Louise A. Tilly, eds. 1986. *Computer chips and paper clips: Technology and women's employment*. Vol. 1. Washington, DC: National Academy Press.

Haskell, Molly. 1989. Hers: He drives me crazy. *New York Times Magazine*, 24 September, 6, 28.

Hyde, Janet Shibley. 1990. Meta-analysis and the psychology of gender differences. *Signs: Journal of Women in Culture and Society* 16:55–73.

Jaggar, Alison M. 1983. *Feminist politics and human nature*. Totowa, NJ: Rowman & Allanheld.

Kessler, Suzanne J. 1990. The medical construction of gender: Case management of intersexed infants. *Signs: Journal of Women in Culture and Society* 16:3–26.

Kessler, Suzanne J., and Wendy McKenna. [1978] 1985. *Gender: An ethnomethodological approach*. Chicago: University of Chicago Press.

Kolata, Gina. 1992. Track federation urges end to gene test for femaleness. *New York Times*, 12 February.

Kramer, Pamela E., and Sheila Lehman. 1990. Mismeasuring women: A critique of research on computer ability and avoidance. *Signs: Journal of Women in Culture and Society* 16:158–72.

Laqueur, Thomas. 1990. *Making sex: Body and gender from the Greeks to Freud*. Cambridge, MA: Harvard University Press.

Levesque-Lopman, Louise. 1988. *Claiming reality: Phenomenology and women's experience*. Totowa, NJ: Rowman & Littlefield.

MacKinnon, Catharine. 1987. *Feminism unmodified*. Cambridge, MA: Harvard University Press.

Molotch, Harvey. 1988. The restroom and equal opportunity. *Sociological Forum* 3:128–32.

Money, John, and Anke A. Ehrhardt. 1972. *Man & woman, boy & girl*. Baltimore, MD: Johns Hopkins University Press.

Naftolin, F., and E. Butz, eds. 1981. Sexual dimorphism. *Science* 211:1263–1324.

Perry, Ruth, and Lisa Greber. 1990. Women and computers: An introduction. *Signs: Journal of Women in Culture and Society* 16:74–101.

Richards, Renée, with Jack Ames. 1983. *Second serve*. New York: Stein and Day.

Riley, Denise. 1988. *Am I that name? Feminism and the category of women in history.* Minneapolis: University of Minnesota Press.

Scharff, Virginia. 1991. *Taking the wheel: Women and the coming of the motor age.* New York: Free Press.

Smith, Dorothy E. 1990. *The conceptual practices of power: A feminist sociology of knowledge.* Toronto: University of Toronto Press.

Spelman, Elizabeth. 1988. *Inessential woman: Problems of exclusion in feminist thought.* Boston: Beacon Press.

Wright, Barbara Drygulski, et al., eds. 1987. *Women, work, and technology: Transformations.* Ann Arbor: University of Michigan Press.

Yoder, Janice D. 1989. Women at West Point: Lessons for token women in male-dominated occupations. In *Women: A feminist perspective,* edited by Jo Freeman. 4th ed. Palo Alto, CA: Mayfield.

Zimmerman, Jan, ed. 1983. *The technological woman: Interfacing with tomorrow.* New York: Praeger.

■ ■ ■

## Reading as a Writer: Analyzing Rhetorical Choices

1. In paragraphs 5, 6, and 7, how does Lorber use sports examples to help illuminate her larger argument in this essay? Which examples are most persuasive to you, and why? How might the recent case of the South African runner Caster Semenya fit into Lorber's argument?

2. Find key sentences in Lorber's discussion of technology and the "bathroom problem" that help you understand how these ideas serve her larger point. What does she call for in her final paragraph?

## Writing as a Reader: Entering the Conversation of Ideas

1. In the second half of her essay, Lorber explains some of the implications she sees in male bodies being the standard for universal "humanness" (para. 14). Shari L. Dworkin and Michael A. Messner are similarly fascinated by the standards we use to measure human power, and particularly athletic prowess. Write an essay that places these authors in conversation on the implications of the universal male standard when it comes to sports culture. Feel free to include some recent examples from sports news that help you make your point about these standards and what they tell us about our expectations of "masculinity" and "femininity."

2. Both Lorber and Deborah Tannen examine the gendered habits of moving and speaking that influence our understanding of what it means to be "male" or "female." Both authors also see these gendered habits as learned rather than biological. Compose an essay in which you connect examples and ideas from each essay in order to make a point about the significance of these learned behaviors for our understanding of ourselves. What is at stake in keeping these practices as they are or in changing them?

## SHARI L. DWORKIN AND MICHAEL A. MESSNER

# Just Do . . . What? Sport, Bodies, Gender

Shari L. Dworkin holds graduate degrees in sociology and gender studies and in biostatistics. She is a professor of behavioral medicine at Columbia University, but her wide-ranging scholarship includes interdisciplinary study of domestic and international issues relating to sociology, gender and sexuality, and public health. Dworkin's coauthor, Michael A. Messner, is a professor of sociology and gender studies at the University of Southern California. Messner has published many books and articles on gender as a cultural invention and is well known for his research on understandings of masculinity. His interests include gender and sport, the culture of coaching, and gender and political imagery. This essay is taken from the book *Revisioning Gender* (1998), edited by Myra Marx Ferree, Judith Lorber, and Beth B. Hess.

In this essay, the authors use *The Council of Biology Editors Style Manual* to cite sources. The long list of references at the end of the essay shows that a lot of academics are participating in the conversation about gender and sport culture. Dworkin and Messner's essay builds on the work of many of the scholars who have examined the ways our notions of masculinity and femininity are tested, exhibited, and reinforced through participating in and watching sports.

As you read, pay attention to the different ways Dworkin and Messner contextualize their points. The discussion of Title IX (paras. 5–7), for example, offers legal context. (Do you know what Title IX is? If not, this essay will explain it.) Also adding context are discussions of the media coverage of an incident at the 1996 Olympics (para. 10) and of the burgeoning business of corporate sponsorship of athletes and athletic events (paras. 12–18). The authors look at many specific examples of sporting events, images, and commercials to draw out the larger significance of sport culture to our shifting understanding of what it means to look and act masculine or feminine. They also include in their analysis the additional roles that differences in class, race, and sexuality play in the expected and "approved" athletic performance of players.

You should be able to think of additional examples of celebrity athletes beyond the examples in this selection. Consider how those examples confirm or test the limits of the arguments Dworkin and Messner make. Be sure to read their conclusion carefully as they address the question "What's the big deal about athletics, anyway?" These authors hope we'll see that by looking at sports through the lens of gender and race, we will learn a lot about how flexible or rigid our ideas about gender really are.

■ ■ ■

## Athletic Men: Paying the Price

When we disentangle the historical and contemporary relationship *1* between sport and men's power, we must recognize the distinction between sport as a cultural practice that constructs dominant belief systems and the individual experience of sport as an athletic career. Clearly, for at least the past 100 years, the dominant cultural meanings surrounding athletic masculinity have served mostly to stabilize hegemonic masculinity in the face of challenges by women, working-class men, men of color, and immigrants (Crosset 1990; Kimmel 1990). However, the experience of male athletes is often fraught with contradiction and paradox. Although many male athletes may dream of being the next Michael Jordan, very few ever actually make a living playing sports (Messner 1992). Even for extremely successful male athletes, the rigor of attaining and maintaining athletic stardom often comes at the cost of emotional and interpersonal development (Connell 1990). And although athletic masculinity symbolizes an image of physical health and sexual virility, athletes commonly develop alienated relationships with their bodies, learning to relate to them like machines, tools, or even weapons to be "used up" to get a job done. As a result, many athletes and former athletes suffer from permanent injuries, poor health, and low life expectancy (Sabo 1994; White, Young, and McTeer 1995). In particular, it is disproportionately young men from poor socioeconomic and racial/ethnic backgrounds who pay these costs.

To put it simply, young men from race- or class-subordinated back- *2* grounds disproportionately seek status, respect, empowerment, and upward mobility through athletic careers. Most of them do not make it to the mythical "top," but this majority is mostly invisible to the general public. Instead, those very few who do make it into the limelight—especially those in sports like football or boxing, that reward the most extreme possibilities of large, powerful, and violent male bodies—serve as public symbols of exemplary masculinity, with whom all men can identify *as men*, as separate and superior to women (Messner 1988, 1992). While serving to differentiate "men" from "women" symbolically, top male athletes—especially African American men in violent sports—are simultaneously available to be used by men as cultural symbols of differences among them. African American male athletes—for instance, boxer Mike Tyson—have become icons of an atavistic masculinity, in comparison to whom White middle-class men can construct themselves as kinder, gentler "new men" (Messner 1993a). This imagery of Black men includes a package of sexual potency and muscular power wrapped in danger. Just as African American males have been used in the past to symbolize fears of a "primitive" sexuality unleashed (Hoch 1979; Davis 1981), Americans are increasingly obsessed with documenting the sexual misbehaviors of Black male athletes (Messner 1993b).

Men's sport, then, constructs masculinities in complex and contradic- *3* tory ways. At a time in history when physical strength is of less and less practical significance in workplaces, especially in the professional and managerial jobs of most White, college-educated men, African American, poor, and working-class men have increasingly "taken over" the sports to which they have access. But having played sports is of little or no practical use to most of these young men once their athletic careers have ended. Athletic skills rarely transfer over into nonsports careers. The significance of successful African American male athletes in the current gender order is *not* that they challenge dominant social meanings or power relations. To the contrary, they serve to stabilize ideas of natural difference and hierarchy between women and men *and* among men of different social classes and races.

We can draw two conclusions from this brief discussion of men's 4 sports. First, although we can see African American men's struggles to achieve success and respect through sport as a collective response to class and racial constraints, this agency operates largely to *reproduce*—rather than to *resist* or challenge—current race, class, and gender relations of power. Put another way, Black men's agency in sport is a key element in the current hegemony of the race, class, and gender order. As in the past, men at the bottom of the stratification system achieve limited upward mobility by providing entertainment and vicarious thrills for those more advantaged. Second, we can see by looking at men's sports that *simply* employing a "gender lens" to analyze sport critically is limiting, even dangerous. The current literature supports the claim that men's sport does continue to empower "men," but for the most part, it is not the men who are doing the playing who are being empowered. Clearly, when we speak of "sport and empowerment" for men, we need to ask, Which men? These two points—that "agency" is not necessarily synonymous with "resistance," and that we need to be very cautious about employing a simplistic gender lens to speak categorically about "men and sport"—will inform our examination of women's current movement into sports.

## Sex Equity for "Women in Sport"

Since the passage of Title IX of the Education Act Amendments, adopted 5 by Congress in 1972, girls' and women's sports in the United States have changed in dramatic, but paradoxical, ways. On the one hand, there is no denying the rapid movement toward equity in the number of female participants and programs for women and girls (Cahn 1994; Carpenter 1993). For example, in 1971, only 294,015 U.S. girls, compared with 3,666,917 boys, participated in interscholastic high school sports. By 1996, the number of girls participating had risen to 2,240,000, compared with 3,554,429 boys (Acosta and Carpenter 1996). Opportunities for women to play intercollegiate sports have also continued to rise. In 1978, right before the date for mandatory compliance with Title IX, colleges and universities offered an average of 5.61 women's sports per school. By 1988, the average had risen to 7.31 sports per school, and it continued to rise to an all-time high of 7.53 in 1996 (Acosta and Carpenter 1996). These numerical increases in opportunities to participate in such a masculine-structured institution as school sports prove the effectiveness of organizing politically and legally around the concept "woman." Indeed, the relative success of this post–Title IX liberal strategy of gender equity in sport was premised on the deployment of separate "male" and "female" sports.

On the one hand, at least within the confines of liberalism, a "strategic essentialism" that successfully deploys the category "woman" can result in moves toward greater distributive justice. And in this case, we can see that there are benefits that result when girls' and women's participation in sports increases. Research suggests that girls who play interscholastic sports tend to have higher self-esteem and greater self-confidence, more positive feelings about body image, lower school dropout rates, and lower levels of unwanted pregnancies than girls who do not play sports (Sabo and Women's Sports Foundation 1988; President's Council on Physical Fitness and Sports 1997). And it is likely that boys who play with, or watch, competent and powerful female athletes will develop a broader and more respectful view of women's physical capabilities than did earlier generations of boys and men (Messner and Sabo 1994).

Yet, Title IX has not yet yielded anything close to equity for girls and women within sports—more boys and men still play sports; they still have far more opportunities, from the peewee level through professional sports; and girls and women often have to struggle for access to uniforms, travel money, practice facilities, and scholarships that boys and men routinely take for granted (Lopiano 1993; Women's Sports Foundation 1997). But the dramatic movement of girls and women into sport—and the continued legal basis for challenges to inequities that are provided by Title IX precedents—makes sport an impressive example of a previously almost entirely masculine terrain that is now gender contested. The very existence of skilled and strong women athletes demanding recognition and equal access to resources is a destabilizing tendency in the current gender order.

On the other hand, there are obvious limits in the liberal quest for gender equity in sport. First, as the popularity, opportunities, and funding for women's sports have risen, the leadership positions have markedly shifted away from women to men. For example, in 1972 more than 90 percent of women's college teams had women coaches. By 1996, the proportion had dropped to 47.7 percent. Similarly, in 1972 more than 90 percent of women's college programs were headed by women athletic directors. By 1996, the figure had dropped to 18.5 percent (Acosta and Carpenter 1996). Radical critics of sport have argued that this shift toward men's control of girl and women athletes is but one indicator of the limits and dangers of a gender-blind model of equity that uncritically adopts the men's "military model" of sport (Nelson 1991). To be sure, this shift to men coaches was heroically resisted throughout the 1970s by many women coaches and athletic administrators behind the banner of the Association for

Intercollegiate Athletics for Women (AIAW). The AIAW attempted to defend the idea that women's sports should be controlled by women, and should reflect the values of health, cooperation, and participation, rather than the values of cutthroat competition and star systems that dominated men's sports. But as the economic power of the National Collegiate Athletic Association (NCAA) (and its linkages with television) rapidly brought women's college sports under its aegis, "the AIAW faded quickly from the scene, closing down operations in 1982 and conceding final defeat in 1984 when it lost an antitrust suit against the NCAA" (Cahn 1994:257). Locally, most women's athletic departments were folded into male athletic departments, and the hiring of coaches for women's sports was placed in the hands of male athletic directors.

As women's sports has become controlled by men, it increasingly   9 reflects the most valued characteristics of men's sports: "hierarchy, competitiveness, and aggression" (Hall 1996:91). In the most "feminine" sports, men coaches are simultaneously demanding the aggressiveness of adult men athletes and the submissiveness of little girls—a most complex gender message! A poignant example of these dangers can be seen in women's gymnastics and ice-skating, where very young girls, typically coached mostly by men coaches who are often abusive, learn to practice with painful injuries and often develop severe eating disorders in order to keep their bodies "small, thin, and prepubescent" (Ryan 1995:103).

Most people who followed media coverage of the 1996 Olympics still   *10* hold the image in their minds of a grinning coach Bela Karolyi cradling gymnast Kerri Strug in his arms, her leg in a brace, after she had courageously vaulted with a painful injury, and thus appeared to secure a gold medal for the U.S. team. Strug's deed resulted in a great deal of flag-waving and in numerous endorsement contracts for her, and it was lauded by the media as an act of bravery that symbolized the "arrival" of women's sports. But it can also be seen as an example of the limits and contradictions of the uncritical adoption of the dominant values of men's sports. The image of Karolyi's cradling the much smaller body of the young, injured Strug, so often replayed on television and prominently positioned in print coverage of the Olympics, illustrates two important points. First, the sports media today continue to frame women athletes ambivalently, symbolically denying them their power (Duncan and Hasbrook 1988). After all, it was not Strug's moment of triumphant power as she exploded off the vault, or even her difficult and painful landing on her injured leg that the media etched in all of our memories; instead, it was the aftermath of the actual athletic moment that the media seized upon. Here, an infantilized and vulnerable Strug appeared anything but powerful. It is unlikely that the sports media would frame a male athlete in a similar situation the same way. The second point that this popular image illustrates is that today, young girl and women athletes' bodies are in the literal and symbolic hands of men coaches. As Ryan's powerful book *Little Girls in Pretty Boxes* (1995) illustrates, Karolyi is seen by many as the most egregious in a system of men coaches who systematically submit aspiring young girl athletes to verbal, psychological, and physical abuse. The physical and psychological carnage that results from this professionalized system, whose main aim is to produce gold medalists for the United States every four years, is staggering. Recent discussions of exploitation, sexual harassment, and sexual abuse of young female athletes—especially those competing in the more "feminine" sports, such as swimming and gymnastics—by male coaches add another frightening dimension to this picture (Nelson 1994; Tomlinson and Yorganci 1997).

In short, as girls and women push for equity in sport, they are mov- *11* ing—often uncritically—into a hierarchical system that has as its main goal to produce winners, champions, and profits. Although increased participation for girls and women apparently has its benefits at the lower levels, as the incentives mount for girl and women athletes to professionalize, they increasingly face many of the same limitations and dangers (in addition to some others, such as sexual harassment and rape) as those experienced by highly competitive men.

## "If You Let Me Play . . ."

In recent years, corporate America has begun to awaken to the vast and *12* lucrative potential markets that might be developed within and subsidiary to women's sports. The 1996 Olympics and its aftermath saw unprecedented amounts of money spent on television and magazine ads featuring women athletes. Two new professional women's basketball leagues were begun in 1996 and 1997, and one of them, the Women's National Basketball Association (WNBA), began with a substantial television contract—a factor that today is the best predictor of financial success in pro sports. Although many see these developments as merely the next step in the successful accomplishment of gender equity for women in sport, we argue that the increasingly corporate context of this trend calls for special critical scrutiny.

In recent years, athletic footwear advertisements by Reebok and Nike *13* have exemplified the ways that corporations have made themselves champions of women's athletic participation. In the early 1990s, Reebok was first to seize the lion's share of the female athletic shoe market. But by the mid-1990s, Nike had made great gains with a highly successful advertising campaign that positioned the corporation as the champion of girls' and women's rights inside and outside of sports. One influential TV spot included images of athletically active girls and women, with the voiceover saying things like, "If you let me play, I'll be less likely to drop out of school," and "If you let me play, I'll be better able to say no to unwanted sexual activity." These ads made use of the research findings from such organizations as the Women's Sports Foundation, documenting the positive, healthy, and empowering aspects of athletic participation for girls.

Couching this information in the language of individual empowerment, Nike sold it to girls and women in the form of athletic shoes.

To be sure, the power of these commercials lies partly in the fact that they almost never mentioned shoes or even the Nike name. The message is that individual girls will be happier, healthier, and more in charge of their lives if we "let them play." The Nike "swoosh" logo is subtly displayed in the corner of the ads so that the viewer knows who is the source of these liberating ideas. It is through this kind of campaign that Nike has positioned itself as what Cole and Hribar (1995) call a "celebrity feminist," a corporate liberal entity that has successfully appropriated and co-opted the language of individual empowerment underlying the dominant discourse of opportunity for girls and women in sports. Aspiring athletes are then encouraged by slick advertising campaigns to identify their own individual empowerment—in essence, *their relationship to feminism*—with that of the corporate entity that acts as a celebrity feminist. If "feminist identity" can be displayed most readily through the wearing of the Nike logo on shoes and other athletic apparel, then displaying the Nike "swoosh" on one's body becomes a statement to the world that one is an independent, empowered individual—a successful young woman of the nineties.

There are fundamental limitations to this kind of "empowerment." If radical feminists are correct in claiming that patriarchy reproduces itself largely through men's ability to dominate and exploit women's bodies, we might suggest a corollary: Corporations have found peace and profit with liberal feminism by co-opting a genuine quest by women for bodily agency and empowerment and channeling it toward a goal of physical achievement severely limited by its consumerist context. The kind of collective women's agency that emphasizes the building of institutions such as rape crisis centers, domestic violence shelters, and community women's athletic leagues is a *resistant agency* through which women have empowered themselves to fight against and change the institutions that oppress them. In contrast, individual women's agency expressed as identification with corporate consumerism is a *reproductive agency* that firmly situates women's actions and bodies within the structural gender order that oppresses them.

In addition, Nike's commitment to women's liberation is contradicted by its own corporate practices. In 1996, when it posted its largest profits, and its CEO Phillip Knight's stock was estimated to be worth $5 billion, the mostly women Indonesian workers who manufactured the shoes were paid about $2.25 a day. Workers who attempted to organize for higher pay and better working conditions were fired (Take Action for Girls 1996). Meanwhile, U.S. women's eager consumption of corporate celebrity feminism makes it almost impossible for them to see, much less to act upon, the exploitation of women workers halfway around the globe. In fact, it is likely that the kinds of individual "empowerment" that can be purchased through consumerism seriously reduce women's abilities even to identify their collective interests in changing institutions here within the United States.

Liberal feminism in sport has come full circle: A universalized con-   *17*
cept of "women" was strategically deployed to push—with some impressive but limited success—for equal opportunities for women in sport. As
these successes mounted, a key ideological support for hegemonic masculinity—the naturalized equation of male bodies with athletic ability
and physical strength—was destabilized. But corporations have recently
seized upon the individualist impulse of female empowerment that underlies liberal feminism, and have sold it back to women as an ideology and
bodily practice that largely precludes any actual mobilizing around the
collective concept of "women." Individual women are now implored by
Nike to "Just do it"—just like the men "do it." Undoubtedly, many women
strongly approve of, and feel good about, the Nike ads. But Nike's individu-
alized and depoliticized "feminism" ignores how individuals who "do it"
with Nike are implicated in an international system of racial, gender, and
class exploitation of women workers in less developed nations.

Just as we argued in our discussion of the limits of sports for raising   *18*
the status of working-class and African American men, here, too, gender
analysis alone is not enough. It is not just muscular, or athletic, or "fit"
bodies that must be considered in women's liberation—it is also laboring
bodies as well. In fact, as we will argue next, a danger in contemporary
reductionist understandings of empowerment as being synonymous with
the development of one's body is that concentrating on toning muscles can
easily transfer energies—especially those of women privileged by class
and race—away from collective organizing to change institutions that disadvantage all women, but especially those who are poor, working-class,
and racially disadvantaged.

## Women and Muscles

In addition to the ever-increasing numbers of women who compete in high   *19*
school and college sport, more and more women today engage in fitness
activities, lift weights, and enjoy the power of carrying musculature. Much
of the new emphasis and popularity of fitness and muscular development
among women has emerged outside of organized sport. New bodily ideals
can be said to have broadened from thin and slim to tight and toned, with
an "allowance" for "substantial weight and bulk" (Bordo 1993:191). By
some standards, today's more muscular woman can be viewed as embodying agency, power, and independence in a way that exemplifies resistance
to patriarchal ideals. However, just as within sport, women's bodily agency
in fitness activities can be contradictory. Is this bodily agency resistant
and/or empowering, or is the fit, muscled ideal simply the latest bodily
requirement for women, a form of "self-surveillance and obedience" in
service to patriarchal capitalism (Bartky 1988)?

Some feminists argue that when women exercise their agency to   *20*
develop bodily mobility and muscular power, these activities are self-
affirming for women and antithetical to patriarchal definitions of women

as passive, docile, and weak (MacKinnon 1987; Nelson 1991; Young 1990). By fighting for access to participation in sport and fitness, women have created an empowering arena where the meaning of gender is being contested and renegotiated, and where active rejections of dominant notions of femininity may be forged (e.g., Bolin 1992b; Gilroy 1989; Guthrie and Castelnuovo 1992; Kane and Lenskyj 1998; Lenskyj 1987; McDermott 1996; Theberge 1987). Other feminists, however, offer compelling counterarguments. First, there is the question as to whether bodily "empowerment" is merely a modern version of the "docile body," the intensely limiting and oppressive bodily management and scrutiny with which women learn to be complicit (Bordo 1993). For some women (especially those who are White, middle-class, and married heterosexuals) this complicit agency might result in more work on top of their already stifling "second shift" (Hochschild 1989)—a "third shift" that consists of long doses of effort invested in conforming to the latest touted bodily "requirement." It is these women, whose daily lives in families and careers might leave them feeling less than empowered, who would then respond to advertisements that encourage them to participate in sport and fitness in order to feel a sense of empowerment through their bodies. Couched in the logic of individualism and the Protestant work ethic, it seems that a woman need only enact her free will and "just do it" in order to "have it all." But "doing it" the corporate individualist way involves a radical turning inward of agency toward the goal of transformation of one's own body, in contrast to a turning outward to mobilize for collective political purposes, with the goal of transforming social institutions. Clearly, despite its uplifting tone and seemingly patriotic commitment to American women, corporate slogans such as Nike's beg several questions, such as: Just do *what*? And *for whom*?

Just as the cult of true womanhood excluded numerous women from *21* its "ideal" in the early nineteenth century, a similar conceptual vacuum arises here. After all, the dominant fitness industry message very likely "has no relevance to the majority of working-class women, or to Black women, or those from other ethnic minorities" (Hargreaves 1994:161). Bordo (1993) might disagree as she argues for the power of such messages to "normalize" across different races, classes, and sexualities. However, rather than being prematurely celebratory of bodily agency across categories of women, it may be argued that these newest images are fully compatible with the current "needs" of patriarchal capitalism for (especially and increasingly middle-class) women to be both active laborers and consumers (Bartky 1988).

Just as images of physically powerful and financially successful Afri- *22* can American men ultimately did not challenge, but instead continued to construct a stratified race, class, and gender order, current images of athletic women appear to represent a broadening of the definitional boundaries of what Connell (1987) calls "emphasized femininity" to include more muscular development. But the resistant possibilities in images of athletic women are largely contained by the continued strong assertion of (and commercial rewards for) retaining a link between heterosexual attractiveness and body image. For instance, many lauded Olympic track star Florence Griffith-Joyner's muscularity as a challenge to the dominant image of femininity and to images of men as physically superior. However, Griffith-Joyner's muscularity existed alongside "rapier-like" nails, flowing hair, and spectacular outfits, which ultimately situated her body and its markings firmly within a commercialized modernization of heterosexual femininity (Messner forthcoming). Now more than ever, the commodification of women's bodies may mean that when women "just do it," they are "just doing" 1990s "heterosexy" femininity. In the media, these bodies are not unambiguously resistant images of powerful women, but rather an ambivalent framing or subtle trivialization or sexualization of women's bodies that undermines their muscles and their athletic accomplishments (Duncan and Hasbrook 1988; Messner, Duncan, and Wachs 1996; Kane 1995; Kane and Lenskyj 1998). Female bodybuilders in particular illustrate these gender ambiguities. Research demonstrates that women can and do press and contest the limits of emphasized femininity. However, their agency is contained by the structure, rules, and ideologies of women's bodybuilding. For instance, Bolin (1992a, 1992b) found that the increasing size of the woman bodybuilder "beast" is acceptable only if "tamed" by "beauty." Female bodybuilders have faced penalties from judges for being too muscular, and they are rewarded for appearing with painted fingernails, dyed and highlighted hair, and breast implants. In short, their muscle size and body comportment is expected to be made consistent with emphasized femininity.

Researchers who study women's participation in fitness activities 23 find the same tendency to adhere to emphasized femininity as is shown by women athletes and bodybuilders. They tend to avoid lifting weights "too much" for fear of being "too big." Instead, they engage in long doses of cardiovascular work, which is thought to emphasize tone and leanness (Dworkin forthcoming; Markula 1996). Just as women in male-dominated occupations often hit a glass ceiling that halts their professional advancement, there appears to be a glass ceiling on women's musculature that constrains the development of women's muscular strength. Defined according to the latest commodified eroticization of heterosexual femininity, most women (with differences by race, class, sexuality, age) remain acutely aware of how much muscle is "allowed," how much is "still" attractive.

## Conclusion

Through an examination of gender, bodies, and sport, we have made three 24 main points . . . that may illuminate more general attempts to understand and change the current gender order. First, although sport has been an arena for contesting the status quo by men of color and by White women and women of color, the positive results have been individual rather than collective. A few star athletes have become celebrities, but their popularity has not raised the overall status of disadvantaged men and women (although it may have upgraded the physical potentiality of middle-class White women). Second, whatever sport has accomplished in terms of equity, women's and men's sports are still segregated, and men's sports are still dominant in commercial value and in the media. Third, rather than breaking down conventional concepts of masculinity and femininity, organized sport has overblown the cultural hegemony of heterosexualized, aggressive, violent, heavily muscled male athletes and heterosexualized, flirtatious, moderately muscled female athletes who are accomplished and competitive but expected to be submissive to the control of men coaches and managers.

The link in all these outcomes is that organized sport is a commercial 25 activity first and foremost. Organized sport is financially underwritten by corporations that sell shoes and clothing to a public looking for vicarious thrills and personal "fitness." The corporations capitalize on the celebrity of star athletes, who use individual achievements to make more money, rather than to help upgrade the communities from which they have come. Their endorsements sell individual achievement and conventional beauty and sexuality as well as Nikes and Reeboks. A further negative consequence to the upbeat message of "Just do it" is that many of the appurtenances of sport and fitness are produced by the labor of poorly paid, malnourished, and probably physically unfit women workers.

Does this mean that women's agency in sports and other physical 26 activities is a dead end that should be abandoned by feminist activists? Absolutely not. We think that sport is like any other institution: We cannot abandon it, nor can we escape from it. Instead, we must struggle within it. When liberal reforms such as Title IX are fought for and won, the results—though not revolutionary—are often positive changes in individual lives. And these changes shift the context for current and future struggles over control of resources and over ideologies and symbols that support inequalities. But we think feminists need to fight on two fronts in the battle for equity in sports. On the one hand, we must continue to push for equal opportunities for girls and women in sports. On the other hand, although the research points to benefits for girls and women who play sports at the lower levels, many of the girls and women who are professionalized into corporate sports can expect—just as most of their men counterparts in corporate sports can—to pay emotional and physical costs.

But in challenging women's uncritical adoption of the dominant val- 27 ues of corporate sport, we must be cautious not to fall into the same trap as have past activists for girls' and women's sports. In the 1920s and 1930s, in the wake of two decades of burgeoning athleticism by girls and women, medical leaders and physical educators responded with what now appear to be hysterical fears that vigorous physical activity for girls and women carried enormous physical and psychological dangers (Cahn 1994). The result of these fears was the institutionalization of an "adapted model" (i.e., "tamed down" sports for women) that served to ghettoize women's sports, leaving the hegemonic masculinity of men's sports virtually unchallenged for the next forty years. Given this history, today's advocates of women's sports walk a perilous tightrope: They must assert the positive value of vigorous physical activity and muscular strength for girls and women while simultaneously criticizing the unhealthy aspects of men's sports. A key to the accomplishment of this task must involve the development of a critical analysis of the dominant assumptions, beliefs, and practices of *men's* sports (Thompson 1988; Messner and Sabo 1994). In addition, we need to continue to explore feminist alternatives, for women and for men, to the "military model," with its emphasis on heroism, "playing through pain," and winning at all costs (Birrell and Richter 1987; Nelson 1991; Theberge 1985).

The activist fight for women and girls as a group will not be helped    28 by simplistic scholarship that acts as a cheering section for numerical increases in women's athletic participation, or for the increasing visibility of women's athletics in televised ads. Nor will a simple "gender lens" that views sports uncritically in terms of undifferentiated and falsely universalized categories of "men" and "women" take us very far in framing questions and analyzing data. Different groups of men and of women disproportionately benefit from and pay the costs of the current social organization of sports. We need an analytic framework that appreciates the importance of class, racial, and sexual differences among both men and women while retaining the feminist impulse that places the need to empower the disadvantaged in the foreground.

Data from empirical observation of sports demonstrate the absence of    29 absolute categorical differences between "men" and "women"—instead, there is a "continuum of performance" that, when acknowledged, can radically deconstruct dichotomous sex categories (Kane 1995). Obscuring this continuum are the social processes through which sport constructs and naturalizes differences and inequality between "men" and "women." Does this observation lead us down the path of radical deconstruction? We think the discussion in this chapter [of *Revisioning Gender* (1998)] demonstrates just the opposite. The current poststructuralist preoccupation with deconstructing binary categories like "men and women" (e.g., Butler 1990; Sedgewick 1990) has produced new discourses and practices that disrupt and fracture these binaries (Lorber 1996). Yet simply deconstructing our *discourse* about binary categories does not necessarily challenge the material basis of master categories to which subordinate categories of people stand in binary opposition: the capitalist class, men, heterosexuals, Whites. In fact, quite the contrary may be true (Stein and Plummer 1994). As many feminists have pointed out, although it is certainly true that every woman is somewhat uniquely situated, a radical deconstruction of the concept "woman" could lead to an individualism that denies similarity of experience, thus leading to depoliticized subjects. We would argue that it is currently corporations such as Nike that are in the forefront of the widespread development of this sort of depoliticized individualist "empowerment" among women. Radical deconstruction, therefore, is very much in the interests of the most powerful institutions in our world, as it leaves us feeling (at best) individually "empowered," so long as we are able to continue to consume the right products, while making it unlikely we will identify common interests with others in challenging institutions.

Rather than a shift toward radical deconstruction, the research on gender, bodies, and sport suggests that it is essential to retain and build upon the concept of social structure, with its attendant emphasis on the importance of people's shared positions within social institutions (Duncan 1993; Messner 1992). Such a materialist analysis reveals how differential access to resources and opportunities and the varieties of structured constraints shape the contexts in which people think, interact, and construct political practices and discourse. A critical analysis of gender within a materialist, structural analysis of institutions entails a reassertion of the crucial importance (though not necessarily the primacy) of social class. Interestingly, as recent intellectual trends have taken many scholars away from the study of institutions toward a preoccupation with individuals, bodies, and difference, the literature has highlighted race, gender, and sexual identities in new and important ways, but social class has too often dropped out of the analysis. As we have demonstrated, discussions of the possibilities and limits of women's agency in gender equity struggles in sports, the co-optation of feminism by Nike's "celebrity feminism," and the current encouragement of physical fitness for middle-class women all need to be examined within the context of distributive justice. We also need a clear analysis of the position of women and men as workers in organized sports; as marketable celebrities; as workers in sweatshops making sport shoes, clothing, and equipment; and as consumers of these products and symbols. This analysis must be informed by feminist theories of the intersections of race, class, and gender (e.g., Baca Zinn and Dill 1996). Politically, this work can inform an alliance politics that is grounded simultaneously in a structural analysis of power and a recognition of differences and inequalities between and among women and men.

REFERENCES

Acosta, R. Vivian, and Linda Jean Carpenter. 1996. "Women in Intercollegiate Sport: A Longitudinal Study—Nineteen Year Update, 1977–1996." Brooklyn, NY: Department of Physical Education, Brooklyn College.

Baca Zinn, Maxine, and Bonnie Thornton Dill. 1996. "Theorizing Difference from Multiracial Feminism." *Feminist Studies* 22:321–31.

Bartky, Sandra L. 1988. "Foucault, Femininity, and the Modernization of Patriarchal Power." In *Feminism and Foucault: Reflections on Resistance*, edited by I. Diamond and L. Quinby. Boston: Northeastern University Press.

Birrell, Susan, and Diana M. Richter. 1987. "Is a Diamond Forever? Feminist Transformations of Sport." *Women's Studies International Forum* 10:395–409.

Bolin, Anne. 1992a. "Flex Appeal, Food, and Fat: Competitive Bodybuilding, Gender, and Diet." *Play and Culture* 5:378–400.

———. 1992b. "Vandalized Vanity: Feminine Physique Betrayed and Portrayed." Pp. 79–90 in *Tattoo, Torture, Mutilation, and Adornment: The Denaturalization of the Body in Culture and Text,* edited by Frances E. Mascia-Lees and Patricia Sharpe. Albany: State University of New York Press.

Bordo, Susan. 1993. *Unbearable Weight: Feminism, Western Culture, and the Body.* Berkeley: University of California Press.

Butler, Judith. 1990. *Gender Trouble: Feminism and the Subversion of Identity.* New York: Routledge.

Cahn, Susan K. 1994. *Coming On Strong: Gender and Sexuality in Twentieth Century Women's Sport.* New York: Free Press.

Carpenter, Linda Jean. 1993. "Letters Home: My Life with Title IX." Pp. 79–94 in *Women in Sport: Issues and Controversies,* edited by Greta L. Cohen. Newbury Park, CA: Sage.

Cole, Cheryl L., and Amy Hribar. 1995. "Celebrity Feminism: Nike Style Post-Fordism, Transcendence, and Consumer Power." *Sociology of Sport Journal* 12:347–69.

Connell, R. W. 1987. *Gender and Power.* Stanford, CA: Stanford University Press.

———. 1990. "An Iron Man: The Body and Some Contradictions of Hegemonic Masculinity." Pp. 83–95 in *Sport, Men, and the Gender Order: Critical Feminist Perspectives,* edited by Michael A. Messner and Donald F. Sabo. Champaign, IL: Human Kinetics.

Crosset, Todd W. 1990. "Masculinity, Sexuality, and the Development of Early Modern Sport." Pp. 45–54 in *Sport, Men, and the Gender Order: Critical Feminist Perspectives,* edited by Michael A. Messner and Donald F. Sabo. Champaign, IL: Human Kinetics.

Davis, Angela Y. 1981. *Women, Race, and Class.* New York: Random House.

Duncan, Margaret Carlisle. 1993. "Beyond Analyses of Sport Media Texts: An Argument for Formal Analyses of Institutional Structures." *Sociology of Sport Journal* 10: 353–72.

Duncan, Margaret Carlisle, and Cynthia A. Hasbrook. 1988. "Denial of Power in Televised Women's Sports." *Sociology of Sport Journal* 5:1–21.

Dworkin, Shari L. [2003]. "A Woman's Place Is in the . . . Cardiovascular Room? Gender Relations, the Body, and the Gym." In *Athletic Intruders,* edited by Anne Bolin and Jane Granskog. Albany: State University of New York Press.

Gilroy, S. 1989. "The Embody-ment of Power: Gender and Physical Activity." *Leisure Studies* 8:163–71.

Guthrie, Sharon R., and Shirley Castelnuovo. 1992. "Elite Women Bodybuilders: Model of Resistance or Compliance?" *Play and Culture* 5:378–400.

Hall, M. Ann. 1996. *Feminism and Sporting Bodies: Essays on Theory and Practice.* Champaign, IL: Human Kinetics.

Hargreaves, Jennifer. 1994. *Sporting Females: Critical Issues in the History and Sociology of Women's Sport.* New York: Routledge.

Hoch, Paul. 1979. *White Hero, Black Beast: Racism, Sexism, and the Mask of Masculinity.* London: Pluto.

Hochschild, Arlie R. 1989. *The Second Shift.* New York: Avon.

Kane, Mary Jo. 1995. "Resistance/Transformation of the Oppositional Binary: Exposing Sport as a Continuum." *Journal of Sport and Social Issues* 19:191–218.

Kane, Mary Jo, and Helen Lenskyj. 1998. "Media Treatment of Female Athletes: Issues of Gender and Sexualities." In *MediaSport: Cultural Sensibilities and Sport in the Media Age,* edited by Lawrence A. Wenner. London: Routledge.

Kimmel, Michael S. 1990. "Baseball and the Reconstitution of American Masculinity, 1880–1920." Pp. 55–66 in *Sport, Men, and the Gender Order: Critical Feminist Perspectives,* edited by Michael A. Messner and Donald F. Sabo. Champaign, IL: Human Kinetics.

Lenskyj, Helen. 1987. "Female Sexuality and Women's Sport." *Women's Studies International Forum* 4:381–86.

Lopiano, Donna A. 1993. "Political Analysis: Gender Equity Strategies for the Future." Pp. 104–16 in *Women in Sport: Issues and Controversies,* edited by Greta L. Cohen. Newbury Park, CA: Sage.

Lorber, Judith. 1996. "Beyond the Binaries: Depolarizing the Categories of Sex, Sexuality, and Gender." *Sociological Inquiry* 66:143–59.

MacKinnon, Catharine A. 1987. *Feminism Unmodified: Discourses on Life and Law.* Cambridge, MA: Harvard University Press.

Markula, Pirkko. 1996. "Firm but Shapely, Fit but Sexy, Strong but Thin: The Postmodern Aerobicizing Female Bodies." *Sociology of Sport Journal* 12:424–53.

McDermott, Lisa. 1996. "Towards a Feminist Understanding of Physicality within the Context of Women's Physically Active and Sporting Lives." *Sociology of Sport Journal* 13:12–30.

Messner, Michael A. 1988. "Sports and Male Domination: The Female Athlete as Contested Ideological Terrain." *Sociology of Sport Journal* 5:197–211.

———. 1992. *Power at Play: Sports and the Problem of Masculinity.* Boston: Beacon.

———. 1993a. " 'Changing Men' and Feminist Politics in the United States." *Theory and Society* 22:723–37.

———. 1993b. "White Men Misbehaving: Feminism, Afrocentrism, and the Promise of a Critical Standpoint." *Journal of Sport and Social Issues* 16:136–44.

———. Forthcoming. "Theorizing Gendered Bodies: Beyond the Subject/Object Dichotomy." In *Exercising Power: The Making and Remaking of the Body,* edited by Cheryl L. Cole, John Loy, and Michael A. Messner. Albany: State University of New York Press.

Messner, Michael A., Margaret Carlisle Duncan, and Faye Linda Wachs. 1996. "The Gender of Audience-Building: Televised Coverage of Men's and Women's NCAA Basketball." *Sociological Inquiry* 66:422–39.

Messner, Michael A., and Donald F. Sabo. 1990. "Towards a Critical Feminist Reappraisal of Sport, Men, and the Gender Order." In *Sport, Men, and the Gender Order: Critical Feminist Perspectives,* edited by Michael A. Messner and Donald F. Sabo. Champaign, IL: Human Kinetics.

———. 1994. *Sex, Violence, and Power in Sports: Rethinking Masculinity.* Freedom, CA: Crossing Press.

Nelson, Mariah Burton. 1991. *Are We Winning Yet? How Women Are Changing Sports and Sports Are Changing Women.* New York: Random House.

———. 1994. *The Stronger Women Get, the More Men Love Football: Sexism and the American Culture of Sports.* New York: Avon.

President's Council on Physical Fitness and Sports. 1997. "Physical Activity and Sport in the Lives of Girls." Washington, DC: President's Council on Physical Fitness and Sports.

Ryan, Joan. 1995. *Little Girls in Pretty Boxes: The Making and Breaking of Elite Gymnasts and Figure Skaters.* New York: Warner.

Sabo, Donald F. 1994. "Pigskin, Patriarchy, and Pain." Pp. 82–88 in *Sex, Violence, and Power in Sports: Rethinking Masculinity,* by Michael A. Messner and Donald F. Sabo. Freedom, CA: Crossing Press.

Sabo, Donald F., and Women's Sports Foundation. 1988. *The Wilson Report: Moms, Dads, Daughters, and Sports.* East Meadow, NY: Women's Sports Foundation.

Sedgewick, Eve K. 1990. *Epistemology of the Closet.* Berkeley: University of California Press.

Stein, Arlene, and Ken Plummer. 1994. " 'I Can't Even Think Straight': Queer Theory and the Missing Sexual Revolution in Sociology." *Sociological Theory* 12:178–87.

Take Action for Girls. 1996. "The Two Faces of Nike." *Take Action for Girls Newsletter* 1 (November):2.

Theberge, Nancy. 1985. "Toward a Feminist Alternative to Sport as a Male Preserve." *Quest* 37:193–202.

————. 1987. "Sport and Women's Empowerment." *Women's Studies International Forum* 10:387–93.

Thompson, Shona M. 1988. "Challenging the Hegemony: New Zealand Women's Opposition to Rugby and the Reproduction of Capitalist Patriarchy." *International Review of the Sociology of Sport* 23:205–12.

Tomlinson, Alan, and Ilkay Yorganci. 1997. "Male Coach/Female Athlete Relations: Gender and Power Relations in Competitive Sport." *Journal of Sport and Social Issues* 21:134–55.

White, Philip G., Kevin Young, and William G. McTeer. 1995. "Sport, Masculinity, and the Injured Body." Pp. 158–82 in *Men's Health and Illness: Gender, Power, and the Body,* edited by Donald F. Sabo and Frederick Gordon. Thousand Oaks, CA: Sage.

Women's Sports Foundation. 1997. *The Women's Sports Foundation Gender Equity Report Card: A Survey of Athletic Opportunity in American Higher Education.* East Meadow, NY: Women's Sports Foundation.

Young, Iris M. 1990. *Throwing Like a Girl and Other Essays in Feminist Philosophy and Social Theory.* Bloomington: Indiana University Press.

■ ■ ■

## Reading as a Writer: Analyzing Rhetorical Choices

1. What do Dworkin and Messner mean by "hegemonic masculinity" (para. 1)? Using a dictionary and the context of the essay (see para. 17, in particular), explain in your own words—and with your own examples—what the phrase means. How is this concept important to the argument the authors make about sport culture?

2. Like many authors in this collection, Dworkin and Messner divide their essay into sections. Summarize the purpose of each section, and point to a key sentence or two in each section that best expresses its purpose. How does each section serve the larger argument of the essay? What can you conclude about effective ways to organize complex essays of your own?

## Writing as a Reader: Entering the Conversation of Ideas

1. Like Dworkin and Messner, Franklin Foer is interested in what sports offer those who participate in them, both on and off the field. Drawing on and analyzing the ideas of these writers, compose an essay in which you make an argument about what participation in sports offers (and perhaps fails to offer) and the effect a player's race and gender have on this equation. Provide examples and evidence for your claims.

2. In paragraph 10, Dworkin and Messner analyze the image of gymnast Kerri Strug in the arms of her coach to illustrate a point about women's bodies and athletics. Jean Kilbourne is similarly interested in what images of bodies tell us about our assumptions about gender. Write an essay in which you use these authors' strategies of visual analysis to examine a series of images of female or male athletes. Given these images, what conclusions can you draw about the relationship between gender (and perhaps race) and sports? What is the significance of your findings?

MATTHEW PETROCELLI, TRISH OBERWEIS,
AND JOSEPH PETROCELLI

# Getting Huge, Getting Ripped: A Qualitative Exploration of Recreational Steroid Use

Matthew Petrocelli and Trish Oberweis both hold PhDs in justice studies and are professors of criminal justice studies at Southern Illinois University, Edwardsville. Joseph Petrocelli is a commander and deputy sheriff with the Passaic County (New Jersey) Sheriff's Department and holds two master's degrees. In this article, published in the *Journal of Drug Issues* in 2008, they explore the motivations of recreational steroid users. They identify a "gap" in the research on this issue, noting that while studies have been conducted on steroid use in professional athletes or those in high school or college, few researchers had investigated the "motivations, knowledge, and attitudes toward illegal anabolic steroids" of post-college-age recreational users. They point out that in contrast to professional athletes who have a clear incentive to gain a competitive edge, "it is much more difficult to understand why someone who lifts weights as a hobby would risk arrest and felony conviction, along with a host of medically verified detrimental side effects" (para. 10). Thus, they set out to interview users in this large population group in order to understand why they use steroids and to establish policies that will address this use.

One of the first aspects of this essay that you may notice is that it is structured like a traditional social science article, with an introduction, a literature review, a methods section, analysis, and a conclusion (here labeled "Discussion and Implications"). How does this structure affect the way you read the piece? You might pay particular attention to the authors' method of gathering information through semi-structured interviews after they had established themselves in the culture of particular gyms. What might be the strengths and weaknesses of this approach? Also, listen for the way the authors incorporate the voices of their interviewees, quoting long portions of the interviews and also including short comment in quotation marks. What do these direct voices add to this piece? What can you say about the language of gym culture and the way it reflects on our cultural expectations for masculinity?

Whether you are familiar with gym culture or are an outsider to this kind of bodybuilding, this research might help you think about the ways men are manipulated by media images of impossible body types, just as women are. What is at stake in "getting huge" and "getting ripped" among people you know? The answers to that question, and the ideas raised in this article, should help provoke some interesting conversation about what it means to be a man in the United States today.

# Introduction[1]

Steroid use has exploded into our national consciousness. As a nation, *1*
we slowly began to realize that illegal supplementation had infil-
trated athletics in the late 1980s, when Olympic sprinter Ben Johnson was
stripped of his gold medal after testing positive for a banned steroid. Since
then, it has been impossible to ignore the massive muscular gains and
record-shattering performances of men and women across the athletic
spectrum. NFL players grew to gargantuan proportions, track and field
athletes redefined the limits of human speed and endurance, and baseball
players not only began to resemble bodybuilders but also started hitting
tape measure home runs at a frenetic pace. Indeed, St. Louis Cardinal
Mark McGuire captured the imagination of the sporting world and single-
handedly rejuvenated interest in our "national pastime" in 1998 when he
chased and eventually broke one of the most heralded records in baseball:
the single season home run record. His 70 home runs, 9 more than the
1961 record held by Roger Maris, marked an astounding athletic accomplishment. Yet skeptics raised their eyebrows and questioned the validity
of McGuire's accomplishment. It was impossible to ignore how his physical dimensions had changed in the twilight of his career. McGuire began
his career as a tall, lanky infielder weighing about 200 pounds; by 1998,
at the age of 35, he had added 50 pounds of solid muscle to his frame.
Like other athletes who exhibited such phenomenal growth, he scornfully
denied using steroid, instead attributing his physique to scientific improvements in weight training and dietary regimes, along with legal nutritional
supplements.

That explanation began to unravel on September 3, 2003, when agents *2*
from the Internal Revenue Service, the U.S. Food and Drug Administration, and the San Mateo (CA) Narcotics Task Force raided the Burlingame
Bay Area Laboratory Co-Operation (BALCO). Scientists at the Olympic
drug-testing lab at UCLA had discovered new and powerful steroids in
some athletes and forwarded that information to the Department of Justice, which tracked the new drugs to BALCO. Owned by Victor Conte (a
former rock musician of some notoriety in the 1970s), BALCO's client list
read like a veritable *Who's Who* in American sports. Clients included members of the Miami Dolphins, All Pro NFL linebacker Bill Romanoski, track
and field gold medalist and world record holder Marion Jones, baseball All
Stars Jason Giambi and, most notably, Barry Bonds (who broke McGuire's
record in 2001 with 73 home runs and who, like McGuire, had added
40–50 pounds of muscle to his frame late in his career).

The fallout of the BALCO investigation was both telling and troubling. *3*
Although no athlete was arrested or prosecuted, several were summoned to
appear before a federal grand jury. The confidential testimony of Giambi,
Bonds, and outfielder Gary Sheffield were illegally leaked to the *San Fran-
cisco Chronicle*. On December 2, 2004, that paper ran an article entitled
"Giambi admitted taking steroids" that reported that between 2001–2003,

Giambi verified he took HGH (Human Growth Hormone), Deca-Durabolin (an anabolic steroid), and undetectable BALCO performance-enhancing drugs (Fainaru-Wada & Williams, 2004a). On December 3, 2004, that same paper ran an article entitled "What Bonds told BALCO grand jury," which asserted that Bonds and Sheffield admitted using undetectable BALCO performance-enhancing drugs, although both claimed they had been duped into doing so because they believed the substances were legal (Fainaru-Wada & Williams, 2004b). In March of 2005, Congressional hearings were held to determine the extent and prevalence of steroid use in baseball. Among the ballplayers called to testify were Mark McGuire and All Star Rafael Palmeiro. Under oath, McGuire adamantly refused to discuss whether he had used steroid and Palmeiro angrily denied the charge. In August 2005, Palmeiro received a 10-day suspension for testing positive for steroids. In January 2007, Mark McGuire, previously considered to be a lock for induction into the Baseball Hall of Fame, was snubbed by sportswriters and did not receive enough votes for baseball's highest honor; most speculate that his career statistics will forever be tainted by steroid suspicions. Moreover, recent investigations and research into national steroid use has begun to demonstrate that these drugs are widely used by athletes of all ages and at all levels of competition (Goldberg et al., 2000). The present study explores the use of steroids by amateur bodybuilders.

## Literature Review

Although we are only now recognizing the prevalence of steroid use in pro- 4
fessional athletics, these drugs have been part of the American sporting culture since the 1950s when synthetic testosterone was first produced and marketed (Rashid, 2000). Early academic research into the efficacy of anabolic steroids did much to damage the credibility of medical doctors and scientists as these "experts" made claims that steroids did little or nothing to improve athletic performance (Dawson, 2001; Hoaken & Stewart, 2003). Of course, steroid users learned from direct experience that steroids were effective at enhancing strength and muscle mass and thus began the entrenched belief that neither the government nor the scientific community could be trusted to reliably report the positive or negative effect of anabolic steroids (Kutscher, Lund, & Perry, 2002).

Recent research has attempted to rectify past shortcomings and stud- 5
ies have concentrated on medical evidence of effectiveness, trends, and patterns of usage among adolescent and high school students, college athletes, and professional competitors. In terms of the medical literature, scientists are universal in their agreement that anabolic steroids can lead to a host of ill-effects including acute acne, hypertension, blood clotting, jaundice, tendon damage, reduced fertility, the development of breasts in male users (technically known as gynacomastia but crudely referred to as "bitch tits" in the vernacular of steroid users), and a myriad of psychiatric and

behavioral problems (Boyadjiev, Georgieva, Massaldjieva, & Gueorguiev, 2000; Karila, Hovatta, & Seppala, 2004; Mottram & George, 2000; Nudell, Monoski, & Lipshultz, 2002; Pope, Kouri, & Hudson, 2000; Sirois, 2003; Taylor, 2002). More controversial studies have made the case that protracted steroid use is fatal (Parssinen & Seppala, 2002; Thiblin, Lindquist, & Rajs, 2000).

Studies of adolescent and high school steroid users focus on their 6 motivation to use the drugs and their intended and unintended consequences. Most studies are in agreement that 3–12% of American youths have experimented with steroids (Labre, 2002). The inspiration of these steroid users largely stems from a desire to either better their athletic performance or improve their body image (termed the "Adonis complex," Congeni & Miller, 2002; Yesalis & Bahrke, 2000). In males specifically, teenage steroid use has been attributed and linked to poor self-esteem, elevated rates of depression, attempted suicide, poor knowledge about health, a desire to participate in sports that require great strength, parental concerns about weight, and higher rates of eating disorder (Irving, Wall, Neurmark-Sztainer, & Story, 2002). Increased rates of violent behavior have been noted among these users (Pedersen Wichstrom, & Blekesaune, 2001).

Additionally, some researchers conclude there is a "gateway effect" 7 associated with adolescent steroid use. Namely, there is evidence to suggest that these steroid users are significantly more likely to use other illegal drugs (including inhalants, cannabis, hashish, PCP, sedatives, amphetamines, cocaine, heroin, and opiates), tobacco, and alcohol. Moreover, addictive and compulsive behaviors relating to gambling, vehicular risk taking, sexual activity, and violence have been reported (Bahrke et al., 2000; Estroff, 2001; Goldberg et al., 2000; Miller et al., 2002; Pedersen et al., 2001; Wichstrom & Pedersen, 2001). On the brighter side, there is at least some support for the notion that drug intervention strategies are successful in stemming steroid use in this subset (Congeni & Miller, 2002; Goldberg et al., 2000).

Studies centering on collegiate and professional steroid use demon- 8 strate similar findings. Along with verifying the litany of detrimental side effects noted in clinical trials, the same gateway effect has been found in mature steroid users. Specifically, adult use was significantly associated with higher rates of psychotropic drug use and overall substance dependence, particularly with opiates (Boyadjiev et al., 2000; Kanayama, Pope, Cohane, & Hudson, 2003; Togna, Togna, Graziani, & Franconi, 2003). Additionally, male bodybuilders exhibited an abnormal incidence of eating disorders and obsessive dietary tendencies (Marzano-Parisoli, 2001). Motivations for this group focused on the desire to obtain strength, muscular mass, muscular definition, or a combination of the three (Peters & Phelps, 2001). Interestingly enough, anger management problems and uncharacteristic violence (so called "roid rage") are largely discounted in the literature (Christiansen, 2001; Hoaken & Stewart, 2003; Pope et al., 2000).

It is clear that steroids pose risks to the users that have been identi- 9
fied by experts. Yet the black market for steroids is estimated to generate somewhere between $400–500 million a year (Rashid, 2000). It seems
unlikely that high school students, collegiate athletes, and competitive
bodybuilders comprise the entirety of that marketplace. Thus, it is logical
to assume that there is a group of steroid users that remains unidentified
and unstudied by researchers. We hypothesize that a significant portion of
this segment of the steroids-using population are recreational weightlifters, or individuals who bodybuild as a hobby. Indeed, in our review of the
literature we found only two studies that broached this virtually untapped
population: one that examines steroid usage among gym users in Trinidad
(Maharaj et al., 2000) and another that essentially examines justifications
for steroid use (Monaghan, 2002).

The problem, then, is that there are no studies examining the moti- 10
vations, knowledge, and attitudes of recreational steroid users. From a
social scientific standpoint, we know little to nothing about this potentially large group of steroid users in the United States. Thus, the significance of the present study is apparent. It is much easier to understand why
professional or Olympic athletes would take steroids—namely, to gain a
competitive edge, for the glory of victory, and for the enormous monetary
compensation tied to performance or endorsement deals. However, it is
much more difficult to understand why someone who lifts weights as a
hobby would risk arrest and felony conviction, along with a host of medically verified detrimental side effects. The need for social scientific analysis
of recreational steroid users is crucial to round out our understanding of
the entire spectrum of steroid users and thus to foster policies that address
the entire problem of illegal steroid use, rather than just one subgroup or
another.

## Methods

This project entailed the use of semi-structured interviews and snowball 11
sampling techniques in gyms in California, New Jersey, and Illinois. In
order to tap into the steroid subculture, we trained at gyms rumored to
have steroid access. These were not fitness clubs but rather more dingy
structures that catered to the hardcore weightlifting crowd. There were
massive amounts of free weights, very few (if any) women, blaring music,
and larger than average men. Our access to our original research subjects
was facilitated by the fact that two of the authors are lifelong weightlifters (M. Petrocelli was a fairly successful collegiate powerlifter and J. Petrocelli was a nationally recognized powerlifter); we could hold our own in
the gym, knew the repartee, and gradually built a good rapport with most
other lifters. Over time, as jocular insults and training tips were exchanged,
we broached the subject of steroid use with likely research subjects (chosen for their noticeable strength, size, muscularity, and approachability).

Despite our familiarity with both the subject matter and the potential interviewees, developing a rapport with any individual interviewee took a long period of time.

Initial interviews took place in the gym, usually after a training ses- *12* sion. By that time, most gym members knew we were academics. When we approached our initial subjects we further identified ourselves as researchers interested in discussing various aspects of steroid use, promising complete confidentiality.

The interviews themselves were semi-structured, asking specific ques- *13* tions about types of steroids used, dosages, ingestion methods, motivations, access, side effects, and concerns about legal ramifications. The subjects were given free rein to build upon those questions and themes. More often than not, the user was quite open and seemingly honest about such issues and provided even further insights and clarifications. After completing an interview, we would request that the subject direct us to another user (at either that gym or another), making appropriate introductions and assisting us with assurances of confidentiality. While we did have a snowballing effect, not all interviews produced additional interviewees; thus, our sample developed quite slowly.

Over the course of four years, from 2000–2004, we collected 37 inter- *14* views. Most interviews took place in a private area of the gym (out of earshot) or in the parking lot and lasted approximately one hour. Each interview was recorded (audio only) and later transcribed for analysis.

Our sample proved fairly homogeneous for key demographic vari- *15* ables. All the respondents were men. In terms of race, approximately 90% were white, and all were employed in essentially blue-collar or public service–related professions. Approximately 60% were married with children, 30% were divorced, and the remainder were unmarried. Ages ranged from 19 to 43 years old.

Analytically, we relied on a grounded theory approach. By definition, *16* "grounded theory is an inductive method of theory construction where observations [in this case, interviews] are examined to find underlying and recurring patterns that suggest particular theoretical explanations" (Maxfield & Babbie, 2005, p. 36). Our analysis of these interview data reveals several themes related to steroid use by this particular group of men.

## Analysis

### *Motivations for Use*

In stark contrast to the motivations espoused by adolescent, collegiate *17* athletes, or professional steroid users, we found that frustration seems to be a primary motivator for the recreational steroid user. Essentially, these employed, adult men report having grown up reading muscle magazines their entire lives. They believed what they read and thought that a good diet and hard workouts would get them a "magazine look" (competitive bodybuilder appearance). Naturally, they were bewildered that years of weight training had not yielded that dividend. This quote is typical of their epiphany:

> I grew up idolizing Arnold [Schwarzenegger, former bodybuilding champion and Governor of California] and Lou [Ferrigno, another champion body-builder who starred in *The Incredible Hulk* television series]. I used to train in my basement with my brother and friends all the time. Monster workouts. Dieted like crazy and everything the magazines said, and after five years my build wasn't even close. I couldn't understand it. Finally, I started going to a gym where muscle heads trained and learned what everyone on the inside knew: You gotta use if you want to get huge.[2]

Nearly every research subject we interviewed mirrored this sentiment. [18] They entered into the bodybuilding subculture thinking they could rely on the information presented in professionally produced and endorsed periodicals. They reported feeling duped and subsequently disgusted that their idols had sold them a bill of goods. When dieting, training, and legal supplements all failed to produce the magazine-like results, respondents realized that they would need illegal supplements to achieve their goals. Now, as individuals who had insider knowledge, they reported feeling obligated and compelled to pass on the secret to aspiring weightlifters. As one subject put it:

> If I see a kid training hard, doing all the right things, and asking questions about why he isn't making gains, I'm gonna tell him the truth. I spent too many years busting my ass in the gym like that. I don't tell anyone they should use, but I do tell them they can only get so far without using.

Another major motivation which surfaced in our interviews was the [19] desire to "get huge." Although this is another motive that was almost universally asserted by our subjects, the meaning of "getting huge" varied from person to person. Some reported that they wanted to achieve, at least once in their lives, the kind of "comic book" size proportions they always dreamed of. A few reported having grown up small or being bullied and they wanted to build the type of size and strength that would forever alter those early perceptions or experiences. However, these were mostly men who were either naturally big or who had attained above-average dimensions through years of weight training. Part of their desire to use steroids seems to stem from some sort of internal or external competitive obsession:

> It's addictive. . . . you can never be too big. There's always another guy with more size and you want to outdo him. And you think to yourself, "If I can get this big doing this cycle, I'll be huge if I do that cycle." So you up your cycles and train harder.[3]

Another major motivation we found is the craving to "get ripped." This [20] is a common term among weightlifters and bodybuilders, which has also become part of the popular lexicon. Being ripped means stripping away enough body fat so your muscles are clearly defined and vascular. Most of our research subjects reported the desire to get ripped but realized, like getting huge, they could only achieve their goal through steroid use:

> You can only go so far with diet and exercise. Yeah, there's a guy here or there that has great genetics and has a good build. But most of us don't.

Still others reported that being ripped increased and enhanced their *21* confidence and love life, as they claimed having a defined, muscular physique allowed them to meet and have sexual relations with more partners. Quite simply, most believed that they had become either more attractive to their partner or more desirable in a singles setting, or both.

Lastly, many subjects reported an odd blend of psychological and *22* physical power, or "feeling strong." It seems that for these individuals, the development of material strength via steroids had a profound impact on their psyche:

> When I'm on [steroids], I feel great. Unless you've been on, you don't know what I'm talking about. It just gives you a feeling that you can handle anything. You just feel so powerful and that makes you feel about the rest of your life, like you can do anything.

This theme resounded among most of the users we interviewed, who *23* claim a kind of raw, primitive strength and enthusiasm: "When I'm on, I feel like Superman."

### Usage Patterns

Most users in our study did two or three "cycles" a year. According to our *24* subjects, cycles are tailored to achieve particular gains. For instance, a "bulking cycle," intended to build as much muscular mass as possible, entails using steroids designed for that purpose, lifting very heavy weights with low repetitions, and eating tremendous amounts of food and protein supplements (as many as 6,000 plus calories per day), whereas a "cutting cycle" is meant to achieve the ripped look. "Cutting up" involves using different types of steroids than would be used for "bulking up," as well as training with lighter weights and higher repetitions and eating a stringent, low-fat, calorie-conscious diet. Normally, a bulking cycle is followed by a cutting cycle. As mentioned, a cycle lasted approximately 12 weeks and our subjects were very quick to point out the importance of "cycling." This means doing a steroid cycle and then "cycling off," or refraining from steroid use for at least 12 weeks. The reasons for cycling were varied, but most subjects indicated that they had health concerns if they did not take a break between use cycles (e.g., "It gives your body a rest"). However, most held the belief that the bodybuilders who appeared in magazines never cycled off: "Those guys are always 'on.' They might taper their cycles after a competition, but they're always on."

Another popular reason for cycling on and off was the expense of ste- *25* roids. All of our subjects made less than $77,000 per year (range: 23–77k), so cost was an issue. Steroid cycles varied in cost, depending on type and amount of steroids. Users reported that the amount of money they had on hand for a given cycle would primarily dictate the ingestion method, as steroid users can take steroids via an oral pill or through injections. There are pros and cons to each technique. Using pills is obviously easier in terms of intake. It is also easier to conceal your use in that it does not require the ritual of injection or any subsequent marks, and oral steroids are generally cheaper than injectables. The downside is that they are widely viewed as not being nearly as effective as "the darts." Most users believe that injectable steroids are superior to orals because they make you stronger, bigger, or more cut. The reported negatives to injecting steroids include having to learn to inject yourself, which can be painful:

> Shooting yourself is tough at first. You have to learn the spot on your ass that is best for you, and then you have to learn not to shoot there too often. A lot of guys who start out keep shooting themselves in the same place and you can get like an abscess or something there. It feels like a hard, round golf ball. You can always tell the guys in the gym who have them, because they're always squirming when they sit down. It's pretty funny.[4]

Interestingly, none of the users in our study mentioned any concerns 26 about sharing needles. When queried about this, all those reporting injectable steroid use claimed that getting clean needles was the easiest part of the process, as they are normally sold in bulk by steroid dealers.

All users reported that if they had the money and resources, they 27 would take both oral and injectable steroids in tandem, commonly known as "stacking." This is perceived to be the absolute best way to achieve maximum gains. But whether doing an oral cycle (at a cost of about $300–500), an injectable cycle (at a cost of about $600–800), or stacking (at a cost of about $1,200–1,500), the research subjects were unanimous in their approach to ingestion.[5] Specifically, users employed a "pyramid" technique, in which small amounts are used in the preliminary weeks, increasing amounts in the middle weeks, maximum dosage at the midpoint, and then gradually decreasing portions until the final week where the amount is the same as the start of the cycle.

### Access

Most subjects reported that it is fairly easy to get steroids. A typical 28 response: You go to a gym where you know the muscle heads go. You start training and get to know some of the guys over time. After a while, you can start sniffing around. If everyone is sure you're not a cop or an asshole, then people will start talking to you. Usually, there are at least a few guys who are selling and they'll set you up.

Or, potential users would approach a friend who they know to be on 29 steroids, who would then in turn make the appropriate introductions to his dealer and vouch for the new user. Interestingly, this dynamic mirrors some empirical findings concerning some market distribution systems for other illicit drugs (Adler, 1985; Dorn, Murji, & South, 1992; Rengert, 2003).

Alternatively, a few subjects reported receiving steroids through inter- *30* net sites. Some of these sites are easily found through a Google search (example: "purchase steroids"), but most users reported a high degree of suspicion that these could be law enforcement traps set up by the DEA or the like, and eschewed this method. Still, subjects agreed that there are more reliable sites, but this is considered to be highly classified information known only to a few; even after multiple queries, none of the subjects would divulge the internet address(es). In short, most subjects reported that once a person becomes a known entity at a gym that houses users and dealers, steroids are in abundance, along with needles and all the home-spun advice one wants about ingestion, stacking, or cycling.

### Health Concerns

Amazingly, the steroid users in our study were only minimally, if at all con- *31* cerned about any adverse health risks stemming from their drug use. Their lack of anxiety stemmed from both their experiential reality and a type of adulterated agreement reality. In terms of their own experience, none of our research subjects reported ever having an ill health effect. When asked about such side effects as hair loss, infertility, acne, "roid rage," or liver damage, they universally assailed such empirical findings as unbelievable and intentionally manipulative on the part of the medical community and government. For example:

> That's total bullshit. I've been taking steroids for eight years and I have three kids and a full head of hair. As long as you know what you're doing, they are only going to help you, not hurt you. The government is just totally fucked when it comes to drugs, so I don't pay any attention to their hype. And a lot of those side effect rumors come from Alzado.

Lyle Alzado was an NFL All-Pro defensive lineman for several teams *32* during the 1970s and 1980s. After a career of renown for his size, speed, aggression, and physique, Alzado was diagnosed with brain cancer in the early 1990s. Before his death in 1992, he went on record stating that he had used steroids constantly since 1969. He asserted that although they certainly helped him become the great player he was, they were also directly responsible for his cancer. Before his death, he urged athletes to stop (Alzado & Smith, 1991). When asked about the life and death of Alzado, our research subjects dismissed his deathbed warnings:

> Alzado was a brawler before he ever took steroids. I've never seen anyone snap because of steroids. I mean, look at Arnold [Schwarzenegger]. That guy has been taking buckets of steroids since he was thirteen, and he has movie star good looks, kids, and great health.[6]

Since none of our research subjects reported ever experiencing a *33* significant negative side effect, coupled with the seemingly good health of well-known steroid users from the recent past, their fear was slight. They simply do not believe that steroids will hurt them. While hair loss, development of breasts, and other potential side effects of steroids might be readily identified by users, other potential effects may not be obvious. "Rage" may be present but not attributed to steroids. Kidney or liver damage may go unknown to users for long periods of time. This is not to suggest that the users in our study suffered from these ill effects, but rather to point out that the lack of side effects is the subjects' perception.

### Illegality Concerns

Anabolic steroids have been classified as Schedule III drugs in the Controlled Substances Act since 1991. According to the Drug Enforcement Administration: Simple possession of illicitly obtained anabolic steroids carries a maximum penalty of one year in prison and a minimum $1,000 fine if this is an individual's first drug offense. The maximum penalty for trafficking is five years in prison and a fine of $250,000 if this is the individual's first felony drug offense. For a second felony drug offense, the maximum period of imprisonment and the maximum fine are doubled. While the above-listed penalties are for federal offenses, individual states have also implemented fines and penalties for illegal use of anabolic steroids (http://www.dea.gov/concern/steroids.html). 34

Most users voiced at least some concern about getting caught, although it was clear that their apprehension was not enough to deter them. Users who were married were the most worried about getting caught, but almost all dismissed the possibility and repercussions: 35

> It would suck to get arrested, but it's not like you're going to do time. Talk about a victimless crime. Why is everyone so worried if I take steroids? Why would anyone want to put me in jail for it? It's just stupid.

Others believed that steroid enforcement was such a low law enforcement priority that only either the very stupid or the very brazen need to be concerned. In short, our research subjects exhibited disdain for the laws banning steroids, did not fear law enforcement efforts, and were not particularly worried about receiving a harsh or unmanageable punishment. 36

### Discussion and Implications

There are several key findings in our research and other ideas that merit further thought and discussion. Our study identifies average men of average means who are longtime and dedicated steroid users. First, we found that a user's frustration with their lack of results using natural bodybuilding techniques was critical in terms of understanding their motivation for use. The source of this frustration seems to stem from an earlier belief that competitive bodybuilders are truthful when they assert in muscle magazines that certain diet and training techniques are the keys to their success. Our respondents unanimously believe that they are not. Although our results stem from a nonprobability sample, hence negating generalizability, it is noteworthy that our subjects hail from three different states in distinct regions of America (i.e., the West, the Midwest, and the East Coast) and this finding was consistent across that geography. 37

Moreover, our respondents clearly articulated their disenchantment 38
with the magazines' advertisements for legal supplements. These, our
respondents insist, did not produce the effects promised in words and
pictures, while anabolic steroids do. Longtime dedication to the diets, the
lifting strategeies, and the legal supplementation promising to produce a
huge, ripped physique led our respondents only to disappointment and
frustration. That frustration, in turn, was answered by anabolic steroids.
We think one area for further research would be to examine the content of
muscle magazines and scrutinize the text, the promises, and the images
that are available. Indeed, we believe that such a study could shed light on
an industry that is not known for its truth in advertising.

It was only with the use of anabolic supplements, our respondents sug- 39
gest, that they were finally able to achieve their goals. They got huge. They
got ripped. They got the added bonus of a sense of power that was part
physical and part psychological, yet they did not report feeling the more
well-known side effects of illegal steroids. No one reported uncontrollable
anger, for example. Moreover, our respondents' accounts of their drug use
did not include a concern over the health risks that may be associated with
anabolic steroids. They did not demonstrate any anxiety over the possible
side effects, and they were only minimally worried about any legal ramifications, particularly if they were unmarried. Indeed, another direction
for future research in this arena of study is an examination of our national
steroid policy and possibilities for either more aggressive enforcement or
reform.

Financial concerns posed a larger issue, though these were overcome 40
by use patterns in which users cycled on and off of a variety of substances
to obtain maximum benefits at a minimal cost. "Off" time, or a resting
period between cycles, helped to ease the financial burden without com-
promising results. Friends were a major source of steroids for a new users,
although the internet was mentioned as possibility as well. Already, some
nonprofessional users have found a route to obtaining steroids legally
through choosing medical doctors that specialize in "anti-aging" thera-
pies. Essentially, these doctors measure testosterone levels in middle-aged
men, and then provide anabolic supplementation and HGH to bring these
levels up to those commonly found in much younger men. As one research
subject put it, "It's the newest scam. If you have the cash to pay the doctors, then you can be 'on' legally."

Our research suggests that like most street drugs in the US, steroids are 41
easy to get and used by an array of individuals across the socioeconomic
spectrum. It is hard to deny that they have become part of the American
fabric. Competitive bodybuilding is obviously stacked with hardcore users
who operate in the open. Professional sports teams are only now reluctantly acknowledging the rampant use that most fans and experts have
suspected or known about for decades. Even the entertainment industry
is under suspicion. While it is impossible to empirically verify Hollywood
actors' use of steroids, strong suspicions, bordering on certainty, abound
among recreational users:

Ever see Will Smith? Tall, skinny guy most of the time. But then he decides to play Ali [former heavyweight boxing champ Muhammad Ali] and he slaps on 40 pounds of muscles almost immediately. C'mon. Look at the difference in Stallone's body [Sylvester Stallone] from the first *Rocky* until now. He's got a better build today than he did 30 years ago.[7]

Yet given all the national attention about steroid use, the subjects in our study were universally unfazed by the clamor; they are just getting huge and getting ripped. [42]

## NOTES

1. This information is largely taken from Fainaru-Wada and Williams (2006).

2. From our experience in the gym, this is certainly true. As we trained with the steroid users in our sample, we noted amazing gains in their size, strength, and muscular definition. Even among those users who asserted they were not deriving optimum results (e.g., "The shit's not working great this time around"), we noted incredible development.

3. A "cycle" is traditionally a 12-week period in which you take various steroids, eat a strict diet, and train as hard as you can.

4. Anabolic steroids such as the ones being discussed are injected intramuscularly, not intravenously.

5. For most of the subjects who engaged in stacking, three or four separate steroids were normally used, thus accounting for the cost differential (Standora, 2005).

6. Arnold Schwarzenegger did affirm that he used steroids during the course of his bodybuilding career, before they were deemed illegal (Weise, 2008).

7. Stallone is 60 years old and in May 2007 plead guilty to the illegal importation of Human Growth Hormone into Australia after a search by Australian law enforcement officials. Stallone, who was visiting the country to promote his new film *Rocky Balboa*, called the event a "minor misunderstanding" and will pay approximately $10,000 in fines.

## REFERENCES

Adler, P. (1985). *Wheeling and dealing: An ethnography of an upper-level drug dealing and smuggling community*. New York: Columbia University Press.

Alzado, L., & Smith, S. (1991, July 8). I'm sick and I'm scared. *Sports Illustrated*, pp. 21–27.

Bahrke, M.S., Yesalis, C.E., Kopstein, A.N., & Stephens, J.A. (2000). Risk factors associated with anabolic-androgenic steroid use among adolescents. *Sports Medicine, 29*, 397–405.

Bolding, G., Sherr, L., & Elford, J. (2002). Use of anabolic steroids and associated health risks among gay men attending London gyms. *Addictions, 97*, 195–203.

Bouchard, R., Weber, A., & Geiger, J.D. (2002). Informed decision-making on sympathomimetic use in sport and health. *Clinical Journal of Sport Medicine, 12*, 209–224.

Boyadjiev, N.P., Georgieva, K.N., Massaldjieva, R.I., & Gueorguiev, S.I. (2000). Reversible hypogonadism and azoospermia as a result of anabolic-androgenic steroid use in a bodybuilder with personality disorder. A case study. *Journal of Sports Medicine and Physical Fitness, 40*, 271–274.

Christiansen, K. (2001). Behavioral effects of androgen in men and women. *Journal of Endocrinology, 170*, 39–48.

Congeni, J., & Miller, S. (2002). Supplements and drugs used to enhance athletic performance. *Pediatric Clinics of North America, 49*, 435–462.

Copeland, J., Peters, R., & Dillon, P. (2000). Anabolic-androgenic steroid use disorders among a sample of Australian competitive and recreational users. *Drug and Alcohol Dependence, 60,* 91–96.

Dawson, R.T. (2001). Drugs in sport: The role of the physician. *Journal of Endocrinology, 170,* 55–61.

Donovan, R.J., Egger, G., Kapernick, V., & Mendoza, J. (2002). A conceptual framework for achieving performance enhancing drug compliance in sport. *Sports Medicine, 32,* 269–284.

Dorn, N., Murji, K., & South, N. (1992). *Traffickers: Drug markets and law enforcement.* New York: Routledge.

Estroff, T.W. (2001). Routes of abuse and specific drugs. In T.W. Estroff (Ed.), *Manual of adolescent substance abuse treatment.* Washington, D.C.: American Psychiatric Press.

Fainaru-Wada, M., & Williams, L. (2004a, December 2). Giambi admitted taking steroids. *San Francisco Chronicle,* p. A1.

Fianaru-Wada, M., & Williams, L. (2004b, December 3). What Bonds told BALCO grand jury. *San Francisco Chronicle,* p. A1.

Fianaru-Wada, M., & Williams, L. (2006). *Game of shadows.* New York: Gotham Books.

Goldberg, L., MacKinnon, D., Elliot, D., Moe, E., Clarke, G., & Cheong, J. (2000). The Adolescents Training and Learning to Avoid Steroids Program: Preventing drug use and promoting health behaviors. *Archives of Pediatrics & Adolescent Medicine, 154,* 332–338.

Gonzalez, A., McLachlan, S., & Keaney, F. (2001). Anabolic steroid misuse: How much should we know? *International Journal of Psychiatry in Clinical Practice, 5,* 159–167.

Gray, J.P. (2001). *Why our drug laws have failed and what we can do about it: A judicial indictment of the war on drugs.* Philadelphia: Temple University Press.

Green, G.A., Uryasz, F.O., Petr, T.A., & Bray, C.D. (2001). NCAA study of substance use and abuse habits of college student-athletes. *Clinical Journal of Sport Medicine, 11,* 51–56.

Gruber, A.J., & Pope, H.G., Jr. (2000). Psychiatric and medical effects of anabolic-androgenic steroid use in women. *Psychotherapy and Psychosomatics, 69,* 19–26.

Hoaken, P.N.S., & Stewart, S.H. (2003). Drugs of abuse and the elicitation of human aggressive behavior. *Addictive Behaviors, 28,* 1533–1554.

Inciardi, J. (2002). *The War on Drugs III,* Boston: Allyn and Bacon.

Irving, L.M., Wall, M., Neumark-Sztainer, D., & Story, M. (2002). Steroid use among adolescents: Findings from project EAT. *Journal of Adolescent Health, 30,* 243–252.

Jenkins, P. (2003). The next panic. In L. Gaines & P. Kraska (Eds.), *Drugs, crime, and justice* (2nd ed.). Prospect Heights, IL: Waveland Press.

Kanayama, G., Cohane, R.D., Weiss, G.H., & Pope, H.G. (2003). Past anabolic-androgenic steroid use among men admitted for substance abuse treatment: An under-recognized problem? *Journal of Clinical Psychiatry, 64,* 156–160.

Kanayama, G., Pope, H.G., Cohane, R.D., & Hudson, J.I. (2003). Risk factors for anabolic-androgenic steroid use among weightlifters: A case-control study. *Drug and Alcohol Dependence, 71,* 77–86.

Karila, T., Hovatta, H., & Seppala, T. (2004). Concomitant abuse of anabolic androgenic steroids in human chorionic gonadotrophin impairs spermatogenesis in power athletes. *International Journal of Sports Medicine, 25,* 257–263.

Koziris, L. (2000). Anabolic-androgenic steroid abuse. *Physician and Sports Medicine, 28,* 67–68.

Kutscher, E., Lund, B., & Perry, P.J. (2002). Anabolic steroids: A review for the clinician. *Sports Medicine, 32,* 285–296.

Labre, M.P. (2002). Adolescent boys and the muscular male body ideal. *Journal of Adolescent Health, 30,* 233–242.

Laure, P., Binsinger, C., Lecerf, T., & Ayotte, C. (2003). General practitioners and doping in sport: Attitudes and experience. *British Journal of Sports Medicine, 37,* 335–338.

Maharaj, V., Dookie, T., Mohammed, S., Ince, S., Marsang, B., & Rambocas, N. (2000). Knowledge, attitudes, and practices of anabolic steroid usage among gym users in Trinidad. *West Indian Medical Journal, 49*, 55–58.

Mangweth, B., Pope, H.G., Kemmler, G., Ebenbichler, C., Hausmann, A. & De Col, C. (2001). Body image and psychopathology in male bodybuilders. *Psychotherapy and Psychosomatics, 70*, 38–43.

Marzano-Parisoli, M.M. (2001). The contemporary construction of a perfect body image: Bodybuilding, exercise addiction, and eating disorders. *Quest, 53*, 216–230.

Metzel, J.D. (2002). Performance-enchancing drug use in the young athlete. *Pediatric Annals, 31*, 27–32.

Midgley, S., Heather, N., Best, D., Henderson, D., McCarthy, S., & Davies, J.B. (2000). Risk behaviors for HIV and hepatitis infection among anabolic-androgenic steroid users. *AIDS Care, 12*, 163–170.

Miller, K., Barnes, G., Sabo, D., Melnick, M., & Farrell, M.P. (2002). Anabolic-androgenic steroid use and other adolescent problem behaviors: Rethinking the male athlete assumption. *Sociological Perspectives, 45*, 467–489.

Monaghan, L.F. (2002). Vocabularies of motive for illicit steroid use among bodybuilders. *Social Science & Medicine, 55*, 695–708.

Mottram, D.R., & George, A.J. (2000). Anabolic steroids. *Best Practice & Research in Clinical Endocrinology & Metabolism, 14*, 55–69.

Naylor, A., Gardner, D., & Zaichkowsky, L. (2001). Drug use patterns among high school athletes and nonathletes. *Adolescence, 36*, 627–639.

Nilsson S., Baigi, A., Marklund, B., & Fridlund, B. (2001a). The prevalence of the use of androgenic anabolic steroids by adolescents in a county of Sweden. *European Journal of Public Health, 11*, 195–197.

Nilsson, S., Baigi, A., Marklund, B., & Fridlund, B. (2001b). Trends in the misuse of androgenic anabolic steroids among boys 16–17 years old in a primary health care area in Sweden. *Scandinavia Journal of Primary Health Care, 19*, 181–182.

Nudell, D., Monoski, M., & Lipshultz, L.I. (2002). Common medications and drugs: How they affect male fertitily. *Urologic Clinics of North America, 29*, 965–973.

Parssinen, M., & Seppala, T. (2002). Steroid use and long-term health risks in former athletes. *Sports Medicine, 32*, 83–94.

Pedersen, W., Wichstrom, L., & Blekesaune, M. (2001). Violent behaviors, violent victimization, and doping agents: A normal population study of adolescents. *Journal of Interpersonal Violence, 16*, 808–832.

Peters, M.A., & Phelps, L. (2001). Body image dissatisfaction and distortion, steroid use, and sex differences in college age bodybuilders. *Psychology in the Schools, 38*, 283–289.

Pope, H., Kouri, E., & Hudson, J.I. (2000). Effects of supraphysiologic doses of testosterone on mood and aggression in normal men: A randomized controlled trial. *Archives of General Psychiatry, 57*, 133–140.

Rashid, W. (2000). Testosterone abuse and affective disorders. *Journal of Substance Abuse Treatment, 18*, 179–184.

Rengert, G. (2003). The distribution of illegal drugs at the retail level: The street dealers. In L. Gaines & P. Kraska (Eds.), *Drugs, crime, and justice* (2nd ed.). Prospect Heights, IL: Waveland Press.

Sirois, F. (2003). Steroid psychosis. *General Hospital Psychiatry, 25*, 27–33.

Standora, L. (2005). Arnold doesn't regret "roid use." *Daily News* (New York), News section, p. 4, accessed 1-22-09 from Lexis/Nexis.

Street, C., & Antonio, J. (2000). Steroids from Mexico: Educating the strength and conditioning community. *Journal of Strength and Conditioning Research, 14*, 289–294.

Taylor, W.N. (2002). Anabolic steroids and the athlete (2nd ed.). Jefferson, NC: McFarland and Company, Inc.

Thiblin, I., Lindquist, O., & Rajs, J. (2000). Cause and manner of death among users of anabolic androgenic steroids. *Journal of Forensic Sciences, 45*, 16–23.

Togna, G., Togna, A., Graziani, M., & Fraconi, M. (2003). Testosterone and cocaine: Vascular toxicity of their concomitant abuse. *Thrombosis Research, 109,* 195–201.

Van Breda, E., Keizer, H., Kuipers, H., & Woffenbuttel, B.H.R. (2003). Androgenic anabolic steroid use and severe hypothalamic-pituitary dysfunction: A case study. *International Journal of Sports Medicine, 24* 195–196.

Van Eenoo, P., & Delbeke, F.T. (2003). The prevalence of doping in Flanders in comparison to the prevalence of doping in international sports. *International Journal of Sports Medicine, 24,* 565–570.

Walker, E.T. (2003). Missing the target: How performance-enhancing drugs go unnoticed and endanger the lives of athletes. *Villanova Sports and Entertainment Law Journal, 10,* 181–209.

Weise, E. (2008, December 2). Stallone puts muscle behind human growth hormone, but some doctors doubt its effectiveness, safety. *USA Today.*

Wichstrom, L., & Pederson, W. (2001). Use of anabolic-androgenic steroids in adolescence: Winning, looking good, or being bad? *Journal of Studies on Alcohol, 62,* 5–13.

Wright S., Grogan, S., & Hunter, G. (2001). Body-builders' attitudes toward steroid use. *Drugs: Education, Prevention, and Policy, 8,* 91–95.

Yesalis, C.E., & Bahrke, M.S. (2000). Doping among adolescent athletes. *Best Practices & Research in Clinical Endocrinology & Metabolism, 14,* 25–35.

■ ■ ■

## Reading as a Writer: Analyzing Rhetorical Choices

1. Compare the introductory paragraphs and the concluding paragraphs in this essay, and evaluate how effectively the authors use their new data to fill in the "gap" they see in the existing research. What are the most interesting aspects of their data and conclusions? Be prepared to point to specific passages as you reply.

2. With your classmates, discuss the strengths and weaknesses of the method the authors used to gather their data. What suggestions could you make for improving their strategy of data collection, and what effect do you think those suggested improvements might have on the information they could gather?

## Writing as a Reader: Entering the Conversation of Ideas

1. Petrocelli, Oberweis, and Petrocelli and Sharlene Nagy Hesse-Biber examine different ways men feel pressured to shape their bodies according to particular cultural standards. Compose an essay in which you place these authors in conversation with each other, focusing in particular on Hesse-Biber's sections on men. How do the examples and insights from these authors help build a larger picture of the pressures contemporary men feel to display a particular kind of masculinity? What significance do you see in the kind of masculinity that is being promoted in advertisements and gym culture?

2. Like Petrocelli, Oberweis, and Petrocelli, Michael S. Kimmel is interested in the popularization of a very narrow image of hypermasculinity. Drawing on these authors' insights about the motivations of men who actively shape themselves according to these extreme standards, write an essay

examining the significance you see in the direction in which our ideas about "masculinity" are headed. Refer to examples and ideas in both texts, and explain to your readers what you think is at stake, and for whom, in this conception of masculinity.

## SHARLENE NAGY HESSE-BIBER

# The Spread of the Cult of Thinness: Preteen Girls, Adolescents, Straight Men, Gays, Lesbians, and Ethnic Women

Sharlene Nagy Hesse-Biber is a professor of sociology at Boston College and has directed its Women's Studies Program. She is also the founder and director of the National Association for Women in Catholic Higher Education. She has coedited and coauthored many books and is the author of *Am I Thin Enough Yet?* (1996) and *The Cult of Thinness* (2007). This reading is a chapter from *The Cult of Thinness*. In the introduction to that book, Hesse-Biber explains that her study of body image began when the director of the campus Counseling Center called on her scholarly insights to help figure out why eating disorders were more common among women. This request led Hesse-Biber to conduct surveys and interviews with female and male college students over the course of eight years in order to understand their attitudes toward their own bodies. These research data are included in her book, in which she coins the powerful metaphor of the "Cult of Thinness" to explain the connections she sees between the ritualized behaviors and obsession with an impossible ideal both in cults and in eating disorders.

While much of Hesse-Biber's research focuses on young women, only the first section of this reading examines that particular demographic. The rest of this piece aims to move readers beyond standard examinations of disordered eating. She uses her "cult" metaphor here to examine the way the Cult of Thinness "continues to recruit new members" (para. 32), who fall into the categories listed in her long title. As you read, consider how the evidence and claims in each section are similar to and distinct from other sections of the piece. What main argumentative threads does she pull through this whole selection? Hesse-Biber draws on many different kinds of sources to build her overall argument about the effect of this "cult" of body anxiety in each different cultural context. Pay attention to the evidence that you find most persuasive and most surprising, and prepare to explain why.

The topic of eating disorders is familiar to most of us, but, like most of the writers in this book, Hesse-Biber aims at helping us to see the smaller, fascinating issues within this broad topic and to grasp their complexity and connections to other cultural issues. It is likely that you, or people you know, fit somewhere in this widening context of contemporary body obsession. What tools does Hesse-Biber offer us to see these problems in a new light? What can you do with this knowledge? Given the depth of pain revealed in many of Hesse-Biber's interviews, the answer clearly matters.

■ ■ ■

## Marketing the Cult to Preteen Girls

When I see these twigs of people in the magazines and on TV, I say "I'm going to go on a diet." You almost want to get thin just so you can wear the right clothes. I watch my junior high friends — they look like something out of a magazine.

—DARCEY, age 12

Eating disorders are increasing in the United States. They are no lon- [1] ger confined to a particular class or ethnic group, and are affecting females at younger ages. [1]

The average fashion model is white, 5′9″ tall, and weighs 110 pounds[2] — [2] approximately 32 pounds lighter and five inches taller than the average American woman.[3] Her good looks are relatively rare among the population, yet her image is so pervasive that it is difficult for girls to see themselves as anything but "wrong" in comparison. They are barraged with messages from beauty magazines and TV, and from classmates and parents and doctors, about the value of thinness and the liability of obesity. Many of them, by virtue of being female, white, and middle class, are already primed to join the Cult of Thinness. This population supplies new recruits, at ever-younger ages. Even preadolescents are joining the diet craze, and some are stunting their growth as a result.[4] In one national study, 45% of adolescent girls reported having been on a diet at some point, with 89% giving "to look better" as the reason for dieting.[5] Comparatively, only 20% of the boys indicated they had ever dieted, with 62% motivated by the desire to look better.[6] Why are they all so fearful of fat?

As I have indicated, convincing certain vulnerable groups that they [3] need to purchase goods and services to feel good about their bodies is very profitable. Advertising campaigns for fashion and beauty products are more frequently targeting children.[7] These industries are well aware of the purchasing power of preteens. One market researcher notes, "Today's parents spend more money on their children than any prior generation; children and adolescents have unprecedented amounts of money at their disposal, which they spend on fashion, beauty, and entertainment or leisure products; and children have gained increasing power in a wide range of purchasing decisions made by their parents." [8] Many of these products are directly aimed at promoting body insecurity. Am I fat? Does my hair lack body? Do I have blemishes? At a developmental point in their lives when they are highly sensitive to peer group pressure and media hype, kids seek out "how to" messages. As "guidelines about how to behave, young adolescents may be particularly susceptible to popular media stereotypes, especially those values and ideas presented by entertainment and fashion industries as vital elements of 'youth culture.'"[9] Teen magazines provide a seductive case for body obsession, defining what young girls are supposed to be doing with their lives—what is important and valued. The message is: You must be model beautiful, and attract a boyfriend, to be happy. These magazines exploit newfound interest in the opposite sex and youthful insecurities in order to market countless beauty and clothing trends.

One young woman I interviewed told me:                                       4

> Magazines were the big thing, especially in the teen years. There were always articles talking about how to become thinner and sexier and how to attract the opposite sex.

These media messages link thinness with love and happiness, often solely in terms of having the right body to attract the opposite sex. Diet and weight loss products fill the mail-order section of these magazines.

The slender ideal in magazines also shows up in educational materi-   5
als. In a 1992 study of third-grade textbooks since 1900, girls' body illustrations were progressively thinner in each decade. The study focused on depictions of the child's entire body, where gender could be clearly identified. Conversely, there was no significant trend for the images of boys' bodies.[10]

## Fear of Fat

Some researchers suggest that young girls' problems with weight, body   6
image, and eating are linked to puberty's onset, which brings a 20–30% increase in body fat.[11] Though it is critical to maturity and reproduction,[12] many young teenagers regard this normal increase with horror. My college interview subjects recalled this time in their lives with pain or embarrassment.

> I was 12 when I started getting a chest. I hated it. My sisters weren't developing yet—even my older sister. I guess at first, I thought it was fat. I never wanted it.

The medical establishment may have helped trigger an excessive fear of childhood fat by casting doubt on the old image of a chubby, healthy baby.[13] With 65% of the U.S. population characterized as overweight,[14] adults' weight and dieting preoccupation is transferred to the younger generations. As Seid notes, fear of obesity has spawned a shelf of weight-loss books for younger children as well as kids' weight-loss camps.[15] The "fat camp" promotional literature shows how well they understand the social consequence of being fat—*the* primary issue for kids.

> Erica [15 years old], 215 pounds at 5 foot 4, has checked into Camp Camelot because she hated being fat. She hated being taunted, being called "fatso" and "lardo." She hated looking in the mirror, hated what she saw there so much that she would punch her pillowy face in search for cheekbones and scream at herself inside her head: "I HATE YOU! I HATE YOU! YOU ARE SO FAT!"

The 1995 comedy *Heavyweights*, set at a fact camp, earned box office   7
bucks as adolescent paid to be reminded that fat is something to ridicule and get rid of. The reward of thinness is social acceptance, "a new image—a new you," and better feelings about one's "slimmer, trimmer

self." But by binding self-esteem so closely to weight and physical appearance, this attitude may also set the stage for a psychologically damaging cycle of weight gain and self-hatred. The youngster who loses weight at summer camp and "improves her self-esteem" is in danger of feeling worthless if she regains some weight when she returns home.

Studies show how early the cultural mirror begins to distort girls' perceptions of their body size and weight: one study in 2000 found that 41% of girls ages 9–10 favored a slimmer body shape.[16] Another study asked girls and boys ages 5–11 to choose an "ideal" and an "aspired to" female and male body shape from a group of drawings.[17] Then they were asked to consider their own body shape and to associate different traits with different body shapes.[18] The results showed that "by the age of 5, girls already have a perception of the ideal female as being thin. By age 7 they recognize that this is the body shape they would like, as seen by their 'aspired to' choices. By the time the girls reach 9 years old, some have become aware of a mechanism for pursuing this aspiration and have begun dieting."[19] The study also concluded that "the children ascribed more feminine traits to the thinner female figure, whereas ascription of the masculine traits did not favor any one particular body type."[20]

While there have been some reported cases of preteen anorexia nervosa, eating disorders are not widespread in this younger population. Approximately 1% of adolescent females are anorectic.[21] Four percent of college women have bulimia.[22] Roughly 10% of all people with bulimia and anorexia are men.[23] Studies suggest that the majority of cases of anorexia begin between the ages of 15 and 19.[24] However, severe dieting practices are quite common among preteen girls.[25] In a study of almost 10,000 Connecticut students in their seventh, ninth, and eleventh years of school, 7.5% of the girls and 3.4% of the boys stated that they had made themselves vomit, or taken diet pills, laxatives, or diuretics in the previous week in order to control their weight.[26] Numerous research studies have documented fat fears among normal-size young girls.[27] This fear exists despite their knowledge of nutrition and their own "normal" body weight. More than 50% of the underweight adolescents in one study described themselves as extremely fearful of being fat, and said that they did not apply their basic nutritional awareness to their eating habits.[28] They have the fear without the behavior; this makes them a perfect target for marketing, because they are already susceptible at a young age, primed and ready to join the Cult. Another study found that at age 10, 19.6% of the young adolescent girls questioned indicated a fear of being overweight, and that that number increased to 58.8% by the age of 14.[29] There is also some evidence that young girls who practice extreme dieting risk "nutritional dwarfing"—short stature and delayed puberty.[30] Self-imposed malnutrition has become a health concern in clinical pediatric practice.[31]

Lauren, in one of my college interviews, recalled:

> I was a big for my age and they called me Baby Huey, after the fat cartoon duck. That was always my impression of myself—a real clod. At 6 years old

I can remember feeling big. It was horrible, because in ballet class I wanted to be like the other girls, petite and pretty. I look at those pictures now, and I looked fine. I was a beautiful little girl, but at the time I didn't feel that way.

While the mass media provides young children with images of the cul- *11* turally desirable body, family members and peers also influence positive or negative self-image. . . . The young women I interviewed often referred to criticism from friends, siblings, and parents, especially their mothers. In some cases it had a lasting effect on their self-esteem. One young woman, Sandra, reflected on her mother's critical attitude about her appearance when she was growing up and how this criticism still impacts her life.

She was very critical. I was always the fat one and she was the thin one. She made sarcastic remarks like "you have the fattest thighs in the world." She was always saying "you better watch what you eat, you're going to get fat; you look chunky." This started when I was little. My mom said, "Thin down!" all my life. She's 5' 1" and weighs about 100 pounds. She always fits into size 2 and size 4 clothes. And here I am and I can't fit size 2 on my elbow. I don't even eat dinner with them anymore.

A study of fourth and fifth graders and their parents[32] examines how *12* parents' concerns about their own dieting and body dissatisfaction as well as their concerns about their child's weight and body image are important factors in determining their child's feelings about his or her body. Parents who commented on their child's weight negatively impacted how both daughters and sons felt about their bodies, especially their fear of becoming fat. While a father's attitude about his own weight issues is related to a daughter feeling too fat, it appears that the mother's influence is greater. Some research suggests that where the mother-daughter relationship lacks clear boundaries, and the mother is controlling her daughter's everyday routines, especially her food intake, the daughter may be at greater risk for developing eating issues.[33]

Eating disorders expert Michael Levine [34] stresses the importance of *13* parental self-awareness. Parents should examine their own attitudes and stereotypes about weight and body image and whether they convey negativity about their child's body in what they say and do within the family. To what extent does a parent pressure a child to lose weight or to objectify his or her body? To what extent do parents discuss the unrealistic nature of body images in magazines and commercials, thereby teaching children media literacy skills?

## Peers and Siblings

Another important influence on young girls' attitudes toward their weight *14* and body image comes from their peer group. Peer group comparisons become especially important now, as bodies begin to change and develop. Many women I interviewed remarked that while they did not feel like "one of the boys" during this time, they certainly did not feel like one of the girls. They were simply girls who wanted to do boy things.

> When I was a kid I used to love hanging out with guys, much more than with the girls. I remember one day my mother came to school. I guess she got a call from a teacher. She yanked me off the slide, because I was playing with the guys. She told me never to play with them again. I asked her why, and she said, "Just because."

> She used to put me in dresses for parties, especially when it was my own party. I'd go back into my room, change into my favorite pants and by that time I knew that she couldn't do anything about it, because if she did it would make a scene.

Being a tomboy protects some young girls—it relieves them from being attentive to fashion and body image and from getting caught up in "boy appeal." For most of them it is a phase, a short delay before they succumb to being a "normal" female in this society.  15

Donna's young male peers sent her a powerful negative message about her body. She relates a specific trauma she experienced in seventh grade:  16

> I was going out with a guy who was very cute and I was feeling like the happiest person in the world. His friends started giving him a hard time because I was fat and also the smartest girl in the school, and you don't go out with the fattest and smartest girl in the school. So he broke up with me—even though we had confessed love to each other. To this day, he was the only guy I ever felt that way for and he dumped me, totally unexpectedly. It was real hard because not only did he dump me but he convinced all his friends to give me a hard time, too, I guess so it didn't look like it was just him. So again, I was totally ostracized, this time for being smart and not just for being fat.

One 11-year-old told me "personality and body image" determines whether a guy will like you, and added that boys "don't like overweight people. They want pretty girls. When you're older they probably won't mind as much if you are a little overweight but right now they notice everything." This girl's perception of what males want seems to have been formed not just by magazines and television, but by her own experience.

There is also the pressure young girls feel from their older female peers, including older sisters. Amanda recalls her competitive feelings about her sister Gretchen.  17

> I think my older sister influenced my attitudes about wanting to be thin. I always compared myself with her. She is now 5' 5" but has a very small body frame. My mom is more like me, medium to large frame, well developed and well proportioned. And my father has a medium frame. I was always known as the little one. So I didn't have anything to worry about when I was very young. But then as I developed, I always had to watch my weight. I couldn't eat everything that I wanted; it would go to my stomach. I wanted to be like Gretchen, I always envied her. She had so many boyfriends. She could take one everything. In high school, she was a social butterfly, she had so many friends, yet Gretchen was the valedictorian; she could do it academically and

socially. And I'm looking at her wishing I could do that. But . . . I never had the confidence in myself.

In comparison, Amanda felt she did not measure up. Some recent *18* research suggests that young girls who are deeply involved in teen culture at a young age and are exposed to older girls in school or older sisters at home may be at greater risk for following the Cult of Thinness.[35] An older sister may adversely impact a younger sibling's attitude concerning weight and body image.

Although dieting and weight preoccupation are more common in *19* young girls, many young boys are getting caught up as well. While females feel the pressure to be thin, young boys are increasingly urged to increase muscle size, shape, and tone.[36]

## Adolescent Boys and Adult Males

Research on body image in adolescent boys reveals that at any one time *20* between 20% and 50% of boys want to lose weight, while 20% to slightly over 50% are trying to "bulk up."[37] Many spend time in body work because they link body image to success in their peer group relationships with both genders. One researcher notes: "It would appear that adolescent boys gain greater peer acceptance and popularity with both same-gender and other-gender peers by achieving a more muscular body that demonstrates phys-ical strength and athletic success."[38] Young men often accomplish their desired body through excessive exercise.[39]

Men in general are less concerned with their appearance than women, *21* and less convinced to alter their looks, but the number of men who are dissatisfied with their bodies is growing. In 1984 I interviewed two college-age men, Jim and Ken, and asked, "Do you think women are more weight-conscious than men?"

> **Jim:** Women are more weight-conscious. Men have never had to worry—the only time I think men get really weight-conscious is when they're playing sports. When I swim, I have to be conscious of it, but otherwise I never think of my weight. When I'm not in swim season, I'll just grab a candy bar and not think about it. I don't expect to marry because some woman thinks I look good. Hell, no.

> **Ken:** Traditionally men are more active in athletics, so weight-watching is not a problem. The media and models have placed a lot of pressure on women to be painfully thin, as opposed to the strong and muscular man.

Fifteen years later, their attitudes may not be shared by as many men. *22* Today, the strong, muscular ideal has more guys packing the gyms, per-forming obsessive rituals of exercise, diet, and supplement use. Men have some rigorous standards when it comes to their bodies: rippled muscles from shoulders, arms, and chest, to six-pack, rock-hard abs, all the way to bulging thighs and calves. Toned, buff young men are used by the media to sell everything from paper towels to diet soda to luxury cars. Men struggling to express their masculinity are increasingly concerned about their body image.

## The Rise of Male Consumers

As all Americans are becoming more consumer-oriented, "men as well as   23
women will be evaluated increasingly in terms of how they measure up to
media images of attractiveness rather than their achievement in work."[40] A
1994 study of men's magazine articles over a 12-year period notes "a statistical trend for an increase in weight-loss focus" and suggests that men are
becoming more appearance conscious.[41]

There is huge financial potential in promoting body obsession and   24
anxiety in males, and it is no wonder that the market for men's body products has grown dramatically in recent years. The diet and cosmetics industries have developed marketing strategies that prey on men's weight and
appearance insecurities. Certain diet soft drinks and weight-loss products
are targeting the male market.[42] Women's cosmetics companies, like Estée
Lauder, Inc., Elizabeth Arden, and others, have been offering men's skin
care items for years.

Targeted media like *Men's Health* and *Men's Fitness* capitalize on the   25
trend, urging men to "Build a Beach Ready Body: Sculpt Big Arms, Chisel
a Muscle Chest, Carve Awesome Arms," and "Lose Your Gut for Good: 35
Fat-Burning Meals," Guys—you too can look like the hunky model on the
cover.

## Body Dissatisfaction

There is growing evidence that the market emphasis may be working,   26
as body image surveys published every decade or so in *Psychology Today*
attest. In 1972, 15% of the men surveyed were dissatisfied with their overall appearance.[43] In 1985 this number rose to 34%,[44] and in 1997 it reached
43%,[45] with 22% desiring weight gain.[46]

Men are spending hours in the gym lifting weights and trying to gain   27
muscle and lose fat. I asked Tom, a trainer at a local gym, who these men
compare themselves to, and he answered:

> Each other, I think. But no matter how much they look others or themselves,
> in general, it's never good enough. They are never big enough; they are never
> "cut" enough, so they'll go to any extreme to get to their goals. Attraction is
> the main issue; sexual attraction to the opposite sex—or it's an ego thing . . .
> it's how you look at yourself compared to other people.

Interestingly, one study found that college males "believe females pre-   28
fer larger male bodies than they actually do."[47] Similarly, the study also

found that college women believed men preferred a much smaller female body than they in fact do.[48] So both college men and women are under the misconception that "model-skinny" and "bodybuilder-huge" are the looks that others find most appealing.[49] The changing nature of gender roles offers another reason for men's increasing attention to appearance. Traditionally, "the woman is supposed to be attracted to the man for his social achievements (wealth and power) and simply because he is a man, not because of any special effort on his part to make himself attractive to her."[50] Today, as women are gaining economic resources and positions of authority, they are starting to shift the balance of power within society. Noted psychologist and eating disorder specialist Judith Rodin writes:

> Men's appearance concerns also seem affected by shifting gender roles and expectations. Once a man could be assured of his masculinity by virtue of his occupation, his interests, or certain personality characteristics. According to historian Mark Gerzon in his book, *A Choice of Heroes: The Changing Faces of American Manhood*, there have been five traditional archetypes of masculinity throughout history: soldier, frontiersman, expert, breadwinner, and lord. Frontiersman and lord are no longer available roles for anyone, and expert and breadwinner are no longer exclusively male. Men may be grasping for the soldier archetype—the strong, muscle-armored body—in an exaggerated, unconscious attempt to incorporate what possible options remain of the male images they have held since youth.[51]

Today women can be CEOs of top companies and high-ranking military officers, so men may feel that, more than ever, muscles define manhood.[52] This idea may be an important contributing factor to male eating disorders, muscle dysmorphia, supplement use, and male cosmetic surgery.    29

## Dieting and Eating Disorders

Historically, Roberta Seid notes, "Men could not easily be sucked into dieting because of the persistent belief that a big, strong body was masculine and sexy. Even if it wasn't too strong, a big body gave the illusion of power and sexual vigor."[53] While most men who are dissatisfied with their weight deal with it through exercise,[54] there is evidence that others are taking to dieting.    30

Researchers in the early 1990s noted that "already diet soft drinks, light beers, and other diet products are being marketed by male movie stars and athletes. Men are finally getting hooked into feeling immoral if they eat the wrong foods." They suggested that if this trend continues, "the next ten years will see an explosion of weight problems in males."[55]    31

Indeed, the last 10 years has seen a pronounced jump in reported cases of male eating disorders. As the Cult continues to recruit new members and the gym culture expands, more cases can be predicted. Researchers Drewnowski and Yee found that 29% of men they studied had followed    32 a reduced calorie diet during the previous month and that 66% of them reported more than 30 minutes of exercise per day.[56] This highlights a gender difference: Women tend to diet (64% had dieted in the previous month in the study just mentioned) more than men, while men tend to exercise more.[57] Thus, men who are dissatisfied with their abs (63% of men, according to a 1997 survey conducted by *Psychology Today*)[58] or their muscle tone (45% of men according to that same survey)[59] are sweating and pumping iron at the gym to achieve the ideal body, rather than watching food intake. The researchers agree. A 2001 study by Woodside and others found 2% of their male subjects had full or partial eating disorders, compared to 4.8% of their female subjects.[60] Braun et al. noted that males comprise about 5–10% of anorectics and 10–15% of bulimics.[61] Petrie notes that "approximately 10 percent of individuals with anorexia nervosa and bulimia nervosa and 25 percent of those with binge eating disorder are men."[62] This does not mean, however, that less prevalent male eating disorders are less serious. Eating-disordered males live lives of secrecy and shame, like their female counterparts, but far fewer are receiving treatment due to the heightened stigma attached to a male eating disorder.

Woodside's study found the female to male ratio of patients with at 33 least partial syndrome anorexia nervosa was 2.0:1, and the ratio for bulimia was 2.9:1.[63] Still, researchers are unsure if this number is completely accurate. Judith Rodin observes how men try to conceal their concern with physical appearance: "Perhaps they try to keep their body image concerns a secret. It's less socially acceptable for men to think and worry about their appearance than it is for women to do so. Men experience their body concerns as unmasculine, and therefore embarrassing and shameful."[64]

According to psychologist Harry Gwirtsman, "Bulimia may be more 34 prevalent among males than we though since it's an easy disease to hide and men are reluctant to come in for treatment."[65] In their study of males at the inpatient eating disorders unit at The New York Hospital, Cornell, Braun et al. noted that although there was evidence of an increase in males with eating disorders, the percentage of males admitted into the unit increased from 1984 to 1997.[66] The researchers hypothesized this surge could be explained as "men are beginning to feel a greater degree of comfort in seeking treatment" and/or that "area professionals have become better able to detect eating disorders in males or are more readily referring them for treatment."[67]

When I asked Tom, the fitness trainer I interviewed, if he'd noticed eat- 35 ing disorders among men at his gym he said he felt eating disorders were mostly a female thing.

> I've seen bulimic behavior in one bodybuilder, in a competition. When he'd eat something right before he went on stage, I watched him throw it up . . . because they feel if they hold that water they are not going to be as "cut" on the stage; I've also seen wrestlers throw up to lose weight before going on the scale—I think that's a lot of pressure from the coach.

Both examples Tom mentions come from sports with weight require-ments and this suggests that men at the gym may be dealing with their body image insecurities more covertly. However, it would be erroneous to assume that such pressure does not also stem from the individuals them-selves—who live in a culture where bigger is better (for men anyway). As a sports nutritionist, Nancy Clark notes:

> In our society, muscularity is commonly associated with masculinity. Accord-ing to Olivardia, compared to ordinary men, muscular men tend to command more respect and are deemed more powerful, threatening, and sexually virile. Muscular men perceive others as "backing off" and "taking them seriously." Not surprisingly, men's desire for muscles has manifested itself in a dramatic increase in muscle (and penile) implants.[68]

Some men experience a secret torment when they have an eating dis-order. In their book, *The Adonis Complex*, psychiatrist Harrison Pope and his colleagues studied a variety of body image issues in men and boys, which they coin "The Adonis Complex." This term describes a number of body image distortions they find increasingly prevalent among boys and men. Adonis is a god depicted in Greek mythology as "half man and half god," who was idolized as the ideal masculine form. It was Adonis who gained the love of Aphrodite through his perfect physique. "The Adonis Complex" can present itself in several forms—as a preoccupation with fat that leads to the development of an eating disorder, as well as an obsession with muscle mass. Bill's situation, as recounted in *The Adonis Complex*, captures his lonely struggle with Binge Eating Disorder:

> On his way home from the gym, Bill will purchase two large Italian subma-rine sandwiches, two large bags of Doritos, two cans of onion dip, and a quart of chocolate-chip cookie-dough ice cream. After shutting off the ringer on his phone, he'll begin to eat as fast as he can—sometimes even using both hands to feed himself, grabbing food with his left while eating with his right.[69]

Bill abuses food not to enlarge his physique, but rather to soothe psycho-logical distress.

## Muscle Dysmorphia

Some men with the Adonis Complex become fixated with muscle mass, obsessively bulking up, and being bigger than the next guy. This behavior is now a disorder classified as muscle dysmorphia, "in which individuals develop a pathological preoccupation with their muscularity."[70] In their book, *The Adonis Complex*, psychiatrist Harrison Pope and his colleagues also relate the story of Scott. Scott graduated from business school, but became a personal trainer because "it was the only job I could think of that gave me enough time to do my own training."[71] His body image, his exer-cise routine, and his diet consumed his life: "even on hot summer days, after getting a bad shot of myself in the mirror, I'll put on heavy sweatshirts to cover up my body because I think I don't look big enough."[72] He even lost his girlfriend: "I told her that when we first started living together: the gym comes first, my diet second, and she was third. I guess she couldn't take being in third place anymore."[73] But he thought she would probably leave him for a bigger guy anyway. He didn't see therapy as beneficial: "At first, it was a healthy thing, wanting to pursue a healthy lifestyle and be in shape. But now, it's gotten out of control. It's a trap. I can't get out of it."[74]

Tom, the certified trainer I interviewed, relates a similar story about himself: 38

> It's like I always had to be the best. So I would always train. Even in high school, I'd go to the gym in the morning, I'd go to school, I'd have practice, I'd go to the gym afterwards. I was probably one of the only kids that did that. . . . I was the only one that actually started to train directly off-season. I had coaches that would help me.

Men with muscle dysmorphia have a difficult life. They spend hours at the gym bulking up, but are so afraid that they are too small that they are embarrassed to even take off their shirts at the beach. They cling to their regime of weightlifting, much like an anorectic exercises extreme control over her food intake. To most onlookers, these bodybuilders appear leaner and much more muscular than the average man, yet they feel exactly the opposite. One study found that 71% of the bodybuilders they observed began their careers because they "felt too fat, too thin, and/or not sufficiently masculine."[75] Olivardia, Pope, and Hudson found that 52% of the muscle dysmorphic bodybuilders they studied disagreed with the statement "I really like my body" and 46% of them stated that they were dissatisfied with their body proportion.[76] 39

Men with this disorder often, and quickly, turn to steroids or supplements to enhance and maintain their muscle. Tom, the trainer, revealed to me that he has used supplements. 40

> I'm not going to say I've never taken ephedrine. I do now. I've taken it because I see the results. I'm not the type of person that says I need more, or more is better. I'll take the serving or half a serving; it speeds your metabolism up with just a little bit more energy, and makes you sweat a little bit more. So it's more of a charge, like having a coffee in the morning.

But Tom also knows the risks of using steroids to obtain more muscle. 41

> A friend of my friend's just passed away at 23 years old. He gained 110 pounds of solid muscle in 1 year. That's almost impossible. He didn't understand that his heart is also a muscle that also built to a point where it just burst in his sleep.

Although steroids are illegal, they are attainable at the fringes of the gym scene. However, innumerable weight gain and protein products, diet pills, and supplements *are* legal, marketed, and sold to men yearning for the ideal muscular body. Some researchers note that "the muscular mesomorph is the ideal because it is intimately tied to cultural views of 42 masculinity and the male sex role, which prescribes that men can be powerful, strong, efficacious—even domineering and destructive."[77]

What both these forms of the Adonis Complex—obsession with fat   43
and fixation on muscle mass—share in common is the secrecy of these disorders. While more women have become open about their experiences with food and body image issues over the past several decades, few men are able to talk openly about their eating and body image problems because they perceive them to be "women's" concerns. As Harrison Pope, coauthor of *The Adonis Complex*, notes, "Over the last 20 years, women with eating disorders have become more willing to disclose such problems, but men often remain too embarrassed to do so."[78]

## Under the Knife

Body dissatisfaction has led some men to drastic measures. While women   44
undergoing cosmetic surgery still outnumber men 7 to 1, men are beginning to take this route to good looks. According to the American Society for Aesthetic Plastic Surgery, men had almost 1.2 million cosmetic procedures in 2004, making up 8% of all procedures performed that year,[79] reflecting an 8% increase from 2003.[80] The five most popular surgical procedures were liposuction, eyelid surgery, rhinoplasty, male breast reduction, and hair transplantation.[81] As they age, men who were once secure about their bodies may fear the kind of devaluation aging women experience.

I asked a successful plastic surgeon why there has been an increase in   45
the cosmetic surgery on men. He told me:

> The most common reason is economic. It's the male who is rising up the economic ladder and usually achieves his greatest success in his 50s and 60s. Now he needs a physical appearance that is consistent with his power and his place in society. He must stay physically trim, must not have loose skin, must not have anything that suggests infirmity. His looks maintain his power because we're all being judged by the vigor of our appearance. This is more true for men, because our society continues to economically reward them over women. Even though a 50-year-old woman entering my office might give the same reasons as a man—she wants to maintain a high position in her career and feels that without a youthful appearance, she would lose out—I think for most women it's an issue of self-esteem. With aging, they have diminished self-esteem and they want to regain something that they feel they've lost.

## Male Subgroups

The greatest number of converts to the pursuit of muscular thinness   46
occurs in particular subgroups. Men who are heavily involved in sports

with required weight norms (e.g., wrestling, horse racing) may be more at risk for eating problems.[82] Some studies hint that gay males may be at even greater risk because of the importance of appearance (from body build to clothing) in their culture.[83] David Crawford, in his book *Easing the Ache: Gay Men Recovering from Compulsive Disorders*, highlights the importance of physical attractiveness in gay society: "To some degree, we can identify with the image women have had thrust on them. Seeing ourselves in abject terms of physical attractiveness, we—like many women—are extraordinary self-conscious about our looks."[84] Some research also suggests there is greater body dissatisfaction among gay males. A research study comparing heterosexual and homosexual college men notes that "gay men expressed greater dissatisfaction with body build, waist, biceps, arms, and stomach than did heterosexual men. Homosexual men also indicated a greater discrepancy between their actual and ideal body shapes than did heterosexual men, and showed higher scores on measures of eating regulation, and food and weight preoccupation."[85]

The impact of AIDS and its physical devastation may be changing gay 47 emphasis on thin appearance. Some researchers suggest that instead, a more muscularly powerful body image may be emerging to "avoid the appearance of illness with AIDS. The illness has been described in slang usage as 'slims' in some countries."[86]

## The Spread of the Cult of Thinness to Other Social Classes, Races, and Cultures

The Cult of Thinness occurs primarily in wealthy Western societies among 48 white, upper-middle-class, educated females.[87] Their stories have comprised this book. The excessive pursuit of thinness has been rare among people of color in the United States (e.g., Blacks and Latinos)[88] and in non-Western developing societies such as in Asia, Africa, and South America.[89] In fact, traditionally these societies view obesity quite positively. As psychologist Esther Rothblum writes, "In developing countries, the major causes of death are malnutrition and infectious disease, and thinness is unlikely to be viewed with envy, rather, increased body weight is associated with health and wealth."[90] Furnham and Baguma also note: ". . . to a person living in a poor country an obese body may be considered a healthy body for two reasons: first, fat deposits laid down mean that people may survive 'lean' periods more effectively; second, because one has to be fairly wealthy to afford food and could equally use this wealth to acquire medical treatment."[91]

Emily Bradley Massara's 1989 study, *¡Que Gordita!*, looks at the role of 49 obesity in the day-to-day lives of ethnic women.[92] She wanted to know the cultural causes of weight gain among a small sample of Puerto Ricans living in one Philadelphia neighborhood. Massara investigated the life histories of several first-generation women who "have a distinct sense of social identity as Puerto Ricans"[93] and who were defined as "medically obese." All were married and had children. She found that certain cultural definitions of overweight were important factors. Within this community, fat was not considered a sign of illness, but indicated "tranquility, good appetite, and health."[94] Conversely, to be thin meant to be malnourished and diseased—an undesired condition. In fact, when given a series of photos of body types (thin to obese) to rank in terms of attractiveness, the women in her sample gave a narrower range of acceptable thin weights, but a wider range of acceptable heavier weights. As Massara notes, "one of the ways in which the 'good wife' and mother expresses her love for her husband and children is by presenting family members with large helpings of food and manifesting concern over amounts of food eaten."[95]

Women were expected to gain weight, especially upon marriage. It  50
was a "sign, particularly to her family, that she was adequately provided for."[96] Women who lost weight got negative reactions. One woman whose weight declined from 170 to 140 pounds when she divorced her husband reported: "When I lost weight, people said: 'You're so skinny! What happened to you?' So many people told me fat didn't look bad and I looked better that way because I had a shape."[97]

Massara notes that:                                                       51

> Linguistic terms, such as "pretty little plump one" (*gordita buena*), reinforce
> the notion that a certain degree of heaviness in women is positively valued.
> The plump (*gordita*) woman may also be referred to as a "total woman" (*mujer
> entera*) because she is considered to have a "beautiful body [shape]" and good
> health. . . . "How plump!" (*¡Que gordita!*) is one expression which suggests
> shapeliness and health and is used in a highly complimentary manner.[98]

In Massara's sample, the men appeared more sensitive to their weight than the women, in part from the expectations of the provider role: "Both men and women expressed a belief that men should, as one informant explained, 'be in shape for the work they do,' or, 'they shouldn't let themselves go.'"[99]

Massara found that the men were more likely to diet and were more  52
concerned about their appearance. One man in her sample lamented, "Already I'm 'over the hill!' The girls like someone who is nice and slim."[100]

Massara also observed that American values of female thinness were  53
beginning to appear within this group of first-generation women, as the process of acculturation spread to their children.[101] "For instance, many mothers showed an awareness of Western medical concepts about the dangers of heaviness in children. With regard to adult weight, some children encourage their mothers to reduce so that they will look more attractive. By the same token, some of the more acculturated women actively practiced eating restraint."[102]

What is happening in one Puerto Rican neighborhood is a microcosm  54
of what is happening throughout nonaffluent classes and racial groups in American society, as well as in non-Western societies as a whole.[103]

## Thinness and Black Culture

Some research findings suggest that "cultural loyalty and strong ethnic 55 identity protects black women from the thin ideal standards of American culture."[104] Black women are likely to report feeling underweight, while white women are likely to report feeling overweight.[105] Although black women's ideal body image is larger than the ideal body image for white women, "one might expect that black women who are significantly overweight from their ideal body image might display similar dieting, bingeing, and purging symptoms as white women."[106] As one recent study suggests, "some black women are not buffered against eating disorders as suggested in previous research."[107] The Cult of Thinness has a different context for a woman of color, whose hair texture, skin tone, and build do not conform to Anglo-Saxon standards. One black sociologist writes: "White feminists who write about body image, such as Naomi Wolf, often fail to acknowledge the particular concerns that black women face because of the combination of racism and the beauty myth."[108]

She lists the important appearance issues that came up in discussions 56 with other black women:

> African women are subject to the same pressures to attain an ideal of beauty as are white women in North American society, but efforts to approach the blonde, thin, young ideal are made at an even greater cost for black women. Weight preoccupation is not a central concern for many black women,[109] but weight is one among many factors that preclude black women from attaining "beauty" according to the cultural archetype. Three issues came up again and again when I talked with other black women: skin color, hair texture, and body size.[110]

As one black researcher says, the defining of white beauty depends on the denigrating of what is not white: "Blue-eyed, blond, thin white women could not be considered beautiful without the Other—Black women with classical African features of dark skin, broad noses, full lips, and kinky hair."[111]

Gladys Jennings, Associate Professor of Food Science and Human 57 Nutrition at Washington State University, comments, "There's a cultural standard from our African heritage that allows for more voluptuousness and padding on black women."[112]

Traditionally, the African American community's ideal has been more 58 realistic and sensual: "Women's bodies were substantial. They had breasts and hips and curves and softness."[113] Black psychologist Marva Styles notes that many black women have maintained strong bonds with their cultural roots through soul food: "The essence of Black culture has been handed down through oral history, generation after generation in the African tradition, through the selection and preparation of soul food. The determination to hold on to native foods by bringing seeds into this country may be symbolic of the ever-present determination to preserve the African culture through food."[114]

That preparation becomes a primary definer of a black woman's sense *59* of herself: "The Black woman gains a sense of pride as she watches her extended family—her man, her children, and maybe her grandparents, sisters, nieces, and friends—enjoy the soulful tastes and textures prepared by her skillful hands."[115]

As in the Puerto Rican community, plumpness is a sign of health *60* and prosperity—telling the black woman she is doing a good job. Styles remarks on the generational differences in her attitude toward food compared with her mother's.

> Slimness, however, is not valued by middle aged and older black women. My mom worries about my slimness because at 5'4", I barely weigh 120, and I am a middle-aged woman. She asks me often, "Are you eating properly these days?" Maintaining my weight at 120 pounds is hard for me, because I was taught to enjoy eating and preparing food. If I ate the kind of food my mom prepares consistently, I would probably weigh 150 by now. . . . Staying slim is difficult in a culture that values cooking and eating.[116]

Yet there is reason to believe from current research studies that the *61* Cult of Thinness is spreading beyond the white middle class.[117] Eating disorders are reportedly growing among the black American population.[118] One researcher speculated that "increasing affluence among some blacks, and thus their access to traditional white middle class values, and the homogenization of life style and priorities, perhaps as a result of the increasing influence of the media, have finally penetrated the black culture: the young black female (and perhaps the male) is getting fatter and is becoming more concerned about her fatness."[119] The problem appears particularly acute among persons of color who are upwardly mobile.[120] A case study of anorexia nervosa in seven middle-class black and Hispanic adolescent women elaborated:

> They encountered early our [white] society's conviction that thinness and trimness are the essential ingredients that lead to success. Thus, these girls, who were already feeling different and suffering from a low self-esteem and a powerful need to be accepted, sought integration with society through rigid dieting and an extremist adoption of the current societal standard of slimness.[121]

In general, the rate of obesity among black women is greater than *62* among white women. Research indicates that black women are less concerned with being thin[122] and that eating disorders are less common in black women than in white women.[123] However, one recent study, which compared eating disorder symptoms in a group of black and white girls, found that "black girls had significantly higher bulimia scores than white girls."[124]

Women of color face double jeopardy—they are subject to racial as *63* well as sexual discrimination. If we include discrimination based on social class, they suffer from "triple jeopardy."[125] In my interviews with women of color, I found they used food as a nurturing mechanism to cope with oppressive social and economic conditions. Bingeing can be a "cheap" way to find temporary relief from sexual abuse, poverty, racism, and sexism. Eating large quantities of food in a short time can serve to numb, soothe, and literally "shield" (with fat) some women from physical and emotional trauma.[126]

Compulsive eating was also a coping mechanism for white women in my sample who had experienced sexual abuse—their drive for thinness was secondary. This form of bingeing is an eating disorder, but also a perfectly rational means of dealing with the pain blacks and others also experience living in our society.    *64*

## Lesbians

Some research suggests that gay men and straight women are the most likely groups to engage in eating-disordered behaviors.[127] Even though lesbians are often portrayed as uninterested in their physical appearance, a 1992 study that compares lesbians, heterosexual women, gay men, and heterosexual men notes that lesbians and heterosexual women were most discontented with their body image.[128] Lesbians dieted significantly more than gay or heterosexual males.[129] Although heterosexual women and gay men were found to be more preoccupied with weight than lesbians and heterosexual men, "gender was a more salient factor than sexual orientation on most variables."[130]    *65*

But other research suggests that while lesbians (compared to heterosexual females) are aware of the cultural pressures on women in heterosexual society to look thin, they do not appear to internalize this norm to the same degree.[131] As one lesbian in her early 20s told me:    *66*

> In straight communities, if a girl says "I'm too fat, I'm going to diet," there is support for that. In the queer community, there wouldn't be support. People would challenge it and confront it. I've never met a lesbian on a diet.

I conducted focus group interviews and intensive interviews with white middle-class college-age and postcollege lesbians about body image, weight concerns, eating issues, and general appearance and identity—all in the context of their lesbian lifestyle. They first discussed what it meant be a lesbian in today's society and that their body image seems to be central to their perception of themselves in relation to both the lesbian and heterosexual communities. Just as homosexual males, raised in a heterosexual world, get the clear message that the "real" men are macho and have big muscles, lesbian women are told that "real" women are slim and, in a male-driven world, submissive.    *67*

Martha, a white, lesbian, middle-class college student, told me:    *68*

> I grew up listening to my mother and sister always being on diets. In the straight world, I am not like what every girl is supposed to want to look like. I don't want to say I'm not feminine but I'm not fitting into the mold. . . . I had

the longest hair, but then two summers ago I chopped it off. A friend of my mother's commented that my hair was "just a bit too short."

Those lesbian women I interviewed who were now in the job market  69 spoke about how they had to negotiate their appearance in their workplace. They were keenly aware of how the straight world would stereotype them if they did not conform to the dominant ideals of beauty. Natasha noted:

> People get jobs because of how they look . . . people identify you as pretty, "let's hire her because she'll sell things." . . . I mean, if you want income from the straight world, there's a certain price you pay for not conforming.

Although lesbians are not trying to attract men with their bodies or  70 style of dress, they still may be Cult of Thinness practitioners in order to attract other women. Some of those I interviewed used their bodies as symbols of their rejection of the patriarchal society—refusing to shave their armpits or legs, wear high heels, or apply makeup. Some identify politically with feminists or take on a "butch" role, actively combating the oppressive thinking that torments women into believing they must be thin to be valued. Jennie, a white middle-class professional woman in her late 20s, said, "I feel like being skinny has really been a struggle for me because it's hard to be a powerful woman."

The opposite stereotype is the "lipstick femme" lesbian, who follows  71 the more traditional image of a thin heterosexual woman. Mary, a lesbian I interviewed, talked about lesbians who identify themselves along the butch-femme continuum. She pointed out that these categories are not mutually exclusive and are often imposed by straight culture:

> It depends on how you self-identify. There's an eroticism to a big, fat, butch/ dyke. . . . Or if you're femme, being big breasted and having voluptuousness can be like a way to be more feminine. I think there is a whole other side of the spectrum for those who don't identify in categories. While most lesbians self-identify as queer, that's probably the only commonality we have. In my opinion, queer doesn't necessarily mean I'm a lesbian, I'm a dyke, I'm a butch, and a this or that—it's all of those things.

Caroline noted that she does not want her own lesbian identity to be  72 compartmentalized, but she also feels pressure to live up to her butch appearance when she is out with her lesbian friends:

> When I am out with my gay friends I still don't fit the lesbian mold because I . . . look like this. There is always going to be something, like my hair is not looking perfect, I don't match. I have this look, but I really am not perceived as "butch," since I really don't have that kind of personality.

Dress and public behavior are self-expressions associated with gen-  73 der. Whereas homosexual males may be judged as "twinks" because they are "flamey" or effeminate, in the lesbian community women feel safe to challenge or play with traditional gender roles. Some lesbians "pass" for men and enjoy the strength that image gives them. Weight-related issues may be a concern for some lesbians, but not for others, taking a back seat to these gender-role issues. Their different attitudes about weight-related issues in fact may reflect which role a lesbian primarily identifies with. Some research suggests lesbians who are on the "lipstick femme" end of lesbianism may experience lower body satisfaction than those who identify with the more masculine "butch" role.[132] These differences within lesbian culture help our understanding of the impact of the Cult of Thinness on the lesbian community. In addition, lesbian women who are dissatisfied with their bodies, but who are acutely aware that this dissatisfaction is culturally based, may deal with it in a healthier way than heterosexual women.

## Globalization of Eating Issues

It appears that eating disorder rates are increasing in other Western and non-Western societies. According to a recent *Christian Science Monitor* article, anorexia rates in Argentina surpass those in the United States.  74

> In this beauty-conscious nation, which has the world's second-highest rate of anorexia (after Japan), many are partially blaming the country's clothing industry for offering only tiny sizes of the latest fashions. The result, say many health experts, is a dangerous paradox of girls and women adapting to the clothes rather than clothes adapting to them. Prompted by anecdotal evidence and expert testimony, the Argentine legislature is considering whether to force clothing manufacturers to cover "all the anthropometric measurements of the Argentine woman" up to size 54 (the equivalent of extra large in the United States).[133]

As globalization spreads Western values to other nations, American society's "Cult of Thinness" message promises to envelope these nations' young women in a complex web of eating disorders and eating problems.[134] Satellite television transmits these values across all cultures, regardless of race, class, and level of industrial advancement. Developing societies import Caucasian beauty ideals with every purchase of Western media, clothing styles, and beauty products. As non-Western women attempt to meet the ideal, they may deny the very features that give them their racial and ethnic identities—and their unique beauty.  75

Susie Orbach, author of *Fat Is a Feminist Issue*,[135] notes that  76

> if you want to measure a culture's engagement with globalism, go look at the level of eating problems. It's probably a better indicator than economic ones. In cultures in which a small group of people are allowed to be Westernised the immediate thing is that they try to create a Western body.[136]

A recent study analyzed Western culture's impact on the relatively isolated island of Fiji. Traditionally, Fijians view weight loss as a sign of  77 illness and deteriorating health. When American television programming was introduced to the island in 1995, none of the girls surveyed reported that they practiced self-induced vomiting to lose weight.[137] After 3 years of American TV exposure, that number had jumped to 11.3%.[138] That same year, 1998, 74% of girls reported feeling "'too big or fat' at least some of the time" and 62% stated that they had dieted in the last month.[139] The island's cultural understanding of beauty is drastically changing. What has happened in Fiji may serve as a warning to other global economies that have embraced Western culture.[140]

Unless cultural globalization takes a different turn, rejecting the idealized Western body, the ultra-thin ideal and its effects on young women are likely to spread dangerously throughout the world.

78

## NOTES

1. See: Madeline Altabe, "Ethnicity and Body Image: Quantitative and Qualitative Analysis," *International Journal of Eating Disorders*, 23, no. 2 (1998): 153–59; Declan T. Barry, Carlos M. Grilo, and Robin Masheb, "Gender Differences in Patients with Binge Eating Disorder," *International Journal of Eating Disorders*, 31, no. 1 (2002): 63–70; Renee A. Botta, "The Mirror of Television: A Comparison of Black and White Adolescents' Body Image," *Journal of Communication*, 50, no. 3 (2000): 144–59; Jack Demarest and Rita Allen, "Body Image: Gender, Ethnic, and Age Differences," *Journal of Social Psychology*, 140, no. 4 (2000): 465–72.

2. Karen Schneider, "Mission Impossible," *People Weekly*, June 1996, p. 71.

3. Ibid.

4. L.M. Mellin, S. Scully, and C.E. Irwin, *Disordered Eating Characteristics in Preadolescent Girls*, Paper presented at American Dietetic Association Annual Meeting, Las Vegas, NV, October 28, 1986; David M. Stein and Paula Reichert, "Extreme Dieting Behaviors in Early Adolescence," *Journal of Early Adolescence*, 10, no. 2 (1990): 108–21.

5. Dianne Neumark-Sztainer and Peter J. Hannan, "Weight-Related Behaviors among Adolescent Girls and Boys," *Archives of Pediatrics and Adolescent Medicine*, 154, no. 6 (2000): 570–71.

6. Ibid.

7. R.H. Striegel-Moore, "Prevention of Bulimia Nervosa: Questions and Challenges," in *The Etiology of Bulimia Nervosa: The Individual and Familial Context*, ed. Janis H. Crowther, Daniel L. Tennenbaum, Stevan E. Hobfoll, and Mary Ann Parris Stephens (Washington, D.C.: Hemisphere Publishing, 1992), 203–23.

8. Ibid., 212.

9. I. Attie and J. Brooks-Gunn, "Weight Concerns as Chronic Stressors in Women," in *Gender and Stress*, ed. R.C. Barnett, L. Beiner, and G.K. Baruch (New York: Free Press, 1987), 233. See also: Striegel-Moore, "Prevention of Bulimia Nervosa," 213.

10. Jenifer Davis and Robert Oswalt, "Societal Influences on a Thinner Body Size in Children," *Perceptual and Motor Skills*, 74, no. 3 (1992): 697–98.

11. Attie and Brooks-Gunn, "Weight Concerns as Chronic Stressors In Women," 218–54. See especially: M.P. Levine and L. Smolak, "Toward a Model of the Developmental Psychopathology of Eating Disorders: The Example of Early Adolescence," in *The Etiology of Bulimia Nervosa: The Individual and Familial Context*, ed. J.H. Crowther, D.L. Tennenbaum, S.E. Hobfoll, and M.A.P. Stephens (London: Hemisphere Publishing, 1992), 69–70.

12. See: Deborah Dunlap Marino and Janet C. King, "Nutritional Concerns during Adolescence," *Pediatric Clinics of North America*, 27, no. 1 (1980): 125–39; M.P. Warren, "Physical and Biological Aspects of Puberty," in *Girls at Puberty: Biological and Psycho-*

*social Perspectives,* ed. J. Brooks-Gunn and A.C. Petersen (New York: Plenum, 1983). A certain amount of fat on the body is required for reproduction. Adolescent girls undergo an increase in fat around puberty.

13. S. Shapiro, M. Newcomb, and T.B. Loeb. "Fear of Fat, Disregulated-Restrained Eating, and Body-esteem: Prevalence and Gender Differences among Eight- and Ten-Year-Old Children," *Journal of Clinical Child Psychology,* 26, no. 4 (1997): 358–65.

14. U.S. Department of Health and Human Services, "Prevalence of Overweight and Obesity among Adults: United States, 1999–2002," http://www.cdc.gov./nchs/products/pubs/pubd/hestats/obese/obse99.htm.

15. Roberta Pollack Seid, *Never Too Thin: Why Women Are at War with Their Bodies* (New York: Prentice-Hall Press, 1989), 173.

16. Ellen A. Schur, Mary Sanders, and Hans Steiner, "Body Dissatisfaction and Dieting in Young Children," *International Journal of Eating Disorders,* 27, no. 1 (2000): 74.

17. Karen J. Pine, "Children's Perceptions of Body Shape: A Thinness Bias in Pre-Adolescent Girls and Associations with Femininity," *Clinical Child Psychology and Psychiatry,* 6, no. 4 (2001): 527.

18. Ibid., 528.

19. Ibid., 534.

20. Ibid., 533.

21. Anorexia Nervosa and Related Eating Disorders, Inc. (ANRED), http://www.anred.com.

22. Ibid.

23. Ibid.

24. Cynthia M. Bulik, Lauren Reba, Anna-Marie Siega-Riz, and Ted Reichborn-Kjennerud, "Anorexia Nervosa: Definition, Epidemiology, and Cycle of Risk," *International Journal of Eating Disorders,* 37, no. S1 (2005): S2–S9.

25. L.M. Mellin et al., "Disordered Eating Characteristics in Preadolescent Girls."

26. Dianne Neumark-Sztainer et al., "Disordered Eating among Adolescents: Associations with Sexual/Physical Abuse and Other Familial/Psychosocial Factors," *International Journal of Eating Disorders,* 28, no. 3 (2000): 252.

27. For a discussion of the research literature on "fear of fat" in young children, see: M.H. Thelen, C.M. Lawrence, and A.L. Powell, "Body Image, Weight Control and Eating Disorders among Children," in *The Etiology of Bulimia Nervosa: The Individual and Familial Context,* ed. J.H. Crowther, D.L. Tennenbaum, S.E. Hobfoll, and M.A.P. Stephens (London: Hemisphere Publishing, 1992.), 81–101. A note of caution must be voiced here. Some researchers note that while teenage girls may talk about fear of fat and dieting, these attitudes may not translate into severe dieting behaviors, as some research on adolescents suggests. A recent study by Mark Nichter and Mimi Nichter questioned adolescents about their dieting behavior by asking "What does being on a diet mean?" They noted that, for teens, being on a diet "often constitutes a ritual activity wherein the consumption of token foods is suspended." See: Mark Nichter and Mimi Nichter, "Hype and Weight," *Medical Anthropology,* 13, no.3 (1991): 264. "Fat Talk" among adolescents has important consequences even if these attitudes do not readily translate into severe dieting. Researchers Mimi Nichter and Nancy Vuckovic's longitudinal study of adolescent teens' "fat talk" suggests that "by engaging in fat talk, females present themselves to others as responsible beings concerned about their appearance. . . . Irrespective of what actions girls are taking to achieve their body goals, they are attempting to reproduce the cultural ideal through their discourse." See: Mimi Nichter and Nancy Vuckovic, "Fat Talk: Body Image among Adolescent Girls," in *Many Mirrors: Body Image and Social Relations,* ed. Nicole Sault (New Brunswick, NJ: Rutgers University Press, 1994), 127.

28. N. Moses, M. Banilivy, and F. Lifshitz, "Fear of Obesity among Adolescent Girls," *Pediatrics,* 83, no. 3 (1989): 393–98. Other research studies reveal similar results. For an excellent review of the literature on eating disorders among children, see: M.H. Thelen,

C.M. Lawrence, and A.L. Powell, "Body Image, Weight Control, and Eating Disorders among Children," in *The Etiology of Bulimia Nervosa: The Individual and Familial Context*, ed. J.H. Crowther, D.L. Tennenbaum, S.E. Hobfoll, and M.A.P. Stephens (London: Hemisphere Publishing, 1992), 81–101.

29. Gail McVey, Stacey Tweed, and Elizabeth Blackmore, "Dieting among Preadolescent and Young Adolescent Females," *Canadian Medical Association Journal*, 170, no. 10 (2004): 1560.

30. See: F. Lifshitz, N. Moses, C. Cervantes, and L. Ginsberg, "Nutritional Dwarfing in Adolescents," *Seminars in Adolescent Medicine*, 3 no. 4 (1987): 255–66; F. Lifshitz and N. Moses, "Nutritional Dwarfing: Growth, Dieting, and Fear of Obesity," *Journal of the American College of Nutrition*, 7, no. 5 (1988): 367–76.

31. See: F. Lifshitz et al., "Nutritional Dwarfing in Adolescents," 255.

32. L. Smolak, M.P. Levine, and R. Schermer, "Parental Input and Weight Concerns among Elementary School Children," *International Journal of Eating Disorders*, 25, no. 3 (1999): 263–71.

33. J. Ogden and J. Steward, "The Role of the Mother-Daughter Relationship in Explaining Weight Concern," *International Journal of Eating Disorders*, 28, no. 1 (2000): 78–83.

34. Michael Levine, "10 Things Parents Can Do to Help Prevent Eating Disorders," http://www.nationaleatingdisorders.org.

35. See: Jane Wardle and Rachel Watters, "Sociocultural Influences on Attitudes to Weight and Eating: Results of a Natural Experiment," *International Journal of Eating Disorders*, 35, no. 4 (2004): 589–96.

36. See: Lina A. Ricciardelli, Marita P. MacCabe, and Jennifer Finemore, "The Role of Puberty, Media, and Popularity with Peers on Strategies to Increase Weight, Decrease Weight, and Increase Muscle Tone among Adolescent Boys and Girls," *Journal of Psychosomatic Research*, 52, no. 3 (2002): 145–54.

37. Lina A. Ricciardelli and Marita P. McCabe, "A Longitudinal Analysis of the Role of Biopsychosocial Factors in Predicting Body Change Strategies among Adolescent Boys," *Sex Roles: A Journal of Research*, 48, nos. 7–8 (2003): 349–60.

38. Jacqueline N. Stanford and Marita P. McCabe, "Evaluation of Body Image Prevention Programme for Adolescent Boys," *European Eating Disorders Review*, 13, no. 5 (2005): 360–70.

39. See: Marita P. MacCabe and Lina A. Ricciardelli, "Body Image and Body Change Techniques among Young Adolescent Boys," *European Eating Disorders Review*, 9, no. 5 (2001): 335–47.

40. M. Millman, *Such a Pretty Face: Being Fat in America* (New York: Berkeley, 1981), 224.

41. Carol J. Nemeroff, R.I. Stein, N.S. Diehl, and K.M. Smilack, "From the Cleavers to the Clintons: Role Choices and Body Orientation as Reflected in Magazine Article Content," *International Journal of Eating Disorders*, 16, no. 2 (1994): 167, 173.

42. See: M.E. Mishkind, J. Rodin, L.R. Silberstein, and R.H. Striegel-Moore, "The Embodiment of Masculinity: Cultural, Psychological and Behavioral Dimensions," *American Behavioral Scientist*, 29 (1986); 545–62. See also: "You're So Vain," *Newsweek*, April 1986, pp. 48–55.

43. David M. Garner, "The 1997 Body Image Survey Results," *Psychology Today*, 30, no. 1 (1997): 42.

44. Ibid.

45. Ibid.

46. Ibid., 35.

47. Gordon B. Forbes, Leah E. Adams-Curtis, Brooke Rade, and Peter Jaberg, "Body Dissatisfaction in Women and Men: The Role of Gender-Typing and Self-Esteem," *Sex Roles*, 44, no. 7/8 (2001): 471.

48. Ibid.

49. Ibid.

50. D. MacCannell and J.F. MacCannell, "The Beauty System," in *The Ideology of Conduct: Essays in Literature and the History of Sexuality*, ed. N. Armstrong and L. Tennenhouse (New York: Methuen, 1987), 207.

51. J. Rodin, *Body Traps: Breaking the Binds That Keep You from Feeling Good about Your Body* (New York: William Morrow, 1992), 38–39.

52. Harrison G. Pope, Katherine A. Phillips, and Roberto Olivardia, *The Adonis Complex* (New York: Free Press, 2000), 23–24.

53. Seid, *Never Too Thin*, 116.

54. Adam Drewnowski and Doris K. Yee, "Men and Body Image: Are Males Satisfied with Their Body Weight?" *Psychosomatic Medicine*, 49, no. 6 (1987): 626–34.

55. Rodin, *Body Traps*, 181.

56. Drewnowski and Yee, "Men and Body Image," 632.

57. Ibid.

58. Garner, "The 1997 Body Image Survey Results," 42.

59. Ibid.

60. D. Blake Woodside et al., "Comparisons of Men with Full or Partial Eating Disorders, Men without Eating Disorders, and Women with Eating Disorders in the Community," *American Journal of Psychiatry*, 158, no. 4 (2001): 570–74.

61. Devra L. Braun, Suzanne R. Sunday, Amy Huang, and Katherine A. Halmi, "More Males Seek Treatment for Eating Disorders," *International Journal of Eating Disorders*, 25, no. 4 (1999): 515.

62. Trent A. Petrie and Rebecca Rogers. "Extending the Discussion of Eating Disorders to Include Men and Athletes," *The Counseling Psychologist*, 29, no. 5 (2001): 475.

63. Woodside et al., "Comparisons of Men with Full or Partial Eating Disorders," 571.

64. Rodin, *Body Traps*, 88.

65. Harry Gwirtsman, cited in Judy Folkenberg, "Bulimia: Not for Women Only," *Psychology Today*, 18 (March 1984): 10.

66. Braun et al., "More Males Seek Treatment for Eating Disorders," 421.

67. Ibid.

68. Nancy Clark, "Mirror, Mirror on the Wall . . . Are Muscular Men the Best of All? The Hidden Turmoil of Muscle Dysmorphia—Nutrition," *American Fitness*, January–February 2004, http://www.looksmartfitness.com/p/articles/mi_m0675/is_1_22/ai_112408511.

69. Pope et al., *The Adonis Complex*, 13–14.

70. Roberto Olivardia, Harrison G. Pope, and James I. Hudson, "Muscle Dysmorphia in Male Weightlifters: A Case-Control Study," *American Journal of Psychiatry*, 157, no. 8 (2000): 1291.

71. Pope et al., *The Adonis Complex*, 8.

72. Ibid., 9.

73. Ibid., 10.

74. Ibid.

75. B. Mangweth et al., "Body Image and Psychopathology in Male Bodybuilders," *Psychotheraphy and Psychosomatics*, 70, no. 1 (2001): 41.

76. Olivardia et al., "Muscle of Dysmorphia in Male Weighlifters," 1294.

77. Mishkind et al., "The Embodiment of Masculinity," 549.

78. Harrison G. Pope, "Unraveling the Adonis Complex," *Psychiatric Times*, 18, no. 3 (March 2001), http://www.psychiatrictimes.com/p010353.html.

79. American Society for Aesthetic Plastic Surgery (ASAPS), http://www.surgery.org.

80. Ibid.

81. Ibid.

82. See: M.B. King and G. Mezey, "Eating Behavior of Male Racing Jockeys," *Psychological Medicine*, 17 (1987): 249–53; S.N. Steen, R.A. Oppliger, and K.D. Brownell, "Metabolic Effects of Repeated Weight Loss and Regain in Adolescent Wrestlers," *Journal of the American Medical Association*, 260 (1988): 47–50.

83. Millman, *Such a Pretty Face*, 225.

84. David Crawford, *Easing the Ache: Gay Men Recovering from Compulsive Disorders* (New York: Dutton, 1990), 126.

85. Mishkind et al., "The Embodiment of Masculinity," 455.

86. A.D. Mickalide, "Sociocultural Factors Influencing Weight among Males," in Arnold M. Andersen, *Males with Eating Disorders* (New York: Brunner/Mazel, 1990), 30–39.

87. See: D. Garner and P.E. Garfinkel, "Socio-Cultural Factors in the Development of Anorexia Nervosa," *Psychological Medicine*, 10, no. 4 (1980): 647–56; D.M. Garner, P.E. Garfinkel, D. Schwartz, and M. Thompson, "Cultural Expectations of Thinness in Women," *Psychological Reports*, 47, no. 2 (1980): 483–91; E.D. Rothblum, "Women and Weight: Fad and Fiction," *Journal of Psychology*, 124, no. 1 (1990): 5–24.

88. See: M.P. Warren and R.L. Vande Wiele, "Clinical and Metabolic Features of Anorexia Nervosa," *American Journal of Obstetrics and Gynecology*, 117, no. 3 (1973): 435–49; H. Bruch, "Anorexia Nervosa and Its Differential Diagnosis," *Journal of Nervous Mental Disease*, 141 (1966): 555–66; D.J. Jones, M.M. Fox, H.M. Babigian, and H.E. Hutton, "Epidemiology of Anorexia Nervosa in Monroe County, New York: 1960–1976." *Psychosomatic Medicine*, 42, no. 6 (1980): 551–58.

89. See: Elizabeth Rieger, Stephen Touyz, Tony Swain, and Peter Beaumont, "Cross-Cultural Research on Anorexia Nervosa: Assumptions Regarding the Role of Body Weight, "*International Journal of Eating Disorders*, 29, no. 2 (2001): 205–15; G.A. German, "Aspects of Clinical Psychiatry in Sub-Saharan Africa," *British Journal of Psychiatry*, 121, no. 564 (1972): 461–79; J.S. Neki, "Psychiatry in South East Asia." *British Journal of Psychiatry*, 123, no. 574 (1973): 257–69; B. Dolan, "Cross-Cultural Aspects of Anorexia Nervosa and Bulimia," *International Journal of Eating Disorders*, 10 (1990): 67–78. See also: A. Furnham and P. Baguma, "Cross-Cultural Differences in the Evaluation of Male and Female Body Shapes," *International Journal of Eating Disorders*, 15, no. 1 (1994): 81–89.

90. Rothblum, "Women and Weight," 5. See also: P.S. Powers, *Obesity: The Regulation of Weight* (Baltimore, MD: Williams & Wilkins, 1980).

91. Furnham and Baguma, "Cross-Cultural Differences in the Evaluation of Male and Female Body Shapes," 88. Sobal and Stunkard note: "Obesity may be a sign of health and wealth in developing societies, the opposite of its meaning in developed countries." They also note the importance of evolution: "Through the millennia, obesity was probably not a possibility for most people. Limited supplies of food characterized the lives of many of our ancestors and are present in many developing societies today." See: J. Sobal and A.J. Stunkard, "Socioeconomic Status and Obesity: A Review of the Literature," *Psychological Bulletin*, 105, no. 2 (1989): 226–67.

92. Emily Bradley Massara, *¡Que Gordita! A Study of Weight among Women in a Puerto Rican Community* (New York: AMS Press, 1989).

93. Ibid., 19.

94. Ibid., 12.

95. Ibid., 171.

96. Ibid., 293.

97. Ibid., 141.

98. Ibid., 145.

99. Ibid., 161.

100. Ibid.

101. It is important to point out that the extent of the spread of the Cult of Thinness depends on a variety of factors within a given ethnic community. Within this community there are the beginnings of intracultural variations in terms of the degree of assimilation. As the second generation of Puerto Ricans in this community comes to gain upward mobility, their susceptibility to the Cult of Thinness may grow as well. As one researcher notes: "Among the African-American and Latina women I interviewed, the degree to which thinness was imposed on them as girls depended upon whether their families'

class had changed, the families' geographical location, the schools the children attended, and nationality," See: B. Thompson, "Food, Bodies, and Growing Up Female: Childhood Lessons about Culture, Race, and Class," in *Feminist Perspectives on Eating Disorders*, ed. P. Fallon, M.A. Katzman, and S.C. Wooley (New York: Guilford Press, 1994), 371.

102. Massara, *!Que Gordita!*, 145.

103. Regarding American society, see: J.E. Smith and J. Krejci, "Minorities Join the Majority: Eating Disturbances among Hispanic and Native American Youth,"*International Journal of Eating Disorders*, 10, no. 2 (1991): 179–86; L.K.G. Hsu, "Are the Eating Disorders Becoming More Common in Blacks?" *International Journal of Eating Disorders*, 6 (1987): 113–24. Regarding non-Western societies as a whole, see: M. Nasser, "Comparative Study of the Prevalence of Abnormal Eating Attitudes among Arab Female Students of Both London and Cairo Universities," *Psychological Medicine*, 16, no. 3 (1986): 621–25; Sobal and Stunkard, "Socioeconomic Status and Obesity," 260–75; Furnham and Baguma, "Cross-Cultural Differences in the Evaluation of Male and Female Body Shapes," 81–89; T. Furukawa, "Weight Changes and Eating Attitudes of Japanese Adolescents under Acculturative Stresses: A Prospective Study," *International Journal of Eating Disorders*, 15, no. 1 (1994): 71–79; L.L. Osvold and G.R. Sodowsky, "Eating Disorders of White American, Racial and Ethnic Minority American, and International Women," *Journal of Multicultural Counseling and Development*, 21, no. 3 (1993): 143–54.

104. Marisol Perez and Thomas E. Joiner, Jr., "Body Image Dissatisfaction and Disordered Eating in Black and White Women," *International Journal of Eating Disorders*, 33, no. 3 (2003): 343.

105. Ibid., 342.

106. Ibid., 343.

107. Ibid., 342.

108. K.S. Buchanan, "Creating Beauty in Blackness," in *Consuming Passions: Feminist Approaches to Weight Preoccupation and Eating Disorders*, ed. C. Brown and K. Jasper (Toronto, Ontario, Canada: Second Story Press, 1993), 37.

109. K.K. Abrams, L.R. Allen, and J.J. Gray, "Disordered Eating Attitudes and Behaviors, Psychiatric Adjustment, and Ethnic Identity: A Comparison of Black and White Female College Students," *International Journal of Eating Disorders*, 14, no. 1 (1993): 49–57.

110. Buchanan, "Creating Beauty in Blackness," 37.

111. P. Collins, *Black Feminist Thought: Knowledge, Consciousness, and the Politics of Empowerment* (Boston: Unwin Hyman, 1990), cited in K.S. Buchanan, "Creating Beauty in Blackness," 79.

112. E. White, "Unhealthy Appetites," *Essence*, September 1991, p. 28. See also: C.S.W. Rand and J.M. Kaldau, "The Epidemiology of Obesity and Self-Defined Weight Problems in the General Population: Gender, Race, Age, and Social Class," *International Journal of Eating Disorders*, 9, no. 3 (1990): 329–43.

113. R. Bray, "Heavy Burden," *Essence*, January 1992, p. 54.

114. M.H. Styles, "Soul, Black Women, and Food," in *A Woman's Conflict: The Special Relationship between Women and Food*, ed. Jane Rachel Kaplan (New York: Prentice Hall, 1980), 161–62. The roots of plants are the primary ingredients of soul food: for example, yams, sweet potatoes, turnips, and "greens" such as collards.

115. Ibid., 163.

116. Ibid., 174–75.

117. I. Attie and J. Brooks-Gunn, "The Development of Eating Regulation across the Life Span," in D. Cicchetti and D. Cohen (eds.), *Developmental Psychopathology: Vol. 2: Risk, Disorder, and Adaptation* (New York: Wiley, 1995): 332–68.

118. R. Streigel-Moore and L. Smolak, "The Role of Race in the Development of Eating Disorders," in L. Smolak and M.P. Levine (eds.), *The Developmental Psychopathology of Eating Disorders: Implications for Research, Prevention, and Treatment* (Mahwah, NJ: Lawrence Erlbaum, 1996), 259–84.

119. Hsu, "Are Eating Disorders Becoming More Common in Blacks?," 122.
120. See: Jalmeen K. Makkar and Michael J. Strube, "Black Women's Self-Perceptions of Attractiveness following Exposure to White versus Black Beauty Standards: The Moderating Role of Social Identity and Self-Esteem," *Journal of Applied Social Psychology*, 25, no. 17 (1995): 1547–66.
121. T.J. Silber, "Anorexia Nervosa in Blacks and Hispanics," *International Journal of Eating Disorders*, 5, no. 1 (1986): 127.
122. Perez and Joiner, "Body Image Dissatisfaction and Disordered Eating in Black and White Women," 343.
123. Ibid., 342.
124. Ruth H. Striegel-Moore et al., "Eating Disorder Symptoms in a Cohort of 11 to 16-Year-Old Black and White Girls: The NHLBI Growth and Health Study," *International Journal of Eating Disorders*, 27, no. 1 (2000): 62.
125. J.A. Ladner, *Tomorrow's Tomorrow: The Black Woman* (New York: Doubleday, 1971).
126. See: Becky Thompson, *A Hunger So Wide and So Deep: A Multiracial View of Women's Eating Problems* (Minneapolis: University of Minnesota Press, 1994). Thompson writes,

> Talking with Latina, African-American, and white women—including both heterosexual and lesbian women—reveals that the origins of eating problems have little or nothing to do with vanity or obsession with appearance. In fact, eating problems begin as survival strategies—as sensible acts of self-preservation—in response to myriad injustices including racism, sexism, homophobia, classism, the stress of acculturation, and emotional, physical, and sexual abuse. (12)

Later Thompson describes bingeing as "a creative coping mechanism in the face of terrible odds. . . . As a drug, food worked quickly to help her [respondent] 'stuff back emotions'" (61). For another respondent of Thompson's, bingeing "made her 'disappear,'" which made her feel protected; it began as a way to numb and block painful feelings" (61).
127. Tory DeAngelis. "Body-Image Problems Affect All Groups," *Monitor on Psychology*, 28, no. 3 (1997): 45.
128. Pamela A. Brand, Esther D. Rothblum, and Laura J. Solomon, "A Comparision of Lesbians, Gay Men, and Heterosexuals on Weight and Restrained Eating," *International Journal of Eating Disorders*, 11, no. 3 (1992): 253.
129. Ibid.
130. Ibid.
131. Ibid., 103.
132. Maryanne R. Ludwig and Kelly D. Brownell, "Lesbians, Bisexual Women, and Body Image: An Investigation of Gender Roles and Social Groups Affiliation," *International Journal of Eating Disorders*, 24 (1997): 89–97.
133. Kelly Hearn, "Which Came First, Thin Women or Tiny Sizes?" *Christian Science Monitor* [Electronic version], February 24, 2005, http://www.csmonitor.com/2005/0224/p12s02-lihc.html.
134. See: Amelia J. Lake, Petra K. Staiger, and Huguette Glowinski, "Effect of Western Culture on Women's Attitudes to Eating and Perceptions of Body Shape," *International Journal of Eating Disorders*, 27, no. 1 (2000): 83–89. See also: K.M. Pike and B.T. Walsh, "Ethnicity and Eating Disorders: Implications for Incidence and Treatment," *Psychopharmacology Bulletin*, 32, no. 2 (1996): 265–74; M.A. Katzman and S. Lee, "Beyond Body Image: The Integration of Feminist and Transcultural Theories in the Understanding of Self Starvation," *International Journal of Eating Disorders*, 22, no. 4 (1997): 385–94; J.E. Pate, A.J. Pumariega, C. Hester, and D.M. Garner, "Cross-cultural Patterns in Eating Disorders: A Review," *Journal of the American Academy of Child and Adolescent Psychiatry*, 31, no. 5 (1992): 802–9.
135. See: Susie Orbach, *Fat Is a Feminist Issue* (New York: Berkeley Press, 1978).

136. Susan Flockhart, "Diet Industry Blamed for Obese Society," *Sunday Herald*, September 15, 2002, http://www.sundayherald.com/print27674.

137. Anne E. Becker, Rebecca A. Burwell, Stephen E. Gilman, David B. Herzog, and Paul Hamburg, "Eating Behaviors and Attitudes following Prolonged Exposure to Television among Ethnic Fijian Adolescent Girls," *British Journal of Psychiatry*, 180, no. 6 (2002): 510.

138. Ibid.

139. Ibid., 511.

140. M.N. Miller and A.J. Pumariega, "Culture and Eating Disorders: A Historical and Cross-cultural Review," *Psychiatry: Interpersonal and Biological Processes*, 64, no. 2 (2001): 93–110.

## BIBLIOGRAPHY

Abrams, K.K., L.R. Allen, & J.J. Gray. "Disordered Eating Attitudes and Behaviors, Psychiatric Adjustment, and Ethnic Identity: A Comparison of Black and White Female College Students." *International Journal of Eating Disorders*, 14, no. 1 (1993): 49–57.

Altabe, M. "Ethnicity and Body Image: Quantitative and Qualitative Analysis," *International Journal of Eating Disorders*, 23, no. 2 (1998): 153–159.

American Society for Aesthetic Plastic Surgery. "ASAPS." http://www.surgery.org.

Anorexia Nervosa and Related Eating Disorders, Inc. "ANRED." http://www.anred.com.

Attie, I., & J. Brooks-Gunn. "The Development of Eating Regulation across the Life Span." In *Developmental Psychopathology: Volume 2. Risk, Disorder, and Adaption*, ed. D. Cicchetti & D. Cohen, pp. 332–368. New York: Wiley, 1995.

Attie, I., & J. Brooks-Gunn. "Weight Concerns as Chronic Stressors in Women." In *Gender and Stress*, ed. R.C. Barnett, L. Biener, & G.K. Baruch, p. 218–254. New York: Free Press, 1987.

Barry, D.T., C.M. Grilo, & R. Masheb. "Gender Differences in Patients with Binge Eating Disorder." *International Journal of Eating Disorders*, 31, no. 1 (2002): 63–70.

Becker, A.E., R.A. Burwell, D.B. Herzog, P. Hamburg, & S.E. Gilman. "Eating Behaviors and Attitudes Following Prolonged Exposure to Television among Ethnic Fijian Adolescent Girls." *British Journal of Psychiatry*, 180, no. 6 (2002): 509–514.

Botta, R.A. "The Mirror of Television: A Comparison of Black and White Adolescents' Body Image." *Journal of Communication*, 50, no. 3 (2000): 144–159.

Brand, P.A., E.D. Rothblum, and L.J. Solomon. "A Comparison of Lesbians, Gay Men and Heterosexuals on Weight and Restrained Eating." *International Journal of Eating Disorders*, 11, no. 3 (1992): 253–259.

Braun, D.L., S.R. Sunday, A. Huang, & K.A. Halmi. "More Males Seek Treatment for Eating Disorders." *International Journal of Eating Disorders*, 25, no. 4 (1999): 415–424.

Bray, R. "Heavy Burden," *Essence*, January 1992, p. 52–54, 90.

Bruch, H. "Anorexia Nervosa and Its Differential Diagnosis." *Journal of Nervous and Mental Disease*, 141 (1966): 555–566.

Buchanan, K.S. "Creating Beauty in Blackness." In *Consuming Passions: Feminist Approaches to Weight Preoccupation and Eating Disorders*, ed. C. Brown & K. Jasper pp. 36–52. Toronto, Ontario, Canada: Second Story Press, 1993.

Bulik, C.M., L. Reba, A.-M. Siega-Riz, & T. Reichborn-Kjennerud. "Anorexia Nervosa: Definition, Epidemiology, and Cycle of Risk." *International Journal of Eating Disorders*, 37, no. S1 (2005): S2–S9.

Clark, N. "Mirror, Mirror on the Wall . . . Are Muscular Men the Best of All? The Hidden Turmoil of Muscle Dysmorphia—Nutrition." *American Fitness*, January–February 2004. http://www.looksmartfitness.com/p/articles/mi_m0675/is_1_22/ai_112408511.

Collins, P. *Black Feminist Thought: Knowledge, Consciousness and the Politics of Empowerment* (Boston: Unwin Hyman, 1990), cited in K.S. Buchanan, "Creating Beauty in

Blackness," in *Consuming Passions: Feminist Approaches to Weight Preoccupation and Eating Disorders*, eds. C. Brown and K. Jasper (Toronto, Ontario, Canada: Second Story Press, 1993), 79.

Crawford, D. *Easing the Ache: Gay Men Recovering from Compulsive Disorders*. New York: Dutton, 1990.

Davis, J., & R. Oswalt. "Societal Influences on a Thinner Body Size in Children." *Perceptual and Motor Skills*, 74, no. 3 (1992): 697–698.

DeAngelis, T. "Body-Image Problems Affect All Groups." *Monitor on Psychology*, 28, no. 3 (1997): 45.

Demarest, J. & R. Allen. "Body Image: Gender, Ethnic, and Age Differences." *Journal of Social Psychology*, 140, no. 4 (2000): 465–472.

Dolan, B. "Cross-Cultural Aspects of Anorexia Nervosa and Bulimia." *International Journal of Eating Disorders*, 10 (1990): 67–78.

Drewnowski, A., & D.K. Yee. "Men and Body Image: Are Males Satisfied with Their Body Weight?" *Psychosomatic Medicine*, 49, no. 6 (1987): 626–634.

Flockhart, S. "Diet Industry Blamed for Obese Society." *Sunday Herald*, September 15, 2002 [Electronic version]. http://www.sundayherald.com/print27674.

Folkenberg, J. "Bulimia: Not for women only." *Psychology Today*, 18 (March 1984): 10.

Forbes, G.B., L.E. Adams-Curtis, B. Rade, & P. Jaberg. "Body Dissatisfaction in Women and Men: The Role of Gender-Typing and Self-Esteem." *Sex Roles*, 44, no. 7/8 (2001): 461–484.

Furnham, A. & P. Baguma. "Cross-Cultural Differences in the Evaluation of Male and Female Body Shape," *International Journal of Eating Disorders*, 15, no. 1 (1994): 81–89.

Furukawa, T. "Weight Changes and Eating Attitudes of Japanese Adolescent under Acculturative Stress: A Prospective Study," *International Journal of Eating Disorders*, 15, no. 1 (1994): 71–79.

Garner, D.M. "The 1997 Body Image Survey Results." *Psychology Today*, 30, no. 1 (1997): 30–44.

Garner D., & P.E. Garfinkel, "Socio-Cultural Factors in the Development of Anorexia Nervosa," *Psychological Medicine*, 10, no. 4 (1980): 647–656.

Garner D.M., P.E. Garfinkel, D. Schwartz, & M. Thompson. "Cultural Expectations of Thinness in Women." *Psychological Reports*, 47, no. 2 (1980): 483–491.

German, G.A. "Aspects of Clinical Psychiatry in Sub-Saharan Africa." *British Journal of Psychiatry*, 121, no. 564 (1972): 461–479.

Hearn, K. "Which Came First, Thin Women or Tiny Sizes?" *The Christian Science Monitor* [Electronic version]. http://www.csmonitor.com/2005/0224/p12s02-lihc.html (accessed February 24, 2005).

Hsu, L.K.G. "Are the Eating Disorders Becoming More Common in Blacks?" *International Journal of Eating Disorders*, 6, no. 1 (1987): 113–124.

Jones, D.J., M.M. Fox, H.M. Babigian, & H.E. Hutton, "Epidemiology of Anorexia Nervosa in Monroe County, New York: 1960–1976." *Psychosomatic Medicine*, 42, no. 6 (1980): 551–558.

Katzman, M.A., & S. Lee. "Beyond Body Image: The Integration of Feminist and Transcultural Theories in the Understanding of Self Starvation." *International Journal of Eating Disorders*, 22, no. 4 (1997): 385–394.

King, M.B. & G. Mezey. "Eating Behavior of Male Racing Jockeys," *Psychological Medicine*, 17, no. 1 (1987): 249–253.

Ladner, J.A. *Tomorrow's Tomorrow: The Black Woman*. New York: Doubleday, 1971.

Lake, A.J., P.K. Staiger, and H. Glowinski. "Effect of Western Culture on Women's Attitudes to Eating and Perceptions of Body Shape." *International Journal of Eating Disorders*, 27, no. 1 (2000): 83–89.

Levine, M. "10 Things Parents Can Do to Help Prevent Eating Disorders." http://www.nationaleatingdisorders.org.

Levine, M.P., & L. Smolak, "Toward a Model of the Developmental Psychopathology of Eating Disorders: The Example of Early Adolescence." In *The Etiology of Bulimia*

*Nervosa: The Individual and Familial Context*, ed. J.H. Crowther, D.L. Tennenbaum, S.E. Hobfoll, & M.A.P. Stephens, pp. 59–80. London: Hemisphere Publishing, 1992.

Lifshitz, F., & N. Moses. "Nutritional Dwarfing: Growth, Dieting, and Fear of Obesity." *Journal of the American College of Nutrition*, 7, no. 5 (1988): 367–376.

Lifshitz, F., N. Moses, C. Cervantes, & L. Ginsberg, "Nutritional Dwarfing in Adolescents." *Seminars in Adolescent Medicine*, 3, no. 4 (1987): 255–266.

Ludwig, M.R., & K.D. Brownell. "Lesbians, Bisexual Women, and Body Image: An Investigation of Gender Roles and Social Groups Affiliation." *International Journal of Eating Disorders*, 25, no. 1 (1999): 89–97.

MacCannell, D., & J.F. MacCannell. "The Beauty System." In *The Ideology of Conduct: Essays in Literature and the History of Sexuality*, ed. N. Armstrong & L. Tennenhouse, pp. 206–238. New York: Methuen, 1987.

Makkar, J.K. & M.J. Strube. "Black Women's Self-Perceptions of Attractiveness Following Exposure to White versus Black Beauty Standards: The Moderating Role of Racial Identity and Self-Esteem." *Journal of Applied Social Psychology*, 25, no. 17 (1995): 1547–1566.

Mangweth, B., H.G. Pope, Jr., G. Kemmler, C. Ebenbichler, A. Hausmann, C. De Col, B. Kreutner, J. Kinzl, & W. Biebl. "Body Image and Psychopathology in Male Bodybuilders." *Psychotherapy and Psychosomatics*, 70, no. 1 (2001): 41.

Marino, D.D. & J.C. King. "Nutritional Concerns during Adolescence." *Pediatric Clinics of North America*, 27, no. 7 (1980): 125–139.

Massara, E.B. *¡Que Gordita! A Study of Weight among Women in a Puerto Rican Community*. New York: AMS Press, 1989.

McVey, G., S. Tweed, & E. Blackmore. "Dieting among Preadolescent and Young Adolescent Females." *Canadian Medical Association Journal*, 170, no. 10 (2004): 1559–1561.

Mellin, L.M., S. Scully, & C.E. Irwin. *Disordered Eating Characteristics in Preadolescent Girls*. Paper presented at American Dietetic Association Annual Meeting, Las Vegas, NV, October 28, 1986.

Mickalide, A.D. "Sociocultural Factors Influencing Weight among Males." *Males with Eating Disorders*, ed. A.M. Andersen, pp. 30–39. New York: Brunner/Mazel, 1990.

Miller, M.N., & A.J. Pumariega. "Culture and Eating Disorders: A Historical and Cross-Cultural Review." *Psychiatry: Interpersonal and Biological Processes*, 64, no. 2 (2001): 93–110.

Millman, M. *Such a Pretty Face: Being Fat in America*. New York: Berkeley, 1981.

Mishkind, M.E., J. Rodin, L.R. Silberstein, & R.H. Striegel-Moore. "The Embodiment of Masculinity: Cultural, Psychological, and Behavioral Dimensions." *American Behavioral Scientist*, 29, no. 5 (1986): 545–562.

Moses, N., M. Banilivy, & F. Lifshitz. "Fear of Obesity among Adolescent Girls." *Pediatrics*, 83, no. 3 (1989): 393–398.

Nasser, M. "Comparative Study of the Prevalence of Abnormal Eating Attitudes among Arab Female Students of Both London and Cairo Universities." *Psychological Medicine*, 16, no. 3 (1986): 621–625.

Neki, J.S. "Psychiatry in South East Asia." *British Journal of Psychiatry*, 123, no. 574 (1973): 257–269.

Nemeroff, C.J., R.I. Stein, N.S. Diehl, & K.M. Smilack. "From the Cleavers to the Clintons: Role Choices and Body Orientation as Reflected in Magazine Article Content." *International Journal of Eating Disorders*, 16, no. 2 (1994): 167–176.

Neumark-Sztainer, D., & P.J. Hannan. "Weight-Related Behaviors among Adolescent Girls and Boys." *Archives of Pediatrics and Adolescent Medicine*, 154, no. 6 (2000): 569–577.

Neumark-Sztainer, D., M. Story, P.J. Hannan, T. Beuhring, & M.D. Resnick. "Disordered Eating among Adolescents: Associations with Sexual/Physical Abuse and Other Familial/Psychosocial Factors." *International Journal of Eating Disorders*, 28, no. 3 (2000): 249–258.

Nichter, M., & M. Nichter. "Hype and Weight." *Medical Anthropology*, 13, no. 3 (1991): 249–284.

Nichter, M. & N. Vuckovic. "Fat Talk: Body Image among Adolescent Girls." In *Many Mirrors: Body Image and Social Relations*, ed. N. Sault, pp. 109–131. New Brunswick, NJ: Rutgers University Press, 1994.

Ogden, J., & J. Steward. "The Role of the Mother-Daughter Relationship in Explaining Weight Concern." *International Journal of Eating Disorders*, 28, no. 1 (2000): 78–83.

Olivardia, R., H.G. Pope, & J.I. Hudson. "Muscle Dysmorphia in Male Weightlifters: A Case-Control Study." *American Journal of Psychiatry*, 157, no. 8 (2000): 1291–1296.

Orbach, S. *Fat Is a Feminist Issue*. New York: Berkeley Press, 1978.

Osvold, L.L., & G.R. Sodowsky. "Eating Disorders of White American, Racial and Ethnic Minority American, and International Women." *Journal of Multicultural Counseling and Development*, 21, no. 3 (1993): 143–154.

Pate, J.E., A.J. Pumariega, C. Hester, & D.M. Garner. "Cross-cultural patterns in eating disorders: A review." *Journal of the American Academy of Child and Adolescent Psychiatry*, 31, no. 5 (1992): 802–809.

Perez, M., & T.E. Joiner, Jr. "Body Image Dissatisfaction and Disordered Eating in Black and White Women." *International Journal of Eating Disorders*, 33, no. 3 (2003): 342–350.

Petrie, T.A., & R. Rogers. "Extending the Discussion of Eating Disorders to Include Men and Athletes." *Counseling Psychologist*, 29, no. 5 (2001): 743–753.

Pike, K.M., & B.T. Walsh. "Ethnicity and Eating Disorders: Implications for Incidence and Treatment." *Psychopharmacology Bulletin*, 32, no. 2 (1996): 265–274.

Pine, K.J. "Children's Perceptions of Body Shape: A Thinness Bias in Pre-Adolescent Girls and Associations with Femininity." *Clinical Child Psychology and Psychiatry*, 6, no. 4 (2001): 519–536.

Pope, H.G. "Unraveling the Adonis Complex." *Psychiatric Times*, 18, no. 3 (March 2001) [Electronic version]. http://www.psychiatrictimes.com/p010353.html.

Pope, H.G., K.A. Phillips, and R. Olivardia. *The Adonis Complex: The Secret Crisis of Male Body Obsession*. New York: Free Press, 2000.

Powers, P.A. *Obesity: The Regulation of Weight*. Baltimore, MD: Williams & Wilkins, 1980.

Rand, C.S.W., & J.M. Kuldau. "The Epidemiology of Obesity and Self-Defined Weight Problems in the General Population: Gender, Race, Age, and Social Class." *International Journal of Eating Disorders*, 9, no. 3 (1990): 329–343.

Random House of Canada, Ltd. "Pamela Paul: Author Spotlight." 2005. http://www.randomhouse.ca/catalog/author.pperl?authorid=23378.

Ricciardelli, L.A., & M.P. McCabe. "A Longitudinal Analysis of the Role of Biopsychosocial Factors in Predicting Body Change Strategies Among Adolescent Boys." *Sex Roles: A Journal of Research*, 48, nos. 7–8 (2003): 349–360.

Ricciardelli, L.A., & M.P. McCabe. "Body Image and Body Change Techniques among Young Adolescent Boys." *European Eating Disorders Review*, 9, no. 5 (2001): 335–347.

Ricciardelli, L.A., M.P. McCabe, & J. Finemore. "The Role of Puberty, Media and Popularity with Peers on Strategies to Increase Weight, Decrease Weight and Increase Muscle Tone among Adolescent Boys and Girls." *Journal of Psychosomatic Research*, 52, no. 3 (2002): 145–154.

Rieger, E., S.W. Touyz, T. Swain, & P.J.V. Beumont. "Cross-Cultural Research on Anorexia Nervosa: Assumptions Regarding the Role of Body Weight." *International Journal of Eating Disorders*, 29, no. 2 (2001): 205–215.

Rodin, J. *Body Traps: Breaking the Binds That Keep You from Feeling Good about Your Body*. New York: William Morrow, 1992.

Rothblum, E.D. "Women and Weight: Fad and Friction." *Journal of Psychology*, 124, no. 1 (1990): 5–24.

Schneider, K. "Mission Impossible." *People Weekly*, June 1996, pp. 65–73.

Schur, E.A., M. Sanders, & H. Steiner. "Body Dissatisfaction and Dieting in Young Children." *International Journal of Eating Disorders*, 27, no. 1 (2000): 74–82.

Seid, R.P. *Never Too Thin: Why Women Are at War with Their Bodies*. New York: Prentice-Hall Press, 1989.

Shapiro, S., M. Newcomb, & T.B. Loeb, "Fear of Fat, Disregulated-Restrained Eating, and Body-Esteem: Prevalence and Gender Differences among Eight- to Ten-Year-Old Children." *Journal of Clinical Child Psychology*, 26, no. 4 (1997): 358–365.

Silber, T.J. "Anorexia Nervosa in Blacks and Hispanics." *International Journal of Eating Disorders*, 5, no. 1 (1986): 121–128.

Smith, J.E. & J. Krejci. "Minorities Join the Majority: Eating Disturbances among Hispanic and Native American Youth." *International Journal of Eating Disorders*, 10, no. 2 (1991): 179–186.

Smolak, L., M.P. Levine, & R. Schermer. "Parental Input and Weight Concerns among Elementary School Children." *International Journal of Eating Disorders*, 25, no. 3 (1999): 263–271.

Sobal, J., & A.J. Stunkard. "Socioeconomic Status and Obesity: A Review of the Literature." *Psychological Bulletin*, 105, no. 2 (1989): 260–275.

Stanford, J.N. & M.P. McCabe. "Evaluation of Body Image Prevention Programme for Adolescent Boys." *European Eating Disorders Review*, 13, no. 5 (2005): 360–370.

Steen, S.N., R.A. Oppliger, & K.D. Brownell, "Metabolic Effects of Repeated Weight Loss and Regain in Adolescent Wrestlers." *Journal of the American Medical Association*, 260, no. 1 (1988): 47–50.

Stein, D.M., & P. Reichert. "Extreme Dieting Behaviors in Early Adolescence." *Journal of Early Adolescence*, 10, no. 2 (1990): 108–121.

Striegel-Moore, R.H. "Prevention of Bulimia Nervosa: Questions and Challenges." In *The Etiology of Bulimia Nervosa: The Individual and Familial Context*, ed. J.H. Crowther, D.L. Tennenbaum, S.E. Hobfoll, & M.A.P Stephens, pp. 203–223. Washington, DC: Hemisphere Publishing, 1992.

Striegel-Moore, R.H., G.B. Schreiber, A. Lo, P. Crawford, E. Obarzanek, & J. Rodin. "Eating Disorder Symptoms in a Cohort of 11 to 16-Year-Old Black and White Girls: The NHLBI Growth and Health Study." *International Journal of Eating Disorders*, 27, no. 1. (2000):49–66.

Strigel-Moore, R., & L. Smolak, "The Role of Race in the Development of Eating Disorders." In *The Developmental Psychopathology of Eating Disorders: Implications for Research, Prevention, and Treatment*, ed. L. Smolak & M.P. Levine pp. 259–284. Mahwah, NJ: Lawrence Erlbaum, 1996.

Style, M.H. "Soul, Black Women and Food." In *A Woman's Conflict: The Special Relationship between Women and Food*, ed. J.R. Kaplan pp. 161–176. New York: Prentice-Hall, 1980.

Thelen, M.H., C.M. Lawrence, & A.L. Powell. "Body Image, Weight Control and Eating Disorders among Children." In *The Etiology of Bulimia Nervosa: The Individual and Familial Context*, ed. J.H. Crowther, D.L. Tennenbaum, S.E. Hobfoll, & M.A.P. Stephens, pp. 81–101. London: Hemisphere Publishing, 1992.

Thompson, B. "Food, Bodies, and Growing Up Female: Childhood Lessons about Culture, Race, and Class." In *Feminist Perspectives on Eating Disorders*, ed. P. Fallon, M.A. Katzman, & S.C. Wooley, pp. 355–378. New York: The Guilford Press, 1994.

Thompson, B. *A Hunger So Wide and So Deep: A Multiracial View of Women's Eating Problems*. Minneapolis: University of Minnesota Press, 1994.

U.S. Department of Health and Human Services. "Prevalence of Overweight and Obesity among Adults: United States, 1999–2002." http://www.cdc.gov/nchs/products/pubs/pubd/hestats/obese/obse99.htm.

Wardle, J., & R. Watters. "Sociocultural Influence on Attitudes to Weight and Eating: Results of a Natural Experiment." *International Journal of Eating Disorders*, 35, no. 4 (2004): 589–596.

Warren, M.P. "Physical and Biological Aspects of Puberty." In *Girls at Puberty: Biological and Psychosocial Perspectives*, ed. J. Brooks-Gunn & A.C. Petersen, pp. 3–28. New York: Plenum, 1983.

Warren, M.P., & R.L. Vande Wiele. "Clinical and Metabolic Features of Anorexia Nervosa." *American Journal of Obstetrics and Gynecology*, 117, no. 3 (1973): 435–449.

White, E. "Unhealthy Appetites." *Essence*, September 1991, p. 28.

Woodside, D.B., P.E. Garfinkel, E. Lin, P. Goering, A.S. Kaplan, D.S. Goldbloom, & S.H. Kennedy. "Comparisons of Men with Full or Partial Eating Disorders, Men without Eating Disorders, and Women with Eating Disorders in the Community." *American Journal of Psychiatry*, 158, no. 4 (2001): 570–574.

"You're So Vain." *Newsweek*, April 1986, pp. 48–55.

■ ■ ■

## Reading as a Writer: Analyzing Rhetorical Choices

1. Read back through this selection, and take brief notes on how the evidence and claims in each section are similar to and distinct from those in other sections. Underline a specific sentence or two in each section that helps you explain the relationship between that part and the larger argument of the piece.

2. Hesse-Biber uses different kinds of sources to support her claims, including research done by others and the original data she gathered through surveys and interviews. Choose a section of this reading to examine closely, and use different colored pens to "code" the various kinds of sources you see in that section. Be sure to follow the superscript numbers to the "Notes" section to see what kinds of journals and studies Hesse-Biber uses to enrich her own data. What can you say about the strengths and possible shortcomings of her sources?

## Writing as a Reader: Entering the Conversation of Ideas

1. Both Hesse-Biber and Matthew Petrocelli, Trish Oberweis, and Joseph Petrocelli use interview data to develop arguments about men's increasing obsession with a particular kind of muscular body, but they contextualize their research differently. Write a paper in which you place these authors in conversation, comparing the ways they write about gym culture, including the evidence they use and the conclusions they draw. How might the authors of the two essays contribute to, or refute, each other's ideas? What can you conclude about the significance of gym culture in understanding contemporary masculinity?

2. Hesse-Biber's analysis of body obsessions is interesting to consider in light of Judith Lorber's insights about the ways we learn to incorporate gender expectations into the small gestures of our everyday lives. In an essay that draws on insights from both authors, make an argument about some of the specific ways we learn to enforce gender standards on our bodies. You might analyze examples of these behaviors that are fairly harmless as well as those you consider to be harmful. What significance do you see in the range of behaviors we learn to exhibit in order to display bodies that are clearly marked as "feminine" or "masculine"? How do these practices affect the way we understand who we are?

VIRGINIA L. BLUM

# Love My Neighbors, Hate Myself: The Vicissitudes of Affect in Cosmetic Surgery

Virginia Blum is a professor of English at the University of Kentucky whose research includes nineteenth- and twentieth-century literature and culture. She is fascinated by popular culture, as is evident in her book *Flesh Wounds: The Culture of Cosmetic Surgery* (2005), which focuses on contemporary attitudes toward cosmetic surgery. For that book, Blum interviewed more than fifty plastic surgeons and patients in order to find out how people invested in this body-altering business assess their own aspirations and realities in the context of changing cultural standards. The following essay develops this theme through an examination of popular television shows that feature plastic surgery, including *The Swan, I Want a Famous Face*, and *Extreme Makeover*. It first appeared in a collection of essays on body alteration titled *Bodies in the Making: Transgressions and Transformations* (2006), edited by Nancy N. Chen and Helene Moglen.

In this brief but sometimes challenging essay, Blum opens with an observation about the sudden rise in the number of popular television shows about plastic surgery. She suggests that the public enthusiasm for these shows means that plastic surgery has shifted from being "traditionally seen as a hyper-investment in appearance over substance" and instead is now considered "a route toward glowing self-improvement, not as acts of self-loathing but as evidence of self-esteem" (para. 2). In the rest of the essay, Blum develops her argument about this shift in perceptions of cosmetic surgery by looking at the kinds of stories featured on various plastic surgery shows.

Whether or not you are familiar with the shows Blum describes here, you should be able to weigh the evidence she offers in her examples in the context of her point that cosmetic surgery has come to be an expected and increasingly "normal" way for people to maintain their edge in a culture obsessed with youth and physical perfection. Test Blum's ideas against shows currently running on television and against your own knowledge of and attitude toward surgical makeovers. These shows, even if they seem silly at first, offer a glimpse of a truth that Blum believes has implications for all of us—the connections between self-love and self-loathing in contemporary culture.

■ ■ ■

ABC's reality makeover hit, *Extreme Makeover*, surprised everyone, *1* including the network. Originally intended to be a one-off series aired in fall 2002, *Extreme Makeover* created such a sensation that it soon became a staple of ABC's Thursday night reality programming lineup. This extraordinary series features "everyday people" (often expressly identified as working-class) who undergo radical or extreme revisions to their physical appearance. The show's producers choose from an applicant pool based on a number of criteria, including the viability of the procedures candidates request and their presumed psychological health.[1] Typically, the extreme makeover entails a range of interventions on the part of plastic surgeons, cosmetic dentists, dermatologists, and even ophthalmologists. Their physical transformations are followed up by the less invasive and more conventional makeovers of workout regimes, hair style and color, makeup, and wardrobe. This makeover plastic surgery series was swiftly followed by many others including *The Swan, I Want a Famous Face, Plastic Surgery Before and After, Beverly Hills Plastic Surgeon*, and *Dr. 90210*— indeed, we seem to have a unappeasable appetite for stories of surgical rescue stories.

In order for cosmetic surgery (traditionally seen as a hyper-  2 investment in appearance over substance) to have gone so mainstream, certain conventional cultural values had to be recruited on behalf of representing these surgeries not as vain and superficial but as a route toward glowing self-improvement, not as acts of self-loathing but as evidence of self-esteem, and the patients not as passive victims of consumer beauty culture but as take-charge agents eager to author their lives. Cosmetic surgery is no longer dismissed as a silly and imprudent waste of money, but is now condoned as an investment in your future; nor is it the elite purview of the rich and celebrated, but rather (and this is central to the whole industry) a deeply democratizing option. Just as the *Bachelor* and *Bachelorette* series have both reacted to and participated in carving out mainstream cultural fantasies about soul mates and emotional connections, and just as the *Survivor* series has specialized in distilling resourcefulness in a state of nature, plastic surgery makeover programming latches onto a set of widely held American identity motifs that manage to offset the equally widely held negative assessments of both the practice and the kinds of people who could possibly engage in it.

Television is normalizing plastic surgery in US culture in stages. Once  3 relegated to the "special" or exposé or talk-show revelation or even medical channel documentary, cosmetic surgery now occupies primetime in mid-stride from being outrageous to everyday. Just to offer a sense of how rapidly this normalization process is taking place, consider the following: In a *New York Times* article entitled "How Young Is Too Young to Have a Nose Job and Breast Implants?" the reporter writes the following: "The teenagers were notably realistic in their assessments of the body part they wanted to have changed. . . . Rather than overestimating their physical problem, they typically rated their deformity as less severe than the surgeons did."[2] In other words, the teenager's internalization of what Naomi Wolf once pathologized as the "beauty myth" now renders her an apparently healthy member of the culture.[3]

*Extreme Makeover* is simply one among many makeover programs. On  4 television, and in reality programming as well, it's "normal" to want to look buff and beautiful, normal within the terms of the understood contract between viewers and producers regarding what can and cannot appear within the televisual setting. Indeed, where better to become beautiful but on the air—and thus wonderfully the television, the social site *par excellence* for the experienced insufficiency of the masses, turns into a benefactor, while viewers are encouraged to identify as the potential beneficiaries of television's deep commitment to our self-improvement. This constitutes an ethical transposition whereby plastic surgery, which was until recently widely deplored as a practice dwelling on the superficial and inauthentic, is now increasingly embraced as central to values promoting well being and happiness. Such a transposition happens, I will argue, in part through the reversal of negative affect (or self-loathing) into its apparent opposite—self-love. Moreover, the makeover program's sudden and radical conversion of attacks against the ego into what feels ego-strengthening leads to an intoxicating postoperative experience (the bandages-off moment). This moment is further intensified by its having become a cultural trope.

The participants in *Extreme Makeover* already know exactly what is 5 wrong with them. These ordinary people bring to the plastic surgeons a veritable menu of their surgical requests. The surgeons seem to generously mirror the patients' expectations with a surgical aesthetic that already had been internalized by their patients. The surgeons will confirm the patient's sense of inadequacy (which is inevitably shaming) and yet almost instantly reassure the patient through the promise that they will transform what is ugly and insufficient into what is beautiful. Importantly, because the patients already know what they want, the surgeons appear to serve the patients' best interest. In contrast to representations of surgeons as predators who manipulate the insecurities of (largely) women in order to pay off their mortgages and their children's college tuitions, here they are kindly healers—carefully attending to that delicate combination of wounded bodies and psyches.

During the first two series of *Extreme Makeover* the doctors, train- 6 ers, and style consultants all changed weekly. By its second year, however, every week we started seeing the same surgeons, the same dentist and dermatologist, and the same fashion consultant and trainer. Indeed, the opening credits of the program became reminiscent of the opening credits of another makeover show on Bravo, *Queer Eye for the Straight Guy*. Like *Queer Eye*'s "Fab Five," *Extreme Makeover* refers to its "extreme team." These are surrogate and provisional makeover families in the business of counteracting the shame and degradation set up by the structure of the makeover program itself, especially when it involves the body. Makeover programming subjects need to be rescued from their ugly and disorganized lives, their bad taste and miserable looks, sutured into the glad and radiant world. The makeover team thus becomes a temporary caregiving unit that may indeed humiliate one, but since we know that in the end they will love us and care for us and correct our deficits, they appear to undo the very shame that their presence in our life occasions.

## *I Want a Famous Face*

Like other reality programs, *Extreme Makeover* charts the progress of    7
becoming-celebrity. Ordinary people are suddenly stars—not only in physical appearance but also in the media coverage they receive as a result of
appearing on these reality programs. *Extreme Makeover* shows us people
being made good-looking enough to be on television; it is, in other words,
a kind of ground zero of celebrity-building.

Not long after *Extreme Makeover* first aired, MTV gave us *I Want a*    8
*Famous Face*, which differs from its predecessor in significant ways. Organized around the stories of largely very young people who want surgery
to transform their faces or bodies in the image of a favorite celebrity, *I*
*Want a Famous Face* is more critical of plastic surgery culture. The producers don't pay for the surgeries, they depict the surgery itself as well
as its aftermath more graphically, and they typically incorporate in each
episode negative experiences with plastic surgery, such as botched breast
implants. Repeatedly, the participants on *I Want a Famous Face* express
their conviction that these changes will improve their lives—either they'll
become stars themselves or, like one Ricky Martin wannabe, they hope to
win the heart of someone they secretly adore.

Typically, the young participants on *I Want a Famous Face* bring to the    9
surgeons pictures of what they're after and the surgeons more often than
not promise them a match. Each episode concludes with either a photo
shoot or some other quasi–star turn that confirms the identification with
the star template. What these individuals may hope to achieve through
surgery is complicated. Stars' beautiful appearance can begin to seem like
both cause and effect of their exquisite material lives. Much more than
*Extreme Makeover, I Want a Famous Face* underscores the self-loathing of
the young people pursuing surgery; although most of them are conventionally attractive to begin with, we learn in painful detail how inadequate
they feel in relation to their template celebrity, whose imagined share of
universal love (the love that is celebrity's cultural due) they cheerfully label
"self-esteem."

From a psychoanalytic perspective the ease with which self-loathing    10
gets reversed into the appearance of self-esteem is unsurprising. In the
event of one reversal into its opposite in a dream, Freud observed, one
should be on the lookout for other such reversals.[4] In *Civilization and Its*
*Discontents*, Freud discusses at length one of the central affective reversals of civilization, the commandment to love one's neighbor as one loves
oneself—which, as he notes, "cannot be recommended as reasonable. . . .
Not merely is this stranger in general unworthy of my love; I must honestly confess that he has more claims to my hostility and even my hatred."[5]
Freud ultimately argues that it is precisely because our innate aggressivity
threatens to undo all the ties that bind of civilization that we must erect
into a central tenet of human relationships this improbable formula. In
his seminar on *The Ethics of Psychoanalysis* Jacques Lacan focuses on the
role identification plays, not only in the aggressive relationship among

human beings, but more importantly in producing subjects in endless conflict with ourselves. Lacan's account of subject formation involves visual identifications with other human objects which plunge the subject into an ongoing structural rivalry with an ideal who is simultaneously external and internal; he points out that to love one's neighbor as one loves oneself is easy enough when one considers that this so-called neighbor is no more than the "other" constitutive of the ego. As he puts it, this is "the most neighborly of neighbors who is inside me."[6] Cosmetic surgery thus holds out the uncanny capacity to transform into material reality the subject's complicated identifications, that always involve simultaneously the idealization of love and the equally intense experience of rivalry.

The viewer of the surgical makeover program, who identifies with this *11* radical shift in affect on the part of the patient, experiences gratification through the ways in which our aggressivity (directed at the original "ugly" patient) is transformed into our putative good will (our feelings of joy as a consequence of their successful makeover). That cosmetic surgery is marketed as among the ultimate achievements of modern civilization is ironic, in light of the war it depicts between those counterforces of primitive destructiveness and the injunction to love our neighbor.

Finally, it is this discourse of self-improvement plundering feelings *12* of self-loathing that is ethically squaring plastic surgery with mainstream American practices and values. Surgeons correct perceived mismatches between insides and outsides, adrenalize self-esteem, give aging businessmen a fighting chance in a youth-saturated market, urge that former wallflower to shine at her class reunion, rescue aging housewives from their cruel dowdiness. Surgeons urge us forward into our self-determined corporeal destinies. Ultimately, they promise to make us love-worthy—to the neighbor who is ourself. Those final moments of *Extreme Makeover*, when the patients are returned by their temporary caregiving family to their "real" friends and family, are no less than celebrations of their new love-worthiness—a love-worthiness achieved through vivid acts of self-hatred. What apparently rendered one unloveable, one's appearance, is now transformed into the very source of pleasure as the patient achieves (and the spectator witnesses) those twin poles of American desire, youth and beauty. Ideological conversions yoked to affective conversions makes cosmetic surgery an especially compelling story right now. More, as the distance increasingly narrows between unattractiveness and its "cure," as cosmetic surgery becomes more widely available both economically and ideologically to the middle classes, it will become a less interesting story precisely because the body that diverges from conventional attractiveness will no longer be perceived as at risk—given the high probability that the imperfect feature will be corrected in no time at all.

NOTES

1. Participants need to be healed in time for their celebratory "reveal."
2. Mary Duenwald, "How Young Is Too Young to Have a Nose Job and Breast Implants?" *New York Times*, Sept. 28, 2004, The Consumer section.

3. Naomi Wolf, *The Beauty Myth: How Images of Beauty Are Used Against Women* (New York: William Morrow & Co., 1991).

4. Sigmund Freud, *The Interpretation of Dreams* in *The Standard Edition of the Complete Psychological Works of Sigmund Freud*, vol. 4, ed. James Strachey (London: Hogarth, 1900), p. 288.

5. Sigmund Freud, *Civilization and Its Discontents* in *SE*, vol. 21, ed. James Strachey (London: Hogarth, 1927–1931), p. 110.

6. Jacques Lacan, *The Ethics of Psychoanalysis, Book 7, 1959–1960*, ed. Jacques Alain-Miller, trans. Dennis Porter (New York: Norton, 1986), p. 187.

■ ■ ■

## Reading as a Writer: Analyzing Rhetorical Choices

1. While this is a short and lively essay, Blum uses a challenging vocabulary, and at least some of these words might be new to you. Read back through this essay, circle all the words you either don't know or are uncertain about, and look them up in a dictionary. (Don't neglect the title; *vicissitudes* is worth looking up, as is *affect*, used here as a noun.) You might divide up this task with your peers. Given her vocabulary, who is Blum's audience?

2. In the final three paragraphs, Blum discusses the first part of her title, "Love My Neighbors, Hate Myself." Reread those dense paragraphs carefully, and analyze how the ideas there help to explain the title, as well as her overall argument.

## Writing as a Reader: Entering the Conversation of Ideas

1. Blum analyzes the contradictory love-hate messages she sees in our cultural fascination with cosmetic surgery. Sharlene Nagy Hesse-Biber also analyzes the complex meanings in body obsessions. Write an essay that places these writers in conversation on this issue, considering what each author might say about the other's insights and examples. Given the connections, possible contradictions, and evidence you examine, what significance do you see in our current attitudes toward controlling and shaping our bodies?

2. While Blum interprets television shows and Jean Kilbourne analyzes advertisements, both authors use popular visual culture to provide evidence for their claims about contemporary standards and expectations for bodies. Compose an essay in which you forge connections between each author's examples and analysis in order to draw your own conclusions about what these images of "perfected" bodies tell us about our expectations of and beliefs about ourselves.

NANCY N. CHEN

# Dead Bodies, Violence, and Living On Through Plastination

Nancy N. Chen is a professor of medical anthropology at the University of California, Santa Cruz, who specializes in comparative studies of Chinese and Chinese-diaspora cultures. She studies attitudes toward health and healing, food, and biotechnology, as well as the connection between images and culture. She is the author of *Breathing Spaces: Qigong, Psychiatry, and Healing in China* (2003) and the editor of many books on cultural interpretations of the body. The following essay is taken from a collection she coedited with Helene Moglen titled *Bodies in the Making: Transgressions and Transformations* (2006). In this piece, she examines the popular *BodyWorlds, Inc.* and *The Universe Within* exhibits that have toured worldwide in the past decade. Her interest, as a medical anthropologist, is to reveal what the popularity of these plastinated bodies tells us about our contemporary attitudes toward death, violence, science, and bodily transformation.

Chen's essay is a brief fifteen paragraphs, but she covers a lot of ground. She opens with a brief history of the "medical gaze," from Leonardo da Vinci's anatomical sketches, to Victorian paintings of dissected bodies, to contemporary television shows featuring graphic dissection or surgery scenes. What does it mean, she asks, that we are currently fascinated by plastination as a new "technology of viewing" the human body? Chen describes in detail the look and poses of some of these plastinated bodies and analyzes the responses from visitors. She takes into account the different cultural contexts of these *BodyWorlds* exhibits, such as the history of Nazi medical experimentation that potentially shapes responses to the exhibit when it comes to Berlin, and the anxiety about the violence in the fast-growing organ trade that might be in the minds of Chinese visitors. As you will see, for her sources she uses anthropologists and cultural studies scholars who help her puzzle through the attitudes toward corpses and death that she sees in her own and others' reactions to these graphic exhibits.

If you have not seen one of these exhibits, you can see many plastinated-body images on the Web that will further "flesh out" your ideas about the enormous popularity of these exhibits. In her final paragraphs, Chen raises big questions about ethics, violence, and our desire to use technology to transcend body boundaries—even beyond death. What does this tell us about the living? That is Chen's question for us.

■　■　■

Medicine offers a powerful lens onto the human condition. The medical gaze, in particular, has become a common entry point into the human body. Early anatomical sketches by da Vinci, schematic maps of Chinese acupuncture points, and Victorian paintings of dissected bodies offer medicalized visions that eventually come to represent human bodies to larger lay audiences. Contemporary US television and news media offer an array of medical and forensic dramas with the hospital ward, dissection room, or plastic surgery operating table as primary sites for the viewing of bodies. Vivid images of laboratory dissections or operating techniques are interspersed with ongoing story plots. These ways of seeing, via dead bodies and their parts, offer the perfect body—one that can be dissected, mapped, and reframed. In the past three decades, the literature on bodies addresses lived experience and subjective knowledge through embodiment or rejection of that somatic frame. Few, with the exception of Cartwright (1997) in her analysis of the visible human project, address the impact of dead bodies and how these come to represent the living. This paper examines the stories that are told about dead bodies through new technologies of viewing. In the horror genre, a dead body in daily life often represents evil or an immoral order. However, science and medicine have come to offer a different representation: one that is quite human and accepted as an embodiment of the universal being.

Plastination is a recent technique that enables corpses to be preserved 2 without formaldehyde, which tended to transform the color of tissue and organs in toxic fumes. With plastination, the fat and water in human tissue and various body parts are removed and the body is then slowly injected with polymers. This form of preservation, which slows down decomposition, was patented in the 1970s by Dr. Gunther von Hagens, an eccentric Austrian scientist who then went on to create large-scale exhibits of plastinated bodies. These exhibitions—*Körperweltern* or *BodyWorlds, Inc.*—have traveled across Europe, Asia, and now North America since the 1990s. Von Hagens's process is rarely coded as violent. Instead, it is framed in the medical culture as preservative and in the popular media as a fascinating opportunity to look inside.

In what follows, I attempt to trace the flow of plastinated bodies 3 upstream from the popular exhibition halls, their production in plastination factories and, ultimately, to the donor bodies that enable this circulation. In the process, I address the management of dead bodies and query their different paths from the organ trade. Cadaveric bodies donated to science in order to further medical education live on as social objects of public display in new ways. The procurement and use of cadavers raises questions about what happens to dead bodies that are not necessarily organized by donation. As in Victorian times, there is a concern that lurks behind such exhibits: Have cadaveric bodies originated from questionable sources such as prisons and morgues? Beyond these immediate issues of the ethics of donation or the presumed violence of cadaveric origins, I am also curious about what it is that we see when such bodies are on display and what stories they tell about our culture of medicine. In some displays, disfigurement, dismemberment, and disembowelment are presented as natural forms of representation, while in other exhibits elaborate efforts are made to contextualize the plastinated cadaver in daily life or in practices that disrupt the distancing that takes place between life and afterlife.

## "I See Dead Bodies"

My first encounter with plastinated cadaveric bodies was in 2001. Dra- *4* matic posters of a dissected male body sitting on a dissected horse could be seen all over Berlin. Given the history of medical experimentation during the Nazi regime, it was disconcerting to see these posters advertising "Anatomy Art." Would this be a Barnum and Bailey show of oddities? Repulsed yet curious, I decided to visit the exhibit on a Wednesday evening with Afsaneh Kalantary, a University of California–Santa Cruz graduate student then finishing field work in Berlin. Housed in a former railway station of East Berlin, the exhibit had about 200 preserved bodies, with one horse and eight fetuses. Only two of the figures were female and both were pregnant with the plastinated fetus also visible. Many of the bodies had tattoos still evident on their arms and even more had blackened lungs.

The display of bodies was fascinating to view. Some were posed in *5* various activities, engaged in a sport, for example, or hunched over a keyboard. Having suffered a recent knee injury, I was amazed to see an anterior cruciate ligament (ACL) on one body. More fascinating still were the reactions of other attendees, who were mostly German. The arena was packed on a midweek evening with nearly a thousand persons. A young German couple in their twenties noted that the exhibit was about to close and the show was quite popular. The bodies were not encased behind glass, merely located on stands or sometimes placed behind ropes. This did not prevent viewers from putting their faces only centimeters away from—or even slightly touching—the bodies. One of the more notable images was a figure that presumably held its own flayed skin, a rendition of a Renaissance anatomical drawing. At the end of the display was the ubiquitous museum shop selling items related to the exhibit. I found myself unable to resist buying a videotape, catalog, and T-shirt. Ironically, the videotape had footage from its first show in Japan, another country with a history of wartime medical experimentation on prisoners. In the past four years, the exhibit has traveled extensively in Europe, the United States, and Asia. Despite the sensationalist and vexing ethical concerns that the exhibition raised, it explicitly emphasized the scientific contributions of and the need to learn from such bodies. Still, there remained lingering questions about the different kinds of life that bodies may have beyond death—a social life made possible with plastination—and about ways in which these bodies may come to represent the ideal body.

## Chinese Bodies

I attended the *Universe Within* exhibit of plastinated bodies in Masonic *6* Auditorium of San Francisco in spring 2005. The show followed on the heels of the *BodyWorlds 2* show held earlier in Los Angeles several months ago. At the San Francisco exhibit, I met quite a few viewers who had attended the Los Angeles show several times. Alerted by my colleague, Carla Freccero, that the bodies were clearly Chinese, I went to study how this exhibit compared with the display in Berlin. The show was much smaller with fewer bodies, about fifty, and indeed the plastinated bodies, at least the whole ones, were clearly from non-European donors. Despite the lack of skin, the eyes and facial structure indicated their Chinese origin. A videotape of an interview with Dr. Sui Hongjin confirmed that the bodies indeed originated from China and played continuously at two corners of the exhibit. Extensive attention has been paid to the origin of these bodies on the Chinese website devoted to plastinated bodies.

While race and the ethical procurement of these donor bodies were   7 a critical part of this exhibit, gender was another focus of the display. Despite the removal of skin from some bodies, there were clear efforts to retain the genitalia. Moreover, in one case gender was elaborately tacked onto one figure. An aged female body had high heels and a handbag, ostensibly to illustrate the effects of such shoes on body posture. Near this body, in an unmarked case of body parts, was the plastinated foot of a woman whose feet had been bound.

Similar to the exhibit in Berlin, the end of the show had a small   8 museum shop as well as a comment book. I observed and spoke with participants who chose to enter their thoughts in this book. Many, like myself, also read through prior comments made by other viewers. Several genres were evident: praise, suggestions for improvement, dead-body jokes, and questions about the sources of these bodies. The question "Chinese prisons?" came up a dozen times in the volume that I read. In newspaper accounts about the San Francisco show, two plastinated bodies were described as having what appeared to be bullet holes in the brain. Controversies have emerged at each venue where the plastinated bodies are exhibited. For instance, the San Francisco show was marked by protests from Asian-American groups that claimed the bodies had transgressed "traditional" forms of funerary ritual and offended Buddhist beliefs. The Los Angeles show had a fetus stolen. In a sense, these events increased awareness of the exhibit and offered free publicity.

What follows is background about the origins of two different shows   9 involving plastinated bodies —*BodyWorlds* and *The Universe Within*. Earlier in 2001, the journal *Nature* reported that Dr. Hagens had opened a plastination factory in Dalian, a port city on the Chinese eastern seaboard. This seemed to be a logical move, since the location offered cheap labor to process the plastinated bodies as well as ready access to corpses. Although Chinese state and medical authorities have been quick to disclaim any link to prisoner bodies, many donors may indeed come from morgues with unclaimed bodies and the sources for plastination are therefore not entirely clear.

The story of plastinated bodies and their display takes another twist in   10 China. A display had dramatically opened in Beijing earlier in 2004 with mainly Chinese bodies from the Dalian factory. The proliferation of plastinated bodies from China have produced competing shows with the *Body-*

*Worlds* exhibits, which are officially sanctioned and associated with Dr. Hagens. Once the technique was introduced in Dalian, the lack of trademark protections meant that the techniques could be shared and spread widely across the country's medical schools. Cheap labor will produce not only inexpensive sneakers or toys but also literally cheap bodies.

The circulation of plastinated bodies at times parallels the organic trade, *11* which has established official routes as well as illicit conduits that often intertwine (Scheper-Hughes 2004). In Europe and the United States, elaborate information about the ethical donation process is always provided (Sharp 2005). Similarly, the Chinese medical schools that have undertaken plastination emphasize their ethical procurement of bodies. Such attention to ethical issues indirectly underscores uneasy concerns about whether a donor has truly been a donor. The display of plastinated bodies, whether whole or in parts, raises key questions about aspects of the human condition that dead bodies represent and about the violence that is undertaken to produce them. Unlike organs that are procured mainly from bodies that have been subject to violent accidents, plastination can be applied to bodies in all conditions.

In seeing and thinking about these dead bodies, I find myself asking *12* why I still feel unsettled about their exhibition, a response that many attendees have reported to me. Is it because these dead bodies may once have been animated, were embodied selves, felt the sensations of a delicious meal and the tactility of warm ocean waves? Is it because we think dead bodies are meant to go away and disappear, to be placed in the ground, scattered in ashes, or offered up in a Tibetan sky burial? Is this the other inside? Or closer to home, why does the morbid anthropologist in me insist on witnessing the spectacle and transformation of dead bodies in displays about the human condition?

Plastinated bodies simultaneously confront the senses with corpses *13* while desensitizing viewers to the violence involved in producing them.

Sharon Kaufman's suggestion . . . that we are all potential donors or *14* recipients emphasizes the ability of medicine and technology to extend life through organ transplants and other interventions. These technologies often illuminate illogics of the political economy, which allows 90% of our health care costs to be incurred in the last years of our lives. For you see, death marks the ultimate failure of medicine. Yet, the inevitable sense that we will all become dead bodies one day is disrupted by the possibility that a cadaveric body may actually live on and become a different subject.

This is a story with a transformative ending. A post-human body in *15* the making. Perhaps that is the vexing allure and promise that plastination offers. Rather than relying on cryogenics and revival through future technology, plastination suggests tangible and visible forms of bodily transformation beyond death in the present.

BIBLIOGRAPHY

Cartwright, Lisa, *Screening the Body: Tracing Medicine's Visual Culture.* Minneapolis: University of Minnesota Press, 1995.

Kaufman, Sharon R., Ann J. Russ, and Janet K. Shim. "Aged Bodies and Kinship Matters: The Bioligization of Moral Commitment." *Bodies in the Making: Transgression and Transformation*, eds. Nancy N. Chen and Helene Moglen. Santa Cruz, CA: New Pacific Press, 2006. 126–35.

Scheper-Hughes, Nancy, "Parts Unknown: Undercover Ethnography of the Organs—Trafficking Underworld." *Ethnography* 5(1):29–73. 2004.

———. "The Global Traffic in Organs." *Current Anthropology* 41(2):191–224. 2000.

Scheper-Hughes, Nancy, and Philippe Bourgois, eds. *Violence in War and Peace: An Anthology*. London: Basil Blackwell, 2003.

Sharp, Lesley. *Bodies, Commodities, and Biotechnologies*. The 2004 Leonard Hastings Schoff Memorial Lectures, Columbia University. New York: Columbia University Press, 2006.

Treichler, Paula A., Lisa Cartwright, and Constance Penley, eds. *The Visible Woman: Imaging Technologies, Gender, and Science*. New York: New York University Press, 1998.

■ ■ ■

## Reading as a Writer: Analyzing Rhetorical Choices

1. If you are unfamiliar with the *BodyWorlds, Inc.* and other plastinated-body exhibits, look them up on the Web and analyze some of the images you see. With your peers, evaluate how effectively Chen describes the bodies. Discuss some specific examples of images you find in relation to the ideas in this essay. How do those images coincide with, extend, or refute the descriptions and analysis she makes?

2. In the final four paragraphs, Chen moves from her specific analysis of the plastinated-body exhibits to larger questions about "the human condition." Reread these paragraphs and explain, in your own words, the issues and future implications she sees stemming from our fascination with plastinated corpses. What do *you* think?

## Writing as a Reader: Entering the Conversation of Ideas

1. Chen and Virginia L. Blum are both interested in the normalization of certain kinds of violence done to bodies. Compose an essay in which you draw connections or contrasts between each author's examples and conclusions in order to make a point about our contemporary tolerance for—and even fascination with—bodily violence. Use the concluding paragraphs in each essay as a model for your own concluding paragraphs about what you think this attitude toward bodily violence means, and for whom.

2. Chen looks at our fascination with the human body through the lens of medical anthropology. Similarly, Toine Pieters and Stephen Snelders examine attitudes toward mood-altering drugs throughout medical history. Write an essay in which you make a point about the shifting understandings of how we should treat the human body, based on some of the examples and ideas in both essays that you find most compelling. As these writers do, consider what might be next, and why, in our ever-shifting attitudes toward human bodies.

# 17

# Environmental Studies

*What effects do we have on the natural world?*

I n this chapter, you plunge into high-stakes arguments and very personal conversations about our individual relationships to the planet. In the face of climate change and dwindling resources, you have certainly heard the cacophony of voices—on television, in the movies, in newspapers and magazines—addressing these frightening global problems with "green" or "sustainable" solutions. What do these terms mean? More important, what do they mean for *you* as you go about your daily activities of getting from one place to the next, eating meals, buying things, learning, and occasionally cleaning your living space?

While "environmental studies" may sound mostly scientific, as you will see, thinkers in many disciplines are challenging us to reconsider our relationship to the environment in eye-opening and innovative ways. For example, journalist Pamela Paul invites us to look more closely at the ingredients in household cleaning products and to consider what they might mean for our bodies and the planet, given the evidence available. The visual text "Little Green Lies" reveals the truth about "green-washing"; that is, while the idea of "being green" is a hot seller, the truth is that many "green" products are no better for the environment than their "un-green" alternatives. Jim Tarter reminds us what is at stake in these discussions, as he reflects personally and professionally on the effects of environmental toxins on cancers that have afflicted him and his family. He introduces readers to the concept of environmental justice, a way of looking at environmental issues as human rights issues that often affect those with the least social power in the most destructive ways.

Other writers focus on the politics of food, in a growing chorus of thinkers whose ideas are captured in Anna Lappé's title "The Climate Crisis at the End of Our Fork." What is the connection between your supper plate and our planet? Lappé offers surprising statistics about the food industry's enormous contributions to global warming, as well as solutions you might consider. Many of us may not be willing to make the changes we *should* make, both for the health of the planet and for the sake of ethics, according to philosopher Gary Steiner in his impassioned plea for veganism. (Most of us know that a conversation about vegetarianism—let alone veganism—is a way to get people overheated in a hurry. Why? We have included some letters to the editor in response to Steiner's piece that can help answer this.) A short but powerful list of "Ten Things You Can Do to Fight World Hunger" challenges us to think about personal choices that can have an enormous impact on the environment and human rights. Even if we make the effort to "go organic" in our food purchases, however, the visual text "Buying Organic" reveals that it might be more difficult than we think, given the power of business conglomerates.

Finally, a few of the writers in this chapter critique the way the entire conversation about sustainability and going green has been constructed by scientists and the popular press. Both Curtis White and well-known food writer Michael Pollan illuminate shortcomings in the environmental arguments we hear most often. They suggest, in different ways and with different evidence, that many well-meaning scholars and activists are leaving out crucial aspects of what it means to be human when we focus only on scientific and technological solutions to our environmental crises. They also help us face a common response to the overwhelming problems of global warming—a paralysis that Pollan captures in his title "Why

Bother?" What can we gain not only by changing what we eat but also by altering what Pollan calls our "cheap-energy minds"?

White, Pollan, and other writers in this chapter want to offer us another path besides the destructive one they all agree we are on. These writers propose specific ways of living more wholly, with more emotion, with more delicious food, and with deeper connections to human and nonhuman animals. This is the good news in the host of bad news about our current environmental crises. Wherever you stand on these complex issues, these writers will invite you to see your life and your health as connected to others and to the planet. Given the evidence you are about to read, this news might be frightening, but the authors invite you to see it as empowering as well.

PAMELA PAUL

# Green, If Not Clean

Pamela Paul is an author and journalist who specializes in revealing the quirks and contradictions in consumer culture, family life, and health issues. She is a frequent guest on *Oprah, Politically Incorrect*, and National Public Radio. Her books include *Pornified* (2005), about the way porn culture has saturated our daily lives, and *Parenting, Inc.* (2008), about the "parenting business." She also writes frequently for *Time* magazine, the *New York Times, Self*, and blogs for the Huffington Post. This essay appeared in an anthology titled *Dirt: The Quirks, Habits, and Passions of Keeping House* (2009), edited by Mindy Lewis.

An essay about cleaning products might not sound like an exciting read, but pay attention to how Paul draws in readers with nostalgic and funny details. Unlike some of the writers in this book, she has a casual, conversational style, and you might mark sentences that you think are standouts because of their humor, sheepish self-criticism, or surprising language choices. How does Paul characterize her childhood and contrast it to her present? How does she help us see that cleaning products, and their environmental virtues or vices, might go far beyond our countertops?

In this essay, Paul represents her own frustrations with trying to research the mysterious ingredients in the cleaning products she uses in her home. As most of us know, research doesn't always go smoothly, and her experience of "feeling part angry adult, part chastised child" (para. 9) when she cannot find answers to her questions may be familiar to you, too. Paul presses onward, though, modeling for readers a way to apply research methods to their daily lives. Paul should raise questions about chemicals in your life that you, too, may have come to think of as harmless. Are they? How will you know?

■ ■ ■

Along the neat vs. clean divide, I have historically fallen into the neat *1* camp. As long as things appear orderly on the surface, it's generally been okay by me if a fine layer of dust lies on top. So when I had my first child, I swore I wouldn't become one of those purifier-wielding neurotics who zap binkies and rattles in one of those ludicrous nursery germ-killing devices and refuse to return a fallen lollipop to a child's quivering lips. Who's afraid of a little grime? Life is dirty, I figured; better that kids get used to it. I'd even convinced myself that the four-inch-high dust bunnies lurking in my house were good for my daughter. "She'll grow up accustomed to dirt and won't develop allergies," I reasoned.

But at a certain point, I had to face reality: My house was filthy, and *2* the fact that my desktop displayed relatively neat piles of manila folders didn't obviate the fact. Though I hadn't had time to clean the house myself (or, let's face it, cared to devote myself to the task) and was too stingy to hire someone else to do it, ten months after my daughter's birth, I'd run out of excuses. Besides, the image of her actually confronting one of the bunnies was enough to get me to Costco.

Once there, I found the familiar Donna Reedish brands of my orange- 3 carpeted, Lysol-scented youth oddly soothing. It was as if the good old-fashioned scrubbers and solvents on display could magically transform my home along the lines of my rosiest nostalgia. I grew up in a sparkly environment, back in the seventies suburbs, when normal people could afford live-in help. I imagined an efficient housekeeper buzzing around my house with Ajax, telenovelas humming in the background—something financially impossible but worth fantasizing about nonetheless.

Now that I'm my own matriarch, I told myself, it was time to spruce up. 4 I was even eager to begin a life of responsible motherhood: clean, yes—but not neurotically so. Isn't there something magical, after all, about swiping a truly grimy bathtub or crusty kitchen counter and seeing it turn spar-kly clean within seconds? Ah, the satisfaction of fastidiousness—easier than ever in our ear of turbo disinfectants, HEPA filter-equipped vacuum cleaners, and Handi Wipes. I unloaded the rediscovered cleaning products of my youth and set them down to study the labels, as any responsible mother would do. Like most other new moms, I had become hypercon-scious of everything that could potentially be mouthed, chewed, or suckled in the roving maw of my teething, crawling child.

But here was a mystery: Where were the ingredients? There was noth- 5 ing but an ominous series of *Caution*, *Warning*, and *Danger! Keep Out of Reach of Children*. I turned the bottles every which way but found nothing other than references to harsh-sounding materials like bleach, ammonia, chlorine, and the ever-present "disinfectant." With cereal boxes detailing everything from trans fats to soluble fiber, I expected there to be some description of what I would be spraying on my countertops. Heaven for-bid I didn't rinse the bathtub thoroughly—what kind of residue would my daughter's bottom be resting on?

Surely, Mr. Clean could tell me more. I logged onto the Procter & 6 Gamble website, where I found lots of handy tips about usage but noth-ing about what made the stuff work. It turns out manufacturers aren't required to list ingredients; there is no FDA regulating what goes in and what must stay out of soap-scum spray. It's not easy to get a hold of ingre-dient lists either. The government hosts a website that lists components of many cleaners, gleaned from Material Safety Data Sheets (MSDS), which are posted by law in the factories where products are manufactured, but the Mr. Clean Antibacterial Multi-Purpose Cleaner I held in my hands didn't even show up. Companies frequently update their products, rebrand and rename them, and tweak the formulations. Still I was able to click onto his all-purpose cleaner, and the results weren't encouraging. Some ingredients were unspecified, and the MSDS provided "no information about the [product's] potential for carcinogenicity." I was able to follow the trail of one ingredient, diethylene glycol monobutyl ether, which has an intimidating ring but appears in everything from brake fluid to hair dye. Though the MSDS measures workplace exposure, which can be far greater than the amount one would encounter at home, the foreboding Hazardous Substances Data Bank warned that "results of limited repeated-dose oral work reported suggests that material may be rather toxic when inhaled or absorbed through skin in repeated small doses." Eek. And that was just one ingredient.

Further research didn't assuage my concerns. Companies say they   7 conceal ingredients to maintain trade secrets. It's almost impossible for a trained chemist, never mind the average consumer, to keep up. Environmental organizations and producers of "eco" products told me, not surprisingly, to be wary. A 2005 study by Clean Production Action, an environmental group, found traces of six classes of chemicals in dust taken from seventy homes in seven states (California, Maine, Massachusetts, Michigan, New York, Oregon, and Washington). Chemicals such as phthalates, alkylphenols, polybrominated diphenyl ethers (commonly know as PDBEs), and others linked to adverse effects including hormonal and sexual development impairment were found in every sample evaluated.

When I called the Soap and Detergent Association, a spokesperson for   8 the industry assured me no tests had proven cleansers to be carcinogenic and that alkylphenols, which can imitate estrogen in the body and are commonly used as surfactants, have a "negligible" environmental impact. "All chemicals are toxic at some exposure, including salt and water," he told me, emphasizing, "the most important thing consumers can do to ensure the safe and effective use of a product is to read the label."

"But that's what I did . . . ," I insisted, feeling part angry adult, part chas-   9 tised child. With Beatrice now a cautious toddler who weighs each step to preempt a tumble and her younger brother a fastidious one-year-old ("Uh oh," he'll intone dramatically when spotting a stray crumb on the floor), I see myself reflected in them. Perceptive, wary, even a bit suspicious.

Yes, I like to think I'm a skeptic. Contradictory information abounds:   10 Environmentalists cite risks while industry groups emphasize the sketchy science that proves them. Mostly, the answer is: We don't yet know. Not enough solid research has been done. But the way I see it is this: In a courtroom, you're innocent until proven guilty. When it comes to my family's health, I don't want to wait to be proven wrong after the fact, twenty years from now when my son is unable to impregnate his wife or my daughter suffers from a new strain of cancer. Instead of becoming crazy Purell Mom, I've turned into an environmentalist neurotic. (Why must we all seemingly end up some variant of maternal extremist?) Dirt may not scare me, but potential toxins do.

It seriously ran against my cheapskate instincts to dump the Costco   11 cache and worse, to bid adieu to the admittedly whitewashed fantasy of my Fantastik childhood home. Life in a house stocked with Seventh Generation and its ilk never emits that strangely intoxicating scent that so many of us have come to associate with "clean." Though my house is regularly cleaned, my bathtubs rarely shine, the countertops are sometimes streaky, and the floors need to be washed in vinegar solution rather too frequently. In the end, there are still dust bunnies beneath the stairwell and under my bed. But I figure, hell, if I don't kill them, they won't kill my kids.

■ ■ ■

## Reading as a Writer: Analyzing Rhetorical Choices

1. Find some sentences in which Paul characterizes her childhood, and compare them to her descriptions of her present. How does she build her argument through these contrasting descriptions?

2. Locate places where Paul represents different perspectives on cleaning chemicals in this essay. How does she use this information to help build a case for her own perspective on these chemicals?

## Writing as a Reader: Entering the Conversation of Ideas

1. Both Paul and Jim Tarter are interested in revealing the effects of industrial chemicals on our daily lives. They also describe the challenge of researching the connections between hazardous chemicals and poor health. Compose an essay in which you draw on the ideas and research methods of both authors in order to explain what you think are the most effective research strategies for this issue and the most effective way to help others see the significance of this issue.

2. Paul and Michael Pollan focus on the small changes in our daily habits that are connected to larger issues of personal and planetary health. Drawing on the ideas of both writers, write an essay that uses Pollan's idea as a jumping-off point: "Going personally green is a bet, nothing more or less, though it's one we probably all should make, even if the odds of it paying off aren't great. Sometimes you have to act as if acting will make a difference, even when you can't prove that it will" (para. 16). How does each writer address this complex stance? (Feel free to draw on the information in the "Little Green Lies" visual.) What are the payoffs when we change our behavior this way? Where do you stand in this conversation?

# Little Green Lies — How Companies Erect an Eco-Facade

This image and short list of slogans and reality checks appeared in 2008 in *Wired*, a print and online magazine that examines the impact of technology on culture and politics. How does this visual and textual piece present an argument? What evidence do you find most persuasive? How effectively do you think it addresses skeptical readers?

■ ■ ■

**Comcast Ecobill**

**Slogan:** *PaperLESSisMORE*

**Reality Check:** Sparing trees is is nice, but we suspect the cable behemoth's practice of carpet bombing potential customers with direct-marketing brochures—often after they've already signed up—might off-set the benefits. Can't Comcast just spam people? After all, it works for those environmentally minded v1agr@ sellers.

### Poland Spring Eco-Shape bottle

**Slogan:** *A little natural does a lot of good.*

**Reality Check:** How does selling more $H_2O$ in a bottle made of recycled plastic qualify as doing "a lot of good"? Eight out of 10 empties are landfilled anyway, and producing shipping the 31.8 billion liters of water sold in the US every year requires 17 million barrels of oil. Tap water, anyone?

### Airbus A380

**Slogan:** *A better environment inside and out.*

**Reality Check:** Reducing the carbon footprint per passenger by hauling more of them at a time makes sense. But unless the aviation industry switches to some magic new fuel, it will be spewing 1.4 billion tons of $CO_2$ into the atmosphere per year by 2025. That's gotta make Mother Nature cry, inside and out.

■ ■ ■

## Reading as a Writer: Analyzing Rhetorical Choices

1. Using the tools in the "Analyzing Visual Rhetoric" section of Chapter 9, discuss the relationship between the image and the text in this piece. Where exactly in the image and the text do you see the argument most clearly? What appeals to ethos, pathos, and logos do you see? How effective do you find this piece, and why?

## Writing as a Reader: Entering the Conversation of Ideas

1. How do the ideas presented in this image and text help you contextualize the arguments made by Jim Tarter and Pamela Paul about the effects of chemicals on our daily lives? Write an essay in which you establish the connections you see, and explain the significance to your readers. Why should we care?

2. This image and text reveal aspects of the "green" movement that Curtis White also finds deeply distressing. In an essay, connect what you consider to be the key ideas raised in these two texts. In light of these ideas, make an argument about what you think the most effective strategies for publicizing "green" behaviors should be, and why.

JIM TARTER

# Some Live More Downstream than Others: Cancer, Gender, and Environmental Justice

Jim Tarter is a professor of American literature and cultural studies who specializes in Native American and multiethnic texts. Environmental themes are a consistent focus of his research, as in this essay, published in 2002 in *The Environment Justice Reader*. Tarter is part of a growing group of scholars and activists from different disciplines who study environmental justice, a new field that connects "environmental exploitation and human exploitation" (para. 17) and illuminates the fact that not all citizens enjoy equal protection from environmental health hazards. You may have heard the phrase "not in my backyard" (sometimes shortened to NIMBY) to describe the attitude many people have toward development (such as an airport or a landfill for their garbage): They desire the benefits of the development but want it to be located elsewhere. Of course, dangerous wastes have to go *somewhere*, and environmental justice scholars examine the larger picture: What does it mean that people with less social power often suffer disproportionately from the ill effects of living near hazardous sites?

This essay combines both personal and scholarly insights. You will notice the personal voice right away in this essay; Tarter even begins with the pronoun *I* as he reflects on his own cancer experiences and those of his sister. At other places in the essay, he describes his childhood, including playing in and around the toxic waterways of the Michigan "Rust Belt" city where he grew up. These personal reflections are woven in with his scholarly analysis of the work of Sandra Steingraber, a biologist and cancer survivor whose writing he both praises and faults. As you read, mark the places where you notice Tarter shifting between personal and scholarly modes. What connections is he drawing?

Steingraber's research is in the tradition of the famous American environmentalist writer Rachel Carson. Tarter may assume that readers know a bit about Rachel Carson already, so if her name is new to you, you might look up some information on this scientist who is credited with launching the modern environmental movement with the publication of her book *Silent Spring* (1962). In that book, Carson took on the pesticide industry's use of DDT and warned the nation about the carcinogens that were routinely being used for home products and by the farming industry after World War II as part of Americans' desire for "better living through chemistry." Steingraber's research on the environmental causes of cancer is in this same tradition. As you will see, Tarter praises Steingraber for pushing the research in new directions—for example, looking at data that show how these environmental toxins affect women's bodies differently than men's. Tarter also finds shortcomings in Steingraber's research—particularly, that she avoids examining the effect race has on experiences of cancer and treatment.

In his title, Tarter points out that "some live more downstream than others." This comes from the fable he quotes about a village along a river where "residents . . . began noticing increasing numbers of drowning people caught in the river's swift current and so went to work inventing ever more elaborate technologies to resuscitate them" (para. 10). The fable concludes by noting that in their focus on the drowning victims, the villagers never think "to look upstream to see who was pushing the victims in" (para. 10). This environmental parable should get you thinking about who benefits, and who suffers, from our current environmental policies. This is, Tarter argues, not just an environmental issue but a human rights issue as well. Do you agree?

■  ■  ■

I consider myself a daughter of Rachel.

— SANDRA STEINGRABER, *Rachel's Daughters:*
*Searching for the Causes of Breast Cancer*

I come from one of those "cancer families." Fourteen years ago, at *1* twenty-seven, I was diagnosed with Hodgkin's Disease — a cancer of the lymphatic system. The cancer was in an advanced stage, having metastasized, and according to my doctors I would have to do a year of treatment. Fortunately for me, after World War II some American soldiers had been inadvertently cured of Hodgkin's as a result of exposure to mustard gas. So my oncologists were able to prescribe a treatment of nitrogen mustard in chemotherapy, in combination with surgery and radiation, which had achieved good results. They told me I stood an 80 percent chance of surviving five years.

After a year of high-tech medicine and four years of remission, the *2* doctors pronounced me cured. Happy to be one of the lucky few, I tried to just go on with my life and forget about cancer. But a year later, in 1994, a close friend was diagnosed with metastatic breast cancer. Later that year my sister Karen was diagnosed with an advanced stage of the dreaded ovarian cancer. She had a terrible prognosis — a 10 to 15 percent chance of surviving five years.

Then my aunt, who was born and raised in the same town as us — Bay *3* City, Michigan — was diagnosed with breast cancer. At this point the family began to talk about it. We remembered that our mom's father had died of cancer. Some of us would speculate about "the family" and make vague references to genes. But for years after she was diagnosed, Karen and I would privately ask each other if our cancers were really just genetic, or if something else was involved.

We began trying to ask the environmental question about cancer. Our *4* problem was that we could never face the question itself for long. I now see that this problem was not exclusive to us: In my experience, very few people are willing to talk much about the cancer-environment question. In fact, as I see it, our entire culture is in denial about the link between our toxified environment and cancer. In what follows, I hope to interweave my experience of cancer with Sandra Steingraber's work on cancer to show how and why we have to break the silence.

## Carson's Children

The silence around cancer retained its grip on me for a decade after I was    5
diagnosed, and I have only recently, with the help of others, begun to break
it. For me, the silence was first broken by Audre Lorde, who named the
silence as a problem in her great work, *The Cancer Journals*. Lorde, however, does not address in a direct way the environmental question about
cancer. This particular silence was broken for me by a "mother-daughter"
pair of cancer survivors, Rachel Carson and Sandra Steingraber.

Both Carson's *Silent Spring* (1962) and Sandra Steingraber's *Living*    6
*Downstream: An Ecologist Looks at Cancer and the Environment* (1997) are
essentially environmental justice texts.[1] Environmental justice discourse
argues a connection between environmental exploitation and human
exploitation or social justice. Carson's and Steingraber's texts are unique
in the annals of both environmental literature and the literature of cancer,
and for many of the same reasons: featuring an environmental argument
about the causes of cancer, they are both written in that rare style of scientific prose that is clear, engaging, and accessible, and yet precise, accurate, and well-documented. There is also a similarity in the political and
ethical uses to which Carson and Steingraber apply their science. Both
deliberately set out, not to render objectively the "true" scientific facts, but
to write from a constructed, political perspective as citizens and environmentalists, as well as scientists, in order to change public and corporate
policies. But of all the correlations between Carson's and Steingraber's
texts, the most important one involves cancer.

By claiming Rachel Carson as her mother in the film *Rachel's Daugh-*    7
*ters*, Steingraber is no doubt claiming kinship to Carson's intellectual heritage as environmentalist, scientist, and feminist, and she is acknowledging
the influence of Carson's carefully documented, rhetorically moderate
style of writing. But their kinship, to my mind, has even more to do with
cancer itself. It is now well-established (with the new biographies and the
publication of her letters) that Carson knew she had breast cancer as she
was writing *Silent Spring*. She died of it in 1964, two years after the book
was published, and had carefully kept it a closely guarded secret throughout the debate and publicity that surrounded her after the book appeared.
So although there is only one chapter explicitly devoted to cancer in
*Silent Spring*, with hindsight it is clear that cancer underlies implicitly the
book's whole argument about the danger of the new chemicals we were
releasing into the environment. This same general threat is exactly what
Steingraber's book is about—and like Carson, she writes as a cancer victim. Thus, if anyone is Rachel's daughter, it is Sandra Steingraber.

The big difference between the two, however, is that in public and in her    8
writing, Carson kept her cancer a secret, whereas Steingraber foregrounds
her own personal experience of cancer. In so doing, Steingraber's book
sketches a complex, political interrelationship of cancer, gender, and envi-

ronment, one that I would compare to environmental justice discourse in its connection of social justice issues to the environment. Steingraber does not argue directly on feminist grounds; nor does she use the term "environmental justice," choosing instead to argue on the grounds of human right in general. Nevertheless, she subtly shows us, if we connect the dots, that gender is a category of environmental justice. As I will argue, cancer, as she represents it, may even help bring together ecofeminism (or gender-conscious environmentalism) and environmental justice discourse and practice.

## Facing Living Downstream

Two years ago, after a four-year struggle with ovarian cancer, my sister 9 Karen died. For the last six months of her life, I left my job and moved to Oregon to become her primary, live-in caretaker. Just as I was about to move, a good friend gave me a copy of *Living Downstream*. She had inscribed it, "Here's the book we knew had to be written." It was true; we had been talking about possible environmental connections to cancer for years. But suddenly I couldn't bear to read any further. I almost didn't bring it with me.

At Karen's, my eye fell on a passage in the book's introduction:    10

> There are individuals who claim, as a form of dismissal, that links between cancer and environmental contamination are unproven and unprovable. There are others who believe that placing people in harm's way is wrong — whether the exact mechanism by which this harm is inflicted can be deciphered or not. At the very least, they argue, we are obliged to investigate, however imperfect our scientific tools: with the right to know comes the duty to inquire.
>
> Happily, the latter perspective is gaining esteem as many leading cancer researchers acknowledge the need for an "upstream" focus. . . . This image comes from a fable about a village along a river. The residents . . . began noticing increasing numbers of drowning people caught in the river's swift current and so went to work inventing ever more elaborate technologies to resuscitate them. So preoccupied were these heroic villagers with rescue and treatment that they never thought to look upstream to see who was pushing the victims in. (xvi)

Suddenly I was confronted with what I had secretly feared most. I couldn't stand to look up that river; I threw the book in a corner. Occasionally, during Karen's naps, I'd pick it up, but I just couldn't stick with it. It was beautifully written, but every time I tried to read it, my heart would race and my head would swim. In shock, I'd gaze across the room at my sister on her deathbed, and put the book down. Too scary—and too close to home.

Of course I couldn't forget anything I'd read of the book, either. As a 11 cancer survivor myself, sometimes Steingraber's basic idea was exhilarating; it showed there was something concrete we could do. So now and then I would mention the book to Karen. "Here is this new book," I'd say, "that synthesizes the new information from toxics right-to-know laws with information from the new cancer registries. It confirms what we've suspected about cancer and the environment."

With a look on her pale, drawn face as though she had just tasted   12
something surprisingly bitter, Karen would gulp and nod knowingly, but we could never discuss it further. Any further comments from me would receive silence from her or an awkward change of subject. One time, after I'd made it through a few pages, I repeated to her some of Steingraber's facts, such as the tripling of the general cancer rate in this country in the last fifty years, and the fact that the worst cancer rates, including lymphomas, breast cancer, and ovarian cancer—all the cancers that had recently struck us as a family—were happening mainly in the industrialized nations. She simply cut me off, and at last I understood. She wasn't denying the truth, but the implications were just too much for her to look at from her position. I didn't have to ask why. About these things we had an intuitive bond.

What Steingraber is saying was usually too hard for me to look at too:   13
It meant that Karen might be a *victim*, not an accident, and not (the politically correct term) simply a patient. Steingraber's book confronted us with the bitter injustice of her premature death. Right then it was too much to take in, as Steingraber does, the injustice involved in the pervasive presence of toxins in the general environment, or our lifetimes of minute, repeated exposures to persistent, organic pollutants. And so we never did talk about these things enough. I was thinking about them all the time, but Karen took a serious turn for the worse before we were able to discuss Steingraber's basic argument in a satisfactory way. Now I am left thinking about why so many of us are getting sick—and why as a society we are still not talking seriously about cancer and its environmental roots.

Looking back, I see it wasn't just our own fear of cancer that blocked   14
us. In contemporary American society there are many layers of silence wrapped around cancer, not only because the disease itself is frightening and we have trouble with issues of death and dying in our culture, but also because it is too frightening to contemplate the huge investment of money, power, and emotional capital in toxifying the environment and ourselves in the way we do now. If we are taking seriously the possibility of environmental contamination's role in the near-epidemic of cancer, we are faced with having to talk scientifically and politically about things like industrial capitalism, petrochemicals, corporate agriculture, environmental racism, or patriarchal science and medicine.

Not that I thought all this while I was sick; I just wanted to get on with   15
my life. But Karen's cancer made me face it—and so does *Living Downstream*. Not that reading this book has gotten any easier. It still makes me cry when I read passages, such as this one about the new cancer maps: "Death from cancer is not randomly distributed in the United States. Shades of red consistently light up the Northeast coast, the Great Lakes

area, and the mouth of the Mississippi River. For all cancers combined, these are the areas of highest mortality; they are also the areas of the most intense industrial activity" (63). In other words, although millions are dying, we are not all equally exposed. Some are more at risk, more downstream, than others. Typically, Steingraber doesn't argue this point explicitly, but her information implies it. This map means that cancer is both an environmental issue and an issue that involves social justice. It means, in other words, that cancer is an issue of environmental justice.

Steingraber often suggest environmental injustice with her tone, such    *16* as when she tells the story about the moment she knew that she had not and never would accept her friend Jeannie's death from cancer (39). And when she writes, "None of these 10,940 Americans [a conservative estimate of environmentally caused cancer deaths in the United States per year] will die quick, painless deaths. They will be amputated, irradiated, and dosed with chemotherapy. They will expire privately in hospitals and hospices and be buried quietly. Photographs of their bodies will not appear in newspapers. We will not know who most of them are. Their anonymity, however, does not moderate this violence. These deaths are a form of homicide" (269).

## Environmental Justice and Cancer

Environmental justice writers and activists have consistently made links    *17* between environmental exploitation and human exploitation, attempting to reveal, criticize, and transform relationships between human social practices and environmental issues. The central term in environmental justice discourse and practice has historically been environmental racism. But there are other social categories that are centrally involved in projects of social justice, and Steingraber shows, by example and implication, how to look at gender as a category of environmental justice. Before she does that, however, she first carefully establishes her basic argument that the primary causes of cancer now (i.e., since 1950 or so) are *environmental* in origin.

Federal and state right-to-know laws, established in the past decade,    *18* have made available disturbing information about the extent to which our environment has been polluted by known carcinogens (and many others which are probable, suspected, or untested). Meanwhile, newly established cancer registries make it possible to see historical trends in cancer incidence and mortality, and to see some of the ways cancer is distributed geographically and (to a lesser extent) demographically. In *Living Downstream*, Steingraber maps this new toxic release information onto the new cancer registry information, and synthesizes that with other new studies on cancer and toxins. She shows that the case is now clear enough: Although the research is not totally conclusive, and much work remains to be done, so much of the information indicates danger now, that we cannot ignore environmental links to cancer just because some uncertainties remain. We must make basic policy changes regarding environmental contamination and public health.

Steingraber is much more clearly a feminist than Carson (as we shall see), but like Carson she prefers to remain basically a scientist, avoiding overtly gendered political rhetoric. Despite the fact that her politics are muted, however, Steingraber makes a powerful environmental argument about cancer. One of her most effective strategies in this regard is to adopt an historical perspective: "If heredity is suspected as the main cause of a certain kind of cancer, we would not expect to see its incidence rise rapidly over the course of a few human generations [as all the worst cancers have done in industrialized nations] because genes cannot increase their frequency in the population that quickly" (32). The new historical perspective available from cancer registries makes clear that the main causes of cancer are environmental, not genetic. Supporting this argument are her skills of synthesis and her knack for the telling fact: "All types combined, the incidence of cancer rose 49.3 percent between 1950 and 1991. This is the longest reliable view we have available. . . . More of the overall upsurge has occurred in the past two decades than in the previous two, and increases in cancer incidence are seen in all age groups" (40). Steingraber's argument is not new. Even the World Health Organization has concluded that "at least 80 percent of all cancer [worldwide] is attributable to environmental influences" (60). (Here they use "environmental," like Steingraber, in the broad sense.) But Steingraber's book is most effective when she speaks on the personal level: "As a woman with cancer . . . I am less concerned about whether the cancer in my community is directly connected to the dump sites, the air emissions, the occupational exposures, or the drinking water. I am more concerned that the uncertainty over details is being used to call into doubt the fact that profound connections do exist between human health and the environment. I am more concerned that uncertainty is too often parlayed into an excuse to do nothing until more research can be conducted" (72–73).

That is, all too often a lack of basic information is taken to mean that there is no real evidence of harm, which chemical industry interests and others then try to spin into the assertion that a chemical in question is harmless. And we continue to wait as the bodies pile up. Most importantly, once Steingraber makes the case that cancer is partly environmental in origin, we are confronted with questions such as who gets cancer, and which groups are more exposed than others to toxics in the environment—that is, we are faced with a range of issues that have come to be called environmental justice.

## Looking Upstream from My Hometown

Steingraber also forces each of us to face the question of our own ecological roots. My sister and I grew up in Bay City, Michigan, a Rust Belt city of sixty thousand. Bay City lies at the mouth of the Saginaw River, on Lake

*19*

*20*

*21*

Huron, about a hundred miles north of Detroit. Founded as a sawmill town at the hub of the clear-cutting of the state in the nineteenth century, its basic identity as a city is built upon early- and mid-twentieth-century heavy industry. It was World War II that made our town socioeconomically what it remains to this day, with its focus on automotive, petrochemical, and transportation industries.

We grew up very near where the Saginaw River dumps into Sag-  22 inaw Bay. That river always looked bad, and so did the beaches on the bay. Riding our bikes along the river, peering into the thick, gray-black soup, imagining what sorts of creatures survived in there, we didn't wonder much about why it looked so nasty. It always smelled like metal, oil, and dead fish. The few fish we ever saw were dead suckers and carp. Only now do I realize how many species of plants and animals were endangered or extinct there. The only living things we saw were rats, gulls, and flies. Across the river were the storage tanks and slag piles, and upriver were docks, rail yards, and the General Motors factory, just visible to the west. To the north, the cement factory smokestack kept watch.

As teenagers we would often take off to the water in the summer. A  23 couple of our more well-to-do friends would take us waterskiing, and if the bay was choppy (which was more often than not) we'd ski up the river right past the holding ponds, brownfields, storage tanks, dumps, and factories. Neither my sister nor I had ever seen the river from that perspective before: mile after mile of industrial wasteland. It didn't stop us. We weren't very good, but we tried hard, making sharp turns on the slalom ski and wiping out a lot. Afterwards we would party on the beach at the mouth of the river, swimming and making out with our dates in the gray waters of Saginaw Bay.

Nobody said a thing to us. In those days, nobody seemed to think much  24 about dioxin, or even about the tap water, which was from up the bay, or the fish from the Great Lakes. No one talked about mercury, lead, polychlorinated biphenyls, or persistent organic pollutants. No one seemed to know about the tremendous increases in deformities, cancers, and extinctions of wildlife in the Great Lakes.

Even though I worked one summer in the Chevy factory just upriver,  25 it wasn't until I had left for college that I began to realize how much was upstream from where we had lived. There was Dow Chemical's home base in Midland, on the Tittabawassee River just to the west, which empties into the Saginaw; it had been making napalm and Agent Orange for the Vietnam War and handling millions of tons of chlorinated hydrocarbons the whole time. There were power plants, Defoe Shipbuilding (the biggest Great Lakes shipbuilding factory of World War II), power plants, waste dumps, and many of the Big Three's factories, from the Bay City parts plant just upstream to the massive industrial complexes of Saginaw farther upriver. Only later did we realize that the awesome General Motors factory city we went through along the freeway in Flint, not quite an hour's drive to the south, was also upstream: The Flint River flows into the Saginaw. Later yet, in the mid-1980s, we heard that in Bay City, just a mile upstream from where we grew up, right where we used to water-ski, there was a big industrial waste dump that had just become a Superfund site.

What happened to the Saginaw is not at all exceptional. That is the 26 scary thing; something like it has happened to nearly every major water-way in the industrial Midwest.[2]

Karen and I will never know with any degree of precision why we got 27 cancer. Cancer usually has multiple causes, and many carcinogens take decades to reveal their effects. But all that last summer, as my sister was dying, we had each begun to think that perhaps many of the thousands of people like Karen, who were dying, *didn't* have to. Maybe their deaths were not genetically programmed. We heard that most cancers were not determined by genetics, but that some people who get cancer are, geneti-cally speaking, more sensitive to carcinogens; but that, we reasoned, still involves environmental causes. So we began to wonder if the causes of cancer were not only genetics and lifestyle, as the hospital booklets told us, but environmental carcinogens. Without knowing it, we had become two more of Rachel's many children.

## Cancer and Gender

The last six months of Karen's life, during which I lived in her house as 28 her primary caretaker, taught me a lot about gender politics in cancer. We had always compared notes on our experiences, but at that time we went into much more depth—about her hysterectomy, her sense of physical unattractiveness, her loss of fertility, her issues with past boyfriends and present prospects, her courses of treatment, and her problems with male doctors. At the same time, we had to work through some delicate gender issues on intimate terms, such as how I could help her bathe or change her colostomy bag and bladder catheter. It became clear to me then that my experiences with cancer were differently gendered than my sister's. And now I can understand better what Steingraber is talking about when, in *Rachel's Daughters*, she says something that she never says in *Living Down-stream*: that cancer is a feminist issue.

Steingraber has actually been arguing this point for some time. In 29 her 1991 essay, "We All Live Downwind," Steingraber wrote, "I know as a woman that having cancer alters one's physical and sexual self and is thus a gendered experience which requires a feminist analysis" (38). Six years later in the 1997 documentary film *Rachel's Daughters*, Steingraber makes other kinds of feminist arguments: "Every time we [women cancer patients] go into the doctor's office and sit down we bring our gender with us, which means we also bring the fact that we have less money, we are more poorly insured, and we are more likely to be deferential to authority, perhaps because we've been socialized that way." Here Steingraber con-centrates on issues surrounding treatment. But in that same documentary she also handles other issues in feminist terms:

INTERVIEWER: Why is cancer a feminist issue?

STEINGRABER: It is a feminist issue because the parts of women's bodies that have been affected—our ovaries, our uterus, our breasts—are the parts of the body that have been despised, objectified, fetishized; so what it means to cut off a woman's breast in our society . . . says a lot about our culture, and the way we might value a breast over a woman's mind, or a woman's life, even.

Steingraber, following Audre Lorde here, is arguing that cancer is a feminist issue because it involves the way our society attempts to ideologically code women's bodies.

Given Steingraber's history as a feminist cancer activist, then, it 30 is interesting to me that she never overtly makes such a claim in *Living Downstream*. However, although Steingraber never makes the argument explicitly, there is a complex, detailed gender-related subtext in *Living Downstream*. This subtext takes various forms. One form it takes is the pattern of evidence the book presents on breast cancer, which is by far the most frequently mentioned cancer in the book and the only cancer mentioned in every chapter. The facts she cites about it are among the most suggestive of environmental causes in the entire book. And then there are the issues of persistent organic pollutants concentrating in breast milk and being passed down to infants: clearly women and children are at greater risk than men.

Aside from this accumulation of evidence about breast cancer, there 31 are a number of other lines of suggestion that help make the implicit case about gender and cancer for Steingraber. One is the pattern Steingraber repeatedly points out concerning the way women's cancers are seriously under-researched. To be sure, lack of research into environmental connections to cancer in general is one of the central motifs in Steingraber's book, but very often these are women's cancers she is talking about. So although she never says explicitly that this is a gender issue, the pattern is there.

Another gender issue in cancer is adipose tissue (fat). Again, although 32 she never says it is a feminist issue, she repeatedly shows that some of the most dangerous carcinogens—those that are most persistent in the environment and the most persistent in our bodies—are stored in fatty tissues. Obviously this affects women in a different way than men.

The most complicated and subtle aspect of Steingraber's implicit feminism, 33 however, is the way in which these specific issues (breast cancer, under-research, and fat) relate to her more general levels of analysis, particularly her analysis of the war machine and its relation to the post–World War II "petrochemical economy," as she calls it. She never spells it out, but she does tip her hand: "Seek. Strike. Destroy. Of all the unexpected consequences of World War II, perhaps the most ironic is the discovery that a remarkable number of the new chemicals it ushered in were estrogenic—that is, at low levels inside the human body, they mimic the female hormone estrogen. Many of the *hypermasculine* weapons of conquest and progress are, biologically speaking, emasculating" (109; emphasis mine).

This passage suggests nothing less than an association between the patriarchal war machine and cancer, because it was World War II, as her whole chapter shows, that led to the invention of most of the dangerous new chemicals we use routinely now. Steingraber has been talking at length about the petrochemical economy and the chemicalization of our environment since World War II, but this is the only time she reveals that she might consider the whole war machine—from which the chemicals and the attitudes toward their use derive—to be patriarchal as well as carcinogenic.

In these ways Steingraber implies, with complexity and detail, that 34 women are unfairly exposed to cancer risks. However, she never spells out this point explicitly. Why not? For one thing, her Carsonian rhetorical form involves a subtle masking at the political level, which includes gender (Carson, after all, had to hide her cancer in order to protect herself from personal attacks—she was labeled a hysterical woman and a spinster—by her male enemies in the chemical industry). For another, perhaps she felt that to argue explicitly as a feminist would take away from her status as a scientist or from the book's broad appeal. Most importantly, however, I would argue that she wished to avoid the appearance of bias, limitation, or compromise in her larger argument on behalf of human rights.

## Conclusion: Human Rights and Environmental Justice

In the conclusion of her book, Steingraber goes back to Carson in order 35 to construct her book's basic conclusion around human rights. By claiming explicitly that cancer is a human rights issue, she suggests a linkage between environmental issues and issues of social justice. What pushes Steingraber's conclusion further than Carson—and implicitly suggests that cancer is an environmental justice issue—is the phrase "the right to protection." For Steingraber this is a basic human right. It is the key link in moving toward an environmental justice argument, though, because once she makes it, we are faced with the fact that some people's rights to protection are more well-enforced than others. Another way of saying this is that there is a pattern, at least in this country, of unequal protection from environmental hazards. The pattern largely breaks down along racial and ethnic lines, although class is also involved. This concept is captured well by the title of Robert Bullard's best-known, book-length collection of essays, *Unequal Protection*. Bullard's title displays the essential connection between established environmental justice discourse and Steingraber's book: the issue is one of the right to protection. The human rights argument, as Steingraber articulates it, is thus an issue of social justice—of equal protection—and as such, her argument may be a different way of articulating cancer as an environmental justice issue: "Such an approach recognizes that the current system of regulating the use, release, and disposal of known and suspected carcinogens—rather than preventing their generation in the first place—is intolerable. So is the decision to allow untested chemicals free access to our bodies, until which time they are finally assessed for carcinogenic properties. Both practices show reckless disregard for human life" (268). Passages like this are the reason why I am arguing that Steingraber is close to making an explicit environmental justice argument, and that, as in this case, she may be already doing so—because her book establishes clearly that we have here a question of unjust and intolerable social practices at the environmental level. However, as much as she stresses human rights in general, she doesn't directly confront the fact that some human lives are more recklessly "disregarded" than others, with clear patterns of discrimination along racial and class lines as well as the gender lines she has indicated. Steingraber shows she is aware of the issue when she goes on to say, "we do not all bear equal risks when carcinogens are allowed to circulate within our environment" (268).

In itself, this conclusion and the rhetorical structure of human rights 36 that supports it is plausible, but in the process of making this general case she has lost sight of race and class issues that may have been raised by her original point that "we do not all bear equal risks." Instead, she adopts the political line of Carson on human rights. This is the same line Steingraber sketched out in "We All Live Downwind." The tone has thus shifted; with this formulation she makes an important general point, but by saying no more, she precludes any further exploration of the argument that *some people live more downwind than others*.

In this manner, Steingraber generally avoids dealing with race as an 37 issue in cancer. By way of contrast to this subtle sidestepping of racial issues, Steingraber develops (as we have seen) a complex and detailed structure of argumentation on gender issues in cancer. In fact, this is one of her book's greatest achievements—but it also tells us something about the way she omits considerations of race. I am simply saying that, given some of the information she presents, she could make a clearer connection than she does to race as an issue in cancer. (She could also do more with class, but as the above example about workers suggests, she does work a little with issues of class and labor.) She consistently prefers, like Carson, to pull back and argue at the more general level of human rights.

I find this move somewhat troubling in its similarity to the long history 38 in this country of blindness to racial issues, and to different people's ways of seeing the environment, in mainstream (i.e., white, middle-class) American environmentalism. To be sure, Steingraber does imply that cancer is an issue that involves race and class as well as gender—she just deals with the latter issue in a more complete way. In the end, then, although this book remains a powerful, effective toolkit, it is one which is still incomplete.

My experience with cancer—and some of Steingraber's own informa- 39 tion—shows that we can't separate issues of race, gender, and class from environmental issues of toxicity and public health. In this light, Steingraber's work does suggest a potentially productive convergence of these issues. And if her work suggests that the environmental justice writers and activists haven't done as much with gender as they might, it also shows us how ecofeminists, indeed all environmentalists, need to deal much more with race and ethnicity as environmental issues. Historically, ecofeminists

have been overwhelmingly white in terms of basic demographic composition and in their ways of defining and working on their environmental
issues. One of the most original contributions of Steingraber, in this context,
is the way she shows how cancer may function as a bridge issue between different kinds of environmentalists; she shows that cancer as an environmental issue may function as a principle of alliance between ecofeminists (or
gender-conscious environmentalists) and environmental justice activists,
artists, and scholars. It may even be a link between environmentalists and
multi-cultural, social justice movements.

At the personal level, Steingraber, like Carson, remains one of my    40
heroes. She is a cancer survivor who has become active, taking responsibility for having survived and for the knowledge she has gained. I see
Steingraber's book not only as an heroic achievement in itself, like *Silent
Spring*, but as a powerful toolkit for community activists. Not only does it
help me understand better what happened to my sister, it helps me to be
more effective as an environmental activist. In fact, it compels me to do so,
because now that I have this information—this set of tools—I am responsible for the resolution of the problem it exposes.

This year, my x-ray is clear. I am relieved, at least for the moment,    41
unlike too many others who are getting bad news. And I realize that following Steingraber's act is not going to be easy. Steingraber wrote in 1991,
"For me, dealing with the social implications of cancer can feel like being
forced to look at my own body lying in the street" (47). For me, dealing
with those implications—thanks in large part to Steingraber—is more like
being forced to look at my sister's body. And to look at the millions of dead,
dying, and soon to be cancer-ridden bodies all round us. *And* to look at the
socioeconomic patterns: Who is getting sick? Who benefits?

NOTES

This essay is dedicated to the memory of my sister, Karen Tarter. Thanks to the "Ecologi-
cal Conversations" Program in Association with the University of Oregon's Center for the
study of Women in Society for their financial support in the form of a research grant.
Thanks also to my parents, James and Mary Tarter, and to Rachel Stein, Mei Mei Evans,
Ellen Cantor, Rich Stevenson, Molly Westling, Mary O'Brien, Suzanne Clark, Linda
Rose, and Eldon Haines for their guidance and support.

1. Historically, environmental justice as a term emerged from the practice of community activists protesting environmental racism. It can be traced backed at least to the
1982 protests in Warren County, North Carolina, against the dumping of toxic soil near
black neighborhoods. Ever since then, the key term in the movement has been environmental racism, a basic fact of life in this country, which was demonstrated clearly by the
now-classic 1987 landmark study *Toxic Wastes and Race in the United States*. This study
established race as the most important single factor nationwide in determining the distribution of environmental hazards, more so even than class. In the late 1980s environmental justice as a term began to be used in some regions of the South and Southwest
by activists in networks such as the Southern Organizing Council, and the Southwest
Network for Economic and Environmental Justice. The term was widely accepted after
the first National People of Color Environmental Leadership Summit of 1991, with
their adoption of the now famous "Principles of Environmental Justice" (see Bullard,

*Unequal Protection*). Since that time a small industry of activists, artists, and academics has developed a discourse of environmental justice (see, for example, Bullard, Di Chiro, Hofrichter, LaDuke, Peña, Hamiton, Shiva, and Pulido).

2. The first chapter of Winona LaDuke's recent *All Our Relations* shows how Mohawk people in the Great Lakes region (near Lake Ontario) have been affected disastrously by very similar kinds of industrialization. LaDuke's book shows how many native people in North America are facing environmental racism, health threats, and clear environmental injustices from the same socioeconomic system.

WORKS CITED

Bullard, Robert, D., ed. *Confronting Environmental Racism: Voices from the Grassroots*. Boston: South End, 1993.

———. *Unequal Protection: Environmental Justice and Communities of Color*. San Francisco: Sierra Club Books, 1994.

Carson, Rachel. *Silent Spring*. Boston: Houghton Mifflin, 1962.

Di Chiro, Giovanna. "Nature as Community: The Convergence of Environment and Social Justice." In *Uncommon Ground: Toward Reinventing Nature*, edited by William Cronon, 298–320. New York: Norton, 1995.

Hamilton, Cynthia. "Women, Home, and Community: The Struggle in an Urban Environment." In *A Forest of Voices: Reading and Writing the Environment*, by Chris Anderson and Lex Runciman, 673–80. Mountain View, Calif.: Mayfield, 1995.

Hofrichter, Richard, ed. *Toxic Struggles: The Theory and Practice of Environmental Justice*. Philadelphia: New Society, 1993.

LaDuke, Winona. *All Our Relations: Native Struggles for Land and Life*. Cambridge, Mass.: South End, 1999.

Lorde, Audre. *The Cancer Journals*. 1st ed. Argyle, N.Y.: Spinsters, Ink, 1980.

Peña, Devon, ed. *Chicano Culture, Ecology, Politics: Subversive Kin*. Tucson: University of Arizona, 1998.

Pulido, Laura. *Environmentalism and Economic Justice: Two Chicano Struggles in the Southwest*. Tucson: University of Arizona, 1996.

*Rachel's Daughters: Searching for the Causes of Breast Cancer*. Directed and produced by Allie Light and Irving Saraf. Women Make Movies. New York, 1997. Film/videocassette.

Shiva, Vandana. "Development as a New Project of Western Patriarchy." In *Reweaving the World: The Emergence of Ecofeminism*, edited by Irene Diamond and Gloria Feman Orenstein, 189–200. San Francisco: Sierra Club Books, 1990.

Steingraber, Sandra. *Living Downstream: An Ecologist Looks at Cancer and the Environment*. Reading, Mass.: Addison-Wesley, 1997.

———."We All Live Downwind." In *1 in 3: Women with Cancer Confront an Epidemic*, edited by Judith Brady. Pittsburgh: Cleis, 1991.

United Church of Christ Commission for Racial Justice. *Toxic Wastes and Race in the United States: A National Report on the Racial and Socio-Economic Characteristics of Communities with Hazardous Waste Sites*. New York: Public Data Access, 1987.

■ ■ ■

## Reading as a Writer: Analyzing Rhetorical Choices

1. Along the edge of the text, mark the places in this essay where Tarter uses personal experiences. What can you conclude about the ways he uses personal experience and about the effect of using it in the places he does? How does this material add to the overall impact of his argument?

2. Tarter uses the "mother-daughter" pair of Rachel Carson and Sandra Steingraber to compare the research that has been done on the environmental causes of cancer. (The two women are not literally mother and daughter, but they share a personal and scholarly interest in linking environmental toxins to cancer.) Reread and mark the places where Tarter explains the similarities and differences he sees in their research, and explain how these ideas are connected to the larger point he makes in his piece.

## Writing as a Reader: Entering the Conversation of Ideas

1. Both Tarter and Pamela Paul explore the somewhat murky and yet compelling evidence linking environmental toxins to dangerous—even deadly— illnesses. Compose an essay in which you compare the ways these writers make their cases, through evidence and argument. What can you conclude about the most effective ways to build this kind of argument? What different approaches could you suggest? If you like, draw in the "Little Green Lies" image and text to help you make your point about the most effective persuasive tactics on this issue.

2. Tarter claims that Steingraber writes not from a feminist perspective or an environmentalist perspective, but from a "human rights" perspective (para. 8). Once you have explained to yourself what you think this means within Tarter's essay, consider how this insight could be applied to the ideas Jean Kilbourne presents in her essay on violent images of women in advertising. Write an essay in which you evaluate the ideas raised in these two essays in order to explain what you think are the benefits and possible problems of framing women's experiences of inequity as "human rights" issues. Use examples and ideas from each text as you make your point.

## CURTIS WHITE

## A Good Without Light

Curtis White is a professor of English at Illinois State University who writes fiction, essays, and nonfiction books on American cultural trends. He is well known for making irascible arguments that run counter to popular opinion, which you can hear in the titles of his books, including *The Middle Mind: Why Americans Don't Think for Themselves* (2003) and *The Spirit of Disobedience: Resisting the Charms of Fake Politics, Mindless Consumption, and the Culture of Total Work* (2008). This piece was published in *Tin House*, a literary magazine specializing in lively and provocative writing on current issues.

This essay is a distillation of the argument in his most recent book, *The Barbaric Heart: Faith, Money, and the Crisis of Nature* (2009), which critiques the sustainability movement for relying too much on science as the cure-all for our environmental crisis. Sustainability can mean different things to different people, but it generally involves a focus on renewable resources and the goal of sustaining human and environmental growth and diversity. White takes on current trends in sustainability technology, claiming that science alone cannot counter what he finds most harmful to current culture—what he calls the "Barbaric Heart." He coins this phrase to explain the long human history of admiring violence and competition, from the Punic Wars in ancient Rome to the popular video game Grand Theft Auto. Most approaches to sustainability, he argues, simply rely on this same capitalist race to overcome our problems with better science, better technology. What we are not noticing, he claims, is that "our pursuit of what we want makes us blind to how that pursuit is actually destroying ourselves" (para. 20).

White argues that rather than seeing religion, spirituality, and the arts as the opposite of hard science, we need to open our minds to include these approaches as we try to solve our current problems. White explains, "Science can tell you that global warming puts the polar bear at risk, but it can't tell you why you should care" (para. 16). White links science's reliance on rationality as too limited to address our current crisis, which he sees as a crisis of the human spirit, as well as of the planet. In his final paragraph, he clarifies how our daily lives are steeped in what he sees as the blood of the "Barbaric Heart" approach to living. See what you think of his ideas. And then, see what you think.

■ ■ ■

As so often happens in disasters, the best course always seemed the one for which it was now too late.

— Tacitus, *The Histories*

For environmental, business, and political organizations alike, the term *1* that has come to stand for the hope of the natural world is "sustainable." Sustainable agriculture. Sustainable cities. Sustainable development. Sustainable economies. But you would be mistaken if you assumed that the point of sustainability was to change our ways. It's not, really. The great unspoken assumption of the sustainability movement is the idea that although the economic, political, and social systems that have produced our current environmental calamity are bad, they do not need to be entirely replaced. In fact, the point of sustainability often seems to be to preserve—not overthrow—the economic and social status quo.

This should not be surprising. Sustainability is, after all, a mainstream *2* response to environmental crisis. It may want change, but it does not want what would amount to a fundamental self-confrontation. While it wants to modify existing models of production and consumption, especially of energy, it does not want to abandon what it calls "freedom," especially the freedom to own and use large accumulations of private property. And certainly it does not want to ask, "What went wrong in the great Western experiment with freedom? *Why do we seem to be mostly free to destroy ourselves?*"

What no one is allowed to consider is the distressing possibility that no *3* amount of tinkering and changing and greening and teaching the kindergartners to plant trees and recycle Dad's beer cans will ever really matter if our assumptions about what it means to be prosperous, what it means to be "developed," what it means to live in "progress," and what it means to be "free" remain what they have been for the last four hundred years under the ever-growing weight of capitalist markets and capitalist social relations. As Marx put it, under capitalism we carry our relation to others in our pockets. Marx would now have to add, sadly, that those "others" must now include the animals of the field and the birds of the sky (Daniel 2:38) as well as the fields and sky themselves.[1] But such a line of thought is not tolerated because the very word "capitalism" (not to mention "Marx") is a fighting word.[2] (Or, worse, it is a sort of faux pas to speak of "capitalism" at all; you'd be better off saying "the economy," just as if you were a slave asked to refer to your master as your employment counselor.) Unfortunately, in banishing this word we eliminate from the conversation the very thing we came together to discuss. We can talk about our plans to save the world, but we can't talk about the economic system that put it in jeopardy in the first place. That's off the table.

But I do not believe that capitalism is somehow singularly at fault. I    4
don't even think that it is necessarily bad. It is too reductive to say simply that there are cruel and greedy and violent people among us (capitalists), and that we need somehow to confront them and assert the good in ourselves. The truer problem is that the people who are destructive honestly believe that they are doing good. They are more often than not, or more often than any of us should be comfortable with, an expression of the virtues of what I call the Barbaric Heart.

This is the barbaric calculation: if you can prosper from violence, then    5
you should go ahead and be violent. In short order the Barbaric Heart is led to conclude that, in fact, prosperity is dependent on violence. Therefore, you should be good at violence, for your own sake and the sake of your country. Which is a way of saying that the barbaric itself is a form of virtue, especially if you think that winning, surviving, triumphing, and accumulating great wealth are virtues, just as athletes, Darwinians, military commanders, and capitalists do.

My reader may wonder how I can yoke together virtue and violence. To    6
which I would reply, "How can one remove the claim of virtue from the behavior that is most habitual to a people?" The artful (if ruthless) use of violence is obviously something that we admire in those sectors of the culture that we most associate with success: athletics, the military, entertainment (especially that arena of the armchair warrior, *Grand Theft Auto*), the frightening world of financial markets (where, as the *Economist* put it, there are "barbarians at the vaults"), and the rapacious world we blandly call real estate development. Instead of being "shocked, just shocked" by it, instead of living in bad faith, let's just say that violence (especially *competent* violence, violence that has a skill set and a certain virtuosity) is something that we're rather pleased with ourselves about. As ever, artful violence is the marker of an elite (whether the Persian "Immortals,"

the Spartan 300, the Praetorian Guard, the United States Marines, or the Redeem Team of men's basketball at the 2008 Beijing Olympics).[3]

Violence is an ethical construction that we forward to the rest of the world as an image of our virtue. The idea that we can "move mountains" is an expression of admiration. When it is done with mammoth machines provided by the Caterpillar Company of Peoria, Illinois, it is also a form of violence (as the sheered mountain tops of West Virginia confirm). To any complaints about the disheartening destruction and injustice that comes with such power, the Barbaric Heart need only reply: The strong have always dominated the weak and then instructed them. That is how great civilizations have always been made, from the ancient Egyptians to the British in India to Karl Rove and George Bush.  7

When Scipio Africanus looked over the army of Hannibal in the deciding battle of the second Punic War, he saw not only another long day's work in the phalanx worrying about being stepped on by the Carthaginian elephants. He also saw the end of any limitation on Roman power. One last concerted act of violence and Rome would be history's lone actor for the next five hundred years. As the historian Polybius described it, "The effect of their victory would be not only to make them complete masters of Libya, but to give them and their country the supremacy and undisputed lordship of the world" (302). This is how the American government felt as the Berlin Wall fell: Carthage is no more. After the fall of the Berlin Wall, the Karl Roves of the world (those who soak themselves in the blood of the Barbaric Heart as if it were a marinade) understood that they could use violence any time it was in their interest to do so, and they believed that was a *good*, if bloody, thing.  8

The question becomes, if this is our moral context, violence masquerading as virtue, how is this thing we call sustainability going to work? Sustainability presents itself as a kind of wisdom. It argues that it can reach an understanding, an accommodation with our destructive virtues and our faithfulness to capitalism. The wisdom of the sustainability movement (especially in its most visible activities through the United Nations and NGOs) is that it can make the Barbarian play nice. ("Attila, this is a tea cup. It's fragile. No! Okay, here's another one, now . . . Oh!" And so on.)  9

But I want to be quite uncompromising in saying that the logic of sustainability is also a sort of thoughtlessness. It is not really opposed to the Barbaric Heart. In fact, it participates in the yearning and willfulness of the Barbaric Heart in spite of itself. In spite of the fact that it can feel that this Heart is grasping, pitiful, and a danger to itself and others. The logic of sustainability provides a sort of program of carefully calibrated amendment ("Sure! We can make coal clean and still maintain our lifestyle"). But in the end, it is not an answer to our problems but a surrender to them. Its virtues are dependent on its sins. It is, as Simone Weil put it, a "good without light."  10

What is most menacing about the logic of sustainability is evident to anyone who wishes to look into its language. It will "operationalize"  11 sustainability. It will create metrics and indices. It will create "life-cycle assessments." It will create a sustainability index. It will institute a "global reporting initiative." It will imagine something called "industrial ecology" and not laugh. Most famously, it will measure ecological footprints. What the so-called sustainability movement has accomplished is the creation of "metrics," ways of measuring. It may not have had much impact on the natural world, but it has guaranteed that, for the moment, thinking will remain only technical interpretation. In short, it has brought calipers to the head of a songbird.

But what is most thoughtless about the logic of sustainability, espe-  *12*
cially as it has emerged through the Kyoto and Bali international agreements and protocols, is the assumption that it should allow for continued economic growth and development. In short, sustainability assumes that the reasoning of economics—of economics as a form of reason—must continue to provide the most telling analyses of and prescriptions for any future model for the relationship between human beings and the natural world. But what if the assumptions of economics are nothing more than a form of thoughtlessness? And what if that thoughtlessness's purpose is nothing more than to allow—oh, tragically, we'll all say—the very activities and, more importantly, the very habits of mind that over the last two centuries of industrialization have brought us to this sorry pass? In short, what if the thinking of economics is merely another vestment for the Barbaric Heart?

The idea that economics will aid us in thinking through the problem  *13*
of the destruction of the natural world, will aid us in managing the earth's "carrying capacity," commits us to the assumption that our world ought to be governed and guided by technicians. It is part of the thinking that says, "If only the politicians would listen to what we scientists have to say! Listen to what the climatologists have to say about the sources and consequences of global warming! The scientists will save us if only we'd listen to them, respect their authority, follow their instructions." They can maintain this while gloriously ignoring the fact that the world we presently inhabit was conceived by science, designed by engineers, and implemented by technicians. It starts with the rapidly beating heart of the four-stroke engine inside your automobile, and then radiates out in what is laughably called urban planning, the world as designed for the convenience of the automobile, the sterility of the interstate highway, and the fantastic waste and increasingly fascistic experience of jet travel. Of course, behind all this there is the global energy infrastructure, burning off methane waste, spilling its toxic cargo on land and shore, and destroying the people who have been cursed with "oil wealth." Looming over everything, guaranteeing it, is the grim visage of the warrior, the global oil price known as the military. In short, looming over all this is the Barbaric Heart.

What I want to suggest, not to put too fine a point on it, is that the act  *14*
of trusting these experts—whether economists or scientists—to provide

us with a sustainable future of ever-growing capitalist enterprise is not to place faith in the subtle capacities of the engineer but to indulge in the primitive longing of the barbarian in his moment of despair. After a period of truly grand slaughter and plunder, the barbarian discovers with an audible "uh-oh" that the legions have regrouped, they're moving forward in an orderly and powerful way, and it's going to be murder and mayhem in the barbarian camp for a while. The barbarian sees that his willfulness and violence has become the equivalent of self-defeat. That is his inescapable reality, even if it's one he is constitutionally incapable of understanding. (Rising oceans may make Manhattan the next fabled city of Atlantis. Get that?)

What science should be saying now is not, "Why were we not listened 15 to, respected, followed?" but, "We have wittingly taken common cause with the barbarians and participated in the making of this world, and it is clear now that this making was also our collective unmaking." In other words, science should be looking to something other than science, and certainly something other than barbarians, for ideas that will be a truer response to the disasters it has helped create. This looking elsewhere is not something science is particularly good at, if for no other reason than because, as intellectual victor for the last two centuries, it has contempt for those religious, philosophical, and artistic "elsewheres."

For instance, at the Ecocity World Summit in San Francisco in 2008, 16 climatologist Stephen Schneider commented that science could only demonstrate the "preponderance of evidence" and make suggestions about risk management and the investment of resources. (You see how comfortable science is in the garments of economics?) But it cannot make decisions that depend upon what Schneider called "value judgments." In other words, science can tell you that global warming puts the polar bear at risk, but it can't tell you why you should care.[4] It's as if Schneider were saying that we should take that issue up with the Pope. And maybe what I'm saying is: That's exactly right. We need a common language, not arrogance and then a punt.

The irony here, and it seems to be mostly lost on Schneider, is that 17 *nothing* has been more destructive of value than Western science. It has contempt for the truth claims of religion, obviously, but also the arts and even the so-called "soft" or social sciences. So just where, one might ask, does Schneider expect these "values" to come from when in fact science has done all it could to use its social prestige and intellectual authority to destroy all nonscientific system of value?

From the point of view of the Barbaric Heart, this is all good news. 18 Until science can manage to join its habits of mind to a way of thinking that is genuinely dedicated to the cultivation of value (i.e. a whole, thriving human culture and not the shards that science leaves to us), the Barbaric Heart will only hear in what science says that it can continue to be barbaric, if under a somewhat chastened model. Endless, profligate energy consumption, yes, but we'll pump the $CO_2$ back into the ground. How about that? That should fix it. That's sustainable, ain't it? For the barbarian, so long as someone suggests to him that he can continue to be violent and willful but mitigate the self-destructive consequences if he's shrewd about it, well, he's more than willing to listen and believe. And that is what the logic of sustainability does. "Let us *mitigate* your violence," it tells the barbarian, "so that your heart may retain all those barbaric qualities that have become the envy of the world."[5]

As the Romans knew, empire and wealth attract envy, but in the end    *19* it is envy not of some sort of civilized superiority but of the freedom to behave like barbarians without the consequences.

But perhaps we should say with a breezy sigh, "Thus has it ever been."    *20* What makes such breeziness untenable is the newfound understanding, for which the term "Global Warming" has become a sort of shorthand, that as we pursue our own venal ends, heedless of the consequences that pursuit will have on others, we are "sacking," in the barbarian vernacular, *ourselves*. We are like the barbarians described so aptly by Edward Gibbon in that we are not much conscious of the fact that our energetic pursuit of our own interests has a "blowback" factor (as the CIA puts it). Our pursuit of what we want makes us blind to how that pursuit is actually destroying ourselves. In the midst of its murderous pillaging, the Barbaric Heart discovers with a cry of surprise and animal anguish that it has dug its own grave. This self-defeat is true of our international bungling in places like Iraq, but it is most dramatically true in relation to the destruction of our own environment. Ask the people of New Orleans, or all of the places from Southern Europe to Africa to Australia to Malibu that have been visited by "once in a century" droughts, or places like Shanghai or Mumbai or the tiny island nation of Tuvalu, all of which are about to have the unique opportunity of seeing what it's like to live underwater. The future and its consequences is obviously now.

Which makes it a little easier to see why I would say that we are a cul-    *21* ture dominated by a rationality that is the equivalent of thoughtlessness. We are dominated by a form of logical intelligibility (science) that insists that *what is not intelligible to it is not intelligible at all*. Strangely, what is most dramatically unintelligible to science is *itself*. Especially hidden to it is the degree to which its own habit of logical orderliness prepares the way for the progress of the Barbaric, just as Rome's system of roads proved a great convenience not only to its own legions but to the barbaric armies that for once didn't need to "swarm" but could proceed in an orderly and direct fashion to their bloody destination: the final sacking of Rome.

To say that we live in thoughtlessness is really no more than to say that    *22* for the moment the Barbaric Heart is very comfortable. It does not feel threatened except distantly by things like Islamic terror, which it understands very well since that violence is little more than a reflection of its own conduct. And nothing is working *persuasively* with it, suggesting that it ought not to be what it is. (The intellectual disdain of science keeps all those voices at a distance in their respective communities: the university, the church, the museum, or the downtown art scene.) Rather, it hears only the narcissistic self-congratulation from the "experts" it hires to describe its triumphs and it benevolence on cable news programs. We are not quite yet at the point where the orderly rhythm of violence and plunder have no choice but to stop.

"And why should we stop?" you might ask. After all, the Barbaric Heart produces certain sweet and pleasurable things that we know quite well. The food is abundant, sex is everywhere, and the spectacles are spectacular.[6] (Always a sufficient argument for the *populous Romanus*.) But these sweet things are all produced by procedures that we do not see and do not understand, like the black boxes that run our cars or televisions or computers or, well, our lives. We know the benefits of these things but not their origin and not their procedures and not their ultimate purpose. The finely marbled filet at the supermarket meat counter is shrink-wrapped and looks as if it has been produced by an algorithm. It looks as if it were the Platonic idea of meat and not something hacked from a cow, not something produced by poor people standing in blood. At the far end of a gallon of gasoline is a Marine rolling a hand grenade into a living room in Haditha, Iraq. At the far end of the purchase of a plastic gizmo at Walmart is a Chinese industry dependent on the oil produced by a genocidal regime in Sudan. How that changes the look of the delightfully cheap gizmo! It is steeped in blood!

NOTES

1. In China and India, the commitment to capitalist development has become an international scandal and tragedy. The unthinkable has become commonplace. China seeks to triple the size of its economy by 2020. Expanding cities and industry claim rural areas, and farmers in turn claim ever more animal and plant habitat. At present, nearly 40 percent of all mammal species are endangered. For plants, 70 percent of non-flowering and 86 percent of flowering species are threatened. What the situation will be in 2020, that golden time of universal prosperity, is horrifying to imagine. (NYT A1, December 5, 2007)

2. I once gave a talk at Elliot Bay Book Company in Seattle and during the Q&A was asked, "Did you say you were a Marxist?" I could feel the room lift in anticipation of the wrong answer ("Yes"), as if they were already halfway out of their seats and through the door. I almost had to laugh. They had come expecting a little good-humored and satirical lambasting of the current state of capitalism, but praise Marx? And this was in Seattle!

3. As Freud put it presciently in *Moses and Monotheism*, the inclination to violence is "usually found where athletic development becomes the ideal of the people." (182) Or, as Hank Williams Jr. likes to sing on Monday nights, "*Are you ready for some football!?*"

4. In fact, Schneider commented that the polar bear is already "functionally extinct" because its ecosystem is extinct. The polar bear will survive only in a sort of great northern zoo. The species is sufficiently generalist to scavenge an existence from a variety of food sources, many of which will depend on humans. In short, the polar bear is becoming a big, white, house sparrow.

5. As eco-architect Richard S. Levine has explained, less dramatically, "To the extent that sustainable development agents move from crisis to crisis, using technological fixes to patch up larger structural problems, they tend to strengthen the systematic relations supporting unsustainability—especially when such 'band-aid' solutions lead to instances where these deeper problems fall below the threshold of public attention and the political momentum for more fundamental change dissipates." (Richard S. Levine, "Sustainable

Development," in Christopher Canfield, ed., *Ecocity Conference 1990: Report of the First International Ecocity Conference* (Urban Ecology, 1990), Pg. 24.)

6. The Persian poet Hafiz (1320–1389), one of whose early English translators was Emerson, wrote, "You have built, with so much care, / Such a great brothel / To house all of your pleasures. / You have even surrounded the whole damn place / With armed guards and vicious dogs / To protect your desires / So that you can sneak away / From time to time / And try to squeeze light / Into your parched being / From a source as fruitful / As a dried date pit / That even a bird / Is wise enough to spit out" (5).

■ ■ ■

## Reading as a Writer: Analyzing Rhetorical Choices

1. How would you characterize White's voice in this piece? Point to some specific passages where his voice is most distinctive and clear to you, and consider the benefits and possible shortcomings of this rhetorical approach.

2. As befits his argument, White draws on the ideas of both scientists and literary and philosophical thinkers. Look through his endnotes and discuss what you find most interesting about the kinds of sources he uses to support his argument.

## Writing as a Reader: Entering the Conversation of Ideas

1. The final paragraph of White's essay is linked to the heart of Gary Steiner's argument that veganism is the only ethical dietary practice. Write an essay in which you place these two lively thinkers in conversation with each other, considering how the ideas of one would illuminate the examples and argument of the other. Ultimately, how much crossover do you see in their arguments? What significance do you see in this?

2. In part, White's argument is that we are telling the wrong kinds of stories about sustainability if we really want to change our behaviors and improve the health of the planet. Noël Sturgeon makes a similar argument about the environmental stories being told in popular children's books and films. Compose an essay that brings together the arguments of both writers and considers the relationship between the stories we tell to children and those we tell to adults about our place in the environment. What conclusions can you draw about the changes you think need to be made, if any? Why?

## GARY STEINER

# Animal, Vegetable, Miserable

Gary Steiner is a philosophy professor at Bucknell University who has focused his most recent work on the significance of the ways we understand our relationship with animals. This is the topic of his book *Anthropocentrism and Its Discontents: The Moral Status of Animals in the History of Western Philosophy* (2005) and also his most recent book, *Animals and the Moral Community: Mental Life, Moral Status, and Kinship* (2008). Steiner's key argument is that we should reevaluate the ideas we have inherited from Western philosophy that human animals are morally superior to non-human animals. Using both moral reasoning and statistics about the levels of violence that nonhuman animals suffer at the hands of humans, he attempts to open readers' minds about what we assume is "normal" behavior, such as eating meat or enjoying circuses and zoos.

In this short and pointedly argued guest column in the *New York Times*, Steiner raises questions about the ethics of eating even "humanely" raised meat, and he does so in late November (2009), just when millions of Americans are preparing to tuck into roasted turkey. As you read, pay attention to his word choice and examples as he tries to get us to see what he calls our "meat-crazed" culture through his eyes, the eyes of an "ethical vegan" who avoids *all* animal products—not just in food but in clothing, shoes, and even Band-Aids (para. 13). Steiner knows he is in the minority; how does this knowledge affect his argument, and how does he address what he knows to be the enormous opposition to his perspective?

Where do you stand in this heated conversation about ethics and the treatment of nonhuman animals? Take a look at the letters to the editor that respond to Steiner's piece and that follow Steiner's column here. Again, where do you stand? How you respond will affect the next meal you eat.

■　■　■

L ately more people have begun to express an interest in where the  *1* meat they eat comes from and how it was raised. Were the animals humanely treated? Did they have a good quality of life before the death that turned them into someone's dinner?

Some of these questions, which reach a fever pitch in the days lead- *2* ing up to Thanksgiving, pertain to the ways in which animals are treated. (Did your turkey get to live outdoors?) Others focus on the question of how eating the animals in question will affect the consumer's health and well-being. (Was it given hormones and antibiotics?)

None of these questions, however, make any consideration of whether *3* it is wrong to kill animals for human consumption. And even when people ask this question, they almost always find a variety of resourceful answers that purport to justify the killing and consumption of animals in the name of human welfare. Strict ethical vegans, of which I am one, are customarily excoriated for equating our society's treatment of animals with mass murder. Can anyone seriously consider animal suffering even remotely comparable to human suffering? Those who answer with a resounding no typically argue in one of two ways.

Some suggest that human beings but not animals are made in God's *4* image and hence stand in much closer proximity to the divine than any non-human animal; according to this line of thought, animals were made expressly for the sake of humans and may be used without scruple to satisfy their needs and desires. There is ample support in the Bible and in the writings of Christian thinkers like Augustine and Thomas Aquinas for this pointedly anthropocentric way of devaluing animals.

Others argue that the human capacity for abstract thought makes us  5 capable of suffering that both qualitatively and quantitatively exceeds the suffering of any non-human animal. Philosophers like Jeremy Bentham, who is famous for having based moral status not on linguistic or rational capacities but rather on the capacity to suffer, argue that because animals are incapable of abstract thought, they are imprisoned in an eternal present, have no sense of the extended future, and hence cannot be said to have an interest in continued existence.

The most penetrating and iconoclastic response to this sort of reason-  6 ing came from the writer Isaac Bashevis Singer in his story "The Letter Writer," in which he called the slaughter of animals the "eternal Treblinka."

The story depicts an encounter between a man and a mouse. The man,  7 Herman Gombiner, contemplates his place in the cosmic scheme of things and concludes that there is an essential connection between his own existence as "a child of God" and the "holy creature" scuffling about on the floor in front of him.

Surely, he reflects, the mouse has some capacity for thought; Gom-  8 biner even thinks that the mouse has the capacity to share love and gratitude with him. Not merely a means for the satisfaction of human desires, nor a mere nuisance to be exterminated, this tiny creature possesses the same dignity that any conscious being possesses. In the face of that inherent dignity, Gombiner concludes, the human practice of delivering animals to the table in the form of food is abhorrent and inexcusable.

Many of the people who denounce the ways in which we treat animals in  9 the course of raising them for human consumption never stop to think about this profound contradiction. Instead, they make impassioned calls for more "humanely" raised meat. Many people soothe their consciences by purchasing only free-range fowl and eggs, blissfully ignorant that "free range" has very little if any practical significance. Chickens may be labeled free-range even if they've never been outside or seen a speck of daylight in their entire lives. And that Thanksgiving turkey? Even if it is raised "free range," it still lives a life of pain and confinement that ends with the butcher's knife.

How can intelligent people who purport to be deeply concerned with  10 animal welfare and respectful of life turn a blind eye to such practices? And how can people continue to eat meat when they become aware that nearly 53 billion land animals are slaughtered every year for human consumption? The simple answer is that most people just don't care about the lives or fortunes of animals. If they did care, they would learn as much as possible about the ways in which our society systematically abuses animals, and they would make what is at once a very simple and a very difficult choice: to forswear the consumption of animal products of all kinds.

The easy part of this consists in seeing clearly what ethics requires *11* and then just plain doing it. The difficult part: You just haven't lived until you've tried to function as a strict vegan in a meat-crazed society.

What were once the most straightforward activities become a constant *12* ordeal. You might think that it's as simple as just removing meat, eggs, and dairy products from your diet, but it goes a lot deeper than that.

To be a really strict vegan is to strive to avoid all animal products, *13* and this includes materials like leather, silk, and wool, as well as a panoply of cosmetics and medications. The more you dig, the more you learn about products you would never stop to think might contain or involve animal products in their production—like wine and beer (isinglass, a kind of gelatin derived from fish bladders, is often used to "fine," or purify, these beverages), refined sugar (bone char is sometimes used to bleach it), or Band-Aids (animal products in the adhesive). Just last week I was told that those little comfort strips on most razor blades contain animal fat.

To go down this road is to stare headlong into an abyss that, to para- *14* phrase Nietzsche, will ultimately stare back at you.

The challenges faced by a vegan don't end with the nuts and bolts of *15* material existence. You face quite a few social difficulties as well, perhaps the chief one being how one should feel about spending time with people who are not vegans.

Is it O.K. to eat dinner with people who are eating meat? What do you *16* say when a dining companion says, "I'm really a vegetarian—I don't eat red meat at home." (I've heard it lots of times, always without any prompting from me.) What do you do when someone starts to grill you (so to speak) about your vegan ethics during dinner? (Wise vegans always defer until food isn't around.) Or when someone starts to lodge accusations to the effect that you consider yourself morally superior to others, or that it is ridiculous to worry so much about animals when there is so much human suffering in the world? (Smile politely and ask them to pass the seitan.)

Let me be candid: By and large, meat-eaters are a self-righteous bunch. *17* The number of vegans I know personally is . . . five. And I have been a vegan for almost 15 years, having been a vegetarian for almost 15 before that.

Five. I have lost more friends than this over arguments about animal *18* ethics. One lapidary conclusion to be drawn here is that people take deadly seriously the prerogative to use animals as sources of satisfaction. Not only for food, but as beasts of burden, as raw materials, and as sources of captive entertainment—which is the way animals are used in zoos, circuses, and the like.

These uses of animals are so institutionalized, so normalized, in our *19* society that it is difficult to find the critical distance needed to see them as the horrors that they are: so many forms of subjection, servitude, and—in the case of killing animals for human consumption and other purposes—outright murder.

People who are ethical vegans believe that differences in intelligence *20* between human and non-human animals have no moral significance whatsoever. The fact that my cat can't appreciate Schubert's late symphonies and can't perform syllogistic logic does not mean that I am entitled to use him as an organic toy, as if I were somehow not only morally superior to him but virtually entitled to treat him as a commodity with minuscule market value.

We have been trained by a history of thinking of which we are scarcely   21
aware to view non-human animals as resources we are entitled to employ in whatever ways we see fit in order to satisfy our needs and desires. Yes, there are animal welfare laws. But these laws have been formulated by, and are enforced by, people who proceed from the proposition that animals are fundamentally inferior to human beings. At best, these laws make living conditions for animals marginally better than they would be otherwise—right up to the point when we send them to the slaughterhouse.

Think about that when you're picking out your free-range turkey,   22
which has absolutely nothing to be thankful for on Thanksgiving. All it ever had was a short and miserable life, thanks to us intelligent, compassionate humans.

■ ■ ■

### Reading as a Writer: Analyzing Rhetorical Choices

1. How and where does Steiner make use of ethos, pathos, and logos as he builds his argument in this piece? Discuss the relationship you see between these different strategies. Which is most effective? How do they complement one another?

2. How does Steiner characterize those who are not vegans? Locate some passages and discuss the ways you think this serves, or does not serve, his argument well. How does he characterize himself and other vegans? Again, discuss how you think this serves, or does not serve, his argument well.

### Writing as a Reader: Entering the Conversation of Ideas

1. Steiner and Anna Lappé both make strong appeals for changing the way we eat as a key strategy (perhaps *the* key strategy) to living more humane lives that are healthier for us and healthier for the globe. Compose an essay in which you place these authors in conversation, considering how each describes the problem and solutions. What do you think are the most compelling reasons for changing our lifestyles, and why? You might also analyze the rhetorical strategies each author uses as you consider how best to inspire others to change their daily habits.

2. While they may seem unlikely companions, both Steiner and Jean Kilbourne write about levels of violence we have become accustomed to in our daily lives, whether on our plates or in the images we consume. Write an essay in which you connect the ways each author writes about violence and its effects. What connections do you see in the objectification of and violence to bodies in each text? What solutions does each author offer, and what connections do you see there? Where do you stand?

# The Ethical Choices in What We Eat:
# Responses to Gary Steiner

As you read these varying responses to Gary Steiner's "Animal, Vegetable, Miserable," from the Letters to the Editor section of the *New York Times*, evaluate how effectively these writers use ethos, pathos, and logos as persuasive tactics. Some of the writers have listed their professions, and some have not. How does knowing the writers' professions affect the way you read these letters? What would *your* letter in response to Steiner look like?

* * *

To the Editor:

Re "Animal, Vegetable, Miserable," by Gary Steiner (Op-Ed, Nov. 22):

Mr. Steiner might feel less lonely as an ethical vegan—he says he has 1 just five vegan friends—if he recognized that he has allies in mere vegetarians (like me), ethical omnivores, and even carnivores. Some of us agree with his outlook, but just don't have the fortitude to make every sacrifice he makes.

In fact, a whole lot of semi-vegans can do much more for animals than 2 the tiny number of people who are willing to give up all animal products and scrupulously read labels. Farm animals also benefit from the humane farming movement, even if the animal welfare changes it effects are not all that we should hope and work for.

If the goal is not moral perfection for ourselves, but the maximum ben- 3 efit for animals, half-measures ought to be encouraged and appreciated.

Go vegan, go vegetarian, go humane, or just eat less meat. It's all good 4 advice from the point of view of doing better by animals.

Jean Kazez
Dallas, November 22, 2009
The writer teaches philosophy at Southern Methodist University and is the author of the forthcoming *Animalkind: What We Owe to Animals*.

■ ■ ■

To the Editor:
Soon after I read Gary Steiner's article, my wife asked me to kill a spi- 5 der, which I did. This made me feel guilty. Spiders are living creatures, too; perhaps I should have gently caught it and carried it outdoors?

It is hard to imagine where a line can be drawn. We kill so many living 6 creatures when we build a house, construct a road, drive down that road, or just walk on a path. How far do we go in protecting them?

When we plant and harvest crops that vegans would find acceptable to 7 eat, many animals are killed and their habitats are destroyed.

If we all decide to consider animals as precious as humans, the only *8* logical place for us is back in the jungle. But even then if we were to survive we would have to kill some animals in self-defense.

Alexander Mauskop
New York, November 22, 2009

■ ■ ■

To the Editor:

I am an ethical vegan. Gary Steiner perfectly articulates my feelings, *9* and particularly my frustration, as so many around me obsess about the preparation of their turkeys.

When one "goes vegan," what seems obvious to that person is ridiculed *10* by a large part of society. Mr. Steiner illustrates the disconnect within our culture about eating animals and the righteousness with which people will defend that disconnect.

Alice Walker once said: "The animals of the world exist for their own *11* reasons. They were not made for humans any more than black people were made for white, or women created for men."

I hope that Mr. Steiner's essay will result in people at least stopping for *12* a moment, before carving the birds on their tables, and giving these ideas some serious critical thought.

Chris Taylor
Lawrence, Kansas, November 22, 2009

■ ■ ■

To the Editor:

Gary Steiner's case for veganism founders on the facts. First, the *13* human digestive system has evolved to accommodate an omnivorous diet, not a purely vegetable one.

Indeed, many paleoanthropologists maintain that the evolution of the *14* large, energy-hungry human brains depended on a transition of our ancestors' diets to include meat.

And vegans must tread a very narrow line to avoid all sorts of defi- *15* ciency diseases, while omnivores have very broad latitude in diet, as a survey of world cuisines makes evident.

Second, our food animals have co-evolved with us. Cows, domes- *16* tic sheep, chickens, and many others would not survive if they were not raised for human consumption, protected from malnutrition, disease, and predators.

Professor Steiner is entitled to his beliefs and his tofurkey; most of the *17* rest of us will enjoy our turkey without guilt (but with vegetable stuffing).

Lawrence S. Lerner
Woodside, California, November 22, 2009
The writer is professor emeritus at the College of Natural Sciences and Mathematics at California State University, Long Beach.

■ ■ ■

To the Editor:

Gary Steiner recognizes that many of us justify eating animals because    *18*
we believe we are superior to them. Mr. Steiner rightly rejects this view as
morally flawed.

Humans can acceptably consume animals precisely because we are    *19*
not superior to them at all. Wolves eat sheep. Tuna eat mackerel. We are
animals ourselves—and are no more (or less) than the animals we consume, or than the predators that would otherwise consume them.

If we are not justified in eating mackerel ourselves, are we not also    *20*
morally obligated to stop the slaughter brought on by the tuna?

Such an obligation would make us the protectors of all species, and    *21*
the destroyers of every ecosystem on earth.

L. David Peters
New York, November 22, 2009

■ ■ ■

To the Editor:

As a vegetarian for 18 years, I have been confronted with the same    *22*
questions that Gary Steiner faces from those challenging his dietary habits. I learned an effective response long ago that has benefited both my
blood pressure and friendships.

I say with a big smile: "My vegetarianism is a personal choice that I    *23*
usually don't discuss in detail. I'm happy to eat with nonvegetarians." And
then I'm quiet.

That has pleasantly ended many potentially uncomfortable exchanges.    *24*
Being vegetarian, as with being a member of a political party or a religious
denomination, does not bestow license to convert others to one's own way
of thinking.

On my deathbed, I'll be happy to have lived life as a vegetarian and    *25*
also (I hope) comforted by many who were not alienated through heated
discussions about my dietary choices.

Lisa Dinhofer
Frederick, Maryland, November 22, 2009

■ ■ ■

To the Editor:

I will rise to the challenge Gary Steiner presents. He's right: I don't    *26*
care deeply about the suffering of animals I eat, wear, or otherwise benefit
from. Suffering and injustice are inherent in life, and time is short.

Moreover, I find no way to shine a moral spotlight on one corner with-    *27*
out letting shadows fall on another. I radically limit my conscious sphere
of concern (just as Mr. Steiner must).

My moral boundaries may be rational or reflexive, expansive or self-    *28*
ish—who can judge?

I also recognize that alleviating suffering in one area may cause pain *29* elsewhere. My mind and spirit are continually tested by outrages, from the countless dead innocents in current wars to the limited life prospects of my son's first-grade classmates with drug dealers for parents.

Were I also to internalize the pain experienced by animals, I'd simply *30* shut down. Whose lot could that possibly help?

Sandy Asirvatham
Baltimore, Maryland, November 22, 2009

■ ■ ■

To the Editor:

I was shocked to read that Gary Steiner thinks his cat can't appreciate *31* Schubert's late symphonies. It's not the feline lack of musical discernment that I found disturbing (I don't "get" Schubert's symphonies either), but rather that Mr. Steiner owns a pet.

If he wishes to make no distinction between animal and human life *32* and rights, how does he justify keeping an animal in what amounts to captivity?

And where does he draw the line between keeping a cow for milk and *33* keeping a cat or dog for comfort or gratification?

Alice Desaulniers
Irvington, New York, November 23, 2009

■ ■ ■

## Reading as a Writer: Analyzing Rhetorical Choices

1. Discuss the different argumentative strategies you see these writers using, including the appeals of ethos, pathos, and logos and the evidence they do (or do not) provide. What can you conclude about writing an effective letter to the editor?

## ANNA LAPPÉ

## The Climate Crisis at the End of Our Fork

Anna Lappé is a best-selling author and public speaker who founded—along with her mother, the food activist Frances Moore Lappé—the Small Planet Institute, an international network of scholars, activists, and educators who are interested in the intersections of hunger and poverty. Lappé is a frequent guest writer for the *New York Times*, *Gourmet*, *O: The Oprah Magazine*, and *Body + Soul*, to name a few of the many publications that have featured her writing on food politics. She has also edited and written or cowritten several books, including *Hope's Edge: The Next Diet for a Small Planet* (2002, with Frances Moore Lappé) and *Grub: Ideas for an Urban*

*Organic Kitchen* (2006, with chef Bryant Terry). Her most recent book is *Diet for a Hot Planet: The Climate Crisis at the End of Your Fork and What You Can Do About It* (2010). This essay was published in the anthology *Food Inc.: A Participant Guide: How Industrial Food Is Making Us Sicker, Fatter, and Poorer—And What You Can Do About It* (2009), edited by Karl Weber. The book is a companion to the documentary film *Food, Inc.*, about the ecological and health effects of the industrialization of the food chain.

In this piece, Lappé opens by describing the gasping response of the audience at a talk at which a climate change scholar discussed the enormous impact of the food system on global warming. She throws at readers the same surprising information she learned at this talk, that "the global system for producing and distributing food accounts for roughly *one-third* of the human-caused global warming effect . . . [and] the livestock sector alone is responsible for eighteen percent of the world's total global warming effect—more than the emissions produced by every plane, train, and steamer ship on the planet" (para. 5, emphasis in original). These statistics launch her argument that if the food sector is a critical part of the global-warming problem, then it is also critical to the solution. Lappé wants readers to see that changing the food system is as crucial as—or even more crucial than—any other ecological solutions we commonly think of, such as changing lightbulbs or driving more efficient cars.

As you read, pay close attention to the evidence Lappé offers, in her text and in her copious endnotes. What do you think are the most persuasive examples and statistics she offers to make her point about the problem and how much is at stake? How does she use evidence to propose solutions in her final section?

Lappé is part of a rapidly expanding group of scholars, writers, and activists who are interested in all aspects of food politics. Unlike some forms of consumption that we can avoid—like smoking, for example—we all need to eat to survive. What will we spear on the end of our fork when we take our next bite of food? Lappé argues that our answer will affect not only our bodies but also the fate of the planet.

■ ■ ■

We could hear audible gasps from the two dozen New York state farmers gathered at the Glynwood Center on a cold December day in 2007 when NASA scientist Cynthia Rosenzweig, one of the world's leading experts on climate change and agriculture, explained the slide glowing on the screen in front of us.

The Glynwood Center, an education nonprofit and farm set on 225 acres in the Hudson Valley, had brought Rosenzweig to speak to area farmers about the possible impact of climate change on the region. Pointing to an arrow swooping south from New York, Rosenzweig said: "If we don't drastically reduce greenhouse gas emissions by 2080, farming in New York could feel like farming in Georgia."

"It was all projections before. It's not projections now—it's observa- 3
tional science," said Rosenzweig. We are already seeing major impacts of
climate change on agriculture: droughts leading to crop loss and saliniza-
tion of soils, flooding causing waterlogged soils, longer growing seasons
leading to new and more pest pressures, and erratic weather shifting harvesting seasons, explained Rosenzweig.

When people think about climate change and food, many first think 4
of the aspect of the equation that Rosenzweig focused on that day—the
impact of climate change on farming. But when it comes to how the food
system impacts global warming, most draw a blank.

Challenged to name the human factors that promote climate change, 5
we typically picture industrial smokestacks or oil-thirsty planes and automobiles, not Pop-Tarts or pork chops. Yet the global system for producing
and distributing food accounts for roughly *one-third* of the human-caused
global warming effect. According to the United Nation's seminal report,
*Livestock's Long Shadow*, the livestock sector alone is responsible for
eighteen percent of the world's total global warming effect—more than
the emissions produced by every plane, train, and steamer ship on the
planet.[1]

Asked what we can do as individuals to help solve the climate change 6
crisis, most of us could recite these eco-mantras from memory: Change
our light bulbs! Drive less! Choose energy-efficient appliances! Asked
what we can do as a nation, most of us would probably mention promoting renewable energy and ending our addiction to fossil fuels. Few among
us would mention changing the way we produce our food or the dietary
choices we make.

Unfortunately, the dominant storyline about climate change—its big- 7
gest drivers and the key solutions—diverts us from understanding how
other sectors, particularly the food sector, are critical parts of the *problem*,
but even more importantly can be vital strategies for *solutions*.

If the role of our food system in global warming comes as news to you, 8
it's understandable. Many of us have gotten the bulk of our information
about global warming from Al Gore's wake-up call *An Inconvenient Truth*,
the 2006 Oscar-winning documentary that became the fourth-highest
grossing nonfiction film in American history.[2] In addition to the record-
breaking doc, Gore's train-the-trainer program, which coaches educators
on sharing his slideshow, has further spread his central message about the
threat posed by human-made climate change. But Gore's program offers
little information about the connection between climate change and the
food on your plate.

Mainstream newspapers in the United States haven't done a much bet- 9
ter job of covering the topic. Researchers at Johns Hopkins University analyzed climate change coverage in sixteen leading U.S. newspapers from
September 2005 through January 2008. Of the 4,582 articles published on
climate change during that period, only 2.4 percent addressed the role of

the food production system, and most of those only peripherally. In fact, just half of one percent of all climate change articles had "a substantial focus" on food and agriculture.[3] Internationally, the focus hasn't been much different. Until recently, much of the attention from the international climate change community and national coordinating bodies was also mostly focused on polluting industries and the burning of fossil fuels, not on the food sector.

This is finally starting to change. In the second half of 2008, writers *10* from *O: The Oprah Magazine* to the *Los Angeles Times* started to cover the topic, increasing the public's awareness of the food and climate change connection. In September 2008, Dr. Rajendra Pachauri, the Indian economist serving his second term as chair of the United Nations Intergovernmental Panel on Climate Change, made a bold statement about the connection between our diet and global warming. Choosing to eat less meat, or eliminating meat entirely, is one of the most important personal choices we can make to address climate change, said Pachauri.[4] "In terms of immediacy of action and the feasibility of bringing about reductions in a short period of time, it clearly is the most attractive opportunity," said Pachauri. "Give up meat for one day [a week] initially, and decrease it from there."[5]

Why does our food system play such a significant role in the global *11* warming effect? There are many reasons, including the emissions created by industrial farming processes, such as fertilizer production, and the carbon emissions produced by trucks, ships, and planes as they transport foods across nations and around the world. Among the main sources of the food system's impact on climate are land use changes, especially the expansion of palm oil production, and effects caused by contemporary agricultural practices, including the emissions produced by livestock.

## The Land Use Connection

Let's look at land use first. A full eighteen percent of the world's global *12* warming effect is associated with "land use changes," mostly from the food system.[6] The biggest factors are the destruction of vital rainforests through burning and clearing and the elimination of wetlands and peat bogs to expand pasture for cattle, feed crops for livestock, and oil palm plantations, especially in a handful of countries, Brazil and Indonesia chief among them.[7]

What do Quaker Granola Bars and Girl Scout Cookies have to do with *13* the climate crisis?[8] These processed foods—along with other popular products, including cosmetics, soaps, shampoo, even fabric softeners—share a common ingredient, one with enormous climate implications: palm oil.[9] As the taste for processed foods skyrockets, so does the demand for palm oil, production of which has more that doubled in the last decade.[10] Today, palm oil is the most widely traded vegetable oil in the world, with major growth in the world's top two importing countries, India and China.[11]

As oil palm plantations expand on rainforests and peat lands in Southeast Asia, the natural swamp forests that formerly filled those lands are cut down and drained, and the peat-filled soils release carbon dioxide and methane into the atmosphere. (Methane is a key greenhouse gas with twenty-three times the global warming impact of carbon dioxide.) In a recent study, researchers estimate that producing one ton of palm oil can create fifteen to seventy tons of carbon dioxide over a twenty-five year period.[12]    14

Three of the world's biggest agribusiness companies are major players in the palm oil market, which is concentrated in two countries—Malaysia and Indonesia—where in 2007, forty-three percent and forty-four percent of the world's total palm oil was produced, respectively.[13] Wilmar, an affiliate of the multinational giant Archer Daniels Midland, is the largest palm oil producer in the world;[14] soy behemoth Bunge is a major importer of palm oil into the United States (although at the moment it doesn't own or operate any of its own facilities);[15] and grain-trading Cargill owns palm plantations throughout Indonesia and Malaysia.[16] These three companies and others producing palm oil claim that guidelines from the Roundtable on Sustainable Palm Oil (RSPO), established in 2004 by industry and international nonprofits, ensure sustainable production that minimizes the destruction of forest and peat bogs as well as deleterious effect on the global climate.[17]    15

However, some environmental and human rights groups argue that loopholes in the Roundtable's regulations still leave too much wiggle room. Says Greenpeace, "The existing standards developed by the RSPO will not prevent forest and peat land destruction, and a number of RSPO members are taking no steps to avoid the worst practices of the palm oil industry."[18]    16

We also know from new data that palm plantation expansion on peat land is not slowing. According to Dr. Susan Page from the University of Leicester, deforestation rates on peat lands have been increasing for twenty years, with one-quarter of all deforestation in Southeast Asia occurring on peat lands in 2005 alone.[19]    17

The other side of the land use story is deforestation driven by the increased production of livestock, expanding pasture lands and cropland for feed. In Latin America, for instance, nearly three-quarters of formerly forested land is now occupied by pastures; feed crops for livestock cover much of the remainder.[20] Globally, one-third of the world's arable land is dedicated to feed crop production.[21] Poorly managed pastures lead to overgrazing, compaction, and erosion, which release stored carbon into the atmosphere. With livestock now occupying twenty-six percent of the planet's ice-free land, the impact of this poor land management is significant.[22]    18

Raising livestock in confinement and feeding them diets of grains and other feedstock—including animal waste by-products—is a relatively    19 recent phenomenon. In the postwar period, intensification of animal production was seen as the path to productivity. As livestock were confined in high stocking densities often far from where their feed was grown, a highly inefficient and environmentally costly system was born.

As a British Government Panel on Sustainable Development said in 1997, "Farming methods in the last half century have changed rapidly as a result of policies which have favored food production at the expense of the conservation of biodiversity and the protection of the landscape."[23] Despite these environmental costs, confined animal feeding operations (CAFOs) spread in the 1960s and 1970s into Europe and Japan and what was then the Soviet Union. Today, CAFOs are becoming increasingly common in East Asia, Latin America, and West Asia. 20

As the largest U.S.-based multinational meat companies, including Tyson, Cargill, and Smithfield, set their sights overseas, the production of industrial meat globally is growing.[24] In addition, the increasing supply of meat in developing countries flooded with advertising for Western-style eating habits is leading to a potential doubling in demand for industrial livestock production, and therefore feed crops, from 1997–1999 to 2030.[25] 21

Although the shift from traditional ways of raising livestock to industrial-scale confinement operations is often defended in the name of "efficiency," it's a spurious claim. As a way of producing edible proteins, feedlot livestock production is inherently inefficient. While ruminants such as cattle naturally convert inedible-to-humans grasses into high-grade proteins, under industrial production, grain-fed cattle pass along to humans only a fraction of the protein they consume.[26] Debates about this conversion rate abound. The U.S. Department of Agriculture estimates that it takes seven pounds of grain to produce one pound of beef.[27] However, journalist Paul Roberts, author of *The End of Food*, argues that the true conversion rate is much higher. While feedlot cattle need at least ten pounds of feed to gain one pound of live weight, Roberts states, nearly two-thirds of this weight gain is for inedible parts, such as bones, other organs, and hide. The true conversion ratio, Roberts estimates, is twenty pounds of grain to produce a single pound of beef, 7.3 pounds for pigs, and 3.5 pounds for poultry.[28] 22

The inefficiency of turning to grain-fed livestock as a major component of the human diet is devastating in itself, especially in a world where nearly one billion people still go hungry. But now we know there is a climate cost as well. The more consolidation in the livestock industry—where small-scale farmers are pushed out and replaced by large-scale confinement operations—the more land will be turned over to feed production. This production is dependent on fossil fuel—intensive farming, from synthesizing the human-made nitrogen fertilizer to using fossil fuel–based chemicals on feed crops. Each of these production steps cost in emissions contributing to the escalating greenhouse effect undermining our planet's ecological balance. 23

## The Agriculture Connection

One reason we may have been slow to recognize the impact of the food 24
system on climate change may be a certain "carbon bias." While carbon
dioxide is the most abundant human-made greenhouse gas in the atmosphere, making up seventy-seven percent of the total human-caused global
warming effect, methane and nitrous oxide contribute nearly all the rest.[29]
(Other greenhouse gases are also relevant to the global warming effect, but
are currently present in much smaller quantities and have a less significant
impact.)[30] Agriculture is responsible for most of the human-made methane and nitrous oxide in the atmosphere, which contribute 13.5 percent of
total greenhouse gas emissions, primarily from animal waste mismanage-
ment, fertilizer overuse, the natural effects of ruminant digestion, and to a
small degree rice production[31] (1.5 percent of total emissions come from
methane produced during rice cultivation).[32]

Though livestock only contribute nine percent or carbon dioxide emis- 25
sions, the sector is responsible for thirty-seven percent of methane and
sixty-five percent of nitrous oxide.[33] Here again, recent changes in agricultural practices are a significant factor. For centuries, livestock have been
a vital part of sustainable food systems, providing muscle for farm work
and meat as a vital protein source. Historically, properly grazed livestock
produced numerous benefits to the land: Hooves aerate soil, allowing
more oxygen in the ground, which helps plant growth; their hoof action
also presses grass seed into the earth, fostering plant growth, too; and, of
course, their manure provides natural fertilizer. Indeed, new self-described
"carbon farmers" are developing best management practices to manage
cattle grazing to reduce compaction and overgrazing and, mimicking traditional grazing patterns, increasing carbon sequestration in the soil.[34]

But modern livestock production has steered away from these tradi- 26
tional practices toward the industrial-style production described above and
to highly destructive overgrazing. In sustainable systems tapping nature's
wisdom, there is no such thing as waste: Manure is part of a holistic cycle
and serves to fertilize the same lands where the animals that produce it
live. In CAFOs, there is simply too much waste to cycle back through the
system. Instead, waste is stored in manure "lagoons," as they're euphemis-
tically called. Without sufficient oxygenation, this waste emits methane
and nitrous oxide gas. As a consequence of industrial livestock production,
the United States scores at the top of the world for methane emissions
from manure. Swine production is king in terms of methane emissions,
responsible for half of the globe's total.[35]

The sheer numbers of livestock exacerbate the problem. In 1965, eight 27
billion livestock animals were alive on the planet at any given moment; ten
billion were slaughtered every year. Today, thanks in part to CAFOs that spur
faster growth and shorter lifespan, twenty billion livestock animals are alive
at any moment, while nearly fifty-five billion are slaughtered annually.[36]

Ruminants, such as cattle, buffalo, sheep, and goats, are among the   28
main agricultural sources of methane. They can't help it; it's in their nature.
Ruminants digest through microbial, or enteric, fermentation, which produces methane that is then released by the animals, mainly through belch-
ing. While this process enables ruminants to digest fibrous grasses that we
humans can't convert into digestible form, it also contributes to livestock's
climate change impact. (Enteric fermentation accounts for twenty-five
percent of the total emissions from the livestock sector; land use changes
account for another 35.4 percent; manure accounts for 30.5 percent.)[37]

In addition to the ruminants' digestive process, emissions from live-   29
stock can be traced back to the production of the crops they consume.
Globally, thirty-three percent of the world's cereal harvest and ninety percent of the world's soy harvest are now being raised for animal feed.[38] Feed
crop farmers are heavily dependent on fossil fuels, used to power the on-
farm machinery as well as used in the production of the petroleum-based
chemicals to protect against pests, stave off weeds, and foster soil fertility
on large-scale monoculture fields. In addition, these crops use up immense
quantities of fertilizer. In the United States and Canada, half of all synthetic fertilizer is used for feed crops.[39] In the United Kingdom, the total is
nearly seventy percent.[40] To produce this fertilizer requires tons of natural
gas; on average 1.5 tons of oil equivalents are used up to make one ton of
fertilizer.[41] Yet in the United States, only about half of the nitrogen fertilizer applied to corn is even used by the crop.[42] This needless waste is all
the more alarming because nitrogen fertilizer contributes roughly three-
quarters of the country's nitrous oxide emissions.

Erosion and deterioration of soils on industrial farms is another factor   30
in the food sector's global warming toll. As industrial farms diminish natural soil fertility and disturb soil through tillage, soil carbon is released into
the atmosphere.[43] Because industrialized agriculture also relies on huge
amounts of water for irrigation, these farms will be more vulnerable as
climate change increases drought frequency and intensity and decreases
water availability. Globally, seventy percent of the world's available fresh-
water is being diverted to irrigation-intensive agriculture.[44]

## The Waste and Transportation Connection

The sources of food system emissions on which we've focused so far—   31
including land use changes and agricultural production—are responsible
for nearly one-third of the total human-made global warming effect. That's
already quite a lot, but other sectors include emissions from the food
chain, including transportation, waste, and manufacturing.

For example, 3.6 percent of global greenhouse gas emissions come   32
from waste, including landfills, wastewater, and other waste.[45] The food
production system contributes its share to this total. After all, where does

most of our uneaten food and food ready for harvest that never even makes it to our plates end up? Landfills. Solid waste, including food scraps, produces greenhouse gas emissions from anaerobic decomposition, which produces methane, and from carbon dioxide as a by-product of incineration and waste transportation.[46]

An additional 13.1 percent of the emissions that contribute to the global warming effect come from transportation, toting everything from people to pork chops.[47] The factory farming industry, in particular, demands energy-intensive shipping. CAFOs, for example, transport feed and live animals to feedlots and then to slaughter. Then the meat must be shipped to retail distribution centers and to the stores where it is sold to us consumers. `33`

Americans, in particular, import and export a lot of meat. In 2007, the United States exported 1.4 billion pounds of beef and veal (5.4 percent of our total production of beef)[48] and imported 3.1 billion pounds of the same.[49] One could argue that a lot of that transport is unnecessary from a consumer point of view and damaging from an environmental point of view. `34`

Globally, international trade in meat is rapidly accelerating. As recently as 1995, Brazil was exporting less than half-a-million dollars' worth of beef. A little more than a decade later, the Brazilian Beef Industry and Exporters Association estimates the value of beef exports could reach $5.2 billion and expects revenues of $15 billion from beef exports by 2013.[50] `35`

All of these billions of pounds of meat being shipped around the world add significantly to the carbon emissions from transportation. So do the Chilean grapes shipped to California, the Australian dairy destined for Japan, or the Twinkies toted across the country—all the meat and dairy, drinks, and processed foods shipped worldwide in today's globalized food market. `36`

## The Organic Solution

The globalized and industrialized food system has not only negative health consequences—think of all those Twinkies, that factory-farmed meat, and that chemically raised produce—but a climate change toll as well. But the news is not all bad. Once we gaze directly at the connection between food, farming, and global warming, we see plenty of cause for hope. `37`

First, unlike many other climate change conundrums, we already know many of the steps we can take now to reduce carbon emissions from the food sector. For instance, we know that compared with industrial farms, small-scale organic and sustained farms can significantly reduce the sector's emissions. Small-scale sustainable agriculture relies on people power, not heavy machinery, and depends on working with biological methods, not human-made chemicals, to increase soil fertility and handle pests. As a result, small-scale sustained farms use much fewer fossil fuels and have been found to emit between one-half and two-thirds less carbon dioxide for every acre of production.[51] `38`

We also are just beginning to see results from long-term studies show- [39] ing how organic farms create healthy soil, which has greater capacity to store carbon, creating those all-important "carbon sinks."[52] By one estimate, converting 10,000 medium-sized farms to organic would store as much carbon in the soil as we would save in emissions if we took one million cars off the road.[53]

We're closer than ever to global consensus about the direction in which [40] we need to head. In April 2008, a report on agriculture initiated by the World Bank, in partnership with the United Nations and representatives from the private sector, NGOs, and scientific institutions from around the world, declared that diverse, small-holder sustainable agriculture can play a vital role in reducing the environment impacts of the agriculture sector.

The result of four years of work by hundreds of scientists and review- [41] ers,[54] the International Assessment of Agriculture Science and Technology for Development (IAASTD) calls for supporting agroecological systems; enhancing agricultural biodiversity; promoting small-scale farms; and encouraging the sustainable management of livestock, forest, and fisheries, as well as supporting "biological substitutes for agrochemicals" and "reducing the dependency of the agricultural sector on fossil fuels."[55] A civil society statement timed with the report's release declared that the IAASTD represents the beginning of a "new era of agriculture" and offers "a sobering account of the failure of industrial farming."[56] Said Greenpeace, the IAASTD report recommends a "significant departure from the destructive chemical-dependent, one-size-fits-all model of industrial agriculture."[57]

(Not everyone involved in the process was happy with the final report, [42] which was signed by fifty-seven governments.[58] Chemical giant and agricultural biotechnology leaders Syngenta and Monsanto, for instance, refused to sign on to the final document. No public statements were given at the time.[59] But in an interview, Syngenta's Martin Clough told me, "When it became pretty evident that the breadth of technologies were not getting equal airtime, then I think the view was that there was no point in participating. It's important to represent the technological options and it's equally important to say that they get fair play. That wasn't happening."[60])

Despite the chemical industry holdouts, there is also consensus that [43] sustainable farming practices create more resilient farms, better able to withstand the weather extremes of drought and flooding already afflicting many regions as a result of climate change. In other words, mitigation *is* adaptation. Because organic farms, by their design, build healthy soil, organic soils are better able to absorb water, making them more stable during floods, droughts, and extreme weather changes. In one specific example, conventional rice farmers in a region in Japan were nearly wiped out by an unusually cold summer, while organic farmers in the same region still yielded sixty to eighty percent of their typical production levels.[61]

In ongoing studies by the Pennsylvania-based Rodale Institute, organic [44] crops outperformed nonorganic crops in times of drought, yielding thirty-five to one hundred percent more in drought years than conventional crops.[62] Visiting a Wisconsin organic farmer just after the major Midwest flooding of the summer of 2008, I could see the deep ravines in the surroundings corn fields caused by the recent flooding, while I spent the afternoon walking through a visibly unscathed biodiverse organic farm.

Encouraging sustainable agriculture will not only help us reduce    45 emissions and adapt to the future climate chaos, it will have other beneficial ripples: addressing hunger and poverty, improving public health, and preserving biodiversity. In one study comparing organic and conventional agriculture in Europe, Canada, New Zealand, and the United States, researchers found that organic farming increased biodiversity at "every level of the food chain," from birds and mammals, to flora, all the way down to the bacteria in the soil.[63]

Finally, we know that shifting toward sustainable production need    46 not mean sacrificing production. In one of the largest studies of sustainable agriculture, covering 286 projects in fifty-seven countries and including 12.6 million farmers, researchers from the University of Essex found a yield increase of seventy-nine percent when farmers shifted to sustainable farming across a wide variety of systems and crop types.[64] Harvests of some crops such as maize, potatoes, and beans increased one hundred percent.[65]

Here's the other great plus: we all have to eat, so we can each do our    47 part to encourage the shift to organic, sustainable farming every time we make a choice about our food, from our local market, to our local restaurants, to our local food policies.

I was recently talking with Helene York, director of the Bon Appétit Man-    48 agement Company Foundation, an arm of the Bon Appétit catering company, which serves eighty million meals a year at four hundred venues across the country. York has been at the forefront of educating consumers and chefs about the impacts of our culinary choices on climate change, including leading the charge of the foundation's "Low Carbon Diet," which has dramatically reduced greenhouse gas emissions associated with their food. She summed up the challenge of awakening people to the food and climate change connection this way: "When you're sitting in front of a steaming plate of macaroni and cheese, you're not imagining plumes of greenhouse gases. You're thinking, dinner."

But the truth is those plumes of gases are there nonetheless, in the    49 background of how our dinners are produced, processed, and shipped to our plates. Thankfully, more and more of us eaters and policymakers are considering the climate crisis at the end of our fork and what we can do to support the organic, local, sustainable food production that's better for the planet, more pleasing to the palate, and healthier for people too.

NOTES

1. Henning Steinfeld et al., *Livestock's Long Shadow: Environmental Issues and Options* (Rome: Food and Agriculture Organization of the United Nations, 2006). While

livestock is responsible for eighteen percent of total emissions, transportation is responsible for a total of thirteen percent of the global warming effect.

2. Film stats from Box Office Mojo. Available online at http://www.boxofficemojo.com/movies/?page=main&id=inconvenienttruth.htm.

3. R. A. Neff, I. L. Chan, and K. A. Smith, "Yesterday's Dinner, Tomorrow's Weather, Today's News?: US Newspaper Coverage of Food System Contributions to Climate Change," *Public Health Nutrition* (2008).

4. Rajendra Pachauri, "Global Warning—The Impact of Meat Production and Consumption on Climate Change," paper presented at the Compassion in World Farming, London, September 8, 2008.

5. Ibid.

6. N. H. Stern, *The Economics of Climate Change: The Stern Review* (Cambridge: Cambridge University Press, 2007), 539.

7. Ibid.

8. Ingredients for Quaker Granola Bar available online: https://www.wegmans.com/webapp/wcs/stores/servlet/ProductDisplay?langId=1&storeId=10052&productId=359351&catalogId=10002&krypto=QJrbAudPd0vzXUGByeatog%3D%3D&ddkey=http:ProductDisplay.

9. Marc Gunther, "Eco-Police Find New Target: Oreos," *Money*, August 21, 2008. Available online at http://money.cnn.com/2008/08/21/news/companies/palm_oil.fortune/index.htm?postversion=2008082112.

10. Ibid.

11. USDA FAS, "Indonesia: Palm Oil Production Prospects Continue to Grow," December 31, 2007. Total area for Indonesia palm oil in 2006 is estimated at 6.07 million hectares according to information from the Indonesia Palm Oil Board (IPOB). Available online at http://www.pecad.fas.usda.gov/highlights/2007/12/Indonesia_palmoil/.

12. New Data Analysis Conclusive About Release of $CO_2$ When Natural Swamp Forest Is Converted to Oil Palm Plantation," CARBOPEAT Press Release, December 3, 2007. Dr. Sue Page or Dr. Chris Banks (CARBOPEAT Project Office), Department of Geography, University of Leicester, UK.

13. USDA FAS.

14. "Palm Oil Firm Wilmar Harming Indonesia Forests-Group," Reuters, July 3, 2007. Available at http://www.alertnet.org/thenews/newsdesk/SIN344348.htm.

15. Bunge Corporate Website. Online at http://www.bunge.com/about-bunge/promoting_sustainability.html.

16. See information at Cargill-Malaysia's website, http://www.cargill.com.my/, and Cargill-Indonesia, http://www.cargill.com/news/issues/palm_current.htm.

17. See, for instance, Cargill's position statement: http://www.cargill.com/news/issues/palm_roundtable.htm#TopOfPage. Bunge: http://www.bunge.com/about-bunge/promoting_sustainability.html.

18. Greenpeace. See, for instance, http://www.greenpeace.org.uk/forests/faq-palm-oil-forests-and-climate-change.

19. "New Data Analysis . . ." For more information, see "Carbon–Climate–Human Interactions in Tropical Peatlands: Vulnerabilities, Risks & Mitigation Measures."

20. Steinfield et al., xxi.

21. Ibid., xxi.

22. Ibid.

23. British Government Panel on Sustainable Development, *Third Report*, 1997. Department of the Environment.

24. From company annual reports, Tyson and Smithfield, 2007.

25. Steinfield et al., 45.

26. For further discussion, see Paul Roberts, *The End of Food* (Boston: Houghton Mifflin, 2008), 293. See also Frances Moore Lappé, *Diet for a Small Planet*, 20th anniversary ed. (New York: Ballantine Books, 1991).

27. Conversion ratios from USDA, from Allen Baker, Feed Situation and Outlook staff, ERS, USDA, Washington, D.C.

28. Roberts, quoting "Legume versus Fertilizer Sources of Nitrogen: Ecological Trade-offs and Human Need," *Agriculture, Ecosystems, and Environment* 102 (2004): 293.

29. World GHG Emissions Flow Chart, World Resources Institute, Washington, D.C. Based on data from 2000. All calculations are based on $CO_2$ equivalents, using 100-year global warming potentials from the IPCC (1996). Land use change includes both emissions and absorptions. Available online at http://cait.wri.org/figures.php?page=/World-FlowChart.

30. According to the IPCC, greenhouse gases relevant to radiative forcing include the following ( parts per million [ppm] and parts per trillion [ppt] are based on 1998 levels): carbon dioxide ($CO_2$), 365 ppm; methane ($CH_4$), 1,745 ppb; nitrous oxide ($N_2O$), 314 ppb; tetrafluoromethane ($CF_4$), 80 ppt; hexafluoroethane ($C_2F_6$), 3 ppt; sulfur hexafluoride ($SF_6$), 4.2 ppt; trifluoromenthane ($CHF_3$), 14 ppt; 1,1,1,2-tetrafluoroethane ($C_2H_2F_4$), 7.5 ppt; 1,1-Difluoroethane ($C_2H_4F_2$), 0.5 ppt.

31. IPCC, *Climate Change 2007: Fourth Assessment Report of the Intergovernmental Panel on Climate Change* (New York: Cambridge University Press, 2007). Graphic 13.5.

32. World GHG Emissions Flow Chart, World Resources Institute.

33. Steinfeld et al., 79. See also, for instance, http://www.fao.org/ag/magazine/0612spl.htm.

34. See, for example, Carbon Farmers of Australia. http://www.carbonfarmersofaustralia.com.au.

35. Steinfeld et al.

36. United Nations FAO, quoting Anthony Weis, *The Global Food Economy: The Battle for the Future of Farming* (London: Zed Books, 2007), 19.

37. J. McMichael et al., "Food, Livestock Production, Energy, Climate Change, and Health," *The Lancet* 370 (2007): 1253–63.

38. Pachauri.

39. Steinfeld et al.

40. Ibid.

41. CNN, "All About: Food and Fossil Fuels," March 17, 2008, cnn.com. Available online at http://edition.cnn.com/2008/WORLD/asiapcf/03/16/eco.food.miles/; author communication with Professor Jonathan Lynch, University of Pennsylvania.

42. Author communication with Lynch.

43. Stern.

44. See, for instance, Niles Eldredge, *Life on Earth: An Encyclopedia of Biodiversity, Ecology, and Evolution* (Santa Barbara, Calif.: ABC-CLIO, 2002). Online at http://www.landinstitute.org/vnews/display.v/ART/2002/08/23/439bd36c9acf1.

45. World GHG Emissions Flow Chart, World Resources Institute.

46. For more detail, see Environmental Protection Agency, "General Information on the Link Between Solid Waste and Greenhouse Gas Emissions." Available online at http://www.epa.gov/climatechange/wycd/waste/generalinfo.html#q1.

47. IPCC. See Figure 1, Chapter 2.

48. Most recent data available from USDA/ERS, U.S. Cattle and Beef Industry, 2002–2007. Available online at http://www.ers.usda.gov/news/BSECoverage.htm.

49. Pounds noted here are measured by commercial carcass weight. U.S. Red Meat and Poultry Forecasts. Source: World Agricultural Supply and Demand Estimates and Supporting Materials. From USDA/ERS. See also http://www.ers.usda.gov/Browse/TradeInternationalMarkets/.

50. Data from Brazilian Beef Industry and Exporters Association. Cited in "Brazilian Beef Break Records in September," October 3, 2008, The Beef Site. Available online at http://www.thebeefsite.com/news/24565/brazilian-beef-break-records-in-september.

51. IPCC.

52. http://www.rodaleinstitute.org.

53. See, for instance, studies from the Rodale Institute, found here: http://www
.newfarm.org/depts/NFfield_trials/1003/carbonsequest.shtml.

54. Editorial, "Deserting the Hungry?" *Nature* 451 (17 January 2008): 223–24;
dio:10.1038/451223b; published online January 16, 2008. Available at http://www.nature
.com/nature/journal/v451/n7176/full/451223b.html.

55. Executive Summary, 9. IAASTD, "Summary Report," paper presented at the International Assessment of Agricultural Science and Technology for Development, Johannesburg, South Africa, April 2008.

56. "Civil Society Statement from Johannesburg, South Africa: A New Era of Agriculture Begins Today," April 12, 2008. Available online at http://www.agassessment.org/
docs/Civil_Society_Statement_on_IAASTD-28Apr08.pdf.

57. Greenpeace Press Release, "Urgent Changes Needed in Global Farming Practices
to Avoid Environmental Destruction," April 15, 2008.

58. Fifty-seven governments approved the Executive Summary of the Synthesis
Report. An additional three governments—Australia, Canada, and the United States of
America—did not fully approve the Executive Summary of the Synthesis Report, and
their reservations are entered in the Annex. From the Executive Summary of IAASTD,
"Summary Report."

59. *Nature*, 223–24.

60. Author interview with Martin Clough, head of biotech R & D and president of
Syngenta Biotechnology, Inc., based in North Carolina; and Anne Birch, director with
Corporate Affairs, Syngenta, September 9, 2008.

61. Nadia El-Hage Scialabba and Caroline Hattam, "General Concepts and Issues in
Organic Agriculture," in *Organic Agriculture, Environment and Food Security,* ed. Environment and Natural Resources Service Sustainable Development Department (Rome:
Food and Agriculture Organization of the United Nations, 2002), chapter 1. Available
online at http://www.fao.org/docrep/005/y4137e/y4137e01.htm#P0_3.

62. "Organic crops perform up to 100 percent better in drought and flood years,"
November 7, 2003, Rodale Institute. Online at www.newfarm.org.

63. D. G. Hole et al., "Does Organic Farming Benefit Biodiversity?," *Biological Conservation* 122 (2005): 113–30, quoting James Randerson, "Organic Farming Boosts Biodiversity," *New Scientist*, October 11, 2004. Note: *New Scientist* emphasizes that neither
of the two groups of researchers—from the government agency, English Nature, and
from the Royal Society for the Protection of Birds—"has a vested interest in organic
farming."

64. Jules Pretty, *Agroecological Approaches to Agricultural Development* (Essex: University of Essex, 2006).

65. Ibid.

■ ■ ■

## Reading as a Writer: Analyzing Rhetorical Choices

1. Lappé offers many different forms of evidence in this piece. Mark at least
   three places in the text and three endnotes where you think the evidence
   is especially compelling. Explain the strengths you see in these examples.
   What conclusions can you draw about providing evidence in your own
   persuasive writing?

2. Like Al Gore, Lappé tells us some "inconvenient truths" about our daily
   food habits. How does she coax readers into seeing that there is a problem? What solutions does she offer? Locate some specific places where
   you see her addressing how challenging it can be to acknowledge the

connection between our eating habits and the health of the planet. How and where does she try to bring skeptics to her side? How effective do you think she is, and why?

### Writing as a Reader: Entering the Conversation of Ideas

1.  Both Lappé and Gary Steiner make claims that we should change the way we eat, and not simply based on what tastes good to us. To what extent do these writers' ideas about changing our dietary choices overlap? Write an essay in which you place these writers in conversation, considering the ways their arguments about what we ought to eat are related, even if they may not seem to be at first. How might one author's ideas enhance the other's? What larger point might you make about the connection between what we eat and the larger world? Feel free to draw on the "Buying Organic" visual text as you consider the challenges each writer faces.

2.  Lappé, like Michael Pollan, urges us to see the connections between our supper plates and the planet. Compose an essay that draws on the ideas and examples in both writers' texts to build your own argument about the problems in the ways most Americans eat, and then offer possible solutions. If you like, include material from "Buying Organic" or "Ten Things You Can Do to Fight World Hunger" to support your argument.

## PHIL HOWARD

## Buying Organic

This chart was produced by Phil Howard, a professor of community, agriculture, and recreation and resource studies at Michigan State University. Howard's research focuses on the rapidly changing process of food production and marketing to appeal to consumer interest in organic food. Thus, he is as interested in the labeling and selling of food as in the changes in food itself.

What do you find most and least surprising about this chart? Do you think it makes an argument or just presents facts? How does the presentation—the visual organization of the chart—support your claim that this piece makes or does not make an argument?

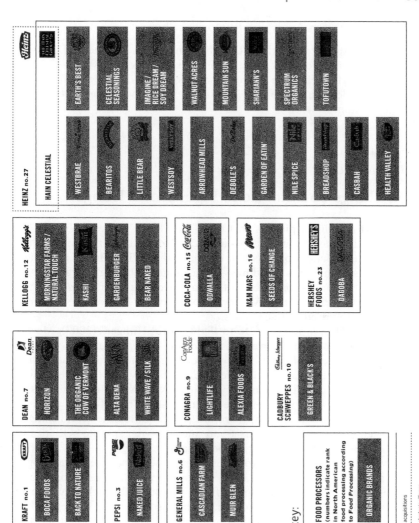

**HEINZ** no.27

HAIN CELESTIAL

EARTH'S BEST
CELESTIAL SEASONINGS
IMAGINE/ RICE DREAM/ SOY DREAM
WALNUT ACRES
MOUNTAIN SUN
SHARIANN'S
SPECTRUM ORGANICS
TOFUTOWN

WESTBRAE
BEARITOS
LITTLE BEAR
WESTSOY
ARROWHEAD MILLS
DEBOLE'S
GARDEN OF EATIN'
NILE SPICE
BREADSHOP
CASBAH
HEALTH VALLEY

**KELLOGG** no.12

MORNINGSTAR FARMS/ NATURAL TOUCH
KASHI
GARDENBURGER
BEAR NAKED

**COCA-COLA** no.15

ODWALLA

**M&M MARS** no.16

SEEDS OF CHANGE

**HERSHEY FOODS** no.23

DAGOBA

**DEAN** no.7

HORIZON
THE ORGANIC COW OF VERMONT
ALTA DENA
WHITE WAVE/SILK

**CONAGRA** no.9

LIGHTLIFE
ALEXIA FOODS

**CADBURY SCHWEPPES** no.10

GREEN & BLACK'S

**KRAFT** no.1

BOCA FOODS
BACK TO NATURE

**PEPSI** no.3

NAKED JUICE

**GENERAL MILLS** no.6

CASCADIAN FARM
MUIR GLEN

key:

FOOD PROCESSORS
(numbers indicate rank in North American food processing according to Food Processing)

ORGANIC BRANDS

---------- acquisitions

············· strategic alliance

Reading as a Writer: Analyzing Rhetorical Choices

1. To what extent do you think this chart makes an argument? Discuss the visual organization and information presented here as you explain your response. How effective do you find this chart, and why? What suggestions would you make to Howard to improve the presentation and information?

---

*THE NATION*

## Ten Things You Can Do to Fight World Hunger

This short and direct piece is part of a "Ten Things" series in *The Nation* magazine designed to give readers a specific "to do" list for acting on staggeringly huge social problems. For example, these "Ten Things" lists have suggested specific ways to address homelessness, the high incarceration rate, one's carbon footprint, or, in this case, world hunger. These lists are composed by writer Walter Mosley, who serves on *The Nation's* editorial board, with research by Rae Gomes.

In "Ten Things You Can Do to Fight World Hunger" (2009), Mosley and Gomes open with a corrective argument—that, contrary to what we might believe, "our planet produces enough food to feed its more than 960 million undernourished people" (para. 1). How can it be, then, that so many people globally are hungry or literally starving to death? Mosley and Gomes claim that if we reframe our understanding of food as a human right instead of a commodity, there are clear solutions to world hunger. They then offer regular citizens—you and me—ten specific activities to help bring about this reframing of food as a human right.

Which of these ideas are you most drawn to? What other issues might be addressable by ordinary citizens through similar means? Mosley and Gomes offer a model for tackling difficult problems through very specific activities. You might decide to look up the resources offered here. They hope you will do far more than just read this list. They have kept it short to give you room to *act*.

■ ■ ■

O ur planet produces enough food to feed its more than 960 million  /
undernourished people. The basic cause of global hunger is not underproduction; it is a production and distribution system that treats food as a commodity rather than a human right. In developing countries huge agribusinesses, fat with government subsidies, sell their unsustainable (and sometimes genetically modified) products at a reduced rate, thus making it impossible for local farmers to compete. Farmers who can't compete can't feed their own families or work their own fields. Hunger becomes both the cause and effect of poverty.

Ruth Messinger, president of American Jewish World Service, says ₂
sending food aid is not a sustainable way to end hunger. Rather, people
must be empowered to raise their own food. She proposes Ten Things we
can do to help solve the world's growing hunger problem (for more info, go
to TheNation.com).

1. Write letters to the editor and op-ed articles in your local paper ₃
calling on the government to cut or end subsidies that encourage large
agribusinesses to overproduce grains and dump their surpluses on the
developing world at sub-market prices. This ultimately places poor communities at the mercy of volatile global commodity prices. Learn more at
tradeobservatory.org/issue_foodSecurity.cfm.

2. Ask your representatives in Congress to demand that more foreign ₄
food aid be in the form of cash and training rather than food. Farmers in
the global South know how to grow food but lack the resources, inputs,
and tools to farm effectively, develop markets, and compete in the world
marketplace.

3. Learn the specifics of what makes products "fair trade." Buy them ₅
where available. Download "Green America's Guide to Fair Trade" for a
definition of "fair trade" and a list of organizations that follow these speci-
fications. Go to coopamerica.org/programs/fairtrade/orderguide.cfm.

4. Conserve energy. With a reduced demand for fuel—which spiked ₆
as the cost of fuel for shipping rose wildly last year—global commodity
prices should stabilize. Although imports are not the solution to hunger,
they have a role to play because First World consumers want a variety of
foods.

5. Pressure the Obama administration to come up with a renewable ₇
energy policy that does not stress ethanol and other biofuels. As demand
for biofuels has grown over the past few years, farmers in the developed
and developing worlds have set aside more and more land for fuel production, degrading the environment and reducing food for human consumption (go to oaklandinstitute.org and click "Agro Fuel Watch").

6. Eat less meat. Every pound of meat produced requires sixteen ₈
pounds of grain; food given to farm animals each year could feed the
world's hungry with plenty to spare. Search "Diet for a Small Planet" and
"We Feed the World" at bullfrogfilms.com.

7. Support grassroots projects that advance sustainable agriculture at ₉
the community level. Organizations like American Jewish World Service
(ajws.org) partner with grassroots organizations in the global South that
use sustainable farming techniques.

8. Persuade your local editorial writers to cover hunger in a way that ₁₀
focuses on economic rights rather than food scarcity. Emphasize that the
underlying causes of poverty are political instability, joblessness, gender

inequality, illiteracy, and limited access to education, loss of land, disenfranchisement, forced migration, and preventable epidemics. These hamper local food production and sustainable development (for examples of current coverage go to tradeobservatory.org and click "Headlines").

9. Demand a worldwide reduction in the sale of pesticides, herbicides, and genetically modified seeds, which benefit large agribusinesses like Monsanto because they do not reproduce, forcing farmers to purchase new seeds year after year. Watch *Future of Food* for more information, available at hulu.com or youtube.com.    *11*

10. Advocate for food security as a human right. Even though the United Nations has declared that nutrition is a universal right, many member nations have adopted policies that reinforce a global system whereby food is treated as a commodity to be bought and sold by speculators.    *12*

Read "The Politics of Hunger" (wfp.org/content/politics-hunger-foreign-affairs). Remember that global hunger is a local problem, a feminist problem (go to land-in-uganda.org), a socioeconomic problem, and, most urgently, a political problem that can be overcome.

■ ■ ■

## Reading as a Writer: Analyzing Rhetorical Choices

1. What are the strengths and shortcomings of this very targeted, brief "to do" list in response to a big issue? Do the strengths outweigh the shortcomings, or vice versa? Why?

2. How does the final sentence apply to the specific suggestions for action in this list?

## Writing as a Reader: Entering the Conversation of Ideas

1. How do the ideas in this list relate to Jim Tarter's argument that environmental rights are human rights? Write an essay in which you connect the ideas in this list to Tarter's insights in order to build your own argument about how health and the environment could be classified as human rights issues. What difference would this perspective make in the way we see the problem and its solutions?

2. This list demonstrates an idea that other authors in this chapter express, too: Small changes in our daily habits can add up to big changes for personal and global health. Compose an essay in which you connect the ideas in this list to the arguments of one or two of the following writers: Gary Steiner, Anna Lappé, Curtis White, or Michael Pollan. You also might draw on the "Buying Organic" visual text to make your point about how you think we can best inspire people to make healthy changes and which changes are most pressing, given the evidence you have found in these selections.

## MICHAEL POLLAN

# Why Bother?

When it comes to the politics of food, Michael Pollan is one of the best-known American public intellectuals on the topic. He is also a professor of journalism at the University of California, Berkeley. Pollan's lively critiques of modern agribusiness and the harms our industrial food chain causes the environment and ourselves have appeared in dozens of top-ranked news and literary magazines, including the *New York Times Magazine* and *Harper's*. His research and writing and dynamic public lectures are interdisciplinary, bringing together history, the sciences, cultural studies, anthropology, sociology, and environmental justice (to name a few) in his focus on food—the ways we think about it, and the ways we do not think about it. His most recent books, *The Omnivore's Dilemma: A Natural History of Four Meals* (2006), *In Defense of Food: An Eater's Manifesto* (2008), and *Food Rules: An Eater's Manual* (2009), are designed to make us far more mindful about what we put into our mouths. Pollan reveals to us the ways every bite of food is connected to politics and practices that we might find unsavory if we knew about them.

This is an excerpt of a longer essay that ran in the *New York Times Magazine* in 2008. Pollan opens with a question that many of us have asked when faced with the overwhelming problem of climate change. Can small differences in our daily lives really make a difference to our planet's health? In this essay, Pollan works through the doubts many of us have that our personal attempts to "go green" will matter very much when, for example, we see our neighbors driving gas-guzzlers or power mowers. For Pollan, the "why bother" question is answered partially by the writing of Wendell Berry, a farmer and writer who for more than thirty years has been arguing that the crisis in our relationship to the land is a "disease of the modern character" in which we have become accustomed to specialists solving our problems and therefore we no longer see our role in the big picture of personal and planet health (para. 9).

Drawing on Berry's insights and his own interest in industrial food production as a key contributor to global warming, Pollan offers a concrete solution: Plant a garden. (If you don't have a yard, Pollan suggests trying to grow some of your food in a planter or buying into a community garden.) Pollan acknowledges that this can seem like too small a gesture in the face of climate change, but he argues that growing even a little of your own food is "one of the most powerful things an individual can do—to reduce your carbon footprint, sure, but more important, to reduce your sense of dependence and dividedness: to change the cheap-energy mind" (para. 18).

Pollan reframes climate change as a call for *personal* change, noting that if we cultivate the ground in a garden, we will be cultivating different "habits of mind" (para. 21). He is part of a growing chorus of scholars who connect our cheap and unhealthy food supply to our increasingly unhealthy planet. Pollan's point is that the solution—changing the way we eat—will be delicious and make us feel better. In the face of so much "feel bad" news about global warming, you might be hungry for his perspective.

Why bother? That really is the big question facing us as individuals hop-  *1*
ing to do something about climate change, and it's not an easy one to
answer. I don't know about you, but for me the most upsetting moment in
*An Inconvenient Truth* came long after Al Gore scared the hell out of me,
constructing an utterly convincing case that the very survival of life on earth
as we know it is threatened by climate change. No, the really dark moment
came during the closing credits, when we are asked to . . . change our light
bulbs. That's when it got really depressing. The immense disproportion
between the magnitude of the problem Gore had described and the puni-
ness of what he was asking us to do about it was enough to sink your heart.

But the drop-in-the-bucket issue is not the only problem lurking  *2*
behind the "why bother" question. Let's say I do bother, big time. I turn my
life upside-down, start biking to work, plant a big garden, turn down the
thermostat so low I need the Jimmy Carter signature cardigan, forsake the
clothes dryer for a laundry line across the yard, trade in the station wagon
for a hybrid, get off the beef, go completely local. I could theoretically do
all that, but what would be the point when I know full well that halfway
around the world there lives my evil twin, some carbon-footprint doppel-
ganger in Shanghai or Chongqing who has just bought his first car (Chinese car ownership is where ours was back in 1918), is eager to swallow
every bite of meat I forswear, and who's positively itching to replace every
last pound of $CO_2$ I'm struggling no longer to emit. So what exactly would
I have to show for all my trouble?

There are so many stories we can tell ourselves to justify doing noth-  *3*
ing, but perhaps the most insidious is that, whatever we do manage to do,
it will be too little too late. Climate change is upon us, and it has arrived
well ahead of schedule. Scientists' projections that seemed dire a decade
ago turn out to have been unduly optimistic: the warming and the melting
is occurring much faster than the models predicted. Now truly terrifying
feedback loops threaten to boost the rate of change exponentially, as the
shift from white ice to blue water in the Arctic absorbs more sunlight and
warming soils everywhere become more biologically active, causing them
to release their vast stores of carbon into the air. Have you looked into the
eyes of a climate scientist recently? They look really scared.

So do you still want to talk about planting gardens?  *4*

I do.  *5*

Whatever we can do as individuals to change the way we live at this  *6*
suddenly very late date does seem utterly inadequate to the challenge.
It's hard to argue with Michael Specter, in a recent *New Yorker* piece on
carbon footprints, when he says: "Personal choices, no matter how virtuous, cannot do enough. It will also take laws and money." So it will. Yet
it is no less accurate or hardheaded to say that laws and money cannot
do enough, either; that it will also take profound changes in the way we
live. Why? Because the climate-change crisis is at its very bottom a crisis
of lifestyle—of character, even. The Big Problem is nothing more or less
than the sum total of countless little everyday choices, most of them made

by us (consumer spending represents 70 percent of our economy), and most of the rest of them made in the name of our needs and desires and preferences.

For us to wait for legislation or technology to solve the problem of how we're living our lives suggests we're not really serious about changing—something our politicians cannot fail to notice. They will not move until we do. Indeed, to look to leaders and experts, to laws and money and grand schemes, to save us from our predicament represents precisely the sort of thinking—passive, delegated, dependent for solutions on specialists—that helped get us into this mess in the first place. It's hard to believe that the same sort of thinking could now get us out of it.

Thirty years ago, Wendell Berry, the Kentucky farmer and writer, put forward a blunt analysis of precisely this mentality. He argued that the environmental crisis of the 1970s—an era innocent of climate change; what we would give to have back that environmental crisis!—was at its heart a crisis of character and would have to be addressed first at that level: at home, as it were. He was impatient with people who wrote checks to environmental organizations while thoughtlessly squandering fossil fuel in their everyday lives—the 1970s equivalent of people buying carbon offsets to atone for their Tahoes and Durangos. Nothing was likely to change until we healed the "split between what we think and what we do." For Berry, the "why bother" question came down to a moral imperative: "Once our personal connection to what is wrong becomes clear, then we have to choose: we can go on as before, recognizing our dishonesty and living with it the best we can, or we can begin the effort to change the way we think and live."

For Berry, the deep problem standing behind all the other problems of industrial civilization is "specialization," which he regards as the "disease of the modern character." Our society assigns us a tiny number of roles: we're producers (of one thing) at work, consumers of a great many other things the rest of the time, and then once a year or so we vote as citizens. Virtually all of our needs and desires we delegate to specialists of one kind or another—our meals to agribusiness, health to the doctor, education to the teacher, entertainment to the media, care for the environment to the environmentalist, political action to the politician.

As Adam Smith and many others have pointed out, this division of labor has given us many of the blessings of civilization. Specialization is what allows me to sit at a computer thinking about climate change. Yet this same division of labor obscures the lines of connection—and responsibility—linking our everyday acts to their real-world consequences, making it easy for me to overlook the coal-fired power plant that is lighting my screen, or the mountaintop in Kentucky that had to be destroyed to provide the coal to that plant, or the streams running crimson with heavy metals as a result.

Of course, what made this sort of specialization possible in the first place was cheap energy. Cheap energy, which gives us climate change, fosters precisely the mentality that makes dealing with climate change in our own lives seem impossibly difficult. Specialists ourselves, we can no longer imagine anyone but an expert, or anything but a new technology or law, solving our problems.

The "cheap-energy mind," as Wendell Berry called it, is the mind    *12* that asks, "Why bother?" because it is helpless to imagine—much less attempt—a different sort of life, one less divided, less reliant. Since the cheap-energy mind translates everything into money, its proxy, it prefers to put its faith in market-based solutions—carbon taxes and pollution-trading schemes. If we could just get the incentives right, it believes, the economy will properly value everything that matters and nudge our self-interest down the proper channels. The best we can hope for is a greener version of the old invisible hand. Visible hands it has no use for.

But while some such grand scheme may well be necessary, it's doubt-    *13* ful that it will be sufficient or that it will be politically sustainable before we've demonstrated to ourselves that change is possible. Merely to give, to spend, even to vote, is not to do, and there is so much that needs to be done—without further delay. In the judgment of James Hansen, the NASA climate scientist who began sounding the alarm on global warming 20 years ago, we have only 10 years left to start cutting—not just slowing—the amount of carbon we're emitting or face a "different planet." Hansen said this more than two years ago, however; two years have gone by, and nothing of consequence has been done. So: eight years left to go and a great deal left to do.

Which brings us back to the "why bother" question and how we might    *14* better answer it. The reasons not to bother are many and compelling, at least to the cheap-energy mind. But let me offer a few admittedly tentative reasons that we might put on the other side of the scale.

If you do bother, you will set an example for other people. If enough    *15* other people bother, each one influencing yet another in a chain reaction of behavioral change, markets for all manner of green products and alternative technologies will prosper and expand. (Just look at the market for hybrid cars.) Consciousness will be raised, perhaps even changed: new moral imperatives and new taboos might take root in the culture.

Going personally green is a bet, nothing more or less, though it's one    *16* we probably all should make, even if the odds of it paying off aren't great. Sometimes you have to act as if acting will make a difference, even when you can't prove that it will.

So what would be a comparable bet that the individual might make    *17* in the case of the environmental crisis? The idea is to find one thing to do in your life that doesn't involve spending or voting, that may or may not virally rock the world but is real and particular (as well as symbolic) and that, come what may, will offer its own rewards. Maybe you decide to give up meat, an act that would reduce your carbon footprint by as much as a quarter. Or you could try this: determine to observe the Sabbath. For one day a week, abstain completely from economic activity: no shopping, no driving, no electronics.

But the act I want to talk about is growing some—even just a little—of 18 your own food. Rip out your lawn, if you have one, and if you don't—if you live in a high-rise, or have a yard shrouded in shade—look into getting a plot in a community garden. Measured against the Problem We Face, planting a garden sounds pretty benign, I know, but in fact it's one of the most powerful things an individual can do—to reduce your carbon footprint, sure, but more important, to reduce your sense of dependence and dividedness: to change the cheap-energy mind.

A great many things happen when you plant a vegetable garden, some 19 of them directly related to climate change, others indirect but related nevertheless. Growing food, we forget, comprises the original solar technology: calories produced by means of photosynthesis. Years ago the cheap-energy mind discovered that more food could be produced with less effort by replacing sunlight with fossil-fuel fertilizers and pesticides, with a result that the typical calorie of food energy in your diet now requires about 10 calories of fossil-fuel energy to produce. It's estimated that the way we feed ourselves (or rather, allow ourselves to be fed) accounts for about a fifth of the greenhouse gas for which each of us is responsible.

Yet the sun still shines down on your yard, and photosynthesis still 20 works so abundantly that in a thoughtfully organized vegetable garden (one planted from seed, nourished by compost from the kitchen, and involving not too many drives to the garden center), you can grow the proverbial free lunch—$CO_2$-free and dollar-free. This is the most-local food you can possibly eat (not to mention the freshest, tastiest, and most nutritious). And while we're counting carbon, consider too your compost pile, which shrinks the heap of garbage your household needs trucked away even as it feeds your vegetables and sequesters carbon in your soil. What else? Well, you will probably notice that you're getting a pretty good workout there in your garden, burning calories without having to get into the car to drive to the gym. Also, by engaging both body and mind, time spent in the garden is time (and energy) subtracted from electronic forms of entertainment.

Still more valuable are the habits of mind that growing a little of your 21 own food can yield. You quickly learn that you need not be dependent on specialists to provide for yourself—that your body is still good for something and may actually be enlisted in its own support. If the experts are right, if both oil and time are running out, these are skills and habits of mind we're all very soon going to need. We may also need the food. Could gardens provide it? Well, during World War II, victory gardens supplied as much as 40 percent of the produce Americans ate.

But there are sweeter reasons to plant that garden, to bother. At least 22 in this one corner of your yard and life, you will have begun to heal the split between what you think and what you do, to commingle your identities as consumer and producer and citizen. Chances are, your garden will re-engage you with your neighbors, for you will have produce to give away and the need to borrow their tools. You will have reduced the power of the cheap-energy mind by personally overcoming its most debilitating weakness: its helplessness and the fact that it can't do much of anything that doesn't involve division or subtraction. The garden's season-long transit from seed to ripe fruit—will you get a load of that zucchini?!—suggests that the operations of addition and multiplication still obtain, that the abundance of nature is not exhausted. The single greatest lesson the garden teaches is that our relationship to the planet need not be zero-sum, and that as long as the sun still shines and people still can plan and plant, think and do, we can, if we bother to try, find ways to provide for ourselves without diminishing the world.

■ ■ ■

### Reading as a Writer: Analyzing Rhetorical Choices

1. Pollan's title indicates that he understands it can be hard to believe that our personal actions can have an effect on the environment. Throughout the essay, he addresses this skepticism in various ways. Mark the places where you see him addressing skeptical readers, and evaluate how effective you find his strategies for inviting readers to see this issue from his perspective.

2. Pollan draws on the ideas of Wendell Berry, a farmer and well-known environmentalist writer, to develop his argument here. Mark the places where he explicitly mentions Berry. How exactly do Berry's concepts help Pollan make his own point in this essay?

### Writing as a Reader: Entering the Conversation of Ideas

1. Both Pollan and Curtis White argue that in order to make an impact on climate change, citizens have to do more than tweak their daily behaviors; they also have to change their values and understand their relationship to the world differently. Write an essay in which you draw on the insights and examples in both texts in order to make your own argument about the ways we could and should live more healthful lives, for ourselves and the planet. What benefits do you see for individuals?

2. Like Pollan, other writers in this chapter argue that changing our daily habits can improve our health and the health of the planet. Compose an essay in which you connect Pollan's ideas about changing our habits to one or more of the following pieces: the essays by Pamela Paul, Gary Steiner, or Anna Lappé; the "Ten Things You Can Do to Fight World Hunger" list; or the "Little Green Lies" and "Buying Organic" visuals. Use key ideas and examples from your chosen texts to build an argument about which changes are most pressing, given the evidence you have gleaned. What challenges do you see, and what benefits?

# Assignment Sequences

The assignment sequences invite different kinds of inquiry from the writing exercises that follow each reading. Those exercises ask you to consider what you have just read, paying attention to specific aspects of the text and seeking new understanding by placing each reading next to others for examination and written response. In contrast, the assignments here are sequences, which define a subject for extended inquiry and offer a series of steps through readings and writing assignments that build on one another. For example, you might write an essay in which you analyze a film about American education through the lens of two authors in this collection. In the next essay, you might examine the same film in light of different readings and research that give context to your ideas by describing the ongoing conversation on the issue you are exploring. Yet another assignment in the sequence might invite you to analyze test cases, such as texts from your own college's promotional materials, to see how the issues raised in the film are played out in those publications.

In other words, instead of writing one essay in response to an assignment and then moving on to a new topic, these assignment sequences allow you to pursue an issue in depth by writing an essay that prepares you to develop an idea in your next essay, considering one central issue from different perspectives and a range of sources. You will be asked to analyze texts from different chapters of the reader, to play a wider range of ideas off one another. As you draw on various combinations of resources over a series of assignments and contribute your own research—from the library or from data you have gathered yourself—your ideas about the issues you examine in these essays will become richer and more complex. Through reading, researching, and writing, you become an academic writer in conversation with other academic writers. In addition, these assignments can help you see the world around you—for example, your daily life at college, a Saturday night at the movies, or your next meal—in unexpected and insightful ways.

As an academic writer, you will need to document your sources carefully, using the guidelines for quoting and citing sources explained in the Appendix. We have not included page-length requirements for these assignments; your instructor will determine this, in accordance with your program's guidelines.

## ■ SEQUENCE ONE: What Do Media Representations Tell Us About American Education? [hooks, Siering, Tannen, Tatum, Edmundson, Talbot, original research]

These assignments address the stories we tell ourselves through the media about American education. The readings in this sequence act as lenses you can use to examine representations of American education, not to label them "true" or "false," "good" or "bad," but to consider what they tell us about the positive possibilities, the anxieties, and maybe the dangers we see played out in schoolrooms. What does it really mean to be educated in America? These assignments begin an inquiry into this always relevant issue.

### ASSIGNMENT 1: Educated by the Movies  [hooks, Siering]

This assignment asks you to interpret the way a film of your choosing represents American education and to make an argument about the film's attitudes toward this subject by paying attention to the role of stereotypes in the film. What key issue is raised in the film, and what resolutions are offered? Who is the intended audience, and how does it shape the film's issues and point?

The film you choose might be one that celebrates teachers' relationships with students (*Stand and Deliver*, *Dangerous Minds*, *Dead Poets' Society*, *Freedom Writers*, or the *Harry Potter* films, for example) or depicts them in vicious or even mortal conflict (*Teaching Mrs. Tingle*, *The Faculty*, *Cheaters*, or the *Harry Potter* films) or somewhere in between. Or you might choose a film that illuminates high school social dynamics, like *Napoleon Dynamite*, *Juno*, or *Charlie Bartlett*. Choose a visual text that really interests you so you can convey that interest through an argument richly supported by details from the film. Describe and analyze specific scenes and images in detail as you build an argument about the significance of the way education is represented in this film.

To help you sharpen your focus and analyze your visual text, use strategies drawn from bell hooks's and Carmen Siering's analysis of stereotypes in films. Both authors show how to look for the unquestioned assumptions about people and to understand how the "invisibility" of those assumptions allows the plot to unfold, often at the expense of the stereotyped characters. Use their methods for a close analysis of particular scenes and images, and then draw your own conclusions about a central issue of interest to you in the film. What is this film teaching us about American education? What do you learn about the function of stereotyping in the process?

### ASSIGNMENT 2: *What Does Gender or Race Have to Do with It?* [Tannen, Tatum]

Return to the media example you used for Assignment 1, but analyze the film through the lens of gender or race dynamics. (Choose a focus you did not take in your first essay.) Draw on Deborah Tannen's or Beverly Daniel Tatum's claims that behaviors we often consider to be intrinsic to a person (gender and race) are actually learned behaviors, and that school is often a place that reinforces these limiting patterns. Using the author whose ideas are most pertinent for your focus, reconsider the scenes you wrote about for Assignment 1 to analyze the way the film confirms or reimagines (or both) stereotypes relating to gender and race in educational settings. What new issues and details come into focus when you apply Tannen's or Tatum's specific insights to the scenes? (You may also draw on scenes you did not discuss in your previous paper.) Write a paper that uses these fresh insights to make a point about the way your film teaches viewers to see education in relation to gender or racial stereotypes.

### ASSIGNMENT 3: *Broadening the Conversation* [Adding scholarly research to Assignment 1 or 2]

Further develop the essay you wrote for Assignment 1 or 2 with research in your college library. What conversations are unfolding among academic writers on the issue you focused on in that essay? Speak with a librarian about which research tools will be most effective for finding two or three recent scholarly articles on this issue. In addition to drawing on resources from education, you might want to use materials from sociology, psychology, or other fields that provide a broader understanding of the dynamics you analyzed in your essay. (Your instructor and librarian can show you library databases that focus on specific disciplines.)

The object of this assignment is not simply to add more secondary sources to your paper but to use those sources to help you reconsider your position and perhaps see significant new details in your film—maybe in the very scenes you have already analyzed. You may need to revise your thesis as you develop a broader understanding of the issue from your research. You also may find that you no longer want to use one or more of the readings from this collection in your final draft if other framing concepts and examples from your new research are more useful for supporting the argument you make in your essay.

### ASSIGNMENT 4: *Focusing on Your Campus* [Edmundson, Talbot, original research]

Analyze representations of your college on its Web site, in promotional videos, and in brochures and student catalogs through the lenses of Mark Edmundson's and Margaret Talbot's texts. For example, how does Edmundson's argument that students expect college to be "lite entertainment," with an emphasis on recreation and enjoyable learning experiences, apply to the images and text in these materials? How does Talbot's analysis of extreme study habits and intense academic pressure apply to these materials?

This assignment asks you to read college materials closely, in the same way you analyzed the film, looking for visual and textual details to help you determine the arguments these promotional materials make about education at your institution. You will need to select specific examples to analyze—perhaps a section of the college's Web site and a brochure, or one promotional film and one brochure. How do these materials make an argument about both the pleasures and the rigors of education at your institution? What do you want to teach your readers about these materials and what they tell us about what we value about American education?

■ SEQUENCE TWO: Reading Bodies [duCille, Blum, Lorber, Dworkin and Messner, McIntosh, original research]

This sequence asks you to analyze bodies as cultural texts, to see what we can find out about cultural beliefs from the ways we learn to appear, move, and act. These readings and assignments ask you to analyze, from different perspectives, how our bodies display cultural values. An awareness of the arguments bodies make may allow you to examine popular culture in a new way, as well as consider the ways your own body is capable of confirming or challenging cultural expectations.

### ASSIGNMENT 1: Plastic Bodies: How Are Our Bodies Commodities? [duCille, Blum]

Read Ann duCille's analysis of multicultural plastic Barbie dolls and Virginia L. Blum's analysis of plastic surgery–themed television shows, and consider what it means that our culture places so much emphasis on buying into—or just buying—a certain kind of body and identity. Although duCille focuses on toy culture, her argument is a broader one about the kinds of bodies that "sell" in American culture. Similarly, Blum sees the popularity of plastic (or cosmetic) surgery–themed television shows as an indication that cultural attitudes have shifted so that we now see the purchase of a new body as a sign of healthy self-improvement.

In your own essay, use duCille's and Blum's ideas to help you think about the significance of these cultural trends in entertainment for children and grown-ups. What are these authors pessimistic or optimistic about, and where do you place yourself in this conversation? These authors focus on female bodies and experiences, but you certainly can choose to apply their insights to male bodies and experiences. Using specific insights and analyzing examples from each text, tell your readers what you find most significant about what you have learned about the bodies we seem to want to buy.

### ASSIGNMENT 2: Sporting Bodies: What Can We Learn from the Games We Play? [Lorber, Dworkin and Messner]

Reconsider the ideas you wrote about for Assignment 1 in the context of sports culture. How do our expectations of what gendered bodies should look like influence our ideas about female and male athletes? What role does money play (in the form of athletic scholarships for students, or salaries and commercial contracts for professional athletes) in demonstrating the kinds of sporting bodies our culture values?

Using concepts from Lorber's text or Dworkin and Messner's text (or both), write an essay in which you address these questions. Incorporating the ideas you explored in your first essay, think about how duCille's and Blum's insights might apply to "sporting" bodies. Use concrete examples to illustrate your claims. (A quick look through any sports magazine should provide you with lots of examples to analyze.) Be sure to anchor your ideas to the concepts you have learned in order to strengthen your argument.

### ASSIGNMENT 3: *What Role Does Race Play?* [McIntosh, duCille, scholarly research]

Return to the essays you wrote for Assignments 1 and 2, and choose one to develop in light of the role race plays in the way we "read" bodies. Peggy McIntosh or Ann duCille should help you think about the ways we "see" (or don't see) race, and how those ideas shift over time. Whichever essay of yours you choose, reread your sources with fresh eyes to find passages that will help you develop your thinking about the role race plays in our interpretations and expectations of bodies.

In addition, investigate the broader scholarly conversation about the significance of the ways we interpret racial differences. Search EBSCO-host, JSTOR, or another resource recommended by a librarian or your instructor to find an article that helps you analyze the role of race in the context of your essay's focus (on "buying" bodies, sports culture, and so on). Work with a librarian to develop search terms that will yield the best results—an article that offers you the analytical tools you need for a fresh focus.

### ASSIGNMENT 4: *Hearing from Your Peers* [Using a focus group to develop your ideas]

Use a focus group to find out what your peers think about an issue you have written about in this sequence. (Refer to the discussion in Chapter 11 about designing and conducting an effective focus group.) Given the topics and issues you have explored in these essays, decide on a specific focus for this final paper that can be enriched with the kind of data you can collect in a focus group. Think carefully about the kinds of information you need as you choose participants for the focus group and write questions for them. (See Chapter 11, too, for a discussion of the kinds of claims you can make based on data from focus groups.) As you consider how best to analyze and contextualize the material you gather in your focus group, return to your previous essays, your library research, and the readings themselves to choose the most useful tools to make sense of your findings. Be sure to shape your essay so that you teach your readers something specific about a body issue and its significance.

■ **SEQUENCE THREE: Visualizing Meaning: How Do Images Make Arguments?** [Kilbourne, Hesse-Biber, Satrapi, images from Chapter 8, original research]

This sequence gives you the opportunity to practice analyzing images in order to examine how visual arguments work. As we discuss in Chapter 8, we are surrounded by images in our culture, so it is crucial to learn to make sense of what these images tell us about cultural values and aspirations. The readings in this sequence offer concrete strategies for analyzing visual arguments in advertisements and graphic novels. You will have the opportunity to pursue areas of interest to you, through both your research and the test cases you analyze. Reading, researching, collecting, and writing about visual arguments will help you see the world around you with new—and perhaps startling—clarity.

*ASSIGNMENT 1: Analyzing Advertising* [Kilbourne, Hesse-Biber]

Consider the strategies Jean Kilbourne and Sharlene Nagy Hesse-Biber use to analyze advertisements, and apply their insights to three advertisements of your choice. Kilbourne and Hesse-Biber argue that images are not neutral but that, like any text, they project perspectives and arguments. Reread the authors' essays to determine their most effective strategies for analyzing the images and language in advertisements. How are their strategies similar? How are they different?

Choose three visual advertisements that share a focus or theme that interests you (as a starting place, you could use the images in Chapter 8). Using tools drawn from Kilbourne, Hesse-Biber, and Chapter 8's "Analyzing Visual Rhetoric" section, write an essay about what these images argue and how they do so. Examine the assumptions the ads make about their audience, as well as the ideas and associations the ads play on in order to sell the product. How does the language of each ad work in relation to the image? As you show your reader how Kilbourne and Hesse-Biber help you analyze these visual arguments, be sure to describe and analyze specific details in the advertisements to illustrate your claims. Be clear about what you want your readers to see in these advertisements, and why these insights matter.

*ASSIGNMENT 2: Examining the Visual Arguments of a Graphic Novel* [Satrapi, Kilbourne or Hesse-Biber]

Marjane Satrapi's graphic novel can be analyzed with at least some of the same tools you used in your first essay. Select a series of frames in Satrapi's text that work interestingly with some of the advertisements you analyzed in your first essay (or you could find a few new ads, if you like), and write a new essay that explains the way visual rhetoric works to build an argument in both the advertisements and the graphic novel. You might consider the way the images are framed, for example, and the relationship between the images and the words.

In your essay, explain the parallels you see between analyzing these two different kinds of visual rhetorics, and the differences as well. What do these similarities and differences tell us about the importance of visual literacy? What kinds of skills do we need for visual analysis? What might be lost in the case of the advertisements and the graphic novel if a reader did not bring these tools of visual analysis to bear on these images? What conclusions can you draw?

### ASSIGNMENT 3: Broadening the Conversation About Visual Arguments [Adding scholarly research to Assignment 1 or 2]

Choose the paper you wrote in response to Assignment 1 or 2 to develop through scholarly research. Which ideas and issues in that paper spark your interest the most? Building on those ideas, use your library's databases to find out what other scholars have said on this topic or issue. For example, you might begin with a general database like EBSCOhost and search on "advertising and gender" or "graphic novels and politics," to name just two of the many possibilities. Your instructor or a librarian can help you narrow your search and find the most useful database for your needs. Read broadly enough in your search results to gain a clear sense of the scholarly conversation on your issue, and select two articles that will help you further develop the ideas you have written about for this sequence.

Depending on the direction your essay takes, you may wish to return to the examples you used in the previous assignments, or you may decide to use fresh passages and examples to support the focus and argument in this essay. Drawing on the broader conversation you have researched and now joined, what new ideas can you present to your readers about the significance of visual rhetoric?

### ASSIGNMENT 4: Working with a Larger Archive [Developing your ideas with test cases]

This assignment requires you to gather a broader archive, or collection, of materials to analyze, using the readings in this sequence and the tools in Chapter 8. So, depending on your interests, collect a larger archive of images (advertisements, graphic novel excerpts, book covers, posters, and the like) to use as your data for this essay. Think carefully about what you would like to learn from this process to be sure that the materials you collect will address your interest. Your instructor and classmates can also help you reflect on how best to develop a collection and how large your collection should be to answer your research question responsibly. (For example, if you wish to examine a particular kind of image on magazine covers, you would need to decide if you will analyze only one magazine or several, and how many issues, and over how many years.)

Draw on the theories and ideas you have read about and learned in the assignments in this sequence, and apply them to the samples in your archive in order to address your focus in this essay. What can you teach your readers about the significance of the patterns you see in these images, using the tools of visual analysis? This essay is your opportunity to contribute to the scholarly conversation on how visual arguments work, because you will be the expert on the collection of materials you use for your essay. Be clear about what you want your readers to learn, and why your ideas about these images matter.

■ SEQUENCE FOUR: The "I" in the "We": Exploring Tensions Between Individual and Group Identities [Anzaldúa, Foer, McIntosh, Lorber, Kimmel, original research]

This sequence gives you an opportunity to reflect on the many ways individuals understand their relationship to their communities, whether those communities are defined by ethnicity, social class, race, religion, or something else. The writers listed here use their personal experiences as they develop their arguments, moving between those experiences and larger arguments. This sequence gives you an opportunity to consider the issues that arise when people think about themselves in relation to community identities. It also asks you to evaluate the rhetorical tactic of drawing on personal experience when making a larger argument: What are the advantages and possible problems of constructing an argument this way? As you explore the ideas of others in this sequence, think carefully about the insights you can apply to yourself in terms of the ways you think about your relation to larger communities and the ways you might wish to use personal experiences in your own writing.

### ASSIGNMENT 1: *Seeing a Community Through the Writer's Eye/"I"*
[Anzaldúa, Foer]

Examine the tensions you see between individuals and communities in the texts by Gloria Anzaldúa and Franklin Foer. While these essays are very different, both writers move between personal experiences and a larger argument. How does this rhetorical strategy shape the impact of the pieces? How do these writers depict themselves as part of their communities? How do they set themselves apart? How do their representations of themselves in the past and the present affect the meaning of their texts?

Write an essay in which you analyze the relationship between the individual and the community in these texts. Choose specific passages to use as your examples. In what ways are these writers' strategies similar? In what ways are they different? What can you conclude about the uses (personal, political, social) of seeing oneself as part of a community or different from a community?

### ASSIGNMENT 2: *Focusing on the Influence of Race and Gender*
[McIntosh, Lorber]

Reconsider Assignment 1 in light of the ideas about race and gender raised by Peggy McIntosh or Judith Lorber. Both McIntosh and Lorber offer readers tools to see race and gender hierarchies that we are often taught to ignore in American culture. How do these additional texts help you see the role that race and gender hierarchies play in the relationship between the self and the community in Anzaldúa's and Foer's texts?

In your essay, draw on passages from McIntosh or Lorber (or both, if you find both useful) that help you think about the role of race or gender (or both) in the individual and community experiences that Anzaldúa and Foer describe. What conflicts or opportunities for coalition do these dynamics provide within each author's sense of community? What further ideas and conclusions can you draw about Anzaldúa's and Foer's arguments—and the strategy of using personal experience to build these arguments—when you focus on race or gender?

**ASSIGNMENT 3: *Researching the Relationship Between Individuals and Their Communities*** [Adding scholarly research to Assignment 1 or 2]

Now that you have written two essays, choose one to develop further with insights drawn from scholarly research on your subject. Using your library's research databases, find two articles that enrich your understanding of the relationship between individuals and their communities. For example, you might use databases through EBSCOhost (be sure to narrow your search to peer-reviewed journals) to search on terms such as "group identity and education and race," "cultural boundaries," or "ethnic groups." You can narrow your search to the United States or to specific areas of the United States. Your librarian will be able to suggest other search strategies and other databases that might be helpful.

The purpose of your research is to find two articles that will help you develop ideas from one of your two previous essays. To this end, search for framing theories and concepts that will allow you to draw a richer analysis from the details and examples in Anzaldúa's and Foer's texts and will help you think about your conclusions in fresh ways. You must be willing to rethink and rewrite your essay substantially as you return to your ideas with a fresh perspective and the new meanings you've discovered in the material. Establish a clear thesis to draw through the whole essay as you explain what your research has led you to discover about the relationship between individual and group identities as this dynamic pertains to Anzaldúa's and Foer's texts.

**ASSIGNMENT 4: *Adding Other Voices Through Original Research***
[Using interviews or a focus group to develop your ideas]

In this assignment, you have the opportunity to use interviews or a focus group (see Chapter 11) to discover how others have negotiated the relationship between their individual and community identities. Look back through your previous three essays and draw out the most compelling issues and ideas from the readings and research you have done. Based on this work, decide on the form your original research should take. That is, are you more likely to obtain useful material for developing your ideas through interviews with individuals who have experience with these issues or through a focus group?

Be sure to make good use of the framing theories and concepts you have explored in the readings and in your research as you plan questions for your interviews or focus group. For example, you might choose to concentrate on the role that education, team sports, ethnicity, or another social category plays in the individual–group relationship.

Whatever the focus of your original research, have a clear goal in mind about the material you want to gather so that you will have rich data to analyze as you develop a thesis for your final essay of this sequence. You may find that you have to do more library research to make sense of your new findings. You may also decide to use passages in the textbook readings that you have not used before; or you may return to familiar passages but use them in new ways to teach your readers something significant about the relationship between individual and community identities.

# APPENDIX:
# Citing and Documenting Sources

You must provide a brief citation in the text of your paper for every quotation or an idea taken from another writer, and you must list complete information at the end of your paper for the sources you use. This information is essential for readers who want to read the source to understand a quotation or an idea in its original context. How you cite sources in the body of your paper and document them at the end of your paper varies from discipline to discipline, so it is important to ask your instructor what documentation style he or she prefers.

Even within academic disciplines, documentation styles can vary. Specific academic journals within disciplines will sometimes have their own set of style guidelines. The important thing is to adhere faithfully to your chosen (or assigned) style throughout your paper, observing all the niceties of form prescribed by the style. You may have noticed small differences in the citation styles in the examples throughout Chapter 7. That's because the examples are taken from the work of a variety of writers, both professionals and students, who had to conform to the documentation requirements of their publication venues or of their teachers.

Here we briefly introduce two common documentation styles that may be useful in your college career: the Modern Language Association (MLA) style for listing bibliographic information in the humanities, and the American Psychological Association (APA) style, in the social sciences. The information is basic, for use when you begin drafting your paper. In the final stages of writing, you should consult either the *MLA Handbook for Writers of Research Papers* (7th ed.) or the *Publication Manual of the American Psychological Association* (6th ed.).

Although you'll need the manuals for complete style information, both the MLA (http://www.mla.org/style_faq/) and the APA (http://www.apastyle.org/learn/faqs/) maintain Web sites for frequently asked questions. Again, before you start your research, check with your instructor to find out whether you should use either of these styles or if there's another style he or she prefers.

MLA and APA styles have many similarities—for example, both require short citations in the body of an essay linked to a list of sources at the end of the essay. But it is their differences, though subtle, that are crucial. To a great extent, these differences reflect the assumptions writers in the humanities and in the social sciences bring to working with sources. In particular, you should understand each style's treatment of the source's author, publication date, and page numbers in in-text citations, and verb use in referring to sources.

*Author.*    MLA style requires that you give the author's full name on first mention in your paper; APA style uses last names throughout. The humanities emphasize "the human element"—the individual as creative force—so MLA style uses the complete name at first mention to imply the author's importance. Because the social sciences emphasize the primacy of data in studies of human activity, in APA style last names are deemed sufficient.

*Publication Date.*    In-text citations using MLA style leave out the date of publication. The assumption is that the insights of the past may be as useful as those of the present. By contrast, APA style gives the date of the study after the author's name, reflecting a belief in the progress of research, that recent findings may supersede earlier ones.

*Page Numbers.*    MLA style requires that page numbers be included with paraphrases and summaries as well as quotations (the written text is so important that a reader may want to check the exact language of the original). By contrast, APA style requires attribution but not page numbers for paraphrases and summaries (it is the findings, not how they are described, that are most important).

*Verb Use.*    MLA style uses the present tense of verbs ("Writer X claims") to introduce cited material, assuming the cited text's timelessness, whether written last week or centuries ago. By contrast, the verbs introducing citations in APA style acknowledge the "pastness" of research ("Writer X claimed" or "Writer Y has claimed") on the assumption that new data may emerge to challenge older research.

Although it is useful to understand that different citation styles reflect different attitudes toward inquiry and research in different disciplines, for the purposes of your writing it is mainly important to know the style you have to follow in your paper, and to stick to it scrupulously. Whenever you

TABLE A.1   Basic Information Needed for Citing Sources

| BOOKS | CHAPTERS IN BOOKS | JOURNAL ARTICLES | ONLINE SOURCES |
|---|---|---|---|
| Author(s) or editor(s) | Author(s) | Author(s) | Author(s) |
| Title and subtitle | Chapter title and subtitle | Article title and subtitle | Document title and subtitle |
| Edition information | Book editor(s) | Journal title | Print publication information, if any |
| Place of publication | Book title | Volume and issue number | Site sponsor |
| Publisher | Edition information | Date of publication | Site title |
| Year of publication | Place of publication | Page numbers | Year of publication |
| Medium of publication | Publisher | Medium of publication | Medium of publication |
| | Year of publication | | Date accessed |
| | Page numbers | | |
| | Medium of publication | | |

consult a source—even if you don't end up using it in your paper—write down complete citation information so that you can cite it fully and accurately if you need to. Table A.1 shows the basic information needed to cite books, chapters in books, journal articles, and online sources. You also should note any other information that could be relevant—a translator's name, for example, or a series title and editor. Ideally, you want to be able to cite a source fully without having to go back to it to get more information.

## THE BASICS OF MLA STYLE

*In-Text Citations.*   In MLA style, you must provide a brief citation in the body of your essay (1) when you quote directly from a source, (2) when you paraphrase or summarize what someone else has written, and (3) even when you use an idea or a concept that originated with someone else.

In the excerpt below, the citation tells readers that the student writer's argument about the evolution of Ebonics is rooted in a well-established source of information. Because the writer does not mention the author in the paraphrase of her source in the text, she gives the author's name in the citation:

> The evolution of US Ebonics can be traced from the year 1557 to the present day. In times of great oppression, such as the beginning of the slave codes in 1661, the language of the black community was at its most "ebonified" levels, whereas in times of racial progress, for example during the abolitionist movement, the language as a source of community identity was forsaken for greater assimilation (Smitherman 119).

The parenthetical citation refers to page 119 of Geneva Smitherman's book *Talkin and Testifyin: The Language of Black America* (1977). Smitherman is a recognized authority on Ebonics. Had the student mentioned Smitherman's name in her introduction to the paraphrase, she would not have had to repeat it in the citation. Notice that there is no punctuation within the parentheses and no *p.* before the page number. Also notice that the citation is considered part of the sentence in which it appears, so the period ending the sentence follows the closing parenthesis.

By contrast, in the example that follows, the student quotes directly from Richard Rodriguez's book *Hunger of Memory: The Education of Richard Rodriguez* (1982):

> Many minority cultures in today's society feel that it is more important to maintain cultural bonds than to extend themselves into the larger community. People who do not speak English may feel a similar sense of community and consequently lose some of the individuality and cultural ties that come with speaking their native or home language. This shared language within a home or community also adds to the unity of the community. Richard Rodriguez attests to this fact in his essay "Aria." He then goes on to say that "it is not healthy to distinguish public words from private sounds so easily" (183).

Because the student mentions Rodriguez in her text right before the quotation ("Richard Rodriguez attests"), she does not need to include his name in the citation; the page number is sufficient.

*Works Cited.*   At the end of your researched essay, and starting on a new page, you must provide a list of works cited, a list of all the sources you have used (leaving out sources you consulted but did not cite). Entries should be listed alphabetically by author's last name or by title if no author is identified. Figure A.1 is a sample works cited page in MLA style that illustrates a few (very few) of the basic types of documentation.

---

### Steps to Compiling an MLA List of Works Cited

**1** Begin your list of works cited on a new page at the end of your paper.

**2** Put your last name and page number in the upper-right corner.

**3** Double-space throughout.

**4** Center the heading ("Works Cited") on the page.

**5** Arrange the list of sources alphabetically by author's last name or by title if no author is identified.

**6** Begin the first line of each source flush left; second and subsequent lines should be indented ½ inch.

**7** Invert the author's name, last name first. In the case of multiple authors, only the first author's name is inverted.

**8** Italicize the titles of books, journals, magazines, and newspapers. Put the titles of book chapters and articles in quotation marks. Capitalize each word in all titles except for articles, short prepositions, and coordinating conjunctions.

**9** For books, list the place of publication, the name of the publisher, and the year of publication. For chapters, list the editors of the book, the book title, and the publication information. For articles, list the journal title, volume and issue numbers, and the date of publication.

**10** List the relevant page numbers for articles and selections from longer works.

**11** Give the medium of publication, such as Print, Web, CD, DVD, Film, Lecture, Performance, Radio, Television, PDF file, MP3 file, or E-mail.

The steps outlined here for compiling a list of works cited apply to printed sources. MLA formats for citing online sources vary, but this is an example of the basic format:

Author. "Document Title." *Name of Site*. Site Sponsor, date posted/revised. Medium. Date you accessed the site.

Things to remember:

- Invert the author's name or the first author's name.
- Italicize the name of the site.
- If the site sponsor—usually an institution or organization—isn't clear, check the copyright notice at the bottom of the Web page.
- MLA style uses the day-month-year format for dates in the works-cited list.
- Notice that there's a comma between the sponsor and the publication date.
- In general, the medium of publication for online sources is "Web."
- Notice that you do not need to include a URL after the date of access.

In addition to online sources, you will likely use other nonprint sources in researching your papers. Our students, for example, regularly analyze films, recordings, television and radio programs, paintings, and photographs. For details on how to format these sources, consult the *MLA Handbook* or go to Purdue University's Online Writing Lab (OWL) site (http://owl.english.purdue.edu/owl/section/2/11).

Eck 10

## Works Cited

Gutiérrez, Kris D., Patricia Baquedano-López, and Jolynn Asato. "English for the Children: The New Literacy of the Old World Order." *Bilingual Review Journal* 24.1&2 (2000): 87-112. Print.

*Online scholarly journal/article, no author*

"History of Bilingual Education." *Rethinking Schools* 12.3 (1998): n. pag. Web. 15 Feb. 2008.

*Article in a scholarly journal*

Lanehart, Sonja L. "African American Vernacular English and Education." *Journal of English Linguistics* 26.2 (1998): 122-36. Print.

*Article in a magazine*

Pompa, Delia. "Bilingual Success: Why Two-Language Education Is Critical for Latinos." *Hispanic* Oct. 1996: 96. Print.

Rawls, John. *Political Liberalism*. New York: Columbia UP, 1993. Print.

*Essay in an edited collection; second source by same writer*

---. "Social Unity and Primary Goods." *Utilitarianism and Beyond*. Ed. Amartya Sen and Bernard Williams. Cambridge, Eng.: Cambridge UP, 1982. 159-85. Print.

Rodriguez, Richard. "Aria." *Hunger of Memory: The Education of Richard Rodriguez*. New York: Bantam, 1982. 11-40. Print.

Schrag, Peter. "Language Barrier." *New Republic* 9 Mar. 1998: 14-15. Print.

*A book*

Smitherman, Geneva. *Talkin and Testifyin: The Language of Black America*. Detroit: Wayne State UP, 1977. Print.

Willis, Arlette. "Reading the World of School Literacy: Contextualizing the Experience of a Young American Male." *Harvard Educational Review* 65.1 (1995): 30-49. Print.

**FIGURE A.1    Sample List of Works Cited, MLA Format**

# THE BASICS OF APA STYLE

*In-Text Citations.*  In APA style, in-text citations identify the author or authors of a source and the publication date. If the author or authors are mentioned in the text, only the publication date is needed:

> Feingold (1992) documented the fact that males perform much better than females in math and science and other "masculine" areas.

Notice that the in-text citation does not include a page number. Because Feingold is only cited, not quoted, no page reference is necessary. If the source is quoted directly, a page number is added in parentheses following the quote:

> Feingold (1992) argued that "men scored significantly higher than women in situations designed to test aptitude in mathematics and hard sciences" (p. 92).

APA style uses the abbreviation *p.* or *pp.* before page numbers, which MLA style does not. If the author is not identified with a signal phrase, the name, year, and page number would be noted parenthetically after the quotation:

> One study found that "men scored significantly higher than women in situations designed to test aptitude in mathematics and hard sciences" (Feingold, 1992, p. 92).

Many studies in the social sciences have multiple authors. In a work with two authors, cite both authors every time:

> Dlugos and Friedlander (2000) wrote that "sustaining passionate commitment to work as a psychotherapist reflects passionate commitment in other areas of life" (p. 298).

Here, too, if you do not identify the authors in a signal phrase, include their names, the year the source was published, and the relevant page number parenthetically after the quotation—but use an ampersand (&) instead of the word *and* between the authors' names:

> Some believe that "sustaining passionate commitment to work as a psychotherapist reflects passionate commitment in other areas of life" (Dlugos & Friedlander, 2000, p. 298).

Use the same principles the first time you cite a work with three to five authors:

> Booth-Butterfield, Anderson, and Williams (2000) tested . . .
> (Booth-Butterfield, Anderson, & Williams, 2000, p. 5)

Thereafter, you can use the name of the first author followed by the abbreviation *et al.* (Latin for "and others") in roman type:

Booth-Butterfield et al. (2000) tested . . .

(Booth-Butterfield et al., 2000, p. 5)

For a work with six or more authors, use *et al.* from the first mention.

These are only some of the most basic examples of APA in-text citation. Consult the APA manual for other guidelines.

*References.* APA style, like MLA style, requires a separate list of sources at the end of a research paper. This list is called "References," not "Works Cited." The list of references starts on a new page at the end of your paper and lists sources alphabetically by author (or title if no author is identified). Figure A.2 shows a sample list of references with sources cited in APA style.

## Steps to Compiling an APA List of References

**1** Begin your list of references on a new page at the end of your paper.

**2** Put a shortened version of the paper's title (not your last name) in all caps in the upper-left corner; put the page number in the upper-right corner.

**3** Double-space throughout.

**4** Center the heading ("References") on the page.

**5** Arrange the list of sources alphabetically by author's last name or by title if no author is identified.

**6** Begin the first line of each source flush left; second and subsequent lines should be indented ½ inch.

**7** Invert all authors' names. If a source has more than one author, use an ampersand (not *and*) before the last name.

**8** Insert the date in parentheses after the last author's name.

**9** Italicize the titles of books, capitalizing only the first letter of the title and subtitle and proper nouns.

**10** Follow the same capitalization for the titles of book chapters and articles. Do not use quotation marks around chapter and article titles.

**11** Italicize the titles of journals, magazines, and newspapers, capitalizing the initial letters of all key words.